T0181853

Lecture Notes in Computer Science

Lecture Notes in Artificial Intelligence   13718

Founding Editor

Jörg Siekmann

Series Editors

Randy Goebel, *University of Alberta, Edmonton, Canada*
Wolfgang Wahlster, *DFKI, Berlin, Germany*
Zhi-Hua Zhou, *Nanjing University, Nanjing, China*

The series Lecture Notes in Artificial Intelligence (LNAI) was established in 1988 as a topical subseries of LNCS devoted to artificial intelligence.

The series publishes state-of-the-art research results at a high level. As with the LNCS mother series, the mission of the series is to serve the international R & D community by providing an invaluable service, mainly focused on the publication of conference and workshop proceedings and postproceedings.

Massih-Reza Amini · Stéphane Canu ·
Asja Fischer · Tias Guns · Petra Kralj Novak ·
Grigorios Tsoumakas
Editors

Machine Learning and Knowledge Discovery in Databases

European Conference, ECML PKDD 2022
Grenoble, France, September 19–23, 2022
Proceedings, Part VI

Springer

Editors
Massih-Reza Amini
Grenoble Alpes University
Saint Martin d'Hères, France

Stéphane Canu
INSA Rouen Normandy
Saint Etienne du Rouvray, France

Asja Fischer
Ruhr-Universität Bochum
Bochum, Germany

Tias Guns
KU Leuven
Leuven, Belgium

Petra Kralj Novak
Central European University
Vienna, Austria

Grigorios Tsoumakas
Aristotle University of Thessaloniki
Thessaloniki, Greece

ISSN 0302-9743 ISSN 1611-3349 (electronic)
Lecture Notes in Artificial Intelligence
ISBN 978-3-031-26421-4 ISBN 978-3-031-26422-1 (eBook)
https://doi.org/10.1007/978-3-031-26422-1

LNCS Sublibrary: SL7 – Artificial Intelligence

Preface

The European Conference on Machine Learning and Principles and Practice of Knowledge Discovery in Databases (ECML–PKDD 2022) in Grenoble, France, was once again a place for in-person gathering and the exchange of ideas after two years of completely virtual conferences due to the SARS-CoV-2 pandemic. This year the conference was hosted for the first time in hybrid format, and we are honored and delighted to offer you these proceedings as a result.

The annual ECML–PKDD conference serves as a global venue for the most recent research in all fields of machine learning and knowledge discovery in databases, including cutting-edge applications. It builds on a highly successful run of ECML–PKDD conferences which has made it the premier European machine learning and data mining conference.

This year, the conference drew over 1080 participants (762 in-person and 318 online) from 37 countries, including 23 European nations. This wealth of interest considerably exceeded our expectations, and we were both excited and under pressure to plan a special event. Overall, the conference attracted a lot of interest from industry thanks to sponsorship, participation, and the conference's industrial day.

The main conference program consisted of presentations of 242 accepted papers and four keynote talks (in order of appearance):

- Francis Bach (Inria), Information Theory with Kernel Methods
- Danai Koutra (University of Michigan), Mining & Learning [Compact] Representations for Structured Data
- Fosca Gianotti (Scuola Normale Superiore di Pisa), Explainable Machine Learning for Trustworthy AI
- Yann Le Cun (Facebook AI Research), From Machine Learning to Autonomous Intelligence

In addition, there were respectively twenty three in-person and three online workshops; five in-person and three online tutorials; two combined in-person and one combined online workshop-tutorials, together with a PhD Forum, a discovery challenge and demonstrations.

Papers presented during the three main conference days were organized in 4 tracks, within 54 sessions:

- Research Track: articles on research or methodology from all branches of machine learning, data mining, and knowledge discovery;
- Applied Data Science Track: articles on cutting-edge uses of machine learning, data mining, and knowledge discovery to resolve practical use cases and close the gap between current theory and practice;
- Journal Track: articles that were published in special issues of the journals *Machine Learning* and *Data Mining and Knowledge Discovery*;

– Demo Track: short articles that propose a novel system that advances the state of the art and include a demonstration video.

We received a record number of 1238 abstract submissions, and for the Research and Applied Data Science Tracks, 932 papers made it through the review process (the remaining papers were withdrawn, with the bulk being desk rejected). We accepted 189 (27.3%) Research papers and 53 (22.2%) Applied Data science articles. 47 papers from the Journal Track and 17 demo papers were also included in the program. We were able to put together an extraordinarily rich and engaging program because of the high quality submissions.

Research articles that were judged to be of exceptional quality and deserving of special distinction were chosen by the awards committee:

– Machine Learning Best Paper Award: "*Bounding the Family-Wise Error Rate in Local Causal Discovery Using Rademacher Averages*", by Dario Simionato (University of Padova) and Fabio Vandin (University of Padova)
– Data-Mining Best Paper Award: "*Transforming PageRank into an Infinite-Depth Graph Neural Network*", by Andreas Roth (TU Dortmund), and Thomas Liebig (TU Dortmund)
– Test of Time Award for highest impact paper from ECML–PKDD 2012: "*Fairness-Aware Classifier with Prejudice Remover Regularizer*", by Toshihiro Kamishima (National Institute of Advanced Industrial Science and Technology AIST), Shotaro Akashi (National Institute of Advanced Industrial Science and Technology AIST), Hideki Asoh (National Institute of Advanced Industrial Science and Technology AIST), and Jun Sakuma (University of Tsukuba)

We sincerely thank the contributions of all participants, authors, PC members, area chairs, session chairs, volunteers, and co-organizers who made ECML–PKDD 2022 a huge success. We would especially like to thank Julie from the Grenoble World Trade Center for all her help and Titouan from Insight-outside, who worked so hard to make the online event possible. We also like to express our gratitude to Thierry for the design of the conference logo representing the three mountain chains surrounding the Grenoble city, as well as the sponsors and the ECML–PKDD Steering Committee.

October 2022

Massih-Reza Amini
Stéphane Canu
Asja Fischer
Petra Kralj Novak
Tias Guns
Grigorios Tsoumakas
Georgios Balikas
Fragkiskos Malliaros

Organization

General Chairs

Massih-Reza Amini   University Grenoble Alpes, France
Stéphane Canu   INSA Rouen, France

Program Chairs

Asja Fischer   Ruhr University Bochum, Germany
Tias Guns   KU Leuven, Belgium
Petra Kralj Novak   Central European University, Austria
Grigorios Tsoumakas   Aristotle University of Thessaloniki, Greece

Journal Track Chairs

Peggy Cellier   INSA Rennes, IRISA, France
Krzysztof Dembczyński   Yahoo Research, USA
Emilie Devijver   CNRS, France
Albrecht Zimmermann   University of Caen Normandie, France

Workshop and Tutorial Chairs

Bruno Crémilleux   University of Caen Normandie, France
Charlotte Laclau   Telecom Paris, France

Local Chairs

Latifa Boudiba   University Grenoble Alpes, France
Franck Iutzeler   University Grenoble Alpes, France

Proceedings Chairs

Wouter Duivesteijn	Technische Universiteit Eindhoven, the Netherlands
Sibylle Hess	Technische Universiteit Eindhoven, the Netherlands

Industry Track Chairs

Rohit Babbar	Aalto University, Finland
Françoise Fogelmann	Hub France IA, France

Discovery Challenge Chairs

Ioannis Katakis	University of Nicosia, Cyprus
Ioannis Partalas	Expedia, Switzerland

Demonstration Chairs

Georgios Balikas	Salesforce, France
Fragkiskos Malliaros	CentraleSupélec, France

PhD Forum Chairs

Esther Galbrun	University of Eastern Finland, Finland
Justine Reynaud	University of Caen Normandie, France

Awards Chairs

Francesca Lisi	Università degli Studi di Bari, Italy
Michalis Vlachos	University of Lausanne, Switzerland

Sponsorship Chairs

Patrice Aknin	IRT SystemX, France
Gilles Gasso	INSA Rouen, France

Web Chairs

Martine Harshé	Laboratoire d'Informatique de Grenoble, France
Marta Soare	University Grenoble Alpes, France

Publicity Chair

Emilie Morvant	Université Jean Monnet, France

ECML PKDD Steering Committee

Annalisa Appice	University of Bari Aldo Moro, Italy
Ira Assent	Aarhus University, Denmark
Albert Bifet	Télécom ParisTech, France
Francesco Bonchi	ISI Foundation, Italy
Tania Cerquitelli	Politecnico di Torino, Italy
Sašo Džeroski	Jožef Stefan Institute, Slovenia
Elisa Fromont	Université de Rennes, France
Andreas Hotho	Julius-Maximilians-Universität Würzburg, Germany
Alípio Jorge	University of Porto, Portugal
Kristian Kersting	TU Darmstadt, Germany
Jefrey Lijffijt	Ghent University, Belgium
Luís Moreira-Matias	University of Porto, Portugal
Katharina Morik	TU Dortmund, Germany
Siegfried Nijssen	Université catholique de Louvain, Belgium
Andrea Passerini	University of Trento, Italy
Fernando Perez-Cruz	ETH Zurich, Switzerland
Alessandra Sala	Shutterstock Ireland Limited, Ireland
Arno Siebes	Utrecht University, the Netherlands
Isabel Valera	Universität des Saarlandes, Germany

Program Committees

Guest Editorial Board, Journal Track

Richard Allmendinger	University of Manchester, UK
Marie Anastacio	Universiteit Leiden, the Netherlands
Ira Assent	Aarhus University, Denmark
Martin Atzmueller	Universität Osnabrück, Germany
Rohit Babbar	Aalto University, Finland

Jaume Bacardit	Newcastle University, UK
Anthony Bagnall	University of East Anglia, UK
Mitra Baratchi	Universiteit Leiden, the Netherlands
Francesco Bariatti	IRISA, France
German Barquero	Universität de Barcelona, Spain
Alessio Benavoli	Trinity College Dublin, Ireland
Viktor Bengs	Ludwig-Maximilians-Universität München, Germany
Massimo Bilancia	Università degli Studi di Bari Aldo Moro, Italy
Ilaria Bordino	Unicredit R&D, Italy
Jakob Bossek	University of Münster, Germany
Ulf Brefeld	Leuphana University of Lüneburg, Germany
Ricardo Campello	University of Newcastle, UK
Michelangelo Ceci	University of Bari, Italy
Loic Cerf	Universidade Federal de Minas Gerais, Brazil
Vitor Cerqueira	Universidade do Porto, Portugal
Laetitia Chapel	IRISA, France
Jinghui Chen	Pennsylvania State University, USA
Silvia Chiusano	Politecnico di Torino, Italy
Roberto Corizzo	Università degli Studi di Bari Aldo Moro, Italy
Bruno Cremilleux	Université de Caen Normandie, France
Marco de Gemmis	University of Bari Aldo Moro, Italy
Sebastien Destercke	Centre National de la Recherche Scientifique, France
Shridhar Devamane	Global Academy of Technology, India
Benjamin Doerr	Ecole Polytechnique, France
Wouter Duivesteijn	Technische Universiteit Eindhoven, the Netherlands
Thomas Dyhre Nielsen	Aalborg University, Denmark
Tapio Elomaa	Tampere University, Finland
Remi Emonet	Université Jean Monnet Saint-Etienne, France
Nicola Fanizzi	Università degli Studi di Bari Aldo Moro, Italy
Pedro Ferreira	University of Lisbon, Portugal
Cesar Ferri	Universität Politecnica de Valencia, Spain
Julia Flores	University of Castilla-La Mancha, Spain
Ionut Florescu	Stevens Institute of Technology, USA
Germain Forestier	Université de Haute-Alsace, France
Joel Frank	Ruhr-Universität Bochum, Germany
Marco Frasca	Università degli Studi di Milano, Italy
Jose A. Gomez	Universidad de Castilla-La Mancha, Spain
Stephan Günnemann	Institute for Advanced Study, Germany
Luis Galarraga	Inria, France

Corrado Loglisci	Università degli Studi di Bari Aldo Moro, Italy
Nuno Lourenço	University of Coimbra, Portugal
Claudio Lucchese	Ca'Foscari University of Venice, Italy
Brian MacNamee	University College Dublin, Ireland
Davide Maiorca	University of Cagliari, Italy
Giuseppe Manco	National Research Council, Italy
Elio Masciari	University of Naples Federico II, Italy
Andres Masegosa	University of Aalborg, Denmark
Ernestina Menasalvas	Universidad Politecnica de Madrid, Spain
Lien Michiels	Universiteit Antwerpen, Belgium
Jan Mielniczuk	Polish Academy of Sciences, Poland
Paolo Mignone	Università degli Studi di Bari Aldo Moro, Italy
Anna Monreale	University of Pisa, Italy
Giovanni Montana	University of Warwick, UK
Gregoire Montavon	Technische Universität Berlin, Germany
Amedeo Napoli	LORIA, France
Frank Neumann	University of Adelaide, Australia
Thomas Nielsen	Aalborg Universitet, Denmark
Bruno Ordozgoiti	Aalto-yliopisto, Finland
Panagiotis Papapetrou	Stockholms Universitet, Sweden
Andrea Passerini	University of Trento, Italy
Mykola Pechenizkiy	Technische Universiteit Eindhoven, the Netherlands
Charlotte Pelletier	IRISA, France
Ruggero Pensa	University of Turin, Italy
Nico Piatkowski	Technische Universität Dortmund, Germany
Gianvito Pio	Università degli Studi di Bari Aldo Moro, Italy
Marc Plantevit	Université Claude Bernard Lyon 1, France
Jose M. Puerta	Universidad de Castilla-La Mancha, Spain
Kai Puolamaki	Helsingin Yliopisto, Finland
Michael Rabbat	Meta Platforms Inc, USA
Jan Ramon	Inria Lille Nord Europe, France
Rita Ribeiro	Universidade do Porto, Portugal
Kaspar Riesen	University of Bern, Switzerland
Matteo Riondato	Amherst College, USA
Celine Robardet	INSA Lyon, France
Pieter Robberechts	KU Leuven, Belgium
Antonio Salmeron	University of Almería, Spain
Jorg Sander	University of Alberta, Canada
Roberto Santana	University of the Basque Country, Spain
Michael Schaub	Rheinisch-Westfälische Technische Hochschule, Germany

Erik Schultheis	Aalto-yliopisto, Finland
Thomas Seidl	Ludwig-Maximilians-Universität München, Germany
Moritz Seiler	University of Münster, Germany
Kijung Shin	KAIST, South Korea
Shinichi Shirakawa	Yokohama National University, Japan
Marek Smieja	Jagiellonian University, Poland
James Edward Smith	University of the West of England, UK
Carlos Soares	Universidade do Porto, Portugal
Arnaud Soulet	Université de Tours, France
Gerasimos Spanakis	Maastricht University, the Netherlands
Giancarlo Sperli	University of Campania Luigi Vanvitelli, Italy
Myra Spiliopoulou	Otto von Guericke Universität Magdeburg, Germany
Jerzy Stefanowski	Poznan University of Technology, Poland
Giovanni Stilo	Università degli Studi dell'Aquila, Italy
Catalin Stoean	University of Craiova, Romania
Mahito Sugiyama	National Institute of Informatics, Japan
Nikolaj Tatti	Helsingin Yliopisto, Finland
Alexandre Termier	Université de Rennes 1, France
Luis Torgo	Dalhousie University, Canada
Leonardo Trujillo	Tecnologico Nacional de Mexico, Mexico
Wei-Wei Tu	4Paradigm Inc., China
Steffen Udluft	Siemens AG Corporate Technology, Germany
Arnaud Vandaele	Université de Mons, Belgium
Celine Vens	KU Leuven, Belgium
Herna Viktor	University of Ottawa, Canada
Marco Virgolin	Centrum Wiskunde en Informatica, the Netherlands
Jordi Vitria	Universität de Barcelona, Spain
Jilles Vreeken	CISPA Helmholtz Center for Information Security, Germany
Willem Waegeman	Universiteit Gent, Belgium
Markus Wagner	University of Adelaide, Australia
Elizabeth Wanner	Centro Federal de Educacao Tecnologica de Minas, Brazil
Marcel Wever	Universität Paderborn, Germany
Ngai Wong	University of Hong Kong, Hong Kong, China
Man Leung Wong	Lingnan University, Hong Kong, China
Marek Wydmuch	Poznan University of Technology, Poland
Guoxian Yu	Shandong University, China
Xiang Zhang	University of Hong Kong, Hong Kong, China

Ye Zhu   Deakin University, USA
Arthur Zimek   Syddansk Universitet, Denmark
Albrecht Zimmermann   Université de Caen Normandie, France

Area Chairs

Fabrizio Angiulli   DIMES, University of Calabria, Italy
Annalisa Appice   University of Bari, Italy
Ira Assent   Aarhus University, Denmark
Martin Atzmueller   Osnabrück University, Germany
Michael Berthold   Universität Konstanz, Germany
Albert Bifet   Université Paris-Saclay, France
Hendrik Blockeel   KU Leuven, Belgium
Christian Böhm   LMU Munich, Germany
Francesco Bonchi   ISI Foundation, Turin, Italy
Ulf Brefeld   Leuphana, Germany
Francesco Calabrese   Richemont, USA
Toon Calders   Universiteit Antwerpen, Belgium
Michelangelo Ceci   University of Bari, Italy
Peggy Cellier   IRISA, France
Duen Horng Chau   Georgia Institute of Technology, USA
Nicolas Courty   IRISA, Université Bretagne-Sud, France
Bruno Cremilleux   Université de Caen Normandie, France
Jesse Davis   KU Leuven, Belgium
Gianmarco De Francisci Morales   CentAI, Italy
Tom Diethe   Amazon, UK
Carlotta Domeniconi   George Mason University, USA
Yuxiao Dong   Tsinghua University, China
Kurt Driessens   Maastricht University, the Netherlands
Tapio Elomaa   Tampere University, Finland
Sergio Escalera   CVC and University of Barcelona, Spain
Faisal Farooq   Qatar Computing Research Institute, Qatar
Asja Fischer   Ruhr University Bochum, Germany
Peter Flach   University of Bristol, UK
Eibe Frank   University of Waikato, New Zealand
Paolo Frasconi   Università degli Studi di Firenze, Italy
Elisa Fromont   Université Rennes 1, IRISA/Inria, France
Johannes Fürnkranz   JKU Linz, Austria
Patrick Gallinari   Sorbonne Université, Criteo AI Lab, France
Joao Gama   INESC TEC - LIAAD, Portugal
Jose Gamez   Universidad de Castilla-La Mancha, Spain
Roman Garnett   Washington University in St. Louis, USA
Thomas Gärtner   TU Wien, Austria

Aristides Gionis	KTH Royal Institute of Technology, Sweden
Francesco Gullo	UniCredit, Italy
Stephan Günnemann	Technical University of Munich, Germany
Xiangnan He	University of Science and Technology of China, China
Daniel Hernandez-Lobato	Universidad Autonoma de Madrid, Spain
José Hernández-Orallo	Universität Politècnica de València, Spain
Jaakko Hollmén	Aalto University, Finland
Andreas Hotho	Universität Würzburg, Germany
Eyke Hüllermeier	University of Munich, Germany
Neil Hurley	University College Dublin, Ireland
Georgiana Ifrim	University College Dublin, Ireland
Alipio Jorge	INESC TEC/University of Porto, Portugal
Ross King	Chalmers University of Technology, Sweden
Arno Knobbe	Leiden University, the Netherlands
Yun Sing Koh	University of Auckland, New Zealand
Parisa Kordjamshidi	Michigan State University, USA
Lars Kotthoff	University of Wyoming, USA
Nicolas Kourtellis	Telefonica Research, Spain
Danai Koutra	University of Michigan, USA
Danica Kragic	KTH Royal Institute of Technology, Sweden
Stefan Kramer	Johannes Gutenberg University Mainz, Germany
Niklas Lavesson	Blekinge Institute of Technology, Sweden
Sébastien Lefèvre	Université de Bretagne Sud/IRISA, France
Jefrey Lijffijt	Ghent University, Belgium
Marius Lindauer	Leibniz University Hannover, Germany
Patrick Loiseau	Inria, France
Jose Lozano	UPV/EHU, Spain
Jörg Lücke	Universität Oldenburg, Germany
Donato Malerba	Università degli Studi di Bari Aldo Moro, Italy
Fragkiskos Malliaros	CentraleSupelec, France
Giuseppe Manco	ICAR-CNR, Italy
Wannes Meert	KU Leuven, Belgium
Pauli Miettinen	University of Eastern Finland, Finland
Dunja Mladenic	Jožef Stefan Institute, Slovenia
Anna Monreale	Università di Pisa, Italy
Luis Moreira-Matias	Finiata, Germany
Emilie Morvant	University Jean Monnet, St-Etienne, France
Sriraam Natarajan	UT Dallas, USA
Nuria Oliver	Vodafone Research, USA
Panagiotis Papapetrou	Stockholm University, Sweden
Laurence Park	WSU, Australia

Andrea Passerini	University of Trento, Italy
Mykola Pechenizkiy	TU Eindhoven, the Netherlands
Dino Pedreschi	University of Pisa, Italy
Robert Peharz	Graz University of Technology, Austria
Julien Perez	Naver Labs Europe, France
Franz Pernkopf	Graz University of Technology, Austria
Bernhard Pfahringer	University of Waikato, New Zealand
Fabio Pinelli	IMT Lucca, Italy
Visvanathan Ramesh	Goethe University Frankfurt, Germany
Jesse Read	Ecole Polytechnique, France
Zhaochun Ren	Shandong University, China
Marian-Andrei Rizoiu	University of Technology Sydney, Australia
Celine Robardet	INSA Lyon, France
Sriparna Saha	IIT Patna, India
Ute Schmid	University of Bamberg, Germany
Lars Schmidt-Thieme	University of Hildesheim, Germany
Michele Sebag	LISN CNRS, France
Thomas Seidl	LMU Munich, Germany
Arno Siebes	Universiteit Utrecht, the Netherlands
Fabrizio Silvestri	Sapienza, University of Rome, Italy
Myra Spiliopoulou	Otto-von-Guericke-University Magdeburg, Germany
Yizhou Sun	UCLA, USA
Jie Tang	Tsinghua University, China
Nikolaj Tatti	Helsinki University, Finland
Evimaria Terzi	Boston University, USA
Marc Tommasi	Lille University, France
Antti Ukkonen	University of Helsinki, Finland
Herke van Hoof	University of Amsterdam, the Netherlands
Matthijs van Leeuwen	Leiden University, the Netherlands
Celine Vens	KU Leuven, Belgium
Christel Vrain	University of Orleans, France
Jilles Vreeken	CISPA Helmholtz Center for Information Security, Germany
Willem Waegeman	Universiteit Gent, Belgium
Stefan Wrobel	Fraunhofer IAIS, Germany
Xing Xie	Microsoft Research Asia, China
Min-Ling Zhang	Southeast University, China
Albrecht Zimmermann	Université de Caen Normandie, France
Indre Zliobaite	University of Helsinki, Finland

Program Committee Members

Amos Abbott	Virginia Tech, USA
Pedro Abreu	CISUC, Portugal
Maribel Acosta	Ruhr University Bochum, Germany
Timilehin Aderinola	Insight Centre, University College Dublin, Ireland
Linara Adilova	Ruhr University Bochum, Fraunhofer IAIS, Germany
Florian Adriaens	KTH, Sweden
Azim Ahmadzadeh	Georgia State University, USA
Nourhan Ahmed	University of Hildesheim, Germany
Deepak Ajwani	University College Dublin, Ireland
Amir Hossein Akhavan Rahnama	KTH Royal Institute of Technology, Sweden
Aymen Al Marjani	ENS Lyon, France
Mehwish Alam	Leibniz Institute for Information Infrastructure, Germany
Francesco Alesiani	NEC Laboratories Europe, Germany
Omar Alfarisi	ADNOC, Canada
Pegah Alizadeh	Ericsson Research, France
Reem Alotaibi	King Abdulaziz University, Saudi Arabia
Jumanah Alshehri	Temple University, USA
Bakhtiar Amen	University of Huddersfield, UK
Evelin Amorim	Inesc tec, Portugal
Shin Ando	Tokyo University of Science, Japan
Thiago Andrade	INESC TEC - LIAAD, Portugal
Jean-Marc Andreoli	Naverlabs Europe, France
Giuseppina Andresini	University of Bari Aldo Moro, Italy
Alessandro Antonucci	IDSIA, Switzerland
Xiang Ao	Institute of Computing Technology, CAS, China
Siddharth Aravindan	National University of Singapore, Singapore
Héber H. Arcolezi	Inria and École Polytechnique, France
Adrián Arnaiz-Rodríguez	ELLIS Unit Alicante, Spain
Yusuf Arslan	University of Luxembourg, Luxembourg
André Artelt	Bielefeld University, Germany
Sunil Aryal	Deakin University, Australia
Charles Assaad	Easyvista, France
Matthias Aßenmacher	Ludwig-Maxmilians-Universität München, Germany
Zeyar Aung	Masdar Institute, UAE
Serge Autexier	DFKI Bremen, Germany
Rohit Babbar	Aalto University, Finland
Housam Babiker	University of Alberta, Canada

Antonio Bahamonde	University of Oviedo, Spain
Maroua Bahri	Inria Paris, France
Georgios Balikas	Salesforce, France
Maria Bampa	Stockholm University, Sweden
Hubert Baniecki	Warsaw University of Technology, Poland
Elena Baralis	Politecnico di Torino, Italy
Mitra Baratchi	LIACS - University of Leiden, the Netherlands
Kalliopi Basioti	Rutgers University, USA
Martin Becker	Stanford University, USA
Diana Benavides Prado	University of Auckland, New Zealand
Anes Bendimerad	LIRIS, France
Idir Benouaret	Université Grenoble Alpes, France
Isacco Beretta	Università di Pisa, Italy
Victor Berger	CEA, France
Christoph Bergmeir	Monash University, Australia
Cuissart Bertrand	University of Caen, France
Antonio Bevilacqua	University College Dublin, Ireland
Yaxin Bi	Ulster University, UK
Ranran Bian	University of Auckland, New Zealand
Adrien Bibal	University of Louvain, Belgium
Subhodip Biswas	Virginia Tech, USA
Patrick Blöbaum	Amazon AWS, USA
Carlos Bobed	University of Zaragoza, Spain
Paul Bogdan	USC, USA
Chiara Boldrini	CNR, Italy
Clément Bonet	Université Bretagne Sud, France
Andrea Bontempelli	University of Trento, Italy
Ludovico Boratto	University of Cagliari, Italy
Stefano Bortoli	Huawei Research Center, Germany
Diana-Laura Borza	Babes Bolyai University, Romania
Ahcene Boubekki	UiT, Norway
Sabri Boughorbel	QCRI, Qatar
Paula Branco	University of Ottawa, Canada
Jure Brence	Jožef Stefan Institute, Slovenia
Martin Breskvar	Jožef Stefan Institute, Slovenia
Marco Bressan	University of Milan, Italy
Dariusz Brzezinski	Poznan University of Technology, Poland
Florian Buettner	German Cancer Research Center, Germany
Julian Busch	Siemens Technology, Germany
Sebastian Buschjäger	TU Dortmund Artificial Intelligence Unit, Germany
Ali Butt	Virginia Tech, USA

Yuqiao Chen	UT Dallas, USA
Yuzhou Chen	Princeton University, USA
Zhennan Chen	Xiamen University, China
Zhiyu Chen	UCSB, USA
Zhqian Chen	Mississippi State University, USA
Ziheng Chen	Stony Brook University, USA
Zhiyong Cheng	Shandong Academy of Sciences, China
Noëlie Cherrier	CITiO, France
Anshuman Chhabra	UC Davis, USA
Zhixuan Chu	Ant Group, China
Guillaume Cleuziou	LIFO, France
Ciaran Cooney	AflacNI, UK
Robson Cordeiro	University of São Paulo, Brazil
Roberto Corizzo	American University, USA
Antoine Cornuéjols	AgroParisTech, France
Fabrizio Costa	Exeter University, UK
Gustavo Costa	Instituto Federal de Goiás - Campus Jataí, Brazil
Luís Cruz	Delft University of Technology, the Netherlands
Tianyu Cui	Institute of Information Engineering, China
Wang-Zhou Dai	Imperial College London, UK
Tanmoy Dam	University of New South Wales Canberra, Australia
Thi-Bich-Hanh Dao	University of Orleans, France
Adrian Sergiu Darabant	Babes Bolyai University, Romania
Mrinal Das	IIT Palakaad, India
Sina Däubener	Ruhr University, Bochum, Germany
Padraig Davidson	University of Würzburg, Germany
Paul Davidsson	Malmö University, Sweden
Andre de Carvalho	USP, Brazil
Antoine de Mathelin	ENS Paris-Saclay, France
Tom De Schepper	University of Antwerp, Belgium
Marcilio de Souto	LIFO/Univ. Orleans, France
Gaetan De Waele	Ghent University, Belgium
Pieter Delobelle	KU Leuven, Belgium
Alper Demir	Izmir University of Economics, Turkey
Ambra Demontis	University of Cagliari, Italy
Difan Deng	Leibniz Universität Hannover, Germany
Guillaume Derval	UCLouvain - ICTEAM, Belgium
Maunendra Sankar Desarkar	IIT Hyderabad, India
Chris Develder	University of Ghent - iMec, Belgium
Arnout Devos	Swiss Federal Institute of Technology Lausanne, Switzerland

Laurens Devos	KU Leuven, Belgium
Bhaskar Dhariyal	University College Dublin, Ireland
Nicola Di Mauro	University of Bari, Italy
Aissatou Diallo	University College London, UK
Christos Dimitrakakis	University of Neuchatel, Switzerland
Jiahao Ding	University of Houston, USA
Kaize Ding	Arizona State University, USA
Yao-Xiang Ding	Nanjing University, China
Guilherme Dinis Junior	Stockholm University, Sweden
Nikolaos Dionelis	University of Edinburgh, UK
Christos Diou	Harokopio University of Athens, Greece
Sonia Djebali	Léonard de Vinci Pôle Universitaire, France
Nicolas Dobigeon	University of Toulouse, France
Carola Doerr	Sorbonne University, France
Ruihai Dong	University College Dublin, Ireland
Shuyu Dong	Inria, Université Paris-Saclay, France
Yixiang Dong	Xi'an Jiaotong University, China
Xin Du	University of Edinburgh, UK
Yuntao Du	Nanjing University, China
Stefan Duffner	University of Lyon, France
Rahul Duggal	Georgia Tech, USA
Wouter Duivesteijn	TU Eindhoven, the Netherlands
Sebastijan Dumancic	TU Delft, the Netherlands
Inês Dutra	University of Porto, Portugal
Thomas Dyhre Nielsen	AAU, Denmark
Saso Dzeroski	Jožef Stefan Institute, Ljubljana, Slovenia
Tome Eftimov	Jožef Stefan Institute, Ljubljana, Slovenia
Hamid Eghbal-zadeh	LIT AI Lab, Johannes Kepler University, Austria
Theresa Eimer	Leibniz University Hannover, Germany
Radwa El Shawi	Tartu University, Estonia
Dominik Endres	Philipps-Universität Marburg, Germany
Roberto Esposito	Università di Torino, Italy
Georgios Evangelidis	University of Macedonia, Greece
Samuel Fadel	Leuphana University, Germany
Stephan Fahrenkrog-Petersen	Humboldt-Universität zu Berlin, Germany
Xiaomao Fan	Shenzhen Technology University, China
Zipei Fan	University of Tokyo, Japan
Hadi Fanaee	Halmstad University, Sweden
Meng Fang	TU/e, the Netherlands
Elaine Faria	UFU, Brazil
Ad Feelders	Universiteit Utrecht, the Netherlands
Sophie Fellenz	TU Kaiserslautern, Germany

Stefano Ferilli	University of Bari, Italy
Daniel Fernández-Sánchez	Universidad Autónoma de Madrid, Spain
Pedro Ferreira	Faculty of Sciences University of Porto, Portugal
Cèsar Ferri	Universität Politècnica València, Spain
Flavio Figueiredo	UFMG, Brazil
Soukaina Filali Boubrahimi	Utah State University, USA
Raphaël Fischer	TU Dortmund, Germany
Germain Forestier	University of Haute Alsace, France
Edouard Fouché	Karlsruhe Institute of Technology, Germany
Philippe Fournier-Viger	Shenzhen University, China
Kary Framling	Umeå University, Sweden
Jérôme François	Inria Nancy Grand-Est, France
Fabio Fumarola	Prometeia, Italy
Pratik Gajane	Eindhoven University of Technology, the Netherlands
Esther Galbrun	University of Eastern Finland, Finland
Laura Galindez Olascoaga	KU Leuven, Belgium
Sunanda Gamage	University of Western Ontario, Canada
Chen Gao	Tsinghua University, China
Wei Gao	Nanjing University, China
Xiaofeng Gao	Shanghai Jiaotong University, China
Yuan Gao	University of Science and Technology of China, China
Jochen Garcke	University of Bonn, Germany
Clement Gautrais	Brightclue, France
Benoit Gauzere	INSA Rouen, France
Dominique Gay	Université de La Réunion, France
Xiou Ge	University of Southern California, USA
Bernhard Geiger	Know-Center GmbH, Germany
Jiahui Geng	University of Stavanger, Norway
Yangliao Geng	Tsinghua University, China
Konstantin Genin	University of Tübingen, Germany
Firas Gerges	New Jersey Institute of Technology, USA
Pierre Geurts	University of Liège, Belgium
Gizem Gezici	Sabanci University, Turkey
Amirata Ghorbani	Stanford, USA
Biraja Ghoshal	TCS, UK
Anna Giabelli	Università degli studi di Milano Bicocca, Italy
George Giannakopoulos	IIT Demokritos, Greece
Tobias Glasmachers	Ruhr-University Bochum, Germany
Heitor Murilo Gomes	University of Waikato, New Zealand
Anastasios Gounaris	Aristotle University of Thessaloniki, Greece

Antoine Gourru   University of Lyon, France
Michael Granitzer   University of Passau, Germany
Magda Gregorova   Hochschule Würzburg-Schweinfurt, Germany
Moritz Grosse-Wentrup   University of Vienna, Austria
Divya Grover   Chalmers University, Sweden
Bochen Guan   OPPO US Research Center, USA
Xinyu Guan   Xian Jiaotong University, China
Guillaume Guerard   ESILV, France
Daniel Guerreiro e Silva   University of Brasilia, Brazil
Riccardo Guidotti   University of Pisa, Italy
Ekta Gujral   University of California, Riverside, USA
Aditya Gulati   ELLIS Unit Alicante, Spain
Guibing Guo   Northeastern University, China
Jianxiong Guo   Beijing Normal University, China
Yuhui Guo   Renmin University of China, China
Karthik Gurumoorthy   Amazon, India
Thomas Guyet   Inria, Centre de Lyon, France
Guillaume Habault   KDDI Research, Inc., Japan
Amaury Habrard   University of St-Etienne, France
Shahrzad Haddadan   Brown University, USA
Shah Muhammad Hamdi   New Mexico State University, USA
Massinissa Hamidi   PRES Sorbonne Paris Cité, France
Peng Han   KAUST, Saudi Arabia
Tom Hanika   University of Kassel, Germany
Sébastien Harispe   IMT Mines Alès, France
Marwan Hassani   TU Eindhoven, the Netherlands
Kohei Hayashi   Preferred Networks, Inc., Japan
Conor Hayes   National University of Ireland Galway, Ireland
Lingna He   Zhejiang University of Technology, China
Ramya Hebbalaguppe   Indian Institute of Technology, Delhi, India
Jukka Heikkonen   University of Turku, Finland
Fredrik Heintz   Linköping University, Sweden
Patrick Hemmer   Karlsruhe Institute of Technology, Germany
Romain Hérault   INSA de Rouen, France
Jeronimo Hernandez-Gonzalez   University of Barcelona, Spain
Sibylle Hess   TU Eindhoven, the Netherlands
Fabian Hinder   Bielefeld University, Germany
Lars Holdijk   University of Amsterdam, the Netherlands
Martin Holena   Institute of Computer Science, Czechia
Mike Holenderski   Eindhoven University of Technology,
                                          the Netherlands
Shenda Hong   Peking University, China

Yupeng Hou	Renmin University of China, China
Binbin Hu	Ant Financial Services Group, China
Jian Hu	Queen Mary University of London, UK
Liang Hu	Tongji University, China
Wen Hu	Ant Group, China
Wenbin Hu	Wuhan University, China
Wenbo Hu	Tsinghua University, China
Yaowei Hu	University of Arkansas, USA
Chao Huang	University of Hong Kong, China
Gang Huang	Zhejiang Lab, China
Guanjie Huang	Penn State University, USA
Hong Huang	HUST, China
Jin Huang	University of Amsterdam, the Netherlands
Junjie Huang	Chinese Academy of Sciences, China
Qiang Huang	Jilin University, China
Shangrong Huang	Hunan University, China
Weitian Huang	South China University of Technology, China
Yan Huang	Huazhong University of Science and Technology, China
Yiran Huang	Karlsruhe Institute of Technology, Germany
Angelo Impedovo	University of Bari, Italy
Roberto Interdonato	CIRAD, France
Iñaki Inza	University of the Basque Country, Spain
Stratis Ioannidis	Northeastern University, USA
Rakib Islam	Facebook, USA
Tobias Jacobs	NEC Laboratories Europe GmbH, Germany
Priyank Jaini	Google, Canada
Johannes Jakubik	Karlsruhe Institute of Technology, Germany
Nathalie Japkowicz	American University, USA
Szymon Jaroszewicz	Polish Academy of Sciences, Poland
Shayan Jawed	University of Hildesheim, Germany
Rathinaraja Jeyaraj	Kyungpook National University, South Korea
Shaoxiong Ji	Aalto University, Finland
Taoran Ji	Virginia Tech, USA
Bin-Bin Jia	Southeast University, China
Yuheng Jia	Southeast University, China
Ziyu Jia	Beijing Jiaotong University, China
Nan Jiang	Purdue University, USA
Renhe Jiang	University of Tokyo, Japan
Siyang Jiang	National Taiwan University, Taiwan
Song Jiang	University of California, Los Angeles, USA
Wenyu Jiang	Nanjing University, China

Zhen Jiang	Jiangsu University, China
Yuncheng Jiang	South China Normal University, China
François-Xavier Jollois	Université de Paris Cité, France
Adan Jose-Garcia	Université de Lille, France
Ferdian Jovan	University of Bristol, UK
Steffen Jung	MPII, Germany
Thorsten Jungeblut	Bielefeld University of Applied Sciences, Germany
Hachem Kadri	Aix-Marseille University, France
Vana Kalogeraki	Athens University of Economics and Business, Greece
Vinayaka Kamath	Microsoft Research India, India
Toshihiro Kamishima	National Institute of Advanced Industrial Science, Japan
Bo Kang	Ghent University, Belgium
Alexandros Karakasidis	University of Macedonia, Greece
Mansooreh Karami	Arizona State University, USA
Panagiotis Karras	Aarhus University, Denmark
Ioannis Katakis	University of Nicosia, Cyprus
Koki Kawabata	Osaka University, Tokyo
Klemen Kenda	Jožef Stefan Institute, Slovenia
Patrik Joslin Kenfack	Innopolis University, Russia
Mahsa Keramati	Simon Fraser University, Canada
Hamidreza Keshavarz	Tarbiat Modares University, Iran
Adil Khan	Innopolis University, Russia
Jihed Khiari	Johannes Kepler University, Austria
Mi-Young Kim	University of Alberta, Canada
Arto Klami	University of Helsinki, Finland
Jiri Klema	Czech Technical University, Czechia
Tomas Kliegr	University of Economics Prague, Czechia
Christian Knoll	Graz, University of Technology, Austria
Dmitry Kobak	University of Tübingen, Germany
Vladimer Kobayashi	University of the Philippines Mindanao, Philippines
Dragi Kocev	Jožef Stefan Institute, Slovenia
Adrian Kochsiek	University of Mannheim, Germany
Masahiro Kohjima	NTT Corporation, Japan
Georgia Koloniari	University of Macedonia, Greece
Nikos Konofaos	Aristotle University of Thessaloniki, Greece
Irena Koprinska	University of Sydney, Australia
Lars Kotthoff	University of Wyoming, USA
Daniel Kottke	University of Kassel, Germany

Anna Krause	University of Würzburg, Germany
Alexander Kravberg	KTH Royal Institute of Technology, Sweden
Anastasia Krithara	NCSR Demokritos, Greece
Meelis Kull	University of Tartu, Estonia
Pawan Kumar	IIIT, Hyderabad, India
Suresh Kirthi Kumaraswamy	InterDigital, France
Gautam Kunapuli	Verisk Inc, USA
Marcin Kurdziel	AGH University of Science and Technology, Poland
Vladimir Kuzmanovski	Aalto University, Finland
Ariel Kwiatkowski	École Polytechnique, France
Firas Laakom	Tampere University, Finland
Harri Lähdesmäki	Aalto University, Finland
Stefanos Laskaridis	Samsung AI, UK
Alberto Lavelli	FBK-ict, Italy
Aonghus Lawlor	University College Dublin, Ireland
Thai Le	University of Mississippi, USA
Hoàng-Ân Lê	IRISA, University of South Brittany, France
Hoel Le Capitaine	University of Nantes, France
Thach Le Nguyen	Insight Centre, Ireland
Tai Le Quy	L3S Research Center - Leibniz University Hannover, Germany
Mustapha Lebbah	Sorbonne Paris Nord University, France
Dongman Lee	KAIST, South Korea
John Lee	Université catholique de Louvain, Belgium
Minwoo Lee	University of North Carolina at Charlotte, USA
Zed Lee	Stockholm University, Sweden
Yunwen Lei	University of Birmingham, UK
Douglas Leith	Trinity College Dublin, Ireland
Florian Lemmerich	RWTH Aachen, Germany
Carson Leung	University of Manitoba, Canada
Chaozhuo Li	Microsoft Research Asia, China
Jian Li	Institute of Information Engineering, China
Lei Li	Peking University, China
Li Li	Southwest University, China
Rui Li	Inspur Group, China
Shiyang Li	UCSB, USA
Shuokai Li	Chinese Academy of Sciences, China
Tianyu Li	Alibaba Group, China
Wenye Li	The Chinese University of Hong Kong, Shenzhen, China
Wenzhong Li	Nanjing University, China

Xiaoting Li	Pennsylvania State University, USA
Yang Li	University of North Carolina at Chapel Hill, USA
Zejian Li	Zhejiang University, China
Zhidong Li	UTS, Australia
Zhixin Li	Guangxi Normal University, China
Defu Lian	University of Science and Technology of China, China
Bin Liang	UTS, Australia
Yuchen Liang	RPI, USA
Yiwen Liao	University of Stuttgart, Germany
Pieter Libin	VUB, Belgium
Thomas Liebig	TU Dortmund, Germany
Seng Pei Liew	LINE Corporation, Japan
Beiyu Lin	University of Nevada - Las Vegas, USA
Chen Lin	Xiamen University, China
Tony Lindgren	Stockholm University, Sweden
Chen Ling	Emory University, USA
Jiajing Ling	Singapore Management University, Singapore
Marco Lippi	University of Modena and Reggio Emilia, Italy
Bin Liu	Chongqing University, China
Bowen Liu	Stanford University, USA
Chang Liu	Institute of Information Engineering, CAS, China
Chien-Liang Liu	National Chiao Tung University, Taiwan
Feng Liu	East China Normal University, China
Jiacheng Liu	Chinese University of Hong Kong, China
Li Liu	Chongqing University, China
Shengcai Liu	Southern University of Science and Technology, China
Shenghua Liu	Institute of Computing Technology, CAS, China
Tingwen Liu	Institute of Information Engineering, CAS, China
Xiangyu Liu	Tencent, China
Yong Liu	Renmin University of China, China
Yuansan Liu	University of Melbourne, Australia
Zhiwei Liu	Salesforce, USA
Tuwe Löfström	Jönköping University, Sweden
Corrado Loglisci	Università degli Studi di Bari Aldo Moro, Italy
Ting Long	Shanghai Jiao Tong University, China
Beatriz López	University of Girona, Spain
Yin Lou	Ant Group, USA
Samir Loudni	TASC (LS2N-CNRS), IMT Atlantique, France
Yang Lu	Xiamen University, China
Yuxun Lu	National Institute of Informatics, Japan

Massimiliano Luca	Bruno Kessler Foundation, Italy
Stefan Lüdtke	University of Mannheim, Germany
Jovita Lukasik	University of Mannheim, Germany
Denis Lukovnikov	University of Bonn, Germany
Pedro Henrique Luz de Araujo	University of Brasília, Brazil
Fenglong Ma	Pennsylvania State University, USA
Jing Ma	University of Virginia, USA
Meng Ma	Peking University, China
Muyang Ma	Shandong University, China
Ruizhe Ma	University of Massachusetts Lowell, USA
Xingkong Ma	National University of Defense Technology, China
Xueqi Ma	Tsinghua University, China
Zichen Ma	The Chinese University of Hong Kong, Shenzhen, China
Luis Macedo	University of Coimbra, Portugal
Harshitha Machiraju	EPFL, Switzerland
Manchit Madan	Delivery Hero, Germany
Seiji Maekawa	Osaka University, Japan
Sindri Magnusson	Stockholm University, Sweden
Pathum Chamikara Mahawaga	CSIRO Data61, Australia
Saket Maheshwary	Amazon, India
Ajay Mahimkar	AT&T, USA
Pierre Maillot	Inria, France
Lorenzo Malandri	Unimib, Italy
Rammohan Mallipeddi	Kyungpook National University, South Korea
Sahil Manchanda	IIT Delhi, India
Domenico Mandaglio	DIMES-UNICAL, Italy
Panagiotis Mandros	Harvard University, USA
Robin Manhaeve	KU Leuven, Belgium
Silviu Maniu	Université Paris-Saclay, France
Cinmayii Manliguez	National Sun Yat-Sen University, Taiwan
Naresh Manwani	International Institute of Information Technology, India
Jiali Mao	East China Normal University, China
Alexandru Mara	Ghent University, Belgium
Radu Marculescu	University of Texas at Austin, USA
Roger Mark	Massachusetts Institute of Technology, USA
Fernando Martínez-Plume	Joint Research Centre - European Commission, Belgium
Koji Maruhashi	Fujitsu Research, Fujitsu Limited, Japan
Simone Marullo	University of Siena, Italy

Elio Masciari — University of Naples, Italy
Florent Masseglia — Inria, France
Michael Mathioudakis — University of Helsinki, Finland
Takashi Matsubara — Osaka University, Japan
Tetsu Matsukawa — Kyushu University, Japan
Santiago Mazuelas — BCAM-Basque Center for Applied Mathematics, Spain
Ryan McConville — University of Bristol, UK
Hardik Meisheri — TCS Research, India
Panagiotis Meletis — Eindhoven University of Technology, the Netherlands
Gabor Melli — Medable, USA
Joao Mendes-Moreira — INESC TEC, Portugal
Chuan Meng — University of Amsterdam, the Netherlands
Cristina Menghini — Brown University, USA
Engelbert Mephu Nguifo — Université Clermont Auvergne, CNRS, LIMOS, France
Fabio Mercorio — University of Milan-Bicocca, Italy
Guillaume Metzler — Laboratoire ERIC, France
Hao Miao — Aalborg University, Denmark
Alessio Micheli — Università di Pisa, Italy
Paolo Mignone — University of Bari Aldo Moro, Italy
Matej Mihelcic — University of Zagreb, Croatia
Ioanna Miliou — Stockholm University, Sweden
Bamdev Mishra — Microsoft, India
Rishabh Misra — Twitter, Inc, USA
Dixant Mittal — National University of Singapore, Singapore
Zhaobin Mo — Columbia University, USA
Daichi Mochihashi — Institute of Statistical Mathematics, Japan
Armin Moharrer — Northeastern University, USA
Ioannis Mollas — Aristotle University of Thessaloniki, Greece
Carlos Monserrat-Aranda — Universität Politècnica de València, Spain
Konda Reddy Mopuri — Indian Institute of Technology Guwahati, India
Raha Moraffah — Arizona State University, USA
Pawel Morawiecki — Polish Academy of Sciences, Poland
Ahmadreza Mosallanezhad — Arizona State University, USA
Davide Mottin — Aarhus University, Denmark
Koyel Mukherjee — Adobe Research, India
Maximilian Münch — University of Applied Sciences Würzburg, Germany
Fabricio Murai — Universidade Federal de Minas Gerais, Brazil
Taichi Murayama — NAIST, Japan

Apostolos Papadopoulos	Aristotle University of Thessaloniki, Greece
Evangelos Papalexakis	UC Riverside, USA
Anna Pappa	Université Paris 8, France
Chanyoung Park	UIUC, USA
Haekyu Park	Georgia Institute of Technology, USA
Sanghyun Park	Yonsei University, South Korea
Luca Pasa	University of Padova, Italy
Kevin Pasini	IRT SystemX, France
Vincenzo Pasquadibisceglie	University of Bari Aldo Moro, Italy
Nikolaos Passalis	Aristotle University of Thessaloniki, Greece
Javier Pastorino	University of Colorado, Denver, USA
Kitsuchart Pasupa	King Mongkut's Institute of Technology, Thailand
Andrea Paudice	University of Milan, Italy
Anand Paul	Kyungpook National University, South Korea
Yulong Pei	TU Eindhoven, the Netherlands
Charlotte Pelletier	Université de Bretagne du Sud, France
Jaakko Peltonen	Tampere University, Finland
Ruggero Pensa	University of Torino, Italy
Fabiola Pereira	Federal University of Uberlandia, Brazil
Lucas Pereira	ITI, LARSyS, Técnico Lisboa, Portugal
Aritz Pérez	Basque Center for Applied Mathematics, Spain
Lorenzo Perini	KU Leuven, Belgium
Alan Perotti	CENTAI Institute, Italy
Michaël Perrot	Inria Lille, France
Matej Petkovic	Institute Jožef Stefan, Slovenia
Lukas Pfahler	TU Dortmund University, Germany
Nico Piatkowski	Fraunhofer IAIS, Germany
Francesco Piccialli	University of Naples Federico II, Italy
Gianvito Pio	University of Bari, Italy
Giuseppe Pirrò	Sapienza University of Rome, Italy
Marc Plantevit	EPITA, France
Konstantinos Pliakos	KU Leuven, Belgium
Matthias Pohl	Otto von Guericke University, Germany
Nicolas Posocco	EURA NOVA, Belgium
Cedric Pradalier	GeorgiaTech Lorraine, France
Paul Prasse	University of Potsdam, Germany
Mahardhika Pratama	University of South Australia, Australia
Francesca Pratesi	ISTI - CNR, Italy
Steven Prestwich	University College Cork, Ireland
Giulia Preti	CentAI, Italy
Philippe Preux	Inria, France
Shalini Priya	Oak Ridge National Laboratory, USA

Ricardo Prudencio	Universidade Federal de Pernambuco, Brazil
Luca Putelli	Università degli Studi di Brescia, Italy
Peter van der Putten	Leiden University, the Netherlands
Chuan Qin	Baidu, China
Jixiang Qing	Ghent University, Belgium
Jolin Qu	Western Sydney University, Australia
Nicolas Quesada	Polytechnique Montreal, Canada
Teeradaj Racharak	Japan Advanced Institute of Science and Technology, Japan
Krystian Radlak	Warsaw University of Technology, Poland
Sandro Radovanovic	University of Belgrade, Serbia
Md Masudur Rahman	Purdue University, USA
Ankita Raj	Indian Institute of Technology Delhi, India
Herilalaina Rakotoarison	Inria, France
Alexander Rakowski	Hasso Plattner Institute, Germany
Jan Ramon	Inria, France
Sascha Ranftl	Graz University of Technology, Austria
Aleksandra Rashkovska Koceva	Jožef Stefan Institute, Slovenia
S. Ravi	Biocomplexity Institute, USA
Jesse Read	Ecole Polytechnique, France
David Reich	Universität Potsdam, Germany
Marina Reyboz	CEA, LIST, France
Pedro Ribeiro	University of Porto, Portugal
Rita P. Ribeiro	University of Porto, Portugal
Piera Riccio	ELLIS Unit Alicante Foundation, Spain
Christophe Rigotti	INSA Lyon, France
Matteo Riondato	Amherst College, USA
Mateus Riva	Telecom ParisTech, France
Kit Rodolfa	CMU, USA
Christophe Rodrigues	DVRC Pôle Universitaire Léonard de Vinci, France
Simon Rodríguez-Santana	ICMAT, Spain
Gaetano Rossiello	IBM Research, USA
Mohammad Rostami	University of Southern California, USA
Franz Rothlauf	Mainz Universität, Germany
Celine Rouveirol	Université Paris-Nord, France
Arjun Roy	Freie Universität Berlin, Germany
Joze Rozanec	Josef Stefan International Postgraduate School, Slovenia
Salvatore Ruggieri	University of Pisa, Italy
Marko Ruman	UTIA, AV CR, Czechia
Ellen Rushe	University College Dublin, Ireland

Dawid Rymarczyk	Jagiellonian University, Poland
Amal Saadallah	TU Dortmund, Germany
Khaled Mohammed Saifuddin	Georgia State University, USA
Hajer Salem	AUDENSIEL, France
Francesco Salvetti	Politecnico di Torino, Italy
Roberto Santana	University of the Basque Country (UPV/EHU), Spain
KC Santosh	University of South Dakota, USA
Somdeb Sarkhel	Adobe, USA
Yuya Sasaki	Osaka University, Japan
Yücel Saygın	Sabancı Universitesi, Turkey
Patrick Schäfer	Humboldt-Universität zu Berlin, Germany
Alexander Schiendorfer	Technische Hochschule Ingolstadt, Germany
Peter Schlicht	Volkswagen Group Research, Germany
Daniel Schmidt	Monash University, Australia
Johannes Schneider	University of Liechtenstein, Liechtenstein
Steven Schockaert	Cardiff University, UK
Jens Schreiber	University of Kassel, Germany
Matthias Schubert	Ludwig-Maximilians-Universität München, Germany
Alexander Schulz	CITEC, Bielefeld University, Germany
Jan-Philipp Schulze	Fraunhofer AISEC, Germany
Andreas Schwung	Fachhochschule Südwestfalen, Germany
Vasile-Marian Scuturici	LIRIS, France
Raquel Sebastião	IEETA/DETI-UA, Portugal
Stanislav Selitskiy	University of Bedfordshire, UK
Edoardo Serra	Boise State University, USA
Lorenzo Severini	UniCredit, R&D Dept., Italy
Tapan Shah	GE, USA
Ammar Shaker	NEC Laboratories Europe, Germany
Shiv Shankar	University of Massachusetts, USA
Junming Shao	University of Electronic Science and Technology, China
Kartik Sharma	Georgia Institute of Technology, USA
Manali Sharma	Samsung, USA
Ariona Shashaj	Network Contacts, Italy
Betty Shea	University of British Columbia, Canada
Chengchao Shen	Central South University, China
Hailan Shen	Central South University, China
Jiawei Sheng	Chinese Academy of Sciences, China
Yongpan Sheng	Southwest University, China
Chongyang Shi	Beijing Institute of Technology, China

Youming Tao	Shandong University, China
Martin Tappler	Graz University of Technology, Austria
Garth Tarr	University of Sydney, Australia
Mohammad Tayebi	Simon Fraser University, Canada
Anastasios Tefas	Aristotle University of Thessaloniki, Greece
Maguelonne Teisseire	INRAE - UMR Tetis, France
Stefano Teso	University of Trento, Italy
Olivier Teste	IRIT, University of Toulouse, France
Maximilian Thiessen	TU Wien, Austria
Eleftherios Tiakas	Aristotle University of Thessaloniki, Greece
Hongda Tian	University of Technology Sydney, Australia
Alessandro Tibo	Aalborg University, Denmark
Aditya Srinivas Timmaraju	Facebook, USA
Christos Tjortjis	International Hellenic University, Greece
Ljupco Todorovski	University of Ljubljana, Slovenia
Laszlo Toka	BME, Hungary
Ancy Tom	University of Minnesota, Twin Cities, USA
Panagiotis Traganitis	Michigan State University, USA
Cuong Tran	Syracuse University, USA
Minh-Tuan Tran	KAIST, South Korea
Giovanni Trappolini	Sapienza University of Rome, Italy
Volker Tresp	LMU, Germany
Yu-Chee Tseng	National Yang Ming Chiao Tung University, Taiwan
Maria Tzelepi	Aristotle University of Thessaloniki, Greece
Willy Ugarte	University of Applied Sciences (UPC), Peru
Antti Ukkonen	University of Helsinki, Finland
Abhishek Kumar Umrawal	Purdue University, USA
Athena Vakal	Aristotle University, Greece
Matias Valdenegro Toro	University of Groningen, the Netherlands
Maaike Van Roy	KU Leuven, Belgium
Dinh Van Tran	University of Freiburg, Germany
Fabio Vandin	University of Padova, Italy
Valerie Vaquet	CITEC, Bielefeld University, Germany
Iraklis Varlamis	Harokopio University of Athens, Greece
Santiago Velasco-Forero	MINES ParisTech, France
Bruno Veloso	Porto, Portugal
Dmytro Velychko	Carl von Ossietzky Universität Oldenburg, Germany
Sreekanth Vempati	Myntra, India
Sebastián Ventura Soto	University of Cordoba, Portugal
Rosana Veroneze	LBiC, Brazil

Yuandong Wang	Tsinghua University, China
Yue Wang	Microsoft Research, USA
Yun Cheng Wang	University of Southern California, USA
Zhaonan Wang	University of Tokyo, Japan
Zhaoxia Wang	SMU, Singapore
Zhiwei Wang	University of Chinese Academy of Sciences, China
Zihan Wang	Shandong University, China
Zijie J. Wang	Georgia Tech, USA
Dilusha Weeraddana	CSIRO, Australia
Pascal Welke	University of Bonn, Germany
Tobias Weller	University of Mannheim, Germany
Jörg Wicker	University of Auckland, New Zealand
Lena Wiese	Goethe University Frankfurt, Germany
Michael Wilbur	Vanderbilt University, USA
Moritz Wolter	Bonn University, Germany
Bin Wu	Beijing University of Posts and Telecommunications, China
Bo Wu	Renmin University of China, China
Jiancan Wu	University of Science and Technology of China, China
Jiantao Wu	University of Jinan, China
Ou Wu	Tianjin University, China
Yang Wu	Chinese Academy of Sciences, China
Yiqing Wu	University of Chinese Academic of Science, China
Yuejia Wu	Inner Mongolia University, China
Bin Xiao	University of Ottawa, Canada
Zhiwen Xiao	Southwest Jiaotong University, China
Ruobing Xie	WeChat, Tencent, China
Zikang Xiong	Purdue University, USA
Depeng Xu	University of North Carolina at Charlotte, USA
Jian Xu	Citadel, USA
Jiarong Xu	Fudan University, China
Kunpeng Xu	University of Sherbrooke, Canada
Ning Xu	Southeast University, China
Xianghong Xu	Tsinghua University, China
Sangeeta Yadav	Indian Institute of Science, India
Mehrdad Yaghoobi	University of Edinburgh, UK
Makoto Yamada	RIKEN AIP/Kyoto University, Japan
Akihiro Yamaguchi	Toshiba Corporation, Japan
Anil Yaman	Vrije Universiteit Amsterdam, the Netherlands

Hao Yan   Washington University in St Louis, USA
Qiao Yan   Shenzhen University, China
Chuang Yang   University of Tokyo, Japan
Deqing Yang   Fudan University, China
Haitian Yang   Chinese Academy of Sciences, China
Renchi Yang   National University of Singapore, Singapore
Shaofu Yang   Southeast University, China
Yang Yang   Nanjing University of Science and Technology,
                             China
Yang Yang   Northwestern University, USA
Yiyang Yang   Guangdong University of Technology, China
Yu Yang   The Hong Kong Polytechnic University, China
Peng Yao   University of Science and Technology of China,
                             China
Vithya Yogarajan   University of Auckland, New Zealand
Tetsuya Yoshida   Nara Women's University, Japan
Hong Yu   Chongqing Laboratory of Comput. Intelligence,
                             China
Wenjian Yu   Tsinghua University, China
Yanwei Yu   Ocean University of China, China
Ziqiang Yu   Yantai University, China
Sha Yuan   Beijing Academy of Artificial Intelligence, China
Shuhan Yuan   Utah State University, USA
Mingxuan Yue   Google, USA
Aras Yurtman   KU Leuven, Belgium
Nayyar Zaidi   Deakin University, Australia
Zelin Zang   Zhejiang University & Westlake University, China
Masoumeh Zareapoor   Shanghai Jiao Tong University, China
Hanqing Zeng   USC, USA
Tieyong Zeng   The Chinese University of Hong Kong, China
Bin Zhang   South China University of Technology, China
Bob Zhang   University of Macau, Macao, China
Hang Zhang   National University of Defense Technology,
                             China
Huaizheng Zhang   Nanyang Technological University, Singapore
Jiangwei Zhang   Tencent, China
Jinwei Zhang   Cornell University, USA
Jun Zhang   Tsinghua University, China
Lei Zhang   Virginia Tech, USA
Luxin Zhang   Worldline/Inria, France
Mimi Zhang   Trinity College Dublin, Ireland
Qi Zhang   University of Technology Sydney, Australia

Qiyiwen Zhang	University of Pennsylvania, USA
Teng Zhang	Huazhong University of Science and Technology, China
Tianle Zhang	University of Exeter, UK
Xuan Zhang	Renmin University of China, China
Yang Zhang	University of Science and Technology of China, China
Yaqian Zhang	University of Waikato, New Zealand
Yu Zhang	University of Illinois at Urbana-Champaign, USA
Zhengbo Zhang	Beihang University, China
Zhiyuan Zhang	Peking University, China
Heng Zhao	Shenzhen Technology University, China
Mia Zhao	Airbnb, USA
Tong Zhao	Snap Inc., USA
Qinkai Zheng	Tsinghua University, China
Xiangping Zheng	Renmin University of China, China
Bingxin Zhou	University of Sydney, Australia
Bo Zhou	Baidu, Inc., China
Min Zhou	Huawei Technologies, China
Zhipeng Zhou	University of Science and Technology of China, China
Hui Zhu	Chinese Academy of Sciences, China
Kenny Zhu	SJTU, China
Lingwei Zhu	Nara Institute of Science and Technology, Japan
Mengying Zhu	Zhejiang University, China
Renbo Zhu	Peking University, China
Yanmin Zhu	Shanghai Jiao Tong University, China
Yifan Zhu	Tsinghua University, China
Bartosz Zieliński	Jagiellonian University, Poland
Sebastian Ziesche	Bosch Center for Artificial Intelligence, Germany
Indre Zliobaite	University of Helsinki, Finland
Gianlucca Zuin	UFM, Brazil

Program Committee Members, Demo Track

Hesam Amoualian	WholeSoft Market, France
Georgios Balikas	Salesforce, France
Giannis Bekoulis	Vrije Universiteit Brussel, Belgium
Ludovico Boratto	University of Cagliari, Italy
Michelangelo Ceci	University of Bari, Italy
Abdulkadir Celikkanat	Technical University of Denmark, Denmark

Tania Cerquitelli	Informatica Politecnico di Torino, Italy
Mel Chekol	Utrecht University, the Netherlands
Charalampos Chelmis	University at Albany, USA
Yagmur Gizem Cinar	Amazon, France
Eustache Diemert	Criteo AI Lab, France
Sophie Fellenz	TU Kaiserslautern, Germany
James Foulds	University of Maryland, Baltimore County, USA
Jhony H. Giraldo	Télécom Paris, France
Parantapa Goswami	Rakuten Institute of Technology, Rakuten Group, Japan
Derek Greene	University College Dublin, Ireland
Lili Jiang	Umeå University, Sweden
Bikash Joshi	Elsevier, the Netherlands
Alexander Jung	Aalto University, Finland
Zekarias Kefato	KTH Royal Institute of Technology, Sweden
Ilkcan Keles	Aalborg University, Denmark
Sammy Khalife	Johns Hopkins University, USA
Tuan Le	New Mexico State University, USA
Ye Liu	Salesforce, USA
Fragkiskos Malliaros	CentraleSupelec, France
Hamid Mirisaee	AMLRightSource, France
Robert Moro	Kempelen Institute of Intelligent Technologies, Slovakia
Iosif Mporas	University of Hertfordshire, UK
Giannis Nikolentzos	Ecole Polytechnique, France
Eirini Ntoutsi	Freie Universität Berlin, Germany
Frans Oliehoek	Delft University of Technology, the Netherlands
Nora Ouzir	CentraleSupélec, France
Özlem Özgöbek	Norwegian University of Science and Technology, Norway
Manos Papagelis	York University, UK
Shichao Pei	University of Notre Dame, USA
Botao Peng	Chinese Academy of Sciences, China
Antonia Saravanou	National and Kapodistrian University of Athens, Greece
Rik Sarkar	University of Edinburgh, UK
Vera Shalaeva	Inria Lille-Nord, France
Kostas Stefanidis	Tampere University, Finland
Nikolaos Tziortziotis	Jellyfish, France
Davide Vega	Uppsala University, Sweden
Sagar Verma	CentraleSupelec, France
Yanhao Wang	East China Normal University, China

Zhirong Yang   Norwegian University of Science and Technology, Norway

Xiangyu Zhao   City University of Hong Kong, Hong Kong, China

Sponsors

Contents – Part VI

Applications

Applications: Transportation

Demo Track

Time Series

Few-Shot Forecasting of Time-Series with Heterogeneous Channels

Lukas Brinkmeyer$^{(\boxtimes)}$ ⓘ, Rafael Rego Drumond$^{(\boxtimes)}$ ⓘ, Johannes Burchert,
and Lars Schmidt-Thieme ⓘ

University of Hildesheim, Hildesheim, Germany
{brinkmeyer,radrumond,burchert,schmidt-thieme}@ismll.uni-hildesheim.de

Abstract. Learning complex time series forecasting models usually requires a large amount of data, as each model is trained from scratch for each task/data set. Leveraging learning experience with similar datasets is a well-established technique for classification problems called few-shot classification. However, existing approaches cannot be applied to time-series forecasting because i) multivariate time-series datasets have different channels, and ii) forecasting is principally different from classification. In this paper, we formalize the problem of few-shot forecasting of time-series with heterogeneous channels for the first time. Extending recent work on heterogeneous attributes in vector data, we develop a model composed of permutation-invariant deep set-blocks which incorporate a temporal embedding. We assemble the first meta-dataset of 40 multivariate time-series datasets and show through experiments that our model provides a good generalization, outperforming baselines carried over from simpler scenarios that either fail to learn across tasks or miss temporal information.

Keywords: Few-shot learning · Time-series forecasting · Meta-learning

1 Introduction

Time-series research is a central area in the field of machine learning and is widely present in real-life problems and applications ranging from health to the financial sector [23,24], with time-series data being an essential modality in all of the industry. In particular, time-series forecasting has been in focus of research as it strives to forecast variables over a future time horizon which applies to most data currently being collected. Forecasts can be made for a complete horizon or just a single point in time. Forecasting on univariate time-series, meaning

---

L. Brinkmeyer and R. Drumond—Equal contribution.

Supplementary Information The online version contains supplementary material available at https://doi.org/10.1007/978-3-031-26422-1_1.

a signal that varies over time and comes without covariates that contain additional information, e.g., the day of the week, is a well-researched area, spanning decades of work with classical approaches being well-studied for all kinds of problem settings [3,41]. Recently, deep learning approaches are becoming more popular in this area, showing to outperform classical approaches when a sufficient amount of training data is available [28]. However, often this is not the case as many time-series datasets are limited in size, giving classical approaches the edge [29]. Specifically, in the case of multivariate time-series data, this is a common problem because datasets have different sets of covariates, making it impossible to learn joint model attributes. Research for time-series shares a lot of commonality with research on image data since both areas are just special cases of structural data. As an example, both benefit from using convolutional networks and transformer-based approaches. However, one main difference in the respective state-of-the-art models is that the best approaches in computer vision rely almost exclusively on a deep feature extractor [13,47]. These models are pretrained on vast amounts of data pooled from various sources with a trend toward ever-larger collections (e.g. Imagenet [8], JFT-300M [16], JFT-3B [5]) to facilitate the ever-growing models, which nowadays consist of several billion parameters [6]. Meanwhile, this is not easily possible on time-series data due to heterogeneous covariates. Thus, virtually all models are just trained on limited single tasks of time-series data. Looking at the state-of-the-art in the area of computer vision, our aim is to enable the training of a single model across a larger pool of various time-series datasets. The M4 competition was held with that objective [28], by assembling a dataset consisting of 100.000 time-series from various datasets and domains, they analyzed the performance of forecasting approaches when applied to various tasks at once. The clear winner was a hybrid deep learning model by Smyl et al. [43] outperforming any statistical model. However, the competition was limited to univariate time-series data to avoid the problem of dealing with heterogeneous channels and did not introduce unseen datasets in the test evaluation. Most real-world applications involve multivariate time-series data since a set of covariates is almost always given, which can aid forecasting greatly. These covariate channels can be, for example, additional sensors or simple information about the respective day and month.

Learning a single model on a set of different tasks can be achieved through meta-learning. Meta-learning has been hugely successful in various areas of machine learning, with a special focus on computer vision and few-shot image recognition in particular. In contrast to classical machine learning, where a model is typically trained on a single dataset for one specific task, meta-learning aims at learning from a distribution of tasks which can vary in their target [12,34] or even their predictors [4,19]. Meta-learning techniques have been successfully applied to various areas of machine learning including few-shot classification [17], hyperparameter optimization [11,20], reinforcement learning [15] and neural architecture search [25]. In particular, research in few-shot learning has seen an immense rise in popularity, with methods undergoing fundamental changes and benchmarks significantly improving over a very short period of time. Motivated by the fact that humans require only a few examples to correctly classify previously unseen objects based on their past experience, few-shot learning strives to learn models which can generalize to novel tasks based on task-agnostic information extracted from a large set of tasks. Most meta-learning approaches still require a homogeneous representation across tasks, rendering them not feasible in the application to multivariate time-series tasks with heterogeneous channels. In recent works, various approaches were published to enable machine learning on sets by introducing permutation-invariant and equivariant layers [30,53]. The work of Iwata et al. [19] incorporated these permutation-invariant layers in a few-shot learning approach to enable learning on vector data with heterogeneous attributes. Encouraged by these findings, we propose the first model for few-shot forecasting on time-series tasks with heterogeneous channels. Our main contributions are as follows:

1. We formalize the problem of few-shot forecasting of time-series with heterogeneous channels for the first time.
2. We develop a model for this new problem that extends prior work on vector data in a principled way.
3. We assemble the first meta-dataset of 40 multivariate time-series datasets and thus provide a public benchmark for future research.
4. We show that our model provides a good generalization, outperforming baselines carried over from simpler scenarios that either fail to learn across tasks or miss temporal information.

2   Related Work

There exists a vast amount of research on time-series forecasting and few-shot learning in literature, but the intersection of the two is still very limited, with no existing approaches dealing with few-shot forecasting for time-series tasks with heterogeneous channels. In this section, we will discuss the research of these related areas in a concise way and point out the most important distinctions.

Time-series forecasting focuses on identifying temporal patterns in given data. Historically this was done with methods like ARIMA [3]. In the field of machine learning, CNN and RNN architectures [39,41] were used to significantly outperform these methods. A further improvement came with the incorporation of attention layers [48] in time-series models [38]. While proving to be very effective, the quadratic complexity of attention comes with a high computational cost. Recent architectures like the Reformer [22], Yformer [27], and Informer [54] focused on reducing this cost by introducing restricted attention layers to effectively approximate the full attention mechanism. Currently, the best performing model architectures are SCINet [26] and N-BEATS [37] on all common datasets and we will compare against them as baselines.

In relation to the problem setting in this work, learning across time-series stemming from different datasets has also been the goal of the popular M4 time-series forecasting competition [28]. However, it was limited to univariate time-series and, more importantly, designed as a classical forecasting problem and not a meta-learning one, meaning that the test set only contained future windows of datasets seen during training. In contrast, our work aims at generalizing to a new time-series dataset during testing, which renders the winning approaches of the M4 competition not applicable to our problem. **Few-Shot Learning** describes a subarea of meta-learning that deals with evaluating tasks of unseen classes or even datasets with very few labeled samples [51]. By learning from a large collection of related tasks, the model is trained to capture task-agnostic knowledge, which can then be used for a fast adaptation to a novel task that shares this similarity. Different approaches have been proposed with this goal in mind. Gradient-based methods rely on second-order gradient information that is passed across tasks to optimize meta-parameters [12, 33, 40]. Neighbor-based approaches learn a metric embedding space to compare novel tasks [44, 49] while memory-based approaches rely on recurrent components to memorize a representation of the previous tasks [31, 42].

All these methods, however, require a homogeneous predictor and target space in order to learn a joint distribution. One of the first methods to attempt few-shot learning on homogeneous predictors was CHAMELEON [4], which used a convolutional encoder to align tasks from similar domains to a common attribute space before utilizing gradient-based few-shot methods. Similarly, other works tried to learn across tasks with varied label spaces [9, 34]. Finally, Iwata et al. [19] proposed a model that uses deep sets [53] based blocks to compute a task-embedding over predictor and targets of training samples (support data), which then can be combined with new unlabeled samples (query data) to perform classification or regression without the need of retraining or fine-tuning, similar to neighbor-based approaches (we will refer to this method as HETNET throughout the rest of the paper). The main advantage of HETNET is that, since it uses the deep sets formalization, it is invariant to the order of attributes and samples in both query and support set. So far, these approaches are limited to simple vector data and not applicable to structural data.

Few-Shot Learning for Time-Series Data. Few works have been published that apply few-shot learning or even meta-learning to time-series data. We argue that this is due to the fact that, in contrast to image data, it is not readily possible to learn a single feature extractor across tasks stemming from different datasets when dealing with multivariate time-series data. Thus, published approaches can be divided into two groups. The first group of approaches utilizes meta-learning techniques to train across slices of the same time-series with homogeneous channels. This includes approaches that combine classical time-series regression with gradient-based meta-learning [1] and approaches that utilize metric-based meta-learning in combination with shapelet learning [46]. These methods are not applicable to our problem setting as they are not equipped to learn across tasks with heterogeneous channels.

Second, there are meta-learning approaches for time-series data that limit their problem setting to univariate time-series tasks in order to learn a single feature extractor without having to deal with heterogeneous channels. Iwata et al. [18] proposed a method to embed tasks through BiLSTM and regular LSTM layers. Narwariya et al. [32] utilized Resnet to embed each time-series to a vector, and then trained across tasks with REPTILE [33] on a meta-dataset of 41 univariate UCR datasets. Lastly, Oreshkin et al. [36] showed how N-BEATS can be used for zero-shot time-series forecasting by rephrasing it in a meta-learning formalization. None of these approaches are capable of dealing with multivariate time-series tasks with heterogeneous channels, which is the focus of this work. Nevertheless, we compare our approach against N-BEATS for zero-shot time-series forecasting by using only the target channel to show that incorporating covariate channels is absolutely necessary for this problem setup. Our method called TIMEHETNET serves as the first few-shot time-series forecasting model for multivariate time-series data that can learn across different tasks with heterogeneous channels.

3 Methodology

In this work, we want to propose the first work in the intersection of few-shot learning and multivariate time-series forecasting. We will first formalize the problem of time-series forecasting on a single task before extending it to a few-shot learning setting across a meta-dataset of tasks with heterogeneous channels.

3.1 Problem Setting

In the **(vanilla) time-series forecasting problem**, a time-series x with C channels is a finite sequence of vectors in $\mathbb{R}^C$. Their space is denoted by $\mathbb{R}^{* \times C} := \bigcup_{T \in \mathbb{N}} \mathbb{R}^{T \times C}$ with time-series length $|x| := T$. Time-series forecasting data with a single univariate target time-series and C predictor channels is then given by:

$$\mathcal{D} := \{(x_1, y_1, x_1', y_1'), ..., (x_N, y_N, x_N', y_N')\} \in \mathcal{X} \times \mathcal{Y} \tag{1}$$

with $x, x' \in \mathbb{R}^{* \times C}$ and $y, y' \in \mathbb{R}^*$, sampled from an unknown distribution p, where x, y are predictors and targets up to a reference time point $t_0 - 1$ and x', y' denote the corresponding future predictors and targets starting from time point t_0 up to T. The predictors can also be described as future covariate information for the target. Given a loss function $l : \mathbb{R}^* \times \mathbb{R}^* \to \mathbb{R}$, we want to learn a function $\hat{y} : \mathbb{R}^{* \times C} \times \mathbb{R}^* \times \mathbb{R}^{* \times C} \to \mathbb{R}^*$ called model with minimal expected loss over the data:

$$\mathbb{E}_{(x,y,x',y') \sim p} \quad l(y', \hat{y}(x, y, x')) \tag{2}$$

Extending this formalization, the problem of **few-shot time-series forecasting across tasks with heterogeneous channels** is then given by a sample $D := \{(\mathcal{D}_1^s, \mathcal{D}_1^q), ..., (\mathcal{D}_m^s, \mathcal{D}_m^q)\}$ called meta-dataset of pairs $\mathcal{D}^s, \mathcal{D}^q \in (\mathcal{X} \times \mathcal{Y})$ from an unknown distribution p_m of dataset pairs, and a function $\mathcal{L} : \mathcal{Y} \times \mathcal{Y} \to \mathbb{R}$. Each pair is called a task and consists of support data D^s for which the full instance (x, y, x', y') is known during prediction time and the query data D^q for which the future target y' is not known during prediction time. The number of predictor channels C varies across tasks between $C_{\min}$ and $C_{\max}$. In few-shot learning, the number of samples N^s in the support data D^s is typically low. We want to find a function $\hat{y} : \mathcal{X} \times (\mathcal{X} \times \mathcal{Y})^* \to \mathcal{Y}$ called meta-model with minimal expected loss:

$$\mathbb{E}_{(\mathcal{D}^s, \mathcal{D}^q) \sim p_m} \frac{1}{|\mathcal{D}^q|} \sum_{(x,y,x',y') \in \mathcal{D}^q} \mathcal{L}(y', \hat{y}(x, y, x', \mathcal{D}^s)) \tag{3}$$

In this work, the loss $\mathcal{L}$ is chosen to be the mean squared error (MSE) averaged over the query datasets of our meta-dataset. By weighting only a single time step of the target y', we can learn a point-forecasting model with a specific focus on that one point.

3.2 Model Formulation

In this work, we extend HETNET [19] which is a permutation-invariant model for few-shot classification on vector data with heterogeneous attributes. Their model relies on nested deep set-blocks [53] which were first published as a means to enable machine learning models to process sets by introducing a family of permutation-invariant functions. Each deep set-block consists of an inner function f that is applied on each element of the set and an outer function g which is applied after aggregating the output of f such that the block is permutation-invariant to the order of elements. The architecture consists of an inference network that extracts latent task-dependent features of the support data D^s, which are then used by the prediction network in conjunction with the query data $(x, y, x') \in D^q$ to generate the forecast for the future targets y' of a given task.

Inference Network. We adapted the formalization of HETNET [19] to our proposed problem setting by extending it from simple vector data to a forecasting task on structural data. A conceptual depiction of our model is shown in Fig. 1. First, using the support data D^s we compute the target embeddings $\bar{w}$ and $\bar{c}$ for y and y' respectively, and a predictor embedding $\bar{v}_i$ for each predictor channel $i \in C$ by aggregating across the instances such that the block is permutation-invariant to their order:

$$\bar{v}_i = g_{\bar{v}} \left(\frac{1}{N} \sum_{n=1}^{N} f_{\bar{v}}([x_{ni}, x'_{ni}]) \right) \quad \forall i \in C \tag{4}$$

$$\bar{w} = g_{\bar{w}} \left(\frac{1}{N} \sum_{n=1}^{N} f_{\bar{w}}(y_n) \right), \quad \bar{c} = g_{\bar{c}} \left(\frac{1}{N} \sum_{n=1}^{N} f_{\bar{c}}(y'_n) \right)$$

Here, $\bar{v} \in \mathbb{R}^{C \times T \times K}$ with K being the latent output dimension of $g_{\bar{v}}$, T the length of the time-series task at hand, N the number of samples in the support data D^s and $[\cdot, \cdot]$ a concatenation. Through concatenation of the embeddings with the respective support data followed by another deep-set block, we can generate an

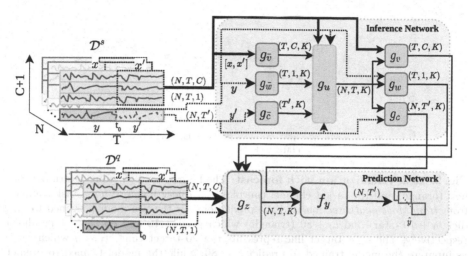

Fig. 1. TIMEHETNET architecture. Values in parenthesis represent the output shape of each layer. x and y represent the predictor and target channels respectively, while x' and y' represent future predictor and targets. N represents the number of samples in the set, T represents the maximum time length, C describes the number of channels/attributes in each sample. K represents the latent space embedding. T' represents the number of future points of y' we want to predict. For readability: Raw predictors are bold, raw targets are dotted, and latent tensors are regular arrows.

embedding for each instance in the support data D^s through aggregation over the predictor channels:

$$u_n = g_u \left(\frac{1}{C} \sum_{i=1}^{C} \left(f_u([x_{ni}, x'_{ni}, \bar{v}_i]) \right) + f_o([y_n, \bar{w}]) + f_p([y'_n, \bar{c}]) \right) \quad \forall n \in N \quad (5)$$

where C is the number of predictor channels of the task and $u \in \mathbb{R}^{N \times T \times K}$. By concatenating these instance-wise embeddings with the respective support data before repeating the block structure of Eq. 4, we can again generate the predictor and target embeddings, only this time they are computed with regard to the entire support set. The embeddings for the future target y' are not aggregated over the number of instances, as they are fed directly into the final network f_y generating the forecast on an instance-level:

$$v_i = g_v \left(\frac{1}{N} \sum_{n=1}^{N} f_v([x_{ni}, x'_{ni}, u_n]) \right) \quad \forall i \in C \quad (6)$$

$$w = g_w \left(\frac{1}{N} \sum_{n=1}^{N} f_w([y_n, u_n]) \right), \quad c = f_c([y'_n, u_n])$$

Prediction Network. The embeddings for the predictors v and the past targets w are concatenated with the predictors x, x', and past target y of the query data

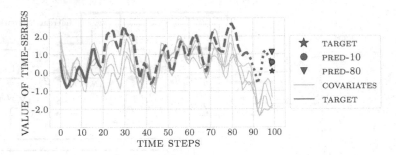

Fig. 2. Task visualization with forecast: The figure shows the four covariate channels (orange) and the target channel (purple) of a query instance for a task sampled from *HandMovementDirection*, and the predictions for the two models trained to predict $t_0 + 10$ (star) and $t_0 + 80$ (triangle) which predict 10 and 80 time steps ahead respectively. The solid target line represents the 20 target time steps y which serve as input to the model trained to predict $t_0 + 80$, while the model trained to predict $t_0 + 10$ receives the target data including the dashed line mark. The dotted line shows the target over the last 10 steps.

D^q. This concatenation is passed to a deep set-block consisting of networks g_z and f_z which compute the per-instance features:

$$z_n = g_z \left(\frac{1}{C} \sum_{i=1}^{I} f_z([x_{ni}, y_n, x'_{ni}, v_i, w]) \right) \quad \forall n \in N^q \qquad (7)$$

where N^q is the number of samples in D^q. Finally, the prediction for a query sample n is made by passing the embedding z of D^q and the embedding c of the future target of D^s to a final network f_y:

$$\hat{y}_n = f_y([z_n, c]) \qquad (8)$$

The full TIMEHETNET then contains the following neural networks $g_{\bar{v}}$, $f_{\bar{v}}$, $g_{\bar{w}}$, $f_{\bar{w}}$, $g_{\bar{c}}$, $f_{\bar{c}}$, g_u, f_u, f_o, f_p, g_v, f_v, g_w, f_w, f_c, g_z, f_z. We share the parameters between the network pairs $(f_{\hat{v}}, f_{\hat{w}}), (g_{\hat{v}}, g_{\hat{w}}), (f_v, f_w), (g_v, g_w)$.

4   Experimental Setup

In order to evaluate TIMEHETNET, we have performed an extensive evaluation by creating a meta-dataset to learn few-shot forecasting on multivariate time-series data and comparing the performance of our method to related baseline methods. In this section, we will describe our meta-dataset construction, our baseline methods, the experimental procedures with observed results, and finally, a discussion of our findings.

4.1   Meta-Dataset

In order to evaluate our approach, we assembled the first meta-dataset for few-shot forecasting on multivariate time-series data. For that purpose, we collected

40 multivariate time-series datasets consisting of popular forecasting datasets like the *ETT* and *ECL* [54], as well as datasets from the *Monash* time series forecasting archive, [14], 3 *Kaggle* datasets [35,45,50], the *UCR* and *UEA* time series archive [2,7], and also the sparse motion capture dataset *PeekDB* [10]. The details on all datasets are summarized in Table 3 (supplementary material). A single task is sampled from a dataset by randomly selecting between C_{min} and C_{max} of the channels, a random slice of the temporal dimension of size T and N_Q+N_S samples for the query and support split of the task. We normalized the channel of each task to mean zero and standard deviation one. In our experiments, we set the number of query and support instances to 20 each, the time length to 100, and varied the number of channels between 5 and 10. In case a dataset has only a single instance, we sample multiple temporal slices for a single task. Furthermore, one channel is selected to be the target channel, with the remaining channels serving as covariate information (during sampling, we make sure that the target channel is not included in the covariates). Finally, the last time step $t = 100$ of the target channel for a given instance is chosen as the future target y', while the last p time steps of the target channel y are removed, thus creating a multivariate time-series forecasting task with covariate information with the aim of forecasting p steps ahead. We evaluated our approach for $p = 1, 10, 80$ and 100, where $p = 1$ corresponds to forecasting the next time step $t + 1$ with the target channel y including the first 99 steps, and $p = 80$ to forecasting the time step $t + 80$ with the target channel including the first 20 time steps. The experiments with $p = 100$ demonstrate an uncontrolled scenario where only covariate channels are given in addition to the future target y' for the support instances. A visualization of a single task is given in Fig. 4 including the forecast of our approach.

4.2   Experimental Details

We conducted a 5-fold cross-validation with each fold having 8 datasets in meta-test, 8 in meta-validation, and 24 in meta-training. During each epoch of meta-training, we sample 10 meta-batches, where each meta-batch includes one task per dataset: 24 tasks in meta-training and 8 in meta-validation. For the sake of comparability, we generated 11.000 tasks for each dataset in meta-testing beforehand (1.000 tasks per channel size 5 to 10). The final meta-test performance can then be computed by evaluating the model on each of the 440.000 tasks in the fixed test set while guaranteeing comparability between different models. Instead of evaluating our model for the average loss over all time steps, we evaluate the model for individual time steps. By doing this, we want to emphasize the concrete performance differences for close and far events without overlap. For our approach TIMEHETNET, all networks f and g in the deep set-blocks consist of three layers. In all configurations, f_y is a feed-forward network. After optimizing the concrete architecture on the validation tasks, we selected GRU layers for the deep-set blocks formalized in Eqs. 4 and 7 and convolutional layers for 5 and 6. All hyperparameters for all approaches were optimized via grid search. Our model was trained with Adam [21] for a maximum number of 15.000 epochs with

Table 1. Experimental results across all folds. All scores represent mean squared error. Standard deviation is computed over 5 repeated experimental runs. Oracle channel gives the best possible performance if the best control channel is known. Bold-faced results represent the best scores.

Category	Method	$t_0 + 1$	$t_0 + 10$	$t_0 + 80$	$t_0 + 100$
Proposed	TIMEHETNET	**0.148**	**0.389**	**0.509**	**0.579**
	(ours)	**±0.003**	**±0.007**	**±0.006**	**±0.004**
Meta-Learning	HETNET[19]	0.178	0.413	0.524	0.582
		±0.002	±0.003	±0.003	±0.006
	ZERO PREDICTION	1.006	1.006	1.006	1.006
Heuristic	LAST TIME STEP	0.215	0.899	1.404	×
	AVG TIME STEP	0.867	0.867	0.867	0.867
	GRU	0.531	0.692	0.699	0.712
Single task	FCN [52]	0.631	0.791	0.806	0.871
	1D-FF	0.484	0.726	0.845	0.947
No covariates	N-BEATS [36]	0.193	0.677	0.924	×
		±0.002	±0.005	±0.006	×
	SCINET [26]	0.192	0.594	0.718	×
		±0.003	±0.006	±0.006	×
Oracle	Best Channel*	0.353	0.353	0.353	0.353

early stopping over the validation tasks. More details on our experimental setup and the concrete hyperparameters can be found in our supplementary material.

4.3   Baseline Methods

We evaluated our approach against baselines from different related problem settings since there is no approach that can learn across multivariate time-series tasks with heterogeneous channels to the best of our knowledge: a set of heuristics consisting of predicting the constant zero (ZERO PREDICTION) as our data is normalized to mean zero, predicting the last observed time step of the target channel (LAST TIME STEP), and predicting the average of the last time steps over the covariate channels (AVG TIME STEP). Moreover, we evaluate a set of models on each individual task in meta-test, namely a stacked GRU network (GRU), a fully-convolutional model (FCN) [52] and a feed-forward neural network which relies only on the last observed time step (1D-FF). Note that these models have a lower model complexity than the other approaches, as they are only trained on the support data of a single task without incorporating any other tasks. Additionally, we show the performance of a hypothetical oracle which gives the mean squared error between the target and the last time step of the closest covariate channel (ORACLE). This model can be used as a point of orientation for the upper limit of the information within the covariate channels and is not a feasible model.

Moreover, we evaluate a set of time-series forecasting models by training them across all datasets without using the covariate channels. Here, we select only the target channel y and the future target y' per task, similar to the setup of Oreshkin

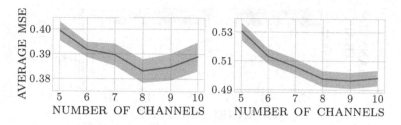

Fig. 3. Varying number of channels: Mean-squared error over the test tasks with fixed number of channels. Results are averaged over all five folds and five repetitions with the corresponding standard deviation (shade) for the experiment $t_0 + 10$ (left) and $t_0 + 80$ (right).

et al. [36]. In this setup we evaluate the current best model for time-series forecasting on *PapersWithCode*, SCINET, and the popular time-forecasting model N-BEATS [37] as it is shown as a successful model for zero-shot time-series forecasting on univariate data [36]. Evaluating the state-of-the-art forecasting models on the single-task level has proven to be infeasible, as a single task is too small for these architectures to train on, as well as too computationally expensive for all tasks in the test set. Lastly, we evaluate HETNET by feeding the last time-steps of x' and y of the time-series as it is the only few-shot learning model which can learn with heterogeneous attributes. The details on all baseline approaches and the training setup can be found in the supplementary material.

4.4   Results

The results for our main experiments can be seen in Table 1 stating the mean-squared error averaged over the test tasks of each fold. It is not useful to compute the standard deviation over cross-validation folds as each fold includes different datasets for which the expected losses naturally vary. Instead, we repeated the full 5-fold cross-validation experiment five times to compute a standard deviation. However, this was too computationally expensive for the models trained on each task from scratch. Thus it is only given for the approaches that train across tasks. Note that heuristical approaches have no standard deviation since they are completely deterministic, and the test tasks are pre-generated. This is the same reason why ZERO PREDICTION, AVG TIME STEP and ORACLE have the same performance for all experiments, as the test tasks only vary in what part of the target channel is given.

   Our approach is shown to outperform all of our baselines in all 4 scenarios. As expected, LAST TIME STEP yields competitive results for the $t_0 + 1$ experiments since oftentimes the next time step does not deviate too much. The closest baseline is HETNET which learns across tasks and utilizes the heterogeneous channels but does not incorporate any past temporal information. The approach is still significantly worse than our proposed model for $t_0 + 1$, $t_0 + 10$ and $t_0 + 80$ when looking at the standard deviation, suggesting that especially existing

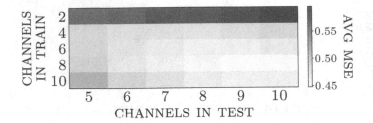

Fig. 4. Heatmap over channels: Performance of our approach for $t_0 + 80$ when trained and evaluated on a fixed task size. Results are averaged over five repetitions of the 5-fold cross validation. Train channels include $[2, 4, 6, 8, 10]$.

temporal information for the target channel aids the prediction. The models trained on a single task from scratch show an expected subpar performance as they can only learn from a single limited few-shot task. Moreover, the state-of-the-art time-series forecasting methods show a good performance on $t_0 + 1$ and $t_0 + 10$, but degrade a lot for $t_0 + 80$, which is the consequence of only relying on the target channel, while especially for $t_0 + 80$ the covariates are shown to be crucial. This fact is emphasized when evaluating the performance of ORACLE as it gives an upper limit on the achievable score when only considering the predictor channels. Note that there are no scores listed for approaches that rely solely on the target channel for $t_0 + 100$ as there is no past target y given in that setting.

4.5   Ablations

We conducted several ablation studies to analyze the robustness of our model with respect to the number of channels across tasks and to show the performance of different architectural choices. First, we analyzed the performance of our approach for $t_0 + 10$ and $t_0 + 80$ with respect to the number of predictor channels for a given novel test task. We show the aggregated results for this experiment in Fig. 2. We can see that the performance of our approach increases with the number of predictor channels up to 8 channels. Note that c channels here refer to one target channel and $c - 1$ predictor channels for each task. This suggests that our model successfully learned to process tasks independently of their number of channels. It can benefit from the fact that tasks with a higher number of randomly sampled channels are more likely to feature covariates that correlate to the target channel up to a certain point. In the case of predicting 10 steps ahead, the performance slightly degrades for tasks with more than 8 channels.

To investigate the robustness of our model to the number of predictor channels of the tasks in training, we repeated our experiments while limiting the tasks sampled in training to a fixed number of channels. In Fig. 3 we show the performance of our model for $t_0 + 80$ trained only on tasks with 2, 4, 6, 8 and 10 channels respectively, while evaluating it again for a fixed number of channels in

Table 2. Architectures ablation: Comparison of four different architecture setups.

Experiment	GRU-Corner	Conv-Corner	All GRU	All Conv
$t_0 + 80$	**0.509**	0.538	0.512	0.522
$t_0 + 10$	**0.389**	0.397	**0.389**	0.395

test. One can see that the model is generally robust to the number of channels in training, with the exception of training on tasks with only 2 channels, meaning only one predictor and one target channel. This is most likely due to the number of sampled training tasks that will not have a predictor channel that is sufficiently correlated to the target task. In accord with the previous ablation, there seems to be a slight performance optimum around tasks with 8 channels, while training on tasks with 10 channels and evaluating on tasks with 2 channels also degrades the performance.

Finally, we compare the performance of our model when changing the network design within the deep set blocks. Namely, we evaluate different combinations of convolutional and GRU layers to the one chosen in this work after optimizing the hyperparameters on the validation data. The results are shown in Table 2. The best architecture which is used throughout all our experiments utilizes stacked GRU layers in first the deep-set blocks formalized in Eq. 4 which receive the raw data input as well as the one before the final output layer in Eq. 7 which output the final embedding, while using 1D-convolutional layers in the intermediate blocks (*GRU-Corner*). Using only GRU layers (*All GRU*) degrades the performance by a slight margin while using convolutional layers at the beginning and end of the network is shown to be significantly worse (*Conv-Corner*). This indicates that the GRU blocks are adapting more easily to the very heterogeneous time-series tasks. For comparison reasons, we make our code available at https://github.com/radrumond/timehetnet.

5   Conclusion

In this work, we presented the first multivariate time-series forecasting model that works across tasks with heterogeneous channels. Currently, to the best of our knowledge, this is the first work to build a multivariate time-series meta-dataset for this type of meta task. Our model significantly outperforms all related baselines, which either fail to incorporate covariate information or cannot learn across tasks. This approach serves as a benchmark for future research in this area. In future work, we would like to explore the effects of different deep-set blocks and how the model behaves with different types of models and problems.

Acknowledgements. This work was supported by the Federal Ministry for Economic Affairs and Climate Action (BMWK), Germany, within the framework of the IIP-Ecosphere project (project number: 01MK20006D).

References

1. Arango, S.P., Heinrich, F., Madhusudhanan, K., Schmidt-Thieme, L.: Multimodal meta-learning for time series regression. In: Lemaire, V., Malinowski, S., Bagnall, A., Guyet, T., Tavenard, R., Ifrim, G. (eds.) AALTD 2021. LNCS (LNAI), vol. 13114, pp. 123–138. Springer, Cham (2021). https://doi.org/10.1007/978-3-030-91445-5_8
2. Bagnall, A., et al.: The UEA multivariate time series classification archive (2018). arXiv preprint arXiv:1811.00075 (2018)
3. Box, G.E.P., Jenkins, G.M.: Some recent advances in forecasting and control. J. R. Stat. Soc. Ser. C (Applied Statistics) 17(2), 91–109 (1968). http://www.jstor.org/stable/2985674
4. Brinkmeyer, L., Drumond, R.R., Scholz, R., Grabocka, J., Schmidt-Thieme, L.: Chameleon: learning model initializations across tasks with different schemas. arXiv preprint arXiv:1909.13576 (2019)
5. Chollet, F.: Xception: deep learning with depthwise separable convolutions. In: Proceedings of the IEEE Conference on Computer Vision and Pattern Recognition, pp. 1251–1258 (2017)
6. Dai, Z., Liu, H., Le, Q., Tan, M.: Coatnet: marrying convolution and attention for all data sizes. Advances in Neural IHou, R., Chang, H., Ma, B., Shan, S., and Chen, X. (2019). Cross attention network for few-shot classification. Advances in Neural Information Processing Systems, 32. Information Processing Systems 34 (2021)
7. Dau, H.A., et al.: The UCR time series archive. IEEE/CAA J. Automatica Sinica 6(6), 1293–1305 (2019)
8. Deng, J., et al.: Imagenet: A large-scale hierarchical image database. In: 2009 IEEE Conference on Computer Vision and Pattern Recognition, pp. 248–255. IEEE (2009)
9. Drumond, R.R., Brinkmeyer, L., Grabocka, J., Schmidt-Thieme, L.: Hidra: Head initialization across dynamic targets for robust architectures. In: Proceedings of the 2020 SIAM International Conference on Data Mining, pp. 397–405. SIAM (2020). https://epubs.siam.org/doi/abs/10.1137/1.9781611976236.45
10. Drumond, R.R., Marques, B.A., Vasconcelos, C.N., Clua, E.: Peek-an lstm recurrent network for motion classification from sparse data. In: VISIGRAPP (1: GRAPP), pp. 215–222 (2018)
11. Feurer, M., Springenberg, J., Hutter, F.: Initializing bayesian hyperparameter optimization via meta-learning. In: Proceedings of the AAAI Conference on Artificial Intelligence, vol. 29 (2015)
12. Finn, C., Abbeel, P., Levine, S.: Model-agnostic meta-learning for fast adaptation of deep networks. In: International Conference on Machine Learning, pp. 1126–1135. PMLR (2017)
13. Foret, P., Kleiner, A., Mobahi, H., Neyshabur, B.: Sharpness-aware minimization for efficiently improving generalization. arXiv preprint arXiv:2010.01412 (2020)
14. Godahewa, R., Bergmeir, C., Webb, G.I., Hyndman, R.J., Montero-Manso, P.: Monash time series forecasting archive. arXiv preprint arXiv:2105.06643 (2021)
15. Gupta, A., Mendonca, R., Liu, Y., Abbeel, P., Levine, S.: Meta-reinforcement learning of structured exploration strategies. In: Advances in Neural Information Processing Systems 31 (2018)
16. Hinton, G., Vinyals, O., Dean, J., et al.: Distilling the knowledge in a neural network. arXiv preprint arXiv:1503.02531 2(7) (2015)

17. Hou, R., Chang, H., Ma, B., Shan, S., Chen, X.: Cross attention network for few-shot classification. In: Advances in Neural Information Processing Systems, vol. 32 (2019)
18. Iwata, T., Kumagai, A.: Few-shot learning for time-series forecasting. arXiv preprint arXiv:2009.14379 (2020)
19. Iwata, T., Kumagai, A.: Meta-learning from tasks with heterogeneous attribute spaces. Adv. Neural Inf. Process. Syst. **33**, 6053–6063 (2020)
20. Jawed, S., Jomaa, H., Schmidt-Thieme, L., Grabocka, J.: Multi-task learning curve forecasting across hyperparameter configurations and datasets. In: Oliver, N., Pérez-Cruz, F., Kramer, S., Read, J., Lozano, J.A. (eds.) ECML PKDD 2021. LNCS (LNAI), vol. 12975, pp. 485–501. Springer, Cham (2021). https://doi.org/10.1007/978-3-030-86486-6_30
21. Kingma, D.P., Ba, J.: Adam: A method for stochastic optimization. arXiv preprint arXiv:1412.6980 (2014)
22. Kitaev, N., Kaiser, L., Levskaya, A.: Reformer: the efficient transformer. arXiv preprint arXiv:2001.04451 (2020)
23. Krollner, B., Vanstone, B.J., Finnie, G.R., et al.: Financial time series forecasting with machine learning techniques: a survey. In: ESANN (2010)
24. Lim, B., Zohren, S.: Time-series forecasting with deep learning: a survey. Philos. Trans. R. Society A **379**(2194), 20200209 (2021)
25. Liu, H., Simonyan, K., Yang, Y.: Darts: Differentiable architecture search. arXiv preprint arXiv:1806.09055 (2018)
26. Liu, M., Zeng, A., Xu, Z., Lai, Q., Xu, Q.: Time series is a special sequence: forecasting with sample convolution and interaction. arXiv preprint arXiv:2106.09305 (2021)
27. Madhusudhanan, K., Burchert, J., Duong-Trung, N., Born, S., Schmidt-Thieme, L.: Yformer: u-net inspired transformer architecture for far horizon time series forecasting. arXiv preprint arXiv:2110.08255 (2021)
28. Makridakis, S., Spiliotis, E., Assimakopoulos, V.: The m4 competition: results, findings, conclusion and way forward. Int. J. Forecast. **34**(4), 802–808 (2018)
29. Makridakis, S., Spiliotis, E., Assimakopoulos, V.: Statistical and machine learning forecasting methods: concerns and ways forward. PLoS ONE **13**(3), e0194889 (2018)
30. Maron, H., Ben-Hamu, H., Shamir, N., Lipman, Y.: Invariant and equivariant graph networks. arXiv preprint arXiv:1812.09902 (2018)
31. Munkhdalai, T., Yu, H.: Meta networks. In: International Conference on Machine Learning, pp. 2554–2563. PMLR (2017)
32. Narwariya, J., Malhotra, P., Vig, L., Shroff, G., Vishnu, T.: Meta-learning for few-shot time series classification. In: Proceedings of the 7th ACM IKDD CoDS and 25th COMAD, pp. 28–36 (2020)
33. Nichol, A., Achiam, J., Schulman, J.: On first-order meta-learning algorithms. arXiv preprint arXiv:1803.02999 (2018)
34. Oh, J., Yoo, H., Kim, C., Yun, S.Y.: BOIL: towards representation change for few-shot learning. In: International Conference on Learning Representations (2021). https://openreview.net/forum?id=umIdUL8rMH
35. Oliveira, E.M.: Quality prediction in a mining process. https://www.kaggle.com/datasets/shasun/tool-wear-detection-in-cnc-mill?select=README.txt
36. Oreshkin, B.N., Carpov, D., Chapados, N., Bengio, Y.: Meta-learning framework with applications to zero-shot time-series forecasting. arXiv preprint arXiv:2002.02887 (2020)

37. Oreshkin, B.N., Carpov, D., Chapados, N., Bengio, Y.: N-beats: Neural basis expansion analysis for interpretable time series forecasting. In: International Conference on Learning Representations (2020). https://openreview.net/forum?id=r1ecqn4YwB
38. Qin, Y., Song, D., Chen, H., Cheng, W., Jiang, G., Cottrell, G.: A dual-stage attention-based recurrent neural network for time series prediction. arXiv preprint arXiv:1704.02971 (2017)
39. Rangapuram, S.S., Seeger, M.W., Gasthaus, J., Stella, L., Wang, Y., Januschowski, T.: Deep state space models for time series forecasting. In: Bengio, S., Wallach, H., Larochelle, H., Grauman, K., Cesa-Bianchi, N., Garnett, R. (eds.) Advances in Neural Information Processing Systems. vol. 31. Curran Associates, Inc. (2018). https://proceedings.neurips.cc/paper/2018/file/5cf68969fb67aa6082363a6d4e6468e2-Paper.pdf
40. Rusu, A.A., Rao, D., Sygnowski, J., Vinyals, O., Pascanu, R., Osindero, S., Hadsell, R.: Meta-learning with latent embedding optimization. arXiv preprint arXiv:1807.05960 (2018)
41. Salinas, D., Flunkert, V., Gasthaus, J., Januschowski, T.: Deepar: probabilistic forecasting with autoregressive recurrent networks. Int. J. Forecast. **36**(3), 1181–1191 (2020)
42. Santoro, A., Bartunov, S., Botvinick, M., Wierstra, D., Lillicrap, T.: Meta-learning with memory-augmented neural networks. In: International Conference on Machine Learning, pp. 1842–1850. PMLR (2016)
43. Smyl, S.: A hybrid method of exponential smoothing and recurrent neural networks for time series forecasting. Int. J. Forecast. **36**(1), 75–85 (2020)
44. Snell, J., Swersky, K., Zemel, R.: Prototypical networks for few-shot learning. In: Advances in Neural Information Processing Systems, vol. 30 (2017)
45. Sun, S.: Cnc mill tool wear. https://www.kaggle.com/datasets/shasun/tool-wear-detection-in-cnc-mill?select=README.txt
46. Tang, W., Liu, L., Long, G.: Interpretable time-series classification on few-shot samples. In: 2020 International Joint Conference on Neural Networks (IJCNN), pp. 1–8. IEEE (2020)
47. Tolstikhin, I.O., et al.: Mlp-mixer: an all-mlp architecture for vision. In: Advances in Neural Information Processing Systems (2021)
48. Vaswani, A., et al.: Attention is all you need. In: Advances in Neural Information Processing Systems, pp. 5998–6008 (2017)
49. Vinyals, O., Blundell, C., Lillicrap, T., Wierstra, D., et al.: Matching networks for one shot learning. In: Advances in Neural Information Processing Systems, vol. 29 (2016)
50. Von Birgelen, A., Buratti, D., Mager, J., Niggemann, O.: Self-organizing maps for anomaly localization and predictive maintenance in cyber-physical production systems. Procedia cirp **72**, 480–485 (2018)
51. Wang, Y., Yao, Q., Kwok, J.T., Ni, L.M.: Generalizing from a few examples: a survey on few-shot learning. ACM Comput. Surv. (CSUR) **53**(3), 1–34 (2020)
52. Wang, Z., Yan, W., Oates, T.: Time series classification from scratch with deep neural networks: a strong baseline. In: 2017 International joint conference on neural networks (IJCNN), pp. 1578–1585. IEEE (2017)
53. Zaheer, M., Kottur, S., Ravanbakhsh, S., Poczos, B., Salakhutdinov, R.R., Smola, A.J.: Deep sets. In: Advances in Neural Information Processing Systems, vol. 30 (2017)
54. Zhou, H., et al.: Informer: beyond efficient transformer for long sequence time-series forecasting. In: Proceedings of AAAI (2021)

Online Adaptive Multivariate Time Series Forecasting

Amal Saadallah[✉], Hanna Mykula, and Katharina Morik

Artificial Intelligence Group, Department of Computer Science, TU Dortmund,
Dortmund, Germany
{amal.saadallah,hanna.mykula,katharina.morik}@tu-dortmund.de

Abstract. Multivariate Time Series (MTS) involve multiple time series
variables that are interdependent. The MTS follows two dimensions,
namely spatial along the different variables composing the MTS and
temporal. Both, the complex and the time-evolving nature of MTS data
make forecasting one of the most challenging tasks in time series analysis. Typical methods for MTS forecasting are designed to operate in a
static manner in time or space without taking into account the evolution
of spatio-temporal dependencies among data observations, which may
be subject to significant changes. Moreover, it is generally accepted that
none of these methods is universally valid for every application. Therefore, we propose an online adaptation of MTS forecasting by devising
a fully automated framework for both adaptive input spatio-temporal
variables and adequate forecasting model selection. The adaptation is
performed in an informed manner following concept-drift detection in
both spatio-temporal dependencies and model performance over time. In
addition, a well-designed meta-learning scheme is used to automate the
selection of appropriate dependence measures and the forecasting model.
An extensive empirical study on several real-world datasets shows that
our method achieves excellent or on-par results in comparison to the
state-of-the-art (SoA) approaches as well as several baselines.

Keywords: Multivariate time series · Forecasting · Automated model
selection · Spatio-temporal dependencies · Concept-drift

1 Introduction

Time series forecasting is an important task in time series analysis to study the
behavior of temporal data and forecast its future values [19, 20]. It is widely applied

This work is supported by the Deutsche Forschungsgemeinschaft (DFG) within the
Collaborative Research Center SFB 876 and the Federal Ministry of Education and
Research of Germany as part of the competence center for machine learning ML2R
(01-S18038A).

Supplementary Information The online version contains supplementary material
available at https://doi.org/10.1007/978-3-031-26422-1_2.

in various fields, including weather forecasts, energy demand/consumption predictions, and stock market prices forecasting, to name but a few [18–20]. In nowadays' rapidly growing digital environments and Internet-of-Things systems, the representation of time series data often involves multiple interdependent variables, thus creating Multivariate Time Series (MTS) data [25]. On the one hand, this data represents an enriched form of information about the application. On the other hand, the number of these variables can increase drastically and might include irrelevant and redundant ones. This may heighten the curse of dimensionality. Therefore, it is necessary to carefully select the most important time series variables. The evolution of MTS is spatio-temporal, along with the different variables and over time, respectively. However, this spatio-temporal data may involve multiple non-stationary processes and the dependencies along its composing variables may also follow a non-stationary process. As a result, the relationship between some time series variables and the target one might change significantly over time. This phenomenon is broached in the machine learning literature as concept drift [8]. Hence, previously learned concepts about data become no longer valid, making the offline input variable selection procedures inappropriate for making future predictions. Therefore, the selection of time series variables should cope with the evolving nature of the spatio-temporal dependencies in the MTS data.

Various Machine Learning (ML) models have already been successfully applied to solve the forecasting task either by dealing with the MTS data as a collection of ordered sequences of observations in an offline [25] or a streaming fashion [19], or by using an embedding of the MTS to reformulate the forecasting task as a regression task [20]. However, it is generally accepted that none of the ML methods is universally valid for every task, in particular for forecasting [20]. Therefore, in addition to adaptive time-dependent spatial variables selection, adequate model selection is required to cope with the characteristics of the MTS. Most of the existing MTS forecasting models operate in a static manner, i.e. the model is trained offline using some collection of historical data and a fixed selection of input variables. Its parameters are optimized once at training time. At test time, the model is deployed with fixed learned parameters and fixed information about temporal and spatial data [25]. Methods for online MTS forecasting focus either on very specific application/setting [9] or use a very specific family of ML models, such as Deep Neural Networks [21,26]. More recently, a drift-aware Vector Autoregressive (VAR) model has been proposed in [19]. In contrast to the classic VAR model which takes as input, all the variables of the MTS [25], an adaptive selection procedure of a subset of input variables is done in the drift-aware VAR. The update of this subset depends on a change in the Pearson-Correlation (PC) [15] measured between two variables over a time-sliding window, which we assume has occurred due to concept drift. Even though the proposed method is online and adaptive, it focuses only on a particular model, namely the VAR. In addition, the time series variables selection is done by ranking them according to their relevance to the target time series using PC. No further analysis is carried out to investigate the redundancy in the selected subset. The relevance/similarity to the target is measured using the PC coefficient. However, it has been proven that there is no single universal measure for the similarity between two time series either for relevance or redundancy analysis [15]. The quality of the achieved results in this context depends to a large extent on the used time series measure [15].

In this work, we propose an online adaptive framework for MTS forecasting which performs both input variable time series selection and adequate forecasting model selection. Input variables selection is done on two stages using relevance and redundancy analysis. The selection is made dynamically and adaptively in an informed manner following concept drift detection. The concept drift detection covers the two MTS dimensions, namely spatial and temporal. Spatial dependencies indicate the similarity between the input variables at one time instant. We monitor the change of the similarity values over time. Temporal dependencies indicate the patterns discovered within the same spatial dimension over time. The drift detection within the temporal dimension is ensured by tracking the change in the estimated model's performance on a given target time series variable over time. In addition, the choice of the adequate relevance and redundancy measures, as well as the forecasting model is done in an automated fashion using meta-learning on well-devised MTS meta-features. Our framework is denoted in the rest of the paper, OAMTS: Online Adaptive Multivariate Time series forecasting. We further conduct a comprehensive empirical analysis to validate our method using 66 real-world MTS datasets from different domains. We have created separate meta-data which cover a collection of real-world and synthetic MTS with various characteristics for the meta-learning task. The obtained results show that our method achieves excellent results in comparison to the SoA approaches for MTS forecasting. We note that all experiments are fully reproducible and that both the code and datasets are publicly available[1].

The main contributions of this work can be summarized as follows: We present a novel method for online drift-aware input time series variables selection using relevance and redundancy analysis; The drift detection mechanism is devised to operate on both spatial and temporal dimensions; We fully automate the choice of relevance and redundancy measures for MTS, as well as forecasting model selection using meta-learning; We provide a comparative empirical study with SoA methods, and discuss their implications in terms of predictive performance and scalability.

2   Literature Review

In contrast to univariate time series forecasting, i.e. the forecast of a single time series, where several methods for online adaptive single model selection [18] or ensemble learning [19,20] have been proposed, most of existing methods for MTS forecasting are devised to operate in a static manner [9,25,26]. In other words, the models in these methods are learned offline using a collection of historical MTS data, their parameters are optimized using these datasets and stored to be used at test time to make the predictions. In addition, most of these methods

---

[1] https://www.dropbox.com/sh/z2g0us0nti3nqzg/AAAJ6_6JcGZHN_y10q8XDYa_a?dl=0.

are either application specific [9] or model specific, i.e. use an arbitrary selected machine learning model family [25]. The most widely used models are VAR [19,25] or DNNs [21,26]. In [9], MTS for energy forecasting in smart buildings is transformed into a standard regression task using time series embedding, and then, different types of feature selection methods for regression tasks are applied. The features are extracted offline once and kept static at test time.

More recently, some works have exploited the success of some DNNs architectures in computer vision-related applications and successfully transferred and adapted them to MTS forecasting by treating the temporal and the spatial dimensions in MTS as the 2d-dimension in images. Some of other works focused on introducing some improvements or adaptations over existing DNNs to cope with the characteristics of MTS [21,26]. In [21], authors argued that the random weights initialization in Recurrent Neural Networks (RNNs), disallows the neurons from learning the latent features of the correlated variables of the MTS. Therefore, they suggest using a pre-trained LSTM combined with a stacked auto-encoder to replace the random weight initialization strategy adopted in deep RNNs. In [26], Graph Neural Networks (GNNs) are adapted to MTS forecasting by adding a mix-hop propagation layer and a dilated inception layer to capture the spatial and temporal dependencies within the MTS. This is done to make GNN capable of handling relational dependencies that are not known in advance like in the case of MTS. Even though dependencies between the variables of the MTS may change significantly over time, most of the aforementioned works do not consider a time-dependent selection of the input time series variables to the MTS forecasting model. The choice of the model is most often arbitrary or transferred from another domain like computer vision or regression. In addition, once the model is chosen, its corresponding parameters are kept fixed. It is important to note that there exist methods for model adaptation to data changes and model performance, more particularly to concept drift in the context of streaming data classification [13,14] and univariate time series forecasting [20]. These methods can be grouped into two main families, namely blind adaptation and informed adaptation. In blind adaptation, the model is retrained either at each time instant with each upcoming observation or over a fixed period in time without any consideration of possible data or model performance changes. However, this family of methods is known to be time-intensive, resource-consuming, and unpractical for online forecasting [18,20]. Informed adaptation methods use some statistical information about the data or model performance to inform the model about the occurrence of concept drift and, if necessary, trigger input data update using adaptive time-windowing approaches and input re-selection [13,14,20] and subsequently, model retraining [19] or new model selection [18]. In this work, we propose an informed adaptation for MTS forecasting. This is done by monitoring the changes in spatio-temporal dependencies in the MTS and the model performance over time. Since the results achieved in various time series tasks such as clustering and classification depend to a large extent on the used measures for evaluating time series dependencies/similarities [15], we suggest automating the choice of the adequate dependencies measures as well as the selection of the adequate model for a particular application by means of meta-learning.

3   Methodology

In this section, we present our framework and its main components. For given MTS data, the input time series variables to be used for forecasting are determined in a timely manner by computing their *relevance* to the target time series variable. Once the most relevant variables are identified, *redundancy* analysis through time series clustering is carried out to remove redundant variables. The choice of adequate time series measures for *relevance* and *redundancy* is determined beforehand by the meta-learning component that decides as well which model to be used for particular MTS data. Both input time series variables and model updates are triggered once a concept drift in the spatio-temporal dependencies among these variables or/and model performance is detected. Basically, either new variables are selected or time windows are adjusted to update the time series variables with recent observations. This depends on the nature of detected concept drift, i.e. whether it is on variables dependencies or model performance or on both.

3.1   Preliminaries

A time series variable X^i with $i \in \mathbb{N}$, is a temporal sequence of values, where $X^i_{1:t} = \{x^i_1, x^i_2, \cdots, x^i_t\}$ denotes the sequence of X^i recorded until time t and x^i_j is the value of X^i at a time instant j. A MTS $\mathbf{X}$ consists of multiple time series variables, i.e. $\mathbf{X} = \{X^1, X^2, \cdots, X^N\}$, that are interdependent. The variables are assumed in this work to be recorded simultaneously with the same frequency. The MTS $\mathbf{X}_{1:t}$ recorded until a time instant t can be formally described as $N \times t$-dimensional matrix, with $\mathbf{X}_j = \{x^1_j, x^2_j, \cdots, x^N_j\}$ which represent the *spatial* dimension of $\mathbf{X}$ for a fixed time instant j and $X^i_{1:t}$ represents the evolution of $\mathbf{X}$ over the *temporal* dimension across the variable i.

Given a target time series variable X^r, the goal of online input variable selection is to determine which time series variables $X^i, i \in [1, N] \backslash \{r\}$ should be fed into the forecasting model at time t to forecast the next value at time $t+1$. It is important to note that in MTS, each time series variable can play the role of the target variable and be predicted using the remaining variables, as it may be that only one or some variables need to be predicted. This is application dependent. However, the reasoning applied to one target variable can be generalized to all the remaining variables. We denote by $X^i_{t_s:t_e}$ the subsequence of X^i starting at time instant t_s and ending at time instant t_e. We divide the MTS $\mathbf{X}$ into $\mathbf{X}^{train}_\omega = \{X^1_{1:t-\omega}, X^2_{1:t-\omega}, \cdots, X^N_{1:t-\omega}\}$ and $\mathbf{X}^{val}_\omega = \{X^1_{t-\omega+1:t}, X^2_{t-\omega+1:t}, \cdots, X^N_{t-\omega+1:t}\}$, with ω a provided window size. $\mathbf{X}^{train}_\omega$ is used for training the forecasting model and $\mathbf{X}^{val}_\omega$ is used to compute the *relevance* and *redundancy* measures, since both input and target time series variables are required to be known.

3.2   Forecasting Models Learning

Standard approaches for addressing MTS forecasting tasks include traditional techniques for MTS analysis, such as the popular Vector Autoregressive VAR family of methods [25], or ARIMAX [3] which is the extension of Autoregressive Integrated Moving Average model (ARIMA) to MTS where some input time series variables are provided as exogenous variables to forecast the dependent variable, i.e. target variable. These models take as an input multiple time series sequences $\mathbf{X}_{1:t}$. In addition, regression models can be employed in the context of MTS forecasting by using a time-delayed embedding that maps a set of observations from the target time series variable $X^r \in \mathbf{X}$ to a $l \times N$-dimensional feature space corresponding to the l past lagged values of each observation in each time series variable in $\mathbf{X}$. Each observation is composed of a feature vector $z_i \in \mathbf{Z} \subset \mathbb{R}^{l \times N}$, which denotes the previous l values of each variable, and a target vector $x_i \in \mathbf{X} \subset \mathbb{R}$, which represents the value we want to predict. The objective is to construct a model $f : \mathbf{Z} \to \mathbf{X}$, where f denotes the regression function. In this work, we aim to select an adequate model given the characteristics of MTS data in question. This is done by the meta-learning components in Sect. 3.5. Therefore, we consider a pool of candidate forecasting models $\mathbb{P}$ which is designed to contain a set of various and *heterogeneous* models, such as VAR, Gaussian processes, support vector regression, and DNNs. The candidate models are trained on $\mathbf{X}_\omega^{train}$ using the same number l of lagged values for each variable in the MTS as input to model the following value in the time series.

3.3   Adaptive Input Time Series Variables Selection

Given a target time series $X^r \in \mathbf{X}$, in order to forecast its value at a future time instant $t + h, h \geq 1$ (for simplicity of notation, we assume $h = 1$), the selection of the time series variables $X^i, i \in [1, N] \backslash \{r\}$ whose l-lagged values will be used as input for the forecasting model in addition to the l-lagged values of target time series X^r, has to be determined in a timely-manner at t. The selection is decided by measuring how much each of $X^i, \forall i \in [1, N] \backslash \{r\}$ is relevant to X^r and whether X^i is redundant in the presence of the other variables.

Relevance. The relevance of each $X^i, \forall i \in [1, N] \backslash \{r\}$ to X^r is measured by computing the similarity between them on $T_\omega^{val} = [t - \omega + 1, t]$, denoted $s_t^{i,r} = sim(X_{t-\omega+1:t}^i, X_{t-\omega+1:t}^r)$. The time series variables $X^i, \forall i \in [1, N] \backslash \{r\}$ are sorted according to their $s_t^{i,r}$ and the top-n most similar variables to X^r are selected. There is no single universal similarity measure between time series that is valid for every application. The choice of the adequate similarity measure is done by considering the characteristics of the MTS at question.

Redundancy. The top-n selected input time series variables may include some redundant variables that would lead to increasing the dimensionality of the MTS forecasting task without contributing to the model's accuracy. Relying on the computed similarity measures is not sufficient since they are measured over a time window of observations T_ω^{val}. For instance, two candidate variables can have the same level of similarity to the target variables while being effectively similar to it on two distinct time intervals included within T_ω^{val}. Therefore, we suggest removing redundancies by clustering the top-n variables and selecting only one-time series representative per cluster. To compute clusters for time series, several techniques are proposed in the literature which can be classified based on the way they treat the data and how the underlying grouping is performed [1]. One classification depends on whether the whole series, a subsequence, or individual time points are to be clustered. In our case, we cluster the subsequences $\{X_{t-\omega+1:t}^1, X_{t-\omega+1:t}^2, \cdots, X_{t-\omega+1:t}^N\}$. On the other hand, the clustering itself may be shape-based, feature-based, or model-based. The choice of time-series representation and the clustering algorithm has a big impact on performance with respect to cluster quality and execution time [22]. Again, no single clustering method is universally valid and the success of the method depends on the characteristics of the time series data [1]. Denote with the $c_t^{i,j}$ the clustering measure used for computing the distance between the two sequences $X_{t-\omega+1:t}^i$ and $X_{t-\omega+1:t}^j$, with $i, j \in TOP_n$ and Top_n denotes the subset of selected input time series variables,i.e. $|TOP_n| = top_n$. The choice of the clustering algorithm together with the corresponding distance measure is decided by the meta-learning component. Further details are provided in Sect. 3.5.

Drift-Aware Variables Selection Adaptation. Both relevance and redundancies are monitored continuously over time. For relevance, with each upcoming data observation at $t + h, h \geq 1$, we slide T_ω^{val} by one step, i.e. to include the observation at $t + h$, and we measure $s_{t+h}^{i,r}, \forall i \in [1, N]\backslash\{r\}$. Then, we computed: $s_{t+h}^{min} = \min_{i\in[1,N]\backslash\{r\}} s_{t+h}^{i,r}$ in order to determine the distance between the target sequence and the most dissimilar sequence within the $N - 1$ input variables. Then, we compare it to the initial calculated distance $s_{t_i}^{min}$. In our case, $t_i = t$ indicates the start of the online forecasting stage. The distance is treated as time series where s_{t+h}^{min} is its value at time $t + h$.

Definition 1 (_Weak stationary Similarity_). _The similarity structure between a set of input time series variables and a target time series is said to be weakly stationary if the true mean of Δ^s is 0, with:_ $\Delta_{t+h}^s = \left| s_{t+h}^{min} - s_{t_i}^{min} \right|$

Following this definition, we can assume that the distance between the target time series sequence and the most dissimilar input sequence sets its boundary under a form of a logical _diameter_. If this boundary diverges in a significant way over time, a drift is assumed to take place. We propose to detect the validity of such an assumption using the well-known Hoeffding Bound, which states that after ω independent observations of a real-value random variable with range R, its true mean has not diverged if the sample mean is contained within $\pm\zeta$: $\zeta = \sqrt{\frac{R^2 \ln(1/\mu)}{2\omega}}$ with a probability of $1 - \mu$ (a user-defined hyperparameter). Once the condition of the _weak stationary similarity_ presented in Definition 1 is violated at t_d, a drift is assumed to take place at t_{d_s}. A relevance re-computation is then triggered. A re-clustering is also performed, the selection of the variables is updated and the reference diameter $s_{t_i}^{min}$ is reset by setting $t_i = t_{d_s}$. This drift type is denoted `Drift Type I`.

Similarly for the redundancy, we monitor continuously the distance measure used for clustering $c_{t+h}^{i,j}, \forall X^i, X^j \in TOP_n$, which results in the similarity matrix $\mathcal{C}_{t+h} = (c_{t+h}^{i,j})_{1 \leq i, j \geq top_n} \in \mathbb{R}^{top_n \times top_n}$ and we place all the elements of $\mathcal{C}_{t+h}$ in a vector ς_{t+h}, where $\varsigma_{j,t+h} \geq \varsigma_{j-1,t+h}, \forall j \in \{1, \cdots, top_n^2\}$. Let ς_{t_i} denote the value of ς at the initial instant $t_i = t$ of the generation of $\mathcal{C}$. We monitor the deviation $\Delta_{t+h}^\varsigma = |\varsigma_{t+h} - \varsigma_{t_i}|$ similarly to Δ_{t+h}^s. We test the occurrence of concept drift within the clusters following the same condition defined in Definition 1. If a concept drift is detected at t_{d_c}, both relevance and redundancies re-computation are triggered and a re-selection of input variables is performed. We reset then $\varsigma_{t_i} = \varsigma_{t_{d_c}}$. This drift type is denoted `Drift Type II`.

3.4 Forecasting Models Adaptation

The increase in the forecasting error may indicate a possible change in the relationship between the input variables and the target time series or outdated model parameters due to outdated time series observations that were used for training. Therefore, necessary measures such as input variables re-selection and/or model re-training with recently acquired data have to be taken. To do so, the forecasting error ϵ is estimated using the Root Mean Square Error (RMSE) and is monitored over the sliding window of the recent observations T_ω^{val}. The error can be viewed as a time series, and at $t + h$ $\epsilon_{t+h}^\omega = \frac{1}{\omega} \sum_{j=t+h-\omega}^{t+h-1} (x_j^r - \hat{x}_j^r)^2$, with $\hat{x}_j^r$ the predicted value of X^r at time j. Naturally, with time-evolving data, the model's error changes over time and may follow non-stationary concepts. Let ϵ_{t_i} denote ϵ value at the initial instant of its generation $t_i = t$. Since the forecasting error is directional, the drift-detection using the absolute value of the error deviation with the Hoeffding-bound can be misleading. Therefore, we suggest using the Page-Hinkley Test [19] to detect a significant increase in the forecasting error. We present the pseudo-code of the Page-Hinkley Test in the supplementary materials. ν and ϱ are user-defined hyper-parameters, where ν is the tolerable change in the estimated error and ϱ is a threshold. A larger ϱ avoids detecting false drift alarms, but can also lead to missing true drifts [8]. The error drift detection is denoted `Drift Type III`. An alert at time t_{d_ϵ} declares the occurrence of `Drift Type III` and triggers the update of the input variables through new selection, i.e. new relevance and redundancy re-computation and updates the current model with the new input and the recent observations. It also restarts the Page-Hinkley Test from the beginning. The model gets also updated with the update of the input triggered by `Drift Type I` or `Drift Type II`.

3.5 Online Automated MTS Forecasting

As discussed above, there are no single universal similarity measures for relevance and redundancies. Similarly, for the forecasting model, adequate model selection has to be performed to cope with the characteristics of the MTS in question. Once the model is selected, the online adaptation scheme in our framework (See Sect. 3.4) takes care of the update of the model in an informed manner to the real-time changes in the data and the performance. To automate the choice of the measures and the model, we use meta-learning. Let $\mathbb{S}$ and $\mathbb{C}$ be the spaces of the relevance and redundancy measures, respectively. Denote with $\mathbb{M}$ the space of the candidate models to solve the MTS forecasting task. Using a set of m MTS characteristics represented here by the so-called meta-features, the goal of the meta-task is to fit model $f_{meta} : \mathbb{R}^m \to \mathbb{S} \times \mathbb{C} \times \mathbb{M}$ to predict the best combination of relevance and redundancies measures and forecasting model choice given a vector of m MTS meta-features as input.

MTS Meta-features. Several works have been proposed for extracting Univariate Time Series (UTS) meta-features [24]. Therefore, most of the existing works that tackled the same task for MTS use the same features developed for UTS to extract meta-features from each time series variable in the MTS and concatenate them in one feature vector [9]. In this work, in addition to the transfer of the most often used meta-features in the context of univariate time series to the MTS domain, we propose to add MTS-specific meta-features. We additionally adapted the concept of *land-marking* developed for meta-tasks in classification and regression [12] to MTS data. The extracted meta-features can be grouped into three main families.

UTS-Specific Features. For each time series variable in the MTS, we extract different time series-specific features that can be grouped into three families, including descriptive statistics, frequency domain, and auto-correlation features [11]. The list of these features includes then trend, skewness of series, turning points, kurtosis of series, step changes, length of series, non-linearity measure, the standard deviation of de-trended series, power spectrum: maximal value, no. of peaks not lower than 60% of the max, auto- and partial correlations at lags one and two, seasonality. Since the number of variables in the MTS can be very big, we compute the mean and the standard deviation of each extracted feature over the different variables from a subset.

MTS-Specific Features. We suggest investigating the relationships/dependence among the MTS variables. To do so, we compute several similarity measures [15], including Pearson Correlation, Euclidean distance, Dynamic time warping distance, Mahalanobis distance, Amplitude and Phase differences of the Fourier Transform (FT), and Shape similarity based on derived FT amplitude and phase differences, between each pair of variables. These similarities computations result in similarity matrices for each measure. Instead of concatenating all the coefficients of all the matrices in one feature vector and increasing the meta-task input dimensionality, we suggest computing diversity in similarity/dependence along with all the variables pairs for each similarity matrix. Denote with $\mathcal{S} \in \mathbb{R}^{N \times N}$ the resulting similarity matrix of a given similarity/distance s between all the

N MTS variables. We define the diversity as (note the similarity values are normalized between -1 and 1) : $div(\mathcal{S}) = 1 - \frac{1}{\sum_{1 \leq i \neq j, \leq N}} \sum_{1 \leq i \neq j, \leq N} s(X^i, X^j)$

Landmarking-Based Features. This type of meta-features are designed to describe the performance of some learning algorithms, called *landmarkers*, in various learning contexts on the same data. *Landmarkers* are machine learning models that are computationally relatively cheap either in training or testing compared to other models. So far, all the proposed *landmarkers* and corresponding meta-features have been proposed for classical meta-learning applications to classification problems and one work has added the extension of this concept to regression [12], whereas we focus on *landmarkers* integration for MTS forecasting. In regression, the process starts by creating one landmarking model over the entire training set. A small artificial neighborhood for each training example is created using Gaussian noise. Then descriptive statistics of the models' output, mean, stdev., 1st/3rd quantile, are extracted. In our case, we use, LASSO, 1NN, MARS and CART, as *landmarkers* [12] and train them on $\mathbf{X}_\omega^{train}$. We can distinguish three types of Landmarking features:

- *Global landmarking*: We evaluate each model on each time $\mathbf{X}_\omega^{val}$ and we extract the descriptive statistics of the models' output.
- *Performance-based local landmarking*: we split $\mathbf{X}_\omega^{val}$ into equally-sized non-overlapping time windows of size n_ω. We evaluate each model on each time window and we extract for each window the descriptive statistics of the models' output.
- *Model-based local landmarking*: This type of local landmarking is designed to characterize the *landmarkers* within a particular time series region, in our case each time window of size n_ω. To do so, we extract the knowledge that the *landmarkers* have learned about each window. In addition to the prediction of each *landmarker* on each window, we compute the depth of the leaf which makes the prediction and the number of examples in that leaf and variance for each window for CART, the average over each window of the width and mass of the interval in which each time value falls, and the average over each window of absolute distance to the nearest neighbor for 1NN.

4 Experiments

We present the experiments carried out to validate OAMTS and to answer these research questions: **Q1:** How does OAMTS perform compared to the SoA and existing online methods for MTS forecasting?; **Q2:** To which extent is it necessary to automate the choice of adequate relevance and redundancies measures, as well as the forecasting model choice? **Q3:** What is the importance of each component, namely relevance and redundancy, in the input time series variables selection on the performance? **Q4:** What is the benefit of each drift type detection for the performance of OAMTS? **Q5:** How scalable is OAMTS in terms of computational resources compared to the most competitive online model selection methods? and what is the computational advantage of **drift-aware** adaptation of the framework?

4.1 Experimental Setup

The methods used in the experiments were evaluated using the root mean squared error (RMSE). We collected a total of 166 MTS from various real-world applications. 100 MTS are exclusively used for the meta-learning task, while the remaining 66 MTS are used for testing the meta-model which recommends which relevance and redundancy measures and forecasting model from the pool of candidate models that we have devised, to use. Following the recommendation of the meta-model, these 66 MTS are used to validate the online forecasting performance of OAMTS. Each of the 66 MTS was split using 50% for training (X_ω^{train}), and 25% for validation (X_ω^{val}) and 25% for testing. Note that in each MTS, we have chosen one variable as the target one depending on the application and the remaining variables as different input variables. However, for some applications like taxi demand forecasting, all the variables can play the role of the target one and change the role between variables. A full list of the used datasets, together with a description, is given in the code repository[2] and in the supplementary materials.

Candidate Models Set-Up. We construct the pool $\mathbb{P}$ of candidate models. We mentioned earlier that there is no single method for forecasting that outperforms all the other methods on every time series. Hence, we incorporate and test different families of models. Traditional time series forecasting models like **VAR** [25] is included. Regression models are also included in $\mathbb{P}$ and are applied after using MTS embedding of dimension $N \times l$. These models include Gradient Boosting Machines **GBM** [5], Support Vector Regression **SVR** [4], Random Forest **RF** [2], Projection Pursuit Regression **PPR** [6], MARS **MARS** [7], and Partial Least Squares Regression **PLS** [16]. Neural networks based models that are designed for time series forecasting task are introduced to $\mathbb{P}$ such as Multi-Layer Perceptron **MLP** [10], Bidirectional LSTM **bi-LSTM** [23]. More recently, **CNN-LSTM** [27] and Convolutional LSTM **Conv-LSTM** [27] are suggested to solve MTS forecasting tasks. Using different parameter settings for each family, we generate a pool of 20 candidate models.

Meta-learning Task Set-Up. The list of similarity measures considered to measure the variables relevance includes Pearson Correlation, Spearman correlation, Euclidean distance, Dynamic time warping distance, Manhattan distance, and Fourier-based distance. A detailed description of each measure can be found in [15] (Table 1). For redundancies, we have chosen K-means [17] as the clustering algorithm with distance measure either Euclidean distance or Dynamic time warping distance. For the models, we consider the selection from the pool $\mathbb{P}$. Note for the meta-data labelling, we consider all the possible combinations of relevance, redundancy measures and model type and we evaluate our framework performance on each MTS dataset in the meta set by splitting it into 80% for training the framework and 20% for testing. Even though, the meta-task is performed fully offline (only meta-model predictions are output online), this

---

[2] https://www.dropbox.com/sh/z2g0us0nti3nqzg/AAAJ6_6JcGZHN_y10q8XDYa_a?dl=0.

annotation is very resource-consuming because of the big number of combinations. That is why we restrained the size of the metadata to 100 MTS. However, we aim to enlarge this data in the future. There are different options on how to tackle the meta-learning task. One possible option would be to encode all the combinations of relevance, redundancy measures, and model type which would lead to a high number of classes compared to the size of the meta-data. Another option is to consider it as a multi-label classification task. However, a classifier's performance on different labels can vary significantly. Therefore, we have chosen to split the task into three learning tasks. The first one is for relevance measure prediction and is a multi-class classification task solved with SVM [4]. The second task is for redundancy measure prediction and is a binary classification task solved with SVM [4]. The third task is for model selection and is a multi-class classification task solved with RF [2]. The choice of the learning algorithm is decided using a cross-validation evaluation of the accuracy on the meta-data.

OAMTS Set-Up: OAMTS has also a number of hyper-parameters that are summarized in Table 1 in the supplementary materials. We compare **OAMTS** against the following approaches which include SoA methods for MTS forecasting. Some of them operate in an online fashion.

SoA Forecasting Models: ARIMAX [3]: Auto-Regressive Moving Average model with exogenous variables, **LSTM** [18]: Long Short Term Memory Network which has shown better performance than the remaining neural networks such as MLP and CNN-LSTM and comparable performance with bi-LSTM, **VAR** [25]: Traditional Vector Autoregressive model. Its order is tuned using Akaike Information Criterion (AIC) using the R-package 'vars', **Drift-aware VAR** [19] A recent framework that selects the relevant variables using Pearson-Correlation for the VAR model and update them following concept-drift detection. It uses also L1-regularization to prevent over-fitting. However, redundancies are not removed.

OAMTS Variants: OAMTS-Ran: The variant of OAMTS that is computed using a random selection of Relevance and Redundancies measures and model, **OAMTS-VAR**: The variant of OAMTS that uses VAR as the forecasting model instead of the automatic model selection. Relevance and Redundancies are selected by the meta-model, **OAMTS-Rel**: The variant of OAMTS that performs adaptive input selection by considering only the relevance, **OAMTS-Red**: The variant of OAMTS that performs adaptive input selection by considering only the redundancy, **OAMTS-DI-II**: The variant of OAMTS that performs model adaptation following concept drift in the input structure (Drift type I and Drift type II, **OAMTS-DIII**: The variant of OAMTS that performs model adaptation following in the changes in the error (Drift type III), **OAMTS-Per**: The variant of OAMTS that performs model adaptation periodically without any consideration of concept drift occurrence, with each upcoming 10% data points, **OAMTS-BG**: The variant of OAMTS where we assume we know the background truth of which Relevance and Redundancies measures to use and which model to select. This is done by evaluating all the possible combinations on the test set. This variant is used as a reference model to know how well the meta-learning component performs.

4.2 Results

Table 1 presents the average ranks and their deviation for all methods. For the paired comparison, we compare our method OAMTS against each of the other methods. We counted wins and losses for each dataset using the RMSE scores. We use the non-parametric Wilcoxon Signed Rank test to compute significant wins and losses (significance level 0.05). In the results in Table 1, OAMTS outperforms the baseline methods in terms of wins/loses in pairwise comparison. The online MTS forecasting methods, e.g., Drift-aware VAR [19] and OAMTS-VAR show inferior performance compared to OAMTS. VAR and LSTM, SoA methods for forecasting, are considerably worse in average rank compared to OAMTS. The most competitive SoA approach to OAMTS is ARIMAX. Nevertheless, it has a higher average rank and a lower performance than our method. VAR is considered to be the most widely used method of MTS forecasting but it can be seen from OAMTS-VAR that it is not always the best model choice. This is also confirmed by the Drift-aware VAR performance. It can also be seen that none of OAMTS-Rel and OAMTS-Red is able on its own to reach the performance of OAMTS which shows the importance of both relevance and redundancies

Table 1. Comparison of OAMTS to different SoA for 66 time series. The rank column presents the average rank and its standard deviation across different time series. A rank of 1 means the model was the best performing on all time series. We report only significant wins and losses of OAMTS against remaining methods.

Method	Our method		
	Wins	Losses	Avg. rank
VAR	40	0	7.7 ± 0.9
ARIMAX	20	20	3.0 ± 2.2
LSTM	40	0	7.8 ± 1.4
Drift-aware VAR	40	0	6.7 ± 0.9
OAMTS-VAR	40	0	7.6 ± 0.7
OAMTS-Ran	40	0	5.0 ± 0.9
OAMTS-Rel	40	0	5.9 ± 1.3
OAMTS-Red	40	0	6.3 ± 0.6
OAMTS-Per	39	1	4.3 ± 0.8
OAMTS-DI-II	30	10	3.2 ± 1.2
OAMTS-DIII	7	33	2.9 ± 0.7
OAMTS	–	–	$\mathbf{2.2 \pm 0.5}$
OAMTS-BG	–	–	$\mathbf{1.9 \pm 0.6}$

consideration in the input selection. These results address the research questions **Q1-Q2**.

Table 2 presents some examples where we show the ground truth of which are the best relevance and redundancies measures, as well as the model choice for some data sets. It is clear from Table 2 that there is no one single best relevance and redundancies measures, as well as one optimal model choice, even for MTS data sets extracted from the same data source like Taxi1,2,3 that are extracted from NYC Trip Record Data (Yellow taxi 2021). This justifies the necessity of automating these choices. Random choices would lead to considerably worse performance which is reflected in the performance of OAMTS-Ran in Table 1. In addition, comparing OAMTSto OAMTS-BG, we can see a slight difference in the ranks in favor of course of OAMTS-BG but it highlights the usefulness of the meta-learning component in our framework for automating all the choices. These results address the research question **Q3**.

Table 2. Ground truth of the best model and relevance/redundancy measures for some datasets.

Dataset	Model	Similarity measure	Clustering method
Taxi-1	PLS	Pearson correlation	DTW
Taxi-2	MARS	Euclidean distance	DTW
Taxi-3	PLS	Spearman correlation	DTW
Chengdu-city-3	MARS	Spearman correlation	Euclidean

From Table 1, we can also see that none of the drift adaptation methods is able on its own to perform as well as OAMTSwhich deploys the three drift types to monitor changes in the input dependence structure as well as the model performance. In addition, OAMTS which relies on the informed adaption of the framework using concept drift detection is better than OAMTS-Per. This can be explained by the fact that unnecessary updates are not always beneficial. This answers the research question **Q4**.

In the next experiment, we compare the runtime of OAMTS and its variants against some SoA methods in Table 3.

All the reported runtimes concern only the online predictions and any operation computed offline is not taken into account. The results demonstrate that OAMTS has lower runtime than OAMTS-Per. This is due to using drift detection to update only when necessary. This results in faster predictions and less computational requirements. The high deviation of the runtime of OAMTS is due to the different numbers of drifts per time series. This answers question **Q5**.

4.3 Discussion and Future Work

The empirical results indicate that OAMTS has performance advantages compared to popular MTS forecasting methods. We show that our method, for adaptively selecting input MTS variables and performing the model update, is able

Table 3. Empirical runtime comparison between different methods in seconds.

Method	OAMTS	OAMTS-Per	LSTM
Avg. runtime	34.26	72.12	150.09
±	94.51	35.29	29.26

to gain excellent and reliable empirical performance in our setting. The informed adaptation following concept drift detection makes our method in addition to better predictive performance, computationally cheaper than blind adaptation methods like periodic ones. In future work, we plan to enhance further the meta-learning components by adding more datasets and annotating them, and establishing a direct mapping to the best combination of measures and model choice as target label as we assume that there is a link in addition to the MTS characteristics that we tried to cover from different perspectives, between relevance and redundancies measures and the chosen forecasting model. This investigation will make the scope of our future work. In addition, we've thought about adding more time series clustering algorithms so that we change the mapping to the clustering algorithm directly instead of the relevance measure. We may also think about enlarging the pool $\mathbb{P}$.

5   Concluding Remarks

This paper introduces OAMTS: a novel, practically useful online adaptive framework for multivariate time series forecasting. OAMTS uses adaptive input selection by investigating relevance and redundancies. Both input variables and learning models are updated in an informed manner following different types of concept drift detection. The choice of the relevance and redundancies measure, as well as the model, is automated using meta-learning. An exhaustive empirical evaluation, including several real-world datasets and multiple comparison algorithms, showed the advantages of OAMTS in terms of performance and scalability.

References

1. Aghabozorgi, S., Seyed Shirkhorshidi, A., Ying Wah, T.: Time-series clustering-a decade review. Inf. Syst. **53**, 16–38 (2015)
2. Breiman, L.: Bagging predictors. Mach. Learn. **24**(2), 123–140 (1996)
3. Dissanayake, B., Hemachandra, O., Lakshitha, N., Haputhanthri, D., Wijayasiri, A.: A comparison of ARIMAX, VAR and LSTM on multivariate short-term traffic volume forecasting. In: Conference of Open Innovations Association, FRUCT, pp. 564–570. No. 28, FRUCT Oy (2021)
4. Drucker, H., Burges, C.J., Kaufman, L., Smola, A.J., Vapnik, V.: Support vector regression machines. In: Advances in Neural Information Processing Systems, pp. 155–161 (1997)

5. Friedman, J.H.: Greedy function approximation: a gradient boosting machine. Ann. Stat. **29**, 1189–1232 (2001)
6. Friedman, J.H., Stuetzle, W.: Projection pursuit regression. J. Am. Stat. Assoc. **76**(376), 817–823 (1981)
7. Friedman, J.H., et al.: Multivariate adaptive regression splines. Ann. Stat. **19**(1), 1–67 (1991)
8. Gama, J., Žliobaitė, I., Bifet, A., Pechenizkiy, M., Bouchachia, A.: A survey on concept drift adaptation. ACM Comput. Surv. (CSUR) **46**(4), 1–37 (2014)
9. González-Vidal, A., Jiménez, F., Gómez-Skarmeta, A.F.: A methodology for energy multivariate time series forecasting in smart buildings based on feature selection. Energy Build. **196**, 71–82 (2019)
10. Goodfellow, I., Bengio, Y., Courville, A.: Deep Learning. MIT Press (2016). www.deeplearningbook.org
11. Hyndman, R.J., Wang, E., Laptev, N.: Large-scale unusual time series detection. In: 2015 IEEE International Conference on Data Mining Workshop (ICDMW), pp. 1616–1619. IEEE (2015)
12. Khiari, J., Moreira-Matias, L., Shaker, A., Ženko, B., Džeroski, S.: MetaBags: bagged meta-decision trees for regression. In: Berlingerio, M., Bonchi, F., Gärtner, T., Hurley, N., Ifrim, G. (eds.) ECML PKDD 2018. LNCS (LNAI), vol. 11051, pp. 637–652. Springer, Cham (2019). https://doi.org/10.1007/978-3-030-10925-7_39
13. Klinkenberg, R., Joachims, T.: Detecting concept drift with support vector machines. In: ICML, pp. 487–494 (2000)
14. Klinkenberg, R., Rüping, S.: Concept drift and the importance of examples. In: Text Mining-Theoretical Aspects and Applications. Citeseer (2002)
15. Lhermitte, S., Verbesselt, J., Verstraeten, W.W., Coppin, P.: A comparison of time series similarity measures for classification and change detection of ecosystem dynamics. Remote Sens. Environ. **115**(12), 3129–3152 (2011)
16. Mevik, B.H., Wehrens, R., Liland, K.H.: PLS: partial least squares and principal component regression (2018). CRAN.R-project.org/package=pls
17. Priebe, F.: Dynamic model selection for automated machine learning in time series (2019)
18. Saadallah, A., Jakobs, M., Morik, K.: Explainable online deep neural network selection using adaptive saliency maps for time series forecasting. In: Oliver, N., Pérez-Cruz, F., Kramer, S., Read, J., Lozano, J.A. (eds.) ECML PKDD 2021. LNCS (LNAI), vol. 12975, pp. 404–420. Springer, Cham (2021). https://doi.org/10.1007/978-3-030-86486-6_25
19. Saadallah, A., Moreira-Matias, L., Sousa, R., Khiari, J., Jenelius, E., Gama, J.: Bright-drift-aware demand predictions for taxi networks. IEEE Trans. Knowl. Data Eng. **32**, 234–245 (2018)
20. Saadallah, A., Priebe, F., Morik, K.: A drift-based dynamic ensemble members selection using clustering for time series forecasting. In: Brefeld, U., Fromont, E., Hotho, A., Knobbe, A., Maathuis, M., Robardet, C. (eds.) ECML PKDD 2019. LNCS (LNAI), vol. 11906, pp. 678–694. Springer, Cham (2020). https://doi.org/10.1007/978-3-030-46150-8_40
21. Sagheer, A., Kotb, M.: Unsupervised pre-training of a deep LSTM-based stacked autoencoder for multivariate time series forecasting problems. Sci. Rep. **9**(1), 1–16 (2019)
22. Sardá-Espinosa, A.: Comparing time-series clustering algorithms in R using the dtwclust package. R Package Vignette **12**, 41 (2017)

23. Sun, Q., Jankovic, M.V., Bally, L., Mougiakakou, S.G.: Predicting blood glucose with an LSTM and Bi-LSTM based deep neural network. In: 2018 14th Symposium on Neural Networks and Applications (NEUREL), pp. 1–5. IEEE (2018)
24. Talagala, T.S., Hyndman, R.J., Athanasopoulos, G., et al.: Meta-learning how to forecast time series. Monash Econometrics Bus. Stat. Work. Papers **6**(18), 16 (2018)
25. Tsay, R.S.: Multivariate Time Series Analysis: with R and Financial Applications. John Wiley & Sons (2013)
26. Wu, Z., Pan, S., Long, G., Jiang, J., Chang, X., Zhang, C.: Connecting the dots: multivariate time series forecasting with graph neural networks. In: Proceedings of the 26th ACM SIGKDD International Conference on Knowledge Discovery & Data Mining, pp. 753–763 (2020)
27. Xingjian, S., Chen, Z., Wang, H., Yeung, D.Y., Wong, W.K., Woo, W.C.: Convolutional LSTM network: a machine learning approach for precipitation nowcasting. In: Advances in Neural Information Processing Systems, pp. 802–810 (2015)

U-Net Inspired Transformer Architecture for Far Horizon Time Series Forecasting

Kiran Madhusudhanan[1]([⊠])(ORCID), Johannes Burchert[1], Nghia Duong-Trung[2],
Stefan Born[2], and Lars Schmidt-Thieme[1](ORCID)

[1] Institute for Computer Science, University of Hildesheim, Hildesheim, Germany
{madhusudhanan,burchert,schmidt-thieme}@ismll.uni-hildesheim.de
[2] Technische Universität Berlin, Berlin, Germany
nghia.duong-trung@tu-berlin.de, born@math.tu-berlin.de

Abstract. Time series data is ubiquitous in research as well as in a wide variety of industrial applications. Effectively analyzing the available historical data and providing insights into the far future allows us to make effective decisions. Recent research has witnessed the superior performance of transformer-based architectures, especially in the regime of far horizon time series forecasting. However, the current state of the art sparse Transformer architectures fail to couple down- and upsampling procedures to produce outputs in a similar resolution as the input. We propose a U-Net inspired Transformer architecture named Yformer, based on a novel Y-shaped encoder-decoder architecture that (1) uses direct connection from the downscaled encoder layer to the corresponding upsampled decoder layer in a U-Net inspired architecture, (2) Combines the downscaling/upsampling with sparse attention to capture long-range effects, and (3) stabilizes the encoder-decoder stacks with the addition of an auxiliary reconstruction loss. Extensive experiments have been conducted with relevant baselines on three benchmark datasets, demonstrating an average improvement of 19.82, 18.41% MSE and 13.62, 11.85% MAE in comparison to the baselines for the univariate and the multivariate settings respectively.

Keywords: Time series forecasting · Transformer · U-Net

1 Introduction

In the most simple case, time series forecasting deals with a scalar time-varying signal and aims to predict or forecast its values in the near future; for example, countless applications in finance, healthcare, production automatization, etc. [4,27,29] can benefit from an accurate forecasting solution. Often not just a single scalar signal is of interest, but multiple at once, and further time-varying

Supplementary Information The online version contains supplementary material available at https://doi.org/10.1007/978-3-031-26422-1_3.

signals are available and even *known for the future*. For example, suppose one aims to forecast the energy consumption of a house, it likely depends on the social time that one seeks to forecast for (such as the next hour or day), and also on features of these time points (such as weekday, daylight, etc.), which are known already for the future. This is also the case in model predictive control [3], where one is interested to forecast the expected value realized by some planned action, then this action is also known at the time of forecast. More generally, time series forecasting, nowadays deals with quadruples (x, y, x', y') of known past predictors x, known past targets y, known future predictors x' and sought future targets y' (Fig. 1).

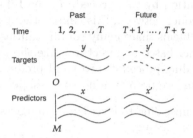

Fig. 1. General time series setting illustrating the quadruples (x, y, x', y') denoting the *past predictors, past targets, future predictors* and *future targets* respectively. Given the history information (x, y) until time $t = T$ and the future predictors (x') for the next τ time steps, time series forecasting predicts the target y' from $t = T + 1, \ldots, \tau$ time steps. In the figure, O and M represents the respective channels of the targets and the predictors.

Time series problems can often be addressed by methods developed initially for images, treating them as 1-dimensional images. Especially for time-series classification many typical time series encoder architectures have been adapted from models for images [33,37]. Time series forecasting then is closely related to image outpainting [32], the task to predict how an image likely extends to the left, right, top or bottom, as well as to the more well-known task of image segmentation, where for each input pixel, an output pixel has to be predicted, whose channels encode pixel-wise classes such as vehicle, road, pedestrian say for road scenes. Time series forecasting combines aspects from both problem settings: information about targets from shifted positions (e.g., the past targets y as in image outpainting) and information about other channels from the same positions (e.g., the future predictors x' as in image segmentation). One of the most successful, principled architectures for the image segmentation task are U-Nets introduced in [26], an architecture that successively downsamples/coarsens its inputs and then upsamples/refines the latent representation with deconvolutions also using the latent representations of the same detail level, tightly coupling down- and upsampling procedures and thus yielding latent features on the same resolution as the inputs.

Following the great success in Natural Language Processing (NLP) applications, attention-based, esp. transformer-based architectures [30] that model pairwise interactions between sequence elements have been recently adapted for time series forecasting. One of the significant challenges, is that the length of the time series, are often one or two magnitudes of order larger than the (sentence-level) NLP problems.

Plenty of approaches aim to mitigate the quadratic complexity $O(T^2)$ in the sequence/time series length T to at most $O(T \log T)$. For example, the Informer architecture [35], adapts the transformer with a sparse attention mechanism and a successive downsampling/coarsening of the past time series. As in the original transformer, only the coarsest representation is fed into the decoder. Possibly to remedy the loss in resolution by this procedure, the Informer feeds its input a second time into the decoder network, this time without any coarsening.

While forecasting problems share many commonalities with image segmentation problems, transformer-based architectures like the Informer do not involve coupled down- and upscaling procedures to yield predictions on the same resolution as the inputs. Thus, we propose a novel Y-shaped architecture that

1. Couples downscaling/upscaling to leverage both, coarse and fine-grained features for time series forecasting,
2. Combines the coupled scaling mechanism with sparse attention modules to capture long-range effects on all scale levels, and
3. Stabilizes encoder and decoder stacks by reconstructing the recent past.

2   Related Work

Time Series Forecasting: While Convolutional Neural Network (CNN) and Recurrent Neural network (RNN) based architectures [25,28] outperform traditional methods like ARIMA [2] and exponential smoothing methods [10], the addition of attention layers [30] to model time series forecasting has proven to be very beneficial across different problem settings [7,16,24,34]. Attention allows direct pair-wise interaction with eccentric events (like holidays) and can model temporal dynamics inherently unlike RNNs and CNNs that fail to capture long-range dependencies directly. Recent work like Reformer [14], Linformer, [31], Triformer [5] and Informer [35] have focused on reducing the quadratic complexity of modeling pair-wise interactions to a lower complexity with the introduction of restricted attention layers. Consequently, they can predict for longer forecasting horizons but are hindered by their capability of aggregating features and maintaining the resolution required for far horizon forecasting.

U-Net: The Yformer model is inspired by the famous U-Net architecture introduced in [26] originating from the field of medical image segmentation. The U-net architecture is capable of compressing information by aggregating over the inputs and up-sampling embeddings to the same resolutions as that of the inputs from their compressed latent features. While there exist U-Net based transformer architectures within the vision community [23,36], to the best of our knowledge U-Net based transformer architecture for time series forecasting remains unexplored. Current transformer architectures like the Informer [35] do not utilize up-sampling techniques even though the network produces intermediate multi-resolution feature maps. Our work aims to capitalize on these multi-resolution feature maps and use the U-net shape effectively for the task of time series forecasting. In [22], the authors have successfully applied U-Net architecture for the task of time series segmentation, illustrating superior results in the task. These motivate the use of a U-Net-inspired architecture for time series forecasting as current methods fail to couple sparse attention mechanism with the U-Net shaped architecture for time series forecasting.

Reconstruction Loss: Reconstruction loss is widely used in the domain of time series outlier detection [13] and is less popular within the Time Series Forecasting community. Although recent time series forecasting architecture like the N-Beats [21] tries to reconstruct part of the past time steps (backcasting) as an effective method to improve model performance, the majority of transformer-based time series forecasting architectures [7,16,19] fail to utilize the reconstruction loss as an auxiliary target to improve performance. In [12], the authors demonstrate a multi-task approach for time series forecasting that couples an auxiliary task of predicting known channels along with the target channel for improved regularization. Additionally, recent studies [17] have shown that the addition of the reconstruction term to any loss function generally provides uniform stability and bounds on the generalization error, therefore leading to a more robust model overall with no negative effect on the performance.

3 Problem Formulation

By a **time series** x **with** M **channels**, we mean a finite sequence of vectors in $\mathbb{R}^M$, denote their space by $\mathbb{R}^{*\times M} := \bigcup_{T\in\mathbb{N}}\mathbb{R}^{T\times M}$, and their length by $|x| := T$ (for $x \in \mathbb{R}^{T\times M}, M \in \mathbb{N}$). We write $(x,y) \in \mathbb{R}^{*\times(M+O)}$ to denote two time series of same length with M and O channels for the predictors and targets, respectively. We model a **time series forecasting instance** as a quadruple $(x,y,x',y') \in \mathbb{R}^{*\times(M+O)} \times \mathbb{R}^{*\times(M+O)}$, where x,y denote the past predictors and targets until a reference time point T and x',y' denote the future predictors and targets from the reference point T to the next τ (forecast horizon) time steps.

For a **Time Series Forecasting Problem**, given (i) a sample $\mathcal{D} := \{ (x_1,y_1,x_1',y_1'), \ldots, (x_N,y_N,x_N',y_N')\}$ from an unknown distribution p of time series forecasting instances and (ii) a function $\ell : \mathbb{R}^{*\times(O+O)} \to \mathbb{R}$ called loss, we attempt to find a function $\hat{y} : \mathbb{R}^{*\times(M+O)} \times \mathbb{R}^{*\times M} \to \mathbb{R}^{*\times O}$ (with $|\hat{y}(x,y,x')| = |x'|$) with minimal expected loss

$$\mathbb{E}_{(x,y,x',y')\sim p}\ \ell(y', \hat{y}(x,y,x')) \tag{1}$$

The loss ℓ usually is the mean absolute error (MAE) or mean squared error (MSE) averaged over future time points:

$$\ell^{\mathrm{mae}}(y',\hat{y}) := \frac{1}{|y'|} \sum_{t=1}^{|y'|} \frac{1}{O} ||y'_t - \hat{y}_t||_1, \quad \ell^{\mathrm{mse}}(y',\hat{y}) := \frac{1}{|y'|} \sum_{t=1}^{|y'|} \frac{1}{O} ||y'_t - \hat{y}_t||_2^2 \quad (2)$$

Furthermore, if there is only one target channel and no predictor channels ($O = 1, M = 0$), the time series forecasting problem is called **univariate**, otherwise **multivariate**.

4 Background

Our work incorporates restricted attention based Transformer in a U-Net inspired architecture. For this reason, we base our work on the current state of the art sparse attention model Informer, introduced in [35]. We provide a brief overview of the *ProbSparse* attention and the *Contracting ProbSparse Self-Attention Blocks* used in the Informer model for completeness.

ProbSparse **Attention:** The *ProbSparse* attention mechanism restricts the canonical attention [30] by selecting a subset u of dominant queries from available sequence length L_Q having the largest variance across all the keys. Consequently, the dense query matrix $Q \in \mathbb{R}^{L_Q \times d}$ in the canonical attention is replaced by a sparse query matrix $\overline{Q} \in \mathbb{R}^{L_Q \times d}$ consisting of the u dominant queries. *ProbSparse* attention can hence be defined as:

$$\mathcal{A}^{\mathrm{PropSparse}}(\overline{Q}, K, V) = \mathrm{Softmax}(\frac{\overline{Q}K^T}{\sqrt{d}})V \quad (3)$$

where d denotes the input dimension to the attention module. For more details on the *ProbSparse* attention mechanism, we refer the reader to [35].

Contracting ProbSparse Self-attention Blocks: The Informer model uses *Contracting ProbSparse Self-Attention Blocks* to distill out redundant information from the long history input sequence (x, y) in a pyramid structure motivated from the image domain [20]. The sequence of operations within a block begins with a *ProbSparse* self-attention that takes as input the hidden representation h_i from the ith block and projects the hidden representation into query, key and value for self-attention. This is followed by convolution operations (Conv1d) [15], and finally the Max-Pooling (MaxPool) [15] operation reduces the latent dimension by effectively distilling out redundant information at each block as summarized in Algorithm 1. Here, ELU represents the ELU activation function [6] and LayerNorm is the Layer Normalization operation [1]. The encoder block in the Informer model [35] stacks multiple *Contracting ProbSparse Self-Attention Block* blocks and produce multi-resolution encoder embeddings following a pyramid structure.

Algorithm 1. Contracting ProbSparse Self-Attention Block

$Input : h_i$
$Output : h_{i+1}$
$h_{i+1} \leftarrow \text{ProbSparseAttn}(h_i, h_i)$
$h_{i+1} \leftarrow \text{Conv1d}(h_{i+1})$
$h_{i+1} \leftarrow \text{LayerNorm}(h_{i+1})$
$h_{i+1} \leftarrow \text{MaxPool}(\text{ELU}(\text{Conv1d}(h_{i+1})))$

---

5   Methodology

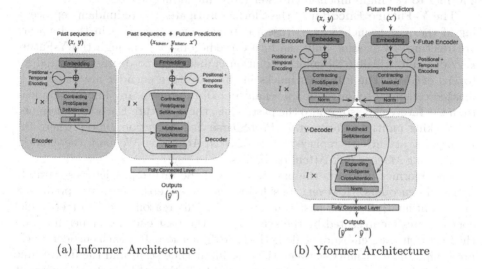

(a) Informer Architecture   (b) Yformer Architecture

Fig. 2. Comparison of Informer and Yformer architecture highlighting the three key differences. (1) The Informer architecture process part of the past input data (x, y) within the decoder as $(x_{\text{token}}, y_{\text{token}})$ along with the future predictors (x'). The Yformer avoids this redundant reprocessing of (x, y) and uses a masked self-attention network for embedding the only the future predictors (x'). (2) The Informer uses the final encoder embedding as the input to the decoder. The Yformer passes a concatenated ($+$) representation (e_i) of the ith Y-Past and Y-Future Encoder embedding to the $I - i^{\text{th}}$ layer of the Y-Decoder, forming a U-Net connection (represented in red) between the encoder and the decoder. (3) The Yformer architecture predicts both the input reconstruction $\hat{y}^{\text{past}}$ and future predictions $\hat{y}^{\text{fut}}$.

The Yformer model is a Y-shaped symmetric encoder-decoder architecture that is specifically designed to take advantage of the multi-resolution embeddings generated by the *Contracting ProbSparse Self-Attention Blocks*. The fundamental design consideration is the adoption of U-Net-inspired connections to extract encoder features at multiple resolutions and provide a direct connection to the corresponding symmetric decoder block. The Yformer additionally utilizes reconstruction loss to learn generalized embeddings that better approximate the data generating distribution. Figures 2a and 2b compares the Informer architecture with the Yformer and Fig. 3 illustrates the U-Net connections employed by the Yformer model.

The **Y-Past Encoder** of the Yformer is designed using a similar encoder structure as that of the Informer (Fig. 2a). The Y-Past Encoder embeds the past sequence (x, y) into a scalar projection along with the addition of positional and temporal embeddings. Multiple *Contracting ProbSparse Self-Attention Blocks* are used to generate encoder embeddings at various resolutions following a con tracting pyramid structure. The Informer model uses the final low-dimensional embedding as the input to the decoder whereas, the Yformer retains the embeddings at multiple resolutions to be passed on to the decoder. This allows the Yformer to use high-dimensional lower-level embeddings effectively.

The **Y-Future Encoder** of the Yformer mitigates the redundant reprocessing of the past sequence (x, y) (used as tokens (x_{token}, y_{token}) in the Informer architecture) by passing only the future predictors (x') through the Y-Future Encoder and utilizing the multi-resolution embeddings to dismiss the need for tokens entirely. The attention blocks in the Y-Future encoder are based on a masked canonical self-attention mechanism [30] to prevent any information leak from the future time steps into the past. Thus, the Y-Future Encoder is designed by stacking multiple *Contracting ProbSparse Self-Attention Blocks* where the *ProbSparse* attention is replaced by the *Masked Attention*. We name these blocks *Contracting Masked Self-Attention Blocks*.

The Yformer processes the past inputs and the future predictors separately within its encoders. However, considering the time steps, the future predictors are a continuation of the past time steps. For this reason, the Yformer model concatenates (represented by the symbol $\mathbin{+\!\!+}$) the past encoder embedding and the future encoder embedding along the time dimension after each encoder block, preserving the continuity between the past input time steps and the future time steps. Let i represent the index of an encoder block, then e_{i+1}^{past} and e_{i+1}^{fut} represent the output from the past encoder and the future encoder respectively. The final concatenated encoder embedding (e_{i+1}) is calculated as,

$$e_{i+1}^{past} = \text{ContractingProbSparseSelfAttentionBlock}(e_i^{past})$$
$$e_{i+1}^{fut} = \text{ContractingMaskedSelfAttentionBlock}(e_i^{fut}) \qquad (4)$$
$$e_{i+1} = e_{i+1}^{past} \mathbin{+\!\!+} e_{i+1}^{fut}$$

The encoder embeddings represented by $\mathcal{E} = [e_0, \ldots, e_I]$ (where I is the number of encoder layers) contain the combination of past and future embeddings at multiple resolutions.

The **Y-Decoder** of the Yformer consists of two parts. The first part takes as input the final concatenated low-dimensional embedding (e_I) of the encoders and performs a multi-head canonical self-attention mechanism. Since the canonical self-attention layer is separated from the repeating attention blocks within the decoder, the Yformer complexity from this full attention module does not increase with an increase in the number of decoder blocks. The U-Net architecture inspires the second part of the Y-Decoder. Consequently, the decoder is

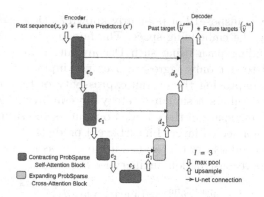

Fig. 3. U-Net connections for effectively utilizing embeddings at multiple resolutions in the Yformer. The Y-Past Encoder embeddings and the Y-Future Encoder embeddings are concatenated within the Yformer encoder. A direct connection is allowed between the contracting encoder embedding (e_i) and the corresponding expanding decoder embedding (d_{I-i}). (++ denotes concatenation)

structured in a symmetric expanding path identical to the contracting encoder (Fig. 3). We realize this idea by introducing *Expanding ProbSparse Cross-Attention Block* for symmetric upsampling.

The ***Expanding ProbSparse Cross-Attention Block*** within the Yformer decoder performs two tasks: (1) upsample the compressed encoder embedding e_I and (2) perform restricted cross attention between the expanding decoder embedding d_{I-i} and the corresponding encoder embedding e_i as shown below.

Algorithm 2. Expanding ProbSparse Cross-Attention Block

$Input : d_{I-i}, e_i$
$Output : d_{I-i+1}$
$d_{I-i+1} \leftarrow \text{ProbSparseCrossAttn}(d_{I-i}, e_i)$
$d_{I-i+1} \leftarrow \text{Conv1d}(d_{I-i+1})$
$d_{I-i+1} \leftarrow \text{LayerNorm}(d_{I-i+1})$
$d_{I-i+1} \leftarrow \text{ELU}(\text{ConvTranspose1d}(d_{I-i+1}))$

The *Expanding ProbSparse Cross-Attention Blocks* within the Yformer decoder uses a ProbSparseCrossAttn to construct direct connections between the lower levels of the encoder and the corresponding symmetric higher levels of the decoder. Direct connections from the encoder to the decoder are an essential component for the majority of models within the image domain. For example, ResNet [8], and DenseNet [9] have demonstrated that direct connections between previous feature maps, strengthen feature propagation, reduce parameters, mitigate vanishing gradients and encourage feature reuse. However, current transformer-based architectures fail to utilize these direct connections.

We utilize ConvTranspose1d or popularly known as Deconvolution for incrementally increasing the embedding space. The famous U-Net architecture uses a symmetric expanding path using such Deconvolution layers. This property enables the model to not only aggregate over the input but also upscale the latent dimensions, improving the overall expressivity of the architecture. The decoder of Yformer follows a similar strategy by employing Deconvolution to expand the embedding space of the encoded output as shown in Fig. 3.

Finally, a fully connected layer (LinearLayer) predicts the future time steps $\hat{y}^{\text{fut}}$ from the final decoder layer (d_I) and additionally reconstructs the past input targets $\hat{y}^{\text{past}}$ for the reconstruction auxiliary loss.

$$[\hat{y}^{\text{past}}, \hat{y}^{\text{fut}}] = \text{LinearLayer}(d_I) \tag{5}$$

The addition of reconstruction loss to the Yformer as an auxiliary loss serves two significant purposes. Firstly, the reconstruction loss acts as a data-dependent regularization term that reduces overfitting by learning embeddings that are more general [11]. Secondly, the reconstruction loss helps in producing future output in a similar distribution as the inputs. For far horizon forecasting, we are interested in learning a future-output distribution, however, the future-output distribution and the past-input distribution arise from the same data generating process. Therefore having an auxiliary reconstruction loss would direct the gradients to a better approximate of the data generating process. Consequently, the Yformer model is trained on the combined loss ℓ,

$$\ell = \alpha \, \ell^{\text{mse}}(y, \hat{y}^{\text{past}}) + (1 - \alpha) \, \ell^{\text{mse}}(y', \hat{y}^{\text{fut}}) \tag{6}$$

where the first term tries to learn the past targets y and the second term learns the future targets y'. We use the reconstruction factor (α) to vary the importance of reconstruction and future prediction and tune this as a hyperparameter.

6   Experiments

6.1   Datasets

We compare the experimental results of our proposed YFormer architecture, with that of the Informer on three real-world public datasets.

ETTh1 and ETTh2 (Electricity Transformer Temperature[1]): These real-world datasets for the electric power deployment introduced by [35] combine short-term periodical patterns, long-term periodical patterns, long-term trends, and irregular patterns. The data consists of load and temperature readings from two transformers at two different stations with varying load conditions. The ETTm1 dataset is generated by splitting ETTh1 dataset into 15-minute intervals. The dataset has six features and 70,080 data points in total. For easy comparison, we kept the splits for train/val/test consistent with the published results in [35],

---

[1] https://github.com/zhouhaoyi/ETDataset.

where the available 20 months of data is split as 12/4/4. For the Univariate setting, 'OT' (Oil Temperature) was set as the target value.

ECL (Electricity Consuming Load[2]): This electricity dataset represents the electricity consumption from 2011 to 2014 of 370 clients recorded in 15-minutes periods in Kilowatt (kW). We split the data into 15/3/4 months for train, validation, and test respectively as in [35]. For the Univariate setting, 'MT 320' was set as the target value.

6.2   Experimental Setup

Baseline: Our main baseline is the Informer architecture. As a second baseline, we also compare the second-best performing model which is the Informer that uses canonical attention module [35] represented as Informer[†]. Furthermore, we also compare against DeepAR [28], and LogTrans [18] for the univariate setting, and LSTnet [16] for the multivariate setting as they outperform the Informer baseline for certain forecasting horizons. For a quick analysis, we present the percent improvement achieved by the Yformer over the current best results as the final column in Tables 1, 2.

For a fair comparison, we retain the design choices from the Informer baseline like the history input length (T) for a particular forecast length (τ), so that any performance improvement can exclusively be attributed to the architecture of the Yformer model and not to an increased history input length. We performed a grid search for learning rates of $\{0.001, 0.0001\}$, α-values of $\{0, 0.3, 0.5, 0.7, 1\}$, number of encoder and decoder blocks $I = \{2, 3, 4\}$ while keeping all the other hyperparameters the same as the Informer. Furthermore, Adam optimizer and an early stopping criterion with a patience of three epochs was used for all experiments. To counteract overfitting, we tried dropout with varying ratios but interestingly found the effect to be minimal in the results. Therefore, we adopt weight-decay for our experiments with factors $\{0, 0.02, 0.05\}$ for additional regularization. We select the optimal hyperparameters based on the lowest validation loss.

For easy comparison, we choose two commonly used metrics for time series forecasting to evaluate the Yformer architecture, the MAE and MSE in Eq. 2. We performed our experiments on GeForce RTX 2080 Ti GPU nodes with 32 GB ram and provide results as an average of three runs. The source code[3] and optimal hyperparameter configurations are made public for reproducibility.

6.3   Results and Analysis

This section compares our results with the results reported in the Informer baseline both in uni- and multivariate settings for the multiple datasets and horizons. A direct comparison with the reported results [35] is possible as the experimental setup and the problem settings are kept the same. The best-performing and the second-best models are highlighted in bold and in underline, respectively.

---

[2] https://archive.ics.uci.edu/ml/datasets/ElectricityLoadDiagrams20112014.
[3] https://github.com/18kiran12/Yformer-Time-Series-Forecasting.

Table 1. Univariate results for three datasets (four cases) with different prediction lengths $\tau \in \{24, 48, 96, 168, 288, 336, 672, 720, 960\}$.

Methods		Yformer		Informer		Informer[†]		LogTrans		DeepAR		Improvement%	
Metric		MSE	MAE	MSE	MAE	MSE	MAE	MSE	MAE	MSE	MAE	MSE	MAE
ETTh$_1$	24	**0.082**	**0.230**	0.098	0.247	_0.092_	_0.246_	0.103	0.259	0.107	0.280	10.87	6.50
	48	**0.139**	**0.308**	_0.158_	_0.319_	0.161	0.322	0.167	0.328	0.162	0.327	12.03	3.45
	168	**0.111**	**0.208**	_0.183_	_0.346_	0.187	0.355	0.207	0.375	0.239	0.422	39.34	22.54
	336	**0.195**	**0.365**	0.222	0.387	_0.215_	_0.369_	0.230	0.398	0.445	0.552	09.30	1.08
	720	**0.226**	**0.394**	0.269	0.435	_0.257_	_0.421_	0.273	0.463	0.658	0.707	12.06	6.41
ETTh$_2$	24	**0.082**	**0.221**	_0.093_	_0.240_	0.099	0.241	0.102	0.255	0.098	0.263	11.83	7.92
	48	0.172	0.334	**0.155**	**0.314**	_0.159_	_0.317_	0.169	0.348	0.163	0.341	−10.97	−6.37
	168	**0.174**	**0.337**	_0.232_	_0.389_	0.235	0.390	0.246	0.422	0.255	0.414	25.00	13.37
	336	**0.224**	**0.391**	0.263	_0.417_	_0.258_	0.423	0.267	0.437	0.604	0.607	13.18	6.24
	720	**0.211**	**0.382**	_0.277_	_0.431_	0.285	0.442	0.303	0.493	0.429	0.580	23.83	11.37
ETTm$_1$	24	**0.024**	**0.118**	_0.030_	_0.137_	0.034	0.160	0.065	0.202	0.091	0.243	20.00	13.87
	48	**0.048**	**0.173**	0.069	0.203	_0.066_	_0.194_	0.078	0.220	0.219	0.362	27.27	10.82
	96	**0.143**	**0.311**	0.194	_0.372_	_0.187_	0.384	0.199	0.386	0.364	0.496	23.53	16.40
	288	**0.150**	**0.316**	_0.401_	0.554	0.409	_0.548_	0.411	0.572	0.948	0.795	62.59	42.34
	672	**0.305**	**0.476**	_0.512_	_0.644_	0.519	0.665	0.598	0.702	2.437	1.352	40.43	26.09
ECL	48	**0.194**	**0.322**	0.239	0.359	0.238	0.368	0.280	0.429	_0.204_	_0.357_	4.90	9.80
	168	**0.260**	**0.361**	0.447	0.503	0.442	0.514	0.454	0.529	_0.315_	_0.436_	17.46	17.20
	336	**0.269**	**0.375**	0.489	0.528	0.501	0.552	0.514	0.563	_0.414_	_0.519_	35.02	27.75
	720	**0.427**	**0.479**	_0.540_	_0.571_	0.543	0.578	4.891	4.047	0.563	0.595	20.93	19.50
	960	0.595	**0.573**	**0.582**	_0.608_	0.594	0.638	7.019	5.105	0.657	0.683	−2.23	16.11
Count		37		3		0		0		0			
Average												19.82	13.62

Univariate: The proposed Yformer model is able to outperform the Informer baseline in 37 out of the 40 available tasks across different datasets and horizons by an average of 19.82% MSE and 13.62 % of MAE. Table 1 illustrates that the superiority of the Yformer is not just limited to a far horizon but even for the shorter horizons and in general across datasets. Considering the individual datasets, the Yformer surpasses the baselines by 8, 6.8, 21.9, and 18.1% of MAE for the ETTh1, ETTh2, ETTm1, and ECL datasets respectively. MSE results illustrates an improvement of 16.7, 12.6, 34.8, and 15.2% for the ETTh1, ETTh2, ETTm1, and ECL datasets respectively. We observe that the MAE for the model is greater at horizon 48 than the MAE at horizon 168 for the ETTh1 dataset. This may be a case where the reused hyperparameters from the Informer paper are far from optimal for the Yformer. The other results show consistent behavior of increasing error with increasing horizon length τ. Additionally, this behavior is also observed in the Informer baseline for ETTh2 dataset (Table 2), where the loss is 1.340 for horizon 336 and 1.515 for a horizon of 168.

Table 2. Multivariate results for three datasets (four cases) with different prediction lengths $\tau \in \{24, 48, 96, 168, 288, 336, 672, 720, 960\}$.

Methods		Yformer		Informer		Informer†		LogTrans		LSTnet		Improvement%	
Metric		MSE	MAE	MSE	MAE	MSE	MAE	MSE	MAE	MSE	MAE	MSE	MAE
ETTh$_1$	24	**0.485**	**0.492**	<u>0.577</u>	<u>0.549</u>	0.620	0.577	0.686	0.604	1.293	0.901	15.94	10.38
	48	**0.530**	**0.537**	<u>0.685</u>	<u>0.625</u>	0.692	0.671	0.766	0.757	1.456	0.960	22.63	14.08
	168	**0.866**	**0.684**	<u>0.931</u>	<u>0.752</u>	0.947	0.797	1.002	0.846	1.997	1.214	06.98	09.04
	336	**1.041**	**0.803**	1.128	0.873	<u>1.094</u>	<u>0.813</u>	1.362	0.952	2.655	1.369	04.84	01.23
	720	**1.098**	**0.803**	<u>1.215</u>	<u>0.896</u>	1.241	0.917	1.397	1.291	2.143	1.380	09.63	10.38
ETTh$_2$	24	**0.412**	**0.498**	<u>0.720</u>	<u>0.665</u>	0.753	0.727	0.828	0.750	2.742	1.457	42.78	25.11
	48	**1.171**	**0.865**	<u>1.457</u>	<u>1.001</u>	1.461	1.077	1.806	1.034	3.567	1.687	19.63	13.59
	168	**2.171**	**1.218**	3.489	<u>1.515</u>	3.485	1.612	4.070	1.681	<u>3.242</u>	2.513	33.04	19.60
	336	**2.260**	**1.283**	2.723	1.340	2.626	<u>1.285</u>	3.875	1.763	<u>2.544</u>	2.591	11.16	0.16
	720	**2.595**	**1.337**	<u>3.467</u>	<u>1.473</u>	3.548	1.495	3.913	1.552	4.625	3.709	25.15	9.23
ETTm$_1$	24	**0.289**	**0.363**	0.323	<u>0.369</u>	<u>0.306</u>	0.371	0.419	0.412	1.968	1.170	05.56	1.63
	48	<u>0.486</u>	**0.457**	0.494	0.503	**0.465**	<u>0.470</u>	0.507	0.583	1.999	1.215	-4.52	2.77
	96	**0.569**	**0.567**	<u>0.678</u>	0.614	0.681	<u>0.612</u>	0.768	0.792	2.762	1.542	16.08	7.35
	288	**0.649**	**0.593**	<u>1.056</u>	<u>0.786</u>	1.162	0.879	1.462	1.320	1.257	2.076	38.54	24.55
	672	**0.772**	**0.656**	<u>1.192</u>	<u>0.926</u>	1.231	1.103	1.669	1.461	1.917	2.941	35.23	29.16
ECL	48	**0.306**	**0.390**	0.344	<u>0.393</u>	<u>0.334</u>	0.399	0.355	0.418	0.369	0.445	08.38	0.76
	168	**0.317**	**0.387**	0.368	0.424	<u>0.353</u>	<u>0.420</u>	0.368	0.432	0.394	0.476	10.20	7.86
	336	**0.323**	**0.394**	0.381	<u>0.431</u>	0.381	0.439	<u>0.373</u>	0.439	0.419	0.477	15.22	8.58
	720	**0.312**	**0.384**	0.406	0.443	<u>0.391</u>	<u>0.438</u>	0.409	0.454	0.556	0.565	20.20	12.33
	960	**0.315**	**0.388**	<u>0.460</u>	<u>0.548</u>	0.492	0.550	0.477	0.589	0.605	0.599	31.52	29.20
Count		39		0		1		0		0			
Average												18.41	11.85

Multivariate: We observe a similar trend in the multivariate setting. Here the Yformer model outperforms the baseline method in almost all of the 40 tasks across the three datasets by a margin of 18.41 % MSE and 11.85% of MAE. There is a clear superiority of the proposed approach, especially for the longer horizons. Across the different datasets, the Yformer improves on the baseline results by 9, 13.5, 13.1, and 11.7% of MAE, and 12, 26.3, 13.9, and 17.1% of MSE for the ETTh1, ETTh2, ETTm1, and ECL datasets respectively. We attribute the improvement in performance to superior architecture and the ability to approximate the data distribution due to the addition of auxiliary loss.

7   Ablation Study

Additional experiments were performed on the ETTm1 datasets to analyze the different components of the Yformer model. Similar ablation experiment results for ETTh2 dataset are reported in the Appendix section for reference.

7.1   Y-Former Architecture

In this section, we attempt to understand (1) the improvement brought about by the Y-shaped model architecture, and (2) the impact of the reconstruction loss on the superiority of the Yformer model. Firstly, Fig. 5c compares the model complexity for the proposed Yformer model with the Informer baseline model and demonstrates the advantage offered by the Yformer model for longer horizons. Secondly, Figs. 4a, 4b, show that the Yformer architecture performs better or is comparable to the Informer throughout the entire horizon range. Moreover, for the larger horizons, the Yformer architecture without the reconstruction loss i.e. $\alpha = 0$, has a clear advantage over the Informer baseline. We attribute this improvement in performance to the additional direct U-Net inspired connections within the Yformer architecture. Using feature maps at multiple resolutions offers a clear advantage by eliminating vanishing gradients and encouraging feature reuse. Figures 4a, 4b also clearly delineates the advantage offered by adding reconstruction loss as an auxiliary task for the model, by comparing Yformer with Yformer ($\alpha = 0$) results. Such a multi-task approach offers regularization to the model by learning parameters that do not overfit on the future target distribution and propels the gradients towards a general distribution that can predict the history along with the future time steps.

7.2   Effectiveness of the U-Net Based Skip Connections

To analyze the impact of U-Net based skip-connections, we conduct an ablation study on the Y-former architecture by removing the U-Net skip connections from the encoder to the decoder. We denote this model as Yformer*. Figures 4c, 4d provides a summary of the results obtained after hyperparameter tuning the Yformer* and comparing it with the proposed Yformer model. The skip connections from the encoder to the decoder improve the performance throughout the entire horizon range for the multivariate setting and offers partial improvement for the univariate setting. Within the multivariate setting, the skip connections have a considerable impact on larger horizons and a smaller impact on the shorter horizons. This observation can be reasoned by considering the fact that long-range forecasting can utilize the additional multi-resolution encoder feature maps encoded by the U-Net based skip connections. Similar reason can be applied to the fact that U-Net based skip connections improve the performance of the multivariate setting more than that of the univariate settings.

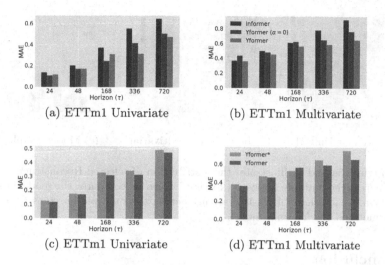

(a) ETTm1 Univariate

(b) ETTm1 Multivariate

(c) ETTm1 Univariate

(d) ETTm1 Multivariate

Fig. 4. (top) Figs. 4a, 4b illustrates the reduction in MAE loss (y-axis) by the Yformer architecture in comparison with the Informer baseline for the univariate and multivariate settings respectively. The Yformer ($\alpha = 0$) represent the Yformer architecture without the reconstruction loss. (bottom) Figs. 4c, 4d demonstrate the reduction in MAE loss (y-axis) brought by the addition of U-Net based skip connections (Yformer) to the Yformer architecture without the skip connections (Yformer*).

7.3   Reconstruction Factor

How impactful is the reconstruction factor α from the proposed loss in Eq. 6? We aggregated the optimal value chosen by hyperparameter tuning α across different datasets and summarized the distribution in Figs. 5a and 5b. Interestingly, α value of 0.7 is the predominant optimal setting across most horizons. Consequently, this shows that a high weight for the reconstruction loss helps the Yformer to achieve a lower loss for the future targets. Moreover, we can observe a trend that α is on average larger for short forecasting horizons signifying the importance of auxiliary loss for the shorter horizons. One possible reason could be that the reconstruction loss generalizes the output distribution better and avoids overfitting on short-horizon lengths. For the longer horizon forecasts, optimal α values are distributed on the lower and upper range of α's evenly, indicating that for long horizons, the reconstruction loss from long history helps for some datasets and does not for other datasets. This could be a characteristic of the dataset having a domain shift within the forecast horizon.

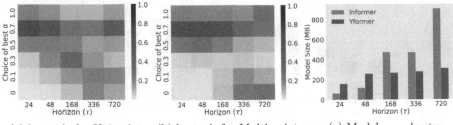

(a) best α's for Univariate   (b) best α's for Multivariate   (c) Model complexity

Fig. 5. Figures 5a and 5b illustrates the distribution of selected Reconstruction factor (y-axis) across the multiple horizons (x-axis). Figure 5c, compares the model size complexity (y-axis) for the multivariate setting across the multiple horizons (x-axis) for the Informer and the Yformer model.

8   Conclusion

Time series forecasting is an important business and research problem that has a broad impact in today's world. This paper proposes a novel Y-shaped architecture, specifically designed for the far horizon time series forecasting problem. The study shows the importance of direct connections from the multi-resolution encoder to the decoder and reconstruction loss for the task of time series forecasting. The Yformer couples the U-Net architecture from the image segmentation domain on a sparse transformer model and empirically demonstrates superior performance across multiple datasets for both univariate and multivariate settings. We believe that our work provides a base for future research in the direction of using efficient U-Net based skip connections and the use of reconstruction loss as an auxiliary loss within the time series forecasting community.

Acknowledgements. This work was supported by the Federal Ministry for Economic Affairs and Climate Action (BMWK), Germany, within the framework of the IIP-Ecosphere project (project number: 01MK20006D).

References

1. Ba, L.J., Kiros, J.R., Hinton, G.E.: Layer normalization. CoRR (2016)
2. Box, G.E.P., Jenkins, G.M.: Some recent advances in forecasting and control. Journal of the Royal Statistical Society. Series C (Appl. Stat.) **17**, 91–109 (1968)
3. Camacho, E.F., Alba, C.B.: Model Predictive Control. Springer, Heidelberg (2013)
4. Cao, W., Wang, D., Li, J., Zhou, H., Li, L., Li, Y.: Brits: bidirectional recurrent imputation for time series. In: NeurIPS (2018)
5. Cirstea, R.G., Guo, C., Yang, B., Kieu, T., Dong, X., Pan, S.: Triformer: Triangular, variable-specific attentions for long sequence multivariate time series forecasting. In: IJCAI (2022)
6. Clevert, D., Unterthiner, T., Hochreiter, S.: Fast and accurate deep network learning by exponential linear units (ELUS). In: ICLR (2016)

7. Fan, C., et al.: Multi-horizon time series forecasting with temporal attention learning. In: SIGKDD (2019)
8. He, K., Zhang, X., Ren, S., Sun, J.: Deep residual learning for image recognition. In: CVPR (2016)
9. Huang, G., Liu, Z., Van Der Maaten, L., Weinberger, K.Q.: Densely connected convolutional networks. In: CVPR (2017)
10. Hyndman, R.J., Athanasopoulos, G.: Forecasting: principles and practice. In: OTexts (2018)
11. Jarrett, D., van der Schaar, M.: Target-embedding autoencoders for supervised representation learning. In: ICLR (2020)
12. Jawed, S., Rashed, A., Schmidt-Thieme, L.: Multi-step forecasting via multi-task learning. In: IEEE Big Data (2019)
13. Kieu, T., Yang, B., Guo, C., S. Jensen, C.: Outlier detection for time series with recurrent autoencoder ensembles. In: IJCAI (2019)
14. Kitaev, N., Kaiser, L., Levskaya, A.: Reformer: The efficient transformer. In: ICLR (2020)
15. Krizhevsky, A., Sutskever, I., Hinton, G.E.: ImageNet classification with deep convolutional neural networks. In: NeurIPS (2012)
16. Lai, G., Chang, W.C., Yang, Y., Liu, H.: Modeling long-and short-term temporal patterns with deep neural networks. In: SIGIR (2018)
17. Le, L., Patterson, A., White, M.: Supervised autoencoders: Improving generalization performance with unsupervised regularizers. In: NeurIPS (2018)
18. Li, S., et al.: Enhancing the locality and breaking the memory bottleneck of transformer on time series forecasting. In: NeurIPS (2019)
19. Lim, B., Arık, S.Ö., Loeff, N., Pfister, T.: Temporal fusion transformers for interpretable multi-horizon time series forecasting. Int. J. Forecast. **37**, 1748–1764 (2021)
20. Lin, T.Y., Dollár, P., Girshick, R., He, K., Hariharan, B., Belongie, S.: Feature pyramid networks for object detection. In: CVPR (2017)
21. Oreshkin, B.N., Carpov, D., Chapados, N., Bengio, Y.: N-BEATS: neural basis expansion analysis for interpretable time series forecasting. In: ICLR (2020)
22. Perslev, M., Jensen, M., Darkner, S., Jennum, P.J., Igel, C.: U-time: a fully convolutional network for time series segmentation applied to sleep staging. In: NeurIPS (2019)
23. Petit, O., Thome, N., Rambour, C., Themyr, L., Collins, T., Soler, L.: U-net transformer: self and cross attention for medical image segmentation. In: International Workshop on MLMI (2021)
24. Qin, Y., Song, D., Chen, H., Cheng, W., Jiang, G., Cottrell, G.W.: A dual-stage attention-based recurrent neural network for time series prediction. In: IJCAI (2017)
25. Rangapuram, S.S., Seeger, M.W., Gasthaus, J., Stella, L., Wang, Y., Januschowski, T.: Deep state space models for time series forecasting. In: NeurIPS (2018)
26. Ronneberger, O., Fischer, P., Brox, T.: U-net: convolutional networks for biomedical image segmentation. In: Navab, N., Hornegger, J., Wells, W.M., Frangi, A.F. (eds.) MICCAI 2015. LNCS, vol. 9351, pp. 234–241. Springer, Cham (2015). https://doi.org/10.1007/978-3-319-24574-4_28
27. Sagheer, A., Kotb, M.: Time series forecasting of petroleum production using deep lstm recurrent networks. Neurocomputing **323**, 203–213 (2019)
28. Salinas, D., Flunkert, V., Gasthaus, J., Januschowski, T.: Deepar: Probabilistic forecasting with autoregressive recurrent networks. Int. J. Forecast. 36, 1181–1191 (2020)

29. Sezer, O.B., Gudelek, M.U., Ozbayoglu, A.M.: Financial time series forecasting with deep learning: a systematic literature review: 2005–2019. Appl. Soft Comput. **90** 106181(2020)
30. Vaswani, A., et al.: Attention is all you need. In: NeurIPS (2017)
31. Wang, S., Li, B.Z., Khabsa, M., Fang, H., Ma, H.: Linformer: Self-attention with linear complexity. ArXiv (2020)
32. Wang, Y., Tao, X., Shen, X., Jia, J.: Wide-context semantic image extrapolation. In: CVPR (2019)
33. Wang, Z., Yan, W., Oates, T.: Time series classification from scratch with deep neural networks: a strong baseline. In: IJCNN (2017)
34. Wu, H., Xu, J., Wang, J., Long, M.: Autoformer: decomposition transformers with auto-correlation for long-term series forecasting. In: NeurIPS (2021)
35. Zhou, H., et al.: Informer: beyond efficient transformer for long sequence time-series forecasting. In: AAAI (2021)
36. Zhou, H.Y., Guo, J., Zhang, Y., Yu, L., Wang, L., Yu, Y.: nnFormer: interleaved transformer for volumetric segmentation. ArXiv (2021)
37. Zou, X., Wang, Z., Li, Q., Sheng, W.: Integration of residual network and convolutional neural network along with various activation functions and global pooling for time series classification. Neurocomputing **367**, 39–45 (2019)

Learning Perceptual Position-Aware Shapelets for Time Series Classification

Xuan-May Le[1], Minh-Tuan Tran[2], and Van-Nam Huynh[1(✉)]

[1] School of Knowledge Science, Japan Advanced Institute of Science and Technology, Nomi, Japan
{xuanmay,huynh}@jaist.ac.jp
[2] School of Computing, Korea Advanced Institute of Science and Technology, Daejeon, Korea
tmtuan@kaist.ac.kr

Abstract. Shapelets are time series subsequences that effectively distinguish time series classes. Recently, time series classifiers based on shapelets have gained interest from the community thanks to their high accuracy and interpretable results. However, these shapelet-based methods still have some problems in both shapelet initialization and learning shapelet phases that limit their performances. In this paper, we propose a novel shapelet-based classifier, called Perceptual Position-aware Shapelet Network (PPSN), to effectively discover and optimize the shapelets. Our method effectively utilizes the perceptually important points to extract a small number of high-quality shapelet candidates and leverages the position-aware subsequence distance for evaluating these candidates. In the learning shapelet phase, our model applied the fixed normalization on each shapelet's transformed values to address the negative impact of their different value ranges. It also uses the stop-gradient connection in the first few epochs to reduce the unwelcome effect of the non-optimal weights of the final linear layer. Experimental results on 112 UCR datasets demonstrate that our model is state-of-the-art compared to existing non-ensemble methods and competitive with the current most accurate classifier, HIVE-COTE 2.0, while retaining the advantage of low computational time and the power of interpretation.

Keywords: Time series classification · Shapelet discovery · Efficiency

1 Introduction

Time series classification (TSC) has been receiving a great attention from the research community due to its importance in many real-world applications. In 2009, Ye et al. [1] introduced a novel concept of shapelets for TSC. Intuitively, shapelets are time series subsequences that can effectively discriminate the classes. It has been demonstrated to be a superb success in leveraging for TSC tasks since various classes are generally recognized by local patterns

---

X.-M. Le and M.-T. Tran—Equal contribution.

© The Author(s), under exclusive license to Springer Nature Switzerland AG 2023
M.-R. Amini et al. (Eds.): ECML PKDD 2022, LNAI 13718, pp. 53–69, 2023.
https://doi.org/10.1007/978-3-031-26422-1_4

rather than global structures. Furthermore, shapelet-based approaches can convey interpretable results. Two first shapelet-based classifiers searched all possible shapelet candidates from the dataset and selected the final shapelets by their information gain. After that, they build the shapelet decision tree with the optimal shapelet at each of their nodes [1] or transform a target time series by its distance to shapelets and then leverage several standard methods to classify transform values instead of the original time series [6]. On the other hand, shapelets and learning algorithms have been integrated into recent research [2–4] to directly train shapelets that can identify time series of distinct classes.

In general, almost the shapelet-based classifiers contain two main phases: (i) shapelet initialization phase that discovers shapelet candidates from training time series and then selects the final shapelets by using quality evaluations like information gain, Kruskal-Wallis statistic or F-statistic; (ii) learning shapelet phase that optimizes shapelets through a gradient descent algorithm with the neural network model. Nevertheless, there are shortcomings in both phases of the existing shapelet-based methods.

In the shapelet initialization phase, the first shapelet-based methods [1,6] use a so-called Full Extractor to find all possible shapelet candidates and then utilize the Euclidean Distance to define the distance between the shapelet candidates and the target time series, it yields a good performance while suffering from high computational complexity. To avoid this problem, in [2], the authors proposed to use the Fixed-Length Extractor that only draws out all the candidates of the same length. Then, they apply k-Mean for clustering these candidates and use the k-Mean centroids as initial shapelets. However, this means that the shapelet length must be fixed while there can be shapelets of different lengths in the dataset. Recently, several attempts have been made to shorten the time for the process of shapelet extractor and automatically tune cumbersome parameters (e.g., the number and length of shapelets) by exploiting piecewise aggregate approximation (PAA), potentially resulting in loss of detailed data characteristics [5,7,8]. On the other hand, leveraging Euclidean Distance to calculate subsequence distance between shapelet candidates and original long time series instances takes significant time and inadvertently ignores the position of shapelets.

In the learning shapelet phase, the previous methods learn directly from the subsequence distances (transformed values) of shapelets and target time series. However, this makes the model challenging to train and converge when some shapelets give an extremely high values, and others provide values that are considered small. On the other hand, during the first training epochs, the linear layer in the final network usually generates very unsatisfactory predictions due to its non-optimal weights. Both problems may limit the model's performance.

In this paper, we propose a novel method called the Perceptual Position-aware Shapelets Network (PPSN) for time series classification in order to tackle the aforementioned issues. In the shapelet initialization phase, we construct a perceptual shapelet extractor that automatically extracts a few prominent shapelet candidates by using three consecutive important points. Next, we use position-aware subsequence distance for shapelet evaluation, which calculates the distance of the shapelet candidate and its corresponding time series by leveraging its position information rather than comparing it with the entire original time series, leading to both achieving better performance and reducing the computation time. Finally, high-quality shapelets with various lengths are retained effectively. In the learning shapelet phase, our model applied the fixed normalization on each shapelet's transformed values to address the negative impact of their different value ranges. Furthermore, the proposed method uses the stop-gradient connection in the first few epochs (stop-gradient epochs) to reduce the unwelcome effect of the non-optimal weights of the final linear layer.

Our contributions can be summarized as follows: (i) We propose the novel shapelet-based approach, PPSN, that combines the effective shapelet extractor and effectively applies position information to calculate subsequence distance; (ii) We also introduce the fixed normalization and stop-gradient epochs techniques that increase the model's accuracy; (iii) Extensive experiments on 112 UCR datasets show that our PPSN achieves state-of-the-art performance to non-ensemble methods while still having the power of interpretation and low computational time.

2 Relative Works

2.1 State-of-the-Art Time Series Classifiers

During the late decades, numerous algorithms have been developed for TSC, among them the ensemble-based and feature-based methods are currently the state-of-the-art. Some popular ensemble-based methods include HIVE-COTE [13] and the most accurate TSC model, HIVE-COTE 2.0 [12], that combine four highly different classifiers, each of which is designed to capture a separate discriminatory feature. InceptionTime [16] is the best deep learning model for TSC. It is proposed to reduce the variance of the sub-model by using an ensemble of five Inception-based convolutional neural networks. On the other hand, many feature-based methods have been demonstrated to be successful in the task. Specifically, ROCKET [11] feeds the target time series into convolutional kernels and then classifies their transformed features by a simple linear classifier, e.g. ridge regression. MiniRocket [14] is a reformulated version of ROCKET, which makes a few adjustments in their kernels and highly optimizes the convolutional process. Thus, MiniROCKET achieves the state-of-the-art compared to non-ensemble classifiers. Shapelet-based classifiers [1,6] are also the feature-based approaches. However, since essential local patterns (shapelets) obtained from original time series are employed to designate their class, shapelet-based approaches can deliver more interpretable decisions.

2.2 Perceptually Important Points

Perceptually Important Points (PIPs) method was first proposed [9] in order to extract important points from a price series. PIPs are then mainly used in time series data mining for many tasks such as data representation or dimension reduction. Assume we have a time series $T = [t_1, ..., t_n]$, where k is the number of salient points to be extracted. To begin, we create a list of PIPs ($PIPs = [1, n]$) with the first and last indexes of T. The maximum Perpendicular Distance (PD) from the line created from two preceding elements added to PIPs is then determined by recursively finding the index in T with the highest PD. Equation 1 is used to compute the PD between one position pos and PIPs.

$$PD(pos, PIPs) = \frac{a * P_{pos} - T_{pos} + c}{\sqrt{a^2 + 1}} \tag{1}$$

where, $a = \frac{T_e - T_s}{P_e - P_s}$, $c = T_e - a * P_e$ and $P = z\_norm([1, ..., n])$ is a z-normalized list of positions. In which, given g where $1 \leq g \leq k$ and $PIPs_g < pos < PIPs_{g+1}$, define $s = PIPs_g$ and $e = PIPs_{g+1}$. The Fig. 1 shows an example of finding the first six PIPs from the target time series.

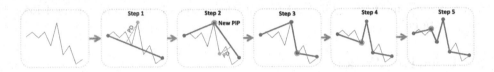

Fig. 1. The process of extracting first 6 PIPs. In that, PD is calculated by Eq. 1.

3 Preliminaries

In this section, we provide all of the essential definitions and notations.

Definition 1. Time Series. *A time series T is a sequence of real numbers collected at regular intervals over a period of time: $T = [t_1, .., t_n]$, where $n \in N$ is length of T.*

Definition 2. Time Series Dataset. *A time series dataset D consists of m time series: $D = [T_1, ..., T_m]$, where T_i is the $i - th$ time series in D with Y_i is label of T_i. Note that, $Y_i \in Y$ is label of dataset and $|Y|$ is indicated as number of classes in dataset D.*

Definition 3. Subsequence. *Given a time series T of length n, a time series subsequence $T_{i,i+l-1} = [t_i, ..., t_{i+l-1}]$ is a consecutive subsequence of time series T, where i is a starting position and l is length of S with $l \leq n$.*

Definition 4. Time Series Distance Measure. *Time series distance measure is a crucial function for determining the similarity of two time series.*

Complexity Invariant Distance. *Complexity Invariant Distance (CID) [17] is motivated on the notion that complex time series are frequently seen to be* *more comparable to simple time series than to other complex time series. The complexity-invariant estimate, $CI(Q) = \sqrt{\sum_{i=1}^{n-1}(q_{i+1} - c_i)^2}$, is used to calculate the CID of Q and C as follows:*

$$CID(Q,C) = ED(Q,C) * \frac{max(CI(Q), CI(C))}{min(CI(Q), CI(C))}, \tag{2}$$

where ED is Euclidean Distance:

$$ED(Q,C) = \sqrt{\sum_{i=1}^{n}(q_i - c_i)^2} \tag{3}$$

Definition 5. Subsequence Distance (SubDist). *Given a time series $T = [t_1, ..., t_n]$ of length n, and a subsequence $S^i = [s_1^i, ..., s_l^i]$ of length l, with $l \leq n$, the subsequence distance of T and S^i (SubDist) is determined as:*

$$SubDist(T, S^i) = \min_{j=1}^{n-l+1} \left(ED(T_{j,j+l-1}, S^i) \right) \tag{4}$$

In this work, we utilize the CID to calculate the SubDist between T and S^i, called CID_SubDist, the formulation for determining CID_SubDist is given by:

$$CID\_SubDist(T, S^i) = \min_{j=1}^{n-l+1} \left(CID(T_{j,j+l-1}, S^i) \right) \tag{5}$$

Definition 6. Information Gain (Infogain). *Given a time series dataset D with two labels A and B, where p(A) and p(B) represent the percentage of instances in each class. Given a split strategy sp that divides D into two sub-datasets D1 and D2. This splitting's information gain is determined as follows:*

$$IG(sp) = E(D) - \left(\frac{|D_1|}{|D|} E(D_1) + \frac{|D_2|}{|D|} E(D_2) \right) \tag{6}$$

where $|D|$ denotes the number of instances in dataset D, and E(D) denotes the entropy of D, which is calculated as follows:

$$E(D) = -p(A)log(p(A)) - p(B)log(p(B)) \tag{7}$$

Definition 7. Optimal Split Point (OSP). *Give time series dataset D and a subsequence S^i, we first compute SubDist between S^i and all instances of D, and then sort the distance collection. For separating D into D_1 and D_2, we pick certain distance thresholds d_t. For instance, $SubDist(S^i, T_i) \leq d_t$ if $T_i \in D_1$, while $SubDist(S^i, T_i) > d_t$ if $T_i \in D_2$. An Optimal Split Point (OSP), $OSP(S^i)$, is a set of thresholds with the best information gain when compared to other thresholds d_t^*.*

$$IG(S^i, OSP(S^i)) \geq IG(S^i, d_t^*) \tag{8}$$

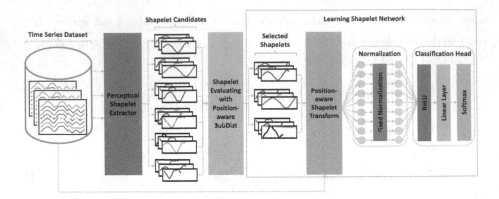

Fig. 2. General Architecture of Perceptual Position-aware Shapelet Network.

Definition 8. Shapelet. *Given a shapelet candidate S^i of class Y_i with its corresponding $OSP(S^i)$. It is considered as a shapelet when it has the highest information gain compared to any other candidates S^*.*

$$IG(S^i, OSP(S^i)) \geq IG(S^*, OSP(S^*)) \tag{9}$$

As a result, it can discriminate a class Y_i from other classes $Y \backslash \{Y_i\}$.

Definition 9. Soft-minimum Function. *Arcoding to [2], the minimum functions in 4 and 5 are not differentiable. We therefore use the soft-minimum function instead of original minimum function. Given a time series T of length n, and a shapelet S^i of length l. The CID_SubDist of T and S^i is calculated as Eq. 10. In that, when $\alpha \to \infty$ the soft-minimum approaches the true minimum.*

$$CID\_SubDist(T, S^i) = \frac{\sum_{i=1}^{n-l+1} CID_{i,l} e^{\alpha CID_{i,l}}}{\sum_{i=1}^{n-l+1} e^{\alpha CID_{i,l}}} \tag{10}$$

where, $CID_{i,l} = CID(T_{i,i+l-1}, S^i)$

4   Perceptual Position-Aware Shapelet Network

In this section, we propose the novel Perceptual Position-aware Shapelet Network (PPSN). Specifically, our method uses the Perceptually Important Points to extract the shapelet candidates (Perceptual Shapelet Extractor at Sect. 4.1) and leverages the position information on calculating SubDist (Position-aware SubDist at Sect. 4.2) for evaluating these shapelet candidates. Then, we also introduce two techniques for better classifying, namely Fixed Normalization (Sect. 4.3) and Stop-Gradient Epochs (Sect. 4.3). The general architecture of PPSN is shown in Fig. 2.

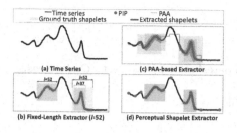

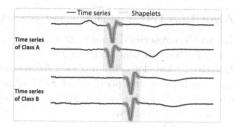

Fig. 3. Shapelets in beef dataset selected by compared extractors. Ground truths are the most infogain shapelets.

Fig. 4. Two classes in CinCECGTorso dataset have a same shapelet in different positions.

Table 1. Average information gains of PSE with different number of continuous PIPs on 10 first UCR datasets.

Number of continuous PIPs	2	**3 (Default)**	4	5	Full extractor
Avg. Information Gain	0.501	**0.631**	0.601	0.581	0.652

4.1 Perceptual Shapelet Extractor

Extracting shapelet candidates is the most critical component of shapelet-based classifiers. From that, the high-quality shapelets can increase the model's performance [5,7]. However, the current extractors have their own problems. The Full Extractor used in [1,6], for instance, draws out all possible candidates from the dataset that can provide the highest quality after evaluation, but its complexity is the significant problem. To avoid the problem, Fixed-Length Extractor [2] draws out the same length l candidates. However, the method requires the length of shapelet as its parameter, while finding the optimal fixed length is challenging. Furthermore, time series often has shapelets with various lengths; therefore, constraining shapelets' length can hurt the accuracy. For instance, the most infogain Fixed-Length Extractor (with $l = 52$) cannot draw out the shapelets that perfectly cover the second ground truth of length 37. Note that, the ground truths are the most infogain shapelets extracted by Full Extractor. [5,7,8] proposed to use the PAA-based extractor to reduce the complexity. However, this may make the methods suffer from the loss of detailed data characteristics. In Fig. 3(c) the extracted shapelet is bigger on both sides compared to the ground truths since they only use the reduced-information segments.

We propose to use Perceptual Shapelet Extractor (PSE), which leverages the PIPs to efficiently pick out the high-quality shapelet candidates of various lengths. We conduct the experiment in Table 1 to show that 3 continuous PIPs provide the highest infogain which is close to Full Extractor's score (0.631 compared to 0.652). The Algorithm 1 shows the pseudo-code of PSE. Specifically, with each new extracted PIPs, p, three new possible candidates are checked and added into the candidate pool if they exist (Line 9 → 15). Figure 3(d) demonstrates that our PSE can extract perfectly similar shapelets with ground truths.

Algorithm 1. Perceptual Shapelet Extractor

Input: Time series data set: $D = [T_1, ..., T_m]$, number of important points: k, and n is length of all time series in D
Output: Shapelet candidates set SCs, candidates' start position set SC_start_pos, and candidates' end position set SC_end_pos
01: $SCs = SCs\_start\_pos = SCs\_end\_pos = []$
02: **for** $i - 1$ to $|D|$ **do**
03:       $PIPs = [1, n]$
04:       **for** $j = 1$ to $k - 2$ **do**
05:             Find p from 1 to n with max $PD(T_i[pos], PIPs)$ where $p \notin PIPs$
06:             $PIPs$.append(p)
07:             $PIPs$.sort()
08:             **for** $z = 0$ to 2 **do**
09:                 # Check if the candidate is valid, if yes add it into SCs
10:                 **if** $p - z \geq 1$ **and** $p + 2 - z \leq |PIPs|$ **then**
11:                     $start\_pos = PIPs[p - z]$, $end\_pos = PIPs[p + 2 - z]$
12:                     SCs.append($T_i[start\_pos : end\_pos]$)
13:                     SCs_start_pos.append($start\_pos$)
14:                     SCs_end_pos.append(end_pos)
15: **return** $SCs, SCs\_start\_pos, SCs\_end\_pos$

4.2 Position-Aware Sub-Distance for Shapelet Evaluating

Position-Aware Sub-Distance (PSD). Subsequence distance (SubDist) is the distance of shapelet and the best matching location in the time series instance. Typically, ED is used to calculate the SubDist of the shapelet candidate to the entire target time series, which ignores the position information of the shapelet. As a result, it significantly elevates their computing cost and renders them susceptible when the major difference between time series of various classes is the location of the shapelet. In Fig. 4, two first time series belong to the same class A, and two last ones come to class B. Obviously, four time series share a similar subsequence, but differ in their occurrence position. To address this issue, we use a Position-aware SubDist (PSD), which only computes the SubDist between the shapelet and the subsequence in target time series with the original position of the shapelet, but enlarges on both sides with a window size w. Given time series T of length n, shapelet S^i with its start position s_i and end position e_i, and window size w. The Position-aware SubDist (PSD) of T and S^i is calculated as Eq. 11. Note that, instead of ED, we use the CID for the SubDist (as Eq. 5).

$$PSD(T, S^i) = CID\_SubDist(T[s\_pos_i : e\_pos_i], S^i), \tag{11}$$

$$s\_pos_i = \begin{cases} s_i - w + 1, & s_i - w + 1 \geq 1 \\ 1, & \text{otherwise} \end{cases} ; \quad e\_pos_i = \begin{cases} e_i + w, & e_i + w \leq n \\ n, & \text{otherwise} \end{cases}$$

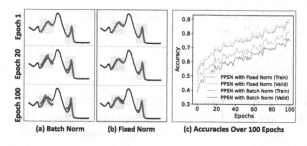

Fig. 5. (a,b) The changing of shapelets after 1, 20 and 100 epochs. (c) Average accuracies over 5 runs in Beef dataset of compared methods.

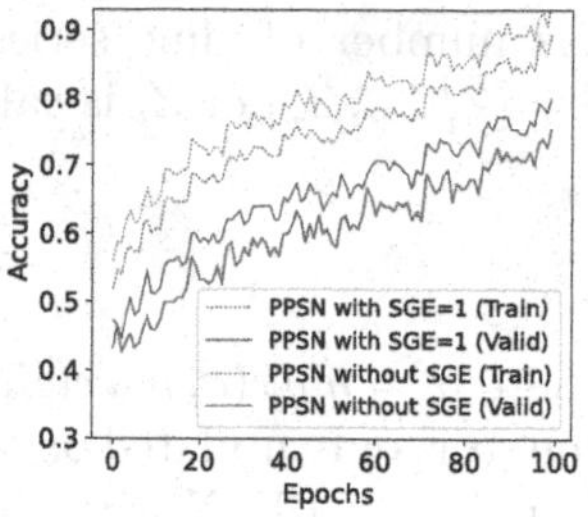

Fig. 6. Average accuracies over 5 runs in Beef dataset of compared methods.

Shapelet Evaluating with PSD. Given the shapelet candidates set $SCs = [S^1, ..., S^c]$, we find OSP of them with PSD between each S^i and all instances of D. Then, the top highest infogain g shapelet candidates are considered as selected shapelets $S = [S^i, ..., S^g]$. Given S^* is any instance in $SCs \backslash S$.

$$IG(S^i, OSP(S^i)) \geq IG(S^*, OSP(S^*))$$

4.3 Learning Shapelet Network

The ground truth shapelets have better discriminant capabilities that may not occur in the training time series instance. In this module, we use the set of selected shapelets as the learnable parameters and try to optimize it by the learning shapelet network. The model includes four modules: Position-aware Shapelet Transform, Fixed Normalization, Classification Head, and Stop-Gradient Epochs.

Position-Aware Shapelet Transform. With the utility of PSD mentioned at Sect. 4.2, our method transforms the time series by the PSD (Eq. 11) instead of original SubDist. Given the set of shapelet $S = [S^i, ..., S^g]$ and the input time series T. The transformed vector, $Z = [Z_i, ..., Z_g]$ of T is computed as follows:

$$Z_i = PSD(T, S^i), \quad \forall i \in [1, .., g] \tag{12}$$

Fixed Normalization. Each shapelet has a different OSP to classify its class and others. This makes the shapelet generate the different ranges of SubDist values. Consequently, it makes the model challenging to train and converge when some shapelets generate extremely high SubDist values, and others provide significantly small values. We proposed the fixed normalization on each shapelet's transformed values to address this problem. Given the vector of transformed Position-ware SubDist of Shapelet S^i over a mini-batch: $\mathcal{B} = [Z_i^1, ..., Z_i^b]$ with

b is number of time series instances in the batch. The normalization vector $\bar{B} = [\bar{Z}_i^1, ..., \bar{Z}_i^b]$ of Z_i is calculated as follows:

$$\bar{Z}_i^j = 1 - \frac{Z_i^j}{\sigma}, \quad \forall j \in [1, .., b] \tag{13}$$

where $\sigma = max(\sigma, max(Z_i))$ is the learned parameter. Unlike batch normalization, σ is only updated on the first epoch. In Fig. 5, by stopping the σ update, the shapelets of PPSN with fixed normalization are not changing excessively, while its accuracies are higher than that of batch normalization. It demonstrates the utility of fixed normalization.

Classification Head. After normalizing the transform value, we use the simple neural network containing a ReLU activation and a single Linear Layer to optimize the shapelets. Softmax function is then used for calculating the predicted label. Given the normalization vector $V = [V_1, ..., V_g]$, the predicted label $\hat{y} = [\hat{y}_1, ..., \hat{y}_{|Y|}]$ is predicted as follows:

$$h_i = W_{i,0} + \sum_{j=1}^{g} W_{i,j} ReLU(V_j), \quad \forall i \in [1, .., |Y|] \tag{14}$$

$$\hat{y}_i = \frac{e^{h_i}}{\sum_{j=1}^{|Y|} e^{h_j}}, \quad \forall i \in [1, .., |Y|] \tag{15}$$

where $W_{i,j}$ and $W_{i,0}$ denote the weights and bias of Linear Layer respectively, and ReLU is the activation function computed as follows: $ReLU(V_j) = max(0, V_j)$. We use the cross-entropy loss function for this model:

$$Loss = - \sum_{i=1}^{|Y|} y_i * log(\hat{y}_i) \tag{16}$$

Stop-Gradient Epochs. Our Perceptual Shapelet Extractor provides very high-quality shapelets for classifying time series. However, during the first training epochs, the linear layer in the final network usually generates very unsatisfactory predictions due to its non-optimal weights. Therefore, we apply the stop-gradient epochs for our model in which the shapelet is not updated. As can be seen in Fig. 6, PPSN without SGE has a significant drop in validation accuracies in the first few epochs, it makes the gap of the model far bigger than that of PPSN with SGE. That demonstrates the negative impact on the accuracy of non-optimal weights and the benefit of stop-gradient epochs.

5   Experimental Results

In this work, we follow to [12] perform experiments on 112 datasets UCR Time Series Archive [10] in the original train/test split (which does not include unequal

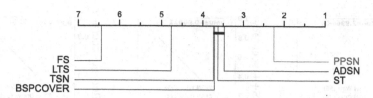

Fig. 7. Critical different diagram shows the average ranks of PPSN and 6 shapelet-based methods on 85 UCR Dataset. Solid lines indicate the group in which there is no significant difference (p-value > 0.05)

length and missing values datasets). They vary by the dataset types, number of classes, number of instances, and time series lengths.

To compare multiple classifiers on multiple datasets, we follow the recommendation in [11] and report the result on a critical different diagram that contains average ranks instead of error rates. A black horizontal line connects methods whose pairwise classification accuracy difference is not statistically significant using a two-sided Wilcoxon signed-rank test ($\alpha = 5\%$). Holm correction is used as the post-hoc test to the Friedman test [11] for all comparison.

In order to reproduce our experiments, we built a website[1] containing all results on 112 UCR datasets and the source code.

5.1 Hyperparameter Setting

The number of Stop-Gradient Epochs and PIPs are fixed at 1 and 0.3 of time series length, respectively. The number of shapelets g is searched over $\{0.1, 0.2, 0.5, 1, 2, 5, 10\}$ of time series length. We use the simple heuristic approach for searching the window size w from $\{5, 10, 20, 30, 50, 100, 200\}$. In that, with each number of shapelets g, we calculate information gain for shapelet candidates for all $w \in \{5, 10, 20, 30, 50, 100, 200\}$. We then choose the window size w, which has the highest average information gain of top g selected shapelets. From that, PPSN has only one parameter g that needs to tune.

We conduct the experiments on Pytorch and use the AdamW optimizer with learning rate at 0.01 and momentum at 0.9. For all datasets, we use the Smoothing Label at 0.1, and the Batch size depends on the size of datasets. Specifically, the batch size is chosen from $\{16, 32, 64, 128, 256\}$ if the number of training instances is higher than $\{0, 100, 200, 400, 800\}$, respectively. For example, if the number of training instances is 500, the batch size is then set at 128.

5.2 Compared with Shapelet Methods

In this section, we conduct the experiment to compare our PPSN with 6 state-of-the-art shapelet-based classifiers, including Learning Time Series Shapelet (LTS) [2], Shapelet Transform (ST) [6], Fast Shapelet (FS) [8], BSPCOVER [7],

---

[1] https://github.com/xuanmay2701/ppsn.

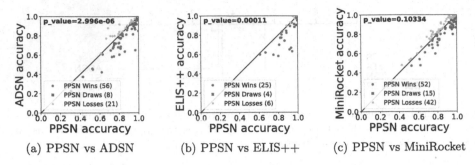

(a) PPSN vs ADSN   (b) PPSN vs ELIS++   (c) PPSN vs MiniRocket

Fig. 8. Scatter charts compare the accuracy of our PPSN and ADSN, ELIS++, and MiniRocket. Each point represents the accuracy over dataset. We only conduct the comparison on the datasets they reported (85, 35, and 109 datasets for ADSN, ELIS++, and MiniRocket, respectively)

Triple-Shapelet Network (TSN) [3] and Adversarial Dynamic Shapelet Network (ADSN) [4]. We follow the protocol in [3,4,7], we only report the result on 85 UCR datasets. We do not compare to ELIS++ [5] since they only provide the results on 35/85 datasets. Figure 7 shows the critical different diagram for comparing our model and baseline classifiers. It is clear that our PPSN achieves the highest rank and significantly outperforms all other shapelet-based classifiers. We also provide a pair-wise comparison with ADSN in Fig. 8(a) and the ELIS++ [5] in Fig. 8(b). The charts show that PPSN is superior (including equal) to ADSN and ELIS++ in most datasets (64/85 and 29/35 datasets, respectively).

5.3   Compared with Current State-of-the-Art Methods

PPSN is compared with 7 SOTA methods including: (i) 4 ensemble-based methods HIVE-COTE (HC1) [13], HIVE-COTE 2.0 (HC2) [12], TS-CHIEF [15], InceptionTime [16]; (ii) 2 feature-based methods Rocket [11], MiniRocket [14]; (iii) interval-based algorithms DrCIF [12]. They are chosen since they are currently the most accurate approaches for time series classification.

We conduct the experiment on all 112 datasets but only report the results of 109 datasets to follow the protocol at [14]. The average rank of our model (PPSN) and other state-of-the-art classifiers is shown in Fig. 9. PPSN is more accurate than MiniRocket, InceptionTime on average, and comparatively less accurate than the most accurate existing ensemble classifiers, especially TSCHIEF, HIVE-COTE, and HIVE-COTE 2.0, although the differences are not statistically significant. However, please note that InceptionTime, HIVE-COTE, TS-CHIEF and HIVE-COTE 2.0 are ensemble methods that combime many different models including several shapelet-based classifiers. Furthermore, our model is considerably faster than those ensemble methods in terms of computational time. We also provide the scatter chart to pair-wise compare our PPSN and the best non-ensemble methods MiniRocket (see Fig. 8(c)). The chart demonstrates that our

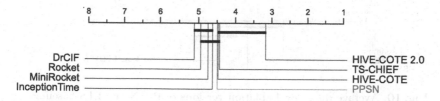

Fig. 9. Critical different diagram shows the average ranks of PPSN and 7 SOTA methods on 109 UCR datasets. Note that InceptionTime, HIVE-COTE, TS-CHIEF and HIVE-COTE 2.0 are ensemble methods that combime many different models including several shapelet-based classifiers.

Table 2. Run time (in hours) to train 109 UCR datasets. We run the shapelet initialization phase on the single thread on a cluster using AMD EPYC 7H12 2.6GHz CPU and learning shapelet phase threads on NVIDIA A40 GPU.

Methods	MiniRocket	Rocket	DrCIF	InceptionTime	HC1	HC2	TS-CHIEF
Total train time	0.25	2.85	45.4	86.58	340.21	427.18	1016.87
Our methods	PPSN (1 thread)		PPSN (32 threads)		PPSN (64 threads)		
	Shapelet Initialization	Learning Shapelet	Shapelet Initialization	Learning Shapelet	Shapelet Initialization	Learning Shapelet	
Total train time	13.73	0.62	4.23	0.62	2.47	0.62	

PPSN is superior (including equal) to MiniRocket on most datasets (68/109 datasets) with p-value at 0.10334.

5.4 Computation Time Comparison

As shown in Table 2, PPSN takes 14.35 h to train all 109 UCR datasets, it is far faster than all of the state-of-the-art methods except Rocket and MiniRocket. Especially, PPSN is two order of magnitude faster than TS-CHIEF and 34 times faster than HC2. In addition, executing PPSN with multiple threads significantly speeds up the computational time. For instance, if we train PPSN on 32 threads and 64 threads, the running time is reduced to only 4.23 and 2.47 h, respectively. Note that, almost of PPSN's running is taken by the shapelet initialization phase, 13.73 h compared to only 0.62 h of the learning shapelet phase (on single threads). This also means that the testing time of our PPSN is really fast, approximately 10 min for all 109 UCR datasets. The results indicate the advantage of our proposed method in terms of computational time.

5.5 Ablation Study and Sensitivity Study

We conduct several experiments on the first 30 UCR datasets to evaluate the effect of proposed components and the key parameter choice for PPSN.

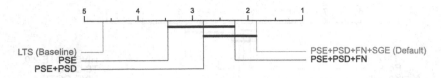

Fig. 10. Average ranks for 4 ablation versions of PPSN and LTS baseline.

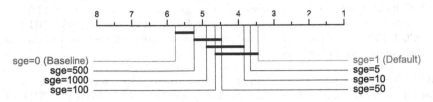

Fig. 11. Average ranks for PPSN with different number of Stop-Gradient Epochs.

Component Evaluation. We first evaluate the impact of four proposed components of our PPSN: Perceptual Shaplet Extractor at Sect. 4.1 (PSE), Position-aware SubDist at Sect. 4.2 (PSD), Fixed Normalization at Sect. 4.3 (FN), and Stop-Gradient Epochs at Sect. 4.3 (SGE). In that, the components are added one-by-one to measure their effect on final accuracy. As can be seen in Fig. 10, all four components have a positive impact on increasing the results of the final proposed model.

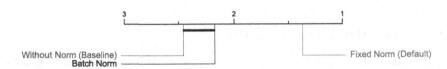

Fig. 12. Average ranks for our Fixed Normalization and Batch Normalization.

Number of Perceptually Important Points. We conduct experiments to execute our PPSN with different number of PIPs values and measure the average information gain (Eq. 4.2) of selected shapelets. We use the parameter related to the length of time series. This means that given n is length of time series, so $k = n * npips$. As shown in Table 3, the average of information gain of PPSN with $npips = 0.3$ (our default parameter) is approximately equal to $npips = 0.4$ and $npips = 0.5$, while the number of extracted candidates is considerably smaller. In addition, the information gain from our PPSN with $npips = 0.3$ is very close to that of Full Extractor, at 0.633 and 0.652, respectively, while only extracting 280 candidates compared to 102380 candidates of Full Extractor.

Table 3. The comparison of our PPSN with different number of PIPs.

Number of PIPs (npips)	0.1	0.2	**0.3 (Default)**	0.4	0.5	Full extractor
Avg. information gain	0.592	0.611	**0.631**	0.633	0.635	0.652
Avg. no. extracted candidates	100.1	195.2	**280.2**	370.5	475.5	102380.9

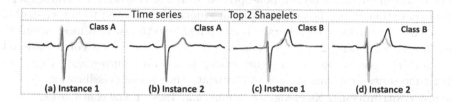

Fig. 13. Selected shapelets by PPSN for ECGFiveDays dataset.

Number of Stop-Gradient Epochs. Figure 11 shows the effect of our PPSN model with different numbers of Stop-Gradient Epochs (SGE), ranging from 1 to 1000. While all PPSN with different number of SGE outperforms the baseline, there is almost no benefit for increasing the number of SGE. Finally, PPSN with SGE at 1 gains the most performance.

Normalization. Figure 12 indicates the comparison of our proposed Fixed Normalization, Batch Normalization, and Baseline (without Norm). It is clear that while there are improvements when applied normalization for PPSN, Fixed Normalization shows a significantly superior result to its counterparts.

5.6   Experiments on Interpretability

One of the great capabilities of shapelets is the power of interpretability, which can effectively provide data comprehension. Figure 13 illustrates that the shapelets can discriminate between two classes of the ECGFiveDays dataset [10]. Electrocardiography (ECG) is a term that refers to the study of the heart. Two time series instances in Fig. 13 (a) (b) come from Class A, and those of Fig. 13 (c) (d) come from Class B. It is clear that selected shapelets by PPSN (orange lines) indicate the major differences between segments in the two classes. Specifically, the first shapelet presents a QRS complex, while the second one is a T wave of ECG. Intuitively, the T wave gained a larger peak compared to the QRS complex in Class A. In medicine, it is known as a hyperacute T wave when it occurs as a result of certain diseases such as ischemia or hyperkalemia.

6   Conclusion

This paper has proposed a novel Perceptual Position-aware Shapelet Network for time series classification, namely PPSN, including two phases. For shapelet initialization phase, we introduce an effective shapelet candidates extractor using perceptually important points and evaluate them based on position-aware subsequence distance. For learning shapelet phase, we introduce two techniques called fixed normalization and stop-gradient epochs in order to mitigate the detrimental impact of various subsequence distance ranges and diminish the unpleasant effect of the final linear layer's non-optimal weights, respectively. Our experiments show that PPSN is a state-of-the-art method compared to non-ensemble approaches. In addition, its accuracy is comparable to the current most accurate classifier, HIVE-COTE 2.0, while maintaining the benefits of low computational time and interpretive power. In future work, we intend to investigate PPSN to other time series problems such as multivariate time series classification.

Author contributions. Xuan-May Le, Minh-Tuan Tran : Equal contribution

References

1. Chung, F.L.K., Fu, T.C., Luk, W.P.R., Ng, V.T.Y.: Flexible time series pattern matching based on perceptually important points. In: Workshop on Learning from Temporal and Spatial Data in IJCAI (2001)
2. Grabocka, J., Schilling, N., Wistuba, M., Schmidt-Thieme, L.: Learning time-series shapelets. In: Proceedings of the 20th ACM SIGKDD international Conference On Knowledge Discovery And Data Mining. pp. 392–401 (2014)
3. Ma, Q., Zhuang, W., Cottrell, G.: Triple-shapelet networks for time series classification. In: 2019 IEEE International Conference on Data Mining (ICDM), pp. 1246–1251. IEEE (2019)
4. Ma, Q., Zhuang, W., Li, S., Huang, D., Cottrell, G.: Adversarial dynamic shapelet networks. In: Proceedings of the AAAI Conference on Artificial Intelligence, vol. 34, pp. 5069–5076 (2020)
5. Zhang, H., Wang, P., Fang, Z., Wang, Z., Wang, W.: Elis++: a shapelet learning approach for accurate and efficient time series classification. World Wide Web **24**(2), 511–539 (2021)
6. Lines, J., Davis, L.M., Hills, J., Bagnall, A.: A shapelet transform for time series classification. In: Proceedings of the 18th ACM SIGKDD International Conference on Knowledge Discovery and Data Mining, pp. 289–297 (2012)
7. Li, G., Choi, B.K.K., Xu, J., Bhowmick, S.S., Chun, K.P., Wong, G.L.: Efficient shapelet discovery for time series classification. IEEE Trans. Knowl. Data Eng. (2020)
8. Rakthanmanon, T., Keogh, E.: Fast shapelets: A scalable algorithm for discovering time series shapelets. In: Proceedings of the 2013 SIAM International Conference on Data Mining, pp. 668–676. SIAM (2013)
9. Chung, F.L.K., Fu, T.C., Luk, W.P.R., Ng, V.T.Y.: Flexible time series pattern matching based on perceptually important points. In: Workshop on Learning from Temporal and Spatial Data in International Joint Conference on Artificial Intelligence (2001)
10. Dau, H., et al.: Batista & Hexagon-ML The UCR Time Series Classification Archive. (October 2018). www.cs.ucr.edu/~eamonn/time_series_data_2018/
11. Dempster, A., Petitjean, F., Webb, G.I.: Rocket: exceptionally fast and accurate time series classification using random convolutional kernels. Data Min. Knowl. Disc. **34**(5), 1454–1495 (2020)

12. Middlehurst, M., Large, J., Flynn, M., Lines, J., Bostrom, A., Bagnall, A.: Hivecote 2.0: a new meta ensemble for time series classification. Mach. Learn. **110**(11), 3211–3243 (2021)
13. Lines, J., Taylor, S., Bagnall, A.: Time series classification with hive-cote: The hierarchical vote collective of transformation-based ensembles. ACM Trans. Knowl. Disc. Data **12**(5) (2018)
14. Dempster, A., Schmidt, D.F., Webb, G.I.: Minirocket: A very fast (almost) deterministic transform for time series classification. In: Proceedings of the 27th ACM SIGKDD Conference on Knowledge Discovery & Data Mining, pp. 248–257 (2021)
15. Shifaz, A., Pelletier, C., Petitjean, F., Webb, G.I.: Ts-chief: a scalable and accurate forest algorithm for time series classification. Data Min. Knowl. Disc. **34**(3), 742–775 (2020)
16. Ismail Fawaz, H., et al.: Inceptiontime: Finding alexnet for time series classification. Data Mining Knowl. Disc. **34**(6), 1936–1962
17. Batista, G.E., Wang, X., Keogh, E.J.: A complexity-invariant distance measure for time series. In: Proceedings of the 2011 SIAM International Conference on Data Mining, pp. 699–710. SIAM (2011)

Finding Local Groupings of Time Series

Zed Lee[1]([✉]), Marco Trincavelli[2], and Panagiotis Papapetrou[1]

[1] Stockholm University, Stockholm, Sweden
{zed.lee,panagiotis}@dsv.su.se
[2] H&M Group, Milan, Italy
marco.trincavelli@hm.com

Abstract. Collections of time series can be grouped over time both globally, over their whole time span, as well as locally, over several common
time ranges, depending on the similarity patterns they share. In addition,
local groupings can be persistent over time, defining associations of local
groupings. In this paper, we introduce Z-Grouping, a novel framework for
finding local groupings and their associations. Our solution converts time
series to a set of event label channels by applying a temporal abstraction function and finds local groupings of maximized time span and time
series instance members. A grouping-instance matrix structure is also
exploited to detect associations of contiguous local groupings sharing
common member instances. Finally, the validity of each local grouping is
assessed against predefined global groupings. We demonstrate the ability
of Z-Grouping to find local groupings without size constraints on time
ranges on a synthetic dataset, three real-world datasets, and 128 UCR
datasets, against four competitors.

Keywords: Local groupings · Temporal abstractions · Time series

1 Introduction

Groupings of time series can be found in several application domains where multiple time series instances are collected and monitored. These groupings comprise
sets of time series of high similarity over a time period (e.g., in terms of concurrently similar values or trends). Such groupings can span the whole time
series length, defining *global* groupings, or shorter time periods, defining *local*
groupings. Furthermore, some instances may persist being grouped together in
consecutive local groupings over a longer time period, possibly separated by
short time gaps, hence forming *associations* of local groupings. For example,
Fig. 1-left shows two time series with four consecutive local groupings (red-blue-
red-blue), forming an *association* (green box). Moreover, Fig. 1-right shows six
associations of local groupings each depicted by a different color, and each containing several local groupings (bold color) separated by short time gaps (light

---

Supplementary Information The online version contains supplementary material
available at https://doi.org/10.1007/978-3-031-26422-1_5.

color). Note that all local groupings and associations have different lengths and member instances. Such local groupings and associations can be of high utility in various application domains, including retail monitoring [11] or stock price prediction [10]. More concretely:

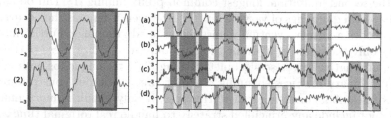

Fig. 1. An example of locally similar time series with four local groupings (left) and six associations (right) each containing several local groupings separated by short time gaps indicated by a lighter color.

- **Retail monitoring:** Product sales may follow different patterns over time, while a particular set of products can show a common local trend, e.g., high sales over the Christmas week, forming a "high sales" local grouping. After Christmas some sales in this grouping may drop, while some may still be maintained. This results in the "high sales" grouping to continue expanding over time and a new "low sales" grouping to be formed. If multiple local sales trends are shared by the same set of products, e.g., high sales over Christmas (1st local trend), followed by low sales in Feb-March (2nd local trend) and high sales over Easter (3rd local trend), they form an *association*.
- **Investing portfolio management:** Sets of stocks exhibit similar fluctuations from time to time. Local groupings represent stocks with similar fluctuation trends over fixed time periods. Moreover, at some time point some stocks from a local grouping may start showing different fluctuations and are, hence, placed into another grouping. Finally, *associations* are formed by growth stocks or sectors following consistently common fluctuation patterns, e.g., rising and dropping concurrently over the same time periods, and can be used for improving the portfolio over time or suggesting new portfolios.

In this paper, we study two problems: given a set of time series instances, we want to identify (1) local groupings of high similarity with maximized time span and number of member instances, (2) associations of maximum number of common local groupings and number of member instances. One solution is clustering (e.g., kmeans under the Euclidean distance) over a fixed-length sliding window. Nonetheless, such approach has two limitations: (1) noise or outliers can distort distance values, (2) as local groupings continuously evolve based on the similarity in each grouping, some instances in one grouping may become more similar to instances in another grouping, hence swapping groupings. As a result, detecting local groupings becomes even harder since groupings change over time both in length (i.e., time duration) and size (i.e., number of member instances).

One way to mitigate the first limitation is to resort to *temporal abstractions*, widely used to for time series summarization [14,19]. A temporal abstraction compresses a time series by converting its original values into a set of *event labels* that are no longer sensitive to noise or outliers, and are no longer distorted by minor fluctuations, thus they tend to favor the formation of patterns over time.

For the second limitation, longest common prefix mining [18] can be applied for finding local groupings of varying length. However, it ignores the occurrences of smaller ones and may eventually miss many local groupings. Furthermore, it considers only the ordering of events, hence failing to localize these patterns in time. An alternative way is semigeometric tiling [9], a technique for finding local patterns in binary matrices spanning different ranges without constraining the number of neighbors or a time range. However, it only handles binary matrices and does not include any principled strategy to handle real (original time series) or categorical (abstraction) values. One way to apply semigeometric tiling is to binarize the original time series values by converting them to 1 if the original value is greater than, e.g., the mean of the time series values. Nonetheless, such solution is unable to capture all granularity levels in the data and the formed groupings will be sparse. In addition, this solution cannot identify associations.

1.1   Related Work

There have been several attempts to cluster time series by employing different distance functions [6,13], exploiting temporal features of high utility (e.g., shapelets [15], temporal abstractions [20]), or hybrid solutions [3]. However, they focus only on finding global groupings [2]. Subsequence clustering finds clusters of subsequences within a single time series, but not across different time series [22]. The problem of finding patterns from subsets of a dataset has been addressed in diverse ways including segmentation [8], bi-clustering [5]. However, all previous attempts have focused on finding common patterns between data examples without placing any constraints to the ordering of the features (i.e., both data rows and columns can be re-ordered), making it infeasible to be applied to time series. Column-coherent bi-clustering [12] clusters time series keeping their column order, but the problem formulation and its solutions are still not free from placing specific constraints on the column order. Although semigeometric tiling [9] imposes column order to the problem, it assumes a binary data representation and suffers from generating small tiles that are not practically useful for identifying local groupings of maximum time span. Longest common prefix mining [18] can be applied to extracting temporal patterns of time series; nonetheless, it is not directly applicable to our problem setup as it fails to detect concurrent patterns, since it only focuses on the longest patterns per time series, hence missing many local patterns shared by time series instances. Maximum correlation algorithms [16,17] find the local segment with the maximum correlation between pairs of time series under a minimum subsequence length threshold. This setup is orthogonal to ours since we are interested in finding all local groupings with the maximum number of instances and time span under a similarity measure. In contrast to maximum correlation algorithms, local maximum correlation algorithms [21] identify the longest gapped time interval between two time series with the maximum correlation. This outputs the pair of regions with the highest correlation across the two time series. This problem differs from the problem studied in this paper, since we aim to find groupings of time series subsequences with high similarity over the same time period. Time series motif discovery [4] aims to find motifs, i.e., repetitive patterns in one time series. However, this paper focuses on detecting different time ranges where high similarity of time series instances can be detected, thus creating a grouping that is not repetitive throughout time, unlike motifs. Applying motif discovery across time series instances over a fixed-length sliding window would identify some local groupings, but it would fail to find local groupings of variable time ranges.

1.2 Contributions

To the best of our knowledge, none of the existing formulations and solutions is directly applicable and comparable to our problem, since we aim to find all maximized time spans of groupings of locally similar time series without a specific time range as a constraint. Our main contributions include:

- **Novelty.** We propose Z-Grouping, an effective algorithm for finding *local groupings* of time series with high similarity and their *associations* in four steps by: (a) exploiting the notion of *temporal abstraction*, (b) generating local groupings based on the abstraction labels, (c) generating associations using a *grouping-instance matrix*, (d) validating the local groupings and associations against predefined global groupings.
- **Effectiveness.** We benchmark the effectiveness of Z-Grouping against four competitors on one synthetic and three real-world datasets. Effectiveness is measured in terms of the ability of extracted local groupings to identify highly similar local regions in unseen instances. Z-Grouping achieves lower mean squared error (MSE) up to 59.2% compared to the four competitors on our synthetic dataset, and up to 44.3% on three real-world datasets.
- **Generalizability.** We additionally benchmark Z-Grouping on 128 UCR time series datasets to demonstrate its ability to find valid local groupings with lower errors than the four competitors.

2 Problem Definition

Let $t = \{t_1, \ldots, t_m\}$ be a *time series instance* of length $|t| = m$. A *time series collection* $\mathcal{T} = \{t_1, \ldots, t_n\}$ is a collection of $|\mathcal{T}| = n$ time series instances.

Definition 1. (Event sequence) *An event sequence* $e = \{e_1, \ldots, e_l\}$ *of length* $|e| = l$ *is a collection of event labels, with* $\forall i \leq n, e_i \in \Sigma$, *where* Σ *is a set of discrete event labels of size* λ.

Definition 2. (Temporal abstraction) *A temporal abstraction of a time series instance* t *is an event sequence* e *obtained by applying a mapping function* f *to* t, *such that* $e = f(t)$, *with* $e \in \Sigma^{|e|}$ *and* $|t| = |e|$.

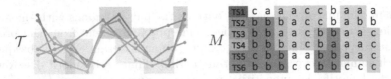

Fig. 2. An example of a time series collection T of size 6 (left) and its event sequence matrix M (right) with $\lambda = 3$ with six candidates for local groupings.

Function f can be any time series summarization technique, such as discrete Fourier transform (DFT) [20] or symbolic aggregate approximation (SAX) [14]. For example, given $\mathbf{t} = \{1, 3, 3, 4, 5\}$, f converts $\mathbf{t}$ to an event sequence $\mathbf{e} = \{a, b, b, c, c\}$ with $\lambda = 3$. Applying temporal abstraction to a time series collection T results in an $n \times m$ event sequence matrix $M = \{\mathbf{e}_1, \ldots, \mathbf{e}_n\}$ where $\mathbf{e}_i = f(\mathbf{t}_i)$.

Definition 3. (Local grouping) *A local grouping $\rho = \{r_\rho, T_\rho\}$ is defined by a time range $\boldsymbol{r_\rho} = [r_s, r_e]$ and a subset of time series instances $T_\rho \in T$ that are similar over time range $\boldsymbol{r_\rho}$.*

The time series instances in T_ρ are called *member instances* of ρ, where $|\rho| = (\mathbf{r}_\rho.r_e - \mathbf{r}_\rho.r_s + 1) \times |T_\rho|$ is the *size* of ρ. A set of local groupings is denoted as $\mathcal{R} = \{\rho_1, \ldots, \rho_{|\mathcal{R}|}\}$.

Example. Figure 2 depicts a time series collection T with $|T| = 6$, and an event sequence matrix M abstracting T. In M we define six local groupings (colored areas) of sizes $|5 \times 3|, |4 \times 2|, |4 \times 2|, |4 \times 2|, |5 \times 2|$, and $|4 \times 1|$.

Definition 4. (Association) *An association $\gamma = \{r_\gamma, T_\gamma, \mathcal{R}_\gamma\}$ is a merger of local groupings $\mathcal{R}_\gamma$ with a time range spanning all $\rho \in \mathcal{R}_\gamma$, while containing the* **intersection** *of the member instances, i.e.:*

$$r_\gamma = \{min(\mathbf{r}_\rho.r_s : \rho \in \mathcal{R}_\gamma), max(\mathbf{r}_\rho.r_e : \rho \in \mathcal{R}_\gamma)\}, T_\gamma = \{T_{\rho_1} \cap T_{\rho_2} \cap \cdots \cap T_{\rho_k}\}\}.$$

The *cardinality* of an association $|\gamma|$ is the number of comprised local groupings. The purpose of an association is to identify time series instances with maximum commonalities over time, by sharing many adjacent local groupings not easily detected globally, due to their negligible time spans or noise and outliers.

Based on the above definitions, we formulate our two problems.

Problem 1. **(Detecting local groupings maximizing the time span and the number of member instances)** Given T and a threshold $\theta \in \mathbb{R}$, find $\mathcal{R}$ with maximum instance size, maintaining the internal pairwise distance between the raw times series members below θ. That is, for each $\rho = \{\mathbf{r}_\rho, T_\rho\} \in \mathcal{R}$:

$$\mathbf{max} \ |\rho|, \ \mathbf{s.t.} \ \forall \mathbf{t}_i, \mathbf{t}_j \in T_\rho : dist(\mathbf{t}_i[\mathbf{r}_\rho.r_s : \mathbf{r}_\rho.r_e], \mathbf{t}_j[\mathbf{r}_\rho.r_s : \mathbf{r}_\rho.r_e]) \leq \theta.$$

Problem 2. **(Detecting associations maximizing the number of common local groupings and member instances)** Given T and a threshold $\theta' \in$

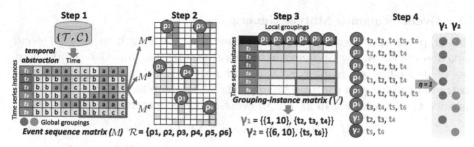

Fig. 3. An example of the four steps of Z-Grouping.

Algorithm 1: Z-Grouping

Input : $\mathcal{T}$, λ, $\mathcal{G}$: global groupings, α: purity, η: global grouping density
Result: $\mathcal{R}$: local groupings, Γ: associations, $\mathcal{Z}$: validity matrix

1   $\mathcal{R} \leftarrow \{\}$, $M \leftarrow \text{SAX}(\mathcal{T}, \lambda)$
2   **for** $M^k \in \text{generateChannels}(M, \lambda)$ **do**
3   **for** $\rho \in \text{generateLocalGroupingCandidates}(M^k)$ **do**
4   **if** $\dfrac{\sum_{t \in \mathcal{T}_\rho} (M^k[t, \mathbf{r}_\rho.r_s : \mathbf{r}_\rho.r_e])}{\sum_{t \in \mathcal{T}_\rho} |M^k[t, \mathbf{r}_\rho.r_s : \mathbf{r}_\rho.r_e]|} \geq \alpha$ **then** $\mathcal{R} \leftarrow \mathcal{R} \cup \rho$
5   $\Gamma \leftarrow \text{createAssociations}(\mathcal{T}, \mathcal{R}, \alpha)$
6   $\mathcal{Z} \leftarrow \text{validateGroupings}(\mathcal{R}, \mathcal{G}, \Gamma, \eta)$
7   **return** $\mathcal{R}$, Γ, $\mathcal{Z}$

$\mathbb{R}$, find the set of associations $\Gamma = \{\gamma_1, \ldots, \gamma_{|\Gamma|}\}$ of maximum cardinality and number of instance members, keeping the internal pairwise distance between the raw instance members below θ'. That is, for each $\gamma = \{\mathbf{r}_\gamma, \mathcal{T}_\gamma, \mathcal{R}_\gamma\} \in \Gamma$:

$$\max \ |\gamma| \times |\mathcal{T}_\gamma|, \ \textbf{s.t.} \ \forall \mathbf{t}_i, \mathbf{t}_j \in \mathcal{T}_\gamma : dist(\mathbf{t}_i[\mathbf{r}_\gamma.r_s : \mathbf{r}_\gamma.r_e], \mathbf{t}_j[\mathbf{r}_\gamma.r_s : \mathbf{r}_\gamma.r_e]) \leq \theta'.$$

Constraining time to a specific range makes it difficult to spot local groupings that can be wider or narrower than the specified range. An exhaustive search with any distance function to optimize *Problems* 1, 2 is computationally prohibitive.

3   The Z-Grouping Algorithm

Z-Grouping is a four-step algorithm for solving *Problems* 1, 2. The first step converts a time series collection into an event sequence matrix by applying a temporal abstraction function. The second step generates local groupings on the abstractions (*Problem* 1), while the third step identifies associations of local groupings using a *grouping-instance matrix* (*Problem* 2). Finally, local groupings and associations are validated against predefined global groupings. These steps, also outlined in Fig. 3 and Algorthim 1, are described below.

3.1 Event Sequence Matrix Generation

This step converts a collection $\mathcal{T}$ of n time series of length m into an *event sequence matrix* M by applying a temporal abstraction function f. Without loss of generality, we employ SAX as our abstraction function, but different abstraction techniques can also be applied. SAX is applied to each time series instance $\mathbf{t}_i \in \mathcal{T}$ resulting in an $n \times m$ event sequence matrix M, such that

$$M = \{\mathbf{e}_i \mid \forall i \leq n, \mathbf{e}_i = SAX(\mathbf{t}_i, \lambda)\} ,$$

and λ corresponds to the event label size parameter of SAX (Algorithm 1, line 1). Next, we split M into λ subsets, which we refer to as *event label channels*, where each channel M^k corresponds to the kth event label in Σ and records its occurrence in the form of binary values, indicating whether an event is assigned with the abstraction label of that channel (line 2); i.e., $\forall i \in \{1, \ldots, n\} \ \forall j \in \{1, \ldots, m\}(M_{ij} = k \rightarrow M_{ij}^k = 1) \wedge (M_{ij} \neq k \rightarrow M_{ij}^k = 0)$. Note that the channels do not contain duplicate values, hence always satisfying $M_{ij}^k \neq M_{ij}^{k'}$ if $k \neq k'$.

Example. An example of this transformation is depicted in Fig. 3 (Step 1), where we obtain matrix M with event labels $\{a, b, c\}$, i.e., $\lambda = 3$. Next, we divide M into three event label channels $\{M^1, M^2, M^3\}$, one per event label.

3.2 Local Grouping Generation

The second step reduces *Problem 1* to finding λ separate sets of local groupings, one set per channel M^k. Since by definition the active events in each channel (indicated by 1s) share the same temporal abstraction label, they also fall in the same value range in their original representation. This implies that each channel can be used to extract local groupings, creating subsets of the channel by selecting time series instances and a time range. We apply semigeometric tiling [9] to each channel to generate candidates for local groupings (Algorithm 1, line 3). The algorithm employs a priority queue to store the counts of active labels for every combination of time ranges $\mathbf{r} = \{r_s, r_e\}$ in each channel M^k. It then iteratively selects the time range with the maximum count from the priority queue and adds rows from the one with the highest number of active labels until a given threshold α is satisfied. α controls *label purity* of each subset, which we define as the proportion of active events in the subset of the channel (see Eq. 1).

More concretely, we create optimal subsets by optimizing the trade-off between two scores: *recall* (i.e., the number of active labels in the subset divided by the total number of active labels in M^k) and α. The algorithm keeps expanding the size of each subset by maximizing the recall while satisfying a given constraint of the subset. Since for each M^k we have a binary problem setup, recall is submodular [9], thus the generated subsets are at least $1 - \frac{1}{e}$ times the optimal recall. A local grouping ρ is defined by a candidate channel subset with a time range $\mathbf{r}_\rho$ and a subset of time series instances $\mathcal{T}_\rho$. Each ρ can be added to $\mathcal{R}$ when the following condition on α is satisfied:

$$accept(\rho, M^k) = \frac{\sum_{\mathbf{t} \in \mathcal{T}_\rho}(M^k[\mathbf{t}, \mathbf{r}_\rho.r_s : \mathbf{r}_\rho.r_e])}{\sum_{\mathbf{t} \in \mathcal{T}_\rho}|M^k[\mathbf{t}, \mathbf{r}_\rho.r_s : \mathbf{r}_\rho.r_e]|} \geq \alpha \tag{1}$$

Algorithm 2: createAssociations

Input : $\mathcal{T}$, $\mathcal{R}$, α

1   $\Gamma = \{\}$, $V \leftarrow \mathbb{0}||\mathcal{T}| \times |\mathcal{R}||$, $\mathcal{R} \leftarrow \text{sort}(\mathcal{R}, \text{by}=\{\mathbf{r}_\rho.r_s : \forall \rho \in \mathcal{R}\})$

2   $\forall j \leq |\mathcal{R}| \; \forall i \leq |\mathcal{T}_{\rho_j}| \; (\mathbf{t}_i \in \mathcal{T}_{\rho_j} \rightarrow V_{ij} = 1) \wedge (\mathbf{t}_i \notin \mathcal{T}_{\rho_j} \rightarrow V_{ij} = 0)$

3   **for** $\bar{\gamma} = \{\mathbf{r}_{\bar{\gamma}}, \mathcal{T}_{\bar{\gamma}}\} \in \text{generateAssociationCandidates}(V)$ **do**

4   **if** $\dfrac{\sum_{t \in \mathcal{T}_{\bar{\gamma}}} (V[t, \mathbf{r}_{\bar{\gamma}}.r_s : r_{\bar{\gamma}}.r_e])}{\sum_{t \in \mathcal{T}_{\bar{\gamma}}} |V[t, \mathbf{r}_{\bar{\gamma}}.r_s : r_{\bar{\gamma}}.r_e]|} \geq \alpha$ **then**

5        $r_s^{min} \leftarrow min(\{\mathbf{r}_{\rho_j}.r_s : \forall j \in \mathbf{r}_{\bar{\gamma}}\})$

6        $r_e^{max} \leftarrow max(\{\mathbf{r}_{\rho_j}.r_e : \forall j \in \mathbf{r}_{\bar{\gamma}}\})$

7        $\Gamma \leftarrow \Gamma \cup \{(r_s^{min}, r_e^{max}), \mathcal{T}_{\bar{\gamma}}, \{\rho_j : \forall j \in \mathbf{r}_{\bar{\gamma}}\})$

8   **return** Γ

---

where $M^k[\mathbf{t}, \mathbf{r}_\rho.r_s : \mathbf{r}_\rho.r_e]$ corresponds to the subset of M^k that matches time series $\mathbf{t}$ within $\mathbf{r}_\rho$, and *accept* is a function that computes the proportion of active labels in ρ on its corresponding channel M^k. We keep the continuous order of time, but we can include any time series instances to $\mathcal{T}_\rho$ regardless of their order.

Next, we proceed by extracting a set of local groupings from each channel and store all local groupings in a list $\mathcal{R}$, which is used in the next steps (line 4).

Example. Figure 3 (Step 2) shows six local grouping candidates with $\alpha = 0.75$ allowing 25% of impurity in each candidate. Using Eq. 1, ρ_1, ρ_2, and ρ_3 return $0.75 \geq \alpha$, so they are added to $\mathcal{R}$, while ρ_6 returns 1 and is also added.

3.3 Association Generation

This step solves *Problem* 2 by reducing it to the problem of associating adjacent local groupings represented by time-ordered local groupings. An association of local groupings is generated following Definition 4 requiring minimized internal pairwise distances between the time series instances, while expanding cardinality, i.e., the number of local groupings included in the association. Computing all pairwise distances of all possible instances over time would be computationally prohibitive. We solve this problem by defining a *grouping-instance matrix* V, i.e., a binary matrix of size $|\mathcal{T}| \times |\mathcal{R}|$ recording the memberships of time series instances to each local grouping, where the columns are sorted by start time of each local grouping to keep their temporal order (Algorithm 2, lines 1-2).

Matrix V allows us to easily find consecutive local groupings even if they are not continuous (i.e., gaps between them are allowed) in time. We first generate local groupings of V as candidate associations, each denoted by $\bar{\gamma} = \{\mathbf{r}_{\bar{\gamma}}, \mathcal{T}_{\bar{\gamma}}\}$ (line 3). Using Eq. 1 with each candidate $\bar{\gamma}$, we accept the candidate if $accept(\bar{\gamma}, V) \geq \alpha$, by checking which instances belong to which local groupings, with α being the degree of proximity between local groupings in $\bar{\gamma}$ (line 4). Then we create an association γ by extracting the minimum start and maximum end time from the involved local groupings in the candidate $\bar{\gamma}$, alongside the time series instances sharing those groupings (lines 5-7). In this way, local groupings are merged into the association, if they are consecutive in V. Depending on α, non-consecutive but close local groupings in V can also be added. Since associations maintain the longest time span (Definition 4), time gaps are also covered by the associations. As the main goal of associations is to find contiguous groupings of locally similar time series instances, we only store the intersecting instances; thus an association contains fewer instances than merged local groupings.

Example. In Figure 3 (Step 3), six local groupings are generated in Step 2. Using these groupings and their member instances, we create V, marking if the grouping contains the corresponding members. We find two associations γ_1 with range $[1, 10]$ and γ_2 with $[6, 10]$. Each association only contains the intersecting instances, so γ_1 contains $\{t_2, t_3, t_4\}$, excluding t_5 and t_6. Associations can contain non-consecutive groupings based on α, e.g., ρ_3, ρ_5 in γ_1, and ρ_4, ρ_6 in γ_2.

3.4   Validation of Local Groupings

In this last step, we validate the obtained local groupings by assuming a set of global groupings on the same time series collection $\mathcal{T}$, obtained either by time series clustering or provided by a domain expert. Hence, each time series $t \in \mathcal{T}$ can belong to a global grouping as well as to multiple local groupings. Our goal is to assess how related the global groupings are to local groupings and how can local groupings help us assess the similarity of these global groupings.

Let $\mathcal{G} = \{g_1, \ldots, g_x\}$ be a list of global groupings and consider a local grouping ρ, with its member instances $\mathcal{T}_\rho$. For each $t \in \mathcal{T}_\rho$, we can extract the corresponding global grouping g and its member instances $\mathcal{T}_g$, hence $t \in \mathcal{T}_\rho \cap \mathcal{T}_g$. If the majority of $\mathcal{T}_\rho$ also belong to $\mathcal{T}_g$, we can assume such global grouping follows a similarity pattern of ρ over the time span $\mathbf{r}_\rho$ of the grouping. However, some instances in $\mathcal{T}_\rho$ may belong to different global groupings, and all these groupings may not always follow the similarity pattern of ρ, as small number of global grouping instances can be included by chance. Therefore, it is important to check the validity of a local grouping for each global grouping having its members in $\mathcal{T}_\rho$. This is achieved by a *validity score* δ for g and ρ calculated as:

$$\delta_\rho^{g,\eta} = \lceil s_\rho \cdot s_g \cdot \eta \rceil, \text{ where } s_\rho = \frac{|\mathcal{T}_\rho|}{|\mathcal{T}|}, \; s_g = |\mathcal{T}_g|.$$

A *global grouping density* parameter η controls the required proportion of the member instances of g in $\mathcal{T}_\rho$ for ρ to be valid for g. If $\eta = 1$, ρ is valid when the proportion of $\mathcal{T}_g \cap \mathcal{T}_\rho$ in $\mathcal{T}_\rho$ is equal to the proportion of $\mathcal{T}_g$ in $\mathcal{T}$. For example, if $|\mathcal{T}| = 100$, $|\mathcal{T}_\rho| = 10$, and $|\mathcal{T}_g| = 90$, we need at least 9 members satisfying $t \in \mathcal{T}_\rho \cap \mathcal{T}_g$ to accept ρ for g. If $\eta = 0$, we accept all $\{\rho : \forall t \in \mathcal{T}_\rho, \exists t \in \mathcal{T}_g\}$ since δ becomes 0. If $\eta = 2$, the same calculation of δ would require at least 18 members. Using δ, we create a *validity matrix* $\mathcal{Z}$ of size $|\mathcal{G}| \times |\mathcal{R}|$ to record the validity between local and global groupings, where $\forall i \leq |\mathcal{G}| \; \forall j \leq |\mathcal{R}| \; (\sum_{t \in \mathcal{T}_{\rho_j}} \llbracket t \in \mathcal{T}_{g_i} \rrbracket \geq \delta_{\rho_j}^{g_i,\eta} \rightarrow \mathcal{Z}_{ij} = 1) \wedge (\sum_{t \in \mathcal{T}_{\rho_j}} \llbracket t \in \mathcal{T}_{g_i} \rrbracket < \delta_{\rho_j}^{g_i,\eta} \rightarrow \mathcal{Z}_{ij} = 0)$.

Example. Figure 3 (Step 4) shows the valid groupings with $\eta = 1$. We first calculate δ for each $\rho_i \in \mathcal{R}$ and $g_j \in \mathcal{G}$. For groupings of size 4 ($\{\rho_2 . \rho_3, \rho_4, \rho_6\}$),

Table 1. Summary of the datasets used in this paper.

Dataset	$|\mathcal{T}|$	$|t|$	$|\mathcal{G}|$	avg($|\mathcal{T}_g|$)	max($|\mathcal{T}_g|$)	min($|\mathcal{T}_g|$)
SYNTHETIC	1,000	365	20	50	50	50
GARMENT	3,963	365	50	79.26	282	29
STOCK	505	503	11	45.91	84	3
COVID	191	618	6	31.83	53	11

we need at least $\lceil \frac{4}{6} \cdot 2 \cdot 1 \rceil = 2$ instances of g_1 and $\lceil \frac{4}{6} \cdot 4 \cdot 1 \rceil = 3$ of g_2 to be valid. Since ρ_2, ρ_3, ρ_4 contain two instances of g_1 and two instances of g_2, they are only valid for g_1 On the other hand, ρ_6 has three of g_2 and one of g_1 so it is only valid for g_2.

3.5   Complexity of Z-Grouping

Given an $n \times m$ time series collection $\mathcal{T}$ and λ, the time complexity for creating the groupings for one event label follows the complexity of semigeometric tiling $O(m^2 n \log n)$ [9], leading to $O(\lambda m^2 n \log n)$ as the total complexity of Steps 1–2. For creating associations (Step 3), since, in the extreme case, the number of local groupings can be the same as the count of all data points ($|\mathcal{R}| = mn$), the worst case complexity becomes $O(m^2 n^3 \log n)$. The validation (Step 4) takes $O(n^2 m)$ since Z-Grouping checks every grouping and all time series instances for each grouping in the worst case. However, in practice, we can relax the complexity of Steps 1–3 by limiting the number of local groupings and associations Z-Grouping finds. For example, the complexity can be reduced to $O(kn \log n)$ by picking top k local groupings and associations, as they are chosen in descending order. Extremely small local groupings which have either few time points or few member instances may have no meaningful information and can be ignored. It may also be possible to give other constraints such as minimum length or size.

4   Experiments

4.1   Setup

Datasets. We use three real-world datasets from (1) retail industry (GARMENT), (2) stock market (STOCK), and (3) COVID-19 epidemics (COVID). A summary of the properties of these datasets is provided in Table 1, while a detailed description and sources can be found in our repository [1]. We also generated a synthetic dataset (SYNTHETIC) for extensive parameter investigation. It contains 1,000 instances and 20 global groupings that resemble the presence of local similarity. Each global grouping comprises a sinusoidal pattern with a different frequency and amplitude. The number of inserted patterns is smaller than the number of global groupings, hence some of them can share the same pattern, which can be detected as local groupings. To simulate a realistic scenario, noise and outliers are imputed. We also tested on 128 UCR datasets [7], excluding the cases where at least one algorithm cannot find any valid groupings (17 cases) and where the dataset length is shorter than the smallest window size parameter (6 cases). Our datasets and code including synthetic data generator are available online [1].

Competitors. While, to the best of our knowledge, there exists no direct competitor for the problem solved by Z-Grouping, we benchmark on the closest approach, i.e., semigeometric tiling and three additional baselines.

- Semigeometric: We employ a simple modification of semigeometric tiling [9]. First, we generate a binary matrix with its values set to 1 for the standardized time series values above the boundary found by SAX with $\lambda = 2$. Second, to make it directly comparable to Z-Grouping, we apply α (Eq. 1).
- kmeans: We divide each instance $\mathbf{t}$ into r partitions of time range w, such that $w \cdot r = |\mathbf{t}|$. For each partition, we apply kmeans; the resulting k clusters per partition correspond to the local groupings.
- kmeans-FLEX: We define a flexible version of kmeans with a sliding window of width w and slide step $\frac{w}{2}$ as a brute-force solution to finding local groupings of multiple fixed window lengths. We repeat for different values of w and k, and for each window, clusters with an average silhouette above a cutoff threshold s are accepted as groupings.
- kNN: Using the same partitioning approach as kmeans, and given a global grouping (see Experiment protocol), for each partition, we identify k instances belonging to that global grouping. For each instance, we apply kNN, retrieving the k nearest instances under the Euclidean distance resulting in k^2 samples, which correspond to a local grouping.

Note that kNN, kmeans, and kmeans-FLEX are also tested on the SAX abstracted space with $\lambda = 5$ to directly compare to Z-Grouping running on the abstracted space to detect maximized time spans. The results on the raw time series are in favor of the competitors since they can find more accurate neighbors but still only find fixed-length groupings. Also, as we are after local similarity synced in time, we do not explore elastic measures such as dynamic time warping.

Experiment Protocol. Assuming a set of predefined global groupings $\mathcal{G}$ on a given time series collection $\mathcal{T}$, we divide $\mathcal{T}$ into a training set $\mathcal{T}^{train}$ and a test set $\mathcal{T}^{test}$, and create local groupings on $\mathcal{T}^{train}$. Our goal is to investigate if the local groupings detected by each algorithm can identify potential local similarity on unseen instances. More concretely, for each unseen sample $\mathbf{t}_i \in \mathcal{T}^{test}$, we retrieve its global grouping $\bar{g}$. Our assumption is that the values of $\mathbf{t}_i$ are unseen, so the only information available for choosing valid local groupings is $\bar{g}$. For example, this simulates the scenario where we have a new product ready for market and we would like to identify potential local similarity patterns of its upcoming sales with existing products. In this case, $\bar{g}$ corresponds to a predefined product type and its features (e.g., color, size, material type).

Hence, for each unseen sample $\mathbf{t}_i \in \mathcal{T}^{test}$ and its corresponding global grouping $\bar{g}$, our evaluation is as follows. For kmeans, we choose the cluster with the

Table 2. Average test errors of the algorithms on SYNTHETIC (CV: Coverage (%)).

α	Semigeometric									Z-Grouping ($\lambda = 3$)								
	$\eta = 1$			$\eta = 1.5$			$\eta = 2$			$\eta = 1$			$\eta = 1.5$			$\eta = 2$		
	MSE	MAE	CV	MSE	MAE	CV	MSE	MAE	CV	MSE	MAE	CV	MSE	MAE	CV	MSE	MAE	CV
0.8	1.30	0.79	72	1.28	0.78	41	1.24	0.74	15	1.22	0.75	88	1.08	0.68	55	1.09	0.68	29
0.9	1.18	0.73	61	1.16	0.72	44	1.14	0.72	21	1.08	0.69	68	1.09	0.69	43	0.97	0.63	30
1.0	1.11	0.71	40	1.16	0.72	22	1.09	0.68	7	0.97	0.73	40	0.95	0.62	24	0.89	0.61	15

α	Z-Grouping ($\lambda = 5$)									Z-Grouping ($\lambda = 10$)								
0.8	1.00	0.65	45	0.93	0.62	27	0.85	0.57	15	0.88	0.56	20	0.88	0.56	12	0.78	0.52	10
0.9	0.95	0.60	30	0.94	0.59	20	0.87	0.55	10	0.84	0.56	14	0.86	0.55	10	0.81	0.52	5
1.0	0.87	0.57	21	0.87	0.56	15	0.77	0.52	8	0.73	0.51	8	0.89	0.56	5	0.97	0.61	2

w	kNN-SAX									kNN								
	$k = 3$			$k = 5$			$k = 10$			$k = 3$			$k = 5$			$k = 10$		
30	1.30	0.77	-	1.41	0.83	-	1.59	0.92	-	1.31	0.77	-	1.40	0.83	-	1.58	0.91	-
60	1.23	0.74	-	1.34	0.80	-	1.54	0.90	-	1.22	0.73	-	1.33	0.80	-	1.53	0.90	-
180	1.12	0.68	-	1.22	0.72	-	1.40	0.82	-	1.10	0.67	-	1.20	0.72	-	1.40	0.83	-

w	kmeans-SAX									kmeans								
30	1.49	0.88	-	1.51	0.89	-	1.51	0.88	-	1.51	0.89	-	1.53	0.90	-	1.53	0.90	-
60	1.59	0.93	-	1.59	0.93	-	1.58	0.92	-	1.60	0.93	-	1.60	0.93	-	1.59	0.93	-
180	1.57	0.91	-	1.56	0.91	-	1.55	0.90	-	1.58	0.92	-	1.58	0.91	-	1.57	0.91	-

kmeans-FLEX-SAX		MSE	MAE	CV	kmeans-FLEX		MSE	MAE	CV
	$s = 0.1$	1.44	0.84	100		$s = 0.1$	1.45	0.85	100
	$s = 0.2$	1.48	0.85	100		$s = 0.2$	1.47	0.85	100
	$s = 0.3$	1.56	0.93	100		$s = 0.3$	1.53	0.89	100
	$s = 0.4$	1.79	1.01	36		$s = 0.4$	1.79	1.01	36

highest number of instances of $\bar{g}$ for each time window. For kNN we employ the k^2 chosen samples. For Z-Grouping and Semigeometric, we choose the groupings based on δ (see Sect. 3.4). Next, for each ρ, we extract all global groupings $\{g : \forall \mathbf{t}_j \in \mathcal{T}_\rho, \exists \mathbf{t}_j \in \mathcal{T}_g\}$ except for the target global grouping $\bar{g}$. Then we calculate the errors (MSE and mean absolute error (MAE)) over the active time range $\mathbf{r}_\rho$ between the test time series $\mathbf{t}_i[\mathbf{r}_\rho.r_s : \mathbf{r}_\rho.r_e]$ and $\{\mathbf{t}_j[\mathbf{r}_\rho.r_s : \mathbf{r}_\rho.r_e] \mid \forall \mathbf{t}_j \in \mathcal{T}^{train} \wedge \mathbf{t}_j \notin \mathcal{T}_{\bar{g}}\}$, i.e., all the instances in the local grouping that belong to the chosen global groupings. This way we explore if these global groupings show local similarity and benchmark the robustness of each algorithm to randomness and noise. For Z-Grouping, Semigeometric, and kmeans-FLEX, we report *coverage*, i.e., the fraction of time series covered by the groupings. kmeans and kNN have 100% coverage since they always find similar instances based on the distance function. The ability of Z-Grouping can be shown by lower errors than the competitors since this confirms Z-Grouping can find groupings of different lengths showing better local similarity than fixed-size clusters.

4.2 Results

Results on the Synthetic Dataset. For Z-Grouping, we test $\alpha = \{0.8, 0.9, 1\}$, $\lambda = \{3, 5, 10\}$, and $\eta = \{1, 1.5, 2\}$. For Semigeometric, we apply the same α and η. For kmeans and kNN, we test different time ranges of $w = \{30, 60, 180\}$ and $k = \{3, 5, 10\}$. For kmeans-FLEX, we apply a silhouette cutoff from 0.1 until it fails to detect any valid groupings. All results are 10-fold cross-validated.

Table 2 shows the average test errors of Z-Grouping and its four competitors. Z-Grouping always succeeds in finding valid local groupings of low errors. Z-Grouping's lowest MSE is at least 33.0% lower than the competitors' lowest MSE (23.9% in MAE), and up to 59.2% lower (49.5% in MAE) than the worst score of the competitors. Semigeometric shows lower errors in general than kmeans and kNN, but it still has higher errors than Z-Grouping while covering smaller areas in the same parameter setting, as it suffers from its lack of representation power with a strong binary assumption, outperformed by Z-Grouping to a great extent up to 33.0% (25.0% in MAE). Except for two cases ($\alpha = \{0.8, 0.9\}, \eta = 1$), Semigeometric even fails to cover more than 50% of the dataset. This confirms the effectiveness of Z-Grouping in finding local groupings compared to its binary competitor; Z-Grouping with only one more abstraction label ($\lambda = 3$) achieves substantially better results than Semigeometric achieving from 6.0% to 18.3% lower MSEs while covering larger areas.

Since our synthetic data is designed to have clear local groupings, distance-based methods do not show noticeable differences in errors on both abstracted and original spaces. kNN achieves its best score with $\{w : 180, k : 3\}$ in both spaces, but its MSE is still 50.7% higher than Z-Grouping's best error (31.4% in MAE). It achieves lower errors with smaller window sizes, as it is easier to identify local groupings within the window. kmeans does not show remarkable differences with various parameter settings; it is generally worse than its competitors. Kmeans-FLEX has its lowest MSE being only 3.4% lower than the lowest error of kmeans (4.6% in MAE) but 97.3% higher than the lowest error of Z-Grouping (64.7% in MAE). This means giving a few options for the length of local groupings can be worse than fixed-size search, as well as far worse than Z-Grouping's ability to detect a maximized time range for local groupings. None of the competitors detect groupings of similar quality to Z-Grouping, which means an exhaustive search is required to find meaningful groupings, while Z-Grouping can find more flexible groupings with more valid local similarity.

Effect of the Parameters. All three parameters (λ, α, and η) of Z-Grouping control the trade-off between coverage and error. Since the abstraction label size is directly related to the sparsity of the channels, higher λ can lead to lower coverage, making Z-Grouping difficult to find the same event labels adjacent to each other, while detecting better local groupings with lower errors. Highe3 α leads to purer groupings allowing a smaller number of different event labels. If we increase flexibility with small α, the error increases due to the formation of many impure groupings. Higher η requires more samples in the local grouping for validity, leading to smaller number of groupings. This results in lower error scores but reduces coverage too. Associations of the groupings help increase coverage by filling the gaps created by high values of the parameters. However, under the highest parameter values, the algorithm loses its ability to grow over a substantial area, only showing less than 10% coverage and the error also gets higher since there is no meaningful amount of data points to compare to.

Relationship between θ, θ' and α. Z-Grouping solves *Problems* 1, 2 by transforming θ, θ' to the purity parameter α while maximizing the same space, assuming

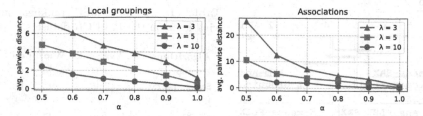

Fig. 4. Relation between α and the average pairwise distance of time series instances in local groupings (left) and associations (right) on SYNTHETIC.

Table 3. Best average test errors of the algorithms on three real-world datasets.

Datasets	Z-Grouping			Semigeometric			kNN-SAX			kNN		
	MSE	MAE	CV	MSE	MAE	CV	MSE	MAE	CV	MSE	MAE	CV
GARMENT	0.83	0.65	88	1.76	0.96	67	1.64	0.92	100	1.64	0.92	100
STOCK	0.99	0.74	77	1.49	0.84	70	1.21	0.83	100	1.20	0.83	100
COVID	0.84	0.49	40	2.17	0.92	74	1.37	0.70	100	1.37	0.71	100
Datasets	kmeans-SAX			kmeans			kmeans-FLEX			kmeans-FLEX-SAX		
GARMENT	1.65	0.90	100	1.67	0.92	100	1.49	0.87	100	1.51	0.92	100
STOCK	1.37	0.89	100	1.37	0.89	100	1.49	0.92	100	1.50	0.92	100
COVID	1.49	0.73	100	1.49	0.73	100	0.99	0.55	38	0.99	0.55	37

that θ, θ' are dependent on our choice of α. Hence, it is important to validate the relation between θ and α. Figure 4 shows the relation between α and the average pairwise distance of time series instances in the estimated groupings (left) and the associations (right) on SYNTHETIC. This confirms higher α leads to smaller θ, hence Z-Grouping approximately solves *Problems 1, 2*, while the actual thresholds (θ, θ') are dependent on α, and we maximize $|\rho_l|$ and $|\gamma_l| \times |\mathcal{T}_{\gamma_l}|$ keeping α. The same analysis on the real-world datasets is in the supplement (Sec. A).

Results on Three Real-World Datasets. Table 3 shows the average test errors of Z-Grouping and the competitors on three real-world datasets. We explore the same parameter settings as for the synthetic experiment. We report the best case in MSE covering more than 30% of the datasets, while Z-Grouping also gets lower errors with lower coverage. Overall, Z-Grouping achieves the best score on every dataset. On GARMENT and STOCK, Z-Grouping is a clear winner by having 44.3% lower MSE (25.2% in MAE) on GARMENT and 17.5% lower MSE (10.9% in MAE) on STOCK than the MSE under the best competitor, with at least 70% coverage. On COVID, Z-Grouping shows 15.2% lower MSE (11.0% in MAE) compared to the best of four competitors (kmeans-FLEX), but only covers 40% of the dataset as the COVID-19 patterns in one continent have not always been similar. It appears that the goal of finding consistent local similarity across continents has not been well met compared to the other two cases. Semigeometric

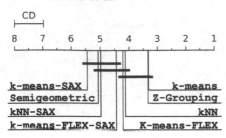

Fig. 5. Nemenyi post hoc test on the 128 UCR datasets.

Table 4. Average MSE rankings and wins/loses on the 128 UCR datasets.

Algorithms	Avg.rank	Win	Lose
Z-Grouping	3.34	48	9
Semigeometric	5.45	9	45
kNN	4.13	8	0
kNN-SAX	5.07	0	8
kmeans	3.32	20	1
kmeans-SAX	4.98	6	22
kmeans-FLEX	4.21	8	5
kmeans-FLEX-SAX	4.44	9	4

performs the worst on every dataset, even outperformed by the baselines. Full results for each parameter setting are available in our repository [1].

Results on the UCR Datasets. We test Z-Grouping and its competitors on 128 UCR datasets using the parameter settings yielding average performance in our synthetic experiments. Since the UCR datasets contain general cases and do not always have clear local similarity, the experiment shows a different perspective from our synthetic and three real-world data experiments as described in Fig. 5 and Table 4. First, the solutions on the abstracted space show significantly worse results than the ones on the original space, while Z-Grouping still outperforms them. Second, kmeans performs well on the UCR datasets showing the lowest average rank in terms of MSE and MAE while it shows the worst performance in our synthetic experiment, due to some datasets entirely missing valid local groupings; this can be confirmed by kmeans-FLEX underperforming even though it is also the same distance-based solution.

Z-Grouping in itself requires temporal abstraction to maximize the time span of the local groupings and the associations given α, thus losing some of the original information. This might make the detection process harder when local groupings are not distinct in the dataset as some cases in the UCR datasets. However, Z-Grouping still succeeds in finding valid local groupings of variable time span from these cases. This can be confirmed by noticing that Z-Grouping wins in 48 cases and only loses in nine cases, while two competitors capable of searching for local groupings of varying lengths (Semigeometric and kmeans-FLEX) show significantly worse results. Our main state-of-the-art competitor (Semigeometric) loses in 45 cases, even underperforming the baselines and Z-Grouping .

While losing information due to SAX, Z-Grouping achieves statistically equivalent average rank to its competitors running on the original space, despite the fact that it is harder to identify local groupings in some of the UCR datasets. Moreover, this also means we show our effectiveness over the baselines, since the competitors are still limited to only finding the fixed area (i.e., window size) while Z-Grouping finds maximized length areas for the groupings with similar or lower errors. Z-Grouping loses (1) when there are completely no valid local groupings in the dataset, (2) when there are more than two different local similarities in the same period with enough support in one class, and (3) when the original values have only slight fluctuations, so the SAX space loses all this information and as a result distance-based clustering outperforms. Examples of losing cases can be found in the supplementary material (Sec. B).

5   Conclusion

We proposed Z-Grouping, a novel framework for detecting local groupings of locally similar time series and their associations. We benchmarked Z-Grouping on three real-world datasets and a synthetic dataset as well as 128 UCR datasets against four competitor methods. Our experiments showed that Z-Grouping could achieve lower error rates than its competitors while successfully retrieving local groupings without size constraints on time ranges, which is infeasible by using traditional methods. Future work includes exploring alternative temporal abstractions, applying global optimization to create the local groupings, studying multivariate time series, i.e., creating multidimensional groupings.

References

1. Z-Grouping repository. www.github.com/zedshape/zgrouping/
2. Aghabozorgi, S., Shirkhorshidi, A.S., Wah, T.Y.: Time-series clustering-a decade review. ISJ **53**, 16–38 (2015)
3. Aghabozorgi, S., Wah, T.Y.: Clustering of large time series datasets. IDA **18**(5), 793–817 (2014)
4. Alaee, S., Mercer, R., Kamgar, K., Keogh, E.: Time series motifs discovery under dtw allows more robust discovery of conserved structure. DAMI **35**(3), 863–910 (2021)
5. Cheng, Y., Church, G.: Biclustering of expression data. ISMB **8**, 93–103 (2000)
6. Cuturi, M., Blondel, M.: Soft-dtw: a differentiable loss function for time-series. In: ICML, pp. 894–903. PMLR (2017)
7. Dau, H.A., et al.: The ucr time series archive. JAS **6**(6), 1293–1305 (2019)
8. Gionis, A., Mannila, H., Terzi, E.: Clustered segmentations. In: TDM. Citeseer (2004)
9. Henelius, A., Karlsson, I., Papapetrou, P., Ukkonen, A., Puolamäki, K.: Semi-geometric tiling of event sequences. In: Frasconi, P., Landwehr, N., Manco, G., Vreeken, J. (eds.) ECML PKDD 2016. LNCS (LNAI), vol. 9851, pp. 329–344. Springer, Cham (2016). https://doi.org/10.1007/978-3-319-46128-1_21
10. Huang, C.F.: A hybrid stock selection model using genetic algorithms and support vector regression. Appl. Soft Comput. **12**(2), 807–818 (2012)
11. Jiang, Y., Liu, Y., Wang, H., Shang, J., Ding, S.: Online pricing with bundling and coupon discounts. IJPR **56**(5), 1773–1788 (2018)
12. Lee, J.H., Lee, Y.R., Jun, C.H.: A biclustering method for time series analysis. IEMS **9**(2), 131–140 (2010)
13. Li, H., Liu, J., Yang, Z., Liu, R.W., Wu, K., Wan, Y.: Adaptively constrained dynamic time warping for time series classification and clustering. Inf. Sci. **534**, 97–116 (2020)

14. Lin, J., Keogh, E., Wei, L., Lonardi, S.: Experiencing sax: a novel symbolic representation of time series. DMKD **15**(2), 107–144 (2007)
15. Luo, L., Lv, S.: An accelerated u-shapelet time series clustering method with lsh. In: Journal of Phys. Conference Series, vol. 1631, pp. 12–77. IOP (2020)
16. Mueen, A., Hamooni, H., Estrada, T.: Time series join on subsequence correlation. In: ICDM, pp. 450–459. IEEE (2014)
17. Mueen, A., Nath, S., Liu, J.: Fast approximate correlation for massive time-series data. In: SIGMOD, pp. 171–182 (2010)
18. Raza, A., Kramer, S.: Accelerating pattern-based time series classification: a linear time and space string mining approach. KAIS **62**(3), 1113–1141 (2020)
19. Ruta, N., Sawada, N., McKeough, K., Behrisch, M., Beyer, J.: Sax navigator: Time series exploration through hierarchical clustering. In: VIS, pp. 236–240 (2019)
20. Schäfer, P.: The boss is concerned with time series classification in the presence of noise. DAMI **29**(6), 1505–1530 (2015)
21. Wu, J., Wang, Y., Wang, P., Pei, J., Wang, W.: Finding maximal significant linear representation between long time series. In: ICDM, pp. 1320–1325. IEEE (2018)
22. Zolhavarieh, S., Aghabozorgi, S., Teh, Y.W.: A review of subsequence time series clustering. The Scientific World Journal 2014 (2014)

TS-MIoU: A Time Series Similarity Metric Without Mapping

Azim Ahmadzadeh[1]($\boxtimes$), Yang Chen[1], Krishna Rukmini Puthucode[1], Ruizhe Ma[2], and Rafal A. Angryk[1]

[1] Department of Computer Science, Georgia State University, Atlanta, Georgia
aahmadzadeh1@gsu.edu
[2] Department of Computer Science, University of Massachusetts Lowell, Lowell, USA

Abstract. Quantifying the similarity or distance between time series, processes, signals, and trajectories is a task-specific problem and remains a challenge for many applications. The simplest measure, meaning the Euclidean distance, is often dismissed because of its sensitivity to noise and the curse of dimensionality. Therefore, elastic mappings (such as DTW, LCSS, ED) are often utilized instead. However, these measures are not metric functions, and more importantly, they must deal with the challenges intrinsic to point-to-point mappings, such as pathological alignment. In this paper, we adopt an object-similarity measure, namely Multiscale Intersection over Union (MIoU), for measuring the distance/similarity between time series. We call the new measure TS-MIoU. Unlike the most popular time series similarity measures, TS-MIoU does not rely on a point-to-point mapping, and therefore, circumvents all respective challenges. We show that TS-MIoU is indeed a metric function, especially that it holds the triangle inequality axiom, and therefore can take advantage of indexing algorithms without a lower bounding. We further show that its sensitivity to noise is adjustable, which makes it a strong alternative to the Euclidean distance while not suffering from the curse of dimensionality. Our proof-of-concept experiments on over 100 UCR datasets show that TS-MIoU can fill the gap between the unforgiving strictness of the ℓ_p-norm measures, and the mapping challenges of elastic measures.

Keywords: Time series · Similarity · Distance

1 Introduction

Signals, processes, time series, and trajectories are data types which despite their differences have a lot in common. They all are ordered—and often equally spaced in time—values of a random variable recorded in time. With the advances in machine learning algorithms and computational power at our disposal, these high-dimensional data types have become ubiquitous. Since our primary focus in this study is on their spatiotemporal similarities, we use the name "time series" as an umbrella term for all such data types.

© The Author(s), under exclusive license to Springer Nature Switzerland AG 2023
M.-R. Amini et al. (Eds.): ECML PKDD 2022, LNAI 13718, pp. 87–102, 2023.
https://doi.org/10.1007/978-3-031-26422-1_6

One of the primary challenges in dealing with these data types is in the way the similarity notion is defined. Similarity is a subjective concept, so much so that often different applications require very different or even contradictory criteria to define similarity. For example, two trajectories sampled from the Australian Sign Language dataset [15] may be considered 'similar' despite the absence of any spatial alignment, whereas in the Taxi Service Trajectory dataset [25], a significant spatial alignment is essential for trips to be considered 'similar'. Therefore, the *no-free-lunch* theorem applies; there is no general-purpose, universal similarity measure that outperforms all others in all applications. This subjectivity has given rise to the invention of an array of effective and elegant measures, each with its own strengths and shortcomings. Because of this diversity, a degree of expertise is almost always expected for the user to be able to appropriately utilize them and achieve the optimal gain.

In this paper, we entertain a new idea that claims, in the context of similarity measures, time series can be treated as *objects* with unique shapes and structures, as opposed to spatiotemporal data types. Time series have been treated as objects before (e.g., as fractals [27]), primarily to extract their complex features. But to the best of our knowledge, the similarity notion has almost always been tied to a mapping function of some sort, which requires time series to be considered what they actually are; sequences of points.

Although the mapping-based strategies are ideal for a large pool of time series applications, it should not be generalized as the *only* way of defining and quantifying their similarity. Borrowing from the computer vision domain, this is analogous to the pixel-to-pixel similarity measures (e.g., Mean Square Error), as opposed to other strategies such as a patch-to-patch comparison or Histogram of Oriented Gradients (HOG) [21]. We bring this up because it was shown that the pixel-to-pixel similarity measures, despite their popularity, are not the best choices for, for example, an objective similarity evaluation [26]. Compared to images, time series are much less intuitive data points, and therefore, we might not be able to always perceive the inadequacy of some measures' mapping strategy.

Our non-mapping perspective has two fundamental advantages. Firstly, it circumvents the real challenges caused by different point-to-point mapping strategies. Secondly, it builds (adjustable) resistance against noise. The latter will be more clear after we define the measure. Regarding the former, the mapping strategy generally divides the similarity measures into two main groups: those which do not allow local time shifting, such as the ℓ_p norm family, and those which do, such as the Edit Distance on Real Sequence (EDR) [6], Longest Common Subsequence (LCSS) [34], and Dynamic Time Warping (DTW) [4,17,30], and their many variants. The first group of measures are very sensitive to noise, and moreover, they require time series to be of the same length. Among the measures in the second group, one of the most prominent issues is the occurrence of pathological alignments, i.e., when a single point is mapped onto a large subsection of another time series—a known issue of DTW and some of its variants [30]. Several constraints have been proposed to control for such undesirable mappings, such as *windowing, slope weighting,* and *step patterns* (see [29] and references therein).

In addition, methods such as feature mapping/segmentation have also been proposed to avoid pathological warpings [13,22]. Another complication that comes with this approach lies in the mapping of some key points (e.g., peaks or dips of time series). In addition to the possibility of pathological mappings of these key points, the detection of peaks and dips is often a challenge of its own, as peaks and dips are also subjective and task-specific concepts [22]. There are also assumptions in the mapping functions that may or may not be desirable in some applications. For example, DTW is restricted by assumptions such as *continuity* and/or *monotonicity*. The continuity assumption forbids 'jumps', meaning that every point on each time series must be mapped onto at least one other point on the other time series. The monotonicity assumption forbids going back in time, i.e., connecting a point of one time series to a processed point in another time series. Because of these restrictions, an optimal mapping may exist well outside such a confined space. A good example in which discontinuity is allowed is LCSS, however, its mapping is still monotonic. A similarity measure that does not require a mapping is entirely free of such challenges—while of course subject to some other challenges.

2   Background

The literature on the similarity measures for time series is as rich and diverse as the time series application itself. A thorough review of these measures, even when limited to a particular application, requires a dedicated study on its own. Therefore, in the present work, which should not be seen as anything other than a proof of concept, we do not go beyond a quick review of the most popular similarity measures (in Sect. 2.1). Instead, we review a few other measures which, at some level, bear some resemblance to our proposed measure (in Sect. 2.2).

2.1   Popular Distance/Similarity Measures

The simplest approach for measuring the distance between two time series is by seeing them as high-dimensional data points in the Euclidean space, and measuring their distance with the Euclidean distance (a.k.a. ℓ_2 norm). This measure, as well as the Manhattan distance (ℓ_1 norm) and Chebyshev distance (ℓ_∞ norm), are special cases of a more generalized distance function called the Minkowski distance (ℓ_p norm). Euclidean distance, the most popular of the ℓ_p norm family, is very sensitive to noise. Meaning small variations on the time axis or any spatial misalignment may significantly impact the distance. Moreover, it cannot be used for time series of different lengths and sampling rates due to its static pairwise mapping between the time series elements. For applications such as GPS tracking, where the spherical coordinates system might be preferred over a Cartesian coordinate system, Haversine distance can be used instead. Haversine distance is the angular distance between two points on a surface of a sphere. Haversine distance is also sensitive to noise, but what makes these measures popular, in addition to their simplicity and cheap computation (i.e., a linear time complexity), is the fact that they are metric functions. A metric function holds the triangle inequality axiom, which makes it a natural choice for indexing and tree-based search algorithms (as discussed in Sect. 3.5).

The fact that ℓ_p norm does not allow local time shifting—it restricts the mapping of the i-th element of one time series to only the i-th element of the other time series—gave rise to a number of other distance/similarity measures of which we only review some of the most popular. Inspired by the Edit Distance (ED) measure used for string comparisons [19], the ED with Real Penalty (ERP) was introduced for quantifying the time series similarity with local time shifting [5]. Although ERP is a metric, it was shown that (like DTW) it is sensitive to noise [6]. As a remedy, a modified version of it, namely the ED on Real Sequence (EDR), was proposed [6]. EDR defines the distance between two time series in terms of the number of modifications (i.e., insertion, deletion, and replacement) one time series may need to change into the other. EDR reduces the impact of noise the same way LCSS does; by quantizing pairwise distances to either 0 or 1. This advantage comes at the cost of violating the triangle inequality which makes EDR a non-metric [5]. Among several ED-based measures, the Time Warp ED with Stiffness Adjustment (TWED) was tailored to (1) hold the triangle inequality while being an elastic metric and (2) provide a parameter to control the elasticity of the mapping function [24]. All these measures have a quadratic time complexity.

The LCSS measure can also be seen as a special case of ED. The key difference for LCSS is that unlike DTW and ED-based measures (which require all elements of time series to be matched), it allows partial comparisons, i.e., parts of time series can be left unmatched. This is advantageous because it allows tolerance of some noise. This unique feature, from a different angle, limits the application of LCSS, since the unmatched elements are entirely ignored and do not contribute to the final value of the distance. LCSS is not a metric as it violates the triangle inequality. It is also worth mentioning that LCSS, as well as DTW and ED-based measures, cannot be *directly* used for 2D time series (with time as the third dimension). Interested readers in multidimensional time series can read about some proposed approaches in [9].

DTW searches through a 2D space to find an optimal mapping between the two given time series and then defines the distance as the sum of the Euclidean distance between all matched elements. In principle, DTW requires quadratic computation time, it is not a metric [5], and it remains sensitive to noise. That said, DTW seems to have become the most popular elastic measure for time series data mining community thanks to the several lower bounding methods (including the lower bounding based on warping constraints, i.e., 4S), which significantly sped up its computation time [28].

2.2   Measures with Comparable Ideas

A grid-based approach for measuring the distance between two trajectories was introduced by Lin et al. [20]. The authors talked about the applications such as animal migration patterns and city traffic monitoring, in which the similarity of interest is primarily determined by the trajectories' spatial patterns, and the temporal aspect (e.g., timestamp and velocity) is not seen as critical. Given a query trajectory Q and an arbitrary trajectory T, their method superimposes a grid over T and Q, and then computes the one-way distance (OWD) of Q from T. The OWD is computed by first identifying the so-called "local min points" on T (one local min point relative to each point on Q) and then summing up the Euclidean distances between each point on Q and its corresponding local min point on T. The main purpose of their grid representation is to build an efficient indexing method that speeds up the similarity search. The authors recommended building multiple grid representations of trajectories with different granularity levels to confine the search space. This is done by starting the search algorithm from the coarsest representation of trajectories and iteratively passing forward the k-most similar trajectories, as the granularity of the grid increases. This approach is similar to ours in that they both use a 2-dimensional grid-based segmentation. However, it is only in our approach that the hierarchical representation of time series directly contributes to the measure of similarity. In the method proposed by Lin et al., the hierarchical representation is part of their retrieval algorithm and not the similarity measure.

The Complexity-Invariant Distance (CID) is a method for adding a complexity sensitivity to distance measures [3]. CID has a somewhat similar motivation as ours; without taking into account this new invariance property, similarity search algorithms may not be able to differentiate between 'complex' and 'simple' time series because of their overall similarities, hence ignoring their difference in 'complexity'. Although the authors did not define 'complexity', they explained it intuitively, that the complexity of a time series is proportional to the total sum of its line segments' length. This is generally how the *correction factor* is computed. Their notion of complexity is identical to what is known in fractal geometry as *fractal dimension* [23]. Our measure of similarity takes full advantage of the definition of fractal dimension to account for time series' complexity (see Sect. 3).

The Hausdorff distance [2] is another measure that—if carefully examined— is somewhat similar to our approach. To quantify the distance between two time series (originally between two shapes), Hausdorff distance finds the smallest radius of the disk needed that if each point of either of the time series is replaced with that disk, the union of those disks contains all points of the other time series. This 'thickening' process is in principle similar to the change of resolution in our proposed measure, as we explain in Sect. 3.2. Hausdorff distance is a metric, but unlike our measure, it is sensitive to noise. This is because the computed distance is always determined by the single farthest point from the other time series, and therefore, a single outlier can heavily impact the distance.

Although not a distance measure, the indexing technique used in [17] bears some resemblance to our proposed measure, in that they both treat time series as shapes. The authors introduced LB_PAA—a modified version of the Piecewise Aggregate Approximation [35]—for reducing the dimensionality of time series (from n to 16) and therefore speeding up the indexing process for DTW. Instead of comparing a candidate time series T to a query time series Q, they compare a 16-dimensional version of T, denoted as $\bar{T}$, to the 16-dimensional lower and upper bounds of Q. Then, when building the tree structure for indexing, they compute the distance of Q from a minimum bounding rectangle (MBR) of $\bar{T}$ instead of T itself. This is where a time series is treated as a shape and estimated by an MBR. Our proposed measure uses a similar spatial estimate of time series to compare them without a mapping.

3   Multiscale IoU (MIoU) for Time Series

Since we are borrowing a region-based similarity measure, namely MIoU [1], and re-purposing it for time series analysis, we first review the original idea, and then discuss the specific modifications needed for this adoption[1][2].

3.1   MIoU Recap

Intuitively, MIoU [1] is the marriage of two concepts: *Intersection over Union* (IoU) [10] and the *fractal dimension* [23]. IoU (a.k.a. the Jaccard Index [14]) is a widely used object-similarity measure that quantifies the degree of which a ground-truth object is detected (i.e., intersection) relative to the area occupied by both of the ground-truth and detected objects (i.e., union). The fractal dimension was originally proposed to quantify the complexity of self-similar objects, called *fractals*. Among several methods that compute the fractal dimension the *box-counting* method utilizes grids of varying cell sizes in order to capture the complexity of fractals' geometry (see [33] and the references therein). Figure 1 illustrates the general idea behind MIoU for two different proposed objects representing a solar filament.

The motivation behind introducing MIoU for measuring objects' similarity is to compensate for the limited sensitivity of IoU (as well as other area-based measures such as f_1 score, precision, and recall) to the fine details visible in objects' structures—a highly informative feature present in many scientific computer vision applications (see examples in [1]). MIoU achieves this through a multiscale approach: for noticeably misaligned objects, either spatially or structurally, MIoU is able to capture major misalignments early on, at lower resolution levels, whereas for well-aligned objects, MIoU can identify the subtle misalignments at higher resolution levels.

Formally, the MIoU measure is formulated using three functions. Let O denote a set of all valid objects (represented as binary masks of regions), and $\Delta \subset \mathbb{N}$ denote a finite set of box sizes. The first function, $s : O \times \Delta \longrightarrow O$, performs a grid-based segmentation on the object $o \in O$, with a given box size $\delta_i \in \Delta$, and downsamples the region. The second function, $|\cdot| : O \longrightarrow \mathbb{N}$, computes the area of a given region by counting the number of pixels (or grid

---

[1] MIoU repository: https://bitbucket.org/gsudmlab/multiscale_iou/.
[2] TS-MIoU repository: https://bitbucket.org/gsudmlab/ts_miou_ecmlpkdd22/.

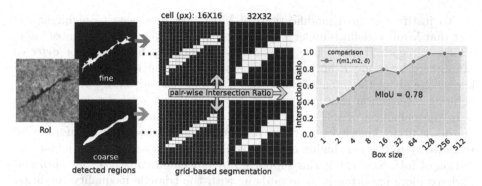

Fig. 1. The graphic reviews how MIoU measures the similarity between a fine (top) and coarse (bottom) region (each of size 512×512 pixels). The box sizes of the grid varies from 1 pixel (highest resolution) to 512 pixels (lowest resolution). The line plot shows the intersection ratios, and the area under its curve (0.78) which defines the similarity between two regions.

cells after it was downsampled by s) o's boundary spans over. The last function, $r : O^2 \times \Delta \longrightarrow [0, 1]$, called *intersection ratio*, computes the intersection between the boundaries of a region o and its estimate $\tilde{o}$, in terms of the number of $\delta_i \times \delta_i$ boxes they share, and normalizes it by the number of boxes o's boundary spans over. More precisely, $r(o, \tilde{o}, \delta_i) = \frac{|s(o,\delta_i) \cap s(\tilde{o},\delta_i)|}{|s(o,\delta_i)|}$.

Having r calculated for all different box sizes in Δ, MIoU is then computed by measuring the area under the curve formed by r. This curve is shown in Fig. 1, and can be formulated as follows: $\text{MIoU}(o, \tilde{o}) = \int_0^1 r(o, \tilde{o}, \delta) \, d\delta$, which is the total area of $|\Delta| - 1$ trapezoids. MIoU varies within the interval $[0, 1]$ if $d\delta = \frac{1}{|\Delta|-1}$. As a similarity measure, greater values indicate greater similarity, 1 means a perfect alignment, and no overlap is represented by 0. It is worth noting that although $1 - \text{MIoU}$ can be considered a distance (dissimilarity) measure, it is not a *metric*. We will discuss this shortly in Sect. 3.5.

3.2 TS-MIoU: MIoU for Time Series

We claim that MIoU is an effective measure for quantifying time series similarity. In many applications, the implicit or explicit definition of similarity for time series is indistinguishable from that for objects. In such cases, while we want similar time series to have similar shapes and patterns, we expect them to generally stay within a close distance along the time dimension, regardless of their individual sampling rate. Trajectory of moving objects [20] is just one of such cases. As we discuss in this section, with some minor changes and appropriate (task-specific) segmentation strategies, time series can be treated as objects and shapes. Needless to say that neither this nor any other realization of similarity can be used universally for all applications.

To justify our main modifications of MIoU, we first need to highlight the fact that MIoU is defined under a specific assumption; the given regions of interest are categorized into either *ground truth* (annotated by human) or *detected* (annotated by an algorithm) regions. This subtle assumption gives away a priori knowledge about the intended comparison, and to take advantage of that, when defining intersection ratio, the authors replaced the *area of the union*—which is in the definition of IoU—with the *area of the ground-truth*. In the absence of this a priori knowledge (e.g., in unsupervised approaches and information retrieval systems), it is highly advantageous for us to revert to the original definition of IoU. Not only is this supported by our empirical study, but also, and perhaps more importantly, it rewards us with the triangle inequality condition (see Sect. 3.5). The reverted definition of the intersection ratio that we used for TS-MIoU is given in Eq. 1.

$$r(T_1, T_2, (\delta_{x,i}, \delta_{y,i})) = \frac{|s(T_1, (\delta_{x,i}, \delta_{y,i})) \cap s(T_2, (\delta_{x,i}, \delta_{y,i}))|}{|s(T_1, (\delta_{x,i}, \delta_{y,i})) \cup s(T_2, (\delta_{x,i}, \delta_{y,i}))|} \qquad (1)$$

Another minor change is that compared to the intersection ratio in MIoU, TS-MIoU's intersection ratio benefits from a tuple, i.e., $(\delta_{x,i}, \delta_{y,i})$, determining the box sizes, instead of a single value of δ. Consequently, TS-MIoU$(T_1, T_2) = \int_0^1 r(T_1, T_2, (\delta_x, \delta_y)) d\delta_x \delta_y$. This allows us to build segmentations grids with non-squared cells in order to tackle the ill-definedness of the time series space. We further discuss these topics in Sects. 3.3 and 3.4.

3.3   Ill-Definedness of Space

TS-MIoU transforms time series into binary masks. This procedure requires quantisation (binning) on both of the dimensions. In doing so caution must be taken in using shape-based similarity metrics on time series. For a time series to be considered a 2-dimensional object with a well-defined geometry, both dimensions must be of the same unit. This incommensurability of the axes of time series plots makes the geometrical aspect ratio of this artificially-made space ill-defined. One direct consequence of this ill-definedness is the arbitrariness of measures such as the fractal dimension. Such measures depend on the arbitrariness of the aspect ratios of time series plots. In fact, time series' patterns and motifs might be partially or completely obscured by choosing an inappropriate aspect ratio of the axes in the binning process.

This is certainly a concern for the box-counting method incorporated in TS-MIoU. Theoretically, the $\delta \times \delta$ boxes used by the box-counting method do not represent any meaningful geometric area on time series space. However, similarity is a *relative* concept. For example, a retrieval algorithm looks for the most similar instances relative to a query instance. Therefore, this ill-defined space can still be explored as long as (1) the sides of the boxes used for segmentation can be adjusted independently to account for the different resolutions needed for each dimension of the time series space, and (2) the conditions determining the space remain constant for all comparisons. We elaborate in these conditions in the following sections.

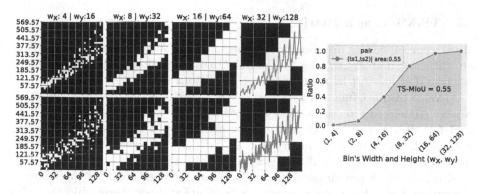

Fig. 2. Segmentation with proportional binning is illustrated for computing TS-MIoU on two time series (blue and purple). For visibility purposes, only four of the six representations of time series are shown, corresponding to the bin sizes in $\Delta_{x,y} = \{(1,4),(2,8),(4,16),(8,32),(16,64),(32,128)\}$. (Color figure online)

3.4 Segmentation with Proportional Binning

As mentioned before, TS-MIoU treats time series like objects through the use of grid-based segmentation while remaining completely agnostic to the segmentation method used. The simplest approach for segmentation is to set an upper bound for the number of cells, k, and then carry out hierarchical segmentation with all integers from 1 to k. The upper bound can be axis-specific as well. A slightly more dynamic strategy is to define non-square boxes with widths and heights proportional to the ranges of values on the x and y axes, respectively. These boxes will then be used to form the segmentation grids representing varying resolutions. The latter is the strategy we use in our experiments, and we call it *segmentation with proportional binning*.

Suppose we have a dataset of N time series, $\mathcal{T} = \{T\}_{i=1}^{N}$, each of length n. Note that this assumption of fixed length is not a requirement for TS-MIoU as it does not rely on any types of mapping between time series. Let m and M denote the global minimum and maximum values in $\mathcal{T}$ (per variate, for multivariate time series), respectively. The width and height of the largest $(\delta_x \times \delta_y)$-box used for segmentation can then be determined by $\delta_x = \frac{n}{c_x}$ and $\delta_y = \frac{(M-m)}{c_y}$, respectively, where $c_x, c_y \in (0,1]$ are user-defined parameters. Appropriate choices of c_x and c_y can guarantee that TS-MIoU does not overlook the interesting structures of the time series. Each of the upper bounds δ_x and δ_y determine the rest of the corresponding box sizes using a linear or logarithmic function, starting from 1, representing the original time series. In Sect. 4, we use powers of two, inspired by the original definition of fractal dimension [23]. An example of such a segmentation strategy is illustrated in Fig. 2.

In this paper, we will not address an optimum binning strategies as it heavily depends on the data, the time series' patterns, and structures. An efficient, data-driven methodology for determining the optimal set $\Delta_{x,y}$ seeks a thorough investigation of its own, which belongs to our future work.

3.5   TS-MIoU as a Metric

MIoU's corresponding distance function, $d_{\text{MIoU}} = 1 - \text{MIoU}$, is not a metric. But we will show that $d_{\text{TS-MIoU}} = 1 - \text{TS-MIoU}$ satisfies all conditions of a metric function. Let us start by reviewing these conditions.

Given a distance function $d : \mathcal{X} \times \mathcal{X} \longrightarrow \mathbb{R}$ where $\mathcal{X}$ is the universe of all valid objects (time series in our case), d is called a *metric* if the following properties hold for all $x, y, z \in \mathcal{X}$: (1) *positiveness*, $d(x, y) \geq 0$; (2) *strict positiveness*, $x \neq y \Rightarrow d(x, y) > 0$; (3) *symmetry*, $d(x, y) = d(y, x)$; (4) *reflexivity*, $d(x, x) = 0$; and (5) *triangle inequality*, $d(x, z) \leq d(x, y) + d(y, z)$.

d_{MIoU} is by definition asymmetric. Moreover, it does not hold the triangle inequality. A simple counterexample can be made with any three objects A, B, and $|A| = |C|$, $A \cap C = \emptyset$, and $A \cup C = B$. This gives us $\text{MIoU}(A, C) = 0$, $\text{MIoU}(A, B) = 1$, and $\text{MIoU}(B, C) = 0.5$. Consequently, d_{MIoU} of those pairs are 1, 0, and 0.5, respectively. The triangle inequality $d_{\text{MIoU}}(A, C) \leq d_{\text{MIoU}}(A, B) + d_{\text{MIoU}}(B, C)$ yields the contradiction $1 \leq 0 + 0.5$. Therefore, d_{MIoU} is not a metric function.

It is easy to see that $d_{\text{TS-MIoU}}$ satisfies the positiveness condition as the area under the intersection-ratio curve is non-negative and less than or equal to 1. The strict positiveness also holds as long as $(1, 1) \in \Delta$. This guarantees the inclusion of the original time series in all comparisons, i.e., by computing $r(T_1, T_2, (1, 1))$; If $T_1 \neq T_2$, no matter how subtle their differences might be, $r(T_1, T_2, (1, 1)) > 0$, and hence $d_{\text{TS-MIoU}} > 0$. The generalization discussed in Sect. 3.2 propagates the symmetry property of IoU to $d_{\text{TS-MIoU}}$. The reflexivity condition is trivial. And lastly, $d_{\text{TS-MIoU}}$'s triangle inequality is inherited from the triangle inequality of d_{IoU} (see the proofs in [11, 18]); since TS-MIoU is the sum of a finite number of IoUs, it therefore preserves the IoU's triangle inequality condition. Therefore, $d_{\text{TS-MIoU}}$ is indeed a metric function.

3.6   Time Complexity of TS-MIoU

A pseudo-code of TS-MIoU is given in Algorithm 1. Outside the loop, the **area** can be computed in linear time ($O(n)$, n being the number of iterations) using the Riemann sum. Inside the loop, the **segmentize** method is responsible for binning on the axes of a given time series. One possible implementation of this (e.g., see the **digitize** method in the *NumPy* package [12]) can be achieved through a binary search (with $O(log(n))$, where n is the number of bins). The logical **and** and **or** operations on 2D arrays require $O(r \times c)$, where r and c are the number of rows and columns of the binary matrices m_1 and m_2. This is the bottleneck of TS-MIoU's time complexity. If the proportional binning strategy discussed in Sect. 3.4 is adopted, the number of **and** (or **or**) operations at the i-th iteration will be $(r \cdot c)/4^i$. The overall complexity of the algorithm is then equivalent to the sum of the geometric series $\sum_{i=0}^{\infty} (r \cdot c)/4^i$ which converges to $4/3(r \cdot c)$. Therefore, the current implementation of TS-MIoU has a quadratic time complexity. This is similar to the time complexity of the most popular similarity measures such as DTW, EDR, and LCSS without any additional constraints.

Algorithm 1: TS-MIoU Distance Metric

   Input : T_1, T_2, Δ
   output: TS-MIoU
1 **function** $ts\_miou(t_1$: array, t_2: array, Δ: array) : float
2 | $ratios = [\,]$
3 | **for** $\delta_x, \delta_y \in \Delta$:
4 | | $m_1 = \text{segmentize}(T_1, \delta_x, \delta_y)$
5 | | $m_2 = \text{segmentize}(T_2, \delta_x, \delta_y)$
6 | | $union = m_1 \vee m_2$ /* logical or */
7 | | $inters = m_1 \wedge m_2$ /* logical and */
8 | | $ratios.\text{append}(\text{sum}(inters)\,/\,\text{sum}(union))$
9 | $tsmiou = 1 - \text{area\_under\_curve}(ratios)$
10 | **return** $tsmiou$
11 **end**

---

4 Experiments and Results

4.1 Experimental Settings

We conducted our experiments on 105 (out of 128) datasets of the UCR Time Series Archive [7]. We excluded the 11 datasets with varying lengths of time series because each similarity measure handles the varying length (if at all) differently, and this would have introduced a confounding factor to our experiments. We excluded another set of 12 datasets which contain very lengthy time series (> 900 elements). This decision was made primarily because for such long time series, a full-size comparison of time series has limited application in the real world, and failure or success of a similarity measure on such time series does not reveal much about its weaknesses or strengths.

As a proof of concept, we compared TS-MIoU with Euclidean distance (EuD), DTW, and LCSS. For the time series segmentation of TS-MIoU, we determined the bin sizes (i.e., δ_x and δ_y) as discussed in Sect. 3.4. Except for 16 datasets, for all other datasets, we defined the upper bounds of the bin sizes on the x and y axes by setting $c_x = 2.5$ and $c_y = 0.025$, respectively. This difference compensates for the difference in the range of the values on the two axes. For the 16 datasets in which the ratio $n/(M-m)$ was lower than 10, we noticed that setting $c_y = 0.025$ would make our segmentation method generate significantly imbalanced bin-size sets (i.e., $|\delta_y| - |\delta_x| \geq 4$). For these datasets, we increased c_y to 0.25 to reduce the difference. In all cases, we handled the imbalanced bin-size sets (of x and y axes) by clipping the head of the longer sets.

Regarding DTW, for the results shown in Figs. 3 and 4, we used the best values reported in the UCR official web site [8] (under the column DTW (learned_w)). For LCSS, we used the *tslearn* Python package [32] and we set the *maximum matching distance* threshold ϵ to one, i.e., the default value in the package.

4.2 Accuracy Gain of TS-MIoU

To fairly assess the overall quality of TS-MIoU, we use the so-called "Texas sharpshooter plot", as suggested in [3,7]. We compute the accuracy of the 1-NN classifier, using leave-one-out cross-validation, on the training set D^{train} of each UCR dataset, using an arbitrary distance function μ. We repeat the experiment but this time we classify time series of the respective test set D^{test}. The former gives us the *expected* performance, denoted as $\widehat{\text{acc}}_\mu$, and the latter gives us the *actual* performance, denoted as acc_μ. Using these quantities, we calculate the *expected gain* $(\widehat{g}_{\mu,\text{ref}})$ and the *actual gain* $(g_{\mu,\text{ref}})$ of using the distance function μ (i.e., TS-MIoU) over another distance function μ_{ref} (i.e., DTW or EuD), for each dataset. Precisely, $\widehat{g}_{\mu,\text{ref}} = \dfrac{\widehat{\text{acc}}_\mu(D^{\text{train}})}{\widehat{\text{acc}}_{\mu_{\text{ref}}}(D^{\text{train}})}$ and $g_{\mu,\text{ref}} = \dfrac{\text{acc}_\mu(D^{\text{test}})}{\text{acc}_{\mu_{\text{ref}}}(D^{\text{test}})}$.

The aggregated results illustrated in Fig. 3 show that TS-MIoU (with $\text{acc}_{\text{TS-MIoU}} = 0.72 \pm 0.19$, $\widehat{\text{acc}}_{\text{TS-MIoU}} = 0.73 \pm 0.20$) can indeed make 1-NN classifier to achieve a performance similar to that of DTW (with $\text{acc}_{\text{DTW}} = 0.76 \pm 0.19$, $\widehat{\text{acc}}_{\text{DTW}} = 0.75 \pm 0.21$) and EuD (with $\text{acc}_{\text{EuD}} = 0.71 \pm 0.20$, $\widehat{\text{acc}}_{\text{EuD}} = 0.73 \pm 0.22$). Note that in this comparison, DTW's parameter, the *warping window size*, was already optimized for each dataset, whereas for TS-MIoU a generic set of bin sizes were used. 1-NN with LCSS performed significantly worse than the others, which shows its sensitive dependence on its parameter ϵ. Because of LCSS's significantly lower accuracy values which resulted in outside-the-range accuracy gain of TS-MIoU, we had to remove its corresponding points from the Texas sharpshooter plot for better visibility.

There are four partitions in Fig. 4, namely true positive (TP), true negative (TN), false positive (FP), and false negative (FN). The TP region represents datasets on which TS-MIoU claimed to make improvements, and it did. In the TN region, TS-MIoU made no such claims and no improvements were made either. In the FN region, TS-MIoU improved 1-NN's performance despite making no claim about it. The worst cases lie in the FP region, where TS-MIoU falsely claimed to achieve an improvement. Overall, TS-MIoU wins on 42 datasets (41% of all datasets) over EuD, on 87 datasets (83%) over LCSS, and on 14 datasets (13%) over DTW with learned window sizes. Although these numbers paint a convincing picture of TS-MIoU's effectiveness in many applications, this is not the most informative way to analyze the outcome; even a handful of datasets could be enough to show the unique value of a measure.

Looking at the distribution of the red and blue points in these regions, we are interested in a few different angles. One is the magnitude of accuracy gain 1-NN benefits from. By recognizing all the points in the TP region, which are not close to the center, it is evident that the improvement is not just marginal. For example see the Worms dataset (marked in Fig. 4) on which TS-MIoU improved 1-NN's performance significantly compared to both EuD and DTW, in both the expected and actual cases. This shows TS-MIoU can in fact make a significant contribution to the similarity search and retrieval applications. Another interesting angle to consider is the reason as to why TS-MIoU significantly underperforms in several cases, precisely in 51% of datasets compared to DTW and

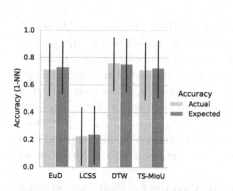

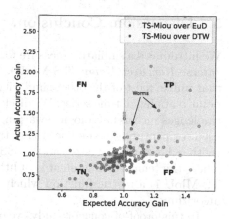

Fig. 3. The average expected and actual accuracy values of 1-NN on the UCR datasets, using four different distance functions.

Fig. 4. The Texas sharpshooter plot showing the accuracy gain of 1-NN on UCR datasets, using TS-MIoU as the distance function over Euclidean distance and DTW.

40% compared to EuD. Our analysis reveals that in most of these cases our generic binning strategy resulted in too large or too small bin sizes which could not capture the discriminatory characteristics of time series. For example, time series in `TwoPatterns` dataset have two distinct patterns; a white noise pattern and a clear min-max binary pattern. Based on the class labels, it seems that only the second pattern has discriminatory power. DTW did an excellent job on this dataset ($acc_{DTW} \simeq 1.00$) which makes it perhaps the most difficult dataset to compete against DTW on. This nearly perfect performance is owed to DTW's learned window size and its success in the mapping of the binary peaks and dips. The added distance corresponding to the (correct or incorrect) mapping of the noisy patterns is almost constant across all pairwise comparisons and does not have a significant impact on the 1-NN's performance. Regarding TS-MIoU, our generic binning strategy on the y-axis returns the bin size set $\{0.01, 0.02, 0.04, 0.08, 0.16, 0.32\}$ (since we set c_y to 0.025). These disproportionately small bin sizes results in $acc_{TS\text{-}MIoU} = 0.57$. Upon a quick grid-search on c_y, we found that changing the bin sizes to a much smaller but more effective set, i.e., $\{0.5, 1.0\}$ (by setting c_y to 1.25), significantly boosts the performance of 1-NN to 0.94. It might be interesting to note that the range of the noisy pattern of `TwoPatterns`'s time series lies almost always within the range of 0.5 to 1.0, the bin sizes corresponding to $c_y = 1.25$. This example is a strong evidence supporting the power and flexibility of TS-MIoU when appropriate bin sizes are used.

5   Discussion, Conclusion, and Future Work

We introduced a similarity measure for time series, called *Time Series Multiscale Intersection over Union* (TS-MIoU). The novelty of TS-MIoU lies in the fact that unlike most of the other similarity measures, it does not require a point-to-point mapping of time series. We discussed that this approach circumvents many challenges such as pathological warping. TS-MIoU, however, is not intended to be used for capturing non-co-occurring trends between time series. DTW measure (with a large window size) and LCSS are more suitable for these applications where the temporal alignment is of little or no importance. We also showed that TS-MIoU is a metric function which makes it an excellent choice for indexing algorithms.

In this proof-of-concept study, we only focused on the feasibility and applicability of TS-MIoU in time series similarity analysis. One avenue that we wish to explore is its pruning and further indexing potential. Sequential scan algorithms can be used to illustrate the pruning power, independent of the actual indexing structure [5]. The next natural step is to investigate the indexing of the TS-MIoU algorithm in detail. Other than taking advantage of the triangle inequality condition, another method for indexing is to apply the GEMINI framework where lower-bounding is used. Since the TS-MIoU is based on box-counting, we could adapt it for lower-bounding, similar to the Piecewise Aggregate Approximation used in LB_Keogh [16]. Another avenue of our future work is to adapt TS-MIoU for streaming time series data. We will investigate the various dynamic normalization methods, such as the ones based on z-normalization and min-max normalization (e.g., [31] among many). Real-time processing combined with early abandoning can greatly enhance TS-MIoU in real-world applications.

Acknowledgment. This project has been supported in part by funding from CISE, MPS and GEO Directorates under NSF award #1931555, and by funding from the LWS Program, under NASA award #80NSSC20K1352.

References

1. Ahmadzadeh, A., Kempton, D.J., Chen, Y., Angryk, R.A.: Multiscale iou: A metric for evaluation of salient object detection with fine structures. In: 2021 IEEE International Conference on Image Processing (ICIP), pp. 684–688 (2021). https://doi.org/10.1109/ICIP42928.2021.9506337
2. Alt, H.: The computational geometry of comparing shapes. In: Efficient Algorithms, Essays Dedicated to Kurt Mehlhorn on the Occasion of His 60th Birthday. LNCS, vol. 5760, pp. 235–248. Springer (2009). https://doi.org/10.1007/978-3-642-03456-5_16
3. Batista, G.E.A.P.A., Wang, X., Keogh, E.J.: A complexity-invariant distance measure for time series. In: Proceedings of the Eleventh SIAM International Conference on Data Mining, SDM 2011, 28–30 April 2011, Mesa, Arizona, USA, pp. 699–710. SIAM / Omnipress (2011). https://doi.org/10.1137/1.9781611972818.60

4. Berndt, D.J., Clifford, J.: Using dynamic time warping to find patterns in time series. In: Knowledge Discovery in Databases: Papers from the 1994 AAAI Workshop, Seattle, Washington, USA, July 1994. Technical Report WS-94-03, pp. 359–370. AAAI Press (1994)

5. Chen, L., Ng, R.T.: On the marriage of lp-norms and edit distance. In: (e)Proceedings of the Thirtieth International Conference on Very Large Data Bases, VLDB 2004, Toronto, Canada, 31 August - 3 September 2004, pp. 792–803. Morgan Kaufmann (2004). https://doi.org/10.1016/B978-012088469-8.50070-X, https://www.vldb.org/conf/2004/RS21P2.PDF

6. Chen, L., Özsu, M.T., Oria, V.: Robust and fast similarity search for moving object trajectories. In: Proceedings of the 2005 ACM SIGMOD International Conference on Management of Data, SIGMOD 2005, pp. 491–502. Association for Computing Machinery, New York, NY, USA (2005). https://doi.org/10.1145/1066157.1066213

7. Dau, H.A., et al.: The UCR time series archive. IEEE CAA J. Autom. Sinica **6**(6), 1293–1305 (2019)

8. Dau, H.A., et al.: The ucr time series classification archive (October 2018). https://www.cs.ucr.edu/~eamonn/time_series_data_2018/

9. Frentzos, E., Gratsias, K., Theodoridis, Y.: Index-based most similar trajectory search. In: Proceedings of the 23rd International Conference on Data Engineering, ICDE 2007, The Marmara Hotel, Istanbul, Turkey, 15–20 April 2007, pp. 816–825. IEEE Computer Society (2007). https://doi.org/10.1109/ICDE.2007.367927

10. Ge, F., Wang, S., Liu, T.: Image-segmentation evaluation from the perspective of salient object extraction. In: 2006 IEEE Computer Society Conference on Computer Vision and Pattern Recognition (CVPR 2006), vol. 1, pp. 1146–1153. IEEE (2006)

11. Gilbert, G.: Distance between sets. Nature **239**, 174–174 (1972)

12. Harris, C.R., Millman, K.J., et al.: Array programming with NumPy. Nature **585**(7825), 357–362 (2020)

13. Hong, J.Y., Park, S.H., Baek, J.G.: Ssdtw: Shape segment dynamic time warping. Expert Syst. Appl. **150**, 113291 (2020)

14. Jaccard, P.: The distribution of the flora in the alpine zone. New Phytologist **11**, 37–50 (1912)

15. Kadous, W., Taylor, S.A.: Grasp: Recognition of australian sign language using instrumented gloves (1995)

16. Keogh, E.J.: Exact indexing of dynamic time warping. In: Proceedings of 28th International Conference on Very Large Data Bases, VLDB 2002, Hong Kong, 20–23 August 2002, pp. 406–417. Morgan Kaufmann (2002). https://doi.org/10.1016/B978-155860869-6/50043-3, www.vldb.org/conf/2002/S12P01.pdf

17. Keogh, E.J., Ratanamahatana, C.A.: Exact indexing of dynamic time warping. Knowl. Inf. Syst. **7**(3), 358–386 (2005)

18. Kosub, S.: A note on the triangle inequality for the jaccard distance. Pattern Recognit. Lett. **120**, 36–38 (2019)

19. Levenshtein, V.I., et al.: Binary codes capable of correcting deletions, insertions, and reversals. In: Soviet Physics Doklady. vol. 10, pp. 707–710. Soviet Union (1966)

20. Lin, B., Su, J.: Shapes based trajectory queries for moving objects. In: 13th ACM International Workshop on Geographic Information Systems, ACM-GIS 2005, 4–5 November 2005, Bremen, Germany, Proceedings, pp. 21–30. ACM (2005). https://doi.org/10.1145/1097064.1097069

21. Lowe, D.G.: Distinctive image features from scale-invariant keypoints. Int. J. Comput. Vis. **60**(2), 91–110 (2004)

22. Ma, R., Ahmadzadeh, A., Boubrahimi, S.F., Angryk, R.A.: Segmentation of time series in improving dynamic time warping. In: 2018 IEEE International Conference on Big Data (Big Data), pp. 3756–3761 (2018). https://doi.org/10.1109/BigData. 2018.8622554
23. Mandelbrot, B.B.: The fractal geometry of nature. 1982, San Francisco, CA (1982)
24. Marteau, P.: Time warp edit distance with stiffness adjustment for time series matching. IEEE Trans. Pattern Anal. Mach. Intell. **31**(2), 306–318 (2009)
25. Moreira-Matias, L., Gama, J., Ferreira, M., Mendes-Moreira, J., Damas, L.: Predicting taxi-passenger demand using streaming data. IEEE Trans. Intell. Transp. Syst. **14**(3), 1393–1402 (2013)
26. Mrak, S., et al.: Reliability of objective picture quality measures. J. Electr. Eng. **55**(1–2), 3–10 (2004)
27. Pilgrim, I., Taylor, R.P.: Fractal analysis of time-series data sets: Methods and challenges (2019)
28. Ratanamahatana, C.A., Keogh, E.: Everything you know about dynamic time warping is wrong. In: Third workshop on Mining Temporal And Sequential Data, vol. 32. Citeseer (2004)
29. Ratanamahatana, C.A., Keogh, E.J.: Making time-series classification more accurate using learned constraints, pp. 11–22 (2004). https://doi.org/10.1137/1. 9781611972740.2
30. Sakoe, H., Chiba, S.: Dynamic programming algorithm optimization for spoken word recognition. IEEE Trans. Acoust. Speech Signal Process. **26**(1), 43–49 (1978). https://doi.org/10.1109/TASSP.1978.1163055
31. Sukhanov, S., Wu, R., Debes, C., Zoubir, A.M.: Dynamic pattern matching with multiple queries on large scale data streams. Signal Process. **171**, 107402 (2020)
32. Tavenard, R., et al.: Tslearn, a machine learning toolkit for time series data. J. Mach. Learn. Res. 21, 118:1–118:6 (2020)
33. Theiler, J.: Estimating fractal dimension. J. Optical Soc. Am. A-optics Image Sci. Vis. **7**(6), 1055–1073 (1990)
34. Vlachos, M., Kollios, G., Gunopulos, D.: Discovering similar multidimensional trajectories. In: Proceedings 18th International Conference On Data Engineering. pp. 673–684. IEEE (2002)
35. Yi, B., Faloutsos, C.: Fast time sequence indexing for arbitrary lp norms, pp. 385–394 (2000), www.vldb.org/conf/2000/P385.pdf

Financial Machine Learning

Distributional Correlation–Aware Knowledge Distillation for Stock Trading Volume Prediction

Lei Li[1,2], Zhiyuan Zhang[1,2], Ruihan Bao[3(✉)], Keiko Harimoto[3], and Xu Sun[1,2(✉)]

[1] MOE Key Lab of Computational Linguistics, Peking University, Beijing, China
lilei@stu.pku.edu.cn, {zzy1210,xusun}@pku.edu.cn
[2] School of Computer Science, Peking University, Beijing, China
[3] Mizuho Securities Co., Ltd., Tokyo, Japan
{ruihan.bao,keiko.harimoto}@mizuho-sc.com

Abstract. Traditional knowledge distillation in classification problems transfers the knowledge via class correlations in the soft label produced by teacher models, which are not available in regression problems like stock trading volume prediction. To remedy this, we present a novel distillation framework for training a light-weight student model to perform trading volume prediction given historical transaction data. Specifically, we turn the regression model into a probabilistic forecasting model, by training models to predict a Gaussian distribution to which the trading volume belongs. The student model can thus learn from the teacher at a more informative distributional level, by matching its predicted distributions to that of the teacher. Two correlational distillation objectives are further introduced to encourage the student to produce consistent pairwise relationships with the teacher model. We evaluate the framework on a real-world stock volume dataset with two different time window settings. Experiments demonstrate that our framework is superior to strong baseline models, compressing the model size by 5× while maintaining 99.6% prediction accuracy. The extensive analysis further reveals that our framework is more effective than vanilla distillation methods under low-resource scenarios. Our code and data are available at https://github.com/lancopku/DCKD.

Keywords: Knowledge distillation · Trading volume prediction

1 Introduction

Large deep neural networks (DNNs) like Transformer [30] have achieved superior performance in various areas like computer vision [6], natural language processing [5] and time series forecasting problems like stock trading volume prediction [32]. However, the increase of model parameters demands more computational resources, limiting their applicability in latency-sensitive scenarios like high-frequency trading (HFT). The pursuit of a better performance-efficiency

© The Author(s), under exclusive license to Springer Nature Switzerland AG 2023
M.-R. Amini et al. (Eds.): ECML PKDD 2022, LNAI 13718, pp. 105–120, 2023.
https://doi.org/10.1007/978-3-031-26422-1_7

trade-off promotes an active research field toward compressing large DNNs while maintaining promising model performance. Pilot model compression techniques include pruning [8], quantization [11, 28] and knowledge distillation [9, 24]. Pruning improves the parameter efficiency by de-activating redundant structures in the network, and quantization focuses on exploring fewer bits for representing the model weights. While effective in reducing the model size, these two methods require hardware-specific support for actually gaining the speed-up. On the other hand, knowledge distillation (KD), trains a much smaller student model by utilizing the learned knowledge from a large teacher model. It has been prove successful in various classifications problems like natural language understanding [26, 29] and image classification [9, 24], and recent studies have demonstrated that KD can obtain a compact student model that matches or even outperforms the teacher model [7, 13, 24].

Traditional knowledge distillation works relatively well for classification problems, as it can transfer the *dark knowledge*, i.e., the softened logits of the teacher prediction, to the student. The softened logits contain richer supervision signals than the vanilla one-hot class label, reflecting the semantic correlation between different classes and thus boosting student performance. However, this advantage cannot hold in regression problems like stock trading volume prediction, as the teacher model only produces real-valued predictions which have an identical characteristic to the oracle label. Without an optimal carrier for the learned knowledge in the teacher, the effects of KD are limited in regression problems.

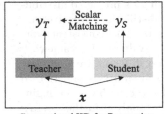
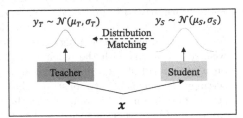

Conventional KD for Regression   Distributional KD for Regression

Fig. 1. Distributional knowledge distillation for regression problems. While conventional KD for regression problems only transfers the knowledge by matching the scalar y_S to y_T, our proposed distributional KD operates on the distributional level and provides more informative supervision for the student.

To remedy this, in this paper, we propose a distributional knowledge distillation framework for regression problems, as illustrated in Fig. 1. Specifically, we first turn the problem into a probabilistic forecasting problem. We cast the trading volume prediction problem as a conditional probability distribution modeling problem given the historical data. The teacher and the student are both probabilistic forecasting models trained by minimizing the log-likelihood of the training data. The learned knowledge from the teacher model is then transferred to the student by minimizing the discrepancy between the predicted distributions.

Besides, recent studies have shown that the capacity gap between the teacher model and the student model may harm the distillation effect [15,21], which is also observed in our vanilla distributional KD framework. To alleviate this, we design two correlations between different samples regarding the output distributions. The student is then trained to predict pair-wise correlations consistently with the teacher model, by incorporating the correlation congruence objectives into the distillation process. These objectives serve as auxiliary objectives to provide more informative supervision for alleviating the capacity gap problem. We validate our proposal by distilling a multiple-layer Transformer model into a single layer student model. Experiments on a real-world stock volume prediction dataset show that our framework can reduce the number of model parameters by 5 times while maintaining 99.6% prediction accuracy. Further analysis shows that our framework is more effective under low-resource settings and can make the student produce more calibrated predictions.

2   Methodology

In this section, we first formulate the stock trading volume prediction problem and introduce the metrics defined for evaluation. Followingly, we introduce conventional knowledge distillation for classification problems. We then elaborate the proposed distributional correlation-aware knowledge distillation framework for the regression problem.

2.1   Task Formulation

Stock trading volume prediction aims at predicting the market trading volume given historical transaction data. Specifically, given training dataset consists of N data samples $\mathcal{D} = \{(\mathbf{x}_1, y_1), \ldots, (\mathbf{x}_N, y_N)\}$, where $\mathbf{x}_i$ denotes the transaction data including open, closing, lowest, highest price and the trading volume in the past time windows, and y_i is the target volume of the i-th sample. Our goal is training a light-weight student model S, to predict the trading volume $\hat{y}$, by learning from a larger teacher model T. The student performance is measured by the mean squared error (MSE), mean absolute error (MAE) and prediction accuracy (ACC):

$$
\begin{aligned}
\mathrm{MSE} &= \mathbb{E}_{(\mathbf{x},y)\sim\mathcal{D}}(\hat{y} - y)^2, \\
\mathrm{MAE} &= \mathbb{E}_{(\mathbf{x},y)\sim\mathcal{D}}|\hat{y} - y|, \\
\mathrm{ACC} &= \mathbb{P}_{(\mathbf{x},y)\sim\mathcal{D}}\left((\hat{y} - y_{\text{last}}) \times (y - y_{\text{last}}) > 0\right),
\end{aligned}
\tag{1}
$$

where y_{last} is the volume of the most last time slot. Thus, ACC is the accuracy of whether the volume increases or decreases compared to the last time slot.

2.2   Conventional Knowledge Distillation for Classification

Knowledge distillation is a classic framework for transferring the knowledge of a larger teacher model to a light-weight student model. The main idea behind is training the student model to mimic the outputs of the teacher model. Specifically, in a classification problem, given the one-hot label $\mathbf{y}$, the student prediction $\mathbf{O}_S$ and the teacher prediction $\mathbf{O}_T$ over the class set, KD is usually achieved by minimizing both the hard label error and a soft label error between the student and the teacher predictions:

$$\mathcal{L}_{KD} = \alpha \mathcal{H}\left(\mathbf{y}, \mathbf{O}_S\right) + (1 - \alpha)\mathcal{H}\left(\mathbf{O}_T, \mathbf{O}_S\right), \tag{2}$$

where $\mathcal{H}(\cdot, \cdot)$ denotes the cross-entropy objective and α is a tuning parameter controlling the relative contribution of cross-entropies. As $\mathbf{O}_T$ usually contains rich information regarding the semantic relationships between classes, the student can capture more fine-grained structured information from the teacher predictions than directly learning from the ground-truth label. However, this characteristic cannot hold in regression problems like stock trading volume prediction, as the teacher predictions are also real-valued scalars. The predicted scalars of the teacher cannot convey more information to benefit the student, motivating us to explore a better distillation framework for regression problems.

2.3   Distributional Knowledge Distillation for Regression Problems

To facilitate the distillation effect, we propose to cast the trading volume prediction problem as a probabilistic forecasting problem, thus the information can be transferred at the distribution level. Specifically, following DeepAR [25], instead of directly predicting the scalar, we assume that the predicted trading volume follows a Gaussian distribution $\mathcal{N}(\mu, \sigma)$, turning the regression problem into a likelihood model as:

$$p(y \mid \mu, \sigma) = \frac{1}{\sqrt{2\pi\sigma^2}} \exp\left(-\frac{(y - \mu)^2}{2\sigma^2}\right). \tag{3}$$

The Gaussian distribution is parameterized by a mean μ and a standard deviation σ, which can be obtained by applying affine transformations on the model encoding $\mathbf{h}$ of the input transaction data $\mathbf{x}$:

$$\begin{aligned} \mu\left(\mathbf{h}\right) &= \mathbf{w}_\mu^T \mathbf{h} + b_\mu \\ \sigma\left(\mathbf{h}\right) &= \log\left(1 + \exp\left(\mathbf{w}_\sigma^T \mathbf{h} + b_\sigma\right)\right), \end{aligned} \tag{4}$$

where $\mathbf{w}_\mu$, b_μ, $\mathbf{w}_\sigma$ and b_σ are learnable parameters of the affine transformation. Note that the standard deviation is wrapped with a softplus activation to ensure the value is positive. With this formulation, a model M can be trained by minimizing the negative log-likelihood of the ground-truth data:

$$\begin{aligned} \mathbf{h}_i &= M(\mathbf{x}_i) \\ \mathcal{L}_{\mathrm{NLL}} &= -\sum_{i=1}^{N} \log p\left(y_i \mid \mu\left(\mathbf{h}_i\right), \sigma\left(\mathbf{h}_i\right)\right). \end{aligned} \tag{5}$$

We first train a teacher model with the above objective, and then transfer the learned knowledge into the student model by minimizing the Kullback-Leibler (KL) divergence between the Gaussian distributions [22] predicted by the teacher and the student model:

$$
\begin{aligned}
\mathcal{L}_{\text{DKD}} &= -\sum_i^N \text{KL}\left(\mathcal{N}\left(\mu_i^T,\sigma_i^T\right) \| \mathcal{N}\left(\mu_i^S,\sigma_i^S\right)\right) \\
&= -\sum_i^N \left(\log \frac{\sigma_i^S}{\sigma_i^T} + \frac{\left(\sigma_i^T\right)^2 + \left(\mu_i^T - \mu_i^S\right)^2}{2\left(\sigma_i^S\right)^2} - \frac{1}{2}\right),
\end{aligned}
\tag{6}
$$

where μ_i^S, μ_i^T, σ_i^S and σ_i^T are the mean and standard deviation outputs of the student model and the teacher model of the i-th data sample, respectively.

2.4 Transferring Knowledge via Correlation Consistency

Directly minimizing the KL-divergence between distributions can be challenging for the student model, as revealed by recent studies regarding the capacity gap between the teacher model and the student model [15,21]. To remedy this, we introduce correlational knowledge distillation objectives which capture the pairwise relationships between the examples for alleviating this issue. Specifically, given the outputs distributions of the teacher models and the students model on m data samples:

$$
\begin{aligned}
\boldsymbol{N}_T &= [\mathcal{N}_1^T, \ldots, \mathcal{N}_m^T] \\
\boldsymbol{N}_S &= [\mathcal{N}_1^S, \ldots, \mathcal{N}_m^S].
\end{aligned}
\tag{7}
$$

A mapping function ψ is introduced for mapping the outputs to a pairwise correlation matrix $\boldsymbol{C}$:

$$
\psi : \boldsymbol{N} \to \boldsymbol{C} \in \mathbb{R}^{m \times m}.
\tag{8}
$$

The element in $\boldsymbol{C}$ denotes the correlation between distributions on two sample $\mathbf{x}_i$ and $\mathbf{x}_j$:

$$
\boldsymbol{C}_{ij} = \varphi\left(\mathcal{N}_i, \mathcal{N}_j\right), \quad \boldsymbol{C}_{ij} \in \mathbb{R}.
\tag{9}
$$

The function φ denotes a correlation metric that captures the relationship between two Gaussian distributions, and the two options we designed for the function will be elaborated later. The correlational knowledge in the teacher then can be transferred by training student to minimize the congruence objective:

$$
\begin{aligned}
\mathcal{L}_{\text{DCKD}} &= \frac{1}{m^2} \|\psi\left(\boldsymbol{N}_S\right) - \psi\left(\boldsymbol{N}_T\right)\|_2^2 \\
&= \frac{1}{m^2} \sum_{i,j} \left(\varphi\left(\mathcal{N}_i^S, \mathcal{N}_j^S\right) - \varphi\left(\mathcal{N}_i^T, \mathcal{N}_j^T\right)\right)^2.
\end{aligned}
\tag{10}
$$

In this way, the student can learn to predict the correlation between instances consistently with the teacher model. The correlational distillation objective serves as an auxiliary objective. The student can first learn the correlations

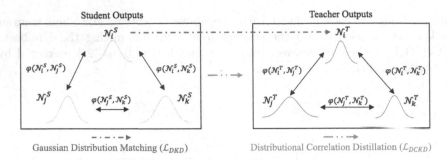

Fig. 2. The main idea illustration of the proposed distributional correlation-aware distillation, which transfers the knowledge in the teacher model by matching the predicted Gaussian distributions, with correlational consistency distillation objectives for improving the student performance.

between its own predictions according to the teacher predictions, then make efforts towards predicting exactly the same as the teacher model. Followingly, we introduce two correlation metrics regarding the distance-wise and the angle-wise similarity between samples.

Distance-Wise Correlation. Given two Gaussian distributions, a straightforward correlation metric is the distance between these two distributions. Specifically, we adopt the Jeffreys divergence (JSD) as the distance between $\mathcal{N}_i(\mu_i, \sigma_i)$ and $\mathcal{N}_j(\mu_j, \sigma_j)$ since it is symmetrized:

$$
\begin{aligned}
\varphi_{\text{Dist}}(\mathcal{N}_i, \mathcal{N}_j) &= \frac{1}{2} \left(\text{KL}\left(\mathcal{N}_i \| \mathcal{N}_j\right) + \text{KL}\left(\mathcal{N}_j \| \mathcal{N}_i\right) \right) \\
&= \frac{1}{2} \left(\frac{1}{\sigma_i^2} + \frac{1}{\sigma_j^2} \right) \left((\sigma_i - \sigma_j)^2 + (\mu_i - \mu_j)^2 \right).
\end{aligned}
\tag{11}
$$

We note that the JSD can be replaced with alternative distance measurements like Wasserstein distance. As our goal is developing a distributional distillation framework for regression problems and the JSD works well in practice, we leave the explorations on the choices of distance metrics for future work.

Angle-Wise Correlation. Another commonly adopted similarity measurement is the angle-wise correlation, which is a higher-order relationship than the vanilla distance metric and thus can be more effective for transferring information [23]. In the Euclidean space, cosine similarity is a commonly adopted for evaluating the angle-wise correlation between two vectors:

$$
\cos\langle \mathbf{u}, \mathbf{v} \rangle = \frac{(\mathbf{u}, \mathbf{v})}{\sqrt{(\mathbf{u}, \mathbf{u})(\mathbf{v}, \mathbf{v})}},
\tag{12}
$$

where $(\mathbf{u}, \mathbf{v})$ denotes the inner-product in the Euclidean space of two vectors. We extend this idea to Gaussian distributions and design a corresponding angle-wise cosine similarity metric for probabilistic distributions. Specifically, we define $(\mathcal{N}_i, \mathcal{N}_j)$ as the inner-product in the Hilbert space:

$$(\mathcal{N}_i, \mathcal{N}_j) = \int_{-\infty}^{+\infty} \mathcal{N}_i(t \mid \mu_i, \sigma_i) \mathcal{N}_j(t \mid \mu_j, \sigma_j) dt . \tag{13}$$

The cosine similarity thus can be calculated as:

$$\varphi_{\text{Cosine}}(\mathcal{N}_i, \mathcal{N}_j) = \frac{(\mathcal{N}_i, \mathcal{N}_j)}{\sqrt{(\mathcal{N}_i, \mathcal{N}_i)(\mathcal{N}_j, \mathcal{N}_j)}} = \sqrt{\frac{2\sigma_i\sigma_j}{\sigma_i^2 + \sigma_j^2}} \exp\left(-\frac{(\mu_i - \mu_j)^2}{2(\sigma_i^2 + \sigma_j^2)}\right).$$
$$\tag{14}$$

We refer readers to Appendix A for the detailed proof of the inner-dot and the cosine similarity of Gaussian distributions.

By combining the correlation metrics with the distillation objective, the student model finally is trained by minimizing the following loss function:

$$\mathcal{L} = \lambda_{\text{NLL}}\mathcal{L}_{\text{NLL}} + \lambda_{\text{DKD}}\mathcal{L}_{\text{DKD}} + \lambda_{\text{Dist}}\mathcal{L}_{\text{Dist-CKD}} + \lambda_{\text{Cosine}}\mathcal{L}_{\text{Cosine-CKD}}, \tag{15}$$

where λ_{NLL}, λ_{DKD}, λ_{Dist} and λ_{Cosine} are hyper-parameters for tuning the relative contribution of the proposed correlational distillation objectives. We name the methods that setting $\lambda_{\text{Dist}} = 0$ and $\lambda_{\text{Cosine}} = 0$ as Cosine-CKD and Dist-CKD, respectively. Figure 2 gives an overview of our proposed framework.

3   Experiments

In this section, we conduct experiments on a real-world stock trading volume prediction dataset for evaluating the effectiveness of our framework. We first introduce the dataset used for evaluation, followed by the details of compared baseline models and implementation details for reproducible results. Finally, we present the main results compared with strong baseline models.

Table 1. The statistics of the TPX500 datasets used in our paper. The training and validation datasets have no time window overlapping with the test dataset to avoid potential data leakage.

Dataset	Hourly			Daily		
Split	Training	Validation	Test	Training	Validation	Test
# of Samples	49,712	16,571	26,841	81,950	27,317	38,316

3.1   Datasets

We conduct our experiments by collecting trading data from the largest 500 stock names traded at Tokyo Exchange known as TPX500. For our research, we construct two datasets with different time windows, i.e., an hourly intra-day trading volume prediction dataset and a daily trading volume prediction dataset. The two datasets are both extracted from the price and trading volume data of the TPX500 between Jan. 2017 and June. 2018. Each data sample consists of the open, closing, lowest, highest price and trading volume in the past time windows and a target trading volume. We adopt the data of 2017 as the training set and development set, and the samples between Jan. 2018 and Jun. 2018 are adopted as the test set, making sure that the test set and the training dataset are non-overlapping. The dataset statistics can be found in Table 1.

3.2 Baselines

We compare our methods to the following baseline models, including:

Moving average methods, which adopts the averaged last 20-day transaction data as the predictions. We implement (1) Simple Moving Average (SMA), where the predictions are the averaged trading volume of the last 20 days at the same time slot, i.e., $\hat{x} = \frac{1}{T}\sum_{i=1}^{T} x_i$, and (2) Exponential Moving Average (EMA), which pays more attention to the nearest values, by setting $y_1 = x_1$ and $y_t = \rho x_t + (1-\rho)y_{t-1}$. y_T is adopted as the prediction. We set $\rho = 0.04$ following [32].

Teacher-free methods, which requires no teacher model for training the student. We implement two methods: (1) Min-MSE, where the student minimizes the mean-square error between the prediction and the ground-truth volume, and (2) DeepAR [25], which models the prediction as a conditional probability distribution and maximizes the log-likelihood of the oracle data.

Distillation methods, which utilizes the teacher model for enhancing the student model. Specifically, we implement (1) Vanilla KD [9], where the mean-square error of the student predictions and teacher predictions and the objective of the Min-MSE method are both optimized, similar to the original knowledge distillation in the classification problem, and (2) Attentive Imitation Loss (AIL) [27], where the supervision from imitating the teacher prediction is adaptively adjusted according to the relative correctness of the teacher model.

3.3 Implementation Details

Without loss of generality, we adopt the Transformer [30] model as the backbone model due to its powerful modeling ability. The teacher model consists of 6 Transformer layer, which contains a self-attention module and a feed-forward network layer. We omit the description of the Transformer layer due to the space limit and refer readers to the original Transformer paper [30] for details. The student is a much smaller Transformer model with only one layer. The number of input, number of hidden units and the output dimension are all set to 200, and the hidden states are split into 8 heads for capturing sub-space relations. The teacher and the student only differ from the layer number. The resulting numbers of model parameters of the student and the teacher model are 0.3M and 1.5M, respectively. To eliminate the influence of model capacity, all the teacher-free models are of the same architecture with the student model in distillation methods. For a fair comparison, we set the λ_{NLL} and λ_{DKD} to

0.5, which is consistent with the α in Vanilla KD. We perform grid search over the hyper-parameter λ_{Dist} and λ_{Cosine} in $\{1.0, 2.0, 5.0, 10.0\}$ and select the best performing parameters according to the validation performance. We adopt the Adam [20] optimizer and initialize the learning rate with 0.001. The batch size is set to 32 and the consistency matrix is computed in the mini-batch. We evaluate the model performance on the validation set every 1000 steps, and test the best model on the test set. We repeat every experiment with 7 random seeds and report the averaged results with a GeForce GTX 1080Ti GPU.

3.4   Main Results

Table 2. Experimental results on two different time window settings comparing with different baseline models. The best results are shown in **bold**. * denotes the results are statistically significant compared with the best performing baseline with $p < 0.05$.

Dataset	Hourly			Daily		
Model	MSE ($\downarrow$)	MAE ($\downarrow$)	ACC ($\uparrow$)	MSE ($\downarrow$)	MAE ($\downarrow$)	ACC ($\uparrow$)
Teacher model	0.195	0.335	0.731	0.124	0.265	0.665
20-day SMA	0.249	0.385	0.709	0.169	0.321	0.634
20-day EMA	0.288	0.413	0.696	0.196	0.344	0.632
Min-MSE	0.206	0.348	0.719	0.137	0.284	0.630
DeepAR [25]	0.204	0.347	0.721	0.139	0.288	0.627
Vanilla KD [9]	0.200	0.342	0.725	0.132	0.277	0.645
AIL [27]	0.202	0.344	0.722	0.134	0.282	0.634
DKD	0.201	0.342	0.724	0.133	0.279	0.639
w/Dist-CKD	0.202	0.344	0.726	0.129	0.272	0.652
w/Cosine-CKD	**0.197***	**0.339***	**0.728***	**0.128***	**0.271***	**0.656***
w/Dist-CKD + Cosine-CKD	0.199	0.340	0.727	0.129	0.273	0.652

The main results on the TPX500 dataset with two different time-window settings can be found in Table 2. It can be found that:

(1) Naïve moving average methods like 20-day SMA achieves high prediction accuracy, even better than DNN-based models on the daily dataset. This reflects a strong consistency of stock trading volume in time series, i.e., stocks with larger trading volumes in the last 20 days will also have more active trading in the future. However, regarding the absolute prediction error metrics MSE and MAE, averaging methods fall far behind the DNN-based methods, which indicates that the powerful DNNs are capable of capturing more complex data patterns behind the time series data and thus making closer predictions. (2) Distillation methods like Vanilla KD and AIL consistently outperform methods without a teacher model. This validates the effectiveness of KD by transferring the learned knowledge from a larger teacher model into the student model to help improve the student performance. (3) Our proposed correlation-aware distillation framework

Table 3. Experimental results on two settings. The best results are shown in **bold**.

Dataset	Hourly			Daily		
Model	MSE ($\downarrow$)	MAE ($\downarrow$)	ACC ($\uparrow$)	MSE ($\downarrow$)	MAE ($\downarrow$)	ACC ($\uparrow$)
Vanilla KD [9]	0.200	0.342	0.725	0.132	0.277	0.645
DKD	0.201	0.342	0.724	0.133	0.279	0.639
w/Dist-CKD	0.202	0.344	0.726	0.129	0.272	0.652
w/Cosine-CKD	**0.197**	**0.339**	**0.728**	**0.128**	**0.271**	**0.656**
Only Dist-CKD	0.223	0.364	0.717	0.132	0.278	0.647
Only Cosine-CKD	0.199	0.341	0.726	0.138	0.286	0.633

achieves the best performance. For example, on the hourly dataset, conducting distributional KD with the cosine similarity correlation objective achieves 99.6% prediction accuracy of the teacher model, while reducing the model size by 5×. It indicates that conducting KD on the distribution level and incorporating the correlation objectives are effective for enhancing the KD effect. (4) Interestingly, we observe that the angle-wise objective consistently outperforms the distance-wise correlation, which we attribute to the fact the angle correlation is higher-order information, thus is more effective for the student model to gain knowledge. Besides, combining two correlation objectives together cannot bring further performance gain, indicating that the knowledge in the two correlations can be overlapped to some extent. We leave the exploration towards better incorporating different correlation objectives as future work.

4 Analysis

In this section, we conduct experiments for probing the property of our proposed framework, by exploring the interplay between the distillation objectives, investigating the performance gain under low-resource settings and examining the pair-wise relationship with different distillation methods.

4.1 Interplay Between Distributional KD and Correlational KD

In our framework, there are two types of distillation objectives: individual distributional distillation objective, i.e., the DKD distillation objective, and pair-wise correlational distillation objectives, i.e., Dist-CKD or Cosine-CKD objective. However, the interplay between these two distillation objectives remains unclear. To investigate this, we examine the performance without the DKD distillation objective in Eq. 6 by setting the λ_{DKD} to 0. The results are listed in Table 3. We find that DKD alone performs worse than Vanilla KD, indicating that directly mimicking the distributional level outputs of teacher models is more challenging for the student than minimizing the discrepancy between single trading volume values. On the other hand, the correlational distillation objective alone, i.e., only

Dist-CKD and only Cosine-CKD also under-perform the Vanilla KD baseline, as only learning the relative correlation of output distributions is not sufficient for the student to predict accurately. It can be found that only when combined with the correctional distillation objectives, distributional knowledge distillation can achieve the best performance. These findings suggest that our proposed framework is holistic, where the two types of distillation objectives are complementary to each other to achieve optimal distillation performance.

4.2   Correlational Objectives Boost More with Fewer Data

As our framework can provide more informative supervision than conventional KD, it can be more effective under low-resource settings. To investigate this, we conduct experiments to compare the performance gain over the non-distillation training methods, i.e., Vanilla KD and AIL over Min-MSE and our methods over DeepAR. We vary the size of the training dataset from 10% to 100%, and plot the performance gain regarding the reduction of the MSE and the MAE with varying training dataset sizes in Fig. 3.

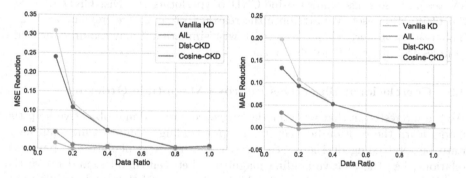

Fig. 3. The MSE (left) and MAE (right) reduction curve over the non-distillation methods with varying dataset sizes of different distillation objective on the hourly dataset. Our distributional correlation-aware distillation boosts the performance more significantly under low-resource settings. Best viewed in color.

Our findings are: (1) The performance gain of distillation vanishes as the data size becomes larger. It is reasonable as the small training dataset cannot provide comprehensive supervision, while the extra information in the teacher predictions can alleviate this problem. As the size of the training dataset increases, the training samples cover more diverse data patterns, thus the student can directly learn from the supervision provided by the original data samples instead of relying on the teacher predictions. This is consistent with previous studies which observe that KD brings more performance boost on small datasets [17,29]. (2) Compared with distillation methods solely based on the predicted scalar values, the proposed Dist-CKD and Cosine-CKD boost the performance more significantly under low-resource settings. We attribute the success to the more

Table 4. Examining the Error Ranking Number of different methods on datasets with different time window settings. The best results are shown in **bold**.

Dataset	Hourly	Daily
Model	Error ranking number ($\downarrow$)	Error ranking number ($\downarrow$)
Min-MSE	20,545,150	14,781,916
Vanilla KD [9]	20,011,092	14,369,730
AIL [27]	20,026,808	14,580,932
DeepAR [25]	20,042,538	14,490,082
DKD	20,036,694	14,363,378
w/Dist-CKD	**19,841,196**	**14,294,670**
w/Cosine-CKD	19,930,742	14,393,534

informative supervision brought by the distributional correlational-aware distillation objectives, which helps the student make more accurate predictions even with few training samples. (3) Dist-CKD reduces prediction error more under low-resource settings while Cosine-CKD outperforms the Dist-CKD with the full training dataset. We attribute the reason to that the cosine similarity is a higher-order property than the distance-wise similarity, it may require more data samples to fully exploit its effectiveness.

4.3   Correlational Objectives Improve Magnitude Ordering

We are interested in that whether the proposed correlational objective help the model learn the relation between the output trading volumes, which can facilitate better trading decisions. To investigate this, we calculate the pair-wise relations, i.e., the relative trading magnitude between samples, and probe the relation consistency between the model predictions and the oracle trading volume. Specifically, given N data samples and the corresponding oracle volume $y_1, \ldots, y_N$, we define the error ranking score as:

$$\text{Error Ranking Number} = \sum_{i=1}^{N} \sum_{j=1, j\neq i}^{N} \text{ErrorSign}\left((y_i - y_j) \times (\hat{y}_i - \hat{y}_j)\right),$$

$$\text{ErrorSign}(x) = \begin{cases} 1 & \text{if } x \leq 0, \\ 0 & \text{otherwise.} \end{cases}$$

(16)

This metric indicates how many pairs of data samples whose relative trading volume magnitude are mispredicted by the model. We randomly sampled $12,000$ data samples from the test set and calculate the metric. The results are shown in Table 4. Our observations are: (1) Distillation methods are effective for improving the prediction consistency with the oracle model. Compared with training the student model with the original mean-square error loss objective, Vanilla KD and AIL both greatly reduce the error ranking number. This shows that transferring the knowledge from the teacher model to the student not only improves the student prediction accuracy, but also makes the student become more aware of the relative magnitude between predictions. (2) Our methods achieve the best performance on both datasets. For example, on the hourly dataset, compared with the Min-MSE method, Dist-CKD reduces the Error Ranking Number by 3.4%, which verifies that our proposed correlational distillation objectives can help the model learn the relative trading volume magnitude better. Besides, Dist-CKD performs consistently better than Cosine-CKD regarding the trading volume magnitude relationship, which we attribute to the fact that the distance correlation defined in Eq. 11 is a more explicit modeling of the magnitude relation than the angle-wise objective.

5   Related Work

5.1   Knowledge Distillation

Neural network compression can produce light-weight models for efficient deployments, and it has been an active research area towards green and sustainable deep learning [14, 16, 31]. Knowledge distillation [9, 24] transfers the knowledge of a larger teacher to a smaller student model, achieving a better trade-off between model performance and inference efficiency. Recent studies show that KD is effective in computer vision [21, 23] and natural language processing [13, 29], successfully training a compact student model to perform on par with the large teacher model. While previous studies focus on classification problems, in this paper, we explore knowledge distillation for obtaining a compact student model to perform time series forecasting. We build a distributional level knowledge distillation framework for trading volume prediction and propose two correlation-aware distillation objectives. Our work is partially inspired by [23], which aligns the pair-wise correlations of data representations in the teacher and the student model. However, our framework focuses on the relationship of output distributions. Their method thus is orthogonal to our method and can be incorporated into our framework for further performance boost. Besides, to the best of our knowledge, we are the first to conduct knowledge distillation for the trading volume prediction problem and prove it is effective for obtaining light-weight and well-performing models.

5.2   Volume Prediction

Stock trading volume prediction has a significant role in algorithmic trading systems [2–4], which aims to predict the stock trading volume based on preceding transaction data. Recently, progresses have been made towards more accurate volume prediction via various machine learning techniques. Specifically, [19] propose to adopt support vector machine (SVM) for the regression problem to predict the changes of volume percentage. [18] exploit long short-term memory (LSTM) models [10] for its capability of modeling long-range dependency.

Besides, temporal mixture ensemble models [1], Bayesian auto-regressive models [12] and graph neural networks [33] are also explored in volume prediction. [32] train a Transformer model [30] with adversarial objectives to improve the model performance and robustness at the same time. In this paper, we focus on distilling a more efficient trading volume prediction model and adopt the powerful Transformer as the backbone model for distillation. Our framework is generalizable and can be easily extended to other backbone models.

6   Conclusion

In this paper, we present a distributional knowledge distillation framework for training light-weight trading volume prediction models. The learned knowledge of the teacher model is transferred to the student model at the distributional level, by minimizing the KL-divergence between the predicted Gaussian distributions and the distance-wise and angle-wise correlation distillation objectives. Experiments on the TPX500 dataset with two different time window settings show that our framework can effectively compress the model while maintaining accurate predictions. Further analysis shows that the correlational objectives significantly boost the student performance under low-resource settings and make the predictions more consistent with the oracle labels. In the future, we are hoping to explore this framework for more general regression tasks.

Acknowledgements. We thank all the anonymous reviewers for their constructive comments. This work is supported by a Research Grant from Mizuho Securities Co., Ltd. We sincerely thank Mizuho Securities for valuable domain expert suggestions and the experiment dataset.

A   Cosine Similarity of Gaussian Distributions

Proof. The inner-dot and the cosine similarity of $\mathcal{N}_i\left(\mu_i, \sigma_i\right)$ and $\mathcal{N}_j\left(\mu_j, \sigma_j\right)$ are:

$$
\begin{aligned}
(\mathcal{N}_i, \mathcal{N}_j) &= \int_{-\infty}^{+\infty} \mathcal{N}_i(t \mid \mu_i, \sigma_i) \mathcal{N}_j(t \mid \mu_j, \sigma_j) dt \\
&= \int_{-\infty}^{+\infty} \frac{1}{2\pi\sigma_i^2\sigma_j^2} \exp\left(-\frac{(t-\mu_i)^2}{2\sigma_i^2} - \frac{(t-\mu_j)^2}{2\sigma_j^2}\right) dt \\
&= \int_{-\infty}^{+\infty} \frac{1}{2\pi\sigma_i\sigma_j} \exp\left(-\frac{(t-\mu')^2}{2\frac{\sigma_i^2\sigma_j^2}{\sigma_i^2+\sigma_j^2}} - \frac{(\mu_i-\mu_j)^2}{2(\sigma_i^2+\sigma_j^2)}\right) dt \\
&= \frac{1}{\sqrt{2\pi(\sigma_i^2 + \sigma_j^2)}} \exp\left(-\frac{(\mu_i-\mu_j)^2}{2(\sigma_i^2+\sigma_j^2)}\right)
\end{aligned}
$$

where $\mu' = \frac{\mu_i \sigma_j^2 + \mu_j \sigma_i^2}{\sigma_i^2 + \sigma_j^2}$, $(\mathcal{N}_i, \mathcal{N}_i) = \frac{1}{\sqrt{4\pi\sigma_i^2}}$, $(\mathcal{N}_j, \mathcal{N}_j) = \frac{1}{\sqrt{4\pi\sigma_j^2}}$,

$$
\begin{aligned}
\varphi_{\text{Cosine}}\left(\mathcal{N}_i, \mathcal{N}_j\right) &= \frac{(\mathcal{N}_i, \mathcal{N}_j)}{\sqrt{(\mathcal{N}_i, \mathcal{N}_i)(\mathcal{N}_j, \mathcal{N}_j)}} \\
&= \frac{\sqrt{(4\pi\sigma_i^2)^{\frac{1}{2}}(4\pi\sigma_j^2)^{\frac{1}{2}}}}{\sqrt{2\pi(\sigma_i^2 + \sigma_j^2)}} \exp\left(-\frac{(\mu_i - \mu_j)^2}{2(\sigma_i^2 + \sigma_j^2)}\right) \\
&= \sqrt{\frac{2\sigma_i \sigma_j}{\sigma_i^2 + \sigma_j^2}} \exp\left(-\frac{(\mu_i - \mu_j)^2}{2\left(\sigma_i^2 + \sigma_j^2\right)}\right)
\end{aligned}
$$

References

1. Antulov-Fantulin, N., Guo, T., Lillo, F.: Temporal mixture ensemble models for intraday volume forecasting in cryptocurrency exchange markets. arXiv Trading and Market Microstructure (2020)
2. Białkowski, J., Darolles, S., Le Fol, G.: Improving vwap strategies: a dynamic volume approach. J. Bank. Finan. **32**(9), 1709–1722 (2008)
3. Brownlees, C.T., Cipollini, F., Gallo, G.M.: Intra-daily volume modeling and prediction for algorithmic trading. J. Finan. Econ. **9**(3), 489–518 (2011)
4. Cartea, Á., Jaimungal, S.: A closed-form execution strategy to target volume weighted average price. SIAM J. Finan. Math. **7**(1), 760–785 (2016)
5. Devlin, J., Chang, M.W., Lee, K., Toutanova, K.: BERT: pre-training of deep bidirectional transformers for language understanding. In: NAACL-HLT, pp. 4171–4186 (2019)
6. Dosovitskiy, A., et al.: An image is worth 16×16 words: transformers for image recognition at scale. In: ICLR (2020)
7. Furlanello, T., Lipton, Z.C., Tschannen, M., Itti, L., Anandkumar, A.: Born-again neural networks. In: ICML. Proceedings of Machine Learning Research, vol. 80, pp. 1602–1611 (2018)
8. Han, S., Mao, H., Dally, W.J.: Deep compression: compressing deep neural networks with pruning, trained quantization and huffman coding. arXiv preprint arXiv:1510.00149 (2015)
9. Hinton, G., Vinyals, O., Dean, J.: Distilling the knowledge in a neural network. arXiv preprint arXiv:1503.02531 (2015)
10. Hochreiter, S., Schmidhuber, J.: Long short-term memory. Neural Comput. **9**(8), 1735–1780 (1997)
11. Hubara, I., Courbariaux, M., Soudry, D., El-Yaniv, R., Bengio, Y.: Binarized neural networks. In: NeurIPS, pp. 4107–4115 (2016)
12. Huptas, R.: Point forecasting of intraday volume using bayesian autoregressive conditional volume models. J. Forecast. (2018)
13. Jiao, X., et al.: Tinybert: distilling bert for natural language understanding. In: Findings of the Association for Computational Linguistics: EMNLP 2020, pp. 4163–4174 (2020)
14. Li, L., et al.: CascadeBERT: accelerating inference of pre-trained language models via calibrated complete models cascade. In: Findings of the Association for Computational Linguistics: EMNLP, pp. 475–486 (2021)

15. Li, L., Lin, Y., Ren, S., Li, P., Zhou, J., Sun, X.: Dynamic knowledge distillation for pre-trained language models. In: EMNLP, pp. 379–389 (2021)
16. Li, L., et al.: Model uncertainty-aware knowledge amalgamation for pre-trained language models. arXiv preprint arXiv:2112.07327 (2021)
17. Liang, K.J., et al.: MixKD: towards efficient distillation of large-scale language models. In: ICLR (2021)
18. Libman, D.S., Haber, S., Schaps, M.: Volume prediction with neural networks. Front. Artif. Intell. **2** (2019)
19. Liu, X., Lai, K.K.: Intraday volume percentages forecasting using a dynamic svm-based approach. J. Syst. Sci. Complex. **30**(2), 421–433 (2017)
20. Loshchilov, I., Hutter, F.: Decoupled weight decay regularization. In: ICLR (2019)
21. Mirzadeh, S., Farajtabar, M., Li, A., Levine, N., Matsukawa, A., Ghasemzadeh, H.: Improved knowledge distillation via teacher assistant. In: AAAI, pp. 5191–5198 (2020)
22. Pardo, L.: Statistical Inference Based on Divergence Measures. Chapman and Hall/CRC, Boca Raton (2018)
23. Park, W., Kim, D., Lu, Y., Cho, M.: Relational knowledge distillation. In: CVPR, pp. 3967–3976 (2019)
24. Romero, A., Ballas, N., Kahou, S.E., Chassang, A., Gatta, C., Bengio, Y.: Fitnets: hints for thin deep nets. In: ICLR (2015)
25. Salinas, D., Flunkert, V., Gasthaus, J., Januschowski, T.: Deepar: probabilistic forecasting with autoregressive recurrent networks. Int. J. Forecast. **36**(3), 1181–1191 (2020)
26. Sanh, V., Debut, L., Chaumond, J., Wolf, T.: DistilBERT, a distilled version of BERT: smaller, faster, cheaper and lighter. In: NeurIPS Workshop on Energy Efficient Machine Learning and Cognitive Computing (2019)
27. Saputra, M.R.U., de Gusmão, P.P.B., Almalioglu, Y., Markham, A., Trigoni, N.: Distilling knowledge from a deep pose regressor network. In: ICCV, pp. 263–272 (2019)
28. Shen, S., et al.: Q-BERT: hessian based ultra low precision quantization of BERT. In: AAAI, pp. 8815–8821 (2020)
29. Sun, S., Cheng, Y., Gan, Z., Liu, J.: Patient knowledge distillation for BERT model compression. In: EMNLP-IJCNLP, pp. 4323–4332 (2019)
30. Vaswani, A., et al.: Attention is all you need. In: NeurIPS, pp. 5998–6008 (2017)
31. Xu, J., Zhou, W., Fu, Z., Zhou, H., Li, L.: A survey on green deep learning. arXiv preprint arXiv:2111.05193 (2021)
32. Zhang, Z., Li, W., Bao, R., Harimoto, K., Wu, Y., Sun, X.: ASAT: adaptively scaled adversarial training in time series. arXiv preprint arXiv:2108.08976 (2021)
33. Zhao, L., Li, W., Bao, R., Harimoto, K., Wu, Y., Sun, X.: Long-term, short-term and sudden event: trading volume movement prediction with graph-based multi-view modeling. In: Zhou, Z. (ed.) IJCAI, pp. 3764–3770 (2021)

Banksformer: A Deep Generative Model for Synthetic Transaction Sequences

Kyle Nickerson[1]([✉]), Terrence Tricco[1], Antonina Kolokolova[1],
Farzaneh Shoeleh[2], Charles Robertson[2], John Hawkin[2], and Ting Hu[3]

[1] Memorial University of Newfoundland, St. John's, NL, Canada
`kln870@mun.ca`
[2] Verafin Inc., St. John's, NL, Canada
[3] Queen's University, Kingston, ON, Canada

Abstract. Synthetic data are generated data that closely model real-world measurements, and can be a valuable substitute for real data in domains where it is costly to obtain real data or privacy concerns exist. Synthetic data has traditionally been generated using computational simulations, but deep generative models (DGMs) are increasingly used to create high-quality synthetic data. In this work, we tackle the problem of generating synthetic, multivariate sequences of banking transactions.

A key challenge in modeling transactional sequences with DGMs is that transactions occur at irregular intervals and may depend on timestamp-based features, such as the time of day or day of the week. Relationships between date-based features are often poorly represented in data generated using state-of-the-art sequence DGMs, such as DoppelGANger [17] and TimeGAN [31]. To remedy this, we propose a novel DGM, called Banksformer (Code available at github.com/BigTuna08/Banksformer_ecml_2022), which is able to emulate date-based patterns found in transactional data significantly better than other DGMs. We demonstrate Banksformers' ability to generate high-quality synthetic sequences of banking transactions by conducting a multi-faceted evaluation that compares synthetic data generated by Banksformer to data from other comparable DGMs, across two datasets of banking transactions.

Keywords: Synthetic data · Deep generative models · Transaction sequences

1 Introduction

Synthetic data are becoming an increasingly important component in machine learning systems. Recent work has demonstrated the ability of deep genera-

We wish to acknowledge the support of Mitacs through Accelerate funding for applied research.

Supplementary Information The online version contains supplementary material available at https://doi.org/10.1007/978-3-031-26422-1_8.

tive models (DGMs) to produce high-quality synthetic data in domains such as images [10], text [3], and audio [6]. Each of these domains has presented unique challenges, which were addressed by modifying model architectures from previous tasks to be more suited to the target task. Success in these general domains has led to the creation of focused, domain-specific models. One domain that has received considerable recent interest is financial data.

Financial data is a broad category, however most existing work on DGMs in finance focuses on modeling price sequences for stocks and other financial instruments [13,25,29]. Another important type of financial data is transactional data; that is, data that contains sequences of records or transactions recorded at arbitrary intervals. Transactional data is common in finance but also occurs in other domains. For example, both a sequence of purchase records from a credit card and a sequence of entries in electronic health records are transactional. In general, modeling transactional data is more challenging than other time-series data, as we must learn to model the intervals between transactions in addition to the transaction features. This can be particularly challenging in a domain such as banking, where the date and time of a transaction can be strongly related to the transaction type and amount. Further, certain types of dates, such as the weekends or the end of the month, can significantly influence what transactions occur.

Evaluating the quality of synthetic data is a difficult problem without a single clear solution [1,9,26]. Ideally, we would like to measure a distance between the real and synthetic data distributions; however, this is not feasible for multidimensional sequence data. A seemingly general approach would be to use the log-likelihood the generative model assigns to validation data. Unfortunately, this approach is known to have issues [26], and also depends on the model being able to assign likelihood scores, which is possible for transformers but not generative adversarial networks (GANs) [8]. Existing work generating financial time series is limited but commonly evaluates the quality of generated data by comparing univariate features distributions [13,29]. However, these univariate metrics only give a rough picture of the synthetic data quality. These metrics cannot measure how well the synthetic data captures feature interactions and interactions between sequence elements.

The main goal of this work is to produce high-quality synthetic financial transaction sequence datasets, with the same statistical properties as real data upon which they are based. We propose Banksformer (BF), a novel transformer-based DGM designed to model transactional data with date-based patterns. GANs have typically been used as the generative model in previous work generating sequential financial data [13,25,29]. To demonstrate the benefits of our approach, we compare BF against two high-quality GAN models – TimeGAN (TG) [31] and DoppelGANger (DG) [17] – on two datasets of banking transaction sequences.

2   Datasets

We used two datasets of banking transactions to compare the quality of synthetic data produced by BF with data produced by TG and DG. The first is a set of real banking data from the Czech Republic in the 1990s[1] (*czech*), and the second is a synthetic dataset of transactions from the UK in 2017[2] (*uk*). Both datasets contain transaction records from many different bank accounts, with the *uk* dataset containing 5 000 unique accounts, and the *czech* containing 4 500 accounts. Each transaction contains the dollar value of the transaction, multiple categorical codes that have information about the transaction type, and a timestamp indicating when the transaction occurred. To create a uniform representation between datasets, we concatenate together all categorical codes into a single field called the *tcode* (transaction code). In the *czech* data there are 16 unique tcodes, and the *uk* dataset has 44 (Table 1). The timestamp in the *czech* dataset only contains the transaction date, and not the specific time of day. Because of this, we do not use the time of day information in the *uk* dataset and focus only on modeling the transaction dates.

Table 1. Dataset Summary. Properties of the *czech* and *uk* data sets. Columns show the number of unique accounts (Accts), total number of transactions (Total Trans), statistics on the number of transactions per account (Trans per Acct), number of unique transcations codes (Tcodes), and the date range.

	Accts	Total trans	Trans per Acct			Tcodes	Date range	
	Count	Count	Min	Max	Mean	Count	Start	End
Czech	4500	1.06×10^6	9	675	235	16	01/01/1993	31/12/1998
UK	5000	10^5	2	50	20	44	01/04/2017	25/05/2017

We are primarily interested in the *czech* dataset, which was initially made available as part of the Discovery Challenge at the 1999 PKKD conference [23]. This dataset is likely to lead to more meaningful results than the *uk* dataset for three main reasons. First, the *czech* dataset contains real banking data. This is in contrast to the *uk* dataset, which is a synthetic dataset. Second, the *czech* dataset contains over 1 M transactions, making it over ten times larger than the *uk* dataset, which has only 100K transactions. Because the datasets have a similar number of unique accounts, this means there are comparatively fewer transactions per account in the *uk* dataset (Table 1). Finally, the *uk* data is also from a much smaller range of dates, containing less than two months' data, whereas the *czech* dataset spans five years. Transactional banking data often contains date-based patterns, which can be difficult for DGMs to emulate. In the *uk* dataset, the most significant date-based patterns are related to the day of the week. In that dataset, transactions never occur on Sunday. Further, certain types of transactions are related to the day of the week, and happen more or less often on certain days. Because the *uk* dataset spans less than two full months,

---

[1] https://data.world/lpetrocelli/czech-financial-dataset-real-anonymized-transactions.

[2] https://pub.towardsai.net/generating-synthetic-sequential-data-using-gans-a1d67a7752ac; this blog post explores using DG to create synthetic data.

we do not consider patterns related to the day of the month. In contrast, the *czech* dataset does not contain any apparent relationships involving the day of the week. However, in the *czech* data there are clear patterns related to the day of the month, with certain types of transactions only occurring at the month's end, and others only happening early in the month.

We transform this dataset of transactions into transaction sequences by grouping together transactions by account, and then sorting the transactions for each account by date (and time in the *uk* dataset). In order to create more uni form datasets, we filtered out sequences shorter than a minimum length parameter l_{min} (5 for *uk* and 20 for *czech*), and split sequences longer than l_{max} (20 for *uk* and 80 for *czech*) into multiple contiguous subsequences, so that all sequences used for training and validation have length in the range $[l_{min}, l_{max}]$. In addition to the features present in each transaction, there is also meta-data information associated with each sequence. This meta-data contains the starting account balance, start date of the sequence, and for the *czech* dataset, the customers' age at the start of the sequence. To preprocess the data for the generative models, continuous features are linearly scaled to have a variance of 1, and categorical features are encoded with a one-hot encoding. In the generic preprocessing step used by all models, we follow the method of [17] and represent time information by providing the start date as meta-data and including a time delta feature with each transaction that indicates the amount of time that has passed between transactions. When using BF, we perform a further preprocessing step (detailed in Sect. 5.1) to create additional date-based features which BF requires.

3   Methods

3.1   Generative Adversarial Networks (GANs)

GANs [8] are a commonly used generative model, and are capable of generating high-quality synthetic data in many domains [3,6,10]. TG [31] and DG [17] are two GAN models that have been successful at generating complex multivariate sequence data. Each of these models has unique innovations that allow them to generate high-fidelity synthetic sequences. In TG, an embedding scheme is used so that the generator and discriminator are operating in an embedded space, and a supervised loss based on predicting the next sequence element is used in addition to the standard GAN training objective. In DG, there are many innovations, including *batch generation* to better capture long-term dependencies, a conditional generation mechanism to deal with relationships between metadata and sequences, and a custom *auto-normalization* scheme that reduces mode collapse.

3.2   Transformers

The *transformer* architecture [27] was designed to perform sequence modeling tasks without a recurrence, instead relying on an attention mechanism and positional encoding scheme to model sequence ordering. While originally proposed as a language model [27], transformers have since been applied to modeling many types of sequences [14,30]. In this work, we use the *transformer-decoder* (TD) [18] variant of the transformer, as this is most appropriate for generating novel sequences. TD is designed as an auto-regressive model that can model probability distributions over sequences. The main innovations in the transformer and TD architectures are *positional encodings* (PEs) and *multi-head attention* (MHA). Since transformers do not use recurrence, and process all sequence elements simultaneously, the PEs are designed to allow the model to learn ordered sequences by adding a PE vector to the initial embedding. While there are many possible options for creating PE vectors, a standard choice for d-dimensional PE vectors is for the ith dimension, corresponding to input position t, to be $\sin(t/10000^{i/d})$ if i is even, and $\cos(t/10000^{i/d})$ otherwise. The MHA mechanism allows the model to create multiple sequence representations by projecting the encoded sequences into multiple sub-spaces. Scaled dot-product attention [27] is then applied separately in each sub-space. When TD models are applied to sequences of discrete symbols, including language, they are trained using the maximum-likelihood objective of minimizing the negative log-likelihood of observed sequences, $-log(P(seq; \Theta))$, with parameters Θ. The probability of a length n sequence, $s = (x_1, ..., x_n)$, is computed using the auto-regressive factorization $p(seq; \Theta) = \prod_{i=1}^{n} p(x_n | x_1, ..., x_{n_1}; \Theta)$, which is implemented by the TD.

4   Related Work

There are several different approaches to creating and evaluating synthetic financial time series. Here, we give a brief overview of the most relevant works.

4.1   Synthetic Financial Time Series

Traditionally, agent-based models were used to generate synthetic sequences of financial banking data [2,19], similar to the type of data modeled in our work, as well as for generating synthetic stock-market data [4,12,21].

Methods based on DGMs have recently begun to outperform agent-based approaches in generating realistic, univariate financial sequences [11,24,25,29]; however, there is less research on generating multivariate financial data. A GAN model for generating multivariate sequences of stock option prices was proposed in [28]. The work most similar to ours is StockGAN [13], which generates synthetic stock-market order-stream data, where each sequence item contains information about the order price, quantity, type, and date.

Methods based on DGMs have recently begun to outperform agent-based approaches in generating realistic, univariate financial sequences [11,24,25,29]. There is less research on generating multivariate financial sequences; however, [28] introduced a GAN model for generating multivariate sequences of stock option prices, and [13] proposed StockGAN, which generates synthetic stock-market order-stream data.

A critical difference between the banking data we are interested in and the datasets used in these works on financial time series is the transactional nature of our data. The previously mentioned works all aim to model sequences where measurements are taken at regular intervals, such as daily stock prices. In our transactional data, the time between transactions varies, and the timing information plays a critical role influencing the transactional properties. Existing work on modeling transactional data with DGMs is limited, and we are not aware of other works which have solely focused on this task. In the papers which introduced both TG [31] and DG [17], the authors briefly discuss how their models can be used on data with irregular time intervals. In both cases, the authors suggest adding a time delta feature to indicate the time between elements and modeling this like a typical continuous feature. However, neither of these works attempts to show that their models can learn patterns based on dates or times.

To the best of our knowledge, transformers have not yet been applied to the task of generating synthetic financial time-series data. Originally proposed as a language model, transformer models such as GPT-3 can generate novel text with narrative structure [3]. Transformers have also been applied to modeling other types of time series data, including influenza prevalence [30], as well as electricity usage and traffic [7,14,16].

4.2   Evaluation of Synthetic Sequence Data

The evaluation of synthetic data depends upon its planned use. If synthetic data is planned to augment training data, then one approach is to train the model on synthetic data and evaluate its predictive performance on real data [17,31]. If it can achieve comparable accuracy on real data to a model trained on real data, then this is taken as evidence of the quality of the synthetic data. This approach is less valuable when the use of the synthetic data is not known a priori.

Continuous Data. A simple way to evaluate synthetic financial time-series data is to compare univariate distributions, using metrics such as the 1-Wasserstein distance [29] or Kolmogorov-Smirnov distance [2,13]. For multivariate data, these distances can be computed separately for each feature of interest [13]. A limitation is that these metrics do not consider interactions between features, nor sequence order. Due to the limited work in generating multivariate banking data, there are no domain-specific metrics we are aware of. In works on financial sequences of asset prices, such as [13,29], domain-specific metrics were used that focused on well-documented features that occur in real market data known as *stylized-facts* [5].

Categorical Data. [13] studied synthetic financial time-series that generates data with both categorical and continuous-valued features, however, their evaluation only focused on continuous features. [32] use a randomly initialized LSTM model to generate a dataset of discrete sequences that were used to train their sequence generator. The LSTM model was then used to evaluate the likelihood of the data produced by the generator. [15] adopt a similar approach, performing additional validation experiments on real text sequences. To evaluate the quality of the generated text, they use BLEU scores [22], which measure the proportion of N-grams in the generated data that also occur in the real data.

5   Banksformer

We have created a modified TD model, called Banksformer (BF), to generate multivariate sequences of banking transactions. There are two main innovations in the design of BF. First, a preprocessing step allows BF to model sequences of items that contain multiple features of different types, including continuous and categorical features, as well as dates. Second, BF uses a novel method for generating multivariate time series data, in which each field of a transaction is generated sequentially. Our results indicate that this allows BF to better learn the joint distribution, such as $p(amount, tcode)$ as the product of two simpler distributions $p(amount, tcode) = p(tcode)p(amount|tcode)$.

5.1   Date Mechanism

The unique way Banksformer handles dates involves two parts – encoding and prediction. In BF, we create multiple features based on the timestamp to facilitate learning date-based patterns. Specifically, the day of the month (DoM), the number of days until the months' end (DTME), the day of the week (DoW), and the month of the transaction are each represented using two features. The two features are $f_1 = \sin(2\pi i/n_i)$ and $f_2 = \cos(2\pi i/n_i)$, where i is an ordering index and n_i is the number of possible indices (e.g., $i = 0$ and $n_i = 12$ when encoding the month of January). Additionally, BF also models a time delta (Δ_t) feature, as is done in TG and DG.

The way we have chosen to encode the date information helps BF learn date patterns; however, it also clearly contains redundancy. When generating data with BF, we first generate a probability distribution over the result for each date feature, and then create a distribution over the transaction date as

$$p(date) = \frac{1}{Z} \prod_{field \in \{DoM, DTME, DoW, month, \Delta_t\}} p_{field}(date[field]), \quad (1)$$

where Z is a normalizing constant.

We implement this with the following approach. First, a maximum time between transactions is set to make the approach feasible. The distribution over the time delta feature is modeled with a truncated Gaussian distribution, covering the range from 0 to the maximum time. BF outputs two features for the time delta, which are interpreted as the mean and variance to the truncated Gaussian. For each of the other features, BF outputs a categorical distribution over the options, which is created by a softmax layer. To compute the normalizing constant for the distribution, we sum the normalized probabilities of all dates between 0 and the maximum number of days from the current date. We then sample a date from this distribution, and then convert the selected date back into the separate date features.

5.2   Architecture

Figure 1 outlines the architecture of BF, which is composed of 3 main parts. The input layer takes a sequence of multivariate transactions and maps it to a d_{model}

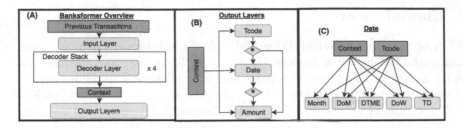

Fig. 1. An illustration of BF. (A) An overview of BFs architecture. (B) A zoomed-in view of the output layers, showing how BF sequentially handles transaction parts. When generating data, the * boxes indicate a sampling operation that samples a value from the input distribution. During training, teacher forcing is used, and the * boxes indicate the true value which should have been produced by the input distribution. (C) A further zoomed-in view of the date layer, showing that each piece of date information is predicted independently from the context, which encodes the sequence of previous transactions and the true value of the tcode for the current transaction.

dimensional sequence to which the positional encoding is added. The decoder stack then processes the encoded sequence and emits a context sequence that encodes predictions about the next element in the sequence. Finally, the output layers process each context and transform them into transaction predictions.

Input Layer. The input layer in BF is fully connected and simply maps the input data with dimension d_{input} to a representation with dimension d_{model}, which is used throughout the decoder stack.

Decoder Stack. After the input layer, BF contains a stack of 4 identical decoder layers, following a similar design as the decoder layers used in [27]. Each decoder layer is composed of two sub-layers. The first is a masked multi-head self-attention layer. This layer allows the network to attend to all sequence positions less than i when predicting the ith element. This design follows the decoder stack in [18]. The final decoder layer emits a vector with size d_{model}. Our BF synthetic datasets were created using $d_{model} = 128$ (see Supplementary materials for a complete list of parameters).

Output Layer. In BF, the output contains multiple important pieces of information. This work focuses specifically on three: a categorical tcode, a transaction date, and a real-valued amount. The output layer of BF contains a conditional generation mechanism, which generates each of these values sequentially, and conditions each value on all previous ones. In the end, our model represents the probability distribution of the kth transaction $(trans_k)$ in a sequence as $p(trans_k|hist) = p(tcode_k|hist) \cdot p(date|hist, tcode_k) \cdot p(amount|hist, tcode_k, date)$, where $hist$ is the transaction history up to the kth element of the sequence.

Loss Function. The loss function used for training BF treats each piece of information within a transaction separately, with the overall loss a weighted sum of individual losses. For continuous features, BF outputs predictions as parameters to a normal distribution, and the loss is the negative log probability of the data under the distribution. For categorical features, categorical cross-entropy is used.

5.3 Generating Data

BF generates synthetic data in the following way. The first element of the sequence contains the metadata, transformed into a vector with the same dimensionality as the feature dimension of the training sequences. A sequence of l transactions is then iteratively generated. At each step, the current generated sequence is passed as input, and the next element in the sequence is output. This element is then concatenated to the existing generated sequence. When generating a transaction, BF generates each attribute in a predefined order, conditioning each attribute on all previous attributes. Each generated attribute is output by a unique, fully connected layer. For categorical attributes, the raw output from the associated layer is passed through a softmax function to create a probability distribution over possible values, and the generated value is randomly sampled from this distribution. For continuous attributes, BF outputs two features, which are treated as the mean and variance of a normal distribution, and the generated value is sampled from this distribution. The transaction date is sampled from the distribution in Eq. 1, following the method detailed in Sect. 5.1.

6 Results

In this section, we present a comparison of synthetic data generated by BF, TG, and DG on both the *czech* and *uk* datasets. Due to space limitations, the figures in this section focus on results from the *czech* dataset; however, we have included additional figures further detailing our results on the *uk* dataset as a supplementary PDF. For BF and TG, all synthetic sequences had an equal number of transactions (20 for *uk*, 80 for *czech*), and the start dates (plus ages for the *czech* data) were randomly sampled from the empirical distribution in the real datasets. In contrast, DG generates sequence lengths and meta-data along with the transaction sequences. To better understand the quality of our generated data, we use a set of metrics to evaluate multiple aspects of our synthetic data.

6.1 Univariate Distributions

The most straightforward metrics are based on comparing univariate feature distributions for the continuous and categorical features. We use the Wasserstein-1 distance for distributions of continuous variables and the Jensen Shannon divergence (JSD) for discrete variables to quantify the difference in univariate distributions. For continuous variables, we compare the distributions of transaction amounts and monthly cash flow. The monthly cash flow of an account is simply the sum of all credits and debits (positively and negatively-valued transaction amounts) in a given month. We are interested in cash flow distributions because, unlike the transaction amount, cash flow is not directly modeled as a variable in the training data. However, cash flow is still an important facet of bank data. If synthetic data can capture the cash flow patterns from the real training data, this will support the claim that the model is learning the actual data distribution. As we can see from Fig. 2, the synthetic data generated by BF best captured the monthly cash flow patterns from the real data. This is supported quantitatively as well (Table 2). The amount distribution produced by BF was quantitatively worse than both TG and DG on the *czech* data (Table 2). However, when viewed on a log scale, BF appears to better capture the three modes of the real amount distribution Fig. 2. On the *uk* dataset, BFs' amount distribution was closest to the real data. The data generated by BF also performs best at emulating the tcode distribution in the *czech* data, which can be seen in Fig. 2 and Table 2. DG does nearly as well as BF at capturing the tcode distribution on the *czech* data, and slightly better than BF on the *uk* data.

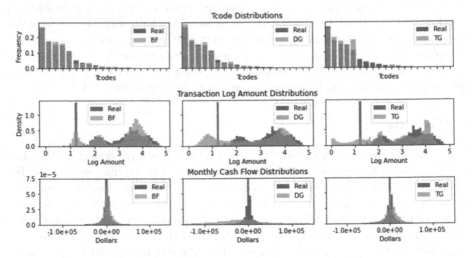

Fig. 2. Comparison of univariate distributions in *czech* data. This figure shows a comparison of the distributions for the tcode (top), log amount (middle), and monthly cash flow (bottom) in the synthetic datasets produced by BF, DG, and TG.

6.2   N-grams

We also compare N-gram distributions for the categorical feature to measure the models' ability to capture sequence orderings. Here we focus on 3-grams, and use the JSD to quantify differences in these distributions. We experimented with other values of N and the results did not change significantly. However, the JSD becomes harder to estimate as N increases because the empirical N-gram distributions become worse estimates of the true N-gram distributions

Table 2. Results Summary. The first 2 score columns are the Wasserstein-1 distances comparing the univariate amount (Amt) and monthly cash flow (CF) distributions respectively. The next two columns are JSD results comparing the univariate distributions of the tcode (Tcode) and transaction day of the month (DoM). The final columns are also JSD results. The Tcode 3G column show the JSD between the distributions of tcode 3-grams. And finally, the (Tcode, Date*) column compares the joint distributions of tcode and the most significant categorical date feature, which is DoM for the *czech* data, and DoW for the *uk* data. The bottom three results for the *czech* dataset show the results of ablation experiments; ablation results for the *uk* dataset can be found in the supplementary PDF.

Data	Model	Amt	CF	Tcode	DoM	Tcode 3G	Tcode, Date*
Czech	BF	2102	**2738**	**0.004**	0.011	**0.042**	**0.251**
	DG	1939	57800	0.007	0.090	0.132	0.660
	TG	**1931**	4980	0.075	0.059	0.337	0.638
	BF-ND	3705	4191	0.009	0.059	0.059	0.595
	BF-NC	3580	4775	0.158	**0.006**	0.411	0.542
	TF-V	4726	4138	0.185	0.059	0.445	0.674
UK	BF	**42.6**	**541.8**	0.015	**0.024**	0.156	**0.008**
	DG	179.0	1051	**0.011**	0.034	**0.135**	0.061
	TG	116.0	1460	0.237	0.087	0.622	0.077

due to the curse of dimensionality. We attempted to mitigate this with *additive smoothing* [20], however this did not significantly change the results, so the results we present are based solely on comparing empirical distributions. Figure 3 compares the distributions of the most common N-grams, and shows both BF and DG produce more accurate N-gram distributions on the *czech* data than TG. This is supported by quantitative results in Table 2, which also show that BF outperforms DG in terms of the JSD metric on the *czech* dataset. This metric also shows DG performs slightly better than BF on the *uk* dataset.

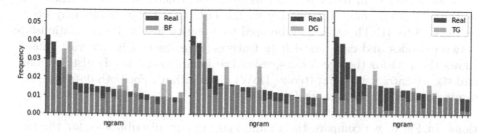

Fig. 3. 3-gram frequency comparison. This figure compares the frequency of the 25 most commonly occurring 3-grams in the real *czech* data, for each of the synthetic datasets.

6.3 Joint Distributions

One limitation of the previous metrics is that they do not account for how well feature interactions are modeled in the synthetic data. To get a sense of the overall joint distribution, we can visually compare the distributions of two-dimensional projections of the datasets (Fig. 4). To create this visualization, we follow the approach of [31], The sequences were first flattened along the temporal dimension and then a PCA model was fit to the real data. All data sets are projected into 2D using this PCA fit. Figure 4 shows that there are multiple peaks in the real *czech* data, and that BF reproduces these peaks on the whole. DG only poorly reproduces the real data, yielding a bimodal distribution, and TG focuses on a single mode.

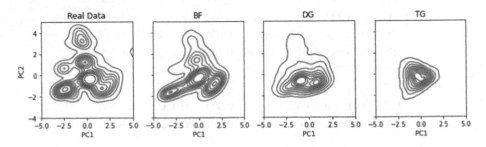

Fig. 4. PCA visualization of *czech* data. The two principal components of the data distributions obained using PCA. The generated data are projected using the PCA model that was fit to the real data.

Figure 5 shows the distribution over the day of the month for two specific tcodes that only occur at specific times of the month. The top row is for interest credited to the account, which only happens on the last day of the month, and the bottom row is a type of debit transaction that only occurred between the 5th and 14th of the month. BF is the only model able to learn the date pattern associated with these tcodes. In particular, our model can correctly generate transactions at the end of the month, even though the last day of the month may occur on days 28 to 31. The JSD may be used to quantify how well the relationship between tcodes and categorical date features were learned in general. Table 2 shows the JSD for the *czech* data, using the joint (tcode, DoM) distributions, and the *uk* data, using joint (tcode, DoW) distributions. For both data sets, BF significantly outperforms both DG and TG.

Different transaction types also have different associated amount distributions. In Fig. 6, we compare the conditional amount distributions for the two most common tcodes in the *czech* dataset. In this figure, we can see that BF, TG and DG all appear to have approximately learned the relationship between amount and tcode. Additionally, this figure also shows qualitative differences in the conditional amount distributions produced by the different models. BF tends to produce narrower, symmetric distributions, which are centered near the

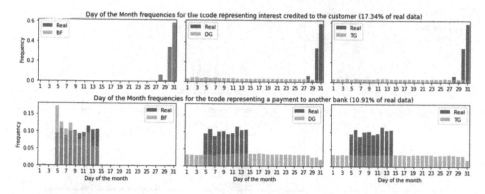

Fig. 5. Date, tcode relationship in *czech* data. This figure shows the conditional distribution of the transaction day of the month, given the tcode, for two tcodes that are strongly related to the date. This figure shows that BF (left) is the only model which has learned the relationship between these tcodes and the date.

mean of the real data; whereas both DG and TG tend to produce much wider, asymmetric distributions.

6.4 Ablation

To illustrate the impact of the innovations behind BF, we perform ablation experiments on conditional generation and date generation mechanisms. Specifically, we create the following three ablated versions of BF:

- A version without the date mechanism (BF-ND). In this implementation, we model the date using only the time delta feature, as is done in TG and DG.
- A version without conditional generation (BF-NC). In this implementation, we generate all transaction fields simultaneously.
- A basic transformer model with neither mechanism (TF-V).

The results from these experiments are shown in Table 2, which validate that both mechanisms introduced to the architecture of BF led to improved performance on most metrics. This was particularly true for the metrics that measured joint distributions, as well as metrics related to the amount, where BF scored much better than the ablated versions, and TF-V scored noticeably worse. For other metrics, different ablations had different impacts. The BF-NC version did worse than BF-ND on comparisons of both the tcode and tcode 3-gram distributions, with BF-NC being comparable to TF-V on these metrics. Similarly, BF-ND does worse than BF-NC and is comparable to TF-V on the DoM metric, which compares the distributions of transaction day of month.

Overall, these results are in line with expectations. It is somewhat surprising that the conditional generation mechanism improved the distributions of tcodes and tcode 3-grams, as the tcode is the first feature produced when generating conditionally. It may be that without conditional generation, the other features

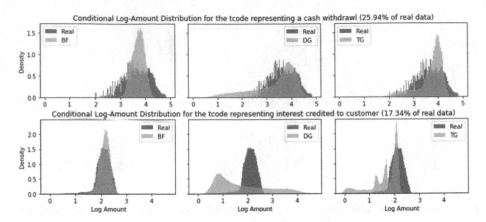

Fig. 6. Amount, tcode relationship in *czech* data. This figure shows a comparison of the conditional distributions $p(amount|tcode)$ produced by BF, DG and TG, against real data for the two most common tcodes in the real data.

become more difficult to model, causing the model to spend more effort learning those relationships, and less on the tcodes. We plan to investigate this further in future work.

7   Discussion

Our experiments show that the design of BF led to a clear improvement over TG and DG in modeling financial transactional sequences. Qualitatively, the most significant area of gain is in modeling the joint relationship between dates and transaction types, as only BF was able to learn these. Quantitatively, BF also created data that better matched the statistical properties of real data, according to the majority of the metrics we considered. Through ablation experiments, we demonstrated that both of BFs' innovations, the date mechanism and conditional generation for the individual transaction fields, improved synthetic data quality. We believe a promising future direction for this work is to explore hybrid models and combine innovations from BF, TG, and DG. There are multiple approaches we have in mind to explore this idea, including adapting the date mechanism from BF to GAN models based on TG and DG, and adding an adversarial training step to BF.

Another critical area for future work is to examine the privacy implications of these models. One major motivation for studying synthetic banking transaction data is to minimize reliance on real private data. However, before these models can be used to generate synthetic data to replace real data with genuine privacy concerns, users must be aware of any potential information which could be leaked through synthetic datasets.

Reproducible Research Statement. Code for Banksformer is available at github.com/BigTuna08/Banksformer_ecml_2022, as well as copies of the datasets and links to the other models used in this work. The synthetic datasets we have generated are available upon request.

References

1. Alaa, A.M., van Breugel, B., Saveliev, E., van der Schaar, M.: How faithful is your synthetic data? sample-level metrics for evaluating and auditing generative models. CoRR abs/2102.08921 (2021)
2. Assefa, S., Dervovic, D., Mahfouz, M., Balch, T., Reddy, P., Veloso, M.: Generating Synthetic Data in Finance: Opportunities, Challenges and Pitfalls. InfoSciRN: Data Protection (Topic) (2020)
3. Brown, T., Mann, B., Ryder, N., et al.: Language models are few-shot learners. In: Advances in Neural Information Processing Systems, vol. 33, pp. 1877–1901. Curran Associates, Inc. (2020)
4. Byrd, D., Hybinette, M., Balch, T.H.: ABIDES: towards high-fidelity market simulation for AI research. ArXiv abs/1904.12066 (2019)
5. Cont, R.: Empirical properties of asset returns: stylized facts and statistical issues. Quant. Finan. **1**, 223–236 (2001)
6. Engel, J., Agrawal, K.K., Chen, S., Gulrajani, I., Donahue, C., Roberts, A.: Gansynth: adversarial neural audio synthesis. arXiv:1902.08710 (2019)
7. Farsani, R.M., Pazouki, E.: A transformer self-attention model for time series forecasting. J. Electr. Comput. Eng. Innov. (JECEI) **9**(1), 1–10 (2021)
8. Goodfellow, I., et al.: Generative Adversarial Networks. ArXiv abs/1406.2661 (2014)
9. Jordon, J., Yoon, J., van der Schaar, M.: Measuring the quality of synthetic data for use in competitions. arXiv:1806.11345 (2018)
10. Karras, T., Laine, S., Aittala, M., Hellsten, J., Lehtinen, J., Aila, T.: Analyzing and improving the image quality of stylegan. CoRR abs/1912.04958 (2019)
11. Koshiyama, A., Firoozye, N., Treleaven, P.: Generative adversarial networks for financial trading strategies fine-tuning and combination. Quant. Finan. **21**(5), 797–813 (2021)
12. LeBaron, B.: Chapter 24 agent-based computational finance. In: Handbook of Computational Economics, vol. 2, pp. 1187–1233. Elsevier (2006)
13. Li, J., Wang, X., Lin, Y., Sinha, A., Wellman, M.: Generating realistic stock market order streams. In: Proceedings of the AAAI Conference on Artificial Intelligence, vol. 34, no. 01, pp. 727–734 (2020)
14. Li, S., Jin, X., Xuan, Y., et al.: Enhancing the locality and breaking the memory bottleneck of transformer on time series forecasting. In: Advances in Neural Information Processing Systems, vol. 32. Curran Associates, Inc. (2019)
15. Li, Z., Xia, T., Lou, X., et al.: Adversarial discrete sequence generation without explicit neural networks as discriminators. In: The 22nd International Conference on Artificial Intelligence and Statistics, pp. 3089–3098. PMLR (2019)
16. Lim, B., Arık, S., Loeff, N., Pfister, T.: Temporal Fusion Transformers for interpretable multi-horizon time series forecasting. Int. J. Forecast. **37**(4), 1748–1764 (2021)

17. Lin, Z., Jain, A., Wang, C., Fanti, G., Sekar, V.: Using GANs for sharing networked time series data: challenges, initial promise, and open questions. In: Proceedings of the ACM Internet Measurement Conference, IMC 2020, pp. 464–483. Association for Computing Machinery, New York (2020)
18. Liu, P.J., Saleh, M., Pot, E., et al.: Generating Wikipedia by Summarizing Long Sequences. ArXiv abs/1801.10198 (2018)
19. Lopez-Rojas, E.: Applying Simulation to the Problem of Detecting Financial Fraud. Ph.D. thesis, Blekinge Institute of Technology (2016)
20. Manning, C.D., Raghavan, P., Schütze, H.: Introduction to Information Retrieval. Cambridge University Press, Cambridge (2008)
21. Panayi, E., Harman, M., Wetherilt, A.: Agent-based modelling of stock markets using existing order book data. In: MABS (2012)
22. Papineni, K., Roukos, S., Ward, T., Zhu, W.J.: BLEU: a method for automatic evaluation of machine translation. In: Proceedings of the 40th Annual Meeting on Association for Computational Linguistics, pp. 311–318 (2002)
23. Berka, P., Sochorova, M.: PKKD 1999 Discovery Challenge (1999). Accessed 01 Apr 2022
24. Silva, B.D., Shi, S.S.: Towards Improved Generalization in Financial Markets with Synthetic Data Generation (2019)
25. Takahashi, S., Chen, Y., Tanaka-Ishii, K.: Modeling financial time-series with generative adversarial networks. Physica A: Stat. Mech. Appl. **527**, 121261 (2019)
26. Theis, L., Oord, A.V.D., Bethge, M.: A note on the evaluation of generative models. arXiv preprint arXiv:1511.01844 (2015)
27. Vaswani, A., et al.: Attention is all you need. In: Proceedings of the 31st International Conference on Neural Information Processing Systems, NIPS 2017, pp. 6000–6010. Curran Associates Inc., Red Hook (2017)
28. Wiese, M., Bai, L., Wood, B., Buehler, H.: Deep hedging: learning to simulate equity option markets. arXiv preprint arXiv:1911.01700 (2019)
29. Wiese, M., Knobloch, R., Korn, R., Kretschmer, P.: Quant GANs: deep generation of financial time series. Quant. Finan. **20**(9), 1419–1440 (2020)
30. Wu, N., Green, B., Ben, X., O'Banion, S.: Deep transformer models for time series forecasting: the influenza prevalence case. CoRR abs/2001.08317 (2020)
31. Yoon, J., Jarrett, D., van der Schaar, M.: Time-series generative adversarial networks. In: Advances in Neural Information Processing Systems, vol. 32 (2019)
32. Yu, L., Zhang, W., Wang, J., Yu, Y.: SeqGAN: sequence generative adversarial nets with policy gradient. In: Proceedings of the Thirty-First AAAI Conference on Artificial Intelligence, AAAI 2017, pp. 2852–2858. AAAI Press (2017)

Stock Trading Volume Prediction with Dual-Process Meta-Learning

Ruibo Chen[1], Wei Li[2], Zhiyuan Zhang[1], Ruihan Bao[3(✉)], Keiko Harimoto[3], and Xu Sun[1(✉)]

[1] Peking University, Beijing, China
{ruibochen,zzy1210,xusun}@pku.edu.cn
[2] Beijing Language and Culture University, Beijing, China
liweitj47@blcu.edu.cn
[3] Mizuho Securities Co., Ltd., Chiyoda-ku, Japan
{ruihan.bao,keiko.harimoto}@mizuho-sc.com

Abstract. Volume prediction is one of the fundamental objectives in the Fintech area, which is helpful for many downstream tasks, e.g., algorithmic trading. Previous methods mostly learn a universal model for different stocks. However, this kind of practice omits the specific characteristics of individual stocks by applying the same set of parameters for different stocks. On the other hand, learning different models for each stock would face data sparsity or cold start problems for many stocks with small capitalization. To take advantage of the data scale and the various characteristics of individual stocks, we propose a dual-process meta-learning method that treats the prediction of each stock as one task under the meta-learning framework. Our method can model the common pattern behind different stocks with a meta-learner, while modeling the specific pattern for each stock across time spans with stock-dependent parameters. Furthermore, we propose to mine the pattern of each stock in the form of a latent variable which is then used for learning the parameters for the prediction module. This makes the prediction procedure aware of the data pattern. Extensive experiments on volume predictions show that our method can improve the performance of various baseline models. Further analyses testify the effectiveness of our proposed meta-learning framework.

Keywords: Volume prediction · Meta-learning · Dual-process

1 Introduction

Stock trading volume prediction is one of the fundamental objectives in the Fintech area, which plays a crucial role in various downstream tasks, e.g., algorithmic trading. Volume prediction aims to predict the absolute volume value or the movement trend within a certain period of time based on the historical trading-related information. Considering the importance of volume prediction, many researchers have been devoted to predicting the volume. Both classical machine learning models and deep learning models have been applied in volume prediction. For instance,

© The Author(s), under exclusive license to Springer Nature Switzerland AG 2023
M.-R. Amini et al. (Eds.): ECML PKDD 2022, LNAI 13718, pp. 137–153, 2023.
https://doi.org/10.1007/978-3-031-26422-1_9

Liu and Lai [13] propose to predict the volume with the dynamic SVM method. Chen, Feng, and Palomar [2] propose to adopt a Kalman filter approach. While Libman, Haber, and Schaps [10] first propose to apply the LSTM models in volume pre-diction, which is popularly used for sequence prediction.

Although these methods have produced practicable prediction results, they basically model different stocks with one universal set of parameters. This kind of approach omits the individual characteristics of each stock. For example, the volumes of stocks with different scales of capitalization or from different industries can follow quite different movement patterns. On the other hand, learning different sets of parameters for each stock would face severe data sparsity and cold start problems, especially for newly listed stocks.

Based on the above observations, we propose to introduce the meta-learning framework into volume prediction. Under the proposed meta-learning framework, we propose to treat each stock as one individual task, while a meta-learner is responsible for learning the general pattern from the whole market. The meta-learner is updated according to the learning process of each task, so that its parameters can stay sensitive to individual tasks.

Apart from the pattern variation among different stocks, we assume that the pattern of one stock from different time spans can vary too. Therefore, we propose a dual meta-learning process that makes the parameters not only sensitive to different stocks (tasks), but also sensitive to different time spans. To model the movement pattern of each stock at a specific period, we propose to learn a latent variable for each sampled batch from that period of time with an encoder. This latent variable is then fed into a decoder to produce the actual prediction parameters. Note that the encoder-decoder framework instead of the prediction model plays the role of meta-learner in our method. This dual meta-learning process makes the latent variable sensitive to different time periods inside given the given stock while the decoder sensitive to different stocks (tasks).

To test the effectiveness of our proposed dual meta-learning process method, we conduct experiments on the TPX500 volume prediction dataset. Extensive analyses show that our dual meta-learning process outperforms the traditional methods and neural network baselines on five-minute and ten-minute dataset. Our codes have been made public.[1]

We conclude our contributions as follows:

- We propose to introduce the meta-learning framework into the volume prediction task to take advantage of both the general pattern and the individual stock patterns. In order to model the specific patterns of each stock, we apply an encoder-decoder framework, which encodes the volume variation trend into a latent variable.
- We propose a dual meta-learning process method to make the meta-learner sensitive to both the task-specific pattern and the time-specific pattern.
- Experiment results show that our proposed method can significantly improve the performance of various popularly applied baseline models.

---

[1] https://github.com/RayRuiboChen/DPML.

2   Related Work

2.1   Stock Market Prediction

As deep learning techniques developed rapidly in recent years, much effort has been made in the finance area, such as stock market prediction. Existing methods are mainly based on classic models, such as Feedforward Neural Networks (FNN) [1,24], Convolutional Neural Networks (CNN) [20,22], Recurrent Neural Networks (RNN), including Gated Recurrent Unit model (GRU) [12] and Long-Short Term Memory model (LSTM) [16,21]. Liu et al. [11] first use Capsule Network based on Transformer Encoder to predict stock movements. Ding et al. [3] propose several enhancements to the basic Transformer in stock movement prediction.

2.2   Meta-Learning

Recent meta-learning approaches can be basically classified into three categories, metric-based, model-based and optimization-based techniques.

Metric-based methods like Siamese networks [8] use neural networks to map the input into a feature space, and predict labels by comparing the similarity between features from support sets and query sets. Matching networks [27] absorbs the same idea and learns a network to map the support sets and unlabelled examples to their labels. Cosine similarity is used and they are trained in the few-shot setting. Prototypical networks [23] generate a prototype for each class in the feature space for comparing, increasing the robustness and reducing the time for inference. Relation networks [25] propose to use a network to work as the similarity function, which breaks the limits of pre-defined similarity metrics and exploits the task-specific information.

Model-based techniques usually use a fixed neural network at test time, and use various memory techniques to store the information from previously seen inputs or tasks. Meta Networks [15] use fast weights and slow weights to generate task-specific weights. SNAIL [14] use the temporal convolution and attention mechanisms to improve memory capacity.

Optimization-based techniques are aimed at learning new tasks quickly with optimization methods and they mostly view meta-learning as a bi-level optimization problem. In the inner level(usually described as the inner loop), a base learner is proposed to make task-specific adjustments and the outer level(the outer loop) is concerned with performance across tasks. Model Agnostic Meta-Learning (MAML) [4] uses second-order derivatives to find the most sensitive parameters in the parameter space for fast adaptation to new tasks. A large number of variations [5,6,17,18] are proposed afterwards. Meta-SGD [9] learns a learning rate vector and aims to adapt to the given task in one optimization step. Latent Embedding Optimization [19] proposes an encoder-decoder architecture and optimizes in the latent embedding space under the few-shot setting.

However, previous methods mostly concentrate on classification tasks and are more suitable for few-shot learning. When presented with a larger dataset, they often cannot perform well and are computationally expensive [7]. Thus, we propose the dual meta-learning process, which are able to solve both classification and regression problems and can deal with the few-shot setting as well as large support set scenarios.

Algorithm 1. Meta-Train

Require: Stocks S, Encoder e, Decoder d, prediction model f, learning rates α, β, γ

Initialize encoder parameters ϕ_e, decoder parameters ϕ_d

for i=1,2,... **do**

 For $S_i = (D_i^{train}, D_i^{test})$, z_i is the latent variable of S_i

 $\phi_{d_i} = \phi_d$

 for a few steps

  Sample a time span t_1 with batch $\{x_{t_1}, y_{t_1}\}$ from D_i^{train}

  $z = e(\phi_e, x_{t_1})$

  for a few steps:

   $\theta' = d(\phi_{d_i}, z)$

   $\mathcal{L}_1 = loss(f(\theta', x_{t_1}), y_{t_1})$

   $z = z - \alpha \nabla_z \mathcal{L}_1$

  end for

  $z_i = z_i + \beta(z - z_i)$

  $\theta_i = d(\phi_{d_i}, z_i)$

  Sample another time span t_2 with batch $\{x_{t_2}, y_{t_2}\}$ from D_i^{train}

  $\mathcal{L}_2 = loss(f(\theta_i, x_{t_2}), y_{t_2})$

  Update ϕ_e, ϕ_{d_i} using $\mathcal{L}_2$

 end for

 $\phi_d = \phi_d + \gamma(\phi_{d_i} - \phi_d)$

end for

3　Approach

In this paper, we propose the dual meta-learning approach on top of the encoder-decoder framework. The encoder-decoder framework is responsible for extracting the patterns behind the data and learning latent variables z representing the task data distribution, while the dual meta-learning process is to keep the model parameters sensitive to different stocks from different time spans. Our model first generates latent variables z for each stock with the help of the encoder, which represent the characteristics of the stocks. Then we calculate the parameters θ for actual prediction models through the decoder using latent variables z. A dual meta-learning process with two layers is proposed to endow the encoder-decoder framework with the ability to learn the features and similarities among stocks regarding both stock level and time scale level. The inner meta-learning layer optimizes z for each stock by learning different time spans while the outer layer focuses on different stocks and meta-learn through the encoder-decoder framework, making the parameters sensitive to changes, such that the model can quickly adapt to different tasks. Figure 1 visualizes the whole optimization steps illustrated in Algorithm 1.

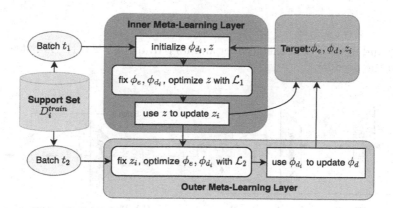

Fig. 1. An overview of the optimization steps in the dual meta-learning process.

3.1 Encoder-Decoder Framework

Instead of learning high-dimensional prediction module parameters θ directly, we propose to apply the encoder-decoder framework to learn the pattern behind stock data with latent variables z, which is represented in the form of low-dimensional vectors for each stock. The encoder maps the input data x to z in the latent space, and z serves as the input of the decoder. Note that the parameters θ for the prediction module f are produced by the decoder, and the final prediction result y' can be computed as $y' = f(\theta, x)$.

Encoder. The encoder can effectively capture the patterns behind data and transform the knowledge into low-dimensional latent variables. It takes input data x as input and generate latent variables. Given a batch of data x, y, the encoder e together with its parameters ϕ_e, we calculate the latent variable z as:

$$z = e(\phi_e, x) \tag{1}$$

The latent variables contain local information and patterns for each batch with unique time spans, and they will then be generalized in the inner meta-learning layer process to produce the latent variable for the whole stock.

Decoder. The decoder is designed to output proper prediction model parameters θ based on different latent variables for different stocks. Instead of treating all stocks uniformly, the proposed decoder makes every stock attached with its own prediction model parameters, which makes the prediction module sensible to the pattern of individual stocks. The decoder works as:

$$\theta = d(\phi_d, z) \tag{2}$$

where d and ϕ_d represent the decoder and its parameters, z is the latent variable fed into the decoder.

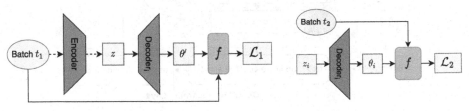

(a) The inner meta-learning layer   (b) The outer meta-learning layer

Fig. 2. A visualization of how the encoder-decoder framework interacts with the dual meta-learning process. Note that in the inner layer, the encoder is only used to initialize the latent variable z, linked by dashed line. In the outer layer, the encoder is not involved. The gradients of the encoder parameters ϕ_e can be backpropagated through z.

3.2   Dual Meta-Learning Process

Different stocks and different time spans compose two major challenges for the stock volume prediction task. Stocks are heavily influenced by the companies' actual performance, while time span features can vary according to accidental events or policies. Thus, we propose the dual meta-learning process to make our model better utilize the specific characteristics of different stocks and time periods.

Intuitively, we separate the process into two layers. The inner meta-learning layer is intended to learn the pattern behind different time spans and to make the model more precise and robust when handling new time spans in the future. The outer layer focuses on different patterns behind different stocks and makes sure the model gains sufficient global knowledge while learning individual features.

Note that our dual meta-learning process is fundamentally different from the traditional bi-level setting in optimization-based techniques, as the inner layer uses a meta-learning approach to meta-learn inside a single task, and the outer layer resembles the classic bi-level problem. A tri-level setting among instance level(time span), task level(single task) and task distribution level(all tasks) is actually proposed and processed.

As we store latent variables z_i for stocks, and optimize the model in the latent space for z_i and the parameter space for the encoder-decoder framework, which will be shown in the following sections, our dual meta-learning process has the feature for both model-based techniques and optimization-based techniques. The detailed architectures of the dual-process meta-learning are shown in Fig. 2.

Inner Meta-Learning Layer. The inner meta-learning layer mainly functions inside different time spans in one stock. To generate a stock latent variable that is sensitive to time spans, we do not use the whole training data in the support set, which can be large, time consuming and can omit the information for small time scales. Instead, we sample a batch of data $\{x_{t_1}, y_{t_1}\}$ which are continuous in time and represent the stock pattern during the given time span t_1.

The inner layer works by incorporating the characteristics of latent variables z for each batch into the stock latent variable z_i. For each z initialized by the encoder, we first optimize it by using inner meta-train loss $\mathcal{L}_1$, which is computed as:

$$\theta' = d(\phi_d, z) \tag{3}$$

$$\mathcal{L}_1 = loss(f(\theta', x_{t_1}), y_{t_1}) \tag{4}$$

Note that all other parameters like ϕ_e, ϕ_d are kept fixed in the inner layer's meta-learning procedure.

After a few steps, we add the underlying information for the certain time span in optimized z into the latent variable for the i-th stock z_i by:

$$z_i = z_i + \beta(z - z_i) \tag{5}$$

Outer Meta-Learning Layer. In contrast to the inner layer meta-learning process, the outer layer is designed to learn the pattern behind different stocks. The encoder-decoder framework and distinctive stock latent variables introduce a large amount of uniqueness, and the outer meta-learning layer secures enough global knowledge by learning and generalizing comprehensive patterns between stocks, allowing quick adaptation to new tasks.

We keep global encoder parameters ϕ_e and decoder parameters ϕ_d across different stocks in the outer meta-learning layer. To obtain the similarities in different stocks, in every epoch we create unique decoder parameters ϕ_{d_i} for the i-th stock and initialize it with ϕ_d. Similar to the inner layer, the outer layer also uses optimized ϕ_{d_i} to carry stock-specific knowledge.

Note that in the outer meta-learning layer, we sample another batch of data $\{x_{t_2}, y_{t_2}\}$ from a different time span t_2. We do not directly use $\{x_{t_1}, y_{t_1}\}$ sampled in the inner layer in order to avoid overfitting on the same time span and enhance the generalization ability of the model. Given ϕ_{d_i} and optimized z_i, the outer meta-train loss $\mathcal{L}_2$ is computed as:

$$\theta_i = d(\phi_{d_i}, z_i) \tag{6}$$

$$\mathcal{L}_2 = loss(f(\theta_i, x_{t_2}), y_{t_2}) \tag{7}$$

In the outer meta-learning layer, we only update ϕ_e, ϕ_{d_i} using $\mathcal{L}_2$ and keep z_i fixed. The alternate optimization separated in two layers similar to Generative Adversarial Networks helps layers to reach local optima in each step and finally move to global optima during the meta-training procedure.

After ϕ_{d_i} is optimized, we tune ϕ_d towards ϕ_{d_i} in the parameter space by:

$$\phi_d = \phi_d + \gamma(\phi_{d_i} - \phi_d) \tag{8}$$

In this process, ϕ_d meta-learn the differences between different stocks with the help of first-order gradients and become sensitive in the parameter space, minimizing the expected loss across task distribution as Nichol et al. [17] discussed.

3.3 Inference

The meta-learning setup consists of meta-training, meta-development and meta-test stages. Tasks for meta-development and meta-test are not seen during the meta-train stage, thus evaluating the generalization ability of the trained model. Considering the tri-level setting proposed in our dual meta-learning process, the dataset segmentation can be done from the task level and instance level, and different inference algorithms are proposed as follows.

Segmentation in the task level coincides with traditional settings, and in the stock market prediction area, we can simply view different stocks as different tasks. During meta-training, only part of the stocks are available, and the meta-test stage focuses on results on unseen stocks. In this time, inner layer must first be applied to acquire the latent variable z_i for the new task, which can be efficiently initialized by using the mean of latent variables of meta-training tasks.

However, in application, the stock market prediction problems are mostly time series analysis problems, where all stocks are available, but time spans are restricted. We propose instance level dataset segmentation for this kind of data, that all stocks are available but time spans are divided for meta-train, meta-evaluate and meta-test in chronological order. This is more suitable in real work application and we are more concerned with the performance on the unknown, future time spans.

The inference algorithm is given in Algorithm 2. The meta-train process provides a proper representation for each stock as different latent variables and globally effective parameters for encoder and decoder. As ϕ_d are meta-learned and sensitive to changes in the parameter space, we optimize the ϕ_d using the support set for the corresponding stock for a few steps to make it quickly adapt to the given task. Then we use the prediction model parameters produced by the tuned decoder to evaluate and get the final prediction result. This process is similar to meta-learning techniques like MAML and Meta-SGD.

Algorithm 2. Inference

Require: Stocks S, Decoder d, model f

  For $S_i = (D_i^{train}, D_i^{test})$

  $\phi_{d_i} = \phi_d$

  for a few steps

    Sample a time span t with batch $\{x_t, y_t\}$ from D_i^{train}

    $\theta' = d(\phi_{d_i}, z_i)$

    $\mathcal{L}_t = loss(f(\theta', x_t), y_t)$

    Update ϕ_{d_i} using $\mathcal{L}_t$

  end for

  $\theta_i = d(\phi_{d_i}, z_i)$

  Compute $\mathcal{L}_{test} = loss(f(\theta_i, x), y)$ for x, y in D_i^{test}

3.4 Model Agnostic

An important feature of the encoder-decoder framework is that it can be easily applied to any models. For example, we can replace the last fully-connected (FC) layer with the encoder-decoder framework, where input data x are the input vectors for the original last FC layer. In this situation, the given model like LSTM or Transformer can be viewed as a feature extractor. The feature can then be fed into the encoder-decoder framework to be processed. This makes our approach model-agnostic, which means that existing models can leverage our dual meta-learning process to improve performance. If a feature extractor network F is used, we first pre-train the feature extractor on the meta-training dataset. Then the input batch can be presented as $\{F(x_t), y_t\}$ given time span t. The feature extractor can be optimized in the outer layer using $\mathcal{L}_2$ during meta-training stage.

4 Experiment

4.1 Tasks and Datasets

Dataset and Data Preprocessing. In this paper, we adopt five-minute and ten-minute intra-day volume prediction dataset. The two datasets are extracted from the Topix500 dataset with volumes and open, close, high, low prices. The input data consists of log volumes and prices of the previous 12 time slots(in the same day) and the same time slots in the previous 20 trading days. We dropped the data instances which have missing volumes or prices. The target of our prediction task is to regress the log volume.

Our data were collected between *2017* and *2018*. We choose the proposed instance level data segmentation to simulate the application scene. We adopt the data of *2017* for meta-training set and meta-development set, and the data of *Jan.2018* and *Feb.2018* as the test set. The training set and development set are split by time. The statistics of the two datasets are shown in Table 1.

Table 1. Statistic information on the two datasets

Dataset	Five-minute			Ten-minute		
Split	Meta-train	Meta-dev	Meta-test	Meta-train	Meta-dev	Meta-test
Samples	106139	35359	27189	318383	81562	76418

Evaluation Metrics. We adopt three evaluation metrics for our volume prediction task: mean squared error(MSE), mean absolute error(MAE) and accuracy(ACC). Given input data pair $\{x, y\}$, prediction result $\hat{y} = f(\theta, x)$, the three metrics are defined as: $MSE = \mathbb{E}_{(x,y)\sim\mathcal{D}}(\hat{y} - y)^2$, $MAE = \mathbb{E}_{(x,y)\sim\mathcal{D}}|\hat{y} - y|$, $ACC = \mathbb{P}_{(x,y)\sim\mathcal{D}}((\hat{y} - v_{last})(y - v_{last}) > 0)$.

Here v_{last} represents the volume of the last time slot and ACC is the accuracy of whether the predicted volumes vary in accordance with the ground truth compared with the last time slot.

4.2 Baselines

Traditional Methods

- **Naive forecasting.** In our experiment, the naive forecasting algorithm uses volumes of last time slot or the same slot in yesterday.
- **Simple moving average (SMA).** The simple moving average algorithm calculates the naive average value. In our experiment, we adopt the 12-slot average, 20-day average, and 12-slot and 20-day average.
- **Exponential moving average (EMA).** Given a series of data $\{x_1, x_2, ...\}$, the EMA series $y_n(y_1 = x_1)$ are computed by $y_n = \frac{2x_n + (n-1)y_{n-1}}{n+1}$. In our experiments, we tried 20-day EMA and 12-slot EMA.

Linear. Given input data x and model parameters $\theta = (w, b)$, the linear model is formulated as $f(\theta, x) = w^T x + b$. We use the concatenation of 12-slot and 20-day history as x in our experiments.

LSTM. Following the widely use of LSTM [16,21] in stock market prediction task, we implement two one-layer LSTM models for previous 12-slot and 20-day history respectively. First, we project the input data to a feature space using an FC layer. Then the features are fed into the LSTM models, followed by an attentive pooling layer. Then another FC layer is used to get the prediction result.

Transformers. We also implement a six-layer Transformer Encoder [26] model as a baseline. The input data consists of a special *[CLS]* token and the concatenation of the 12-slot and 20-day data. The Positional Encoding is enabled. The prediction result is computed by using the output vector of *[CLS]* token to feed into a FC layer.

Table 2. Experimental results

Dataset	Five-minute			Ten-minute		
Model	MSE↓	MAE↓	ACC↑	MSE↓	MAE↓	ACC↑
Yesterday	1.203	0.797	0.665	0.517	0.532	0.719
20-day Average	0.698	0.607	0.709	0.433	0.503	0.720
20-day EMA	0.689	0.600	0.713	0.427	0.498	0.727
Last Time Slot	1.118	0.742	0.500	0.653	0.602	0.500
12-slot Average	0.982	0.710	0.630	0.975	0.782	0.445
12-slot EMA	0.888	0.668	0.642	0.846	0.718	0.457
20-day and 12-slot Average	0.689	0.581	0.713	0.377	0.469	0.698
Linear	0.694	0.638	0.681	0.303	0.419	0.740
Linear+ours	0.623	0.585	0.710	0.266	0.381	0.760
LSTM	0.623	0.583	0.706	0.272	0.391	0.745
LSTM+ours	**0.586**	0.556	**0.724**	**0.252**	**0.370**	**0.765**
Transformer	0.611	0.573	0.711	0.270	0.389	0.748
Transformer+ours	0.589	**0.555**	**0.724**	0.255	0.372	0.764

4.3   Settings and Hyperparameters

We repeat every experiment for 5 times and report the result on the meta-test dataset on the checkpoint with the lowest meta-development MSE loss. For hyperparameters in Algorithm 1, we set $\alpha = 1\text{e-}4$, $\beta = 1\text{e-}4$, $\gamma = 1$ and the stock latent variables are initialized to zeros. We adopt the SGD optimizer to optimize encoder parameters ϕ_e and decoder parameters ϕ_{d_i} with the learning rate set to 1e-5. For encoder e, decoder d, we adopt Multilayer Perceptron(MLP) with 3 layers. For prediction model f, we use a linear model. The loss function we used in Algorithm 1 and Algorithm 2 is MSE loss. For baseline models and pre-train stage for feature extractors, we adopt the Adam optimizer with the learning rate initialized to 1e-4. The batch size we used is 32. In meta-development and meta-test stages, we only conduct 10 steps in tuning ϕ_{d_i} and we use the SGD optimizer with the learning rate set to 1e-6.

4.4   Experimental Results

After selecting the best hyperparameter configurations based on the results on the meta-development set, the experimental results on meta-test set are shown in Table 2. As the result illustrated, our methods successfully improves the performance on three neural network baselines in both five-minute and ten-minute tasks. They also remarkably outperform the traditional baseline results.

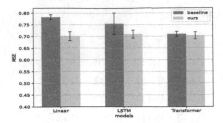

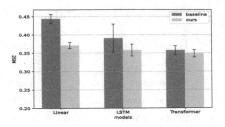

(a) Small market capitalization stocks on five-minute dataset

(b) Large market capitalization stocks on five-minute dataset

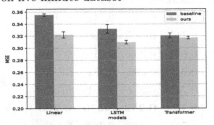

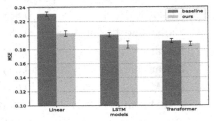

(c) Small market capitalization stocks on ten-minute dataset

(d) Large market capitalization stocks on ten-minute dataset

Fig. 3. MSE loss on simulation of newly listed stocks. On both dataset our dual meta-learning process enhance the performance of three baselines. Note that the loss for stocks with small market capitalization is significantly higher than those with large market capitalization, indicating that they are more sensitive and difficult to predict.

5 Analysis

5.1 Effectiveness of Meta-Learning

In Table 3, we show the experiment results on whether treating different stocks as different tasks in the meta-learning framework(w/o tasks). We can see that modeling different stocks with stock-specific parameters yield large gain on all the metrics in both five-minute and ten-minute datasets. This testifies the assumption that different stocks vary in the volume variation trend. Therefore, modeling stocks with stock-specific parameters is necessary.

To test whether our meta-learning method can improve the model performance on newly listed stocks, where the number of historical volume data is small, we conduct experiments to simulate those cases on five-minute and ten-minute datasets. We randomly sample 50 stocks with relatively large market capitalization or small market capitalization and only keep their last 10% data in chronological order. We report the meta-test MSE loss with lowest meta-development MSE loss.

From the results shown in Fig. 3, we can see that applying the meta-learning framework can indeed enhance the model performance on few-shot cases especially for less effective baseline models, linear and LSTM. Whereas the performance of the Transformer baseline also improves. Furthermore, the gap between stocks with large and small market capitalization proves that different patterns exist in different stocks, which can be seized by the dual meta-learning process.

Table 3. Ablation study: Effectiveness of meta-learning

Dataset	Five-minute			Ten-minute		
Model	MSE↓	MAE↓	ACC↑	MSE↓	MAE↓	ACC↑
Linear	0.694	0.638	0.681	0.303	0.419	0.740
+our approach	**0.623**	**0.585**	**0.710**	**0.266**	**0.381**	**0.760**
w/o tasks	0.745	0.669	0.669	0.315	0.430	0.731
LSTM	0.623	0.583	0.706	0.272	0.391	0.745
+our approach	**0.586**	**0.556**	**0.724**	**0.252**	**0.370**	**0.765**
w/o tasks	0.635	0.592	0.701	0.271	0.391	0.745
Transformer	0.611	0.573	0.711	0.270	0.389	0.748
+our approach	**0.589**	**0.555**	**0.724**	**0.255**	**0.372**	**0.764**
w/o tasks	0.608	0.572	0.713	0.269	0.389	0.748

5.2 Effectiveness of Encoder-Decoder Framework

To test whether the encoder can extract useful information for volume prediction, we remove the encoder, where latent variables are initialized by the input features. From the results in Table 4, we can see that without the encoder module, all the metrics decline, which shows the effectiveness of our proposed encoder structure.

We further remove the design for latent variables in Eq. 2, where parameters θ are generated by the input data using the decoder directly. The performance drop indicates that latent variables z are more informative in the latent space, which may work by denoising the raw input and extracting important features. On ten-minute dataset the Transformer model performance gets slightly better. It may be caused by data homogeneity in ten-minute dataset and the Transformer model may partially learn the role of the encoder.

To examine whether the design for producing prediction parameters based on the latent variables can help volume prediction, we further remove the decoder in addition to the encoder. In this case, only first-order gradients for the parameters of prediction model f are exploited, degenerate into simple Reptile. In this case, performance deteriorates greatly, proving the effectiveness of the encoder-decoder framework.

Table 4. Ablation study: effectiveness of encoder-decoder framework

Dataset	Five-Minute			Ten-Minute		
Model	MSE↓	MAE↓	ACC↑	MSE↓	MAE↓	ACC↑
Linear	0.694	0.638	0.681	0.303	0.419	0.740
+our approach	**0.623**	**0.585**	**0.710**	**0.266**	**0.381**	**0.760**
w/o encoder	0.700	0.642	0.681	0.288	0.405	0.748
w/o encoder, latent variables	0.661	0.610	0.697	0.272	0.387	0.758
w/o encoder, decoder	0.718	0.656	0.673	0.292	0.406	0.747
LSTM	0.623	0.583	0.706	0.272	0.391	0.745
+our approach	**0.586**	**0.556**	**0.724**	**0.252**	**0.370**	**0.765**
w/o encoder	0.630	0.587	0.704	0.265	0.383	0.755
w/o encoder, latent variables	0.614	0.576	0.711	0.270	0.384	0.756
w/o encoder, decoder	0.620	0.581	0.722	0.266	0.383	0.757
Transformer	0.611	0.573	0.711	0.270	0.389	0.748
+our approach	**0.589**	**0.555**	**0.724**	0.255	0.372	0.764
w/o encoder	0.610	0.573	0.712	0.260	0.378	0.760
w/o encoder, latent variables	0.599	0.564	0.719	**0.252**	**0.370**	**0.768**
w/o encoder, decoder	0.603	0.566	0.718	0.265	0.381	0.760

5.3 Analyzing Dual Meta-Learning Process

In Table 5, we analyze the effectiveness of the dual meta-learning process. We first remove the inner meta-learning layer(w/o inner meta-learning) by generating the latent variable z_i with the entire D_i^{train} from stock S_i. Results show that it reduces the performance on both five-minute and ten-minute dataset. It proves that different time spans have distinct patterns and the inner meta-learning process successfully captures and exploits the features behind a small time scale.

For the outer meta-learning layer, if it is fully removed, the situation can be viewed as there is only one single task and results collapse as we have discussed before. We further probe the influence of unique decoders(w/o unique decoder). Recall that in outer meta-learning layer, we implement stock-specific decoder parameter ϕ_{d_i} in meta-training stage. If we replace it with a universal decoder parameter, it can be seen that on five-minute dataset, all the metrics degrade, showing that on this time scale stock-specific information can be valuable and unique decoders are influential. But on ten-minute dataset, the accuracy metric and the more effective Transformer model showed a marginal improvement in performance, which may be caused by less noise and uncertainty in the data.

Table 5. Ablation study: Analyzing dual meta-learning process

Dataset	Five-minute			Ten-minute		
Model	MSE↓	MAE↓	ACC↑	MSE↓	MAE↓	ACC↑
Linear	0.694	0.638	0.681	0.303	0.419	0.740
+our approach	**0.623**	**0.585**	**0.710**	**0.266**	**0.381**	0.760
w/o inner meta-learning	0.664	0.599	0.705	0.284	0.398	0.751
w/o unique decoder	0.644	0.599	0.705	**0.266**	0.382	**0.763**
LSTM	0.623	0.583	0.706	0.272	0.391	0.745
+our approach	**0.586**	**0.556**	**0.724**	**0.252**	**0.370**	0.765
w/o inner meta-learning	0.588	0.557	0.723	0.253	0.371	0.764
w/o unique decoder	0.594	0.561	0.720	0.256	0.372	**0.766**
Transformer	0.611	0.573	0.711	0.270	0.389	0.748
+our approach	**0.589**	**0.555**	**0.724**	0.255	0.372	0.764
w/o inner meta-learning	0.664	0.611	0.699	0.256	0.374	0.761
w/o unique decoder	0.597	0.561	0.721	**0.253**	**0.370**	**0.769**

6 Conclusion

In this work, we propose the dual meta-learning process for stock trading volume prediction, which are model agnostic and can be implemented on given models without a meta-learning procedure to improve performance. We use the inner meta-learning layer to mine the pattern behind different time spans and learn a stock-specific latent variable. The outer meta-learning layer gains generalization ability across stock (task) distributions. The dual meta-learning process successfully models the characteristics of stock data and outperforms various baselines. Extensive analyses further show the effectiveness of each component of the dual meta-learning process.

Acknowledgements. We thank all the anonymous reviewers for their valuable suggestions. This work is supported by Mizuho Securities Co., Ltd. We sincerely thank Mizuho Securities for the domain expert suggestions and the experiment dataset. Ruihan Bao and Xu Sun are the corresponding authors.

References

1. Chen, H., Xiao, K., Sun, J., Wu, S.: A double-layer neural network framework for high-frequency forecasting. ACM Trans. Manag. Inf. Syst. (TMIS) **7**(4), 1–17 (2017)
2. Chen, R., Feng, Y., Palomar, D.: Forecasting intraday trading volume: a Kalman filter approach (2016). SSRN 3101695
3. Ding, Q., Wu, S., Sun, H., Guo, J., Guo, J.: Hierarchical multi-scale Gaussian transformer for stock movement prediction. In: IJCAI, pp. 4640–4646 (2020)

4. Finn, C., Abbeel, P., Levine, S.: Model-agnostic meta-learning for fast adaptation of deep networks. In: International Conference on Machine Learning, pp. 1126–1135. PMLR (2017)
5. Finn, C., Rajeswaran, A., Kakade, S., Levine, S.: Online meta-learning. In: International Conference on Machine Learning, pp. 1920–1930. PMLR (2019)
6. Grant, E., Finn, C., Levine, S., Darrell, T., Griffiths, T.: Recasting gradient-based meta-learning as hierarchical Bayes. arXiv preprint arXiv:1801.08930 (2018)
7. Hospedales, T., Antoniou, A., Micaelli, P., Storkey, A.: Meta-learning in neural networks: a survey. arXiv preprint arXiv:2004.05439 (2020)
8. Koch, G., Zemel, R., Salakhutdinov, R., et al.: Siamese neural networks for one-shot image recognition. In: ICML Deep Learning Workshop, vol. 2, Lille (2015)
9. Li, Z., Zhou, F., Chen, F., Li, H.: Meta-SGD: learning to learn quickly for few-shot learning. arXiv preprint arXiv:1707.09835 (2017)
10. Libman, D., Haber, S., Schaps, M.: Volume prediction with neural networks. Frontiers Artif. Intell. **2**, 21 (2019)
11. Liu, J., et al.: Transformer-based capsule network for stock movement prediction. In: Proceedings of the First Workshop on Financial Technology and Natural Language Processing, pp. 66–73 (2019)
12. Liu, J., Lu, Z., Du, W.: Combining enterprise knowledge graph and news sentiment analysis for stock price prediction. In: Proceedings of the 52nd Hawaii International Conference on System Sciences (2019)
13. Liu, X., Lai, K.K.: Intraday volume percentages forecasting using a dynamic SVM-based approach. J. Syst. Sci. Complex. **30**(2), 421–433 (2017)
14. Mishra, N., Rohaninejad, M., Chen, X., Abbeel, P.: A simple neural attentive meta-learner. arXiv preprint arXiv:1707.03141 (2017)
15. Munkhdalai, T., Yu, H.: Meta networks. In: International Conference on Machine Learning, pp. 2554–2563. PMLR (2017)
16. Nelson, D.M., Pereira, A.C., De Oliveira, R.A.: Stock market's price movement prediction with LSTM neural networks. In: 2017 International Joint Conference on Neural Networks (IJCNN), pp. 1419–1426. IEEE (2017)
17. Nichol, A., Schulman, J.: Reptile: a scalable metalearning algorithm. arXiv preprint arXiv:1803.02999 2(3), 4 (2018)
18. Rajeswaran, A., Finn, C., Kakade, S.M., Levine, S.: Meta-learning with implicit gradients. In: Advances in Neural Information Processing Systems, vol. 32 (2019)
19. Rusu, A.A., et al.: Meta-learning with latent embedding optimization. arXiv preprint arXiv:1807.05960 (2018)
20. Sezer, O.B., Ozbayoglu, A.M.: Algorithmic financial trading with deep convolutional neural networks: time series to image conversion approach. Appl. Soft Comput. **70**, 525–538 (2018)
21. Siami-Namini, S., Tavakoli, N., Namin, A.S.: A comparative analysis of forecasting financial time series using ARIMA, LSTM, and BILSTM. arXiv preprint arXiv:1911.09512 (2019)
22. Sim, H.S., Kim, H.I., Ahn, J.J.: Is deep learning for image recognition applicable to stock market prediction? Complexity **2019**, 1–10 (2019)
23. Snell, J., Swersky, K., Zemel, R.: Prototypical networks for few-shot learning. In: Advances in Neural Information Processing Systems, vol. 30 (2017)
24. Song, Y., Lee, J.W., Lee, J.: A study on novel filtering and relationship between input-features and target-vectors in a deep learning model for stock price prediction. Appl. Intell. **49**(3), 897–911 (2019)

25. Sung, F., Yang, Y., Zhang, L., Xiang, T., Torr, P.H., Hospedales, T.M.: Learning to compare: relation network for few-shot learning. In: Proceedings of the IEEE Conference on Computer Vision and Pattern Recognition, pp. 1199–1208 (2018)
26. Vaswani, A., et al.: Attention is all you need. In: Advances in Neural Information Processing Systems, vol. 30 (2017)
27. Vinyals, O., Blundell, C., Lillicrap, T., Wierstra, D., et al.: Matching networks for one shot learning. In: Advances in Neural Information Processing Systems, vol. 29 (2016)

Uncertainty Awareness for Predicting Noisy Stock Price Movements

Yun-Hsuan Lien, Yu-Syuan Lin, and Yu-Shuen Wang[✉]

National Yang Ming Chiao Tung University, Hsinchu, Taiwan
yushuen@cs.nctu.edu.tw

Abstract. Predicting stock price movements is challenging because financial markets are noisy – signals and patterns in different periods are dissimilar and often conflict with each other. Consequently, irrespective of whether the price rises or falls, none of the previous methods achieve high prediction accuracy in this binary classification task. In this study, we consider aleatoric uncertainty and model uncertainty when training neural networks to forecast stock price movements. Specifically, aleatoric uncertainty is known as statistical uncertainty. It indicates that similar historical price trajectories may not lead to similar future price movements. On the other hand, model uncertainty is caused by the model's mathematical structures and parameter values, which can be used to estimate whether the models are familiar with the testing sample. Considering that most of the existing uncertainty estimation methods focus on model uncertainty, we transform the aleatoric uncertainty in financial markets to model uncertainty by removing samples with similar historical price trajectories and different future movements. The Bayesian neural network is then adopted to estimate the model uncertainty during inference. Experiment results demonstrated that the networks achieved high accuracy when they were certain about their predictions.

Keywords: Stock price movement prediction · Aleatoric uncertainty · Model uncertainty · Uncertainty quantification

1 Introduction

Stock price movement prediction has attracted intense attention in the research field and the financial industry because investors can manage their portfolios to earn substantial profits from price fluctuations. The prediction can be considered as a binary classification problem, in which the inputs are historical prices, news, and company statistics, and the output is a rise or a fall in price at the next period (e.g., tomorrow). Theoretically, although price movements could exhibit a trend, in practice, a high level of uncertainty remains. The trend also changes over time so that knowledge learned from the past could be insufficient to predict future

---

Supplementary Information The online version contains supplementary material available at https://doi.org/10.1007/978-3-031-26422-1_10.

price movements. In fact, even the state-of-the-art method [8] achieved accuracy that was only slightly higher than a random guess in this binary classification task when taking historical prices as inputs.

In this study, we aim to quantify the uncertainty of stock price movement prediction, which is helpful for later investment strategies. On the one hand, stocks that have similar price trajectories in the past may not result in similar movements in the future, and we refer to the phenomenon as *aleatoric uncertainty* [30]. Aleatoric uncertainty is known as statistical uncertainty, which indicates that the outcomes of an experiment in different runs can be different because of unknown or inherently random effects. A typical example is coin-flipping. In other words, the price movement cannot be accurately predicted due to currently unavailable information. On the other hand, mathematical structures and parameter values of a model that are used to map inputs to outputs result in *model* uncertainty. It is known that neural networks are composed of tremendous parameters, and the networks can be considerably dissimilar if they are trained from different initializations, although on the same dataset and using the same loss. In other words, given an input, particularly an input that is dissimilar to all samples in the training set, networks trained from different initializations are likely to output different results. This model uncertainty should also be considered when predicting stock price movements.

We transform the aleatoric uncertainty of stock price movements to model uncertainty for quantification. Specifically, since similar historical price trajectories do not necessarily lead to similar future movements, we treat rises and falls in price in the next period as noisy labels. The noisy label training is then applied to remove such samples from the training set. It deserves noting that, when removing the samples with noisy labels, the aleatoric uncertainty becomes model uncertainty because the network does not learn from these samples. We then apply the Bayesian neural network to quantify model uncertainty – whether the networks are familiar with a testing sample or they just guess the solution. Unlike general neural networks, a Bayesian neural network takes a single sample as input but outputs a label distribution. The variance of the distribution implies the level of uncertainty. We exploit the depth structure of neural networks to quantify uncertainty [2]. Our network contains multiple branches of different depths and outputs multiple labels to forecast future price movements. Since different branches imply different prediction functions, the predictions are likely diverse if inputs are dissimilar to any training sample. For this reason, we measure prediction entropy and variance to elucidate how certain the network is about its output.

We estimate the uncertainty of stock price movement prediction. We argue that our network is *uncertainty-aware* because it not only outputs the prediction but also reveals the level of uncertainty. For evaluation, we trained neural networks to predict stock price movements on the next day and after ten days on the *KDD17* and *ACL18* benchmark datasets. We also evaluated the prediction accuracy in terms of the network's prediction uncertainty on our collected dataset that contains bull, flat, and bear markets. Experiment results showed that high certainty of our network's prediction indeed leads to high accuracy. Below, we summarize our contributions:

- We estimate each prediction's level of uncertainty, which can assist investors to develop flexible investment strategies.
- We transform the aleatoric uncertainty of stock price movements to model uncertainty by removing samples with noisy labels. Then, we apply the Bayesian neural network to quantify model uncertainty.
- Our experiment results verified that high certainty of a network prediction indeed leads to high accuracy.

2 Related Work

Financial Forecasting. Recently, neural networks gained considerable attention in financial forecasting [13]. They are trained to predict stock prices [1], stock movements [5,24,27], and currency exchange rates [32]. Most of the networks considered historical prices and technical analysis [6] when making predictions because of "the market discounts everything theory", i.e., the price reflects all information in the market. Considering that financial markets are noisy and non-stationary, Feng et al. [7] applied adversarial training [16] to help networks learn robust representations and facilitate generalization. In addition to prices, several methods additionally considered limit order books [28,31,38], news events [4], and texts from social media [26,34] for prediction. Their experiment results confirmed the benefits of these metadata. Rather than predicting future trends, Feng et al. [8] temporally captured stock relations and ranked the stocks according to their return ratios. The back-test results demonstrated that trading based on stock ranking were more effective than that based on future trends.

Uncertainty Estimation. In time series forecasting applications, training and testing data are from different periods and are likely to contain varied properties. Since standard networks are trained by maximum likelihood estimation (MLE), they are frequently over-confident with unfamiliar samples [25]. Due to the non-stationarity of financial markets, it is essential to extend a standard network to a Bayesian network with posterior inference from a probabilistic perspective. Under this formulation, the output becomes a distribution rather than a single point. When the network takes a novel observation as input, its output's distribution will have a large variance. Generally, the posterior inference can be approximated by dropout [9,10], model ensembles [17], subspace inference [14], and depth [2]. The high variance of the outputs implies high uncertainty.

Noisy Labels. Since neural networks can fit even random variables [36], their robustness easily degenerates when training data contain noisy labels. To ease the problem, one of the directions taken was sample selection. These methods train two networks with the same architecture and select samples according to output disagreement [22], smaller loss values [12], and their combinations [35], to update network parameters. Besides sample selection, Wei et al. [33] pointed out that networks are likely to have the same outputs if the labels are correct. Hence, they updated the network by label loss and distance loss, and expected the two networks to become the same.

3   Method

Price movement prediction can be considered to be a binary classification problem, which takes historical price movements as inputs and forecasts price rises or price falls at the next period. Specifically, let the stock market data be $\mathcal{D} = \{(\mathbf{X}_t, y_{t+1})\}_{t=1}^N$, where $\mathbf{X}_t = [x_{t-T+1}, ..., x_t] \in \mathcal{R}^{F \times T \times W}$ with F-dimensional features (e.g., high and low prices of a period, and the corresponding technical analysis) in the lag of the past T time-steps, W is the number of moving averages, and y_{t+1} denotes the actual price movement at the next period. The goal is to build a network $f(\cdot)$ with $\mathcal{D}$. Specifically, $f(\mathbf{X_t})$ forecasts the price movement y_{t+1} based on the currently available features $\mathbf{X_t}$.

3.1   Transforming Aleatoric Uncertainty to Model Uncertainty

Financial market prices constitute non-stationary time series data. The price movements are drifting, and their distributions change over time. In addition, when the market does not have a clear direction, the price moves up and down in a small range, bringing many meaningless labels. In other words, although price movements could exhibit a trend, they contain aleatoric uncertainty. Considering that most existing methods focus on quantifying model uncertainty, we attempt to transform aleatoric uncertainty into model uncertainty by removing samples with noisy labels for quantification. Specifically, samples with noisy labels are those with similar $\mathbf{X}_t$ but different y_{t+1}. Since the network does not learn from the samples with aleatoric uncertainty, it can only guess the results when such samples appear during inference, and the uncertainty can thus be quantified.

Consistent and Inconsistent Labels. Differentiating correct and incorrect labels in a traditional classification problem is simple. However, in financial markets, there is no clear definition between them. All labels can be considered correct because the stock price movements indeed happen. Since prediction implies choosing the price movement that likely occurs, financial data can be partitioned into two groups: samples with consistent and inconsistent labels. Consistent labels are those that appear more frequently than others under the condition of similar historical patterns. This new definition fulfills the assumption in the noisy label training that correct labels are the majority, and networks can learn these labels at the early stage of training.

Let $\mathbf{X}_i$, $\mathbf{X}_j$ be the price features in consecutive days with $\|\mathbf{X}_i - \mathbf{X}_j\|_2 \leq \varepsilon$, and y_i, y_j be the corresponding ground truth labels. Li et al. [19] defined that the labels of $\mathbf{X}_i$ and $\mathbf{X}_j$ are inconsistent if $\|y_i - y_j\| \geq \delta$. They also proved that the network $f(\cdot)$ with randomly initialized parameters has to traverse a long distance to fulfill inconsistent labels. In other words, in the early iterations, models updated by the gradient descent method only fit samples with consistent labels, essentially ignoring the inconsistent ones. This motivates us to remove samples with inconsistent labels when training since they contain aleatoric uncertainty.

Sample Selection. Previous experiment results show that deep neural networks tend to learn correct labels at the early stage of training and then memorize the incorrect ones [3]. In other words, at the early stage of training, the loss of correct labels decreases quickly, whereas the loss of incorrect labels remains high. Therefore, removing inconsistent labels is equivalent to removing samples that have a large training loss [15,29]. In our implementation, we adopt the co-teaching strategy in [12] and train two neural networks simultaneously. Each network selects samples with a small loss to train the other. Let f and g be the two networks with parameters ω_f and ω_g, respectively. Each mini-batch B will be reduced to

$$\tilde{B}_i = arg \min_{|\tilde{B}_i|=r|B|} \ell(B,i), \tag{1}$$

where $i \in \{f,g\}$, ℓ is the loss function and r is the ratio of data that we want to keep. To avoid accumulated error from the sample-selection bias, we train the network f using samples in $\tilde{B}_g$ and the network g using samples in $\tilde{B}_f$.

Deep neural networks tend to learn easy patterns first and gradually memorize hard samples as the number of training epoch increases. Therefore, we keep more samples at the early stage of training and gradually increase the filter out ratio. Let $R(n) \in [1-\tau, 1]$ be the proportion of the mini-batch samples that will be kept at the nth training iteration. We formulate the proportion as

$$R(n) = 1 - \min\left\{\frac{n}{n_k}\tau, \tau\right\}, \tag{2}$$

where $n \in [1, N]$, $n_k \leq N$, N is the total number of epochs, and τ and n_k are hyperparameters. Therefore, we select samples

$$\tilde{B}_i = arg \min_{|\tilde{B}_i|=R(n)|B|} \ell(i, B) \tag{3}$$

at every iteration for network training.

3.2 Model Uncertainty Estimation

Experiments have shown that deep neural networks frequently suffer from erroneous predictions with high confidence [11,25]. To remedy this problem in practice, methods were presented to estimate whether networks have learned how to handle a testing sample or they just guess the solution. The idea is based on the theory of Bayesian neural networks, and the output distribution can be used to quantify model uncertainty.

While a standard network considers the input sample and determines one predictive value, the Bayesian network computes a prediction distribution by

$$p(y|X, \mathcal{D}) = \int p(y|X, \theta)p(\theta|\mathcal{D})d\theta, \tag{4}$$

where X and y are the input sample and the corresponding label, respectively, θ indicates the network parameters, and $\mathcal{D}$ is the data set. Specifically, $p(y|X, \theta)$ tells us how well the network parameters θ explain the observation. The prediction $p(y|X, \mathcal{D})$ considers all possible parameter configurations weighted by the their posterior probabilities $p(\theta|\mathcal{D})$. Apparently, computing the exact posterior distribution $p(\theta|\mathcal{D})$ is difficult due to the complexity of deep neural networks. In practice, the distribution can be approximated by training multiple models, and the disagreement of the models yields the uncertainty [17].

Bayesian Approximation. We adopt the method in [2] and exploit the network's depth to quantify uncertainty because of its accurate approximation and computational efficiency. The main idea is to add an auxiliary output layer at the back of each intermediate block. Then, we view each output as a sub-network's prediction result. This enables us to estimate uncertainty by checking the consistency of the predictions. An intuitive explanation to this Bayesian approximation is that the sub-networks' outputs would be consistent if they have learned the sample. Otherwise, the outputs would be diverse. To perform a Bayesian inference on the depth of a neural network, we consider the network's depth to be a random variable. Let a categorical prior over network's depth d be $p_\beta(d = i) = \beta_i = 1/D$, where i is the layer index and D is the number of network layers. The marginal log likelihood of the model can be written as follows:

$$\log p(\mathcal{D}; \theta) = \log \sum_{i=1}^{D} \left(p_\beta(d = i) \cdot \prod_{t=1}^{N} p(y_t|\mathbf{X}_t, d = i, \theta) \right), \tag{5}$$

where θ indicates the network parameters and $p(y|\mathbf{X}, d = i, \theta)$ is the output of the ith layer. The posterior over depth, $p(d|\mathcal{D}; \theta) = p(\mathcal{D}|d; \theta)p_\beta(d)/p(\mathcal{D}; \theta)$, represents how well each layer explains the data.

Training. An intuitive approach to train the network is to maximize the marginal log likelihood through stochastic gradient descent. However, the approach does not work because each layer is weighted by the depth posterior. It leads gradients to vanish when the posterior collapses to a delta function. Therefore, we adopt the strategy in [2] and optimize the network by stochastic gradient variational inference. Let $q_\alpha(d = i) = \alpha_i$ be an approximate posterior. The evidence lower bound (ELBO) is written as

$$\log p(\mathcal{D}; \theta) = \sum_{t=1}^{N} \mathbb{E}_{q_\alpha(d)}[\log p(y_t|\mathbf{X}_t, d; \theta)] - KL(q_\alpha(d)||p_\beta(d)).$$

Let B and N be the batch size and the dataset size, respectively. We maximize the ELBO of each mini-batch by using

$$\frac{N}{B} \sum_{t=1}^{B} \sum_{i=1}^{D} (\log p(y_t|\mathbf{X}_t, d = i; \theta) \cdot \alpha_i) - \sum_{i=1}^{D} \left(\alpha_i \log \frac{\alpha_i}{\beta_i} \right). \tag{6}$$

Inference. After network training, we marginalize depth with the variational posterior to predict price movements. For each new sample $\mathbf{X}^*$, the prediction is computed using Bayesian model averaging [21]:

$$p(y^*|\mathbf{X}^*, \mathcal{D}; \theta) = \sum_{i=1}^{D} p(y^*|\mathbf{X}^*, d = i; \theta)q_\alpha(d = i). \tag{7}$$

Regarding the uncertainty of the network's output, we implement predictive entropy and variance because they are common measures of the uncertainty inherent in a distribution of possible outcomes. Then, we test their performances on predicting stock price movements. Specifically, predictive entropy is defined as

$$\mathbb{H}(y^*|\mathbf{X}^*, \mathcal{D}; \theta) = \sum_{c=0}^{1} p(y^* = c|\mathbf{X}^*, \mathcal{D}; \theta) \log p(y^* = c|\mathbf{X}^*, \mathcal{D}; \theta) \tag{8}$$

where $c \in \{0,1\}$ is the class label. Moreover, the prediction's variance is formulated as

$$\sigma^2(y^* = 0|\mathbf{X}^*, \mathcal{D}; \theta) = \mathbb{E}_{q_\alpha(d)}\left(p(y^* = 0|\mathbf{X}^*, d; \theta)^2\right) - $$
$$\mathbb{E}_{q_\alpha(d)}\left(p(y^* = 0|\mathbf{X}^*, d; \theta)\right)^2. \tag{9}$$

For a binary classification problem $p(y^* = 0|\mathbf{X}^*, d; \theta) = 1 - p(y^* = 1|\mathbf{X}^*, d; \theta)$ and $\sigma^2(y^* = 0|\mathbf{X}^*, \mathcal{D}; \theta) = \sigma^2(y^* = 1|\mathbf{X}^*, \mathcal{D}; \theta)$. Therefore, we only compute $\sigma^2(y^* = 0|\mathbf{X}^*, \mathcal{D}; \theta)$.

3.3 Implementation Details

Features. Recall that the input of our network is a tensor $\mathbf{X}_t = [x_{t-T+1}, ..., x_t] \in \mathcal{R}^{F \times T \times W}$, where F is the number of features, T indicates the past period that the network considers, and W is the number of moving averages. In our implementation, $F = 6$, $T = 30$, and $W = 4$. The feature x_t is composed of six price attributes, including *high, low, open, close, adjust close*, and *volume*. For each attribute, we computed the moving average according to four window sizes. Specifically, the attributes of the past 1, 3, 7, and 14 days were averaged. We also normalized the values in each sample individually to $[0, 1]$ in the pre-processing stage.

Network Architecture. We built a convolutional neural network (CNN) to forecast stock price movements. The network contained four convolutional layers and then two fully connected layers. The first three convolutional layers consider features along the temporal dimension, whereas the fourth layer exchanges information at the same period. In addition, we link the output of every convolutional layer to the shared fully connected layers to implement the depth uncertainty network. Figure 1 illustrates the detailed network architecture.

Parameters and Network Training. We initialized network parameters using the Xavier initialization and set the batch size and the learning rate to 4096 and 0.003 for the *KDD17* dataset, and 1024 and 0.001 for the *ACL18* and our collected datasets, respectively. Since price movement data of an individual stock are rare, we followed the strategy in previous works and mixed samples of different stocks for training networks. The AdamW [20] optimizer was adopted to minimize binary cross-entropy loss. We repeated the training process for 300 epochs in our implementation. Subsequently, we selected the model that performed the best on the validation data and tested it on the testing data for evaluation.

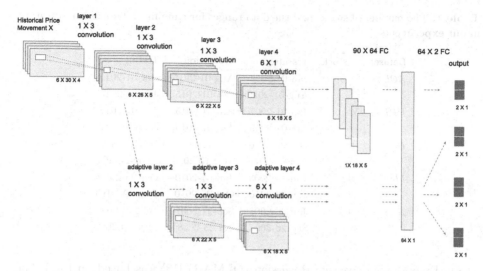

Fig. 1. The network architecture used in our study. Each intermediate layer has an auxiliary output. The adaptive layer is set to adjust the resolution. By exploiting the network's depth, we obtain the approximation of a Bayesian inference by one forward.

4 Results and Evaluations

4.1 Comparison to Baselines

We evaluated the performance of our method on five datasets: the first two are benchmark datasets *ACL18* [34] and *KDD17* [37], and the last three are our collected datasets in which the testing periods are *bull*, *flat*, and *bear* markets, respectively. We selected the stocks from the U.S. stock market that have the highest trading volumes for evaluation. Specifically, they are GOOG, NVDA, AMZN, AMD, QCOM, INTC, MSFT, AAPL, and BIDU. Table 1 shows the description, and the ranges used for training, validation, and testing. Let x_t and x_{t+1} be the closing prices of consecutive days. We computed the movement percent by $p_{t+1} = (x_{t+1}/x_t) - 1$. Typically, the label $y_{i+1} = 1$ if $p_{t+1} > 0$ and $y_{i+1} = 0$ otherwise. However, to compare with the state-of-the-art methods, we followed the setting of [8] and additionally defined the label $y_{i+1} = 1$ if $p_{t+1} \geq 0.55\%$ and $y_{i+1} = 0$ if $p_{t+1} \leq -0.5\%$. In other words, the samples with flat price movements were ignored in the experiment.

Baselines. We briefly describe the baselines in the following paragraph. Two of them were traditional technical analysis, and the others were the latest neural networks.

– Time Series Momentum Strategy (MOM) [23] was based on the belief that the current market trend will continue by taking the sign of returns over the last period. We used the trend in the last 10 days as the momentum indicator.

Table 1. The number of stocks and the data ranges for training, validation, and testing in our experiments.

Dataset	# stocks	Training	Validation	Testing
ACL18	88	Jan-01-2014– Aug-01-2015	Aug-01-2015– Oct-01-2015	Oct-01-2015– Jan-01-2016–
KDD17	50	Jan-01-2007– Jan-01-2015	Jan-01-2015– Jan-01-2016	Jan-01-2016– Jan-01-2017
Bull	9	Oct-20-2006– Jun-20-2012	Jun-21-2012– Mar-10-2013	Mar-11-2013 –Nov-20-2013
Flat	9	Jun-19-2003– Jan-03-2010	Jan-04-2010– Oct-25-2010	Oct-26-2010- Aug-19-2010
Bear	9	Jan-20-2001– Sep-26-2007	Sep-27-2007– Jul-23-2008	Jul-24-2008– May-20-2009

- On-Line Moving Average Reversion (OLMAR) [18] was based on the belief that prices will revert to the long-term mean by taking the opposite sign of the difference between the last price and the moving average. We used the 30 days moving average as the mean reversion indicator.
- StockNet [34] was a variational autoencoder exploiting text and price signals to capture the market stochasticity. In the comparison, we discarded the text signals because they are often unavailable in practice.
- ADV-ALSTM [7] applied adversarial training to improve the generalization of a prediction model. They generated additional samples by adding small perturbations on input features and trained the model on both the origin and perturbed samples.

Table 2. Mean accuracy of the baselines on the ACL18 and KDD17 datasets. All of the methods performed only slightly better than a random guess. However, the mean accuracy considerably increases if the top 10% certain samples are evaluated. We highlight the highest accuracy in boldface.

	Removing flat		Containing flat	
	ACL18	KDD17	ACL18	KDD17
MOM	46.61	49.12	47.92	48.84
OLMAR	52.7	49.85	52.21	50.23
StockNet	54.96	51.93	–	–
ADV-ALSTM	**57.2**	53.05	52.03	51.95
Ours	54.96	**53.49**	**53.5**	**52.69**
ADV-ALSTM (10%)	55.37	53.58	50.54	54.26
Ours (10%)	**64.98**	**55.81**	**60.8**	**55.37**

Experiment Results. Table 2 shows the comparison results on ACL18 and KDD17 datasets. The reported statistics were the mean testing accuracy of five different runs. From the numbers, one can realize that predicting stock

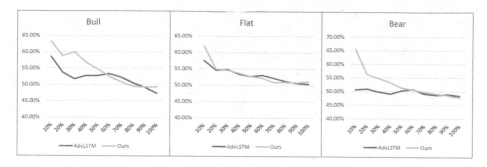

Fig. 2. We compared our method to ADV-LSTM-Dropout on our collected datasets. The testing periods are bull, flat, and bear markets, respectively. We report the prediction accuracy from the cumulative lowest to highest uncertain samples for evaluation.

price movements is extremely difficult. Even the state-of-the-art, ADV-LSTM [7], achieved an accuracy slightly higher than a random guess. Since, to the best of our knowledge, there are no stock price prediction methods built upon deep neural networks and consider uncertainty, we extend ADV-LSTM and selected the top 10% certain samples for comparison. Because ADV-LSTM's network cannot exploit depth structures for uncertainty estimation, we apply the dropout approach to approximate the posterior inference [9]. The final result is the average of its five predictions. We named the extended ADV-LSTM as ADV-LSTM-Dropout. In our implementation, we set the dropout rate to 0.8; we also repeated the experiments five times to estimate the output's variance since our network contains five branches. As indicated in Table 2, our selected top 10% certain samples have higher prediction accuracy than the remains, whereas the samples selected by ADV-LSTM do not. We suspect the reasons could be: (1) dropout reduces the prediction accuracy during inference, and (2) the network cannot learn effective knowledge from the training data that contain aleatoric uncertainty. However, without theoretical proofs and thorough experiments, they may not truly explain the phenomenon.

We additionally compared our method with ADV-LSTM-Dropout regarding different degrees of uncertainty on our collected datasets. The testing periods are bull, flat, and bear markets, respectively. We mixed all stocks in the testing data and ranked the data based on the uncertainty of each sample in ascending order. The mean accuracy of the cumulative lowest 10% to 100% uncertain samples was computed. As indicated in Fig. 2, the mean accuracy of our results gradually decreased as the uncertainty increased, which implies that our network can achieve higher accuracy when it is more certain about its prediction. Although ADV-LSTM-Dropout had a similar trend, it was not as clear as ours.

In the following sections, we evaluated the system on the whole testing set (i.e., containing flat movements) since removing them is unachievable in practice. Namely, $y_{i+1} = 1$ if $p_{t+1} > 0$ and $y_{i+1} = 0$ otherwise.

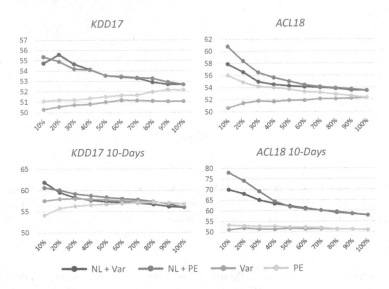

Fig. 3. The mean prediction accuracy of networks trained on a variety of conditions. We evaluated the accuracy of predictions from the cumulative lowest to highest uncertain samples. *NL*, *Var*, and *PE* are the abbreviations of noisy label training, uncertainty estimated by variance, and uncertainty estimated by predictive entropy, respectively. The line charts indicate the effectiveness of uncertainty awareness prediction. This phenomenon appeared both in the predictions of the next day and the next ten days.

4.2   Uncertainty Estimation Using Variance and Predictive Entropy

We estimated the prediction uncertainty by computing the output's variance and predictive entropy. To evaluate the performance of these two strategies, we compare the accuracy regarding different degrees of uncertainty. In this experiment, we trained the network to predict the price movement of the next day and the next 10 days and plotted the results in Fig. 3. All stocks in the testing data are mixed and then ranked for evaluation. As indicated, the mean accuracy of the stocks gradually decreased as the uncertainty increased. This phenomenon appeared both in predictions of the next day and the next 10 days, irrespective of whether variance or predictive entropy was used to represent uncertainty. Overall, the predictive entropy slightly performs better than the variance on the *ACL18* dataset, yet this advantage is not clear on the *KDD17* dataset.

In addition to mixing all stocks together, we evaluated each stock's mean prediction accuracy under the ranking of uncertainty. Let h_r^i be the mean accuracy of the $r\%$ lowest uncertain samples of stock i, where $r = \{0.1, 0.2, ..., 1.0\}$. We compute the Pearson correlation coefficient between r and h_r^i of each stock. The coefficient ranges from -1 to 1, which indicates negative and positive correlations, respectively. Figure 4 shows the correlation histogram results on the *KDD17* [37] and *ACL18* [34] datasets. The x and y axes represent the Pearson correlation coefficient and the number of stocks within each range, respectively. As indicated, most of the stocks have negative coefficients, which fulfilled the

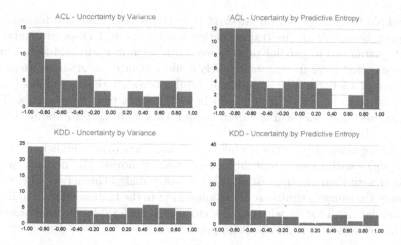

Fig. 4. The Pearson correlation coefficient between prediction uncertainty and accuracy. The x and y axes represent the range of the coefficient and the frequency, respectively. Clearly, in most stocks, low prediction uncertainty leads to high accuracy.

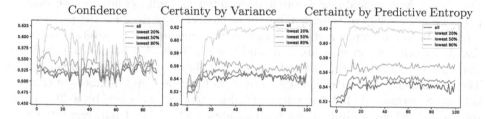

Fig. 5. Comparison of the mean accuracy of the samples selected according to confidence and two variants of certainty estimations. The lowest 20%, 50%, and 80% non-confident and uncertain samples, and all samples, in the testing data set during network training, were compared.

expectation, i.e., the lower is the uncertainty, the higher is the accuracy. Different from the results of mixing all stocks together, the variance in this experiment performs slightly better than the predictive entropy since samples in the bin of 0.8–1.0 are few.

4.3   The Effectiveness of Removing Aleatoric Uncertainty

We remove samples with aleatoric uncertainty by applying the noisy label training. In addition to the benefits of uncertainty quantification, this strategy improves network's generalization because it was not forced to memorize samples with inconsistent labels. To evaluate the effectiveness, we trained the networks with and without removing inconsistent samples and compared their predictive accuracy on the benchmark datasets. The lines in Fig. 3 verify that removing aleatoric uncertainty was effective. The improvement was about 1% accuracy if the whole testing set is evaluated. It is worth noting that the testing data were noisy. Even though the trained network achieved perfect generalization, it was not guaranteed to predict price movements accurately. In addition, removing samples that have inconsistent labels could advance uncertainty awareness of network predictions. The experiment results revealed that networks trained to fulfill all training data did not learn how to predict price movements. Their prediction accuracy was still low even though they were certain about the predictions of the selected samples.

Removing aleatoric uncertainty helps networks learn price trends in a dataset. Since samples with inconsistent labels have been removed, the network will be unfamiliar with them during testing. This strategy makes the network be certain about only the samples similar to those appearing in the training data and having consistent labels. That is why our system can considerably increase accuracy when the network is certain about its prediction.

4.4   Confidence v.s. Certainty

Neural networks output the probability of each label to represent their prediction. Since high probability is often interpreted as high confidence, we compare the relationship of these two measures to accuracy. Because the predicted probability in our implementation was a vector weighted from several outputs (Eq. 7), which was an ensemble, we additionally trained a standard network that has the same depth, but did not contain branches, for the comparison. The parameters, such as kernel size, activation functions, and numbers of channels were unchanged. Let the output of this standard network be a 2D vector (p_ℓ, p_f), where p_ℓ and p_f are the probability of rise and fall, respectively, $0 \leq p_\ell, p_f \leq 1$, and $p_\ell + p_f = 1$. We computed the non-confidence of a prediction by $\min(1 - p_\ell, 1 - p_f)$. Overall, low values indicate high confidence. We then ranked the testing data based on the non-confidence of each sample in ascending order, and computed the mean accuracy of the lowest 20%, 50%, and 80% non-confident, and all samples. The accuracy of samples selected according to confidence and certainty estimations was compared.

Figure 5 shows the mean test accuracy during network training. As indicated, the accuracy lines of different uncertainties are clearly separated, while the lines of different non-confidence are not. Moreover, the high certainty samples enjoy high accuracy. This means that sample selection based on certainty was markedly reliable. It is also worth noting that the selected samples in each epoch were different because the network changed when training.

4.5   Compatibility to Other Network Structures

Our uncertainty framework is compatible with all types of network structures. In our implementation, we build a CNN with multiple branches to approximate a Bayesian network because of the balance between accurate approximation and computational efficiency. The Bayesian approximation, however, can be achieved by ensemble models [17] or dropouts [9,10]. Regarding the noisy label training, we utilize two networks with the same structure to remove samples with inconsistent labels [12]. This training strategy is irrelevant to network structures. Therefore, new uncertainty measures and noisy label training methods can be seamlessly integrated into our system to improve prediction accuracy further.

4.6 Limitations and Future Works

Although our experimental results indicate that considering uncertainty when forecasting stock price movements is effective, there is still a large space for improvement. After all, financial markets are noisy and uncertain. In addition, the amounts of daily stock price data are rare. While ancient samples could be useless for predicting future price movements, removing samples with aleatoric uncertainty would further reduce the data size. In our implementation, we mixed samples of different stocks to enlarge the data set. However, since stocks are of different properties, networks trained on the mixed data could be insufficient to predict the price movements of a specific stock. Therefore, in the future, we will consider stock relationships to overcome the problems caused by data mixing.

5 Conclusions

In this study, we consider aleatoric and model uncertainty when predicting stock price movements. The uncertainty estimation allows the network to know how certain the prediction is, which provides a high degree of freedom for investment strategies. While estimating aleatoric uncertainty during inference is challenging, we transform aleatoric uncertainty to model uncertainty by removing samples with inconsistent labels. The Bayesian inference is then applied to evaluate whether networks are familiar with a testing sample for estimating model uncertainty. In addition, removing samples with aleatoric uncertainty improves the network's generalization because networks only learn from samples with consistent labels. They are only certain about samples that have been seen in the training set and contain consistent labels. Experiment results verified that the high certainty of our network prediction indeed results in high accuracy.

Acknowledgments. We thank the anonymous reviewers for their constructive comments. This work was supported by E. SUN Bank and the Ministry of Science and Technology, Taiwan (110-2221-E-A49 -062 - and 109-2221-E-009 -097 -).

References

1. Adebiyi, A.A., Adewumi, A.O., Ayo, C.K.: Comparison of Arima and artificial neural networks models for stock price prediction. J. Appl. Math. **2014**, 1–7 (2014)
2. Antorán, J., Allingham, J., Hernández-Lobato, J.M.: Depth uncertainty in neural networks. In: Advances in Neural Information Processing Systems, vol. 33 (2020)
3. Arpit, D., et al.: A closer look at memorization in deep networks. In: International Conference on Machine Learning, pp. 233–242 (2017)

4. Ding, X., Zhang, Y., Liu, T., Duan, J.: Using structured events to predict stock price movement: an empirical investigation. In: Conference on Empirical Methods in Natural Language Processing, pp. 1415–1425 (2014)
5. Dixon, M., Klabjan, D., Bang, J.H.: Classification-based financial markets prediction using deep neural networks. Algorithmic Finan. **6**(3–4), 67–77 (2017)
6. Edwards, R.D., Magee, J., Bassetti, W.C.: Technical Analysis of Stock Trends. CRC Press (2018)
7. Feng, F., Chen, H., He, X., Ding, J., Sun, M., Chua, T.S.: Enhancing stock movement prediction with adversarial training. In: International Joint Conference on Artificial Intelligence, pp. 5843–5849 (2019)
8. Feng, F., He, X., Wang, X., Luo, C., Liu, Y., Chua, T.S.: Temporal relational ranking for stock prediction. ACM Trans. Inf. Syst. **37**(2), 1–30 (2019)
9. Foong, A.Y., Burt, D.R., Li, Y., Turner, R.E.: Pathologies of factorised Gaussian and MC dropout posteriors in Bayesian neural networks. STAT **1050**, 2 (2019)
10. Gal, Y., Ghahramani, Z.: Dropout as a Bayesian approximation: representing model uncertainty in deep learning. In: International Conference on Machine Learning, pp. 1050–1059 (2016)
11. Goodfellow, I., Shlens, J., Szegedy, C.: Explaining and harnessing adversarial examples. In: International Conference on Learning Representations (2015). https://arxiv.org/abs/1412.6572
12. Han, B., et al.: Co-teaching: robust training of deep neural networks with extremely noisy labels. In: Advances in Neural Information Processing Systems, pp. 8527–8537 (2018)
13. Heaton, J.B., Polson, N.G., Witte, J.H.: Deep learning for finance: deep portfolios. Appl. Stoch. Model. Bus. Ind. **33**(1), 3–12 (2017)
14. Izmailov, P., Maddox, W.J., Kirichenko, P., Garipov, T., Vetrov, D., Wilson, A.G.: Subspace inference for Bayesian deep learning. In: Uncertainty in Artificial Intelligence, pp. 1169–1179 (2020)
15. Jiang, L., Zhou, Z., Leung, T., Li, L.J., Fei-Fei, L.: MentorNet: learning data-driven curriculum for very deep neural networks on corrupted labels. In: International Conference on Machine Learning (2018)
16. Kurakin, A., Goodfellow, J.I., Bengio, S.: Adversarial machine learning at scale. In: International Conference on Learning Representations (2017)
17. Lakshminarayanan, B., Pritzel, A., Blundell, C.: Simple and scalable predictive uncertainty estimation using deep ensembles. In: Advances in Neural Information Processing Systems, pp. 6402–6413 (2017)
18. Li, B., Hoi, S.C.: On-line portfolio selection with moving average reversion. arXiv preprint arXiv:1206.4626 (2012)
19. Li, M., Soltanolkotabi, M., Oymak, S.: Gradient descent with early stopping is provably robust to label noise for overparameterized neural networks. In: International Conference on Artificial Intelligence and Statistics (2020)
20. Loshchilov, I., Hutter, F.: Decoupled weight decay regularization. arXiv preprint arXiv:1711.05101 (2017)
21. Maddox, W., Garipov, T., Izmailov, P., Vetrov, D., Wilson, A.G.: A simple baseline for Bayesian uncertainty in deep learning. arXiv preprint arXiv:1902.02476 (2019)
22. Malach, E., Shalev-Shwartz, S.: Decoupling "when to update" from "how to update". In: Advances in Neural Information Processing Systems, pp. 960–970 (2017)
23. Moskowitz, T.J., Ooi, Y.H., Pedersen, L.H.: Time series momentum. J. Financ. Econ. **104**(2), 228–250 (2012)

24. Nelson, D.M., Pereira, A.C., de Oliveira, R.A.: Stock market's price movement prediction with LSTM neural networks. In: International Joint Conference on Neural Networks, pp. 1419–1426 (2017)
25. Nguyen, A., Yosinski, J., Clune, J.: Deep neural networks are easily fooled: high confidence predictions for unrecognizable images. In: IEEE Conference on Computer Vision and Pattern Recognition, pp. 427–436 (2015)
26. Nguyen, T.H., Shirai, K., Velcin, J.: Sentiment analysis on social media for stock movement prediction. Expert Syst. Appl. **42**(24), 9603–9611 (2015)
27. Niaki, S.T.A., Hoseinzade, S.: Forecasting s&p 500 index using artificial neural networks and design of experiments. J. Ind. Eng. Int. **9**(1), 1 (2013)
28. Ntakaris, A., Magris, M., Kanniainen, J., Gabbouj, M., Iosifidis, A.: Benchmark dataset for mid-price forecasting of limit order book data with machine learning methods. J. Forecast. **37**(8), 852–866 (2018)
29. Ren, M., Zeng, W., Yang, B., Urtasun, R.: Learning to reweight examples for robust deep learning. In: International Conference on Machine Learning (2018)
30. Shaker, M.H., Hüllermeier, E.: Aleatoric and epistemic uncertainty with random forests. In: Berthold, M.R., Feelders, A., Krempl, G. (eds.) IDA 2020. LNCS, vol. 12080, pp. 444–456. Springer, Cham (2020). https://doi.org/10.1007/978-3-030-44584-3_35
31. Tsantekidis, A., Passalis, N., Tefas, A., Kanniainen, J., Gabbouj, M., Iosifidis, A.: Using deep learning to detect price change indications in financial markets. In: European Signal Processing Conference, pp. 2511–2515 (2017)
32. Walczak, S.: An empirical analysis of data requirements for financial forecasting with neural networks. J. Manag. Inf. Syst. **17**(4), 203–222 (2001)
33. Wei, H., Feng, L., Chen, X., An, B.: Combating noisy labels by agreement: a joint training method with co-regularization. In: IEEE Conference on Computer Vision and Pattern Recognition, pp. 13726–13735 (2020)
34. Xu, Y., Cohen, S.B.: Stock movement prediction from tweets and historical prices. In: Annual Meeting of the Association for Computational Linguistics, pp. 1970–1979 (2018)
35. Yu, X., Han, B., Yao, J., Niu, G., Tsang, I.W., Sugiyama, M.: How does disagreement help generalization against label corruption? arXiv preprint arXiv:1901.04215 (2019)
36. Zhang, C., Bengio, S., Hardt, M., Recht, B., Vinyals, O.: Understanding deep learning requires rethinking generalization. arXiv preprint arXiv:1611.03530 (2016)
37. Zhang, L., Aggarwal, C., Qi, G.J.: Stock price prediction via discovering multi-frequency trading patterns. In: ACM SIGKDD International Conference on Knowledge Discovery and Data Mining, pp. 2141–2149 (2017)
38. Zhang, Z., Zohren, S., Roberts, S.: DeepLOB: deep convolutional neural networks for limit order books. IEEE Trans. Signal Process. **67**(11), 3001–3012 (2019)

A Prescriptive Machine Learning Approach for Assessing Goodwill in the Automotive Domain

Stefan Haas[1]([envelope]) and Eyke Hüllermeier[2]([envelope])

[1] BMW Group, Munich, Germany
stefan.sh.haas@bmwgroup.com
[2] Institute of Informatics, University of Munich (LMU), Munich, Germany
eyke@lmu.de

Abstract. Car manufacturers receive thousands of goodwill requests for vehicle defects per year. At BMW, these requests for repair-cost contributions are either assessed automatically by a set of fixed rules or manually by human experts. To decrease manual effort, which is still around 50%, we propose a machine learning approach with the goal to discover so far unknown assessment patterns in human decisions. Since the assessment contribution data is heavily imbalanced, we structure the learning task hierarchically: The first layer's task is to predict the main rank of the request (no contribution, partial contribution, or full contribution). Then, in the case where partial contribution is suggested, the second layer predicts the concrete percentage using a regression model. To optimize our model and tailor it to certain strategies (e.g., customer friendly or more cost oriented), we make use of a custom-defined cost matrix. We also outline how the model can be used in a scenario in which it prescribes appropriate monetary contributions for requested repair-costs. This can initially happen in the form of a decision support system (DSS) and, in the next step, through automated decision making (ADM), where a certain part of goodwill requests is processed automatically by the prescriptive model.

Keywords: Prescriptive machine learning · Decision support systems · Automated decision making · Cost-sensitive learning · Hierarchical learning

1 Introduction

Rule-based expert systems are used widely in many fields, for example in industry to assess financial credit risks or in medicine to detect diseases such as breast cancer or diabetes [1,8]. They arguably constitute the simplest form of artificial intelligence (AI), storing rules carefully assembled by domain-knowledge in the form of if-then-else statements. They do not require any data and are *naturally interpretable* [2]. This makes them a natural fit for automating decision processes that need to be auditable, 100% accurate, and which comprise a certain risk, either financially or for life and limb.

© The Author(s), under exclusive license to Springer Nature Switzerland AG 2023
M.-R. Amini et al. (Eds.): ECML PKDD 2022, LNAI 13718, pp. 170–184, 2023.
https://doi.org/10.1007/978-3-031-26422-1_11

One such financial rule-based expert system is the central Goodwill system of BMW. In cases of vehicle defects, dealers carry out goodwill repair on behalf of customers and in turn get compensated by the original equipment manufacturer (OEM) for their spare parts and labor efforts. Whether or not customers are eligible for goodwill compensation is decided automatically on the basis of a fixed set of expert rules. This automatic rule based assessment is only done in countries where no legal restrictions against it apply. In case the goodwill request is rejected in the first place, the final decision is transferred to a so-called *assessor*, a human after-sales goodwill expert, who manually looks at the individual case and determines the monetary contribution of the OEM, if any. Although a decision matrix to support this manual process is in place in many sales markets, it is still often a commercial gut decision and not standardized across markets.

The need for human intervention is due to several problems of a rule-based approach, notably the difficulty to maintain a coherent set of deterministic rules capturing all eventualities of a complex commercial use case. Therefore, the data-driven design of decision models by means of machine learning (ML) appears to be an appealing alternative to increase the degree of automation. Over the years, a good amount of historic human decision data has been collected, which can be leveraged in this regard. The goal hereby is to deduce so far unknown assessment patterns from observed human decisions that might be too complex to be put into rules in the first place. Supervised machine learning models can be trained on the observed decision data and later used in the manual decision process to *prescribe* certain monetary contributions. This can either happen in the form of a *decision support system* (DSS) or, if trust in the models is high enough, through *automated decision making* (ADM), which helps decrease manual human assessment effort and save costs in the long run.

The goodwill use case qualifies as what has recently been coined *prescriptive* machine learning [7]. In contrast to the common setting of *predictive* machine learning, the goal is not to predict some underlying ground-truth, but rather to learn models that stipulate appropriate decisions or actions to be taken in order to achieve a certain goal (i.e., to answer the question "How to make something happen?" rather than "What will happen?"). In fact, in the case of goodwill, there is nothing like a "right" monetary contribution. Instead, a decision is more or less appropriate, fair for the customer and strategically opportune for the company. Such decisions are supposed to ensure customer satisfaction while remaining economically reasonable from a manufacturer's perspective. In addition to increasing the degree of automation, prescriptive models may also contribute to the standardization, consistency, and objectivity of the decision process.

The main contribution of this paper is a prescriptive ML approach to goodwill assessment, which is based on real human decision data. In the next section, we describe the goodwill assessment problem in more detail. Next, we outline how prescriptive ML could be incorporated into the existing process. Then, we propose an ML method for goodwill assessments, which is specifically tailored to the use case and properties of the data. Finally, we conclude with related work, identify challenges and outline directions of future work.

2 The Vehicle Goodwill Assessment Process

Assessing goodwill requests is an important topic for manufacturers. In case of
BMW, dealers yearly submit thousands of goodwill requests for vehicles that
must be assessed. The question whether goodwill is granted or not, and which
amount, is far from trivial. It is an individual *commercial decision* that must balance customer satisfaction and financial impact. In this regard, it is important
to distinguish between *warranty*, which is a legal obligation for manufacturers,
and *goodwill*, which is a non-obligatory service manufacturers provide to customers outside the *warranty* time window (usually after 3–5 years). The goal of
compensating customers for product failures outside the *warranty* time window
is primarily to safeguard customer satisfaction and loyalty with the brand.

At the OEM, handling goodwill on system level is currently a hybrid approach
based on automatic and human manual assessment. The UML Use-Case diagram
in Fig. 1 depicts the process and its actors.

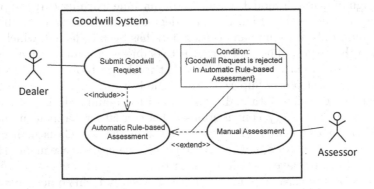

Fig. 1. UML use case diagram for the classic goodwill process.

The standard use case is as follows. Customers arrive at a dealership with
a vehicle defect and request a repair from the dealer. Next, the dealer checks
whether the manufacturer would grant goodwill for this particular defect by
submitting a goodwill request on the behalf of the customer. The data the dealer
has to enter ranges from certain vehicle information like vehicle mileage and
age to estimated labor and parts costs for the repair itself. On system side,
the request is first evaluated against a fixed set of rules (automatic rule-based
assessment). If it goes through and goodwill is granted, the process is finished
and the dealer will be compensated for the repair. If not, the goodwill request is
further processed through a *manual assessment*. In this case, a human goodwill
after-sales expert checks the request and makes the final decision. The manual
assessment step only extends the automatic rule-based assessment in case of an
automatic rejection in the first place but cannot be requested right from the
beginning. In case of a manual assessment, the dealer also has the possibility

to send attachments (e.g., a video of rattling engine) and a free text comment along with the request.

In tangible terms, the result of the goodwill process is a percentage of the labor and parts cost contributions the dealer requests and the manufacturer is willing to pay. The set of possible contribution percentages ranges from 0 to 100% in steps of 10%: $C = \{0, 10, 20, \ldots, 100\}$. For instance, if the dealer has labor and parts costs of €1,149.82 and €903.30, respectively, and requests labor and parts cost contributions of 100%, the assessor decides which percentage of contribution is appropriate by taking all the provided information into account. He or she might first check the mileage and age of the vehicle, then the respective defect, whether the vehicle was regularly serviced, and so on. Based on these checks, he or she decides for a contribution, e.g., 50% for labor and 100% for parts. In our example, this would lead to a monetary compensation of the dealer of €574.91 for labor and €903.30 for parts.

To get an idea about the dimensions of automatic vs. manual goodwill assessments, Fig. 2 shows the overall proportion of automatic and manual goodwill assessments of some selected sales markets.

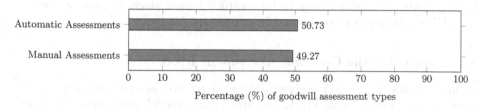

Fig. 2. Overall portions (%) of manual and automatic assessments.

Note that the period of data selection is veiled to allow no conclusions. The portion of goodwill requests that need to be assessed manually is almost as high (49.27%) as the portion of automatically processed goodwill requests (50.73%). In total numbers, 688,879 goodwill requests have been created so far, 349,488 of which were processed automatically by rules and 339,391 manually by a human expert.

Table 1 breaks down the goodwill numbers per selected National Sales Company (NSC). The NSC names have been anonymized here by letters (A to E), to prevent conclusions about goodwill strategies per country. The size of the sales market naturally influences the number of goodwill cases. From an assessment perspective it makes sense to look at the goodwill cases on a per sales market basis, since sales markets have their own goodwill strategies. Therefore, goodwill compensations is very market specific.

Table 1. Goodwill assessment numbers by National Sales Company (NSC).

NSC	Goodwill requests	Automatic	Manual	Degree of automation
A	35,624	20,998	14,626	58.94
B	76,461	48,666	27,795	63.65
C	84,030	47,278	36,752	56.26
D	437,656	200,831	236,825	45.89
E	55,108	31,715	23,393	57.55
Σ	688,879	349,488	339,391	∅ 50.73 %

3 Prescriptive Machine Learning for Goodwill Assessment

In this section, we propose to extend the standard goodwill assessment process as outlined in the previous section, with prescriptive ML models. First, we describe how ML models could be integrated into the existing goodwill use case. Subsequently, we evaluate how well a complex human decision process such as goodwill assessment can be covered by supervised ML.

3.1 Enhancing the Goodwill Assessment Process

Figure 3 shows a goodwill use case extended by ML in comparison with the classic use case outlined in Fig. 1. The *prescriptive model assessment* can either be included in the *manual assessment* process or extend the *automatic rule-based assessment*.

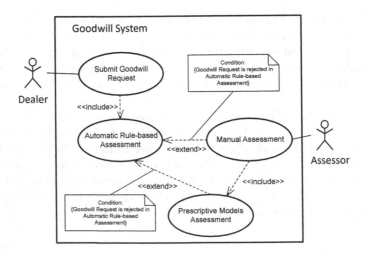

Fig. 3. UML use case diagram for the ML-enhanced goodwill process.

In the inclusion scenario, the prescriptive model supports the manual assessment through goodwill contribution suggestions that guide the assessor in his or her decision process. The prescriptive model serves as a *decision support system* (DSS) and only informs the assessor about the presumably most appropriate decision. Accepting the decision is not compulsory for the assessor, who still possesses the sovereignty over the goodwill decision. Nevertheless, the model suggestions could help to harmonize and standardize decisions from a business perspective. Including the prescriptive model assessment in the manual assessment might be a good starting point for making use of ML in the goodwill process, as the risk of wrong assessments is low and the final decision is still in the hands of an expert.

In the extension scenario, the model extends the automatic rule-based assessment and takes over cases not decidable by rules. The model assesses goodwill decisions automatically and supports the process through *automated decision making* (ADM). From a business perspective, this is the ultimate goal to aim for, as it will directly reduce process costs. However, this approach also comes with the greatest risk, as there is no human expert involved anymore who supervises the final decisions. Customer satisfaction and financial impact for the manufacturer are left to the machine. Leaving the final goodwill decision to a prescriptive model requires trust that can only be built through an evaluation by business experts over a long term period.

A combination of inclusion and extension is also conceivable. While ADM might be feasible in less complex cases, it might be advisable to just integrate the model as a DSS in more complex scenarios, leaving the final decision to a human expert. What exactly distinguishes less and more complex goodwill scenarios is still an open research question.

3.2 Prescriptive Machine Learning

The setting of prescriptive ML deviates from the standard setting of predictive ML in various ways [7]. This also includes the process of supervision. As already mentioned, in prescriptive ML, there is not necessarily something like a "ground-truth" or correct decision, and even if decisions might be compared in terms of quality or desirability of their implications, there is no guarantee that decisions made by human experts in the past were optimal. Therefore, taking them directly as targets for a supervised learning method might not be advisable [11]. In the case of goodwill, for example, a decision of 50% contribution appears to be somewhat overrepresented (cf. Fig. 4), letting one suspect that this is often taken as a default choice for a partial cost coverage, even if it might not necessarily be the most appropriate percentage. In the following, we will nevertheless assume that mimicking the expert is a reasonable strategy, at least as a first step toward a data-driven goodwill assessment, leaving more elaborate approaches for future work.

Under this premise, the problem is essentially reduced to a supervised learning task, with the observed human goodwill decisions

$$\mathcal{D} = \{(\boldsymbol{x}_1, y_1), \ldots, (\boldsymbol{x}_n, y_n)\}$$

as training data. Instances are goodwill requests entered by the dealer and represented as a *feature vector* $\boldsymbol{x} \in \mathcal{X} \subseteq \mathbb{R}^m$. These instances are labeled by assessed contribution percentages, which serve as the target variable $y \in \mathcal{Y} \subseteq \mathbb{R}$. The goal of the ML task is to learn a decision model $h^* \in \mathcal{H}$, where $\mathcal{H}$ is the class of candidate models (referred to as hypothesis space in the common setting of supervised learning). This model is a mapping $\mathcal{X} \rightarrow \mathcal{Y}$ supposed to approximate the training data and, more importantly, generalize well to new decision problems. Like in supervised learning, we model the performance of a model h in terms of a loss (error) function $l : \mathcal{Y} \times \mathcal{Y} \rightarrow \mathbb{R}_+$, so that $l(y, \hat{y})$ denotes the penalty incurred by the learner for prescribing $\hat{y}$ when the expert decides y. The choice of a presumably optimal model h^* is commonly guided by the empirical risk

$$R(h) := \frac{1}{n} \sum_{i=1}^{n} l(y_i, h(\boldsymbol{x}_i)) \tag{1}$$

as an estimate of a model's performance. This measure is normally not minimized directly by the learner, however, because the empirical risk minimizer $h^* = \arg\min_{h \in \mathcal{H}} R(h)$ is knowingly prone to overfitting the training data, and hence to suboptimal generalization.

3.3 Human Goodwill Decision Data

Table 2 shows the features used for the ML task. In the first step, we will only look at the *hard facts*, such as vehicle mileage, vehicle age, the defect code, the costs, and the requested labor and part contributions. The raw data entered by the dealer will be enriched with further vehicle data that can be derived from the vehicle identification number (VIN), including the vehicle model type, the series, the motor series, the order country of the vehicle, the sales country of the vehicle, and whether the vehicle is a car or motorbike. The free-text dealer comment and attachments will be ignored for now, because they can be considered as "soft" facts. Besides, they are not immediately usable and require sophisticated post-processing techniques such as NLP. The rest of the data is a mixture of categorical and numerical data and qualifies as tabular data.

The features are pre-processed as follows: Numeric data is scaled using *min-max-scaling* (e.g., Parts, Labor and Total Costs), low cardinality categorical features are encoded using *one-hot-encoding* (e.g., Customer Type or Requested Labor and Parts Contributions), and high cardinality features are *hashed* (e.g., Defect Code or Vehicle Series).

Turning our attention to the target variable, Fig. 4 shows how the overall contributions are distributed over the possible percentages $\mathcal{Y} = \{0, 10, 20, \ldots, 100\}$. Obviously, the data is heavily imbalanced, and contributions other than 0% and 100% are rarely used. Among the rare contributions, the 50% decision sticks out and appears a bit more frequently, whereas 90% is the least frequent contribution. As already said, this may reflect a common human pattern: If not being exactly sure what to grant, people tend to opt for a compromise in the middle. Another pattern one can observe is a kind of "generous rounding" to

Table 2. Features used for model training.

Attribute	Data type	Description
Vehicle Mileage	Numeric (continuous)	12,500
Vehicle Age	Numeric (continuous)	48
Enquiry Indicator	Categorical (ordinal)	Request after or before the repair
Warranty Stage	Categorical (nominal)	Standard or Extended Goodwill
Product Type	Categorical (nominal)	Car or Motorbike
Regular Service	Categorical (nominal)	Yes or No
Sales Country	Categorical (nominal)	NL
Order Country	Categorical (nominal)	BE
External Guarantee	Categorical (nominal)	Yes or No
Vehicle registered to customer	Categorical (nominal)	Yes or No
Vehicle Model Type	Categorical (nominal)	FG81
Vehicle Series	Categorical (nominal)	G21
Motor Series	Categorical (nominal)	N57T
Mobility provided	Categorical (nominal)	Yes or No
Defect Code	Categorical (nominal)	1178031500
Defect Code (Main and sub group only)	Categorical (nominal)	1178
Shared last expenses	Categorical (nominal)	Yes or No
Customer Type	Categorical (nominal)	Regular, Transit or International
Requested Labor Contribution (per cent)	Categorical (nominal)	60%
Requested Parts Contribution (per cent)	Categorical (nominal)	60%
Dealer Labor Contribution (per cent)	Categorical (nominal)	40%
Dealer Parts Contribution (per cent)	Categorical (nominal)	40%
Parts Costs	Numeric (continuous)	€903.30
Labor Costs	Numeric (continuous)	€1,149.82
Requested Open Time Units	Numeric (discrete)	5
Dealer Open Time Units	Numeric (discrete)	2
Additional service costs, e.g., replacement car	Numeric (continuous)	€460.30
Total Costs	Numeric (continuous)	€3,682.89

"meaningful" contributions, namely, 0%, 30%, 50%, 70%, 100%. Other contributions, such as 10% and 90%, are even more rare, probably because these are considered somewhat pedantic. In any case, the rare contributions are likely to carry important information, as they reflect subtle human instinct, and they are key to safeguard customer satisfaction. There is also an apparent tendency to contribute rather than not contribute from manufacturer's perspective, as the 100% bar is noticeably higher than the 0% bar. This is the case for labor as well as parts. However, for parts the tendency is stronger than for labor.

3.4 Hierarchical Cost-Sensitive Learning

From the description of the task and the data, it becomes clear that goodwill assessment comes with a number of important challenges from a machine learning perspective. First, looking at the scale of the target variable (contribution in percentage), the problem is somehow in-between ordinal classification and

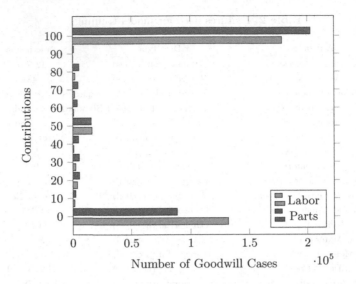

Fig. 4. Distribution of goodwill contributions for Labor and Parts at BMW.

regression: In principle, the target is numerical, but not all numbers between 0 and 100 are deemed valid prescriptions. Therefore, one may also think of tackling the task as a problem of ordinal classification with 11 class labels sorted in increasing order from lowest (0%) to highest (100%).

Related to the interpretation of the scale is the question of how a suitable loss function should look like. Obviously, a standard measure such as misclassification rate (0/1 loss) is inappropriate, even if the task is treated as a classification problem, because the loss function should take the linear structure of the contribution scale into account. Squared or absolute error as commonly used in regression do not appear to be perfect choices either, as one may argue that there is not only a quantitative but also a *qualitative* difference between the 0% decision, the 100% decision, and the decision of a partial contribution. This suggests a cost-sensitive approach, in which a cost (loss) function $\mathcal{Y} \times \mathcal{Y} \rightarrow \mathbb{R}_+$ is explicitly defined in "tabular" form. As an additional advantage, this allows for incentivising the learner in a strategic way, e.g., to constructing more customer-friendly or more cost-oriented decision models.

Another challenge is the class imbalance. Imbalanced data makes learning more difficult, and many algorithms have a tendency to compromise the accuracy of small classes in favor of bigger classes [12]. This would be especially problematic in the case of goodwill assessment, enforcing extreme decisions at the cost of partial contributions. Common approaches to deal with imbalanced data include up-sampling of the minority classes or down-sampling of the predominant classes in order to balance the data [13]. Similar effects can be achieved by adding weights to the training examples, making the underrepresented examples more important and the overrepresented less.

To tackle both problems, cost-sensitivity and imbalance, we propose a hierarchical approach with a qualitative (categorical) first layer and a quantitative second layer. In the first layer, we solve an ordinal 3-class classification (or ranking) problem, distinguishing between classes NO (no contribution, rank 1), PARTIAL (partial contribution, rank 2), and FULL (full contribution, rank 3). Obviously, this problem is more balanced, because all contributions between 10% and 90% are collected in a single class.

In the case where an instance is assigned to PARTIAL in the first layer, it is forwarded to the second layer, where the concrete percentage of contribution is determined. Thus, while an instance x is mapped to a rank $r(x) \in \{1, 2, 3\}$ in the first layer, x is mapped to any of the numbers $\{10, 20, \ldots, 90\}$ in the second layer. The latter task can be formalized as a (constrained) regression problem.

The first problem, where an example (x, y) consists of an input vector $x \in \mathcal{X}$ and an ordinal label $y \in \mathcal{Y} = \{1, 2, ..., K\}$ (in our case $\{\text{NO}, \text{PARTIAL}, \text{FULL}\}$, i.e., $K = 3$), provides us with the opportunity to use the cost-sensitive ranking framework presented in [9]. This framework allows one to specify a *cost matrix* in a flexible way, which is especially convenient in our case. In fact, by utilizing a custom defined $K \times K$ cost matrix $\mathcal{C}$, we can configure the mislabeling cost according to our strategy, e.g., rather customer-friendly or more cost-oriented from manufacturer's perspective. The cost of predicting an example (x, y) as rank k is given by the entry $\mathcal{C}_{y,k}$ in the cost matrix. Table 3 shows two distinct strategies for goodwill assessments. The cost matrix on the left side shows a customer-friendly strategy, where the learner is strongly penalized when prescribing NO instead of FULL ($\mathcal{C}_{3,1} = 30$). On the right side, the cost matrix implements a more cost-orientated approach, where the learner is penalized the most for the decision FULL instead of NO ($\mathcal{C}_{1,3} = 30$). Note that the result of the regression model for the PARTIAL values ($k = 2$) will be mapped back to the interval $\mathcal{C}_{2,2} = [0, 5]$ to also integrate the regression into the overall cost-sensitive ranking framework. By the width of the interval, we can configure how much importance we give to the exact prediction of the values of the regression layer. Figure 5 visualizes the structure of the proposed hierarchical approach.

Table 3. Different assessment strategies specified by different cost functions: customer-oriented with higher penalization of contributions that are loo low (left) vs. manufacturer-oriented with higher penalization of contributions that are too high (right).

		Prescribed					Prescribed		
		NO	PARTIAL	FULL			NO	PARTIAL	FULL
Actual	NO	0	5	10	*Actual*	NO	0	10	30
	PARTIAL	10	[0,5]	5		PARTIAL	5	[0,5]	10
	FULL	30	10	0		FULL	10	5	0

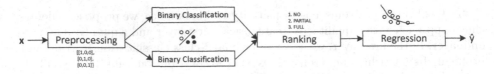

Fig. 5. Overview of the hierarchical cost-sensitive approach.

The approach [9] to ordinal classification is based on a reduction to weighted binary classification. More specifically, a binary classifier

$$f : \mathcal{X} \times \{1, \ldots, K-1\} \to \{0, 1\}$$

is trained that accepts *extended* instances $(\boldsymbol{x}, k)$ as input. As output, the classifier is supposed to produce 1 (answer "yes") if the true rank of $\boldsymbol{x}$ exceeds k and 0 (answer "no") otherwise. The actual rank of a query instance can then be determined by applying the following ranking rule:

$$r(\boldsymbol{x}) = 1 + \sum_{k=1}^{K-1} f(\boldsymbol{x}, k). \tag{2}$$

To train the classifier, the original data is extended as follows: Each original example $(\boldsymbol{x}, y)$ is turned into extended examples $(\boldsymbol{x}^k, y^k)$ with weights $w_{y,k}$, where[1]

$$\boldsymbol{x}^k = (\boldsymbol{x}, k), \quad y^k = [\![k < y]\!], \quad w_{y,k} = |\mathcal{C}_{y,k} - \mathcal{C}_{y,k+1}|.$$

The weights $w_{y,k}$ control the importance of an example during the training phase of the binary classifier. The higher the cost difference between two adjacent ranks, the larger the weights and therefore the importance of a particular example.

Incorporating domain knowledge, we propose the following small modification of the ranking rule (2): As the proposed contribution essentially never exceeds the contribution q requested for $\boldsymbol{x}$, we set

$$r(\boldsymbol{x}) = \min\left\{1 + f(\boldsymbol{x}, 1) + f(\boldsymbol{x}, 2), q\right\}. \tag{3}$$

For the second layer of our model, any regression method can in principle be used. For the exact inference of the partial contribution values, we round and constrain the regression model's output to the set of possible contributions $\{10, \ldots, 90\}$. Also, like for the prescription of ranks, we make sure that the prescription does not exceed the requested contribution q:

$$\hat{y} = \min\left\{\lfloor \frac{f(\boldsymbol{x})}{10} \rceil \cdot 10, q\right\} \tag{4}$$

---

[1] $[\![\cdot]\!]$ denotes the indicator function returning 1 if the argument is true and 0 otherwise.

4   Evaluation and Results

In this section, we evaluate our hierarchical cost-sensitive approach on BMW's goodwill data sets. For training the classifier f (and ranker r) in the first layer, a learning algorithm is needed that is able to handle weighted examples. In our experimental study, we used extreme gradient boosting (XGBoost) [3], a versatile method that proved to work very well on tabular data and also outperforms deep neural networks in this context [10]. Another advantage is that XGBoost can be used for both classification and regression, hence we could use it for training the first as well as the second layer of our model.

Tables 4 and 5 show the results of a ten-fold cross validation in terms of the mean and standard deviation of various performance metrics. The first metric of interest is the cost of the model's prescriptions according to the underlying cost function — here, we present results for the cost matrix (a) in Table 3 (those for matrix (b) look very similar). The middle part of the matrix, i.e., the cost for assessments involving a partial contribution, is filled with the absolute error of the regression model scaled to the specified interval (in this case [0, 5]). As the cost values are measured on an abstract scale without interpretable dimension, we also report the mean accuracy (ACC) for the ranking part and the mean absolute error (MAE) for the regression model (on a scale from 10 to 90), thereby making the results more tangible. Overall, our model shows a quite satisfactory performance.

Table 4. Evaluation metric results obtained for Labor.

	Ranking		Regression		Costs	
NSC	ACC	SD	MAE	SD	C	SD
A	0.887	0.032	0.942	0.24	1.133	0.303
B	0.904	0.014	5.094	0.524	1.018	0.221
C	0.926	0.028	4.519	0.454	0.725	0.271
D	0.857	0.009	1.306	0.19	1.321	0.09
E	0.881	0.047	7.161	1.755	1.064	0.398
Mean	**0.891**	0.026	**3.8044**	0.6326	**1.0522**	0.2566
Median	**0.887**	0.028	**4.519**	0.454	**1.064**	0.271

As already explained, the cost function can be used to tailor a decision model to certain strategies, e.g., making it more customer-friendly or more manufacturer-friendly (cost-oriented). To evaluate this feature, we looked at the confusion matrices obtained for the cost functions in Table 3. As can be seen in Table 6, the confusion matrix for the customer-friendly cost matrix is indeed more geared to the right, showing a tendency toward higher ranks and consequently higher contributions. In contrast, the matrix for the cost-oriented strategy is more geared towards the left side, with lower ranks and thus less contributions.

Table 5. Evaluation metric results obtained for Parts.

NSC	Ranking		Regression		Costs	
	ACC	SD	MAE	SD	C	SD
A	0.889	0.035	1.265	0.249	1.059	0.452
B	0.869	0.016	5.691	0.485	1.215	0.158
C	0.949	0.023	6.522	0.711	0.552	0.183
D	0.872	0.011	4.625	0.313	1.154	0.078
E	0.887	0.055	7.041	1.732	1.001	0.51
Mean	**0.8932**	0.028	**5.0288**	0.698	**0.9962**	0.2762
Median	**0.887**	0.023	**5.691**	0.485	**1.059**	0.183

Table 6. Different parts ranking confusion matrix depending on the assessment strategy (for NSC A): customer-oriented (left) vs. manufacturer-oriented (right).

		Prescribed		
		NO	PARTIAL	FULL
Actual	NO	494	47	45
	PARTIAL	0	286	34
	FULL	2	13	541

		Prescribed		
		NO	PARTIAL	FULL
Actual	NO	526	40	20
	PARTIAL	6	295	19
	FULL	11	34	511

5   Conclusion and Future Work

In this paper, we described the existing rule-based and manual goodwill assessment process at BMW and how it can be extended through prescriptive machine learning models. This can either happen in the form of a decision support system, automated decision making, or a combination of both. Furthermore, we proposed a hierarchical, cost-sensitive approach for learning prescriptive models from human goodwill decisions, which accounts for the specific structure of the decision space, counteracts class imbalance, and allows for tailoring strategies to different value systems and market situations (e.g., customer friendly vs. cost oriented).

Motivated by our encouraging results, we plan to address the following challenges in future work.

- *Trust and Explanation*: We noticed that business experts do not immediately trust a prescriptive ML solution. Therefore, involving business experts in the development and evaluation process is important, not only to improve the ML solution itself, but also to foster trust in it. Explainability will play a key role in this regard, making machine learning more transparent and accessible to all stakeholders involved [5]. In fact, decisions need to be explained, and different parties may have different needs for explanation. For a dealer, feedback about the most important attribute that led to the rejection of the request might be enough, whereas an auditor needs to understand the whole reasoning process in detail.

- *Uncertainty*: Although the decision models we trained perform very well, showing the high potential of automated decision making, not all decisions appear to be perfect all the time. Therefore, it would be desirable to increase the uncertainty-awareness of decision models, so that final decisions could be transferred to the human expert in cases of high uncertainty [6].
- *Weak supervision*: As already mentioned, human goodwill decisions might be biased in one way or the other and should not necessarily be taken as a gold standard. Additionally, the data may contain concept drift due to strategy changes in the assessment process over time. Therefore, past decisions should be considered and modeled as *weak* information about the target rather than an incontestable ground truth, suggesting the use of methods for weakly supervised learning [14] in prescriptive modeling.
- *Fairness:* Another important question concerns the notion of fairness in the goodwill decision process. There might be different strategies toward fairness, depending on the sales market. For instance, some markets might want to treat all customers equally, independently of the money they spent for a vehicle, whereas others might want to prefer customers with higher priced vehicles in the goodwill process. It needs to be investigated whether or not models can be tailored to such strategies automatically, or if a manual intervention is required [4].

References

1. Abu-Naser, S.S., Bastami, B.G.: A proposed rule based system for breasts cancer diagnosis. World Wide J. Multidisc. Res. Dev. **2**(5), 27–33 (2016)
2. Burkart, N., Huber, M.F.: A survey on the explainability of supervised machine learning. J. Artif. Intell. Res. **70**, 245–317 (2021)
3. Chen, T., Guestrin, C.: XGBoost: a scalable tree boosting system. In: Proceedings of the 22nd ACM SIGKDD International Conference on Knowledge Discovery and Data Mining, pp. 785–794 (2016)
4. Friedler, S.A., Scheidegger, C., Venkatasubramanian, S., Choudhary, S., Hamilton, E.P., Roth, D.: A comparative study of fairness-enhancing interventions in machine learning. In: Proceedings of the Conference on Fairness, Accountability, and Transparency (FAT*), pp. 329–338. Association for Computing Machinery, New York, NY, USA (2019)
5. Hong, S.R., Hullman, J., Bertini, E.: Human factors in model interpretability: industry practices, challenges, and needs. Proc. ACM Hum. Comput. Interact. (CSCW1). **4**, 1–26 (2020)
6. Hüllermeier, E., Waegeman, W.: Aleatoric and epistemic uncertainty in machine learning: an introduction to concepts and methods. Mach. Learn. **110**(3), 457–506 (2021). https://doi.org/10.1007/s10994-021-05946-3

7. Hüllermeier, E.: Prescriptive machine learning for automated decision making: Challenges and opportunities. CoRR abs/2112.08268 (2021). https://arxiv.org/abs/2112.08268
8. Karthikeyan, R., Geetha, P., Ramaraj, E.: Rule based system for better prediction of diabetes. In: 3rd International Conference on Computing and Communications Technologies (ICCCT), pp. 195–203 (2019)
9. Li, L., Lin, H.T.: Ordinal regression by extended binary classification. In: Schölkopf, B., Platt, J., Hoffman, T. (eds.) Advances in Neural Information Processing Systems, vol. 19. MIT Press (2006)
10. Shwartz-Ziv, R., Armon, A.: Tabular data: deep learning is not all you need. Inf. Fusion **81**, 84–90 (2022)
11. Swaminathan, A., Joachims, T.: Counterfactual risk minimization: learning from logged bandit feedback. In: Proceedings of ICML, International Conference on Machine Learning, pp. 814–823 (2015)
12. Van Hulse, J., Khoshgoftaar, T.M., Napolitano, A.: Experimental perspectives on learning from imbalanced data. In: Proceedings of ICML 24th International Conference on Machine Learning, pp. 935–942. NY, USA, New York (2007)
13. Zhang, N.N., Ye, S.Z., Chien, T.Y.: Imbalanced data classification based on hybrid methods. In: Proceedings of ICBDR 2nd International Conference on Big Data Research, pp. 16–20. Association for Computing Machinery, New York, NY, USA (2018)
14. Zhou, Z.: A brief introduction to weakly supervised learning. Natl. Sci. Rev. **5**, 44–53 (2018)

Risk-Aware Reinforcement Learning for Multi-Period Portfolio Selection

David Winkel(✉) ⓘ, Niklas Strauß ⓘ, Matthias Schubert ⓘ, and Thomas Seidl ⓘ

LMU Munich, Munich, Germany
{winkel,strauss,schubert,seidl}@dbs.ifi.lmu.de

Abstract. The task of portfolio management is the selection of portfolio allocations for every single time step during an investment period while adjusting the risk-return profile of the portfolio to the investor's individual level of risk preference. In practice, it can be hard for an investor to quantify his individual risk preference. As an alternative, approximating the risk-return Pareto front allows for the comparison of different optimized portfolio allocations and hence for the selection of the most suitable risk level. Furthermore, an approximation of the Pareto front allows the analysis of the overall risk sensitivity of various investment policies. In this paper, we propose a deep reinforcement learning (RL) based approach, in which a single meta agent generates optimized portfolio allocation policies for any level of risk preference in a given interval. Our method is more efficient than previous approaches, as it only requires training of a single agent for the full approximate risk-return Pareto front. Additionally, it is more stable in training and only requires per time step *market* risk estimations *independent* of the policy. Such risk control per time step is a common regulatory requirement for e.g., insurance companies. We benchmark our meta agent against other state-of-the-art risk-aware RL methods using a realistic environment based on real-world Nasdaq-100 data. Our evaluation shows that the proposed meta agent outperforms various benchmark approaches by generating strategies with better risk-return profiles.

Keywords: Portfolio selection · Multi-objective optimization · Deep RL

1 Introduction

The modern financial system offers investors the possibility to store wealth over long time horizons. Typically, wealth is accumulated in times of productivity and is then consumed in times of need. This can for example allow a private investor to retire or allow an institutional investor, such as an insurance company, to distribute funds to its clients at a later point in time. Thereby arises the fundamental question of how to manage the stored wealth while it is not needed for consumption. The task of portfolio management addresses this question and deals with the most suitable selection of assets out of a basket of available assets.

M.-R. Amini et al. (Eds.): ECML PKDD 2022, LNAI 13718, pp. 185–200, 2023.
https://doi.org/10.1007/978-3-031-26422-1_12

Besides the obvious goal of maximizing the expected economic return, often, the investor's capacity to bear risk, i.e., the uncertainty in his economic returns, has to additionally be taken into account. This bearing capacity of risk for an investor is summarized in his individual risk preference level. The individual risk preference level can depend on various factors, such as the investor's investment horizon, his return expectations as well as his individual risk appetite.

While there are various works on short-term *trading* such as [3,30], we focus on the long-term task of *portfolio selection* which brings multiple practical challenges for investors. According to requirements for many institutional investors from regulatory frameworks, such as Solvency II[1], the risk in returns needs to be considered on a per time step basis. Professional investors are furthermore generally evaluated by their customers on their periodical performance, including the periodical risk taken on. The aforementioned individual risk preference of an investor can be difficult to quantify. In practice, the identification of a risk preference parameter is therefore often done by comparing alternative risk-return optimized allocation policies to one another and by then selecting the allocation policy fitting best. However, the identification of various optimized allocation policies on the Pareto front is computationally expensive, especially in multi-period settings which allow the investor to dynamically adjust his asset allocation during the trajectory. A typical example for the high computational demand is the extensive use of Monte Carlo simulations in the field of Asset Liability Management (ALM) applications, which can be seen as a specific type of the portfolio selection task, as discussed e.g., in [1].

In this paper, we frame the task of portfolio selection as a Markov decision process (MDP) which we set up to allow the modelling of a complex multi-period stochastic financial environment. To solve the MDP, we propose a risk-aware RL approach, which is able to control the risk in returns for each time step over the entire investment horizon. We choose to estimate the risk independently from the agent's current policy, making it only dependent on a market risk estimator as well as on the agent's current action. Contrary to policy dependent estimators in RL, such as critics, which can suffer from a moving target problem, our proposed risk estimator does not suffer from this issue, thereby allowing for sample efficiency and accelerated convergence. We propose a *meta agent* which uses the risk preference level as an inference parameter rather than as a hyperparameter. This allows for the agent to be trained over an interval of risk preference levels. In contrast, previous approaches have relied on training different agents for each level of risk preference, which has the drawback of requiring separate computationally expensive trainings, separate model networks and separate sets of hyperparameters. The usage of the risk preference level as an inference parameter further allows for approximating the Pareto front in a computationally efficient manner. One single trained meta agent is able to generate optimized asset allocation policies for any risk preference level within the specified interval during inference time. The implementation of our agent is based on PPO by [26], using a Dirichlet action distribution. In our experiments,

---

[1] https://www.eiopa.europa.eu/browse/solvency-2_en.

our PPO based approach is able to outperform three alternative approaches: firstly, a simple Equal Weight Buy and Hold strategy; secondly, a DDPG based risk-aware RL approach by [1] and thirdly, a TD3 based risk-aware RL approach by [32].

We benchmark all approaches in two different settings: on previously not known data from the training environment and on a full year of unseen real world Nasdaq-100 data in a backtesting setting.

The main contributions of this paper are:

- A computationally efficient way to approximate the risk-return Pareto front for a continuous interval of risk preference levels by training only a single meta agent
- A method that allows estimating the risk of returns independently from the agent's current policy
- A PPO based approach with a Dirichlet action distribution suitable for the task of multi-period portfolio selection

2   Related Work

The related work to our approach can be categorized into four main areas: risk measures in risk-aware RL, portfolio optimization, RL applications to financial tasks, approximation of the Pareto front.

The related work on **risk measures in risk-aware RL** considers several different risk measures. Early works use the *standard deviation* as a measure of risk such as [29] who proposed a risk-adjusted objective function by subtracting the standard deviation from the cumulated discounted rewards. However, this formulation violates the temporal persistence property necessary to guarantee the convergence to an optimum for policy iteration algorithms. Alternative approaches such as [10] use the *CVaR* as a risk measure, thereby addressing the risk of small probability events with high impact. Recent approaches have recognized the importance of measuring dispersion not solely in cumulated returns, i.e., over the entire trajectory, but of also addressing the variability in rewards per time step which can be highly relevant, e.g., for economic tasks such as trading or portfolio construction. A risk measure addressing this issue is the *reward volatility* defined by [6] which captures the variability of rewards between steps. [32] too proposed a framework optimizing the *variance of a per-step reward*. Another risk measure aiming to capture the variability per time step was published by [1] where it is defined as the *variance in rewards per time step observed in the current trajectory*. In contrast to the approaches mentioned above, we exploit the fact that in our setting, the risk of a step can be computed based solely on the current action and the market risk which is estimated independently from the policy. This in turn allows for the estimation of the risk in a very sample efficient way.

The foundations for **portfolio optimization** in financial literature were laid by the work of [16] who formulated the modern portfolio theory which is the basis of many works such as the one by [7]. They too used a mean-variance (MV) optimization approach in order to find the optimal weightings of investments in a portfolio offering the best risk-return trade-off. Thereby, the risk is measured as the variance in economic returns for a single time step. A more recent approach by [11] introduces a regime-switching factor model which – while still in the MV setup – allows for a single period optimization under different market regimes. Such different market regimes correspond to different states of the market, e.g., optimistic and pessimistic market sentiments. Other works such as the one by [8] introduce a framework extending the MV single-period optimization to a MV multi-period optimization.

The area of **RL applications to financial tasks** has become more popular in recent years, as RL methods can naturally handle multi-period problems as well as different states, such as different market regimes, in the context of a MDP and are thus well suited to tackle the requirements of financial tasks. Many of the correspondingly published works, such as [3,30] focus on trading which is characterized by a rather short term view. Other authors use RL methods to find long term strategies to solve a portfolio selection task. [25] apply a policy iteration algorithm to the portfolio selection problem in combination with a risk-adjusted objective function. In order to model the actions of an investor in a MV setup, [4] use a policy gradient method and propose the usage of the Dirichlet distribution. [1] propose the usage of the DDPG algorithm to optimize the risk-reward trade-off faced in a portfolio selection task for a life insurance company. In contrast to the approaches mentioned above, our approach allows a single meta agent to be trained over a continuous interval of risk preference levels, instead of training different agents for each level of risk preference individually.

The **approximation of a Pareto front** multi-objective optimization (MOO) is discussed by authors such as [18]. In contrast to our approach, they focus on a supervised MOO problem instead of a RL one. Other authors such as [22] propose the approximation of the Pareto front in a RL MOO setting. However, in their setting, they deal with a MOMDP with multiple reward functions, while we formulate the task as an MDP using a scalarized objective function by linearly combining the economic return objective and the economic risk objective. Thus, our method computes all Pareto optimal solutions on the convex hull but neglects those being Pareto optimal for non-linear scalarization functions [24]. Though this restriction systematically reduces the number of found Pareto optimal policies, we argue that the approximation generated by our method yields a sufficiently large and intuitive set of user options.

3   Background

A discrete-time MDP is described by a five tuple $(\mathcal{S}, \mathcal{A}, R, P, \gamma)$, consisting of the state space $\mathcal{S}$, the action space $\mathcal{A}$, a reward R which will be treated as a random variable as well as the transition probability function $P(s'|s,a) \in [0,1]$ for $s, s' \in \mathcal{S}$ and $a \in \mathcal{A}$ and a discount factor γ discounting future rewards.

The random variables for the next state S' and for the reward R are determined jointly and depend only on the preceding state s and action a. Their joint probability distribution is described by

$$p(s', r | s, a) = Pr(S' = s', R = r | S = s, A = a).$$

In the case that R is a continuous reward random variable, we obtain

$$\hat{R}(s, a) := \underset{s', r \sim p(\cdot, \cdot | s, a)}{\mathbb{E}[R | S = s, A = a]} = \int_r \int_{s'} r \, p(s', r | s, a) ds' dr.$$

A trajectory $\tau = (s_0, a_0, r_1, s_1, a_1, ...)$ is a sequence of states and actions. Let

$$P(\tau | \pi) = \mu_0(s_0) \prod_{t=0}^{T-1} p(s_{t+1}, r_{t+1} | s_t, a_t) \pi(a_t | s_t)$$

represent the probability of observing the trajectory τ given policy π. The term $\mu_0(s_0)$ describes the probability of observing s_0 as the initial state, i.e., $s_0 \sim \mu(\cdot)$.

We define the return as the observed discounted cumulative rewards for the trajectory τ, i.e.,

$$G(\tau) := \sum_{t=0}^{T-1} \gamma^t r_{t+1}$$

where r_{t+1} are the observed rewards from time step t, given s_t, a_t and s_{t+1}.

The objective function is then defined as the expected return for a given policy π and thus

$$J(\pi) := \underset{\tau \sim P(\tau | \pi)}{\mathbb{E}(G)} = \int_\tau P(\tau | \pi) G(\tau) d\tau.$$

4   Risk-Aware Portfolio Optimization

We consider an agent (i.e., investor) with a fixed investment horizon T who wants to allocate his wealth into different assets in order to maximize the trade-off between the expected return and the individual preference for risk for the periods $t = 0, \ldots, T$. The investable asset universe contains N assets. The **discount factor** is set to $\gamma = 1$.

We define the **state space** of the MDP as $\mathcal{S} = \mathcal{T} \times \mathcal{W} \times \mathcal{V} \times \mathcal{U}$. Here, the space $\mathcal{T} \subseteq \mathbb{R}$ is populated by the parameter λ which is used to represent the agent's individual risk preference level. In contrast to other approaches [1, 32], we thus use λ as an inference parameter, rather than as a hyperparameter. This parameter is crucial in enabling the agent to learn an interval of different risk preference levels by being randomly sampled at the beginning of each trajectory during training and then remaining constant until the end of the trajectory. $\mathcal{W} \subseteq \mathbb{R}_0^+$ represents the current absolute wealth level of the agent while the standard-simplex $\mathcal{V} = \left\{ v \in \mathbb{R}^N : \sum_{i=0}^{N-1} v_i = 1, v_i \geq 0 \text{ for } i = 0, \ldots, N-1 \right\}$ represents the current relative portfolio allocation. $\mathcal{U} \subseteq \mathbb{R}^N$ represents all the observed single asset returns from the previous time step.

The **action space** $\mathcal{A}$ is also defined as a standard-simplex to represent the weighting vector chosen by the agent as action $a_t = [a_{t,0}, \ldots, a_{t,N-1}] \in \mathcal{A}$ at time step t. The choice of the action space $\mathcal{A}$ as a standard-simplex represents the need of the agent to allocate all available funds into its portfolio within each period, i.e., $a_t^\mathsf{T} \mathbb{1} = 1$, whereby short-selling of assets is not permitted, i.e., $a_i \geq 0 \; \forall i$.

The random vector $\Theta = [\Theta_0, \ldots, \Theta_{N-1}] \in \mathcal{U}$ models the economic return of each asset individually for each time step. The portfolio return is a random variable with an expected value denoted as

$$\mathbb{E}\left[\Theta_{PF}\right] = \mathbb{E}\left[a^\mathsf{T}\Theta\right] = a^\mathsf{T}\mathbb{E}\left[\Theta\right].$$

Changes in the portfolio weightings a_t in period t by the agent cause transaction costs, defined by

$$tc_t = (|a_t - v_t|)^\mathsf{T} c$$

where the vector $c = [c_0, \ldots, c_{N-1}]$ contains the asset-specific transaction costs caused by a trade of the respective asset. Note that the transaction costs are non-stochastic and fully determined by action a_t.

We then define the observed economic reward r as a combination of the transaction costs tc and a realization ϑ_{PF} of the random variable of the portfolio's economic return Θ_{PF}, i.e.,

$$r = \vartheta_{PF} - tc. \tag{1}$$

To include the element of risk awareness in the **reward** of the MDP, we shape the reward to include the economic reward as well as a risk measure weighted by a penalty term:

$$r'(s, a) := r(s, a) - \lambda f_{risk, \Theta_{PF}}(s, a).$$

The term λ is the risk penalty factor which reflects the agent's individual preference to take on risk. Note that the risk in the reward, i.e., $f_{risk, \Theta_{PF}}(s, a)$, is measured per time step, cannot be observed directly and therefore has to be estimated.

Subsequently, the risk-aware return is defined as:

$$G'(\tau) := \sum_{t=0}^{T-1} \gamma^t \left(r_{t+1} - \lambda \hat{f}_{risk, \Theta_{PF}}(s_t, a_t) \right)$$

where $\hat{f}_{risk, \Theta_{PF}}(s_t, a_t)$ is an estimated function to measure the risk in r_{t+1} and only depends on the state-action pair of time step t. With our approach, $\hat{f}_{risk, \Theta_{PF}}$ can therefore be estimated over different trajectories regardless of the agent's current policy.

4.1   Risk Measure

Based on the financial setting, we use the standard deviation as a risk measure. This risk measure is widely accepted in finance, as e.g., discussed by [13]. Thus, our approach requires estimating the risk per time step, i.e., the standard deviation in returns associated with each state-action pair. In our setting and in line with other authors such as [8], the returns of financial assets are assumed to be independent between time steps. The only source of stochasticity in the estimator for the portfolio's risk is the market risk of the individual assets, while the action is a deterministic component of the estimator function.

The variance of the economic portfolio return is defined as:

$$Var(\Theta_{PF}) = a^\mathsf{T} \Sigma_\Theta a$$

where Σ_Θ is the covariance matrix for asset-wise economic returns Θ and a describes the weightings in the individual assets – which in our setting is the action selected by the agent. Note that the standard deviation is a risk measure free from assumptions about the underlying distribution. The $N \times N$ covariance matrix Σ_Θ can be rewritten in terms of the first and second moment of Θ:

$$\Sigma_\Theta = \mathbb{E}[\Theta\Theta^\mathsf{T}] - \mathbb{E}[\Theta]\mathbb{E}[\Theta]^\mathsf{T} .$$

The covariance matrix can be estimated independently from both the agent's action as well as from his current policy and solely depends on the state of the market environment from which the estimator receives the latest observable information $u \in \mathcal{U}$ which is included in $s \in \mathcal{S}$, and thus

$$\hat{f}_{Cov}(s) := \widehat{\Sigma_\Theta} .$$

Including action a in our estimator function, the estimator for the risk of the portfolio return in a single time step is defined as

$$\hat{f}_{risk,\Theta_{PF}}(s,a) := \sqrt{a^\mathsf{T}\widehat{\Sigma_\Theta}a} = \sqrt{a^\mathsf{T}\hat{f}_{Cov}(s)a} .$$

We use two neural networks, $\hat{M}_1$ and $\hat{M}_2$, to estimate the first and second moment of Θ. Due to our multivariate setting with N individual assets, $\hat{M}_1$ has to estimate N values. For the second moment, $\hat{M}_2$ has to estimate the unique elements present in the symmetric matrix, i.e., $(N+1) \cdot N \cdot 0.5$ elements. These moment estimators are trained simultaneously with the agent's policy.

4.2   Policy

As a policy function for our PPO based implementation, we use the Dirichlet distribution as proposed in a similar context by [4]. The Dirichlet distribution is a multivariate probability distribution governed by the concentration parameter vector $\alpha = [\alpha_0, \ldots, \alpha_{N-1}]$ where $\alpha_i > 0$ with $i = 0, \ldots, N - 1$. Its probability density function for a random vector is defined as

$$f(x; \alpha) = \frac{1}{B(\alpha)} \prod_{i=0}^{N-1} x_i^{\alpha_i - 1}$$

where $B(\alpha)$ is the multivariate beta function. A sample $x = [x_0, \ldots, x_{N-1}]$ drawn from a Dirichlet distribution satisfies the properties $\sum_{i=0}^{N-1} x_i = 1$ and $x_i > 0$, and is thus a member of a standard simplex fulfilling the requirements imposed on actions in the context of portfolio selection. In the experimental part, we further examine for comparison purposes a DDPG based as well as a TD3 based implementation of our method. For both implementations, the natural way of enforcing the sampled outputs to be members of a standard simplex is by applying a softmax function in the output layer. The exploration is done by adding the explorational noise to the parameters in the hidden layers of the policy network, which is an approach described by [23].

4.3   Algorithm

The algorithm for the PPO based implementation can be found in Algorithm 1. Note that in our setting the ability of the meta agent to learn asset allocation policies for any level of risk preference on a continuous interval is enabled through (a) the formulation of a policy independent risk measure and (b) the treatment of the risk preference parameter λ as an inference parameter by inclusion in the state $s \in \mathcal{S}$. During training, at the beginning of each trajectory, the risk preference parameter λ is sampled from a continuous uniform distribution. Within each trajectory i the initially sampled λ_i remains constant.

4.4   Network Architectures

For our PPO based framework, we have four different models: an actor network $\pi(a|s, \theta)$, a critic network $v(s)$ and two moment estimating neural networks $\hat{M}_1$ and $\hat{M}_2$, responsible for the estimation of the first and second moments of the individual assets to form an estimated covariance matrix. The architecture of the actor network and the critic network share the same body network of four fully connected hidden layers of size 512, 256, 128 and 64 with ReLU activation functions. These layers are followed by an attention based GTrXL architecture by [21] allowing for also handling tasks requiring memory. The use of a GTrXL element instead of the standard transformer architecture improves the architecture's optimization properties in RL settings significantly. The GTrXL element consists of a single transformer unit with one encoder layer as well as one decoder layer with four attention heads and an embedding size of 64. The network's body is then split into two heads, in which the actor network's output layer utilizes an exponential activation function. This enforces the output to be in the value range

---

Algorithm 1. Risk controlling PPO

Input: environment ϵ

1: **init** parameters: $\theta_0, \phi_0,\ \gamma_0,\ \delta_0$ # policy, value function, 1st & 2nd moment estimate
2: **for** $k = 0, 1, \ldots$ **do**
3:     sample trajectories $\mathcal{D}_k = \{\tau_i\}$ with policy $\pi_k = \pi(\theta_k)$ in ϵ for T time steps; at each trajectory start sample risk preference $\lambda_i \sim U(a, b)$.
4:     Update risk estimator function $\hat{f}_k(\cdot, \cdot) = \sqrt{\hat{M}_{2,\delta_k}(\cdot, \cdot) - \left(\hat{M}_{1,\gamma_k}(\cdot, \cdot)\right)^2}$.
5:     Calculate the est. risk $\hat{f}_k(s_t, a_t)$ and then the risk adjusted reward r'_{t+1}.
6:     Calculate advantage estimates, $\hat{A}_t$ based on the current value function V_{ϕ_k}.
7:     Update policy by maximizing the PPO-Clip objective:

$$\theta_{k+1} = \arg\max_{\theta} \frac{1}{|\mathcal{D}_k|T} \sum_{\tau \in \mathcal{D}_k} \sum_{t=0}^{T}$$

$$\min\left(\frac{\pi_\theta(a_t|s_t)}{\pi_{\theta_k}(a_t|s_t)} A^{\pi_{\theta_k}}(s_t, a_t),\ g(\epsilon, A^{\pi_{\theta_k}}(s_t, a_t))\right).$$

8:     $\phi_{k+1} = \arg\min_{\phi} \frac{1}{|\mathcal{D}_k|T} \sum_{\tau \in \mathcal{D}_k} \sum_{t=0}^{T} \left(V_\phi(s_t) - r'_{t+1}\right)^2$. # update ϕ
9:     $\gamma_{k+1} = \arg\min_{\gamma} \frac{1}{|\mathcal{D}_k|T} \sum_{\tau \in \mathcal{D}_k} \sum_{t=0}^{T} \left(\hat{M}_{1,\gamma_k}(s_t, a_t) - r_{t+1}\right)^2$. # update γ
10:    $\delta_{k+1} = \arg\min_{\delta} \frac{1}{|\mathcal{D}_k|T} \sum_{\tau \in \mathcal{D}_k} \sum_{t=0}^{T} \left(\hat{M}_{2,\delta_k}(s_t, a_t) - r_{t+1}^2\right)^2$. # update δ
11: **end for**

---

of $\mathbb{R}^+$, to meet the requirements of the parameter input of the Dirichlet distribution. The head of the critic network on the other hand is a basic linear layer without activation function. We further need to estimate the covariance matrix in order to estimate the risk associated with an action by estimating the elements of the multivariate expressions of the first and second moment, i.e. $\mathbb{E}[\Theta]$ and $\mathbb{E}[\Theta\Theta^{\mathsf{T}}]$. Since this is a standard supervised learning problem, we apply a standard transformer architecture to estimate a multivariate time series as described by [31]. In our setting, this architecture consists of four encoder layers and four decoder layers, each utilizing eight attention heads with an embedding size of 512. Note that the actor and critic network are trained together, having a joint loss function using the Adam optimizer with a learning rate of $5.0 \cdot 10^{-5}$. The moment estimating networks use a separate loss function and utilize the Adam optimizer with a learning rate of $1.0 \cdot 10^{-3}$.

5   Experiments

5.1   Environment

We use the qlib package[2] to fetch and process real-world financial data for the US market contained in the Nasdaq-100. The Nasdaq-100 is a modified market value-weighted index containing the shares from the 100 largest non-financial companies traded on the Nasdaq stock exchange. Over time, the composition of the index changes. This is due to the (de)listing of shares and changes in the market value of companies, which can then – according to the guidelines of the Nasdaq-100 – lead to removal from or addition to the Nasdaq-100. We consider the monthly single share closing prices for the period from January 1, 2010 to December 31, 2020. In order to avoid having to deal with missing data, we filter out the companies that were not included in the Nasdaq-100 throughout the entire period. From the remaining 35 companies, we randomly choose 16 to represent the investable universe in the RL environment.

In literature, there is a multitude of approaches modelling the dynamics in the time series of financial returns. One such approach is the application of classical time series models, e.g., by [5,17]. Another approach is the usage of deep learning based methods, e.g., by [15,20]. Furthermore, hidden markov models (HMMs) are applied, e.g., by [14,19]. In our setup, we decide to model the market dynamics by applying a HMM. However, any method capable of modelling the dynamics in a time series of financial returns could be used interchangeably.

To choose the HMM fitting best, we follow [19] and use two criteria, namely the Akaike information criterion (AIC) by [2] and the Bayesian information criterion (BIC) by [27]. Both criteria suggest the use of a two state HMM. In our environment, we set the length of a trajectory to twelve time steps, reflecting the investment horizon of a year. The transaction costs are set to 0.2% of the traded volume.

5.2   Experimental Setup

The implementation of our approach is based on the RLlib framework[3] and the agents were trained on a cluster utilizing various types of commercially available single GPUs. For each evaluation step, we sample 1000 trajectories to calculate the corresponding statistics.

For the implementation of our benchmark RL algorithms, we base [32] on the publicly available GitHub code[4] while for the approach proposed by [1], we rebuild the architecture as described in their paper.

5.3   Evaluation

Benchmarking with Other Approaches. For our evaluation setup, we compare our approach with three alternative approaches. The first one is an Equal

---

[2] https://github.com/microsoft/qlib/tree/main.
[3] https://docs.ray.io/en/master/rllib/index.html.
[4] https://github.com/ShangtongZhang/DeepRL.

Table 1. Evaluation results of 1000 trajectories from the environment (I) and backtesting on the Nasdaq-100 data trajectory of 2021 (II).

	Sharpe Ratio (ex-post)	Total Econ. Payoff	Est. Std. Dev.
(I) Environment			
Equal Weight B&H	1.232	0.218	0.177
Ours	**1.347**	**0.240**	0.178
Zhang et al. (2021)	1.283	0.229	0.178
Abrate et al. (2021)	1.158	0.209	0.180
(II) Backtesting			
Equal Weight B&H	1.968	0.336	0.171
Ours	**2.039**	**0.344**	0.168
Zhang et al. (2021)	1.921	0.335	0.174
Abrate et al. (2021)	1.908	0.331	0.173

Weight Buy and Hold (Equal Weight B&H) policy, which is a simple investment heuristic. At the beginning of the investment horizon, the funds are distributed equally to all available assets. After buying the assets they are held until the end of the investment horizon without any allocation adjustments. Despite its low complexity, an Equal Weight policy is considered to be a performant allocation policy. The second approach is a risk-aware RL DDPG based method described by [1] which in their paper is specifically applied to the task of generating an optimized asset allocation policy for a single level of risk preference. In the following, we will refer to their approach as Abrate et al. (2021). The third approach is MVPI-TD3 by [32]. It is a state-of-the-art risk-aware RL method based on the TD3 algorithm, originally introduced by [12]. In the following, we will refer to the third approach as Zhang et al. (2021).

We evaluate two different settings: in setting (I) we evaluate the policies' performances for 1000 unseen trajectories generated by the environment. Setting (II) follows a backtesting approach by evaluating the policies' performances for the unseen historical trajectory of the Nasdaq-100 data for the entire year of 2021. To allow for a consistent comparison of the asset allocation policies, every approach needs to be adjusted to bear a comparable amount of risk. All of our evaluated RL approaches are able to control the risk of the optimized asset allocation policy by adjusting their specific risk preference level parameter λ. In contrast, the Equal Weight B&H approach does not have this feature, resulting in the use of the risk level of the Equal Weight B&H approach as the baseline level of risk to which the other approaches have to adapt. Accordingly, the λ in the other approaches are set in such a way to generate strategies with a standard deviation in returns comparable to the one produced by the Equal Weight B&H approach.

For (I), the policies' standard deviations in returns over the entire trajectory are estimated as the empirical standard deviations. To estimate the standard

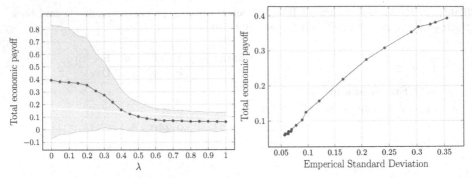

(a) Approx. Pareto front of strategies' mean total economic payoff and their respective 90% confidence interval in relation to the risk preference level λ.

(b) Approx. Pareto front of strategies' mean total economic payoff in relation to their empirical standard deviation.

Fig. 1. Evaluation of a single PPO based meta agent for different levels of risk preference.

deviations in returns in (II), a different approach is needed, since the real-world data offer only a single observation per month, which makes it difficult to estimate the monthly variances in returns. To address this issue, we use the daily observations within a month. After estimating the daily variance, this value is scaled up by the number of trading days within the month in order to estimate the assets' monthly variance – a method commonly used in finance [9]. The root of the sum of the monthly variances is then used to obtain an estimate for the policies' standard deviations in returns in the backtesting evaluation setting.

Table 1 provides the evaluation results of our experiments. We evaluate the approaches in regards to their ex-post Sharpe ratio, an evaluation metric commonly used in finance to compare investment performances [8,28]. In addition, Table 1 shows the individual components of the Sharpe ratio, which in our setting are the total economic payoff and the estimated standard deviation. In both evaluation settings (I) and (II), our approach is able to provide the asset allocation policy scoring the highest Sharpe ratio and – under an approximately equal level of risk – therefore also the highest total economic payoff.

Note that the risk preference parameters λ of the different risk-aware RL approaches cannot be compared directly, due to different definitions of risk and different objective functions. For Zhang et al. (2021) we use a risk preference parameter value of 0.55, for Abrate et al. (2021) a risk preference parameter value of 0.3 and for our own approach a risk preference parameter value of 0.34.

Approximation of the Pareto Front. A multi-period asset allocation policy for a given level of risk preference incorporates a suggested asset allocation for each single time step. Our meta agent approach generates an entire set of asset allocation policies, whereby each single one is linked to a specific level of risk preference within a continuous interval. Figure 1a shows the performance of our

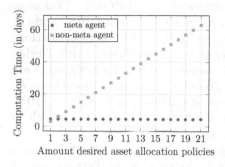

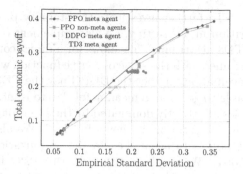

Fig. 2. Computation time required for training.

Fig. 3. Comparison of meta agent approaches and PPO non-meta agents.

approach with respect to different levels of risk preference λ. Each point represents an entire asset allocation policy evaluated over twelve time steps of the trajectory. The y-axis shows the economic return including the transaction costs, as defined in Eq. 1, cumulated over the entire trajectory. In the following, this value will be referred to as the *total economic payoff*. In Fig. 1a we are evaluating 21 different asset allocation strategies with corresponding risk preference levels in the interval of 0.0 to 1.0 in steps of 0.05 generated by the same meta agent. The figure shows that our method is capable of approximating a monotonic decreasing Pareto front with increasing levels of risk preference. In order to illustrate the measured uncertainty of the total economic payoff, Fig. 1a also includes the empirical 90% confidence interval. As in Fig. 1a, in Fig. 1b the 21 asset allocation strategies, evaluated in relation to their empirical standard deviation, form a Pareto front.

Stability During Training. In order to find a suitable asset allocation policy, the RL based approaches use their model specific risk preference parameter λ. To allow for a consistent comparison of the approaches, each approach needs to generate a policy with a comparable level of risk, i.e., a comparable level of standard deviation in returns measured over the trajectory. From this arises the need to identify for each approach the corresponding individual risk preference parameter λ which produces a certain level of standard deviation. For the non-meta agent approaches by Zhang et al. (2021) and Abrate et al. (2021), the identification of a suitable risk preference parameter is done manually via an iterative interval search. Thereby, single agents need to be trained and evaluated. Both the DDPG and TD3 based approaches require a considerable amount of hyperparameter tuning for each single agent. When a suitable set of hyperparameters is found, it is then often not transferable between agents with different levels of risk preference. This leads to unstable training results combined with repeatedly extensive hyperparameter tuning.

To further investigate the stability properties of the DDPG and TD3 algorithm in our setting, we also implement our meta agent for the DDPG and the TD3 algorithm. This allows for a direct comparison of all three implementations trained with the *same* objective function with the *same* definition of risk. During evaluation, neither the DDPG nor the TD3 implementation of a meta agent are able to generate a meaningful Pareto front. Their proposed asset allocation policies are strictly dominated by the asset allocation policies generated by the PPO implementation as shown in Fig. 3. We also apply the PPO based approach to a non-meta agent, i.e., to the optimization of a single level of risk preference solely. We emphasize that for this PPO based approach, we are able to use a single set of hyperparameters for training, thereby transferable between agents for different levels of risk preference. Figure 3 further shows the comparison to the PPO meta agent. Due to computational limitations, we only train and evaluate 11 optimized allocation policies with PPO non-meta agents. Nevertheless, it can be seen that for the PPO based methods, both the meta agent as well as the non-meta agents are able to approximate a Pareto front, with the non-meta agents performing slightly worse. We hypothesize that the superior stability in hyperparameters for a PPO based approach over the DDPG and the TD3 based approaches plays an important role when successfully training a meta agent.

Efficiency. One advantage of our method when approximating the Pareto front is its computational efficiency. Once the meta agent has been trained, we are able to generate any number of optimized asset allocation strategies by simply changing the risk preference levels as an inference parameter. Thereby, the respective asset allocation strategies can be evaluated without further training. In contrast, previous approaches would need to train a different agent for each level of risk preference. Figure 2 shows the training time required to generate different optimized asset allocation strategies on the machine used for our experiments. While the time required to train a single agent for an optimized asset allocation using one single level of risk preference takes roughly 3 days, the training of a meta agent for an interval of levels of risk preference takes roughly 4.5 days on a system with an NVIDIA RTX 8000. When training multiple agents, the cumulative computation time increases linearly with the amount of desired optimized asset allocation strategies. In contrast, the training time of our approach stays constant due to the need of only training a single meta agent to cover an entire interval of risk preference levels.

Performance of Risk Measure Estimation. With our approach, we further introduce a method to estimate the risk per time step, which can be done independently from the agent's current policy. The experiments show fast convergence for both the first and the second moment estimators after roughly 6% of the total training time, i.e., after 150 out of a total of 2500 training iterations.

6   Conclusion

In this paper, we train an agent to invest a given amount of wealth into a set of assets on a monthly basis. In order to control the risk of the investment, the agent receives a risk preference parameter constraining the standard deviation in the financial returns received per time step. This in turn also indirectly controls the risk of the financial returns over the entire trajectory. Our method of estimating the risk in a time step is independent of the agent's current policy and only requires the agent's current action as well as an estimate of the market risk. In our approach a single meta agent is trained for any risk preference level within a continuous interval, enabling a computationally efficient approximation of the Pareto front. We evaluate our PPO based approach combined with a Dirichlet action distribution against other state-of-the-art risk-aware RL approaches in a setting based on real-world Nasdaq-100 data. The results show that our new method outperforms compared approaches w.r.t. stability during training as well as generating asset allocation policies with better risk-return profiles. For future work, we want to explore the setting of multiple competing meta agents able to influence the market prices and their resulting interactions.

Acknowledgments. This work has been funded by the German Federal Ministry of Education and Research (BMBF) under Grant No. 01IS18036A. The authors of this work take full responsibility for its content.

References

1. Abrate, C., et al.: Continuous-action reinforcement learning for portfolio allocation of a life insurance company. In: Dong, Y., Kourtellis, N., Hammer, B., Lozano, J.A. (eds.) ECML PKDD 2021. LNCS (LNAI), vol. 12978, pp. 237–252. Springer, Cham (2021). https://doi.org/10.1007/978-3-030-86514-6_15
2. Akaike, H.: A new look at the statistical model identification. IEEE Trans. Autom. Control **19**(6), 716–723 (1974)
3. Almahdi, S., Yang, S.Y.: An adaptive portfolio trading system: a risk-return portfolio optimization using recurrent reinforcement learning with expected maximum drawdown. Expert Syst. Appl. **87**, 267–279 (2017)
4. André, E., Coqueret, G.: Dirichlet policies for reinforced factor portfolios. arXiv preprint arXiv:2011.05381 (2020)
5. Ariyo, A.A., Adewumi, A.O., Ayo, C.K.: Stock price prediction using the Arima model. In: 2014 UKSim-AMSS 16th International Conference on Computer Modelling and Simulation, pp. 106–112. IEEE (2014)
6. Bisi, L., Sabbioni, L., Vittori, E., Papini, M., Restelli, M.: Risk-averse trust region optimization for reward-volatility reduction. In: Twenty-Ninth International Joint Conference on Artificial Intelligence Special Track, pp. 4583–4589. International Joint Conferences on Artificial Intelligence Organization (2020)
7. Black, F., Litterman, R.: Global portfolio optimization. Finan. Analy. J. **48**(5), 28–43 (1992)
8. Boyd, S., et al.: Multi-period trading via convex optimization. Found. Trends Optim. **3**(1), 1–76 (2017)
9. Brigham, E.F., Ehrhardt, M.C.: Financial Management: Theory & Practice. Cengage Learning (2019)
10. Chow, Y., Ghavamzadeh, M., Janson, L., Pavone, M.: Risk-constrained reinforcement learning with percentile risk criteria. J. Mach. Learn. Res. **18**(1), 6070–6120 (2017)

11. Costa, G., Kwon, R.: A regime-switching factor model for mean-variance optimization. J. Risk (2020)
12. Fujimoto, S., Hoof, H., Meger, D.: Addressing function approximation error in actor-critic methods. In: International Conference on Machine Learning, pp. 1587–1596. PMLR (2018)
13. Guercio, D.D., Reuter, J.: Mutual fund performance and the incentive to generate alpha. J. Financ. **69**(4), 1673–1704 (2014)
14. Hassan, M.R., Nath, B.: Stock market forecasting using hidden Markov model: a new approach. In: 5th International Conference on Intelligent Systems Design and Applications (ISDA 2005), pp. 192–196. IEEE (2005)
15. Hiransha, M., Gopalakrishnan, E.A., Menon, V.K., Soman, K.: NSE stock market prediction using deep-learning models. Procedia Comput. Sci. **132**, 1351–1362 (2018)
16. Markowitz, H.: Portfolio selection. J. Finan. **7**(1), 77–91 (1952)
17. Munim, Z.H., Shakil, M.H., Alon, I.: Next-day bitcoin price forecast. J. Risk Finan. Manag. **12**(2), 103 (2019)
18. Navon, A., Shamsian, A., Fetaya, E., Chechik, G.: Learning the pareto front with hypernetworks. In: International Conference on Learning Representations (2021)
19. Nguyen, N.: Hidden Markov model for stock trading. Int. J. Finan. Stud. **6**(2), 36 (2018)
20. Pang, X., Zhou, Y., Wang, P., Lin, W., Chang, V.: An innovative neural network approach for stock market prediction. J. Supercomput. **76**(3), 2098–2118 (2020)
21. Parisotto, E., et al.: Stabilizing transformers for reinforcement learning. In: International Conference on Machine Learning, pp. 7487–7498. PMLR (2020)
22. Pirotta, M., Parisi, S., Restelli, M.: Multi-objective reinforcement learning with continuous pareto frontier approximation. In: Twenty-Ninth AAAI Conference on Artificial Intelligence (2015)
23. Plappert, M., et al.: Parameter space noise for exploration. arXiv preprint arXiv:1706.01905 (2017)
24. Roijers, D.M., Vamplew, P., Whiteson, S., Dazeley, R.: A survey of multi-objective sequential decision-making. J. Artif. Intell. Res. **48**, 67–113 (2013)
25. Sato, M., Kobayashi, S.: Variance-penalized reinforcement learning for risk-averse asset allocation. In: Leung, K.S., Chan, L.-W., Meng, H. (eds.) IDEAL 2000. LNCS, vol. 1983, pp. 244–249. Springer, Heidelberg (2000). https://doi.org/10.1007/3-540-44491-2_34
26. Schulman, J., Wolski, F., Dhariwal, P., Radford, A., Klimov, O.: Proximal policy optimization algorithms. arXiv preprint arXiv:1707.06347 (2017)
27. Schwarz, G.: Estimating the dimension of a model. Ann. Statist. **6**, 461–464 (1978)
28. Sharpe, W.F.: The sharpe ratio. Streetwise Best J. Portfolio Manag. **3**, 169–185 (1998)
29. Sobel, M.J.: The variance of discounted Markov decision processes. J. Appl. Probab. **19**, pp. 794–802 (1982)
30. Wang, H., Zhou, X.Y.: Continuous-time mean-variance portfolio selection: a reinforcement learning framework. Math. Financ. **30**(4), 1273–1308 (2020)
31. Wu, N., Green, B., Ben, X., O'Banion, S.: Deep transformer models for time series forecasting: the influenza prevalence case. arXiv preprint arXiv:2001.08317 (2020)
32. Zhang, S., Liu, B., Whiteson, S.: Mean-variance policy iteration for risk-averse reinforcement learning. In: AAAI (2021)

Applications

Waypoint Generation in Row-Based Crops with Deep Learning and Contrastive Clustering

Francesco Salvetti[1,2,3]($\boxtimes$), Simone Angarano[1,2], Mauro Martini[1,2],
Simone Cerrato[1,2], and Marcello Chiaberge[1,2]

[1] Politecnico di Torino, Turin, Italy
{francesco.salvetti,simone.angarano,mauro.martini,
simone.cerrato,marcello.chiaberge}@polito.it
[2] PIC4SeR (PoliTo Interdepartmental Centre for Service Robotics), Turin, Italy
[3] SmartData@PoliTo, Turin, Italy

Abstract. The development of precision agriculture has gradually introduced automation in the agricultural process to support and rationalize all the activities related to field management. In particular, service robotics plays a predominant role in this evolution by deploying autonomous agents able to navigate in fields while executing different tasks without the need for human intervention, such as monitoring, spraying and harvesting. In this context, global path planning is the first necessary step for every robotic mission and ensures that the navigation is performed efficiently and with complete field coverage. In this paper, we propose a learning-based approach to tackle waypoint generation for planning a navigation path for row-based crops, starting from a top-view map of the region-of-interest. We present a novel methodology for waypoint clustering based on a contrastive loss, able to project the points to a separable latent space. The proposed deep neural network can simultaneously predict the waypoint position and cluster assignment with two specialized heads in a single forward pass. The extensive experimentation on simulated and real-world images demonstrates that the proposed approach effectively solves the waypoint generation problem for both straight and curved row-based crops, overcoming the limitations of previous state-of-the-art methodologies.

Keywords: Deep learning · Clustering · Global path planning · Precision agriculture

1 Introduction

Agriculture 4.0 is introducing digital tools and technologies in precision farming. According to this innovative paradigm, Big Data, Artificial Intelligence and robotics play a key role in increasing the economic, environmental and social sustainability of agricultural processes, thanks to the efficient and automatic data collection and the processing tools they provide. In the last years, Deep Learning (DL) research has been substantially contributing to the development of

M.-R. Amini et al. (Eds.): ECML PKDD 2022, LNAI 13718, pp. 203–218, 2023.
https://doi.org/10.1007/978-3-031-26422-1_13

new technologies for precision agriculture applications [12,13,33,38]. In particular, several computer vision techniques have proven effective in supporting visual agricultural tasks such as fruit detection and counting [23], plant disease identification [11,25], land coverage and vegetation index classification from satellite and Unmanned Aerial Vehicles (UAVs) imagery [15,21,22].

Besides image processing systems, self-driving machines represent a crucial component to reduce the costs of agricultural processes by providing autonomous, full-time and weather-independent operators. In this regard, the confidence in solutions based on autonomous Unmanned Ground Vehicles (UGVs) and UAVs is drastically increasing [30,31], considering the competitive advantage they can provide supporting tasks such as crop monitoring [35], spraying [8], grasping [14], and harvesting [19]. In this context, designing a reliable autonomous navigation system in constrained row-based crops such as vineyards and orchards is fundamental. So far, many works proposed local planners combining deep learning with computer vision [1,2] or other sensor processing methods [3,4,28]. However, local planners provide a solution for intra-row navigation only, and therefore a global path generator is always needed. In a complex scenario such as a row-based environment, where traversing each row is the practical navigation goal, the problem of developing an efficient global path planner has been quite neglected by the research community. Existing solutions usually tackle the problem by clustering visual data obtained from satellites or UAVs. For example, in [39] authors use a classical clustering method to identify vineyard rows from a 3D model of the terrain reconstructed from UAV data and then compute the path accordingly. However, as pointed out in [34], the extraction of relevant information about rows geometry from images can be a complex task, in addition to being extremely computationally expensive. This limitation also holds considering other approaches besides clustering. For instance, in [7] authors adopted 3D point cloud aerial photogrammetry to detect the structure of vineyards.

Recently, the DeepWay method [24] has been proposed to efficiently combine deep learning and clustering for the generation of start and end row waypoints given an occupancy grid of the vineyard. Moreover, novel contributions adopted the same paradigm and training procedure to extend the coverage to arbitrary unstructured environments [17]. Despite being an important baseline for row-based path generation, DeepWay leaves substantial space for improvement. In particular, it applies DBSCAN clustering [9], followed by a complex heuristic geometrical post-processing heavily based on angle estimation, to discriminate start waypoints from end waypoints. However, this method performs poorly in a wide range of real-world situations, including curved crops and rows of different lengths.

In this work, we propose a novel solution for waypoint generation in row-based crops, combining deep learning with a contrastive clustering approach. To this end, we conceive a new DNN architecture to simultaneously predict the position of the navigation waypoints for each row and cluster them in a single forward step. Hence, we train our model with an additional contrastive loss on a synthetic dataset of top-view vineyard maps and test it on manually-labeled real satellite images. Our extensive experimentation demonstrates that the proposed solution successfully predicts precise waypoints also in real-world crop maps. We also consider complex conditions such as curved rows, differently from previous solutions based on classical clustering algorithms.

The contributions of this work can be therefore summarized as follows:

- we propose a novel deep learning model to simultaneously predict the position of navigation waypoints and cluster them in a unique forward step;
- we solve the limitations of classical clustering methodologies by adopting a contrastive loss function;
- we present a method for synthetic generation of realistic curved occupancy grids for row-based crops;
- we demonstrate that our model trained on synthetic data successfully generalizes to challenging real-world satellite images.

The article is organized in the following sections. In Sect. 2, we introduce our methodology, describing the backbone design, the waypoint estimation and the contrastive clustering separately. In Sect. 3, we propose a thorough description of our experimentation, defining the settings and procedures used to generate the synthetic dataset and train the DNN. In Sect. 4, we report and discuss the obtained results, comparing our solution with classical clustering baselines, and, in Sect. 5, we draw some conclusions.

2 Methodology

Due to its intrinsic nature, every row-based crop is characterized by a set of lines or curves that identify two regions comprising the starting and ending points of each row, respectively. In this scenario, a robotic path should cover the whole field, and it can be divided into intra-row segments, that connect the starting region to the ending region, and inter-row segments, that connect two starting or two ending points. Given an optimal estimation of these starting and ending waypoints, it is possible to plan a full-coverage path in the row-based environment simply by alternating intra-row and inter-row segments. Therefore, the planning process heavily relies on two main steps: waypoint estimation, which identifies candidates for the points of interest, and waypoint clustering, which assigns each estimated point to one of the two regions.

Following the same approach presented in [24], we frame the waypoint generation process as a regression problem, in which we estimate the coordinates of the points with a deep neural network, starting from a top-view map of the environment. The map consists of a 1-bit single-channel occupancy grid that identifies with 1 the plant rows and with 0 the free terrain. Therefore, this kind of estimation process can be easily applied to geo-referenced segmented masks of the target fields obtained from satellites or UAV imagery. The waypoints and the planned path can then be converted from the image reference system to a Global Navigation Satellite System (GNSS) reference frame to be used in real-world navigation. In addition to waypoint detection, differently from classical

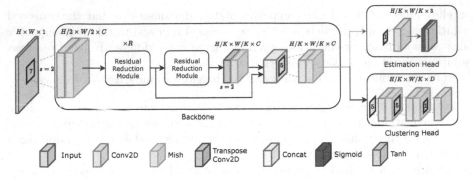

Fig. 1. Architecture of the backbone and the two regression heads. The number of residual reduction modules in the main block R determines the backbone compression factor $K = 2^{R+1}$.

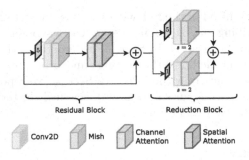

Fig. 2. Residual reduction module architecture. The channel and spatial attentions are implemented as in [36].

unsupervised methodologies for point clustering, we propose a supervised app-roach based on a contrastive loss to perform point assignment. Therefore, the proposed model simultaneously performs both estimation and clustering with a single forward pass, without the need for complex post-processing operations based on heuristic geometrical-based rules.

2.1   Backbone Design

We implement the model as a convolutional neural network characterized by a feature extraction backbone, followed by two specialized heads. A head is responsible for the estimation task, while the other deals with clustering.

The backbone is designed following the same architecture used in [24]. The basic block of the network is the residual module, characterized by a stack of a 2D convolution and spatial and channel attention [36]. Each residual block is followed by a reduction module characterized by convolutions with stride 2 that progressively halve the spatial dimensions. The backbone is a stack of R resid-ual reduction modules, made by combining a residual module and a reduction module. The final part of the network is made by an additional downsampling

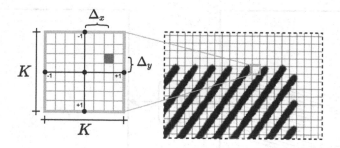

Fig. 3. The input occupancy grid is subdivided into a grid of $K \times K$ cells. For each cell, the waypoint estimation head outputs the probability p of a waypoint presence, as well as the relative horizontal and vertical displacements with respect to the cell center $\Delta = (\Delta x, \Delta y)$.

block, followed by a transposed convolution upsampling stage, all arranged in a residual fashion. This combination of compression and expansion has been proved very effective for different computer vision tasks such as segmentation [29] and representation learning [32]. Overall, the model performs a dimensionality compression of a factor of 2^{R+1}, where R is the number of residual reduction modules in the main block. The complete backbone structure is detailed in Fig. 1 and Fig. 2.

2.2 Waypoint Estimation

The waypoint estimation is framed as a regression problem, similarly to object detection approaches in computer vision [27]. In particular, given an input occupancy grid map X with dimensions $H \times W$, we subdivide it into a grid of $K \times K$ cells. Each cell is responsible for predicting the probability p that a waypoint falls in that region, as well as its relative horizontal and vertical displacements with respect to the cell center $\Delta = (\Delta x, \Delta y)$. The displacements are defined in the range $[-1, +1]$ and represent a shift relative to half of the cell dimension, with -1 identifying the left/top borders and $+1$ the right/bottom ones. An example of prediction with its correspondent displacements is shown in Fig. 3. Given a prediction $\hat{p}_{out} = (\hat{x}_{out}, \hat{y}_{out})$ in the output reference frame, the waypoint coordinates in the input reference frame $\hat{p}_{in}$ can be reconstructed with the following equation:

$$\hat{p}_{in} = \hat{p}_{out}\, K + \frac{K}{2} + \Delta \frac{K}{2} \tag{1}$$

The waypoint estimation head maps the high-level features extracted with the backbone to the output space with a 1×1 convolution. The backbone compression factor 2^{R+1} corresponds to the grid dimension K. Therefore, the output tensor of the estimation branch has a dimension of $H/K \times W/K \times 3$. We apply a sigmoid activation to the probability output and a tanh activation to the displacement outputs. We optimize the network for the waypoint estimation task

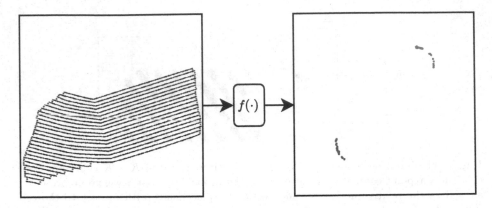

Fig. 4. In the latent space mapped by $f(\cdot)$, points of the same cluster appear closer together with respect to points of the other cluster. The mapping function $f(\cdot)$ is implemented with the backbone and the clustering head together. In this example, the latent space has a dimensionality $D = 2$.

with a weighted mean squared error loss. For each output cell $u_{i,j}$, the estimation loss is therefore computed as:

$$l_{i,j}^{\text{est}} = \mathbb{1}_{i,j}^{\text{wp}}\lambda\|u_{i,j} - \hat{u}_{i,j}\|_2 + (1 - \mathbb{1}_{i,j}^{\text{wp}})(1 - \lambda)\|u_{i,j} - \hat{u}_{i,j}\|_2 \tag{2}$$

where $\mathbb{1}_{i,j}^{\text{wp}} \in \{0, 1\}$ is an indicator Boolean function evaluating 1 if a waypoint is present in that cell, and λ is the relative constant that weights differently positive and negative cells.

At inference time, we get the list of predicted waypoints by considering all the cells with probability p over a certain threshold t_p. As in standard object detection methodologies, we also apply a suppression algorithm to decrease the number of redundant predictions that typically occur when multiple adjacent cells detect the same waypoint. The algorithm identifies all the groups of predictions with Euclidean distance within a certain threshold t_{sup} in the input reference frame. For each group, the point with highest confidence p is selected, while the remaining predictions are discarded.

2.3   Contrastive Clustering

Once the waypoints are detected, they should be assigned to starting or ending regions. This task can be seen as a simple binary classification, in which the labels represent the two clusters. However, in this scenario the actual assigned label is not relevant, as the only fundamental aspect is whether points of the same group are assigned the same label. The aim is to discriminate the points of the two regions without caring about which of them is classified as starting or ending. Indeed, an optimal path can be successfully planned regardless of the choice of the starting cluster. This invariance cannot be guaranteed by supervised classification.

For this reason, we model the clustering problem as a supervised representation learning process. Given the two sets of points $A = \{p \mid p \in \text{first cluster}\}$ and $B = \{p \mid p \in \text{second cluster}\}$, we want to find a non-linear mapping $f(\cdot)$ such that

$$d\big(f(p_i), f(p_j)\big) \ll d\big(f(p_i), f(p_k)\big) \quad \text{for} \quad p_i, p_j \in A \, , \, p_k \in B \tag{3}$$

and vice versa, where d is a distance measure. In the latent space mapped by $f(\cdot)$, points of different clusters are well-separated according to distance d. This means that a simple clustering method such as K-means [20] can successfully discriminate the two groups in the latent space, as shown in Fig. 4. Inspired by the contrastive framework used for unsupervised learning in [6], we select as distance metric d the inverse of the cosine similarity:

$$\text{sim}(u, v) = \frac{u^\top v}{\|u\|_2 \, \|v\|_2} \tag{4}$$

For each image, we consider the N ground-truth waypoints as independent samples. Given a point p_i, we consider as positive examples all the other $N/2 - 1$ points in the same cluster, and as negative examples the $N/2$ points of the other cluster. Therefore, we define the clustering loss contribution for the sample i as:

$$l_i^{\text{clus}} = \frac{1}{N-1} \sum_{\substack{j=1 \\ j \neq i}}^{N} \Bigg[\, \mathbb{1}_{\substack{p_i, p_j \in A \\ \vee \, p_i, p_j \in B}} \, \log\Big(\text{sig}\left(\text{sim}\left(f(p_i), f(p_j)\right)\right)\Big)$$

$$+ \left(1 - \mathbb{1}_{\substack{p_i, p_j \in A \\ \vee \, p_i, p_j \in B}}\right) \log\Big(1 - \text{sig}\left(\text{sim}\left(f(p_i), f(p_j)\right)\right)\Big) \Bigg] \tag{5}$$

where $\mathbb{1}_{\substack{p_i, p_j \in A \\ \vee \, p_i, p_j \in B}} \in \{0, 1\}$ is an indicator function evaluating 1 if p_i and p_j are in the same cluster and 0 otherwise, while 'sig' represents the sigmoid function. Basically, this loss computes the binary cross-entropy of the cosine similarity in the latent space mapped by $f(\cdot)$ for the pair (p_i, p_j). $f(\cdot)$ is optimized to push the cosine similarity towards the maximum $+1$ if the points are in the same cluster and towards the minimum -1 otherwise. The final loss is computed over all the pairs (i, j) as well as (j, i) for each input image. This loss can be seen as a variation of the one used in [6,26,37], but instead of N groups with 2 elements each, optimized with categorical cross-entropy and softmax, we have 2 groups with $N/2$ elements each, optimized with binary cross-entropy and sigmoid.

The mapping $f(\cdot)$ is modeled by the clustering head in the output space reference system. The head is composed of two convolutional layers with Mish activation and one final 1×1 convolution with linear activation. The output tensor of the clustering branch has a dimension of $H/K \times W/K \times D$, where D is the latent space dimensionality.

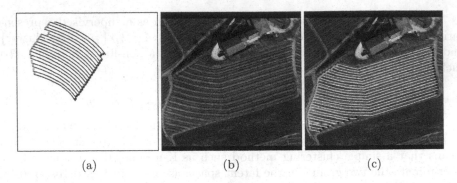

(a)   (b)   (c)

Fig. 5. Examples of curved occupancy grids: synthetic (a) and real-world from Google Maps satellite database without (b) and with (c) manual annotation. Red and blue points are the ground-truth waypoints divided in the two clusters. (Color figure online)

At inference time, for each waypoint detected in the estimation phase, we select the correspondent feature from the clustering head output. We can predict the clustering assignment by fitting a K-means predictor with two centroids on the selected features. Since we use the cosine similarity in the loss computation, we are optimizing the clustering in the normalized latent space. For this reason, the features should be divided by their Euclidean norm before clustering. This normalization decreases by one the latent space dimensionality, and therefore the minimum number of dimensions D for the clustering head is 2.

3   Experimental Setting

In this section, we present all the details of our experimentation. We describe the datasets used for network training and testing as well as the main hyperparameters adopted during the training phase.

3.1   Dataset Description

Considering the lack of open datasets of row crops bird-eye maps and the time required to manually annotate a large set of real images, we define a method to build realistic synthetic occupancy grids to train the model. We modify the method presented in [24] to extend it to both straight and curved occupancy grids. The generation process can be summarized as follows:

1. sample a uniformly random number of rows $n \in [10, 50]$ and angle $\alpha \in [-\pi/2, \pi/2]$;
2. generate row centers with a random inter-row distance, along the line perpendicular to α and passing through the image center;
3. generate random field borders and find starting and ending points for each row with orientation α;

4. to create curved maps, add a random displacement to the row centers and compute a quadratic Bézier curve with the starting, ending and center points as control points; this ensures that the curves are continuous and smooth;
5. generate the occupancy grid by drawing circles with random radius $r \in [1, 2]$ pixels to model irregularities in the row width
6. create random holes in the rows to emulate segmentation errors or missing plants;
7. compute the $N = 2n$ ground-truth waypoints as the mean points of the lines connecting the ending points of the rows with the adjacent ones.

To further increase variability, we randomly add displacement noise every time we sample a point coordinate during the generation process. We select $H = W = 800$ pixels as input dimension for all the generated images. To investigate the effect of including synthetic curved images in the training set, we randomly generate two independent datasets, one with straight rows only, the other with both straight and curved rows. Overall, each dataset contains 3000 images for training, 300 for validation, and 1000 for testing. In addition to the synthetic data, we manually annotate real row-based images of vineyards and orchards from Google Maps (100 straight and 50 curved). These satellite images are fundamental to test the ability of the network to generalize to real-world scenarios and to prove the effectiveness of the synthetic generation process. Figure 5 shows examples of both synthetic and manually-annotated images.

3.2 Network Training

To select the best hyperparameters, we perform a random search over a set of reasonable values. For all the convolutional layers, we set a kernel size of 5 and channel dimension $C = 16$. For the main block of the backbone, we set the number of residual reduction modules $R = 2$. Therefore, the backbone compression factor and output cell dimension is $K = 2^{(R+1)} = 8$. We set the clustering space dimensionality to $D = 3$. Thus, the output tensors have both a dimension of $100 \times 100 \times 3$. The resulting network is a lightweight model with less than 73,000 parameters. We select Adam [16] as optimizer with a constant learning rate of $\eta = 3e-4$ and batch size of 16. Experimentally, we find more effective to first train the estimation head and the backbone together with the loss of Eq. 2. We set the loss weight to $\lambda = 0.7$ to compensate for the high imbalance in the number of positive and negative cells and stabilize the training. We then freeze the backbone weights and train the clustering head only with the loss of Eq. 5. To highlight the challenge posed by curved scenarios, we independently train the model on both the straight and curved training sets. We train each model for a total of 200 epochs on an Nvidia 2080 Ti GPU using the TensorFlow 2 framework. To obtain significant statistics, we run each training session three times, so that the results can be described in terms of mean and standard deviation.

Table 1. Performance of waypoint estimation on both straight and curved test datasets. We first test the model on our synthetic datasets (Straight Synth, Curved Synth) and then validate the results on manually annotated occupancy grids obtained from real satellite images (Straight Real, Curved Real). For each test set, we compare the results of the model trained on straight rows with those obtained training on curved rows. We report the mean and standard deviation for the Average Precision AP_r, where r is the maximum accepted distance in pixels between predicted and ground-truth waypoints.

Test	Train	AP_2	AP_3	AP_4	AP_6	AP_8
Straight synth	Straight	0.6404 ± 0.0171	0.9284 ± 0.0088	0.9856 ± 0.0021	0.9991 ± 0.0001	0.9993 ± 0.0001
	Curved	0.5751 ± 0.0241	0.8921 ± 0.0107	0.9743 ± 0.0022	0.9979 ± 0.0001	0.9984 ± 0.0001
Straight real	Straight	0.5191 ± 0.0288	0.8155 ± 0.0109	0.9116 ± 0.0032	0.9482 ± 0.0017	0.9507 ± 0.0024
	Curved	0.4597 ± 0.0166	0.7634 ± 0.0076	0.8788 ± 0.0089	0.9391 ± 0.0052	0.9433 ± 0.0049
Curved synth	Straight	0.5143 ± 0.0193	0.8224 ± 0.0236	0.9232 ± 0.0166	0.9726 ± 0.0078	0.9768 ± 0.0065
	Curved	0.5664 ± 0.0226	0.876 ± 0.0066	0.9632 ± 0.0009	0.9937 ± 0.0006	0.9949 ± 0.0006
Curved real	Straight	0.4685 ± 0.0906	0.7110 ± 0.0625	0.8125 ± 0.0625	0.8802 ± 0.0374	0.8891 ± 0.0355
	Curved	0.5327 ± 0.0269	0.8010 ± 0.0095	0.8881 ± 0.0094	0.9333 ± 0.0026	0.9374 ± 0.0033

4   Results

In this section, we report and comment the main results regarding both waypoint detection and clustering. Visual examples are included as well, to give a qualitative idea of the performance of our model. We extensively test our approach on both straight and curved rows, including a final evaluation on real satellite data. All the related code is open source and available online[1].

4.1   Waypoint Estimation

As regards waypoint estimation, we use Average Precision (AP_r) as principal metric, considering different values of the range threshold r, such that a waypoint is considered correctly detected if its Euclidean position error in pixels is smaller than r. In this way, we can highlight the precision of the model at different levels of proximity. The AP is commonly used for evaluating object detection tasks [10,18] and is computed as the area-under-the-curve of the precision-recall plot obtained varying the confidence threshold t_p. The waypoint estimation results are reported in Table 1, where each value is detailed with its mean and standard deviation. All the tests are performed setting a waypoint suppression threshold equal to the minimum inter-row distance of the synthetic datasets, $t_{sup} = 8$ pixels.

The first important result is the model trained on curved crops being able to reach an AP_8 of about 94% on all four test scenarios. This achievement confirms the effectiveness of our model far beyond the synthetic training scenario, as real satellite data does not seem to create substantial performance drops (5.7% at worst). Looking at lower values of r, the synthetic-to-real gap rises to 11.5%,

---

[1] www.github.com/fsalv/ClusterWay.

Table 2. Performance of waypoint clustering on both straight and curved datasets, comparing our approach with K-means and the DBSCAN pipeline proposed by [24]. We first test models on our synthetic datasets (Straight Synth, Curved Synth) and then validate the results on real occupancy grids obtained from satellite images (Straight Real, Curved Real). For each test, we compare the results of models trained on straight rows with those obtained training on curved rows. We report the mean adjusted accuracy and clustering error with their standard deviations.

Test	Method	Train	Adjusted accuracy	Clustering error
Straight synth	K-means	Straight	**1.0000 ± 0**	**0 ± 0**
		Curved	0.9913 ± 0.0076	0.6667 ± 0.5774
	DBSCAN	Straight	**1.0000 ± 0**	**0 ± 0**
		Curved	0.9724 ± 0.0240	2.0000 ± 1.7321
	Ours	Straight	0.9994 ± 0.0003	0.0187 ± 0.0114
		Curved	0.9985 ± 0.0006	0.0527 ± 0.0219
Straight real	K-means	Straight	0.4243 ± 0.1037	26.3333 ± 7.0238
		Curved	0.4635 ± 0.0873	26.0000 ± 5.1962
	DBSCAN	Straight	0.9532 ± 0.0429	2.3333 ± 2.0817
		Curved	0.9585 ± 0.0026	2.0000 ± 0
	Ours	Straight	0.9707 ± 0.0135	1.0400 ± 0.5197
		Curved	**0.9716 ± 0.0123**	**0.7700 ± 0.3012**
Curved synth	K-means	Straight	0.9714 ± 0.0336	1.0000 ± 1.0000
		Curved	0.9885 ± 0.0199	0.3333 ± 0.5774
	DBSCAN	Straight	0.9563 ± 0.0757	1.3333 ± 2.3094
		Curved	0.8898 ± 0.0337	3.0000 ± 1.0000
	Ours	Straight	0.9823 ± 0.0138	0.3414 ± 0.3278
		Curved	**0.9992 ± 0.0006**	**0.0127 ± 0.0038**
Curved real	K-means	Straight	0.2443 ± 0.0984	73.3333 ± 29.2632
		Curved	0.2721 ± 0.1493	70.0000 ± 19.5192
	DBSCAN	Straight	0.7247 ± 0.2734	27.0000 ± 25.5343
		Curved	0.5181 ± 0.1061	45.3333 ± 6.6583
	Ours	Straight	0.8571 ± 0.0924	3.4667 ± 2.4437
		Curved	**0.9344 ± 0.0116**	**1.1933 ± 0.1858**

showing how the model is able to estimate synthetic waypoints with higher precision. The model trained on straight crops achieves excellent performance on its corresponding test set and even on real satellite data, but generalizes poorly on curved rows: the precision drop reaches 11% on AP_8 and even 22% considering AP_3. On the contrary, the model trained on curved crops scales very well on straight scenarios. This outcome confirms the importance of training on curved crops to obtain robust models able to cope with challenging situations.

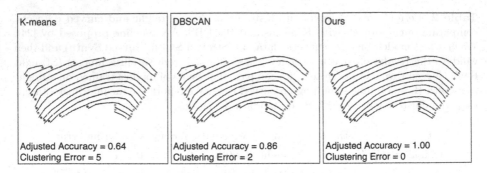

Fig. 6. Examples of clustering on a real-world curved sample: K-means and DBSCAN pipeline [24] are not able to correctly cluster the predicted waypoints; on the other hand, the proposed method correctly assigns the points.

4.2   Waypoint Clustering

As regards waypoint clustering, we adopt two separate metrics. The first is an adjusted binary accuracy, assigning a score of 0 to the worst outcome (all the points in the same cluster, meaning 50% of the points correctly clustered) and 1 to perfect clustering. However, the number of waypoints in a crop is variable and accuracy alone does not give an insight of the distribution of errors among different samples. For example, crops with a small number of waypoints tend to be easier to cluster than dense ones. Considering the fact that full-coverage path planning is possible only if every waypoint is correctly clustered, we add a clustering error metric computing the average number of wrongly labeled points per image. The results are detailed in Table 2. To have a baseline, we compare our approach with the K-means algorithm directly applied in the image reference system and the DBSCAN clustering with geometrical assignment approach proposed by [24]. All the clustering tests are performed setting the confidence threshold to $t_p = 0.4$ and the waypoint suppression threshold to $t_{sup} = 8$ pixels. As for the previous results, each value is reported with its mean and standard deviation.

Our methodology achieves remarkable results, outperforming or at least matching existing solutions in all the testing scenarios. In particular, both the training strategies (based on straight and curved crops) approach perfect clustering on the synthetic straight dataset and generalize well to real crops. On the contrary, K-means, which perfectly works for the well-separated synthetic samples, loses more than half of its adjusted accuracy and presents a very high clustering error when switching to real test rows, mainly due to the irregular shapes typical of real-world vineyards. The DBSCAN pipeline, instead, is able to generalize to straight satellite crops, since the methodology was specifically designed to cope with real-world straight rows.

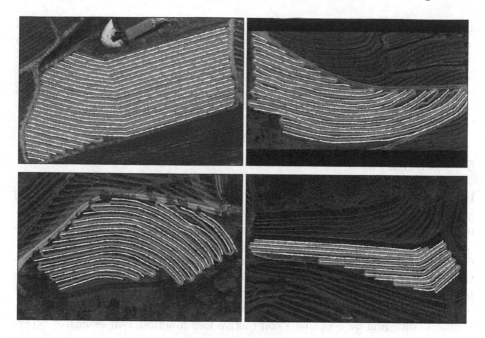

Fig. 7. Examples of full-coverage path planning in real-world curved vineyards taken from Google Maps satellite database.

As regards curved test sets, K-means clustering is totally unable to generalize to the real dataset. At the same time, also the DBSCAN pipeline results drop significantly when switching to real samples, due to its heavy dependence on angle estimation. Our model, trained on straight rows, obtains 0.98 adjusted accuracy and 0.34 clustering error on synthetic data, outperforming both the baselines. However, it struggles to generalize to real crops, reaching an adjusted accuracy of 0.86. On the other hand, the model trained on curved data outperforms the baselines in synthetic and real data, where it achieves an adjusted accuracy of 0.93. This result can be considered extremely positive, taking into account the strong challenges present in satellite data. In particular, a clustering error of 1.19 is remarkably smaller than those obtained by K-means and DBSCAN. In conclusion, these results confirm how the proposed methodology, combined with a well-devised generation process of curved synthetic samples, allows path planning even in challenging scenarios.

4.3 Qualitative Results

To give further insight into the performance of the proposed methodology, we present some qualitative examples on real-world curved samples. Figure 6 shows a comparison between the three clustering methodologies. K-means and the DBSCAN pipeline are clearly unable to correctly assign points in challenging scenarios. Finally, Fig. 7 shows some examples of full-coverage path planning.

The planning is performed by selecting the points in an A-B-B-A fashion and using the planner proposed by [5]. With geo-referenced maps, the planned path can be converted from the image reference system to a Global Navigation Satellite System (GNSS) reference frame to be used in real-world navigation. All the tests are performed with the model trained on the curved dataset and setting the confidence threshold to $t_p = 0.4$ and the waypoint suppression threshold to $t_{sup} = 8$ pixels.

5 Conclusions

In this work, we propose a novel solution for global path generation in row-based crops using deep learning and contrastive clustering. The problem of path planning in geometrically constrained environments such as vineyards and orchards has been solved through the identification of waypoints at the end of each row. Our deep learning model can simultaneously predict the position of navigation waypoints and cluster them in a unique feed-forward step. To this aim, we train the network on a synthetic dataset of top-view occupancy grids and test it on real-world satellite images, outperforming previous methodologies based on classical clustering by adopting a contrastive loss function. Our extensive experimentation demonstrates that this model successfully generalizes to challenging realistic conditions, including curved and incomplete rows.

Future works may seek the integration of the proposed waypoint generator in a complete pipeline for row-based vineyard and orchard navigation, composed of a first segmentation step to obtain the occupancy grid of the parcel from satellite or UAV imagery and a local planner for intra-row navigation.

Acknowledgements. This work has been developed with the contribution of the Politecnico di Torino Interdepartmental Centre for Service Robotics (PIC4SeR) and SmartData@Polito.

References

1. Aghi, D., Mazzia, V., Chiaberge, M.: Autonomous navigation in vineyards with deep learning at the edge. In: Zeghloul, S., Laribi, M.A., Sandoval Arevalo, J.S. (eds.) RAAD 2020. MMS, vol. 84, pp. 479–486. Springer, Cham (2020). https://doi.org/10.1007/978-3-030-48989-2_51
2. Aghi, D., Mazzia, V., Chiaberge, M.: Local motion planner for autonomous navigation in vineyards with a RGB-D camera-based algorithm and deep learning synergy. Machines 8(2), 27 (2020)
3. Astolfi, P., Gabrielli, A., Bascetta, L., Matteucci, M.: Vineyard autonomous navigation in the echord++ grape experiment. IFAC-PapersOnLine 51(11), 704–709 (2018)
4. Barawid, O.C., Jr., Mizushima, A., Ishii, K., Noguchi, N.: Development of an autonomous navigation system using a two-dimensional laser scanner in an orchard application. Biosyst. Eng. 96(2), 139–149 (2007)

5. Cerrato, S., Aghi, D., Mazzia, V., Salvetti, F., Chiaberge, M.: An adaptive row crops path generator with deep learning synergy. In: 2021 6th Asia-Pacific Conference on Intelligent Robot Systems (ACIRS), pp. 6–12. IEEE (2021)
6. Chen, T., Kornblith, S., Norouzi, M., Hinton, G.: A simple framework for contrastive learning of visual representations. In: International Conference on Machine Learning, pp. 1597–1607. PMLR (2020)
7. Comba, L., Biglia, A., Aimonino, D.R., Gay, P.: Unsupervised detection of vineyards by 3D point-cloud UAV photogrammetry for precision agriculture. Comput. Electron. Agric. **155**, 84–95 (2018)
8. Deshmukh, D., Pratihar, D.K., Deb, A.K., Ray, H., Bhattacharyya, N.: Design and development of intelligent pesticide spraying system for agricultural robot. In: Abraham, A., Hanne, T., Castillo, O., Gandhi, N., Nogueira Rios, T., Hong, T.-P. (eds.) HIS 2020. AISC, vol. 1375, pp. 157–170. Springer, Cham (2021). https://doi.org/10.1007/978-3-030-73050-5_16
9. Ester, M., Kriegel, H.P., Sander, J., Xu, X., et al.: A density-based algorithm for discovering clusters in large spatial databases with noise. In: KDD, vol. 96, pp. 226–231 (1996)
10. Everingham, M., Van Gool, L., Williams, C.K., Winn, J., Zisserman, A.: The pascal visual object classes (voc) challenge. Int. J. Comput. Vision **88**(2), 303–338 (2010)
11. Ferentinos, K.P.: Deep learning models for plant disease detection and diagnosis. Comput. Electron. Agric. **145**, 311–318 (2018)
12. Kamilaris, A., Kartakoullis, A., Prenafeta-Boldú, F.X.: A review on the practice of big data analysis in agriculture. Comput. Electron. Agric. **143**, 23–37 (2017)
13. Kamilaris, A., Prenafeta-Boldú, F.X.: Deep learning in agriculture: a survey. Comput. Electron. Agric. **147**, 70–90 (2018)
14. Kang, H., Zhou, H., Wang, X., Chen, C.: Real-time fruit recognition and grasping estimation for robotic apple harvesting. Sensors **20**(19), 5670 (2020)
15. Khaliq, A., Mazzia, V., Chiaberge, M.: Refining satellite imagery by using UAV imagery for vineyard environment: a CNN based approach. In: 2019 IEEE International Workshop on Metrology for Agriculture and Forestry (MetroAgriFor), pp. 25–29. IEEE (2019)
16. Kingma, D.P., Ba, J.: Adam: a method for stochastic optimization. arXiv preprint arXiv:1412.6980 (2014)
17. Lei, T., Luo, C., Jan, G., Bi, Z.: Deep learning-based complete coverage path planning with re-joint and obstacle fusion paradigm. Front. Robot. AI **9**, 843816 (2022). https://doi.org/10.3389/frobt
18. Lin, T.-Y., et al.: Microsoft COCO: common objects in context. In: Fleet, D., Pajdla, T., Schiele, B., Tuytelaars, T. (eds.) ECCV 2014. LNCS, vol. 8693, pp. 740–755. Springer, Cham (2014). https://doi.org/10.1007/978-3-319-10602-1_48
19. Luo, L., Tang, Y., Lu, Q., Chen, X., Zhang, P., Zou, X.: A vision methodology for harvesting robot to detect cutting points on peduncles of double overlapping grape clusters in a vineyard. Comput. Ind. **99**, 130–139 (2018)
20. MacQueen, J., et al.: Some methods for classification and analysis of multivariate observations. In: Proceedings of the Fifth Berkeley Symposium on Mathematical Statistics and Probability, Oakland, CA, USA, pp. 281–297 (1967)
21. Martini, M., Mazzia, V., Khaliq, A., Chiaberge, M.: Domain-adversarial training of self-attention-based networks for land cover classification using multi-temporal sentinel-2 satellite imagery. Remote Sens. **13**(13), 2564 (2021)
22. Mazzia, V., Comba, L., Khaliq, A., Chiaberge, M., Gay, P.: UAV and machine learning based refinement of a satellite-driven vegetation index for precision agriculture. Sensors **20**(9), 2530 (2020)

23. Mazzia, V., Khaliq, A., Salvetti, F., Chiaberge, M.: Real-time apple detection system using embedded systems with hardware accelerators: an edge AI application. IEEE Access **8**, 9102–9114 (2020)
24. Mazzia, V., Salvetti, F., Aghi, D., Chiaberge, M.: Deepway: a deep learning waypoint estimator for global path generation. Comput. Electron. Agric. **184**, 106091 (2021)
25. Mohanty, S.P., Hughes, D.P., Salathé, M.: Using deep learning for image-based plant disease detection. Front. Plant Sci. **7**, 1419 (2016)
26. Van den Oord, A., Li, Y., Vinyals, O., et al.: Representation learning with contrastive predictive coding, vol. 2, no. 3, p. 4. arXiv preprint arXiv:1807.03748 (2018)
27. Redmon, J., Divvala, S., Girshick, R., Farhadi, A.: You only look once: unified, real-time object detection. In: Proceedings of the IEEE Conference on Computer Vision and Pattern Recognition, pp. 779–788 (2016)
28. Riggio, G., Fantuzzi, C., Secchi, C.: A low-cost navigation strategy for yield estimation in vineyards. In: 2018 IEEE International Conference on Robotics and Automation (ICRA), pp. 2200–2205. IEEE (2018)
29. Ronneberger, O., Fischer, P., Brox, T.: U-Net: convolutional networks for biomedical image segmentation. In: Navab, N., Hornegger, J., Wells, W.M., Frangi, A.F. (eds.) MICCAI 2015. LNCS, vol. 9351, pp. 234–241. Springer, Cham (2015). https://doi.org/10.1007/978-3-319-24574-4_28
30. Sparrow, R., Howard, M.: Robots in agriculture: prospects, impacts, ethics, and policy. Prec. Agric. **22**(3), 818–833 (2021)
31. Tripicchio, P., Satler, M., Dabisias, G., Ruffaldi, E., Avizzano, C.A.: Towards smart farming and sustainable agriculture with drones. In: 2015 International Conference on Intelligent Environments, pp. 140–143. IEEE (2015)
32. Tschannen, M., Bachem, O., Lucic, M.: Recent advances in autoencoder-based representation learning. arXiv preprint arXiv:1812.05069 (2018)
33. Ünal, Z.: Smart farming becomes even smarter with deep learning-a bibliographical analysis. IEEE Access **8**, 105587–105609 (2020)
34. Vidović, I., Scitovski, R.: Center-based clustering for line detection and application to crop rows detection. Comput. Electron. Agric. **109**, 212–220 (2014)
35. Virlet, N., Sabermanesh, K., Sadeghi-Tehran, P., Hawkesford, M.J.: Field scanalyzer: an automated robotic field phenotyping platform for detailed crop monitoring. Funct. Plant Biol. **44**(1), 143–153 (2017)
36. Woo, S., Park, J., Lee, J.Y., So Kweon, I.: CBAM: convolutional block attention module. In: Proceedings of the European conference on computer vision (ECCV), pp. 3–19 (2018)
37. Wu, Z., Xiong, Y., Yu, S.X., Lin, D.: Unsupervised feature learning via nonparametric instance discrimination. In: Proceedings of the IEEE Conference on Computer Vision and Pattern Recognition, pp. 3733–3742 (2018)
38. Zhai, Z., Martínez, J.F., Beltran, V., Martínez, N.L.: Decision support systems for agriculture 4.0: survey and challenges. Comput. Electron. Agric. **170**, 105256 (2020)
39. Zoto, J., Musci, M.A., Khaliq, A., Chiaberge, M., Aicardi, I.: Automatic path planning for unmanned ground vehicle using UAV imagery. In: Berns, K., Görges, D. (eds.) RAAD 2019. AISC, vol. 980, pp. 223–230. Springer, Cham (2020). https://doi.org/10.1007/978-3-030-19648-6_26

Grasping Partially Occluded Objects Using Autoencoder-Based Point Cloud Inpainting

Alexander Koebler[1,5(✉)], Ralf Gross[5], Florian Buettner[1,2,3,4,5], and Ingo Thon[5]

[1] Department of Computer Science, Goethe University Frankfurt,
Frankfurt, Germany
[2] Department of Medicine, Goethe University Frankfurt, Frankfurt, Germany
[3] German Cancer Consortium, Frankfurt, Germany
[4] German Cancer Research Center Heidelberg, Heidelberg, Germany
[5] Siemens AG, Munich, Germany
{alexander.koebler,ralf.gross,buettner.florian,ingo.thon}@siemens.com

Abstract. Flexible industrial production systems will play a central role in the future of manufacturing due to higher product individualization and customization. A key component in such systems is the robotic grasping of known or unknown objects in random positions. Real-world applications often come with challenges that might not be considered in grasping solutions tested in simulation or lab settings. Partial occlusion of the target object is the most prominent. Examples of occlusion can be supporting structures in the camera's field of view, sensor imprecision, or parts occluding each other due to the production process. In all these cases, the resulting lack of information leads to shortcomings in calculating grasping points.

In this paper, we present an algorithm to reconstruct the missing information. Our inpainting solution facilitates the real-world utilization of robust object matching approaches for grasping point calculation. We demonstrate the benefit of our solution by enabling an existing grasping system embedded in a real-world industrial application to handle occlusions in the input. With our solution, we drastically decrease the number of objects discarded by the process.

Keywords: Autoencoder · Robotic grasping · Inpainting

1 Introduction

Recent research efforts are paving the way towards robotic grasping of randomly positioned known [10] or unknown objects [12,13], with the potential to substan-

---

F. Buettner—Work done for Siemens AG.

Supplementary Information The online version contains supplementary material available at https://doi.org/10.1007/978-3-031-26422-1_14.

tially increase the efficiency of many production processes. However, key challenges inhibiting the utilization of robot grasping in real-world production seem to receive limited attention in research so far. For example, in settings where not the entire target object is visible in the input scene, state-of-the-art approaches for unknown objects can only sample grasping points in sub-regions of the object captured by the vision system. Conventional object matching approaches for known objects are even more affected by the lack of information and might not be able to determine any grasping point. Missing parts of the object in the input lead to a decline in the accuracy of the used surface or feature matching algorithms [4]. Nevertheless, given complete input, conventional 3D object matching approaches have proven themselves in many real-world applications and offer a highly reliable calculation of grasping points. Their deterministic generation of the grasping points is often crucial for precise actions in pick and place applications. Thus, we aim to use machine learning (ML) to impute the missing information in the input such that robust conventional methods for grasping point detection can be used in more application areas. Most often, the cause for missing information in the input data is the partial occlusion of the target object during the recording phase. A simple remedy is re-scanning the input scene after removing the cause of the occlusion. However, in many real-world applications, re-scanning is either undesirable as it usually causes an unproductive process prolongation or might even be impossible due to existing process constraints.

In industrial applications, 3D models of the processed objects are commonly available as computer-aided design (CAD) models created in the own or the suppliers' product design process. In addition to their use in object matching approaches, these models can be utilized in combination with a simulation environment to generate a synthetic dataset. In this work, we propose to use such generated data to train an auxiliary autoencoder to inpaint occluded areas of objects for robotic grasping. Our approach drastically reduces the impact on the downtime of the real-world assembly machine during the design and training phase.

Our main contribution consists of the development and real-world demonstration of a novel algorithm to recover occluded object information in robotic grasping settings. This method enables the usage of established object matching algorithms for stable grasping point calculation without re-scanning the product or redesigning the production process.

We make the following technical contributions:

- We introduce a new algorithm to process unordered single-view point cloud data generated by an industrial laser scanner with 2D convolutional networks.
- We evaluate the use of style- and perceptual loss functions [9,11] for autoencoder-based inpainting networks in the context of robotic grasping.
- We demonstrate how we bridge the gap between training the model on simulated data and deploying it in the real world.

2   Related Work

Our work combines the two research areas of robotic grasping and machine learning-based inpainting. To our knowledge, there are only a few approaches [29] towards this combination. Therefore, we will first introduce current methods for robotic grasping and discuss their robustness to occlusions in the input. Afterward, we will briefly introduce ML-based image inpainting and the issues associated with transferring those methods to point cloud data.

Robustness of Grasping Algorithms to Occlusions: Data-driven methods to determine grasping points vary widely in terms of their build-in robustness to missing information in the input scene.

Known approaches can be distinguished by the required knowledge about the objects that should be grasped [2]. If the exact object shape is known, common solutions rely on manually labeling optimal grasping points for specific objects. This can, for example, be done with the help of CAD models. The 3D models of the objects and thereby the predetermined grasping points can then be matched to input point clouds by various conventional algorithms or a combination of them [4]. Examples include relying on a subset of the points as features such as RANSAC [6] or the entirety of the point cloud such as ICP [20]. These matching algorithms are heavily affected by missing information in the input point cloud with respect to the object of interest since this can cause a lack of matching key features between the recorded point cloud and the available 3D models. This issue has motivated research efforts towards increasing the robustness of those methods to occlusions and cluttered environments [16,17] as well as the development of more recent ML-based pose estimation methods [23].

Recent approaches for handling unknown objects select grasping point candidates on the visible areas based on local attributes and subsequently classify the most promising grasping point by a trained ML model [12,13]. Although these methods might be more robust in the case of cluttered and occluded scenes, they lack the robustness of conventional matching algorithms in non-occluded cases. For example, they do not generate deterministic grasping points for known objects. Those, however, are required for subsequent processing steps, such as the precise placing of known objects.

Inpainting Approaches for Point Clouds: Our solution aims to enhance existing object matching solutions by an auxiliary autoencoder-based inpainting step. This preprocessing step ensures that an object's complete shape is present in the point cloud.

The reconstruction of missing information in natural images or videos is a well-researched task relying on ML- [11,24] and non-learning-based inpainting [3].

Per-pixel reconstruction loss functions such as mean-squared-error (MSE) or mean-average-error (MAE) in the ML-based inpainting methods often do not satisfy the complicated semantic structure of the images. Thus, [9] utilizes a loss network trained on a supervised classification task to evaluate high-level abstractions of the reconstructed image. By using autoencoder architectures for super-resolution and style-transfer [9] as well as for inpainting [11,24] of natural images, these loss terms resulted in significant improvements in the removal of image artifacts and in the visual perception of the results. Other approaches [8,28] use additional adversarial loss functions, which are inspired by generative adversarial networks (GANs) [7], to include higher-level abstractions in the reconstruction objective.

Using generative models for unordered 3D point clouds instead of images is a less researched field [14,26]. The non-equidistant grid and irregular format of the recorded point clouds do not allow for directly applying convolutional neural networks (CNNs) [18], which are often used in vision use-cases. The authors in [30] are concerned with reconstructing small holes in point clouds rather caused by noise than by occlusions. This does not satisfy our requirement of reconstructing significant coherent portions of more than 80% of the object point cloud.

3   Problem Description

In the context of a real-world assembly machine that includes a grasping application, we face the following problem: During the process, pairs of associated objects drop onto a conveyor belt. The objects have a size of about 30 mm × 25 mm and form the front and back parts of the assembled product. The objects are transported towards a robot arm and should subsequently be grasped with a suction gripper. For this purpose, a laser scanner prior to the robot arm scans the objects on the conveyor belt as they pass through the beam. Re-scanning the scene after the execution of a grasping process is not viable. It would require a time-consuming retraction of the conveyor belt to pass the object through the laser beam repeatably. The laser scanner generates unordered point clouds from a single point of view. The geometry of the objects is known, and a system capable of determining appropriate grasping points on the objects is in place. In the following, this system will be referred to as the perception system. The perception system uses a surface-based 3D matching algorithm and predefined deterministic grasping points for the known objects. The system works reliably if the laser scanner captures the entire geometry of the target objects.

When the objects drop on the conveyor belt, they can end up laying upon each other. Thus in some cases, one object partly occludes the other one. The resulting degree of occlusion is random and varies widely. The perception system can not determine grasping points for a large majority of occurring occlusions.

Our objective, shown in Fig. 1, is to develop a solution to reconstruct the missing parts of the lower object after the scanning process. The reconstruction quality of object parts must be sufficient for the subsequent surface-matching algorithm to match the object with acceptable accuracy. The perception system requires well-restored key features of the objects, such as edges and corners. These are often not sufficiently captured by common reconstruction metrics such as the MSE or the MAE. For this reason, we evaluate the reconstruction quality in a task-specific manner. Our final evaluation criterion for the overall system is the rate of successful grasps in the case of occlusions. In addition, a visual inspection of the reconstruction can offer an estimation of its quality and the later gasping success rate.

The event that objects occlude each other in the input scene is frequent enough that it causes a significant amount of discarded objects. However, gathering a huge dataset for training a reconstruction model would require a long-term operation of the production machine in a sub-optimal state. Therefore, the amount of available real-world data is limited. Furthermore, collecting the point cloud of the non-occluded lower object in the same pose and orientation in the regular process is not possible. This is because the scanning of the input scene and the grasping of the robot are locally separated. Moreover, after the robot grasped the top object, re-scanning the scene with the no more occluded lower object would not yield the ground truth for the previously occluded object but a scan of the now isolated object after the robot operation or the conveyor retraction potentially impacted its positioning.

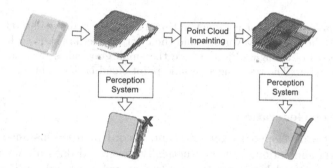

Fig. 1. Investigated problem setting for point cloud inpainting. As shown on the left, the laser scanner can only capture a small portion of the geometry of the occluded object. This is insufficient for the 3D matching algorithm that calculates the grasping points. Our inpainting solution outputs the complete point cloud on the right with the reconstructed lower object. With that, the surface-based matching algorithm can estimate the pose and orientation of both objects and determine corresponding grasping points.

4 Methodology

We propose using a processing pipeline including an autoencoder-based inpainting step to reconstruct missing information in partially occluded point clouds. In this section, we will elaborate on the components of the pipeline and substantiate our design decisions.

The scanned scene's height with two objects is less than 15 mm, even if the objects fall on top of each other. This results in only small deviations in the height-dependent spacing of the grid generated by the scanner. Thus, we consider the information loss by interpolating the point clouds to an equidistant grid in the (x, y)-coordinates as negligible. The representation of the object on an equidistant grid allows for using regular image processing approaches such as CNNs. Thus, we can circumvent the use of more complicated methods that can handle unordered point clouds on non-equidistant grids [18]. In our case, the considered objects are relatively simple, with only a few defining structures that must be preserved. For this reason, we decided on an autoencoder U-Net architecture [19] for the image inpainting process.

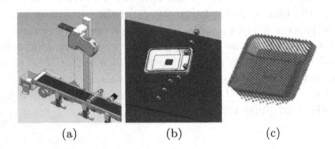

(a)   (b)   (c)

Fig. 2. Simulation environment for generating a synthetic training dataset of occluded scenes. In (a), the green conveyor belt and the laser scanner are shown. (b) depicts the scanning process of a single object, where the small grey cubes illustrate the beams of the laser scanner. The resulting synthetic point cloud is shown in (c). (Color figure online)

4.1 Dataset Generation

A method was developed to generate and record realistic instances of object occlusions via simulation. This synthetically generated data allows us to train the autoencoder model without the need to record a ground truth point cloud of the complete lower object in the real process. The considered machine was already available as a digital twin in a product lifecycle management software with an integrated simulation toolkit. The relevant components shown in Fig. 2, consisting of the conveyor belt, the laser scanner, and the product objects, could be utilized to generate the training dataset. During the simulation, the objects are placed upon each other in random relative positions within a predefined design space. The integrated physics simulation subsequently causes objects to fall into physically valid positions. This allows for realistic occlusion patterns. The dataset is generated by recording the scene where both objects are present, and parts of the lower object are hidden from the scanner's view. Afterward, the top object is removed and the scene only consisting of the lower object is re-scanned, generating a ground truth point cloud of the complete lower object in the corresponding pose. Furthermore, an assignment between points and objects is generated for the point cloud with both objects.

4.2 Data Processing Pipeline

We aimed to simplify the inpainting task and thereby reduce the performance gap we have to cross when we deploy our solution solely trained in simulation to the real-world process. Hence, we split the overall task into multiple simpler sub-tasks, which results in the processing pipeline depicted in Fig. 3.

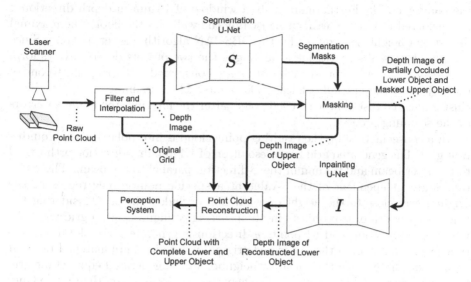

Fig. 3. Data processing pipeline with resulting in- and outputs of the deployed point cloud inpainting solution

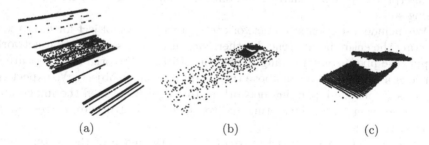

(a)   (b)   (c)

Fig. 4. Filtering steps for the real point clouds. The laser scanner captures different forms of noise and distractions in the raw input point cloud (a), such as the floor on the lower right and the wall on the left side. After cropping the distractions from the recorded view, sparse noise on the conveyor belt is left (b). By removing the sparse noise, only the dense clusters of the objects themselves remain (c).

The in Fig. 4 depicted point clouds recorded by the real laser scanner suffer from two kinds of noise. We apply predefined cropping windows to remove dense clusters from the point cloud that are caused by the conveyor rails, the floor, or the wall. The remaining noise after this step appears sparsely spread. Therefore, a clustering algorithm is used to remove points that do not correspond to the dense clusters formed by the objects. We use the DBSCAN algorithm [5] for this purpose. The required parameters for the filtering operations are tuned manually on a small amount of real input point clouds. The cropping boundaries in the x-direction orthogonal to the conveyor are set to a frame of 92 mm to remove the conveyor rails. Furthermore, only a window of 18 mm in depth direction z is considered to remove artifacts caused by the wall and the floor. The maximal distance of neighboring points for the DBSCAN algorithm is set to 4 mm. Since the top objects often protrude at an angle, the two objects do not always form one coherent cluster. Found sub-clusters are considered to correspond to one of the objects if they include at least 500 points. The remaining complete object cluster must consist of at least 6000 points after the filtering step to detect errors in the scanning process.

In a consecutive step, the resulting point cloud is interpolated to an equidistant grid. The generated grid has a resolution of 1.1 mm in y-direction orthogonal to the laser beam and 0.3 mm in the x-direction parallel to the beam. These distances are independent of the z-value at a specific point. They represent the original grid close to the height of a flat non-occluded object. Considering the height and width of two objects in all occurring configurations, a grid with 256 points in x-direction and 64 points y-direction is generated. For the interpolation step, the points in the unordered original point cloud are matched by their (x, y)-coordinates with their nearest-neighbor in the generated equidistant grid by using a k-d-tree algorithm [1]. The generated pairs between the (x, y)-values of the original and the equidistant grid are subsequently used to interpolate the z-values for the point cloud on the equidistant grid. The resulting point clouds are interpreted as depth images, and only the z-values are used for further processing steps.

We include a segmentation network to extract the top object for later reconstructing the entire input scene. Furthermore, using the segmentation network's output, the pixels corresponding to the top object in the original image are set to a constant value of 15 mm above the height of a single object. We expect this step to support the inpainting network to distinguish between the image areas that are relevant for the inpainting and to identify the structures corresponding to the lower object.

After the inpainting model outputs the depth image of the reconstructed lower object, a post-processing step is necessary to recombine the entire point cloud.

The pixels in the output depth image that correspond to the occluded object and not to the background or interpolation artifacts are identified by a dynamic thresholding algorithm [15]. The top object segmented from the original depth image and the reconstructed lower object are subsequently mapped back to the original non-equidistant grid. For this purpose, the pixel-to-position mapping generated by the k-d-tree in the interpolation step is reused. The resulting point cloud can further on be processed by the perception system.

4.3 Segmentation

For the segmentation task, a commonly used approach is utilized and implemented based on [27]. For the segmentation network we decided for a U-Net architecture with an EfficientNetB2-backbone model [22]. For training, we only use synthetic point clouds. The depth image of the scene where parts of the lower object are occluded is provided as input. The labels are the simulated point-to-object assignments that are also mapped to the generated equidistant grid. This results in 2D segmentation maps with the three categories: top object, occluded object, and background.

4.4 Inpainting

We also used a U-Net architecture with a VGG16-like [21] backbone for the inpainting model. Especially if significant parts of key features such as edges or corners are occluded and missing in the reconstruction, we assume that simple per-pixel loss functions such as MSE do not capture those differences sufficiently. However, these features are essential for the perception system's 3D matching algorithm. Thus, we have evaluated the style and perceptual loss functions applied for super-resolution and style-transfer in [9] and image inpainting in [11].

The proposed loss function relies on high-level intermediate representations extracted from a pretrained loss-network in addition to a per-pixel difference in the input space. In contrast to [9, 11] we do not apply these losses to natural images similar to common public datasets. Thus, for our loss-network, we can not use a model that is trained on a supervised classification task on a dataset such as ImageNet.

For this reason, we train our VGG16 loss-network as an autoencoder in an unsupervised manner. The autoencoder is trained such that the input and the expected output are the synthetic depth images of the ground truth lower object. The unsupervised task does not necessarily result in relevant features for a classification task. However, we expect the bottleneck to capture coherent high-level features of the object, such as edges and corners. Those features should then be represented by the intermediate representations generated by the network.

As shown in Fig. 5, the representations ψ_p^X used in the style and perceptual loss are the output of the max-pooling layers. In particular, the first four convolutional blocks p of the VGG16 loss-network are used. The perceptual loss is the sum of the norm of the difference of the first four intermediate representations for the ground truth image X_{gt} and the by the inpainting network generated image X_{out}:

$$\mathcal{L}_{perceptual} = \sum_{p=1}^{P} ||\psi_p^{X_{out}} - \psi_p^{X_{gt}}||_1 \cdot \frac{1}{C_p H_p W_p} \tag{1}$$

The feature maps ψ_p^X are of size $C_p \times H_p \times W_p$.

For the style loss, the auto-correlation matrix of the representations is calculated first. The norm of the resulting gram matrices of size $C_p \times C_p$ is normalized by the size of the feature maps

$$\mathcal{L}_{style} = \sum_{p=1}^{P} \frac{1}{C_p C_p} \cdot ||\frac{1}{C_p H_p W_p} \cdot ((\psi_p^{X_{out}})^T \cdot (\psi_p^{X_{out}}) - (\psi_p^{X_{gt}})^T \cdot (\psi_p^{X_{gt}}))||_1. \tag{2}$$

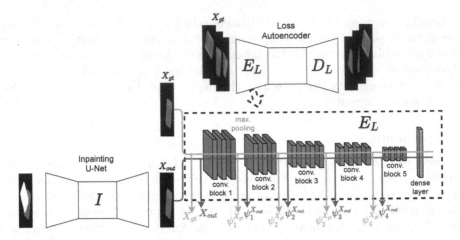

Fig. 5. Training architecture for the inpainting model using a VGG16 loss-network. The loss-network E_L is trained unsupervised by learning equivalence on the depth image of the complete lower object. The inpainting model I is trained to reconstruct the complete lower object from the depth image, including the masked top object and the partially occluded lower object. The intermediate representations of the ground truth image $\psi_p^{X_{gt}}$ and the reconstructed image $\psi_p^{X_{out}}$ for the style and perceptual loss are taken after the first four convolutional blocks.

During our experiments we considered this loss with and without the normalization factor of $\frac{1}{C_p C_p}$. As in [11] and different to [9] we have used the L_1-norm in the style and perceptual loss terms and the per-pixel loss component

$$\mathcal{L}_{pixel} = \frac{1}{CHW} \cdot ||X_{out} - X_{gt}||_1. \tag{3}$$

If we normalize the perceptual loss by the size of the feature maps and the style loss by the size of the gram-matrix, we also have to normalize the per-pixel loss term by the size of the image in input space $C \times H \times W$ to keep all terms in the same order of magnitude. The combined perceptual and style-based loss (PSBL) results as:

$$\mathcal{L}_{psbl} = \mathcal{L}_{pixel} + \alpha \mathcal{L}_{perceptual} + \beta \mathcal{L}_{style} \tag{4}$$

The weight of the perceptual and style loss is determined by the hyperparameters α and β, respectively.

5   Experiments

In the experiments section, we want to focus on the performance of the inpainting network before we end with a performance analysis of the entire pipeline on the real machine.

5.1 Training Procedure

We first pretrain all models with MSE loss for 200 epochs to establish a proper initialization of the network weights. Subsequently, we fine-tune the models for the same amount of epochs on the evaluated loss functions. We use an Adam optimizer and a learning rate of 0.0001 for both training phases.

The loss-network is trained for 300 epochs with MSE loss. The bottleneck dimension for the autoencoder-based unsupervised pretraining is set to 16. This value is empirically set so that the autoencoder can still learn sufficient equality but must learn high-level abstractions to handle the narrow bottleneck at the same time.

The generated synthetic dataset consists of 21 000 examples. It is split into 16 800 training samples and 4 200 test samples. Of the 16 800 training samples 3 360 are used as a validation set to find the best checkpoint based on the peak signal-to-noise ratio (PSNR) during training. This results in an actual training dataset of 13 440 samples.

5.2 Sensitivity to Initialization

We receive very unstable results for training the models from scratch with random initialization. In case of a training collapse, the model's outputs converge within the first ten epochs to an empty image which can easily be detected programmatically. For the different losses, this happens for a different subset of random seeds. When we evaluate using the same 25 random seeds, the models trained with MAE loss collapse in 80% of the time, with MSE loss in 50%, with PSBL loss without normalization in 60%, and with layer-wise loss normalization in 80%, we assume this is due to the high ratio of empty background in most images. If the models are initialized by pretraining on MSE, they do not collapse using other losses during the fine-tuning step.

5.3 Performance on Synthetic Data

In this section, we will compare the performance of the models trained on MSE, MAE, and the PSBL loss. $\mathcal{L}_{psbl}$ is evaluated with and without the per-layer normalization. The parameters α and β are determined by random search in the range $[0.1, 1000]$, optimizing for the best PSNR on the evaluation set. With and without normalization, the best loss function is given by:

$$\mathcal{L}_{psbl} = \mathcal{L}_{pixel} + 0.715\mathcal{L}_{perceptual} + 6.21\mathcal{L}_{style} \tag{5}$$

The visual comparison of the models' outputs in Fig. 6 shows that the reconstruction on synthetic point clouds is sufficient for all loss functions. However, the performance of the models trained solely with MSE loss is worse than the others, followed by the performance of the model with PSBL loss and layer-wise loss normalization. MAE and PSBL loss without normalization generate very similar results. The lack in performance by the models with MSE loss is also

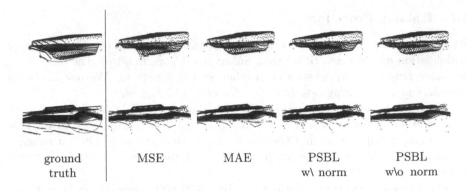

| | ground
truth | MSE | MAE | PSBL
w\ norm | PSBL
w\o norm |

Fig. 6. Examples for the reconstruction performance of models trained on different losses on synthetic point clouds if significant parts of key features are occluded. The first column shows the ground truth point clouds from the same view. The key features are marked with a red circle. The visual performance on the synthetic images is very similar for all losses. The model trained with MSE loss shows small artifacts, e.g., on the lower left side of the upper example. The model with the normalized loss function lacks behind its counterpart without normalization regarding the ramp-like edge in the bottom example, which is flatter compared to the ground truth. The best visual reconstruction is given by the models trained with the MAE and the PSBL loss function without normalization. (Color figure online)

Table 1. Comparison of the performance of the models trained with different loss functions evaluated on per-pixel metrics. The table shows the mean and variance using different random seeds. The models trained on MAE and MSE loss generate the best performance on the corresponding metric. The best mean PSNR is achieved with the model trained on the PSBL loss with layer-wise loss-normalization. The best SSIM index is achieved by the model trained with PSBL without layer-wise loss-normalization.

	MSE	MAE	PSBL w\ norm	PSBL w\ o norm
MSE	**7.63e-4 ± 1.6e-10**	7.84e-4 ± 1.9e-10	7.68e-4 ± 2.0e-12	7.69e-4 ± 1.9e-10
MAE	3.93e-3 ± 3.3e-7	**3.16e-3 ± 2.9e-11**	3.78e-3 ± 2.1e-7	3.2e-3 ± 7.5e-9
PSNR	33.11 ± 2.0e-3	32.94 ± 7.5e-3	**33.14 ± 3.8e-3**	33.13 ± 9.8e-3
SSIM	0.958 ± 2.5e-5	**0.963 ± 6.4e-6**	0.961 ± 5.8e-6	**0.963 ± 4.1e-7**

captured by the per-pixel metrics in Table 1. The visually perceived lower reconstruction quality of the model trained with PSBL loss with normalization is only indicated by the structural similarity (SSIM) index [25]. The per-pixel metrics lack expressiveness as an evaluation metric. However, these are the most suitable options for preselecting the best hyperparameters and model checkpoints with reasonable effort. We decided to optimize our setup based on the PSNR.

5.4   Performance on Real Data

For the evaluation on the real data, no ground truth point clouds of the complete lower objects in the proper position exist. For this reason, the per-pixel metrics can not be evaluated. In Fig. 7 we show visual examples of the reconstruction performance of the different models on real point clouds. The reconstruction errors and performance differences are more significant than those on the synthetic data.

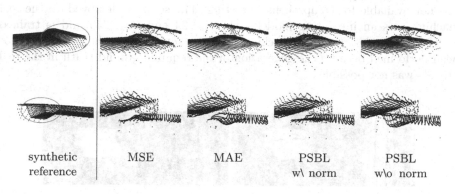

| synthetic reference | MSE | MAE | PSBL w\ norm | PSBL w\o norm |

Fig. 7. Examples for the reconstruction performance of models trained on different losses on real point clouds if significant parts of key features are occluded. The first column shows synthetic reference point clouds of the lower object. The key features are marked with a red circle. The reference point clouds are generated by manually positioning a synthetic object. The model trained with MSE loss performs worth in reconstructing the marked key features in both shown examples. Especially in the lower example, the quality of the reconstruction of the model with PSBL loss without normalization outperforms the one with normalization. (Color figure online)

Although the models trained with MAE loss and with PSBL loss without normalization have a very similar SSIM index on synthetic images, the latter significantly outperforms the other models in the visual reconstruction quality of the occluded features on real examples with severe occlusions. This difference is expected to impact the capability of the perception system to match the 3D objects. This directly transfers to the success rate for the calculation of the grasping points and, finally, the grasping process. The performance on most simpler examples with less severe occlusion is good for all models.

5.5   Performance of the Pipeline on the Real Process

We deployed our solution consisting of the processing pipeline and the models for segmentation and inpainting to the real process. This enabled the grasping application to also pick objects in configurations such as shown in Fig. 8 that would previously be discarded. The deployed version is tested on 100 grasping trials with varying occlusions. The occlusions are manually created by placing one object upon the other in random configurations. In 76% of the examples both objects could be grasped successfully. This shows that we can reduce the amount of discarded objects by 76%, thereby drastically increasing the efficiency of the process. The errors in the remaining 24% are distributed across all components, mainly the segmentation model, the inpainting model, and the matching algorithm. We observed that the matching algorithm produces most errors if the surfaces of the reconstructed object and the top object are very close. This happens if the upper object does not stand out at an angle. The real machine was not available for comprehensive testing. The solution deployed on the real machine uses an inpainting model with $\alpha = 24$ and $\beta = 240$ and is trained on 16 800 samples. Detailed tracking of the exact cause of the errors has not been performed because the generation of the required ground truth in the real process was not possible.

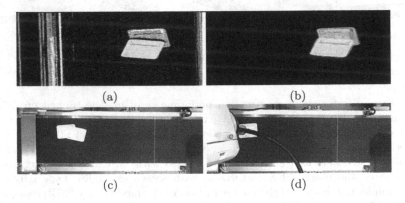

(a)   (b)

(c)   (d)

Fig. 8. Our solution deployed on the real machine. (a) shows the output of the perception system before the inpainting is executed. In this case, only the yellow 3D shape of the top object is matched. The process detects this and our inpainting solution is triggered and executed. Our pipeline returns the inpainted point cloud (b), where both 3D shapes can be matched. (c) shows the overlapping objects on the conveyor belt. In (d), the grasping process of the lower object is illustrated after matching both objects successfully. (Color figure online)

6   Conclusion

Conventional real-world grasping applications often face shortcomings if very strict requirements are not met. With the discussed solution, we could solve one of these shortcomings by inpainting missing information caused by occlusions in single-view point clouds. We developed an auxiliary autoencoder model and a sophisticated data processing pipeline. By reducing the task complexity, we could train our model solely on synthetic data. The deployed solution achieved to pick 76% of otherwise discarded objects in a real-world process.

We see many opportunities for facilitating well-established applications in manufacturing environments using ML to handle cases they currently fall short. At the same time, one could still rely on the tested performance of the established methods in those cases where they already work reliably.

Acknowledgements. We would like to thank Robert Schmeisser, Harald Funk, and all associated colleagues for making the project possible. We are especially grateful to them for setting up the simulation and helping deploy the solution on a real machine.

References

1. Bentley, J.L.: Multidimensional binary search trees used for associative searching. Commun. ACM. **18**(9), 509–517 (1975). https://doi.org/10.1145/361002.361007
2. Bohg, J., Morales, A., Asfour, T., Kragic, D.: Data-driven grasp synthesis-a survey. IEEE Trans. Rob. **30**(2), 289–309 (2013)
3. Criminisi, A., Perez, P., Toyama, K.: Region filling and object removal by exemplar-based image inpainting. IEEE Trans. Image Process. **13**(9), 1200–1212 (2004). https://doi.org/10.1109/TIP.2004.833105
4. Dantanarayana, H.G., Huntley, J.M.: Object recognition and localization from 3D point clouds by maximum-likelihood estimation. R. Soc. Open Sci. 4(8), 160693 (2017). https://doi.org/10.1098/rsos.160693
5. Ester, M., Kriegel, H.P., Sander, J., Xu, X.: A density-based algorithm for discovering clusters in large spatial databases with noise. In: Proceedings of the Second International Conference on Knowledge Discovery and Data Mining, pp. 226–231. KDD 1996, AAAI Press, Portland, Oregon (1996)
6. Fischler, M.A., Bolles, R.C.: Random sample consensus: a paradigm for model fitting with applications to image analysis and automated cartography. Commun. ACM **24**(6), 381–395 (1981). https://doi.org/10.1145/358669.358692
7. Goodfellow, I., et al.: Generative adversarial nets. In: Advances in Neural Information Processing Systems, vol. 27 (2014)
8. Iizuka, S., Simo-Serra, E., Ishikawa, H.: Globally and locally consistent image completion. ACM Trans. Graph. **36**(4), 1–14 (2017). https://doi.org/10.1145/3072959. 3073659
9. Johnson, J., Alahi, A., Fei-Fei, L.: Perceptual losses for real-time style transfer and super-resolution. In: Leibe, B., Matas, J., Sebe, N., Welling, M. (eds.) ECCV 2016. LNCS, vol. 9906, pp. 694–711. Springer, Cham (2016). https://doi.org/10. 1007/978-3-319-46475-6_43
10. Li, Y., Saut, J.P., Cortés, J., Siméon, T., Sidobre, D.: Finding enveloping grasps by matching continuous surfaces. In: 2011 IEEE International Conference on Robotics and Automation, pp. 2825–2830 (2011). https://doi.org/10.1109/ICRA. 2011.5979614
11. Liu, G., Reda, F.A., Shih, K.J., Wang, T.-C., Tao, A., Catanzaro, B.: Image inpainting for irregular holes using partial convolutions. In: Ferrari, V., Hebert, M., Sminchisescu, C., Weiss, Y. (eds.) ECCV 2018. LNCS, vol. 11215, pp. 89–105. Springer, Cham (2018). https://doi.org/10.1007/978-3-030-01252-6_6
12. Mahler, J., et al.: Dex-net 2.0: Deep learning to plan robust grasps with synthetic point clouds and analytic grasp metrics. arXiv preprint arXiv:1703.09312 (2017)

13. Mahler, J., Matl, M., Liu, X., Li, A., Gealy, D., Goldberg, K.: Dex-net 3.0: Computing robust vacuum suction grasp targets in point clouds using a new analytic model and deep learning. In: 2018 IEEE International Conference on robotics and automation (ICRA), pp. 5620–5627. IEEE (2018)

14. Mandikal, P., Radhakrishnan, V.B.: Dense 3d point cloud reconstruction using a deep pyramid network. In: 2019 IEEE Winter Conference on Applications of Computer Vision (WACV), pp. 1052–1060. IEEE (2019)

15. Otsu, N.: A threshold selection method from gray-level histograms. IEEE Trans. Syst. Man Cybern. **9**(1), 62–66 (1979). https://doi.org/10.1109/TSMC.1979.4310076

16. Papazov, C., Burschka, D.: An efficient RANSAC for 3D object recognition in noisy and occluded scenes. In: Kimmel, R., Klette, R., Sugimoto, A. (eds.) ACCV 2010. LNCS, vol. 6492, pp. 135–148. Springer, Heidelberg (2011). https://doi.org/10.1007/978-3-642-19315-6_11

17. Papazov, C., Haddadin, S., Parusel, S., Krieger, K., Burschka, D.: Rigid 3d geometry matching for grasping of known objects in cluttered scenes. The International Journal of Robotics Research **31**(4), 538–553 (2012)

18. Qi, C.R., Su, H., Mo, K., Guibas, L.J.: Pointnet: deep learning on point sets for 3d classification and segmentation. In: Proceedings of the IEEE Conference on Computer Vision and Pattern Recognition, pp. 652–660 (2017)

19. Ronneberger, O., Fischer, P., Brox, T.: U-net: convolutional networks for biomedical image segmentation. In: Navab, N., Hornegger, J., Wells, W.M., Frangi, A.F. (eds.) MICCAI 2015. LNCS, vol. 9351, pp. 234–241. Springer, Cham (2015). https://doi.org/10.1007/978-3-319-24574-4_28

20. Schoenemann, P.H.: A generalized solution of the orthogonal procrustes problem. Psychometrika **31**(1), 1–10 (1966). https://doi.org/10.1007/BF02289451

21. Simonyan, K., Zisserman, A.: Very deep convolutional networks for large-scale image recognition. arXiv preprint arXiv:1409.1556 (2014)

22. Tan, M., Le, Q.: EfficientNet: rethinking model scaling for convolutional neural networks. In: International Conference on Machine Learning, pp. 6105–6114. PMLR (2019)

23. Thalhammer, S., Patten, T., Vincze, M.: SyDPose: object detection and pose estimation in cluttered real-world depth images trained using only synthetic data. In: 2019 International Conference on 3D Vision (3DV), pp. 106–115 (2019). https://doi.org/10.1109/3DV.2019.00021

24. Vo, H.V., Duong, N.Q.K., Pérez, P.: Structural inpainting. In: Proceedings of the 26th ACM International Conference on Multimedia. ACM, October 2018. https://doi.org/10.1145/3240508.3240678

25. Wang, Z., Bovik, A., Sheikh, H., Simoncelli, E.: Image quality assessment: from error visibility to structural similarity. IEEE Trans. Image Process. **13**(4), 600–612 (2004). https://doi.org/10.1109/TIP.2003.819861

26. Xie, J., Xu, Y., Zheng, Z., Zhu, S.C., Wu, Y.N.: Generative pointnet: deep energy-based learning on unordered point sets for 3d generation, reconstruction and classification. In: Proceedings of the IEEE/CVF Conference on Computer Vision and Pattern Recognition, pp. 14976–14985 (2021)

27. Yakubovskiy, P.: Segmentation models (2019). https://github.com/qubvel/segmentation_models

28. Yu, J., Lin, Z., Yang, J., Shen, X., Lu, X., Huang, T.S.: Free-form image inpainting with gated convolution. In: Proceedings of the IEEE/CVF International Conference on Computer Vision, pp. 4471–4480 (2019)

29. Yu, Y., Cao, Z., Liang, S., Geng, W., Yu, J.: A novel vision-based grasping method under occlusion for manipulating robotic system. IEEE Sens. J. **20**(18), 10996–11006 (2020). https://doi.org/10.1109/JSEN.2020.2995395

30. Zhao, Y., Xie, J., Qian, J., Yang, J.: PUI-net: a point cloud upsampling and inpainting network. In: PRCV (2020)

Is This Bug Severe? A Text-Cum-Graph Based Model for Bug Severity Prediction

Rima Hazra[(✉)], Arpit Dwivedi, and Animesh Mukherjee

Indian Institute of Technology Kharagpur, Kharagpur, India
{to_rima,arpitdwivedi}@iitkgp.ac.in,
animeshm@cse.iitkgp.ac.in

Abstract. Repositories of large software systems have become commonplace. This massive expansion has resulted in the emergence of various problems in these software platforms including identification of (i) bug-prone packages, (ii) critical bugs, and (iii) severity of bugs. One of the important goals would be to mine these bugs and recommend them to the developers to resolve them. The first step to this is that one has to accurately detect the extent of severity of the bugs. In this paper, we take up this task of predicting the severity of bugs in the near future. Contextualized neural models built on the text description of a bug and the user comments about the bug help to achieve reasonably good performance. Further information on how the bugs are related to each other in terms of the ways they affect packages can be summarised in the form of a graph and used along with the text to get additional benefits.

1 Introduction

Large software systems have become increasingly commonplace. As these repositories grow, they become more and more complex. Malfunctions (aka bugs) in such systems need to be tackled in a timely fashion. Such bugs can be reported by the end-users (who are using the service), the developers or the testers. Since these bugs need to be attended in a pipelined fashion, an important step is to understand and prioritize the bug reports as per their severity. For instance, the security related bug reports should possibly get more priority than any other types of reports. Here, the term "severity" corresponds to the important bugs. The importance can be of security, privacy, affecting users etc. Though the actual definition of "severity" and "priority" from a business perspective is different, the term "severity" has been used here to represent the critical bugs. Since the number of bugs in a large software system could be in millions, it is difficult for the developers to manually go through the list of bug reports and identify the most important bug from that list. Not only is this a very tedious task but also is prone to mistakes. Thus automatic methods to predict the severity of a bug is very crucial. Such models can predict the bugs that are going to soon become severe based on certain early indicators like the description and the comments about the bug plus the number of packages that it already affects.

M.-R. Amini et al. (Eds.): ECML PKDD 2022, LNAI 13718, pp. 236–252, 2023.
https://doi.org/10.1007/978-3-031-26422-1_15

Bug severity prediction is a task of predicting the severity/impact of each bug from a huge list of bugs. Bug severity prediction task has been performed on many software platforms such as mozilla[1], eclipse[2], GCC[3] etc. by past researchers [1–4]. Most earlier models for bug severity detection assumes it to be a classification problem whereby the task is to predict one of the severity states – critical, major, normal, minor, trivial, enhancement. None of the datasets contains actual parameter based scores of the bugs. The other issue is that none of these models leverage the usefulness of both text and graph information jointly. Even while the state of a bug is predicted by earlier models, there might still be many bugs that need to be manually sorted within each class. Hence in this paper, we present a regression model that generates the rank of each bug in the list, allowing the developers to set their priorities accurately. To this purpose, we curate a new dataset consisting of bugs mapped to the Ubuntu packages that affect those packages over time. This new dataset allows us to perform the experiments in the regression setup. Further, unlike earlier models, we use sophisticated neural architectures that suitably blend text and graph information to harvest the benefits from both of these information sources.

Our Contributions and Results —

A New Dataset: We curate a new dataset[4] consisting of ∼280K bugs along with their meta data (e.g., the textual description of the bug, etc.). Further the ground-truth severity scores of these bugs have been collected in two different time points to facilitate the prediction experiments. In addition, we have also curated the list of packages affected by these bugs over time.

Bug Severity Prediction: As noted earlier we perform the experiments in the regression setup. In particular, we develop different neural models based on the text obtained from the bug description and user/developer/maintainer comments. We also use graph information in the form of how the bugs are related to each other in terms of the packages they co-affect. This is one of the most unique points of our approach. Of particular interest is the observation that the use of the text-cum-graph based models outperform the text based models in low training data settings. A summary of the key results are as follows – with 70% training data the most competing text based method SBERT outperforms the text-cum-graph based methods like GAT and GCN. However, in this setting GRAPHSAGE performs the best. For the low data setting (≤ 25% training data), the text-cum-graph based models largely outperform the purely text based models. Notably, for 5% training data, while SBERT achieves an MAE, MSE and MAPE of 1.178, 2.268 and 0.1778 respectively while GAT reports an MAE, MSE and MAPE of 0.849, 1.415 and 0.1101 respectively.

---

[1] https://bugzilla.mozilla.org/home.
[2] https://bugs.eclipse.org/bugs/.
[3] https://gcc.gnu.org/bugzilla/.
[4] https://doi.org/10.5281/zenodo.5554974.

2   Related Work

Due to the large-scale of software project, many significant problems require auto-mated systems. Some of the major problems of large-scale software systems include identifying high impact bugs (security bug reports), recommending appropriate developers to packages (/modules), identifying bug-prone packages, retrieving duplicate bugs, predicting high priority bugs, predicting severe bugs. Most of these problems were/are handled manually by developers/maintainers in the past, but as the data increases, the automated system is the need of the hour. Some of these problems have been studied for a long time. Researchers have used various meta-data, textual information, underlying graph structures to build systems that can solve certain problems. There are very few datasets available for each of the prob-lems. In this section, first, we will discuss the datasets available, then we briefly discuss the various earlier proposed methods into two parts – text based methods and graph based methods. For high impact bug reports (security bug prediction), there are four datasets – Ambari, Camel, Derby, and Wicket had been first manu-ally labelled by [5] and then further relabelled (only mislabelled data) by [6,7]. Two large scale projects – Chromium, and OpenStack datasets[5] were constructed by Wu *et al.* [6]. In [2], the authors collected bug reports and their severity levels from GCC, OpenOffice, Eclipse, NetBeans, and Mozilla for bug severity prediction. For predicting the severity of bug reports, Ramay *et al.* [8] used the bug reports of seven open-source products – Platform, CDT, JDT, Core, Firefox, Thunderbird, and Bugzilla from the repository created by [9]. So, the datasets available for severity prediction are mostly around these open-source projects, and the severity has only the label but not the scores. For most of the problems [3,4,7], researchers have used textual information such as title, descriptions to solve problems like bug severity prediction. In different papers [3,7,8], authors have used TF-IDF, word2vec [10], glove embeddings, doc2vec, BM25 to represent the text. The bug severity predic-tion is tackled as a classification problem in earlier works [3,4,11]. Authors have used various classification algorithms like SVM, logistic regression, random forest and XGboost to solve the problem. These studies have been performed on differ-ent platforms like Mozilla, eclipse, GCC etc. In [2], the authors proposed a method based on logistic regression to predict the severity of bugs. They used data from all the above three platforms for their experiments. Ramay *et al.* [8] proposed a deep learning approach to predict the severity of software bugs based on the text present in the bug report. Umer *et al.* [1] proposed an emotion-based approach to predict the priority of bug reports. There is very little research on the utility of graphs in the software domain to solve major software system problems. In [12], the authors studied in detail the problem of bug urgency ranking and developer rec-ommendation with the help of underlying graph structures. The authors curated a dataset from the Ubuntu platform for their experiments and developed various machine learning models for the ranking and recommendation problems. Our work is unique in two different ways. The first and possibly simple point of difference is that we formulate the problem in a regression setup and curate a new dataset

---

[5] https://github.com/wuxiaoxue/cve-assisted.

Table 1. Released metadata of a bug.

Field	Information
Bug Id	1663552
Reported On	mysql-5.7
Description	Hi, on one of our servers we noticed that under certain conditions mysql-server can be caused to go berserk, i.e. run with 400% CPU load, spit out extrem tons of log messages and denial it's work completely when contacted by a client, that is not (!) authorized to connect...
Comments	[2017-02-10 20:37:45 UTC] Thanks for the bug user; I'm marking this public so that administrators can more quickly learn that using tcpwrappers for access control has the potential ... [2017-03-06 11:19:44 UTC] user, could you report the package version number of mysql-5.7 in which you are seeing this please? ... [2017-03-06 23:22:02 UTC] user, I did not keep the virtual machine. On a host where the problem occured first we have ...
Affected packages	[10-02-2017]mysql-5.7 [30-03-2017] mysql server
Bug heat score	16

for this purpose. The second and the most unique point is that we propose a novel graph formulation of the problem that allows us to do reasonably good predictions even when very low training data points are available.

3   Dataset

We collect ∼280K bug reports related to Ubuntu repositories reported within the time span of 2004 to 2019. These bug reports are collected from the launchpad[6] bug tracking system. Each bug page consists of various meta information such as the title, the description, the name of the bug reporter, reporting timestamp, comments with timestamp, activity log[7], packages affected by the bug with timestamp and the bug heat[8] (or severity). Bug description consists of textual information written by the bug reporter. Given a bug, activity log keeps track of each and every activity that are made on the bug. 'Affected' packages are the packages that were affected by the given bug at a given time point. The bug heat is the accumulated score based on factors like privacy issue, security issue, duplicate nature, affected users and subscribers. This bug heat score is a representative of the severity/urgency of a bug. The bug heat calculation score is given in Table 2. An example of a bug entry is given in Table 1.

High bug heat represents a more severe bug. In our experiment, we have considered only those bugs which have at least one comment. We have collected the bug heat of the bugs at two different time points – in November 2019 and

---

[6] https://launchpad.net/.

[7] https://bugs.launchpad.net/ubuntu/+source/linux/+bug/1945590/+activity.

[8] https://bugs.launchpad.net/+help-bugs/bug-heat.html.

Table 2. Bug heat score calculation strategy

Attribute	Calculation
Private	Adds 150 points
Security issue	Adds 250 points
Duplicates	6 points per duplicate bug
Affected users	4 points per affected user
Subscribers[a]	2 points per subscriber

(a) (incl. subscribers to duplicates)

Table 3. Dataset statistics.

Basic information	Count
Total number of bugs	273,544
Average number of comments	5.241
Average number of words in description	80.93
Maximum number of words in description	4967
Average number of words in comments	10.959
Maximum number of words in comments	436
Average number of affected packages	1.28

again in November 2020. Table 3 notes the basic statistics of the data collected. In Fig. 3, we show the distribution of bugs having a particular bug heat value. The distribution is highly skewed with most bugs having low severity and a few bugs with very high severity.

Bug-Package Network: From our dataset, we can conceive a bipartite network where one set contains the list of bugs (B) and the other set contains the list of packages (P). A bug $b \in B$ can have a directed edge to a package $p \in P$ if the bug b affects the package p. An example of such a bipartite network shown in Fig. 1. Given a bug, affected packages are added typically along with a timestamp. However, in a few cases, this timestamp is not available. In such cases we replace the unavailable timestamp with the time of the bug creation assuming that the package is being affected since the creation of the bug report.

Degree Distribution: In Fig. 4, we illustrate the distribution of bugs affecting the different number of packages while in Fig. 5 we show the distribution of packages affected by the different number of bugs. Both these distributions exhibit a scale-free behaviour.

Bug-Bug Network: From the bug-package bipartite network we construct an one-mode projection, i.e., a bug-bug network where B is the set of nodes in this network and two nodes b_i and b_j are connected if they co-affect a package. Figure 2 shows the corresponding of bug-bug network constructed from Fig. 1.

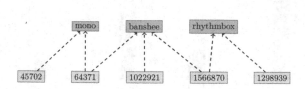

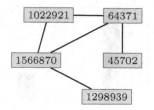

Fig. 1. Bipartite network between set of bugs and set of packages. B ={45702, 64371, 1022921, 1566870 and 1298939}. P ={'mono', 'banshee', 'rhythmbox'} are the affected packages.

Fig. 2. Bug-bug network.

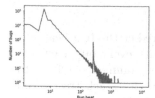

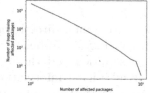

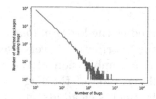

Fig. 3. Distribution of bugs having a specific bug heat.

Fig. 4. Distribution of bugs affecting a given number of packages.

Fig. 5. Distribution of packages affected by a given number of bugs.

For instance, in this figure bug 45702 and 64371 are connected because both of them affect the same package 'mono'. We shall use the information from this network for all our learning algorithms in the subsequent sections.

To understand how the bug-bug network structure is correlated with the bug heat ranks, we analyze a few known network properties of 100 top and bottom-ranked bugs based on bug heat rank. First, we compute three node centric measures: degree centrality, clustering coefficient, and PageRank. We have chosen these measures because they will give us an idea of the neighbourhood quality (i.e., how dense it is and how many neighbours a node has). Given a node centrality measure, we rerank the bugs based on these measures and compute the Spearman's rank correlation with the actual 100 top-ranked and bottom-ranked bugs based on bug heat. In Fig. 6, we plot the correlation values for the top 100 and bottom 100 bugs for all three measures. In all cases we observe that the top ranked bugs are more strongly correlated with the network properties. This gives us the first indication that it is important to leverage the network structure in order to efficiently perform bug severity prediction.

4   Bug Severity Prediction

Given a set of bugs (B), our objective is to predict their ranks based on the bug heat score. In particular, as is usual in a regression setup we are interested to

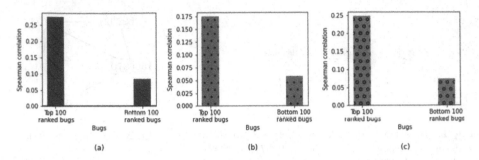

Fig. 6. (a) Spearman's rank correlation between the (a) degree centrality, (b) clustering coefficient and (c) PageRank and bug heat ranks for top 100 ranked bugs and bottom 100 ranked bugs based on bug heat.

predict the $\log(rank(bug\text{-}heat))$. We do not directly predict the bug heat since the distribution is very skewed (see Fig. 3). To begin with every bug is encoded as a combination of the text description and the user comments. Often, the description of the bug contains additional information like stack traces, code fragments email ids and urls. We remove these pieces of information using some simple heuristics.

Text Based Approach: In case of text based approach, we primarily use the textual description and the user comments for a bug for the purpose of prediction.

Doc2Vec: Doc2Vec [13] algorithm is used to generate representation for a document. It follows the same architecture as word2vec [10] along with a new vector called paragraph id. This paragraph id is used to represent each document uniquely. While training, along with the word vectors, a document vector is also trained and at the end it generates the representation of documents. We train the doc2vec [13] model on our corpus. We construct 100 dimension embeddings for the descriptions and the comments separately. Finally, a bug is a concatenation of these two vectors. This is passed through an MLP to obtain the regression scores. The MLP has one hidden layer followed by the output layer and the activation function is RELU.

SBERT: SBERT [14] has the BERT [15] like architecture which can capture better semantics in the sentence. It is the fine tuned BERT sentence embedding model which can correctly capture the the semantic textual similarity (STS) between a pair of sentences. We use the pretrained sentence BERT [14] model (SBERT) to generate embeddings. For each bug, we pass the preprocessed description text and the comment text through the model and obtain separate embeddings for each of these. We then concatenate these two embeddings and pass it through the same MLP model discussed earlier to obtain the regression scores.

Graph Based Approaches:

GAT: Graph attention network (GAT) [16] algorithm can again be used for node classification where the input features are linearly transformed to some output features which is further followed by a self-attention layer on the nodes. This self-attention mechanism captures the importance of one node on another. For our purpose once again the bug-bug network is used as the input graph and each node is initially encoded as a concatenated vector of the SBERT representations of the bug description and the comments. Finally, the regression scores are once again obtained using a linear layer and a RELU activation. Here again the model is only shown the labels of the training nodes.

GCN: Graph convolution network (GCN) [17] is a transductive method for node classification. For our purpose we have used the bug-bug network as the input graph. To begin with each node is featurised as a concatenation of the SBERT representations of the description and the comments. Finally, as earlier, to obtain the regression scores, we pass the output features of the GCN layer to a linear layer with RELU activation. Like before, we show the model only the labels of the training nodes.

GRAPHSAGE: GRAPHSAGE [18] is a graph based algorithm for classifying nodes. In this method, neighbourhood aggregation has been done using uniformly sampled neighbours and aggregating their features. In our case we use the bug-bug network and feed it to GRAPHSAGE. The initial representation of every bug (read node) is a concatenated vector of the SBERT embeddings of the description and the comments. For the purpose of training we provide the label of the nodes (i.e., their $\log(rank(bug\text{-}heat))$) that are part of the training set only (we shall discuss more about this in the following section on experimental setup). We obtain the final predictions using a linear layer with RELU activation.

5 Experiments and Results

Experimental Setup

Training: In order to train the models, we consider all the bugs that have been posted in between January 2017–June 2017. We have considered only the bugs which has at least one comment. This results in a total of 5835 bugs. Given a bug in this time period, all comments posted about the bug in between January 2017–June 2018 are considered to compute the comment based embedding. This ensures that each bug has at least one year span of comments for the computation of the features. The ground truth bug heat scores that we use have been crawled in November 2019. Out of the 5835 bugs obtained, we use different training set sizes for our experiments ranging from 70% to 5%. The rest of the data is used for validation in each case. For each of the training and the validation sets the bugs selected are re-ranked within that set based on their heat scores.

Evaluation: In the test set, we consider all the bugs posted in between July 2018–December 2018. Comments have been considered if it is posted in between July 2018–December 2019. This results in a total of 5302 bugs. Also, we have considered only the bugs which has at least one comment. Once again this ensures that each bug has one year of commenting time. Here, we use ground truth bug heat scores crawled in November 2020. The bugs in the test data are ranked based on these scores. We used the same test data across all the methods.

Graph Setup: While building the graph, we have considered only those packages which were reported to be affected in time periods reported above. The graph setup is transductive, i.e., we consider all the bugs in the training and the test data to construct the graph. Thus the graph consists of around 11137 nodes and ~ 1205682 edges. However, the model is made to observe the ground truth ranks of the nodes present in the training data only. The ground truth ranks for all the other nodes are hidden from the model.

Evaluation Metrics: In our experiments, we use three standard metrics to evaluate all our models. These are MAE (mean absolute error), MSE (mean squared error) and MAPE (mean average percentage error). Mean absolute error (MAE) is calculated as the average of absolute difference between the true scores and the predicted scores. Mean squared error (MSE) is calculated as the average of the squared differences between true scores and predicted scores. Mean average percentage error (MAPE) is calculated as the average of the absolute difference between ground truth and predicted values expressed as a percentage of the ground-truth value.

Hyperparameters – Text Based Approaches: In text based approaches, we have run the models on 70% training data. Further, we choose the text based model which performs best among all the text based models and compare it with the graph based models.

Doc2Vec: In our experiment, the input feature is a concatenation of the 100 dimensional vector representations of the description and the comments. The hyperparameters of the MLP for the regression task are set as follows. The learning rate, ϵ are set to $5e-4$, $1e-5$ respectively. The batch size and weight decay are set to 64 and 0.01 respectively. The number of neurons in hidden layer is 128 unit. We run the model for 20 epochs and saved the model where the current validation loss is better than the current best validation loss.

SBERT: Here, we have used the pretrained SBERT model called 'paraphrase-mpnet-base-v2'. We have generated the embeddings for the description and comments of each bug separately. The dimension for each embedding is 768. The two embeddings are then concatenated to construct the feature. For 70% setup, the MLP learning rate, ϵ, batch size and weight decay are set to $5e-3$, $2e-5$, 64 and 0.3 respectively. We have used one hidden layer with 1024 unit neurons and one output layer. For both the layers, we used RELU activation function. We observed that SBERT performs better than Doc2Vec (see Sect. 5). We therefore use SBERT as the competing text-based baseline. Therefore we had to carry out experiments on SBERT for other training data setup (50%–5%). We use grid search to obtain the best parameter for the different training setups. For a 50% training setup, the learning rate is $1e-3$. The weight decay and ϵ remains the same as that of the 70% training setup. The hidden layer and batch size remains the same for all the setups, i.e., 1024, $2e-5$, and 64 respectively. The ϵ value of 50% and 5% setups is the same as 70% setup. For 25% and 10% setups, the ϵ value is $1e-5$. In the 25% and 5% training data setup, the learning rate is $4e-3$. In the 50% and 10% training data setup, the learning rate is set to $1e-3$. For 25%, 10% and 5%, the value of weight decay is 0.01. The weight decay value for the 50% setup is the same as the 70% setup.

Table 4. Results from the text based models for 70% training setup. Best results are marked in boldface.

Methods	Text based		
	MAE	MSE	MAPE
Doc2Vec	7.585	58.503	$3.42e-16$
Sbert	**1.081**	**1.56**	**0.1649**

Results from Text Based Approaches: The key results obtained from the text-based models are noted in Table 4. The results show that the Sbert based model outperforms the other models. Hence we have used this model to compare the different graph-based approaches in the next section. The results of 50%–5% data setup for the Sbert model are presented in Table 5.

Hyperparameters – Graph Based Approaches: In our graph based approaches, we perform the experiments for different proportions of training data: 70%, 50%, 25%, 10%, 5%. In each case, the rest of the data is used for validation.

GAT: In this experiment, we use Adam optimizer, MAE, as the loss function and patience of early stopping at 15 in all the setups. We use grid search again to obtain the best parameters. For 70% and 5% setup, the attention head size is 32. For 25% and 10%, the size of the attention head is 64. In the case of 50% setup, the attention head size remains 16. For 70%, 50% and 5% training data, the GAT layer sizes are 32, 16 and 32 respectively, and for other setups, it remains at 64. The best learning rate for 70%, 25% and 10% training data setup are 0.01. The best learning rate for 50% and 5% training data is 0.015, respectively. The parameter in_dropout is 0.5 for 50% and 25% training setup, respectively. For 70%, 10% and 5% training data, the in_dropouts are 0.9, 0.85 and 0.6 respectively. The attention dropout parameter is 0.1 for 10% training setup. For other setups, it is 0.3. For all the setups, the activation function used in GAT layer is ELU.

GCN: For all the setup, we have used Adam optimizer, MAE as loss function, patience is 15 for early stopping and ELU activation for GCN layer. We use grid search to obtain the best parameters. For 70%, 25% and 5% setup, we have set the learning rate at 0.01. For 50% and 10% setup, the learning rate is set to 0.015 and 0.008, respectively. For all the setup except 5% setup, GCN layer size is kept at 64. For the 5% setup, the GCN layer size is 32. For 70% and 5% training setup, the dropout value is set at 0.85. For 25% and 10% training setup, the dropout is set to 0.8. For 50% setup, the dropout is 0.9.

GRAPHSAGE: For all the setup, we use Adam optimizer, MAE as loss function and the early stopping patience at 15. Activation function used in GRAPH-SAGE layer is ELU. In the last layer, we have used RELU activation function, and bias is set to true. The batch size is set to 64. For each training proportion, we use grid search to obtain the best parameter setting. For 70% setup, the size of the GRAPHSAGE layer is 64, and for other setups, the size of the GRAPH-SAGE layer is 128. For 70% and 10%, the learning rate is $1e-2$. For 50%, 25% and 5%, the learning rate is $15e-3$. For 70% and 5% setup, the number of nodes sampled in each GRAPHSAGE layer is 5. For 50%, 25% and 10% setup, the number of nodes sampled in GRAPHSAGE layer is 6. For 50% setup, the dropout in GRAPHSAGE layer are 0.6 and for other setups the dropout in GRAPHSAGE layer is 0.9.

Table 5. Results of the bug severity prediction using graph based methods. For each node the initial feature is a concatenation of the SBERT embeddings of the **description** and the **comments**. The best results are indicated in boldface and second best are underlined.

Training data	Text based			Graph based								
	SBERT			GAT			GCN			GRAPHSAGE		
	MAE	MSE	MAPE	MAE	MSE	MAPE	MAE	MSE	MAPE	MAE	MSE	MAPE
70%	**1.081**	**1.56**	**0.1649**	1.151	1.722	0.1736	1.183	1.83	0.1804	<u>1.148</u>	<u>1.796</u>	<u>0.1752</u>
50%	0.908	1.19	0.1334	<u>0.812</u>	<u>0.998</u>	<u>0.1131</u>	0.831	1.038	0.1165	**0.795**	**0.94**	**0.1129**
25%	1.069	1.688	0.1622	**0.757**	**1.11**	**0.1007**	<u>0.833</u>	<u>1.256</u>	<u>0.1148</u>	1.062	1.436	0.1569
10%	1.282	2.565	0.2070	**0.812**	**1.124**	**0.1096**	<u>1.034</u>	<u>1.885</u>	<u>0.1461</u>	1.756	3.658	0.3001
5%	1.178	2.268	0.1778	**0.849**	**1.415**	**0.1101**	<u>1.089</u>	<u>2.09</u>	<u>0.1532</u>	2.242	5.721	0.4213

Results from Graph Based Approaches: Table 5 summarises the main results of this section. We observe that for larger training data setup (70% and 50%), the text based model performs better than GCN and GAT. However, in this setting GRAPHSAGE performs the second best in terms of all the evaluation metrics. For the low training data setup (5%–25%), the graph based models GCN and GAT outperform the text based model. In fact, in this setup, GAT performs the best in terms of all the evaluation metrics. This shows that enabling self-attention on the neighbourhood of a bug in the bug-bug network could be very beneficial for predicting bug severity when the number of training data points are severely low.

6   Ablation Study

In our experiments, we have used a concatenation of representations of both the description and the comments. This section investigates the importance of each of these separately for the text and graph-based methods. The results obtained by using only the description are reported in Table 6. The results for both the text-based and graph-based models obtained using only the comments are reported in Table 7.

Only Description: We execute the text-based model (SBERT) and graph-based models (GAT , GCN , GRAPHSAGE) on only the description feature. In both types of models, we have used the text of the description as a feature. Further, we compute the results for all the training data setups (70%–5%). We wanted to observe whether one can obtain the additional support from graph information even if (s)he uses only one feature (i.e., description in this case).

Observations: Out of all the setups, SBERT has performed slightly better than one of the graph-based models in the 70% setup. However, as the training data reduces, the performance of SBERT drops. For the 50% setup, GRAPHSAGE model outperforms the other models, and GAT is the second best. However, the MAE score difference between the best model (GRAPHSAGE) and the SBERT is negligible ($\sim$0.09). For 25% setup, GRAPHSAGE is again the top performer and GAT is the second best. The difference in MAE scores of SBERT and GRAPHSAGE models now are pretty large ($\sim$0.27). For the 10% setup, GAT model performs better than other models. The MAE score difference between SBERT and GAT is as large as 0.38. For 5% setup, once again GAT performs better than other models. Here the second-best model is GCN. It is visible that if the training data is reduced, then the text-based model does not perform well as was also observed in our original results (see Table 5). Nevertheless, the additional graph structure helps the model to predict better in a low training data setup.

Table 6. Ablation study: MAE, MSE and RMSE values are reported to compare best text based methods with different graph based methods. Only **description** of the bugs are used to generate the embedding.

Training data	Text based			Graph based								
	SBERT			GAT			GCN			GRAPHSAGE		
	MAE	MSE	MAPE	MAE	MSE	MAPE	MAE	MSE	MAPE	MAE	MSE	MAPE
70%	**1.035**	**1.474**	**0.1530**	1.152	1.735	0.1738	1.194	1.931	0.1841	<u>1.093</u>	<u>1.629</u>	<u>0.1635</u>
50%	0.905	1.205	0.1294	<u>0.821</u>	<u>1.03</u>	<u>0.114</u>	0.85	1.081	0.1193	**0.812**	**1.019**	**0.1125**
25%	0.987	1.555	0.144	<u>0.784</u>	<u>1.119</u>	<u>0.1049</u>	0.934	1.465	0.1341	**0.717**	**0.954**	**0.0949**
10%	1.275	2.458	0.2082	**0.892**	**1.607**	**0.1164**	<u>1.067</u>	<u>2.026</u>	<u>0.154</u>	1.677	3.286	0.2782
5%	1.183	2.401	0.1731	**0.87**	**1.54**	**0.1153**	<u>1.057</u>	<u>2.004</u>	<u>0.1531</u>	2.213	5.566	0.412

Table 7. Ablation study: MAE, MSE and RMSE values are reported to compare best text based methods with different graph based methods. Only **comments** of the bugs are used to generate the embedding.

| Training data | Text based | | | Graph based | | | | | | | | |
| | SBERT | | | GAT | | | GCN | | | GRAPHSAGE | | |
	MAE	MSE	MAPE	MAE	MSE	MAPE	MAE	MSE	MAPE	MAE	MSE	MAPE
70%	**0.958**	**1.208**	**0.1414**	1.103	1.621	0.1651	1.195	1.89	0.1838	1.107	1.66	0.1660
50%	0.908	1.196	0.1337	0.802	0.984	0.1109	0.806	0.996	0.112	**0.782**	**0.925**	**0.1113**
25%	1.018	1.677	0.1537	**0.743**	**1.044**	**0.0984**	0.871	1.334	0.1226	1.081	1.489	0.1603
10%	1.431	3.35	0.2348	**0.924**	**1.322**	**0.1305**	1.122	2.128	0.1682	1.724	3.518	0.2916
5%	1.485	3.601	0.2618	**1.004**	**1.809**	**0.1420**	1.171	2.244	0.1794	2.205	5.531	0.4099

Only Comments: Here we carry out the experiments using only one feature, i.e., comments. Once again the idea is to verify whether the graph structure is useful even when one of the feature types are available. We have taken the texts of the comments in this experiment. We ran the experiments for all the text-based and graph-based models. We perform these experiments for all the training setups (70%-5% training data).

Observations: For 70% training setup, like in the previous experiment (Subsect. 6), SBERT is performing well than other graph-based models. But the MAE score difference between the SBERT and best performing graph model (GAT) is quite less ($\sim$0.145). For the 50% training setup, all the three graph models are performing better than the SBERT model. Out of three graph models, GRAPHSAGE performed best (MAE 0.782), and SBERTis performs the worst (MAE 0.908). For the 25% setup, the GAT model outperforms other models, and the MAE difference between the SBERTand GATmodel is quite high ($\sim$0.275). Here, the GRAPHSAGE performs the worst, and SBERT performs better than the GRAPHSAGEmodel. For 10% setup, again GAT model tops the list and GCN comes as second best. For 5% setup, GAT outperforms other models, and GCN is the second in the list. Overall once again we observe that the graph structure is always helpful whatever be the text feature especially in the low data setting.

Table 8. Outcomes of the error analysis. Results are only shown for the low data setup to investigate the importance of the graph neighborhood.

Training data	ΔGAT $< \Delta$SBERT	ΔGAT $< \Delta$SBERT (has neighbor in training)	#nodes in training
25%	3485 (65.72%)	2609 (74.86%)	1458
10%	3712 (70.01%)	2359 (63.55%)	583
5%	3324 (62.69%)	1998 (60.10%)	291

7 Error Analysis

In this section, we will test our models for various cases and identify which models fail when and why. First, we shall test the importance of the graph structure. Second, we shall study some cases where SBERT fails, but GAT wins and vice versa. From the description+comments results, we observe that for low data, the GRAPHSAGE performs poorer than GAT (best) model. Hence we shall consider some use cases to analyze this fact first.

Testing the Importance of Graph Structure: We perform error analysis for low training data setup (5%–25%) to understand the importance of the graph structure. Among all the models, GAT performs better for low training data setup. In order to carry out the analysis, given a model, we first calculate the absolute difference (i.e., Δ) between the predicted rank and the true rank of the bugs. Further, we compute the number of bugs where absolute difference (ΔGAT) in GAT is lesser (i.e., better) than (ΔSBERT) in SBERT. The results of this analysis are summarised in Table 8. As we can observe, for 5% data, in 62.69% of test cases, ΔGAT < ΔSBERT. Out of these, 60.10% of the test bugs have a neighbor in the bug-bug network that was part of the training node of GAT. Similar results hold for the other cases. This shows that the graph structure indeed helps in improving the predicted ranks in low data settings.

Usecase: Gat Wins Sbert Fails: In Table 9, we present a few example test bugs where the GAT model predicts a better rank value than the SBERT model. For this analysis, we use the prediction value from the models trained with 5% training data. We have chosen 5% training data because, especially for low data, the graph-based method outperforms the text-based model. For each of the test bugs, we calculate the number of neighbours present in training set. We observe that in case of test bugs with a large number of neighbours in the training set for GAT predicts nearer ranks to the ground truth rank compared to SBERT. In these examples, most of the test bugs have 27–29 neighbouring nodes in training data (note: the total number of nodes in training data is 291).

Table 9. Few test examples where the GAT model predicts a nearer value to the true rank compared to SBERT. In all these cases the instances have a lot of neighbors present in training data.

Bug Id	True rank	Prediction SBERT	Prediction GAT	ΔSBERT	ΔGAT	#neighbors (in training)
1799406	7.669	8.450	8.050	0.780	0.380	29
1792783	7.920	5.804	8.048	2.116	0.128	28
1798690	7.920	6.086	8.251	1.833	0.330	28
1788045	8.338	7.354	8.252	0.983	0.085	27

Usecase: Sbert Wins Gat Fails: Converse to the data points in the previous section, here we find that there are a set of test points for which GAT fails even in the low (i.e., 5%) training data setup, i.e., the ranks predicted by GAT are further from the ground truth compared to SBERT. In all these cases we observe that the number of nodes in the training set for each of these test points is 0 (see Table 10). The absence of neighbours of these points in the training set does not allow the GAT model to take the advantage of the graph structure and hence the worse rank.

Table 10. Few test examples where the SBERT model predicts a nearer value to the true rank compared to GAT. In all these cases the instances have 0 neighbors present in training data.

Bug Id	True rank	Prediction SBERT	Prediction GAT	ΔSBERT	ΔGAT	#neighbors (in training)
1797179	7.397	8.332	9.005	0.934	1.607	0
1788706	6.772	7.881	8.511	1.108	1.738	0
1810154	6.050	7.127	7.759	1.076	1.708	0
1791333	8.338	8.556	7.509	0.218	0.828	0

Usecase: Gat Wins GraphSage Fails: In Table 11, we list a few test cases where the GAT wins but GRAPHSAGE fails for low data setup (5%). We list those cases where there is a sufficient number of neighbours in training data, but still, the performance of GRAPHSAGE is poor. The ΔGAT is much lesser than the ΔGRAPHSAGE for all the cases. We pick up every instance and try to understand the 1.5 hop neighbourhood structure. We focus on those neighbours specifically who are present in the training set. So, for each test bug (say the anchor node), we build a 1.5 neighbourhood (taking only those neighbours which are present in the training data) graph. 1.5 neighbourhood graph contains the anchor node and its neighbours and connection among themselves (i.e., anchor to neighbours as well as among neighbours). We observe that the degree centrality of the neighbours vary. Thus one can hypothesize that all the neighbours (present in training set) are not equally important for the prediction of the rank of the anchor node. In the GAT architecture, the model provides different attention coefficients to different neighbours of each anchor node to compute the representation of the node. Also, the feature aggregation has been done based on the importance

Table 11. Test examples where the GAT model predicts ranks closer to the ground truth compared to the GRAPHSAGE model.

Bug Id	True rank	Prediction GRAPHSAGE	Prediction GAT	ΔGRAPHSAGE	ΔGAT	#neighbors (in training)
1799406	7.669	5.609	8.050	2.060	0.380	29
1793137	8.338	5.564	8.055	2.773	0.282	28
1798690	7.920	5.614	8.251	2.305	0.330	28
1788045	8.338	5.619	8.252	2.718	0.085	27

(attention coefficient) of immediate neighbours of the anchor node. However, in case of the GRAPHSAGE model, a certain number of nodes has been uniformly sampled from the set of neighbours. Further, the feature aggregation for each anchor node is done based on the sampled neighbourhood. Using the differences in the attention coefficients the GAT model possibly leverages more information from the high degree neighbors in order to predict the rank of the anchor node thus outperforming the GRAPHSAGE model which gives uniform importance to all the neighbors of the anchor node.

8 Conclusion

In this paper, we presented a new dataset comprising bugs, its metadata and ground truth severity scores (i.e., bug heat) from two time points. Further, we collected the list of affected packages by a bug along with the timestamp. We build regression models for bug severity prediction which is one of the well known problems in the software community. We performed the experiments using two type of models – (i) text based models, and (ii) graph based models. We observed that the SBERT model performed better (/similar) for high training data (70%, 50%) setup than graph based models. However, for low training data setup, the GAT model outperformed SBERT by a large margin. Error analysis shows that the performance of GAT is due to the nodes in the training set of the model that are in the neighbourhood of the bug-bug network of the test bugs. In future, we would like to carry out the studies such as how the packages are being affected temporally using our new dataset.

References

1. Umer, Q., Liu, H., Sultan, Y.: Emotion based automated priority prediction for bug reports. IEEE Access **6**, 35743–35752 (2018)
2. Tan, Y., Xu, S., Wang, Z., Zhang, T., Xu, Z., Luo, X.: Bug severity prediction using question-and-answer pairs from stack overflow. J. Syst. Softw. **165**, 110567 (2020)
3. Arokiam, Jude and Bradbury, Jeremy S.: Automatically predicting bug severity early in the development process. In: Proceedings of the ACM/IEEE 42nd International Conference on Software Engineering: New Ideas and Emerging Results, pp. 17–20 (2020)
4. Wu, X., Zheng, W., Chen, X., Yu, Z., Yu, T., Mu, D.: Improving high-impact bug report prediction with combination of interactive machine learning and active learning. Inf. Softw. Technol. **133**, 106530 (2021)
5. Ohira, M., et al.: A dataset of high impact bugs: manually-classified issue reports. In: 2015 IEEE/ACM 12th Working Conference on Mining Software Repositories, pp. 518–521 (2015)
6. Wu, X., Zheng, W., Chen, X., Wang, F., Mu, D.: CVE-assisted large-scale security bug report dataset construction method. J. Syst. Softw. **160**, 110456 (2020)
7. Peters, F., Tun, T.T., Yu, Y., Nuseibeh, B.: Text filtering and ranking for security bug report prediction. IEEE Trans. Softw. Eng. **45**, 615–631 (2019)

8. Ramay, W.Y., Umer, Q., Yin, X.C., Zhu, C., Illahi, I.: Deep neural network-based severity prediction of bug reports. IEEE Access **7**, 46846–46857 (2019)

9. Lamkanfi, A., Pérez, J., Demeyer, S.: The eclipse and mozilla defect tracking dataset: a genuine dataset for mining bug information. In: Proceedings of the 10th Working Conference on Mining Software Repositories, pp. 203–206 (2013)

10. Mikolov, T., Chen, K., Corrado, G., Dean, J.: Efficient estimation of word representations in vector space. In: 1st International Conference on Learning Representations (ICLR) (2013)

11. Goseva-Popstojanova, K., Tyo, J.: Identification of security related bug reports via text mining using supervised and unsupervised classification. In: 2018 IEEE International Conference on Software Quality, Reliability and Security (QRS), pp. 344–355 (2018)

12. Hazra, R., Aggarwal, H., Goyal, P., Mukherjee, A., Chakrabarti, S.: Joint autoregressive and graph models for software and developer social networks. In: Advances in Information Retrieval (ECIR), pp. 224–237 (2021)

13. Le, Q., Mikolov, T.: Distributed representations of sentences and documents. In: Proceedings of the 31st International Conference on Machine Learning, vol. 32, pp. 1188–1196 (2014)

14. Reimers, N., Gurevych, I.: Sentence-BERT: sentence embeddings using Siamese BERT-networks. In: Proceedings of the 2019 Conference on Empirical Methods in Natural Language Processing (EMNLP) (2019)

15. Devlin, J., Chang, M.-W., Lee, K., Toutanova, K.: BERT: pre-training of deep bidirectional transformers for language understanding. In: Proceedings of the 2019 Conference of the North American Chapter of the Association for Computational Linguistics: Human Language Technologies, vol. 1, pp. 4171–4186 (2019)

16. Veličković, P., Cucurull, G., Casanova, A., Romero, A., Liò, P., Bengio, Y.: Graph attention networks. In: International Conference on Learning Representations (2018)

17. Kipf, T.N., Welling, M.: Semi-Supervised classification with graph convolutional networks. In: International Conference on Learning Representations (ICLR) (2017)

18. Hamilton, W.L., Ying, R., Leskovec, J.: Inductive representation learning on large graphs. In: NIPS (2017)

Physically Invertible System Identification for Monitoring System Edges with Unobservability

Jingyi Yuan🆔 and Yang Weng$^{(\boxtimes)}$🆔

Arizona State University, Tempe, AZ 85281, USA
{jyuan46,Yang.Weng}@asu.edu

Abstract. Nowadays, the data collected in physical/engineering systems allows various machine learning methods to conduct system monitoring and control, when the physical knowledge on the system edge is limited and challenging to recover completely. Solving such problems typically requires identifying forward system mapping rules, from system states to the output measurements. However, the forward system identification based on digital twin can hardly provide complete monitoring functions, such as state estimation, e.g., to infer the states from measurements. While one can directly learn the inverse mapping rule, it is more desirable to re-utilize the forward digital twin since it is relatively easy to embed physical law there to regularize the inverse process and avoid overfitting. For this purpose, this paper proposes an invertible learning structure based on designing parallel paths in structural neural networks with basis functionals and embedding virtual storage variables for information preservation. For such a two-way digital twin modeling, there is an additional challenge of multiple solutions for system inverse, which contradict the reality of one feasible solution for the current system. To avoid ambiguous inverse, the proposed model maximizes the physical likelihood to contract the original solution space, leading to the unique system operation status of interest. We validate the proposed method on various physical system monitoring tasks and scenarios, such as inverse kinematics problems, power system state estimation, etc. Furthermore, by building a perfect match of a forward-inverse pair, the proposed method obtains accurate and computation-efficient inverse predictions, given observations. Finally, the forward physical interpretation and small prediction errors guarantee the explainability of the invertible structure, compared to standard learning methods.

Keywords: Inverse system identification · Invertible neural network · System edge · System unobservability

1 Introduction

Monitoring is essential for the sustainable operation of physical systems. However, physical knowledge may be partially unknown, and sensor measurements

© The Author(s), under exclusive license to Springer Nature Switzerland AG 2023
M.-R. Amini et al. (Eds.): ECML PKDD 2022, LNAI 13718, pp. 253–269, 2023.
https://doi.org/10.1007/978-3-031-26422-1_16

are limited for system identification on the system edges [10,11,19,22]. Such weak knowledge on the edge challenges traditional monitoring approaches based on accurate physical models. To bridge the gap, there are works on machine learning models using collected data for system identification [1,4,36]. However, although the data-driven method can mimic the behavior of a physical system, they are not indeed a digital twin to be used for system operation at any operating point [5], e.g., at new operating points never happened in the past. The problems have two causes. One is the lack of physical interpretation, and the other is the mismatch between forward and inverse mapping. These two are natural properties when the physical governing function is available. Therefore, it is essential to build the digital twin with both logical check (consistency of two-way mappings) and physics for an actual replica of the physical counterpart. This paper looks into the inverse learning for state estimation that is consistent with the forward mapping and has physics embedded.

Specifically, an intuitive way for inverse learning is to directly learn the inverse mapping rule from collected data in a discriminative manner. However, it easily causes poor performance due to overfitting. Even worse, the inverse mapping is usually more complex than the forward. For example, unlike the physical priors of the forward system model, the inverse model usually does not have a pre-defined physical form as a reference. Therefore, it is hard to maintain high accuracy directly using fitting models like deep neural networks (DNNs), especially in the extrapolation scenario.

Therefore, this paper aims to learn an accurate forward system with physical regularization while enforcing invertibility. As the prior physical knowledge is embedded into the forward mapping, the physics will regularize the inverse process automatically against overfitting in the second. Such an idea has some similarities to the (variational) auto-encoder [13,15,25,33]. However, the forward-inverse pair in the auto-encoder is forced by the reconstruction loss instead of the interoperability. So, the auto-encoder has neither a decoder providing a perfect inverse nor a physical interpretability. Thus, we would like to build a forward mapping with physics and inverse the forward DNN if possible.

For invertible transformation, we propose splitting the input variables into two groups with a swap of DNN links in the forward mapping to invert the forward DNN for system states. Such a method is much better than auto-encoder, as it can create a perfect pair of encoder and decoder without the approximation errors in typical auto-encoder [7,8]. Now that we know the principles of designing invertible DNN, we want to systematically embed physicals with three considerations. First, we aim to embed physical functionals to reveal similar forms as the physical laws. Second, we aim to embed the physical size of input/output variables into the functionals. Third, we aim to have a unique solution, since the current system state is unique no matter how many possible algebraic solutions there can be according to the mathematical function.

To achieve the first goal, we split the input into a twin set so that we not only provide all possible candidates as input to the physical DNN to maximize the physical gains but also preserve the structural requirement of having separated inputs for the invertible DNN. For the second goal, we propose to add storage variables into the output of the forward mapping rule. This step is to ensure no physical information loss, e.g., when the output of the forward mapping is with a smaller dimension than the input. But, how to pick up the correct output size in the forward mapping? The answer is the network size. The minimum number of states is the network size according to the definition of state estimation. For the third goal, we will utilize the Bayesian framework and the maximum likelihood estimation, for which we use the historical indicator to select the best outcome and avoid the confusion of multiple solutions [14,18]. For example, Fig. 1 shows the collected data in a power system case. The curves of power generation, consumption loads, and node voltages indicate the standard data pattern during system operations. Different quantities stay within the standard operation limit of physical systems. We incorporate such a pattern in the inverse learning problems to ensure a feasible solution and physical uniqueness.

The proposed model can be implemented on various physical/engineering systems for monitoring with unobservability, including manipulator inverse kinematics, structural health monitoring of high-rise buildings, position estimation of robotic system, state estimation of power and water system, etc. [11,14,18,27,29,32,35]. For example, photovoltaic (PV) and electric vehicle (EV) penetrations change the power distribution system dramatically, where a fast-monitoring tool like state estimation (SE) is necessary for operation. Nevertheless, it is hard to conduct traditional SE due to unavailable power system modeling, and partial observability [6,20]. Thus, we conduct experiments to demonstrate how the designed invertibility efficiently infers hidden system states of interest and how the embedded physics in the forward system identification leads to consistently better performance compared to the state-of-art learning methods.

Our main contributions include 1) designing an invertible system that can ensure strict consistency between forward and inverse mapping for edge systems with unobservability; 2) embedding the physical information in the forward mapping to indirectly regularize the inverse learning and avoid overfitting so that the state estimation can be conducted at an arbitrary operating point; and 3) showing how to embed the physical property comprehensively (functionals and variable size) so that information won't get lost due to dimension reduction for some use cases on the system edge.

2   Related Work

2.1   Solve the Inverse Problem of Physical Systems

It has been a basic task of interest to analyze the inverse process of physical/engineering system, which is to extract true states from observations for system operation and control [3,9]. In traditional works, researchers solve such problems by iterative simulations or algorithms based on models. These methods typically require prior system knowledge, e.g., solving power flow using the Newton-Raphson method with a detailed system model and estimating unknown states using Kalman Filter with system dynamics model [17,28,30,34]. However,

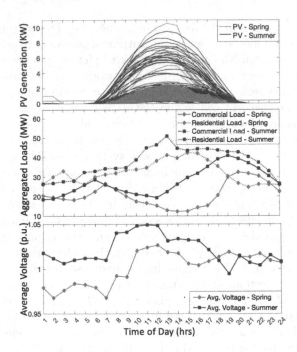

Fig. 1. Example of power distribution system to show the standard data pattern in spring and summer operations: (Top) generation of system-wide photovoltaics (PVs), (middle) aggregated commercial and residential loads, and (bottom) average voltage per unit values.

the complete system information can often be unavailable or inaccurate in complex physical/engineering systems, especially on the system edge [10,11,19,22]. While traditional methods are limited, some studies propose to leverage machine learning tools, approximating the (inverse) mapping rule with data observations [14,23,26,35,37]. However, the data-driven methods either oversimplify the complex physical model or directly use intractable black-box approximation, lacking the interpretability and correctness for system operators to understand and trust. This calls for an invertible structure for learning the forward and inverse processes together with one-to-one mapping.

2.2   Enforce Inverse in Representation Learning

For the idea of unifying the forward and inverse learning, we trace back to the early work in conventional NN inversion that iteratively finds the optimal solutions [21,31]. However, inverting the highly nonlinear and implicit NN for optimum is difficult and computationally inefficient. Therefore, the family of representation learning uses a similar criterion but approximates inference instead of extensive optimization iterations. For example, the popular auto-encoders [15] connect two neural network models in sequence and in symmetry to approximate the inverse correlation while simultaneously training the forward NN.

Specifically, the auto-encoder minimizes the reconstruction mismatch of inputs to enforce an imperfect decoder that approximately inverts the encoder. In fact, the approximation error is unavoidable so that the true inverse counterpart cannot be reached in training. Moreover, as both the forward and inverse functions are black-box models, there is 1) no physical guarantee over implicit learning and 2) no physical meaning of the quantities in latent space.

In contrast, the flow-based models [7,8] construct a sequence of invertible transformations as the forward mapping. Compared to auto-encoders, they leverage the change of variable theorem to ensure a deterministic inverse of the forward mapping without any approximation. Previous work usually uses such a model for complex density estimation tasks like image generation, which are quite different from our target cases. To better represent complex image data, they map images to latent space with a simple distribution in the forward process first and then obtain an "easy" inverse. These models are trained by maximizing the likelihood, in an unsupervised learning manner, to find the solution in a high-density region, which can be viewed as the inverse of dataset [2]. Though the models show good performance in image generation, the design has a strong requirement for splitting the input and output, which is hard to be satisfied fully in physical systems. Also, the design doesn't reveal any physical interpretability, which is necessary for physical system identification. Finally, the design does not consider the unobservability issue, either. Such problems require a comprehensive way to embed all possible physics knowledge from different perspectives.

3 Problem Formulation for Two-Way System Monitoring with Unobservability

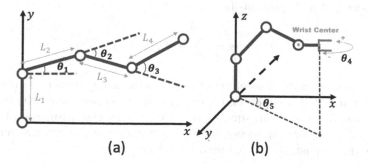

Fig. 2. Example: (a) geometry of the 3-DOF kinematics system in 2D space and (b) geometry of the 5-DOF kinematics system in 3D space.

The physical system identification is a supervised learning task to recover the forward system model f in $y = f(x)$, mapping input variables $x \in \mathcal{X}$ to output variables $y \in \mathcal{Y}$. Subsequently, to infer desired states of physical systems, we aim to find an inverse mapping $g : \mathcal{Y} \to \mathcal{X}$ that satisfies

$x = g(y) = f^{-1}(y)$, $\forall y \in \mathcal{Y}$. For instance, Fig. 2 shows the end-effector position of a robot arm following forward kinematics functions of joint degrees of freedom. The inverse kinematics is to control the joint motions to reach the desired end-effector positions. For such a system, system information is usually required to understand the forward process, e.g., physical function types. When system information is unavailable, one can use machine learning to approximate the forward mapping in a data-driven manner. Unlike the forward mapping, state estimation is another monitoring tool based on inverse learning. However, the inverse learning process is even harder for problems like (1) hard to embed physical law, (2) can have multiple solutions, and (3) information loss due to uneven dimensions between input and output.

To solve these problems, we propose unifying the learning of two-way mappings in an invertible system identification. The two-way mappings indicate learning the forward-inverse pair. Specifically, we aim to learn the function of inverse mapping $x = g(y)$ so that it work in a pair with the forward mapping $y = f(x)$. Therefore, our goal is to let $y = g^{-1}(x)$ approximate the analytical model $y = f(x)$. invertible structure in the approximation model $g^{-1}(\cdot)$ to enforce an automatic inverse $x = g(y)$ for state inference. In this learning process, we have two major targets: 1) to obtain a forward mapping rule that accurately approximates the system model and preserves physical interpretation as much as possible, and 2) to find a perfectly matched forward-inverse pair and estimate the most possible states under the partially observable scenario.

3.1   Optimization Objectives to Identify Invertible System Model

To reach the first goal, we form an optimization problem to find $g^{-1}(\cdot)$ as close as possible to the ground truth of the forward model $f(\cdot)$. For simple notation, we represent g^{-1} as hypothesis function h,

$$h^* = \underset{h \in \mathcal{H}}{\arg\min} \sum_{i=1}^{N} \ell_1(h(x_i), y_i), \tag{1}$$

where $\mathcal{H}$ is a predefined class of hypothesis functions, e.g., parameterized neural networks. Since it is a supervised learning task, $\ell_1(\cdot)$ represents the regression loss function. We use mean square error to measure the mismatch in forward system model recovery. Moreover, for a perfect match of the two-way mappings, we follow the reconstruction loss used by auto-encoder,

$$h^* = \underset{h \in \mathcal{H}}{\arg\min} \sum_{i=1}^{N} \ell_2(x_i, h^{-1}(h(x_i))), \tag{2}$$

where $\ell_2(\cdot)$ is the square loss and $h^{-1}(h(x_i))$ denotes the reconstructed x_i at the output of inverse mapping.

While the supervised learning loss penalizes errors in point estimates during training, it can not easily bypass the ill-conditioned problem for the inverse. Fortunately, physical/engineering systems have operation standards, as the power system example in Fig. 1 shows. Only one solution is feasible to stay within the operating limits or satisfy specific patterns. To promote physically feasible solutions as the second target, we leverage the common criterion for statistical inference. In particular, estimating the probabilistic states x is to maximize likelihood of the posterior probability density [7], which is

$$\hat{x} = \underset{x}{\operatorname{argmax}}\, p(x|y). \tag{3}$$

This process is to learn the invertible representation of real dataset. As long as we design an invertible function hypothesis function h, increasing the likelihood as in (3) contracts the original output data space to the high-density regions. Namely, it tends to locate a high-density data region and estimates the states that stay within the standard operation limit of physical systems

3.2 Virtual Storage Variables to Compensate System Unobservability

For system identification, the recovery of the forward model is sensitive to the data availability in the system. Unfortunately, modern physical/engineering systems are hard to guarantee full observability. Even worse, limited sensors behind the unobservability may lead to information reduction in the forward mapping, making inverse mapping with insufficient knowledge. Therefore, we propose adding virtual storage variables to the output of the forward mapping. All the input knowledge is preserved in the storage variables in the output of the forward mapping. For example, we propose using the network size to decide the number of storage variables. This is because the number of system states indicates the size of the minimum number of variables in a system that can recreate all the measurements in the network, according to the definition of state estimation. And, the number of state variables is typically the same as the network size. Using these variables will not only preserve information, but also format the physical units in the latent layer, which is due to a perfect match on the number of state variables. To exhibit such inherent properties in invertible system identification, we introduce virtual variables y' on the output side. y' is used to compensate the dimension reduction caused by unobservability while imitating the hidden quantities for homogeneous units in the final expression.

During training, the virtual quantities y' are generated from simple orthogonal random variables, e.g., samples from standard isotropic Gaussian distributions. We observed that, compared to directly using Gaussian random variables, it's better to update the generation by a parameterized neural network. Specifically, we convert the virtual variables via a fully-connected NN and update this NN simultaneously with minimizing the reconstruction error in (2). It can better compensate for the information loss caused by unobservability. Thus, the inverse model changes to $x = g(y, y')$. y' are independent from observable y and serve as factorial prior of system uncertainties to estimate the posterior.

4   Physically Invertible System Identification

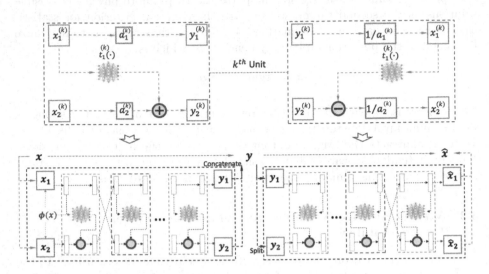

Fig. 3. Illustrate invertible transformation (top) and the structure of the proposed INN.

4.1   Invertible Transformation

To unify the learning of forward and inverse mappings, the key idea is to provide an invertible structure for system identification that find a pair of matched mappings. Enforcing the inversion of $g(\cdot)$ and $g^{-1}(\cdot)$, we consider change of variables, shown below. With $x = g(y, y')$, the change of variables theorem shows

$$p(y') = p(x = g(y, y')|y)|\det \frac{\partial g(y, y')}{\partial y, y'}|,$$

$$p(x|y) = p(y')|\det \frac{\partial g(y, y')}{\partial y, y'}|^{-1}, \tag{4}$$

where $\dfrac{\partial g(y, y')}{\partial y, y'}$ is the Jacobian matrix of function $g(\cdot)$ at x and $\det(\cdot)$ represents the determinant of Jacobian. (4) serves as the theoretical basis of invertible function design. And, we need to find easily invertible functions with non-zero Jacobian determinant.

One intuitive way of invertible design is the linear and addictive function, e.g., the forward $y = ax + b$ and the inverse $x = \frac{1}{a}y - \frac{b}{a}$. The determinant of Jacobian is constant a to ensure invertibility. Motivated by the simple inverse, we follow the invertible design in [7] to split the multi-variate inputs and outputs and construct the following transformation unit:

$$y_1^* = a_1 x_1, y_2^* = a_2 x_2 + t_1(x_1), \tag{5}$$

$$x_1 = \frac{1}{a_1}(y_1^*), x_2 = \frac{1}{a_2}(y_2^* - t_1(x_1)), \tag{6}$$

where $y^* = [y, y']$ for simple notation. Similar to the linear and addictive function, the inverse mapping (6) is easy to derive and the determinant of Jacobian is $a_1 a_2$. Such a split formula is flexible that the nonlinear functions $t_1(\cdot)$ can be arbitrarily complex for representation, without affecting the invertible property.

The unit transforms one part of inputs for invertibility and leaves the other untouched. To enable complete coupling of all dimensions, we composite several units and transform each part in turn. We show in the following Proposition 1 that more than three compositions are necessary to completely transform all inputs dimensions and coupling with the output.

Proposition 1. *With each transformation unit in* (5), *more than three compositions are necessary to completely transform all input dimensions and coupling with the output.*

The proof is intuitive by deriving the Jacobian matrix of the composited invertible functions. For the kth unit, the Jacobian is

$$J_k = \begin{bmatrix} \frac{\partial y_1^{(k)}}{\partial x_1^{(k)}} & \frac{\partial y_1^{(k)}}{\partial x_2^{(k)}} \\ \frac{\partial y_2^{(k)}}{\partial x_1^{(k)}} & \frac{\partial y_2^{(k)}}{\partial x_2^{(k)}} \end{bmatrix} = \begin{bmatrix} a_1^{(k)} I_1 & 0 \\ \frac{\partial t_1^{(k)}(x_1)}{\partial x_1^{(k)}} & a_2^{(k)} I_2 \end{bmatrix}. \tag{7}$$

For every other layer, the columns exchange due to the in-turn transformation. Using the chain rule, the Jacobian of the composited function is $\Pi_k J_k$. Only when $k \geq 3$, the 0's are eliminated from Jacobian matrix and thus indicate a full transformation of all dimensions.

Figure 3 (top) illustrates the invertible transformation. As for the NN structure in the bottom, with each unit to be invertible, the sequence of composited units is invertible, and the Jacobian determinant is easily computed for optimizing (3).

4.2 Building Invertible NN Structure for Physical Interpretability

The sequence of invertible transformations is trained to maximize the likelihood of the training data. However, the unsupervised learning manner performs poorly in generalizing to the out-of-range dataset and reaching global optimum [16]. Furthermore, unlike image density estimation, extrapolation is often the primary concern in the physical system when new operation points occur and have never been recorded in the historical data. In such cases, an accurate inverse solution requires perfect forward mapping learning to recover the governing function of a physical system. Thus, we aim to find a hypothesis that not only minimizes the empirical prediction error (1) but also reveals the underlying analytical function.

However, it is challenging to meet the latter target as any large physical systems (e.g., power, water, traffic systems) have limited sensor deployment for full observability. For these cases, we need to simultaneously recover governing functions in the observable region and approximate hidden correlation in data whenever physical recovery is impossible. According to [36], we express the ground truth $f(\cdot)$ in the form $y = f(x) = f_1(x) + f_2(x) = W_1\phi(x) + f_2(x)$. $f_1(\cdot)$ denotes the recoverable physical law of the observable, and $f_2(\cdot)$ denotes the mapping regarding the unobservable region. Learning $f_1(x)$ only is a system identification problem, where $\phi(x)$ are the physical features of specific systems (e.g., coupling of quadratic and sinusoidal terms for power system) and W_1 represents unknown system parameters to be recovered. To enable physical interpretability, we embed $\phi(x)$ into the invertible hypothesis function (5). In this way, the invertible unit can reveal physics and match the underlying model during learning.

Thus, the proposed invertible NN structure unifies the forward and inverse mappings. The model is trained by optimizing two loss functions simultaneously to reach the optimal inverse solution. On one hand, using the supervised learning loss aims to minimize the mismatch of sample predictions and makes the forward mapping as close to the governing function as possible. On the other hand, using the unsupervised learning loss focuses on a high-density region to avoid ill-conditioned problems in an inverse process. In practice, we observe a trade-off between the two loss terms. Therefore, a hyperparameter is adopted to balance the penalization. The hyperparameter is chosen through cross-validation in the experiments. By training the invertible NN structure, if we find the optimal forward mapping that reveals physics, we naturally obtain the inverse following physical laws.

5   Experiments

The proposed invertible NN is applicable for various inverse problems in physical systems. We validate the algorithm on kinematics systems, power systems, robotic systems, and high-rise buildings (structural health). The results are similar, so we focus on the two most representative systems for in-depth evaluation with respect to each of the proposed designs. They are the inverse kinematics, where hidden states follow one-way cascading correlation, and the inverse power flow, where states yield two-way interactive correlation.

Evaluation Criteria: Learning the inverse mapping in physical system can be seen as a regression problem. Therefore, we use the evaluation metric mean square error (MSE) for state estimation. For the physical system analysis, the interpretability is essential so that we evaluate by the accuracy of learning system parameters for the forward system model. The higher the accuracy, the more reducible is the learned model.

Baselines: We compare the proposed model with the following state-of-the-art baselines on learning the inverse system mapping: support vector regression (SVR) with polynomial kernel or RBF kernel [35], residual neural network (ResNet) [12], variational autoencoder (VAE) to approximate the forward-inverse pair [15], NICE/RealNVP to learn the invertible transformation [7,8]. The first two methods directly learn the inverse mapping while the other two methods enforce the inverse model from forward model to obtain inverse solutions [13,37]. In particular, we use the same architecture (depth, width, and activation) for the NN $t_1(\cdot)$ in invertible structure, ResNet, and auto-encoder. We showed previously that at least three invertible units are required to completely transform all dimensions. Therefore, the depth of NNs is a hyper-parameter selected from $3-10$ layers in validation, and the width depends on the problem size of the test system.

The Adam optimizer is used to train NNs for 200 epochs for each experiment, where we set up a learning rate hyper-parameter set $\{0.001, 0.0002, 0.00005\}$, and momentum parameters $\beta_1 = 0.5, \beta_2 = 0.999$. All the experiments are implemented on a computer equipped with Inter(R) Core(TM) i7-9700k CPU and Nvidia Geforce RTX 3090 GPU.

Table 1. The prediction errors (MSE$\times10^{-3}$) of invertible kinematics system identification: the inverse solution and forward mapping recovery.

Case	Model	Joint angle prediction	Forward model prediction
3-DOF	SVR	0.0004 ± 0.00	N/A
	ResNet	0.001 ± 0.00	N/A
	VAE	0.001 ± 0.01	0.0015 ± 0.00
	RealNVP	0.0005 ± 0.00	0.0004 ± 0.00
	Proposed INN	0.0002 ± 0.00	0.0001 ± 0.00
5-DOF	SVR	0.19 ± 0.07	N/A
	ResNet	0.12 ± 0.03	N/A
	VAE	0.10 ± 0.04	0.09 ± 0.02
	RealNVP	0.08 ± 0.01	0.04 ± 0.02
	Proposed INN	0.06 ± 0.02	0.02 ± 0.00

5.1 Inverse Kinematics Problem

To test the applicability of the proposed model on physical inverse process, we start with a basic inverse kinematics problem, where instruments are not fully equipped to collect all the data. As shown in Fig. 2(a), the movement of end-effectors is determined by multiple degrees of freedom (DOF) chains in the robotic systems. The manipulator in 2D space moves with the rotations of three joints (3 DOFs) that connect 4 rigid parts. The task is to find the most likely joint motions to reach the desired end-effector position. Given the configuration of joint angles, the forward kinematics equations describe the motion of the hierarchical skeleton structure. However, the system parameters, e.g., joint lengths, are unknown. We aim to identify the possible rotation angles of three joints given the expected end-effector coordinates. In this case, 1000 different configurations are sampled for training and random Gaussian noises are added ($\mathcal{N}(0, 0.01)$).

For a more complex setup, we consider the manipulator in 3D space with 5 DOFs (Fig. 2(b)). The new DOFs in the added dimension are intractable where measurements of θ_4 and θ_5 are unavailable. In this case, we evaluate the prediction of joint rotations in inverse process. Moreover, we evaluate the partial recovery of the governing function on observable parts in the forward system identification. Table 1 compares the numerical results of the proposed physics-interpretable invertible NN with the baselines.

For the 3-DOF setup, both SVR and the proposed model have good estimation results. Specifically, our physics-interpretable invertible NN outperforms the original RealNVP due to the physics embedding in the forward mapping. It can also be verified by the accuracy of system parameter recovery, where the proposed INN reaches near 100% for this fully observable case. For the 5-DOF case that has some unobservables, the variational auto-encoder and RealNVP have much lower errors than the first two models that directly approximate the inverse process. Although the proposed invertible neural network can not recover all the system parameters due to the unobservability, it shows a generally lower error in estimating inverse solution than the original RealNVP.

5.2   Inverse Power Flow Problem: Distribution System State Estimation

After the demonstration of the basic kinematics problem, we test the proposed model on more complex and larger systems. Different from the single link in the manipulator, the standard power system can be seen as a graph with many internal couplings. The real utility feeder usually has more complex connections and a larger scale. For an N-node power system, the governing physical law is the classic power flow equations (PF) [35]. The power system state estimation (SE) is of great interest for many downstream operation applications [24,37]. Estimating voltage phasor states from standard measurements (e.g., power injections, branch power flows, and current magnitudes) is an inverse process of power flow analysis. Test feeders IEEE 8- and 123-bus networks, and a utility feeder (2721 nodes with 371 active ones) are used for experiments, shown as 8-bus, 123-bus, and Utility in Table 2. Since ground truth data is not directly available, we conduct traditional simulations with one-year real power data (15-min interval) in MATPOWER [38]. The model information is only available to prepare the dataset and remains unknown during training. The real-world measurements usually have errors due to communication issues. We add random Gaussian noise with a 1%–2% standard deviation to simulate the measurement errors (as usually used by state estimation). Moreover, we prepare out-of-range data (3× PV generation and loads) to validate extrapolation capability.

Table 2. The prediction errors (MSE×10^{-3}/p.u.) of power system cases: the inverse state estimation and the forward power flow mapping.

(a) Testing on the in-range data scenario.

Scenario	Case	SVR	ResNet	VAE	RealNVP	Proposed INN
SE (In-Range)	8-bus	0.08 ± 0.02	0.04 ± 0.00	0.03 ± 0.01	0.008 ± 0.00	$\mathbf{0.006 \pm 0.00}$
	123-bus	0.21 ± 0.04	0.17 ± 0.02	0.13 ± 0.03	0.09 ± 0.01	$\mathbf{0.05 \pm 0.03}$
	Utility	0.27 ± 0.12	0.23 ± 0.05	0.16 ± 0.03	0.13 ± 0.07	$\mathbf{0.11 \pm 0.02}$
PF (In-Range)	8-bus	N/A	N/A	0.05 ± 0.01	0.007 ± 0.00	$\mathbf{0.002 \pm 0.00}$
	123-bus	N/A	N/A	0.11 ± 0.06	0.06 ± 0.03	$\mathbf{0.02 \pm 0.01}$
	Utility	N/A	N/A	0.15 ± 0.01	0.13 ± 0.02	$\mathbf{0.04 \pm 0.03}$

(b) Testing on the out-of-range data scenario for extrapolation.

Scenario	Case	SVR	ResNet	VAE	RealNVP	Proposed INN
SE (Extrapolation)	8-bus	0.14 ± 0.04	0.09 ± 0.03	0.09 ± 0.02	0.03 ± 0.01	$\mathbf{0.009 \pm 0.00}$
	123-bus	0.29 ± 0.11	0.22 ± 0.06	0.25 ± 0.02	0.15 ± 0.03	$\mathbf{0.07 \pm 0.02}$
	Utility	0.43 ± 0.19	0.35 ± 0.02	0.31 ± 0.09	0.19 ± 0.06	$\mathbf{0.15 \pm 0.04}$
PF (Extrapolation)	8-bus	N/A	N/A	0.07 ± 0.03	0.04 ± 0.02	$\mathbf{0.004 \pm 0.00}$
	123-bus	N/A	N/A	0.21 ± 0.03	0.18 ± 0.07	$\mathbf{0.06 \pm 0.03}$
	Utility	N/A	N/A	0.24 ± 0.06	0.22 ± 0.05	$\mathbf{0.11 \pm 0.05}$

The numerical results of estimation are included in Table 2 and Fig. 4 to compare different methods. As we explained, SE denotes the inverse process while PF denotes the forward mapping recovery. First, we observe a general decrease in MSEs for forward-inverse learning methods compared to the direct inverse learning methods (SVR and ResNet).

While the errors of inverse solutions are small, we look back to the forward learning. VAE has a relatively poor result as the reconstruction errors cannot reach zeros in approximation. Although RealNVP naturally has the perfect correspondence to learn an explicit forward, the proposed INN outperforms it by a large margin for forward mapping recovery. This could also be explained by the ablation study of our proposed model. For the observable region, the governing PF function can be recovered by the proposed INN. The ablation study results (Table 3) demonstrate how physics embedding greatly impacts the forward model recovery. Without physics consistency in learning model, both the MSEs of inverse estimation and forward output prediction are higher. Further, the comparison of state estimation given in-range and out-of-range inputs in Fig. 4a and Fig. 4b reveals a better extrapolation capability of the proposed INN. During the experiments, we observe that, when there is no physics embedding, increasing the weight of the density estimation loss can lower the MSE slightly.

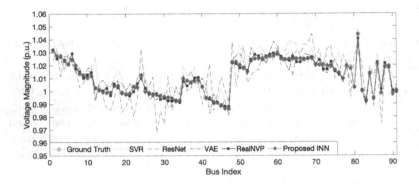

(a) Estimated voltage magnitudes given in-range inputs (generation and load)

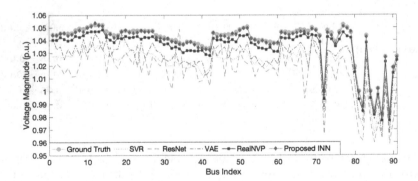

(b) Estimated voltage magnitudes given out-of-range inputs for extrapolation evaluation.

Fig. 4. Validating estimation results of all the nodes (from feeder head to end) on one phase of 123-bus system.

Table 3. Ablation study of the proposed invertible neural network.

Scenario	Case	Proposed INN	W/o physics embedding	W/o virtual variables
SE (In-Range)	8-bus	**0.006 ± 0.00**	0.01 ± 0.00	0.02 ± 0.01
	123-bus	**0.05 ± 0.03**	0.08 ± 0.02	0.07 ± 0.01
	Utility	**0.11 ± 0.02**	0.15 ± 0.05	0.17 ± 0.03
PF (In-Range)	8-bus	**0.002 ± 0.00**	0.003 ± 0.00	0.002 ± 0.00
	123-bus	**0.02 ± 0.01**	0.05 ± 0.02	0.02 ± 0.01
	Utility	**0.04 ± 0.03**	0.15 ± 0.06	0.05 ± 0.02
SE (Extrapolation)	8-bus	**0.009 ± 0.00**	0.04 ± 0.01	0.04 ± 0.00
	123-bus	**0.07 ± 0.02**	0.13 ± 0.05	0.16 ± 0.03
	Utility	**0.15 ± 0.04**	0.23 ± 0.03	0.23 ± 0.07
PF (Extrapolation)	8-bus	**0.004 ± 0.00**	0.03 ± 0.02	0.005 ± 0.00
	123-bus	**0.06 ± 0.03**	0.21 ± 0.05	0.08 ± 0.02
	Utility	**0.11 ± 0.05**	0.26 ± 0.02	0.15 ± 0.04

6 Conclusion

In this paper, we propose a physics-interpretable inverse learning method to tackle the challenge of solving the inverse process of physical systems. Rather than a direct approximation, we unify the forward and inverse learning, and simultaneously optimize over the pair of mappings. The proposed method takes advantage of the flexible NN structure and the recent advances in density estimation to guarantee a perfect forward-inverse pair and solve the ill-conditioned physical systems problem. Moreover, since the generative model has limitations in the adversarial task of physical system identification, we embed physics into the invertible structure to enable interpretability and further enforce the inverse solution following physical laws. Numerical experiments have been conducted on physical/engineering systems with typical couplings to evaluate the proposed method. Our model outperforms the baseline methods on both the inverse process learning and the forward model recovery and output prediction.

References

1. Abdel-Majeed, A., Tenbohlen, S., Schöllhorn, D., Braun, M.: Development of state estimator for low voltage networks using smart meters measurement data. In: IEEE Grenoble Conference, pp. 1–6 (2013)
2. Bengio, Y., Mesnil, G., Dauphin, Y., Rifai, S.: Better mixing via deep representations. In: International Conference on Machine Learning, pp. 552–560. PMLR (2013)
3. Benning, M., Burger, M.: Modern regularization methods for inverse problems. arXiv preprint arXiv:1801.09922 (2018)
4. Bhela, S., Kekatos, V., Veeramachaneni, S.: Enhancing observability in distribution grids using smart meter data. IEEE Trans. Smart Grid **9**(6), 5953–5961 (2018). https://doi.org/10.1109/TSG.2017.2699939

5. Botín-Sanabria, D.M., et al.: Digital twin technology challenges and applications: a comprehensive review. Remote Sens. **14**(6), 1335 (2022)
6. Deka, D., Backhaus, S., Chertkov, M.: Learning topology of the power distribution grid with and without missing data. In: European Control Conference, pp. 313–320 (2016)
7. Dinh, L., Krueger, D., Bengio, Y.: NICE: non-linear independent components estimation. arXiv preprint arXiv:1410.8516 (2014)
8. Dinh, L., Sohl-Dickstein, J., Bengio, S.: Density estimation using Real NVP. arXiv preprint arXiv:1605.08803 (2016)
9. Engl, H.W., Hanke, M., Neubauer, A.: Regularization of Inverse Problems, vol. 375. Springer, Heidelberg (1996)
10. Hamdan, S., Ayyash, M., Almajali, S.: Edge-computing architectures for internet of things applications: a survey. Sensors **20**(22), 6441 (2020)
11. Haque, M.E., Zain, M.F., Hannan, M.A., Rahman, M.H.: Building structural health monitoring using dense and sparse topology wireless sensor network. Smart Struct. Syst. **16**(4), 607–621 (2015)
12. He, K., Zhang, X., Ren, S., Sun, J.: Deep residual learning for image recognition. In: Proceedings of the IEEE Conference on Computer Vision and Pattern Recognition (2016)
13. Hu, X., Hu, H., Verma, S., Zhang, Z.L.: Physics-guided deep neural networks for powerflow analysis. arXiv preprint arXiv:2002.00097 (2020)
14. Karlik, B., Aydin, S.: An improved approach to the solution of inverse kinematics problems for robot manipulators. Eng. Appl. Artif. Intell. **13**(2), 159–164 (2000)
15. Kingma, D.P., Welling, M.: Auto-encoding variational bayes. arXiv preprint arXiv:1312.6114 (2013)
16. Kirichenko, P., Izmailov, P., Wilson, A.G.: Why normalizing flows fail to detect out-of-distribution data. arXiv preprint arXiv:2006.08545 (2020)
17. Kucuk, S., Bingul, Z.: Robot kinematics: Forward and inverse kinematics. INTECH Open Access Publisher (2006)
18. Kuo, Y.L., Tang, S.C.: Dynamics and control of a 3-dof planar parallel manipulator using visual servoing resolved acceleration control. J. Low Freq. Noise Vib. Active Control, 1461348419876154 (2019)
19. Liao, L., Fox, D., Hightower, J., Kautz, H., Schulz, D.: Voronoi tracking: location estimation using sparse and noisy sensor data. In: Proceedings 2003 IEEE/RSJ International Conference on Intelligent Robots and Systems (IROS 2003)(Cat. No. 03CH37453), vol. 1, pp. 723–728. IEEE (2003)
20. Liao, Y., Weng, Y., Liu, G., Zhang, Z., Tan, C.W., Rajagopal, R.: Unbalanced three-phase distribution grid topology estimation and bus phase identification. IET Smart Grid **2**(4), 557–570 (2019)
21. Linden, A., Kindermann, J.: Inversion of multilayer nets. In: Proceedings of International Joint Conference on Neural Networks, vol. 2, pp. 425–430 (1989)
22. Liu, M.Z., et al.: Grid and market services from the edge: using operating envelopes to unlock network-aware bottom-up flexibility. IEEE Power Energy Maga. **19**(4), 52–62 (2021)
23. Liu, Y., Zhang, N., Wang, Y., Yang, J., Kang, C.: Data-driven power flow linearization: a regression approach. IEEE Trans. Smart Grid **10**(3), 2569–2580 (2019)
24. Mestav, K.R., Luengo-Rozas, J., Tong, L.: Bayesian state estimation for unobservable distribution systems via deep learning. IEEE Trans. Power Syst. **34**(6), 4910–4920 (2019)
25. Mnih, A., Gregor, K.: Neural variational inference and learning in belief networks. In: International Conference on Machine Learning, pp. 1791–1799 (2014)

26. Müller, H.H., Rider, M.J., Castro, C.A.: Artificial neural networks for load flow and external equivalents studies. Electr. Power Syst. Res. **80**(9), 1033–1041 (2010)
27. Pan, S., Bonde, A., Jing, J., Zhang, L., Zhang, P., Noh, H.Y.: Boes: building occupancy estimation system using sparse ambient vibration monitoring. In: Sensors and Smart Structures Technologies for Civil, Mechanical, and Aerospace Systems 2014, vol. 9061, p. 90611O. International Society for Optics and Photonics (2014)
28. Pei, Y., Biswas, S., Fussell, D.S., Pingali, K.: An elementary introduction to kalman filtering. Commun. ACM **62**(11), 122–133 (2019)
29. Schmidt, M., Lipson, H.: Distilling free-form natural laws from experimental data. Science **324**(5923), 81–85 (2009)
30. Tinney, W.F., Hart, C.E.: Power flow solution by newton's method. IEEE Trans. Power Apparat. Syst. **11**, 1449–1460 (1967)
31. Varkonyi-Koczy, A.R., Rovid, A.: Observer based iterative neural network model inversion. In: The 14th IEEE International Conference on Fuzzy Systems, FUZZ 2005, pp. 402–407 (2005)
32. Vitus, M.P., Tomlin, C.J.: Sensor placement for improved robotic navigation. In: Robotics: Science and Systems VI, p. 217 (2011)
33. Wang, L., Zhou, Q., Jin, S.: Physics-guided deep learning for power system state estimation. J. Mod. Power Syst. Clean Energy **8**(4), 607–615 (2020)
34. Weng, Y., Negi, R., Ilić, M.D.: Historical data-driven state estimation for electric power systems. In: 2013 IEEE International Conference on Smart Grid Communications (SmartGridComm), pp. 97–102. IEEE (2013)
35. Yu, J., Weng, Y., Rajagopal, R.: Robust mapping rule estimation for power flow analysis in distribution grids, pp. 1–6 (2017)
36. Yuan, J., Weng, Y.: Physics interpretable shallow-deep neural networks for physical system identification with unobservability. In: IEEE International Conference on Data Mining (ICDM) (2021)
37. Zamzam, A.S., Sidiropoulos, N.D.: Physics-aware neural networks for distribution system state estimation. IEEE Trans. Power Syst. **35**, 4347–4356 (2020)
38. Zimmerman, R.D., Murillo-Sánchez, C.E., Thomas, R.J.: Matpower: steady-state operations, planning, and analysis tools for power systems research and education. IEEE Trans. Power Syst. **26**(1), 12–19 (2011)

GALG: Linking Addresses in Tracking Ecosystem Using Graph Autoencoder with Link Generation

Tianyu Cui[1,2], Gang Xiong[1,2], Chang Liu[1,2(✉)], Junzheng Shi[1,2], Peipei Fu[1,2], and Gaopeng Gou[1,2]

[1] Institute of Information Engineering, Chinese Academy of Sciences, Beijing, China
{cuitianyu,xionggang,liuchang,shijunzheng,fupeipei,gougaopeng}@iie.ac.cn
[2] School of Cyber Security, University of Chinese Academy of Sciences, Beijing, China

Abstract. Online tracking technology is a critical tool for user-centric platform practitioners to link users across multiple web pages and make detailed user profiles for the improvement of recommender systems like targeted advertising. Recently, due to the dynamic address allocation and security upgrade, mitigations indirectly make prior tracking techniques unreliable. To overcome the problem, traffic-based tracking techniques are proposed to link users' dynamic addresses through similarity learning of user behaviors in their traffic interaction. However, prior work either provides poor similarity learning ability or is impractical when applied to a large scale. In this paper, we propose GALG, a graph-based artificial intelligence approach to link addresses for user tracking on TLS encrypted traffic. GALG uses the framework of graph autoencoder and adversarial training to learn the user embedding with semantics and distributions. Employing a new theory – link generation, GALG could link all the addresses of target users based on the knowledge of address-service links. When evaluated on real-world user datasets, GALG outperforms existing approaches in both performance and practicality.

Keywords: Online tracking · Graph neural networks · Link prediction

1 Introduction

Websites and third-party services such as search engines, advertising networks, and network providers collect user interests across multiple web pages to improve the quality of recommender systems and user experiences in the area including targeted advertising and content personalization. Under the background, online tracking has been ubiquitous on the web [3]. The tracking mechanism could link records of a user's browsing activity across numerous websites to make inferences about the user's demographics and interests, or observe the conversion that whether an advertisement on a website leads to the desired user activity on another website [17]. Until recently, over four-fifth of websites have enabled tracking systems [25]. Big players like Google and Facebook leverage the widespread

© The Author(s), under exclusive license to Springer Nature Switzerland AG 2023
M.-R. Amini et al. (Eds.): ECML PKDD 2022, LNAI 13718, pp. 270–285, 2023.
https://doi.org/10.1007/978-3-031-26422-1_17

use of their advertising networks and social plugins to track users across websites and gain detailed user profiles.

The core objective of online tracking is to link historical users across multiple contexts. Refer to Fig. 1. When a user generates browsing records on a website, the tracking system could utilize the information in the incoming records to search all records linking to the user in a tracking database. The database is a knowledge base owned by a tracker that contains numerous user records on multiple websites. The linked records of each user are finally used in user profiling for a better recommendation. In this setting, the traceable information in records is critical for the tracking system.

Promoted by the huge tracking ecosystem, researchers have
tried to leverage types of information to track real-world users,
including IP addresses, cookies,
and browser fingerprints. Tracking based on IP addresses is the
primary tracking method because
all online behaviors must come
from users' client addresses. However, the dynamic address allocation causes frequent changes of
users' addresses, making address-

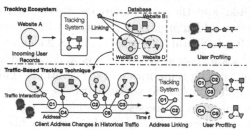

Fig. 1. The illustration of the tracking ecosystem. The traffic-based tracking method links users' addresses across multiple traffic interactions.

to-user correlation unreliable. Tracking based on cookies [19] and browser fingerprints [7] could produce and store the identifier and features of user browsers. Nevertheless, as users are increasingly aware of privacy protection, they start to encrypt communication sessions with Transport Layer Security (TLS) [20], use private browsing modes, and enable privacy-friendly browser extensions to obfuscate traceable features. Although the majority of users only intend to protect their sensitive information rather than deliberately confronting recommender systems, the situation indeed leads to data loss and model failure in the tracking ecosystem. Microsoft reported that they could no longer track 32% of users under their services due to these mitigations [24].

To address these problems, recently, traffic-based user tracking techniques [1,4,8,14] have been proved to have a strong performance by analyzing the patterns in the traffic. As a worldwide information system, the Internet maintains users' daily online activities through traffic transmission. Though the critical payload consisting of user data is encrypted in the TLS session under HTTPS communication, the traffic contains considerable meta-information associated with user behaviors and online interaction. In Fig. 1, banding the address with these traffic characteristics, researchers could link multiple client addresses to achieve long-term user tracking. However, the extensive knowledge hidden in the traffic raises the questions that how to effectively leverage the complicated information to reach high tracking accuracy, and, separately, how to fast link the real-world users in such a huge knowledge volume. Previous works either could only track a specific subset of users on a closed-world dataset due to the unreliable similarity learning [1,8,14], or expense considerable time with an unsuitable framework [4], remaining the problem that the traffic-based tracking technique is impractical when applied to a large scale.

In this paper, we develop a more sophisticated approach to overcome these limitations, juggling performance and practicality. In particular, we introduce **GALG, a graph-based artificial intelligence approach** to link addresses for user tracking on TLS encrypted traffic. GALG is short for "Graph Autoencoder with Link Generation". The framework of our approach consists of three steps as follows. First, GALG constructs a graph with client address-to-online service links and the user preference distribution of each client address to model the traceable information. Second, for better similarity learning, using the theory of Graph Neural Networks [12,13,18,23] and adversarial training, GALG employs a stack attention-based encoder and a discriminator to learn the latent embedding of jointing semantics and distributions. Third, innovating from the task of link prediction [16] in social networks, we propose **link generation**, which could learn from address-service links to generate address-address links. Benefiting from the new theory, GALG could achieve effective few-shot learning, finally taking large-scale user tracking to reality.

In summary, our contributions can be summarized as follows:

- **Application.** We implement reliable user tracking in the tracking ecosystem to link addresses through address embedding learning with a traffic-based tracking system.
- **Theory.** We propose link generation to generate a new type of links from the original type of links in heterogeneous graphs, which is more effective in user tracking tasks than link prediction.
- **Models.** We introduce two novel tracking models GALG and VGALG, which could jointly learn semantics and distributions through an adversarial architecture with a graph autoencoder.
- **Experiments.** We conduct experiments on real-world datasets. Results indicate that GALG outperforms the state-of-the-art tracking techniques and link prediction-based methods in both performance and practicality.

2   Related Work

We overview the related work of our paper from the objective and technical perspectives, including the prior work of user tracking and link prediction.

2.1   User Tracking

User tracking on the Internet could come in various forms. Over the past years, through HTTP cookies [19] and browser fingerprinting [7]. However, recently, traffic-based tracking techniques have been proved to have stronger performance and longer tracking time, which can be extensively applied in various scenarios.

Kumpost et al. [14] used the target IP addresses of each user to build user profiles for tracking them in the future. Banse et al. [10] trained a Bayesian classifier with DNS requests to track users on a university network. Following the deployment of HTTPS, the interaction between users and websites tends to be protected under the wide-used TLS traffic. Anderson et al. [1] extracted field values in TLS ClientHello messages to build traceable fingerprints, which could be easily enhanced with machine learning. Nonetheless, due to the strong variation of different users in the open-world scenarios, these approaches usually perform a poor generalization on unseen users. To address the problem, Cui et al. [4] proposed a knowledge graph-based approach SiamHAN to track users on TLS encrypted traffic. Since the approach requires calculating the similarity between every two addresses, the time cost is impractical at scale. Different from prior work, GALG aims to provide a better learning framework of user embeddings, which could work on unseen users with less time cost.

2.2   Link Prediction

Link prediction [16] is a critical task for graph-structured data. By predicting the relationship of two nodes in a graph, the task has many applications such as recommendation and graph reconstruction. The prior approaches for link prediction mainly include heuristic methods, latent feature methods, and explicit feature methods. Heuristic methods [16] are a class of simple yet effective approaches to calculating node similarity scores with heuristic assumption. Latent feature methods such as spectral clustering [21] and node2vec [9], have been proposed to use the knowledge of graph structure for graph embedding learning. Using the powerful performance of GNNs [12,13,18,23] , explicit feature methods [12,18] could aggregate node attributes built from side information to obtain more meaningful knowledge from the graph. While the techniques for link prediction have many variants, the theory of the task is never changed – using the known links to predict the same type of unknown links. The framework limits that link prediction requires learning considerable annotation links to supplement the lost links in one specific graph. In the tracking database, there is a large ratio of test user nodes and we cannot always keep enough labels in a graph. In this paper, we employ link generation to overcome the limitation in the tracking ecosystem.

3   Preliminaries

This section introduces the definition of the problem and the link generation theory to help readers understand this paper.

3.1   Problem Definition

On the Internet, users could use clients to access various online services. The manifestation in the traffic is that the client address and the server address establish connections. However, to facilitate the address acquisition process, network administrators have widely deployed dynamic address allocation policies like DHCP [5]. Within a period of time, a user might use multiple client addresses for external communication. The relationship between users and addresses cannot be detected using payloads due to TLS encryption.

In the tracking ecosystem, a tracker aims to link user across multiple web pages to make detailed user profiles. To obtain the user traffic, the tracker could be a network provider with a vantage traffic observation point, an advertising network provider with wide-used traffic plugins deployed in numerous Apps and websites, or a content provider like Google owning multiple websites. Using the meta-information in the traffic, tracking systems could link multiple client addresses to find out the target user. Given a period of TLS historical traffic as background knowledge K_t, the set of all client addresses in the traffic is S, the set of client addresses of a target user is $Y = \{y_0, y_1, ..., y_n\}$. A tracking system F could use one client address y_0 to trace the whole address set Y:

$$F((S, y_0)|K_t; \theta) = Y \tag{1}$$

where θ is the parameters of the tracking model. After obtaining the address set Y, researchers could master all activities associated with these addresses to analyze the target user. Holding the long sequences across websites, trackers could infer global user demographics for service policy updates or use the interaction records between addresses and accounts for targeted recommendations.

3.2 Link Generation

The link generation task we proposed is innovated from the link prediction.

Definition 1. Link Prediction. Given a graph G, which contains at least one type of node and one type of link. The link prediction task requires learning a type of links and complementing the missing links of this type in graph G. If A_i is the adjacency matrix of the links with type i, the goal of a model F for link prediction could be shown as follows:

$$A_i \xrightarrow{F(G;\theta)} \widetilde{A_i} \tag{2}$$

where θ is the trained parameters. $\widetilde{A_i}$ is the ground truth of the type-i links.

Definition 2. Link Generation. Given a heterogeneous graph G_h, which contains at least two types of nodes and one type of link. The link generation task requires learning a type of links and generating a new type of links in graph G_h. If A_i is the adjacency matrix of the links with type i, the goal of a model F for link generation could be shown as follows:

$$A_i \xrightarrow{F(G_h;\theta)} A_j \tag{3}$$

where $i \neq j$. A_j is the ground truth of the type-j links. Unlike link prediction, link generation tasks can generate types of links that never appear in the graph. In this paper, we show that link generation is more effective and practical than link prediction by using address-service links to generate address-address links.

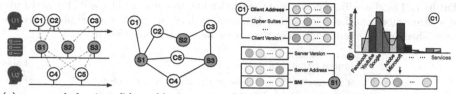

(a) user behaviors (b) address-service (c) client and service (d) user preference
with client addresses. graph construction. fingerprints. distributions.

Fig. 2. The address-service graph and user preference distributions: (a) Users might
use multiple client addresses (c1, c2, and c3 for user u1; c4 and c5 for user u2) to
access online services (s1, s2, and s3) in a period of time; (b) The connection relationship between c and s could build the address-service graph; (c) Each node c/s uses
client/service fingerprints built from TLS traffic as the node attribute; (d) The cumulative visits of a client address to each service could build the preference distribution.

4   Design of GALG

This section proposes the overall framework of GALG, including (1) graph and
distribution construction and (2) GALG's model architecture.

4.1   Graph and Distribution Construction

To implement traffic-based tracking technology, GALG extracts two kinds of
knowledge from the traffic to help track real-world users – an address-service
graph and user preference distributions.

Address-Service Graph. To model the user activities behind the traffic,
GALG uses a heterogeneous graph to capture the meta-information in the traffic. Figure 2(a)-(c) shows the detail of building the address-service graph. In the
historical traffic over a period of time, since users use multiple client addresses to
access online services, the connection relationship between these addresses and
services could be used to build the heterogeneous graph. The graph contains
two types of nodes and one type of link – address node c, service node s, and
address-service link c-s. Whenever a user accesses a web service over HTTPS,
their communication will generate many available data in TLS traffic such as
ClientHello, ServerHello, and Certificate message. GALG extracts client fingerprints and service fingerprints from these messages to model the attributes of
the address nodes and the service nodes in the graph. Table 1 shows the notions
of these fingerprints. In each TLS connection, the fingerprints are bound to an
address node and a service node respectively. The client address and the server
name identifier (SNI) are used as the node identifier to distinguish different
address nodes and service nodes. Finally, these node attributes are learned by
doc2vec [15] to obtain the semantic representation of fingerprints under the feature space.

Table 1. The client fingerprints and the service fingerprints used to build the attributes of address nodes and service nodes. Different address nodes or service nodes are distinguished by the client address or the server name identifier (SNI).

Type	Fingerprint name	Notion	Label
Address node c	Client address*	The address of the client in the TLS traffic	Fc1
	Record version	The TLS version employed by the client	Fc2
	Client version	The version by which the client wishes to connect	Fc3
	Cipher suites	A list of the cryptographic options supported	Fc4
	Compression	A list of the compression methods supported	Fc5
Service node s	SNI*	The domain name that the client wants to reach	Fs1
	Server address	The address of the server in the TLS traffic	Fs2
	Record version	The TLS version employed by the server	Fs3
	Server version	The version finally chosen by the server	Fs4
	Cipher suite	The single cipher suite selected	Fs5
	Algorithm ID	The identifier for the cryptographic algorithm	Fs6
	Issuer	The entity that has signed and issued the certificate	Fs7
	Subject	The entity associated with the public key stored	Fs8

User Preference Distributions. In addition to knowing which services the user accessed in the horizontal analysis, a vertical eye to master how much the user prefers these services could also contribute to identifying the user. GALG uses the cumulative access volume of a client address to each service to build its user preference distribution. Figure 2(d) shows the detail of building the distribution. For each client address, we collect the number of TLS connections of the address to each service to build a distribution vector. The length of the vector is the total number of service nodes in the address-service graph. Finally, to reduce the overlong dimension of the vector, GALG employs PCA [6] to obtain the representation of the distribution for each address node in the graph.

4.2 Model Architecture

Figure 3 shows the overall architecture of GALG. GALG employs an adversarial architecture with a graph autoencoder to implement reliable user tracking.

Encoder Learning. In the task of user tracking, the heterogeneous graph G_h built from TLS traffic contains address-service links A and node attributes X. By learning the meta-information, the goal of the encoder in GALG is to obtain the latent embedding Z of the address nodes for address-address link generation.

To implement the encoder model, GALG leverages stack attention to integrate complex semantic knowledge into the embeddings of the address nodes. The stack attention contains two levels – fingerprint-level attention (FA) and service-level attention (SA). The fingerprint-level attention first learns the weights of all fingerprints in a node attribute X_u and aggregates them to obtain the

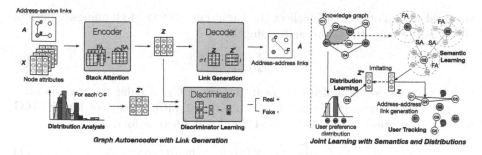

Fig. 3. The overall architecture of GALG. The encoder aggregates meta-information in the knowledge graph to obtain the latent embedding through stack attention. The discriminator distinguishes between the representation of real preference distributions and the latent embedding. The decoder finally generates the address-address links.

first-level node embedding. The fingerprint importance α_u and the first-level node embedding Z_u^1 of a node u are shown as follows:

$$\alpha_{ui} = \frac{\exp(h_{ui}^\top W_h)}{\sum_{i=1}^{|X_u|} \exp(h_{ui}^\top W_h)}, \text{ here } h_{ui} = \tanh(W_w X_{ui} + W_b)$$

$$Z_u^1 = \sum_{i=1}^{|X_u|} \alpha_{ui} X_{ui} \qquad (4)$$

where W_w, W_b, and W_h are the parameter matrices. X_{ui} is a client fingerprint of an address node c or a service fingerprint of a service node s in the heterogeneous graph G_h. Using these fingerprints, the fingerprint attention aims to learn the unique client or service representation from the client or service profiles.

The service-level attention then employs a Graph Attention Network (GAT) [23] based approach to learn the latent embedding of the address nodes. For an address node c_i, S_{c_i} includes node c_i and the service nodes linked to it. The service-level attention could calculate the importance of the services to identifying the user behind the address node c_i and aggregates them to obtain the latent embedding $Z_{c_i}^2$ of the address node:

$$\beta_{c_i s_j} = \frac{\exp(h_{c_i s_j})}{\sum_{s_j \in S_{c_i}} \exp(h_{c_i s_j})}, \text{ here } h_{c_i s_j} = \text{LeakyReLU}(W_s[Z_{c_i}^1 \| Z_{s_j}^1])$$

$$Z_{c_i}^2 = \overset{K}{\underset{k=1}{\|}} \text{ELU}(\sum_{s_j \in S_{c_i}} \beta_{c_i s_j} Z_{s_j}^1) \qquad (5)$$

where W_s is the parameter matrix. $\|$ represents the concatenation operation. K is the number of heads using the multi-head attention mechanism [22]. Using the first-level embeddings, the service-level attention aims to capture the semantics of the user behavior through the communication relationships.

Finally, the stack attention of GALG realizes stacking the two-level semantics into the latent embedding. Through semantic learning, the three-layer meta-information of fingerprints, services, and client addresses are orderly squeezed in the final representation. We collect the latent embedding of all address nodes in the graph to form the latent embedding Z:

$$Z = \prod_{c_i \in V_c} Z_{c_i}^2 \tag{6}$$

where V_c is the set of address nodes in the graph G_h. Similar to previous work [12,18], GALG could be extended to a variational autoencoder version VGALG for link generation. The encoder of VGALG is defined as follows:

$$Z = \prod_{c_i \in V_c} \mathcal{N}(z_{c_i} | \mu_{c_i}, \mathrm{diag}(\sigma^2)) \tag{7}$$

where $\mu = Z^2$ and $\log \sigma = Z^{2'}$ are the matrices of the mean and log variance vectors output by two stack attention networks. Using the two vectors, the model is modified to sample the latent embedding Z to improve the robustness.

Decoder Learning. Using the latent embedding Z, GALG's decoder aims to generate the address-address links $\hat{A}$ for tracking. We could predict whether two client addresses belong to the same user by judging whether there is a link between the two address nodes. The work is implemented by an inner product between their latent embeddings:

$$\hat{A}_{ij} = \prod_{c_i \in V_c} \prod_{c_j \in V_c} \mathrm{sigmoid}(Z_{c_i}^\top Z_{c_j}) \tag{8}$$

where c_i and c_j are two address nodes in the graph G_h.

Adversarial Training. To model the complex user behaviors behind the client addresses, in addition to the semantic knowledge, GALG is also required to use the distribution knowledge to fully grasp the users' activities. Using a multi-layer perceptron (MLP) based discriminator, GALG employs adversarial training to embed the distribution knowledge into the latent embedding Z.

Through the distribution analysis for each address node c, GALG obtain the user preference distribution Z^*. The goal of discriminator is to distinguish whether an input is from the prior distribution or from GALG's encoder.

During the adversarial training, GALG's discriminator aims to identify the real distribution and classify the latent embedding into the fake class. Therefore, we could optimize the discriminator by minimizing the cross-entropy cost J_D:

$$J_D = -\mathbb{E}_{z \sim p_z} \log D(Z^*) - \mathbb{E}_{z \sim F_{en}} \log(1 - D(Z)) \tag{9}$$

where p_z is the real user preference distribution formed by all client addresses in the historical TLS traffic. $D(Z)$ is the discrimination score. To deceive the discriminator, in addition to minimizing the error between the ground truth A^* and the adjacency matrix $\hat{A}$ generated from the latent embedding Z, the encoder is also required to imitate the real preference distributions. Therefore, the cost of the encoder J_E during the adversarial training could be defined as follows:

$$J_E = \mathbb{E}_{\hat{A} \sim F_{en}} \log|\hat{A} - A^*| - \mathbb{E}_{z \sim F_{en}} \log D(Z) \tag{10}$$

Table 2. The composition of graphs built from three datasets.

Dataset	Nodes c	Nodes s	Links c-s	Users
P-AllService	1,016	5,597	7,022	450
P-Google	723	313	4,134	550
CSTNET	958	5,517	6,840	685

where the ground-truth adjacency matrix A^* only contains links between training nodes. The encoder cost J_E' of the variational autoencoder variant VGALG could also be defined as follows:

$$J_E' = \mathbb{E}_{\hat{A} \sim F_{en}} \log |\hat{A} - A^*| - \mathbb{E}_{z \sim F_{en}} \log D(Z) - \text{KL}[Z \| q(z)] \qquad (11)$$

where KL is the Kullback-Leibler divergence. $q(z) = \prod_{c_i} \mathcal{N}(z_{c_i} | 0, \text{I})$ is a Gaussian prior that we followed Kingma et al. [11]. Finally, we use the adjacency matrix $\hat{A}$ to track users in the tracking ecosystem.

5   Experiment Setup

Datasets. In this work, our evaluation datasets consist of a public dataset CSTNET and two participant datasets P-AllService and P-Google generated from 1k participants in two months in our experiments. Table 2 provides the graph composition built from the three datasets.

(1) **CSTNET.** CSTNET is a public dataset collected from March to July 2018 on China Science and Technology Network. Cui et al. [4] monitored the traffic on a vantage point to achieve tracking on IPv6 networks. In the network, 80% of IPv6 users change their client addresses at least once a month. We use the dataset to track real-world users from the perspective of a network provider.

(2) **P-AllService and P-Google.** To conduct extensive experiments, we invited 1k participants to join the traffic collection work under mobile networks. We installed the traffic plugin in participants' devices to record their daily online behaviors with consent. The participants are divided into two groups. For one group, we recorded all the TLS interaction traffic generated by participants to imitate a third party who tracked users with traffic plugins deployed on numerous Apps and build the P-AllService dataset. For the other group, the participants are required to access Google services following their online habits. These activities cannot be fully tracked by Google accounts since many services or web pages are not required to log in for browsing, such as Google Scholar and blogs. We recorded the traffic to form the P-Google dataset to track users from the perspective of a content provider like Google.

Baselines. The baselines in our experiments for comparison mainly include representative link prediction approaches and tracking techniques.

(1) **Link Prediction Approaches.** We compare types of link prediction approaches in this paper. **Common Neighbors (CN)** [16], **Jaccard** [16], and **Preferential Attachment (PA)** [2] are three heuristic methods to determine a link between two nodes. **Spectral Clustering (SC)** [21] and **node2vec** [9] are two latent feature methods to learn graph embeddings. **GAE** [12], **VGAE** [12], **ARGA** [18], and **ARVGA** [18] are four explicit feature methods to aggregate node features through graph autoencoder or its variational version.

(2) **Tracking Techniques.** We implement four representative tracking techniques, which use multiple characteristics in the TLS traffic. **User IP Profiling** [14] and **User SNI Profiling** [8] are methods to build user profiles through the destination IPs of the client addresses or the SNIs and track users through a Bayesian classifier. **Client Fingerprinting** [1] is a method to extract fields in ClientHello messages as client fingerprints and learn the fingerprints through Random Forest. **SiamHAN** [4] is a method to build graphs for each client address and learn the similarity of each two graphs through siamese networks.

Implementation. During the data preprocessing, we limit the maximum fingerprint length to 50. To train the doc2vec model, we set the vector size as 50 and the window size as 5 to obtain the representations of the fingerprints. The output dimension of PCA is 32 for the representations of the distributions. When training GALG, we randomly initialize parameters and optimize the model with the Adam algorithm. The learning rate is set as 0.005. The number of e-steps is 5 and the number of d-steps is 1. The number of attention head K is 4. We use four metrics including TPR, FPR, AUC, and AP to evaluate the models.

6   Evaluation

This section presents all experimental results to implement online user tracking.

6.1   Distribution Analysis

We provide the result of distribution analysis to indicate the effectiveness to leverage the distribution knowledge. Figure 4 shows the representation of distributions in P-AllService dataset. Results indicate that the preference distributions of the client addresses belonging to the same user are similar, demonstrating that exploiting this knowledge could help distinguish the client addresses of different users to a certain degree. For instance, Address0

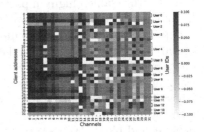

Fig. 4. The preference distributions of client addresses coming from 15 users.

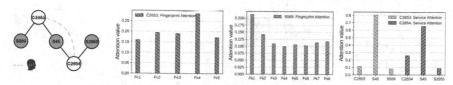

(a) a graph case for attention analysis.   (b) c2653's fingerprint attention.   (c) s569's fingerprint attention.   (d) service attention of c2653 and c2654.

Fig. 5. A case study of stack attention to help track users through semantic knowledge.

and `Address1` keep similar distribution representations because they both belong to `User0`. While the representation of `Address2` belonging to `User1` is obviously different from the former addresses in visual. With deeper analysis, we find that `Address0` and `Address1` have accessed many common domains with similar visit volumes, including `google`, `cloudflare`, `eroimg`, and `share-videos`. While `Address2` has never accessed these domains. GALG could embed the distribution knowledge into the embedding to help link the client addresses.

6.2   Attention Analysis

Figure 5(a) shows a knowledge graph case, including two address nodes (`c2653` and `c2654`), three service nodes (`s569`, `s45`, and `s2655`), and the address-service links between them. In this setting, `c2653` and `c2654` both belong to the user `u1`. Figure 5(b) and Fig. 5(c) show the fingerprint attention of the address node `c2653` and the service node `s569` respectively. The label corresponding to each fingerprint is shown in Table 1. For the client fingerprints of `c2653`, `Fc4` contributes more to the task obviously since it is the significant browser parameter that could be used to identify the client used by a user. Due to the change of the client address, `Fc1` surely obtains the lowest attention for tracking users. For the service fingerprints of `s569`, `Fs1` becomes the critical service fingerprint to indicate the attribute of the service accessed by users. The fingerprint-level attention finally obtains unique client and service embeddings through learning semantic information. The service attention of `c2653` and `c2654` is illustrated in Fig. 5(d). The high attention value of `s45` indicates that service attention could find the same service accessed by both two client addresses to help link them to the same user. Finally, the service-level attention could learn the semantics of address-service communication and obtain the meaningful embeddings.

6.3   Link Generation

To explore the effectiveness, we first measure the link generation performance by evaluating the correctness of the links generated between the test nodes.

Few-shot Learning. In Fig. 6(a), we show GALG's performance on the P-AllService dataset with different ratios of training users. With only 20% training users, GALG could obtain an acceptable performance with 81% AUC.

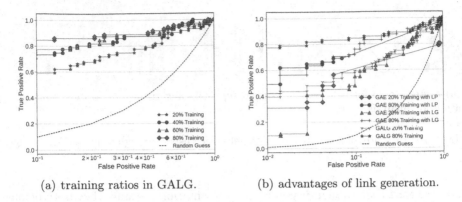

(a) training ratios in GALG.   (b) advantages of link generation.

Fig. 6. The link generation performance of GALG on different training ratios and the advantage of link generation (LG) compared to link prediction (LP) methods.

This advantage comes from the graph structure of address-service links to propagate the knowledge of labeled address nodes to the other non-labeled address nodes. Finally, GALG could achieve 92% AUC with an 80% training ratio. To demonstrate the advantage of link generation, we implement two frameworks of a representative model GAE under link prediction and link generation. Figure 6(b) shows the performance of the two frameworks on 20% and 80% training ratios compared with GALG. With 20% training users, the link prediction method could only obtain 55% AUC. However, with the link generation framework, GAE could achieve 75% AUC under this training ratio. Since link prediction methods require learning the graph with address-address links, when limiting the number of the labeled address nodes, the graph will lose considerable links to propagate the label knowledge. For link generation methods, since the address-service links of each address node are easy to obtain regardless of whether the nodes are labeled, the always complete graph structure help link generation more effective.

Overall Performance. Finally, we modify link prediction baselines with the link generation framework and show the performance of all link prediction baselines under the frameworks of link prediction and link generation in Table 3. Results indicate that the performance of link generation is better than link prediction for all baselines on the three user datasets. It demonstrates that learning the online behaviors behind the address-service links is more effective than inferring the neighbor relationships through address-address links. Our two models GALG and VGALG outperform all baselines using the theory of link generation.

6.4   User Tracking

To test the tracking performance, we set one address node of each test user as the known nodes to evaluate whether we could link all address nodes belonging to the same users with the known nodes.

Table 3. The overall performance of all link prediction baselines under the frameworks of link prediction and link generation.

Method	Link prediction						Link generation					
	CSTNET		P-AllService		P-Google		CSTNET		P-AllService		P-Google	
	AUC	AP	AUC	AP	AUC	AP	AUC	AP	AUC	AP	AUC	AP
CN	0.528	0.515	0.619	0.606	0.600	0.596	0.632	0.617	0.623	0.615	0.728	0.724
Jaccard	0.502	0.495	0.610	0.605	0.582	0.577	0.619	0.611	0.632	0.606	0.759	0.763
PA	0.524	0.524	0.470	0.508	0.595	0.653	0.526	0.557	0.593	0.594	0.603	0.661
SC	0.648	0.680	0.490	0.641	0.396	0.547	0.661	0.687	0.615	0.686	0.589	0.635
node2vec	0.511	0.516	0.514	0.532	0.444	0.476	0.516	0.539	0.633	0.686	0.626	0.641
GAE	0.888	0.887	0.840	0.850	0.933	0.942	0.978	0.985	0.920	0.942	0.941	0.955
VGAE	0.842	0.840	0.850	0.857	0.893	0.901	0.970	0.977	0.929	0.946	0.930	0.951
ARGA	0.918	0.924	0.915	0.937	0.889	0.931	0.938	0.949	0.934	0.945	0.940	0.950
ARVGA	0.867	0.879	0.881	0.909	0.881	0.887	0.886	0.889	0.916	0.936	0.902	0.904
GALG	–	–	–	–	–	–	0.980	0.984	0.957	0.969	0.940	0.959
VGALG	–	–	–	–	–	–	0.988	0.990	0.937	0.954	0.965	0.974

Table 4. The overall tracking performance and the inference time of all tracking techniques to predict 1 million link relationships from 0.5k users

Method	CSTNET		P-AllService		P-Google		One	Total
	AUC	AP	AUC	AP	AUC	AP	Inference	Time
User IP Profiling	0.563	0.001	0.611	0.000	0.596	0.000	0.0006 s	623.0840 s
User SNI Profiling	0.611	0.001	0.645	0.000	0.535	0.000	0.0005 s	592.0129 s
Client Fingerprinting	0.790	0.005	0.740	0.001	0.755	0.001	0.0091 s	9157.4099 s
SiamHAN	0.948	0.723	0.967	0.824	0.976	0.727	0.0013 s	1323.6057 s
GALG - Attention	0.967	0.230	0.968	0.479	0.949	0.201	0.1604 s	0.1604 s
GALG - Distribution	0.990	0.890	0.975	0.889	0.966	0.826	0.1893 s	0.1893 s
GALG	0.995	0.925	0.981	0.906	0.982	0.911	0.1923 s	0.1923 s
VGALG	0.996	0.896	0.982	0.926	0.971	0.844	0.2030 s	0.2030 s

Overall Tracking Performance. The overall tracking performance of all existing tracking techniques is shown in Table 4. Results indicate that the former three methods obtain bad performance on the AP metric since they can not be applied to the open-world dataset to track the users who are not in the training set. When replacing the stack attention layer in the encoder with a 1-d convolutional layer and a graph convolutional layer (GALG - Attention) or removing the discriminator in GALG (GALG - Distribution), the performance drastically degrades. Compared with the state-of-the-art tracking approach SiamHAN, GALG and VGALG could outperform the method by significant margins. For a deeper analysis, Fig. 7(a) and Fig. 7(b) show the ROC curves of GALG, link generation-based methods, and existing tracking techniques. Using the link generation framework, explicit feature methods like GAE and ARGA could reach the similar performance of SiamHAN. For a target FPR $= 2 \times 10^{-2}$, GALG

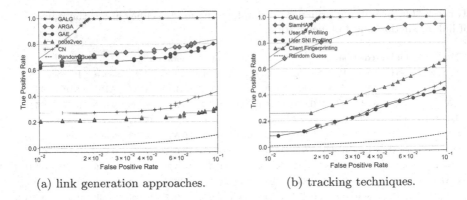

(a) link generation approaches.　　　　(b) tracking techniques.

Fig. 7. The tracking performance of the state-of-the-art tracking techniques and the link prediction baselines with the link generation framework.

could provide a TPR of 0.99. To explore the inference time, we measure the performance on a single GeForce GTX 1080 Ti GPU. Since GALG is to output the whole adjacency matrix, the inference time for one link is equal to the time for all links. However, prior techniques expense considerable time to infer links between every two nodes in the graph. Therefore, the advantage of our framework helps GALG track 0.5k users in 1 s, which is dramatically faster than the state-of-the-art approach SiamHAN in half an hour.

7 Conclusion

In this work, we explore the implementation to track users on TLS encrypted traffic. We propose GALG, a graph-based artificial intelligence approach to link changed client addresses for finding out the target user. Using the adversarial architecture with a graph autoencoder, GALG could jointly learn the user embedding with semantics and distributions. With a new theory - link generation, GALG could more effectively infer address-address links than the framework of link prediction. Extensive experiments indicate that the performance of our models outperform state-of-the-art methods by significant margins. We published the source code of GALG at https://github.com/CuiTianyu961030/GALG.

Acknowledgements. This work is supported by the National Key Research and Development Program of China No. 2020YFE0200500 and the Strategic Priority Research Program of Chinese Academy of Sciences, Grant No. XDC02040400.

References

1. Anderson, B., McGrew, D.A.: OS fingerprinting: new techniques and a study of information gain and obfuscation. In: CNS, pp. 1–9 (2017)

2. Barabási, A.L., Albert, R.: Emergence of scaling in random networks. Science (5439), 509–512 (1999)
3. Bashir, M.A., Farooq, U., Shahid, M., Zaffar, M.F., Wilson, C.: Quantity vs. quality: evaluating user interest profiles using ad preference managers. In: NDSS (2019)
4. Cui, T., Gou, G., Xiong, G., Li, Z., Cui, M., Liu, C.: SiamHAN: IPv6 address correlation attacks on TLS encrypted traffic via siamese heterogeneous graph attention network. In: USENIX Security, pp. 4329–4346 (2021)
5. Droms, R.E.: Dynamic host configuration protocol. RFC **2131**, 1–45 (1997)
6. Dunteman, G.H.: Principal components analysis (1989)
7. Gómez-Boix, A., Laperdrix, P., Baudry, B.: Hiding in the crowd: an analysis of the effectiveness of browser fingerprinting at large scale. In: WWW, pp. 309–318 (2018)
8. Gonzalez, R., Soriente, C., Laoutaris, N.: User profiling in the time of HTTPS. In: IMC, pp. 373–379 (2016)
9. Grover, A., Leskovec, J.: node2vec: scalable feature learning for networks. In: KDD, pp. 855–864 (2016)
10. Herrmann, D., Banse, C., Federrath, H.: Behavior-based tracking: exploiting characteristic patterns in DNS traffic. In: Computer Security, pp. 17–33 (2013)
11. Kingma, D.P., Welling, M.: Auto-encoding variational bayes. In: ICLR (2014)
12. Kipf, T.N., Welling, M.: Variational graph auto-encoders. CoRR (2016)
13. Kipf, T.N., Welling, M.: Semi-supervised classification with graph convolutional networks. In: ICLR (2017)
14. Kumpost, M., Matyas, V.: User profiling and re-identification: case of university-wide network analysis. In: TrustBus, pp. 1–10 (2009)
15. Le, Q., Mikolov, T.: Distributed representations of sentences and documents. In: ICML, pp. 1188–1196 (2014)
16. Liben-Nowell, D., Kleinberg, J.M.: The link-prediction problem for social networks. J. Am. Soc. Inf. Sci. Technol. **7**, 1019–1031 (2007)
17. Mayer, J.R., Mitchell, J.C.: Third-party web tracking: policy and technology. In: SP, pp. 413–427 (2012)
18. Pan, S., Hu, R., Long, G., Jiang, J., Yao, L., Zhang, C.: Adversarially regularized graph autoencoder for graph embedding. In: IJCAI, pp. 2609–2615 (2018)
19. Papadopoulos, P., Kourtellis, N., Markatos, E.P.: Cookie synchronization: everything you always wanted to know but were afraid to ask. In: WWW, pp. 1432–1442 (2019)
20. Rescorla, E.: The transport layer security (TLS) protocol version 1.3. RFC 8446, pp. 1–160 (2018)
21. Tang, L., Liu, H.: Leveraging social media networks for classification. Data Mining Knowl. Disc. **3**, 447–478 (2011)
22. Vaswani, A., et al.: Attention is all you need. In: NeurIPS, pp. 5998–6008 (2017)
23. Velickovic, P., Cucurull, G., Casanova, A., Romero, A., Liò, P., Bengio, Y.: Graph attention networks. In: ICLR (2018)
24. Yen, T., Xie, Y., Yu, F., Yu, R.P., Abadi, M.: Host fingerprinting and tracking on the web: privacy and security implications. In: NDSS (2012)
25. Yu, Z., Macbeth, S., Modi, K., Pujol, J.M.: Tracking the trackers. In: WWW, pp. 121–132 (2016)

Automatic Grading of Student Code with Similarity Measurement

Dongxia Wang, En Zhang, and Xuesong Lu[✉]

East China Normal University, Shanghai, China
{dxwang,zhangen}@stu.ecnu.edu.cn, xslu@dase.ecnu.edu.cn

Abstract. Nowadays, online judges are extensively used for automatically grading student code. However, they grade code by only counting the number of passed test cases, which is not fair for assessing the overall quality of a code snippet. On the other hand, existing studies have used machine learning techniques for code grading. However, they usually require large amounts of labeled code to enable supervised learning and heavily rely on feature engineering. In this work, we design SIM-GRADER, a code grading system that grades student code based on the measurement of similarity to the "good" code, and thus save the effort for code labeling. We extract three types of features to capture the overall quality of a code snippet, and design specific methods to enhance the feature discrimination, which facilitates the similarity measurement. We conduct extensive experiments to show the superiority of SIMGRADER over existing methods and justify the effect of the its system components. We deploy SIMGRADER to grade the student code submitted in an introductory programming course.

Keywords: Code grading · Discriminative feature · Contrastive learning · Tree edit distance

1 Introduction

Online judge (OJ) systems [23] have been extensively used in programming education [7,10,21,22,27]. The systems can automatically assess the correctness of student code by executing them with a set of pre-defined test cases, which greatly reduces teachers' burden of grading student code. However, for students, grading their code by simply counting the number of passed test cases is less informative and sometimes unfair with respect to the quality of the code. For instance, a code snippet passing all test cases may have awful code style or high time/space complexity, whereas a nearly correct code snippet may fail all test cases only due to one variable misuse. A good programming education should encourage students not only to write correct programs, but also to write concise programs with good style. As such, a fair code grading system should consider as many of the above factors as possible and give students a composite score to guide them in optimizing their code. A potential solution is to extract a set of code features

M.-R. Amini et al. (Eds.): ECML PKDD 2022, LNAI 13718, pp. 286–301, 2023.
https://doi.org/10.1007/978-3-031-26422-1_18

pertaining to the grading factors and train machine learning models based on the features to predict the code grade.

Several related studies have investigated automatic code grading with machine learning techniques [14,18–20]. However, there exist following issues in these methods. First, they mainly construct the semantic features reflecting the functionality of a code snippet for grade prediction, e.g., expression features and data-dependency features [19,20], and rarely consider the features related to code style such as variable naming and indent use. These style features are actually crucial for assessing the quality of source code in terms of readability and ease of maintenance. Second, most existing methods manually construct the semantic features of source code, e.g., by counting the occurrences of key expressions and tokens [18,20], or calculating the number of specific nodes in the abstract syntax tree of a code snippet [14]. Manual feature engineering is ad-hoc for each programming question and may introduce noise into the features. Last, existing methods build supervised grading models and therefore require large amounts of labeled source code [11,14,16,18–20]. This not only imposes a lot of human labors but also leads to the underuse of massive unlabeled source code in the OJ system.

In this work, we implement the SIMGRADER system, which grades student code based on the measurement of similarity to the "good" code and therefore avoids the overhead of labeling the student code. For each programming question, "good" code is defined as a concise code snippet with good style to solve the question. Compared to labeling the student code, preparing the good code is much cheaper because the number of questions in an OJ system is often limited and we may find the good code from correct student submissions. For newly added questions, standard code snippets have to be composed for generating the test cases, which can be used as the good code. Note that each programming question may have multiple good code snippets. Then, we can generate the grade for a student code snippet based on its similarity (or distance) to the nearest good code. This is motivated by the human grading process where the teachers often compare a student code snippet with the nearest standard solution and give the grade based on the defects in the student code.

To implement SIMGRADER, at the core of the system is extracting the discriminative feature vector of student code that is used for code similarity measurement. We propose to extract the following three types of features. The first type are the static features such as the number of blank lines, improper spaces and indents, and the ratio of improperly named variables. This type of features mainly reflect whether a code snippet is concise and has good style. The second type of features are the runtime statistics such as execution time, memory usage and the percentage of passed test cases. This type of features mainly capture the efficiency and correctness of a code snippet. The last type are the semantic features of a code snippet, which reflect the functionality of a code snippet and thus are important for evaluating whether the code complies with the requirements of the programming question. Inspired by the recent advances in program representation learning [1,5,12,25], we propose to learn the features from massive student code using deep learning techniques rather than manually constructing them as in previous studies. To improve the discrimination of semantic features, we further design a contrastive learning task followed by a fine-tuning task to obtain the final semantic feature vectors. The above three types of features are concatenated to form the complete feature vector. Finally, we calculate the similarity between the complete feature vector of a student code snippet and that of the nearest good code, based on which the code is graded. We deploy SIM-GRADER in the OJ system used for an introductory programming course and demonstrate how we use it to grade student code.

Our contribution is summarized as follows:

- We design SIMGRADER, a system that grades student code based on the measurement of similarity to the "good" code and therefore avoids the expensive code labeling overhead. For similarity measurement, we propose to extract three types of code features including the static feature, runtime feature and semantic feature, which capture not only the functional information of a code snippet but also the conciseness and the style information. Moreover, the semantic feature is automatically learned from massive student code, avoiding the ad-hoc feature engineering and possible human-injected noise (See Sect. 3.1).
- To improve the discrimination of semantic features, we design a contrastive learning task to train the semantic feature vectors, so that the vectors of more similar code snippets are closer to each other. We further fine-tune the semantic feature vectors by predicting the closeness of each pair of code snippets, where the closeness is calculated based on the tree edit distance between the abstract syntax trees (ASTs) of the snippets (See Sect. 3.2).
- We conduct extensive experiments to show the effectiveness of SIMGRADER. We compare it with existing grading systems using the similarity measurement strategy as well as by training supervised prediction models with a small labeled dataset. We also conduct ablation studies to show the effect of the contrastive learning and fine-tuning sub-steps. The experimental results not only show the superiority of the extracted features but also justify the component design of SIMGRADER (See Sect. 4). We deploy SIMGRADER in an OJ system used for an introductory programming course and demonstrate some use cases (See Sect. 5).

2   Related Work

Existing studies mainly design supervised learning models for automatic code grading and heavily rely on feature engineering. For instance, Srikant and Aggarwal [19] construct six types of code semantic features by counting corresponding patterns. The patterns are extracted from the token sequence, the ASTs, the control flow graphs (CFG) and data dependency graphs (DDG) of a code snippet, and depend on each programming question. Based on the features, they train three regression models to predict code grade, including ridge, SVM and random forests. Later, Singh et al. [18] extend this work and propose a question independent method for code grading. They design a transformation which would transform a question specific feature matrix pertaining to a set of code snippets into a structure invariant feature matrix. This matrix is further used as input to learn a question independent grading model. They use the similar feature engineering method with [19] and still need to label large amounts of code for learning the transformation. A related study [20] attempts to grade uncompilable code. Their focus is how to use feature engineering to extract semantic features from uncompilable code snippets.

Recent studies develop deep learning solutions for code grading. For instance, Orr and Russell [14] use feed-forward neural networks to predict code grade. However, they still use manually constructed features and need to label the code for supervised learning. Qin et al. [16] adopt a Bi-GRU network to learn from the intermediate code representation obtained using LLVM. They design a selection function to pick important features from the intermediate representation. The model is trained with labeled code snippets. A related but different study is conducted by Johnson-Yu et al. [9], where they design a model to find the unmarked code submissions that are mostly similar to the submissions that have been marked by a grader. Then they assign the unmarked submissions to the graders based on the similarity distribution, so that the efficiency of manual grading can be improved.

3   The SIMGRADER System

Fig. 1 shows the overview of the SIMGRADER system consisting of three main steps. In the first step as shown in Fig. 1(a), three types of features are extracted for each code snippet, including static features, runtime features and semantic features. Section 3.1 describes the details of feature extraction. In the second step as shown in Fig. 1(b), two sub-steps including contrastive learning and fune-tuning are designed to enhance the discrimination of the semantic features. Section 3.2 describes the details of these two sub-steps. In the final step as shown in Fig. 1(c), the concatenation of the three types of features is used to output the grading score for a code snippet based on similarity measurement with the good code. Section 3.3 describes this strategy. In the experiments, we also invite two experts to grade a small set of student code and show the results of supervised learning using the dataset.

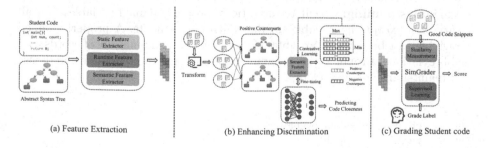

(a) Feature Extraction   (b) Enhancing Discrimination   (c) Grading Student code

Fig. 1. Overview of the SIMGRADER system.

3.1   Feature Extraction

Static Features. We construct the static features by traversing the text and the AST of a code snippet, without executing the code. The AST of a code snippet is an tree-based abstract representation of the grammatical structure, which is composed of semantic structure (internal) nodes and token (leaf) nodes. Figure 2(a) shows a simple code snippet and Fig. 2(b) shows the corresponding AST. It can be observed that the leaf nodes correspond to the tokens in the code text, and the internal nodes indicate the semantic structure of (i.e., relationship between) the tokens. We use *pycparser*[1] to obtain the ASTs of student code. In addition, we also use static analysis tools such as *cpplint*[2] and *cppcheck*[3] to obtain some of the features. The static features obtained by traversing the code text and AST mainly capture the conciseness and style information of the code. The details of the features are described as follows:

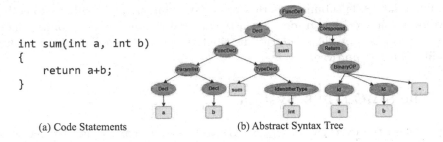

```
int sum(int a, int b)
{
    return a+b;
}
```

(a) Code Statements   (b) Abstract Syntax Tree

Fig. 2. A Code Snippet and its AST.

- **Special lines:** Count the number of comments and blank lines. The intuition is that a code snippet with good style should have a certain number of comments and few blank lines.
- **Improper spaces and indents:** Count the number of improperly used spaces or indents (including too many or too few indents). We use *cpplint* to calculate the numbers.
- **Variables:** Count the number of variables and the number of times each variable is used. The intuition is that a concise code snippet should not have too many unnecessary and repeatedly used variables.
- **Variables naming:** Calculate the ratio of properly named variables over all variables, except the variables in the control statements. A properly named variable can be a word, an abbreviation, or the combination of words and abbreviations. Proper variable naming can enhance the readability and ease of maintenance of code [8,15].

---

[1] https://github.com/eliben/pycparser.
[2] https://github.com/cpplint.
[3] https://cppcheck.sourceforge.io/.

- **Unused elements:** Count the number of unused variables and non-executed code lines. These elements commonly present in the code written by novice students. We use *Cppcheck* to calculate the numbers.
- **Cyclomatic complexity:** Count the number of judgement nodes in an AST. Common judgement nodes include *ForStatement, WhileStatement, IfStatement, BinaryOp* of boolean logic, etc. Cyclomatic complexity measures the complexity of code logic. For each programming question, a higher cyclomatic complexity indicates that the code is less concise and readable.
- **Halstead metrics:** Count the number of unique and total operators and operands, and use them in the Halstead formulas to calculate the metrics. These metrics mainly capture the static complexity of a code snippet.

Runtime Features. The runtime features of the statistics obtained by executing student code with the test cases. The features capture the correctness and efficiency of the code pertaining to a specific programming question, which are described as follows:

- **Test cases:** Calculate the ratio of passed test cases over all test cases.
- **Execution time:** Calculate the maximum, average and minimum execution time of all test cases. The feature captures the time efficiency of code.
- **Memory usage:** Calculate the maximum, average and minimum memory usage of all test cases. The feature captures the space efficiency of code.

Semantic Features. In previous studies [18–20], the semantic features pertaining to the functionality of a code snippet are obtained with feature engineering. This strategy needs to construct ad-hoc features for each question and may introduce noise into the features. A recent study [16] uses a Bi-GRU model [24] to learn from the token sequence of source code and output a distributed vector to represent the semantic features. However, learning from the token sequence leads to a significant effort to learn the syntactic nature of source code from scratch, which reduces the efficiency of learning the semantic features. Inspired by recent studies in program representation learning [1,5,12,25], we choose to learn the semantic features from the AST of a code snippet. The AST structure is shown to preserve the syntactic nature of a code snippet and therefore significantly lower the learning effort of semantic features [2,3]. In the current study, we experiment with two representative models, namely, TBCNN [12] and ASTNN [25], respectively. TBCNN applies tree-based convolution kernels on an AST to gather the information of child nodes into the parent nodes, and uses dynamic pooling to aggregate the feature vectors of all nodes. The resulted vector is used to represent the entire code snippet. ASTNN splits an AST into a set of subtrees corresponding to the statements in the code snippet. The subtrees are organized into a sequence in accordance with the order of the corresponding statements in the original code. Then it adopts a Bi-GRU network to encode the sequence and uses max pooling to aggregate all hidden states to form the semantic feature vector.

3.2   Enhancing the Discrimination of Semantic Features

Since we grade student code based on the measurement of similarity to the good code, the discrimination of the code feature is critical, i.e., the feature vectors of similar code snippets should be close to each other and the feature vectors of dissimilar code snippets should be far away from each other. To enhance feature discrimination, we design two sub-steps after extracting the semantic features for obtaining the final semantic feature vectors.

Contrastive Learning. The first sub-step is to train more discriminative semantic feature vectors using contrastive learning [6]. Contrastive learning represents a category of self-supervised learning methods whose optimization objective is to simultaneously maximize the similarity among positive (close) data points and minimize the similarity among negative (distant) data points. As such it can be used to increase the discrimination of feature vectors. Our design of contrastive learning is as follows. For each code snippet in a random batch, we first construct its positive counterpart based on small random transformation to the source code. We adopt the method in [4] and transform the original source code into a code snippet with equivalent semantic. The transformation has four types including variable renaming, statement swapping, statement insertion and for-while interchanging. Figure 3 shows an example of the transformations, where Fig. 3(a) is the original code snippet, and Fig. 3(b)–(e) show the transformed elements in red for all the transformation types. Note that none of the transformations changes the semantic of the original code snippet. For each code snippet, we transform it with the four types and randomly choose a transformed snippet as its positive counterpart during training.

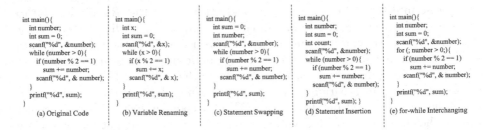

Fig. 3. An example of the code transformation.

The construction of the negative counterpart is relevant to the contrastive loss used for optimization. We experiment with two types of loss functions in the current study, namely, the InfoNCE loss [13] and the Triplet loss [17]. In the former case, for each code snippet, we use all other code snippets in the same batch as the negative counterparts. In the latter case, each code snippet is just paired with one negative counterpart, selected as follows. We first use TBCNN or ASTNN to obtain the encodings of the code snippets. Then for each snippet, we calculate the L2 distances between its encoding and all other encodings and sort all the distances in either order. We pick the distance in the middle and use the other snippet in the distance calculation as the negative counterpart, as suggested in [17]. Denote by c_i, pos_i and neg_i the ith code snippet in a batch, the corresponding positive counterpart and negative counterpart, respectively. For both types of contrastive loss, the objective function of contrastive learning c_i is depicted as follows:

$$\mathcal{L}_{con}^i = -\log \frac{exp(\frac{e_{c_i} \cdot e_{pos_i}}{\tau})}{exp(\frac{e_{c_i} \cdot e_{pos_i}}{\tau}) + \sum_{neg_i \in batch} exp(\frac{e_{c_i} \cdot e_{neg_i}}{\tau})}, \tag{1}$$

where e_{c_i} denotes the encoding of c_i, $\cdot$ denotes the dot product and τ is the temperature parameter. Note that for the Triplet loss, there is only one neg_i for each c_i and the $\sum$ symbol could be omitted.

Predicting Code Closeness Based on Tree Edit Distance. The second sub-step is to further fine-tune the feature vectors obtained in the contrastive learning sub-step using a supervised prediction model. Remember that in contrastive learning, we form a random batch from the student code submitted to all programming questions. As a result, for each code snippet, we equally treat the negative counterparts of the same question and those of a different question. Because the code snippets of the same question are semantically similar, the resulted feature vectors of the same question are still very close to each other. Therefore, we consider to further separate the feature vectors of the code snippets submitted to the same question.

To this end, we train a supervised model to predict the closeness of each pair of code snippets for the same question. We define the closeness of two code snippets as the ratio of the tree edit distance [26] between their ASTs to the number of nodes in the AST with more nodes. Once we obtain the closeness between every pair of code snippets, we set a threshold 0.05 according to the distribution. The pairs with a closeness below the threshold are labeled with 1 (close pairs), and the other pairs are labeled with 0 (non-close pairs). Note that the labels are automatically calculated and do not require any manual labeling effort. Then we train a three-layer fully-connected neural network to predict the labels of the pairs. Each input is a pair of code feature vectors obtained from the contrastive learning sub-step. Because most code pairs are non-close pairs, we use focal loss as the loss function to mitigate the imbalanced distribution problem. Denote by p_i and y_i the predicted probability and label of the ith code pair. The focal loss is depicted as follows:

$$\mathcal{L}_{foc}^i = \begin{cases} -\alpha(1 - p_i)^\gamma \log(p_i), & \text{if } y_i = 1 \\ -(1 - \alpha)p_i^\gamma \log(1 - p_i), & \text{if } y_i = 0, \end{cases} \tag{2}$$

where the α is weighting factor and the γ is the focusing parameter.

At inference time, the output layers of the contrastive learning model and the fine-tuning model are discarded, and the remaining architectures are connected to generate the semantic feature vector for each code snippet.

3.3 Grading Student Code

The above three types of features are concatenated to form the complete feature vector, where each type of feature vector is normalized in the range $[0, 1]$ before concatenation. When grading a code snippet, we first calculate the cosine similarity between its feature vector and the nearest feature vector of a "good" code snippet of the same programming question. Since the similarity score is between -1 and 1, we convert it by adding 1 and then dividing 2 to obtain a score between 0 and 1. To show the grade to the student, we further multiply the score by 100 as the final grade. Denote by v_s and v_g the feature vector of the code snippet and the nearest feature vector of a "good" snippet, respectively. The final grade is calculated as:

$$\text{Grade} = \frac{sim(v_s, v_g) + 1}{2} \times 100, \tag{3}$$

where $sim(v_s, v_g) = v_s^T v_g / \|v_s\| \|v_g\|$ is the cosine similarity between v_s and v_g.

4 Performance Evaluation

We conduct four experiments to determine the model settings, evaluate feature discrimination, evaluate the performance of similarity-based and learning-based grading strategies, respectively. We implement SIMGRADER using Python 3.7.6 and Pytorch 1.7.0. All source code is available at https://github.com/wangDxia/SimGrader.

4.1 The Datasets and Evaluation Metrics

Datasets. We collect 46,949 compilable C code snippets from an OJ system used for an introductory programming course in our university. They are submitted by 146 fresh students in one semester to solve 479 programming questions. We use all the code snippets for feature extraction, contrastive learning and grading.

For the fine-tuning sub-step that predicts code closeness, we extract 73 questions with more than 200 submissions and obtain in total 27,462 code snippets. We form the code pairs for each question and obtain 219000 code pairs, where 41011 pairs are labeled with 1 (close pairs) and 177989 pairs are labeled with 0 (non-close pairs). We randomly divide the pairs with proportion 3:1:1 to form the training, validation and testing set, respectively.

To verify the effectiveness of SIMGRADER, we construct a small dataset that are labeled by experts. We randomly select 30 questions among the 73 questions with more than 200 submissions, and randomly select 15 submissions for each question. As such we obtain a small dataset with 450 code snippets. We invite two teachers of C programming courses and ask them to independently grade each code snippet on a scale between 1 and 5, which is depicted below. If the two teachers give different grades to a snippet, we ask them to further discuss and make an agreement on the final grade.

- **5 - Correct and graceful:** The code passes all test cases, and the style is clean and clear. There are no redundant variables and code lines, and the variable names are very standardized.
- **4 - Correct with some flaws:** A correct implementation but often accompanied by poor style or complex solution.
- **3 - Nearly correct and neat:** The code does not pass all test cases, but the overall logic is the same as the correct solution, and the code style is clean and clear.
- **2 - Incorrect and confusing:** The code is incorrect and very different from the correct solution. The code style is not good and the logic seems confusing.
- **1 - Incorrect and awful:** The code is incorrect and the code style is awful.

Evaluation Metrics. We use multiple metrics to evaluate SIMGRADER. First, we use the fine-tuning sub-step to determine the best settings for the semantic feature extraction model (i.e., TBCNN or ASTNN) and the contrastive loss (i.e., InfoNCE or Triplet loss). We choose the settings when the model has the best prediction performance on the validation set. The evaluation metric is the accuracy of code closeness prediction.

Second, to evaluate the discrimination of the feature vectors, we cluster the vectors and use two internal metrics to assess the clustering results, namely, Davies-Bouldin Index (DBI) and Silhouette Coefficient (SC). DBI finds for each cluster the most similar cluster based on their diameters, and then computes the average similarity over all the clusters. A smaller DBI value means the clusters are less similar to each other, therefore indicating the vectors are more discriminative. SC is a measure of how similar an object is to the objects within the same cluster compared to the objects outside the cluster. A higher SC value means each object is better matched to the objects inside the same cluster and less matched to the objects outside the cluster, therefore indicating the vectors are more discriminative.

Third, to evaluate the grading performance using similarity measurement, we calculate the correlation between the grades produced by SIMGRADER and the grades marked by the two experts, on the 450 labeled source code. The used correlation metrics are the Pearson correlation coefficient (PCC) and the Spearman's rank correlation coefficient (SRCC). Furthermore, we use the 450 labeled source code to train and evaluate several supervised models, so that we can compare with existing code grading systems. The evaluation metrics are precision, recall and F1 score.

4.2   The Comparative Methods

We compare SIMGRADER with three existing supervised learning methods. The LASSO [18,20] method uses feature engineering and trains a LASSO regression model. The Ensemble [14] method trains an ensemble of feed-forward neural networks on the manually constructed features. The SCG_FBS[16] method trains a Bi-GRU network using the intermediate representation of source code.

4.3   The Hyperparameter Setting

In the contrastive learning sub-step, the output embedding size is set to 64 and the temperature parameter τ is set to 0.1. When training, we set the batch size to 32, the learning rate to 0.001. We use Adamax for optimization. In the fine-tuning sub-step, we set α in the focal loss to 0.25 and γ to 0.98. In the supervised models, the Neural Network model has 4 layers, the number of GBDT's estimators is set to 150, and the SVM kernel is set to linear.

4.4   Experiment 1: Predicting Code Closeness

Table 1 shows the performance of predicting code closeness on the testing set in the fine-tuning sub-step for different model settings. We observe that ASTNN with InfoNCE contrastive learning yields the highest accuracy. In particular, the ASTNN variants perform better than the TBCNN variants. This may be because ASTNN uses the order information of the source code in addition to the AST structural information. The InfoNCE variants perform better than the Triplet variants, which may indicate using more negative counterparts improves the discrimination of the feature vectors. All in all, we use the variant of ASTNN with InfoNCE loss in the subsequent experiments.

Table 1. The performance of different settings for predicting code closeness.

Model	TBCNN		ASTNN	
Variants	InfoNCE	Triplet	InfoNCE	Triplet
Accuracy	0.8265	0.8220	**0.8551**	0.8360

4.5   Experiment 2: Evaluating Feature Discrimination

After the fine-tuning sub-step, the three types of features are concatenated for grading student code. Before we use them for grading, we evaluate their discrimination since the property is critical for similarity measurement. We cluster the 27,462 code snippets of the 73 questions with more than 200 submissions and use DBI and SC to evaluate the clustering performance. We use k-means and set $k = 73$. We compare the results of SIMGRADER (Full) with the results obtained using the feature vectors produced by the three comparative methods. Also, we remove the contrastive learning (w/o CL) and fine-tuning (w/o FT) sub-step from SIMGRADER, respectively, and evaluate the features produced by the remaining system. Note that the comparative methods have only a full model, since they do not have a contrastive learning or fine-tuning step as ours. Table 2 shows the results. Remember that a lower DBI and a higher SC indicate the better performance. We observe that SIMGRADER constantly performs much better than existing methods for both metrics. Moreover, the clustering performance of SIMGRADER drops when either sub-step for enhancing feature discrimination is removed. This shows the effect of these two sub-steps. Note that we need at least one of the sub-steps to train the semantic features.

Table 2. The performance of clustering the code feature vectors.

Metrics	DBI			SC		
Model Variants	w/o CL	w/o FT	Full	w/o CL	w/o FT	Full
Ensemble [14]	–	–	1.145	–	–	0.257
SCG_FBS[16]	–	–	1.7718	–	–	0.1644
LASSO [18]	–	–	0.4844	–	–	0.5435
SimGrader	0.3243	0.3233	**0.2948**	0.7059	0.7058	**0.7471**

4.6 Experiment 3: Grading with Similarity Measurement

Our primary contribution is to grade student code based on the measurement of similarity to the good code, so that we don't need large amounts of labeled code and may sufficiently use the massive unlabeled code. To evaluate the accuracy of the grades, we calculate the correlation between the grades produced by SIMGRADER and the grades marked by the two experts on the 450 code snippets. Table 3 shows the results. We observe that SIMGRADER constantly performs much better than existing methods for both correlation metrics. Note that for both correlations, a value greater than 0.8 indicates strong correlation. The results indicate the grades produced by SIMGRADER are very reliable. Moreover, the correlation drops when either contrastive learning or fune-tuning sub-step is removed.

Table 3. The correlation between the grades marked by SIMGRADER and the experts.

Metrics	PCC			SRCC		
Model Variants	w/o CL	w/o FT	Full	w/o CL	w/o FT	Full
Ensemble [14]	–	–	0.652	–	–	0.645
SCG_FBS[16]	–	–	0.7518	–	–	0.7363
LASSO [18]	–	–	0.8238	–	–	0.8027
SimGrader	0.8701	0.8626	**0.8723**	0.8168	0.7867	**0.8438**

4.7 Experiment 4: Grading with Supervised Learning

Finally, we compare SIMGRADER with existing supervised learning solutions using the 450 labeled code snippets. We feed the feature vectors produced by SIMGRADER into different supervised models and pick the best one for comparison. For the comparative solutions, we also use the best settings reported in the original papers [14, 16, 18]. Table 4 shows the results. We observe that GBDT performs better than other models. For each model, we observe the performance drop when either contrastive learning or fine-tuning sub-step is removed.

Table 4. Performance of different supervised models using code features extracted by SimGrader.

Models	w/o CL			w/o FT			Full		
	Precision	Recall	F-score	Precision	Recall	F-score	Precision	Recall	F-score
Neural Network	0.7334	0.7388	0.7329	0.7514	0.7455	0.7377	0.7548	0.7466	0.7408
SVM	0.7420	0.7311	0.7293	0.7446	0.7444	0.7415	0.7357	0.7311	0.7320
DecisionTree	0.6963	0.6888	0.6918	0.6649	0.6688	0.6620	0.7005	0.7044	0.7014
RandomForest	0.7936	0.7833	0.7840	0.7238	0.7333	0.7329	0.7843	0.7844	0.7747
GBDT	**0.7970**	**0.7988**	**0.7918**	**0.7677**	**0.7733**	**0.7666**	**0.8197**	**0.8222**	**0.8194**

We use GBDT (Full) to compare with existing supervised learning solutions. Table 5 shows the results. We observe that SimGrader performs much better than comparative methods, which indicates that the features extracted by SimGrader can better capture the static, runtime and semantic property of student code.

Table 5. Comparing SimGrader with existing supervised learning solutions.

	Precision	Recall	F-score
SimGrader (GBDT)	**0.8197**	**0.8222**	**0.8194**
Ensemble [14]	0.5438	0.5511	0.5491
LASSO [18]	0.6285	0.6177	0.6094
SCG_FBS[16]	0.6048	0.5977	0.5827

5   Application: Using SimGrader in an OJ System

We deploy SimGrader in the online judge system used for an introductory C programming course in our university. Originally, whenever a code snippet is submitted for a programming question, the OJ executes it with the pre-defined test cases and gives the feedback in one of the five main types: accepted, wrong answer, time limit exceeded, memory limit exceeded, runtime error. After the deployment of SimGrader, the OJ can in addition give out a grade score to show the overall quality of the code. Figure 4 shows an example, where four code snippets submitted to the same question are graded. The question is to read three integer values as the side lengths of a triangle and calculate the area of the triangle using Heron's formula.

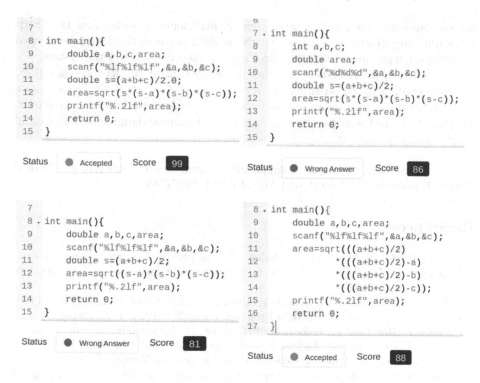

Fig. 4. An example of four code snippets graded by SIMGRADER.

In the top-left corner, we observe a concise and correct code snippet and SIMGRADER gives a grade score 99. In the top-right corner, the code snippet is nearly correct except that it fails to convert the integer type into the double type before division (line 9). As such it fails most of the test cases. However, SIMGRADER finds it very close to the good code and gives a grade score 86. In the bottom-left corner, although the code may pass some cases, it has severe semantic errors. As such SIMGRADER only grades it as 81. Finally in the bottom-right corner, although the code passes all test cases, SIMGRADER finds it not concise enough and grades it as 88.

6   Conclusion and Future Work

We design a code grading system, SIMGRADER, to grade student code based on the measurement of similarity to the good code. As such, we save the expensive overhead to label large amounts of student code required by existing methods. We extract the static features, runtime features and semantic features to capture the overall quality of each code snippet. To enhance the discrimination of the features, we design the contrastive learning and fine-tuning sub-steps to learn more discriminative semantic features. Finally, the three types of features are concatenated for grading prediction. Experimental results show that SIM-GRADER outperforms existing methods in both unsupervised and supervised learning settings, and justify the effect of each step designed in the system.

The current study shows that the discrimination of the features is critical for code grading based on similarity measurement. As such, we will investigate other methods to produce more discriminative code features in future. Moreover, we plan to collect student code in other programming languages and extend SIMGRADER to support multiple languages.

Acknowledgement. This work is supported by the grants from the National Natural Science Foundation of China (Grant No. 62137001, 62072185).

References

1. Alon, U., Brody, S., Levy, O., Yahav, E.: code2seq: generating sequences from structured representations of code. In: International Conference on Learning Representations (2018)
2. Alon, U., Zilberstein, M., Levy, O., Yahav, E.: code2vec: learning distributed representations of code. Proc. ACM Program. Lang. **3**(POPL), 1–29 (2019)
3. Bielik, P., Raychev, V., Vechev, M.: PHOG: probabilistic model for code. In: International Conference on Machine Learning, pp. 2933–2942. PMLR (2016)
4. Bui, N.D., Yu, Y., Jiang, L.: Self-supervised contrastive learning for code retrieval and summarization via semantic-preserving transformations. In: Proceedings of the 44th International ACM SIGIR Conference on Research and Development in Information Retrieval, pp. 511–521 (2021)
5. Bui, N.D., Yu, Y., Jiang, L.: TreeCaps: tree-based capsule networks for source code processing. In: Proceedings of the AAAI Conference on Artificial Intelligence, vol. 35, pp. 30–38 (2021)
6. Chen, T., Kornblith, S., Norouzi, M., Hinton, G.: A simple framework for contrastive learning of visual representations. In: International Conference on Machine Learning, pp. 1597–1607. PMLR (2020)
7. Dong, Yu., Hou, J., Lu, X.: An intelligent online judge system for programming training. In: Nah, Y., Cui, B., Lee, S.-W., Yu, J.X., Moon, Y.-S., Whang, S.E. (eds.) DASFAA 2020. LNCS, vol. 12114, pp. 785–789. Springer, Cham (2020). https://doi.org/10.1007/978-3-030-59419-0_57
8. Hofmeister, J., Siegmund, J., Holt, D.V.: Shorter identifier names take longer to comprehend. In: 2017 IEEE 24th International Conference on Software Analysis, Evolution and Reengineering (SANER), pp. 217–227. IEEE (2017)
9. Johnson-Yu, S., Bowman, N., Sahami, M., Piech, C.: SimGrade: using code similarity measures for more accurate human grading. In: Proceedings of the 14th International Conference on Educational Data Mining, EDM 2021, virtual, 29 June–2 July 2021 (2021)
10. Kim, S., Park, J., Jeon, S., Seo, D.: Web-based online judge system for online programming education. In: 2022 IEEE International Conference on Consumer Electronics (ICCE), pp. 1–3. IEEE (2022)
11. Li, Z., Li, L., Wu, Y., Liu, Y., Chen, X.: Automated student code scoring by analyzing grammatical and semantic information of code. In: 2021 16th International Conference on Computer Science & Education (ICCSE), pp. 963–968. IEEE (2021)

12. Mou, L., Li, G., Zhang, L., Wang, T., Jin, Z.: Convolutional neural networks over tree structures for programming language processing. In: Proceedings of the AAAI Conference on Artificial Intelligence. vol. 30 (2016)
13. Van den Oord, A., Li, Y., Vinyals, O.: Representation learning with contrastive predictive coding. arXiv e-prints pp. arXiv-1807 (2018)
14. Orr, J.W., Russell, N.: Automatic assessment of the design quality of python programs with personalized feedback. In: Proceedings of the 14th International Conference on Educational Data Mining, EDM (2021)
15. Peruma, A., Arnaoudova, V., Newman, C.D.: Ideal: an open-source identifier name appraisal tool. In: 2021 IEEE International Conference on Software Maintenance and Evolution (ICSME), pp. 599–603. IEEE (2021)
16. Qin, Y., Sun, G., Li, J., Hu, T., He, Y.: Scg_fbs: a code grading model for students' program in programming education. In: 2021 13th International Conference on Machine Learning and Computing, pp. 210–216 (2021)
17. Schroff, F., Kalenichenko, D., Philbin, J.: FaceNet: a unified embedding for face recognition and clustering. In: Proceedings of the IEEE Conference on Computer Vision and Pattern Recognition, pp. 815–823 (2015)
18. Singh, G., Srikant, S., Aggarwal, V.: Question independent grading using machine learning: the case of computer program grading. In: Proceedings of the 22nd ACM SIGKDD International Conference on Knowledge Discovery and Data Mining, pp. 263–272 (2016)
19. Srikant, S., Aggarwal, V.: A system to grade computer programming skills using machine learning. In: Proceedings of the 20th ACM SIGKDD International Conference on Knowledge Discovery and Data Mining, pp. 1887–1896 (2014)
20. Takhar, R., Aggarwal, V.: Grading uncompilable programs. In: Proceedings of the AAAI Conference on Artificial Intelligence, vol. 33, pp. 9389–9396 (2019)
21. Wang, G.P., Chen, S.Y., Yang, X., Feng, R.: OJPOT: online judge & practice oriented teaching idea in programming courses. Eur. J. Eng. Educ. **41**(3), 304–319 (2016)
22. Wang, M., Han, W., Chen, W.: MetaOJ: a massive distributed online judge system. Tsinghua Sci. Technol. **26**(4), 548–557 (2021)
23. Wasik, S., Antczak, M., Badura, J., Laskowski, A., Sternal, T.: A survey on online judge systems and their applications. ACM Comput. Surv. **51**(1), 1–34 (2018)
24. Yang, Z., Yang, D., Dyer, C., He, X., Smola, A., Hovy, E.: Hierarchical attention networks for document classification. In: Proceedings of the 2016 Conference of the North American Chapter of the Association for Computational Linguistics: Human Language Technologies, pp. 1480–1489 (2016)
25. Zhang, J., Wang, X., Zhang, H., Sun, H., Wang, K., Liu, X.: A novel neural source code representation based on abstract syntax tree. In: 2019 IEEE/ACM 41st International Conference on Software Engineering (ICSE), pp. 783–794. IEEE (2019)
26. Zhang, K., Shasha, D.: Simple fast algorithms for the editing distance between trees and related problems. SIAM J. Comput. **18**(6), 1245–1262 (1989)
27. Zhou, W., Pan, Y., Zhou, Y., Sun, G.: The framework of a new online judge system for programming education. In: Proceedings of ACM Turing Celebration Conference, China, pp. 9–14 (2018)

Meta Hierarchical Reinforced Learning to Rank for Recommendation: A Comprehensive Study in MOOCs

Yuchen Li[1], Haoyi Xiong[2], Linghe Kong[1(✉)], Rui Zhang[1], Dejing Dou[2], and Guihai Chen[1]

[1] Shanghai Jiao Tong University, Shanghai, China
{yuchenli,linghe.kong,zhang_rui}@sjtu.edu.cn, gchen@cs.sjtu.edu.cn
[2] Baidu Inc., Beijing, China
{xionghaoyi,doudejing}@baidu.com

Abstract. The rapid development of Massive Open Online Courses (MOOCs) surges the needs of advanced models for personalized online education. Existing solutions successfully recommend MOOCs courses via deep learning models, they however generate weak "course embeddings" with original profiles, which contain noisy and few enrolled courses. On the other hand, existing algorithms provide the recommendation list according to the score of each course while ignoring the personalized demands of learners. To tackle the above challenges, we propose a *Meta hierarchical Reinforced Learning to rank* approach **MRLtr**, which consists of a Meta Hierarchical Reinforcement Learning pre-trained mechanism and a gradient boosting ranking method to provide accurate and personalized MOOCs courses recommendation. Specifically, the end-to-end pre-training mechanism combines a user profile reviser and a meta embedding generator to provide course embedding representation enhancement for the recommendation task. Furthermore, the downstream ranking method adopts a LightGBM-based ranking regressor to promote the order quality with gradient boosting. We deploy **MRLtr** on a real-world MOOCs education platform and evaluate it with a large number of baseline models. The results show that **MRLtr** could achieve $\Delta NDCG_4 = 7.74\%-16.36\%$, compared to baselines. Also, we conduct a 7-day A/B test using the realistic traffic of Shanghai Jiao Tong University MOOCs, where we can still observe significant improvement in real-world applications. **MRLtr** performs consistently both in online and offline experiments.

Keywords: Online education · MOOCs recommendation · Meta learning · Hierarchical reinforcement learning · Learning to rank

This work was supported in part by National Key R&D Program of China (No. 2021ZD0110303), NSFC grant 62141220, 61972253, U1908212, 72061127001, 62172276, 61972254, the Program for Professor of Special Appointment (Eastern Scholar) at Shanghai Institutions of Higher Learning, Open Research Projects of Zhejiang Lab No. 2022NL0AB01.

M.-R. Amini et al. (Eds.): ECML PKDD 2022, LNAI 13718, pp. 302–317, 2023.
https://doi.org/10.1007/978-3-031-26422-1_19

1   Introduction

With the rapid development of online education, many Massive Open Online Courses (MOOCs) platforms (e.g., Coursera, edX and Udacity) have been built around the world to offer convenient and low-cost opportunities to access high qualified courses from elite universities. The rapid development of MOOCs surges the needs of advanced models and algorithms for personalized course recommendation. Nowadays, deep learning techniques have made significant achievements in many areas, such as computer vision, natural language processing and recommendation system. The MOOCs recommendation can be considered as a sequential recommendation problem. We can formulate the problem as recommending the most probable course to be enrolled by certain user (the user's preference) at time $t+1$, given a set of historical enrolled courses (the user's profile) before time t. To tackle such issue, existing works have proposed various methods to model users' preferences. For example, factored item similarity model (FISM) [1] represents each course as an embedding vector and averages the embedding of all historical courses as the user's preference without capturing the order of the courses. In order to use the order of historical courses, [2] proposes a gated recurrent unit model adding a temporal sequence of the historical courses, whose output is the last vector of the user preference. However, its performance is compromised by assigning all the historical courses with the same weight when calculating the similarity between the target course and the user profile. To distinguish the weights of different courses, two attention-based models (neural attentive item session-based recommendation (NASR) [3] and neural attentive item similarly (NAIS) [4]) are proposed. NAIS and NASR can estimate the attention coefficient of each enrolled course as the importance indicator.

While existing attempts have made significant progress, there still exists three technical challenges as follows. Firstly, existing solutions using deep learning models could fit the original user profiles well, they however contain noises. For instance, there are some enrolled courses whose watching duration is terribly short in a user profile, which represents that the user shows little interest in the courses or enrolls them mistakenly. Once these noisy courses are fed into deep learning models, they will dilute the importance of the contributing courses, which will make the recommendation model performance poorly. Secondly, existing solutions successfully extract features from course materials for recommendation via "course embeddings", they however fail to extract informative features for recommendation when the training data is limited (e.g., cold-start courses). For some courses with many enrolled users, their features will be learned sufficiently. In such case, it will be a higher chance for them to be recommended. On the contrary, for new courses with relatively few enrollments, their special features will be ignored, which leads to lower recommendation probability. Moreover, for cold-start case, when a new course is added into the platform, or the trained model is deployed on a new platform, the recommendation accuracy will be compromised significantly since the embeddings of the new courses can not be represented well. Finally, existing course recommendation systems usually score the courses and provide the recommendation order directly according to the scores [1]. However, this pointwise method only considers a single course at a time in the loss function, which essentially recasts the problem as a regression task. The score of each candidate course is independent without contemplating the potential relationship between the courses. For the MOOCs recommendation, it is necessary to provide more accurate and personalized recommendation order for students.

In order to tackle the above three issues, we propose a three-step approach: (1) *Reinforced User Profiling with Items Filtering*; (2) *End-to-end Pre-training with Meta Enhancing*; (3) *Gradient Boosting with Order Promoting*. Specially, the first step adopts a hierarchical reinforcement learning method to conduct a user profile reviser, which aims to avoid deep learning models overfitting the noise courses. To enhance the representation of course embeddings, a meta embedding generator is proposed, which can not only adapt fast for new courses, but also perform well on few-shot enrolled data. Instead of using the original course embeddings directly, **MRLtr** fuses the features learned from the user profile reviser and the meta embedding generator to provide an end-to-end pre-training for the downstream recommendation models. After the basic recommendation model, the final step replaces the pointwise loss function with a LightGBM [17]-based Learning To Rank (LTR) model, which chooses the listwise loss function to capture the comprehensive user-course relevance for the sake of promoting more accurate and personalized course order for student users.

We conduct extensive offline and online experiments on a real-world MOOCs platform. The results show the effectiveness of **MRLtr** and the consistent performance in the real-world MOOCs platform. To the best of our knowledge, this is the first work to propose an end-to-end pre-trainning mechanism with a LTR promoting method for the MOOCs recommendation task. Our main contributions can be summarized as follows:

- We study the problem of online recommendation in the context of Online Education, where we particularly focus on the technical challenges on embedding representation and order promotion. To the best of our knowledge, this work is the first to investigate course embedding representation with an end-to-end pre-traininng mechanism and order promotion with a LightGBM-based ranking regressor.
- We design and implement **MRLtr**, incorporating the end-to-end pre-training mechanism and the order promotion model in the basic recommendation task. Specifically, **MRLtr** consists of three steps: (1) *Reinforced User Profiling with Item Filtering* that removes the noisy courses with hierarchical reinforcement learning, (2) *End-to-end Pre-training with Meta Enhancing* that adopts a gradient-based meta learning approach to search a better embedding representation and average the embeddings generated from step (1) to feed recommendation models, (3) *Gradient Boosting with Order Promoting* that promotes the course recommendation order via a ranking regressor.
- We deploy **MRLtr** on the Shanghai Jiao Tong University (SJTU) MOOCs and evaluate it using both offline experiments and online A/B tests in comparison with baseline algorithms. The experiment results show that, com-

pared to the state of the art algorithms, **MRLtr** could achieve $\Delta NDCG_4 = 7.74\% \sim 16.36\%$ in offline experiments and significant improvement in online A/B tests under fair comparisons. Extensive ablation studies further confirm the effectiveness of **MRLtr** for the MOOCs recommendation.

2 Background and Formulation

In this section, we introduce the background of the basic MOOCs recommendation problem and formulate the basic MOOCs recommendation model.

2.1 Background

Like all the recommendation tasks, users and items are two basic elements in MOOCs recommendation problem. We use $U = \{u_1, \cdots, u_{|U|}\}$ to denote the user set and $C = \{c_1, \cdots, c_{|C|}\}$ to denote the course set of a MOOCs platform. The set of historical enrolled courses is defined as $\mathcal{E}^u = (e_1^u, \cdots, e_{t_u}^u)$, which also denotes the user profile. We formulate the problem as recommending the most probable course u to be enrolled at $t_u + 1$, given a set of user's historical enrolled courses $\mathcal{E}^u$ before time t.

2.2 Formulations

Like all general recommendation tasks, characterizing the user's preference based on its profile $\mathcal{E}^u$ is critical. We utilize a valued low dimensional embedding vector $\mathbf{p}_t^u$ to represent each historical enrolled course e_t^u. User u's preference is denoted as $\mathbf{q}_u$, which aggregates the embeddings of all historical enrolled courses. An embedding vector $\mathbf{p}_i$ is utilized to represent the target course c_i. The probability p of recommending c_i to u can be represented as

$$p = P\left(y = 1 \mid \mathcal{E}^u, c_i\right) = \sigma_\theta\left(\mathbf{q}_u^T \mathbf{p}_i\right), \tag{1}$$

where $\sigma_\theta\left(\cdot\right)$ is the sigmoid function which transforms the input embedding vectors into a probability, θ is its parameters. The key issue for solving the recommendation task is to calculate $\mathbf{q}_u$, i.e., the aggregated embedding. There are some existing methods to obtain $\mathbf{q}_u$. For example, we can average the embeddings of all the historical enrolled courses. However, this method treats all historical enrolled courses equally, which neglects the importance of different courses and cannot represent the real interest of users. Hence, an existing work utilizes the attention mechanism to estimate an attention coefficient a_{it}^u for each course e_t^u [4]. Moreover, there is also a method using attentive recurrent neural network to capture the order of historical courses [3].

In this paper, we adopt the method that parameterizes the attention coefficient a_{it}^u as a function, whose inputs are $\mathbf{p}_t^u$ and $\mathbf{p}_i$. Then the embeddings are calculated based on their attentions as,

$$\mathbf{q}_u = \sum_{t=1}^{t_u} a_{it}^u \mathbf{p}_t^u, \quad a_{it}^u = z\left(\mathbf{p}_t^u, \mathbf{p}_i\right), \tag{2}$$

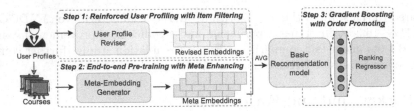

Fig. 1. The pipeline of MRLtr. Firstly, we pre-train the basic recommendation model. Then, we train *Step 1* with the basic recommendation model. Next, we train *Step 2* with the basic recommendation model. Finally, we jointly train all the parts together with the frozen parameters of *Step 2*.

where $z\left(\cdot\right)$ can be instantiated by a multi-layer perception on the concatenation or the element-wise product of the two embeddings $\mathbf{p}_t^u$ and $\mathbf{p}_i$.

3   Methodology

In this section, we present the technical details of **MRLtr**. As illustrated in Fig. 1, **MRLtr** consists of three steps: (1) *Reinforced User Profiling with Item Filtering*, (2) *End-to-end Pre-training with Meta Enhancing*, and (3) *Gradient Boosting with Order Promoting*. We first introduce *Reinforced User Profiling with Item Filtering* which adpots a hierarchical reinforcement learning algorithm to remove the noisy courses. Second, we propose the *End-to-end Pre-training with Meta Enhancing* which utilizes a gradient-based meta learning algorithm to enhance the representation of course embeddings. Finally, we introduce *Gradient Boosting with Order Promoting* which deploys a LightGBM-based ranking regressor to replace the pointwise loss function for the course recommendation.

3.1   Reinforced User Profiling with Item Filtering

The whole profile revising process can be formulated as a hierarchical Markov Decision Process (MDP), which contains a high-level task and a low-level task. The training process of the profile reviser is shown in Fig. 2.

Formulating the Item Filtering Task as a Hierarchical MDP. An MDP can be represented as a 5-tuple $\langle \mathcal{S}, \mathcal{A}, \pi, \mathcal{P}, \mathcal{R} \rangle$, with $\mathcal{S}$ denoting the state space, $\mathcal{A}$ denoting the action space, π denoting the policy, $\mathcal{P}$ denoting the state transition probability matrix, and $\mathcal{R}$ denoting the reward. Specifically, the agent observes an environment state $s \in \mathcal{S}$, takes an action $a \in \mathcal{A}$ based on a certain policy $\pi(a|s)$, which is the conditional probability density of choosing action a under state s. After applying a, the agent receives a reward $r \in \mathcal{R}$, then the state transfers to s' with probability $p(s'|s, a) \in \mathcal{P}$. The proposed approach reformulates the profile revising task as an MDP $\langle \mathcal{S}, \mathcal{A}, \pi, \mathcal{P}, \mathcal{R} \rangle$, which is given as:

1) **state** $\mathcal{S}$. We catrgorize $\mathcal{S}$ into the low-level task and the high-level task:
- low-level task: For each historical course e_t^u, the state feature $\mathbf{s}_t^l$ contains four aspects: the effort taken in the course e_t^u, cosine similarity and element-wise product between the embedding vectors of e_t^u and c_i, and the average of the previous features over all historical courses in $\mathcal{E}^u$. Notice that the embedding vector is obtained from a pre-trained basic recommendation model.
- high-level task: For each user profile, the state feature of high-level task $\mathbf{s}^h$ contains: the average cosine similarity and element-wise product between the embedding vectors of all e_t^u in $\mathcal{E}^u$ and c_i, the probability of recommending e_t^u to user u obtained by a basic recommendation model.

2) **action** $\mathcal{A}$. We categorize $\mathcal{A}$ into the low-level task and the high-level task:
- low-level task: The low-level action $a_t^l \in \{0, 1\}$ for each historical course e_t^u is defined as a binary value to indicate whether to remove it or not.
- high-level task: The high-level action $a^h \in \{0, 1\}$ is defined as a binary value to indicate whether to revise the profile $\mathcal{E}^u$ of user u or not.

3) **policy** π. We utilize policy networks parameterized by θ^l and θ^h for low-level policy $\pi(\mathbf{s}_t^l, a_t^l | \theta^l)$ and high-level policy $\pi(\mathbf{s}^h, a^h | \theta^h)$, respectively.

4) **reward** $\mathcal{R}$. We first define a delayed reward for each low-level action as

$$r(a_t^l, \mathbf{s}_t^l) = \begin{cases} \log p(y = 1 | \widehat{\mathcal{E}}^u, c_i) - \log p(y = 1 | \mathcal{E}^u, c_i), & \text{if } t = t_u \\ 0 & \text{otherwise} \end{cases}, \quad (3)$$

where $\widehat{\mathcal{E}}^u$ is the revised profile. The delayed reward shows the difference between the log-likelihood of recommending c_i after and before the profile is revised.

- high-level task: A delayed reward is used to evaluate the high-level action, $R^h = r(a_t^l, \mathbf{s}_t^l)$. When the high-level task determines to revise the user profile, R^h will be received after the last low-level action is performed.
- low-level task: An internal reward $g(a_t^l, \mathbf{s}_t^l)$ is defined as follows: First, obtain the average cosine similarity between each historical course e_t^u and c_i after and before the profile is revised. Then, calculate the difference between them as $g(a_t^l, \mathbf{s}_t^l)$. Finally, the reward for low-level task is obtained by $R^l = r(a_t^l, \mathbf{s}_t^l) + g(a_t^l, \mathbf{s}_t^l)$.

Algorithm Workflow. With the formulated hierarchical MDP above, the task of profile reviser is to find a set of optimal parameters $\theta = \{\theta^l, \theta^h\}$ to maximize the expected reward as

$$\theta^* = \text{argmax}_\theta \sum_\tau p_\theta(\tau) R(\tau), \quad (4)$$

where τ is the sampled sequence (i.e., $\tau = \{\mathbf{s}_1^l, a_1^l, \mathbf{s}_2^l, \cdots, \mathbf{s}_t^l, a_t^l, \cdots \mathbf{s}_{t_u}^l, a_{t_u}^l\}$ for low-level tasks, and $\tau = \{\mathbf{s}^h, a^h\}$ for high-level tasks), $p_\theta(\tau)$ denotes the sampling probability, and $R(\tau)$ denotes the reward for τ.

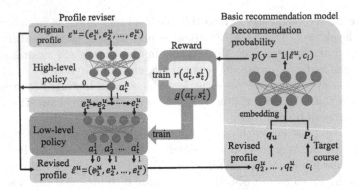

Fig. 2. The training process of the profile reviser.

We invoke monto-carlo policy gradient method to solve the above profile revising task, which is trained jointly with the basic recommendation model. First, we pre-train the basic recommendation model based on the unrevised user profile. With the pre-trained recommendation model, we then train an initialized profile reviser. Specifically, for each user profile $\mathcal{E}^u$ in one training episode, we first execute the high-level task to get a^h. If the high-level task determines to revise the user profile (i.e., $a^h = 1$), the low-level task will be performed. Then, We sample a low-level sequence τ, and compute $r(a_t^l, s_t^l)$ and $g(a_t^l, s_t^l)$. After collecting M trajectories, we update θ^l according to the loss function as

$$L_{\theta^l} = \frac{1}{m} \sum_{m=1}^{M} \sum_{t=1}^{t_u} \nabla_{\theta^l} \log \pi_{\theta^l}(s_t^m, a_t^m) R^l, \tag{5}$$

while the loss function for updating θ^h is given as

$$L_{\theta^h} = \frac{1}{m} \sum_{m=1}^{M} \nabla_{\theta^h} \log \pi_{\theta^h}(s^m, a^m) R^h. \tag{6}$$

Finally, based on the revised profile, we train the recommendation model and start another training episode.

3.2 End-to-End Pre-training with Meta Enhancing

In this section, we first propose the meta embedding generator that captures the skill of learning course embeddings through meta-learning. Then, we describe the end-to-end pre-training mechanism with feature fusion.

View of Meta Learning. The essence of MOOCs recommendation is to learn the function $\sigma(\cdot)$ with inputs of the course embedding vectors as shown in (1).

Before learning the function $\sigma(\cdot)$, we need to transform the course into a real-valued vector. From a meta-learning perspective, we reintroduce the notation of the MOOCs recommendation model as

$$p = h\left(c_i\right) = \sigma_\theta\left(\phi_{\mathbf{i}}, c_i\right), \tag{7}$$

where θ is the parameters of function $\sigma(\cdot)$ and $\phi_{\mathbf{i}}$ is the embeddings for course c_i. Actually, $h(\cdot)$ is the same function as $\sigma_\theta(\cdot)$. Then we can recast the MOOCs recommendation as a meta-learning problem via viewing each course as a distinguished task. Specifically, for course $\mathbf{i} = \{1, 2, \cdots\}$, each task $t_{\mathbf{i}}$ corresponds to a specific function $h(\cdot)$. Each task has its own parameters $\phi_{\mathbf{i}}$ and shares the same parameters θ of the basic recommendation model. We aim to train the model to learn how to learn $\phi_{\mathbf{i}}$. This is the analysis that we recast the MOOCs recommendation as meta-learning.

Train the Meta Embedding Generator. We choose some courses as the prior tasks with many training samples to pre-train the MOOCs recommendation model. In this way, we can get a well-trained parameter set θ and task-specific parameters $\phi_{\mathbf{i}}$ for each prior task. In order to train the meta embedding generator to learn how to learn course embeddings, we choose a course with few enrollments as the new task $\hat{i}$. Due to the fact that the task-specific parameter $\phi_{\mathbf{i}}$ can not be shared with a new task, we have to train a meta embedding generator to replace its place. For a new course (i.e., a new task $t_{\hat{i}}$), we use $\phi_{\mathbf{i}}^{\text{init}}$ as the initial embedding

$$\phi_{\hat{\mathbf{i}}}^{\text{init}} = f_v(c_{\hat{i}}), \tag{8}$$

where v is the meta-parameter and $f_v(\cdot)$ is the meta embedding generator. The recommendation problem can be shown as

$$\hat{p} = h_{meta}\left(c_{\hat{i}}\right) = \sigma_\theta\left(\phi_{\hat{\mathbf{i}}}^{\text{init}}, c_{\hat{i}}\right). \tag{9}$$

As for each task $t_{\mathbf{i}}$ (i.e., course $c_{\mathbf{i}}$), we can get the training set as $\mathcal{D}_{\mathbf{i}} = \{c_{\mathbf{i}}\}_{j=1}^{N_{\mathbf{i}}}$ with $N_{\mathbf{i}}$ samples. We choose two disjoint mini-batches such as $\mathcal{D}_{\mathbf{i}}^1$ and $\mathcal{D}_{\mathbf{i}}^2$, each with K samples. To simulate the course with relatively few enrollments, we assume the mini-batch size K is far less than half of $N_{\mathbf{i}}$. Then we take a two-step strategy to train the meta embedding generator and get the meta-parameter v: (1) We use $h_{meta}(\cdot)$ on the first mini-batch $\mathcal{D}_{\mathbf{i}}^1$ and get the recommendation result as

$$\hat{p}_1 = h_{meta}\left(c_{\mathbf{i}}\right) = \sigma_\theta\left(\phi_{\mathbf{i}}^{\text{init}}, c_{\mathbf{i}}\right). \tag{10}$$

Meanwhile, we obtain the average loss as

$$l_1 = \frac{1}{K}\sum_{k=1}^{K}\left[-y_1\log\hat{p}_1 - (1 - y_1)\log\left(1 - \hat{p}_1\right)\right], \tag{11}$$

where k is of the k-th sample from batch $\mathcal{D}_{\mathbf{i}}^1$. (2) We execute the learning process with the second batch of data $\mathcal{D}_{\mathbf{i}}^2$ and then compute the gradient of l_1 and take a step of gradient descent,

$$\phi_i' = \phi_i^{\text{init}} - \alpha \frac{\partial l_1}{\partial \phi_i^{\text{init}}}, \tag{12}$$

where α is the learning rate. Next, we test the trained model on the second batch $\mathcal{D}_i^2$. Specifically, we obtain the recommendation result as

$$\hat{p}_2 = h'_{\text{meta}}(c_i) = \sigma_\theta(\phi_i', c_i). \tag{13}$$

Meanwhile, we obtain the average loss as

$$l_2 = \frac{1}{K} \sum_{k=1}^{K} [-y_2 \log \hat{p}_2 - (1 - y_2) \log (1 - \hat{p}_2)]. \tag{14}$$

Next we propose the final loss function l_{final} unified l_1 and l_2 as

$$l_{\text{final}} = al_1 + bl_2, \tag{15}$$

where $a, b \in [0, 1]$ are the weight coefficients of the loss functions and the sum of a and b is 1 (i.e., $a + b = 1$). The aims for defining the final loss function as (15) is summarized as: (1) For the new courses, we aim to reduce the error of the MOOCs recommendation. Hence, we calculate l_1 in the final loss function different from MAML, which takes l_2 as the final loss function. (2) For the courses with few enrollments (i.e., small number of labeled data), we aim to make them learn fast through gradient updates. Then we calculate the gradient by the chain rule:

$$\frac{\partial l_{\text{final}}}{\partial v} = \frac{\partial l_{\text{final}}}{\partial \phi_i^{\text{init}}} \frac{\partial \phi_i^{\text{init}}}{\partial v} = \frac{\partial l_{\text{final}}}{\partial \phi_i^{\text{init}}} \frac{\partial f_v}{\partial v}, \tag{16}$$

where

$$\frac{\partial l_{\text{final}}}{\partial \phi_i^{\text{init}}} = a \frac{\partial l_1}{\partial \phi_i^{\text{init}}} + b \frac{\partial l_2}{\partial \phi_i'} - ab \frac{\partial l_2}{\partial \phi_i'} \frac{\partial^2 l_1}{\partial \phi_i^{\text{init}^2}}. \tag{17}$$

Eventually, we propose the training algorithm for the meta embedding generator as shown in Algorithm 1. Specifically, we design a neural network as the meta embedding generator. The inputs of the generator is the course features. In our work, we use the embedding layers of the basic recommendation model in the generator instead of training it from scratch. In order to reduce the number of parameters, we use the parameters of reused layers directly. Then the embeddings from different fields are aggregated by average pooling. Eventually, we use a fully connected layer to get the outputs.

End-to-end Pre-training with Feature Fusion. In this section, we propose a simple yet useful design to fuse the embeddings from the meta embedding generator and the user profile reviser. First, we make sure the output embedding from the profile reviser and the meta embedding generator have the same dimension. If a historical course is revised by the profile reviser, the corresponding item of the original output of the profile reviser will be set as 0. Then we average the sum of the corresponding parts of the profile reviser and the meta embedding generator to obtain the new course embedding.

Algorithm 1. Training Meta Embedding Generator

Input: The base model σ_θ, course dataset C, hyper-parameter a,b, learning rate α,β.

1: Randomly initialize v;
2: **while** not done **do**
3:     Randomly samples n courses $\{i_1, i_2, \ldots, i_n\}$ from C;
4:     **for** i $\in \{i_1, i_2, \ldots, i_n\}$ **do**
5:         Generate the initial embedding: $\phi_i^{init} = f_v(c_i)$;
6:         Sample mini-batch $\mathcal{D}_i^1$ and $\mathcal{D}_i^2$ each with K samples;
7:         Evaluate loss l_1 on $\mathcal{D}_i^1$;
8:         Compute adapted embedding: $\phi_i' = \phi_i^{init} - \alpha \frac{\partial l_1}{\partial \phi_i^{init}}$;
9:         Evaluate loss l_2 on $\mathcal{D}_i^2$;
10:        Compute loss: $l_{final} = al_1 + bl_2$;
11:    **end for**
12:    $v \leftarrow v - \beta \sum_{i \in \{i_1, \ldots, i_n\}} \frac{\partial l_{final}}{\partial v}$;
13: **end while**

3.3 Gradient Boosting with Order Promoting

Given the new fusion embedding to the basic recommendation models, **MRLtr** replaces the fully connected layer of the basic recommendation model with a LightGBM-based ranking regressor, which adpots the listwise loss function. We denote a set of user-course pairs with the ranking score as a set of triple such as $\mathcal{T} = \{(u_1, e_1, \boldsymbol{y}_1), (u_2, e_2, \boldsymbol{y}_2), (u_3, e_3, \boldsymbol{y}_3), \ldots\}$. We aim to gain a LTR scoring function f_s. Therefore, the goal is recast to learn a scoring function f which minimizes the loss as

$$L(f) = \frac{1}{|\mathcal{T}|} \sum_{i=1}^{|\mathcal{T}|} \left(\frac{1}{|e_i|} \sum_{j=1}^{|e_i|} \ell(\boldsymbol{y}_j^i, f_s(u_j^i, e_j^i)) \right), \tag{18}$$

where ℓ represents the loss of the ranking prediction of course e_j^i of user u_i against the ground truth $\boldsymbol{y}_j^i$.

4 Experiments

To demonstrate the effectiveness of **MRLtr**, we present extensive experiments on the SJTU MOOCs platform comparing with a large number of baseline methods. Firstly, we detail the experimental settings. Then, we introduce the results of offline experiments. Finally, the performance of online A/B Test shows the effectiveness of **MRLtr**.

4.1 Experimental Settings

Dataset and Evaluation Methodology. We collect the dataset from SJTU MOOCs, a large MOOCs platform with significant number of users. Specifically, we collect a portion of the student users who enrolled courses from September 1st, 2016 to September 1st, 2021. Moreover, we make some standardized processing, such as defining the courses with the same name in different years as the same one. For instance, we unity "Computer Network" from 2016 to 2020 into the same course named "Computer Network". The collected dataset consist of 1,452 courses, 65,649 users, 313,492 users enrolled behaviors, and 23 categories.

To evaluate the performance of **MRLtr**, we use Normalized Discounted Cumulative Gain (NDCG) [16], which has been widely adopted to evaluate the ranking performance. Before introducing NDCG, we first introduce the Discounted Cumulative Gain (DCG) as

$$DCG_N = \sum_{i=1}^{N} \frac{G_i}{\log_2(i+1)}, \tag{19}$$

where G_i denotes the weight assigned to the item's label at position i. A higher G_i indicates that the item is more relevant to the user and correspondingly a better LTR model. However, due to the different lengths of various users, it makes no sense to compare the DCG among them. Then, we utilize the following implementation of NDCG to take a mean across all scores as

$$NDCG_N = \frac{DCG_N}{IDCG_N}, \tag{20}$$

where $IDCG_N$ is the ideal order to normalize the scores. Moreover, the value of NDCG is in the range of $[0, 1]$. Similarly, a higher $NDCG_N$ indicates a better LTR model. In this paper, we consider the NDCG of top 10 and 4 ranking results, i.e., $NDCG@10$ and $NDCG@4$.

Experiment Setups. In this work, all the offline experiments are implemented on a server with 32G Memory, 1 NVIDIA Tesla V100 GPU and 2T Disk. The online experiments are deployed on SJTU MOOCs platform. In order to evaluate the effectiveness of **MRLtr** comprehensively, we adopt seven related models proposed by previous researches as competitors:

- **Bayesian Personalized Ranking (BPR).** This model uses a Bayesian method to optimize the pairwise ranking loss in recommendation tasks.
- **Multi-layer Perception (MLP).** The model use a multi-layer perceptron on a pair of user and course embeddings to learn the probability of recommending the course to the user.
- **Factorization Machine (FM).** FM is a principled approach that can easily incorporate any heuristic features.
- **Factored Item Similarity Model (FISM).** FISM is an item-to-item collaborative filtering (CF) algorithm which recommends courses via averaging embedding of all enrolled courses and embedding of the target courses.
- **Gated Recurrent Unit (GRU).** GRU is a gated recurrent unit model that receives a sequence of historical courses as input, then output the last hidden vector as the representation of a user's preference.

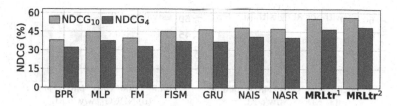

Fig. 3. Offline comparative results of MRLtr and baselines on $\Delta NDCG_{10}$ **and** $\Delta NDCG_4$**. We use MRLtr* and MRLtr** to represent the MRLtr+NAIS and MRLtr+NASR, respectively.**

- **Neural Attentive Item Similarity (NAIS).** NAIS is a collaborative filtering algorithm which utilizes an attention mechanism to distinguish the weights of different historical enrolled courses.
- **Neural Attentive Session-based Recommendation (NASR).** NASR is an improved model GRU model that estimates attention coefficients for historical enrolled courses based on the corresponding hidden vector outputs.

4.2 Offline Experimental Results

To comprehensively evaluate **MRLtr**, we conduct experiments to answer the following research questions:

RQ1: How does **MRLtr** perform compared with state-of-the-art models for MOOCs recommendation tasks?

RQ2: Is the *Reinforced User Profiling with Item Filtering* in **MRLtr** necessary for improving performance?

RQ3: Is the *End-to-end Pre-training with Meta Enhancing* in **MRLtr** vital for improving performance?

RQ4: How does the *Gradient Boosting with Order Promoting* impact the performance of **MRLtr**?

Comparative Results: RQ1. In Fig. 3, we report the offline performance of **MRLtr** compared with other baselines on $NDCG_{10}$ and $NDCG_4$. In order to represent the combination of **MRLtr** with two basic recommendation models briefly, we use **MRLtr**[1] and **MRLtr**[2] to represent the combination of **MRLtr** with NAIS and NASR, respectively. Intuitively, we could see that **MRLtr** gains the best performance compared with other baselines on both two metrics. Specifically, **MRLtr**[2] improves the performance of the baseline models from 7.74% to 16.36% on $NDCG_4$ and from 8.24% to 18.24% on $NDCG_{10}$. Moreover, there are some findings from the comparative experiments. Firstly, all the user-to-item based collaborative models (i.e., BPR, MLP and FM) show poor performance since most of the users in our dataset enrolled a few courses, and the embeddings can not be extracted from the sparse data. Secondly, item-to-item based

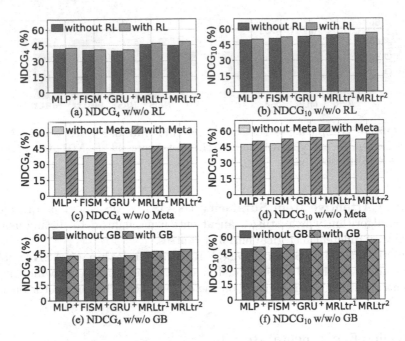

Fig. 4. Ablation studies of *Reinforced User Profiling with Item Filtering* (RL), *End-to-end Pre-training with Meta Enhancing* (Meta) and *Gradient Boosting with Order Promoting* (GB) for **MRLtr** on $NDCG_4$ and $NDCG_{10}$. To briefly represent the models, we use MLP[+], FISM[+], GRU[+], **MRLtr**[1] and **MRLtr**[2] to represent the combinations of **MRLtr** with MLP, FISM, GRU, NAIS, and NASR, respectively. Moreover, "w/w/o" is the abbreviation of "with or without".

collaborative filtering models (i.e., FISM and GRU) perform better than user-to-item based collaborative models, but they still perform worse than the attention models. Because FISM and GRU treat all historical courses equally. As for NAIS and NASR, we find that they perform better than all the above collaborative filtering models, as they can distinguish the importance of different courses via attention mechanism.

Ablation Study: RQ2. We conduct a series of ablation studies to prove the effectiveness of *Reinforced User Profiling with Item Filtering*, *End-to-end Pre-training with Meta Enhancing* and *Gradient Boosting with Order Promoting* for **MRLtr**. Figure 4 (a) and (b) illustrates that all the models with the *Reinforced User Profiling with Item Filtering* based user profile reviser could obtain better performance compared with the models without the user profile reviser. As shown in Fig. 4 (a), *Reinforced User Profiling with Item Filtering* achieves the improvement with 3.91% for **MRLtr**[2] on $NDCG_4$, which is the largest improvement in this study.

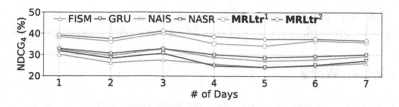

Fig. 5. Online comparative performance on $NDCG_4$ of MRLtr and baselines for 7 d. (t-test with $p < 0.05$ over the baseline).

Ablation Study: RQ3. In order to demonstrate the usefulness of *End-to-end Pre-training with Meta Enhancing*, we conduct a serious of ablation studies. As shown in Fig. 4 (c) and (d), the chosen models with *End-to-end Pre-training with Meta Enhancing* (Meta) based the meta embedding generator perform better than the models without the meta embedding generator. Specifically, the meta embedding generator obtains the largest margin with 4.72% on $NDCG_{10}$. These phenomenons prove that *End-to-End Pre-training with Meta Enhancing* could enhance the representation of course embdeddings. There are many users enrolled few courses in the dataset. The meta embedding generator can not only adapt fast for new courses, but also perform well on few-shot enrolled data.

Ablation Study: RQ4. In Fig. 4 (e) and (f), we report the ablation study of *Gradient Boosting with Order Promoting* of **MRLtr**. Similarity, all the models with the *Gradient Boosting with Order Promoting* based ranking regressor could obtain better performance compared with the models without the ranking regressor. As depicted in Fig. 4 (f), *Gradient Boosting with Order Promoting* achieves the improvement of 5.48% for GRU^+ on $NDCG_{10}$. These results demonstrate that the listwise-based ranking regressor performs better. The listwise function treats the whole document list as a sample and directly optimizes the evaluation metrics, such as the utilized metric $NDCG$ in this work.

4.3 Online Experimental Results

To demonstrate the effectiveness of **MRLtr**, we conduct a series of online A/B tests with real-world web traffics and compare it with the baseline models on SJTU MOOCs platform. According to the offline experimental results, we conduct the online experiments with full real-world web traffic, which last for 7 d. Figure 5 illustrates the comparison of **MRLtr** with the baselines on $\Delta NDCG_4$. Firstly, **MRLtr** could boost the performance compared with the online base system in all days, which demonstrates that **MRLtr** is practical for improving the performance of SJTU MOOCs. Furthermore, we can find that **MRLtr** achieves significant improvements on the real-world MOOCs platform. Specifically, we observe that **MRLtr** outperforms the online base model (FISM) by a large margin on $\Delta NDCG_4$ with 13.8% relative improvement, which reveals the effectiveness of **MRLtr**. Finally, we observe that **MRLtr** performs stably in all days, which demonstrates the soundness and usefulness of our proposed model. Basically, the online performance is consistent with offline experiment results.

5   Related Work

CF has been widely used in sequential recommendation problems, where each user-item interaction data naturally forms a sequence for being associated with timestamp information. For example, bayesian personalized ranking [5], matrix factorization [6] and factorization machine [7] are all user-to-item based CF methods. However, the performances of the above models are limited when data is sparse. By contrast, the item-to-item CF models can handle the above problem. [1] is proposed to calculate the item similarity via dot product of item embeddings. To retrieve the main preference in the sequential data, attention mechanism was proposed in NASR [3] and NAIS [4]. Moreover, RNN [8] and GRU [2] are used to capture the temporal factor of the user-item iteration data.

Recently, some researches attempt to adapt meta-learning algorithm to solve issues. Meta-learning aims to adapt a trained model to new tasks quickly and effectively by using the prior experience learned from the related tasks [9]. For example, Model-Agnostic Meta-Learning (MAML) are proposed to solve the cold-start problem [10]. Recently, motivated by the aforementioned benefits of meta-learning, it has been invoked into the recommendation tasks [11]. Moreover, λOpt [12] is proposed to optimize regularization hyper-parameters based on validation performance.

According to the loss function, we could categorize the LTR models into three families: pointwise [13], pairwise [14]and listwise [15]. The listwise model treats the whole document list as a sample and directly optimizes the evaluation metrics, such as the utilized metric in this work, i.e., NDCG.

6   Conclusion

In this paper, we design, implement and deploy a novel MOOCs recommendation approach **MRLtr** on a real-world MOOCs platform to address the problems which contains course data noises, weak representation for few enrolled courses and the poor recommendation order. **MRLtr** contains three steps: (1) *Reinforced User Profiling with Item Filtering* that removes the noisy courses with hierarchical reinforcement learning, (2) *End-to-end pre-training with Meta Enhancing* adopts a gradient-based meta learning approach to search a better embedding representation, and (3) *Gradient Boosting with Order Promoting* promotes the course recommendation order via a LightGBM-based ranking regressor. To verify the effectiveness of **MRLtr**, we conduct extensive offline and online experiments compared with a large number of baseline methods. Offline experiment results show that **MRLtr** could achieve significant gain over baselines on $NDCG_4$ compared with other baselines. Furthermore, **MRLtr** significantly boosts the online MOOCs recommendation performance in real-world applications, which is consistent with the offline results.

References

1. Kabbur, S., Ning, X., Karypis, G.: Fism: factored item similarity models for top-n recommender systems. In: Proceedings of the 19th ACM SIGKDD International Conference on Knowledge Discovery and Data Mining, pp. 659–667 (2013)
2. Hidasi, B., Karatzoglou, A., Baltrunas, L., Tikk, D.: Session-based recommendations with recurrent neural networks. CoRR abs/1511.06939 (2016)
3. Li, J., Ren, P., Chen, Z., Ren, Z., Lian, T., Ma, J.: Neural attentive session-based recommendation. In: Proceedings of the 2017 ACM on Conference on Information and Knowledge Management, pp. 1419–1428 (2017)
4. He, X., He, Z., Song, J., Liu, Z., Jiang, Y.G., Chua, T.S.: Nais: neural attentive item similarity model for recommendation. IEEE Trans. Knowl. Data Eng. **30**(12), 2354–2366 (2018)
5. Rendle, S., Freudenthaler, C., Gantner, Z., Schmidt-Thieme, L.: Bpr: bayesian personalized ranking from implicit feedback. arXiv preprint arXiv:1205.2618 (2012)
6. Koren, Y., Bell, R., Volinsky, C.: Matrix factorization techniques for recommender systems. Computer **42**(8), 30–37 (2009)
7. Rendle, S.: Factorization machines with libfm. ACM Trans. Intell. Syst. Technol. (TIST) **3**(3), 1–22 (2012)
8. Tan, Y.K., Xu, X., Liu, Y.: Improved recurrent neural networks for session-based recommendations. In: Proceedings of the 1st Workshop on Deep Learning for Recommender Systems, pp. 17–22 (2016)
9. Finn, C., Abbeel, P., Levine, S.: Model-agnostic meta-learning for fast adaptation of deep networks. In: International Conference on Machine Learning, pp. 1126–1135. PMLR (2017)
10. Bharadhwaj, H.: Meta-learning for user cold-start recommendation. In: 2019 International Joint Conference on Neural Networks (IJCNN), pp. 1–8 (2019)
11. Ren, Y., Chi, C., Jintao, Z.: A survey of personalized recommendation algorithm selection based on meta-learning. In: Xu, Z., Choo, K.-K.R., Dehghantanha, A., Parizi, R., Hammoudeh, M. (eds.) CSIA 2019. AISC, vol. 928, pp. 1383–1388. Springer, Cham (2020). https://doi.org/10.1007/978-3-030-15235-2_191
12. Chen, Y., et al.: λopt: learn to regularize recommender models in finer levels. In: Proceedings of the 25th ACM SIGKDD International Conference on Knowledge Discovery & Data Mining, pp. 978–986 (2019)
13. Li, P., Wu, Q., Burges, C.: Mcrank: Learning to rank using multiple classification and gradient boosting. In: Advances in Neural Information Processing Systems, pp. 65–72 (2008)
14. Zheng, Z., Chen, K., Sun, G., Zha, H.: A regression framework for learning ranking functions using relative relevance judgments. In: Proceedings of the 30th Annual International ACM SIGIR Conference on Research and Development in Information Retrieval, pp. 287–294 (2007)
15. Taylor, M., Guiver, J., Robertson, S., Minka, T.: Softrank: optimizing non-smooth rank metrics. In: Proceedings of the 2008 International Conference on Web Search and Data Mining, pp. 77–86 (2008)
16. Jarvelin, K., Kekalainen, J.: IR evaluation methods for retrieving highly relevant documents. In: ACM SIGIR Forum, vol. 51, pp. 243–250. ACM New York, NY, USA (2017)
17. Ke, G., et al.: Lightgbm: a highly efficient gradient boosting decision tree. In: Advances in Neural Information Processing Systems, vol. 30 (2017)

Recognizing Cognitive Load by a Hybrid Spatio-Temporal Causal Model from Multivariate Physiological Data

Zirui Yong[1], Guoxin Su[2], Xiaohu Li[1], Lingyun Sun[3], Zejian Li[3], and Li Liu[1(✉)]

[1] School of Big Data and Software Engineering, Chongqing University,
Chongqing, China
{yongzirui,xhlee,dcsliuli}@cqu.edu.cn
[2] School of Computing and Information Technology, University of Wollongong,
Wollongong, Australia
guoxin@uow.edu.au
[3] International Design Institute, Zhejiang University, Hangzhou, China
{sunly,zejianlee}@zju.edu.cn

Abstract. Cognitive load recognition is challenging due to the inherent diversity and causality of multivariate physiological changes, with each of its instances having its own style of physiological events and their spatio-temporal causal dependencies. This leads us to define a hybrid model that employs Granger causality (GC) and Gramian angular difference fields (GADF) to discover diverse varieties of multivariate physiological events. In particular, our model introduces a GC network to explicitly characterize the unique temporal causal configurations of a particular cognitive state as a variable number of nodes and links . In addition, GADF maps are constructed to capture the inherit spatio-temporal dependency among multivariate signals in a 2D structural space. A capsule network is designed to merge these two heterogenous types of features together in a uniform way, and as a result, all local causal and spatio-temporal dependencies are globally consistent. Empirical evaluations on one benchmark dataset and two in-house datasets collected by ourselves in virtual reality learning environment suggest our model significantly outperforms the state-of-the-art approaches.

Keywords: Cognitive load recognition · Physiological signal · Granger causality · Gramian angular difference fields

1 Introduction

Cognitive load recognition, aiming to estimate the amount of an individual's mental labor when a specific task is imposed on her/his cognitive system [21], has

The original version of this chapter was revised: the name of the author Li Liu has been corrected. The correction to this chapter is available at https://doi.org/10.1007/978-3-031-26422-1_53

Supplementary Information The online version contains supplementary material available at https://doi.org/10.1007/978-3-031-26422-1_20.

become an active field, given its role in facilitating a broad range of applications. Although psychological experiment-based approaches are becoming mature to estimate cognitive load by adopting various subjective scales, they are still limited to obtain the objective states of cognitive load changes in real time. Since an individual's cognitive load state is often accompanied by the changes of physiological characteristics such as EEG, ECG, EMG, blood pressure and respiration, it is possible to achieve a deeper understanding of the correlations between long-term measurements of physiological features and cognitive loads. The main focus of this work is on causal learning of multiple physiological features, since a fundamental assumption for research on cognitive load assessment is the causal relationship between the physiological characteristics and cognitive load states.

Despite being a very challenging problem, in recent years there has been a rapid growth of interest in physiologically-based cognitive load recognition. One popular paradigm might be that of the knowledge-driven approaches, which are capable of representing rich relations among physiological events. These approaches are often semantically clear, logically elegant, and easy to interpret. However, physiological features and their causal relations need to be manually defined and extracted, and subsequently they are limited to scale up. For instance, an alarm of a physiological event (e.g., heart rate deviation from a normal range) is triggered by setting a threshold obtained from the psychological domain knowledge or expert experience. It could be rather difficult to handcraft all the signs of features accurately for many practical scenarios where such knowledge embedded in signals are intricate. In addition, these knowledge-driven models are sensitive to sensor noise or body movement, which occurs frequently when performing a task.

On the other hand, data-driven approaches, especially the deep learning-based models, which may overcome the aforementioned shortcomings by automating feature extraction from raw physiological signals. As the fundamental issue in machine learning, current techniques are becoming mature to analyze physiological time series. We refer interested readers to a recent comprehensive review of varied representative physiological data-driven algorithms [20]. With the great success being achieved, these data-driven models are capable of handling an astonishing number of correlations between features and are often robust to errors caused by incorrect physiological detection. However, these conventional approaches have the assumption that physiological features are independent without taking into account the causality between them. Their results are hard to interpret, and therefore, they are rather limited in further uncovering rich cause-effect relationships among features. For instance, the variation of *the amplitudes of ECG P-QRS-T waves* (P-QRS-T) or *the EEG based zero-phase phase-locking value* (PLV) is the reaction of *high load state* in cognitive processes [5]. In fact, most of existing data-driven models may find that there is a heavy correlation between P-QRS-T and PLV but unfortunately cannot discover the further interpretation that the *high load state* is the common cause of these two symptoms, which leads to their extrinsic association. As a result, it could be rather difficult to examine the determinant factors, which is extremely important in cognitive load assessment because a wrong release of an individual can have bad consequences in some vital scenarios such as aerospace manipulation, surgical rescue, nuclear control and air traffic command. Moreover, since a single channel of physiological sensor data is often not faithful in cognitive load assessment, e.g., a student may learn in a physical environment with high level of noise or high temperature, it is nonetheless difficult for these algorithms to specify only one kind of physiological signals like heart rate for desired load levels. This inspires us to recognize cognitive load states by discovering casual features from multivariate physiological sensor data.

To address these issues in cognitive load recognition, we present a hybrid spatio-temporal causal model by employing *Granger causality* (GC) and *Gramian angular difference fields* (GADF) to discover and combine multivariate physiological features. In particular, our approach considers a principled way of dealing with the inherent spatio-temporal causal variability within physiological signals. Briefly speaking, to discover causal structures in a single physiological channel such as heart rate, we present to introduce a temporal causal network (or *GC network*) generated from Granger causality test among physiological events. Now each resulting casual network contains its unique set of directed links together with their weights that represent cause-effect relations, characterizing a certain instance of a single channel that possess similar physiological features and their temporal causal dependencies. In addition, to combine the representative physiological features from multiple channels, we treat multivariate physiological signals as video-like continuous 2D objects (or called *GADF map*) by adopting GADF to characterize the inherit spatio-temporal dependency among different signals. Specifically, a capsule network is designed to merge the two heterogenous types of features, i.e., GC network and GADF map, together by leveraging the *encoder-classifier* mechanism to efficiently capture their spatio-temporal causal relations in a uniform way. In this way, our hybrid model is more capable of characterizing the inherit causal structural variability together with the spatio-temporal dependencies in cognitive load recognition when compared to existing methods, which is also verified during empirical evaluations on one publicly-available dataset and two in-house datasets under virtual reality (VR) environment collected by ourselves to be detailed in later sections.

2　Related Work

2.1　Knowledge-driven Associations Between Physiological Signals and Cognitive Load

There has been a fair amount of work on learning and recognizing cognitive load states by employing physiological signal data, much of them addressed from a "univariant" perspective. The first study can be traced back to 1963 when Kalsbeek [12] used ECG to analyze cognitive load. Nowadays, a variety of physiological events are studied to associate with the cognitive load states. For instance, different frequency bands in EEG spaces can achieve cognitive load discrimination within tasks [4,25]. The ECG median absolute deviation and median heat flux are found to be the most accurate measurements at distinguishing levels of cognitive load [10]. HRV and PPG that reflect the states of heart activity and blood vessels behave different trends under different levels of cognitive load [27].

Other physiological signals such as galvanic skin response (GSR), respiration (RESP) and electrodermal activity (EDA) have also been used as a measurement criterion for cognitive load assessment [2]. These approaches are capable of capturing rich relations, but unfortunately the semantic rules and their weights are typically hand-coded or based on domain knowledge. In particular, it is not practicable to handcraft the rules whose relations among physiological events are intricate especially for the multivariate signals.

2.2 Data-driven Models for Cognitive Load Assessment

Feature selection-based methods utilize features extracted from one or more specific signals to detect cognitive load. Most of these methods [22,28] use traditional machine learning methods such as SVM and KNN as classifiers. Moreover, these methods need prior knowledge to decide which features are appropriate in cognitive load recognition. Currently, deep network-based approaches have been at the forefront of this research field. RNN [15] and LSTM [11] are widely implemented for cognitive load assessment, which are adopted to capture the temporal features. However, neither of them takes into account the spatio-temporal connections between physiological signals, and they are computationally expensive and difficult for parallel computing due to their sequential structures. To fully exploiting spatio-temporal dependencies, a series of CNN-based model and its variants such as FCN [24], MCDCNN [30], MCNN [6], CNN-LSTM [13] and MLSTM-FCN [13] are introduced to manage both spatial relationship from physiological signals. However, these approaches are limited to capture the spatio-temporal features from multiple physiological signals and ignore the causality among physiological events.

2.3 Granger Causality

As aforementioned in the previous section, currently either knowledge-driven models or data-driven models are rather limited in further uncovering rich cause-effect relationships. Granger causality [9] is a way that can investigate causality between two physiological events that combines temporal relations with probabilistic description. GC-based model can capture event interactions and their temporal dependencies. Especially, it demonstrates the effectiveness in exploring causal event sets. In the field of cognitive load assessment existing GC-based models [18] exploit temporal dependencies between time series from raw physiological signals and use them to detect physiological events. However, they usually lack the expressive power to capture and propagate rich temporal dependencies in physiological events. Most importantly, since cause and effect are unidirectional, these models have to check triangle relationships to maintain causal consistency, which implies temporal consistency in the meantime. These methods often uses GC as a tool to discover temporal dependencies but fail to maintain causal consistency, which are computationally expensive or even intractable in discovering causal dependencies, where the event size is large. Moreover, it is difficult or even meaningless to understand the causes and effects that are learned from raw time series. It is worth clarifying that Granger causality does not imply "true" causality since the question of "true causality" is deeply philosophical. It can be thought of as a tool of specifying a necessary condition for a temporal causal relation. To address the problems in these models, we present our hybrid model to explicitly capture the inherent causal structural varieties by combining physiological event-based causal networks together with spatio-temporal dependency map of multivariate physiological signals under consistency.

3   Problem Formulation

Given a dataset $\mathcal{D}$ collected from C channels of physiological signals, a hybrid model is constructed with respect to the temporal causal relations as well as spatio-temporal maps among multivariate physiological events. Each sample is a sequence of T physiological events, denoted by $S =< s_1, s_2, \ldots, s_T >$. A *physiological event* (or *event* for short) s_t is a vector of C attributes at time interval t, with each being associated with a certain physiological channel. We denote it as $s_t = (s_{t1}, s_{t2}, \ldots, s_{tC})$, where s_{tc} is a vector of K data points collected from the c-th channel measured within the t-th time interval, written by $s_{tc} =< s_{tc}(1), \ldots, s_{tc}(K) >$. In addition, a sequence of k ($k \leq K$) continuous observations in an individual channel event s_{tc} is denoted by $\bar{s}_{tc}(k) =< s_{tc}(1), \ldots, s_{tc}(k) >$. It is worth noting that all events are synchronized for any channel and are spaced at a uniform time interval of length K.

GC Network. For each individual channel c, a GC network can be used to represent the temporal causal relationships between physiological events, where a node v_{tc} represents the corresponding physiological event s_{tc} and a directed link describes the temporal causality between two related events. In what follows, we ignore the subscript c in the network for simplicity. Denote a GC network $\mathbf{X}_{gc} = (\mathbf{V}, \mathbf{E})$ the corresponding network of a sample S, where $\mathbf{V}$ is a set of T nodes. An event s_i is a direct cause of s_j if there is a directed link from v_i to v_j in $\mathbf{E}$, denoted by $v_i \rightarrow v_j$, where $v_i, v_j \in \mathbf{V}$. Any link $v_i \rightarrow v_j$ in a GC network $\mathbf{X}_{gc}$ must satisfy *Granger causality test*, which defines v_i as the cause of v_j if the past values of v_i contain helpful information for predicting the future value of v_j. More formally, for each channel c, given the sequences of k observations of s_{ic} and s_{jc} ($k < K$), v_i is the cause of v_j with respect to data point k if $P(s_{jc}(k+1) \mid \bar{s}_{ic}(k), \bar{s}_{jc}(k)) \neq P(s_{jc}(k+1) \mid \bar{s}_{jc}(k))$, and also states that v_i is not the cause of v_j if $P(s_{jc}(k+1) \mid \bar{s}_{ic}(k), \bar{s}_{jc}(k)) = P(s_{jc}(k+1) \mid \bar{s}_{jc}(k))$. Since causality is transitive, irreflexive and anti-symmetric, it can be verified that the resulting GC network is a directed acyclic graph. A GC network should be *consistent* that the temporal causal relations on every triangle of nodes $\triangle ijk$ in the network satisfy the transitivity property such that if $v_i \rightarrow v_j$ and $v_j \rightarrow v_k$ then $v_k \nrightarrow v_i$. In this way, for each channel a network can characterize only a possible style (or an instance) of a cognitive load state.

GADF Map. To capture the spatio-temporal correlation between physiological events, a unique feature map $\mathbf{X}_{gadf}$ is generated for each event s_{tc}. Here, each data point $s_{tc}(i)$ can be represented in polar coordinates by encoding its corresponding angular cosine value $\phi(i) = \arccos(s_{tc}(i))$ with the radius $\rho(i) = \frac{i}{I}$, where I is a constant factor to regularize the span of the polar coordinate system. Due to the monotonicity of the cosine function in $[0, \pi]$, each channel of an event can be used to generate a unique polar map. Moreover, the temporal dependence between elements in a event can be preserved through the property of the varying radius $\rho(i)$. In this way, for any physiological event, we can readily identify spatial-temporal correlations by measuring the trigonometric differences between any pair of its corresponding points, i.e., a GADF map, defined as $\mathbf{X}_{gadf} = [\sin(\phi(i) - \phi(j))]_{i,j=1,...,T}$, which is a $T \times T$ matrix.

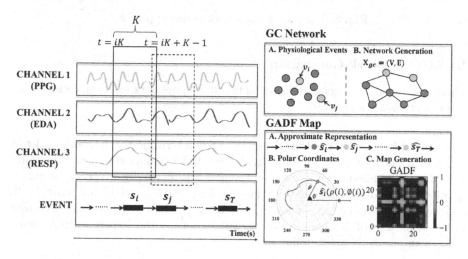

Fig. 1. Illustration of physiological events and their corresponding GC network and GADF map.

As shown in Fig. 1, GC network and GADF map can form a mixing feature space that describes a unique cognitive load states. This inspires us to present in what follows a hybrid model where these temporal causal and spatio-temporal features can be systematically discovered and combined to characterize the cognitive states of interests.

4 Our Approach

Let us consider a dataset $\mathcal{D}$ of M samples $\{(\boldsymbol{S}_m, y_m)\}$ over Y classes (i.e. different levels of cognitive load states), where y_m is the label of the sample $\boldsymbol{S}_m$, $1 \leq m \leq M$. Here each sample $\boldsymbol{S}_m \in \mathcal{D}$ is associated with C-channel sequences of T physiological events $s_t = \{s_{tc}\}_{c=1}^{C}$, $1 \leq t \leq T$. Our objective is to construct GC networks and GADF maps and encode them in a uniform way from these physiological events for cognitive load recognition tasks. The overview of our approach is illustrated in Fig. 2.

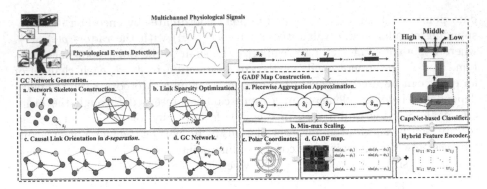

Fig. 2. The overall framework of our approach.

4.1   GC Network Generation

There are two steps to generate a GC network, i.e., network skeleton construction and causal link orientation.

Network Skeleton Construction. We first determine the network skeleton, i.e., which pairs of nodes (events) and their links (temporal causal relations) should be considered as candidates in the network. Formally, given two events of K observations of data points of c-th channel s_{ic} and s_{jc}, which are individually and jointly stationary, s_{jc} causes s_{ic} if adding s_{jc} helps predict s_{ic}, according to the definition of *Granger causality*. Subsequently, the jointly autoregressive model can be expressed as follows:

$$s_{ic}(k) = \sum_{\tau=1}^{L} b_{ii}(\tau)s_{ic}(k-\tau) + \sum_{\tau=1}^{L} b_{ij}(\tau)s_{jc}(k-\tau) + \beta_{ki}, \quad \beta_{ki} \sim \mathcal{N}(0, \Sigma_i), \quad (1)$$

$$s_{jc}(k) = \sum_{\tau=1}^{L} b_{jj}(\tau)s_{jc}(k-\tau) + \sum_{\tau=1}^{L} b_{ji}(\tau)s_{ic}(k-\tau) + \beta_{kj}, \quad \beta_{kj} \sim \mathcal{N}(0, \Sigma_j), \quad (2)$$

where $b_{ii}(\tau)$, $b_{jj}(\tau)$, $b_{ij}(\tau)$ and $b_{ji}(\tau)$ are regression coefficients, β_{ki} and β_{kj} are regression estimation residuals, and $\Sigma_i = var(\beta_{ki})$ and $\Sigma_j = var(\beta_{kj})$. L is a finite value called lag order, which can generally determined by Akaike Information Criterion (AIC).

More generally, for an individual channel c, we define the vector autoregression model regarding all pairs of physiological events (or nodes) as follows:

$$s(k) = \sum_{\tau=1}^{L} \mathbf{B}(\tau)s(k-\tau) + \beta_k, \quad (3)$$

where $\mathbf{B}(\tau)$ is the $T \times T$ coefficient matrix at lag τ where its entry $b_{ji}(\tau) \in \mathbf{B}(\tau)$ is the regression coefficient that indicates the effect on link $v_i \rightarrow v_j$, and β_k is its corresponding residual vector of size T. We adopt the LASSO *algorithm* [1] to estimate these parameters as follows:

$$\hat{\mathbf{b}}_j = \arg\min_{\mathbf{b}_j} \sum_{k=L+1}^{K} \|s_{jc}(k) - \sum_{i=1}^{T} \mathbf{b}_{ji}^{\mathsf{T}}\dot{\mathbf{s}}(k,L)\|_2^2 + \lambda\|\mathbf{b}_j\|_1$$

$$= \arg\min_{\mathbf{b}_j} \sum_{k=L+1}^{K} \|s_{jc}(k) - \sum_{i=1}^{T}\sum_{\tau=1}^{L} b_{ji}(\tau)s_{ic}(k-\tau)\|_2^2 + \lambda\|\mathbf{b}_j\|_1 \quad (4)$$

where $\mathbf{b}_{ji}$ is the i-th vector of coefficients $\mathbf{b}_j$, i.e., $\mathbf{b}_{ji} = [b_{ji}(1), \ldots, b_{ji}(L)]$, and $\dot{\mathbf{s}}(k,L)$ is the concatenated vector of L lagged observations, i.e. $\dot{\mathbf{s}}(k,L) = [s_{jc}(k-L), \ldots, s_{jc}(k-1)]$. In this way, the links that have little influence between any pair of events (i.e., $b_{ji} \approx 0$) can be eliminated by the regularization in LASSO algorithm, and thereby ensuring the sparsity in the network, avoiding the exhaustive computation. Now we can construct the initial network skeleton $\mathbf{X}_{gc}^*$ by setting $v_i \to v_j \in \mathbf{E}$ if and only if $\hat{\mathbf{b}}_{ji}$ is a nonzero vector.

Causal Link Orientation. Now there still exists the awkward situations where bidirectional links such as $v_i \leftrightarrow v_j$ or cyclic triangles (e.g., $v_i \to v_j \to v_k \to v_i$) exist in $\mathbf{X}_{gc}^*$, which may lead to causal inconsistence. To this end, we further orientate the links in $\mathbf{X}_{gc}^*$ through the *d-separation* criterion, that is, if v_i and v_j are *d-separated* by v_k, then v_i and v_j are independent given v_k; otherwise, v_i and v_j are interdependent given v_k. Here, we consider four types of *d-separation* based on the orientation rules [17]. After applying these rules, we can finally obtain a resulting GC network $\mathbf{X}_{gc}$ that is causally inconsistent.

Besides, the weight on each link $v_i \to v_j$ can be estimated in terms of its causal power, as defined by:

$$w_{ij} = \begin{cases} \ln(\Phi_j/\Psi_{ij}), & \text{if } v_i \to v_j \in \mathbf{E} \text{ and } i \neq j \\ 0, & \text{otherwise.} \end{cases} \quad (5)$$

where Φ_j measures the prediction accuracy of v_j based on its own previous values, and Ψ_{ij} measures it from the previous values of both v_i and v_j. If $\Psi_{ij} < \Phi_j$, which means v_i have a causal influence on v_j. Theoretically, the larger w_{ij}, the stronger the causal influence.

4.2   GADF Map Construction

It is straightforward to construct a GADF map from an individual channel of an event s_{tc}. Specifically, an approximate representation of s_{ic}, written as $\hat{s}_{tc}$, can be calculated by applying a simple *piecewise aggregation approximation* [14], that is, $\hat{s}_{tc} = \frac{1}{K}\sum_{j=1}^{K} s_{tc}(j)$ $(t = 1, \ldots, T)$. Here, each $\hat{s}_{tc}$ is normalized within the range of $[-1, 1]$. Next, we transform each event representation $\hat{s}_{tc}$ to a pair $(\phi(t), \rho(t))$ in the polar coordinate system. Formally, a GADF map $\mathbf{X}_{gadf}$ is a $T \times T$ matrix with its entry being calculated as:

$$\mathbf{X}_{gadf}(i,j) = \sin(\phi(i) - \phi(j)) = (\hat{s}_{ic} - \hat{s}_{jc})\sqrt{1 - \hat{s}_{ic}^2}\sqrt{1 - \hat{s}_{jc}^2}. \quad (6)$$

It is verified that GADF maps can provide intuitive spatio-temporal details as well as a cross-boundary division [23].

4.3 Capsule Network-Based Recognition Model

Now we are ready to build a hybrid model that can merge these two types of encoded features (i.e., $\mathbf{X}_{gc}$ and $\mathbf{X}_{gadf}$) together as new inputs for cognitive load state recognition. Here we design an encoder-classifier model, which consists of two parts: a hybrid feature encoder that discovers the deep features by combining GC network and GADF maps, and a capsule network-based classifier to achieve the tasks of classifying different levels of cognitive load states [29].

Hybrid Feature Encoder. The input feature tensor $\mathbf{X}$ is a concatenation of $\mathbf{X}_{gc}, \mathbf{X}_{gadf} \in \mathbb{R}^{C \times T \times T}$ of all the channels, and thus $\mathbf{X} \in \mathbb{R}^{C \times 2 \times T \times T}$. First, a convolution layer F_{conv} aims to transform these causal and spatio-temporal information jointly into a higher-level feature space, where the output feature tensor is denoted by $\mathbf{Z} \in \mathbb{R}^{C' \times 2 \times T \times T}$ $(C' < C)$, as defined:

$$\text{Layer } \textcircled{1}: \quad \mathsf{F}_{conv} : \mathbf{X} = (\boldsymbol{x}_1, \dots, \boldsymbol{x}_C) \mapsto \mathbf{Z} = (\boldsymbol{z}_1, \dots, \boldsymbol{z}_{C'})$$
$$\text{with } \boldsymbol{z}_{c'} = \kappa_{c'} * \mathbf{X} = \sum_{c=1}^{C} \kappa_{c'} * \boldsymbol{x}_c, c' = 1, \dots, C', \tag{7}$$

where $\kappa_{c'}$ is a filter kernel and $*$ is the convolution operator.

Next, we compress the global spatial information from several separate channels by adopting the global average pooling (gap) layer, and its output is fed into two fully-connected (fc) layers with ReLU activation function and sigmoid function σ, as formulated:

$$\text{Layers } \textcircled{2} - \textcircled{4} : \boldsymbol{\omega} = \mathsf{F}_{fc}^2(\mathsf{F}_{gap}(\mathbf{Z})) = \sigma(\boldsymbol{W}_2 \cdot \text{ReLU}(\boldsymbol{W}_1 \cdot (\text{avg}(\boldsymbol{z}_c))_{c=1,\dots,C'})) \tag{8}$$

where $\boldsymbol{W}_1, \boldsymbol{W}_2 \in \mathbb{R}^{C' \times C'}$ are the corresponding weights.

The last layer of our encoder is defined by a *channel-wise soft-threshold operation*:

$$\text{Layer } \textcircled{5}: \quad \boldsymbol{M} = \mathbf{X} + \mathbf{Z} \downarrow \boldsymbol{\tau}$$
$$\text{with } \boldsymbol{\tau} = \boldsymbol{\omega} \odot \mathsf{F}_{gap}(\mathbf{Z}), \mathbf{Z} \downarrow \boldsymbol{\tau} = (\boldsymbol{z}_c \downarrow \tau_c)_{1 \leq c \leq C'} \tag{9}$$

where $\odot$ is the element-wise product, and $\downarrow$ is the soft-threshold operation. In this way, $\boldsymbol{\omega}$ and $\boldsymbol{\tau}$ contain the scaling weights and the thresholds for all the channels, respectively.

CapsNet-Based Classifier. The capsule network is used as a classifier of cognitive load levels, where it takes the previous encoder's output $\boldsymbol{M} \in \mathbb{R}^{C' \times T \times T}$ as its input and output a vector of size Y indicating the different levels of cognitive load states. Our classifier consists of three layers: a standard convolutional layer, a primary capsule layer and a cognitive capsule layer.

In details, the standard convolutional layer has 64 different 3×3 filters with a stride of 2 and a ReLU activation function. The primary capsule layer has 64 types of primary capsules U_i $(i = 1, \ldots, 64)$. Each U_i is generated by a convolutional operation with 8 different 2×2 filters and then is reshaped as a tensor of 8D vectors $\tilde{U}_i = [\tilde{u}_{i,1}, \ldots, \tilde{u}_{i,d}]$ where $d = 8K^2$. Last, the cognitive capsule layer transforms these vectors to Y different 16D vectors by employing a specific *weighting* and *routing* procedure as follows:

$$\mathsf{F}_{wr} : \tilde{U} = (\tilde{u}_{i,k})_{i=1,\ldots,64,k=1,\ldots,d} \mapsto Y = (y_j)_{j=1,\ldots,Y} \tag{10}$$

More specifically, F_{wr} includes two steps. First, for each i $(i = 1, \ldots, 64)$, the primary capsules in $\tilde{U}_i = (\tilde{u}_{i,1}, \ldots, \tilde{u}_{i,d})$ pass through a shared 8×16 weight matrix $W_{i,j}$ to generate $\hat{U}_{j|i} = (\hat{u}_{j|i,1}, \ldots, \hat{u}_{j|i,d})$ $(j = 1, \ldots, Y)$. Next, a *dynamic routing procedure* routes each primary capsule output $\hat{u}_{j|i,k}$ to the j-th cognitive capsule and produces the output y_j for all $i = 1, \ldots, 64$ and $k = 1, \ldots, d$. A squashing function is employed to ensure that short vectors get shrunk to almost zero length while long vectors get shrunk to almost a unit length, as defined as follows:

$$y_j = \mathrm{squash}(e_j) = \frac{\|e_j\|^2}{1 + \|e_j\|^2} \times \frac{e_j}{\|e_j\|}, \tag{11}$$

where $e_j = \sum_{i,k} \frac{\exp(q_{j|i,k})}{\sum_{j=1}^n \exp(q_{j|i,n})} \cdot \hat{u}_{j|i,k}$ and $q_{j|i,k}$ is an internal parameter which is updated by $q_{j|i,k} \leftarrow q_{j|i,k} + \hat{u}_{j|i,k} \cdot y_j$ at each iteration. The loss function of our CapsNet-based classifier is defined below:

$$\mathrm{Loss}_j = \mathrm{I}_j \max\left(0, m^+ - \|y_j\|\right)^2 + \gamma(1 - \mathrm{I}_j) \max\left(0, \|y_j\| - m^-\right)^2 \tag{12}$$

where I_j is an indicator function that indicates whether the true label of a sample is class j, m^+ (*resp.* m^-) refers to the upper (*resp.* lower) boundary, and γ is a regularization weight. $\|y_j\| \in [0, 1]$ and $\hat{j} = \max_j\{\|y_j\|\}$ indicates the final result is recognized as the class of $\hat{j}$.

5   Empirical Evaluations

5.1   Datasets and Preprocessing

Three cognitive load assessment datasets are considered in our experiments, including one publicly-available cognitive load datasets and two in-house dataset on VR learning environment collected by ourselves.

CLAS [16]: This is a publicly-available dataset, which contains synchronized ECG, PPG, and EDA signals (256 Hz) captured from 62 subjects with each 30-minute recording involved in purposely designed interactive or perceptive task indicating two cognitive load states. According to the description of related paper, when the subjects were in the sub-task session, the cognitive load was high, while in the neutral stimulus session, the cognitive load was low. For a better comparison with our data set, we set the original CLAS dataset as a sample set with a sliding window size of 5 s.

3s-COGSET and **5s-COGSET**: To our best knowledge, the above mentioned dataset is so far the only one publicly available and suitable for deep learning methods in the field of cognitive load assessment. In particular, the instances of the cognitive tasks in the experiments of CLAS are relatively simple without considering the practicality of the test scenario. To this end, we conducted a new experiment, which is still an ongoing effort, and at the moment 16 subjects (8 male and 8 are female) with their ages ranging from 18 to 24 were recruited to learn 50 modules of courses that are designed by ourselves in VR environment. Each module is performed 10 runs by each participant. Three types of physiological signals, i.e., PPG, RESP and EDA, were recorded during performing the tasks by means of wearable sensors with the sampling rate 64 Hz. Our experiment contains around 5, 000 annotated samples about three levels of cognitive load states (i.e., low, medium and high.) on VR learning environment. A subset of samples are provided in the supplementary material, and once ready we plan to share the entire dataset in the community. Considering the different settings of physiological events, our records were divided into two new datasets by using the event sizes K of 3 s and 5 s, respectively.

5.2   Experimental Set-Ups

Our model is implemented by Keras with backend of Tensorflow. It is optimized by Adam optimizer ($\beta_1 = 0.9$ and $\beta_2 = 0.999$) with the learning rate of 1×10^{-4} and the step size of $e^{-0.1}$ on one GeForce GTX 750Ti GPU. We set the parameter $K = 28$, $m^+ = 0.9$, $m^- = 0.1$, $\gamma = 0.5$. The batch size is fixed to 14. We compare the classification performance of our model with 7 conventional models and 11 deep models. To make a fair comparison, we did not use any data augmentation or pre-trained weights to improve performance. The ratio of training and testing sequences is 4 : 1. Accuracy was used as the evaluation metric, which is calculated as the proportion of true results among the total number of samples.

5.3   Experimental Results

Comparison Against Conventional Models. Table 1 depicts the comparison results under different settings of physiological channels. In order to integrate various existing feature extraction methods, we extracted 787 features (e.g. Fast Fourier Transformation coefficients, etc.) in total, which however need to be manually encoded from prior knowledge. Generally, our model outperforms these models by a large margin. This is because our hybrid model is capable of capturing causal dependencies and spatio-temporal features among multivariate physiological events.

Comparison Against Other Deep Models. Table. 2 shows the comparison results with other deep models that recognize cognitive load states directly from

Table 1. Accuracy comparisons on three datasets under different settings of physiological channels.

Conventional models	Accuracy							
	LR	SVM	GNB	DT	RF	XGBoost	KNN	Ours
CLAS	0.60	0.61	0.59	0.55	0.60	0.64	0.66	**0.75**
3s-COGSET	0.49	0.58	0.57	0.55	0.67	0.63	0.70	**0.86**
5S-COGSET	0.58	0.65	0.51	0.61	0.54	0.75	0.77	**0.92**
under different combinations of physiological signals								
5S-COGSET (PPG)	0.49	0.49	0.54	0.51	0.48	0.54	0.57	**0.70**
5S-COGSET (RESP)	0.48	0.50	0.54	0.56	0.55	0.60	0.59	**0.65**
5S-COGSET (EDA)	0.49	0.50	0.49	0.48	0.51	0.55	0.58	**0.62**
5S-COGSET (PPG+EDA)	0.60	0.54	0.54	0.46	0.63	0.70	0.69	**0.79**
5S-COGSET (PPG+RESP)	0.60	0.60	0.62	0.66	0.65	0.64	0.70	**0.76**
5S-COGSET (RESP+EDA)	0.62	0.60	0.64	0.59	0.67	0.66	0.74	**0.81**

raw physiological signals. Apparently, it can be observed that our model can is significantly more accurate than other models with around 5%–30% performance boost. Notably, MLP and MCDCNN get relatively acceptable results of identifying states. This is mainly due to their abilities to take advantage of the rich hierarchical and temporal dependency information between various physiological events. It is also clear that our model is superior to other models including those that combine CNN and LSTM (or RNN) structures that can also capture spatio-temporal dependencies among multivariate signals. This is mainly due to the reason that GC network can describe the temporal causal relation between any pair of events.

Table 2. Accuracy comparisons against other deep models. The percentage in the bracket shows the accuracy change taken our approach as a baseline.

Deep models	Accuracy		
	CLAS	3s-COGSET	5s-COGSET
MLP [24]	0.67(−0.08)	0.80(−0.06)	0.85(−0.07)
FCN [24]	0.69(−0.06)	0.57(−0.29)	0.58(−0.34)
ResNet [24]	0.70(−0.05)	0.61(−0.25)	0.56(−0.36)
Inception [8]	0.61(−0.14)	0.67(−0.19)	0.70(−0.22)
MCDCNN [30]	0.60(−0.15)	0.76(−0.10)	0.84(−0.08)
MCNN [6]	0.54(−0.21)	0.57(−0.29)	0.56(−0.36)
1D-CapsNet [3]	0.50(−0.25)	0.75(−0.11)	0.60(−0.32)
Parallel CNN-LSTM [13]	0.63(−0.12)	0.76(−0.10)	0.83(−0.09)
Serial CNN-LSTM [19]	0.56(−0.19)	0.50(−0.46)	0.49(−0.43)
MLSTM-FCN [13]	0.61(−0.14)	0.57(−0.29)	0.61(−0.31)
Grid-CNNs [26]	0.45(−0.30)	0.49(−0.37)	0.56(−0.36)
Ours	**0.75**	**0.86**	**0.92**

Convergence Speed. Figure 3(a) displays the training time of our model. It can be seen that our model converges after 30 epochs. Figure 3(b) reports the comparison results of convergence speeds among different models. Notably, our model converges faster than other methods, which is beneficial to the training and optimization process. Theoretically, the time complexity of our models consists of three parts $O(MTK^2)$, $O(MTK^2)$ and $O(\sum_{l=1}^{H} M_l^2 K_l^2 H_{l-1} H_l)$, indicating the GC network generation, GADF map construction and capsule network-based classifier, respectively. H represents the number of layers of the classifier, and H_{l-1} and H_l refer to the sizes of input and output feature tensors at the l-th layer, respectively.

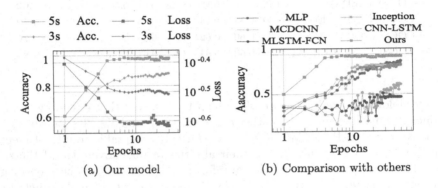

(a) Our model   (b) Comparison with others

Fig. 3. Convergence speed comparison.

5.4 Ablation Study

In this section, we conduct three ablation studies to measure the effectiveness of the modules in our model.

Feature Encoding. We compared our hybrid features of GC network and GADF map with other three commonly used encoded features, i.e., Markov Transition Fields (MTF) [23], Recurrence Plot(RP) [26] and a simple grid structure (Grid) [7]. Figure 4(a) shows that our hybrid features clearly outperform other encoded features in accuracy on the two in-house datasets. This is because the hybrid features contain not only the temporal causal configurations of a particular cognitive state but also the inherit spatio-temporal dependency among multivariate signals.

Optimum Parameter Selection. We also compared various settings of lag order L in our model. Here we increase the lag order L from 1 to 10 with a step of 1. The result shows that changing the lag order cannot lead to negative effects on the performance of our model on the datasets. This is mainly because the duration of cognitive load responses in a subsequence is very short. For instance,

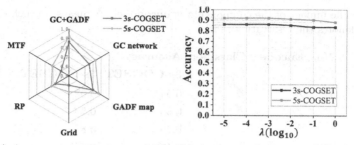

(a) Accuracy comparisons of fea- (b) Accuracy changes on different
ture encoding methods λ $(L = 3)$

Fig. 4. Convergence speed comparison.

there are instantaneous loads, which fluctuate every moment from the beginning
to the end of performing a task or set of tasks, such as cognitive dissonance and
cognitive overload in a certain subsequence, so the variation of L is limited to
affect the final results. Although the selection of lag order still remains an open
issue, we suggest to set the lag order with a value that is slightly larger than the
ordinary length of physiological events. Note that a very large value of L may
result in computational burden.

The sparsity regularization parameter λ in Eq. (4) is an important parameter
for link sparsity optimization. Its effect on classification performance on the three
datasets is shown in Fig. 4(b) by fixing the lag order to $L = 3$. It is clear that
increasing the value of λ strengthens the regularization effect. On the other hand,
a small value of λ will bring about a great number of noisy links in the network,
which may also be unfavorable to the recognition results.

Encoder-Classifier Component Effectiveness. The effectiveness of different
components in encoder-classifier mechanism are separately evaluated by removing or replacing them with other conventional models. We evaluated two types
of modules, including the encoder (i.e., remove the encoder and directly use
the raw GC network and GADF map as input) and the classifier (i.e. remove
the CapsNet-based classifier and only adopt a one-dense-layer for classification).
Table 3 reports the comparison results on the two in-house datasets, which indicates that changing the components may have a negative impact on the performance of our model. Obviously, classification performance degrades when either
component is removed. This might be due to the hybrid encoding of both causal
and spatio-temporal information in a uniform way in our model. Besides, when
removing both components, the model gives worse performance than that using
either our encoder or classifier, which indicates that our model is more effective to capture causal and spatio-temporal dependencies at the same time than
obtaining either of them individually.

Table 3. The impact of the components in our model. ✗ means no such component, while ✓ denotes the reservation of it.

No.	Encoder	Classifier	Accuracy	
			3s-COGSET	5s-COGSET
1	✗	✗	0.54	0.52
2	✓	✗	0.55	0.53
3	✗	✓	0.76	0.85
4	✓	✓	**0.86**	**0.92**

6 Conclusion and Future Work

In this paper, we present a hybrid cognitive load recognition model by merging Granger causality network and Gramian angular difference fields map together for multivariate physiological data, which can capture the inherit causal and spatio-temporal varieties of physiological events in a uniform way. It is more efficient and flexible than existing methods on cognitive load recognition. As for future work, we will explore the applications of our model on more VR learning classes, and we will consider extending our model to detect multiple cognitive states with probabilities and will instead learn a model under uncertainty.

Acknowledgement. This work was supported by grants from the National Major Science and Technology Projects of China (grant no. 2018AAA0100703), the National Natural Science Foundation of China (grant nos. 61977012, 61977054), the Central Universities in China (grant no. 2021CDJYGRH011).

References

1. Arnold, A., Liu, Y., Abe, N.: Temporal causal modeling with graphical granger methods. In: Proceedings of the 13th ACM SIGKDD International Conference on Knowledge Discovery and Data Mining, pp. 66–75 (2007)
2. Barua, S., Ahmed, M.U., Begum, S.: Towards intelligent data analytics: a case study in driver cognitive load classification. Brain Sci. **10**(8), 526 (2020)
3. Butun, E., Yildirim, O., Talo, M., Tan, R.S., Acharya, U.R.: 1d-CADCapsNet: one dimensional deep capsule networks for coronary artery disease detection using ECG signals. Phys. Med. **70**, 39–48 (2020)
4. Chakladar, D.D., Dey, S., Roy, P.P., Dogra, D.P.: EEG-based mental workload estimation using deep BLSTM-LSTM network and evolutionary algorithm. Biomed. Signal Process. Control **60**, 101989 (2020)
5. Critchley, H.D., Garfinkel, S.N.: The influence of physiological signals on cognition. Current Opin. Behav. Sci. **19**, 13–18 (2018)
6. Cui, Z., Chen, W., Chen, Y.: Multi-scale convolutional neural networks for time series classification. arXiv preprint arXiv:1603.06995 (2016)
7. Eckmann, J.P., Kamphorst, S.O., Ruelle, D., et al.: Recurrence plots of dynamical systems. World Sci. Ser. Nonlinear Sci. Ser. A **16**, 441–446 (1995)

8. Fawaz, H.I., et al.: InceptionTime: finding Alexnet for time series classification. Data Min. Knowl. Disc. **34**(6), 1936–1962 (2020)

9. Granger, C.W.J.: Investigating causal relations by econometric models and cross-spectral methods. Econometrica **37**(3), 424–438 (1969)

10. Haapalainen, E., Kim, S., Forlizzi, J.F., Dey, A.K.: Psycho-physiological measures for assessing cognitive load. In: Proceedings of the 12th ACM International Conference on Ubiquitous Computing, pp. 301–310 (2010)

11. Hefron, R.G., Borghetti, B.J., Christensen, J.C., Kabban, C.M.S.: Deep long short-term memory structures model temporal dependencies improving cognitive workload estimation. Pattern Recogn. Lett. **94**, 96–104 (2017)

12. Kalsbeek, J., Ettema, J.: Continuous recording of heart rate and the measurement of perceptual load. Ergonomics **6**(3), 306–307 (1963)

13. Karim, F., Majumdar, S., Darabi, H., Harford, S.: Multivariate LSTM-FCNS for time series classification. Neural Netw. **116**, 237–245 (2019)

14. Keogh, E.J., Pazzani, M.J.: Scaling up dynamic time warping for datamining applications. In: Proceedings of the sixth ACM SIGKDD International Conference on Knowledge Discovery and Data Mining, pp. 285–289 (2000)

15. Kuanar, S., Athitsos, V., Pradhan, N., Mishra, A., Rao, K.R.: Cognitive analysis of working memory load from EEG, by a deep recurrent neural network. In: 2018 IEEE International Conference on Acoustics, Speech and Signal Processing (ICASSP), pp. 2576–2580. IEEE (2018)

16. Markova, V., Ganchev, T., Kalinkov, K.: CLAS: a database for cognitive load, affect and stress recognition. In: 2019 International Conference on Biomedical Innovations and Applications (BIA), pp. 1–4. IEEE (2019)

17. Meek, C.: Causal inference and causal explanation with background knowledge. arXiv preprint arXiv:1302.4972 (2013)

18. Ning, Y., et al.: Assessing cognitive abilities of patients with shift work disorder: insights from RBANS and granger causality connections among resting-state networks. Front. Psych. **11**, 780 (2020)

19. Oord, A., et al.: Wavenet: A generative model for raw audio. arXiv preprint arXiv:1609.03499 (2016)

20. Rim, B., Sung, N.J., Min, S., Hong, M.: Deep learning in physiological signal data: a survey. Sensors **20**(4), 969 (2020)

21. Sweller, J.: Cognitive load during problem solving: effects on learning. Cogn. Sci. **12**(2), 257–285 (1988)

22. Wang, C., Guo, J.: A data-driven framework for learners' cognitive load detection using ECG-PPG physiological feature fusion and xgboost classification. Proc. Comput. Sci. **147**, 338–348 (2019)

23. Wang, Z., Oates, T.: Imaging time-series to improve classification and imputation. In: Twenty-Fourth International Joint Conference on Artificial Intelligence (2015)

24. Wang, Z., Yan, W., Oates, T.: Time series classification from scratch with deep neural networks: a strong baseline. In: 2017 International Joint Conference on Neural Networks (IJCNN), pp. 1578–1585. IEEE (2017)

25. Xiong, R., Kong, F., Yang, X., Liu, G., Wen, W.: Pattern recognition of cognitive load using EEG and ECG signals. Sensors **20**(18), 5122 (2020)

26. Ye, Y., Jiang, J., Ge, B., Dou, Y., Yang, K.: Similarity measures for time series data classification using grid representation and matrix distance. Knowl. Inf. Syst. **60**(2), 1105–1134 (2019)

27. Yu, J., Liu, G.Y., Wen, W.H., Chen, C.W.: Evaluating cognitive task result through heart rate pattern analysis. Healthc. Technol. Lett. **7**(2), 41–44 (2020)

28. Zhang, X., et al.: Photoplethysmogram-based cognitive load assessment using multi-feature fusion model. ACM Trans. Appl. Percept. (TAP) **16**(4), 1–17 (2019)
29. Zhao, M., Zhong, S., Fu, X., Tang, B., Pecht, M.: Deep residual shrinkage networks for fault diagnosis. IEEE Trans. Industr. Inf. **16**(7), 4681–4690 (2019)
30. Zheng, Y., Liu, Q., Chen, E., Ge, Y., Zhao, J.L.: Time series classification using multi-channels deep convolutional neural networks. In: Li, F., Li, G., Hwang, S., Yao, B., Zhang, Z. (eds.) WAIM 2014. LNCS, vol. 8485, pp. 298–310. Springer, Cham (2014). https://doi.org/10.1007/978-3-319-08010-9_33

Placing (Historical) Facts on a Timeline: A Classification Cum Coref Resolution Approach

Sayantan Adak[✉][iD], Altaf Ahmad[iD], Aditya Basu[iD],
and Animesh Mukherjee[iD]

Indian Institute of Technology Kharagpur, Kharagpur, India
sayantanadak.skni@kgpian.iitkgp.ac.in, {altafahmad3037045,
aditya.basu1}@iitkgp.ac.in, animeshm@cse.iitkgp.ac.in

Abstract. A timeline provides one of the most effective ways to visualize the important historical facts that occurred over a period of time, presenting the insights that may not be so apparent from reading the equivalent information in textual form . By leveraging generative adversarial learning for important sentence classification and by assimilating knowledge based tags for improving the performance of event coreference resolution we introduce a two staged system for event timeline generation from multiple (historical) text documents. We demonstrate our results on two manually annotated historical text documents. Our results can be extremely helpful for historians, in advancing research in history and in understanding the socio-political landscape of a country as reflected in the writings of famous personas. The dataset and the code are available at https://github.com/sayantan11995/Event-Timeline-Generation-from-Documents.

1 Introduction

Timeline serves as one of the most effective and easiest means to contextualize and visualize a complex situation ranging from grasping spatio-temporal facts in historical studies to critical decision making in businesses. With the stupendous increase of textual resources for many historical contents in several online platforms it has become imperative for the history researchers to understand the chronological orderings of the incessant historical phenomenon. The fact timeline can be an extremely useful aid to highlight the temporal and causal relationships among several facts and the interactions of the characters over time, that results in identifying common themes that arise over the period of interest in a historical document (see Fig. 2 in Appendix A.1).

In this paper we present a full pipeline to build a chronology of facts extracted from historical text. Our contributions are as follows.

Supplementary Information The online version contains supplementary material available at https://doi.org/10.1007/978-3-031-26422-1_21.

M.-R. Amini et al. (Eds.): ECML PKDD 2022, LNAI 13718, pp. 335–352, 2023.
https://doi.org/10.1007/978-3-031-26422-1_21

- We curate a first of its kind dataset from two different historical texts – the *Collected Works of Mahatma Gandhi* (CWMG) and the *Collected Works of Abraham Lincoln* (CWAL) for our experiments. For each of these datasets we manually annotate sentences that correspond to important facts. Next for each of these annotated sentences we also further annotate the coreferences to the same fact; we call these fact coreferences. Upon acceptance we shall release this data for future research.
- We introduce a novel divide-and-conquer based approach to generate fact timeline from timestamped historical texts. In the first step, we classify sentences as containing facts or not using a generative adversarial learning setup. In the subsequent step we compute fact coreferences using both unsupervised and supervised methods. The main novelty here is that inclusion of world knowledge in the form of tag embeddings results in higher performance gains.
- We present a rigorous evaluation of both the steps as well as the full system which was absent in previous literature [7]. Further we compare our results to the closely related fact timeline summarization tasks by suitably adapting them so that the comparison is fair.
- In order to determine the readability and usefulness of the timeline, we conduct an online crowd-sourced survey. 93% survey participants found it to be effective in summarizing historical timeline of facts.
- We also show that our method is generic by evaluating it against a COVID-19 news related dataset which is not a historical text per se.

2   Related Work

Important Sentence Classification and Sentence Coreference Resolution: Our proposed approach combines important sentence classification, filtering historically important sentences from a bunch of texts, and sentence coreference resolution, merging factually similar sentences. [39] used CNN to analyse sensitivity for text classification. [27] and [38] introduced virtual adversarial training methods for robust text classification from a small number of training data points.

Recent works like [10, 18] have used neural network based architecture to train their model on benchmark coreference dataset (ECB+ [12]). [21] attempted to create an end-to-end event coreference resolution system based on the standard KBP dataset[1].

Timeline of Historical Facts: [5] proposed an unsupervised generative model to construct the timeline of biographical life-facts leveraging encyclopaedic resources such as Wikipedia. [3] also uses Wikipedia for timeline construction of historical facts. [7] attempted to construct a fact timeline from history textbooks considering the sentences having temporal expressions. [29] proposed an automatic approach to capture and visualize temporal ordering of interactions between multiple actors. [2] created an AI-enabled web portal based on CWMG dataset.

---

[1] https://www.ldc.upenn.edu/collaborations/past-projects/tac-kbp.

Timeline Summarization (TLS): The timeline summarization task aims to summarize time evolving documents. [15] evaluated existing state-of-the-art methods for news timeline summarization and proposed *datewise* and *clustering* based approaches on the TLS datasets. [8] demonstrated the potential of employing several IR methods on TLS tasks based on a large news dataset. [20] proposes a new approach by generating date level summaries, and then selecting the most relevant dates for the timeline summarization.

The Present Work: Our paper is closest in spirit to the work done by [7]. In this paper the authors outlined the challenges related to fact coreference for timeline generation; however, they did not suggest ways to effectively tackle these challenges and, thereby, solve the problem. We close this gap in our paper by proposing an efficient approach to resolve fact coreference. Our work has also close parallels with the fact timeline summarization (TLS) task. Nevertheless, previous TLS researchers mostly worked on the documents containing multiple news articles, which are rich in facts. These works have not focused much on prior fact detection and have not addressed how they can be effectively generalized in historical text documents such as biographies. Our work for the first time shows that fact detection could largely benefit TLS tasks in the context of historical texts.

3   Data Preparation

In this section we present the details of the datasets that we prepare for our experiments. We also outline the overall annotation process of these datasets.

3.1   Datasets

Collected Works of Mahatma Gandhi: We leverage the Collected Works of Mahatma Gandhi (CWMG) available at [32], an assortment of 100 volumes consisting of the books, letters, telegrams written by Mahatma Gandhi and also the compiled writings of the speeches, interviews engaging Gandhi. This data covers many important historical facts within the time period of 1884–1948 in British colonised India.

Collected Works of Abraham Lincoln: The second dataset we have use to demonstrate our system is based on the life-long writings of the 16th president of the United States, Abraham Lincoln, formally known as the Collected Works of Abraham Lincoln (CWAL)[2] comprising a total of 8 volumes.

COVID-19 Fact Dataset: In addition, to establish the generalizability of the approach, we collect 140 major facts, that happened in India during the COVID-19 pandemic from different sources such as *Wikipedia*[3], *Who.int*[4] to be placed on a timeline for elegant visualisation using our system.

---

[2] https://quod.lib.umich.edu/l/lincoln/.

[3] https://en.wikipedia.org/wiki/COVID-19_pandemic_in_India.

[4] https://www.who.int/india/emergencies/coronavirus-disease-(covid-19)/india-situation-report.

3.2 Pre-processing

From the 100 volumes of text files from CWMG we first extract all the letters containing the publication dates and recipients name. There were a total of 28531 letters in the entire CWMG. We primarily use the letters for our experiments as we observe that they contain the best temporal account of the facts. From the overall set of letters, we select the year range 1930–1935 since this range has the largest collection of letters. In order to further choose the right data sample, we categorize the letters into *formal* and *informal* types based on the recipients of the letters. A simple heuristic that we follow is – the letters written to government officials and famous historic personalities can be categorized as formal while those written to the family members can be classified as informal ones. We collect the list of Mahatma Gandhi's family member names from Gandhian experts for identifying the informal letters. We manually notice that the formal letters contain much more useful historic information than the informal ones. We therefore only consider the formal letters for manually annotating the useful sentences. In addition, we only consider the letters which have more than 1000 words in its content. This results in 41 letters with substantial content (Table 1).

Table 1. Sample list of sentences from CWMG after the sentence classification. The explicit temporal expression inside the sentence is highlighted.

Doc creation time (Initial reference time)	Important sentences	Updated reference time
May 4, 1930	He was arrested at 12.45 a.m. on May 5.	May 5, 1930
May 4, 1930	In Karachi, Peshawar and Madras the firing would appear to have been unprovoked and unnecessary	May 4, 1930

3.3 Annotation

In this section we outline the data annotation procedure for the two phases. Recall that our method has two important steps – fact classification and coreference resolution. While the fact classification phase is supervised (Level I annotations), the coreference resolution is done using both unsupervised and supervised techniques. The annotations for the coreference resolution (Level II annotations) are therefore required to (a) train the supervised approach and (b) test the efficacy of both the unsupervised and the supervised approaches.

Level I – Important Sentences: Finally, out of these filtered letters we manually annotate all the sentences of 18 letters (i.e., 979 sentences in all). The remaining sentences (i.e., 1689 in total) from the rest of the letters were left unlabelled. Both of these labelled and unlabelled sentences were used for training the classifier. The classes in which the sentences were classified were based on their historical importance. In specific, we identify two such important classes – (a) the *facts* or factful sentences, which typically represent that some important historical phenomena or event [33] happened or took place , e.g., '*A vegetable market in Gujarat has been raided because the dealers would not sell vegetables to officials*'[5], (b) the *demands*, which represent the demands Mahatma Gandhi had made to the British government through his writings, e.g., '*The terrific pressure of land revenue, which furnishes a large part of the total, must undergo considerable modification in an independent India.*' and (c) others (i.e., not important). As the examples suggest, each individual sentence is annotated as important (i.e., containing a fact/demand) or not. In order to further enrich the dataset we collect gold standard facts related to Mahatma Gandhi from an additional reliable and well maintained resource[6]. We obtain 86 additional sentences thus making a total of 1065 (i.e., 979 + 86) important sentences (see Table 2 for the classwise distribution.).

Table 2. Sample list of sentences from CWMG after the sentence classification. The explicit temporal expression inside the sentence is highlighted.

Classes	Count	
	CWMG	CWAL
Fact	716	242
Demand	81	96
Other	268	382

For the CWAL we simply extract all the sentences from volume 2 and follow similar approaches to annotate important sentences as in the case of CWMG. Without considering any filtering criteria we consider all the 111 articles of volume 2 including his letters and propositions which consist of a total of 1386 sentences. Out of these 720 sentences were manually annotated (see Table 2).

Annotator Details and Annotation Guidelines: For both the datasets three annotators annotated the sentences. The annotation process was led by one PhD student along with two undergraduate students. The PhD student had substantial experience in historical text analysis and will be referred to as the expert annotator henceforth. The first level of annotation was carried out for each of the sentences and based on the assumption that a full sentence corresponds to a fact/demand. All the annotators annotated the sentences independently. For the training of the two undergraduate annotators, they were provided with the examples of 25 gold standard facts and demands each. The gold standard facts

---

[5] Such sentences would typically consist of participants and locations.
[6] https://www.gandhiheritageportal.org/.

were collected from the reliable resource mentioned in the earlier paragraph and the gold standard demands were collected from the formal letters of Mahatma Gandhi which were first annotated by the expert annotator and verified by a Gandhian scholar (see Table 9 in Appendix A.2 for example annotations). The inter-annotator agreements, i.e., Cohen's κ were 0.66 and 0.58 for the former and the latter datasets respectively. Table 2 shows the category distribution for both the datasets. The Level I annotation was not carried out for the COVID-19 dataset because, each sentence collected were presented as facts in the mentioned portals and thus we considered all the sentences as important facts.

Level II – Coreference Resolution: The second round of annotation was carried out for evaluating the fact coreference detection task on the same dataset. For this case we only annotate the texts which were marked important during the Level I annotation. In addition, the Level II annotation was also carried out for the COVID-19 fact dataset.

Annotator details and annotation guidelines: The same annotators annotated for the Level II phase. The annotators were provided with sentences, the reference documents (letters) from which the sentences were extracted and the reference time (document publication date). Based on the perception of the annotators, the sentences that potentially referred to the same fact were placed in the same cluster. The coreferences have been placed by the annotators in different clusters based on different factors like the commonness of the mentioned times, entities and the fact name/composition. Consider these two sentences - '*The crowd that demanded restoration of the flag thus illegally seized is reported to have been mercilessly beaten back.*' and '*Bones have been broken, private parts have been squeezed for the purpose of making volunteers give up, to the Government valueless, to the volunteers precious salt*'. Although there is no explicit mention of time in either of the sentences, both of them are from the same document and thus their reference dates would be the same as the publication date of the document. Also both of them refer to similar types of atrocities. So these two sentences should be placed in the same cluster. We first carried out a trial round for the two undergraduate annotators by using 100 randomly chosen important sentences from the Level I phase and the trial annotations were verified by the expert annotator. Finally for the complete Level II annotations, the inter-annotator agreements were 0.74, 0.61, and 0.78 for the CWMG, the CWAL and the COVID-19 dataset respectively using MUC [37] based F1-score [14] (see Table 10 in Appendix A.2 for example annotations and Appendix A.3 for other agreement metrics.).

4   Methodology

Our method consists of three major components (see Fig. 1): (i) important sentence extraction, (ii) sentence coreference resolution, and (iii) timeline visualization. The arrows represent the direction of data flow. In this section we describe in detail the methods used for each of these components.

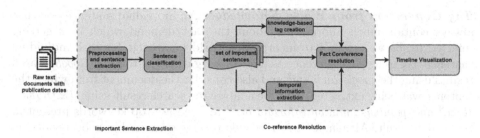

Fig. 1. The overall architecture for generating the timeline.

4.1 Important Sentence Extraction

Baselines: As baselines, we use *SVM* [16] and *Multinomial Naïve Bayes* [19] on simple bag-of-words feature. For *SVM* we use linear kernel. For the evaluation of the classifiers we use a 70:30 train-test split of the annotated data.

Fine-Tuned BERT: Apart from the above two baselines, we try BERT [13] neural network based framework for the classification. We train the model using the PyTorch [30] library, and apply *bert-base-uncased* pre-trained model for text encoding. We use a batch size of 32, sequence length of 80 and learning rate of $2e-5$ as the optimal hyper-parameters for training the model.

GAN-BERT Text Classifier: In search for further enhancement of the performance based on our limited sets of labelled data, we employ the *GAN-BERT* [11] deep learning framework for classifying the important sentences. It uses generative adversarial learning to generate augmented labelled data for semi-supervised training of the transformer based BERT model. It improves the performance of BERT when training data is scarce and is therefore highly suited for our case. Here we also feed the unlabeled data sample, as discussed in Sect. 3.3, to help the network to generalize the representation of input texts for the final classification [11].

4.2 Sentence Coreference Resolution

Once the classification was done we end up with 'factful' sentences linked to its corresponding document creation time in the format noted in Table 2.

Time Within Sentences: For generating the accurate fact timeline we need to assign a valid date to a particular sentence (i.e. fact/demand). For example, in the first sentence in Table 2, although the document publication time is mentioned to be May 4, 1930, the sentence clearly has embedded in it the exact fact date May 5, 1930 apparent from the snippet *'arrested on May 5'*. Therefore, if the explicit time is present in the sentence we use it directly, else we use the creation/publication date of the document. We extract the explicit mention of time in the text using the *HeidelTime* [36] tool. This tool is capable of identifying embedded mentions of temporal expressions such as *'yesterday'*, *'next day'* etc..

Tag Generation from World Knowledge: An individual sentence does not always contain much information about the fact/demand which it is getting referred to. So we attempt to incorporate world knowledge for each individual sentence. By using each sentence as a query we gather the top five *Google* search results using the *googlsearch* api[7] and also consider the document from which the sentence was being extracted. Next we analyse the search result using *TextRank*[8], *Rake*[9] and *pointwise mutual information*[10] to generate top keywords present in the search result. Although these methods produce reasonably good results, in many cases we needed to manually filter out certain noisy tags. For each sentence we therefore land up with one or more tags. We retain the top ten tags for every sentence which means that the number of tags for a sentence could vary between one and ten. The details of the tag generation procedure mentioned in Appendix A.4. We do not use encyclopaedic resources such as Wikipedia to get the search results because the datasets we are using, are only available in a few very specific websites. We fed the list of keyword(s) or tag(s) obtained for a sentence to the pre-trained *sentence-bert* model for obtaining a 768 dimensional embedding representation of the keywords.

Unsupervised Sentence Clustering: We employ several unsupervised approaches for sentence coreference resolution. As baselines, we choose two commonly used approaches for coreference resolution – (a) *Lemma:* It attempts to put the sentence pairs in same coreference chain which share the same head lemma, (b) *Lemma-δ*: In addition to same head lemma as a feature, it also computes the cosine similarity (δ) between the sentence pair based on *tf-idf* features, and only places the sentence pairs in the same coreference chain if δ exceeds some threshold. Then the sentence clusters were created using agglomerative clustering method. To extract the head lemma of a sentence, we use the *SpaCy* dependency parser.

Apart from these two common baselines, we vectorize the sentences using *tf-idf* vectorization technique and then apply different clustering techniques such as *Gaussian-Mixture*[11] model, *agglomerative clustering* to cluster the sentences corresponding to similar facts. We also use the pre-trained *sentence-bert* [35] model to encode the sentences and apply similar clustering techniques. Finally, we concatenate the sentence embedding with the tag embedding generated from that particular sentence. We again cluster the sentences based on this new representation. This, as we shall later see, significantly improves the performance of the clustering phase. We evaluate the clustering results on the basis of the annotated data which had been obtained in the second phase of data annotation. We used the *elbow* method to find the optimal number of clusters in case of Gaussian-Mixture and used *dendogram* to select the optimal distance threshold for the suitable number of clusters in case of agglomerative clustering. The

---

[7] https://github.com/MarioVilas/googlesearch.
[8] https://github.com/DerwenAI/pytextrank.
[9] https://pypi.org/project/rake-nltk/.
[10] https://www.nltk.org/howto/collocations.html.
[11] https://scikit-learn.org/stable/modules/mixture.html.

distance threshold we selected were 0.25, 0.6 and 0.6 for CWMG, CWAL and COVID-19 data respectively.

Supervised Fact Mention-Pair Model: A *fact mention* is a sentence or phrase that defines a fact and one fact may contain multiple *fact mentions* [9]. We first create a dataset containing all the possible pairs of *factful* (i.e., fact or demand) sentences from the ground-truth annotations. We set the coreference label to 1 if the sentence pair is contained in the same cluster as per the Level II annotation and 0 otherwise. Here we again use a 70:30 split to generate training and test instances. The overall architecture is inspired from [6] (see Appendix A.5). The inputs to the model are the two sentences (i.e. S_1 and S_2) and their corresponding *actions* (i.e., A_1 and A_2), *time* (i.e., T_1 and T_2) and *tags* (i.e., K_1 and K_2). We extract *actions* (i.e., A_i) for each of the sentences using *SpaCy* dependency parser[12].

Mention Pair Construction: We used *Tensorflow* [1] tokenizer to vectorize each feature (i.e., sentences, actions, time and tags) to convert it into sequence of integers after restricting the tokenizer to use only the top most common 5000 words. For the sentences we limit the sequence length to 64. For the other features - actions, time and tags - we limit the sequence length to 10. We always use zero padding for smaller sequences. We next encode the words present in each of these sequences using a pre-trained *GloVe* [31] embedding (100 dimensions). Thus each sentence comes out as a $64 * 100$ size vector representation while each of the other features come out as a $10 * 100$ size vector representation. Now each of these vectors are separately passed through a LSTM [17] layer with default hyperparameters to transform them into 128 size vectors each. Next each of these 128 size vectors are passed through separate dense layers to obtain 32 size vectors. Finally, these 32 size vectors are concatenated using a concatenation layer. The output of the concatenation layer is what we term as a *mention representation*. Two mention representations are concatenated to get a pairwise representation (i.e., an *fact mention pair*) and passed through a feed forward network to return a score denoting the likelihood that two mentions are coreferent (see Fig. 3 in Appendix A.5). Based on the predicted pairwise score on the test instances we used a threshold (0.5 in our case) to generate a similarity matrix of the mentions, and then applied agglomerative clustering to partition the similar mentions into the same clusters.

4.3   Timeline Visualization

Once the sentence coreference resolution phase was successfully executed, we generated visualization for the given fact/demand sequence using *vis-timeline*[13], a dynamic, browser based visualization library.

---

[12] We consider the root verb as action for a sentence.

[13] https://visjs.github.io/vis-timeline/docs/timeline/.

Table 3. Results (accuracy and macro F1-score) for the important sentence classification using our approaches on the two datasets. MNB: Multinomial Naïve Bayes. Best results are marked in boldface and highlighted in green cells.

Dataset	Model	Evaluation metric	
		Accuracy	F1
CWMG	MNB	0.74	0.45
	SVM	0.79	0.5
	Fine-tuned BERT	0.8	0.57
	GAN-BERT	**0.9**	**0.69**
CWAL	MNB	0.6	0.3
	SVM	0.6	0.34
	Fine-tuned BERT	0.61	0.56
	GAN-BERT	**0.7**	**0.65**

5   Experiments

5.1   Evaluation Metrics

We have used separate evaluation metrics for the two phases.

Important Sentence Classification: In this case we use the standard *accuracy* and *F1-score* values.

Sentence Coreference Resolution: Here we conduct the evaluation based on the widely used coreference resolution metrics – (a) *MUC* [37], (b) B^3 [4], (c) *CEAF* [22], and (d) *BLANC* [34]. Due to the inconsistency of each of these evaluation metrics [28] we shall also report the average outcomes of all the metrics.

5.2   Results

We evaluate the two different phases separately. Ground-truth data was used from each phase for respective evaluations.

Important Sentence Classification: The key results for the two datasets (CWMG and CWAL) are summarised in Table 3. Our approach based on GAN-BERT by far outperforms the standard baselines. For the CWMG dataset, the macro F1-score shoots from 0.50 (SVM) to 0.69 on the three class classification task. Likewise for the CWAL dataset, the macro F1-score shoots from 0.34 (Naïve Bayes) to 0.65.

Evaluation of Coreference Resolution: For the evaluation of coreference resolution we use several coreference resolution metrics to analyse the model performance. It is apparent from Table 4 that the approach based on clustering with *sentence-bert* embeddings by far outperforms the baselines *lemma* and *lemma-δ*. For the CWMG dataset, *sentence-bert* + agglomerative clustering is

Table 4. Sentence coreference results before and after tag embedding. GM: Gaussian Mixture based clustering; AC: Agglomerative Clustering; s-bert: sentence-bert; m-pair: supervised mention-pair model. Best results including the tag embedding are marked in boldface and highlighted in green cells. Best results excluding the tag embedding are marked by underline and highlighted in blue cells.

Dataset	System	MUC F1	B³ F1	CEAF_E F1	BLANC F1	Avg (overall) Recall	Precision	F1	Time taken
CWMG	Lemma	0.45	0.38	0.20	0.49	0.39	0.38	0.38	45 s
	Lemma-δ	0.53	0.41	0.19	0.48	0.48	0.40	0.41	7 min 22 s
	tf-idf + GM	0.53	0.53	0.36	0.60	0.49	0.52	0.50	26 min 14 s
	tf-idf + AC	0.55	0.50	0.42	0.57	0.50	0.53	0.51	5 min 13 s
	s-bert + GM	0.61	0.54	0.41	0.60	0.54	0.54	0.54	29 min 34 s
	s-bert + AC	0.63	0.57	0.40	0.61	0.55	0.56	0.55	7 min 42 s
	+ tag embedding								
	tf-idf + GM	0.64	0.57	0.45	0.64	0.57	0.60	0.58	28 min 19 s
	tf-idf + AC	0.62	0.61	0.51	0.66	0.58	0.63	0.60	6 min 57 s
	s-bert + GM	0.65	0.62	0.48	0.66	0.60	0.60	0.60	30 min 28 s
	s-bert + AC	0.75	**0.70**	0.52	**0.73**	0.65	**0.71**	0.68	8 min 36 s
	m-pair model	**0.91**	0.59	**0.83**	0.53	**0.83**	0.69	**0.72**	2 hr 10 min 32 s
CWAL	Lemma	0.28	0.11	0.17	0.49	0.26	0.27	0.27	58 s
	Lemma-δ	0.31	0.15	0.14	0.48	0.28	0.27	0.18	9 min 41 s
	tf-idf + GM	0.53	0.37	0.35	0.49	0.42	0.45	0.43	41 min 25 s
	tf-idf + AC	0.57	0.42	0.38	0.49	0.45	0.49	0.46	8 min 5 s
	s-bert + GM	0.43	0.39	0.40	0.54	0.43	0.46	0.44	46 min 18 s
	s-bert + AC	0.51	0.42	0.40	0.54	0.46	0.48	0.47	11 min 15 s
	+ tag embedding								
	tf-idf + GM	0.74	0.52	0.40	0.63	0.56	0.59	0.57	43 min 23 s
	tf-idf + AC	0.72	0.51	0.48	0.64	0.57	0.61	0.59	9 min 27 s
	S-bert + GM	0.74	0.41	0.34	0.67	0.51	0.57	0.54	47 min 12 s
	s-bert + AC	0.82	**0.53**	0.44	**0.72**	0.60	**0.66**	0.63	11 min 42 s
	m-pair model	**0.96**	0.42	**0.78**	0.35	**0.82**	0.65	**0.64**	2 hr 11 min 40 s
COVID-19	Lemma	0.55	0.39	0.28	0.55	0.51	0.42	0.44	9 sec
	Lemma-δ	0.34	0.29	0.25	0.51	0.35	0.34	0.35	1 min 8 s
	tf-idf + GM	0.56	0.41	0.36	0.60	0.47	0.50	0.48	6 min 37 s
	tf-idf + AC	0.59	0.45	0.36	0.62	0.49	0.54	0.51	1 min 44 s
	s-bert + GM	0.63	0.45	0.32	0.57	0.47	0.51	0.49	8 min 41 s
	s-bert + AC	0.61	0.44	0.35	0.57	0.48	0.50	0.49	2 min 25 s
	+ tag embedding								
	tf-idf + GM	0.44	0.33	0.28	0.54	0.39	0.40	0.39	7 min 31 s
	tf-idf + AC	0.44	0.34	0.32	0.44	0.4	0.42	0.41	2 min 38 s
	s-bert + GM	0.57	0.41	0.35	0.59	0.47	0.49	0.48	9 min 35 s
	s-bert + AC	0.63	0.46	0.39	0.59	0.51	0.52	0.52	3 min 19 s
	m-pair model	**0.86**	**0.80**	**0.97**	**0.65**	**0.80**	**0.84**	**0.82**	29 min 18 s

the best overall; for the other two datasets no single method is a clear winner. However, the primary point that we wish to emphasize in the table is the result after incorporating tag embedding. It can be clearly observed that this intuitive, albeit hitherto unreported, technique almost always produces better results (see Appendix A.4 and the Table 12 therein describing the tag generation process in more details). In fact, the assimilation of the tag embeddings with the *sentence-bert* embeddings boosted the overall F1-score by 13%, and 16% for the CWMG and the CWAL datasets respectively. Note that these results hold even if the manual filtering step in the tag generation is completely omitted (see Table 7). An interesting observation is that the benefit of the tag embedding is best leveraged by the sentence-bert + agglomerative clustering. For the COVID-19 dataset, since search results are generic, the benefit of tag embedding is less. Furthermore, the supervised model consistently outperforms the unsupervised results across all three datasets. Note that the tag generation is done only once and therefore takes a fixed amount of time. It took 3.26 s, 3.47 s, and 1.96 s per sentence on average to generate knowledge-based tags for CWMG, CWAL, and COVID-19 datasets respectively. The time that the model takes to inference in presence of the tag embeddings is negligible as compared to the model without these embeddings (see the last column of Table 4). For the supervised models though, the major chunk of time is required for the mention pair generation.

Full System Evaluation: So far, the assessment for the two components was carried out separately, i.e., the evaluation for the important sentence extraction was based on Level I annotated data while the evaluation for sentence coreference resolution was on the basis of Level II annotations independently. We also conduct the full system evaluation for CWMG and CWAL datasets, i.e., the complete evaluation was only dependent on Level II annotated data. For this case we trained the GAN-BERT classifier with 30% of the labeled data along with the unlabeled data (discussed in Sect. 3.3), and had predictions for the rest of 70% data. Now, we consider only the *true positives* (labeled as important, and also predicted important), before performing the coreference resolution. This task is evaluated based on the Level II annotated data. The primary reasons for considering only true positive samples are - (1) we do not have ground-truth Level II annotated data for the non-important sentences (i.e., the false positives), (2) for all practical purposes we are only interested in the coreferences present in the positive predictions (i.e., in the predicted important sentences). Table 5 shows the comparison between the full system evaluation result and the standard result (see Appendix A.8 for results w/o tags). The results shown here are the average value of the four different standard metrics (MUC, B^3, CEAF_E and BLANC) corresponding to the best performing unsupervised model as well as the mention-pair based supervised model.

Comparison with TLS: Since our method has some parallels with TLS, in this section we perform a thorough comparison with state-of-the-art TLS systems. Note that the output of our system is not similar to that of the standard TLS output. In order to make the comparison possible and fair we added a simple summarization step at the end of our pipeline. We used the BERT extractive summarizer [26] to extract the two most important sentences as the summary for each of the fact clusters generated by our method. We evaluated the summaries using the alignment-based ROUGE (AR) F-Score [24]. Unlike [15], we did not use any date ranking method to rank the dates of the predicted timeline and compared the ground-truth with the top-k predicted timeline. We tested all

Table 5. Full system evaluation result. Type: Coref-resolution type, MA: Important sentences obtained through manual annotation, MP: Important sentences obtained from model prediction, Su: Supervised, Un: Unsupervised. Appendix A.8 shows the same results without using tag embeddings.

Dataset	Type	M	R	P	F1
CWMG	Su	MA	0.83	0.69	0.72
		MP	0.74	0.63	0.64
	Un	MA	0.65	0.71	0.68
		MP	0.62	0.65	0.63
CWAL	Su	MA	0.82	0.65	0.64
		MP	0.74	0.59	0.60
	Un	MA	0.60	0.66	0.63
		MP	0.55	0.59	0.57

the approaches using our Level I annotated data as the ground-truth reference. Table 6 shows the detailed comparison of our approach with few of the existing state-of-the-art TLS approaches on two of our datasets. In order to perform these experiments we considered pre-selected 41 formal letters from CWMG in the time period 1930–1935 with more than 1000 words and all the documents of volume 2 from CWAL (from which the Level I annotations were performed) and directly passed through the TLS pipeline using the codes provided by the respective authors. In order to make the comparison further fair, we also performed an experiment by first carrying out important sentence classification using our method and then feeding the filtered data into the TLS pipeline provided by the authors. In order to benefit the TLS models the fact detection for this pre-filtering was performed using the model fine-tuned on our dataset. This modification results in superior performance of the TLS. In fact, fact detection prior to summarization always helps – our method as well as one of the baseline methods [15] where fact detection can be easily incorporated show significantly[14] improved performance. In Table 13 of Appendix A.6 we also show that this fact detection step brings benefits to a standard TLS dataset which has not been built from historical text. The reason for this inferior performance could be that the summary in the standard TLS approaches are highly sensitive to the keywords used for the particular dataset and generating quality keywords for a dataset consisting of diverse facts like ours requires domain-expertise (see Table 14 in Appendix A.7).

6 Ablation Study

We performed two ablation studies - first, to check the effectiveness of manual filtering of noisy tags, second, to assess the added value of each component in the mention-pair model.

---

[14] Statistical significance were performed using Mann-Whitney U test [23].

Table 6. Comparison of our method for the with the existing state-of-the-art TLS methods - (1) MM (submodularity based method): [25] and (2) DT: datewise and (3) CLUST: clustering based TLS by [15], FD: Fact detection. †, *, • show that our results are significantly different from MM, FD + DT, FD + CLUST respectively. In turn, any method with FD (*, •) is significantly better than MM.

System	CWMG Dataset		CWAL Dataset	
	AR1-F	AR2-F	AR1-F	AR2-F
MM	0.023	0.001	0.052	0.024
DT	0.008	0.001	0.022	0.002
FD (our) + DT	0.015*	0.006*	0.026*	0.002
CLUST	0.028	0.02	0.055	0.040
FD (our) + CLUST	0.034•	0.025•	0.086•	0.071•
Our method	**0.062†*•**	**0.043†*•**	**0.069†*•**	**0.042†*•**

Sentence Coreference Resolution Results Without Manual Filtering of Tags: Table 7 shows result obtained from different coreference resolution techniques when we do not include any manual filtering steps to the generated tags. It can be noticed that there is not much difference in the results even when we omit this step.

Added Value of Each Element in the Mention-Pair Model: Table 8 shows the added value of each feature in the mention-pair model. For both the historical texts we observe that inclusion of each feature improves the overall performance. The best improvement is observed on the inclusion of the external knowledge in the form of tag embeddings.

7   Timeline Visualization

Generating a timeline would not be that impactful unless it is visualized in an interpretable and convenient way. We incorporate an elegant visualization for the generated fact/demand timelines using *vis-timeline* javascript library (Appendix A.9 shows an example timeline).

Survey: In order to understand the effectiveness of the interface we ran an online crowd-sourced survey. Out of 33 participants with different educational backgrounds, overall 93% agreed that the interface was very useful for summarization of historical timeline of facts. 88% participants found some information which would have been hard for them to fathom just by reading the CWMG plaintext (more results in Appendix A.10).

Table 7. Sentence coreference results without using manual filtering for the tags. D: dataset, M: model, GM: Gaussian Mixture based clustering; AC: Agglomerative Clustering; s-bert: sentence-bert, m-pair: mention-pair model, B: BLANC, C: CEAF_E. The results mostly remain unaffected.

D	M	MUC	B³	C	B	Avg (overall)		
		F1	F1	F1	F1	R	P	F1
CWMG	tf-idf+GM	0.61	0.55	0.51	0.58	0.62	0.57	0.56
	tf-idf+AC	0.64	0.59	0.51	0.66	0.58	0.64	0.60
	s-bert+GM	0.68	0.61	0.44	0.63	0.62	0.60	0.59
	s-bert+AC	0.76	0.71	0.50	0.72	0.65	0.72	0.67
	m-pair	0.92	0.61	0.85	0.53	0.85	0.70	0.73
CWAL	tf-idf+GM	0.76	0.51	0.44	0.65	0.55	0.59	0.59
	tf-idf + AC	0.75	0.50	0.49	0.65	0.56	0.63	0.59
	S-bert+GM	0.76	0.40	0.35	0.69	0.51	0.59	0.55
	s-bert+AC	0.81	0.59	0.47	0.70	0.63	0.72	0.64
	m-pair	0.95	0.43	0.76	0.36	0.81	0.67	0.62
COVID-19	tf-idf+GM	0.40	0.33	0.26	0.55	0.39	0.44	0.38
	tf-idf+AC	0.42	0.35	0.34	0.43	0.41	0.39	0.38
	s-bert+GM	0.56	0.43	0.36	0.57	0.44	0.49	0.48
	s-bert+AC	0.65	0.44	0.37	0.59	0.52	0.50	0.51
	m-pair	0.84	0.80	0.95	0.66	0.79	0.82	0.81

Table 8. Added value of each component in the mention-pair model for each dataset; F: features, S: considering sentence embedding as the only feature, D: date, A: action, T: tag.

D	F	Avg F1	Inc
CWMG	S	0.613	-
	S+D	0.657	0.044
	S+D+A	0.688	0.031
	S+D+A+T	0.720	0.038
CWAL	S	0.394	-
	S+D	0.544	0.15
	S+D+A	0.560	0.016
	S+D+A+T	0.640	0.008
Covid-19	S	0.791	-
	S+D	0.778	−0.013
	S+D+A	0.811	0.033
	S+D+A+T	0.820	0.009

8   Conclusion

In this work we presented a framework to generate fact timeline from any times-tamped document. The entire pipeline has two parts – important sentence detection and sentence coreference resolution. We achieve very encouraging results for both these tasks. While it is true that our evaluations are based on two historical texts, our methods are generic and can be easily extended to other datasets. The system that we developed is not limited to any actor specific fact (human or location) which, in fact, made the coreference resolution task even more challenging. We believe that our work will open up new and exciting opportunities in history research and education.

References

1. Abadi, M., Agarwal, A., et al.: TensorFlow: large-scale machine learning on heterogeneous systems (2015). https://www.tensorflow.org/
2. Adak, S., et al.: Gandhipedia: A one-stop AI-enabled portal for browsing Gandhian literature, life-events and his social network. In: JCDL, pp. 539–540, New York, NY, USA (2020)
3. Aprosio, A., Tonelli, S.: Recognizing biographical sections in Wikipedia, pp. 811–816, January 2015
4. Bagga, A., Baldwin, B.: Entity-based cross-document coreferencing using the vector space model. In: Coling, vol. 1, p. 79 (2000)
5. Bamman, D., Smith, N.A.: Unsupervised discovery of biographical structure from text. Trans. Assoc. Comput. Linguist. 2, 363–376 (2014)
6. Barhom, S., Shwartz, V., Eirew, A., Bugert, M., Reimers, N., Dagan, I.: Revisiting joint modeling of cross-document entity and event coreference resolution (2019)
7. Bedi, H., Patil, S., Hingmire, S., Palshikar, G.: Event timeline generation from history textbooks. In: Proceedings of the 4th Workshop on Natural Language Processing Techniques for Educational Applications (NLPTEA 2017), pp. 69–77. Asian Federation of Natural Language Processing, Taipei, Taiwan, December 2017
8. Born, L., Bacher, M., Markert, K.: Dataset reproducibility and IR methods in timeline summarization. In: LREC 2020 (2020)
9. Chen, Z., Ji, H., Haralick, R.: A pairwise event coreference model, feature impact and evaluation for event coreference resolution. In: Proceedings of the Workshop on Events in Emerging Text Types, pp. 17–22. Association for Computational Linguistics, Borovets, Bulgaria, September 2009
10. Choubey, P.K., Huang, R.: Event coreference resolution by iteratively unfolding inter-dependencies among events. In: Proceedings of the 2017 Conference on Empirical Methods in Natural Language Processing, pp. 2124–2133. Association for Computational Linguistics, Copenhagen, Denmark, September 2017
11. Croce, D., Castellucci, G., Basili, R.: GAN-BERT: generative adversarial learning for robust text classification with a bunch of labeled examples. In: Proceedings of the 58th Annual Meeting of the Association for Computational Linguistics, pp. 2114–2119. Association for Computational Linguistics, July 2020
12. Cybulska, A., Vossen, P.: Using a sledgehammer to crack a nut? Lexical diversity and event coreference resolution. In: Proceedings of the Ninth International Conference on Language Resources and Evaluation (LREC 2014), pp. 4545–4552. European Language Resources Association (ELRA), Reykjavik, Iceland, May 2014

13. Devlin, J., Chang, M.W., Lee, K., Toutanova, K.: BERT: pre-training of deep bidirectional transformers for language understanding (2019)
14. Ghaddar, A., Langlais, P.: Wikicoref: an English coreference-annotated corpus of Wikipedia articles. In: Chair, N.C.C., et al. (eds.) Proceedings of the Tenth International Conference on Language Resources and Evaluation (LREC 2016). European Language Resources Association (ELRA), Paris, France, May 2016
15. Gholipour Ghalandari, D., Ifrim, G.: Examining the state-of-the-art in news timeline summarization. In: Proceedings of the 58th Annual Meeting of the Association for Computational Linguistics, pp. 1322–1334. Association for Computational Linguistics, July 2020
16. Hearst, M.A.: Support vector machines. IEEE Intell. Syst. **13**(4), 18–28 (1998)
17. Hochreiter, S., Schmidhuber, J.: Long short-term memory. Neural Comput. **9**(8), 1735–1780 (1997)
18. Kenyon-Dean, K., Cheung, J.C.K., Precup, D.: Resolving event coreference with supervised representation learning and clustering-oriented regularization (2018)
19. Kibriya, A.M., Frank, E., Pfahringer, B., Holmes, G.: Multinomial naive Bayes for text categorization revisited. In: Webb, G.I., Yu, X. (eds.) AI 2004. LNCS (LNAI), vol. 3339, pp. 488–499. Springer, Heidelberg (2004). https://doi.org/10.1007/978-3-540-30549-1_43
20. La Quatra, M., Cagliero, L., Baralis, E., Messina, A., Montagnuolo, M.: Summarize dates first: a paradigm shift in timeline summarization, pp. 418–427. Association for Computing Machinery, New York, NY, USA (2021)
21. Lu, Y., Lin, H., Tang, J., Han, X., Sun, L.: End-to-end neural event coreference resolution. Artif. Intell. **303**, 103632 (2020)
22. Luo, X.: On coreference resolution performance metrics, January 2005
23. Mann, H.B., Whitney, D.R.: On a test of whether one of two random variables is stochastically larger than the other. Ann. Math. Stat. **18**(1), 50–60 (1947)
24. Martschat, S., Markert, K.: Improving ROUGE for timeline summarization. In: Proceedings of the 15th Conference of the European Chapter of the Association for Computational Linguistics, vol. 2, Short Papers, pp. 285–290. Association for Computational Linguistics, Valencia, Spain, April 2017
25. Martschat, S., Markert, K.: A temporally sensitive submodularity framework for timeline summarization. In: Proceedings of the 22nd Conference on Computational Natural Language Learning, pp. 230–240. Association for Computational Linguistics, Brussels, Belgium, October 2018
26. Miller, D.: Leveraging BERT for extractive text summarization on lectures (2019)
27. Miyato, T., Dai, A.M., Goodfellow, I.: Adversarial training methods for semi-supervised text classification (2017)
28. Moosavi, N.S., Strube, M.: Which coreference evaluation metric do you trust? A proposal for a link-based entity aware metric. In: Proceedings of the 54th Annual Meeting of the Association for Computational Linguistics, vol. 1, Long Papers, pp. 632–642. Association for Computational Linguistics, Berlin, Germany, August 2016
29. Palshikar, G., Pawar, S., Patil, et al.: Extraction of message sequence charts from narrative history text. In: Proceedings of the First Workshop on Narrative Understanding, pp. 28–36. Association for Computational Linguistics, Minneapolis, Minnesota, June 2019
30. Paszke, A., Gross, S., et al.: PyTorch: an imperative style, high-performance deep learning library. In: Wallach, H., Larochelle, H., Beygelzimer, A., d'Alché-Buc, F., Fox, E., Garnett, R. (eds.) Advances in Neural Information Processing Systems, vol. 32, pp. 8024–8035. Curran Associates, Inc. (2019)

31. Pennington, J., Socher, R., Manning, C.D.: Glove: global vectors for word representation. In: Empirical Methods in Natural Language Processing (EMNLP), pp. 1532–1543 (2014)
32. Preservation, S.A., Trust, M.: The Collected Works of Mahatma Gandhi (2013). https://www.gandhiheritageportal.org/the-collected-works-of-mahatma-gandhi. Accessed 22 Feb 2020
33. Pustejovsky, J., et al.: TimeML: robust specification of event and temporal expressions in text, pp. 28–34, January 2003
34. Recasens, M., Hovy, E.: Blanc: Implementing the rand index for coreference evaluation. Nat. Lang. Eng. **17**, 485–510 (2011)
35. Reimers, N., Gurevych, I.: Sentence-BERT: sentence embeddings using Siamese BERT-networks (2019)
36. Strötgen, J., Gertz, M.: HeidelTime: high quality rule-based extraction and normalization of temporal expressions. In: Proceedings of the 5th International Workshop on Semantic Evaluation, pp. 321–324. Association for Computational Linguistics, Uppsala, Sweden, July 2010
37. Vilain, M., Burger, J., Aberdeen, J., Connolly, D., Hirschman, L.: A model-theoretic coreference scoring scheme, pp. 45–52, January 1995
38. Zhang, W., Chen, Q., Chen, Y.: Deep learning based robust text classification method via virtual adversarial training. IEEE Access **8**, 61174–61182 (2020)
39. Zhang, Y., Wallace, B.: A sensitivity analysis of (and practitioners' guide to) convolutional neural networks for sentence classification (2016)

'John Ate 5 Apples' != 'John Ate Some Apples': Self-supervised Paraphrase Quality Detection for Algebraic Word Problems

Rishabh Gupta[✉], V. Venktesh, Mukesh Mohania, and Vikram Goyal

Indraprastha Institute of Information Technology, Delhi, India
{rishabh19089,venkteshv,mukesh,vikram}@iiitd.ac.in

Abstract. This paper introduces the novel task of scoring paraphrases for Algebraic Word Problems (AWP) and presents a self-supervised method for doing so. In the current online pedagogical setting, paraphrasing these problems is helpful for academicians to generate multiple syntactically diverse questions for assessments. It also helps induce variation to ensure that the student has understood the problem instead of just memorizing it or using unfair means to solve it. The current state-of-the-art paraphrase generation models often cannot effectively paraphrase word problems, losing a critical piece of information (such as numbers or units) which renders the question unsolvable. There is a need for paraphrase scoring methods in the context of AWP to enable the training of good paraphrasers. Thus, we propose ParaQD, a self-supervised paraphrase quality detection method using novel data augmentations that can learn latent representations to separate a high-quality paraphrase of an algebraic question from a poor one by a wide margin. Through extensive experimentation, we demonstrate that our method outperforms existing state-of-the-art self-supervised methods by up to 32% while also demonstrating impressive zero-shot performance.

1 Introduction

Algebraic Word Problems (AWPs) describe real-world tasks requiring learners to solve them using mathematical calculations. However, providing the same problem multiple times may result in the learner memorizing the mathematical formulation for the corresponding questions or exchanging the solution approach during exams without understanding the problem. Hence, paraphrasing would help prepare diverse questions and help to evaluate whether the student can arrive at the correct mathematical formulation and solution[1].

---

[1] https://cutt.ly/MWqHsN8.

R. Gupta and V. Venktesh—Contributed equally.

Supplementary Information The online version contains supplementary material available at https://doi.org/10.1007/978-3-031-26422-1_22.

M.-R. Amini et al. (Eds.): ECML PKDD 2022, LNAI 13718, pp. 353–369, 2023.
https://doi.org/10.1007/978-3-031-26422-1_22

The paraphrasing task can be tackled using supervised approaches like in [3] or self-supervised approaches like in [8]. As shown in Fig. 1, we observed that the generated paraphrases are of low quality as critical information is lost and the solution is not preserved. Some common issues that arose for the paraphrasing models were replacement or removal of numerical terms, important entities, replacement of units with irrelevant ones and other forms of information loss. These issues result in the generated question having a different solution or being rendered impossible to solve. Thus, there exists a need to automatically evaluate if a paraphrase preserves the semantics and solution of the original question. This is a *more challenging problem* than detecting similarity for general sentences. The existing state-of-the-art semantic similarity models give a relatively high score even to very low-quality paraphrases of algebraic questions (where some critical information has been lost), as seen in Fig. 1 and Table 1. In Fig. 1, our approach ParaQD assigns the cosine similarity as −0.999, thereby preventing the low-quality paraphrases from getting chosen. There is a need for solutions like ParaQD because poor paraphrases of algebraic questions cannot be given to the students as they are either unsolvable (as observed in the figure) or do not preserve the original solution.

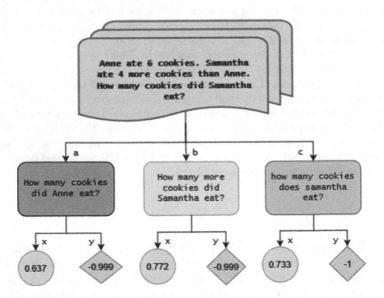

Fig. 1. Paraphrases by SOTA generation models. *a* is output from PEGASUS fine-tuned on PAWS, *b* is from T5 fine-tuned on Quora Question Pairs dataset and *c* is from PARROT paraphraser built on T5. *x* represents the cosine similarity scores assigned by the pretrained encoder MiniLM, while *y* represents the scores with our proposed approach, ParaQD.

To tackle the issues mentioned above, we need a labelled dataset for training a proper scoring model. However, there does not exist a dataset for AWP with labelled paraphrases. Therefore, we propose multiple unsupervised data augmentations to generate positive and negative paraphrases for an input question.

To model our negative augmentations, we identify crucial information in AWPs like numbers, units and key entities and design operators to perturb them. Similarly, for the positive augmentations, we design operators that promote diversity and retain the crucial information, thereby yielding a semantically equivalent AWP. On the other hand, existing augmentation methods like SSMBA [9] and UDA [15] do not capture the crucial information in AWPs. Using the positive and negative paraphrases, we train a paraphrase scoring model using triplet loss. It explicitly allows for the separation of positives and negatives to learn representations that can effectively score paraphrases. In summary, our core contributions are:

- We formulate a novel task of *detecting paraphrase quality for AWPs*, which presents a different challenge than detecting paraphrases for general sentences.
- We propose a new unsupervised data augmentation method that drives our paraphrase scoring model, *ParaQD*.
- We demonstrate that our method leads to a scoring model that surpasses the existing state-of-the-art text augmentation methods like SSMBA and UDA.
- We evaluate ParaQD using test sets prepared using operators disjoint from train augmentation operators and observe that ParaQD demonstrates good performance. We also demonstrate the zero-shot performance of ParaQD on new AWP datasets.

Code and Data are available at: https://github.com/ADS-AI/ParaQD.

2   Related Work

This section briefly discusses prior work in text data augmentation methods. One of the notable initial works in data augmentation for text [19] replaced words and phrases with synonyms to obtain more samples for text classification. In the work [16], the authors propose noising methods for augmentations where words are replaced with alternate words based on unigram distribution, but it introduces a noising parameter. A much easier text augmentation method, EDA, was proposed in the work [14]. The authors propose several operators such as random word deletion and synonym replacement to generate new sentences. The above works are based on heuristics and depend on a hyperparameter for high-quality augmentations.

More recently, self-supervised text augmentation methods have provided a superior performance on multiple tasks. In UDA [15], the authors propose two text augmentation operators, namely backtranslation and TF-IDF based word replacement, where words with low TF-IDF scores are replaced. In SSMBA [9], the authors propose a manifold-based data augmentation method where the input sentences are projected out of the manifold by corrupting them with token masking, followed by a reconstruction function to project them back to the manifold. Another self-supervised augmentation method named InvDA (Inverse Data Augmentation) was proposed in Rotom [8] which was similar to SSMBA in that it tried to reconstruct the original sentence from the corrupted version. Several rule-based text augmentation methods have also been proposed, like [5] which uses Natural Language Inference (NLI) for augmentation, and [1] leverages linguistic knowledge for the question-answering task.

3 Methodology

In this section, we describe the proposed method for paraphrase quality detection for algebraic word problems. The section is divided into two components: Data Augmentation and Paraphrase Quality Detection.

3.1 Data Augmentation

For data augmentation, we define 10 distinct operators to generate the training set. Out of the 10, 4 are positive (i.e. information preserving) transformations, and 6 are negative (information perturbing) transformations. Our negative operators are carefully chosen after observing the common mistakes made by various paraphrasing models to *explicitly teach* the quality detection model to assign a low score for incorrect paraphrases.

Let $Q = \{Q_1, Q_2, Q_3, \ldots Q_n\}$ denote the set of questions. Each question Qi can be tokenized into sentences $Q_{i1}, Q_{i2} \ldots Q_{ip}$ where p denotes the number of sentences in question Q_i. Let an augmentation be denoted by a function f, such that $f_i(Q_j)$ represents the output of the ith augmentation on the jth question.

The function $\lambda : Q \times Q \mapsto \{0, 1\}$ represents a labelling function which returns 1 if the input (Q_i, Q'_i) is a valid paraphrase, and 0 if not. Based on the design of our augmentations (explained in the next section), we work under the following assumption for the function f:

$$\lambda(Q_a, f_i(Q_a)) = \begin{cases} 1, & 1 \leq i \leq 4 \\ 0, & 5 \leq i \leq 10 \end{cases}$$

For the purposes of explanation, we will use a running example with question $\mathbf{Q_0} = $ *Alex travelled 100 km from New York at a constant speed of 20 kmph. How many hours did it take him in total?*

3.2 Positive Augmentations

f_1: **Backtranslation.** Backtranslation is the procedure of translating an example Q_i from language A to language B, and then translating it back to language A, yielding a paraphrase Q'_i. In our case, given an English question Q_i comprised of precisely p sentences $Q_{i1} \ldots Q_{ip}$, we translate each sentence Q_{ij} to German Q^*_{ij}, and then translate Q^*_{ij} back to English yielding $Q'_{ij} \ \forall j \in \{1, 2, \ldots p\}$. Further details are provided in Appendix A.

$$f_1(Q_i) = concat(Q'_{i1}, Q'_{i2} \ldots Q'_{ip})$$

$f_1(Q_0)$: *Alex was driving 100 km from New York at a constant speed of 20 km / h. How many hours did it take in total?*

f_2: **Same Sentence.** Inspired by SimCSE [4], we explicitly provide the same sentence as a positive augmentation as the standard dropout masks in the encoder act as a form of augmentation.

$f_2(Q_0)$: *Alex travelled 100 km from New York at a constant speed of 20 kmph. How many hours did it take him in total?*

f_3: **Num2Words.** Let α be a function that converts any number to its word form. Given a question Q_i, we extract all the numbers $N_i = \{n_{i1}, n_{i2} \ldots n_{ik}\}$ from Q_i. For each number $n_{ij} \in N_i$, we generate its word representation $\alpha(n_{ij})$, and replace n_{ij} by $\alpha(n_{ij})$ in Q_i to get $f_3(Q_i)$. This is done because paraphrasing models can replace numbers with their word form, and thus to ensure the scoring model does not consider it as a negative, we explicitly steer it to consider it a positive.

$f_3(Q_0)$: *Alex travelled one hundred km from New York at a constant speed of twenty kmph. How many hours did it take him in total?*

f_4: **UnitExpansion.** Let v be a function that converts the abbreviation of a unit into its full form. We detect all the abbreviated units $U_i = \{u_{i1}, u_{i2} \ldots u_{ik}\}$ from Q_i (using a predefined vocabulary of units and regular expressions). For each unit $u_{ij} \in U_i$, we generate its expansion $v(u_{ij})$, and replace u_{ij} by $v(u_{ij})$ in Q_i. This transformation helps the model to learn the units and their expansions, and consider them as the same when scoring a paraphrase.

$f_4(Q_0)$: *Alex travelled 100 kilometre from New York at a constant speed of 20 kilometre per hour. How many hours did it take him in total?*

3.3   Negative Augmentations

f_5: **Most Important Phrase Deletion.** The removal of unimportant words like stopwords (the, of, and) from an algebraic question will not perturb the solution or render it impossible to solve.

Thus, to generate hard negatives, we chose the most critical phrase, p_{imp} in any question, deleting which would generate Q'_i such that $\lambda(Q_i, Q'_i) = 0$. Let $\Psi : Q \mapsto P$ denote a function which returns the set of k most critical phrases $(p_1, p_2, \ldots, p_k)$ in the input Q_i.

$$p_{imp} = \underset{p}{\operatorname{argmin}}(cossim(Q_i, Q_i \backslash p)) \qquad \forall p \in \Psi(Q_i)$$

$$f_5(Q_i) = Q_i \backslash p_{imp}$$

where *cossim* denotes cosine similarity and $Q_i \backslash p$ denotes the deletion of p from Q_i. Further details are present in Appendix A.

$f_5(Q_0)$: *Alex travelled 100 km from New York at a constant speed of 20 kmph. How did it take him in total?*

f_6: **Last Sentence Deletion.** When using existing paraphrasing models such as Pegasus, the last few words or even the complete last sentence of the input question got deleted in the generated paraphrase in some cases. Thus, to account for this behaviour, we use this transformation as a negative. More formally, let the input Q_i be tokenized into p sentences $Q_{i1}, Q_{i2} \ldots Q_{ip}$ and the sentence Q_{i1} be tokenized into k tokens $Q_{i11}, Q_{i12} \ldots Q_{i1k}$. Then,

$$f_6(Q_i) = \begin{cases} concat(Q_{i11}, Q_{i12} \ldots Q_{i1(k-3)}) & p = 1 \\ concat(Q_{i1}, Q_{i2} \ldots Q_{i(p-1)}) & p > 1 \end{cases}$$

$f_6(Q_0)$: *Alex travelled 100 km from New York at a constant speed of 20 kmph.*

f_7: **Named Entity Replacement.** Since named entities are an important part of questions, we either replace them with a random one of the same category (from a precompiled list) or with the empty string (deletion). Let $\epsilon : Q \mapsto E$ denote a function which returns a set of all named entities present in the input Q_i, such that $(e_1, e_2, \ldots, e_k) = \epsilon(Q_i)$. We randomly sample w elements $E_i = (e_a, e_b \ldots e_w)$ from $(e_1, e_2, \ldots, e_k)$ and replace/delete the entities. We set $w = rand(1, min(3, k))$ where $rand(a, b)$ represents the random selection of a number from a to b (inclusive). This restricts w from being more than 3, thus increasing the difficulty of the generated negative.

$f_7(Q_0)$: *Sarah travelled 100 km from at a constant speed of 20 kmph. How many hours did it take him in total?*

f_8: **Numerical Entity Deletion.** Since numbers are critical to algebraic questions, their removal perturbs the solution and helps generate hard negatives. Let $\nu : Q \mapsto N$ represent a function which returns a set of all numbers present in the input Q_i, such that $(n_1, n_2, \ldots, n_k) = \nu(Q_i)$. We randomly sample a subset of numbers N_i from $(n_1, n_2, \ldots, n_k)$, and sample a string s from $S = ($*"some"*, *"a few"*, *"many"*, *"a lot of"*, *""*$)$. For each number $n_j \in N_i$, we replace it by s in Q_i. We set $|max(N_i)| = 2$. Similar to f_7, this makes it more challenging for the scoring model as we don't necessarily delete all the numbers, thereby generating harder negatives. This allows the model to learn that even the loss of one number renders the resultant output as an invalid paraphrase, thus getting assigned a low score.

$f_8(Q_0)$: *Alex travelled some km from New York at a constant speed of some kmph. How many hours did it take him in total?*

f_9: **Pegasus.** Pegasus [18] is a transformer-based language model, fine-tuned on PAWS [20] for our purpose. Pegasus consistently gave poor results for paraphrasing algebraic questions, as shown in Fig. 1. This provided the impetus for using it to generate hard negatives.

$f_9(Q_0)$: *= The journey from New York to New Jersey took Alex 100 km at a constant speed.*

f_{10}: **UnitReplacement.** Paraphrasing models sometimes have a tendency to replace units with similar ones (such as *feet* to *inches*). Since this would change the solution to an algebraic question, we defined this transformation to replace a unit with a different one from the same category. We identified 5 categories, $C = [Currency, Length, Time, Weight, Speed]$ to which most units appearing in algebraic problems belong. Our transformation was defined such that a unit u_a belonging to a particular category C_i is replaced with a unit u_b, such that $u_b \in C_i$ and $u_a \neq u_b$. For instance, *hours* could get converted to *minutes* or *days*, *grams* could get converted to *kilograms*.

Let C be the set of identified unit categories and $\Upsilon : U \mapsto U$ be a function that takes as input unit $u_a \in C_i$ and returns a different unit $u_b \in C_i$, where $C_i \in C$. Given the input Q_i containing units $U_i = (u_a, u_b \ldots u_n)$, we sample a set of units $U_{is} = \{u_x, \ldots u_z\}$ and replace them with $\{\Upsilon(u_i) \; \forall u_i \in U_{is}\}$ to generate $f_{10}(Q_i)$.

$\mathbf{f_{10}(Q_0)}$: *Alex travelled 100 m from New York at a constant speed of 20 kmph. How many hours did it take him in total?*

In the next section, we will detail our approach to training a model to detect the quality of paraphrases and how it can be used to score paraphrases.

3.4 Paraphrase Quality Detection

For detecting the quality of the paraphrases, we use MiniLM [13] as our base encoder (specifically, the version with 12 layers which maps the input sentences into 384-dimensional vectors)[2]. We utilize the implementation from Sentence-Transformers [11], where the encoder was trained for semantic similarity tasks using over a billion training pairs and achieved high performance with a fast encoding speed[3].

We train the model using triplet loss. For each question Q_i, let the positive transformation Q_i^+ be denoted by $pos(Q_i)$ and the negative transformation Q_i^- by $neg(Q_i)$ where $pos \in (f_1, \ldots f_4)$ and $neg \in (f_5, f_6 \ldots f_{10})$. Let the vector representation of any question Q_i when passed through the encoder be denoted as $ENC(Q)$. Then the loss is defined as

$$Loss(Q, Q^+, Q^-) = \sum_i max(0, \alpha - dist(Q_i, Q_i^-) + dist(Q_i, Q_i^+))$$

where α is the margin parameter, $dist(Q_i, Q_i^l) = 1 - cossim(ENC(Q_i), ENC(Q_i^l))$ and $l \in \{+, -\}$. The loss ensures that the model yields vector representations such that the distance between Q_i and Q_i^+ is smaller than the distance between Q_i and Q_i^-.

At inference time, to obtain the paraphrase score of Q_i and Q_i', we use cosine similarity. Let $score : Q \times Q \mapsto [-1, 1]$ denote the scoring function, then for a pair of questions (Q_i, Q_i'):

---

[2] https://bit.ly/3F2c9vH.
[3] https://sbert.net/docs/pretrained_models.html.

$$\rho_i, \zeta_i = ENC(Q_i), ENC(Q'_i)$$
$$score(Q_i, Q'_i) = cossim(\rho_i, \zeta_i) = \frac{\rho_i \cdot \zeta_i}{|\rho_i| \cdot |\zeta_i|}$$

4 Experiments

All the experiments were performed using a Tesla T4 and P100. All models, including the baselines, were trained for 9 epochs with a learning rate of 2e−5 using AdamW as the optimizer with seed 3407. We used a linear scheduler, with 10% of the total steps as warm-up having a weight decay of 0.01.

4.1 Datasets

The datasets used in the experiments are:

AquaRAT [6] (Apache, V2.0) is an algebraic dataset consisting of 30,000 (post-filtering) problems in the training set, 254 problems for validation and 220 problems for testing. After applying the test set operators to yield paraphrases, we get 440 samples for testing with manual labels.

EM_Math is a dataset consisting of mathematics questions for students from grades 6–10 from our partner company ExtraMarks. There are 10,000 questions in the training set and 300 in the test set. After applying the test operators, we get 600 paraphrase pairs.

SAWP (Simple Arithmetic Word Problems) is a dataset that we collected (from the internet) consisting of 200 algebraic problems. We evaluate the proposed methods in a zero-shot setting on this dataset by using the model trained on the AquaRAT dataset. After applying the test set operators, we get 400 paraphrase pairs.

PAWP (Paraphrased Algebraic Word Problems) is a dataset of 400 algebraic word problems collected by us. We requested two academicians from the partnering company (paid fair wages by the company) to manually write paraphrases (both valid and invalid) rather than using our test set operators. We use this dataset for zero-shot evaluation to demonstrate the performance of our model on human-crafted paraphrases.

Our data can also be used as a **seed set** for the task of paraphrase generation for algebraic questions.

4.2 Test Set Generation

For generating the synthetic test set (for AquaRAT, EM_Math and SAWP), we define a different set of operators to generate positive and negative paraphrases to test the ability of our method to generalize to a different data distribution. For any question Q_i in the test set, we generate two paraphrases and manually annotate the question-paraphrase pairs with the help of two annotators. The annotators were instructed to mark valid paraphrases as 1 and the rest as 0. We observed Cohen's Kappa values of **0.79**, **0.84** and **0.70** on AquaRAT, EM_Math and SAWP, respectively, indicating a substantial level of agreement between the annotators.

Operator Details. We defined two positive (f_a, f_b) and three negative (f_c, f_d, f_e) test operators. For each question, we randomly chose one operator from each category for generating paraphrases. These functions are:

f_a: **Active-Passive**: We noticed that most algebraic questions are written in the active voice. We used a transformer model for converting them to passive voice[4], followed by a grammar correction model[5] on top of this to ensure grammatical correctness.

f_b: **Corrupted Sentence Reconstruction**: We corrupt an input question by shuffling, deleting and replacing tokens, similar to ROTOM [8] but with additional leniency (Appendix A). We then train a sequence transformation model (t5-base) to reconstruct the original question from the corrupted one, which yields a paraphrase.

f_c: **TF-IDF Replacement**: Instead of the usual replacement of words with low TF-IDF score [15], we replace the words with high TF-IDF scores with random words in the vocabulary. This helps us generate negative paraphrases as it removes the meaningful words in the original question rendering it unsolvable.

f_d: **Random Deletion**: Random deletion is the process of randomly removing some tokens in the input example [14] to generate a paraphrase.

f_e: **T5**: We used T5 [10] fine-tuned on Quora Question Pairs to generate negatives as it was consistently resulting in paraphrases with missing information (Fig. 1).

4.3 Baselines

We compare against two SOTA data augmentation methods, UDA and SSMBA. For all the baselines, we use the same encoder (MiniLM) as for our method to maintain consistency across the experiments and enable a fair comparison.

UDA: UDA uses backtranslation and TF-IDF replacement (replacing words having a low score) to generate augmentations for any given input.

SSMBA: SSMBA is a data augmentation technique that uses corruption and reconstruction functions to generate the augmented output. The corruption is performed by masking some tokens in the input and using an encoder (such as BERT [2]) to fill the masked token.

Since the baselines are intended to generate positive paraphrases, we consider other questions in the dataset (in-batch) as negatives to train using the triplet loss. Alongside the direct implementation of UDA and SSMBA, we also compare pseudo-labelled versions of these baselines. The version of baselines without pseudo-labelling is used in all the experiments unless stated with suffix *(with pl)*. The details of pseudo labelling are provided in Appendix B.

---

[4] https://bit.ly/3FbPIEu.
[5] https://bit.ly/3HGOMcQ.

Table 1. Precision, Recall, F1 and Separation across all methods and datasets.

Dataset	Method	Macro			Weighted			μ^+	μ^-	μ^s
		P	R	F1	P	R	F1			
AquaRAT	Pretrained	0.658	0.502	0.569	0.784	0.318	0.453	0.977	0.897	0.080
	UDA	0.661	0.512	0.577	0.786	0.332	0.467	0.995	0.966	0.029
	UDA (w pl)	0.659	0.507	0.573	0.785	0.325	0.460	0.996	0.973	0.023
	SSMBA	0.645	0.554	0.596	0.757	0.395	0.520	0.965	0.829	0.137
	SSMBA (w pl)	0.663	0.522	0.584	0.787	0.345	0.480	0.997	0.928	0.069
	ParaQD (ours)	0.678	0.695	**0.687**	0.762	0.625	**0.687**	0.770	-0.010	**0.780**
EM_Math	Pretrained	0.694	0.534	0.604	0.773	0.415	0.540	0.955	0.796	0.158
	UDA	0.648	0.523	0.579	0.716	0.403	0.516	0.991	0.912	0.079
	UDA (w pl)	0.683	0.587	0.631	0.751	0.485	0.589	0.963	0.751	0.213
	SSMBA	0.615	0.564	0.588	0.669	0.470	0.552	0.871	0.729	0.142
	SSMBA (w pl)	0.655	0.586	0.619	0.716	0.492	0.583	0.937	0.629	0.308
	ParaQD (ours)	0.665	0.665	**0.665**	0.708	0.622	**0.662**	0.667	0.012	**0.655**
SAWP	Pretrained	0.162	0.500	0.245	0.106	0.325	0.159	0.964	0.896	0.068
	UDA	0.557	0.514	0.535	0.636	0.358	0.458	0.958	0.912	0.046
	UDA (w pl)	0.667	0.519	0.583	0.783	0.350	0.484	0.990	0.929	0.061
	SSMBA	0.662	0.594	0.626	0.763	0.460	0.574	0.929	0.758	0.172
	SSMBA (w pl)	0.649	0.537	0.588	0.757	0.378	0.504	0.978	0.864	0.115
	ParaQD (ours)	0.636	0.645	**0.640**	0.709	0.582	**0.640**	0.656	0.068	**0.589**
PAWP	Pretrained	0.749	0.502	0.602	0.751	0.500	0.600	0.948	0.905	0.042
	UDA	0.558	0.507	0.532	0.559	0.505	0.530	0.960	0.948	0.012
	UDA (w pl)	0.668	0.510	0.578	0.669	0.507	0.577	0.988	0.961	0.026
	SSMBA	0.536	0.512	0.524	0.536	0.510	0.523	0.874	0.853	0.021
	SSMBA (w pl)	0.551	0.510	0.530	0.552	0.507	0.529	0.939	0.913	0.026
	ParaQD (ours)	0.703	0.669	**0.685**	0.703	0.668	**0.685**	0.749	0.076	**0.673**

4.4 Metrics

Our main goal is to ensure the separation of valid and invalid paraphrases by a wide margin. This allows for extrapolation to unseen and unlabelled data (the distribution of scores for positive and negative paraphrases is unknown, thus threshold can be set to the standard 0.5 or a nearby value due to wider margins). It allows for the score to be used as a selection metric using maximization strategies like Simulated Annealing [7] or as reward using Reinforcement Learning [12,17] to steer generation. To this end, along with Precision, Recall, and F1 (both macro and weighted), we compute the separation between the mean positive and mean negative scores. More formally, let the score of all (Q_i, Q_i^+) pairs be denoted by $score(Q, Q^+)$ and the score of all (Q_i, Q_i^-) pairs be denoted by $score(Q, Q^-)$ where $\lambda(Q_i, Q_i^+) = 1$ and $\lambda(Q_i, Q_i^-) = 0$. Then,

$$\mu^s \ (separation) = \mu^+ - \mu^-$$
$$\mu^l = E[score(Q, Q^l)] \ \forall \ l \in \{+, -\}$$

4.5 Test Set Details

The number of positive and negative pairs are (139, 301) in AquaRAT, (223, 377) in EM, (130, 270) in SAWP and (199, 201) in PAWP. The details of the success of test set operators are shown in the form of confusion matrices in Fig. 6 (supplementary). The average precision, recall and accuracy of the operators across the datasets are 0.4, 0.59 and 0.56. The low precision is due to the inability of positive operators to generate valid paraphrases consistently, as the task of effectively paraphrasing algebraic questions is challenging. This further demonstrates the usefulness of a method like ParaQD that can be effectively used to distinguish the paraphrases as an objective to guide paraphrasing models (4.4).

Table 2. Summarizing the top-2 positive (Op+) and negative (Op−) operators across datasets.

Dataset	Op+		Op−	
	1	2	1	2
AquaRAT	f_3	f_1	f_9	f_5
EM_Math	f_4	f_1	f_9	f_8
SAWP	f_2	f_1	f_9	f_6
PAWP	f_1	f_2	f_{10}	f_9

5 Results and Analysis

The performance comparison and results of all methods are shown in Table 1. Across all datasets, for the measures macro-F1, weighted-F1 and separation, ParaQD outperforms all the baselines by a significant margin. For instance, the margin of separation in ParaQD is 5.69 times the best baseline SSMBA. To calculate the precision, recall and F1 measures, we threshold the obtained scores at the standard $\tau = 0.5$. Since this is a self-supervised method, there are no human-annotated labels available for the training and validation set. This means that the distribution of scores is unknown, and thus, the threshold can not be tuned on the validation set.

5.1 Performance

Our primary metric is separation (for reasons detailed in 4.4). Weighted F1 is more representative of the actual performance than macro F1 due to imbalanced data (4.5), and the results are discussed further.

AquaRAT and EM_Math. ParaQD outperforms the best-performing baseline by 32.1% weighted F1 on AquaRAT and 12.4% weighted F1 on EM_Math. The separation achieved by ParaQD on AquaRAT is 0.78 while the best performing baseline achieves 0.137, and on EM_Math, our method achieves a separation of 0.655 while the best performing baseline achieves a separation of 0.308.

SAWP: Evaluating zero-shot performance on SAWP, ParaQD outperforms the best performing baseline by 11.5% weighted F1 and achieves a separation of 0.589 as compared to the 0.172 achieved by the best baseline. This demonstrates the ability of our method to perform well even on zero-shot settings, as the distribution of this dataset is not identical to the ones that the model was trained on.

PAWP: Our method beats the best performing baseline by 14% weighted F1 on the manually created dataset PAWP, which also consists of a zero-shot setting. It demonstrates an impressive separation of 0.673, while the best performing baseline only has a separation of 0.042. This is practically applicable as it highlights that our method can also be used to evaluate paraphrases that have been manually curated by academicians (especially on online learning platforms) instead of only on automatically generated paraphrases.

To analyze and gain a deeper insight into these results, we plotted the confusion matrices (Fig. 4), and observed that ParaQD is able to consistently recognize invalid paraphrases to a greater extent than the baselines as it learns to *estimate the true distribution of negative samples* more effectively through our novel data augmentations.

5.2   Embedding Plots

To qualitatively evaluate ParaQD, we use t-SNE to project the embeddings into a two-dimensional space (Appendix C) as seen in Fig. 2. We observe that the separation between anchors and negatives of triplets is minimal for the baselines, while ParaQD is able to separate them more effectively. Perhaps a more interesting insight from Fig. 2a is that our method is able to cluster negatives together, which is not explicitly optimized by triplet loss as it does not account for inter-sample interaction. We note that our negative operators (with the possible exception of f_7 and f_{10}) are designed to generate unsolvable problems serving as good negatives for training the scoring model (ParaQD).

5.3   Operator Ablations

To measure the impact of all operators, we trained the model after removing each operator one by one. The summary of the results is in Table 2 (complete in Table 4 (supplementary)). We note that f_1 (defined in Sect. 3.2) seems to be the most consistently important operator amongst the positives, while f_9 (defined in Sect. 3.3) is the most consistently important operator amongst the negatives. One possible reason for the success of f1 could be that it is the only

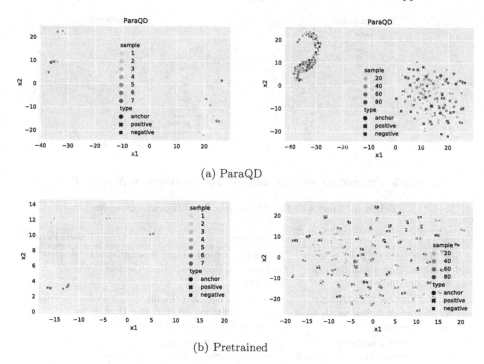

(a) ParaQD

(b) Pretrained

Fig. 2. Embedding plots on AquaRAT. Figure 5 in supplementary covers remaining plots.

positive operator that actually changes the words and sentence structure, which is replicated by our test operators and by the human-generated paraphrases.

Also, for the synthetically generated test sets (for AquaRAT, EM_Math and SAWP), since f_9 is a transformer model, it might generate paraphrases with a closer distribution (especially to f_e), but it also performs well on the human crafted paraphrases on PAWP. f_4 performs really well on EM_Math as the dataset involves more mathematical symbols, and thus the distribution of the data is such that technical operators (like f_4 and f_8) would have a more profound impact on the dataset.

The results also show that operator importance depends on the data, as certain data distributions might possess patterns that are more suitable to a certain set of operators. We also note that all operators are critical as removing any operator reduces performance for multiple datasets, thus demonstrating the usefulness of the combination of augmentations as a general framework.

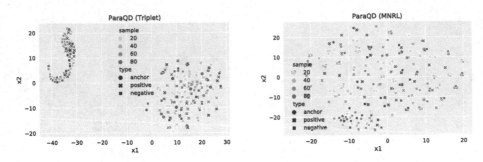

Fig. 3. Embedding plots for different loss functions on AquaRAT

Table 3. Analysis of model scores for different examples

Original	Paraphrase	Label	ParaQD
A bag of cat food weighs 7 pounds and 4 ounces. How much does the bag weigh in ounces?	A bag of cat food weighs 7 pounds and ounces. How much does the bag in ounces?	0	−0.922
A cart of 20 apples is distributed among 10 students. How much apple does each student get?	20 hats in a cart are equally distributed among 10 students. How much apple does each student get?	0	−0.999
A cart of 20 apples is distributed among 10 students. How much apple does each student get?	20 hats in a cart are equally distributed among 10 students. How many hats does each student get?	1	0.999
John walked 200 kilometres. How long did he walk in terms of metres?	John walked 200 centimetres. How long did he walk in terms of metres?	0	−0.999
John walked 200 kilometres. How long did he walk in terms of metres?	John walked 200 km. How long did he walk in terms of metres?	1	0.999

5.4 Effects of Loss Functions, Encoder and Seed

We analyzed the impact of the loss function by performing an ablation with Multiple Negative Ranking Loss (MNRL) (Appendix D) when training ParaQD. Since MNRL considers inter-sample separation, rather than explicitly distancing the generated hard negative, it is not able to provide a high margin of separation between the positives and negatives ($\mu^s = 0.416$) as high as the triplet loss ($\mu^s = 0.78$) but does result in a minor increase in the F1 scores. This can be observed in Fig. 3 and Table 5 (supplementary). We also analyzed the effects of the encoder and seed across methods on AquaRAT (Tables 6 and 8; detailed analysis in Appendix F) to demonstrate the robustness of our approach. We observe that we outperform the baselines on all the metrics for three encoders we experimented with, namely MiniLM (12 layers), MiniLM (6 layers) and MPNet for different seeds.

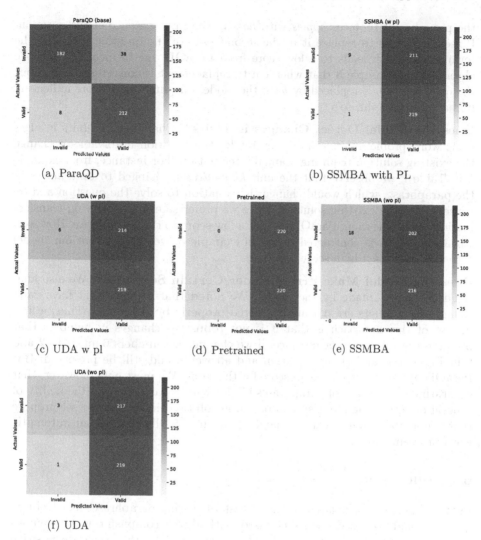

Fig. 4. Confusion matrices for all methods on AquaRAT. Others can be found in supplementary (Figs. 9 and 10)

5.5 Error Analysis and Limitations

Does the Model Check for the Preservation of Numerical Quantities?: From example 1 in Table 3, we observe that the number **4** is missing in the paraphrase rendering the problem unsolvable. Our model outputs a negative score, indicating it is a wrong paraphrase. This general phenomenon is observed in our reported results.

Does the Model Check for Entity Consistency?: We also observe that our model checks for entity consistency. For instance, in example 2, we observe that the paraphraser replaces *apples* with *hats* in the first sentence of the question. However, it fails to replace it in the second part of the question retaining the term *apple* which leads to a low score from ParaQD due to inconsistency. We observe from example 3 that when entity replacement is consistent throughout the question (*apple* replaced by *hats*, the model outputs a high score indicating it is a valid paraphrase.

Does the Model Detect Changes in Units?: Changing the units in algebraic word problems sometimes may render the question unsolvable or change the existing solution requiring manual intervention. For instance, from example 4 in Table 3, we observe that the unit *kilometres* is changed to *centimetres* in the paraphrase, which would change the equation to solve the question and by consequence the existing solution. Since we prefer solution preserving transformation of the question, ParaQD assigns a low score to this paraphrase. However, when *kilometres* is contracted to *km* in example 5, we observe that our model correctly outputs a high score.

Does the Model Make Errors Under Certain Scenarios?: We also analyzed the errors made by the model. We noted that samples that have valid changes in numbers are not always scored properly by the model. Thus, a limitation of this approach is that it is not robust to changes in numbers that preserve the solution. For instance, if we change the numbers 6 and 4 to 2 and 8 in Fig. 1, the underlying equation and answer would still be preserved. But ParaQD may not output a high score for the same. We must note, however, that generating these types of paraphrases is something that is beyond the ability of general paraphrasing models. As a potential solution (in the future), we propose that numerical changes can be handled through feedback from an automatic word problem solver.

6 Conclusion

In this paper, we formulated the novel task of scoring paraphrases for algebraic questions and proposed a self-supervised method to accomplish this. We demonstrated that the model learns valuable representations that separate positive and negative paraphrases better than existing text augmentation methods and provided a detailed analysis of various components. In the future, we plan to use the scoring model as an objective to steer language models for paraphrasing algebraic word problems and also investigate the usage of our method for the novel task of solvable problem detection.

Acknowledgements. We would sincerely like to thank Extramarks Education India Pvt. Ltd., SERB, FICCI (PM fellowship) and TiH Anubhuti (IIITD) for supporting this work.

References

1. Asai, A., Hajishirzi, H.: Logic-guided data augmentation and regularization for consistent question answering (2020)

2. Devlin, J., Chang, M., Lee, K., Toutanova, K.: BERT: Pre-training of deep bidirectional transformers for language understanding. arXiv:1810.04805 (2018)
3. Egonmwan, E., Chali, Y.: Transformer and seq2seq model for paraphrase generation. In: Proceedings of the 3rd Workshop on Neural Generation and Translation, pp. 249–255. Association for Computational Linguistics, Hong Kong (2019). https://doi.org/10.18653/v1/D19-5627,https://aclanthology.org/D19-5627
4. Gao, T., Yao, X., Chen, D.: Simcse: Simple contrastive learning of sentence embeddings (2021)
5. Kang, D., Khot, T., Sabharwal, A., Hovy, E.: Adventure: Adversarial training for textual entailment with knowledge-guided examples (2018)
6. Ling, W., Yogatama, D., Dyer, C., Blunsom, P.: Program induction by rationale generation: Learning to solve and explain algebraic word problems (2017)
7. Liu, X., Mou, L., Meng, F., Zhou, H., Zhou, J., Song, S.: Unsupervised paraphrasing by simulated annealing. In: Proceedings of the 58th Annual Meeting of the Association for Computational Linguistics, pp. 302–312. Association for Computational Linguistics (2020). https://doi.org/10.18653/v1/2020.acl-main.28, https://aclanthology.org/2020.acl-main.28
8. Miao, Z., Li, Y., Wang, X.: Rotom: A Meta-Learned Data Augmentation Framework for Entity Matching, Data Cleaning, Text Classification, and Beyond, pp. 1303–1316. Association for Computing Machinery, New York (2021). https://doi.org/10.1145/3448016.3457258
9. Ng, N., Cho, K., Ghassemi, M.: Ssmba: Self-supervised manifold based data augmentation for improving out-of-domain robustness (2020)
10. Raffel, C., et al.: Exploring the limits of transfer learning with a unified text-to-text transformer (2020)
11. Reimers, N., Gurevych, I.: Sentence-BERT: Sentence embeddings using Siamese BERT-networks. In: Proceedings of the 2019 Conference on Empirical Methods in Natural Language Processing and the 9th International Joint Conference on Natural Language Processing (EMNLP-IJCNLP). Association for Computational Linguistics, Hong Kong (2019)
12. Stiennon, N., et al.: Learning to summarize from human feedback (2020)
13. Wang, W., Wei, F., Dong, L., Bao, H., Yang, N., Zhou, M.: Minilm: Deep self-attention distillation for task-agnostic compression of pre-trained transformers (2020)
14. Wei, J., Zou, K.: Eda: Easy data augmentation techniques for boosting performance on text classification tasks (2019)
15. Xie, Q., Dai, Z., Hovy, E., Luong, M.T., Le, Q.V.: Unsupervised data augmentation for consistency training (2020)
16. Xie, Z., et al.: Data noising as smoothing in neural network language models (2017)
17. Yasui, G., Tsuruoka, Y., Nagata, M.: Using semantic similarity as reward for reinforcement learning in sentence generation. In: Proceedings of the 57th Annual Meeting of the Association for Computational Linguistics: Student Research Workshop, pp. 400–406. Association for Computational Linguistics, Florence (2019). https://doi.org/10.18653/v1/P19-2056, https://aclanthology.org/P19-2056
18. Zhang, J., Zhao, Y., Saleh, M., Liu, P.J.: Pegasus: Pre-training with extracted gap-sentences for abstractive summarization (2019)
19. Zhang, X., Zhao, J., LeCun, Y.: Character-level convolutional networks for text classification (2016)
20. Zhang, Y., Baldridge, J., He, L.: Paws: Paraphrase adversaries from word scrambling (2019)

Looking Beyond the Past: Analyzing the Intrinsic Playing Style of Soccer Teams

Jeroen Clijmans, Maaike Van Roy$^{(\boxtimes)}$, and Jesse Davis

Department of Computer Science, Leuven.AI, KU Leuven, Leuven, Belgium
jeroen.clijmans@student.kuleuven.be,
{maaike.vanroy,jesse.davis}@kuleuven.be

Abstract. Analyzing the offensive playing style of teams is an important task within soccer analytics that has various applications in match preparation and scouting. Existing data-driven approaches typically quantify style by looking at individual events that occur during a match in isolation. This approach has two shortcomings. First, it ignores the sequential aspect of the game, as patterns of play are a crucial aspect of playing style. Second, it fails to generalize over the limited amount of data in order to model slight variations of the observed patterns that a team may employ in the future. This is particularly important when considering rare actions like shots and goals, which are the key success criteria of an offensive style. This paper proposes a novel approach for analyzing playing style that addresses these shortcomings. First, it captures the sequential patterns of a team's style by modeling the observed behavior of a team as a discrete-time Markov chain. Second, it characterizes the offensive style of teams in a number of features that are based on domain knowledge. It applies a combination of analytical techniques and probabilistic model checking to reason about a team's model in order to extract values for these features. As the model allows for a generalization of a team's past behavior, the extracted style is less influenced by the rarity of shots and goals. Using event stream data of the 2019/20 English Premier League, we empirically show that the proposed approach can capture a team's positional and sequential style, as well as reason about the style's efficiency and similarities with other teams.

Keywords: Markov model · Probabilistic model checking · Playing style · Soccer analytics

1 Introduction

Analyzing the in-game behavior of teams (i.e., their playing style) has several important use cases in professional soccer. For example, identifying a team's typical patterns of movement or strategies can be used to aid match preparations such as designing a game plan that exploits the weaknesses of the opponent, or scheduling pre-tournament friendlies based on the similarity between the pre-tournament and in-tournament opponent's playing styles.[1] Additionally, it can also be used for player acquisition, where a club may be interested in targeting players that currently play for a team that is stylistically similar.

Consequently, an important question is how to characterize a team's style of play. One way to do this is based on manual video analysis of matches. However, this is inherently subjective and time-consuming, making it impossible to do this for a large number of matches or teams. Hence, a data-driven approach can play a role by, for example, identifying a shortlist of teams most similar to an upcoming opponent or identifying insights that are difficult for humans to pick up on. Existing approaches mainly focus on quantifying style at the level of individual events in a match [3,5,7]. This has two important limitations. First, it ignores the sequential nature of the game which is crucial for modeling patterns of play. Second, it fails to generalize over the limited amount of data in order to capture slight variations of the observed patterns that a team may employ in the future. As a season is relatively short and players rarely perform the exact same actions multiple times, the data is inherently limited. Using data of previous seasons is often not useful, as changes in players and management, and thus in style, happen regularly. Especially when analyzing the offensive style of teams, in which rare actions such as shots and goals play an important role, being able to generalize over the limited amount of data and capturing the *intrinsic* playing style of teams becomes particularly important.

This paper proposes a novel approach for playing style analysis based on a learned model that captures a team's intrinsic offensive behavior from historical event stream data.[2] In particular, we model the behavior of a team as a discrete-time Markov chain (DTMC). This has the inherent advantages that the sequential nature of the game is taken into account and observed patterns are interleaved allowing for generalization beyond past behavior. Additionally, we define a number of features that characterize playing style based on domain knowledge. Intuitively, these features capture how often teams employ certain stylistic parameters and how effective they are doing so. Then, we show how a combination of analytical techniques and probabilistic model checking can be used to reason about each team's learned model to obtain values for the features we defined, thereby characterizing their intrinsic playing style.

We illustrate our approach on event stream data of the 2019/20 English Premier League. Our approach indicates that Manchester City is the least likely to launch a counterattack and the most likely to eventually arrive at a shot by using combination play; Bournemouth should have considered using their left side more often, as the model considers it a side from which much more danger could have been created than the right side; and Leicester City's playing style was, out of all smaller teams, the most similar to the possession-based playing style that is often employed by big clubs such as Manchester City and Liverpool.

---

[1] https://www.reuters.com/article/socccer-euro-bel/soccer-belgium-coach-martinez-outlines-euro-2020-warm-up-plans-idUKL8N29V0Q4.

[2] The implementation is publicly available: https://github.com/JeroenClijmans/MarkovSoccer.

2 Capturing Team Behavior as a DTMC

The goal of this work is to capture and characterize the intrinsic playing styles of soccer teams. To this end, we propose to model the in-game offensive behavior of each team using a team-specific discrete-time Markov Chain (DTMC). Specifically, this model represents the behavior of the team during a possession sequence and will be learned from the team's historical on-the-ball actions. Next, we describe the data set used and outline the models and how they can be learned from historical data.

2.1 Data Set

The models are constructed using historical event stream data. This type of data typically contains all on-the-ball actions (e.g., passes, dribbles, shots) that occur during a match and records various features about these actions such as location, involved players, timestamp, etc. In this work, we use event stream data from the 2019/20 English Premier League, which consists of 380 matches. We encode this data set to SPADL[3], which is a vendor-independent format to describe on-the-ball player actions and which facilitates the analysis [4].

2.2 Retrieving Possession Sequences

As a first step, before constructing the models, we extract all possession sequences from the data. We exclude possession sequences resulting from corners, crossed free-kicks, goal attempts from free-kicks and penalties, as these often involve custom tactics that are beyond the scope of this work.

We define a possession sequence as a maximal uninterrupted sequence of consecutive actions by the same team that either 1) starts with an action bringing the ball into play (e.g., a throw-in), or 2) involves three or more deliberate ball-moving actions[4] by the team under consideration. The former indicates that the team surely has control over the ball as it signifies the start of a possession sequence. The latter indicates that the team has *established* ball control during the sequence, otherwise they would be unable to execute these actions.

2.3 Constructing Team-Specific DTMCs

The extracted possession sequences of each team are used as input to learn each team's model. Specifically, the proposed model captures (1) how and where the ball is gained, (2) where the team tends to move the ball to, and (3) how and where the possession sequence eventually ends. The model is schematically sketched in Fig. 1 and is defined by the following set of states and transitions:

---

[3] https://github.com/ML-KULeuven/socceraction.
[4] We define a deliberate ball-moving action as an action in which the main objective is to *deliberately move the ball to a certain position*. This includes actions such as passes, crosses, carries, and shots, but excludes actions such as clearances.

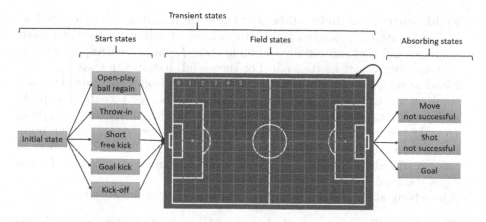

Fig. 1. Schematic overview of the states and transitions of the DTMC used to model the in-game offensive behavior of a team.

Transient States $\mathcal{T}$. This set of states can be entered and exited during a possession sequence. We define two types of transient states: *start states* and *field states*. *Start states* represent how possession of the ball is gained. We include five types: a throw-in, a short free-kick, a goal kick, a kick-off, and an open-play ball regain. *Field states* represent the particular locations on the pitch in which the ball can be situated during the possession sequence. We use discretized locations and divide the field up into 192 field states using a 12×16 grid.

Absorbing States $\mathcal{A}$. This set of states cannot be left once entered and indicates how a possession sequence can end. We include a *move not successful* (*mns*), a *shot not successful* (*sns*), and a *goal* (*g*) state, which represent losing the ball when trying to move it to another location, an unsuccessful shot and a successful shot, respectively.

Transitions. How a team moves the ball from one state to another during a possession sequence is modelled by the transitions. Each transition is associated with a probability, which corresponds to the frequency of the corresponding action in the extracted sequences of the team. Concretely, we include the below transitions and calculate the probabilities as follows:

- **Initial state** *init* **to start state** s_t: These probabilities are calculated as $P(s_t|init) = c_{seq,s_t}/c_{seq}$ where c_{seq,s_t} is the number of sequences starting with an action corresponding to the start state of type t and c_{seq} is the total number of sequences.
- **Start state** s_t **to field state** f_i: These probabilities are calculated as $P(f_i|s_t) = c_{s_t,f_i}/c_{s_t}$ where c_{s_t,f_i} is the number of actions that correspond to the start state of type t and after which the ball ends up in state f_i, and c_{s_t} is the total number of actions that correspond to the start state of type t.

- **Field state f_i to field state f_j:** These probabilities are calculated as $P(f_j|f_i) = c_{f_i,f_j}/c_{f_i}$ where c_{f_i,f_j} is the number of ball-moving actions starting in state f_i that successfully end up in state f_j, and c_{f_i} corresponds to the total number of actions (i.e., failed or successful) initiated in state f_i.
- **Field state f_i to an absorbing state:** Actions from field states can also result in the end of the sequence (i.e., failed actions or a goal). The probabilities for these transitions are calculated as $P(mns|f_i) = c_{f_i,mns}/c_{f_i}$, $P(sns|f_i) = c_{f_i,sns}/c_{f_i}$, and $P(g|f_i) = c_{f_i,g}/c_{f_i}$. Here, $c_{f_i,mns}$ is the number of unsuccessful ball-moving actions from state f_i, $c_{f_i,sns}$ is the number of unsuccessful shots from f_i, $c_{f_i,g}$ is the number of goals scored from f_i, and c_{f_i} is the total number of actions initiated in f_i.
- **Absorbing state:** This is equal to a self loop with probability one.

Using a DTMC confers several advantages for trying to capture a team's style of play. First, DTMCs go beyond considering a single action in isolation by modeling sequences of consecutive actions. As interplay between actions is important, this gives a more comprehensive perspective on a team's style. Second, they are able to generalize over the different actions that a team has performed in the past. Thus, these models allow us to reason about ways in which the team could combine different actions during a possession sequence, even though it was not explicitly observed in the data. This also means that the model is less influenced by the rarity of events such as shots or goals.

3   Characterizing a Team's Playing Style

From a soccer perspective, there are a number of potential behavioral patterns and characteristics of play that are relevant and indicative of style such as:

Preference for Certain Locations. Teams like to work the ball through certain zones on the pitch. This may arise due to tactical instructions, such as Manchester City's use of half spaces, or because teams have strong players in certain positions, which may manifest itself as preference for using one side of the pitch.

Preference for Certain Sequences. Teams like to use and reuse various combinations of actions which allow them to move the ball between locations. Some teams have a preference for playing the ball wide and down the flanks, while other teams predominantly use sequences going through the center of the field.

Directness of Play. Some teams like Manchester City will employ a patient and structured style that methodologically tries to build up to a goal scoring opportunity. Other teams like Everton like to sit deeper and rely on a more direct counter attacking style of play.

Ability to Create Shots. Generating (high-quality) shots is extremely important and is often done by employing particular patterns of play. Capturing how effective teams are at generating shots from various locations on the pitch can give some indications of style.

For each of the aforementioned categories we define a number of different features that can be computed by reasoning about our learned model of a team's behavior. Intuitively, each feature either captures how often a team employs a strategy or how effective a team is at applying a given strategy. These features can also capture relative strengths of a team such as their effectiveness of generating shots when attacking from the left vs. right flank. Next, we describe for each category the different features we defined and how they can be computed using the model.

3.1 Features Regarding a Team's Preference for Certain Locations

One indicator of style of play is a team's preference for working the ball into certain locations. We consider a team's locational preferences in two situations: general possession sequences, and more promising possession sequences that end with a shot. These two situations provide insights into both a team's regular playing style and their style when playing in a more successful manner. Using these situations, we derive six features that allow us to characterize a team's playing style based on their preferred locations. We compute these features in two steps. First, we construct heatmaps containing the expected number of times a team will possess the ball in each location of the pitch during both situations. Second, using these heatmaps, we derive three concrete features for each situation indicating a team's preference for the left, right, and middle part of the pitch.

Step 1: Constructing Heatmaps: We compute the expected number of visits to each location using the fundamental matrix N of the model:

$$N = \sum_{k=0}^{\infty} Q^k = (I - Q)^{-1}. \tag{1}$$

Here, I is the identity matrix and each entry q_{ij} of Q is the transition probability from transient state i to transient state j. Each entry n_{ij} is equal to the expected number of visits to transient state j when starting the possession sequence from state i. We compute this matrix both for general possession sequences as well as for only those ending with a shot. Computing the fundamental matrix $\hat{N}$ that solely generates those sequences of the original model which end in a shot requires a slight alteration to the model. More specifically, we restrict the set of absorbing states $\hat{A}$ to only include the *shot not successful* and *goal* states. The fundamental matrix $\hat{N}$ of the new model can be computed as in Eq. 1 with the new transition probabilities from transient to transient states given by the matrix $\hat{Q}$:

$$\hat{Q} = D_0^{-1} Q D_0. \tag{2}$$

Here, D_0 is the diagonal matrix with, for each transient state i, an entry $b_{i\hat{a}}$:

$$b_{i\hat{a}} = \sum_{j \in \hat{A}} b_{ij} \tag{3}$$

$$B = NR \tag{4}$$

with N the fundamental matrix of the original model and R the matrix containing the original transition probabilities from transient to absorbing states.

The entries of the fundamental matrix yield a heatmap which is already interesting in its own right because it allows us to analyze which exact locations teams prefer to use. Additionally, contrasting a team's preference during general possession sequences with their preference during more promising ones will allow us to identify locations from which a team is more/less efficient.

Step 2: Computing Features: Second, we derive three concrete features from each of the two heatmaps. More precisely, we derive a team's preference for the left side, the right side, and the central part of the field by calculating the relative percentage that the team uses each zone (illustrated in Fig. 2), as given by the heatmaps. This gives an indication of which parts of the field a team tends to use more often (e.g., left side over the right side, or predominantly through the center), both during general play and when playing more successfully.

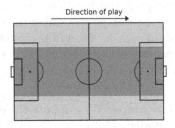

Fig. 2. Illustration of the three zones used to compute a team's locational preference. The left and right sides of the field (yellow) have a width equal to a quarter of the field. The remaining part of the field (blue) is defined as the central zone. (Color figure online)

3.2   Features Regarding a Team's Preference for Certain Sequences

A second indicator of style of play is a team's preference for combinations of consecutive locations, i.e., sequences. This provides insights into which locations of the pitch are often used together to move the ball from one location to the next. For example, whether a team prefers to move the ball wide and attack down the flanks or move it more centrally. We capture this aspect in two steps.

First, we generate the 200 most likely two-action sequences. The number of sequences to generate was empirically determined, and using more than 200 does not influence the results. The likelihood of a sequence is computed by multiplying the transition probabilities between the states of the sequence and weighing it by the expected number of visits to the first state of the sequence starting from the initial state. This weight is given by the fundamental matrix.

Second, we define two concrete features: *inward/outward preference*, which is the fraction of the 200 most likely sequences that move the ball inwards towards the middle of the pitch/outwards towards the touchlines.

3.3 Features Regarding the Directness of Play

A third indicator of style is the directness of play. Namely, how fast a team tends to go from recovering the ball to creating a shooting opportunity, and how directly they do this. While some teams prefer a steady build up from the back using many short on-the-ball actions, other teams prefer to utilize long balls or to sit back and counter. We capture this aspect of style in four concrete features.

The first feature captures the team's speed of play during dangerous attacking sequences by measuring the average number of actions in a sequence that ends in a shot according to the model. We compute this feature in two steps. First, a new model is constructed which only takes into account possession sequences that end in a shot (see Sect. 3.1). Second, we use probabilistic model checking techniques (i.e., PRISM [10]) to compute the average number of actions in such sequences. The higher the number of actions needed, the more a team prefers a slower possession-based style over a faster direct style of play.

The second feature captures the team's probability of performing long goal kicks, which we define as goal kicks that end in the opponent half. This provides insights into a team's directness of build up play. We compute the probability of a team performing these long goal kicks by a summation over all transition probabilities that originate from the *goal kick* start state and end in any field state that is in the opponent's half.

The third feature captures the team's probability of performing long balls. We define these as actions that originate from the defensive half, bypass midfield, and end up in the final third of the pitch. The probability of a team performing these long balls can be computed by a weighted summation over all transition probabilities from states in the defensive half to states in the final third of the pitch. The weight assigned to each state is the relative usage of each location, given by the fundamental matrix. This is scaled so that the entries corresponding to the own half sum to 1, yielding a probability.

The fourth feature captures the team's probability of performing a successful counterattack. We define these as possession sequences that start in the team's own half, after an open-play ball regain, and yield a shot within eight actions. To calculate this probability, we first use a probabilistic model checker to compute the probability of arriving at a shot within eight actions for all locations in the own half. Next, we weight these locations by the probability of recovering the ball there, scaled so that these sum to 1.

3.4 Features Regarding the Ability to Create Shots

A final indicator of style that we consider is the team's ability to create shots. More specifically, we capture the team's probability of creating *non-opportunistic* shots. We define these as shots in a possession sequence that started in the team's own half. In contrast to generating a shot after recovering the ball in the opponent's half after they made a mistake, these shots better capture a team's ability to generate shots via smart ball movements. We capture this in two steps.

First, we compute a heatmap in which each entry is equal to the team's probability of generating a shot later on in the possession sequence when starting from the corresponding location on the field. This heatmap is computed using the formula $B = NR$, where N is the fundamental matrix and R the matrix containing all the transition probabilities from transient to absorbing states. As there are two absorbing states that entail that a shot has happened in our model (i.e., the *shot not successful* and *goal* state), the values of these two absorbing states are summed to calculate the final probability for each possible start state.

Second, we capture the non-opportunistic shot probability in one feature by means of a weighted average over all obtained probabilities for states in the team's own half. The weight of each location is the relative usage of that location, given by the fundamental matrix of the model and scaled so that the entries corresponding to the own half sum to 1.

Teams who lose the ball often will achieve a lower score because there is a higher probability of being absorbed in the *move not successful* state. This is influenced by both the technical ability of a team as well as their behavior. While the influence of the technical ability is obvious, the influence of the behavior can be seen by means of an example. Consider a team that often attempts long balls. The probability of losing the ball when executing these passes will be higher because these tend to be more difficult. On the other hand, if these succeed, then the team is much closer to the shooting area and the likelihood of eventually arriving at a shot increases in this case. This is a trade-off that a team makes by adopting a specific playing style.

4   Use Cases

The previously defined features can be used to easily characterize and compare the intrinsic playing styles of teams. Using the event stream data of the 2019/20 English Premier League (EPL), we illustrate their use on three use cases: finding teams with similar playing styles, identifying mismatches in the relative efficiency of a team's style, and performing a more in-depth analysis of a teams' style.

4.1   Finding Similar Teams

Identifying teams with similar playing styles can be useful during match preparation, e.g., for measuring how similar your next opponent is to a team that you have played before and for scheduling pre-tournament friendlies against teams that behave similarly to in-tournament opponents. We propose three different options of combining the features into playing style vectors. For each of these options, we visualize the vectors in a 2D-plane using t-SNE [17]. Similar data points will lie close to each other, allowing us to visually identify similar teams.

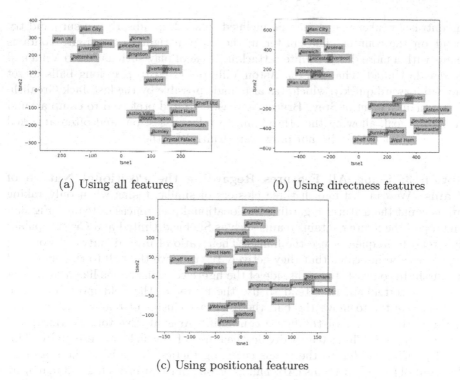

(a) Using all features

(b) Using directness features

(c) Using positional features

Fig. 3. t-SNE visualization of all teams of the 2019/20 EPL using the three different options of combining the features. Teams which are visualized close to each other have a similar playing style.

Option 1: Using All Features. We can distinguish two clusters of teams when combining all 13 features defined in Sect. 3 into one playing style vector for each team (Fig. 3a). One clear cluster is visible in the bottom right of the figure with teams like Sheffield United and Newcastle. These teams tend to have a more direct playing style and like to use their flanks. More possession-based teams like Manchester City can be found in the top part of the figure. Leicester City can be found the closest from all smaller teams to the big teams like Manchester City, Chelsea, and Liverpool. In the analyzed season, Leicester had a possession-based build up with quality players that were good at creating shooting opportunities. This resulted in them finishing in 5th place and playing the Europa League.

Option 2: Using All Features Regarding Directness of Playing Style. We can distinguish two clear clusters of teams when only taking into account the features regarding the directness of play (Fig. 3b). The cluster in the upper left corner contains teams that tend to have more possession, possibly because their styles of play focus on trying to maintain it. Manchester City is the extreme example, but teams such as Leicester and Brighton also preferred to maintain possession. Additionally, the majority of teams in this cluster have strong players.

In contrast, weaker teams may be inclined to sit deep, absorb pressure and try to hit on the counter. The cluster in the bottom right of the figure contains teams with a more direct counter attacking style of play such as Aston Villa and Newcastle United. That season, Aston Villa preferred to play long balls to get the ball forward quickly, which was also made possible by the fast Jack Grealish. Under management of Steve Bruce, Newcastle United preferred to camp around their own goal, allowing the other team to take possession, and often attacked on the counter, which did not prove very fruitful for them.

Option 3: Using All Features Regarding the Positional Nature of Teams. We can distinguish three clusters of similar teams when only taking into account the features regarding the locational preferences of teams (Fig. 3c). The top of the figure contains teams such as Sheffield United and Crystal palace that tend to frequently use the flanks. Their ratio of inward/outward pointing sequences also indicates that they actively try to move the ball to the outside of the pitch. In contrast, the right side of the figure contains teams like Manchester City and Tottenham that tend to use the center of the field most often and also actively try to move the ball there. A last cluster of teams can be found in the bottom center of the figure containing Arsenal, Everton, Watford, and Wolverhampton. These teams divide their use of the field more equally. This could possibly be due to the teams changing tactics throughout the season as three out of these four teams (Arsenal, Everton, and Watford) changed managers mid-season.

4.2   Assessing Mismatch in Efficiency of the Sides

Identifying possible mismatches in the efficiency of a team's playing style can be useful to create a game plan when playing against them, or to propose improvements when analyzing one's own style. To illustrate this, we inspect whether Bournemouth's expected usage of the sides and center of the field match up with their expected efficiency. Bournemouth use their flanks slightly more often than the league average (56.9% vs. 54.2%) and have a preference for the left over right flank with 21% more ball movements taking place on the former during their regular possession sequences (Fig. 4a). However, when only considering possession sequences that end in a shot, there are 64% more actions taking place on their left vs. right side, which is much more than the 21% that would be expected if the sides were equally efficient (Fig. 4b). Perhaps the team should have considered focusing even more on the left side when trying to attack. This could have been useful, as Bournemouth was relegated after the 2019/20 season.

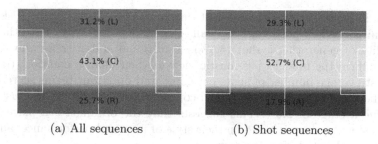

| (a) All sequences | (b) Shot sequences |

Fig. 4. Relative use of the left side, right side and central zone for Bournemouth according to their model when (a) all sequences and (b) only the sequences that end in a shot are taken into account.

4.3 In-depth Analysis of Playing Style

Finally, we perform an in-depth analysis of the identified playing styles of Manchester City and Sheffield United.

Regarding locational preference, City seems to prefer utilizing the half spaces during their build-up play, with a particular preference for the left half space (Fig. 5). Their usage of the central zone is further emphasized when aggregating their usage of the left, right, and central zones (Fig. 6). City uses the central zone more often (54.1%) than any other team with the league average being 45.8%. Consequently, they are also the team that is the least likely to use the sides, and when they do, they prefer the left side over the right side. On the other hand, Sheffield predominantly prefers the flanks and uses them more than any other team. This corresponds with their 3-5-2 formation where the outside center backs would overlap the wing backs to overload situations on the flanks.[5]

Regarding directness of play, City has the most elaborate buildup of all teams, with no other team having a higher average number of actions in sequences ending in a shot (14.2), or with lower probabilities of performing a long goal kick (4.3%) or using a long ball in the own half (0.9%). In contrast, Sheffield is one of the teams with the most direct playing style according to the model. Only Bournemouth has a lower average number of actions in possession sequences ending in a shot (7.2 vs. 8.0), and no team has a higher probability of performing a long goal kick (43.0%) or using a long ball in their own half (2.8%).

Regarding the ability to create shots, City has the highest probability of creating a shooting opportunity when possessing the ball in their own half (15.7%), with the league average being 9.0%. There is also no clear mismatch visible in their efficiency of the sides (Fig. 6), which is not the case for all teams (see Sect. 4.2). Interestingly, City is the least likely team to generate a shot on a counterattack (1.7%) after regaining the ball in their own half. This emphasizes that they are extremely picky about when to launch a counterattack and do not risk losing the ball as they know how adept they are at generating shots with a patient

---
[5] https://themastermindsite.com/2020/08/29/overlapping-centre-backs-tactical-analysis/.

build up. In contrast, Sheffield does not turn out to be good at creating shooting opportunities. When possessing the ball in their own half, they have the worst probability of generating a shot (5.6%). Traditional statistics for the 2019/20 season confirm the model's pessimistic view of their chance creation: they had the lowest average number of shots per game and only four teams scored fewer goals. Their ability to create successful counterattacks (2.2%) is also just below the league average of 2.3%. This suggests that the obtained 9th place during that season was generous based on their style of play and performance, and they were indeed relegated after the next season.

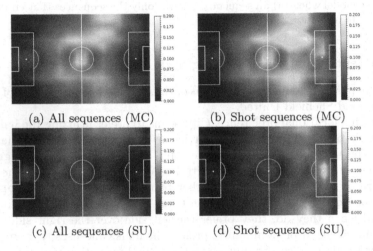

(a) All sequences (MC)   (b) Shot sequences (MC)

(c) All sequences (SU)   (d) Shot sequences (SU)

Fig. 5. Average number of visits to each location in a possession sequence for Manchester City (top row) and Sheffield United (bottom row) according to their model when all sequences (left column) and only the sequences that end in a shot (right column) are taken into account.

5   Related Work

Playing style analysis has already been approached from many different angles. Some works simply aim to retrieve the most common action patterns of a team by e.g., a combination of clustering and pattern mining [6,19] or inductive logic programming [18]. Other works adopt a more generalized view of playing style. For example, some apply clustering methods to the team's (ball) movements to identify the different behavior styles or prototypical actions that are used [1,7,8]. Other works aim to utilize compression methods such as Principal Component Analysis or non-negative matrix factorization to identify factors in the data of players that represents their playing style [2,5,9,11]. More recently, deep learning techniques have also been used to characterize a player's passing style [3].

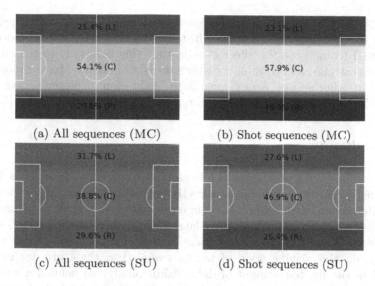

(a) All sequences (MC) (b) Shot sequences (MC)

(c) All sequences (SU) (d) Shot sequences (SU)

Fig. 6. Relative use of the left side, right side and central zone for Manchester City (top row) and Sheffield United (bottom row) according to their model when all sequences (left column) and only the sequences that end in a shot (right column) are taken into account.

Most of these methods do not only try to analyze the playing style of teams, but also identify the different types of style. This is in contrast to the approach adopted in this paper. The identification of the different types of style according to the discussed techniques has two main disadvantages: 1) the identified categories are not always interpretable, and 2) the categorization ultimately depends on the choice of included features, and whether each feature is as significant to get a classification according to the intuitive and practical notion of playing style is often ignored. In contrast, we first define high-level indicators of playing style, break these down into a set of concrete features and then use analytical approaches and model checking techniques to derive values for these features. This has the advantage that the features are and remain interpretable from the start. Additionally, computing the feature values based on a model of the team's intrinsic offensive behavior yields values that are less influenced by rare actions.

Regarding the use of Markov models for soccer analytics tasks, there are many different applications with playing style analysis being the least researched. Rudd [14] first introduced the use of Markov models to the field of soccer analytics by using them to value player actions. The general idea was built upon by others [16,23]. In particular, the Expected Threat (xT) framework of Singh has been illustrated to be useful for analyzing the playing style of teams based on where teams generate threat from [16]. Our work encompasses this framework, as the same xT values can be computed using our proposed models. Peña [12] discusses how Markov models can be used to model possession sequences which yield faithful approximations of the distribution of passing sequences. Van Roy et al. [20–22] use a Markov Decision Process instead to model possession sequences in which the policy reflects a team's historical action behavior. These models can be used to measure the effect of adjusting this behavior, to reason about defensive strategies, and to value a player's decision making. Markov models are also used in other sports. An example is the valuation of player actions in the National Hockey League using a model representing ice hockey games [13,15].

6   Conclusion

This paper proposed a novel approach to carry out playing style analysis. Instead of carrying out data analysis based directly on historical data, it first learns an intermediate team-specific Markov chain representing the offensive behavior of a team. These models can both capture the sequential patterns of a team's style as well as generalize over a team's historical behavior. That is, they capture slight variations on the playing style of teams, even when these are not explicitly observed in the limited amount of data. Additionally, we defined a number of features that characterize playing style and showed how analytical approaches and probabilistic model checking can be used to reason about each team's learned model to obtain values for these features. We illustrated our approach on teams in the 2019/20 English Premier League and showed how our approach can be used to 1) find teams with similar playing styles, 2) find inefficiencies in the playing style, and 3) perform an in-depth analysis of the playing style. The resulting insights can be used to guide coaches and managers when preparing for their next opponent or when scouting new players. Future work can propose more fine-grained models by including temporal information, additional states, and the intentions of actions, and by distinguishing between different action types.

Acknowledgements. This work was supported by the Research Foundation - Flanders under EOS No. 30992574. We thank the RBFA Knowledge Centre for their valuable feedback.

References

1. Bialkowski, A., Lucey, P., Carr, P., Yue, Y., Sridharan, S., Matthews, I.: Identifying team style in soccer using formations learned from spatiotemporal tracking data. In: IEEE International Conference on Data Mining Workshop, pp. 9–14 (2014)
2. Castellano, J., Aguilar Pic, M.: Identification and preference of game styles in Laliga associated with match outcomes. Int. J. Environ. Res. Publ. Health **16**(24), 5090 (2019)
3. Cho, H., Ryu, H., Song, M.: Pass2vec: Analyzing soccer players' passing style using deep learning. Int. J. Sports Sci. Coach. **17**(2), 355–365 (2021)
4. Decroos, T., Bransen, L., Van Haaren, J., Davis, J.: Actions speak louder than goals: Valuing player actions in soccer. In: Proceedings of the 25th ACM SIGKDD International Conference on Knowledge Discovery & Data Mining, pp. 1851–1861 (2019)

5. Decroos, T., Davis, J.: Player vectors. Characterizing soccer players' playstyle from match event streams. In: Joint European Conference on Machine Learning and Knowledge Discovery in Databases, pp. 569–584 (2019)
6. Decroos, T., Van Haaren, J., Davis, J.: Automatic discovery of tactics in spatio-temporal soccer match data. In: Proceedings of the 24th ACM SIGKDD International Conference on Knowledge Discovery & Data Mining, pp. 223–232 (2018)
7. Decroos, T., Van Roy, M., Davis, J.: Soccermix: Representing soccer actions with mixture models. In: Proceedings of the 2020 Joint European Conference on Machine Learning and Knowledge Discovery in Databases, pp. 459–474 (2020)
8. Diquigiovanni, J., Scarpa, B.: Analysis of association football playing styles: An innovative method to cluster networks. Statist. Model. **19**(1), 28–54 (2019)
9. Fernandez-Navarro, J., Fradua, L., Zubillaga, A., Ford, P.R., McRobert, A.P.: Attacking and defensive styles of play in soccer: Analysis of Spanish and English elite teams. J. Sports Sci. **34**(24), 2195–2204 (2016)
10. Kwiatkowska, M., Norman, G., Parker, D.: PRISM 4.0: Verification of probabilistic real-time systems. In: Gopalakrishnan, G., Qadeer, S. (eds.) CAV 2011. LNCS, vol. 6806, pp. 585–591. Springer, Heidelberg (2011). https://doi.org/10.1007/978-3-642-22110-1_47
11. Lago-Peñas, C., Gómez-Ruano, M., Yang, G.: Styles of play in professional soccer: An approach of the Chinese soccer super league. Int. J. Perform. Anal. Sport **17**(6), 1073–1084 (2017)
12. Peña, J.L.: A markovian model for association football possession and its outcomes. arXiv preprint arXiv:1403.7993 (2014)
13. Routley, K., Schulte, O.: A Markov game model for valuing player actions in ice hockey. In: Uncertainty in Artificial Intelligence Conference, pp. 782–791 (2015)
14. Rudd, S.: A framework for tactical analysis and individual offensive production assessment in soccer using Markov chains. In: New England Symposium on Statistics in Sports (2011). https://nessis.org/nessis11/rudd.pdf
15. Schulte, O., Khademi, M., Gholami, S., Zhao, Z., Javan, M., Desaulniers, P.: A Markov game model for valuing actions, locations, and team performance in ice hockey. Data Mining Knowl. Discov. **31**(6), 1735–1757 (2017)
16. Singh, K.: Introducing expected threat (2019). https://karun.in/blog/expected-threat.html
17. Van Der Maaten, L., Hinton, G.: Visualizing data using t-SNE. J. Mach. Learn. Res. **9**, 2579–2625 (2008)
18. Van Haaren, J., Dzyuba, V., Hannosset, S., Davis, J.: Automatically discovering offensive patterns in soccer match data. In: Proceedings of the 14th International Symposium on Intelligent Data Analysis, IDA, vol. 9385, pp. 286–297 (2015)
19. Van Haaren, J., Hannosset, S., Davis, J.: Strategy discovery in professional soccer match data. In: KDD-16 Workshop on Large-Scale Sports Analytics, pp. 1–4 (2016)
20. Van Roy, M., Robberechts, P., Yang, W.C., De Raedt, L., Davis, J.: Learning a Markov model for evaluating soccer decision making. In: RL4RealLife Workshop at ICML (2021)
21. Van Roy, M., Robberechts, P., Yang, W.C., De Raedt, L., Davis, J.: Leaving goals on the pitch: Evaluating decision making in soccer. In: Proceedings of the 15th Annual MIT Sloan Sports Analytics Conference (2021)
22. Van Roy, M., Yang, W.C., De Raedt, L., Davis, J.: Analyzing learned Markov decision processes using model checking for providing tactical advice in professional soccer. In: AI for Sports Analytics (AISA) Workshop at IJCAI (2021)
23. Yam, D.: Attacking contributions: Markov models for football (2019). https://statsbomb.com/2019/02/attacking-contributions-markov-models-for-football/

Recognizing Non-small Cell Lung Cancer Subtypes by a Constraint-Based Causal Network from CT Images

Zhengqiao Deng[1], Shuang Qian[1], Jing Qi[2], Li Liu[1(✉)], and Bo Xu[2,3]

[1] School of Big Data and Software Engineering, Chongqing University,
Chongqing 401331, China
{20161630,202024131068,dcsliuli}@cqu.edu.cn

[2] Department of Biochemistry and Molecular Biology, Key Laboratory of Cancer
Prevention and Therapy, National Clinical Research Center for Cancer, Tianjin's
Clinical Research Center for Cancer, Tianjin Medical University Cancer Institute
and Hospital, Tianjin 300060, China

[3] Center for Intelligent Oncology, Chongqing University Cancer Hospital,
Chongqing University School of Medicine, Chongqing 401331, China

Abstract. The primary goal of non-small cell lung cancer (NSCLC) recognition from CT images is to discover representative features, with each being responsible for NSCLC diagnosis. A key challenge in CT image feature selection is the fact that rich causal dependencies are often neglected among either radiomics or deep learning-based features. This leads us to present a constraint-based model to construct a causal network that explicitly discovers and leverages the inherent local causal variability of these deep and radiomics features under a global view. In particular, an identified network skeleton is generated to characterize a unique causal configuration of a particular NSCLC subtype as a variable number of nodes and links, and as a result, the resulting causal network satisfies the causal Markov property and all local cause-effect dependencies are globally consistent. Furthermore, a representative node selector is devised to select the most representative causal features from the causal network for NSCLC subtype recognition. Empirical evaluations on one benchmark dataset and one in-house dataset suggest our model significantly outperforms the state-of-the-art methods.

Keywords: Non-small cell lung cancer recognition · Constraint-based network · Cause-effect dependency · Feature selection

1 Introduction

Non-small cell lung cancer (NSCLC), a leading cause of cancer deaths all over the world, has different characteristics such as adenocarcinoma (ADC) and squamous

Supplementary Information The online version contains supplementary material available at https://doi.org/10.1007/978-3-031-26422-1_24.

cell carcinoma (SCC), and thus its subtype recognition has become an important research field, given its role in guiding the subsequent treatment for patients with lung cancer. The golden standard for NSCLC diagnosis is pathological diagnosis, which has not yet been fully elucidated and are commonly expensive and time-consuming. Although experienced doctors can make an initial diagnosis from radiographic data, there are still urgent needs for data-driven models that can detect different subtypes from CT images. Currently, these models can be divided into two categories: conventional models which are required to manually encode radiological features, and deep models which can automatically discover features from images. However, these image data generally has the properties of high-dimensional but small samples, which may bring about degradation in accuracy and efficiency of recognition model by curse of dimensionality and overfitting [8]. In addition, most features of CT images are unrelated to NSCLC subtypes and have no effect on their diagnosis or even have negative impacts. Therefore, feature selection is especially significant for the recognition of NSCLC subtypes [9].

Current techniques are becoming mature to select features. Here, a review [17] reports a repository of near 40 representative feature selection algorithms, which have been used in the field of radiomics, such as LASSO [2], PCA [2], RFE [27], mutual information [23] and other deep-based features. It is worth noting that these approaches commonly assume that features are independent without consideration of their causal relationships [10]. However, rich causal relations exist among radiological features in CT images with their unique values in cancer diagnosis [7,18]. For example, as illustrated in Fig. 1, it is known that *pleural tag* or *air bronchogram* is the cause of the NSCLC subtype *adenocarcinoma* in CT image-based detection. In fact, most of the existing data-driven models may find that there is a heavy correlation between *pleural tag* and *air bronchogram* but unfortunately cannot discover the further interpretation that the *adenocarcinoma* is the common effect of these two symptoms, which leads to their extrinsic association. As a result, it could be rather difficult to determine the significant factors, which is extremely important to NSCLC diagnosis because a wrong release of a patient can have bad consequences. The main focus of this paper is on causal discovery of features in CT images, since an important assumption for lung cancer diagnosis is the causal relationships between the radiological imaging data and cancer types [4].

Despite being a very challenging problem, there has been a rapid growth of interest in selecting causal features in recent years. The most popular modeling paradigm might be that of the graphical causal modeling, where the Bayesian network is the most commonly used structure in causal discovery that calculates the relationships of all features by constructing nodes (e.g., imaging features or NSCLC subtypes) and edges (i.e. their causal relations) as well as their joint probability distributions under certain constraints, often entailed by Markov blanket property. In a typical manner, they can be divided into two main categories, *score-based* models which maximize a score criterion to learn a causal network, and *constraint-based* models which use conditional independence and dependence constraints to discovery causal structures of observed variables [11]. However, imaging features are often not causally sufficient (i.e. there exist unobserved causes for two observed variables [26]). If without assuming causal sufficiency, score-based

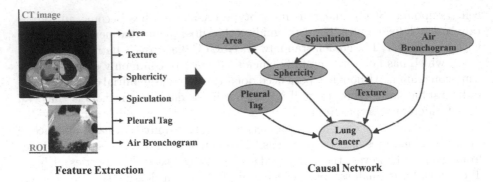

Fig. 1. An example of a causal network representing lung cancer and features of CT images.

models must require a predeterminate number of such latent variables, which is almost unavailable in CT images. In contrast, the constraint-based algorithms are more capable of handling the awkward situation of the lack of such prior knowledge. Moreover, constraint-based algorithms are more computationally efficient than score-based methods, which are NP-hard in terms of complexity [6].

In this work, we adopt a constraint-based model to discover causal features in CT images for NSCLC recognition. Normally, most of such models construct causal structures under Markov blanket property among features by leveraging exhaustively global search to learn from a complete graphical network. Unfortunately, the main challenge is their computational cost as the number of such relations and possible causal networks is super-exponential to the number of variables (i.e., node) [11]. In fact, checking Markov blanket consistency becomes intractable with the growth of network size. Besides, since Bayesian network structure is a directed acyclic graph, some highly correlated relations has to be removed from the network in order to maintain causal consistency, which nevertheless would result in information loss. For example, *air bronchogram* is the most relevant feature of *adenocarcinoma*, which is important in NSCLC diagnosis, but it cannot be identified as a causal variable by existing constraint-based approaches due to the Markov blanket inconsistency. Subsequently, these approaches are rather limited in identifying feature variables with meaningful cause-effect relationships between them in the network [5].

To address these aforementioned issues, we present a constraint-based causal network model for NSCLC subtypes recognition. Specifically, our model considers a principled way of discovering and applying causal relations of CT imaging features associated with NSCLC subtypes. In short, by generating from an identified network skeleton with highly correlated nodes (features) under the constraint of causal Markov property, a causal network is constructed to discover representative causal features from CT images. Note that the node set in the identified network is composed of both deep-based features and representative radiomics features. Now each resulting causal network contains its unique set of directed links that represent cause-effect relations, together with other commonly used radiomics features such as shape, texture and statistical information of the tumor lesion. Moreover, we design a *representative node selector* to choose the most representative causal features from the causal network for NSCLC subtype recognition. In this way, our causal network-based method is more capable of characterizing the inherit cause-effect dependencies of CT imaging features in a non-invasive NSCLC diagnosis when compared to existing approaches, which is also verified during empirical evaluations to be detailed in later sections.

2   Related Work

Existing approaches for NSCLC recognition can be divided into two categories.

2.1   Conventional Models with Radiomics Features

It is commonly known that conventional models can be adopted for diagnosis of lung cancer with radiomics features, which include high-throughput quantitative metrics from medical images related to tumor pathobiology and the creation of minable high dimensional database [13,14,19]. Since radiomics data contains a large number of features describe intensity distribution, spatial relationships between the various intensity levels, texture heterogeneity patterns, shape and the relations of the tumour with the surrounding tissues, it is necessary to apply feature selection to eliminate redundant features that are not relevant to the label [15]. Wang et al. [22] compared the performance of several conventional machine learning methods in predicting the prognostic recurrence of NSCLC using PCA to select features. Zhu et al. [28] successfully performed a radiomics analysis with LASSO logistic model to distinguish ADCs from SCCs. Han et al. [12] evaluated ten feature selection techniques as well as ten conventional models for NSCLC classification. These studies demonstrated that the manually encoded radiological features are capable of characterizing properties as potential biomarkers for recognizing NSCLC subtypes. However, such features are normally hand-coded or defined based on domain knowledge, which would be not practicable since tumor pathobiology in NSCLC is not completely elucidated and its corresponding radiomics images are often intricate. Moreover, the causal relationships between features cannot be exploited by these conventional methods, leading to the significant information loss.

2.2   Deep Model-Based Recognition from Raw CT Images

Different from conventional models, deep models have been at the forefront of this research field, which can automatically quantify radiographic characteristics of tumor and its surroundings without handcraft from CT images for NSCLC diagnosis. Among them, CNNs have achieved excellent performance, and not surprisingly an increasing amount of CNN-based variants are presented in CT image-based classification. These algorithms provide a great aid in the diagnosis of lung cancer, including segmentation of the lung and tumor area, prediction of invasiveness and survival analysis, etc. [20,21,24]. Aonpong et al. [3] found that the deep models such as ResNet can achieve better result in the diagnosis of NSCLC compared to conventional models using radiomics features. However, deep models only take raw CT images as input, which are limited to manage radiomics information such as texture, shape and density. Several recent studies attempted to merge such radiomics features in deep models instead of merely using CT images. Han et al. [12] designed a fusion algorithm that can combine radiomic and deep-based features to help radiologists to differentiate the subtypes of NSCLC via PET/CT images. Aonpong et al. [2] embedded selected radiomics features in a deep network for recurrence prediction of NSCLC. It was shown that these fusion models can achieve better performance than deep models that use raw images alone. However, a major limitation of these deep models concerns that the relationships that are learned from raw images are often hard to understand by human beings, which are extremely crucial in cancer diagnosis. In addition, they usually lack the expressive power to characterize and propagate rich causal dependencies in NSCLC recognition, and thus they are limited to capture the inherent causal variability of radiological image features in a global view. To address the issues, we present a constraint-based causal network to discover and utilize the cause-effect relations of both radiomics features and deep features extracted from CT images to discriminate NSCLC subtypes.

3   Preliminaries

3.1   Data Acquisition

In this study two NSCLC datasets are considered, including one in-house dataset and one publicly-available benchmark dataset.

A public dataset named NSCLC-Radiomics-Lung (P-NSCLC) [1], which includes 422 NSCLC patients is used in this study. It contains CT images with manually segmented gross tumor volumes and contour annotations for each patient. A number of 203 patients were eventually selected in our study (51 patients were diagnosed with ADC, and 152 patients were diagnosed with SCC).

To our best knowledge, the above mentioned dataset is so far the only ones publicly available for the field of NSCLC recognition. To this end, we propose a new NSCLC dataset (named I-NSCLC) collected from a hospital between May 2018 and September 2019, which includes 466 NSCLC patients' computed tomography scans. The inclusion criteria were as follows: (1) Patients were diagnosed with a primary NSCLC subtype, i.e., ADC or SCC; (2) Patients received no treatment before pathological diagnosis; (3) Patients were considered with available thoracic enhanced CT images. In the entire dataset, 368 patients were diagnosed with ADC, and 98 patients were diagnosed with SCC. The collected CT images are consecutive thoracic series in *digital imaging and communications in medicine* (DICOM) format. The corresponding CT system we used in this study is a 64-channel multi-detector CT scanning system (64-slice Light-Speed VCT, GE Medical Systems, Milwaukee, WI, USA), with the same scanning parameters (120 kV; 400 mAs; detector coverage: 40 mm; rotation time: 0.6 s; matrix size: 512 × 512). A subset of samples are provided in the supplementary material, and once ready we plan to share the entire dataset in the community.

3.2 CT Image Preprocessing

All the CT images of the enrolled patients in both the in-house and public-available NSCLC dataset were manually annotated by an experienced radiologist using ITK-snap software using a standard clinical delineation protocol. Each single CT image was checked for delineating the corresponding tumor solid lesions. Then regions of interest (ROI) of those patients were stored separately as the mask information of the original CT image.

For each raw CT image, an intensity normalization was applied to rescale the pixel intensity to [0, 255]. Combined with the mask information, each CT image with tumor lesion was center cropped to 128 × 128 pixels. Radiomics features were extracted from the ROIs of the CT images. These features were divided into the following seven categories: 19 first order statistics features, 16 shape-based (3D) features, 10 shaped-based (2d) features, 34 gray level co-occurrence matrix (GLCM) features, 16 gray level run length matrix (GLRLM) features, 16 gray level size zone matrix (GLSZM) features and 14 gray level dependence matrix (GLDM) features. All the features were extracted from the raw CT images except for shape that are independent of gray value. For each raw image, a set of filters were leveraged to generate derived images, which could also be used for feature extraction. In particular, most of the features are consistent with the standard definitions as described by the *Imaging Biomarker Standardization Initiative* (IBSI) [29].

3.3 Problem Formulation

Given a NSCLC dataset $\mathcal{D}$ of N samples from a set of C subtypes, with each sample representing a patient consisting of a series of CT images of size $C \times W \times H$ (indicating channels, width and height, respectively) and a mask of tumor lesion. Each sample consists of M features extracted from patients' CT images and a corresponding NSCLC subtype. A causal network $\mathbf{G} = (\mathbf{X}, \mathbf{E})$ indicates the causal dependencies of a variable set (including NSCLC feature variable and label variable), where a node in $\mathbf{X}$ represents a variable and a link in $\mathbf{E}$ between any two nodes represents their causal relationship [25]. There are two types of link in $\mathbf{E}$: directed links ($\rightarrow$) and undirected links ($\leftrightarrow$) (can also be seen as two-way links). A directed link ($\rightarrow$) in $\mathbf{E}$ describes that the head node x_i is a direct cause of the tail one, denoted by $x_i \rightarrow x_j$, where $x_i, x_j \in \mathbf{X}$. An undirected link $x_i \leftrightarrow x_j$ means that there exist two Markov equivalence class of $\mathbf{G}$ containing $x_i \rightarrow x_j$ and $x_j \rightarrow x_i$ respectively, indicating a cause-effect relation between x_i and x_j with uncertain direction.

A causal network is a fully *completed partially directed acyclic graph* (i.e., its directed subgraphs does not contain a directed cycle) because causality is transitive, irreflexive and anti-symmetric. For any $\{x_i, x_j\} \in \mathbf{V}$, x_i and x_j are conditionally independent if there is a set of variables $\mathbf{X}' \subseteq \mathbf{X} \backslash \{x_i, x_j\}$ over the dataset $\mathcal{D}$ satisfying $P(x_i, x_j \mid \mathbf{X}', \mathcal{D}) = P(x_i \mid \mathbf{X}', \mathcal{D}) P(x_j \mid \mathbf{X}', \mathcal{D})$, denoted by $x_i \perp\!\!\!\perp x_j \mid (\mathbf{X}', \mathcal{D})$.

A causal network $\mathbf{G}$ must satisfy *causal Markov condition*. That is, give a node $x_i \in \mathbf{X}$ and its parents $\mathbf{Pa}(x_i)$, if x_i is not a cause of x_j, then x_i is conditionally independent of x_j given $\mathbf{Pa}(x_i)$, i.e., $x_i \perp\!\!\!\perp x_j \mid \mathbf{Pa}(x_i)$, where $x_j \in \mathbf{V} \backslash \{x_i, \mathbf{Pa}(x_i)\}$. There are three important structures on a triplet $\langle x_i, x_j, x_k \rangle$ in the causal network, *v-structure*, *chain* and *fork*, as illustrated in Table 1. The *d-separation* criterion captures exactly the conditional independence relationships that are implied by the Markov condition. Let $\mathbf{A}$, $\mathbf{B}$ and $\mathbf{C}$ be disjoint subsets of the nodes of $\mathbf{X}$. $\mathcal{P}$ is a acyclic path between node x_i and x_j, where $x_i \in \mathbf{A}$, $x_j \in \mathbf{B}$. We say $\mathcal{P}$ is *blocked* by the subset $\mathbf{C}$ if and only if (1) there is a *chain* $x_i \rightarrow x_k \rightarrow x_j$ or a *fork* $x_i \leftarrow x_k \rightarrow x_j$ such that $x_k \in \mathbf{C}$; or (2) $\mathcal{P}$ contains a *v-structure* $x_i \rightarrow x_k \leftarrow x_j$ and neither x_k nor any of its descendants are in $\mathbf{C}$. The causal networks constructed according to the conditional independence determined by *d-separation* are not unique, they are Markov equivalence classes of the real Bayesian network with the same skeleton and *v-structures*.

Table 1. Orientation rules in *d-separation*. Adj(nonAdj) means two nodes do(not) have a link

Structure	Probability	Definition
v-structure $x_i \rightarrow x_k \leftarrow x_j$	$P(x_k \mid x_i, x_j) = P(x_k \mid x_i) P(x_k \mid x_j)$	x_k is a common effect of x_i and x_j. x_k is called a *collider*
chain $x_i \rightarrow x_k \rightarrow x_j$	$P(x_k \mid x_i, x_j) = P(x_k \mid x_i)$	x_i is an indirected cause of x_k
fork $x_i \leftarrow x_k \rightarrow x_j$	$P(x_j \mid x_k, x_i) = P(x_j \mid x_i)$	x_k is a common cause of x_i and x_j

Generally, the constraint-based algorithms consist of two key steps to determine a causal network: (1) identifying the network skeleton (the candidate nodes and links); (2) orienting links as many as possible. Notice that we assume the node set $\mathbf{X}$ (observed variables) is causal sufficient, i.e., all the relevant features in the network have been observed and there is no unobserved common cause. A causal network characterizes the relationships between variable features and labels. This inspires us to present in what follows a constraint-based method where these networks can be systematically discovered to construct the final causal network characterizes the causal relationships among various radiomics and deep features for the NSCLC subtypes.

4   Our Model

To generate a causal network for histologic subtypes of NSCLC, two types of features (nodes) are considered in our model. That is, deep features are learned from a deep model while representative radiomics are selected as the nodes of the skeleton. A causal network is then generated by causal link orientation. Finally, the most important causal features are selected for the classification of NSCLC histologic subtypes. The main procedure of our approach is illustrated in Fig. 2.

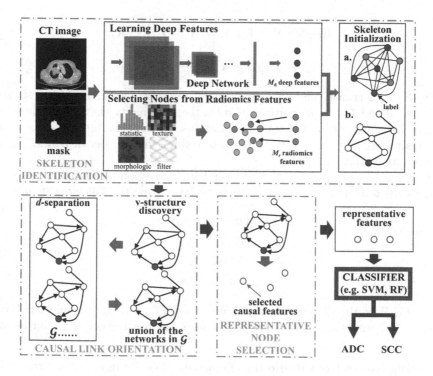

Fig. 2. The framework of our approach.

4.1   Skeleton Identification

To discover causal relationships between features using a constraint-based approach, a network skeleton consist of candidate nodes and links of the final causal network needs to be extracted first.

Learning Deep Features. A homogeneous deep model is constructed to extract deep features related to NSCLC subtypes from CT images automatically. It consists of two main components: convolution layer and residual block. First, a convolution layer is defined as:

$$\text{ConvLayer: } \boldsymbol{Y} = \mathsf{F}_c(\boldsymbol{A}) = \text{ReLu}(\mathbf{W} \cdot \text{BN}_{\gamma,\beta}(\text{Conv}(\boldsymbol{A}))), \tag{1}$$
$$\text{with } \text{Conv}(\boldsymbol{A}) : \boldsymbol{A} = (\mathbf{a}_1, ..., \mathbf{a}_{in}) \mapsto \boldsymbol{Y} = (\mathbf{y}_1, ..., \mathbf{y}_{out}),$$

where $\mathbf{W}$ is the corresponding weight vector of the ReLu function, γ and β are the internal parameters in the BatchNorm function. Conv is the convolution function with the sizes of the input channels in and output channels out. Note that $\mathbf{y}_c = \mathcal{K}_c^s * \boldsymbol{A}$ ($c = 1, ..., out$), where $\mathcal{K}_c^s$ is the c-th convolution kernel of the size s and $*$ is the convolution operator. Subsequently, a residual block is constructed as follows:

$$\text{ResBlk: } \boldsymbol{Y} = \mathsf{F}_r(\boldsymbol{A}) = \boldsymbol{A} + \sum_{i=1}^{Cad} \mathsf{F}_\mathcal{T}(\boldsymbol{A}), \tag{2}$$
$$\text{with } \mathsf{F}_\mathcal{T}(\boldsymbol{A}) = \mathsf{F}_c^3(\boldsymbol{A}),$$

where $\mathsf{F}_\mathcal{T}$ is a transformation including 3 *ConvLayers* with the kernel sizes of 1×1, 3×3 and 1×1 consecutively. *Cad* is the cardinality that is introduced to control the number of complex transformations. In this way, the split-transform-merge strategy is exploited in the block to reduce the number of parameters in an easy and extensive way.

Given a CT image $\mathcal{I} \in \mathbb{R}^{C \times W \times H}$ and its corresponding label c, our deep model aims to discover the deep features by leveraging the following structures:

$$\begin{aligned}
\mathcal{I}_1 &= \text{MaxPool}(\mathsf{F}_c(\mathcal{I})), \\
\mathcal{I}_2 &= \mathsf{F}_r^4(\mathcal{I}_1), \\
\mathbf{V}_{M_d} &= \mathsf{FC}(\text{GAP}(\mathcal{I}_2)), \\
c &= \text{softmax}(\mathsf{FC}(\mathbf{V}_{M_d})),
\end{aligned} \tag{3}$$

where GAP is the global average pooling and FC is a fully connected layer. Finally, $\mathbf{V}_{M_d}$ represents the vector of M_d deep features learned from our model.

Selecting Nodes from Radiomics Features. Now let us consider a radiomics feature set $\mathcal{R} = \{(s_1, c_1), ..., (s_i, c_i), ..., (s_N, c_N)\}$ where s_i is the i-th sample composed of R radiomics features denoted by $[s_{i1}, ..., s_{iR}]$, $c_i \in \{1, ..., C\}$ is its corresponding NSCLC subtype and N is the number of samples. Our goal is to find a weighting vector $\mathbf{w}$ that reflects the importance of each feature to the corresponding label. The weighting vector could be denoted as $\mathbf{w} = [w_1, ..., w_R]$, where w_r represent the importance weight of the r-th feature.

Here, the probability P_{ij} of s_i and s_j with the same NSCLC subtype can be defined as follows:

$$p_{ij} = \begin{cases} \frac{\mathcal{K}(d_\mathbf{w}(\mathbf{x}_i, \mathbf{x}_j))}{\sum_{k \neq i} \mathcal{K}(d_\mathbf{w}(\mathbf{x}_i, \mathbf{x}_k))}, & \text{if } i \neq j \\ 0, & \text{if } i = j \end{cases} \tag{4}$$

where $\mathcal{K}(z) = \exp\left(-\frac{z}{\sigma}\right)$ is a kernel function with a kernel width of σ and $\mathsf{d}_{\mathbf{w}}(s_i, s_j) = \sum_{r=1}^{R} w_r^2 |s_{ir} - s_{jr}|$ is a weighting distance function. To this end, the optimal radiomics feature weight vector $\hat{w}$ over dataset $\mathcal{R}$ can be computed:

$$\hat{\mathbf{w}} = \underset{\mathbf{w}}{\text{argmin}}\{\mathcal{L}(\mathbf{w}, \mathcal{R})\} = \underset{\mathbf{w}}{\text{argmin}} \left\{ \frac{1}{N} \sum_{i=1}^{N} \sum_{j=1, j \neq i}^{N} P_{ij} (1 - c_{ij}) + \lambda \sum_{r=1}^{R} w_r^2 \right\},$$

(5)

where $\lambda > 0$ is regularization parameter to alleviate overfitting, and $c_{ij} = 1$ when s_i and s_j are of the same class, otherwise $c_{ij} = 0$. A gradient based optimizer can be used to optimize the above objective function, such as delta-bardelta or conjugate gradients. It is worth noting that the larger the weight value in $\hat{w}$, the greater the importance it has in NSCLC classification task. We select top M_r features with the largest weight values as the skeleton nodes of radiomics features.

Skeleton Initialization. A complete undirected graph $\mathbf{G}_1 = (\mathbf{X}, \mathbf{E}_1)$ is constructed to initial the skeleton for causal link orientation, where $\mathbf{X}$ composed of M_d deep features nodes, M_r radiomics features nodes and their corresponding NSCLC subtype label, and $K = |\mathbf{V}| = M_d + M_r + 1$. Then, conditional independence test is performed for each edge $x_i \leftrightarrow x_j$ in the graph. x_i and x_j are not independent given any subset of nodes in $\mathbf{X}$ except x_i and x_j, i.e., $\mathbf{E}_1 = \{x_i \leftrightarrow x_j : \forall \mathbf{U} \subseteq \mathbf{V} \setminus \{x_i, x_j\}, x_i \not\perp x_j \mid \mathbf{U}\}$. In consequence, all links that with two conditionally independent nodes are removed from the graph to satisfy causal Markov condition.

4.2   Causal Link Orientation

Now we have a causal network skeleton $\mathbf{G}_1$ which is an undirected graph without any determined causal relation. We continue to direct the links in $\mathbf{G}_1$. First we construct a network $\mathbf{G}_2 = (\mathbf{X}, \mathbf{E}_2)$ by analyse the *v-structures* in $\mathbf{G}_1$. For any triplets $\langle x_i, x_j, x_k \rangle$ with the structure of $x_i \leftrightarrow x_k \leftrightarrow x_j$ in $\mathbf{E}_1$, if $\mathbf{E}_1$ dose not contain such a link $x_i \leftrightarrow x_j$ and x_k dose not belong to any subset $\mathbf{U} \subseteq \mathbf{V} \setminus \{x_i, x_j\}$ so that $x_i \perp\!\!\!\perp x_j \mid \mathbf{U}$, then we add the link $x_i \rightarrow x_k \leftarrow x_j$ to $\mathbf{E}_2$; otherwise, we still keep the undirected link $x_i \leftrightarrow x_k \leftrightarrow x_j$ in $\mathbf{E}_2$. After analysing all *v-structures* in $\mathbf{E}_1$, we get a partially directed acyclic graph $\mathbf{G}_1$, which satisfies causal Markov condition.

Next, we further orientate other undirected links in $\mathbf{G}_2$ according to the *d-separation* criterion, where if x_i and x_j are *d-separated* by x_k. then x_i and x_j are independent given x_k; otherwise, x_i and x_j are interdependent given x_k. Four orientation rules of the corresponding sub-graph are illustrated in Fig. 3. With these rules, we get a set of different networks $\mathcal{G}$ by orientating specific undirected links. These networks in $\mathcal{G}$ are Markov equivalent due to their same skeleton and same *v-structures*.

The final causal network $\mathbf{G} = (\mathbf{X}, \mathbf{E})$ is the union of the networks in $\mathcal{G}$, where a directed link $x_i \rightarrow x_j$ exists in $\mathbf{E}$ if and only if it exists in every network in $\mathcal{G}$,

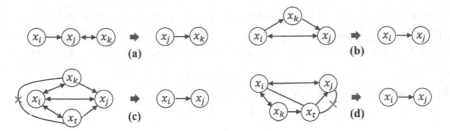

Fig. 3. Four types of orientation rules in *d-separation*. A red cross means there does not exist any link between the two nodes.

otherwise $x_i \leftrightarrow x_j$ remains in $\mathbf{E}$. Note that $\mathbf{G}$ is a completed partially directed acyclic graph representing a Markov equivalence class of $\mathcal{G}$ and thus satisfies causal Markov condition. Besides, the causal probability ξ_{ij} of any two nodes x_i and x_j can be calculated in term of standard deviations:

$$\xi_{ij} = \frac{\sigma^2_{a\mathbf{x}_i+b\mathbf{x}_j} - \sigma^2_{a\mathbf{x}_i-b\mathbf{x}_j}}{\sigma^2_{a\mathbf{x}_i+b\mathbf{x}_j} + \sigma^2_{a\mathbf{x}_i-b\mathbf{x}_j}}, \tag{6}$$

where $\sigma_{\mathbf{X}} = \sqrt{\mathrm{Var}(\mathbf{X})}$.

4.3   Representative Node Selection

To estimate the cause-effect level of each feature node on label node in the causal network $\mathbf{G}$, we introduce a representative node selector that estimates the regression coefficients [16] defined as follows:

$$\mathcal{L}_s\left(\mathbf{w}_s, \lambda_1, \lambda_2\right) = \|\mathbf{C} - \mathbf{S}\mathbf{w}_s\|_2^2 + \lambda_1 \|\mathbf{w}_s\|_1 + \lambda_2 \mathbf{w}_s^T \Phi \mathbf{w}_s, \tag{7}$$

where $\mathbf{w}_s = [w_{s1}, \ldots, w_{sK}]$ is a vector, referred as to causal weights, representing the cause-effect level of each feature node in $\mathbf{G}$. $\mathbf{S} \in \mathbb{R}^{N \times K}$ is a sample matrix from dataset $\mathcal{D}$ where its (i, m)-th entry is the m-th feature of i-th sample s_{im} and $\mathbf{C} \in \mathbb{R}^N$ is its corresponding vector of labels of the NSCLC subtypes. $\Phi \in \mathbb{R}^{K \times K}$ is a Laplacian matrix for the network $\mathbf{G}$ with the (i, j)-th element defined by:

$$\Phi_{ij} = \begin{cases} 1/\deg_i, & \text{if } i = j \text{ and } \deg_i \neq 0 \\ -\xi_{ij}/\sqrt{\deg_i \deg_j}, & \text{if } \mathrm{Adj}\,(x_i, x_j) \in \mathbf{E} \\ 0, & \text{otherwise,} \end{cases} \tag{8}$$

where $\deg_i = \sum_{\mathrm{Adj}(x_i, x_k) \in \mathbf{E}} \xi_{ik}$ and $\mathrm{Adj}\,(x_i, x_k)$ means that there exists a link between the two nodes. The first term in $\mathcal{L}_s$ only seeks to minimize regression errors by regrading each node (variable) individually. The last term considers the coefficient and correlation of two neighboring variables having cause-effect relations. The tuning parameters λ_1, λ_2 control the amount of regularization for sparsity and smoothness, respectively.

Now we are ready to evaluate the causal weights by minimizing the following function using the sparse Laplacian shrinkage with the graphical Lasso estimator:

$$\widehat{\mathbf{w}}_s = \underset{\mathbf{w}_s}{\arg\min} \, \mathcal{L}_s\left(\mathbf{w}_s, \lambda_1, \lambda_2\right) = \left(\mathbf{C} - \mathbf{S}\mathbf{w}_s\right)^T \left(\mathbf{C} - \mathbf{S}\mathbf{w}_s\right) +$$

$$\lambda_1 \sum_i |w_{si}| + \lambda_2 \sum_{\mathrm{Adj}(x_i, x_j) \in \mathbf{E}} \left(\frac{w_{si}}{\sqrt{\deg_i}} - \frac{w_{sj}}{\sqrt{\deg_j}}\right)^2 \xi_{ij}. \tag{9}$$

To recognize NSCLC subtypes, we select the features whose causal weight $\widehat{w}_s$ is greater than a threshold θ_1 as well as the features whose important weight $\widehat{w}$ is greater than a threshold θ_2.

5   Experiments

In our experiments, all the competing models for NSCLC histologic subtypes are evaluated over accuracy, sensitivity, specificity and area under the curve (AUC) of receiver operating characteristic (ROC). The accuracy measures the proportion of the correctly classified samples among the total tested samples. The sensitivity and specificity show the ability to correctly identify samples with ADC or with SCC. The AUC is employed to measure the quality of the model's predictions.

5.1   Comparison Results Against Other Competing Models

Three types of models for NSCLC classification have been taken into account in this part, i.e., five conventional classifiers merely using radiomics (LR, KNN, SVM, RF and GBDT), two deep models directly learning from raw CT images (VGG16 and ResNet) and two fusion models that combine the radiomics and deep features (ResNet_Fusion [2] and VGG16_Fusion [12]). Table 2 shows the accuracy, sensitivity, specificity and AUC performance. Our approach clearly outperforms other NSCLC classification methods on both datasets with a more stable performance with around 2% − 20% boost. This is mainly due to our approach utilized a combination of deep and radiomics features to generate the causal skeleton and subsequently take advantage of the causal-effect dependency information. Also, it is obvious that the two fusion models that merge deep network (for image features) and conventional models (for radiomics features) have better performance than either of them. This might explain why our approach achieves the best performance by a large margin with nearly 20% boost at most compared with LR on I-NSCLC dataset where a large number of features exist but only a few causal features are discovered, which are extremely significant for NSCLC recognition.

Table 2. Performance of different models in NSCLC Classification. The value in the bracket shows the metric change taken our model as a baseline.

Dataset	Method	Metrics (%)			
		Accuracy	Sensitivity	Specificity	AUC
P-NSCLC	LR	74.5(−9.1)	76.9(−7.7)	70.6(−12.6)	76.8(−8.9)
	KNN	75.9(−7.7)	78.3(−6.3)	68.6(−14.6)	77.5(−8.2)
	SVM	70.8(−12.8)	72.4(−12.2)	66.7(−16.5)	74.6(−11.1)
	RF	74.2(−9.4)	76.3(−8.3)	68.8(−14.4)	76.1(−9.6)
	GBDT	72.1(−11.5)	73.7(−10.9)	70.6(−12.6)	75.4(−10.3)
	VGG16	76.5(−7.1)	80.3(−4.3)	65.9(−17.3)	78.3(−7.4)
	ResNet	79.4(−4.2)	81.4(−3.2)	73.8(−9.4)	82.5(−3.2)
	VGG16_Fusion	78.8(−4.8)	80.2(−4.4)	75.1(−8.1)	80.2(−5.5)
	ResNet_Fusion	81.7(−1.9)	82.5(−2.1)	79.7(−3.5)	83.3(−2.4)
	Ours	**83.6**	**84.6**	**83.2**	**85.7**
I-NSCLC	LR	86.9(−3.5)	70.1(−19.9)	91.3(+0.8)	90.0(−2.1)
	KNN	86.1(−4.3)	84.2(−5.8)	86.4(−4.1)	86.3(−5.8)
	SVM	85.2(−5.2)	82.7(−7.3)	86.0(−4.5)	87.5(−4.6)
	RF	86.9(−3.5)	86.5(−3.5)	88.7(−1.8)	90.9(−1.2)
	GBDT	88.7(−1.7)	73.9(−16.1)	92.3(+1.8)	90.0(−2.1)
	VGG16	85.9(−4.5)	77.3(−12.7)	89.1(−1.4)	88.6(−3.5)
	ResNet	87.1(−3.3)	73.9(−16.1)	92.3(+1.8)	90.6(−1.5)
	VGG16_Fusion	88.9(−1.5)	72.2(−17.8)	96.5(+6.0)	90.1(−2.0)
	ResNet_Fusion	87.7(−2.7)	78.9(−11.1)	90.1(−0.4)	90.9(−1.2)
	Ours	**90.4**	**90.0**	**90.5**	**92.1**

5.2 Comparison Results Against Other Radiomics Feature Selection Approaches

To further explore the role of constraint-based method on feature selection, we compared the performance of four commonly used feature selection approaches in radiomics (i.e., LASSO, RFE, PCA, MI) [2,23,27]. Since the features selected by these approaches including ours can be employed in arbitrary classifiers. They were evaluated in several individual classifiers. The results are reported in Fig. 4. Overall, the constraint-based model outperforms other conventional approaches as being capable to capture causal features. This is mainly because the other approaches are greatly affected by outliers, including confounding factors and hidden variables, which often appear in medical datasets. Note that other approaches mainly consider the correlation between features, while ignoring those causal relationships. In addition, it can be seen that the samples generated by our approach are more classifier-agnostic than those of other approaches, which can be adopted by various classifiers. Theoretically, the time complexity of our model is $O(K^3 + NK^2) + O(N^2 RM_r) + O_{df}$, where the first value represents the complexity of causal network construction, while the latter two values indicate the complexity of radiomics feature selection and deep feature learning, respectively, and thus it is affordable for practical usage in NSCLC recognition.

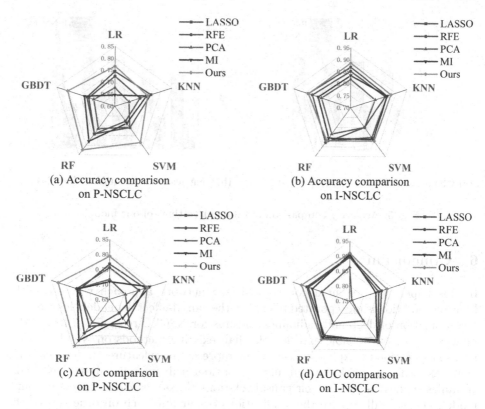

Fig. 4. Accuracy and AUC comparison against other feature selection methods.

5.3 Ablation Study

In this section, we conducted ablation studies to measure the effectiveness of the modules in our model. We evaluate the impact of the respective sizes of deep and radiomics feature nodes in the network skeleton on causal relation discovery and final classification performance. As shown in Fig. 5, it is clear that the combination of both types of features can achieve better classification performance than merely the usage of either of them. It is worth noting that $M_d = 0$ (*resp.* $M_r = 0$) represents that the skeleton is completely composed of radiomics features (*resp.* deep features). There is an improvement in accuracy when M_d and M_r grow to 32 and 24 on I-NSCLC, respectively. Similarly, it can be seen that the best setting on P-NSCLC is $M_d = 24$ and $M_r = 24$. In addition, a large value of M_d and M_r will bring about a very complicated network structure with a great number of nodes (features), which results in a huge computational complexity.

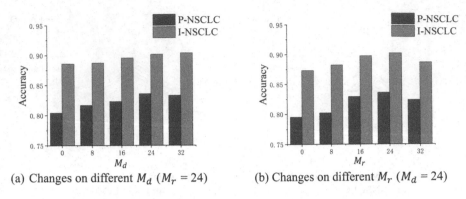

(a) Changes on different M_d ($M_r = 24$)   (b) Changes on different M_r ($M_d = 24$)

Fig. 5. Accuracy comparison of different settings of our model.

6 Conclusion

In this paper, we present a constraint-based network approach where causal Markov condition is incorporated to exploit the causal-effect dependencies among a combination of deep and radiomics features for NSCLC recognition from CT images. It is more reliable and flexible than existing methods on NSCLC sub-type classification by explicitly discovering representative features under a causal view. As for future work, we will further consider utilizing not only the selected variables (nodes) but also their causal relations (links) as features to train our model, and we will explore the applications of our approach on other types of cancers.

Acknowledgements. This work was supported by grants from the National Major Science and Technology Projects of China (grant no. 2018AAA0100703), the National Natural Science Foundation of China (grant nos. 61977012, 61977054), the Central Universities in China (grant no. 2021CDJYGRH011).

References

1. Aerts, H.J., et al.: Decoding tumour phenotype by noninvasive imaging using a quantitative radiomics approach. Nat. Commun. **5**(1), 1–9 (2014)
2. Aonpong, P., Iwamoto, Y., Han, X.H., Lin, L., Chen, Y.W.: Genotype-guided radiomics signatures for recurrence prediction of non-small cell lung cancer. IEEE Access **9**, 90244–90254 (2021)
3. Aonpong, P., Iwamoto, Y., Wang, W., Lin, L., Chen, Y.-W.: Hand-crafted and deep learning-based radiomics models for recurrence prediction of non-small cells lung cancers. In: Chen, Y.-W., Tanaka, S., Howlett, R.J., Jain, L.C. (eds.) Innovation in Medicine and Healthcare. SIST, vol. 192, pp. 135–144. Springer, Singapore (2020). https://doi.org/10.1007/978-981-15-5852-8_13
4. Castro, D.C., Walker, I., Glocker, B.: Causality matters in medical imaging. Nat. Commun. **11**(1), 1–10 (2020)

5. Chaudhary, M.S., et al.: Causality-guided feature selection. In: Li, J., Li, X., Wang, S., Li, J., Sheng, Q.Z. (eds.) ADMA 2016. LNCS (LNAI), vol. 10086, pp. 391–405. Springer, Cham (2016). https://doi.org/10.1007/978-3-319-49586-6_26

6. Coumans, V., Claassen, T., Terwijn, S.: Causal discovery algorithms and real world systems. Ph.D. thesis, Masters thesis (2017)

7. Debbi, H.: Causal explanation of convolutional neural networks. In: Oliver, N., Pérez-Cruz, F., Kramer, S., Read, J., Lozano, J.A. (eds.) ECML PKDD 2021. LNCS (LNAI), vol. 12976, pp. 633–649. Springer, Cham (2021). https://doi.org/10.1007/978-3-030-86520-7_39

8. Duangsoithong, R., Phukpattaranont, P., Windeatt, T.: Bootstrap causal feature selection for irrelevant feature elimination. In: The 6th 2013 Biomedical Engineering International Conference, pp. 1–5. IEEE (2013)

9. Fan, X., Wang, Y., Tang, X.Q.: Extracting predictors for lung adenocarcinoma based on granger causality test and stepwise character selection. BMC Bioinformatics **20**(7), 83–96 (2019)

10. Feng, X., et al.: Selecting multiple biomarker subsets with similarly effective binary classification performances. JoVE (J. Visual. Exp.) **140**, e57738 (2018)

11. Guo, R., Cheng, L., Li, J., Hahn, P.R., Liu, H.: A survey of learning causality with data: Problems and methods. ACM Comput. Surv. (CSUR) **53**(4), 1–37 (2020)

12. Han, Y., et al.: Histologic subtype classification of non-small cell lung cancer using pet/CT images. Eur. J. Nucl. Med. Molecul. Imaging **48**(2), 350–360 (2021)

13. Kumar, V., et al.: Radiomics: The process and the challenges. Magnet. Resonan. Imaging **30**(9), 1234–1248 (2012)

14. Lambin, P., et al.: Radiomics: The bridge between medical imaging and personalized medicine. Nat. Rev. Clin. Oncol. **14**(12), 749–762 (2017)

15. Lambin, P., et al.: Radiomics: Extracting more information from medical images using advanced feature analysis. Eur. J. Cancer **48**(4), 441–446 (2012)

16. Li, C., Li, H.: Variable selection and regression analysis for graph-structured covariates with an application to genomics. Ann. Appl. Stat. **4**(3), 1498 (2010)

17. Li, J., et al.: Feature selection: A data perspective. ACM Comput. Surv. **50**(6), 1–45 (2017)

18. Raghu, V.K., et al.: Feasibility of lung cancer prediction from low-dose CT scan and smoking factors using causal models. Thorax **74**(7), 643–649 (2019)

19. Shayesteh, S., et al.: Treatment response prediction using MRI-based pre-, post-, and delta-radiomic features and machine learning algorithms in colorectal cancer. Med. Phys. **48**(7), 3691–3701 (2021)

20. Shaziya, H., Shyamala, K., Zaheer, R.: Automatic lung segmentation on thoracic CT scans using u-net convolutional network. In: 2018 International Conference on Communication and Signal Processing (ICCSP), pp. 0643–0647. IEEE (2018)

21. Wang, X., et al.: Predicting the invasiveness of lung adenocarcinomas appearing as ground-glass nodule on CT scan using multi-task learning and deep radiomics. Transl. Lung Cancer Res. **9**(4), 1397 (2020)

22. Wang, X., Duan, H.H., Nie, S.D.: Prognostic recurrence analysis method for non-small cell lung cancer based on CT imaging. In: 2019 International Conference on Image and Video Processing, and Artificial Intelligence, vol. 11321, p. 113211T. International Society for Optics and Photonics (2019)

23. Wang, Y., et al.: Comparison study of radiomics and deep learning-based methods for thyroid nodules classification using ultrasound images. IEEE Access **8**, 52010–52017 (2020)

24. Wu, Y., Ma, J., Huang, X., Ling, S.H., Su, S.W.: Deepmmsa: A novel multimodal deep learning method for non-small cell lung cancer survival analysis. In: 2021 IEEE International Conference on Systems, Man, and Cybernetics (SMC), pp. 1468–1472. IEEE (2021)
25. Yan, X., Liao, J., Luo, H., Zhang, Y., Liu, L.: Predicting cancer risks by a constraint-based causal network. In: 2020 IEEE International Conference on Multimedia and Expo (ICME), pp. 1–6. IEEE (2020)
26. van der Zander, B., Liśkiewicz, M., Textor, J.: Separators and adjustment sets in causal graphs: Complete criteria and an algorithmic framework. Artif. Intell. **270**, 1–40 (2019)
27. Zhang, Y., et al.: Radiomics analysis for the differentiation of autoimmune pancreatitis and pancreatic ductal adenocarcinoma in 18f-fdg pet/ct. Med. Phys. **46**(10), 4520–4530 (2019)
28. Zhu, X., et al.: Radiomic signature as a diagnostic factor for histologic subtype classification of non-small cell lung cancer. Eur. Radiol. **28**(7), 2772–2778 (2018)
29. Zwanenburg, A., Leger, S., Vallières, M., Löck, S.: Image biomarker standardisation initiative. arXiv preprint arXiv:1612.07003 (2016)

Detection of ADHD Based on Eye Movements During Natural Viewing

Shuwen Deng[1]($\boxtimes$), Paul Prasse[1], David R. Reich[1], Sabine Dziemian[2],
Maja Stegenwallner-Schütz[1,3], Daniel Krakowczyk[1], Silvia Makowski[1],
Nicolas Langer[2], Tobias Scheffer[1], and Lena A. Jäger[1,4]

[1] Department of Computer Science, University of Potsdam, Potsdam, Germany
shuwen.deng@uni-potsdam.de
[2] Department of Psychology, University of Zurich, Zurich, Switzerland
[3] Department of Inclusive Education, University of Potsdam, Potsdam, Germany
[4] Department of Computational Linguistics, University of Zurich, Zurich, Switzerland

Abstract. Attention-deficit/hyperactivity disorder (ADHD) is a neurodevelopmental disorder that is highly prevalent and requires clinical specialists to diagnose. It is known that an individual's viewing behavior, reflected in their eye movements, is directly related to attentional mechanisms and higher-order cognitive processes. We therefore explore whether ADHD can be detected based on recorded eye movements together with information about the video stimulus in a free-viewing task. To this end, we develop an end-to-end deep learning-based sequence model which we pre-train on a related task for which more data are available. We find that the method is in fact able to detect ADHD and outperforms relevant baselines. We investigate the relevance of the input features in an ablation study. Interestingly, we find that the model's performance is closely related to the content of the video, which provides insights for future experimental designs.

Keywords: ADHD detection · Eye movements · Free-viewing · Deep learning · Deep sequence models

1 Introduction

Attention-deficit/hyperactivity disorder (ADHD) is one of the most common neurodevelopmental disorders of childhood affecting approximately 5 to 13 percent of the children of an age cohort, depending on the diagnostic procedure used [26,37,42]. ADHD is characterized by persistent inattention, high levels of hyperactivity, and impulsivity [2].

The diagnosis of ADHD requires clinical assessment by specialists and typically involves self- and informant reports through clinical interviews and the use of rating scales. Informant reports can be obtained from close family members, teachers, or partners, depending on the age of the candidate. Since the clinical assessment is heavily influenced by subjective reports and ratings, it also

M.-R. Amini et al. (Eds.): ECML PKDD 2022, LNAI 13718, pp. 403–418, 2023.
https://doi.org/10.1007/978-3-031-26422-1_25

incurs the risk to reflect social or cognitive biases. The *Strengths and Weaknesses of ADHD-Symptoms and Normal-Behavior (SWAN) rating scale* [36] is a well-established screening tool based on a questionnaire that has to be filled out by parents or teachers. The SWAN scale registers symptoms of inattention, hyperactivity, and impulsivity yielding the so-called SWAN score. Specifically, the SWAN rating scale probes behaviors according to the full spectrum of symptom severity, which ranges from functionality to dysfunctionality [5,36].

The lack of comprehensive, objective assessment tools, developmental changes in the presentation of symptoms [4], and the high rates of co-morbidities [2] present a major challenge to ADHD assessment and ultimately increases the risk of under- or overdiagnosis. While a false negative can lead to the denial of treatment, a false positive can lead to inappropriate treatment, both of which may have detrimental effects on an individual's ability to function at school, professionally and socially as well as on their overall well-being. This motivates the development of fully automatic screening tools that can be applied at large to people at-risk or with a suspicion of having ADHD, thereby increasing the accessibility of ADHD screening opportunities as well as the objectivity of the screening method prior to specialist assessment.

Eye movements can be classified into so-called oculomotor events. These include fixations ($\approx$200–300 ms), during which the eye is relatively still and visual information is obtained, and saccades, which are fast relocation movements of the eye gaze between any two fixations ($\approx$30–80 ms) [12]. A sequence of fixations is referred to as a *scanpath*. As eye movements are known to reflect cognitive processes including attentional mechanisms [10,17], they are considered a *window on mind and brain* [40]. For several decades, they have been used as a gold-standard measure in cognitive psychology [27]. Researchers from the field of cognitive psychology typically treat eye movements as the dependent variable to investigate the effect of experimental manipulation of the stimulus and hence model it as the target variable. By contrast, more recent research has demonstrated the potential of treating eye movements as the independent variable (i.e., the model input) to infer the properties of the viewer. For example, it has been shown that eye-tracking data can be used to discriminate between different cognitive states [11], personal traits [13], or cognitive load [31]. A major challenge in using eye movements to make inferences about a viewer is the high degree of individual variability in the eye-tracking signal. The dominance of individual characteristics in the eye-tracking data explains why machine-learning methods for viewer identification perform very well [22,24], whereas models for other inference tasks typically perform at best at a proof-of-concept level or slightly above chance level. Another major challenge for the development of machine learning methods for the analysis of eye-tracking data is data scarcity. Since the collection of high-quality eye-tracking data is resource-intensive, only very few large data sets exist.

Differences in viewing behavior between individuals with and without ADHD have been found using eye-tracking tasks in which participants were required to make voluntary eye movements towards or away from a stimulus (so-called pro- or anti-saccade tasks) [18,25]. These findings motivate our approach of developing a screening tool that processes each individual's eye movements and simultaneously takes into account information about the visual stimulus.

The contribution of this paper is fourfold. First, we provide a new state-of-the-art model to detect ADHD from eye movements in a natural free-viewing task and evaluate the performance of this model and relevant reference methods on a real-world data set. Second, we provide an extensive investigation of the relevance of the different input features in i) an ablation study and ii) by computing feature importances. Third, we demonstrate that transfer learning bears the potential to overcome the problem of data scarcity in eye-tracking research. Last but not least, we release a preprocessed free-viewing eye-tracking data set for the detection of ADHD.

The remainder of this paper is structured as follows. Section 2 discusses related work and Sect. 3 lays out the problem setting. We develop a model architecture for the detection of ADHD in Sect. 4 and introduce the dataset in Sect. 5. In Sect. 6 we present the experimental findings while in Sect. 7, we discuss the results. Section 8 concludes.

2   Related Work

Machine learning methods have been applied for the purpose of ADHD detection to different types of diagnostic data; e.g., data of Conners' Adult ADHD Rating Scales [6], EEG signals [38], and functional Magnetic Resonance Imaging (fMRI) data [8] recorded in resting state. The rapid development of affordable eye-tracking hardware offers new possibilities for non-invasive, rapid, and even implicit screenings that do not have to rely on self-, parent-, or teacher reports. In the following section, we briefly review the work related to the use of machine learning methods with the purpose of identifying individuals with ADHD, with a particular focus on eye movement data.

ADHD detection has been conducted based on eye movements collected during different types of tasks, such as reading [7], a reading span task [14], or continuous performance tests [21]. These tasks impose certain requirements on the participants in order to ensure the validity of the measurement; e.g., participants need to have already acquired a certain level of reading skills or have to understand and comply with complex task instructions. Moreover, it has been shown that under instructed conditions, eye movements are less affected by the type of content (e.g., emotional content) that is displayed than in natural viewing [19]. In order to reduce such limitations, first attempts have been made to detect ADHD on the basis of their eye movements in task-free viewing. In contrast to previous methods, this approach bears the potential to be applied already to very young children, which, in turn, allows them to gain access to treatment from a young age onwards. Early identification and treatment are crucial for mitigating the development of ADHD and its negative long-term consequences on individuals' functioning and overall well being [15,28].

Galgani *et al.* [9] proposed three methods for ADHD detection through an image viewing task that they evaluated on participants with a comparatively wide age range (9–59 years). Among these methods, the best-performing approach is based on the Levenshtein distance. This method uses regions of interest (ROI)-based alphabet encoding, which transforms a sequence of fixations into a sequence of symbols by assigning symbols to different ROIs. To classify a new instance, they compute the Levenshtein distance of the corresponding symbol sequence to instances in the ADHD group and the control group. A smaller average distance to a group indicates greater similarity to that group, and thus the corresponding group label is assigned to the instance. While this approach takes into account the spatial information of the sequence of fixations, it fails to consider the temporal information of fixations; i.e., the fixation duration.

Instead of using a binary classifier for ADHD detection only, Tseng *et al.* [39] proposed a three-class classifier to differentiate between children with ADHD, children with fetal alcohol spectrum disorder, and control children, based on eye movements recorded during watching video clips of 15 min. They combined gaze features with visual saliency information of the stimulus computed with a saliency model. However, they rely on engineered features that aggregate the eye gaze events over time (e.g., median saccade duration or saccade peak velocity) at the cost of the sequential information in the eye gaze signal not being used.

More research has focused on using machine learning to detect other neurodevelopmental disorders [16,41]. For example, Jiang *et al.* [16] proposed to detect autism spectrum disorder (ASD) from eye-tracking data collected while viewing images, in which they used a neural network to explicitly model the differences in eye movement patterns between two groups. The main limitation of this method is that for each image only a fixed number of fixations are analyzed, which potentially causes information loss.

3   Problem Setting

We study the problem of ADHD detection. While watching a video, the eye gaze of the j-th individual is recorded as a sequence of fixations, denoted as $P_j = \{(x_1, y_1, t_1), \ldots, (x_M, y_M, t_M)\}$, where x_m, y_m are the m-th fixation location, t_m is the fixation duration, and M is the total number of recorded fixations. Provided a fixed video frame rate, we can use the temporal information to map the fixations to the corresponding video frames V, such that semantic information can be associated with eye-gaze. The training set consists of $\mathcal{D} = \{(P_1, V, c_1), \ldots, (P_J, V, c_J)\}$, where P_j and V represent the j-th individual's aligned fixation sequences and video frames, and c_j is the label for whether an individual has ADHD. The objective is to train a classifier that identifies individuals with ADHD, which is a binary classification problem.

By varying the decision threshold for a learned model, we can plot the receiver operating characteristic (ROC) curve of the true positive rates versus false-positive rates, and finally compute the area under the curve (AUC) which is the area under the ROC curve and is used as a quantitative indicator of classification performance. We use the AUC as the evaluation metric, which is insensitive to the uneven distribution of classes.

4   Method

In this section we introduce our model and the pre-training task used to initialize the weights for the final task of ADHD classification.

4.1   Model

We propose an end-to-end trained neural sequence model to classify gaze sequences as belonging to an individual with or without ADHD. Figure 1 shows an overview of our proposed method. We preprocess the raw eye-tracking, which consists of horizontal and vertical screen coordinates recorded with a sampling rate of 60 120 Hz into sequences of fixations using the Dispersion-Threshold Identification algorithm [29]. The model takes as input the eye gaze sequence (scanpath) and the video clip on which this scanpath has been generated.

Based on our review of the literature, we hypothesized that the eye gaze of individuals with ADHD interacts differently with the visual stimulus in comparison to typically developing controls. We therefore use saliency maps to highlight possible regions of interest in a scene. We use a state-of-the-art saliency model, DeepGaze II [20], to compute saliency maps for our video stimuli. DeepGaze II uses VGG-19 features that were trained on an object recognition task [34] and feeds them into a second network that is trained to predict a probability distribution of fixation locations on a given image.

For each video frame i of size (W, H), the pre-trained DeepGaze II model generates a saliency map $S^{(i)} \in \mathbb{R}^{H \times W}$. We then apply min-max normalization to transform $S^{(i)}$ to the range of $[0, 1]$. To extract the normalized saliency value of each fixation location, we create an extraction mask, $E_m^{(i)} \in \mathbb{R}^{H \times W}$, for the m-th fixation on the i-th video frame. More specifically, $E_m^{(i)}$ is generated by setting the fixation location to one and all other cells to zero. We then smooth the extraction mask with a Gaussian kernel (standard deviation $\sigma = 1.5°$) and normalize it. The Gaussian kernel is applied to account for the parafoveal information intake around the center of the fixation [12]. Eventually, the saliency value for the m-th fixation is given by:

$$s_m = \mathbf{1}_H \left(E_m^{(i)} \odot S^{(i)} \right) \mathbf{1}_W^T, \tag{1}$$

where $\odot$ is the Hadamard product and $\mathbf{1}_d$ is an all-ones row vector of dimension d. In case a fixation spans multiple frames, we use the central frame for the saliency computation. The extracted sequence of saliency values is concatenated with the fixation locations (represented in degrees of visual angle) and the fixation durations (see Fig. 1). Finally, we apply z-score normalization to each of these feature channels.

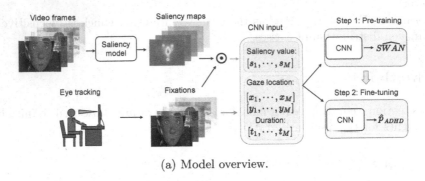

(a) Model overview.

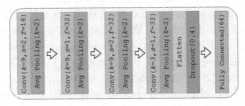

(b) Detailed view of the CNN.

Fig. 1. Proposed network architecture. Panel (a) shows the complete architecture and Panel (b) shows the 1D-CNN denoted as "CNN" in Panel (a). The model is pre-trained to predict the viewer's SWAN score (regression task) and fine-tuned for ADHD classification.

We then feed these feature channels into a 1D-convolutional neural network (CNN) to perform the ADHD classification. Panel (b) of Fig. 1 depicts the details of the CNN architecture. The CNN consists of four one-dimensional convolutional layers with rectified linear unit (ReLU) activation functions, followed by two linear fully-connected layers. We apply ReLU to the first layer and sigmoid to the last layer. Each convolutional layer is followed by a batch normalization layer and an average pooling layer with a pooling size of 2. The parameters k, s and f, specify the kernel size, the stride size, and the number of filters for the convolutions, respectively. A dropout layer with a rate of 0.4 is added before the first dense layer to prevent over-fitting. Finally, the neural network is optimized using the binary cross-entropy metric.

4.2   Pre-training

The number of data points from individuals with diagnosed ADHD and negatively-diagnosed controls in the dataset is limited. We therefore pre-train our model on a relevant task for which more data is available. Specifically, we pre-train our neural network on a regression task predicting an individual's SWAN score. An individual's SWAN score is highly relevant to the diagnosis of ADHD; using the SWAN score to classify individuals with and without ADHD yields an

AUC of 0.878 (standard error = 0.007). We therefore capitalize on the SWAN score to enable the model to detect ADHD-related patterns in the eye movements and perform pre-training on the *SWAN prediction dataset* (see Sect. 5 for details on the datasets).

For pre-training, we replace the sigmoid output unit with a linear output unit for the regression setting. We apply the mean squared error as loss function. The pre-trained weights are then used to initialize the ADHD classification model.

5   Datasets

The data for this study is part of the ongoing Healthy Brain Network (HBN)[1] initiative by the Child Mind Institute [1], establishing a biobank of multi-modal data of children and adolescents. The data analyzed here includes all participants of the HBN up to the 6th release. Participants from the 7th release were included if their data acquisition took place until the end of the season "Spring 2019".

Naturalistic Stimuli Paradigm. The tasks analyzed in this study include all free-viewing naturalistic stimuli paradigms of the test battery. Participants were shown four different age-appropriate videos with audio track: (1) an educational video clip (*Fun with Fractals*, 2:43 min), (2) a short animated film (*The Present*, 3:23 min), (3) a short clip of an animated film (*Despicable Me*, 2:50 min), and (4) a trailer for a feature-length film (*Diary of a Wimpy Kid*, 1:57 min). There were no instructions given for watching the videos. The order of the videos within the test battery was randomized for each participant except for *The Present* always being shown last.

Eye-Tracking. Monocular eye gaze data of the right eye was recorded with an infrared video-based eye tracker (iView-X Red-m, SensoMotoric Instruments [SMI] GmbH, spatial resolution: 0.1°, accuracy: 0.5°). The eye gaze was recorded at a sampling rate 60 Hz 120 Hz, depending on the testing site. In between each task, the eye tracker was calibrated using a 5-point grid.

Participants. The recruited participants were initially screened for having symptoms of any mental disorder. Clinical diagnoses were provided in accordance with the current edition of the Diagnostic and Statistical Manual of Mental Disorders (DSM-V) [2], and based on a consensus by multiple licensed clinicians. A total of 1,246 participants were included in the study, whose tracker loss was less than 10%. 232 participants (178 were male and 54 were female) with an age range of 6–21 years (mean age 9.97 years ± 3 years) were selected on the basis of having received an ADHD diagnosis (including the predominantly inattentive presentation, predominantly hyperactive-impulsive presentation, and combined presentation of ADHD) and having no past or current co-morbidity according

---

[1] https://healthybrainnetwork.org/.

to the DSM-V. These participants were assigned to the ADHD group. A group of 152 participants (71 were male and 81 were female) with an age range of 6–21 years (10.42 years ± 3.31 years) were assigned to the control group whose psychological assessment indicated no past or current presence of any mental disorder according to the DSM-V. All remaining 862 participants are included for hyperparameter tuning and pre-training the models. Hereafter, we refer to the subset of the data that contains recordings from the ADHD and control groups as *ADHD classification dataset* and the subset used for hyperparameter tuning and pre-training as *SWAN prediction dataset*. Note that for some participants recordings are available only from a subset of the four videos, as detailed in Table 1. In addition to the diagnostic assessment, SWAN scores for participants were obtained through the SWAN scale as a measure of ADHD-related symptom severity [36].

Table 1. Number of individuals in the data. Numbers in parentheses show the number of ADHD (A) and healthy controls (C).

Video	ADHD classification dataset	SWAN prediction dataset
Fun with Fractals	67 (48 A, 19 C)	276
The Present	159 (111 A, 48 C)	444
Despicable Me	315 (187 A, 128 C)	656
Diary of a Wimpy Kid	340 (202 A, 138 C)	736

6 Experiments

In this section, we describe the experiments we conducted to evaluate our proposed approach and compare it with relevant reference methods. The code and data are available online.[2]

6.1 Evaluation Protocol

We perform 10 resamplings of 10-fold cross-validation while splitting the data by individuals. That means we test the model on the gaze sequence of unknown individuals, while the video stimulus has already been seen during training. We use the same data splits for all models to ensure a fair comparison.

To evaluate the different models for different videos, we train a separate model for each video with and without pre-training. All neural network models are trained, using the Keras and Tensorflow libraries with the Adam optimizer on an NVIDIA A100-SXM4-40GB GPU.

---

[2] https://github.com/aeye-lab/ecml-ADHD.

6.2   Reference Methods

We compare our model with two relevant baseline methods. The first is the Levenshtein distance-based method proposed by Galgani *et al.* [9] (see Sect. 2). This method was originally intended for the image domain, which is not directly applicable to our video-based data. Therefore, instead of considering only the fixation sequences on a single image, we adapt it to a video-based classifier by calculating the Levenshtein distance based on the fixation sequences across the whole video.

Our second reference method is an approach proposed by Tseng *et al.* [39], in which a support vector machine (SVM) classifier is trained on aggregated engineered features extracted from eye gaze data collected while watching a 15-min video composed of 2–4 s unrelated clip snippets. Tseng *et al.* focuses on ADHD detection in young children only, while the data collected from young adults is used as a reference to compute group-based features. Due to the lack of young individuals in the control group, we are not able to compute these group-based features and thus exclude them in our implementation. Nevertheless, we implement all the remaining saliency- and gaze-based features and report the results of the model that is trained with recursive feature elimination as proposed by Tseng *et al.* [39]. To extract the saliency maps used by Tseng *et al.* we use the publicly available toolkit[3].

6.3   Hyperparameter Tuning

To find the optimal parameter setup for the architecture introduced in Sect. 4.1 we perform a random grid search using 5-fold cross-validation on the SWAN prediction dataset. Table 2 shows the search space for the parameters used during hyperparameter optimization where we restrict the kernel size of the convolutional layers to be less than or equal to the kernel size of the previous layer and the number of filters to be greater than or equal to the number of filters in the previous layer. Furthermore, the stride size is set to 1 when the kernel size is less than or equal to 5, and is restricted to be smaller than or equal to 2 when the kernel size is equal to 7. We use the data from the SWAN prediction dataset and predict the SWAN score to evaluate the stated hyperparameter configurations. The best performing configuration can be found in Fig. 1 and is used for all subsequent experiments.

6.4   Results

In Table 3, we present the evaluation results of our proposed models and the reference methods on all available videos. Except for the video *Diary of a Wimpy Kid*, our proposed method (with and without pre-training) performs significantly above chance level ($p < 0.05$). The best results are achieved for the video *Fun with Fractals*. With regard to this video, the model trained from scratch achieves

---

[3] http://ilab.usc.edu/toolkit/.

Table 2. Parameter used for hyperparameter optimization.

Parameter	Search space
# conv layers	{3, 4, 5, 6, 7, 8, 9}
Kernel size	{3, 5, 7, 9, 11}
# filters	{8, 16, 32, 64}
Stride size	{1, 2, 3}
# fully connected layers	{1, 2, 3}
# hidden units	{8, 16, 32, 64}
Dropout rate	{0.2, 0.3, 0.4, 0.5, 0.6}
Pooling layer type	{max pooling, average pooling}

an AUC of around 0.58, and the pre-training further increases the performance by around 10%. Also for the *Fun with Fractals* video, the results show that the proposed method with pre-training outperforms both baselines. The comparison between the four videos further shows that all methods except for the model by Galgani *et al.* [9] perform best on the *Fun with Fractals* video. This may indicate that certain properties of the stimulus video have an impact on how well the models can distinguish between individuals with ADHD and controls.

To characterize the differences between the videos, we extracted content-related features from each video which arguably quantify the video's degree of contingency [30]: scene cut frequency, the proportion of frames showing at least one face, and the total number of characters that appear in the video (see Fig. 2). The movie trailer *Diary of a Wimpy Kid* has a large number of character appearances, a higher proportion of frames showing faces, and more frequent scene transitions. This arguably renders the video more engaging also for the ADHD group, which, in turn, may make their viewing behavior similar to the control group. The educational video *Fun with Fractals*, by contrast, shows a low level of exciting content: The video mostly consists of relatively static scenes. According to the distinction between intact contingency-shaped and impaired predominantly self-regulatory processes of sustained attention among individuals with ADHD [3], their viewing behavior should be impacted by the video characteristics. Since the educational video contains less contingency, eye movements of individuals with ADHD may display more distinctive information for this video.

6.5   Ablation Study and Feature Importance

In this section, we investigate the impact of each input feature of the proposed model with pre-training (CNN@Pre-tr) on the performance of the four different videos (see Table 4). In a second experiment, we look into the distribution of attribution scores using the attribution method DeepLIFT [32], which is designed to explain model predictions.

Table 3. AUC values ± standard error for ADHD detection of the CNN model with (CNN@Pre-tr.) and without (CNN@Scratch) pre-training. Galgani *et al.* and Tseng *et al.* refer to our re-implementation and adaptation to the data of their proposed method (see Sect. 6.2). The asterisk * indicates that the performance is significantly better than random guessing. The dagger † shows models significantly worse than the best model.

Method	Fun with fractals	The present	Despicable me	Diary of a Wimpy kid
CNN@Scratch	0.583 ± 0.026*	0.553 ± 0.017*	0.55 ± 0.01*	0.486 ± 0.01
CNN@Pre-tr	**0.646 ± 0.025***	**0.554 ± 0.016***	0.544 ± 0.01*	0.503 ± 0.01
Galgani *et al.* [9]	0.33 ± 0.022†	0.526 ± 0.017	0.523 ± 0.012*	**0.515 ± 0.01**
Tseng *et al.* [39]	0.608 ± 0.023*	0.418 ± 0.015†	**0.561 ± 0.011***	0.465 ± 0.01

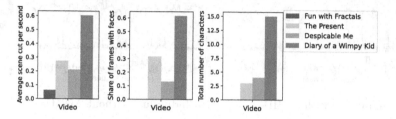

Fig. 2. Video features of different video stimuli.

Our proposed model consumes three different types of inputs: saliency, fixation duration, and fixation location. Table 4 shows the results for models trained without the saliency, fixation duration, and fixation location input in comparison to the model using all inputs. From Table 4 we can conclude that removing any of the input channels lowers the model's performance for the *Fun with Fractals* video. The drop in AUC is similar for each of the three components. Despite the drop in performance, we see that our model still outperforms both the model trained from scratch (CNN@Scratch) and the baseline models (see Table 3), which underlines the benefit of pre-training as well as the advantage of using multiple input channels. For the other three videos, we observe that removing one of the input channels does not have a systematic impact on the model's performance.

In the second set of experiments, we investigate the feature importance of each input channel. To this end, we employ the post-hoc attribution method DeepLIFT [32], which belongs to the family of reference-based attribution methods. For each model prediction, these methods explain the difference in model output with respect to a previously chosen reference input. The explanations are provided as attribution values for each input feature and quantify the relevance to the model output. The resulting attributions can then be interpreted as a computationally less expensive approximation of SHAP values [23]. Figure 3 displays two example instances for an individual with and without ADHD, respectively. These examples indicate that i) the attributions are spread relatively evenly over

Table 4. Results of the ablation study. The table shows AUC values ± standard error for our proposed model (CNN@Pre-tr.) trained with and without specific input features.

Model	Fun with fractals	The present	Despicable me	Diary of a Wimpy kid
Complete	**0.646 ± 0.025***	0.554 ± 0.016*	0.544 ± 0.01*	0.503 ± 0.01
w/o saliency	0.623 ± 0.026*	**0.556 ± 0.016***	**0.545 ± 0.01***	0.494 ± 0.011
w/o fix. duration	0.619 ± 0.027*	0.534 ± 0.016*	0.536 ± 0.011*	0.51 ± 0.01
w/o fix. location	0.622 ± 0.026*	0.551 ± 0.015*	0.542 ± 0.01*	**0.526 ± 0.009***

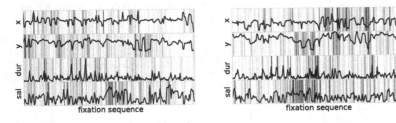

(a) Individual with ADHD.   (b) Individual without ADHD.

Fig. 3. Example attributions for individual instances (ADHD and control group). The black lines represent the values of the input channel labelled on the y-axis. Red background colors show attribution relevance for ADHD, blue background colors show attribution relevance for the control group. Dark colors represent a high relevance, light colors a low relevance. (Color figure online)

time and ii) the model uses all the available input channels. This is in line with our observation from the first part of the ablation study and confirms that all the input channels add valuable information.

To determine the overall importance of each input channel we compute attributions for all instances of the ADHD classification dataset. We take the absolute values of the attributions and normalize the attributions for each instance to the range from zero to one. Figure 4 depicts the resulting box plot grouped by channels and videos. For all videos, the saliency channel is attributed with the highest relevance overall. While for the videos *Despicable Me* and *Diary of a Wimpy Kid* the fixation location channels are about as relevant as fixation duration, the relevance is noticeably higher for the *Fun with Fractals* video. Fixation duration is among the lowest attributed channels for all four videos. Note that the attribution of the two individual positional channels for the fixation location will add up to more relevance when not treated individually.

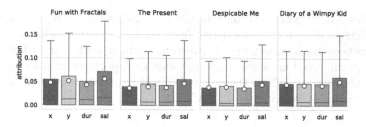

Fig. 4. Attribution box plot. Each video has a separate column with boxes for all four channels. Median value is represented by the horizontal black line in each box, mean value by the centered white dot. Whiskers are set to a 1.5 IQR value.

7 Discussion

Our proposed model achieves state-of-the-art results in the detection of ADHD from eye movements. We developed a deep neural network that integrates a sequential stimulus, a video clip, with the corresponding gaze sequence. In contrast to previous research, we do not aggregate the eye gaze sequence over time, but rather developed a sequence model, that processes the unaggregated scanpath together with the saliency information of the visual stimulus that is currently around the center of the visual field (parafoveal vision). Our investigation of feature attributions revealed that the unaggregated information in the data is indeed used by the model. We have further demonstrated the advantage of pre-training the model on a different task with additional data obtained from individuals diagnosed with other neurodevelopmental disorders. Whereas transfer learning approaches for *predicting* eye movements exist [35], to the best of our knowledge, this is the first transfer learning approach processing eye-tracking data as input. As the recording of eye-tracking data is resource-intensive, data scarcity poses a major challenge to the development of machine learning methods for the analysis of eye movements. Our work demonstrates that transfer learning approaches with pre-training on a different domain or a different task offers the potential to fully exploit the information that is available in eye-tracking data.

The task-free nature of the viewing setting allows us to interpret eye movements to reflect differences in visual attention allocation between individuals with and without ADHD [19]. With regard to clinical implications for ADHD-specific behavior, the model's successful prediction of ADHD group membership corroborates previous reports of distinctive eye movements displayed by individuals with ADHD in contrast to typically developing individuals. This interpretation is also supported by comparisons between the different videos. When comparing the model's performance for the different videos, we noted a substantial improvement for the educational *Fun with Fractals* video in comparison to the other three video clips. According to a distinction between intact contingency-shaped and impaired predominantly self-regulatory processes of sustained attention among individuals with ADHD [3], their viewing behavior should be impacted by the video characteristics. Since the educational video contains less contingency, eye movements from individuals with ADHD should exhibit a larger degree of dissimilarity from controls on this video. Our finding that differences in eye movements between individuals with and without ADHD are most pronounced on a less engaging video supports previous clinical findings [33], according to which the demand of self-regulatory functioning impacts the performance of individuals with ADHD.

8 Conclusion

We developed a neural sequence model that reaches state-of-the-art performance in the classification of viewers with and without ADHD based on their eye gaze on a given video stimulus. Our method is widely applicable for the analysis of eye gaze data: It can be applied to any inference task that uses eye movements and a static or moving visual stimulus as input. We have further demonstrated that the problem of data scarcity in eye-tracking research can be alleviated by pre-training on a different task for which more labeled data is available and by fine-tuning on the target setting. In conclusion, our method bears the prospective advantage of systematically exploiting eye movements in naturalistic settings for diagnostic purposes that includes, but is not limited to ADHD detection, and at the same time broadens our behavioral understanding of the disorder.

Acknowledgements. This work was partially funded by the German Federal Ministry of Education and Research (grant 01|S20043) and a ZNZ PhD grant.

References

1. Alexander, L.M.: An open resource for transdiagnostic research in pediatric mental health and learning disorders. Sci. Data **4**(1), 1–26 (2017)
2. American Psychiatric Association: Diagnostic and Statistical Manual of Mental Disorders, 5th edn. Arlington, VA (2013)
3. Barkley, R.A.: Behavioral inhibition, sustained attention, and executive functions: constructing a unifying theory of ADHD. Psychol. Bull. **121**(1), 65–94 (1997)
4. Biederman, J., Mick, E., Faraone, S.V.: Age-dependent decline of symptoms of attention deficit hyperactivity disorder: impact of remission definition and symptom type. Am. J. Psychiatry **157**(5), 816–818 (2000)
5. Brites, C., Salgado-Azoni, C.A., Ferreira, T.L.L., Lima, R.F., Ciasca, S.M.: Development and applications of the SWAN rating scale for assessment of attention deficit hyperactivity disorder: a literature review. Braz. J. Med. Biol. Res. **48**, 965–972 (2015)
6. Christiansen, H., et al.: Use of machine learning to classify adult ADHD and other conditions based on the Conners' adult ADHD rating scales. Sci. Rep. **10**(1), 1–10 (2020)
7. De Silva, S., et al.: A rule-based system for ADHD identification using eye movement data. In: MERCon 2019, pp. 538–543 (2019)
8. Deshpande, G., Wang, P., Rangaprakash, D., Wilamowski, B.: Fully connected cascade artificial neural network architecture for attention deficit hyperactivity disorder classification from functional magnetic resonance imaging data. IEEE Trans. Cybern. **45**(12), 2668–2679 (2015)

9. Galgani, F., Sun, Y., Lanzi, P.L., Leigh, J.: Automatic analysis of eye tracking data for medical diagnosis. In: IEEE CIDM 2009, pp. 195–202 (2009)

10. Henderson, J.M.: Human gaze control during real-world scene perception. Trends Cogn. Sci. **7**(11), 498–504 (2003)

11. Henderson, J.M., Shinkareva, S.V., Wang, J., Luke, S.G., Olejarczyk, J.: Predicting cognitive state from eye movements. PloS ONE **8**(5) (2013)

12. Holmqvist, K., Nyström, M., Andersson, R., Dewhurst, R., Jarodzka, H., Van de Weijer, J.: Eye Tracking: A Comprehensive Guide to Methods and Measures. Oxford University Press, Oxford (2011)

13. Hoppe, S., Loetscher, T., Morey, S.A., Bulling, A.: Eye movements during everyday behavior predict personality traits. Front. Hum. Neurosci. **12** (2018)

14. Jayawardena, G., Michalek, A., Jayarathna, S.: Eye tracking area of interest in the context of working memory capacity tasks. In: IEEE IRI 2019, pp. 208–215 (2019)

15. Jensen, P.S., et al.: Findings from the NIMH multimodal treatment study of ADHD (MTA): implications and applications for primary care providers. J. Dev. Behav. Pediatr. **22**, 60–73 (2001)

16. Jiang, M., Zhao, Q.: Learning visual attention to identify people with autism spectrum disorder. In: IEEE ICCV, pp. 3267–3276 (2017)

17. Just, M.A., Carpenter, P.A.: Eye fixations and cognitive processes. Cogn. Psychol. **12**(4), 441–480 (1976)

18. Klein, C., Raschke, A., Brandenbusch, A.: Development of pro- and antisaccades in children with attention-deficit hyperactivity disorder (ADHD) and healthy controls. Psychophysiology **40**(1), 17–28 (2003)

19. Kulke, L., Pasqualette, L.: Emotional content influences eye-movements under natural but not under instructed conditions. Cogn. Emot. **36**(2), 332–344 (2022)

20. Kummerer, M., Wallis, T.S., Gatys, L.A., Bethge, M.: Understanding low-and high-level contributions to fixation prediction. In: IEEE ICCV, pp. 4789–4798 (2017)

21. Lev, A., Braw, Y., Elbaum, T., Wagner, M., Rassovsky, Y.: Eye tracking during a continuous performance test: utility for assessing ADHD patients. J. Atten. Disord. **26**(2), 245–255 (2022)

22. Lohr, D., Griffith, H., Aziz, S., Komogortsev, O.: A metric learning approach to eye movement biometrics. In: IEEE IJCB 2020, pp. 1–7 (2020)

23. Lundberg, S., Lee, S.I.: An unexpected unity among methods for interpreting model predictions. arXiv preprint arXiv:1611.07478 (2016)

24. Makowski, S., Prasse, P., Reich, D.R., Krakowczyk, D., Jäger, L.A., Scheffer, T.: Deepeyedentificationlive: oculomotoric biometric identification and presentation-attack detection using deep neural networks. IEEE Trans. Biometrics Behav. Identity Sci. (2021)

25. Munoz, D.P., Everling, S.: Look away: the anti-saccade task and the voluntary control of eye movement. Nat. Rev. Neurosci. **5**(3), 218–228 (2004)

26. Polanczyk, G., De Lima, M.S., Horta, B.L., Biederman, J., Rohde, L.A.: The worldwide prevalence of ADHD: a systematic review and metaregression analysis. Am. J. Psychiatry **164**(6), 942–948 (2007)

27. Rayner, K.: Eye movements in reading and information processing: 20 years of research. Psychol. Bull. **124**(3), 372–422 (1998)

28. Rubia, K., Alegria, A., Brinson, H.: imaging the adhd brain: disorder-specificity, medication effects and clinical translation. Expert Rev. Neurother. **14**(5), 519–538 (2014)

29. Salvucci, D.D., Goldberg, J.H.: Identifying fixations and saccades in eye-tracking protocols. In: ETRA 2020, pp. 71–78 (2000)

30. Schwenzow, J., Hartmann, J., Schikowsky, A., Heitmann, M.: Understanding videos at scale: how to extract insights for business research. J. Bus. Res. **123**, 367–379 (2021)
31. Shojaeizadeh, M., Djamasbi, S., Paffenroth, R.C., Trapp, A.C.: Detecting task demand via an eye tracking machine learning system. Decis. Support Syst. **116**, 91–101 (2019)
32. Shrikumar, A., Greenside, P., Kundaje, A.: Learning important features through propagating activation differences. In: ICML 2017, pp. 3145–3153 (2017)
33. Silverstein, M.J., Faraone, S.V., Leon, T.L., Biederman, J., Spencer, T.J., Adler, L.A.: The relationship between executive function deficits and DSM-5-defined ADHD symptoms. J. Atten. Disord. **24**, 41–51 (2020)
34. Simonyan, K., Zisserman, A.: Very deep convolutional networks for large-scale image recognition. In: International Conference on Learning Representations (ICLR) (2015)
35. Sood, E., Kögel, F., Müller, P., Thomas, D., Bace, M., Bulling, A.: Multimodal integration of human-like attention in visual question answering. arXiv 2109.13139 (2021)
36. Swanson, J.M., et al.: Categorical and dimensional definitions and evaluations of symptoms of ADHD: history of the SNAP and the SWAN rating scales. Int. J. Educ. Psychol. Assess. **10**(1), 51 (2012)
37. Thomas, R., Sanders, S., Doust, J., Beller, E., Glasziou, P.: Prevalence of attention-deficit/hyperactivity disorder: a systematic review and meta-analysis. Pediatrics **135**(4), e994–e1001 (2015)
38. Tor, H.T., et al.: Automated detection of conduct disorder and attention deficit hyperactivity disorder using decomposition and nonlinear techniques with EEG signals. Comput. Methods Programs Biomed. **200**, 105941 (2021)
39. Tseng, P.H., Cameron, I.G., Pari, G., Reynolds, J.N., Munoz, D.P., Itti, L.: High-throughput classification of clinical populations from natural viewing eye movements. J. Neurol. **260**(1), 275–284 (2013)
40. van Gompel, R.P.G., Fischer, M.H., Murray, W.S., Hill, R.L. (eds.): Eye Movements: a Window on Mind and Brain. Elsevier, Amsterdam (2007)
41. Wang, S., et al.: Atypical visual saliency in autism spectrum disorder quantified through model-based eye tracking. Neuron **88**(3), 604–616 (2015)
42. Willcutt, E.G.: The prevalence of DSM-IV attention-deficit/hyperactivity disorder: a meta-analytic review. Neurotherapeutics **9**(3), 490–499 (2012)

FFBDNet: Feature Fusion and Bipartite Decision Networks for Recommending Medication Combination

Zisen Wang[1,2], Ying Liang[1]([✉]), and Zhengjun Liu[1,2]

[1] Research Center for Ubiquitous Computing Systems, Institute of Computing Technology, Chinese Academy of Science, Beijing, China
liangy@ict.ac.cn
[2] School of Computer Science and Technology, University of Chinese Academy of Sciences, Beijing, China

Abstract. Recommending medication combinations for patients is an essential part of artificial intelligence in the healthcare field. Existing approaches improve the effect of recommendations by considering how to make full use of patients' electronic health records or by introducing additional external knowledge, but there is still room for improving the fusion of heterogeneous and diverse knowledge and the effect between accuracy and drug-drug interaction (DDI) rate. To fill this gap, we propose the Feature Fusion and Bipartite Decision Networks (FFBDNet) to leverage external knowledge and improve accuracy and DDI rate. FFBDNet is equipped with a patient feature encoder which extract useful information from current and historical visits of patient to supplement the patient's health status, a medication feature encoder which can easily fuse the heterogeneous and diverse external knowledge of medications as feature, and a bipartite decision module to give medication recommendation results. FFBDNet also has a greedy loss function to improve accuracy and DDI rate. We demonstrate the effectiveness of FFBDNet by comparing with several state-of-the-art methods on a benchmark dataset. FFBDNet outperformed all baselines in all effective measures, reduced relatively the DDI rate by 97.65% from existing EHR data, and also is shown to improve 1.02% on Jaccard similarity.

Keywords: Medication combination prediction · External knowledge · Drug-drug interaction · Data mining · Attention

1 Introduction

Today, abundant health data, such as longitudinal electronic health records (EHR) and massive medical data available on the web enable researchers and doctors to build better predictive models for clinical decision making [1, 2]. Among other things, recommending effective and safe medication combinations is an important task, in particular to help patients with complex medical conditions [3, 4], and the primary objective is to personalize a safe combination of medications for a particular patient based on the patient's electronic health records. In recent years, more and more researchers try to use neural network to model the recommendation process, so as to assist doctors make better and more efficient clinical decisions when facing a large number of patients. There are basically two types of these approaches: 1) Sequential decision-making models that look at recommending medication combinations to patients as a multi-step decision-making task, see [5–8]. However, most decision-making tasks require a predetermined order or an appropriate reward function, which is difficult to define and will eventually affect the effect of the recommendation. 2) Multi-label classification models such as [4, 9–11] that view the medication combination recommendation as a multi-label classification task, so as to avoid the rationality of the order of the medication recommendation in the model prediction. However, they still suffer from the following limitations.

Fuse of External Knowledge. External knowledge refers to the medical data other than EHR, such as age and gender of patients, conflict relationship and molecular structure of medications, and in the medication combination recommendation, it usually refers to the external knowledge of medications. Existing works [4, 12] improve the effect of recommendation by introducing additional external knowledge of medications, but they have poor scalability for new external knowledge. New external knowledge can usually introduce new information for recommendation tasks, and better fusion of external knowledge can better support the model.

Effect Between Accuracy and DDI Rate. In medication combination recommendation, it is very important to avoid unnecessary drug-drug interaction as much as possible, so as to ensure the safety of recommendation results. Some existing works [8, 13] improve the accuracy and DDI rate for recommendation by explicitly or implicitly introducing DDI knowledge into training, such as implicitly adjusting DDI rate through reward function, or directly designing DDI loss to reduce DDI rate. However, there is still room for improvement in the effect between accuracy and DDI rate. Especially for the DDI rate, as the essential factor to measure the safety of medication combination recommendation, the DDI rate of the existing works is still at a high level.

To address these, we propose a Feature Fusion and Bipartite Decision Networks for medication combination recommendation, named FFBDNet, to fuse the external medical knowledge and to improve recommend effect. We believe that different external knowledge can introduce new information to assist recommendation. Our FFBDNet has the following contributions.

We propose a feature fusion module to fuse heterogeneous and diverse knowledge. The attention mechanism is used to extract the previous medical visit information related to the patient's current visit. A variety of non Euclidean space features of medications are encoded by graph convolution network. By concatenating new external knowledge in the feature coding stage, it can easily realize the fusion of external features.

We propose a bipartite decision module to make a joint decision for medication recommendation. It consists of two doctor models: direct doctor and recombination doctor. The direct doctor directly uses the patient's representation for recommendation, and the recombination doctor recombines the medications based on the similarity between the patient and the drugs. Finally, the recommendation results of the two doctor models are fused to complete the joint decision-making.

We design a greedy loss to reduce the DDI rate of medication combination recommendation results. The greedy mask is used to filter high conflict medications in greedy loss, and experiments show that, compared with several state-of-the-art methods on real EHR data, greedy loss can avoid almost all DDI in the medication combination, while still maintaining a good recommendation accuracy.

2 Related Works

2.1 Medication Recommendation

The existing medication combination recommendation methods can be basically divided into two types: sequential decision-making and multi-label classification. Sequential decision-making models decompose one recommendation process into multi-step medication decision-making, see [5–8, 14]. For example, LEAP [6] uses recurrent neural network (RNN) to model the decision-making process, and uses content-based attention mechanism to capture label instance mapping to predict medication at each step. COMP-Net [8] transforms the medication combination recommendation task into a disordered Markov decision process (MDP) problem, and designs a deep Q-learning (DQL) mechanism to learn the correlation and adverse interactions between medications. Multi-label classification models realize medication combination recommendation by predicting multiple labels for patients at one time, see [4, 10–13, 15]. Among them, GAMENet [4] customizes a memory storage module for external knowledge and extract external features from EHR graph and DDI graph by graph convolution network, so as to improve the effect of multi-label classification for medication recommendation. SafeDrug [12] specially designs an encoder to capture drug molecular knowledge, which is composed of global message passing neural network (MPNN) and local bipartite learning module, explicitly models the medication conflict process, and realizes medication recommendation to patients. Despite their initial success, there is still room for improvement in the effect between accuracy and DDI rate, as well as the poor fusion of additional external knowledge caused by structural customization.

In view of the success of the existing works through the use of external knowledge, in this paper, we design a feature fusion module that is easy to fuse the external features for the medication combination recommendation task, and design a greedy loss to optimize the effect between accuracy and DDI rate.

2.2 Medication Representation

The medical data related to medication is often non Euclidean space structure, which is often modeled by graph convolution neural network (GCN) in the existing works. Initializing each node in non Euclidean space data, GCN uses neighbor iterative aggregation to update nodes, and finally obtains the informative latent feature representations of each node [16–20]. At the beginning, it achieved good results in social networks. And with the development, it has been successfully applied in the field of medicine in recent years. For example, Ma et al. [21] use GCN to encode each node in the medical graph to obtain an interpretable embedded representation of the medication. Zitnik et al. [22] construct a two-layer multimodal medication interaction graph, and use GCN to capture the conflict relationship between medications. The representations of medication molecules are commonly modeled by molecular descriptors [23] and medication fingerprint [24], and David et al. [25] use GCN to capture the deep semantic features of medication fingerprint. Huang et al. [26] use medication pairs to capture medical features, and directly model medication molecule graph based GCN [27].

In this paper, we will use GCN to encode a variety of non Euclidean space medical data of medications, so as to capture and utilize the medication feature of different knowledge sources.

3 Problem Formulation

Electrical Health Records (EHR). In longitudinal EHR data, each patient n can be represented as a sequence of multivariate observations: $R^{(n)} = [r_1^{(n)}, r_2^{(n)}, \cdots, r_{T^{(n)}}^{(n)}]$ where $n \in \{1, 2, \cdots, N\}$, N is the total number of patients; $T^{(n)}$ is the number of visits of the n-th patient. To reduce clutter, the algorithms will be described for a single patient and drop the superscript (n) whenever it is unambiguous. Each history record $r_t = [c_t^d, c_t^p, c_t^m](t < T)$ of a patient for t-th visit is concatenation of corresponding diagnoses codes c_t^d, procedure codes c_t^p and medications codes c_t^m. And current record $r_T = [c_T^d, c_T^p]$ of a patient is concatenation of corresponding diagnoses codes c_T^d, procedure codes c_T^p. For simplicity, c_t^* is used to indicate the unified definition for different type of medical codes. $c_t^* \in \{0, 1\}^{|C^*|}$ is a multi-hot vector, where C^* is the medical code set and $|C^*|$ is size of set C^*.

External Knowledge of Medication. In this paper, there are three kinds of external knowledge of medication: EHR graph, DDI graph and molecule graph. EHR graph contains the co-occurrence knowledge of medications, and can be denoted as $G^E = \{V^E, E^E\}$, where $V^E = C^m$ is the node set of all medications and E^E is the edge set of known combination medication in EHR database. DDI graph contains the conflict knowledge between medications, and can be denoted as $G^D = \{V^D, E^D\}$, where $V^D = C^m$ is the node set of all medications and E^D is the edge set of known DDIs between a pair of medications. Molecule graph A contains the molecular composition knowledge of medications, which is similar to the root word in natural language processing, and can be denoted as $G^{m_i} = \{V^{m_i}, E^{m_i}\}$, where V^{m_i} is the node set of all molecular units of medication $m_i \in C^m$ and E^{m_i} is the edge set of known molecular structure of M_i. For simplicity, G^* is used to indicate the unified definition for different type of medical knowledge graphs, and adjacency matrix $A^* \in \mathbb{R}^{|V^*| \times |V^*|}$ is defined to clarify the construction of edge E^*.

Medication Combination Recommendation. Given medical codes of the current visit at time T (excluding medication codes) c_T^d, c_T^p, patient history $[r_1, r_2, \cdots, r_{T-1}]$ and external knowledge graph G^E, G^D, G^{m_t}, we want to recommend multiple medications by predicting multi-label output, while the predicted results are as close to the ground truth as possible and the DDI rate is as low as possible.

4 The FFBDNet

As illustrated in Fig. 1, FFBDNet includes the following components: a patient feature encoder, a medication feature encoder, and a bipartite decision module. Next, we will first introduce these modules and then provide details of training and inference of FFBDNet.

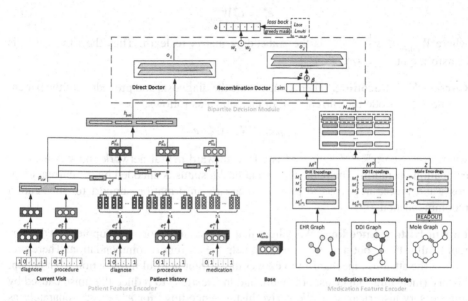

Fig. 1. The FFBDNet: We first encode current visit and patient history by attention mechanism to generate the patient health representation h_{pat} in Eq. (1–5). Then, we encode and concatenate the basic and external knowledge of medications to generate the medication representation H_{med} in Eq. (6–9). Direct doctor model is used to make medication recommendation o_1 based on the patient's representation directly in Eq. (10), and recombination doctor model recombines medications based on the similarity between patient and each medication to generate recommendation result o_2 in Eq. (11–12). Finally, we make a joint decision $\hat{o}$ based on the results of the bipartite doctor model in Eq. (13).

4.1 Patient Feature Encoder

From EHR data, patient health can be encoded by their current visit, which includes diagnosis and procedure information, and patient history, which includes diagnosis, procedure and medication information. Firstly, through EHR embedding, the sparse EHR data is mapped to the dense vector space. Then, current visit encoder is used to encode the patient's current health status. And by taking the patient's current visit code as a query, patient history encoder is used to capture the historical visit information from EHR based on the attention mechanism. Finally, by fusing the patient visit and history code, the patient representation is generated to represent the final medical feature of the patient.

EHR Embedding. As mentioned before, a visit r_t consists of $[c_t^d, c_t^p, c_t^m]$ where each of c_t^* is a multi-hot vector at the t-th visit. The multi-hot vector c_t^* is binary encoded showing the existence of each medical codes recorded at the t-th visit. Like [4] used a linear embedding of the input vector, we derive EHR embeddings for c_t^d, c_t^p, c_t^m separately at the t-th visit as follows.

$$e_t^* = c_t^* W_{emb}^* \tag{1}$$

where $W_{emb}^* \in \mathbb{R}^{|C^*| \times dim}$ is the embedding matrix to learn. Thus the t-th visit r_t is transformed to $\hat{r_t} = [e_t^d, e_t^p, e_t^m]$.

Current Visit Encoding. Then, concatenate the diagnosis and procedure of the patient at time T to encode the current visit of the patient as follows:

$$p_{cur} = NN_{cur}(e_T^d \# e_T^p) \tag{2}$$

where $NN_{cur}(\cdot) : \mathbb{R}^{2dim} \to \mathbb{R}^{2dim}$ is a feed-forward neural network and # is the concatenation operation. The patient's current health status is encoded by the current diagnosis and procedure, so as to provide necessary information support for medication recommendation.

Patient History Encoding. We believe that the patient history can supplement the current health status, but not all history will help the current recommendation. Therefore, we use the attention mechanism to extract the current helpful information from patient history (including diagnosis, procedure and medication) to reduce the noise caused by unnecessary historical data. We derive history encodings for e_t^d, e_t^p, e_t^m separately as follows

$$q^* = NN_{qry}^*(p_{cur}) \tag{3}$$

$$p_{his}^* = \sum_{t=1}^{T-1} NN_{val}^*(e_t^*) \text{Softmax}(NN_{key}^*(e_t^*)q^*) \tag{4}$$

where $NN_{qry}^*(\cdot) : \mathbb{R}^{2dim} \to \mathbb{R}^{dim}$ is the feed-forward neural network of query transform, $NN_{key}^*(\cdot) : \mathbb{R}^{dim} \to \mathbb{R}^{dim}$ is the feed-forward neural network of key transform and $NN_{val}^*(\cdot) : \mathbb{R}^{dim} \to \mathbb{R}^{dim}$ is the feed-forward neural network of value transform.

Patient Representation. The final patient representation is generated by concatenating the current and historical information of the patient. We follow a common and effective approach to first concatenate two vectors as a double-long vector, and then apply a feed-forward neural network as follow,

$$h_{pat} = NN_{pat}(p_{cur} \# p_{his}^d \# p_{his}^p \# p_{his}^m) \tag{5}$$

where $NN_{pat}(\cdot) : \mathbb{R}^{5dim} \rightarrow \mathbb{R}^{dim}$ is a feed-forward neural network and # is the concatenation operation. For the fusion of external knowledge, the existing work usually introduces external knowledge by customizing a feature encoder for specific external knowledge, which leads to poor scalability of new external knowledge. And for our method, it is convenient to expand new useful information sources, such as the patient's age, gender and others that may be helpful to the description of the patient's health, by using the attention mechanism and concatenate operation. Finally, the effect of recommendation will be improved easily by introducing the new and effective external knowledge.

4.2 Medication Feature Encoder

In order to make use of the attributes and dependence of medications to further improve the recommendation effect, we additionally use EHR graph, DDI graph and molecule graph to encode medications and generate the feature representations. Firstly, for base encoding, the medication embedding matrix in the EHR embedding is used to represent the basic information of medication in recommendation. Then, through external knowledge encoding, the non Euclidean space external knowledge of the medication is coded based on the graph convolution network and a readout pooling function. Finally, by fusing the medication base and external code, the medication information table is generated to represent the final medical feature of all medications.

Base Encoding. In order to represent the basic information of medications in the recommendation process, W^m_{emb} is directly used to represent the basic attribute matrix of medications, which is the same as in Eq. (1), and each row vector in the matrix represents one medication.

External Knowledge Encoding. As mentioned before, the external knowledge of medication includes EHR graph, DDI graph and molecule graph, which is represented by A^E, A^D and A^{m_i}. Firstly, each $A^* \in \mathbb{R}^{|V^*| \times |V^*|}$ is preprocessed respectively as follows:

$$\widehat{A}^* = \widehat{D}^{*-\frac{1}{2}}(I + A^*)\widehat{D}^{*-\frac{1}{2}} \tag{6}$$

where $\widehat{D}^*$ is the diagonal matrix of A^* and I is identity matrix. Then we apply GCN on each $\widehat{A}^*$ to learn improved embeddings respectively,

$$M^* = \widehat{A}^* \sigma(\widehat{A}^* W^*_{g1}) W^*_{g2} \tag{7}$$

where σ is a nonlinear activation function and $W^*_{g1} \in \mathbb{R}^{|V^*| \times dim}$, $W^*_{g2} \in \mathbb{R}^{dim \times dim}$ are the graph convolution matrix to learn. And the model depth can be deepened by increasing the number of convolution matrix layers. Then, each node in the external knowledge graph is encoded into M^*, where each row vector of $M^E \in \mathbb{R}^{|C^m| \times dim}$ and $M^D \in \mathbb{R}^{|C^m| \times dim}$ represents one medication, and each matrix represents one medication for $M^{m_i} \in \mathbb{R}^{|V_{m_i}| \times dim}$. In order to get the molecule representation of medications, referring to [12], M^{m_i} is pooled by a readout function to obtain the representation of the molecule knowledge of the medication, which calculates the average of all molecule nodes as follows:

$$z^{m_i} = \text{READOUT}(\{M_j^{m_i} | j = 1, \ldots, |V^{m_i}|\}) \tag{8}$$

where z^{m_i} is the molecule representation of the medication m_i, $M_j^{m_i}$ is the row vector of M^{m_i} and $|V^{m_i}|$ is the total number of the constructed molecule of the medication m_i. Then, the z^{m_i} of all medications are stacked to obtain the molecule matrix $Z = [z^{m_1}, z^{m_2}, \ldots, z^{m_{|C^m|}}]^T$ of medications.

Medication Information Table. Finally, we concatenate the different encodings of medications as the medication information table,

$$H_{med} = NN_{med}(W_{emb}^m \# M^E \# M^D \# Z) \tag{9}$$

where each row vector of $H_{med} \in \mathbb{R}^{|C^m| \times dim}$ is the representation of one medication, $NN_{med}(\cdot) : \mathbb{R}^{4dim} \to \mathbb{R}^{dim}$ is a feed-forward neural network to learn and # is the concatenation operation. For the fusion of external knowledge, similar to the patient representation, it is easy to realize the fusion by adding new external features during vector concatenating.

4.3 Bipartite Decision Module

We use two doctor models to recommend medication combinations. Different doctor models use different encoding features to support the flexible fusion of external knowledge. Firstly, the direct doctor model only considers the patient representation to directly recommend the medication combination. And the recombination doctor model calculates the similarity between patient and each medication based on the patient representation and medication information table, and then recombines the medications based on the similarity calculation results to realize recommendation. Finally, we combine the recommendation results of the two doctor models to make a joint decision and complete the final recommendation for the patient.

Direct Doctor. For this doctor model, we directly use the patient representation for recommendation, and it can work when the feature of medications is missing. We use double-layer feed-forward neural network to project the patient representation and generate the probability of each medication in the recommended combination,

$$o_1 = NN_{o_1}(h_{pat}) \tag{10}$$

where $o_1 \in \mathbb{R}^{|C^m|}$ is directly retrieved using patient representation and $NN_{o_1}(\cdot) : \mathbb{R}^{dim} \to \mathbb{R}^{|C^m|}$ is a feed-forward neural network to learn. When implemented, $NN_{o_1}(\cdot)$ is a two-layer network and its hidden layer is activated by relu.

Recombination Doctor. Recombination doctor calculate the similarity between patient and each medication, recombine medications based on the similarities and patient's representation, and generate the patient's medication combination result. We first use the patient representation h_{pat} and the medication information table H_{med} to calculate the similarity between the patient and each medication,

$$sim = \text{cosine}(H_{med}, h_{pat}) \tag{11}$$

where $sim \in \mathbb{R}^{|C^m|}$ is the similarity of all medications and $\text{cosine}(\cdot)$ is the function of cosine similarity. Then, input the similarity results into a double-layer feed-forward neural network to calculate the recombination, and input the patient representation together to adjust and guide the recombination process, and generate the recommendation results of the recombination doctor,

$$o_2 = NN_{o_2}(\alpha sim \# \beta h_{pat}) \tag{12}$$

where $o_2 \in \mathbb{R}^{|C^m|}$ is the result of recombination based on similarity and $NN_{o_2}(\cdot)$: $\mathbb{R}^{|C^m|+dim} \rightarrow \mathbb{R}^{|C^m|}$ is a feed-forward neural network to learn. $\alpha, \beta \in \mathbb{R}^1$ are trainable fusion weights, which are used to adjust the effect of similarity and patient representation on doctor model decision-making.

Joint Decision-Making. Finally, the attention mechanism is used to adjust the decision weight of the two doctor models to realize joint decision-making,

$$\hat{o} = \text{sigmoid}(w_1 \odot o_1 + w_2 \odot o_2) \tag{13}$$

where $w_1, w_2 \in \mathbb{R}^{|C^m|}$ are trainable weight vectors, which integrate and adjust the importance of two doctors' decisions on different medications.

4.4 Model Training and Inference

In the training phase, the FFBDNet is trained end-to-end. We need to find the optimal parameters to realize medication combination recommendation. In order to improve the accuracy and DDI rate, we propose greedy loss to adjust the process of model training. And in the inference phase, we set a threshold δ, and determine the final medication combination to be recommended by picking those medications whose model prediction probability is greater than δ.

Multi-label Prediction Loss. We view the medication combination recommendation as a multi-label classification task. Therefore, we use two common multi-label classification loss functions as the objective function of our model, namely the binary cross entropy loss L_{bce} and the multi-label margin loss L_{multi}. L_{bce} makes the prediction result of the model closer to the growth truth, and L_{multi} makes the predicted probability of ground truth labels has at least 1 margin larger than others. Thus, threshold value is easier to be fixed when predicting.

$$L_{bce} = \sum_i^{|C^m|} y_i \log(\hat{o}_i) + (1 - y_i)\log(1 - \hat{o}_i) \tag{14}$$

$$L_{multi} = \sum_i^{|C^m|} \sum_{j \in Y} \frac{\max(0, 1 - (\hat{o}_j - \hat{o}_i))}{|Y|} \tag{15}$$

where y is the ground truth of the medication combination and Y is the index set of ground truth label.

Greedy Loss. We achieve greedy loss by multiplying L_{bce} and L_{multi} by greedy mask, which is used to shield high conflict medications,

$$\hat{L}_{bce} = \sum_i^{|C^m|} mask_i y_i \log(\hat{o}_i) + (1 - mask_i y_i)\log(1 - \hat{o}_i) \tag{16}$$

$$\hat{L}_{multi} = \sum_i^{|C^m|} \sum_{j \in Y} \frac{\max(0, mask_j(1 - (\hat{o}_j - \hat{o}_i)))}{|Y|} \tag{17}$$

$$L_{greedy} = \lambda_1 \hat{L}_{bce} + \lambda_2 \hat{L}_{multi} \tag{18}$$

where $\lambda_1, \lambda_2 > 0$ are the mixture weights and $mask_i$ is the greedy mask of the i-th medication of the patient. The essence of greedy loss is to explicitly reduce the co-occurrence frequency of conflict medications, so that the model can reduce the impact of conflict medications on parameters in the back-propagation process when learning statistical knowledge. In detail, the greedy mask can be obtained by Algorithm 1, in which the balance between accuracy and DDI rate can be adjusted by setting different greedy scale.

Inference. In inference phase, we apply a threshold $\delta = 0.5$ on the output in Eq. (13) to predict medication combination.

$$\hat{Y} = \{i | \hat{o}_i > \delta, 1 \le i \le |C^m|\} \tag{19}$$

where $\hat{o}_i$ is the probability of each medication predicted by the model. Before the final inference, based on the loss function of Eq. (18), the model will be calibrated through the back-propagation algorithm to make the predictive scores as close as possible to the probabilities of medications occurrence in the actual scene. The effect of calibration will be affected by the data difference between training samples and actual scene, but it can be alleviated by limiting the number of training iterations or other methods to prevent over fitting. And then, we choose all medications with $\hat{o}_i$ greater than δ as the recommendation result.

Algorithm 1: Greedy mask generation algorithm

Input : Training ground truth $\{y_i, i \in [1,...,|C^m|] \}$, DDI adjancy A^D, greedy scale S
Output: greedy mask $\{mask^{(i)}, i \in [1,...,|C^m|] \}$
1. **initialize** $mask_k^{(i)} = 1$ $\forall k = 1...K$
2. **initialize** $MSet = set()$
3. **for** $i = 1...|C^m|$ **do**
4.   **if** $y_i = 1$ **do**
5. $add(MSet,i)$
6.   **end if**
7. **end for**
8. **while** $True$
9.   **initialize** $M = dict()$
10. **initialize** $fine = True$
11. **for** $\forall pair(n,m)$ in $MSet$ **do**
12.   **if** $A_d[n,m] = 1$ **do**
13. $M[n]\ +=\ 1$
14. $M[m]\ +=\ 1$
15.   **end if**
16. **end for**
17. **if** $\max(M) > S$ **do**
18. $fine = False$
19. **end if**
20. **if** $fine$ **do**
21.   break

---

5 Experiment

We compare FFBDNet with the patient's actual EHR data, take the medication combination actually accepted by the patient as the ground truth, and take the output by FFBDNet as the prediction, and measure the accuracy of recommendations by comparing the differences between the ground truth and prediction. We also calculate the DDI rate in the prediction of FFBDNet by using the real medication confliction. In addition, we evaluate FFBDNet by comparing against other baselines on recommendation accuracy and DDI rate. FFBDNet is implemented in PyTorch [28] and trained with 8GB memory and Nvidia 2060 GPU.

Dataset. The experiments are carried out on MIMIC-III [29]. We follow the procedure similar to [12] to process the medical codes in the experiments. The NDC drug code in MIMIC-III is mapped to third level ATC code as prediction label. The statistics of the postprocessed data is reported in Table 1.

Baselines. We compare our model with the following baseline and state-of-the-art algorithms.

- **Logistic Regression (LR)**, multi-label classification model, is a logistic regression with L2 regularization. Binary relevance technique [30] is used to handle multi-label output.

Table 1. Statistics of the data.

# patients	6,350
# clinical events	15,016
# diagnosis	1,958
# procedure	1,426
# medication	145
avg # of visits	2.36
avg # of diagnosis	10.51
avg # of procedure	3.84
avg # of medication	8.80
# medication in DDI knowledge base	123
# DDI types in knowledge base	40

- **RETain** [14], sequential decision-making model, can integrate recent visits through reverse time attention, and provide sequential prediction of medication combination.
- **Leap** [6], sequential decision-making model, decomposes medication recommendation into a continuous decision-making process, models the decision-making process with a cyclic decoder, and automatically determines the appropriate amount of medications.
- **GAMENet** [4], multi-label classification model, integrates the drug-drug interactions knowledge by a memory module, and models longitudinal patient records as the query. By using query vector to extract the information in the memory module of medications, medication combination recommendation is carried out.
- **CompNet** [8], sequential decision-making model, views the medication combination recommendation as an order-free Markov Decision Process (MDP) problem and designs a Deep Q Learning (DQL) mechanism to learn correlative and adverse interactions between medicines.
- **AMANet** [10], multi-label classification model, integrate both attention and memory to realize asynchronous multi-view learning, and focus on the dual-view sequences. The sequence is saved as the patient's historical memory, and the medication combination is recommended by querying the memory.
- **SafeDrug** [12], multi-label classification model, uses the medications' molecular structure and models DDIs to make safe medication recommendation as much as possible. Finally, the model combines and decodes the medication information for medication combination recommendation.

Metrics. We use five efficacy metrics: DDI rate, Jaccard Similarity Score (Jaccard), Average F1 (F1), Precision Recall AUC (PRAUC), and # of medications to evaluate the recommendation efficacy.

To measure the prediction accuracy, we use Jaccard, F1, PRAUC and # of medications to calculate the gap between the ground truth and the model prediction to describe the treatment efficacy of recommendation [10, 12, 13]. Jaccard is defined as the size of the intersection divided by the size of the union of ground truth and predicted medication set,

$$\text{Jaccard} = \frac{|Y \cap \widehat{Y}|}{|Y \cup \widehat{Y}|} \tag{20}$$

where Y is the index set of ground truth label and $\widehat{Y}$ is the index set of model predicted label. Precision (P), Recall (R), and F1 are defined as:

$$P = \frac{|Y \cap \widehat{Y}|}{|Y|}, R = \frac{|Y \cap \widehat{Y}|}{|\widehat{Y}|} \tag{21}$$

$$F1 = \frac{2PR}{P + R} \tag{22}$$

To measure medication safety, we use DDI Rate and relative DDI Rate ($\triangle$ DDI Rate %),

$$\text{DDI Rate} = \frac{\sum_{i,j} A^m[i,j]}{\sum_{i,j} 1} \tag{23}$$

$$\triangle \text{DDI Rate\%} = \frac{\text{DDI Rate} - \text{DDI Rate (EHR)}}{\text{DDI Rate (EHR)}} \tag{24}$$

where A^m is the adjacency matrix of DDI graph and DDI Rate (EHR) is the DDI rate of the ground truth in EHR. And We randomly divide the dataset into training, validation, and test with ratio 4:1:1 and report the performance from the test set.

Knowledge Source Support. Table 2 lists the support of the baseline methods for different knowledge sources. For these methods that use external knowledge, they customize the feature encoder for specific external knowledge to capture the effective information, which limits the scalability of other external knowledge. For our method, we can support the integration of all different external knowledge of patients and medications, so that we can easily improve the amount of model information by introducing external knowledge, so as to improve the effect of recommendation.

Performance Comparison. Table 3 compares the performance of different approaches on accuracy and DDI rate. Compared with the baselines, FFBDNet can introduce more

Table 2. Knowledge source support of baselines.

Methods	Knowledge source support
LR	EHR
RETAIN	EHR
Leap	EHR
GAMENet	EHR, DDI graph, EHR graph
CompNet	EHR, DDI graph
AMANet	EHR
SafeDrug	EHR, molecule graph

information into the final decision-making process through the fusion of multiple external knowledge, so as to improve the discrimination ability of the model. Results show that FFBDNet has the highest score with respect to Jaccard, PR-AUC and F1. For FFBD-Net(greedy), by using the greedy mask, the co-occurrence frequency of high conflict medications can be reduced. And results show that it can not only avoid almost all DDI while reaching the lowest DDI rate, but also still maintain the accuracy at a high level compared with the SafeDrug that emphasizes security.

As for the baseline, sequential decision-making models such as Leap, Retain and CompNet yield poor results. Similar to the conclusion of previous work [12], multi-label prediction model (GAMENet, AMANet, SafeDrug) might be more straightforward and effective in the medication recommendation task. The accuracy of AMANet can reach a high level, but it does not consider the problem of DDI. Both GAMENet and SafeDrug consider DDI in the process of model training. Although SafeDrug can get low DDI rate, it has low accuracy compared with our greedy method.

Multi Feature Ablation Study. We control the introduction of different knowledge to observe the effect of increasing information sources on the model results. It can be observed in Table 4 that some external knowledge bring new information to the model, so as to improve the final effect. FFBDNet can integrate the medication feature into the recommendation by using the recombination doctor model in the bipartite decision module, and it finally achieves the best results when all the information is used. Thus, in medication combination recommendation task, the effect of introducing new information sources by fusing heterogeneous and diverse external knowledge is verified.

Greedy Ablation Study. We evaluate greedy loss and show that accuracy and DDI rate can be controlled by greedy scale. The ground truth DDI rate in MIMIC-III is 0.0808. Table 5 shows the results of different greedy scales. It can be found that the larger the greedy scale, the greater the accuracy of the model and the greater the DDI rate. When the greedy scale is infinite, the accuracy of the model is the highest. The greedy loss provides a way for doctors to control the tradeoff between accuracy and DDI rate in recommendation.

Table 3. Performance comparison on MIMIC-III (ground truth DDI rate is 0.0808).

Methods	DDI rate	ΔDDI	Jaccard	PRAUC	F1	# of med.	# of parameters
LR	0.0724 ±0.0009	−10.40% ±1.11%	0.4543 ±0.0021	0.7550 ±0.0018	0.6142 ±0.0019	14.23 ±0.09	–
RETAIN	0.0810 ±0.0025	+0.25% ±3.07%	0.4882 ±0.0020	0.7529 ±0.0014	0.6487 ±0.0018	15.83 ±0.31	291,034
Leap	0.0693 ±0.0010	−14.23% ±1.67%	0.4442 ±0.0025	0.6452 ±0.0030	0.6071 ±0.0024	18.83 ±0.17	439,196
GAMENet	0.0798 ±0.0011	−1.24% ±1.32%	0.5146 ±0.0024	0.7657 ±0.0015	0.6694 ±0.0021	19.77 ±0.34	455,002
CompNet	0.0761 ±0.0008	−5.82% ±1.01%	0.4933 ±0.0019	0.7573 ±0.0020	0.6587 ±0.0017	19.33 ±0.21	961,412
AMANet	0.0879 ±0.0023	+8.79% ±2.82%	0.5195 ±0.0021	0.7772 ±0.0027	0.6739 ±0.0020	20.13 ±0.25	1,799,575
SafeDrug	0.0267 ±0.0009	−66.95% ±0.16%	0.4030 ±0.0025	0.6991 ±0.0024	0.5582 ±0.0020	25.56 ±0.11	406,170
FFBDNet(greedy)	**0.0019** ±0.0002	**−97.65%** ±0.28%	0.4361 ±0.0014	0.7061 ±0.0021	0.5978 ±0.0015	14.31 ±0.12	227,750
FFBDNet	0.0717 ±0.0016	−11.26% ±2.01%	**0.5292** ±0.0020	**0.7777** ±0.0010	**0.6833** ±0.0017	19.69 ±0.30	227,750

Table 4. Multi feature ablation study.

Patient	Medication	DDI rate	ΔDDI	Jaccard	PRAUC	F1	# of med.
Current	–	0.0641 ±0.0009	−20.67% ±1.11%	0.5039 ±0.0018	0.7593 ±0.0019	0.6611 ±0.0016	18.95 ±0.24
Current, history	–	0.0771 ±0.0012	−4.58% ±1.48%	0.5173 ±0.0015	0.7661 ±0.0018	0.6732 ±0.0014	20.36 ±0.16
Current, history	Base	0.0735 ±0.0014	−9.03% ±1.72%	0.5204 ±0.0013	0.7712 ±0.0007	0.6751 ±0.0012	19.90 ±0.17
Current, history	Base, EHR	0.0739 ±0.0006	−8.54% ±0.73%	0.5239 ±0.0019	0.7754 ±0.0013	0.6790 ±0.0017	19.65 ±0.16
Current, history	Base, EHR, DDI	0.0726 ±0.0016	−10.15% ±1.98%	0.5241 ±0.0017	0.7761 ±0.0015	0.6816 ±0.0016	19.33 ±0.21
Current, history	Base, EHR, DDI, molecule	**0.0717** ±0.0016	**−11.26%** ±2.01%	**0.5292** ±0.0020	**0.7777** ±0.0010	**0.6833** ±0.0017	19.69 ±0.30

Table 5. Greedy ablation study.

Greedy scale	DDI rate	Jaccard	PRAUC	F1	# of med.
1	0.0019 ± 0.0002	0.4361 ± 0.0014	0.7061 ± 0.0021	0.5978 ± 0.0015	14.31 ± 0.12
2	0.0105 ± 0.0005	0.4748 ± 0.0015	0.7287 ± 0.0014	0.6356 ± 0.0015	16.25 ± 0.18
3	0.0208 ± 0.0004	0.4957 ± 0.0018	0.7421 ± 0.0014	0.6544 ± 0.0016	17.64 ± 0.19
4	0.0277 ± 0.0008	0.5032 ± 0.0021	0.7528 ± 0.0017	0.6608 ± 0.0019	18.09 ± 0.24
5	0.0349 ± 0.0005	0.5072 ± 0.0012	0.7615 ± 0.0013	0.6646 ± 0.0011	18.43 ± 0.20
6	0.0410 ± 0.0006	0.5145 ± 0.0026	0.7694 ± 0.0021	0.6709 ± 0.0023	18.57 ± 0.23
+∞	0.0717 ± 0.0016	0.5292 ± 0.0020	0.7777 ± 0.0010	0.6833 ± 0.0017	19.69 ± 0.30

6 Conclusion

In this paper, we propose FFBDNet for medication combination recommendation, which is equipped with a patient feature encoder, a medication feature encoder and a bipartite decision module. Based on the attention mechanism and the concatenating operation, the feature encoders can easily fuse external knowledge to increase the model information source. With using the encoder results of patient and medications, the bipartite decision module make a joint decision to realize medication combination recommendation through two doctor models. And we design a greedy loss, which uses the greedy mask to filter high conflict medications, to reduce the DDI rate. We evaluated FFBDNet using benchmark data. The experimental results show that FFBDNet outperforms the state-of-the-art methods. Besides, using greedy loss to participate in the model training, FFBDNet can avoid almost all DDI, while still maintaining a good recommendation accuracy. In the future, we will study how to efficiently extract and fuse the multi-feature of medications to further improve the accuracy of representation while ensuring the scalability of external knowledge. Code related to this paper is available at https://github.com/wangzssdwh/FFDBNet.

References

1. Edward, C., Mohammad, T.B., Andy, S., Walter F.S., Sun, J.M.: Doctor AI: predicting clinical events via recurrent neural networks. In: Machine Learning for Healthcare Conference, pp. 301–318 (2016)
2. Xiao, C., Choi, E., Sun, J.M.: Opportunities and challenges in developing deep learning models using electronic health records data: a systematic review. J. Am. Med. Inform. Assoc. 25(10), 1419–1428 (2018)
3. Shang, J.Y., Ma, T.F., Xiao, C., Sun, J.M.: Pre-training of graph augmented transformers for medication recommendation. In: Proceedings of the 28th International Joint Conference on Artificial Intelligence, pp. 1907–1913 (2018)
4. Shang, J.Y., Xiao, C., Ma, T.F., Li, H.Y., Sun, J.M.: GameNet: graph augmented memory networks for recommending medication combination. In: Proceedings of the 33rd AAAI Conference on Artificial Intelligence, pp. 1126–1133 (2019)

5. Li, C., Wang, B.Y., Pavlu, V., Aslam, J.A.: Conditional Bernoulli mixtures for multi-label classification. In: Proceedings of the 33rd International Conference on Machine Learning, pp. 2482–2491 (2016)
6. Zhang, Y., Chen, R., Tang, J., Stewart, W.F., Sun, J.: Leap: learning to prescribe effective and safe treatment combinations for multimorbidity. In: Proceedings of the 23rd ACM SIGKDD International Conference on Knowledge Discovery and Data Mining, pp. 1315–1324 (2017)
7. Le, H., Tran, T., Venkatesh, S.: Dual memory neural computer for asynchronous two-view sequential learning. In: Proceedings of the 24th ACM SIGKDD International Conference on Knowledge Discovery and Data Mining, pp. 1637–1645 (2018)
8. Wang, S., Ren, P., Chen, Z., Ren, Z., Ma, J., Rijke, M.: Order-free medicine combination prediction with graph convolutional reinforcement learning. In: Proceedings of the 28th Conference on Information and Knowledge Management, pp. 1623–1632 (2019)
9. Jacek, M.B., Thomas, A.L.: Predicting medications from diagnostic codes with recurrent neural networks. In: Proceedings of the International Conference on the 5th Learning Representations, pp. 100–119 (2017)
10. He, Y., Wang, C., Li, N., Zeng, Z.: Attention and memory-augmented networks for dual-view sequential learning. In: Proceedings of the 26th ACM SIGKDD International Conference on Knowledge Discovery and Data Mining, pp. 125–134 (2020)
11. Bhoi, S., Lee, M.L., Hsu, W., Fang, H.S., Tan, N.C.: Personalizing medication recommendation with a graph-based approach. ACM Trans. Inf. Syst. $40(3)$, 55–79 (2021)
12. Yang, C., Xiao, C., Ma, F., Glass, L., Sun, J.: SafeDrug: dual molecular graph encoders for recommending effective and safe drug combinations. In: Proceedings of the 30th International Joint Conference on Artificial Intelligence, pp. 3735–3741 (2021)
13. Wang, Y., Chen, W., Pi, D., Yue, L., Wang, S., Xu, M.: Self-supervised adversarial distribution regularization for medication recommendation. In: Proceedings of the Thirtieth International Joint Conference on Artificial Intelligence, pp. 3134–3140 (2021)
14. Choi, E., Bahadori, M.T., Sun, J., Kulas, J., Schuetz, A., Stewart, W.: Retain: an interpretable predictive model for healthcare using reverse time attention mechanism. In: Advances in Neural Information Processing Systems, pp. 3504–3512 (2016)
15. An, Y., Zhang, L., Yang, H.: Prediction of treatment medicines with dual adaptive sequential networks. IEEE Trans. Knowl. Data Eng. 34, 5496–5509 (2021)
16. Kipf, T.N., Welling, M.: Semi-supervised classification with graph convolutional networks. In: International Conference on Learning Representations (2017)
17. Hamilton, W.L., Ying, R., Leskovec, J.: Inductive representation learning on large graphs. In: Proceedings of the 31st Conference on Neural Information Processing Systems, pp. 1024–1034 (2017)
18. Petar, V., Guillem, C., Arantxa, C., Adriana, R., Pietro, L., Yoshua, B.: Graph attention networks. In: International Conference on Learning Representations (2018)
19. Chen, J., Ma, T., Xiao, C.: FastGCN: fast learning with graph convolutional networks via importance sampling. In: International Conference on Learning Representations (2018)
20. Xue, H., Yang, L., Rajan, V.: Multiplex bipartite network embedding using dual hypergraph convolutional networks. In: Proceedings of the 30th Web Conference, pp. 1649–1660 (2021)
21. Ma, T., Xiao, C., Zhou, J., Wang, F.: Drug similarity integration through attentive multi-view graph autoencoders. CoRR abs/1804.10850 (2018)
22. Zitnik, M., Agrawal, M., Leskovec, J.: Modeling polypharmacy side effects with graph convolutional networks. Bioinformatics $34(13)$, 457–466 (2018)
23. Mauri, A., Consonni, V., Pavan, M.: Dragon software: an easy approach to molecular descriptor calculations. Commun. MCC $56(2)$, 237–248 (2006)
24. Rogers, D., Hahn, M.: Extended-connectivity fingerprints. J. Chem. Inf. Model. $50(5)$, 742–754 (2010)

25. David, K.D., et al.: Convolutional networks on graphs for learning molecular fingerprints. In: Proceedings of the 29th Conference on Neural Information Processing Systems (2015)
26. Huang, K.X., Fu, T.F., Xiao, C., Glass, L., Sun, J.M.: DeepPurpose: a deep learning based drug repurposing toolkit. Bioinformatics (2020)
27. Huang, K.X., Xiao, C., Hoang, T., Glass, L., Sun, J.M.: Caster: predicting drug interactions with chemical substructure representation. In: Proceedings of the 34th AAAI Conference on Artificial Intelligence, pp. 702–709 (2020)
28. Paszke, A., et al.: Automatic differentiation in PyTorch (2017)
29. Johnson, A.E., et al.: MIMIC-III, a freely accessible critical care database. Sci. Data $3(1)$, 1–9 (2016)
30. Luaces, O., Díez, J., Barranquero, J., del Coz, J.J., Bahamonde, A.: Binary relevance efficacy for multilabel classification. Progress Artif. Intell. $1(4)$, 303–313 (2012)

Towards Federated COVID-19 Vaccine Side Effect Prediction

Jiaqi Wang[1], Cheng Qian[2], Suhan Cui[1], Lucas Glass[2], and Fenglong Ma[1(✉)]

[1] College of Information Sciences and Technology,
The Pennsylvania State University, State College, USA
{jqwang,sxc6192,fenglong}@psu.edu
[2] Analytics Center of Excellence, IQVIA, Durham, USA
alextoqc@gmail.com, Lucas.Glass@iqvia.com

Abstract. We propose `FedCovid`, a new federated learning system based on electronic health records (EHR), to predict COVID-19 vaccination side effects. Federated learning allows diverse data owners to work together to train machine learning models without sharing data, ensuring the privacy of EHR data. However, because EHR data is unique, directly using existing federated learning models may fail. The EHR data is diverse, with numerical and categorical characteristics as well as consecutive visits. Furthermore, each client's data size is unequal, and the data labels are skewed due to the small number of patients that experience serious side effects. We present an adaptive approach to fuse heterogeneous EHR data and apply data augmentation techniques working with a margin loss to overcome the data imbalance issue in the client model training to address both challenges simultaneously in `FedCovid`. We recommend that when the server is updated, the data size of each client be taken into account to lessen the impact of clients with small data volumes. Finally, in order to train a stable and successful federated learning model, we suggest a new ordinal training technique. Experiments on a real-world dataset reveal that the suggested model is effective at predicting COVID-19 vaccination adverse effects. The performance increases by 14.35%, 17.81%, and 129.36% on the F1 score, Cohen's Kappa, and PR-AUC, respectively, compared with the best baseline (The source code of the proposed `FedCovid` is available at https://github.com/JackqqWang/FedCovid.git).

Keywords: COVID-19 vaccination · Side effect prediction · Federated learning · Electronic health records

J. Wang—This work was done when Jiaqi Wang interned at IQVIA.

Supplementary Information The online version contains supplementary material available at https://doi.org/10.1007/978-3-031-26422-1_27.

1   Introduction

The COVID-19 pandemic has led to 486,761,597 confirmed cases and 6,142,735 deaths globally as of April 1, 2022[1]. One of the preventive measures to reduce the chances of infection is getting vaccinated. There are three widely-applied COVID-19 vaccines, i.e., Moderna, Pfizer-BioNTech, and Johnson & Johnson's Janssen. According to a recent report in [15], during September 22, 2021 to February 6, 2022, approximately 82.6 million U.S. residents aged $\leq$ 18 years had received COVID-19 vaccine doses. Although COVID-19 vaccines are safe and effective, some people may still have a few side effects after receiving the vaccines [3,25,31]. The common side effects include, but are not limited to, swelling, redness, fever, headache, tiredness, muscle pain, chills, and nausea. In fact, these symptoms are normal and are signs that the body is building immunity. A small number of people may experience serious health events after the COVID-19 vaccination, such as anaphylaxis [30], thrombosis with thrombocytopenia syndrome (TTS) [28], myocarditis and pericarditis [9], and Guillain-Barre syndrome (GBS) [27]. These rare yet serious side effects may cause death. Therefore, a challenging but practical question arises: *Is it possible to predict whether people will have COVID-19 vaccine side effects after their vaccination?*

To answer this question, the first challenge that we may face is what kinds of data can be used to learn the vaccine side effect predictor. Existing work shows that the side effects of the COVID-19 vaccine may be related to gender and underline diseases [10]. The Centers for Disease Control and Prevention (CDC) also points out that women over the age of 30–49 years should be aware of the increased risk of the TTS side effect[2]. Thus, the data used for predicting vaccine side effects should contain patient demographics and historical disease information. Fortunately, electronic health records (EHR) consist of patient demographics, historical visit records, and corresponding laboratory results, which have been commonly used for the medical predictive modeling task in recent years [5,19–21]. Each visit record includes multiple diagnosis codes, procedure codes, and medication codes. Each diagnosis code represents a disease, a symptom, or an abnormal finding. Therefore, these characteristics make EHR data suitable for being used for predicting the COVID-19 vaccine side effects.

Due to the privacy issue and the high sensitivity of EHR data, hospitals, health insurance companies, or medical research institutes usually do not allow others to share them with others. The second challenging issue is how to train an accurate predictive model when stakeholders do not share their own data. Towards this end, we propose to use an advanced technique in the machine learning field, i.e., *federated learning* (FL), which enables different clients to work cooperatively to learn a global model by only sharing model parameters, instead of sharing data with others [24,37]. In our case, a local client, e.g., a hospital, a research institute, or a data center in one state, trains its own model with the local patient EHR data. After that, selected clients only need to upload their model parameters to the server for the global model aggregation. After aggregation, the server

---

[1] https://covid19.who.int/.
[2] https://www.cdc.gov/coronavirus/2019-ncov/vaccines/safety/adverse-events.html.

will distribute the global model back to active clients. The active clients will then train their local models starting from the global model they received with their local data. During this iterative process, local clients collaborate to maintain a global model by acquiring concealed information from each client while maintaining data privacy. Although federated learning approaches such as FedAvg [24] have shown their effectiveness on the image datasets such as MNIST[3], CIFAR-10[4], and CIFAR-100[5], they may not work well on the EHR data.

First, **EHR data are heterogeneous**. As we mentioned before, EHR data contains not only demographic information but also visit information. The static demographics include discrete gender and numerical age. The visits are time-ordered sequential data, and each visit consists of a set of unordered discrete codes. Thus, how to automatically integrate these types of data is a challenge. Second, federated learning prevents each client from uploading its EHR data to the central server, and only allows each client to solely update the prediction model with its own data. However, **the size of EHR data stored for each client is unequal**. In other words, the EHR data are not distributed in a uniform and independent manner among customers. Each state in the United States is treated as a data center or client in our work. The amount of EHR data taken from each state varies due to the uneven distribution of the population throughout the 50 states. Clients with limited data may end up with an overfitted model. Aggregating these "poor" client models on the server side may jeopardize the learning of the global predictive model. Third, our goal is to forecast the side effects of the COVID-19 vaccine. The patients who had side effects are labeled as positive cases, whereas those who did not are labeled as negative cases. According to existing research [3,25,31], only a small percentage of persons have side effects. This means that the number of positive cases should be smaller than that of negative cases in the real world. As a result, **the EHR data used for training the predictive model are imbalanced**.

To address these challenges simultaneously, in this paper, we propose a novel **Fed**erated learning framework (named `FedCovid`) for predicting **COVID**-19 vaccine side effects using EHR data extracted from the database of IQVIA[6]. In particular, to address the heterogeneous data challenge, we first map each type of data to a latent representation and then use the proposed adaptive fusion mechanism to obtain the aggregated patient representation. Moreover, to tackle the data imbalance issue, we propose to use the data augmentation technique to increase the number of positive patient representations and incorporate the metric or contrastive learning loss into the client model training. Finally, we designed an ordinary training strategy to deal with the Non-IID issue. In contrast to existing federated learning models such as FedAvg [24] to treat each client equally, we classify clients into two categories according to the amount of EHR data they have. We first train the clients with a larger size to obtain an initialized global model. After the global model becomes stable, we then allow the clients

---

[3] http://yann.lecun.com/exdb/mnist/.

[4] https://www.cs.toronto.edu/~kriz/cifar.html.

[5] https://www.cs.toronto.edu/~kriz/cifar.html.

[6] https://www.iqvia.com/.

with a smaller amount of data to participate in the model training. In addition, we take the size of clients into consideration when aggregating the global model.

To sum up, the contributions of this work are listed as follows:

- To the best of our knowledge, we are the first to investigate the feasibility of using advanced machine learning techniques to predict COVID-19 vaccine side effects with EHR data.
- We propose a novel federated learning framework FedCovid to protect EHR data privacy, fuse different types of EHR data, handle the imbalance data issue, and tackle the Non-IID data distribution challenge simultaneously.
- We conducted extensive experiments to show the effectiveness and efficiency of the proposed framework compared with state-of-the-art baselines. Furthermore, we provide comprehensive results for hyperparameter exploration, ablation study, and convergence analysis.

2   Related Work

Since COVID-19 was declared as a worldwide pandemic, artificial intelligence (AI) has been applied to conduct related research, such as developing novel diagnostic approaches [34], drug discovery [35], spread monitor [14], and e-pharmacy supply chain optimization [23]. There are also several reviews [1,2,26] summarizing the roles of AI during the fight with COVID-19.

There are also several research studies applying federated learning (FL) techniques on COVID-19 related topics. In [13], the authors applied a GAN-augmented FL for COVID-image segmentation. In [8], a fL model was proposed to predict the future oxygen requirements of symptomatic patients with COVID-19 based on chest X-ray images. In [32], a model was trained using dispersed raw clinical data to predict death in COVID-19-infected hospitalized patients.

Current COVID-19-related FL research, however, has a number of limitations. (1) The majority of FL frameworks and models are designed for medical picture data solely, ignoring heterogeneous EHR data. (2) In several previous research, the present centralized machine learning approaches are simply embedded into the FL architecture. Such a simplistic mix overlooks the distributed paradigm's merits and limitations. (3) To our knowledge, no published research effort has investigated the COVID-19 vaccine side effect prediction utilizing distributed EHR data in a FL scenario, specifically to address the problems of imbalanced data and Non-IID concerns in the real-world setting.

3   COVID-19 Vaccine EHR Data

3.1   Dataset Overview

We extracted the EHR data from the health insurance claims database of IQVIA. Similar to other types of data [36,38], EHR data are **heterogeneous**, which include patients' age, gender, zip code, diagnosis codes within each visit, the vaccine brand, and a binary label of the side effects. In this extracted dataset,

Table 1. Data statistics of the extracted EHR dataset.

Patient count	6,526	Moderna	3,355
Positive patient count	1,097	Pfizer-BioNTech	2,159
Negative l	5,429	Janssen	1,012
Male	1,761	ICD code count	803
Female	4,765	State count	29

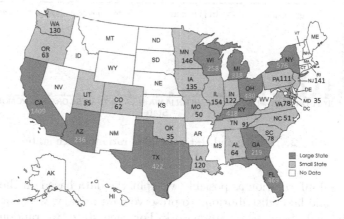

Fig. 1. Patient geographical distribution across states. The states marked in green color are the ones with the total number of data larger than 200. (Color figure online)

there are 6,526 patients with COVID-19 vaccinated. 1,097 of them have side effects who are labeled as 1, and 5429 of them have no side effects who are labeled as 0 on the record. The **imbalanced** label ratio is around 1:5 (# of positive labels : # of negative labels). The vaccine brands include Moderna, Pfizer-BioNTech, and Johnson & Johnson's Janssen. The number of patients with the brands of vaccines is 3,355, 2,159, and 1,012, respectively. The basic statistic of the dataset is shown in Table 1.

The dataset also provides geographic visualization via the zip codes. Based on the zip code information, patients are from 29 states. However, the **data distribution of states** is extremely **unequal**. There are 1,409 patients from CA, while there are only 35 patients in MD, OK, and UT in the dataset. We highlight the 10 states with more than 200 patients in green and visualize the data with geological information in Fig. 1. There are 19 states where the data is less than 200 patients, which raises a **small data challenge**. When we do global model aggregation for federated learning, how we treat the models trained by the small clients appropriately will be a new practical challenge for the COVID-19 vaccine side effect prediction task.

3.2   Training and Test Data Construction

As it is not a benchmark dataset with a well-established training and test split, we will introduce how we create our training and test datasets. To keep as much

Table 2. Training and testing data statistics.

Training		Testing	
# Patient	5,006	# Patient	1,520
# Positive lnt	879	# Positive patient	218
# Negative patient	4,127	# Negative patient	1,302

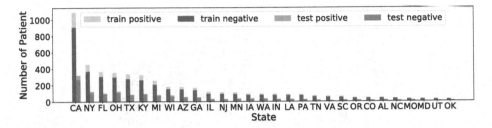

Fig. 2. Training and test data label ratio for each state.

of the original information as possible, we split the data based on the geological information and label distribution. To preserve data privacy, we treat each state as an individual client in our framework. For each state, we randomly sample 80% data for training and 20% data for testing on positive labels and negative labels accordingly.

After that, we keep the training data of each state locally for each client to train the local model. We merge the test data from each state into a large dataset for testing the performance of the global model. In such a way, we preserve the data privacy for each state without sharing patients' data for model training. On the other hand, we construct the training and test data while preserving as much of the geologically similar label distribution as possible. The basic statistics of the training and test data are shown in Table 2. The label ratio of training and test data from different states is visualized in Fig. 2.

4   Task and Notation

In this paper, we focus on a real-world application scenario where each state holds its patients' EHR data and cooperates with other states' data to obtain a COVID-19 vaccine side effect prediction model. Assume that we have K clients or state data centers, and the EHR dataset on the k-th client is denoted as $\mathcal{D}_k = \{X_i^k, y_i^k\}_{i=1}^{N_k}$, where X_i^k represents the EHR data of the i-th patient in the k-th client, y_i^k is the corresponding binary label, and N_k is the number of patient EHR data stored in the k-th client.

As we mentioned before, EHR data are heterogeneous, and $X_i^k :=$ $\{Z_i^k; a_i^k; V_i^k\}$, where Z_i^k is the categorical feature set including gender g_i^k and vaccine brand b_i^k, a_i^k is the numerical feature age, and V_i^k is the time-ordered visit information. $V_i^k = \{x_{i,1}^k, x_{1,2}^k, \cdots, x_{i,M_i}^k\}$, where $x_{i,m}^k$ represents the medical

Table 3. Notations table.

Symbol	Definition and description
$\mathcal{D}_k$	The set of dataset on the k-th client
X_i^k	The EHR record of patient i at client k
$y_i^k \in \{0,1\}$	Vaccine side effect label of patient i on the k-th client
g_i^k	Gender of patient i on the the k-th client
a_i^k	Age of patient i on the the k-th client
b_i^k	Vaccine brand information of patient i on the k-th client
$x_{i,m}^k$	Medical code of patient i at visit m on the the k-th client
K	The number of clients
B	The number of active/selected clients

code set that patient i received at visit m, and M_i denotes the number of visits of patient i.

There are 29 states in our dataset, which are treated as 29 clients in our FL framework. The goal of this paper is to jointly train client models $[\mathbf{w}_1, \cdots, \mathbf{w}_K]$ using the data $\{\mathcal{D}_k\}_{k=1}^K$ stored in all clients, where $K = 29$. Furthermore, we consider the challenges of local model training and global model aggregation raised by the imbalanced labels, Non-IID issue, and small data. We summarize the key notations used in the following sections in Table 3.

5 Methodology

5.1 Model Overview

Figure 3 shows the overview of the proposed federated learning framework FedCovid, which mainly contains the local update and the server update. During the local update, each client k will use the local training data $\mathcal{D}_k$ to update the model parameter $\mathbf{w}_k$. In particular, we propose to learn each patient's embedding by aggregating multiple types of EHR data via an adaptive fusion mechanism. Furthermore, to address the imbalance issue, we propose augmenting the embeddings for the positive patients. Finally, a hybrid fusion loss is used to train the local model $\mathbf{w}_k$. After the local update, active client parameters $[\mathbf{w}_1, \cdots, \mathbf{w}_B]$ will be uploaded to the server. In the server update, the global model $\mathbf{w}_g$ is obtained by aggregating $[\mathbf{w}_1, \cdots, \mathbf{w}_B]$ as well as taking the contribution score β_k of each local model $\mathbf{w}_k$. Note that we first use the clients with larger size to learn the warm-up global model $\mathbf{w}_g$, and then all the clients will be added into the model learning. This new ordinal training strategy aims to alleviate the small data issue. Next, we show the details of each component of the proposed FedCovid framework.

5.2 Local Update: Patient Representation Learning

Patient EHR data contains categorical, numerical, and sequential information. For each type of information, we need to map it to a latent vector representation.

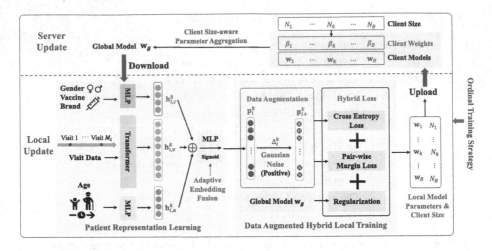

Fig. 3. Overview of the proposed `FedCovid` model.

Embedding Numerical and Categorical Features. We first handle patients' demographic information, including age, gender, and COVID-19 vaccine brand. We treat the age information $a_i k$ as a numerical feature. For the gender g_i^k and COVID-19 vaccine brand information b_i^k, we treat them as the categorical features. We feed these two kinds of features into multi-layer perceptrons (MLP_a and MLP_c) to learn the latent representations for patient i at client k as given by Eq. (1) as follows:

$$\mathbf{h}_{i,a}^k = \text{MLP}_a(a_i^k); \quad \mathbf{h}_{i,c}^k = \text{MLP}_c(g_i^k, b_i^k). \tag{1}$$

Embedding Sequential Visit Data. EHR data also contain the time-ordered sequential visit information $V_i^k = \{x_{i,1}^k, x_{1,2}^k, \cdots, x_{i,M_i}^k\}$. Several approaches [5, 19–22] are proposed to embed the visit data built upon long short-term memory network (LSTM) [16], bidirectional LSTM (Bi-LSTM) [29], convolutional neural network (CNN) [17], and Transformer [33]. Using these backbone models, we can learn the visit embedding as follows:

$$\mathbf{h}_{i,v}^k = \mathcal{M}_b\left(V_i^k\right), \tag{2}$$

where $\mathcal{M}_b$ denotes the backbone approach used for embedding the visit data.

Adaptive Embedding Fusion. The three latent embeddings are obtained from different types of data and models. Here we design an embedding fusion approach to combine the three embeddings in an adaptive approach via a gated linear unit (GLU) [7]. We first concatenate these embeddings as $\mathbf{h}_i^k = [\mathbf{h}_{i,a}^k, \mathbf{h}_{i,c}^k, \mathbf{h}_{i,v}^k]$ and then map $\mathbf{h}_i^k$ to a new representation as follows:

$$\mathbf{h}_i^{k'} = \mathbf{W}_i^k \mathbf{h}_i^k, \tag{3}$$

where $\mathbf{W}_i^k$ is a learnable weight matrix. We then learn a weight for each element in $\mathbf{h}_i^{k'}$ via a Sigmoid function, i.e.,

$$\phi_i^k = \text{sigmoid}(\mathbf{h}_i^{k'}). \tag{4}$$

Finally, the element-wise multiplication $\circ$ is used to generate the patient representation as follows:

$$\mathbf{p}_i^k = \phi_i^k \mathbf{h}_i^{k'}. \tag{5}$$

5.3   Local Update: Data Augmented Hybrid Local Training

Using Eq. (5), we can fuse different types of EHR data together to learn an aggregated patient representation, which can be directly used for prediction. However, as mentioned before, there is another challenge for our setting – imbalanced data. To address this problem, we propose using data augmentation techniques to balance the data, as well as a margin loss to differentiate between positive and negative patient representation learning.

EHR Data Augmentation. Data augmentation approaches have been widely-used for image classification tasks such as rotating, flipping, or mixup technique [4], and natural language processing tasks, e.g., example interpolation techniques and model-based techniques [12]. However, EHR data is heterogeneous, with categorical features, numerical features, and discrete EHR sequence data, making it difficult to directly add small noise to the raw data. To address this issue, we implement the augmentation on the learned embeddings via Eq. (5) rather than the raw input X_i^k. The assumption is that if the patients are similar to each other, then the learned patient representations should also be similar.

Since the number of positive patients is much smaller than that of negative ones, we only need to increase the number of positive cases to make these two classes balanced. In particular, we add a noise vector Δ_i^k generated from a Gaussian distribution with parameters $\{\mu, \sigma\}$ to the learned positive patient embeddings via Eq. (5), where μ is the mean value and σ is the standard deviation for the Gaussian distribution, i.e., $\hat{\mathbf{p}}_{i+}^k = \mathbf{p}_{i+}^k + \Delta_i^k$. Due to the 1:5 ratio of positive and negative labels in our dataset, for each positive data, we will add four randomly generated noise vectors, respectively.

Hybrid Local Training Loss. Let $\hat{\mathbf{P}}_+^k$ represent the representation matrix of the augmented positive data, $\mathbf{P}^k = [\mathbf{P}_+^k, \mathbf{P}_-^k]$ denote the real data representation matrix, where $\mathbf{P}_+^k$ represents the matrix of the real positive data and $\mathbf{P}_-^k$ is the matrix of the real negative data. Using $\hat{\mathbf{P}}_+^k$ and $\mathbf{P}^k$, we can directly train our local model using the cross entropy (CE) loss. To avoid the influence of noise, we will assign different weights to the loss terms of the real data and the augmented data as follows:

$$\mathcal{L}_c^k = \frac{1}{N_k} \text{CE}(f(\mathbf{P}^k), \mathbf{y}^k) + \frac{\lambda_c}{N_k^+} \text{CE}(f(\hat{\mathbf{P}}_+^k), \mathbf{y}_+^k), \tag{6}$$

where λ_c is a hyperparameter, $\mathbf{y}^k = [\mathbf{y}_+^k, \mathbf{y}_-^k]$ is the ground truth label vector of all real data, $\mathbf{y}_+^k$ is the positive label vector, $\mathbf{y}_-^k$ is the negative label vector, and N_k^+ is the total number of augmented data.

To further learn the distinguishable patient representations, we also add a pair-wise margin loss to $\mathcal{L}_c^k$ as follows:

$$\mathcal{L}_m^k = \frac{1}{N_k + N_k^+} \sum_{i=1}^{N_k+N_k^+} \max(d(\tilde{\mathbf{p}}_i^k, \bar{\mathbf{p}}_{j+}^k) - d(\tilde{\mathbf{p}}_i^k, \mathbf{p}_{j'}^k) + \delta, 0), \tag{7}$$

where $d(\cdot, \cdot)$ is the Euclidean distance function, $\tilde{\mathbf{p}}_i^k \in \{\mathbf{P}^k, \hat{\mathbf{P}}_i^k\}$ presents any data representation (i.e., the anchor sample), $\bar{\mathbf{p}}_{j+}^k \in \{\mathbf{P}_+^k, \hat{\mathbf{P}}_+^k\}$ is any positive real or augmented representation, $\mathbf{p}_{j'_-}^k \in \mathbf{P}_-^k$ is a negative patient representation, and δ is the predefined margin value.

These two loss terms $\mathcal{L}_c^k$ and $\mathcal{L}_m^k$ all consider to update the local parameters based on the data. However, when the amount of data on the k-th local client is extremely small, only optimizing these two terms may cause the overfitting problem. To avoid this issue, we add an extra regularization term, which forces the local parameters $\mathbf{w}_k$ to be as close as the global model $\mathbf{w}_g$, i.e., $\|\mathbf{w}_k - \mathbf{w}_g\|^2$. In such a way, we can obtain the final hybrid loss as follows:

$$\mathcal{L}_k = \mathcal{L}_c^k + \lambda_m \mathcal{L}_m^k + \frac{\lambda_w}{N_w} \|\mathbf{w}_k - \mathbf{w}_g\|^2, \tag{8}$$

where λ_m and λ_w are trade-off hyperparameters, and N_w is the number of model parameters. Using Eq. (8), we can learn the local parameter set $\mathbf{w}_k$ and then upload it to the server side.

5.4 Server Update: Client Size-Aware Aggregation

At each communication round, the server side will receive B client models $[\mathbf{w}_1, \cdots, \mathbf{w}_B]$. In general, we can follow FedAvg [24] to directly average them to obtain the global model $\mathbf{w}_g$. As we discussed before, the data size of each local client is unequally. The client with small size may not learn an accurate model by optimizing Eq. (8), and the average operation may destroy the learning of $\mathbf{w}_g$.

To avoid this problem, we propose to upload the size of each client and quantify the contribution of each client according to its size. The larger size, the more reliable, and the greater weight. Let β_k denote the contribution weight of the k-th client, which is defined as follows:

$$\beta_k = \frac{\log(N_k)}{\sum_{i=1}^B \log(N_i)}. \tag{9}$$

Using $[\beta_1, \cdots, \beta_B]$, we can obtain the updated global model as follows:

$$\mathbf{w}_g = \frac{1}{B} \sum_{k=1}^B \beta_k * \mathbf{w}_k. \tag{10}$$

$\mathbf{w}_g$ will be downloaded to each selected or active client for the next round local model training. This procedure will iteratively run until the model converges or achieves the maximum number of communication round.

5.5 Ordinal Training Strategy

As shown in Fig. 2, most of clients only contain a small number of data and they have a higher probability to be selected if we use traditional federated learning training strategy. This may lead to a bad global model learning. To address this issue, we propose to divide the clients into two groups according to their size. We first train the model with the larger size clients. This stage can be considered as model warmup or initialization. After we get the initialized model $\mathbf{w}_g$, we then allow smaller clients to join the training. In particular, we lower the number of epochs and learning rates when training their local models compared with those used for the larger ones. This straightforward training strategy tries to make the negative effect caused by the smaller clients as low as possible.

6 Experiment

6.1 Experiment Setup

Dataset. In our experiments, we use the dataset that is introduced in Sect. 3.

Baselines. We use the following federated learning approaches as baselines:

- **FedAvg** [24] is the classical baseline. Active local clients train their own models and upload the model parameters to the server. The server averages the parameters of local models and re-distributes the updated global model back to active clients for the next round local training.
- **FedProx** [18] adds a reference loss in local training for each client to measure the distances between the local model and the global model, which constrains the local personalized optimization process not to drift excessively.
- **Per-FedAvg** [11] is a personalized federated learning algorithm inspired by meta learning to find an initial shared model that can be easily adapted to local datasets within limited steps of updates.

Implementation Details. We implement all models with Pytorch on Ubuntu 20.04 with NVIDIA RTX A6000 GPU. We leverage the training and testing datasets constructed in Sect. 3.2. The hyperparameters δ, λ_c, λ_m, and λ_w in the loss function Eq. (8) are set to $\frac{1}{5}$, $\frac{1}{2}$, $\frac{1}{6}$, and $\frac{1}{3}$, respectively.

The total communication round is 400, where we set the warmup round as 200 to train the clients' models with larger clients (i.e., CA, NY, FL, OH, TX, KY, MI in Fig. 2). We set the learning rate as 0.001 at the warmup stage and 0.01 after the warmup stage. For the small clients, we set the learning rate as 0.001 after the 200 communication round when they are selected to contribute

Table 4. Performance comparison

Setting	Algorithm	F1 score	Cohen's Kappa	PR-AUC
Central training	CNN	0.4855	0.4279	0.4270
	Transformer	0.4680	0.3842	0.4382
Federated training	FedAvg	0.4081	<u>0.3138</u>	<u>0.1376</u>
	FedProx	<u>0.4083</u>	0.3129	0.1368
	Per-FedAvg	0.3722	0.2669	0.1361
	FedCovid	**0.4669**	**0.3697**	**0.3156**

to the model updates. Baselines do not use the ordinal training strategy, they treat all client equally and use the same learning rate 0.001. In this paper, we apply Transformer as $\mathcal{M}_b$ in Eq. (2) to embed the visit data. In particularly, we employ a two layer Transformer with hidden dimension of 16 and number of heads 8, and apply max-pooling to the output sequence to get the EHR latent embedding. All approaches use Adam as the optimizer, except for Per-FedAvg that uses the SGD optimizer.

6.2 Performance Evaluation

We conduct experiments on the dataset introduced in Sect. 3.2 to validate the proposed approach and baselines. Since the dataset is imbalanced, we use F1 score, Cohen's Kappa, and Area Under the Precision-Recall Curve (PR-AUC) as the evaluation metrics following [6]. We report the average values of the last 10 rounds of the test results at the server side in Table 4.

To explore the performance upper bound of the federated setting, in this experiment, we also put all the training data together to train a prediction model in the central training setting. We use CNN and Transformer as $\mathcal{M}_b$ to embed the visit data. The network structure of Transformer is the same as that of FedCovid. For the CNN model, we use a 1D CNN with kernel size 3 and step size 1. The output channel dimension is set to 2, and we apply a flatten operation to get the visit latent embedding. In Table 4, we can observe that the performance of central training-based approaches is better than that of federated learning approaches.

In the federated setting, FedAvg and FedProx have similar performance, which demonstrates that the reference loss in FedProx may not work for the clients with small size. Due to the unique challenges of the EHR datasets as we discussed in Sect. 3, the personalized federated learning approach Per-FedAvg does not outperform FedAvg and FedProx. We can also observe that the proposed FedCovid achieves the best performance in terms of three metrics. Compared with the best performance of baselines (with underline in Table 4), the performance of our proposed FedCovid model increases 14.35%, 17.81%, and 129.36% on F1 score, Cohen's Kappa, and PR-AUC, respectively.

Table 5. Ablation study

Approach	F1	Cohen's Kappa	PR-AUC
EHR concatenation in Sect. 5.2	0.4365	0.3356	0.2832
CE loss only in Sect. 5.3	0.4150	0.2775	0.2204
Average aggregation in Sect. 5.4	0.4486	0.3093	0.2996
Normal federated training in Sect. 5.5	0.4306	0.3266	0.2817
FedCovid	**0.4669**	**0.3697**	**0.3156**

6.3 Ablation Study

In the proposed FedCovid model, we design several novel mechanisms. To investigate the contribution of each component, we conduct the following ablation study and the results are shown in Table 5. To validate the benefit of the proposed adaptive EHR fusion mechanism in Sect. 5.2, we use the simple **EHR concatenation** operation to learn patient representation. **CE Loss Only** aims to validate the power of data augmentation and the margin loss for handling the imbalance issue in Sect. 5.3. The approach of **Average Aggregation** is to prove the usefulness of the proposed client size-aware aggregation in Sect. 5.4. The goal of **Normal Federated Training** is to show the advantage of ordinal training strategy proposed in Sect. 5.5.

From the results listed in Table 5, we can observe that compared with the proposed FedCovid, the performance of all comparison approaches drops, especially for the CE Loss Only. However, they all outperform the best baselines in Table 4. These results can clearly confirm that each mechanism used in FedCovid is necessary and essential to improve the prediction performance. The contribution descending order in boosting performance is (1) data augmented hybrid loss for training client model, (2) ordinal training strategy, (3) adaptive EHR fusion, and (4) client size-wise model aggregation.

6.4 Convergence Analysis

Figure 4 show the performance changes with regards to each communication round. We can observe that the F1 score also increases dramatically at the beginning and then become stable until 200 communication round. In this warmup stage, we use clients with larger size to train the global model. After the 200th communication round, the performance sharply increases again. This shows that even using the small size of client data, FedCovid can still boost the performance can make the model converge.

6.5 Hyperparameter Sensitivity Analysis

In this subsection, the number of communication rounds for warm-up is very important. To investigate the affect of this parameter on the performance change,

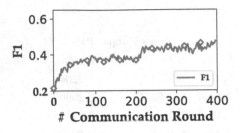

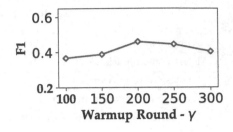

Fig. 4. Model convergence   **Fig. 5.** Hyperparameter analysis

we conduct the following experiment. Let γ controls the warmup round for the large states. Ideally, with the increase of γ, model performance will first increases and then decreases, as there is a trade-off between a well-trained global model and the generalization. To validate this assumption, we alter γ as $\{100, 150, 200, 250, 300\}$, and the results are shown in Fig. 5. We observe that the performance increases first and then decreases with the increase of the warmup round. The reason is that the warmup stage lasts too long, which makes the global model not able to capture enough information from the small states given a fixed communication round and further affects the generalization of the global model. This observation is in accord with our assumption.

7   Conclusion

In this study, we propose FedCovid, a new federated learning model for predicting COVID-19 vaccination side effects. As far as we know, this is the first work to apply a federated learning framework using EHR data to predict COVID-19 side effects. FedCovid solves the following challenges caused by EHR data, including EHR data heterogeneity issue, label imbalanced problem, and client size difference challenge, in a single framework. We conduct experiments on a real world EHR dataset provided by IQVIA. Experimental results show that the proposed FedCovid outperforms baselines in terms of three different metrics, including F1 score, Cohen's Kappa, and PR-AUC. An ablation study demonstrates that all designed mechanisms are useful to improve the prediction performance. Finally, the model insight analysis shows the convergence and hyperparameter sensitivity of the proposed FedCovid model.

References

1. Abiodun, K.M., Awotunde, J.B., Aremu, D.R., Adeniyi, E.A.: Explainable ai for fighting covid-19 pandemic: Opportunities, challenges, and future prospects. In: Computational Intelligence for COVID-19 and Future Pandemics, pp. 315–332. Springer, Heidelberg (2022). https://doi.org/10.1007/978-981-16-3783-4_15

2. Almars, A.M., Gad, I., Atlam, E.-S.: Applications of AI and IoT in COVID-19 vaccine and its impact on social life. In: Hassanien, A.E., Bhatnagar, R., Snášel, V., Yasin Shams, M. (eds.) Medical Informatics and Bioimaging Using Artificial Intelligence. SCI, vol. 1005, pp. 115–127. Springer, Cham (2022). https://doi.org/10.1007/978-3-030-91103-4_7

3. Borriello, A., Master, D., Pellegrini, A., Rose, J.M.: Preferences for a covid-19 vaccine in australia. Vaccine **39**(3), 473–479 (2021)

4. Chlap, P., Min, H., Vandenberg, N., Dowling, J., Holloway, L., Haworth, A.: A review of medical image data augmentation techniques for deep learning applications. J. Med. Imaging Radiat. Oncol. **65**(5), 545–563 (2021)

5. Choi, E., Bahadori, M.T., Schuetz, A., Stewart, W.F., Sun, J.: Doctor AI: predicting clinical events via recurrent neural networks. In: MLHC, pp. 301–318 (2016)

6. Cui, L., Biswal, S., Glass, L.M., Lever, G., Sun, J., Xiao, C.: Conan: complementary pattern augmentation for rare disease detection. In: AAAI, pp. 614–621 (2020)

7. Dauphin, Y.N., Fan, A., Auli, M., Grangier, D.: Language modeling with gated convolutional networks. In: Proceedings of ICML, pp. 933–941. PMLR (2017)

8. Dayan, I., et al.: Federated learning for predicting clinical outcomes in patients with covid-19. Nat. Med. **27**(10), 1735–1743 (2021)

9. Diaz, G.A., Parsons, G.T., Gering, S.K., Meier, A.R., Hutchinson, I.V., Robicsek, A.: Myocarditis and pericarditis after vaccination for covid-19. Jama **326**(12), 1210–1212 (2021)

10. Elnaem, M.H., et al.: Covid-19 vaccination attitudes, perceptions, and side effect experiences in Malaysia: do age, gender, and vaccine type matter? Vaccines **9**(10), 1156 (2021)

11. Fallah, A., Mokhtari, A., Ozdaglar, A.: Personalized federated learning: a meta-learning approach. arXiv preprint arXiv:2002.07948 (2020)

12. Feng, S.Y., et al.: A survey of data augmentation approaches for nlp. arXiv:2105.03075 (2021)

13. Georgiadis, A., Babbar, V., Silavong, F., Moran, S., Otter, R.: St-fl: Style transfer preprocessing in federated learning for covid-19 segmentation. arXiv (2022)

14. Gupta, A., Gharehgozli, A.: Developing a machine learning framework to determine the spread of covid-19. Available at SSRN 3635211 (2020)

15. Hause, A.M., et al.: Safety monitoring of covid-19 vaccine booster doses among adultsâ" United States, september 22, 2021-february 6, 2022. Morb. Mortal. Weekly Rep. **71**(7), 249 (2022)

16. Hochreiter, S., Schmidhuber, J.: Long short-term memory. Neural Comput. **9**(8), 1735–1780 (1997)

17. LeCun, Y., Bengio, Y., Hinton, G.: Deep learning. Nature **521**(7553), 436–444 (2015)

18. Li, T., Sahu, A.K., Zaheer, M., Sanjabi, M., Talwalkar, A., Smith, V.: Federated optimization in heterogeneous networks. Proc. Mach. Learn. Syst. **2**, 429–450 (2020)

19. Luo, J., Ye, M., Xiao, C., Ma, F.: Hitanet: hierarchical time-aware attention networks for risk prediction on electronic health records. In: KDD, pp. 647–656 (2020)

20. Ma, F., Chitta, R., Zhou, J., You, Q., Sun, T., Gao, J.: Dipole: diagnosis prediction in healthcare via attention-based bidirectional recurrent neural networks. In: KDD, pp. 1903–1911 (2017)

21. Ma, F., Gao, J., Suo, Q., You, Q., Zhou, J., Zhang, A.: Risk prediction on electronic health records with prior medical knowledge. In: KDD, pp. 1910–1919 (2018)

22. Ma, F., et al.: A general framework for diagnosis prediction via incorporating medical code descriptions. In: BIBM, pp. 1070–1075. IEEE (2018)

23. Mariappan, M.B., Devi, K., Venkataraman, Y., Lim, M.K., Theivendren, P.: Using AI and ml to predict shipment times of therapeutics, diagnostics and vaccines in e-pharmacy supply chains during covid-19 pandemic. Int. J. Logist. Manag. (2022)
24. McMahan, B., Moore, E., Ramage, D., Hampson, S., y Arcas, B.A.: Communication-efficient learning of deep networks from decentralized data. In: Artificial Intelligence and Statistics, pp. 1273–1282. PMLR (2017)
25. Mohamed, K., et al.: Covid-19 vaccinations: the unknowns, challenges, and hopes. J. Med. Virol. **94**(4), 1336–1349 (2022)
26. Napolitano, F., Xu, X., Gao, X.: Impact of computational approaches in the fight against covid-19: an AI guided review of 17 000 studies. Brief. Bioinf. **23**(1), bbab456 (2022)
27. Rahimi, K.: Guillain-barre syndrome during covid-19 pandemic: an overview of the reports. Neurol. Sci. **41**(11), 3149–3156 (2020)
28. Schultz, N.H.: Thrombosis and thrombocytopenia after chadox1 ncov-19 vaccination. New Engl. J. Med. **384**(22), 2124–2130 (2021)
29. Schuster, M., Paliwal, K.K.: Bidirectional recurrent neural networks. IEEE Trans. Signal Process. **45**(11), 2673–2681 (1997)
30. Shimabukuro, T.T., Cole, M., Su, J.R.: Reports of anaphylaxis after receipt of mrna covid-19 vaccines in the usâ"december 14, 2020-january 18, 2021. Jama **325**(11), 1101–1102 (2021)
31. Sprent, J., King, C.: Covid-19 vaccine side effects: the positives about feeling bad. Science Immunol. **6**(60), eabj9256 (2021)
32. Vaid, A., et al.: Federated learning of electronic health records to improve mortality prediction in hospitalized patients with covid-19: Machine learning approach. JMIR Med. Inf. **9**(1), e24207 (2021)
33. Vaswani, A., et al.: Attention is all you need. In: NeurIPS 30 (2017)
34. Wang, Y., Hu, M., Li, Q., Zhang, X.P., Zhai, G., Yao, N.: Abnormal respiratory patterns classifier may contribute to large-scale screening of people infected with covid-19 in an accurate and unobtrusive manner. arXiv preprint arXiv:2002.05534 (2020)
35. Zhavoronkov, A., et al.: Potential non-covalent sars-cov-2 3c-like protease inhibitors designed using generative deep learning approaches and reviewed by human medicinal chemist in virtual reality (2020)
36. Zhou, Y., He, J.: A randomized approach for crowdsourcing in the presence of multiple views. In: ICDM, pp. 685–694. IEEE Computer Society (2017)
37. Zhou, Y., Wu, J., Wang, H., He, J.: Adversarial robustness through bias variance decomposition: a new perspective for federated learning. arXiv (2020)
38. Zhou, Y., Ying, L., He, J.: Multic^2: an optimization framework for learning from task and worker dual heterogeneity. In: SDM, pp. 579–587. SIAM (2017)

MepoGNN: Metapopulation Epidemic Forecasting with Graph Neural Networks

Qi Cao[1], Renhe Jiang[1(✉)], Chuang Yang[1], Zipei Fan[1], Xuan Song[1,2], and Ryosuke Shibasaki[1]

[1] The University of Tokyo, Tokyo, Japan
{caoqi,jiangrh,chuang.yang,songxuan,shiba}@csis.u-tokyo.ac.jp,
fanzipei@iis.u-tokyo.ac.jp
[2] Southern University of Science and Technology, Shenzhen, China

Abstract. Epidemic prediction is a fundamental task for epidemic control and prevention. Many mechanistic models and deep learning models are built for this task. However, most mechanistic models have difficulty estimating the time/region-varying epidemiological parameters, while most deep learning models lack the guidance of epidemiological domain knowledge and interpretability of prediction results. In this study, we propose a novel hybrid model called MepoGNN for multi-step multi-region epidemic forecasting by incorporating Graph Neural Networks (GNNs) and graph learning mechanisms into Metapopulation SIR model. Our model can not only predict the number of confirmed cases but also explicitly learn the epidemiological parameters and the underlying epidemic propagation graph from heterogeneous data in an end-to-end manner. Experiment results demonstrate our model outperforms the existing mechanistic models and deep learning models by a large margin. Furthermore, the analysis on the learned parameters demonstrates the high reliability and interpretability of our model and helps better understanding of epidemic spread. Our model and data have already been public on GitHub https://github.com/deepkashiwa20/MepoGNN.git.

Keywords: Epidemic forecasting · Hybrid model · Metapopulation epidemic model · Graph Neural Networks · Deep learning · COVID-19

1 Introduction

The coronavirus disease 2019 (COVID-19) pandemic has caused around 500 million confirmed cases and more than 6 million deaths in the global, and it is still ongoing. Due to this circumstance, epidemic forecasting has been a key research topic again as it can guide the policymakers to develop effective interventions and allocate the limited medical resources. Many mechanistic models and deep learning models have been built for the epidemic prediction task. In particular, human mobility is seen as one of the most important factors to understand and forecast the epidemic propagation among different regions. In this study, we

© The Author(s), under exclusive license to Springer Nature Switzerland AG 2023
M.-R. Amini et al. (Eds.): ECML PKDD 2022, LNAI 13718, pp. 453–468, 2023.
https://doi.org/10.1007/978-3-031-26422-1_28

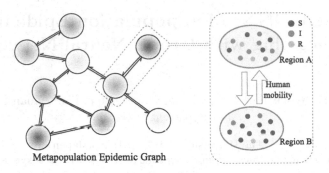

Fig. 1. Illustration of metapopulation epidemic propagation among regions [1].

employ metapopulation SIR model [1,2] as the base model for our task, which extends the most fundamental compartmental model (i.e., SIR [11]) in epidemiology with metapopulation epidemic propagation. As illustrated in Fig. 1, it divides the total population under the epidemic into several sub-populations (e.g., by regions). Each sub-population consists of three compartments, S (susceptible individuals), I (infectious individuals), R (removed individuals, including deaths and recovery cases), and the human mobility between sub-populations is modeled as a directed graph. Thus, it can well model the epidemic propagation in a large-scale area. The metapopulation epidemic models have achieved great success in modeling and analyzing the propagation of epidemic diseases, such as SARS, H1N1, and Malaria [3–5].

However, it is always a non-trivial task to build a metapopulation epidemic model, especially for new emerging epidemics such as the COVID-19 due to the following reasons. First, the epidemiological parameters in metapopulation model keep varying from region to region and time to time. As we all know, the Coronavirus keeps evolving, and the transmissibility and mortality of the variants (e.g., Alpha, Delta, and Omicron) are significantly different. Besides, the intervention policies and the human movements also vary over different periods and regions. Second, due to the mixed factors mentioned above, the epidemic propagation effects via human mobility in metapopulation model are also difficult to be obtained or estimated. In the case of prefecture-level prediction in Japan, we need to collect the large-scale human mobility data of the entire Japan and obtain the amount of human movements between each pair of prefectures. Then how to accurately infer the underlying disease propagation network becomes another intractable task. Third, besides the daily infection data, external features such as date information (e.g., $dayofweek$) and daily movement change patterns should also be involved.

To tackle these challenges, we incorporate deep learning modules into metapopulation SIR model to form a novel hybrid epidemic model. Specifically, we first learn the time/region-varying epidemiological parameters from multiple data features through a spatio-temporal module, which consists of Temporal Convolutional Networks (TCN) and Graph Convolutional Networks (GCN).

Next, we design two types of graph learning module to automatically approximate the underlying epidemic propagation graph based on the countrywide human mobility data. Furthermore, we let the learned latent graph be shared by the spatio-temporal module and the metapopulation SIR module, which further enhances the model interpretability and reliability. Previous deep learning methods [6–10] simply treat the epidemic forecasting as time-series prediction task or spatio-temporal prediction task, which can only output the predicted number of infections in a pure black-box manner. Recent study [29] involves the classical epidemic modeling into deep neural networks, however, it does not explicitly consider the epidemic propagation among regions via metapopulation modeling like ours, which largely limits the model interpretability for multi-region epidemic forecasting. *To the best of our knowledge, our work is the first hybrid model that couples metapopulation epidemic model with spatio-temporal graph neural networks.* In summary, our work has the following contributions:

- We propose a novel hybrid model along with two types of graph learning module for multi-step multi-region epidemic prediction by mixing metapopulation epidemic model and spatio-temporal graph convolution networks.
- Our model can explicitly learn the time/region-varying epidemiological parameters as well as the latent epidemic propagation among regions from the heterogeneous inputs like infection related data, human mobility data, and meta information in a completely end-to-end manner.
- We collect and process the big human GPS trajectory data and other COVID-19 related data that covers the 47 prefectures of Japan from 2020/04/01 to 2021/09/21 for countrywide epidemic forecasting.
- We conduct comprehensive experiments to validate not only the superior forecasting performance but also the high interpretability of our model. Our model and data have already been public on GitHub https://github.com/deepkashiwa20/MepoGNN.git.

2 Related Work

The models for epidemic simulation and forecasting can be divided into two types: *mechanistic approaches* and *deep learning approaches.*

Mechanistic approaches are built based on the domain knowledge of epidemiology which employ pre-defined physical rules to model infectious diseases' transmission dynamics, mainly *classical compartmental models* [11,12], *metapopulation models* [2,13–15] and *agent-based models* [16–18]. The classical compartmental models simulate the spread of infectious diseases in a homogeneous population which are unable to model epidemic spread between regions. The metapopulation models assume the heterogeneity of sub-populations and use the human mobility pattern between regions to model the spread of the epidemic [1,2]. The agent-based models directly use the individual-level movement pattern [16,17] or trajectories [18] to emulate the contagion process. Our work is related to the metapopulation model which is most suitable for multi-region epidemic forecasting task. To implement epidemic modeling, it needs to be calibrated first using historical observations and use the optimized or manually modified parameters to make prediction. These efforts are hardly applicable for multi-step forecasting tasks. The parameters calibration process needs high computational complexity, especially when facing huge parameter state space [13,16]. Moreover, in most mechanistic models, epidemiological parameters keep fixed during forecasting. The variation of parameters through time is not considered which leads to the problem of cumulative error on multi-step prediction.

Deep learning approaches have shown excellent performance in the modeling and forecasting on time series prediction tasks. As a typical time series, several research efforts utilizing deep learning techniques, such as LSTM [6,8], have been conducted for epidemic forecasting over a single region [6,8,19,20]. Nevertheless, the epidemic propagation is often spatially dependent, i.e., co-evolving over regions. Thus, treating epidemic forecasting as a multivariate time-series prediction task, performing collaborative forecasting over multiple geographical units should be a more reasonable choice. For such tasks, a key challenge is to model the complex and implicit spatio-temporal dependencies among the observations, on which much evidence shows that GNN can perform very well for modeling the inter-series relationships. A series of state-of-the-art solutions based on GNN have been proposed for multivariate time-series prediction tasks, such as STGCN [21], DCRNN [22], GraphWaveNet [23], ColaGNN [9], and CovidGNN [10]. In particular, ColaGNN [9] and CovidGNN [10] were explicitly designed for the epidemic prediction. However, these works ignore the domain knowledge of epidemiology and are hard to interpret from the epidemiological perspective. STAN [19] incorporates epidemiological constraints into deep learning models, but it can only predict infections of a single region. CausalGNN [29] embeds single-patched SIRD model into GNN for multi-region epidemic forecasting.

Overall, we distinguish our work from existing ones in the following ways: Compared with the mechanistic models, MepoGNN adopts an end-to-end framework that can predict the dynamic change of epidemiological parameters and use predicted parameters to produce multi-region and multi-step prediction; Compared with the deep learning models for the multi-region prediction task, MepoGNN incorporates the domain knowledge of epidemiology and enhances the interpretability by combining spatio-temporal deep learning model with the metapopulation model; Furthermore, MepoGNN can output the prediction of infections through the metapopulation epidemic model and learn the interpretable epidemiological parameters and the latent graph of epidemic propagation simultaneously.

3 Problem

In this study, we focus on forecasting the number of daily confirmed cases for multi-region and multi-step simultaneously. For a single region, the historical daily confirmed cases from timestep $t - T_{in} + 1$ to t can be represented as $\mathbf{x}^{t-(T_{in}-1):t} \in \mathbb{R}^{T_{in}}$. Then, the historical daily confirmed cases of N regions can be denoted as $\mathbf{X}^{t-(T_{in}-1):t} = \{\mathbf{x}_1^{t-(T_{in}-1):t}, \mathbf{x}_2^{t-(T_{in}-1):t}, ...,$ $\mathbf{x}_N^{t-(T_{in}-1):t}\} \in \mathbb{R}^{N \times T_{in}}$. Besides the historical observations, we also incorporate the external factors to form a multi-channel input as $\mathcal{X}^{t-(T_{in}-1):t} = \{\mathbf{X}_1^{t-(T_{in}-1):t}, \mathbf{X}_2^{t-(T_{in}-1):t}, ..., \mathbf{X}_C^{t-(T_{in}-1):t}\} \in \mathbb{R}^{N \times T_{in} \times C}$. Details of the input features will be introduced in Sect. 5.1. Additionally, human mobility between regions (static flow data $\mathbf{U} \in \mathbb{R}^{N \times N}$ or dynamic flow data $\mathcal{O}^{t-(T_{in}-1):t} \in \mathbb{R}^{N \times N \times T_{in}}$) is used as another type of input. The prediction target is the daily confirmed cases of N regions in next T_{out} timesteps $\mathbf{Y}^{t+1:t+T_{out}} \in \mathbb{R}^{N \times T_{out}}$. The problem can be formulated as follows:

$$\{\mathcal{X}^{t-(T_{in}-1):t}, \mathbf{U}\} \ or \ \{\mathcal{X}^{t-(T_{in}-1):t}, \mathcal{O}^{t-(T_{in}-1):t}\} \xrightarrow{f(\cdot)} \mathbf{Y}^{t+1:t+T_{out}} \quad (1)$$

4 Methodology

We present Metapopulation Epidemic Graph Neural Networks (MepoGNN), demonstrated in Fig. 2, for spatio-temporal epidemic prediction. MepoGNN consists of three major components: metapopulation SIR module, spatio-temporal module and graph learning module. These three components tightly cooperate with each other. Graph learning module learns the mobility intensity between

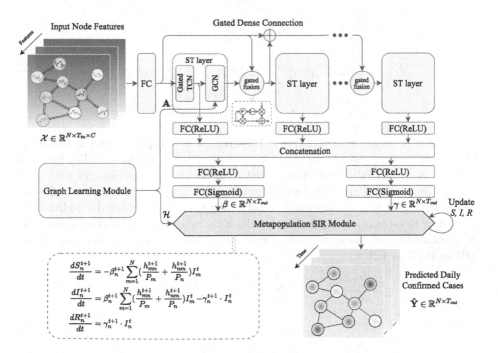

Fig. 2. Proposed metapopulation epidemic graph neural networks (MepoGNN) for spatio-temporal epidemic prediction.

regions as a graph and output it to spatio-temporal module and metapopulation SIR module. Spatio-temporal module captures the spatio-temporal dependency to predict the sequences of parameters for metapopulation SIR module. Then, metapopulation SIR module takes the learned graph and the predicted parameters to produce the multi-step prediction of daily confirmed cases.

4.1 Metapopulation SIR Module

SIR model is one of the most fundamental compartmental models in epidemiology, used for modeling the epidemic spread [11]. However, it can only model the epidemic spread for a homogeneous population, which ignores the epidemic propagation between sub-populations. Metapopulation SIR model [2] fills this gap by assuming the heterogeneity of sub-populations and using human mobility to model the propagation between sub-populations. Metapopulation SIR model, consists of three compartments for each sub-population: S_n^t for number of susceptible individuals, I_n^t for number of infectious individuals, R_n^t for the number of recovered or deceased individuals of sub-population n at time t. P_n represents the size of sub-population n which is assumed to be a constant number, where $P_n = S_n^t + I_n^t + R_n^t$. β is the rate of infection, and γ is the rate of recovery and mortality. Furthermore, it uses h_{nm} to represent the epidemic propagation from sub-population (also called patch) n to m. The original metapopulation SIR model [2] is shown as follows:

$$\frac{dS_n^{t+1}}{dt} = -\beta \cdot S_n^t \sum_{m=1}^{N} (\frac{h_{mn}}{P_m} + \frac{h_{nm}}{P_n}) I_m^t$$

$$\frac{dI_n^{t+1}}{dt} = \beta \cdot S_n^t \sum_{m=1}^{N} (\frac{h_{mn}}{P_m} + \frac{h_{nm}}{P_n}) I_m^t - \gamma \cdot I_n^t \qquad (2)$$

$$\frac{dR_n^{t+1}}{dt} = \gamma \cdot I_n^t$$

In this study, we model population of each region as sub-population in metapopulation SIR model. So, the h_{nm} can be represented by human mobility between regions. Because of different characteristics of regions, policy changes with time and so on, there is spatio-temporal heterogeneity of epidemic spread. In our model, β, γ and h_{nm} are assumed to vary over time and regions. In addition, to prevent β to be extremely small and make it be in a relatively stable magnitude, S_n^t is omitted from the equations. Thus, we extend the original metapopulation SIR in Eq. 2 as follows:

$$\frac{dS_n^{t+1}}{dt} = -\beta_n^{t+1} \sum_{m=1}^{N} (\frac{h_{mn}^{t+1}}{P_m} + \frac{h_{nm}^{t+1}}{P_n}) I_m^t$$

$$\frac{dI_n^{t+1}}{dt} = \beta_n^{t+1} \sum_{m=1}^{N} (\frac{h_{mn}^{t+1}}{P_m} + \frac{h_{nm}^{t+1}}{P_n}) I_m^t - \gamma_n^{t+1} \cdot I_n^t \qquad (3)$$

$$\frac{dR_n^{t+1}}{dt} = \gamma_n^{t+1} \cdot I_n^t$$

With predicted β_n^{t+1}, γ_n^{t+1} and $\mathcal{H}^{t+1}$ (the epidemic propagation matrix formed by $\{h_{nm}^{t+1}|n,m \in \{1,2,...,N\}\}$), S, I, R can be updated iteratively:

$$[S_n^t, I_n^t, R_n^t] \xrightarrow[\beta_n^{t+1},\gamma_n^{t+1},\mathcal{H}^{t+1}]{Eq.(3)} [S_n^{t+1}, I_n^{t+1}, R_n^{t+1}] \tag{4}$$

The final prediction output of daily confirmed cases can be formed as:

$$\hat{y}_n^{t+1} = \beta_n^{t+1} \sum_{m=1}^{N} (\frac{h_{mn}^{t+1}}{P_m} + \frac{h_{nm}^{t+1}}{P_n})I_m^t$$

$$\hat{\mathbf{Y}} = \begin{bmatrix} \hat{y}_1^{t+1} & \cdots & \hat{y}_1^{t+T_{out}} \\ \vdots & \ddots & \vdots \\ \hat{y}_n^{t+1} & \cdots & \hat{y}_n^{t+T_{out}} \end{bmatrix}_{N \times T_{out}} \tag{5}$$

4.2 Spatio-Temporal Module for Epidemiological Parameters

Spatio-temporal module takes the node input features $\mathcal{X} \in \mathbb{R}^{N \times T_{in} \times C}$ and the weighted adjacency matrix $\mathbf{A} \in \mathbb{R}^{N \times N}$ as input and output the predicted parameters $\beta \in \mathbb{R}^{N \times T_{out}}$ and $\gamma \in \mathbb{R}^{N \times T_{out}}$. We use the spatio-temporal layer (ST layer) combining Gated TCN and GCN (same as in GraphWaveNet [23]) to capture the spatio-temporal dependency. Gated TCN [24] is used to capture temporal dependency:

$$\mathcal{Q}_l = g(\Theta_{l1} \star \mathcal{Z}_l + \mathbf{b}_{l1}) \odot \sigma(\Theta_{l2} \star \mathcal{Z}_l + \mathbf{b}_{l2}) \tag{6}$$

where $\mathcal{Z}_l$ is input of l-th layer, Θ_1 and Θ_2 are temporal convolution kernels, $\mathbf{b}_1$ and $\mathbf{b}_2$ are biases, $g(\cdot)$ is tanh activation function for output, $\sigma(\cdot)$ is sigmoid function to form the gate, $\star$ is convolution, $\odot$ is element-wise product. Next, we model the regions and the interactions between regions as a graph and use diffusion graph convolution [22,23] to capture the spatial dependency:

$$\mathbf{P}_f = \mathbf{A}/rowsum(\mathbf{A}), \quad \mathbf{P}_b = \mathbf{A}^{\mathbf{T}}/rowsum(\mathbf{A}^{\mathbf{T}}) \tag{7}$$

$$\tilde{\mathcal{Z}}_l = \sum_{k=0}^{K} \mathbf{P}_f^k \mathcal{Q}_l \mathbf{W}_{lk1} + \mathbf{P}_b^k \mathcal{Q}_l \mathbf{W}_{lk2} \tag{8}$$

where $\mathbf{A} \in \mathbb{R}^{N \times N}$ is weighted adjacency matrix, $\mathbf{P}_f$ is forward transition matrix, $\mathbf{P}_b$ is backward transition matrix, $\tilde{\mathcal{Z}}_l$ is output of l-th layer.

Multiple ST layers can be stacked to capture the spatio-temporal dependency in different scales. We use a gated dense connection to bridge different ST layers. It can extract important information from previous ST layers and pass it to next layer:

$$\mathcal{D}_l = \begin{cases} \mathcal{X}, & \text{if } l = 1, \\ \mathcal{D}_{l-1} + \mathcal{Z}_l, & \text{otherwise.} \end{cases} \tag{9}$$

$$
\mathcal{Z}_{l+1} = \begin{cases} \mathcal{X}, & \text{if } l = 0 \ , \\ \tilde{\mathcal{Z}}_l \odot \sigma(\tilde{\mathcal{Z}}_l) + \mathcal{D}_l \odot (1 - \sigma(\tilde{\mathcal{Z}}_l)), & \text{otherwise.} \end{cases} \tag{10}
$$

where $\mathcal{D}_l$ stores the information from previous layers. Then, we concatenate the output from different layers through skip connections to fuse the information of different scales. Finally, the parameters $\beta \in \mathbb{R}^{N \times T_{out}}$ and $\gamma \in \mathbb{R}^{N \times T_{out}}$ are produced through two fully connected layers, respectively.

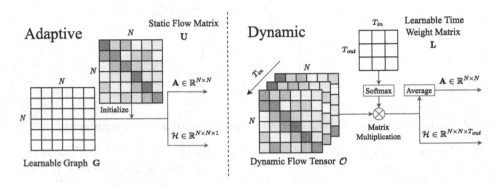

Fig. 3. Two types of graph learning: adaptive and dynamic.

4.3   Graph Learning Module for Epidemic Propagation

There are two different graphs used in metapopulation SIR module and spatio-temporal module, respectively. Unlike the trivial method which input two fixed graphs to each module separately, we make two modules share a single learnable graph. With the shared learnable graph, the spatial dependency used in spatio-temporal module would be consistent with epidemic propagation in metapopulation SIR module which can improve the interpretability of our model. Furthermore, the parameters of graph learning module can be updated by gradients from both spatio-temporal module and metapopulation SIR module which make learned graph more realistic.

As shown in Fig. 3, there are two types of graph learning module to deal with different input data. The first type is adaptive graph learning module which takes the static flow data (e.g., commuter survey data) as input. Intuitively, we initialize an adaptive graph $\mathbf{G}$ with static flow matrix $\mathbf{U}$ and make it learnable through training. Then, the adaptive graph can be output to spatio-temporal module (Eq. 7) as $\mathbf{A} \in \mathbb{R}^{N \times N}$ and to metapopulation SIR module (Eq. 3) as $\mathcal{H} \in \mathbb{R}^{N \times N \times 1}$ (which means we use same h_{nm} for all timesteps). The second type is dynamic graph learning module which takes the dynamic OD flow tensor as input. Although the OD flow and epidemic spread status are both dynamic, but they are not necessarily one-to-one temporally corresponding. Considering the delayed effect, influence of mobility on epidemic spread can be seen as a weighted average of the given past values (T_{in} days). So, we initialize a learnable time weight matrix $\mathbf{L} \in \mathbb{R}^{T_{out} \times T_{in}}$ and normalize it as $\tilde{\mathbf{L}}$ through a softmax function. The normalized time weight matrix can map the historical dynamic flow $\mathcal{O}^{t-(T_{in}-1):t} \in \mathbb{R}^{N \times N \times T_{in}}$ to its influence on future epidemic spread. The output of $\mathcal{H}^{t+1:t+T_{out}} \in \mathbb{R}^{N \times N \times T_{out}}$ and $\mathbf{A} \in \mathbb{R}^{N \times N}$ can be calculated as follows:

$$\tilde{\mathbf{L}} = Softmax_{:,j}(\mathbf{L}) \tag{11}$$

$$\mathcal{H}^{t+1:t+T_{out}} = \tilde{\mathbf{L}}\mathcal{O}^{t-(T_{in}-1):t}, \quad \mathbf{A} = \frac{\sum_{i=1}^{T_{out}} \mathcal{H}^{t+i}}{T_{out}} \tag{12}$$

Why Propose Two Types of Graph Learning? Dynamic graph learning module can illustrate the dynamic change of epidemic propagation. But it requires dynamic flow data which is not available in most cases. To improve the applicability of our model, we propose adaptive graph learning module to address this problem. With two types of graph learning module, our model can handle different situations of data availability in the best way possible.

5   Experiment

5.1   Data

We set 47 prefectures of Japan and 2020/04/01 $\sim$ 2021/09/21 (539 d) as our study area and time period, respectively. The number of daily confirmed cases and cumulative cases and deaths are collected from the NHK COVID-19 database[1]. The number of recovered cases is collected from Japan LIVE Dashboard[2] [25] (original data source is from Ministry of Health, Labour and Welfare, Japan). The population of each prefecture is collected from 2020 census data. With above-mentioned data, daily S, I, R of each prefecture can be calculated. Apart from the number of daily confirmed cases, the input node features also include daily movement change, the ratio of daily confirmed cases in active cases, and $dayofweek$. The movement change data is collected from Facebook Movement Range Maps[3]. It records the change of people movement range compared to a baseline period. Because it is not provided at prefecture level, we use population weighted average to get data at prefecture level. The input static flow data for adaptive graph learning module is the number of commuters between prefectures, which is collected from 2015 census data. The input dynamic flow data for dynamic graph learning module is the daily OD flow data among 47 prefectures, which is generated from human GPS trajectory data provided by

---

[1] https://www3.nhk.or.jp/news/special/coronavirus/data/.
[2] https://github.com/swsoyee/2019-ncov-japan.
[3] https://data.humdata.org/dataset/movement-range-maps.

Blogwatcher Inc. To mitigate the spatio-temporal imbalance in our data, we use stay put ratio (ratio of people staying in a single location all day) in Facebook Movement Range Maps to get the ratio of active users and use it to normalize the OD flow. Finally, the input features of 47 prefectures are generated as a (539, 47, 4) tensor, the static flow is a (47, 47) matrix, and the dynamic flow is a (539, 47, 47) tensor.

5.2 Setting

The input time length T_{in} and output time length T_{out} are both set to 14 d which means we use two-week historical observations to do the two-week prediction of daily confirmed cases. Then, we split the data with ratio 6:1:1 to get training/validation/test datasets, respectively. The fifth wave of infection in Japan is included in test dataset to test the model performance on a real outbreak situation. During training, we use the curriculum learning strategy [26] which increases one prediction horizon every two epochs starting from one day ahead prediction. The batch size is set to 32. The loss function is set as MAE (Mean Absolute Error). Adam is set as the optimizer, where the learning rate is 1e-3 and weight decay is 1e-8. The training algorithm would either be early-stopped if the validation error did not decrease within 20 epochs or be stopped after 300 epochs. PyTorch is used to implement our model. Then experiments are performed on a server with four 2080Ti GPUs. Finally, we evaluate the performance of model on 3 d, 7 d, 14 d ahead prediction and overall 14 steps prediction. The four metrics are used to qualify the performance: $RMSE$ (Root Mean Square Error), MAE (Mean Absolute Error), $MAPE$ (Mean Absolute Percentage Error) and RAE (Relative Absolute Error). To mitigate the influence of randomness, we perform 5 trials for each model and calculate the mean and 95% confidence interval of results. The used random seeds are 0, 1, 2, 3, 4.

5.3 Evaluation

We implement three classes of baselines to compare and evaluate our model on epidemic prediction task:

Mechanistic Models: (1) SIR [11]. SIR model is one of most basic compartmental models in epidemiology. We use optimized β and γ of each regions to produce the prediction. **(2) SIR(Copy)**. Because of weekly periodicity, we copy the β and γ of last week to produce the prediction. **(3) MetaSIR** [2]. Metapopulation SIR model considers the heterogeneity of sub-populations and models the interaction between sub-populations. We use the commuter survey data as $\mathcal{H}$ and optimize β and γ for each region to produce the prediction. **(4) MetaSIR(Copy)**. We copy the β and γ of last week to produce the prediction.

Spatio-Temporal Deep Learning Models: (5) STGCN [21]. STGCN is one of the earliest models which applies GCN and TCN to do spatio-temporal prediction. **(6) DCRNN** [22]. DCRNN proposes a variant of GCN, called diffusion

Table 1. Performance comparison with baselines

Model	3d Ahead				7d Ahead			
	RMSE	MAE	MAPE	RAE	RMSE	MAE	MAPE	RAE
SIR	429.4 ± 23.2	153.9 ± 5.2	83.8 ± 0.7	0.47 ± 0.02	507.5 ± 29.6	191.4 ± 7.7	111.4 ± 3.8	0.57 ± 0.02
SIR(Copy)	248.1	97.4	57.4	0.29	318.5	127.1	67.2	0.38
MetaSIR	336.0 ± 21.6	126.8 ± 3.5	72.2 ± 0.9	0.38 ± 0.01	429.8 ± 25.5	166.9 ± 3.7	92.9 ± 0.8	0.50 ± 0.01
MetaSIR(Copy)	236.5	92.2	54.1	0.28	307.6	120.0	62.7	0.36
STGCN	375.6 ± 18.8	118.6 ± 10.8	45.3 ± 2.8	0.36 ± 0.03	381.1 ± 17.7	128.0 ± 6.6	52.5 ± 3.0	0.38 ± 0.02
DCRNN	305.0 ± 9.8	89.3 ± 4.4	37.3 ± 0.7	0.27 ± 0.01	323.8 ± 15.9	107.6 ± 5.3	47.3 ± 1.4	0.32 ± 0.02
AGCRN	223.5 ± 28.5	80.0 ± 7.8	56.6 ± 13.2	0.24 ± 0.02	253.1 ± 37.7	97.9 ± 7.6	60.8 ± 10.1	0.29 ± 0.02
GraphWaveNet	223.8 ± 46.6	70.6 ± 11.7	35.4 ± 1.2	0.21 ± 0.04	259.9 ± 52.2	89.2 ± 15.2	42.3 ± 1.5	0.27 ± 0.05
MTGNN	297.6 ± 19.2	102.4 ± 6.7	40.6 ± 0.8	0.31 ± 0.02	363.5 ± 37.9	130.9 ± 13.1	49.1 ± 1.7	0.39 ± 0.04
CovidGNN	261.9 ± 55.5	88.4 ± 16.7	43.3 ± 3.8	0.27 ± 0.05	305.4 ± 70.6	116.5 ± 23.8	60.9 ± 5.3	0.35 ± 0.07
ColaGNN	221.7 ± 40.7	72.7 ± 7.2	38.9 ± 1.5	0.22 ± 0.02	300.6 ± 61.2	109.4 ± 16.4	49.3 ± 1.5	0.33 ± 0.05
MepoGNN(Adp)	141.0 ± 7.2	54.3 ± 2.3	34.9 ± 0.8	0.16 ± 0.01	174.6 ± 10.1	69.7 ± 4.2	41.4 ± 1.6	0.21 ± 0.01
MepoGNN(Dyn)	**135.9 ± 17.8**	**52.7 ± 4.6**	**34.2 ± 0.7**	**0.16 ± 0.01**	**160.6 ± 4.5**	**67.6 ± 1.2**	41.7 ± 0.9	**0.20 ± 0.00**
Model	14d Ahead				Overall			
	RMSE	MAE	MAPE	RAE	RMSE	MAE	MAPE	RAE
SIR	890.2 ± 83.8	314.5 ± 16.9	228.3 ± 11.8	0.94 ± 0.05	595.0 ± 43.5	210.0 ± 9.2	128.2 ± 4.7	0.63 ± 0.03
SIR(Copy)	835.5	332.6	183.2	1.00	539.1	190.2	102.7	0.57
MetaSIR	766.1 ± 58.5	279.1 ± 8.2	177.4 ± 4.5	0.84 ± 0.02	500.4 ± 33.9	182.1 ± 4.4	104.9 ± 1.3	0.55 ± 0.01
MetaSIR(Copy)	786.4	302.7	161.9	0.91	503.7	175.6	92.7	0.53
STGCN	430.2 ± 15.8	159.4 ± 6.0	74.7 ± 3.7	0.48 ± 0.02	389.5 ± 7.9	132.0 ± 2.9	55.6 ± 2.4	0.40 ± 0.01
DCRNN	377.9 ± 11.1	146.0 ± 5.0	69.5 ± 4.0	0.44 ± 0.01	335.0 ± 11.8	112.5 ± 4.5	49.5 ± 1.3	0.34 ± 0.01
AGCRN	390.4 ± 105.8	149.0 ± 11.4	88.0 ± 12.8	0.45 ± 0.03	322.7 ± 136.7	108.0 ± 9.9	67.9 ± 15.6	0.32 ± 0.03
GraphWaveNet	389.8 ± 20.8	144.4 ± 7.3	60.2 ± 4.2	0.43 ± 0.02	294.7 ± 40.9	100.1 ± 11.1	44.7 ± 1.4	0.30 ± 0.03
MTGNN	443.5 ± 15.4	168.3 ± 8.1	68.0 ± 2.9	0.50 ± 0.02	363.2 ± 20.5	130.0 ± 8.3	50.7 ± 1.6	0.39 ± 0.03
CovidGNN	414.7 ± 59.8	177.4 ± 15.9	111.2 ± 6.6	0.53 ± 0.05	329.6 ± 59.8	124.2 ± 19.2	66.9 ± 4.2	0.37 ± 0.06
ColaGNN	388.3 ± 23.2	153.4 ± 10.2	75.5 ± 10.8	0.46 ± 0.03	310.7 ± 31.4	110.2 ± 7.2	51.9 ± 3.7	0.33 ± 0.02
MepoGNN(Adp)	261.1 ± 16.0	105.1 ± 7.3	60.1 ± 3.2	**0.32 ± 0.02**	196.2 ± 11.3	75.4 ± 4.7	44.0 ± 1.6	0.23 ± 0.01
MepoGNN(Dyn)	**253.2 ± 7.5**	**107.0 ± 3.0**	62.0 ± 2.0	0.32 ± 0.01	**186.1 ± 5.0**	**74.3 ± 2.0**	44.4 ± 0.8	**0.22 ± 0.01**

convolution and combines it with gated recurrent unit (GRU) to build a spatio-temporal prediction model. **(7) GraphWaveNet** [23]. GraphWaveNet proposes an adaptive learnable graph and uses GCN and TCN to capture spatio-temporal dependency. **(8) MTGNN** [26]. MTGNN uses a graph learning module to learn spatial correlation and fuse different spatial hops and different TCN kernels to enhance the model capacity. **(9) AGCRN** [27]. AGCRN uses GCN and GRU along with a graph learning module and a node adaptive parameter learning module to capture spatio-temporal dependency.

GNN-Based Epidemic Models: (10) CovidGNN [10]. CovidGNN is one of the earliest GNN-based epidemic models. It embeds temporal features on node and uses GCN with skip connections to capture spatial dependency. **(11) ColaGNN** [9]. ColaGNN uses the location-aware attention to extract spatial dependency and uses GCN to integrate the spatio-temporal information.

Performance Evaluation: In Table 1, we compare the performance on three different horizons and overall performance for multi-step prediction among the above-mentioned three classes of baseline models and proposed MepoGNN with two types of graph learning module. Generally, the spatio-temporal deep learning models and GNN-based epidemic models outperform the mechanistic models,

Table 2. Ablation study

Graph	Model	Mean RMSE	Mean MAE	Mean MAPE	Mean RAE
Adaptive	w/o glm	209.51 ± 22.70	81.85 ± 6.69	47.51 ± 2.62	0.25 ± 0.02
	w/o propagation	203.23 ± 24.70	82.05 ± 8.05	45.84 ± 1.68	0.25 ± 0.02
	w/o SIR	318.05 ± 16.30	108.53 ± 5.26	46.07 ± 0.53	0.33 ± 0.02
	MepoGNN	**196.16 ± 11.33**	**75.45 ± 4.65**	**44.02 ± 1.55**	**0.23 ± 0.01**
Dynamic	w/o glm	194.50 ± 17.65	76.84 + 6.04	**43.63 ± 1.59**	0.23 ± 0.02
	w/o propagation	200.55 ± 17.00	80.73 ± 5.54	45.16 ± 1.24	0.24 ± 0.01
	w/o SIR	290.78 ± 33.92	102.00 ± 9.93	45.79 ± 1.61	0.31 ± 0.03
	MepoGNN	**186.07 ± 4.99**	**74.30 ± 1.99**	44.43 ± 0.77	**0.22 ± 0.01**

especially for long horizons. Among all baseline models, GraphWaveNet gets the best performance. However, our proposed two MepoGNN models get the very significant improvement over all baseline models. For two types of graph learning module, dynamic one gets slightly better performance than adaptive one. Figure 4 compares the 7 d ahead prediction results of Tokyo and Hyogo of the top two baseline models and MepoGNN model with dynamic graph learning module. From the prediction results, GraphWaveNet and ColaGNN can not produce accurate predictions for high daily confirmed cases during the outbreak. This phenomenon could be explained by different data distributions of daily confirmed cases in training dataset and test dataset. The test dataset covers the period of fifth epidemic wave in Japan which is much more severe than previous ones. Deep learning models have difficulty to predict these high daily confirmed cases that never happened before the fifth wave. However, with the help of metapopulation SIR module, our proposed MepoGNN model can handle this problem and make significantly better prediction for unprecedented surge of cases. This capability is very crucial for a trustworthy epidemic forecasting model.

Ablation Study: To demonstrate the effect of different components of our model, we conduct an ablation study for MepoGNN models with two different graph learning modules, respectively. The variants are as follows: **(1) w/o glm**: Remove the graph learning module of MepoGNN model; **(2) w/o propagation**: Remove the metapopulation propagation from metapopulaiton SIR module (which means metapopulation SIR model is reduced to SIR model); **(3) w/o SIR**: Remove the metapopulation SIR module completely. Table 2 demonstrates that all three components can bring significant boost of performance for our model. Particularly, it is easy to find that the biggest performance drop happens when removing the metapopulation SIR module. Because the metapopulation SIR module enables the capability of MepoGNN model to handle the unprecedented surge of cases.

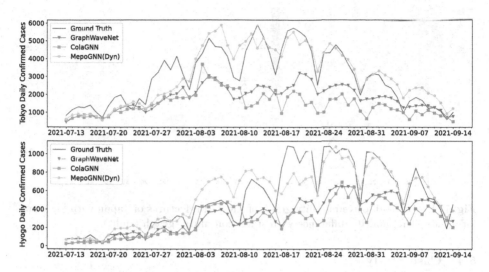

Fig. 4. Predicted daily confirmed cases of Tokyo and Hyogo with horizon = 7.

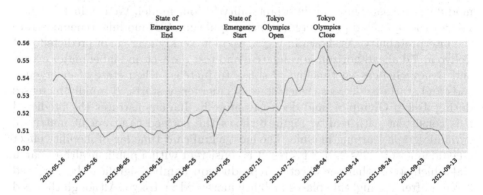

Fig. 5. 7-day moving average of predicted β of Tokyo with horizon = 7.

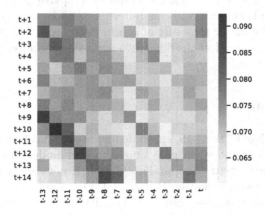

Fig. 6. Learned time weight matrix in dynamic graph learning module.

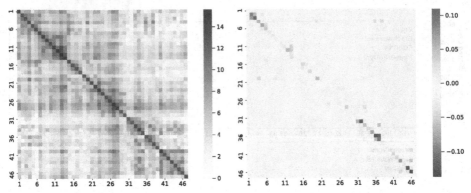

Fig. 7. Learned adaptive mobility graph of the 47 prefectures of Japan with log transformation (left) and its difference with static commuter graph (right).

5.4   Case Study

The final output of MepoGNN model is fully produced by metapopulation SIR module. It brings significant interpretability for our model. We conduct an analysis for the predicted parameters of metapopulation SIR module to demonstrate the interpretability. As shown in Fig. 5, we plot weekly average of predicted β of Tokyo at 7 d ahead horizon in validation and test dataset and label major events and policy changes on timeline. β starts to increase when state of emergency ends and starts to decrease when state of emergency starts. β rapidly increases during Tokyo Olympics, and decreases after it. It demonstrates the predicted β is consistent with reality. Figure 6 shows the learned time weight matrix of dynamic graph learning module. The most significant time lag of mobility effect on epidemic spread is 22 d. This result is consistent with a public health research [28] which states that the effective reproduction number significantly increased 3 weeks after the nightlife places mobility increased in Tokyo. Although the used indicator is different from our research, the mechanisms behind time lag could be similar. Figure 7 shows the learned graph of adaptive graph learning module and the difference between it and commuter graph. The learned adaptive mobility graph keeps the major structure of commuter graph. And the minor change from initialization can reflect the difference between commuter graph and spatial epidemic propagation.

6   Conclusion

Since the outbreak of COVID-19, epidemic forecasting has become a key research topic again. In this study, we propose a novel hybrid model for epidemic forecasting that incorporates spatio-temporal graph neural networks and graph learning mechanisms into metapopulation SIR model. Our model can not only predict the number of confirmed cases but also explicitly learn the time/region-varying epidemiological parameters and the underlying epidemic propagation graph from heterogeneous data in an end-to-end manner. Then, we evaluate our model by using real COVID-19 infection data and big human mobility data of 47 prefectures in Japan. The evaluation results demonstrate the superior performance as well as the high reliability and interpretability of our model.

Acknowledgment. This work was partially supported by JST SICORP Grant Number JPMJSC2104.

References

1. Wang, L., Li, X.: Spatial epidemiology of networked metapopulation: an overview. Chin. Sci. Bull. **59**(28), 3511–3522 (2014)
2. Wang, J., Wang, X., Wu, J.: Inferring metapopulation propagation network for intra-city epidemic control and prevention. In: Proceedings of the 24th ACM SIGKDD International Conference on Knowledge Discovery & Data Mining, pp. 830–838 (2018)
3. Brockmann, D., Helbing, D.: The hidden geometry of complex, network-driven contagion phenomena. Science **342**(6164), 1337–1342 (2013)
4. Hufnagel, L., Brockmann, D., Geisel, T.: Forecast and control of epidemics in a globalized world. Proc. Natl. Acad. Sci. **101**(42), 15124–15129 (2004)
5. Wesolowski, A., Eagle, N., Tatem, A.J., Smith, D.L., Noor, A.M., Snow, R.W., et al.: Quantifying the impact of human mobility on malaria. Science **338**(6104), 267–270 (2012)
6. Venna, S.R., Tavanaei, A., Gottumukkala, R.N., Raghavan, V.V., Maida, A.S., et al.: A novel data-driven model for real-time influenza forecasting. IEEE Access **7**, 7691–7701 (2018)
7. Wu, Y., Yang, Y., Nishiura, H., Saitoh, M.: Deep learning for epidemiological predictions. In: The 41st International ACM SIGIR Conference on Research & Development in Information Retrieval, pp. 1085–1088 (2018)
8. Arora, P., Kumar, H., Panigrahi, B.K.: Prediction and analysis of covid-19 positive cases using deep learning models: a descriptive case study of India. Chaos, Solitons Fractals **139**, 110017 (2020)
9. Deng, S., Wang, S., Rangwala, H., Wang, L., Ning, Y.: Cola-gnn: cross-location attention based graph neural networks for long-term ili prediction. In: Proceedings of the 29th ACM International Conference on Information & Knowledge Management, pp. 245–254 (2020)
10. Kapoor, A., Ben, X., Liu, L., Perozzi, B., Barnes, M., Blais, M., et al.: Examining covid-19 forecasting using spatio-temporal graph neural networks. arXiv preprint arXiv:2007.03113 (2020)
11. Kermack, W.O., McKendrick, A.G.: A contribution to the mathematical theory of epidemics. In: Proceedings of the Royal Society of London. Series A, Containing Papers of a Mathematical and Physical Character, vol. 115, no. 772, pp. 700–721 (1927)
12. Dehning, J., Zierenberg, J., Spitzner, F.P., Wibral, M., Neto, J.P., Wilczek, M., et al.: Inferring change points in the spread of covid-19 reveals the effectiveness of interventions. Science **369**(6500), eabb9789 (2020)
13. Chang, S., Pierson, E., Koh, P.W., Gerardin, J., Redbird, B., Grusky, D., et al.: Mobility network models of covid-19 explain inequities and inform reopening. Nature **589**(7840), 82–87 (2021)
14. Chinazzi, M., Davis, J.T., Ajelli, M., Gioannini, C., Litvinova, M., Merler, S., et al.: The effect of travel restrictions on the spread of the 2019 novel coronavirus (covid-19) outbreak. Science **368**(6489), 395–400 (2020)

15. Jiang, R., et al.: Countrywide origin-destination matrix prediction and its application for covid-19. In: Dong, Y., Kourtellis, N., Hammer, B., Lozano, J.A. (eds.) ECML PKDD 2021. LNCS (LNAI), vol. 12978, pp. 319–334. Springer, Cham (2021). https://doi.org/10.1007/978-3-030-86514-6_20

16. Aleta, A., Martin-Corral, D., Pastore y Piontti, A., Ajelli, M., Litvinova, M., Chinazzi, M., et al.: Modelling the impact of testing, contact tracing and household quarantine on second waves of covid-19. Nat. Hum. Behav. 4(9), 964–971 (2020)

17. Chang, S.L., Harding, N., Zachreson, C., Cliff, O.M., Prokopenko, M.: Modelling transmission and control of the covid-19 pandemic in Australia. Nat. Commun. 11(1), 1–13 (2020)

18. Yang, C., Zhang, Z., Fan, Z., Jiang, R., Chen, Q., Song, X., et al.: Epimob: interactive visual analytics of citywide human mobility restrictions for epidemic control. IEEE Trans. Vis. Comput. Graph. 1 (2022)

19. Gao, J., Sharma, R., Qian, C., Glass, L.M., Spaeder, J., Romberg, J., et al.: Stan: spatio-temporal attention network for pandemic prediction using real-world evidence. J. Am. Med. Inf. Assoc. 28(4), 733–743 (2021)

20. Cui, Y., Zhu, C., Ye, G., Wang, Z., Zheng, K.: Into the unobservables: a multi-range encoder-decoder framework for covid-19 prediction. In: Proceedings of the 30th ACM International Conference on Information & Knowledge Management, pp. 292–301 (2021)

21. Yu, B., Yin, H., Zhu, Z.: Spatio-temporal graph convolutional networks: a deep learning framework for traffic forecasting. In: Proceedings of the 28th International Joint Conference on Artificial Intelligence, pp. 3634–3640 (2018)

22. Li, Y., Yu, R., Shahabi, C., Liu, Y.: Diffusion convolutional recurrent neural network: data-driven traffic forecasting. In: International Conference on Learning Representations (2018)

23. Wu, Z., Pan, S., Long, G., Jiang, J., Zhang, C.: Graph wavenet for deep spatial-temporal graph modeling. In: Proceedings of the 28th International Joint Conference on Artificial Intelligence, pp. 1907–1913 (2019)

24. Dauphin, Y.N., Fan, A., Auli, M., Grangier, D.: Language modeling with gated convolutional networks. In: International conference on machine learning, pp. 933–941. PMLR (2017)

25. Su, W., Fu, W., Kato, K., Wong, Z.S.Y.: "Japan live dashboard" for covid-19: a scalable solution to monitor real-time and regional-level epidemic case data. In: Context Sensitive Health Informatics: The Role of Informatics in Global Pandemics, pp. 21–25. IOS Press (2021)

26. Wu, Z., Pan, S., Long, G., Jiang, J., Chang, X., Zhang, C.: Connecting the dots: multivariate time series forecasting with graph neural networks. In: Proceedings of the 26th ACM SIGKDD International Conference on Knowledge Discovery & Data Mining, pp. 753–763 (2020)

27. Bai, L., Yao, L., Li, C., Wang, X., Wang, C.: Adaptive graph convolutional recurrent network for traffic forecasting. Adv. Neural Inf. Process. Syst. 33, 17804–17815 (2020)

28. Nakanishi, M., Shibasaki, R., Yamasaki, S., Miyazawa, S., Usami, S., Nishiura, H., et al.: On-site dining in Tokyo during the covid-19 pandemic: time series analysis using mobile phone location data. JMIR mHealth and uHealth 9(5), e27342 (2021)

29. Wang, L., Adiga, A., Chen, J., Sadilek, A., Venkatramanan, S., Marathe, M.: Causal-gnn: causal-based graph neural networks for spatio-temporal epidemic forecasting. In: Proceedings of the AAAI Conference on Artificial Intelligence (2022)

EpiGNN: Exploring Spatial Transmission with Graph Neural Network for Regional Epidemic Forecasting

Feng Xie, Zhong Zhang, Liang Li, Bin Zhou[✉], and Yusong Tan

College of Computer, National University of Defense Technology, Changsha, China
{xiefeng,zhangzhong,liliang98,binzhou,ystan}@nudt.edu.cn

Abstract. Epidemic forecasting is the key to effective control of epidemic transmission and helps the world mitigate the crisis that threatens public health. To better understand the transmission and evolution of epidemics, we propose EpiGNN, a graph neural network-based model for epidemic forecasting. Specifically, we design a transmission risk encoding module to characterize local and global spatial effects of regions in epidemic processes and incorporate them into the model. Meanwhile, we develop a Region-Aware Graph Learner (RAGL) that takes transmission risk, geographical dependencies, and temporal information into account to better explore spatial-temporal dependencies and makes regions aware of related regions' epidemic situations. The RAGL can also combine with external resources, such as human mobility, to further improve prediction performance. Comprehensive experiments on five real-world epidemic-related datasets (including influenza and COVID-19) demonstrate the effectiveness of our proposed method and show that EpiGNN outperforms state-of-the-art baselines by 9.48% in RMSE.

Keywords: Epidemic forecasting · Graph neural network · Spatial transmission modeling · Public health informatics

1 Introduction

Epidemics spread through human-to-human interaction and circulate worldwide, seriously endangering public health. The World Health Organization (WHO) estimates that seasonal influenza annually causes approximately 3–5 million severe cases and 290,000-650,000 deaths.[1] Recently, the coronavirus disease 2019 (COVID-19) has spread over more than 200 countries and territories,[2] causing heavy human losses and economic burdens. Accurate prediction of epidemics is the key to effective control of epidemic transmission and plays an essential role in driving administrative decision-making, timely allocating healthcare resources, and helping with drug research.

---

[1] https://www.who.int/en/news-room/fact-sheets/detail/influenza-(seasonal).
[2] https://covid19.who.int/.

A number of studies have investigated epidemic forecasting for decades, aiming to help the world mitigate the crisis that threatens public health. In statistics community, autoregressive (AR) models are widely used in epidemic forecasting [3,15]. In compartment models, the susceptible-infected-recovered (SIR) is the most basic one, many cumulative works in this category are based on its extensions [2,16]. However, the above methods are limited in accuracy and generalization due to their oversimplified or fixed assumptions. Recently, deep learning has achieved tremendous success in many challenging tasks, and various deep learning-based epidemic prediction models [1,7,17] have been proposed, especially models based on emerging graph neural networks (GNNs) [4,11,14]. The core insight behind GNNs is to capture correlations between nodes and model the signal propagation of neighbor nodes. In regional epidemic prediction task, GNN-based approaches model the spread of epidemics by regarding regions as nodes and hidden correlations between regions as edges in a graph structure.

Although both spatial dependencies and temporal information are well exploited, existing methods still face two main challenges. First, the key to GNN-based models is to capture high-quality connections between regions. Using explicit graph structures, such as geographic topology (Fig. 1(a)), does not necessarily reflect the true dependencies or is hard to capture the hidden relationships [19]. Some effective works [11,22] capture potential relationships between regions using specific data (e.g., human mobility) that require struggling with data availability, data accuracy, and data privacy. Due to the excellent feature extraction capability of the attention mechanism [13], several studies [4,7] are mainly dedicated to combining attention mechanism and the latent representation of each region to capture correlations between regions based on similarity. However, owing to the global receptive field of attention mechanism, during aggregating features from other regions, it is prone to causing oversmoothing [9], or bringing noise especially when the data is noisy and sparse in epidemic surveillance [14], which will damage the forecasting performance. Therefore, capturing underlying transmission dependencies between regions reasonably and accurately is crucial to facilitate further improving the prediction performance of GNN-based methods. At the same time, the method we expect should flexibly support both scenarios when rich external information can be collected or not.

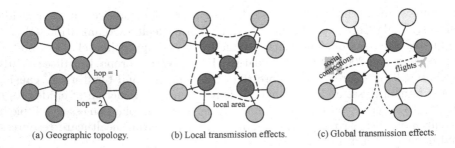

(a) Geographic topology.   (b) Local transmission effects.   (c) Global transmission effects.

Fig. 1. The illustration of geographic topology, local and global spatial transmission effects, where nodes represent regions and edges represent the relationships.

Second, some studies [5,10] have paid much attention to mining the transmission factors of epidemics and assessing the spatial transmission risks of regions, and they suggest transmission risks are meaningful information that provides more practical insights for understanding the spread of epidemics. Spatial transmission risk implies a *potential ability that the epidemic in one region impacts other regions from a spatial perspective*, which is not only important property of regions but also reveals the spatial effects between regions. As shown in Fig. 1, in typical epidemic processes, virus tend to firstly spread in a local range due to intensive mobility of internal elements (e.g., human mobility) between geographically adjacent regions [22] (Fig. 1(b)). Moreover, the epidemic in one region has not only local effects but also spillover effects across regions through complicated social connections [5] (Fig. 1(c)). Thus, modeling spatial effects of regions are beneficial for understanding the spread and evolution of epidemics, which motivates us to investigate how to leverage regional transmission risk to enhance the accuracy and interpretability of epidemic prediction.

To tackle the aforementioned challenges and better understand the spread of epidemics, we propose a novel neural network model, termed EpiGNN, which handles temporal and spatial information through Convolution Neural Network and Graph Convolution Network. In this model, we propose a transmission risk encoding module to characterize spatial effects of regions. Meanwhile, we develop a Region-Aware Graph Learner which takes transmission risk, geographical information, and temporal dependencies into consideration to capture correlations between regions. Our contributions are summarized as follows:

- We design a novel graph neural network-based model for epidemic prediction in which a transmission risk encoding module is proposed that shows how we incorporate local and global spatial effects of regions into the model.
- We introduce a Region-Aware Graph Learner which takes transmission risk, geographical information, and temporal dependencies into account to better explore underlying spatio-temporal correlations between regions.
- We evaluate our model on five epidemic-related datasets. Experimental results show the proposed method achieves state-of-the-art performance and demonstrate the effectiveness of our model. The source code and datasets are available at https://github.com/Xiefeng69/EpiGNN.

The remainder of this paper is organized as follows. We review related works in Sect. 2. Then we explain the details of our contributions in Sect. 3 and present experiments and results in Sect. 4. At last, we conclude in Sect. 5.

2   Related Work

Epidemic Forecasting Methods. As mentioned above, there has been a large body of work focusing on epidemic forecasting. Essentially, the aim of epidemic forecasting is to predict the number of infection cases for a region at a timestamp based on historical data. In statistics community, autoregressive (AR) models are widely used in epidemic forecasting [3,15]. In compartment models, susceptible-infected-recovered (SIR) is the most basic one that divides a population into three groups: susceptible, infected, and recovered, and simulates the variations over time between groups. Many cumulative works in this category are based on its extensions [2,16]. Although these methods have a solid mathematical foundation, their accuracy and generalization are limited due to their oversimplified or fixed assumptions, pre-supposed functional form, and careful feature engineering. In recent years, due to its powerful data learning capability, deep learning has been widely adopted in various fields, including epidemic prediction tasks. Wu et al. [17] proposed CNNRNN-Res that firstly applied deep learning for epidemic forecasting. Adhikari et al. [1] adopted deep clustering to help determine the historical season closest to the predicted time point to aid prediction. Jin et al. [6] introduced an inter-series attention-based model to capture similar progression patterns between time series to assist in COVID-19 prediction. Jung et al. [7] designed a self-attention-based approach that cooperates with Long Short-Term Memory (LSTM) for regional influenza prediction.

Graph Neural Network-Based Models. Graph neural networks (GNNs) have emerged in recent years, such as GCN [8], ST-GCN [20], and demonstrated promising results for extracting the correlation of irregular, non-Euclidean graph data, which make them become powerful tools for understanding the spread and evolution of epidemics. GNN-based epidemic prediction approaches create a graph where nodes correspond to regions of a country, and edge weights correspond to correlations between regions. Deng et al. [4] proposed Cola-GNN that applied an attention mechanism to learn the dependencies between regions based on the latent state of each region learned through Recurrent Neural Networks (RNNs). Panagopoulos et al. [11] took advantage of mobility data across different regions to explore the underlying correlations between regions and adopted message passing neural network (MPNN) combined with LSTM to capture the spatial and temporal evolution of COVID-19. Zhang et al. [22] developed a multi-modal information fusion-powered method that took social connections and demographic information into account to improve COVID-19 forecasting. Wang et al. [14] designed CausalGNN which employed a causal module to provide epidemiological context for guiding the learning of spatial and temporal disease dynamics. Inspired by these works, we aim to explore spatial transmission in typical epidemic processes with GNNs for regional epidemic forecasting.

3   The Proposed Method

3.1   Problem Formulation

We formulate the epidemic prediction problem as a graph-based propagation model. We have a total of N regions (e.g., cities or states). We denote the historical cases data $\mathbf{X} = [\mathbf{x}_1, ..., \mathbf{x}_t]$ as training data, where $\mathbf{x}_z \in \mathbb{R}^N$ represents the observed cases value of N regions at time z. Our goal is to predict the future cases value, i.e. $\mathbf{x}_{t+h}$, where h is a fixed horizon with respect to different tasks (e.g., short- or long-term prediction). For every task, we use $[\mathbf{x}_{t-T+1}..., \mathbf{x}_t] \in \mathbb{R}^{N \times T}$ for a look-back window T to predict $\mathbf{x}_{t+h}$. For a region i, it is associated with a time

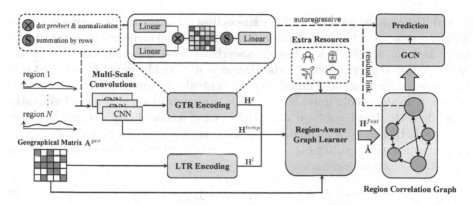

Fig. 2. The overview of our proposed method: EpiGNN.

series $\mathbf{x}_{i:} = [x_{i,t-T+1}, ..., x_{i,t}]$. The proposed method is drawn in Fig. 2. In following sections, we introduce the building blocks for EpiGNN in detail.

3.2 Multi-scale Convolutions

Convolutional Neural Networks (CNNs) have demonstrated strong feature representation ability and efficient parallel computation in grid data and sequence data that apply learnable filters to capture information behind data. Some works [4,18] suggest that using a set of multi-scale convolutions can capture complex temporal patterns simultaneously. Therefore, in this work, we also adopt multi-scale convolutions with different filter sizes and dilated factors as a feature extractor. We denote convolution filter as $\mathbf{f}_{1 \times s, d}$, where s is filter size, d is dilated factor, both s and d are empirically selected. The convolution operation of series $\mathbf{x}_{i:}$ with $\mathbf{f}_{1 \times s, d}$ at step j is represented as:

$$\mathbf{x}_{i:} \star \mathbf{f}_{1 \times s, d}(j) = \sum_{i=0}^{s-1} \mathbf{f}_{1 \times k}(i)\mathbf{x}(j - d \times i), \tag{1}$$

where $\star$ is convolution operator. We use m parallel convolutional layers, each scale with k filters, to generate different feature vectors, and concatenate them after an adaptive pooling layer. We denote $D = (m \times k \times p)$ as the output dimension of multi-scale convolutions, where p is the output dimension of adaptive pooling layer. At last, we obtain the final temporal feature representation $\mathbf{h}_i^{temp} \in \mathbb{R}^D$ for region i.

3.3 Transmission Risk Encoding Module

The epidemic in one region has not only local effects but also spillover effects across regions through complicated social connections [5]. Therefore, We assess local and global transmission risks for regions respectively and encode them as important properties of regions. Essentially, transmission risk encodings indicate spatial structure information which reflects potential spread influence of regions.

Local Transmission Risk (LTR) Encoding. The proximity between regions will lead to a rapid increase in the mobility of internal elements between regions (e.g., human mobility), which will exacerbate local transmission risk. In the geographical network topology, the *degree* is a valuable signal for understanding network structure and describing the centrality of nodes. The more central regions will potentially interact with their surrounding regions more frequently, which leads to significant local spatial effects and is more likely to cause the virus to spread. Hence, we use the degree of each region in geographical topology to measure its local transmission risk. We generate local transmission risk encoding $\mathbf{h}_i^l \in \mathbb{R}^D$ by following equation:

$$\mathbf{h}_i^l = \mathbf{W}^l \cdot d_i + \mathbf{b}^l, \tag{2}$$

where $d_i = \sum_j a_{i,j}^{geo}$ means the degree of region i, and $\mathbf{A}^{geo}$ is the geographical adjacency matrix that indicates the spatial connectivity of regions: $a_{i,j}^{geo} = 1$ means region i and region j are neighbors (by default, $a_{i,i}^{geo} = 1$). $\mathbf{W}^l$ and $\mathbf{b}^l$ are the parameters to transform degree vector $\mathbf{d} \in \mathbb{R}^N$ to encodings.

Global Transmission Risk (GTR) Encoding. Besides geographical adjacent, there are also potential correlations between disjoint regions (e.g., social connections). During the spread of epidemics, it is highly likely that similar progression patterns are shared among related regions because they suffer from the same virus. We believe that if a region has a similar progression pattern to another region, there is probably a dependency between them. Therefore, for global transmission risk assessment, we measure it by the sum of the dynamic correlations based on temporal features of regions, and we call it the *global correlation coefficient* in this paper. Inspired by the self-attention [13], we obtain global correlation coefficients and GTR encodings by following equations:

$$\mathbf{A} = (\mathbf{H}^{temp}\mathbf{W}^q)(\mathbf{H}^{temp}\mathbf{W}^k)^T, \tag{3}$$

$$a_{i,j} = \frac{a_{i,j}}{\max(\|\mathbf{a}_{i:}\|_2, \epsilon)}, \tag{4}$$

$$g_i = \sum_j a_{i,j}, \tag{5}$$

$$\mathbf{h}_i^g = \mathbf{W}^g \cdot g_i + \mathbf{b}^g, \tag{6}$$

where $\mathbf{W}^q$, $\mathbf{W}^k \in \mathbb{R}^{D \times F}$, and $\mathbf{W}^g \in \mathbb{R}^D$ are weight matrices, ϵ is a small value to avoid division by zero. More precisely, we first feed temporal features $\mathbf{H}^{temp}$ to two parallel dense layers and apply a dot product to obtain a correlation distribution matrix $\mathbf{A}$. Then we adopt normalization for each row in $\mathbf{A}$ and calculate global correlation coefficient vector $\mathbf{g} \in \mathbb{R}^N$. At last, we feed g_i to a dense layer to form global transmission risk encoding $\mathbf{h}_i^g \in \mathbb{R}^D$.

3.4   Region-Aware Graph Learner

Capturing correlations between regions by simulating all factors related to the spread of epidemics is troublesome, so we design a Region-Aware Graph Learner (RAGL), which considers both temporal and spatial information to generate a region correlation graph, where nodes correspond to regions, and edge weights correspond to the correlations between regions. We fuse temporal features and transmission risk encodings as nodes' initial attributes $\mathbf{H}^{feat} \in \mathbb{R}^{N \times D}$:

$$\mathbf{h}_i^{feat} = \mathbf{h}_i^{temp} + \mathbf{h}_i^l + \mathbf{h}_i^g. \tag{7}$$

Existing methods for learning correlations based on attention mechanisms are often symmetric or bidirectional [18]. However, the epidemic transmission is often spread from one region to another, or one region impacts another, so we expect that the learned region correlation graph should not be a completely bidirectional graph. First, we extract dynamic temporal relationships by following equations:

$$\mathbf{M}_1 = \tanh(\mathbf{H}^{temp}\mathbf{W}_1 + \mathbf{b}_1), \quad \mathbf{M}_2 = \tanh(\mathbf{H}^{temp}\mathbf{W}_2 + \mathbf{b}_2), \tag{8}$$

$$\hat{\mathbf{A}} = \mathrm{ReLU}(\tanh(\mathbf{M}_1\mathbf{M}_2^T - \mathbf{M}_2\mathbf{M}_1^T)), \tag{9}$$

where $\mathbf{W}_1, \mathbf{W}_2 \in \mathbb{R}^{D \times F}$ are weight matrices. The subtraction term and $\mathrm{ReLU}(\cdot)$ regularize the connectivity of temporal correlation matrix $\hat{\mathbf{A}}$. Next, we capture spatial dependencies utilizing $\mathbf{A}^{geo}$, where we also introduce the *degree* to assess local spatial effects. Specifically, we use the product of the degrees of two adjacent regions as a gate that measures the impacts of local interactions between regions to control spatial dependencies:

$$\mathbf{D}^s = \mathrm{sigmoid}(\mathbf{W}^s \circ \mathbf{dd}^T), \tag{10}$$

$$\tilde{\mathbf{A}} = \mathbf{D}^s \circ \mathbf{A}^{geo} + \hat{\mathbf{A}}, \tag{11}$$

where $\circ$ is element-wise (Hadamard) product, and $\mathbf{W}^s \in \mathbb{R}^{N \times N}$ is a learnable parameter matrix. The spread of epidemics is associated with many factors (e.g., human mobility, climate). RAGL can flexibly take advantage of external resources that are available to extract dependencies between regions more accurately. We denote external resources as $\mathbf{E} = [\mathbf{E}_1, \mathbf{E}_2, ..., \mathbf{E}_t]$ where $\mathbf{E}_z \in \mathbb{R}^{N \times N}$ represents external correlation between regions at time step z (e.g., the weight of edge $e_{i,j}^z$ represents the total number of people that moved from region i to region j), we can calculate external correlation matrix by following equation:

$$\mathbf{A}^e = \mathbf{W}^e \circ \sum_{i=0}^{e-1} \mathbf{E}_{t-e}, \tag{12}$$

where e is the look-back window of external resources, and $\mathbf{W}^e$ is a learnable matrix. At last, we sum them up to obtain the region correlation matrix $\tilde{\mathbf{A}}$.

3.5   Graph Convolution Network

Graph Convolution Networks (GCNs) as a kind of GNNs have been proven to be effective methods for learning node representations. In this work, we apply GCN to investigate the epidemic propagation among different regions [4,8,18]. We apply the following equation to update node representations:

$$\mathbf{H}^{(l)} = \sigma(\tilde{\mathbf{D}}^{-1}\tilde{\mathbf{A}}\mathbf{H}^{(l-1)}\mathbf{W}^{(l-1)}), \tag{13}$$

where $\tilde{\mathbf{D}} = \sum_j \tilde{a}_{i,j}$, $\mathbf{W}^{(l)} \in \mathbb{R}^{D \times D}$ is a layer-specific weight matrix, and $\mathbf{H}^{(l)} \in \mathbb{R}^{N \times D}$ is the node representation matrix at l^{th} layer, with $\mathbf{H}^{(0)} = \mathbf{H}^{feat}$. $\sigma(\cdot)$ is the nonlinear function (e.g., exponential linear unit (ELU)).

3.6   Prediction and Objective Function

Due to the nonlinear characteristics of CNNs and GNNs, the scale of neural network outputs is not sensitive to the input. Moreover, the historical infection cases of each region are not purely nonlinear, especially in COVID-19 datasets, showing linear characteristics on the progression patterns of many regions, which cannot be fully handled well by neural networks [21]. To address these drawbacks, some models [3,12] retain the advantages of traditional linear models and neural networks by combining a linear part to design a more robust prediction framework. Therefore, EpiGNN can optionally integrate a traditional AutoRegressive (AR) component as a linear part to obtain the linear result $\hat{\mathbf{y}}_{t+h}^l \in \mathbb{R}^N$:

$$\hat{y}_{i,t+h}^l = \sum_{m=0}^{q-1} \mathbf{W}_m^{ar} x_{i,t-m} + b^{ar}, \tag{14}$$

where q is the look-back window of AR, and $\mathbf{W}^{ar} \in \mathbb{R}^q$ is the parameters in AR component. We concatenate nodes' initial features and the output of the last layer of GCN together, and feed it to a dense layer to obtain the output:

$$\hat{\mathbf{y}}_{t+h}^n = [\mathbf{H}^{(0)}; \mathbf{H}^{(l)}]\mathbf{W}_n + \mathbf{b}_n, \tag{15}$$

where [;] is concatenation operation, and $\mathbf{W}_n \in \mathbb{R}^{2D}$. The final prediction result $\hat{\mathbf{y}}_{t+h} \in \mathbb{R}^N$ of EpiGNN is obtained by summing $\hat{\mathbf{y}}_{t+h}^l$ and $\hat{\mathbf{y}}_{t+h}^n$:

$$\hat{\mathbf{y}}_{t+h} = \hat{\mathbf{y}}_{t+h}^l + \hat{\mathbf{y}}_{t+h}^n. \tag{16}$$

We employ the Mean Squared Error (MSE) to train the model by minimizing the loss. The loss function can be defined as:

$$\mathcal{L}(\theta) = \|\mathbf{y}_{t+h} - \hat{\mathbf{y}}_{t+h}\|_2^2, \tag{17}$$

where $\mathbf{y}_{t+h}$ is the ground truth value, and θ are all learnable parameters in EpiGNN. The pseudocode of the algorithm is described in Algorithm 1.

Algorithm 1. EpiGNN algorithm

Require: Time series data $\{\mathbf{X}, \mathbf{y}\}$ from multiple regions, geographic adjacent matrix $\mathbf{A}^{geo}$, external resources $\mathbf{E}$ (optional).

Ensure: Prediction result $\hat{\mathbf{y}}$.

1: **for** each *region i* **do**
2:    $\mathbf{h}_i^{temp} \leftarrow$ Multi-Scale Convolutions($\mathbf{x}_{i:}$)
3:    $\mathbf{h}_i^l \leftarrow$ Local Transmission Risk Encoding($\mathbf{A}_{i:}^{geo}$)
4:    $\mathbf{h}_i^g \leftarrow$ Global Transmission Risk Encoding($\mathbf{h}_i^{temp}, \mathbf{H}^{temp}$)
5: **end for**
6: **for** each *region pair* (i,j) **do**
7:    $\tilde{a}_{i,j} \leftarrow$ Region-Aware Graph Learner($\mathbf{h}_i^{temp}, \mathbf{h}_j^{temp}, \mathbf{A}^{geo}, \mathbf{E}$)
8: **end for**
9: **for** each *region i* **do**
10:    $\mathbf{h}_i^{feat} \leftarrow \mathbf{h}_i^{temp} + \mathbf{h}_i^l + \mathbf{h}_i^g$
11:    $\mathbf{h}_i^{(l)} \leftarrow$ Graph Convolution Network($\mathbf{h}_i^{feat}, \tilde{\mathbf{A}}$)
12:    $\hat{y}_i \leftarrow$ Output($\mathbf{x}_{i:}, [\mathbf{h}_i^{feat}; \mathbf{h}_i^{(l)}]$)
13: **end for**
14: **return** $\hat{\mathbf{y}}$

---

4 Experiments and Analysis

4.1 Experimental Settings

Datasets. We conduct experiments on five epidemic-related datasets, three are seasonal influenza datasets and two are COVID-19 datasets. The statistics of datasets are summarized in Table 1. All datasets have been split into training set (50%), validation set (20%), and test set (30%) in chronological order.

Table 1. Statistics of datasets, where SD is standard deviation and granularity means the frequency of epidemic surveillance records.

Datasets	Regions	Length	Min	Max	Mean	SD	Granularity
Japan-Prefectures	47	348	0	26635	655	1711	Weekly
US-Regions	10	785	0	16526	1009	1351	Weekly
US-States	49	360	0	9716	223	428	Weekly
Australia-COVID	8	556	0	9987	539	1532	Daily
Spain-COVID	35	122	0	4623	38	269	Daily

– **Japan-Prefectures.** This dataset is collected from the Infectious Diseases Weekly Report (IDWR) in Japan,[3] which contains weekly influenza-like-illness (ILI) statistics from 47 prefectures from August 2012 to March 2019.

---

[3] https://tinyurl.com/y5dt7stm.

- **US-Regions.** This dataset is the ILINet portion of the US-HHS dataset,[4] consisting of weekly influenza activity levels for 10 Health and Human Services (HHS) regions of the U.S. mainland for the period of 2002 to 2017.
- **US-States.** This dataset is collected from the Center for Disease Control (CDC) (see Footnote 4). It contains the count of patient visits for ILI (positive cases) for each week and each state in the United States from 2010 to 2017. After removing Florida due to missing data, we keep 49 states remaining.
- **Australia-COVID.** This dataset is publicly available at JHU-CSSE.[5] We collect daily new COVID-19 confirmed cases ranging from January 27, 2020, to August 4, 2021, in Australia (including 6 states and 2 territories).
- **Spain-COVID.** This dataset is collected by [11], consisting of daily COVID-19 cases for 35 administrative NUTS3 regions that were mainly affected by pandemic in Spain from February 20, 2020, to June 20, 2020. We also collect human mobility data in Spain from *Data For Good program*.[6]

Metrics. We adopt Root Mean Squared Error ($RMSE = \sqrt{\frac{1}{N}\sum_{i=1}^{n}(\hat{y}_i - y_i)^2}$) and Pearson's Correlation ($PCC = \frac{\sum_{i=1}^{N}(\hat{y}_i - \bar{\hat{y}})(y_i - \bar{y})}{\sqrt{\sum_{i=1}^{N}(\hat{y}_i - \bar{\hat{y}})^2}\sqrt{\sum_{i=1}^{N}(y_i - \bar{y})^2}}$) as metrics. For RMSE lower value is better, while for PCC higher value is better.

Baselines. We compared the proposed model with the following methods:

- **HA:** the historical average number of cases in observation window T.
- **AR:** the standard autoregression model.
- **LSTM:** the recurrent neural networks (RNN) using LSTM cell.
- **TPA-LSTM** [12]: an attention-based LSTM model.
- **ST-GCN** [20]: a spatial temporal graph neural network.
- **CNNRNN-Res** [17]: a deep learning model that combines CNN, RNN, and residual links for epidemiological prediction.
- **SAIFlu-Net** [7]: A self-attention-based model for influenza forecasting.
- **Cola-GNN** [4]: a deep learning model that combines CNN, RNN and GCN for epidemic prediction.

Implementation Details. All programs are implemented using Python 3.8.5 and PyTorch 1.9.1 with CUDA 11.1 in an Ubuntu server with an Nvidia Tesla K80 GPU. For each task we run 5 times with different random initialization. For all tasks, the batch size is set to 128, the look-back window T is set to 20. The horizon h is set to $\{3, 5, 10, 15\}$ and $\{3, 7, 14\}$ for influenza and COVID-19 prediction respectively in turn. We train the model using Adam optimizer with weight decay 5e-4 and perform early stopping to avoid overfitting. We empirically choose 5 filters: $\{\mathbf{f}_{1\times3,1}, \mathbf{f}_{1\times5,1}, \mathbf{f}_{1\times3,2}, \mathbf{f}_{1\times5,2}, \mathbf{f}_{1\times T,1}\}$. The range of

---

[4] https://tinyurl.com/y39tog3h.
[5] https://github.com/CSSEGISandData/COVID-19.
[6] https://dataforgood.fb.com/tools/disease-prevention-maps/.

hidden dimension F is $\{8, 16, 24, 32\}$, the number of CNN filters k is searched from $\{4, 8, 12, 16, 32\}$, the dimension of pooling layer p is chosen in $\{1, 2, 3\}$, the number of GCN layers l is selected from 1 to 5. In COVID-19 task, the model integrates an autoregressive component as a linear part, and the window size q is optimized in $\{10, 20\}$. In Spain-COVID, we denote EpiGNN$_{exter}$ that utilizes human mobility as external resources, and the look-back window e is searched from $\{1, 2, 3\}$.

Table 2. RMSE and PCC performance of different methods on three datasets with horizon = 3, 5, 10, 15. Bold face indicates the best result of each column and underlined the second-best. * represents that the result is reported in the corresponding reference.

Dataset		Japan-Prefectures				US-Regions				US-States			
Methods	Metric	Horizon				Horizon				Horizon			
		3	5	10	15	3	5	10	15	3	5	10	15
HA	RMSE	2129	2180	2230	2242	2552	2653	2891	2992	360	371	392	403
	PCC	0.607	0.475	0.493	0.534	0.845	0.727	0.514	0.415	0.893	0.848	0.772	0.742
AR	RMSE	1705	2013	2107	2042	757	997	1330	1404	204	251	306	327
	PCC	0.579	0.310	0.238	0.483	0.878	0.792	0.612	0.527	0.909	0.863	0.773	0.723
LSTM	RMSE	1246	1335	1622	1649	688	975	1351	1477	180	213	276	307
	PCC	0.873	0.853	0.681	0.695	0.895	0.812	0.586	0.488	0.922	0.889	0.820	0.771
TPA-LSTM	RMSE	1142	1192	1677	1579	761	950	1388	1321	203	247	236	247
	PCC	0.879	0.868	0.644	0.724	0.847	0.814	0.675	0.627	0.892	0.833	0.849	0.844
ST-GCN	RMSE	1115	1129	1541	1527	807	1038	1290	1286	209	256	289	292
	PCC	0.880	0.872	0.735	**0.773**	0.840	0.741	0.644	0.619	0.778	0.823	0.769	0.774
CNNRNN-Res	RMSE	1550	1942	1865	1862	738	936	1233	1285	239	267	260	250
	PCC	0.673	0.380	0.438	0.467	0.862	0.782	0.552	0.485	0.860	0.822	0.820	0.847
SAIFlu-Net	RMSE	1356	1430	1654	1707	661	870	1157	1215	167	195	236	238
	PCC	0.765	0.654	0.585	0.556	0.885	0.800	0.674	0.564	0.930	0.900	0.853	0.852
Cola-GNN*	RMSE	1051	1117	**1372**	1475	636	855	1134	1203	167	202	241	237
	PCC	0.901	0.890	**0.813**	0.753	0.909	0.835	0.717	0.639	0.933	0.897	0.822	0.856
EpiGNN	RMSE	996	1031	1441	1470	589	774	984	1061	160	186	220	236
	PCC	0.904	0.908	0.739	0.773	0.912	0.842	0.749	0.694	0.935	0.907	0.865	0.861

4.2 Prediction Performance

We evaluate each model in short-term (horizon < 10) and long-term (horizon ≥ 10) settings. The experimental results on influenza datasets and COVID-19 datasets are shown in Table 2 and Table 3 respectively. There is an overall trend that the prediction accuracy drops as the prediction horizon increases because the larger the horizon, the harder the problem. The large difference in RMSE across different datasets is due to the scale and variance of the datasets.

We observe that EpiGNN outperforms other models on most tasks. EpiGNN achieves 5.6% and 13.4% lower RMSE than the best baselines in the influenza prediction task and COVID-19 prediction task respectively. In influenza prediction tasks, most deep learning-based models perform better than statistical

Table 3. RMSE performance of different methods on two COVID-19 datasets with horizon = 3, 7, 14. Bold face indicates the best result of each column and underlined the second-best. - means the forecasting results are not available.

Dataset	Spain-COVID			Australia-COVID		
Methods	Horizon			Horizon		
	3	7	14	3	7	14
HA	167.20	189.90	214.19	2948.48	2777.37	2589.61
AR	165.07	179.51	203.13	<u>85.21</u>	237.73	<u>309.03</u>
LSTM	152.79	177.27	<u>184.44</u>	181.97	315.85	338.34
TPA-LSTM	150.74	183.52	227.95	180.14	<u>220.82</u>	462.78
ST-GCN	162.81	186.21	190.13	253.97	443.01	485.12
CNNRNN-Res	163.75	208.85	219.65	210.23	416.90	488.01
SAIFlu-Net	158.06	200.63	229.62	133.85	277.90	351.14
Cola-GNN	138.34	176.52	203.67	127.59	279.56	326.79
EpiGNN	<u>135.54</u>	<u>162.51</u>	186.41	**71.42**	**153.07**	**287.90**
EpiGNN$_{exter}$	**129.90**	**145.33**	**178.73**	–	–	–

Table 4. Runtime (s) and model size (K) comparison on three influenza datasets when horizon = 5. Runtime is the time spent on a single GPU per epoch.

Dataset ($h = 5$)	Japan-Prefectures		US-Regions		US-States	
	Runtime	Params.	Runtime	Params	Runtime	Params.
ST-GCN	0.18	27K	0.16	26K	0.18	27K
CNNRNN-Res	0.05	13K	0.04	5K	0.06	14K
SAIFlu-Net	0.15	35K	0.10	26K	0.14	32K
Cola-GNN	0.14	9K	0.13	7K	0.15	9K
EpiGNN (ours)	0.10	11K	0.14	9K	0.07	12K

models (i.e., HA/AR) since they make effort to deal with nonlinear characteristics and complex patterns behind time series. We also notice that statistical model AR is competitive on COVID-19 prediction tasks, especially on Australia-COVID dataset. This could be because of the strong seasonal effects of influenza datasets, which is obviously not the situation in the COVID-19 historical statistics. During COVID-19 period, due to government interventions (e.g., stay-at-home orders, lockdown), the epidemic situations of regions show significant differences. It turns out that a simple linear aggregation over the past case numbers can achieve relatively good performance. EpiGNN also achieves the best performance in COVID-19 datasets attributed to the integration of a linear model. In Spain-COVID, we conduct EpiGNN$_{exter}$ which considers human mobility data as external information in Eq. 12 to distill the correlations between regions by providing more practical evidence. The results exhibit that EpiGNN$_{exter}$ is better than EpiGNN, pointing out that external information is helpful for capturing correlations between regions. Table 4 shows the runtimes and number of parameters for each model on influenza datasets. EpiGNN has no obvious adverse effect on training efficiency and well controls the model size to prevent overfitting.

4.3   Ablation Study

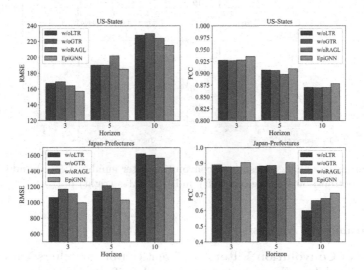

Fig. 3. Results of ablation studies on US-States (top) and Japan-Prefectures (bottom) datasets. For RMSE lower value is better, while for PCC higher value is better.

- **w/oLTR** stands for EpiGNN without local transmission risk encoding.
- **w/oGTR** represents EpiGNN without global transmission risk encoding.
- **w/oRAGL** indicates EpiGNN using self-attention [13] to capture dependencies between regions instead of Region-Aware Graph Learner (i.e., applying $\tilde{\mathbf{A}} = \mathrm{softmax}((\mathbf{H}^{feat}\mathbf{W}_1)(\mathbf{H}^{feat}\mathbf{W}_2)^T))$.

We perform ablation studies on Japan-Prefectures and US-Regions datasets, and the results measured using RMSE and PCC are shown in Fig. 3. We quantitatively show that the complete EpiGNN can yield the most stable and optimal performance compared to other incomplete models. Compared with using self-attention, RAGL can bring performance gains. The fact can be attributed that RAGL well utilizes spatial and temporal information, which affirms the importance of designing a suitable approach to explore the correlations between regions. In addition, since the captured dependencies are not fully bidirectional, it helps GCN to focus on potentially related regions to overcome the oversmoothing phenomenon [9] and avoid noise accumulation. We also notice that both w/oLTR and w/oGTR cause performance drops, which indicates the positive impacts of transmission risk encodings, and exhibits the effectiveness of modeling transmission risks because they emphasize the spatial effects of regions and provide interpretable evidence on risky areas.

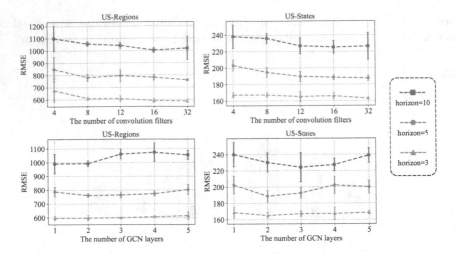

Fig. 4. Parameters analysis results of convolution filter number k (top) and GCN layer number l (bottom) on US-Regions (left) and US-States (right) datasets.

4.4   Parameters Analysis

Number of Convolution Filters. Different convolution filters learn different features behind data. We evaluate k in range $\{4, 8, 12, 16, 32\}$, and the results are shown in Fig. 4. Smaller k results in poor prediction performance due to limited representation ability. As k increases, there are more learnable parameters in model and could bring performance gain to a certain extent. We recommend selecting $k = 12$ to achieve a balance between accuracy and computation.

Number of GCN Layers. More GCN layers stacked tend to aggregate nodes' features from wider neighborhood ranges. We vary the number of GCN layers from 1 to 5, and the results are shown in Fig. 4. We observe that smaller l can reach better performance. However, performance drops when l increases reveals that integrating information from irrelevant/weakly-related nodes may result in oversmoothing [9] or bring noises, which will undermine the performance.

4.5   Visualization

We visualize an example with window $= (2016/46^{th}$–$2017/13^{th})$ and horizon $= 5$ (week) in US-States dataset, meanwhile, we also provide potential risky regions. Figure 5(a) is the distribution of degrees in the United States. We notice that the more central/larger region, the greater the degree. Figure 5(b) is the distribution of global correlation coefficients. Compared with Fig. 5(a), it can be seen that some states (e.g., CA) that are not in the center have high global correlation coefficients. Texas (TX) is the largest and second-most populous state in the U.S. which has a relatively high degree and global correlation coefficient in this case study. We show how Texas is related to other states as drawn in Fig. 5(c). In Fig. 5(c), Texas does not have dependencies with all states. Nevertheless, Texas has relatively significant dependencies with its adjacent regions and also has relationships with some non-adjacent regions.

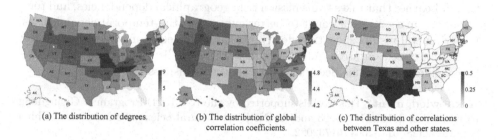

(a) The distribution of degrees.   (b) The distribution of global correlation coefficients.   (c) The distribution of correlations between Texas and other states.

Fig. 5. Visualization of intermediate results.

We visualize the predicted curve of EpiGNN and LSTM in Fig. 6. Compared with LSTM, we observe that EpiGNN fits the ground truth better, and some trends of fluctuation are also predicted better (e.g., WY/DE/VT), while LSTM yields quite inaccurate predictions in some states. We notice that there are similar progression patterns between TX and its adjacent states (e.g., NM/AR/LA), which indicates that local correlations between geographically adjacent regions may be very strong. The correlations drawn in Fig. 5(c) also show that adjacent regions are strongly related, which is consistent with the existing finding [10].

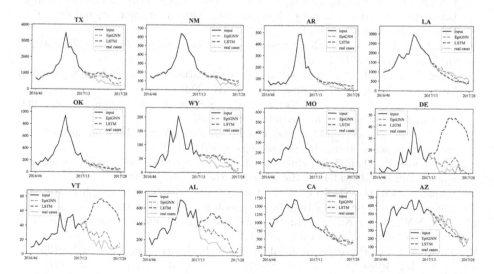

Fig. 6. Predicted curve of EpiGNN (green) and LSTM (blue) for selected states. (Color figure online)

5   Conclusions

In this paper, we develop EpiGNN, a novel model for epidemic prediction. In this model, we design a transmission risk encoding module to characterize local and global spatial effects of each region. Meanwhile, we propose a Region-Aware Graph Learner that takes transmission risk, geographical dependencies, and temporal information into account to better explore spatial-temporal dependencies. Experimental results show the effectiveness and efficiency of our method on five epidemic-related datasets. As for future work, we will devote to better predict by considering the time decay effects of spatial transmission.

Acknowledgment. This work is supported by the Key R&D Program of Guangdong Province No. 2019B010136003 and the National Natural Science Foundation of China No. 62172428, 61732004, 61732022.

References

1. Adhikari, B., Xu, X., Ramakrishnan, N., Prakash, B.A.: EpiDeep: exploiting embeddings for epidemic forecasting. In: Proceedings of KDD (2019)
2. Aron, J.L., Schwartz, I.B.: Seasonality and period-doubling bifurcations in an epidemic model. J. Theor. Biol. **110**, 665–679 (1984)
3. Chakraborty, T., Chattopadhyay, S., Ghosh, I.: Forecasting dengue epidemics using a hybrid methodology. Physica A: Stat. Mech. Appl. (2019)
4. Deng, S., Wang, S., Rangwala, H., Wang, L., Ning, Y.: Cola-GNN: cross-location attention based graph neural networks for long-term ILI prediction. In: Proceedings of CIKM (2020)
5. Han, X., Xu, Y., Fan, L., Huang, Y., Xu, M., Gao, S.: Quantifying Covid-19 importation risk in a dynamic network of domestic cities and international countries. Proc. Natl. Acade. Sci. (2021)
6. Jin, X., Wang, Y.X., Yan, X.: Inter-series attention model for Covid-19 forecasting. In: Proceedings of SDM (2021)
7. Jung, S., Moon, J., Park, S., Hwang, E.: Self-attention-based deep learning network for regional influenza forecasting. IEEE JBHI (2021)
8. Kipf, T.N., Welling, M.: Semi-supervised classification with graph convolutional networks. arXiv preprint arXiv:1609.02907 (2016)
9. Li, Q., Han, Z., Wu, X.M.: Deeper insights into graph convolutional networks for semi-supervised learning. In: Proceedings of AAAI (2018)
10. McMahon, T., Chan, A., Havlin, S., Gallos, L.K.: Spatial correlations in geographical spreading of Covid-19 in the united states. Sci. Rep. (2022)
11. Panagopoulos, G., Nikolentzos, G., Vazirgiannis, M.: Transfer graph neural networks for pandemic forecasting. In: Proceedings of AAAI (2021)
12. Shih, S.Y., Sun, F.K., Lee, H.: Temporal pattern attention for multivariate time series forecasting. Mach. Learn. **108**, 1421–1441 (2019)
13. Vaswani, A., et al.: Attention is all you need. In: Proceedings of NeurIPS (2017)
14. Wang, L., Adiga, A., Chen, J., Sadilek, A., Venkatramanan, S., Marathe, M.: CausalgNN: causal-based graph neural networks for spatio-temporal epidemic forecasting (2022)

15. Wang, Z., Chakraborty, P., Mekaru, S.R., Brownstein, J.S., Ye, J., Ramakrishnan, N.: Dynamic poisson autoregression for influenza-like-illness case count prediction. In: Proceedings of KDD (2015)
16. Won, M., Marques-Pita, M., Louro, C., Gonçalves-Sá, J.: Early and real-time detection of seasonal influenza onset. PLoS Comput. Biol. (2017)
17. Wu, Y., Yang, Y., Nishiura, H., Saitoh, M.: Deep learning for epidemiological predictions. In: Proceedings of SIGIR (2018)
18. Wu, Z., Pan, S., Long, G., Jiang, J., Chang, X., Zhang, C.: Connecting the dots: multivariate time series forecasting with graph neural networks. In: Proceedings of KDD (2020)
19. Wu, Z., Pan, S., Long, G., Jiang, J., Zhang, C.: Graph wavenet for deep spatial-temporal graph modeling. arXiv preprint arXiv:1906.00121 (2019)
20. Yu, B., Yin, H., Zhu, Z.: Spatio-temporal graph convolutional networks: a deep learning framework for traffic forecasting. arXiv preprint arXiv:1709.04875 (2017)
21. Zhang, G.P.: Time series forecasting using a hybrid Arima and neural network model. Neurocomputing (2003)
22. Zhang, H., et al.: Multi-modal information fusion-powered regional Covid-19 epidemic forecasting. In: Proceedings of BIBM (2021)

Applications: Transportation

Route to Time and Time to Route: Travel Time Estimation from Sparse Trajectories

Zhiwen Zhang[2], Hongjun Wang[1], Zipei Fan[1,2(✉)], Jiyuan Chen[1], Xuan Song[1(✉)], and Ryosuke Shibasaki[2]

[1] Southern University of Science and Technology, Shenzhen, China
songx@sustech.edu.cn
[2] The University of Tokyo, Tokyo, Japan
fanzipei@iis.u-tokyo.ac.jp

Abstract. Due to the rapid development of Internet of Things (IoT) technologies, many online web apps (e.g., Google Map and Uber) estimate the travel time of trajectory data collected by mobile devices. However, in reality, complex factors, such as network communication and energy constraints, make multiple trajectories collected at a low sampling rate. In this case, this paper aims to resolve the problem of travel time estimation (TTE) and route recovery in sparse scenarios, which often leads to the uncertain label of travel time and route between continuously sampled GPS points. We formulate this problem as an inexact supervision problem in which the training data has coarsely grained labels and jointly solve the tasks of TTE and route recovery. And we argue that both two tasks are complementary to each other in the model-learning procedure and hold such a relation: more precise travel time can lead to better inference for routes (*Time → Route*), in turn, resulting in a more accurate time estimation (*Route → Time*). Based on this assumption, we propose an EM algorithm to alternatively estimate the travel time of inferred route through weak supervision in E step and retrieve the route based on estimated travel time in M step for sparse trajectories. We conducted experiments on three real-world trajectory datasets and demonstrated the effectiveness of the proposed method.

Keywords: Internet of things · Weakly supervised learning · Graph convolutional network · Travel time estimation · Route recovery

1 Introduction

With advances in the area of the Internet of Things (IoT), GPS modules have been widely used throughout various kinds of mobile devices. These devices collected massive trajectory data and empowered many applications in the intelligent transportation system. Among these applications, travel time estimation

---

Z. Zhang and H. Wang—Equal contribution.

Supplementary Information The online version contains supplementary material available at https://doi.org/10.1007/978-3-031-26422-1_30.

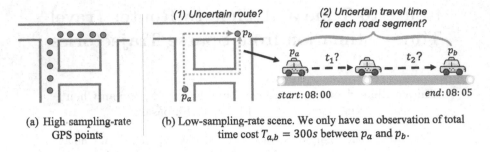

Fig. 1. Comparison between dense and sparse TTE scenarios.

(TTE) is an essential task for route planning, taxi dispatching, and ride-sharing. Subsequently, a large part of relevant approaches ranging from machine learning technologies, such as Bayesian inference [15], to deep learning models [22] have been proposed to solve this task. However, due to the power and communication limitations of the mobile devices, the sampling rate of the trajectories is always low, which leads to a decrease in the accuracy for both travel time and route. Existing efforts need to label the exact travel time and route between two consecutively sampled GPS points, which is used to train the estimation model. We argue that this hypothesis sounds reasonable relying upon the scene of high-sampling-rate. In practice, we have to face a large part of trajectory data with low sampling rates [10, 23].

Motivating Scenario. Figure 1 gives a comparison between two TTE scenarios: dense and sparse. The exact label of travel time in each road segment and the route can be easily obtained from the dense trajectories (Fig. 1a). However, we can not obtain the precise route and travel time label from the sparse trajectories. Figure 1b illustrates a case in low-sampling rate. We are hard to infer the route when given two sampled GPS points p_a and p_b, since there are multiple choices for possible route. Meanwhile, we were also challenged to acquire the exact travel time in each road segment, even though we have the ground truth route marked with a green dotted line, due to the large gap of observation $T_{a,b} = 5$ min. With missing supervision labels, traditional supervised learning is clumsy in giving a fine-grained prediction. This motivates us to model TTE and route recovery from sparse trajectories as a weakly supervised learning problem, more specifically a coarse labeling problem [29].

Unlike conventional supervised learning, where each sample is assigned with a label, coarse labeling annotates the label on a bag of samples. The authors in [29] summarize the task of learning from 1) the mean/sum: the arithmetic mean or the sum of X; 2) the difference/rank: the difference $x_i - x_j$ or the relative order $x_i > x_j$; and 3) the min/max: the smallest/largest value in X. In the task of estimating travel time, the problem can be considered as learning from the mean/sum of X, since the path travel time can be equivalent to the summation of each road pass time within the path, while the exact travel time of each road segment is unknown.

As we know, travel time and route are highly correlated. In addition, the exact routes can result in a better inference of travel time (*Route → Time*), in turn leading to a more precise route recovery (*Time → Route*). In this paper, the Expectation-Maximization (EM) algorithm [4] has been applied to alternatively estimate the travel time and route between any two consecutive GPS points. Technically, the **E step** intends to estimate the travel time of inferred route through weakly supervised learning (WSL), and the **M step** schemes to recover the route by heuristically searching for estimated travel time. Furthermore, to model the time-variant representation of road network, we generate the travel time distributions using the proposed spatio-temporal model. The Lognormal distribution is employed in this paper thanks to the excellent nature of additivity [5] and better performance in fitting real travel time.

The main contributions of this paper can be summarized as follows.

- For the first time, we integrate weakly supervised learning into the problem of TTE, which aims to infer the travel time of each road segment in a *bag* from a large gap of consecutive GPS points.
- The EM algorithm has been designed to alternatively infer the travel time distribution of each road segment and route between two consistent GPS samples (*Route → Time* and *Time → Route*). In addition, we propose a spatio-temporal embedding architecture to forecast the future traffic state that integrates the spatial relational road network and temporal correlations, such as weather conditions and time-of-day.
- We conduct extensive experiments on three real-world large-scale trajectory data sets, which significantly outperform the state-of-the-art baselines for both two tasks - TTE and route recovery.

2 Related Work

Weakly Supervised Learning. Weakly supervised learning focuses on dealing with three kinds of problems [31]: 1) incomplete supervision: only part of the training data is labeled 2) inexact supervision: training data has only coarsely grained labels 3) inaccurate supervision: given labels are not always accurate. Multiple instance learning (MIL), which deals with observed data arranged in sets [7] is a branch of weakly supervised learning belonging to the category of inexact supervision. MIL has been widely applied in many fields, such as image and video classification [3], as well as document and sound classification [32]. This paper expands the concept of MIL to the application of travel time estimation in a highly sparse scenario.

Travel Time Estimation. The loop detectors are firstly used in calculating the travel time by recording the individual road travel speeds and dividing it by the travel distance [13]. However, since traffic lights and left/right turns are omitted, the estimation errors are inaccurate. Therefore, road segment-based methods have been proposed, which can be approximately divided into two types: 1) nearest neighbor search [20], which sets the prediction by averaging the historical trajectory travel time; and 2) trajectory regression methods [9], which predict the travel time of road segment by road features. However, those approaches are based on the assumption that the trajectory's travel time is precise. Moreover, multiple trajectories with low sampling rates exist due to the network communication problem. Although some works try to conduct sparse travel time estimation [10, 23], the uncertain route is also ignored. This paper aims to simultaneously resolve the problem of estimating vehicle travel time and route recovery in a highly sparse scenario.

Route Recovery. The route recovery problem in the low sample rate scenario is vital to reduce the uncertainty of the trajectory, and the TTE problem [17]. As we mentioned, the problems of TTE and route recovery play a role together, and this idea has been considered in previous work. For example, [24] designs a regression TTE model and applies the exact route search to obtain the potential route based on the learned travel time. [19] proposes STGAN to generate a travel time distribution in each road segment throughout the road network based on data from traffic surveillance cameras and update the possible route by posterior estimation in every iteration. Unlike the existing approach, the superior advantage of WSL-TTE is to model the sparse observation problem as weakly supervised learning, which is skilled in coarse labeling problems, and adopt it into the EM framework.

3   Methodology

This section first gives the problem formulation of travel time estimation based on weakly supervised learning and then introduces our proposed weakly supervised learning travel time estimation (WSL-TTE) system.

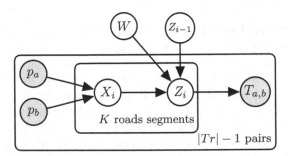

Fig. 2. The graphical model of the data generating process. The grey and white nodes represent the observation and hidden variable, respectively.

3.1   Notation

Let X be the features of the road (e.g., road types, road lanes) and Z **be the unobserved true travel-time distribution of K road segments that we**

want to predict. The goal is to learn a discriminative model f that predicts the true target Z from the feature vector X, so as to maximize the conditional probability $P(Z \mid X)$. Here, the travel time distribution Z highly depends on the real-time traffic condition. Intuitively, we discretize one day into $\mathcal{I}$ time steps (i.e., a specific time window $\Delta t = 30 \min$). So given a trajectory Tr at time step t_s, which can be denoted as sequence of sampled GPS point: $p_1 \to p_2 \to \cdots \to p_{|Tr|}$, $\tilde{r}$ is the most likely route (*bag*) between two continuous GPS points p_a and p_b during Tr, where $|\tilde{r}| = K$ denotes the number of total travelled road segments in $\tilde{r}$. Especially, $X_{1:K}$[1] stands for the *bag* of the travelled road segments' features corresponding to $\tilde{r}$. W is the collection of all weight parameters in the neural network f to learn Z. $T_{a,b}$ is the actual observation of total time cost between p_a and p_b.

Figure 2 illustrates the data generation process with a graphical representation. Given p_a and p_b, we first infer the most likely route $\tilde{r}$ from the road network with $P(\tilde{r} \mid p_a, p_b, Z)$, which is equal to estimate $P(X_{1:K} \mid p_a, p_b, Z_{1:K})$. Subsequently, we generate the conditional probability $P(Z_i \mid 0)$ for each travel time distribution Z_i. Specifically, we here assume that each latent variable Z_i belongs to the Lognormal distribution $Z_i \sim \frac{1}{z\sigma\sqrt{2\pi}} \exp\left(-\frac{(\ln z - \mu)^2}{2\sigma^2}\right)$ [16]. We let the conditional probability $P(Z_i \mid \theta) = P(Z_i \mid (\mu, \sigma) = f(X; W))$, where W and X are the cofactors that generate the parameterized μ and σ of Z_i by the deterministic function f. Consequently, total travel time $T_{a,b}$ can be observed by an aggregate function Q with $T_{a,b} = Q(Z_{1:K}) = \sum_{i=1}^{K} Z_i$.

3.2 Assumptions

Here, we summarize the two basic assumptions used in our paper.

Assumption 1 *(Aggregate observation assumption).* $P(T_{a,b} \mid X_{1:K}, Z_{1:K}) = P(T_{a,b} \mid Z_{1:K})$

We assume that observation $T_{a,b}$ is conditionally independent on $X_{1:K}$ when given $Z_{1:K}$. This assumption is informed by existing studies [2] and conforms to the TTE problem, since given $Z_{1:K}$, observation $T_{a,b}$ can be determined by aggregate function Q.

Assumption 2 *(Markov chain assumption).* $P(Z_{1:K} \mid X_{1:K}) = P(Z_1 \mid X_1) \prod_{i=2}^{K} P(Z_{i+1} \mid X_{i+1}; Z_i)$

We assume that Z_{i+1} are mutually independent except for Z_i. This is under the assumption of a Markov chain and is based on extensive applications in trajectory data mining [1]. Furthermore, since $T_{a,b}$ can be determined by the function Q, the conditional probability can be defined as $P(T_{a,b} \mid Z_{1:K}) = \delta_{Q(Z_{1:K})}(T_{a,b})$, where $\delta(\cdot)$ represents the Dirac delta function.

---

[1] The subscript for example $X_{1:K}$ denotes an abbreviation for the set $\{X_1, X_2, \cdots, X_K\}$.

3.3   Problem Formulation

In summary, the objective function in this paper can be written as follows:

$$\log P(T_{a,b} \mid p_a, p_b, W) = \log \left(\sum_Z P(T_{a,b} \mid p_a, p_b, Z, W) P(Z \mid p_a, p_b, W) \right), \quad (1)$$

which is the maximum of a posterior estimation by taking the Z as latent variables with the observation of sparse travel time $T_{a,b}$. Therefore, we divide the training process into expectation (E step) and maximization (M step) according to the above assumptions.

$$
\begin{aligned}
\textbf{E step:} \quad & \mathbb{E}_Z \left[\log P(T_{a,b}, Z \mid X_{1:K}, W) \mid X_{1:K}^{(i)}; W^{(i)} \right] \\
&= \int_{Z^K} \log P(T_{a,b} \mid Z_{1:K}; X_{1:K}) P(Z_{1:K} \mid X_{1:K}) dZ_{1:K} \\
&= \int_{Z^K} \delta_{Q(z_{1:K})}(T_{a,b}) P(Z_1 \mid X_1) \prod_{i=2}^{K} P(Z_{i+1} \mid X_{i+1}; Z_i) dZ_{1:K} \\
&\approx \mathop{\mathbb{E}}_{\substack{Z_i \sim p(Z_i \mid X_i) \\ i=1,\ldots,K}} \left[\delta_{Q(Z_{1:K})}(T_{a,b}) \right]
\end{aligned}
\quad (2)
$$

$$\textbf{M step:} \quad \tilde{r} = \arg\max_r \log P(T_{a,b} \mid \Omega_{a,b}; \, p_a; \, p_b; \, W) \quad (3)$$

E step aims to estimate the travel time of the most likely route $\tilde{r}$ by learned travel time distribution Z through weakly supervised learning, and **M step** heuristically searches $\tilde{r}$ from the candidate set $\Omega_{a,b} = \{r_1, r_2, \cdots, r_m\}$ to reduce the computational cost. According to the above EM procedure, we obtain the estimated route $\tilde{r}$ for every pair of p_a and p_b, as well as travel time distribution Z. Thus, the final travel time of trajectory Tr can be obtained by summing all the estimation components $\Theta = \{\tilde{T}_1, \tilde{T}_2, \cdots, \tilde{T}_{|Tr|-1}\}$ between every continuous GPS sample with $\tilde{T} = \sum_{i=1}^{|Tr|-1} \tilde{T}_i$, where $\tilde{T}_i$, produced by f, denotes the forecast travel time of p_i and p_{i-1}.

3.4   System Overview

Figure 3 shows our proposed WSL-TTE system with the EM algorithm, which consists of three main components - processor, spatio-temporal model and model training with EM procedure.

(1) **Processor** temporally partitions the low-sampling-rate historical trajectories from the datasets into each time step t_s.
(2) **Spatio-Temporal Model** f estimates the travel time distribution Z of the road segments. We firstly transform a road network into a multi-relational graph $\mathcal{G}$, and encode each time step t_s into a vector. Then we fuse the aforementioned spatial representation and temporal encoding as the time-variant

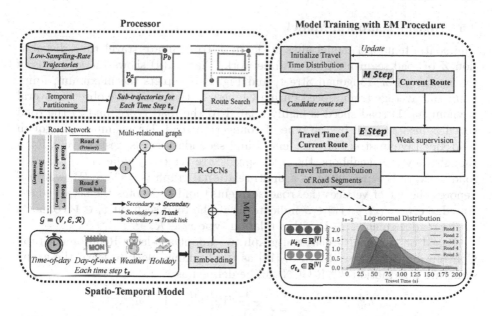

Fig. 3. The system architecture of our proposed WSL-TTE with EM procedure.

vertex representations. In the final, μ_{t_s} and σ_{t_s} of travel time distribution Z are parameterized by two MLPs (Multi-Layer Perception).

(3) **Model Training with EM Procedure** is used to optimize the learned Z in E-step using Eq. (5) and infer route $\tilde{r}$ by Eq. (6). Travel time distribution Z is initially default as $\mu = \frac{L_i}{\mathbf{S}_i}$ and $\sigma = 1$, where L_i and $\mathbf{S}_i$ are the length and speed limits of ith road segment, respectively. The EM algorithm will be finished when the estimated variables Z converge.

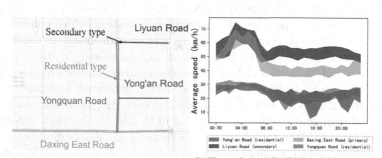

(a) The 1st order neighbors of Yongquan road   (b) The road speed distribution within Chinese National day

Fig. 4. Motivation example of the traffic speed in Xi'an during Chinese National Day. We used high-sampling-rate GPS trajectories to calculate the exact travel speed for these road segments, and observed that the road's speed distribution with adjoining roads is highly related with the road types.

3.5   Spatio-Temporal Model

The spatio-temporal model aims to learn f to estimate travel time distribution Z of road segments from road network. Figure 4(a) shows the locations of the neighbors of Yongquan Street, and Fig. 4(b) depicts the maximum, minimum and average traffic speed during Chinese national day. We observe several phenomena: 1) road speed is highly related to the road types; and 2) the road speed is also affected by the type of connection road. For example, Yongquan road and Liyuan street are residential and secondary roads, respectively. Even though they are neighbors, the road speeds are relatively different. Thus, the road network is represented as a multi-relational graph $\mathcal{G} = (\mathcal{V}, \mathcal{E}, \mathcal{R})$, where $\mathcal{V}$ denotes the set of vertices (i.e. road segments) and $\mathcal{E}$ denotes the set of edges. An edge $\mathbf{e}_{ijk} = (v_i, v_j, \mathbf{r}_k) \in \mathcal{E}$ indicates that the road segment $v_i \in \mathcal{V}$ connects to the road segment $v_j \in \mathcal{V}$ with a relation type $\mathbf{r}_k \in \mathcal{R}$.

Based on this multi-relational graph, we adopt a 3-layer Relational Graph Convolution Networks (R-GCNs) [18] as the building block to learn the graph structure information. l^{th} R-GCN can be defined as

$$h_{v_i}^{(l+1)} = \sum_{\mathbf{r}_k \in \mathcal{R}} \sum_{j \in \mathcal{N}_i^{\mathbf{r}_k}} \frac{1}{c_{i,\mathbf{r}_k}} W_{\mathbf{r}_k}^{(l)} h_j^{(l)} + W_0^{(l)} h_{v_i}^{(l)}, \tag{4}$$

where $h_{v_i}^{(l)} \in \mathbb{R}^{d^{(l)}}$ is the hidden state of road segment v_i in the lth layer of the model with dimension $d^{(l)}$ and $W_{\mathbf{r}_k}^{(l)}, W_0^{(l)}$ present the learnable parameters. $\mathcal{N}_i^{\mathbf{r}_k}$ denotes the set of neighbor indices of node v_i in relation to $\mathbf{r}_k \in \mathcal{R}$. $c_{i,\mathbf{r}_k}$ is the normalization constant. Note that $h_{v_i}^{(0)}$ is the spatial feature X_{v_i} of road segment v_i. We use the embedding layer to encode the following statistical features:

- Road types: for example, primary, primary link, secondary, secondary link;
- Number of lanes: how many marked traffic lanes;
- Whether it is one way or not.

The final output of R-GCNs, represented as $s_{v_i} \in \mathbb{R}^D$, where $v_i \in \mathcal{V}$. But spatial representation s_{v_i} only provides the static representation, which could not show the temporally dynamic correlations for each road segment.

As we mentioned previously, the spatio-temporal model f is to estimate the mean value μ and variance σ of Lognormal distribution for each road segment v_i at each time step t_s. Intuitively, we encode the day-of-week and time-of-day of each time step t_s into $\mathbb{R}^7$ and $\mathbb{R}^{\mathcal{I}}$ using one hot encoding, and concatenate them with the embedding of weather conditions and HolidayID (holiday or not). Then we use one-layer MLP to transform the above temporal embedding vector into a vector $s_{t_s} \in \mathbb{R}^D$, which is equal to the spatial representation s_{v_i}. To obtain the time-variant road segment representations, we fuse the above spatial representation and reconstruct temporal embedding vector: for each road segment s_{v_i} at time step t_s, the spatio-temporal representation is defined as $F_{v_i,t_s} = s_{v_i} + s_{t_s}$, which contains both spatial road structure and temporal information. Based on the spatio-temporal representation $F \in \mathbb{R}^{(|\mathcal{V}| * N_{t_s}) \times D}$, where N_{t_s} denotes the total number of time steps, $\mu_{t_s} \in \mathbb{R}^{|\mathcal{V}|}$ and $\sigma_{t_s} \in \mathbb{R}^{|\mathcal{V}|}$ for each time step $t_s \in \mathbb{R}^{N_{t_s}}$ are parameterized by two-layer MLPs with shared fused representation F.

3.6 Model Training with EM Procedure

Next, we introduce the learning procedure of estimated travel time distribution Z through weakly supervised learning. The aforementioned *expected log-likelihood* in Eq. (2) defines the aggregate expectation from Z to T. Here, we assume the distribution $T_{a,b}$ also under the Lognormal distribution approximated by summation of all $Z_{1:K}$ on route r [5] as

$$
T \sim \text{Lognormal} \left(\mu := \sum_{i=1}^{K} \mu_{t_s}^{(i)}, \sigma^2 := \sum_{i=1}^{K} (\sigma_{t_s}^{(i)})^2 \right)
$$

Thus, the term of expectation in Eq. (2) can be derived to be

$$
L_{\mu,\sigma} = \log p \left(\left\{ x_{t_s}^{(i)}, z_{t_s}^{(i)} \right\}_{i=1}^{K} ; W \right)
$$

$$
= \sum_{i=1}^{K} \frac{\left(z_{t_s}^{(i)} - \mu_{t_s}^{(i)} \right)^2}{2\sigma_{t_s}^2} - \frac{1}{2} \log \left(2\pi \sigma_{t_s}^2 \right)
$$

$$
\approx -\frac{(Q(Z_{1:K}) - Q(\mu))^2}{2\sigma^2} - \frac{1}{2} \log \left(2\pi \sigma^2 \right). \tag{5}
$$

In the final, we introduce how to maximize the conditional probability in Eq. (3). Given two continuous samples p_a, p_b, and the last-step parameters $W^{(i)}$ produced from Eq. (5), our objective is to find the optimal route $\widetilde{r}$ with the travel time closest to the observation $T_{a,b}$. As mentioned in [8], it is natural to assume that the route $\widetilde{r}$ is very likely to be among the top m-shortest paths between p_a and p_b. Therefore, we utilize Yen's algorithm [26] to generate the candidate set $\Omega_{a,b} = \{r_1, r_2, \cdots, r_m\}$ and the optimal route $\widetilde{r}$ can be selected by

$$
\widetilde{r} = \arg\min_{r} | T_{a,b} - \sum_{e_i \in r_j} \mu^{(i)} |, \quad \forall r_j \in \Omega_{a,b}. \tag{6}
$$

We perform Eq. (6) for every pair of continuous samples to update their corresponding route $\widetilde{r}$. Furthermore, to prevent extensive overlap in $\Omega_{a,b}$, this paper leverages the weighted Jaccard ($wJCD$) value to calculate each pair of routes $r_i, r_j \in \Omega_{a,b}$ referring to [8]. The EM algorithm will complete when it reaches the estimated variables μ and σ convergence.

4 Experiments

4.1 Experimental Settings

Data. We validate our proposed methods on three real-world datasets, including Xi'an, Porto and Chengdu dataset. More details can be found in Appendix A.1.

Sampling Rate Setting. According to [27], taxis should report their GPS positions with a low sampling rate to save communication and energy costs. We further vary the sampling ratio of the sets 3.125%, 6.25% and 12.5% to evaluate the robustness of our proposed model. Since the original trajectories are sampled every 15 s, the generated low- sampling-rate trajectories of 3.125%, 6.25% and 12.5% are considered to be as the average time interval of such trajectories is 8 min, 4 min, and 2 min, respectively.

4.2   Baseline Models and Evaluation Metrics

- **DeepTTE:** [22] is an end-to-end deep learning framework, which infers the travel time from both the entire path and each local path simultaneously.
- **DeepGTT:** [11] learns the travel time distribution through the deep generative model, which takes the real-time traffic condition into account.
- **MVSTM:** [14] is a multi-view spatial-temporal model that captures the mutual dependence of spatial-temporal relations and trajectory features.
- **MURAT:** [12] is a multi-task representation learning method by utilizing the underlying road network and the spatio-temporal prior knowledge.
- **DCRNN:** [13] exploits GCN to capture spatial dependency and then uses recurrent neural networks to model temporal dependency.
- **ConSTGAT:** [6] adopts a graph attention mechanism to explore the joint relations of spatio-temporal information.
- **T-GCN:** [30] proposes a temporal GCN model that combines the GCN and GRU to simultaneously extract the spatial and temporal dependencies.

Additionally, three state-of-the-art algorithms STRS [24], MTrajRec [17], and DeepGTT [11] are used as baseline models for route recovery. STRS and Deep-GTT learn the travel time of the road network and conduct the route search for low-sampling-rate trajectories. MtrajRec recoveries the route via a two-stage Seq2Seq model based on coarse grid representation.

Evaluation Metrics. We evaluate the task of TTE with RMSE (radial mean square error), MAE (mean absolute error) and MAPE (mean absolute percentage error). Then the route recovery performance is evaluated by route recovery accuracy, which is defined as the ratio of the length of correctly inferred road segments against the maximum value of the length of the ground truth route R_G and the inferred route R_I, that is, $accuracy = \frac{(R_G \cap R_I).len}{max\{R_G.len, R_I.len\}}$.

4.3   Performance Comparison

Performance on Travel Time Estimation. As reported in Table 1, our WSL-TTE achieves the best results among all baseline methods for three kinds of minute intervals: 2, 4, 8. We summarize the reasons for our model outperforming all baselines by a large margin: 1) The GCN production is used to learn the route's travel time and its travel time distribution for each road segment simultaneously, helping it to yield robust and abundant features. 2) The EM

Table 1. Performance comparison for TTE under three datasets. Here, the units of both RMSE and MAE are minutes, and the unit of MAPE is percentages (%). The best performance is marked in bold font.

Data	Models	2 mins			4 mins			8 mins		
		RMSE	MAE	MAPE	RMSE	MAE	MAPE	RMSE	MAE	MAPE
Xi'an	DeepTTE	2.89	1.74	14.89	3.88	2.57	15.7	3.87	2.79	18.25
	DeepGTT	4.31	3.51	32.16	5.27	4.11	39.85	7.33	6.14	45.31
	MVSTM	4.13	2.59	15.42	4.45	3.68	29.37	5.62	3.84	26.51
	MURAT	8.86	6.87	84.06	9.45	7.76	94.16	11.36	9.23	113.69
	T-GCN	3.24	2.00	14.78	4.23	3.04	15.61	4.43	3.19	18.37
	DCRNN	3.20	1.96	14.6	4.18	2.98	15.43	4.37	3.13	18.16
	ConSTGAT	3.21	1.99	14.41	4.20	3.01	15.22	4.39	3.17	17.91
	Ours	**1.36**	**1.07**	**9.66**	**1.53**	**1.32**	**13.35**	**1.81**	**1.92**	**15.69**
Porto	DeepTTE	2.14	1.46	12.59	2.90	2.10	12.36	3.38	2.48	15.01
	DeepGTT	3.39	2.83	28.58	4.07	3.03	32.05	6.23	5.08	39.34
	MVSTM	3.10	2.27	13.00	3.39	2.75	24.28	4.69	3.18	22.18
	MURAT	6.24	5.35	74.27	7.17	5.63	75.54	9.40	7.39	96.79
	T-GCN	2.04	1.31	12.13	2.85	1.83	11.92	3.16	2.23	14.26
	DCRNN	2.02	1.28	11.99	2.81	1.80	11.78	3.12	2.19	14.09
	ConSTGAT	2.03	1.29	11.83	2.82	1.82	11.62	3.13	2.22	13.90
	Ours	**1.11**	**0.88**	**8.25**	**1.30**	**1.14**	**10.58**	**1.72**	**1.63**	**12.77**
Chengdu	DeepTTE	3.13	1.97	15.11	4.09	2.99	15.96	4.28	3.14	18.79
	DeepGTT	4.97	3.83	34.31	5.75	4.32	41.39	7.89	6.44	49.24
	MVSTM	4.54	3.07	15.61	4.78	3.92	31.36	5.94	4.03	27.77
	MURAT	9.13	7.24	89.17	10.12	8.03	97.57	11.92	9.36	121.16
	T-GCN	2.99	1.77	14.56	4.02	2.61	15.39	4.01	2.83	17.85
	DCRNN	2.95	1.73	14.39	3.97	2.56	15.21	3.96	2.78	17.64
	ConSTGAT	2.97	1.75	14.20	3.98	2.59	15.01	3.97	2.81	17.40
	Ours	**1.89**	**1.31**	**10.15**	**2.14**	**1.93**	**13.98**	**2.55**	**2.21**	**16.28**

Table 2. Performance of our framework and ablation variants for TTE under extremely sparse scenario (8 min).

Models	Xi'an/Porto/Chengdu		
	RMSE	MAE	MAPE
SimpleGCN	1.92/2.09/2.83	2.04/1.74/2.37	15.96/13.09/16.82
GAT	1.96/2.14/2.89	2.15/1.80/2.42	15.92/13.10/16.87
GTN	1.95 /2.10/2.82	2.11/1.78/2.41	15.94/13.07/16.77
Normal Distribution	1.88/2.06/2.79	2.09/1.84/2.56	15.88/13.09/16.89
Variance = 1	2.07 /2.43/3.45	2.71/2.17/2.79	16.12/13.28/17.13
Ours	**1.81/1.72/2.55**	**1.92/1.63/2.21**	**15.69/12.77/16.28**

iteration algorithm has been proposed to update the potential travelled path, which helps our method to learn a more reasonable travel time distribution. Meanwhile, the estimation results among different sampling intervals also reflect that the uncertainty of a sparse GPS trajectory would seriously affect the model performance.

Ablation Study. As is shown in Table 2, in order to validate how the relational GCN modules and weak supervision can effectively capture the spatio-temporal dependencies in WSL-TTE, we first test the effects of relational GCN on modeling road network. Our WSL-TTE removes the relational GCN module and replaces it with a simple GCN, GAT [21] and graph transformer network (GTN) [28] to extract the spatial representation. The experimental results show that using our model with relational GCN can achieve better performance on two datasets. It can be explained that the complex adjacency of the road network needs to model different correlations among different road types. Next, we validate the assumption that the travel time variables belong to the Lognormal distribution. Compared to this setting, we conduct the test of normal distribution and variance=1, respectively. We find that they cannot achieve better performance than the Lognormal distribution. This validates our formulation of weak supervision regarding travel time. In sum, we can conclude that our WSL-based method is effective in travel time estimation.

Performance on Route Recovery. Figure 5 reports the route recovery accuracy and daily divergence over different sampling time intervals. Figure 5(a),

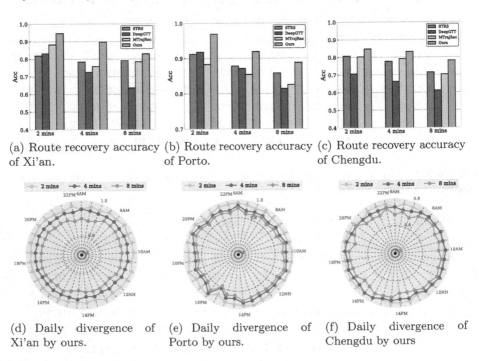

(a) Route recovery accuracy of Xi'an.

(b) Route recovery accuracy of Porto.

(c) Route recovery accuracy of Chengdu.

(d) Daily divergence of Xi'an by ours.

(e) Daily divergence of Porto by ours.

(f) Daily divergence of Chengdu by ours

Fig. 5. Route recovery performance.

Fig. 5(b) and Fig. 5(c) show that our WSL achieves better performance among three sampling intervals, compared to DeepGTT, MTrajRec and STRS. Noted that DeepGTT achieves worse performance at 4 min and 8 min. This is because grid-based traffic condition tensors can not provide efficient road conditions at high sampling intervals. Figure 5(d), Fig. 5(e) and Fig. 5(f) provide the daily divergence of the route recovery accuracy by our proposed WSL. We find that the total recovery performance stays stable from 6:00 AM to 22:00 PM for Xi'an, Porto, and Chengdu. However, the performance of Chengdu is relatively worse than both Xi'an and Porto due to the more complex road network. Furthermore, significantly as the sampling time interval increases, the accuracy of both methods drops, as expected. The reason is that a more extensive sampling time interval leads to more possible candidate routes to be inferred between two sample points. Meanwhile, the daily divergence of our WSL also shows this pattern.

4.4   Case Study

We conducted a real-world case study in Chengdu, which visualizes the learned road conditions using our proposed WSL-TTE. To acquire the road conditions of the road network, we here transform travel time μ estimated by our WSL-TTE into the average speed by $Speed_i = \frac{Length_i}{\mu_i}$ for each road v_i. Four kinds of colors are used to represent the different road states, which can be defined as 1) red - very congested, 2) yellow - congested, 3) orange - slow, and 4) green - unblocked. We equally divide the limiting velocity for each road type and set the speed interval for these four road states. For example, the speed limit of the primary road type is 60 kph, then the speed range that represents very congested is $[0, 15)$,

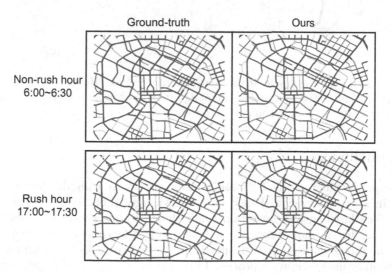

Fig. 6. Traffic condition comparison. We pick two-time steps, i.e., non-rush hour (6:00–6:30) and rush hour (17:00–17:30), and compute the ground truth by original dense trajectories in Chengdu, compared with the transformed speed based on the learned travel time distributions of our WSL-TTE.

congested is $[15, 30)$, slow is $[30, 45)$ and unblocked is $[45, 60)$. We calculate the average speeds by the original dense trajectories as the ground truth. Specifically, we mark them with an unblocked state for the roads without a trajectory. The compared result is shown in Fig. 6, our model can generate approximate road conditions with ground truth for both non-rush and rush hour.

In addition, we provide a visualization example of the route update process in route recovery. As is shown in Fig. 7, our route update process with the EM algorithm can gradually find the approximate route with ground truth, owing to the precise travel time, which demonstrated our previous assumption that: the more precise travel time can lead to a better inference of routes, in turn, resulting in more accurate time estimation.

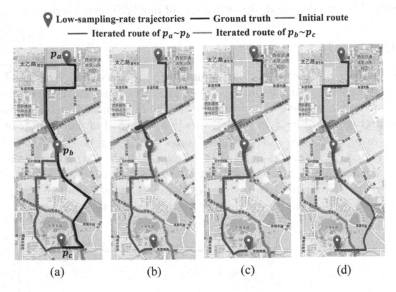

Fig. 7. Visualization example of the route update process. Here, Fig. (a) shows the ground truth and initial route of low-sampling-rate trajectories, and Fig. (b)~(d) shows the intermediate iteration results of route recovery.

5   Conclusion

This paper formulates the TTE and route recovery in a highly sparse scenario as an inexact supervision. Based on the EM algorithm, we solve the inexact travel time labeling and uncertain route choice by alternatively updating the travel time distribution through weakly supervised learning and route searching using the top m-shortest path respectively. Both two tasks are complementary to each other in the iteration process. In future work, we intend to consider more hypotheses of travel time distribution under weakly supervised learning, such as Gamma, Weibull, as well as Burr XII distribution. Source code is available at https://github.com/Dreamzz5/WSL-TTE.

Acknowledgment. This work was partially supported by National Key Research and Development Project (2021YFB1714400) of China and Guangdong Provincial Key Laboratory (2020B121201001).

References

1. Brakatsoulas, S., Pfoser, D., Salas, R., Wenk, C.: On map-matching vehicle tracking data. In: Proceedings of the 31st International Conference on Very Large Data Bases, pp. 853 864 (2005)
2. Carbonneau, M.A., Cheplygina, V., Granger, E., Gagnon, G.: Multiple instance learning: a survey of problem characteristics and applications. Pattern Recogn. **77**, 329–353 (2018)
3. Chen, Y., Bi, J., Wang, J.Z.: Miles: multiple-instance learning via embedded instance selection. IEEE Trans. Pattern Anal. Mach. Intell. **28**(12), 1931–1947 (2006)
4. Dempster, A.P., Laird, N.M., Rubin, D.B.: Maximum likelihood from incomplete data via the EM algorithm. J. Roy. Stat. Soc.: Ser. B (Methodol.) **39**(1), 1–22 (1977)
5. Dufresne, D.: Sums of lognormals. In: Actuarial Research Conference, pp. 1–6 (2008)
6. Fang, X., Huang, J., Wang, F., Zeng, L., Liang, H., Wang, H.: ConSTGAT: contextual spatial-temporal graph attention network for travel time estimation at Baidu maps. In: Proceedings of the 26th ACM SIGKDD International Conference on Knowledge Discovery & Data Mining, pp. 2697–2705 (2020)
7. Frénay, B., Verleysen, M.: Classification in the presence of label noise: a survey. IEEE Trans. Neural Netw. Learn. Syst. **25**(5), 845–869 (2013)
8. He, T., et al.: What is the human mobility in a new city: transfer mobility knowledge across cities. In: Proceedings of The Web Conference 2020, pp. 1355–1365 (2020)
9. Idé, T., Sugiyama, M.: Trajectory regression on road networks. In: Proceedings of the AAAI Conference on Artificial Intelligence, vol. 25 (2011)
10. Jabari, S.E., Freris, N.M., Dilip, D.M.: Sparse travel time estimation from streaming data. Transp. Sci. **54**(1), 1–20 (2020)
11. Li, X., Cong, G., Sun, A., Cheng, Y.: Learning travel time distributions with deep generative model. In: The World Wide Web Conference, pp. 1017–1027 (2019)
12. Li, Y., Fu, K., Wang, Z., Shahabi, C., Ye, J., Liu, Y.: Multi-task representation learning for travel time estimation. In: Proceedings of the 24th ACM SIGKDD International Conference on Knowledge Discovery & Data Mining, pp. 1695–1704 (2018)
13. Li, Y., Yu, R., Shahabi, C., Liu, Y.: Diffusion convolutional recurrent neural network: data-driven traffic forecasting. arXiv preprint arXiv:1707.01926 (2017)
14. Liu, Z., Wu, Z., Wang, M., Zhang, R.: Multi-view spatial-temporal model for travel time estimation. In: Proceedings of the 29th International Conference on Advances in Geographic Information Systems, pp. 646–649 (2021)
15. Mil, S., Piantanakulchai, M.: Modified Bayesian data fusion model for travel time estimation considering spurious data and traffic conditions. Appl. Soft Comput. **72**, 65–78 (2018)
16. Pu, W.: Analytic relationships between travel time reliability measures. Transp. Res. Rec. **2254**(1), 122–130 (2011)

17. Ren, H., et al.: MTrajRec: map-constrained trajectory recovery via seq2seq multi-task learning. In: Proceedings of the 27th ACM SIGKDD Conference on Knowledge Discovery & Data Mining, pp. 1410–1419 (2021)
18. Schlichtkrull, M., Kipf, T.N., Bloem, P., van den Berg, R., Titov, I., Welling, M.: Modeling relational data with graph convolutional networks. In: Gangemi, A., et al. (eds.) ESWC 2018. LNCS, vol. 10843, pp. 593–607. Springer, Cham (2018). https://doi.org/10.1007/978-3-319-93417-4_38
19. Shao, K., Wang, K., Chen, L., Zhou, Z.: Estimation of urban travel time with sparse traffic surveillance data. In: Proceedings of the 2020 4th High Performance Computing and Cluster Technologies Conference & 2020 3rd International Conference on Big Data and Artificial Intelligence, pp. 218–223 (2020)
20. Tiesyte, D., Jensen, C.S.: Similarity-based prediction of travel times for vehicles traveling on known routes. In: Proceedings of the 16th ACM SIGSPATIAL International Conference on Advances in Geographic Information Systems, pp. 1–10 (2008)
21. Veličković, P., Cucurull, G., Casanova, A., Romero, A., Lio, P., Bengio, Y.: Graph attention networks. arXiv preprint arXiv:1710.10903 (2017)
22. Wang, D., Zhang, J., Cao, W., Li, J., Zheng, Y.: When will you arrive? Estimating travel time based on deep neural networks. In: Thirty-Second AAAI Conference on Artificial Intelligence (2018)
23. Wang, Y., Zheng, Y., Xue, Y.: Travel time estimation of a path using sparse trajectories. In: Proceedings of the 20th ACM SIGKDD International Conference on Knowledge Discovery and Data Mining, pp. 25–34 (2014)
24. Wu, H., et al.: Probabilistic robust route recovery with spatio-temporal dynamics. In: Proceedings of the 22nd ACM SIGKDD International Conference on Knowledge Discovery and Data Mining, pp. 1915–1924 (2016)
25. Yang, C., Gidofalvi, G.: Fast map matching, an algorithm integrating hidden Markov model with precomputation. Int. J. Geogr. Inf. Sci. **32**(3), 547–570 (2018)
26. Yen, J.Y.: Finding the K shortest loopless paths in a network. Manag. Sci. **17**(11), 712–716 (1971)
27. Yuan, J., Zheng, Y., Zhang, C., Xie, X., Sun, G.Z.: An interactive-voting based map matching algorithm. In: 2010 Eleventh International Conference on Mobile Data Management, pp. 43–52. IEEE (2010)
28. Yun, S., Jeong, M., Kim, R., Kang, J., Kim, H.J.: Graph transformer networks. In: Advances in Neural Information Processing Systems, vol. 32, pp. 11983–11993 (2019)
29. Zhang, Y., Charoenphakdee, N., Wu, Z., Sugiyama, M.: Learning from aggregate observations. arXiv preprint arXiv:2004.06316 (2020)
30. Zhao, L., et al.: T-GCN: a temporal graph convolutional network for traffic prediction. IEEE Trans. Intell. Transp. Syst. **21**(9), 3848–3858 (2019)
31. Zhou, Z.H.: A brief introduction to weakly supervised learning. Natl. Sci. Rev. **5**(1), 44–53 (2018)
32. Zhou, Z.H., Sun, Y.Y., Li, Y.F.: Multi-instance learning by treating instances as non-IID samples. In: Proceedings of the 26th Annual International Conference on Machine Learning, pp. 1249–1256 (2009)

Attention, Filling in the Gaps for Generalization in Routing Problems

Ahmad Bdeir[✉], Jonas K. Falkner, and Lars Schmidt-Thieme

Hildesheim Universität, Hildesheim, Germany
bdeira@uni-hildesheim.de, {falkner,schmidt-thieme}@ismll.de

Abstract. Machine Learning (ML) methods have become a useful tool for tackling vehicle routing problems, either in combination with popular heuristics or as standalone models. However, current methods suffer from poor generalization when tackling problems of different sizes or different distributions. As a result, ML in vehicle routing has witnessed an expansion phase with new methodologies being created for particular problem instances that become infeasible at larger problem sizes.

This paper aims at encouraging the consolidation of the field through understanding and improving current existing models, namely the attention model by Kool et al. We identify two discrepancy categories for VRP generalization. The first is based on the differences that are inherent to the problems themselves, and the second relates to architectural weaknesses that limit the model's ability to generalize. Our contribution becomes threefold: We first target model discrepancies by adapting the Kool et al. method and its loss function for Sparse Dynamic Attention based on the alpha-entmax activation. We then target inherent differences through the use of a mixed instance training method that has been shown to outperform single instance training in certain scenarios. Finally, we introduce a framework for inference level data augmentation that improves performance by leveraging the model's lack of invariance to rotation and dilation changes.

Keywords: Neural networks · Vehicle routing problems · Generalization

1 Introduction

The vehicle routing problem, first introduced in [4], lends itself as one of the most studied combinatorial optimization problems in the field. It describes the process of optimally serving a set of customers with fixed demands using a fleet of vehicles from a fixed depot. The attention on VRPs has only been bolstered by the more recent explosion of practical applications in the production and delivery of goods whether from local or global sources. This is especially amplified by the global COVID pandemic that forced brick and mortar retail shops to shut down for extended periods of time.

© The Author(s), under exclusive license to Springer Nature Switzerland AG 2023
M.-R. Amini et al. (Eds.): ECML PKDD 2022, LNAI 13718, pp. 505–520, 2023.
https://doi.org/10.1007/978-3-031-26422-1_31

Current approaches to tackling VRPs are divided between classical heuristic methods, machine learning, or a combination of the two. Exact methods do exist for the simpler problem variants however they become infeasible when tackling larger problem instances due to computational constraints [1]. Classical heuristics also suffer from a similar constraint though to a lesser extent. Combing through the solution space becomes very expensive, especially with larger neighborhoods. Additionally, classical heuristics produce a solution for every instance independently. No general model is learned and every further instance will require a reset of the solving time. More time-constrained VRP applications have then come to rely on machine learning to learn a generally applicable model for similar problem types. Despite this trend however, the research has so far been focused on improving performance in smaller problem instances. Scaling the models to even slightly greater sizes has proven inefficient in terms of the training time required and the incurred computation cost. As a result, when targeting these larger VRPs, most methods rely on breaking down the problem into a set of smaller sub-problems and solving them individually. The model would then need components to find optimal route combinations. This is with the earlier approach beginning to gain more traction in the research field [1].

It also seems that the issue of generalization remains somewhat overlooked. There is a rush towards expanding the field with new methods that improve results on the default small instances rather than consolidation of existing research and scaling improvements. This paper will attempt the latter where the second option becomes selecting promising current methods and building on possible flaws so that they can generalize better to large instances. Specifically, we aim at improving one such model by Kool et al. that is based on a combination of reinforcement learning and self-attention [6]. The paper is currently used a base for multiple other models and we hope the improvements derived would extend to those variations as well. Our contribution becomes as follows:

- Identification, classification, and attempted resolution of the model and problem inconsistencies that hinder generalization. Through the proposed solutions we show that the identified issues are valid and we lay the grounds for further research
- Creation of an adapted attention model that improves performance in both upscaling and downscaling scenarios
- Proposition of a modified REINFORCE loss for sparse attention activation functions ($\alpha-entmax$) and a modified VRP training scheme that reduces training time and increases performance
- Proposition of an inference-stage data augmentation method that boosts both regular performance and generalization ability for most ML-based VRP construction methods.

2   Related Work

The attention model (AM) by kool et al. leverages the transformer model and replaces RNN based structures with attention in the encoder and the decoder.

The encoder takes node-wise features and applies a linear projection then updates the resulting embeddings through N attention layers. This is done once at the beginning of the training process. The decoder uses these embeddings as the keys and the values along with a context vector as queries in order to determine the best node to add to the route. The context vector represents the current state of the route and so the problem is solved sequentially, adding one node at a time till completion [6]. This was the first successful transformer model employed for VRPs and the basis for many later works, extending it to VRPs with time windows [5], multi-decoder architectures [15] and off-policy learning [2].

Wu et al. combine the attention approach with classical heuristics to achieve state-of-the-art results in a smaller time frame than using heuristics alone [14]. An initial solution is first generated using nearest insertion, the improvement problem is then formulated into a reinforcement learning process. The state is the current solution, the action is a node pair in the solution to perform a local operator on, and the reward is the difference between the current solution length and the newly generated one. The goal of the model is then to learn an optimal policy for selecting the best local operator pairs. Wu et al. also limit the maximum number of actions that can be performed per iteration to T. Larger Ts lead show better results but slower time performance and as such a balance is made based on the required performance and the training time constraints [14].

To augment the input node features, Wu et al. use self-attention on the encoder and decoder level similar to kool et al. [14]. The model is also trained on a maximum problem graph size of 100. This is because the attention model encoding is computationally expensive at higher sizes. The Wu et al. model is then infeasible when running on larger scale problems even when using smaller T values. In addition, the generalization studies performed by the paper show a drastic increase in the optimality gap when the model is used on different problem size instances. This was true for both downscaling and upscaling respectively [6,14]. Attention models become unable to tackle large, real-world problem instances.

Another method based on the Kool et al. attention model is Policy Optimization with Multiple Optima (POMO). In their paper, Kwon et al. dissect the solution construction problem into the selection of a first node $\pi_1 = p_\theta(a_1|s_1)$ and the selection of the remaining nodes $\pi_t = p_\theta(a_t|s_t, a_{1:t-1})$ where $t \in /2, ..., T/$. When using this formulation the final solution becomes contingent on the first action a_1 similar to a form of bias [7]. The POMO model exploits this lack of consistency to introduce a low variance baseline for REINFORCE applications in VRPs. The model first samples a set of N different nodes as "favorable" starting actions $a_1^1, ..., a_1^N$ and constructs N different trajectories in parallel. The mean cost of N trajectories is used as the baseline when updating the model weights with the REINFORCE algorithm. Kwon et al. show this achieves lower variance and enhances the model's overall performance drastically [7].

Peng et al. criticize another limitation to the attention-based models and present the Adaptive Dynamic Attention for VRPs(ADM-VRP) as a possible solution. They claim that the dynamic nature of the problem is poorly represented in the original Kool et al. model. The graph embedding is only calculated once at the beginning of the solving process [9] and is not updated to reflect the changes in the remaining unserved nodes. To tackle this, ADM instead recomputes the embeddings after every partial solution. The decoder treats the remaining customers as a separate problem w.r.t. the original model and utilizes the encoding of the new subgraph when making decisions. The authors show that ADM performs better on same size problems, and is also able to generalize much better on instances of different sizes [9].

3   Preliminaries

3.1   Problem Definition

We define a CVRP instance of size N over an undirected graph $G(V, E)$ where $V = \{v_0, ..., v_N\}$ is the set of vertices and $E = \{e_{ij} = (v_i, v_j) : v_i, v_j \in V, i < j\}$ is the set of edges connecting the vertices. We also define the symmetric matrix $C = [c_{ij}]$ that corresponds to the cost of traversing edge (e_{ij} as the travel distance between the graph nodes. We fix the node v_0 to the depot node which holds a homogeneous fleet of K vehicles with a carrying capacity of D^N. The goal is to serve the set of customers $V \backslash \{v_0\}$ with individual non-negative demands $d_i > 0$ while minimizing the total travel cost incurred. Each node, except for the depot, is visited exactly once by one vehicle.

The solution for a CVRP instance or tour can then be defined as the sequence $\tau = \{(\tau_0, ..., \tau_T)\}$ where T is the number of individual routes traversed and τ_t is a subset of the graph and begins and ends with the depot node $\tau_t = \{v_0, \subset V \backslash \{v_0\}, v_0\}$. For the CVRPs tackled in this paper, we assume an unconstrained number of vehicles K and as such, an unconstrained number of tours T.

3.2   Original Model

The original Kool et al. model is based on the transformer architecture with an attention encoder-decoder. The main difference is the lack of positional encoding as the input order of the nodes has no significance for the problem representation [6].

Encoder. The encoder first calculates an initial d_h-dimensional graph node embedding through a learned projection:

$$h_i^{(0)} = \begin{cases} W_x x_i + b_x & \text{if } i \neq 0 \\ W_0 x_i + b_0 & \text{if } i = 0 \end{cases} \tag{1}$$

where x_i is the d_x-dimensional node features ($d_x = 3$ for CVRP) and separate weights are used for the depot embedding. We then update these embeddings with $N = 3$ attention layers to compute the final embeddings $h_i^{(N)}$. Here an attention layer is defined as an MHA sublayer and a fully connected feed-forward sub-layer (FF). The MHA layer is used as the message passing algorithm in the graph. It is the standard MHA used in the transformer model with 8 heads. As for the FF layer we use a hidden dimension of 512 and ReLU activations. Both layers also use skip connections and batch normalization:

$$\hat{h}_i^{(l)} = BN^l(h_i^{(l-1)} + MHA_i^{(l)}(h_1^{(l-1)}, ..., h_n^{(l-1)})) \qquad (2)$$

$$FF(\hat{h}_i^{(l)}) = W_1^F ReLU(W_0^F \hat{h}_i^{(l)} + b_0^F) + b_1^F \qquad (3)$$

$$h_i^{(l)} = BN^l(\hat{h}_i + FF^l(\hat{h}_i)) \qquad (4)$$

This gives us the final node embeddings $h_i^{(N)}$. The encoding is done once for the entire solving process and the embeddings are reused statically for every decoding step. We also calculate a graph embedding $\bar{h}$ as an aggregation of the total node embeddings $\bar{h} = \dfrac{1}{n}\sum_{i=1}^n h_i^{(N)}$ to be used for the decoder.

Decoder. The problem is solved sequentially with a node being visited at every construction step $t \in \{1, ..., T\}$. The model uses a context vector h_c and the node embeddings to create a probability distribution over the remaining nodes and sample the next action. The theory behind using a context vector h_c is guiding the decoding process under the current problem state. To calculate h_c we first generate an initial vector h_c' as:

$$h_{(c)}^{(N)} = \begin{cases} [\bar{h}^{(N)}, h_{\pi_{t-1}}^{(N)}, \hat{D}_t], & \text{if } t > 1 \\ [\bar{h}^{(N)}, h_0^{(N)}, \hat{D}_t], & \text{otherwise} \end{cases} \qquad (5)$$

where $\bar{h}^{(N)}$ is the average graph embedding, $h_{\pi_{t-1}}^{(N)}$ is the last visited node, $\hat{D}_t$ is the remaining vehicle capacity and $[.,.,.]$ is used as the concatenation operator.

We then pass h_c' through a single M-head attention layer) to get the final context vector h_c. The parameters are not shared with the encoder layers, and only a single query q_c, the linear transformed h_c' vector, is computed for every head. This gives:

$$q_{(c)}^m = W_q^m h_c', \quad k_j^m = W_k^m h_j^N, \quad v_j^m = W_v^m h_j^N \qquad (6)$$

and the remaining MHA operations are done as discussed in the transformer section. Finally, a single head attention layer is used to calculate probabilities $p(\pi_t | X, \pi_{1:t-1})$:

$$q = W_q h_c, \quad k = W_k h_j^N \qquad (7)$$

$$u_j = \begin{cases} C \cdot \tanh(\dfrac{q_i^T k_j}{\sqrt{d_k}}), & \text{if } d_j < \hat{D}_t \text{ and } x_j \notin \pi_{1:t-1} \\ -\infty, & \text{otherwise} \end{cases} \qquad (8)$$

where C is the clipping operator between $[-10, 10]$. This gives:

$$p_\theta(\pi_t = x_j | X, \pi_{1:t-1}) = \text{softmax}(u_j) \qquad (9)$$

For training, the model samples the next action from the calculated distribution and for inference, it takes a greedy approach and select the node with the highest probability.

4 Targeting Generalization

In order to alleviate the issues with generalization, we first divide the discrepancies between problems of different graph sizes into fixed problem differences and model differences. Fixed differences are discrepancies that are inherent to the problem itself and cannot be changed by altering the model. These include differences in capacities, differences in the action space, differences in the required number of routes, etc. These cannot be changed and instead the model must be altered or trained to accommodate them. As for model differences, they are related to the model's ability to represent the problem properly. The following section discusses the differences tackled in this paper.

4.1 Inherent Differences

In the case of inherent issues, we identify the following key problems:

- **Node Density:** Training data is sampled in the unit square by default. Any increase in the number of nodes generated in the same area will cause an increase in overall node density. This changes the typically expected distances between the nodes and can lead to model confusion when selecting the next best action.
- **Capacity Difference:** Larger problem instances utilize vehicles with greater capacities that can carry more load. When faced with a similar distribution in demands, that leads to a change in the average node-wise route length. We theorize that the model could be learning average route lengths and might tend to have root length bias based on the problem size trained on.

4.2 Model Differences

As for the model differences, we identify:

- **Attention Dilution:** By default, the attention mechanism uses the softmax activation function which is unable to deliver 0 attention to any node [6,10]. By increasing or decreasing the number of nodes we then effectively concentrate or dilute attention and present the model with attention distributions that are unfamiliar to it.
- **Static Encodings:** The Kool et al. model is static in the embedding technique, the encodings are calculated once in the beginning and reused for every subsequent decoding step [6]. It is unable to capture the dynamic changes in the problem as the solution develops [9]. The nodes that have already been visited in a previous route are no longer relevant to the selection of the next node in the current route. Available attention, embedding capacity, and model resources are exhausted.

We realize there are other architectural decisions that could be examined but we recognize the above as more major issues and tackle them in specific.

5   Methodology

5.1   Dynamic Encoder

Kool et al. encode the graph once at the 0-time step and then reuse the encodings in every decoding step until termination [6]. In their paper, Peng et al. state that after a route in the tour is generated, the remaining unvisited nodes form a new subproblem [9]. The static embeddings that were previously calculated become less suited to represent the new structure information. We follow Peng et al. in introducing more frequent encodings to resolve this. Specifically, we re-encode the remaining node features every time a partial solution is found. Formally, the embedding of the problem node i then becomes:

$$h_{(i)}^{(t)} = \begin{cases} ME(h_0^0, ..., h_n^0), & \text{if } \pi_{t-1} = x_{(depot)} \\ h_{(i)}^{(t-1)}, & \text{otherwise} \end{cases} \quad (10)$$

Re-embedding the new subproblem simulates training on smaller graph sizes which would typically help to downscale. However, even for the task of upscaling, breaking down the problem allows it to eventually reach familiar sizes that resemble the training data. This is similar to approaches that rely on the partitioning of the complete problem into smaller subgraphs. The difference here is that problem partitions are done sequentially after a solution route is established. Another difference is that the new problem graph is a subset of the older graph node-set. This is opposed to normal graph partitioning methods where the subproblems are independent, determined in the beginning, and can be solved in parallel (Fig. 1).

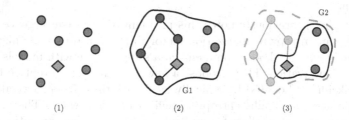

Fig. 1. Problem graph re-encoding at every partial solution found. The new instance G2 is a subgraph of G1 and is encoded as a separate problem.

We follow Peng et al. in their implementation of the re-encoding logic. During the training process, the encoder can only be run for the entire batch, this includes problem instances that have not yet finished their current routes. The model can perform the re-encoding and discard the values but that would be wasteful computationally. To resolve this, a problem instance that has already reached the depot is forced to remain at the depot until all other instances in the batch also finish their partial solutions.

$$\pi_t^b = \begin{cases} x_{depot}, & \text{if } \pi_{t-1}^b = 0 \text{ and } \sum_{b=0}^{B} \pi_{t-1}^b = 0 \\ DECODE, & \text{otherwise} \end{cases} \tag{11}$$

where B is the batch size and $b \in B$.

5.2 α-Entmax Implementation

We recognize two options for the implementation of the α-entmax activation in the place of the softmax activations. This is based on the two roles the softmax plays in the attention model. Internally, the softmax function is used to compute the normalized attention weights in the encoder and the decoder [12]. Applying the entmax function here is straightforward and it is a simple replacement. This has been tried in NLPs and has shown to help remove noise when processing the attention weights by removing the effect of irrelevant data points, see [10].

However, the softmax is also used in order to map the final attention score to a probability distribution for node selection [6]. Introducing the entmax function here is more complicated with the use of the REINFORCE loss. Applying the entmax function without any changes heavily degrades performance. We find that the model converges early to relatively bad actions. We suspect that the high sparsity further exacerbated this by encouraging these overconfident actions and assigning zero values to good actions causing them to be completely ignored early on. Their attention would also be diverted to the remaining actions that are assigned even larger probabilities. This highly limits exploration and the ability to recover good next nodes, which causes the performance to decrease dramatically.

Williams et al. previously notes this problem of early convergence and suggests adding an entropy regularization factor in [13] (entropy maximization). In their paper, Peters et al. also comment on a similar issue with models based on the α-entmax activation. They propose a new loss function to replace the Negative Log-Likelihood Loss (NLL) typically used with the softmax activations. The loss incorporates the Tsallis entropy specific to each α value. They state that "harder" time steps that allow for multiple optimal or close to optimal actions will then lead to a higher entropy that forces the algorithm to better explore the state space [10]. We follow both papers and account for the respective expected entropy for every α. The loss becomes:

$$\nabla \mathbb{L}(\theta|s) = \mathbb{E}_{p_\theta(\pi|s)}[(L(\pi) - b(s))\nabla log\, p(\pi|s) + \beta \nabla \mathcal{H}^\pi)] \tag{12}$$

where β is a hyperparameter to control the entropy regularization amount and $\mathcal{H}^\pi$ is the corresponding entropy for the entmax activation used in policy π. This method allows for the model to learn without any performance issues or instability.

5.3   Mixed Problem Sizes

So far we attempt to address the generalization issue based on the observable heterogeneity between problems of different graph sizes. However, given the black-
box nature of deep learning, the reasoning utilized by the model while tackling
the different sizes is still ambiguous. We acknowledge this and instead attempt
to leverage the model's ability to learn on mixed data.

To do this we generate the training set $F = f_1, ..., f_M$ where f_m is a generated
data subset for a particular problem size, and M is the number of different
problem sizes S to train on. All subsets are equal in size. At every training
iteration i in an epoch, the model samples a batch b_i from f_m where $m =
(i + 1) - \lfloor i/M \rfloor M$ and feeds it into the model. The different problem sizes may
incur different cost magnitudes, and seeing as the objective is minimizing the
cost, this could cause confusion while training. One option would be shifting the
cost formula for the problem to account for the average expected problem cost.

$$cost_{norm}(\tau) = \sum_{t=0}^{T} \frac{cost(\tau_t)}{s_m} \tag{13}$$

where $s_m \in S$ is the size of the problems in the current batch sample set f_m.
However, we found no benefit from this normalization and instead used the
default cost formula.

5.4   Inference Data Augmentation

Kwon et al. introduce the concept of instance augmentation for VRP graph
data. They state that the attention-based model by Kool et al. arrives at a
different solution when reformulating the same problem through small linear
transformations [7]. The POMO model does this by shifting the graphs a certain
amount in 8 different directions before inference. Since the relative position of
graph nodes with respect to each other is conserved, solutions derived from the
augmentations remain valid.

We take this a step further by introducing two new types of instance augmentation, graph dilation, and graph rotation. In the case of the latter the problem is
rotated with respect to $(0.5, 0.5)$, the center of the unit square. Rotation degrees
are determined manually however, intuitively, we only rotate the problem by
multiples of $90°$. This avoids instances where the transformed graph nodes lie
outside the unit square.

$$R_{O,\theta}(x_i, y_i) = \begin{pmatrix} \cos\theta & -\sin\theta \\ \sin\theta & \cos\theta \end{pmatrix} \begin{pmatrix} x_i - a \\ y_i - b \end{pmatrix} + \begin{pmatrix} a \\ b \end{pmatrix} \tag{14}$$

where O is the center of rotation at (a, b) and θ is the rotation degrees in radians.
Tour cost can be calculated directly from the solution of the augmented graphs
since the distances between the nodes remain constant.

The second method, however, graph dilation, relies on scaling the distances
between graph nodes with respect to a center of dilation, also taken as $O =$

(0.5, 0.5). For any augmented node i with coordinates (x_i, y_i) the transformed coordinates become

$$D_{O,k}(x_i, y_i) = (k(x_i - a) + a, \ k(y_i - b) + b) \tag{15}$$

where O is the center of dilation at (a, b) and k is the scale factor. The inference is done on dilated graphs with different scale factors that cater towards fitting the inference problem size to the density of the training problem size. It should be noted that the costs from these solutions cannot be directly computed. Instead, we generate the solutions, apply them to the original data instances and then calculate costs. This is because the inferred cost will scale with the dilation process.

5.5   Model Training and Evaluation

For training, we follow Nazari et al. in their data generation method [8]. The depot node and n customer node coordinates are sampled uniformly in the unit square [0, 1]. The demands δ_i are sampled uniformly in the interval 1, ..., 9 and normalized by the problem vehicle capacity D^n. This gives $\hat{\delta}_i = \delta_i / D^n$, where $D^{20} = 30$, $D^{50} = 40$ and $D^{>100} = 50$.

For testing as well, we follow Nazari et al. in their use of the optimality gap with the best-known solution [8]. The test dataset is also generated based on the distribution above as in [6–9]. Given a large enough test set, this should ensure the ability of reusing the numbers as reported by other papers that also utilize this. We then circumvent the difficulties with typical benchmark evaluations that include a lack of available code, or a lack of trained models (that in turn could lead to deterioration of benchmark performance due to an unknown initialization of benchmark hyperparameters when retraining).

In terms of model time consumption, we rely on the original time values reported by every model's corresponding authors. However, we note that it is difficult to extract meaningful insight from the comparison of these run times. The hardware configurations used in every paper are greatly varied and play a very large role in the overall time consumption. This problem is only exacerbated when models such as LKH-3 are mainly CPU reliant and not only GPU reliant. We find that the field could benefit from a unified routing library that compiles existing literature methodologies. This would facilitate benchmark evaluations in terms of time consumed on the same hardware and a more accurate performance comparisons.

6   Results

6.1   Dynamic Training and Entmax

In the following section, we rely on the 1.5−*entmax* throughout the experiments. The $\alpha = 1.5$ value is used in all heads of the MHA layers during encoding and decoding. It has been shown that allowing for different degrees of sparsity between heads improves performance as different learned features do not necessarily share the same relation sparsity [3]. It is possible to use separate learned α values but this is not done in the paper. At current, the 1.5–*entmax* function has an optimized closed-form solution for both computations and gradients. Other values rely on the bisect method to find a close estimate of the outputs (the degree of accuracy depends on the number of bisections permitted). By allowing the adaptive sparsities we incur a very high computation time and resource cost. Should more efficient methods for estimation become available, we see this as a very promising approach to build upon.

The application of the entmax function happens twofold: once using the function only as an attention normalization mechanism, and once using the function for both normalization and probability distribution mapping. The losses used are vanilla REINFORCE and REINFORCE with expected entropy normalization respectively. All models are trained on the default problem size C_{50} and the results are recorded in Table 1.

Table 1. Performance comparison of the trained C_{50} model with different entmax implementation methods (once with 1.5-entmax as attention normalization only, and once with entmax probability output as well).

	20		50		100	
	Cost	Gap	Cost	Gap	Cost	Gap
LKH-3	6.14	0.00%	10.38	0.00%	15.65	0.00%
ADM-50	6.48	5.54%	10.78	3.85%	16.55	5.75%
SADM - reg. only	6.43	4.72%	10.86	4.62%	16.48	5.30%
SADM - both	6.34	3.26%	10.74	3.47%	16.28	4.03%

Overall we can see that the implementation of the entmax activation for sparse attention leads to a significant increase in the model's generalization ability. We note that when used in conjunction with the softmax activation, the model performance decreases w.r.t. to the original ADM paper on problems of the same training size. We suspect that despite the default loss function implemented allowing training without convergence problems in this scenario, it remains not ideal for use with the entmax activations in general. This is due to the problems stated in the methodology section. When 1.5-entmax is applied for both normalization and in the final output layer, the model is able to exceed the performance of the original ADM model in both the C_{50} test set and the generalization sets.

Based on these results, we deduce that attention dilution is a probable issue in the model encoding and decoding of the problem. The sparse adaptive dynamic model (SADM) is then used as a basis for the final model implemented.

6.2   Final Model

We first compare the C_{50}, C_{100} and $C_{50/100}$ trained models to popular baselines. The baseline results here are reported from the original papers (the models are trained on the graph sizes corresponding to the test set graph sizes) (Table 2).

Table 2. Experimental results on CVRP

Method	Problem size								
	20			50			100		
	Mean	Gap	Time	Mean	Gap	Time	Mean	Gap	Time
LKH3	6.14	0.66%	2 h	10.38	0.00%	7 h	15.65	0.00%	13 h
Kool (greedy)	6.4	4.23%	1 s	10.98	5.78%	3 s	16.8	7.35%	8 s
Kool (sampling 1280)	6.25	1.79%	6 min	10.62	2.31%	28 min	16.23	3.71%	2 h
Wu et. al. (5000 impr. steps)	6.12	−0.33%	2 h	10.45	0.67%	4 h	16.03	2.43%	5 h
POMO	6.17	0.49%	1 s	10.49	1.06%	4 s	15.83	1.15%	19 s
POMO + Aug.	6.14	0.00%	5 s	10.42	0.39%	26 s	15.73	0.51%	2 min
ADM	6.28	2.28%	1 s	10.78	3.85%	7 s	16.4	4.79%	26 s
SADM-50	6.34	3.26%	1 s	10.73	3.37%	5 s	16.28	4.03%	19 s
SADM-100	6.45	5.05%	1 s	10.83	4.34%	5 s	16.23	3.71%	19 s
SADM-Mix	6.34	3.26%	1 s	10.75	3.56%	5 s	16.18	3.39%	19 s
SADM-Mix + Aug.	6.24	1.63%	10 s	10.6	2.12%	38 s	15.99	2.17%	2 min

We see that the model shows competitive performance on all the given problem sizes despite being trained only for specific instance sizes. The model's generalization ability is also able to outperform both the Kool et al. model and the base ADM models when they are trained for the corresponding test size. This is true for both upscaling and downscaling instances. We also notice that the model trained on mixed instances of sizes 50 and 100 (SADM-Mix) seems to outperform the model trained on 100 alone (SADM-100). This is even on C_{100} test instances. Further experiments with other models are required to see if the same behavior is exhibited. If so, this would prove to be a beneficial training method that saves both training time and increases model abilities.

In Table 3, we find that both upscaling and downscaling results have improved dramatically even when compared with the already dynamic attention model proposed by [9]. We extend this to compare with generalization results on significantly greater problem sizes as depicted in Table 4 and Fig. 2.

While the model does seem to remain usable for the C_{200} problem instances, the performance continues to fall off with the increasing sizes. It should be noted that not only does SADM perform better than the Kool et al. model, the falloff between C_{500} and C_{1000} instances is greatly reduced. For Kool et al. the optimality gap increases almost two-fold, this is contrasted with a very slight increase in the gap for the SADM model. We assume that the architectural changes implemented manage to counteract a lot of the model deficiencies with greater scaling. It should also be noted that any lower optimality gap for higher problem sizes could be the result of a fall-off in LKH-3 performance given the time constraint.

Table 3. Generalization comparison with base models trained on C_{50}

	20		100	
	Cost	Gap	Cost	Gap
LKH-3	6.14	0.00%	15.65	0.00%
Kool-50 (greedy)	6.8	10.75%	16.96	8.37%
Kool-50 (sampling)	6.63	7.98%	16.34	4.41%
ADM-50	6.48	5.54%	16.55	5.75%
SADM-50	6.34	3.26%	16.28	4.03%
SADM-Mix	6.34	3.26%	16.18	3.39%
SADM-Mix + Aug.	6.24	1.63%	15.99	2.17%

Table 4. Generalization ability on large graph sizes in table form

	200		500		1000	
	Cost	Gap	Cost	Gap	Cost	Gap
LKH-3	26.8	0.00%	61.87	0.00%	119.02	0.00%
Clarke-Wright	27.69	3.32%	63.1	1.99%	120.2	0.99%
AM (100)	30.23	12.80%	69.08	11.65%	151.01	26.88%
SADM-50	28.95	8.02%	67.05	8.37%	130.58	9.71%
SADM-100	28.5	6.34%	65.1	5.22%	125.66	5.58%
SADM-Mix	28.46	6.19%	64.5	4.25%	123.84	4.05%
SADM-Mix + Aug	28.15	5.04%	64	3.44%	122.99	3.34%

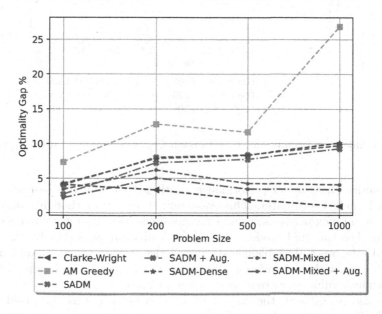

Fig. 2. Comparison of the Generalization ability on large graph sizes

6.3   Graph Augmentation

In terms of data augmentation, we use two main methods of manipulating the inference test set. We are able to rotate the graphs or enlarge and compress them about the center of the unit square they were sampled in. We refer to the process of enlarging and compressing the graphs as dilation. Initially, dilation was only attempted as graph compression, however, an ablation study was conducted to measure any possible benefits from increasing the graph scale. Intuitively, we predicted this would cause a degradation in model performance since graph nodes will no longer be restricted to the trained unit square coordinate space. The graphs were scaled by $k \in [1, 1.8]$ in intervals of 0.1. The results are recorded for the respective validation datasets and reported in the Fig. 3. We record the cumulative performances (take the lowest cost of each instance in the set in different dilations), and single dilation performances.

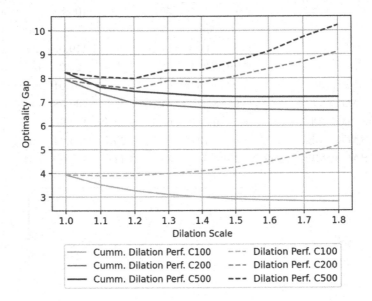

Fig. 3. Model performance for C_{100} through C_{500} using different dilation scales

We notice that model performance continued to benefit when scaling up the graph node coordinates. This was counter to initial thoughts and could prove to be an inexpensive solution to resolving density discrepancies even when upscaling. For the final model, we rely on 5 dilation values $\{1.1, 1.2, 1.6, 1.8\}$ along with the original problem scale. In practice, should the method be applied to graph sizes with high inference time, we can adjust the dilation factors to predetermined values that best suit the target problem size.

As noted in Table 4, the impact of dilation decreases as the problem size grows significantly. Even higher dilation factors are used but no benefit can be drawn which is typically the case as we can see in Fig. 3. We hypothesize that this is due to the very large difference between training and inference densities. In order to mimic the training density, the problem nodes must be dilated too far a distance from the original unit square. The encoder does not have the degree of flexibility required to capture the graph information accordingly at that point. The fall-off in encoder performance counteracts any benefit seen from density dilution.

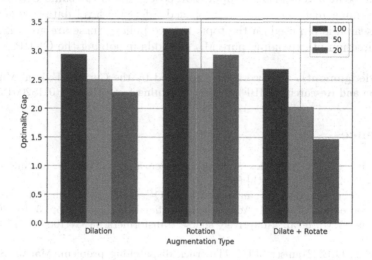

Fig. 4. Model performance for C_{20} through C_{100} using dilation vs rotation

We also find that the larger augmentation benefits come from the dilation operation rather than rotation as can be seen in Fig. 4. This is especially in generalization tasks and likely due to dilation mitigating the graph density issue. However, and with the encoder proving able to handle coordinates slightly outside the unit square, we increase the number of possible rotations from multiples of 90 to multiples of 45. The optimal values of rotation and dilation factors for each problem size should be determined to benefit inference performance while limiting inference time and the number of solving instances. It should be noted, however, that augmented inferences can be done in batches in parallel, this is opposed to the sequential nature of beam search methods. This makes solving a large number of augmentations much faster in comparison.

7   Conclusion

In conclusion, in this paper we provide a series of possible solutions that benefit both the upscaling and downscaling abilities of the attention model by Kool et al. This also inherently verifies our assumptions on the underlying causes of poor performance when moving to other graph sizes. These problems are alleviated but not solved completely as can be seen in the results. The model does perform significantly better than the base attention model and other baselines but the optimality gap still grows as we generalize farther away from the original training set size.

Overall the solutions provided set up a framework for both future works on generalization as well as attention-based models for VRPs in general. Implementing sparse attention, specifically using the α-entmax activation, improves performance at a very small computation cost. This is the same with regard to mixed training instances and the proposed inference level data augmentation. More research is required on the topic but we believe these are good first steps in the direction of expanding pure ML methods in solving the CVRP.

Acknowledgements. This work was supported by the German Federal Ministry of Education and Research (BMBF), project "Learning to Optimize" (01IS20013A:L2O).

References

1. Bai, R., et al.: Analytics and machine learning in vehicle routing research. arXiv:2102.10012 [cs, math] (2021)
2. Bdeir, A., et al.: RP-DQN: an application of Q-learning to vehicle routing problems. In: Proceedings of the KI: Advances in Artificial Intelligence, pp. 3–16 (2021)
3. Correia, G.M., et al.: Adaptively sparse transformers. arXiv:1909.00015 [cs, stat] (2019)
4. Dantzig, G.B., Ramser, J.H.: The truck dispatching problem. Manag. Sci. **6**(1), 80–91 (1959). https://doi.org/10.1287/mnsc.6.1.80
5. Falkner, J.K., Lars, S.-T.: Learning to solve vehicle routing problems with time windows through joint attention. arXiv:2006.09100 [cs] (2020)
6. Kool, W., et al.: Attention, learn to solve routing problems! 25 (2019)
7. Kwon, Y.-D., et al.: POMO: policy optimization with multiple optima for reinforcement learning. arXiv:2010.16011 [cs] (2021)
8. Nazari, M., et al.: Reinforcement learning for solving the vehicle routing problem. arXiv:1802.04240 [cs, stat] (2018)
9. Peng, B., et al.: A deep reinforcement learning algorithm using dynamic attention model for vehicle routing problems. arXiv:2002.03282 [cs, stat] (2020)
10. Peters, B., et al.: Sparse sequence-to-sequence models. arXiv:1905.05702 [cs] (2019)
11. Toth, P., Vigo, D.: Vehicle Routing: Problems, Methods, and Applications. Society for Industrial and Applied Mathematics. SIAM, Philadelphia (2015)
12. Vaswani, A., et al.: Attention is all you need. arXiv:1706.03762 [cs] (2017)
13. Williams, R., Peng, J.: Function optimization using connectionist reinforcement learning algorithms. Connect. Sci. **3**, 241 (1991). https://doi.org/10.1080/09540099108946587
14. Wu, Y., et al.: Learning improvement heuristics for solving routing problems. IEEE Trans. Neural Netw. Learn. Syst. 1–13 (2021). https://doi.org/10.1109/TNNLS.2021.3068828
15. Xin, L., et al.: Multi-decoder attention model with embedding glimpse for solving vehicle routing problems. In: AAAI 2021, pp. 12042–12049 (2021)

Can we Learn from Outliers? Unsupervised Optimization of Intelligent Vehicle Traffic Management Systems

Tom Mertens and Marwan Hassani[✉]⬥

Eindhoven University of Technology, Eindhoven, The Netherlands
m.hassani@tue.nl

Abstract. Vehicle traffic flow prediction is an essential task for several applications including city planning, traffic congestion management and smart traffic light control systems. However, recent solutions suffer in outlier situations where traffic flow becomes more challenging to predict. In this work, we address the problem of predicting traffic flow on different intersections in a traffic network under the realistic assumption of having outliers. Our framework, called OBIS, applies an existing LOF-based approach to detect outliers on each intersection in the network separately. Based on the spatio-temporal interdependencies of these outliers, we infer the correlations between intersections in the network. We use these outlier-based correlations then to improve the predictability of existing traffic flow prediction systems by selecting more relevant inputs for the prediction system. We show that our framework considerably improves the performance of LSTM-based models both under outlier scenarios and also under normal traffic. We test our framework under two real-life settings. In the first, we show how improving the predictability using our framework reduces the overall delays of vehicles on an intersection with a smart traffic light control system. In the second, we demonstrate how OBIS improves the predictability of a real dataset from four trajectories of intersections in the city of The Hague. We share the latter dataset together with an implementation of our framework.

Keywords: Outlier detection · Correlations · Dimensionality reduction · Traffic flow prediction

1 Introduction

Traffic flow modelling is a broad field with many applications, such as enabling city planners to better regulate traffic in a city [16] or reducing and better managing congestion [13]. Next to this, reducing the time spent in traffic jams is time has always been in the interest of researchers and practitioners. In 2014, the US economy lost around 160 billion dollars due to this lost time [15]. Improvements in infrastructure benefit the economy and the well-being of humans. However, upgrading the road capacity by increasing the amount of lanes can be expensive

© The Author(s), under exclusive license to Springer Nature Switzerland AG 2023
M.-R. Amini et al. (Eds.): ECML PKDD 2022, LNAI 13718, pp. 521–537, 2023.
https://doi.org/10.1007/978-3-031-26422-1_32

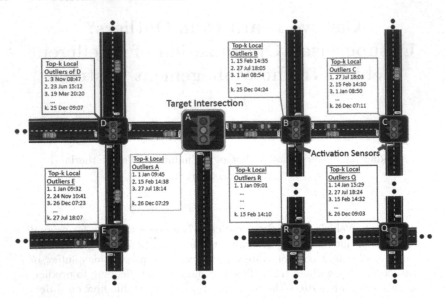

Fig. 1. A traffic network explaining the setting of the problem addressed in this work. Top-k outliers are calculated locally on each intersection. The correlation between the intersections is then checked based on the temporal correlations between their top-k local outliers within a window $w = 1$ h before and after each top-k outlier of the target intersection.

and requires space, something that is often scarce in urban settings. In urban settings, intersections managed by traffic light installations (traffic controllers) are very common, but they are not always optimal. One way of decreasing congestion and optimizing the traffic flow is to increase the efficiency of traffic controllers, the intelligent systems that control the traffic lights [8]. Ineffective traffic controllers can cause unnecessary delays (e.g. when there are less vehicles than predicted on a specific lane). These kinds of problems can cause congestion. If we can introduce more effective traffic controllers, we can reduce congestion, average travel time and average amount of stops required in an intersection, and as such create smoother and faster traffic flows.

In Fig. 1, assume that the task is to predict the traffic flow on the target intersection (A). To count the real number of vehicles flowing on each lane, each intersection is equipped with several activation sensors that continuously collect these values and forward them close to the real time to a prediction model to estimate future traffic flows that are used by the intelligent traffic controller of that intersection. The model used to predict the near-future values of the traffic flow on intersection A can use previous readings on intersection A merely. Obviously this might work, but not as effective as one aims to. The dynamics in the traffic network allow for more connections between intersections. As such, including the traffic flows on neighbouring intersections B, C, D & E while predicting near-future values on A will add more context to the prediction model and should intuitively improve the model prediction accuracy. This is however not a golden rule as some intersection readings might be contributing much more noise to the prediction model than a useful input. Additionally, with slightly complex traffic networks, it becomes almost impossible to know when to stop including further intersections (e.g. is it meaningful to include the readings from the far intersections R & Q?).

The problem we address in this work is how to decide which intersections are "relevant", such that their readings should be included in the prediction model of a target intersection to maximize its accuracy. In Fig. 1, those are intersections marked in green. Due to the connectivity between traffic intersections, deviating traffic situations, or outliers, in the traffic flow in intersection A can propagate to intersection B (or the other way around). We use this propagation of outliers from an intersection to another in our proposed framework to infer the correlating intersections in an unsupervised setting. For each intersection, we find its local outliers individually and in a later step we check the spatio-temporal correlations between the outliers on different intersections. In Fig. 1, the local outliers found on intersection B had a high temporal correlations with the local outliers found on intersection A. Additionally B has a shorter driving time to A than a specified threshold which makes it spatially correlated to A. The outliers found on D are not temporally correlated with the ones found on A, although it is a neighbouring intersection to A. Thus, we assume that D is not a correlating intersection with A. The same applies for Q but the other way around, although the temporal correlation is satisfied, it is not included because the spatial threshold is not satisfied.

Existing traffic prediction models perform relatively well, except when they have to handle an outlier traffic situation. By relaying outlier information to the prediction model, we hope to be able to improve the general performance of traffic prediction flow models. To this end, we propose OBIS, an Outlier-Based Intersection Selection framework which aims to improve an existing intelligent traffic controller that works on real intersections. The existing traffic controller is a product of our industrial partner, Siemens Mobility.

This controller, called DIRECTOR, aims to minimize vehicle traffic delays by using an LSTM-based model for predicting the queues in front of traffic lights. However, it suffers from the limitations mentioned above as it focuses only on the previous readings of the target intersection and the intersections directly preceding it for predicting its future traffic flows. Additionally, it does not perform well under outlier situations. Since both the code of DIRECTOR and the readings from intersections are the ownership of Siemens, we additionally test our method on a large open dataset from 30 real traffic intersections in the city of The Hague collected for 2 years and 3 months and with a total of 7,093,440 readings (cf. Table 1). We share our implementation of OBIS which contains additionally a link to The Hague dataset.

More precisely, the contributions of this work are: (1) we introduce a novel outlier-correlation-based method, called OBIS, for improving the predictability of traffic flows on intersections by selecting more relevant input, (2) we test OBIS on the prediction models of DIRECTOR, a real intelligent traffic controller, (3) we show that the accuracy improvements introduced when using OBIS over DIRECTOR considerably reduces the delay time of vehicles on the intersections to the half, (4) we additionally test OBIS on an open dataset from 30 intersections in the city of The Hague with more than 7 Million readings and show that OBIS increases the accuracy of an LSTM prediction model by 17.9% under outlier situations and by 10.3% in general, and finally, (5) for reproducibility purposes, we share an implementation of OBIS and The Hague dataset too.

The remainder of this paper is organized as follows: Sect. 2 introduces the related work. Preliminaries and some notations are introduced in Sect. 3 after which the main OBIS method is presented in Sect. 4. The applied scenarios are introduced in Sect. 5, and then extensively experimented and evaluated in Sect. 6. Section 7 concludes the paper with an outlook.

2   Related Work

Density-based outlier detection is one of the most common unsupervised ways to detect outliers due to its ability to compare the local outlierness values of data points by using the reachability distance of a data point relative to those of neighbouring data points. There are two main techniques for similarity-based outlier detection and both are based on the nearest neighbours concept. The kNN (k-nearest-neighbours) algorithm and the LOF (Local Outlier Factor) algorithm [5]. There are many dialect techniques which are adapted versions of those two base methods. For example, a kNN based algorithms is: kNN-weight [3] which uses the sum of distances to reduce the variation and sensitivity to the parameter k. Outlier Detection using Indegree Number (ODIN) [9] is a graph based kNN algorithm that defines outlierness as a low number of in-adjacent edges in the graph. An example of a LOF based algorithm is INFLO (Influenced Outlierness) [10] which combats the problem of outlier estimation based on local neighbours that occurs when a dense cluster is close to a data point in a sparse cluster. It does so by considering both neighbours and reverse neighbours of a data point when estimating its density neighbourhood for the LOF. Many more examples of modified kNN and LOF algorithms exist. Research into those different techniques has shown that the original LOF and kNN were still the state of the art in the field of outlier detection [6]. The authors in [17] have designed an LOF-based model that detects outliers over Probability Distributions of traffic flows [17]. A Flow Probability Distribution (FPD) [20] is a stream of multiple values that show what proportion of the traffic happened at which time [17]. The assumption here is that traffic is distributed in certain patterns which can be learned and that a clear deviation from the pattern might mean that we have obtained an outlier. To find these outliers, the work applies the LOF algorithm to the FPDs, creating the FPD-LOF method. In the outlier detection phase of our framework, we will apply an adapted version of FPD-LOF.

Traffic flow modelling has been thoroughly researched. Currently, due to the high effectiveness on time series, LSTM-based architectures are one of the most applied solutions in this field. In [19], several prediction techniques are tested and LSTM neural networks are considered the best option. LSTMs have also been used for trajectory prediction, for all traffic participants (not just cars, but bikes, pedestrians etc. as well) [1,12]. In [11], the authors model traffic using a Recurrent Neural Network that also applies Diffusion Convolution and incorporates random walks on the road graph, better accounting for the spatial structure of traffic modelling, finally leading to a significant increase in prediction accuracy. However, in addition to traffic flow data, this technique requires traffic speed and the distances between the intersections. Particularly the former is not available in the majority of sensor settings on intersections. [14] expected a slightly similar input but applied a hierarchical linear vector autoregressive model and a relatively deep neural network to predict traffic flow. In [18], the authors proposed a neural network based traffic prediction model to capture region-level correlations, temporal periodicity and inter-traffic correlations.

In all of the previous applications, no attention was paid on outlier-based selection of input traffic flow data to the prediction model. The information from all intersections were considered when predicting near-future flow information on any intersection in the network. Our work focuses on finding, for each target intersection, the most relevant other intersections whose traffic flow is correlating with that of the target intersection. For checking the correlations between intersections, we detect the outliers individually on each intersection using an adapted method from the one presented in [17]. Consequently, we check the temporal correlations between the outliers found on different intersections and use that to decide on the list of correlating intersections in general. We show through an extensive experimental evaluation on two real-life scenarios that this considerably improves the predictability of models that blindly include traffic input from all intersections in the network, in general but specifically during outlier situations, where most delays occur. Similar to the most related literature, this work will apply an LSTM-based model in the prediction part without claiming any contribution on the model itself. Also because an LSTM-based architecture that considers the data from the target stream data merely is already in use by Siemens for the traffic flow prediction. This paper extends our proof of concept results presented in [7] by broadening the correlation scope, applying two large real-world datasets and including real KPIs beyond the prediction accuracy.

3   Preliminaries and Notations

The traffic data used in this work are sensor data from inductive loops on any intersection from the set of intersections $\mathbb{I}$. Those sensors are activated when enough metal passes over them, such as a vehicle. Singular activations do not tell us much about the patterns in the traffic, thus these sensor measurements are aggregated every 5 min. The intersection that is controlled by the traffic controller is called the **Target Intersection** and let us call it A (cf. Fig. 1). To control this intersection, models are trained to predict upcoming traffic. A model is trained for each road leading to the target intersection. Intersections that are along those roads form a **trajectory**, denoted as T. The intersections are then formally noted as T_B, with $B \in \mathbb{I}$ being the name of an intersection along trajectory T, and the target intersection is noted as T_A, with $A \in \mathbb{I}$. Thus, only sensors that include data relevant to the trajectory are included in the models, creating **streams** of aggregated activations (x) for each 5 min (h) of relevant sensors at an intersection B. This stream is denoted by x_{hB}.

Flow Probability Distributions (FPDs): to obtain representations of traffic flows that make them comparable with each other, distributions of traffic over a period of time H with a set number of time intervals h within H are created. In this work, $H = 1$ h and $h = 5$ min making 12 time intervals. In short, those FPDs are sets of 12 values, with each value representing the proportion of traffic of that hour within the time interval of 5 min. Let $FPD(H_B)$ be the FPD for time period H on intersection B and let $X_{H_B} = \langle x_{hB1}, x_{hB2}, \cdots, x_{hB\frac{H}{h}} \rangle$ be a collection of aggregated traffic flow values x_{hB} of length $\frac{H}{h}$ for intersection B, the $FPDs$ are calculated as:

$$FPD(H_B) = \langle \frac{x_h}{\sum X_H} \rangle, \forall x_h \in X_H, h = 1, ..., \frac{H}{h} \tag{1}$$

The Bhattacharyya Distance Measure: to compare FPDs, a distance measure that compares two distributions should be applied. We use the Bhattacharyya distance [4]. Given two distributions $p(x)$ and $q(x)$ with $x \in X$, the Bhattacharyya distance $\mathcal{D}_\mathcal{B}$ between $p(x)$ and $q(x)$ is defined as:

$$\mathcal{D}_\mathcal{B}(p(x), q(x)) = -ln(BC(p(x), q(x))) \tag{2}$$

where $BC(p(x), q(x)) = \sum_{x \in X} \sqrt{p(x)q(x)}$ is the Bhattacharyya coefficient for discrete probability distributions. Other distance measures than $\mathcal{D}_\mathcal{B}$ can be also applied [2].

The Weekly Intersection Periodic Pattern: in this work, we used the domain knowledge to decide the length of the period after which a repetitive traffic flow pattern on an intersection is expected. Intuitively, this is one week. In particular, this is suitable when we choose $H = 1$ h. This means that, for instance, the traffic flow on a Tuesday between 9 AM and 10 AM is comparable with all of the traffic flows of Tuesdays in the same period on the same intersection. A reading deviating from the other flows on some Tuesday 9 AM to 10 AM in the measurements on a specific intersection is an indication of an outlier. As such, our task becomes to calculate for each intersection B, the distances between the weekly hour flow probability distributions using $\mathcal{D}_\mathcal{B}$. Note that it is then to be expected that some of the found outliers are caused by holidays, days with extreme weather or special events in the city. We have purposely considered those outliers in our analysis, as we are still interested in how they correlate with other outliers on other intersections under this unusual setting. An important sub-goal of our work is to predict the traffic flow under abnormal scenarios.

Local Outlier Factor over FPDs: the LOF algorithm [5] is used to calculate outlier scores of FPDs within an individual intersection. For an FPD denoted as $\hat{f}$, let us use $reach_k$ to denote the reachability of $\hat{f}$ to $\hat{f}_k$, the k Nearest Neighbour FPD of $\hat{f}$.

The Local Reachability Distance (LRD) of $\hat{f}$ is defined as follows:

$$LRD(\hat{f}) = 1/ \left(\frac{\sum_{\hat{f}_k \in kNN(\hat{f})} reach_k(\hat{f}, \hat{f}_k)}{|kNN(\hat{f})|} \right)$$

with $reach_k(\hat{f}, \hat{f}_k) = max\{\mathcal{D_B}^{kNN}(\hat{f}_k), \mathcal{D_B}(\hat{f}, \hat{f}_k)\}$ where $\mathcal{D_B}^{kNN}(\hat{f}_k)$ is the distance from $\hat{f}_k$ to its kNN for any $\hat{f}_k \in kNN(\hat{f})$. The LOF score of $\hat{f}$ is then defined as:

$$LOF(\hat{f}) = \frac{1}{|kNN(\hat{f})|} \sum_{\hat{f}_k \in kNN(\hat{f})} \frac{LRD(\hat{f}_k)}{LRD(\hat{f})} \tag{3}$$

Outlier Correlations and Intersection Selection: to use these outlier scores for selecting the right intersections, correlations are determined. For each trajectory T, the Pearson correlation C_{AB} is found between the target intersection T_A and all other intersections in that T. Then, to select intersections, a correlation threshold is determined, the intersections that meet the correlation threshold are included in the prediction model. In practice, this means that the intersections that are included in the prediction model often experience similar outliers as the target intersection T_A. Additional spatial filtering is performed such that correlating intersections are considered only if they are spatially closer than ϵ to the target intersection. With ϵ being the spatial threshold for all intersections that are within a driving time of τ of the target intersection. The list of included intersections is noted as $\mathbb{I}^T$. Optimizing the traffic controller can be done by improving its main Key Performance Indicators (KPIs). For a traffic controller, the most important KPIs are the delay and the amount of stops.

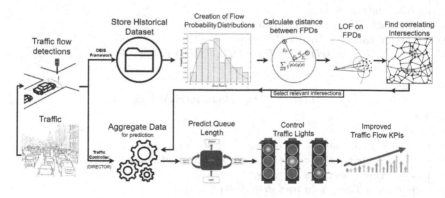

Fig. 2. The context with OBIS framework components in the upper row.

4   OBIS: Outlier-Based Intersection Selection Framework

This section explains each part of the OBIS Framework for traffic controllers, as shown in the upper row of Fig. 2. We will explain each component and introduce all steps taken in the main parts of OBIS framework (not the pre-processing) by referring to the psuedo-code in Algorithm 1. Whose output is a list of most relevant intersections $\mathbb{I}_A^T$ to be included in the prediction model of a target intersection T_A from a Trajectory T. As per Fig. 2, traffic data is recorded and stored as a historical dataset, sets of 1 h with 5 min aggregations, so 12 values x_{hB} for a flow X_{H_B} per hour H. From there, Flow Probability Distributions, $FPDs$ are created as per Eq. 1, in Line 5 of the algorithm. These FPDs are compared with regards to the Bhattacharyya distance between them (Line 10), after which the LOF algorithm is applied to find traffic flows deviating from the norm on that intersection, which receive higher LOF scores than inliers (Line 13). The Pearson correlations between those LOF scores and the LOF scores of A are then calculated to find out which intersections' outliers correlate with those of the target intersection A (Line 17). Intersections that sufficiently correlate are then selected and stored in $\mathbb{I}_A^T$ to be included included in the predictive model of the traffic controller (Line 19) if they are spatially closer than ϵ to the target intersection A.

Algorithm 1: The main components of OBIS

Data: T, $LOFscores_{A_H}$, $Threshold$, ϵ, w
Result: $\mathbb{I}_A^T$

1   $\mathbb{I}_A^T = [\,]$ // Initialization ;
2   **for** *each* $B \in T$ **do**
3      $FPDs_B = [\,]$;
4   **for** $H \in X_{H_i}$ **do**
5 | $FPDs_B += FPD(X_{H_B})$ // Eq. 1
6   **end**
7      $Bha\_matrix = [\,]$;
8   **for** *each* $FPD_i \in FPDs_B$ **do**
9   **for** *each* $FPD_j \in FPDs_B$ **do**
10 | $Bha\_matrix_{ij} += \mathcal{D}_{\mathcal{B}}(FPD_i, FPD_j)$ // Eq. 2
11   **end**
12   **end**
13     $LOFscores_{B_H} = LOF(FPDs_B, Bha\_matrix)$// Eq. 3
14 **end**
15 **for** *each* $B \in T$ **do**
16     $C_{AB} = Pearson(LOFscores_{B_H}, LOFscores_{A_H}, w)$;
17   /* calculate the correlations within a window w before & after each top-k outlier of A */
18   **if** $C_{AB} > Threshold$ **and** $dist(A, B) \leq \epsilon$ **then**
19 | $\mathbb{I}_A^T += B$;
20   **end**
21 **end**

---

5   Applied Scenarios

The OBIS Framework is applied to two scenarios. First with DIRECTOR, the traffic controller system which was provided by Siemens using a dataset collected from a real intersection owned by Siemens. This allows for testing with the use of a traffic simulator that can keep track of important KPIs such as the delay and the number of stops. We refer to this scenario by the DIRECTOR scenario. Second, OBIS is tested on a public dataset, provided by the city of The Hague in a fully reproducible scenario, with the code and dataset publicly provided. For this scenario, to which we refer to by The Hague scenario, only the prediction accuracy can be taken into account, as we cannot test it with the traffic simulator nor the traffic controller developed by Siemens. For both scenarios, the preprocessing and output of the OBIS algorithm are the same, as described above. For both scenarios, LSTM-based neural networks are used for prediction. The goal is to achieve a lower prediction error while using the OBIS framework to decide the input as compared to using input from: (a) all preceding intersections, (b) no other intersections or (c) merely using the directly preceding intersection (the default setting for the DIRECTOR traffic controller).

DIRECTOR Scenario: The target intersection here is called intersection $I00$. A schematic overview of $I00$ is given in Fig. 3. Each white box is an available sensor. The numbers in front of the traffic lights indicate the *signal group*. This is a set of lanes that are controlled by the same signal, e.g. two lanes crossing over belong to the signal group for crossing over. Thus, for the traffic approaching from the left in Fig. 3, Signal Group 03 goes straight while Signal Group 02 goes left. DIRECTOR works by predicting the queues for each lane, with 3 models for the three trajectories for each road approaching the intersection. These are the trajectories for this scenario and along these trajectories are intersections which can be included in the trajectory's model. The available intersections and the trajectories are shown in Fig. 4a. Firstly, the target intersection is intersection $I00$. The first trajectory, Trajectory 0, relates to the queues for Signal Groups 02 and 03 and is shown in green on the map, Trajectory 1 relates to Signal Groups

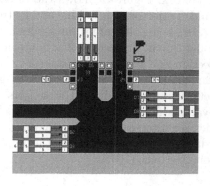

Fig. 3. DIRECTOR: target intersection $I00$ schematic overview.

04 & 06 and is shown in red on the map, lastly Trajectory 2 relates to Signal Groups 07 & 08, is shown in blue on the map. Thus, three prediction models are working simultaneously, predicting queue lengths for each trajectory, for the next 10 s. From these predicted queue lengths, DIRECTOR seeks to optimize a scheme for the traffic lights by minimizing delay. This scheme is simulated in a professional traffic simulator and the KPIs are recorded. The characteristics of the dataset are available in Table 1.

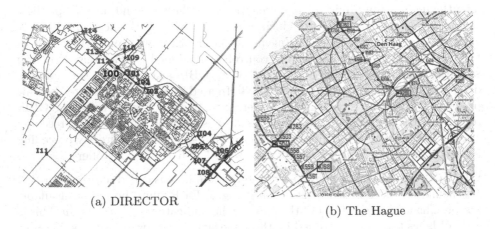

(a) DIRECTOR

(b) The Hague

Fig. 4. Trajectory & intersection maps for DIRECTOR and The Hague scenarios.

The Hague Scenario: The Hague Scenario is meant to provide an additional proof to the utility of the OBIS Framework and is fully reproducible. The dataset features traffic data for 30 intersections, aggregated per 5 min. In this scenario, only the prediction quality is assessed since the traffic controller DIRECTOR and the traffic simulator are owned by Siemens. Two trajectories are formed and traffic data from vehicles heading up and down these trajectories is preprocessed through the OBIS Framework. Figure 4b shows the intersections included and the two trajectories found. Trajectory 1 is in blue and features all intersections in the South-West, with $K198$ being the target intersection for traffic going South and $K504$ for traffic going North. Trajectory 2 is in green, with $K206$ being the Southern target intersection and $K703$ the Northern.

An overview of the datasets used in this work is given in Table 1. Not all data in the datasets could be used, as the sensors used sometimes have noise, such as no activations for a long time or extremely high activations in a short amount of time. We filtered all such noisy data from each dataset. An access to The Hauge dataset is available under the implementation link here: https://github.com/Tom-Mertens/OBIS.

Table 1. The characteristics of the two datasets used in this work.

Name	Intersections	Start	End	Aggregation interval
DIRECTOR	18	15-09-2019	16-09-2020	10 ms
The Hague	30	01-01-2018	31-03-2020	5 min

6 Experimental Results

To evaluate the performance of OBIS, several measures are used. Firstly, the accuracy of the traffic predictions is measured with the Root Mean Squared Error. Furthermore, the eventual performance of the traffic controller in the DIRECTOR scenario is measured with regards to the KPIs: (i) the delay in seconds, and (ii) the amount of required vehicle stops in the intersection. To elaborately test OBIS, it needs to be proven that using it to select intersections is beneficial to the prediction accuracy of the traffic prediction model and that this increase in accuracy can also minimize the delay and amount of stops. Firstly, the parameter tuning of the minimum correlation threshold is discussed, which regulates which intersections will be included in the eventual prediction model. Then, the models for both scenarios are discussed with a general perspective, evaluating the performance in normal settings, before diving deeper into the material and discussing the performance in outlier situations, which are most important for the traffic controller KPIs delay and stops. Lastly, these two KPIs are specifically discussed with regards to the simulated performance of the traffic controller DIRECTOR.

Parameter Tuning. To determine the correlation threshold for including an intersection in the dataset, this section presents the correlations between the LOF scores within Trajectory 1 in The Hague and also those within Trajectory 2 of the DIRECTOR Target Intersection $I00$ from the DIRECTOR dataset. The correlations found in the The Hague dataset for Trajectory 1 (South) are shown in Fig. 5a. Highly correlating intersections are often close to each other. While this result is not surprising, it is confirming the correctness of our concept. The intersection that barely correlates with the rest of the dataset is $K502$, which is also a bit outside of the trajectory; is only connected to the rest of the network through $K504$ (cf. Fig. 4b). The correlation heatmap of Trajectory 2 of the DIRECTOR dataset in Fig. 5b is somewhat surprising. In particular, the total lack of correlation for Intersection $I02$ with any other intersection which is an intersection into the neighboring city. Further analysis indicated that this is because of the reduction in the quality of the data which might be related to noise or absence of the data during several outlier situations. We have chosen to remove data points from $I02$ due to this reduced quality. For many other intersections, the correlations do make sense, for example, $I03$ and $I04$ correlate much more with target Intersection $I00$; these are other major gateways into the city whose readings are almost complete in the dataset.

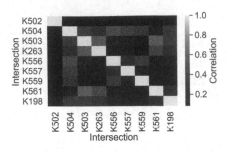

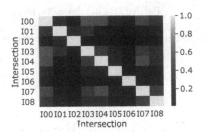

(a) The Hague Trajectory 1 South.   (b) DIRECTOR Trajectory 2.

Fig. 5. Correlations for The Hague (a) and DIRECTOR (b) scenarios.

Table 2. Correlation threshold setting using MSE for The Hague scenario.

Threshold	T 0	T 0.1	T 0.2	T 0.3	T 0.4	T 0.5	T 0.6	T 0.7	T 1.0
Trajectory 1_N	0.310	**0.215**	0.260	0.218	0.218	0.228	0.351	0.351	0.351
Trajectory 1_S	0.230	0.251	0.258	0.258	**0.153**	0.380	0.380	0.380	0.380
Trajectory 2_S	0.318	0.287	0.357	0.304	**0.271**	0.305	0.305	0.354	0.354
Trajectory 2_N	0.303	0.424	0.415	0.415	0.415	0.202	**0.196**	0.196	0.196
Average	0.29	0.29	0.32	0.30	**0.26**	0.29	0.31	0.32	0.32

To decide which intersections to include in the prediction model, a threshold correlation level needs to be selected. The higher the threshold, the fewer intersections to be considered in the model. Thus, for both datasets, many thresholds are selected and models are trained. Eventually the models which perform the best are selected. For the DIRECTOR model, prediction models are trained that are also used by the traffic controller and these are more complex and deal with time intervals of 10 seconds, while for the The Hague dataset, traffic for all incoming lanes of the target intersection is predicted per 5 min by the use of a simple LSTM model. The introduced errors when trying different correlation thresholds over the selected trajectories are listed in Table 2 for The Hague scenario and in Table 3 for the DIRECTOR scenario. As can be seen, a threshold of 0.4 constitutes the best results for the The Hague scenario and a threshold of 0.35 constitutes the best results for the DIRECTOR scenario. We chose those values for the rest of our experiments. Tables 2 and 3 show some non-consistent trends wrt the threshold. This is to be expected as OBIS aims at striking a balance between the one extreme of using the readings of all intersections and the other extreme of using only the readings of the target intersection.

Evaluation Under Normal Settings. Although OBIS is meant to mostly boost performance during outlier situations, the performance in general should not suffer. Thus, for The Hague scenario, the performance is compared to the threshold 1.0 (T 1.0) and threshold 0.0 (T 0.0) scenarios which are: adding no intersections, and adding all intersections respectively. For the DIRECTOR

Table 3. Correlation threshold setting using MSE for DIRECTOR scenario.

Threshold	T 0.35	T 0.5	T 0.6	T 0.7	T 1.0
Trajectory 0	**0.750**	0.812	0.801	1.076	1.127
Trajectory 1	**0.651**	0.806	0.822	0.746	0.772
Trajectory 2	**0.858**	0.934	0.937	0.907	0.910
Average	**0.753**	0.851	0.853	0.910	0.936

scenario, it is compared to the original setting of the traffic controller, adding only the intersection directly preceding the target intersection to the model. As seen in Table 2, the average errors for T 1.0, T 0.0 and T 0.4 are, respectively, 0.32, 0.29 & 0.26. Using OBIS framework in this case yields an improvement of 10.3% over the T 0.0 baseline. Thus, the T 0.4 threshold is significantly better than both baselines, while also being much more efficient than the 0.0 threshold, since less intersections are included.

For the DIRECTOR scenario, the modified director has a mean RMSE of 0.75, a slight improvement compared to the mean RMSE of the original DIREC-TOR (0.79). The RMSEs for the original DIRECTOR and DIRECTOR + OBIS (with T035) are listed in Table 4.

Table 4. RMSEs for DIRECTOR and DIRECTOR + OBIS.

	DIRECTOR	DIRECTOR+OBIS	Difference (%)
Mean	0.791	0.753	4.7%
Trajectory 0	0.960	0.749	22.0%
Trajectory 1	0.661	0.648	2.0%
Trajectory 2	0.751	0.863	−14.8%

Thus, DIRECTOR + OBIS performs especially well on Trajectory 0 but is lacking on Trajectory 2. With this improved prediction accuracy, DIRECTOR should be better able to predict the length of the queue and therefore better optimize the signal schedule to them.

Evaluation Under Outlier Setting. For all 4 trajectories in The Hague scenario, the predictions of T0.4 are compared to the real values, the predictions for T1.0 (Target intersection only) and for T0.0 (all intersections) and the errors are recorded. T1.0 and T0.0 can be considered two baselines for the prediction. To see how well the model is performing during outlier situations, for each model the predictions from all three models are compared to the actual values in terms of MSE, during the 5 largest outlier situations in the test set. The results are shown in Table 5. As can be seen, the 0.4 threshold is performing much better

than both baseline models. The T 0.4 threshold has a **17.9% lower error** than
the best performing baseline, T 0.0. For Trajectory 2, it seems that including
just the target intersection also works quite well, this might be because these
are extreme outliers. On average, the T 0.4 threshold performs better.

Table 5. MSE for baseline models and T 0.4 model under top outliers setting.

Trajectory	T 1.0	T 0.4	T 0.0
T1_North	0.776	**0.371**	0.532
T1_South	0.989	**0.422**	0.720
T2_South	**0.195**	0.704	0.585
T2_North	**0.160**	0.173	0.201
Mean	0.530	**0.418**	0.509

For the DIRECTOR scenario evaluation under outlier settings, one particular
outlier situation is tested and discussed, for which traffic simulations in AIMSUN
8.4 have been used. This is a three hour scenario from 15:00–18:00 on Tuesday
07-01-2019, where outlier traffic behaviour is heavily seen in the middle hour,
which got a high LOF score. The FPD for these hours is shown in Fig. 6.

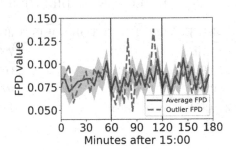

Fig. 6. FPDs for 07-01-2019 15:00–18:00. Outliers in middle flow.

KPIs for DIRECTOR. In Table 6, the upper table shows the mean aggregated
delay in Seconds and the number of stops per model, the lower table sets them
apart per Signal Group (SG), showing the delay in Seconds and the amount of
stops. The OBIS-optimized DIRECTOR only has half the waiting time of the
original DIRECTOR, which is a considerable improvement. Even though the
accuracy in terms of RMSE actually decreased on Trajectory 2 (Signal Groups
7 & 8) as shown in Table 4, the performance in terms of KPIs is much better for
the OBIS-optimized DIRECTOR. The number of stops is not always reduced

Table 6. Aggregate simulation results (delay in seconds), SG = Signal Group.

Means		Delay (s)	Stops	
DIRECTOR		442.7	**186.5**	
DIRECTOR + OBIS		**221.8**	194	

SG	DIR + OBIS Delay (s)	DIR Delay (s)	DIR + OBIS Stops	DIR Stops
02	**10.3**	230.2	162.0	**156.0**
03	**355.4**	628.9	219.0	**205.0**
04	**137.7**	305.9	**171.0**	172.0
06	**401.5**	482.1	192.0	**187.0**
07	**285.5**	635.9	219.0	**197.0**
08	**140.1**	373.1	**201.0**	202.0

because of OBIS. To see how the models perform per hour, the stops and the delay are aggregated per 3 min and for all lanes and signal groups. The results can be seen in Fig. 7a.

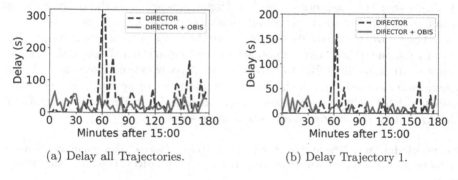

(a) Delay all Trajectories.　　　　　　　(b) Delay Trajectory 1.

Fig. 7. Delay per 3 min for (a) all trajectories and (b) Trajectory 1 alone.

To get a better insight, the means per hour can be found in Table 7. From the table and the figures it becomes clear that the OBIS-optimized DIRECTOR is better prepared to deal with outlier situations in terms of delay.

The outlier was on Trajectory 1, so to get a closer look at those results, Fig. 7b shows the delay per 3 min for Signal Groups 4 and 6 which belong to Trajectory 1. DIRECTOR model incurs a large delay around 16:15, while the OBIS-optimized DIRECTOR incurs much smaller delays for that peak.

Table 7. Mean delay (D) in Seconds and stops (S) per hour for Trajectory 1.

Hour	15:00		16:00		17:00	
Delay: D (s), Stops: S	D (s)	S	D (s)	S	D (s)	S
DIRECTOR	22.8	**20.1**	66.7	**18.4**	43.3	**17.5**
DIRECTOR + OBIS	**26.8**	20.3	**17.6**	18.8	**22.3**	19.2

7   Conclusion and Outlook

In this work, we proposed the OBIS Framework, which applies an existing LOF-based approach to detect outliers on each intersection in the traffic network separately. Based on the spatio-temporal interdependencies of these outliers, we infer the correlations between intersections in the network. We use these outlier-based correlations then to improve the predictability of traffic flow prediction systems by choosing more relevant inputs to the system. We showed through an extensive experimental evaluation that our framework considerably improves the performance of LSTM-based models both under outlier scenarios and also under normal traffic. The prediction accuracy during outlier situations was improved by 19.7% over the baselines in the The Hague scenario and the delay KPI was optimized by 50% in the traffic simulation of the DIRECTOR scenario.

In the future, we would like to investigate the traffic network dynamics and/or the correlation settings that are potentially leading to the increase in the number of stops after applying OBIS to DIRECTOR. Also, we would like to see whether other outlier detection methods or distance metrics can be much more effective than the Bhattacharyya distance. Recent results [2] indicate that the Earth Movers distance is showing more promising results.

Acknowledgment. The authors would like to thank Marco Hennipman and Siemens Mobility for the support with the data, the access to DIRECTOR and the domain expertise.

References

1. Altché, F., de La Fortelle, A.: An LSTM network for highway trajectory prediction. In: ITSC, pp. 353–359 (2017)
2. Andersen, E., Chiarandini, M., Hassani, M., Jänicke, S., Tampakis, P., Zimek, A.: Evaluation of probability distribution distance metrics in traffic flow outlier detection. In: 23rd IEEE International Conference on Mobile Data Management, MDM, Paphos, Cyprus, 6–9 June 2022, pp. 64–69. IEEE (2022). https://doi.org/10.1109/MDM55031.2022.00030
3. Angiulli, F., Pizzuti, C.: Outlier mining in large high-dimensional data sets. IEEE Trans. Knowl. Data Eng. 17(2), 203–215 (2005)
4. Bhattacharyya, A.: On a measure of divergence between two multinomial populations. Sankhyā Indian J. Stat. (1933–1960) 7(4), 401–406 (1946)

5. Breunig, M., Kriegel, H., Ng, R., Sander, J.: LOF: identifying density-based local outliers. In: SIGMOD, Dallas, Texas (2000)
6. Campos, G.O., et al.: On the evaluation of unsupervised outlier detection: measures, datasets, and an empirical study. DMKD **30**, 891–927 (2016)
7. Fitters, W., Cuzzocrea, A., Hassani, M.: Enhancing LSTM prediction of vehicle traffic flow data via outlier correlations. In: COMPSAC, pp. 210–217 (2021)
8. Ghazal, B., et al.: Smart traffic light control system. In: EECEA, pp. 140–145 (2016)
9. Hautamäki, V., Kärkkäinen, I., Fränti, P.: Outlier detection using k-nearest neighbor graph. In: ICPR (2004)
10. Jin, W., Tung, A., Han, J., Wang, W.: Ranking outliers using symmetric neighborhood relationship. In: PAKDD (2006)
11. Li, Y., Yu, R., Shahabi, C., Lui, Y.: Diffusion convolutional recurrent neural network: data-driven traffic forecasting. In: ICLR, Vancouver (2018)
12. Ma, Y., Zhu, X., Zhang, S., Yang, R., Wang, W., Manocha, D.: Trafficpredict: trajectory prediction for heterogeneous traffic-agents. In: AAAI, vol. 33 (2019)
13. Pasquale, C., et al.: Two-class freeway traffic regulation to reduce congestion and emissions via nonlinear optimal control. Transp. Res. **55**, 85–99 (2015)
14. Polson, N.G., Sokolov, V.O.: Deep learning for short-term traffic flow prediction. Transp. Res. Part C Emerg. Technol. **79**, 1–17 (2017)
15. Schrank, D., Eisele, B., Lomax, T., Bak, J.: Urban mobility scorecard. In: Texas A M Transportation Institute (2015)
16. Tanaguchi, E., Thompson, R.G., Yamada, T.: Modelling city logistics. Cairns, Queensland, Australia (1999)
17. Djenouri, Y., Zimek, A., Chiarandini, M.: Outlier detection in urban traffic data. In: ICDM, pp. 935–940 (2018)
18. Yuan, H., et al.: An effective joint prediction model for travel demands and traffic flows. In: ICDE, pp. 348–359 (2021)
19. Zhao, Z., Chen, W., Wu, X., Chen, P.C., Liu, J.: LSTM network: a deep learning approach for short-term traffic forecast. ITS **11**(2), 68–75 (2017)
20. Zimek, A., Djenouri, Y.: Outlier detection in urban traffic data tutorial. In: 8th International Conference on Web Intelligence, Mining and Semantics (2018)

A Bayesian Markov Model
for Station-Level Origin-Destination
Matrix Reconstruction

Victor Amblard, Amir Dib, Noëlie Cherrier[✉], and Guillaume Barthe

CITiO, 22 rue René Boulanger, 75010 Paris, France
{victor.amblard,amir.dib,noelie.cherrier,guillaume.barthe}@cit.io

Abstract. This paper tackles Origin-Destination (OD) matrix reconstruction at a station level, which consists in computing the volume of passengers traveling between two different stations on a public transportation network. This information is critical for the transport operator to compute various indicators concerning the network's state and performance such as vehicle occupancy and travelers' behavior. Trip reconstruction for smart card holders, whose history of validations is available, has been thoroughly investigated in prior work. Conversely, trip reconstruction for non smart card holders has received less attention, mainly due to the difficulty of obtaining ground truth data. Among recent work in this domain, very few contributions have tackled large networks in their entirety, with millions of validations over a month and the computational challenges that come with it.

In this work, we present a new *Bayesian Markov Model* for OD matrix reconstruction. The novelty of our model lies in its scalability and the fact that it uses all available data, including Automated Fare Collection (*i.e.* smart card holders) data and Automatic Passenger Counting data (*i.e.* data from counting sensors), to accurately infer the trips' distribution. Moreover, the proposed approach produces proper OD matrices while taking into account sensor noise and fraud.

We empirically establish the relevance, robustness, and accuracy of the proposed method compared to the popular trip chaining algorithm and a previous Markov based approach on real-world, large-scale industrial datasets for two transportation networks in major cities.

Keywords: Origin destination matrix · Bayesian · Markov model ·
Real world data · Automatic passenger counting data

1 Introduction

Origin-Destination (OD) matrix reconstruction is a key element of public transport management. It provides insights regarding the network's performances and state, which drive strategic decisions regarding the network configuration,

---

Supplementary Information The online version contains supplementary material available at https://doi.org/10.1007/978-3-031-26422-1_33.

such as determining the line routing or evaluating the optimal level of service. OD reconstruction consists in reconstructing the flow of passengers who traveled from one station (origin) to another (destination) during a given period. The OD matrix is defined as the flows for all possible pairs of stations in the network. Since the origin stations are known in most cases (through user ticket validations when boarding the vehicle), accurately reconstructing these flows boils down to reconstructing passengers' alighting stations. For smartcard holders, most current approaches rely on a procedure called *trip chaining* that leverages consecutive validations within a predefined time frame. Each validation is tracked thanks to the related smart card unique identifier, and the associated alighting station is deduced from consecutive boarding stations.

Although very effective, this approach cannot be applied to single-use ticket holders or even smartcard holders whose behavior is not compatible with trip chaining rules based on expert knowledge. These drawbacks motivate the exploration of alternative approaches that use external sensors as additional data to reconstruct passengers' trips. Akin to traffic counts that provide information about vehicles entering and exiting a network of highways, counting cells are sensors installed at the vehicles' doors to count the number of passengers boarding and alighting the vehicle at each station. The availability of data from these detectors can often counterbalance the lack of information about individual passengers. However, the uncertainty associated with these sensors' measurements is significant due to intrinsic sensor noise and high false detection rates (passengers may trigger multiple detections). Hence, filtering and denoising raw sensor data is mandatory for these countings to be used. Finally, these sensors can be costly to install and maintain for transport operators leading to a partial equipment rate of the vehicle fleet. Altogether, these issues make OD reconstruction challenging and call for end-to-end approaches that consider sensor quality, scarcity, and scalability.

In this work, we propose a novel full Bayesian Markov-based model for OD reconstruction that considers all commonly available data sources. Our approach is based on the finding that sampling OD matrices based on Markov chain modeling of agents' behavior amounts to drawing from a multivariate hypergeometric distribution. Moreover, we overcome the short trip problem, which is the main drawback of such an approach, by considering a biased version of the hypergeometric sampling. Subsequently, we tackle two problems that commonly arise when dealing with real-world data: noise and scarcity. We propose a new denoising method for counting sensors that preserve the OD matrix structure and use a time series similarity metric to deal with unequipped vehicles. Finally, we show that this approach can be applied to large-scale networks with real-world data to better reconstruct the flow of passengers.

Section 2 introduces the basic concepts of OD matrix and trip reconstitution along with related works. Then, Sect. 3 presents the various aspects of our approach toward station-level OD reconstruction. Finally, Sect. 4 is devoted to the practical evaluation of our approach on real-world industrial use cases. Detailed proofs and derivations are deferred to the supplementary material.

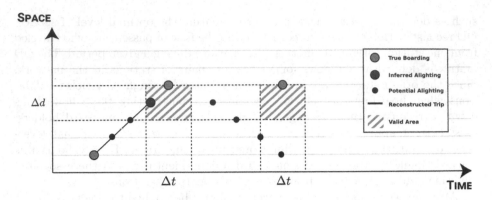

Fig. 1. Illustration of trip chaining with deterministic rules: the first trip is chained since a candidate alighting station lies within the time and distance thresholds Δt and Δd, while the second trip cannot be chained since no candidate alighting station abides by the thresholds.

2   Related Work

Historically, OD matrices were obtained as part of the four-step model [25] for demand modeling using fully deterministic models inspired by physics such as the gravity [32] and the entropy models [31] are the best-known examples.

This work focuses on OD matrix reconstruction in public transport, a subfield of OD reconstruction that presents a few peculiarities, notably considering the amount and quality of available data. Thanks to the recent advancements in technologies, many transportation agencies are now using Automatic Data Collection (ADC) systems, that include Automated Fare Collection (AFC) systems, *i.e.* smart cards most of the time; Automatic Vehicle Location (AVL) systems, giving access to real arrival time of vehicles to stations; and Automatic Passenger Counting (APC) systems, with sensors installed on board the vehicles.

Although these increasingly abundant sources of data have been used for various applications in the last two decades (mining travel patterns, trip purpose detection among others) [5], this work tackles another major application which is station-level OD reconstruction (a review can be found in [13]). More specifically, it focuses on estimating alighting locations from known boarding locations (thanks to smart card validation data).

Until now, the area of OD reconstruction has been dominated by rule-based approaches using smart card data. Notably, *trip chaining* is a method that infers alighting locations from successive boarding locations, supposing the user has not traveled more than a distance threshold during a time threshold between the sought alighting and the next boarding [13,21,29] (see Fig. 1). Other advanced methods are probabilistic [11,12,17] or based on the full user's history [11,18, 19,29].

Recently, increasing attention has been drawn to machine learning approaches [34], notably with neural networks [1,15]. Machine learning is expected to bridge the gap between different data sources, e.g. smartphone location data [9, 33] or land use data [23, 28]. More recent works use graph convolutional networks to infer OD flows [23, 24, 35] but require labeled training data.

Finally, while the vast majority of the literature focuses on exploiting AVL and AFC (*i.e.* vehicle location and smart card) data, only a few studies make use of other sources of data and especially APC data. APC data is mostly used as a scaling factor to the OD matrix extracted from previous methods, using methods such as Iterative Proportional Fitting (IPF) [2, 7, 14, 26]. However, IPF as well as other optimization methods [16, 22] do not enable any uncertainty estimation. On the opposite, statistical frameworks have been proposed and notably Bayesian approaches [10, 20, 36], with the recurrent drawback of being hardly scalable to larger and more complex networks. Also, the work from [3] derived a statistical approach that is inspired by the maximum entropy method, and the study from [14] proposed a Markov-chain Monte Carlo method to infer route OD with large amounts of APC data only.

However, few of these works consider the imprecision associated to APC data: they are usually considered 100% reliable while studies estimated the accuracy of standard infrared sensors to be around 80% [8]. Evaluating the quality and accuracy of the counting instruments is hard, while APC data can cover the entire network and make indicators easy to calculate [4]. In addition, the existing methods often lack validation through real transportation data, and when a validation procedure is proposed it is often on a very small perimeter, missing demonstration of scalability [13]. For instance, [27] validate their approach with an OD survey and a group of volunteers. This work proposes a denoising module for the counting cells data to be used more reliably by a Bayesian Markov model for OD reconstruction. The experiments are conducted on real data collected from Casablanca (Morocco) and Orléans Métropole (France) public transport networks.

3 Origin Destination Matrix Reconstruction Using Ticketing and Count Data

This section describes the different steps of the proposed OD matrix reconstruction procedure. This method is based on a Bayesian Markov model inspired by [20] that takes into account the validations (AFC) and counting cells (APC) data per course. The latter is first denoised to get valid boarding and alighting counts. Then, a biased hypergeometric sampling integrating priors on trip lengths is proposed to simulate trips for each course based on the denoised counts. Finally, the posterior parameters of the Markov model are inferred and extrapolated to courses without counting cells.

In what follows, we consider a network with different routes (*i.e.* lines with specified directions). A course corresponds to a vehicle following a given route with a predefined schedule. For clarity, unless otherwise specified, we focus on a single course that occurs on a specific route. Let us denote by n the number of stations on the route and Y_i, Z_i respectively the number of passengers boarding and alighting at station i and p_{ij} the probability of alighting at station j conditionally to the fact that a passenger boarded at station i. The passengers are assumed to *behave the same way and independently of one another*. The passengers' behavior is described by a non-homogeneous Markov chain valued on a binary state space.

The inference relies on alighting counts, which in this case stem from counting cells measures and are typically tainted with imprecision. The following aims at correcting the counting cells noise before any inference of the model.

3.1   Count Data Preprocessing

This part presents a preprocessing method for counting cells measures. Due to multiple factors, all referred to as noise in what follows, the actual observed boarding counts $\tilde{Y}_i$ (resp. alighting counts $\tilde{Z}_i$) differ from the real ones by a noise $\eta_i^{+,IN} - \eta_i^{-,IN}$ (resp. $\eta_i^{+,OUT} - \eta_i^{-,OUT}$):

$$\tilde{Y}_i = Y_i + \eta_i^{+,IN} - \eta_i^{-,IN}, \quad \eta_i^{+,IN} \sim \mathrm{Bin}(Y_i, p^+), \quad \eta_i^{-,IN} \sim \mathrm{Bin}(Y_i, p^-). \quad (1)$$

The same applies for $(\tilde{Z}_i)_i$ with $\eta_i^{+,OUT}$ and $\eta_i^{-,OUT}$ also following binomial distributions $\mathrm{Bin}(Z_i, p^+)$ and $\mathrm{Bin}(Z_i, p^-)$. Note that the noise is not required to be symmetric, as counting cells may over-count more than they under-count or conversely.

Fraud Removal. In this work, only trips corresponding to passengers who validated their tickets are reconstructed. Counting cells, however, record all passengers entering and exiting the vehicle, regardless of whether they did validate. Therefore, the total passenger count Z_i alighting at station i of a given course must be disaggregated between Z_i^F fraudsters and Z_i^V persons who validated their ticket. To estimate the number of fraudsters on board, a two-step approach first determines the total number of fraudsters during the course and then allocates them to different stations.

Let F be the total number of fraudsters on a given course and S the total number of passengers on the course. $S = F + \mathbb{1}^T Y^V$ is unobserved since neither the true boarding nor alighting counts are known. Nevertheless, two noisy versions of it are observed: $\tilde{S}_Y = \mathbb{1}^T \tilde{Y}$ and $\tilde{S}_Z = \mathbb{1}^T \tilde{Z}$. Therefore, S is the sum of the observed count $\tilde{S}_Y$ plus the sum of the noises for each station measure. Since the $(\eta_i^{+,IN})_i$ and $(\eta_i^{-,IN})_i$ are i.i.d variables, their sum also follows a binomial distribution of parameters $(\sum_i Y_i = S, p^+)$ and (S, p^-) respectively. Formally,

$$\tilde{S}_Y = \sum_{i=1}^{n} \tilde{Y}_i = S + \eta_\Sigma^{+,IN} - \eta_\Sigma^{-,IN}, \quad \eta_\Sigma^{+,IN} \sim \mathrm{Bin}(S, p^+), \quad \eta_\Sigma^{-,IN} \sim \mathrm{Bin}(S, p^-). \quad (2)$$

Thanks to the conditional independence between $\tilde{S}_Y$ an $\tilde{S}_Z$ conditionally to S, the posterior distribution for S is derived and therefore the number of frauding passengers F is sampled from this distribution:

$$\begin{aligned} p(S|\tilde{S}_Y, \tilde{S}_Z) &\propto p(\tilde{S}_Y|S) p(\tilde{S}_Z|S) p(S) \\ &\propto p(\eta_\Sigma^{+,IN} - \eta_\Sigma^{-,IN}|S) p(\eta_\Sigma^{+,OUT} - \eta_\Sigma^{-,OUT}|S) p(S). \end{aligned} \quad (3)$$

In addition, each station i is assigned a predetermined fraud rate f_i. The f_i can either be provided as prior expert knowledge or computed as the average fraud rate from boarding counting and ticketing data over all courses passing by station i in the opposite direction, making the hypothesis that the alighting fraudsters rate in one direction, aggregated over a sufficient number of courses, is approximated by the boarding fraudsters rate in the opposite direction. From there, the F fraudsters of a given course are disaggregated into F_i fraudsters alighting at station i, by sampling them from a Fisher's noncentral hypergeometric distribution with weights f_i and initial number of objects $\tilde{Z}_i$. The F_i are removed from the $\tilde{Z}_i$ to yield adjusted alighting counts denoted as $\tilde{Z}_i^{ad} = \tilde{Z}_i - F_i$.

Alighting Counts Denoising with Gibbs Sampling. The following aims at refining the adjusted alighting counts $\tilde{Z}_i^{ad}$ to obtain a denoised alighting sequence that matches the validations boarding counts Y_i^V. Such an alighting sequence is further referred to as a *feasible alighting sequence*.

Definition 1. *A feasible alighting sequence with respect to a boarding sequence* $Y = (Y_1, ..., Y_{n-1}, 0) \in \mathbb{N}^n$ *is a sequence* $Z = (0, Z_2, ..., Z_n) \in \mathbb{N}^n$ *such that*

$$\sum_{i=1}^{n} Y_i = \sum_{i=1}^{n} Z_i, \quad (4a) \qquad \forall i \in [\![1, n-1]\!], \quad \sum_{k=1}^{i} Y_k \geq \sum_{k=1}^{i} Z_k. \quad (4b)$$

The feasible alighting set *is the set* $\mathcal{S}(Y)$ *of feasible alighting sequences w.r.t.* Y.

Conditions (4a) and (4b) simply enforce the following two physical constraints: the number of boarding passengers must be equal to those alighting during the course, and occupancy must always be nonnegative. The goal is thus to select a feasible alighting sequence close to the observed one ($\tilde{Z}_i$). Although the noise model presented in Eq. (1) is quite simple, the dependencies between the Z_i stemming from constraints (4a) and (4b) make it impossible to sample each count independently and call for a more sophisticated sampling algorithm. Hence, a Gibbs sampler approach is adopted to iteratively sample one of the alighting counts Z_i conditionally to all others sampled so far, so that constraint (4b) is satisfied all the times. Note that to abide by condition (4a), one of the values of the alighting sequence must act as a pivot. Z_1 is arbitrarily chosen to balance the sum of the remaining Z_i. From the noise model defined in Eq. (1), the conditional posterior probability of Z_i given $Z_{-i} = (Z_2, ..., Z_{i-1}, Z_{i+1}, ..., Z_n)$, Y and $\tilde{Z}$ writes

$$\forall k \in \mathbb{N}, \quad p(Z_i = k | Y, \tilde{Z}^{ad}, Z_{-i}) \propto p(\tilde{Z}_i^{ad} | Z_i = k) \, p(Z_i = k)$$

$$p\left(\tilde{Z}_1^{ad} \middle| Z_1 = S - \sum_{k \neq i} Z_k - k\right) p\left(Z_1 = S - \sum_{k \neq i} Z_k - k\right). \tag{5}$$

Algorithm 1. Gibbs sampler

Require: $Y, \tilde{Z}^{ad}, N_{IT}$ the number of sampling iterations, n the number of stops
    $z^0 = (0, Y_1, ..., Y_{n-1})$
    for $t \in [\![1, N_{IT}]\!]$ **do**
      for $j \in [\![2, n]\!]$ **do**

$$m_j = \max_{i \in [\![1,j]\!]} \sum_{k=i+1}^{n} Y_k - \left(\sum_{k=i+1}^{j-1} z_k^t - \sum_{k=j+1}^{n} z_k^{t-1} \right)$$

$$M_j = \mathbb{1}^T Y - \left(\sum_{k=2}^{j-1} z_k^t + \sum_{k=j+1}^{n} z_k^{t-1} \right)$$

        For $k \in [\![m_j, M_j]\!]$, $p_k = p(Z_j = k | \tilde{Z}^{ad}, Z_1 = z_1^t, ..., Z_{j-1} = z_{j-1}^t, Z_{j+1} = z_{j+1}^{t-1}, ..., Z_n = z_n^{t-1})$
        Sample $z_j^t \sim \text{Discrete}([p_{m_i}, ..., p_{M_i}])$
      end for

$$z^t = \left(0, \mathbb{1}^T Y - \sum_{k=2}^{n} z_k^t, z_2^t, ..., z_n^t \right)$$

    end for
    return $Z = z^{N_{IT}}$

One can show that conditions (4a) and (4b) imply that Z_i has a finite support, *i.e.* that there exist two non-negative integers m_i and M_i such that $p(Z_i = k) = 0$ for all k not in $[\![m_i, M_i]\!]$. The full conditional probability is finally derived in closed form, provided that a prior is chosen for the true alighting counts. If no information is available, one could choose a uniform prior over the interval $[\![m_i, M_i]\!]$ for the alighting count Z_i. Finally, Gibbs sampling requires a valid initialization, *i.e.* an initial alighting sequence that belongs to the feasible alighting set. For instance, $z^0 = (0, Y_1^V, ..., Y_{n-1}^V)$ is a feasible alighting sequence w.r.t. Y^V. The full algorithm is presented in Algorithm 1. An improved initialization to reduce the number of iterations is proposed in the supplementary material.

3.2 Trips Sampling and Posterior Estimation

The model presented in this section uses the denoised alighting counts for posterior parameter estimation and trip sampling. A first-order Markov model is first described as a basis for the proposed approach.

Definition 2. *The first-order Markov model is defined by a set of $n-1$ parameters $(\theta_2, ..., \theta_n)$ such that for all $i \in [\![2, n]\!]$,*

$$p(\xi_i = 0 | \xi_{i-1} = 1) = \theta_i, \quad p(\xi_i = 1 | \xi_{i-1} = 1) = 1 - \theta_i, \quad (6)$$

with ξ_i the variable indicating if the passenger is on board as the vehicle departs from station i ($\xi_i = 1$) or not ($\xi_i = 0$).

The above statement conveys that the model is without memory and "forgets" about the passengers' boarding stations, only focusing on whether they were on board the vehicle when it arrived at a station i.

The Markov property allows for simple derivation of the probability p_{ij} for a passenger to alight at a station j provided that they boarded at station i [20]

$$p_{ij} = \theta_j \prod_{k=i+1}^{j-1} (1 - \theta_k). \tag{7}$$

The parameters' likelihood is directly derived from the boarding and alighting counts [20] and writes

$$Z_i|\theta_i \sim Bin\left(\sum_{k=1}^{i-1} Y_k - Z_k, \theta_i\right). \tag{8}$$

Finally, to obtain a full Bayesian model, it is needed to choose a prior distribution over the set of parameters $(\theta_i)_{i=1}^n$. For clarity and simplicity of derivations, we set $\theta_j \sim \text{Beta}(\alpha_j, \beta_j)$ with hyperparameters α, β inferred from the chained trips. Once sampled from the posterior distribution, the model's parameters θ are used in Sect. 3.3 to extrapolate to courses without counting cells.

However, the first-order Markov model's shortcoming lies in that all passengers are considered equal: they all share the same probability to alight at a given station regardless of their boarding station, as long as they are in the vehicle. As a direct consequence, the longer the trip, the less likely it is since $p_{ij} = \theta_j \prod_{k=i+1}^{j-1}(1 - \theta_k) \sim \mathcal{O}(\theta^{j-i})$. The probability of staying in the vehicle for $j - i$ stations decays exponentially. This is far from being realistic and clashes with empirical observations. Indeed, over various networks and cities, it is frequent for the mode of the trip length distribution to be located around a length of 5 with a slow decay followed by a more rapid decay. Therefore, the following proposes a sampling procedure to overcome the short trips issue.

Let us denote by X_{ij} the number of passengers that boarded the vehicle at station i and alighted at station j. Formally we are looking for $(X_{ij})_{i,j}$ given $(Y_k)_k, (Z_k)_k$. Here, $X = (X_{ij})_{i,j}$ is the OD matrix. Although in general the underlying true trip length distribution is unknown, chained trips provide insights into this distribution and prior information. Once estimated, these priors are used to bias our sampling procedure using a Fisher's noncentral hypergeometric distribution for $(X_{ij})_j|Y, Z, L$ where L are the trip length priors. The practical details are deferred to the supplementary material.

This result extends the work of [20] in case priors are available and explores how to leverage biased multivariate hypergeometric distributions to sample directly from the model. As shown in the experiments section, it also alleviates the so-called short trips issue. Algorithm 2 summarizes the different steps to reconstruct the OD matrix from counting cells observations.

Algorithm 2. OD matrix reconstruction for courses with counting cells on a given route

---

Require: $p(\theta)$ prior for the θ parameters of the first-order model, L prior for trips lengths for the considered route, $\mathcal{C}$ all courses, $(f_i)_i$ fraud rates by station i, N_{sim} number of simulations

1: **for** course $c_t \in \mathcal{C}$ **do**
2:      **for** $k \in [\![1, N_{sim}]\!]$ **do**
3:         $\tilde{Z}_{k,t}^{ad} = $ REMOVE FRAUD FROM ALIGHTING COUNTS($Y_t^V, \tilde{Y}_t, \tilde{Z}_t, f_i$) (Section 3.1)
4:         $Z_{k,t} = $ SAMPLE FEASIBLE ALIGHTING COUNTS($\tilde{Y}_{k,t}^{ad}, \tilde{Z}_{k,t}^{ad}, Y_t^V$) (Section 3.1)
5:         $\theta_{k,t} = $ INFER POSTERIOR PARAMETERS($Y_t^V, Z_{k,t}, p(\theta)$) (Section 3.2)
6:         $X_{k,t} = $ SAMPLE FEASIBLE OD MATRIX($Y_t^V, Z_{k,t}, L$) (Section 3.2)
7:      **end for**
8:      $X_t = $ MODE$\left((X_{k,t})_k\right)$
9: **end for**
10: **return** $(X_t)_t, (\theta_{k,t})_{k,t}$

3.3   Extrapolation to Courses Without Counting Cells

Most of the times, due to the high cost of equipping vehicles with counting cells, only a fraction of the fleet operates with them. This is problematic since the proposed approach relies on alighting counts to simulate alighting stations. However, other courses associated to the same route can be used to extrapolate the first-order model's parameters on non-equipped courses.

More specifically, consider a target course $c_{T,r}$ that is associated with route $r \in \mathcal{R}$. The idea is to match the target course to some of the courses with count data on the same route $(c_{t,r})_t$ which are available in the data history.

The proposed method considers a course as a temporal series based on its station-wise validations: $Y_t^V = (Y_{1,t}^V, ...Y_{n-1,t}^V)$. Two courses are said to be similar if their validations are similar, for some time-series similarity metric. Here, Dynamic Time Warping (DTW) [30] is used as the similarity metric. Similar courses are the k-nearest neighbors for the DTW metric with k set experimentally.

$\mathcal{C}(T,r)$ is then the subset of courses $\{c_{t,r}|c_{t,r}$ is similar to $c_{T,r}\}$ that contains all courses matched to $c_{T,r}$ and $\Theta(T,r)$ is the set of parameters of the first-order Markov model for the matched courses: $\Theta(T,r) = \{(\theta_{1,t}, ..., \theta_{n,t})_t | t \in \mathcal{C}(T,r)\}$. Then, the parameters $\theta_{T,i}$ for the target course are sampled as follows for all stations i in $[\![1, n]\!]$:

$$\theta_{T,i} \sim \mathcal{N}(\overline{\theta}, \sigma_\theta), \tag{9}$$

with $\overline{\theta} = (\overline{\theta_1}, ..., \overline{\theta_n})$ the experimental average and $\sigma_\theta = (\sigma_{\theta_1}, ...\sigma_{\theta_n})$ the standard deviation of these parameters over all courses belonging to $\mathcal{C}(T,r)$.

4 Experiments

This section aims at testing the proposed improved Bayesian Markov model. Some considerations on time and space complexity are developed, and the accuracy and robustness of the proposed method are discussed.

4.1 Experimental Setup

The experiments are performed on two different networks. The first one is the Casablanca network with two streetcar lines of 30–40 stations each, totaling more than 100,000 boarding validations per day on average. This network is of high interest since passengers validate when they board but also when they alight, therefore providing ground truth data. However, none of the streetcars are equipped with counting cells, which have been simulated for the experiments (see supplementary material). The Orléans Métropole network is used for scalability assessment. It has a more complex topology than Casablanca's, with more than 50 bus and streetcar lines, numerous connections, and around 70,000 validations and 2,000 courses per day. Counting cells data is available, but this network does not give access to ground truth data since passengers validate only when they board. Both networks are illustrated in the supplementary material.

Five simulations are performed for each course in the dataset to come up with five candidate alighting stations for each passenger. The mode (i.e. the most probable station) is designated as the assigned alighting station. In the simulations, p^+ and p^- the counting cells noise parameters are both set to 0.4. The predefined fraud rates f_i are the same for all stations (the absolute value is not important since they only serve as bias for the hypergeometric sampling). All algorithms are implemented in Python and can run on multiple cores. The *BiasedUrn* library [6] is used for hypergeometric sampling.

4.2 Scalability

Table 1 summarizes and compares the time and space complexity of trip chaining and the proposed model. For trip chaining, passengers without an alighting station are aggregated by boarding station and their alighting stations are inferred simultaneously for the whole batch, which is done in $\mathcal{O}(n^2)$. The proposed model utilizes counting cells at the course level and therefore has a time complexity that is growing linearly with the number of courses $|\mathcal{C}|$. Moreover, the time complexity is directly proportional to the number of simulations N_s. Regarding the space complexity, since all of the passengers' candidate alighting stations are stored, the space complexity is proportional to the number of passengers P and the number of simulations.

However, the implementation still runs comfortably on a laptop: for instance, running 10 simulations on a month of data for the Orléans Métropole network (more than two million validations) takes up to 2 h on an Apple M1 processor. Moreover, if multiples cores are available, courses can be inferred independently on different cores, speeding up the simulation process.

Table 1. Time and space complexity comparison.

Model	Time complexity	Spatial complexity
Trip chaining	$\mathcal{O}(n^2)$	$\mathcal{O}(P)$
Proposed model	$\mathcal{O}(n^2|\mathcal{C}|N_s)$	$\mathcal{O}(PN_s)$

Table 2. Comparison of the proposed method with three baselines along three metrics compared to ground truth in Casablanca network.

	KL divergence	Accuracy	Avg. max. occupancy error
Random model	0.45	6%	5.5%
Trip chaining [29]	0.15	10%	3.8%
Markov model [20] (5 simulations)	0.075	15%	0%
Proposed model (5 simulations)	**0.07**	**17%**	**0%**

4.3   Accuracy of Trips Reconstitution

Three baselines are considered: a random model that assigns to each passenger an alighting station randomly, the popular trip chaining algorithm [29], and the Markov model from [20], to be compared with the proposed improved Bayesian implementation. For trip chaining, passengers whose validation could not be chained are assigned an alighting station following the distribution of chained trips. The Casablanca network is used here with simulated noise-free counting cells and alighting validations removed: the models are run on boarding validations only, and the resulting OD matrices are compared to the true OD matrix obtained from both boarding and alighting validations.

Table 2 compares the proposed model to the baselines according to three metrics: the Kullback-Leibler (KL) divergence between the predicted and the true OD matrices, the accuracy of individual trips (whether the predicted alighting station is correct w.r.t. the ground truth) and the maximum relative error on the occupancy, averaged over all courses. The proposed model outperforms the baselines considering any metric. Both Markov model based approaches obtain a perfect occupancy estimation: indeed, the models are designed to comply with the provided boarding and alighting counts per course. Here, perfect counts are simulated, resulting in errorless occupancy estimation.

Trip Length Distribution. The following experiment evaluates the impact of adding priors and biasing the Hypergeometric distribution to obtain more realistic trip lengths. The same Casablanca dataset as above is used. Figure 2 compares the trip length distribution obtained by the vanilla Markov model (top figure) from [20] to the proposed one with priors over trip lengths (bottom figure). Incorporating priors results in a trip length distribution much closer to the true distribution: the sum of the absolute errors was reduced by over 50%.

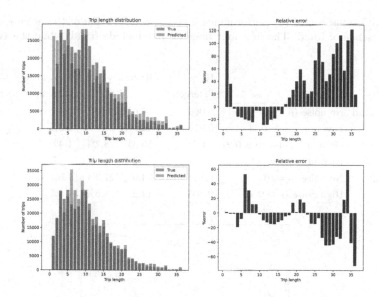

Fig. 2. Top: Markov model without priors. **Bottom**: Markov model with priors on trip length. The left plots display the distribution of trip lengths over all trips, and the right plots show the relative difference between the predicted distribution and the ground truth distribution.

4.4   Robustness

In this part, results are shown for the proposed model only since neither the random model nor trip chaining makes use of counting cells. Moreover, the Markov model from [20] does not deal with situations where count data is not perfect.

Influence of the Noise Level and Fraud. This experiment evaluates how the noise in counting cells data affects the different metrics when considered with and without fraud. The dataset from Casablanca is still used, but counting cells are simulated with a noise level p.

Table 3 presents the same three metrics with respect to Casablanca ground truth with different noise levels and with the presence or absence of fraud. The proposed model is shown resilient to noise: even with significant sensor noise levels, the KL divergence and the accuracy remain almost as high as when there is no noise. However, it is less robust to fraud, even in the absence of noise. This is explained by the fact that the fraud disaggregation algorithm assigns the inferred number of fraudsters to the course stations based on station fraud rates which are given as prior data and may be quite inaccurate. Future work may explore alternate approaches to station-level fraud rate estimation.

Table 3. Comparison of the performance metrics as a function of the noise level and of the presence of fraud. The first four lines do not include fraud, while the two last do.

		KL divergence	Accuracy	Avg. max. occupancy error
No fraud	No noise ($p = 0$)	0.069	16.6%(28.9%)	0%
	Low noise ($p = 0.1$)	0.071	16.5% (28.8%)	1.2%
	Moderate noise ($p = 0.2$)	0.074	16.3% (28.7%)	1.4%
	High noise ($p = 0.4$)	0.077	16.2% (28.4%)	1.6%
Fraud	No noise ($p = 0$)	0.101	14.9% (27.3%)	1.5%
	High noise ($p = 0.4$)	0.105	14.2% (26.6%)	1.8%

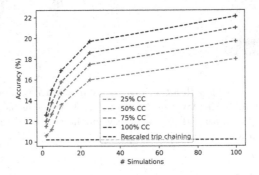

Fig. 3. Alighting station estimation accuracy with respect to the number of simulations of the proposed model, for varying equipment rates (25% CC means 25% of courses are equipped with counting cells), compared to trip chaining.

Influence of Equipment Rate. Here, the sensitivity of the proposed model to lower coverage in counting cells is examined. To this end, counting cells are simulated only for a portion of all vehicles in the Casablanca network.

Figure 3 depicts the accuracy of passenger trip reconstitution (*i.e.* the percentage of correctly inferred alighting stations) as a function of the number of simulations of the proposed model, for different scenarios depending on the percentage of courses equipped with counting cells. One can see that even with low equipment rates, the proposed model consistently outperforms trip chaining (black dotted line). This is particularly important as, for most networks, equipment rates do not exceed 50%. In addition, the accuracy loss resulting from having incomplete data can be compensated by an increased number of simulations at the cost of a linear increase in run time.

5 Conclusion and Perspectives

5.1 Conclusion

This paper aims to reconstruct Origin-Destination matrices to better understand flows in public transport networks. The idea is to infer each passenger's alighting station with the data collected from the operators, the counting cells and the geolocalised stations. While recent statistical approaches may use sophisticated probabilistic models that are not scalable, we started from the model introduced by [20] which allows trips to be directly simulated and the parameters' distribution expressed in a closed form. Our implementation improved this model by using prior knowledge about the OD matrix that a trip chaining algorithm can provide. More importantly, several additions were built on top of this model, allowing us to tackle various phenomena that frequently occur when dealing with large-scale and real data and significantly affect the quality of the resulting OD matrix. Specifically, the objectives of these additions are to denoise count data and take fraudsters into account using a Bayesian approach. Dealing with both at once is challenging because their effects tend to mix and potentially cancel out. In the end, we demonstrated the robustness and accuracy of this approach on two real-world transportation networks. To the best of our knowledge, this approach is a novelty and as of today, extensive tests are performed on multiple networks in cities of different sizes.

5.2 Future Work

Better Understanding of the Sensors. Although the simulation environment enabled us to test different models with real-life phenomena, the lack of true counts to compare on the Orléans' network use case makes it challenging to estimate the correct value of the noise hyperparameters p^+ and p^- or the fraud rates at each station. It could be interesting to collect ground truth data for these sensors by manually counting passengers in vehicles. The value for these hyperparameters could then be estimated using an Expectation-Maximization algorithm.

Multi-source. Although counting cells is very beneficial to OD matrix reconstruction, the problem remains highly uncertain. Indeed, many stations lead to high uncertainty in the resulting OD matrix. Nevertheless, adding other sensors, such as Bluetooth scanners, could reduce the system's underdetermination and increase the reconstruction's reliability.

Denoising Method. The actual statistical denoising method proposed in Subsect. 3.1 is incomplete. Indeed, only observed alighting counts are denoised with respect to the boarding validations, which requires removing fraud beforehand. Thereby, denoising both boarding and alighting counts would give access to the total count of boarding and alighting passengers per station without needing to remove fraudsters, which is useful notably for occupancy estimation.

References

1. Assemi, B., Alsger, A., Moghaddam, M., Hickman, M., Mesbah, M.: Improving alighting stop inference accuracy in the trip chaining method using neural networks. Public Transp. **12**(1), 89–121 (2020)
2. Ben-Akiva, M., Macke, P.P., Hsu, P.S.: Alternative methods to estimate route-level trip tables and expand on-board surveys. No. 1037, Transportation Research Board (1985)
3. Carvalho, L.: A Bayesian statistical approach for inference on static origin-destination matrices in transportation studies. Technometrics **56**(2), 225–237 (2014)
4. Egu, O., Bonnel, P.: Can we estimate accurately fare evasion without a survey? Results from a data comparison approach in Lyon using fare collection data, fare inspection data and counting data. Public Transp. **12**(1), 1–26 (2020)
5. Faroqi, H., Mesbah, M., Kim, J.: Applications of transit smart cards beyond a fare collection tool: a literature review. Adv. Transp. Stud. **45** (2018)
6. Fog, A.: Sampling methods for Wallenius' and Fisher's noncentral hypergeometric distributions. Commun. Stat.-Simul. Comput.® **37**(2), 241–257 (2008)
7. Gordon, J.B., Koutsopoulos, H.N., Wilson, N.H.: Estimation of population origin-interchange-destination flows on multimodal transit networks. Transp. Res. Part C Emerg. Technol. **90**, 350–365 (2018)
8. Grgurević, I., Juršić, K., Rajič, V.: Review of automatic passenger counting systems in public urban transport. In: Knapčíková, L., Peraković, D., Behúnová, A., Periša, M. (eds.) 5th EAI International Conference on Management of Manufacturing Systems. EICC, pp. 1–15. Springer, Cham (2022). https://doi.org/10.1007/978-3-030-67241-6_1
9. Harrison, G., Grant-Muller, S.M., Hodgson, F.C.: New and emerging data forms in transportation planning and policy: opportunities and challenges for "track and trace" data. Transp. Res. Part C Emerg. Technol. **117**, 102672 (2020)
10. Hazelton, M.L.: Network tomography for integer-valued traffic. Ann. Appl. Stat. **9**(1), 474–506 (2015)
11. He, L., Trépanier, M.: Estimating the destination of unlinked trips in transit smart card fare data. Transp. Res. Rec. **2535**(1), 97–104 (2015)
12. Huang, D., Yu, J., Shen, S., Li, Z., Zhao, L., Gong, C.: A method for bus OD matrix estimation using multisource data. J. Adv. Transp. **2020** (2020)
13. Hussain, E., Bhaskar, A., Chung, E.: Transit OD matrix estimation using smart-card data: recent developments and future research challenges. Transp. Res. Part C Emerg. Technol. **125**, 103044 (2021)
14. Ji, Y., You, Q., Jiang, S., Zhang, H.M.: Statistical inference on transit route-level origin-destination flows using automatic passenger counter data. J. Adv. Transp. **49**(6), 724–737 (2015)
15. Jung, J., Sohn, K.: Deep-learning architecture to forecast destinations of bus passengers from entry-only smart-card data. IET Intel. Transp. Syst. **11**(6), 334–339 (2017)
16. Kumar, P., Khani, A., Davis, G.A.: Transit route origin-destination matrix estimation using compressed sensing. Transp. Res. Rec. **2673**(10), 164–174 (2019)
17. Kumar, P., Khani, A., He, Q.: A robust method for estimating transit passenger trajectories using automated data. Transp. Res. Part C Emerg. Technol. **95**, 731–747 (2018)

18. Lee, S., Lee, J., Bae, B., Nam, D., Cheon, S.: Estimating destination of bus trips considering trip type characteristics. Appl. Sci. **11**(21), 10415 (2021)
19. Lei, D., Chen, X., Cheng, L., Zhang, L., Wang, P., Wang, K.: Minimum entropy rate-improved trip-chain method for origin-destination estimation using smart card data. Transp. Res. Part C Emerg. Technol. **130**, 103307 (2021)
20. Li, B.: Markov models for Bayesian analysis about transit route origin-destination matrices. Transp. Res. Part B Methodol. **43**(3), 301–310 (2009)
21. Li, T., Sun, D., Jing, P., Yang, K.: Smart card data mining of public transport destination: a literature review. Information **9**(1), 18 (2018)
22. Liu, X., Van Hentenryck, P., Zhao, X.: Optimization models for estimating transit network origin-destination flows with big transit data. J. Big Data Anal. Transp. **3**(3), 247–262 (2021)
23. Liu, Z., Miranda, F., Xiong, W., Yang, J., Wang, Q., Silva, C.: Learning geo-contextual embeddings for commuting flow prediction. In: Proceedings of the AAAI Conference on Artificial Intelligence, vol. 34, pp. 808–816 (2020)
24. Luca, M., Barlacchi, G., Lepri, B., Pappalardo, L.: A survey on deep learning for human mobility. ACM Comput. Surv. (CSUR) **55**(1), 1–44 (2021)
25. McNally, M.G.: The Four-Step Model. Emerald Group Publishing Limited, Bradford (2007)
26. Mishalani, R.G., Ji, Y., McCord, M.R.: Effect of onboard survey sample size on estimation of transit bus route passenger origin-destination flow matrix using automatic passenger counter data. Transp. Res. Rec. **2246**(1), 64–73 (2011)
27. Munizaga, M., Devillaine, F., Navarrete, C., Silva, D.: Validating travel behavior estimated from smartcard data. Transp. Res. Part C Emerg. Technol. **44**, 70–79 (2014)
28. Simini, F., Barlacchi, G., Luca, M., Pappalardo, L.: A deep gravity model for mobility flows generation. Nat. Commun. **12**(1), 1–13 (2021)
29. Trépanier, M., Tranchant, N., Chapleau, R.: Individual trip destination estimation in a transit smart card automated fare collection system. J. Intell. Transp. Syst. **11**(1), 1–14 (2007)
30. Vintsyuk, T.K.: Speech discrimination by dynamic programming. Cybernetics **4**(1), 52–57 (1968)
31. Wilson, A.G.: The use of entropy maximising models, in the theory of trip distribution, mode split and route split. J. Transp. Econ. Policy 108–126 (1969)
32. Wilson, A.G.: A family of spatial interaction models, and associated developments. Environ. Plan. A **3**(1), 1–32 (1971)
33. Wu, X., Guo, J., Xian, K., Zhou, X.: Hierarchical travel demand estimation using multiple data sources: a forward and backward propagation algorithmic framework on a layered computational graph. Transp. Res. Part C Emerg. Technol. **96**, 321–346 (2018)
34. Yan, F., Yang, C., Ukkusuri, S.V.: Alighting stop determination using two-step algorithms in bus transit systems. Transportmetrica A Transp. Sci. **15**(2), 1522–1542 (2019)
35. Yao, X., Gao, Y., Zhu, D., Manley, E., Wang, J., Liu, Y.: Spatial origin-destination flow imputation using graph convolutional networks. IEEE Trans. Intell. Transp. Syst. **22**(12), 7474–7484 (2020)
36. Zapata, L.P., Flores, M., Larios, V., Maciel, R., Antunez, E.A.: Estimation of people flow in public transportation network through the origin-destination problem for the South-Eastern corridor of Quito city in the smart cities context. In: 2019 IEEE International Smart Cities Conference (ISC2), pp. 181–186. IEEE (2019)

BusWTE: Realtime Bus Waiting Time Estimation of GPS Missing via Multi-task Learning

Yuecheng Rong[1,2(✉)], Jun Liu[1,3], Zhilin Xu[2], Jian Ding[2], Chuangming Zhang[2], and Jiaxiang Gao[2]

[1] College of Computer Science and Technology, Xi'an Jiaotong University, Xi'an, China
[2] Baidu Inc., Beijing, China
{rongyuecheng,xuzhilin01,dingjian01,zhangchuanming,gaojiaxiang}@baidu.com
[3] National Engineering Lab for Big Data Analytics, Xi'an Jiaotong University, Xi'an, China
liukeen@mail.xjtu.edu.cn

Abstract. Realtime bus waiting time is of great importance to the intelligent public transportation system and is beneficial for improving user satisfaction by online map services. While there are limited realtime bus waiting time services in a city, because of the expensive cost of GPS sensor deployment and realtime service operation. To address the above problem, we propose a novel end-to-end multi-task framework named BusWTE, which estimates bus waiting time for those bus routes without GPS sensors deployed. BusWTE utilizes a variety of urban datasets, including historical bus trip data reported by a limited number of GPS equipped buses, road network data, traffic condition data, and mobility data. Specifically, we firstly use a classical BiLSTM architecture to encode the sequence of bus route related features, and employ two fully-connected layers to embed the stop related features and temporal features, respectively. Then a temporal attention mechanism is proposed to capture the dynamic correlation between the route features and temporal features. Furthermore, we employ multi-task learning to estimate the bus waiting time and the bus interval simultaneously, which highly improves the model performance. Finally, extensive experiments conducted on two large-scale real-world datasets demonstrate the effectiveness of BusWTE. In addition, BusWTE has been deployed on Baidu Map app, servicing over twenty major cities in China.

Keywords: Bus waiting time · DNN · LSTM · Attention · Multi-task

1 Introduction

With the rapid expansion of public transportation network, bus navigation has become an essential service for urban residents. As a core function, effective

M.-R. Amini et al. (Eds.): ECML PKDD 2022, LNAI 13718, pp. 554–570, 2023.
https://doi.org/10.1007/978-3-031-26422-1_34

realtime bus waiting time estimation can significantly improve user satisfaction and ultimately optimize the public transportation system [5].

Traditionally, the bus waiting time can be calculated by the estimated travel time and the collected bus realtime location. However, the realtime services with high coverage of bus routes are still limited [3], due to the cost of GPS sensor deployment and maintenance, and the dispersion of operators.

The average waiting time for passengers is considered as a measure of quality for the public transportation service [6,9]. Therefore, it is meaningful yet difficult to estimate the realtime bus waiting time for arbitrary bus stops without GPS sensors in the city. Specifically, the challenges of the above problem lie in two aspects. First, the result of waiting time estimation is affected by many complex factors, including traffic condition, spatial context and temporal dependencies. Existing headway-based methods deduce the static average waiting time as half of the departure interval, assuming that passengers arrive randomly at bus stops and passengers can be served by the earliest arriving bus [2]. However, the static estimation cannot meet the demand for realtime and highly accurate waiting time. Second, staged approaches estimate essential information (e.g., bus departure schedule) separately, which may introduce cumulative error. In practice, the bus schedule information has a great significance on waiting time estimation. However, it is very difficult to reduce the cumulative error while fully leveraging the bus schedule information.

Recent advances of location-acquisition and wireless communication technologies have resulted in massive spatial-temporal data, which provide great potentials to estimate the realtime information in metropolis [11,13,16,17]. To tackle the above challenges, in this paper, we propose BusWTE, a novel end-to-end multi-task framework to estimate bus waiting time for those bus routes without GPS sensors using a variety of urban datasets (e.g., traffic condition data, road network data and mobility data). Specifically, we firstly use a classical BiLSTM architecture to encode the sequence of bus route features and employ two fully-connected layers to embed the stop features and temporal features, respectively. Then, we propose a temporal attention mechanism to capture the dynamic correlation between the bus route features and temporal features. Finally, we employ multi-task learning to estimate the bus waiting time and the bus interval simultaneously, which obviously improves the performance.

To verify the effectiveness of the proposed framework BusWTE, we conduct extensive experiments on two large-scale real-world datasets collected from Baidu Maps. The experimental results demonstrate that BusWTE significantly outperforms the baseline approaches in terms of multiple metrics. In addition, it has already been deployed on Baidu Maps which is one of the world's largest online map services, serving over twenty major cities in China. Figure 1 shows an illustrative example of bus waiting time estimation service on Baidu Maps.

In summary, our main contributions are as follows:

- To the best of our knowledge, we present the first attempt to formally study the problem of estimating waiting time for those bus routes without GPS sensors, in a realtime fashion.

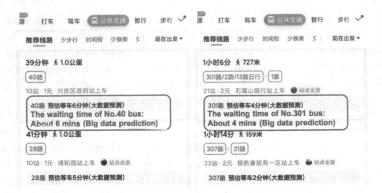

Fig. 1. The bus waiting time application of BusWTE on Baidu Maps. The figure illustrates Baidu Maps provide realtime waiting time estimation service for No. 40 and No. 301 bus without GPS information.

- We propose an end-to-end multi-task framework that learns to estimate the bus waiting time and the bus interval simultaneously, which reduces the cumulative error caused by staged estimation.
- We extract discriminative spatial-temporal related features contributing to our model. Moreover, we design a temporal attention mechanism to adaptively model the dynamic correlation between the bus route features and temporal features, therefore, leading to a high estimation accuracy.
- We conduct extensive experiments on two real-world urban-scale datasets, which demonstrate the effectiveness of BusWTE and its components and features. The successful deployment of BusWTE at Baidu Maps further shows that it is a large-scale practical solution for real-world bus waiting time estimation services.

The rest of this paper is organized as follows. In Sect. 2, we discuss the related work of the proposed approach. Section 3 presents the definitions and problem statement. We elaborate on the detailed methodologies of BusWTE in Sect. 4. Experimental results are presented in Sect. 5. Finally, we conclude this paper and suggest future work in Sect. 6.

2   Related Work

In this section, we mainly discuss the relevant work of bus waiting time estimation. In addition, we also discuss the related work of estimating the realtime information for those entities missing hardware sensors by fusing multi-source spatial-temporal data.

2.1   Bus Waiting Time Estimation

Reliable and realtime waiting time of the bus can help passengers plan their trips better, which would be an effective way to improve the service of public transportation systems. Bus waiting time estimation methods can be organized into the following two categories:

Realtime Location Based Methods: Realtime location based methods acquire the vehicle realtime location using the hardware devices like GPS and then calculate the waiting time by estimating the travel time from the realtime location to the waiting stop. The realtime location-based methods rely on the bus location information, which can be collected by GPS devices or other available sensing resources, including cell tower signals, movement statuses, audio recordings, etc. [18]. However, the realtime bus information is limited due to the expensive cost of GPS sensor deployment and maintenance.

Headway Based Methods: Headway based methods deduce the static average waiting time using the headway distributions through some assumptions, such as passengers arrive randomly at bus stops and passengers can be served by the earliest arriving bus [2]. Under the abovementioned assumptions, the average waiting time is half that of the departure interval. However, sometimes the assumption of regular service cannot be completely reliable and some methods have been proposed to address cases where some degree of irregularity is involved in bus arrivals [1,2]. The static average waiting time is not always applicable, because the punctuality and regularity of bus travel may be heavily affected by traffic and other external fluctuations, which directly impacts the waiting time [10].

It is extremely valuable but hard to estimate the realtime waiting time without directly tracking the bus in real time and timetable information, which is even considered infeasible [3]. However, compared to existing approaches, we propose an end-to-end multi-task learning framework to estimate bus realtime waiting time for those bus routes without GPS sensors.

2.2 Spatial-Temporal Data Estimation

Due to the cost or data constraints, it is a very critical issue to estimate the realtime information by spatial-temporal data without hardware sensors, such as air quality inference [17] and parking difficulty estimation [11,16].

Recently, deep learning techniques have enjoyed considerable success due to their powerful hierarchical feature learning ability in spatial-temporal data estimation [13]. U-Air [17] incorporates a neural network into the co-training framework to inference air quality for any location based on the air pollutant of some monitoring stations and a variety of urban datasets. SHARE [16] employs a semi-supervised hierarchical recurrent graph neural network to predict parking availability for the parking lots without parking sensors, based on historical data reported by a limited number of existing sensors and a variety of datasets observed in the city.

Compared with the prediction tasks of missing sensors at fixed positions, it is more complex to estimate bus realtime waiting time when GPS information is completely missing.

3 Preliminaries

We first introduce some important definitions and formally define the bus waiting time estimation problem.

Definition 1: *Bus Waiting Time.* Consider a set of bus routes $R = R_l \cup R_u = \{r_1, r_2, ..., r_L\}$, where L is the total number of bus routes, R_l and R_u denote a set of bus routes with and without position sensors, respectively. Given current time t, the route $r \in R$, the k-th stop $stop_{rk}$ of the route r, the earliest bus b arrival time $arrtime_{rk}^b$ at $stop_{rk}$ since t, the bus waiting time can be given by $arrtime_{rk}^b - t$.

Let $X_{rkt} \in \mathbb{R}^M$ and $Y_{rkt} \in \mathbb{R}$ denote observed M dimensional feature vectors and bus waiting time for the stop $stop_{rk}$ at time t, respectively.

Definition 2: *Bus Departure Interval.* Bus departure interval is the duration between the departure times of two adjacent buses of the same route. In this paper, we assume that bus departure interval is constant in each time period (e.g., an hour), but may vary in different time periods.

Let $Y_r^{val} = (y_{r1}^{val}, y_{r2}^{val}, ..., y_{rT}^{val}) \in \mathbb{R}^T$ denote the bus departure interval for bus route $r \in R$ at T time intervals in one day.

Problem: *Bus Waiting Time Estimation.* Suppose we have the feature vector set for all bus routes $X_R \subset \mathbb{R}^M$, partially bus waiting times $Y_{R_l} \subset \mathbb{R}$ and partially bus intervals $Y_{R_l}^{val} \subset \mathbb{R}^T$. We aim to estimate the bus waiting time with the given current time t, and the bus stop $stop_{rk}$ of the bus route $r \in R_u$.

4 BusWTE

As shown in Fig. 2, our framework consists of two major parts, feature extraction and waiting time estimation model. We extract discriminative features from the crowdsourcing data, mobility data and transportation network data of Baidu Maps. See Sect. 4.1 for details. The waiting time estimation model is designed as an end-to-end multi-task learning network, as detailed in Sect. 4.2.

4.1 Feature Extraction

We introduce the process of constructing and transforming feature vectors below. Table 1 lists the features we construct with a detailed description.

Bus Route Features. The bus route departure interval has a great influence on the waiting time at the bus stops. In the case of regular bus services, the average waiting time of a bus stop in a time interval is close to half of the departure interval, assuming that the traffic condition remains stable and the time for passengers to arrive at the stop is random [2]. For the route feature extraction, we pay more attention to the bus route departure interval features.

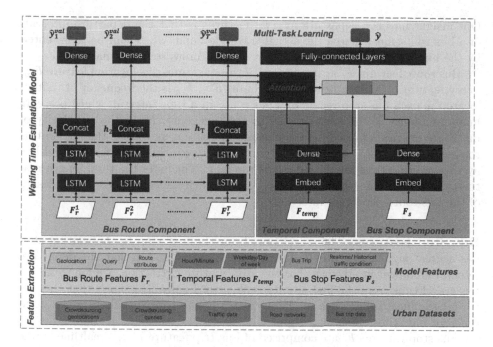

Fig. 2. The framework of BusWTE.

Table 1. The description of features.

Feature type	Feature	Description
Bus route (F_r)	Geolocation (F_{rg})	The popularity of visitors located in the region of a bus route in a time interval
	Query (F_{rq})	The popularity of a bus route search queries in a time interval
	Static attributes (F_{ra})	The length and the number of bus stops in the bus route on the road network
Bus stop (F_s)	Bus Trip (F_{strip})	The length and the number of bus stops in the bus trip from the first stop to the corresponding stop on the road network
	Realtime traffic condition (F_{srtc})	The total current traffic travel time for each road segment in the bus trip
	Historical traffic condition (F_{shtc})	The total Historical traffic travel time for each road segment in the bus trip
Temporal (F_{temp})	Minite (F_{tm})	The corresponding time period in a hour
	Hour (F_{th})	The corresponding time period in a day
	Day of week (F_{td})	The ordinal number of the day in a week
	Workday (F_{tw})	Whether the day is a workday

Our insight into the departure interval features is that the departure intervals of a bus route must match the actual travel demand, which can be represented by the human mobility data in the city, such as crowdsourcing map queries.

Bus route features F_r are comprised of three features: geolocation feature F_{rg}, query feature F_{rq} and route static attributes F_{ra}. F_{rg} is the frequency of visitors located in each bus stop region of a bus route in a time interval, which presents human mobility of the areas crossed by the bus route. F_{rq} is the popularity of bus route queries representing the demand of passengers to take the bus on this route. Figure 3(a) shows a strong correlation between the query feature and bus average waiting time for the same bus route. F_{ra} includes the total length and the total number of stops in each bus route, which are considered in the design of the bus route departure interval.

Bus Stop Features. The travel time from the first stop to the waiting stop has a great significance on the bus waiting time assuming that the departure interval is known in advance. For the stop feature extraction, we focus on the bus travel time from the first stop to each stop. Figure 3(b) shows that there is a very significant difference in the average waiting time distributions between different bus stops on the same route.

Bus stop features F_s are comprised of bus trip feature F_{strip}, realtime traffic condition feature F_{srtc} and historical traffic condition feature F_{shtc}. We use the distance and the stop number of the bus trip as bus trip feature F_{strip}. The bus travel time is highly correlated with the route that bus travels through and the bus stops for the bus trip. We use the realtime traffic travel time as F_{srtc} and the historical average traffic travel time as F_{shtc} to capture the realtime and historical pattern of traffic conditions, respectively.

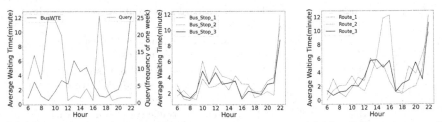

(a) The daily distributions of query feature and average waiting time for the same bus route.

(b) The average waiting time distributions of three the stops in the same route.

(c) The daily average waiting time distributions of three bus routes.

Fig. 3. The correlation between features and bus waiting time on Xiamen City.

Temporal Features. The waiting time of one bus stop could be affected by lots of temporal information. The start waiting time is one of the most important factors. Figure 3(c) shows the strong correlation between time (hour in day) and bus average waiting time. In fact, the average waiting time of the bus stop changes periodically as long as time. We exploit hour of day F_{th}, minute of hour F_{tm}, day of week F_{td} and weekday F_{tw} as the temporal features F_{temp} to estimate bus waiting time.

4.2 Waiting Time Estimation Model

Figure 2 shows the high-level overview of the proposed model, which is comprised of three major components, modeling bus route scheduling patterns, bus stop spatial-temporal information and general temporal factors, respectively.

The route features in each time interval are fed into the route component, which uses the classical BiLSTM to model the temporal dependencies among features at different time intervals. In the stop component and temporal component, the features are fed into a two-layer fully-connected neural network, respectively. Then we propose a temporal attention mechanism to capture the dynamic correlation between the latent representations of the bus route component and temporal component. The outputs of the temporal attention, stop component and temporal component, are concatenated and fed through the fully-connected layer to output the bus waiting time result. Finally, we employ a multi-task mechanism to estimate the bus intervals and the bus waiting time simultaneously, capable of leveraging the operation patterns of bus routes.

Bus Route Component. In this paper, we denote the bus route interval feature at time interval t as $F_r^t = (F_{rg}^t, F_{rq}^t, F_{ra}^t)$. We employ the Bidirectional Long-Short Term Memory (BiLSTM) architecture to encode the sequence of departure features, generating the latent vector representation for each time step feature.

The bus departure interval continuously changes over time, companing the fluctuation of temporal factors that affect it. Intuitively, the previous interval features may influence on the current departure interval, which can be effectively handled by the recurrent neural network (RNN) [12].

Therefore, we employ BiLSTM in the proposed model which can be trained using all the available input temporally-related information from two directions to improve the estimation performance.

A BiLSTM consists of a forward and backward LSTM. The forward $\overrightarrow{f}$ reads the input interval temporally-related feature sequence from F_r^1 to F_r^T and outputs a sequence of forward hidden states $(\overrightarrow{h_1}, \overrightarrow{h_2}, ..., \overrightarrow{h_T})$. The backward LSTM $\overleftarrow{f}$ reads the input feature sequence in the reverse order, i.e., from F_r^T to F_r^1, resulting in a sequence of backward hidden states $(\overleftarrow{h_1}, \overleftarrow{h_2}, ..., \overleftarrow{h_T})$.

We concatenate the forward hidden state $\overrightarrow{h_t}$ and the backward one $\overleftarrow{h_t}$, which becomes the final latent vector representation as $h_t = [\overrightarrow{h_t}; \overleftarrow{h_t}]$.

Bus Stop Component. We use a neural network model, which can effectively capture the relationship among different information, to represent bus stop features. In this paper, the bus stop features is denoted as $F_s = (F_{strip}, F_{srtc}, F_{shtc})$. F_{strip}, F_{srtc} and F_{shtc} are first fed into the embedding layer followed by an activation, respectively. Then we concatenate the output of each sub embedding layer as H_{se}, followed by fully-connected layer as:

$$H_{oslop} = ReLU\left(W_{hse}H_{se} + b_{hse}\right), \tag{1}$$

where W_{hse} and b_{hse} are the parameters to be learned.

Temporal Component. Temporal information is essential for bus waiting time estimation. We use fully-connected neural network component to represent temporal information. In this paper, the temporal features are denoted as $F_{temp} = (F_{th}, F_{tm}, F_{td}, F_{tw})$. Then F_{th}, F_{tm}, F_{td} and F_{tw} are first fed into the embedding layer which is followed by an activation, respectively. Then we concatenate the output of each sub embedding layer as H_{te}, which is followed by fully-connected layer as:

$$H_{otemp} = ReLU\left(W_{hte}H_{te} + b_{hte}\right), \tag{2}$$

where W_{hte} and b_{hte} are the parameters to be learned.

Temporal Attention Mechanism. We employ an attention mechanism to adaptively model the dynamic correlation between the bus route interval features and temporal features. We introduce a temporal attention setting to compute the attention vector for the temporal hidden representation H_{otemp}. In this setting, the temporal hidden representation H_{otemp} is taken as the query of the attention mechanism. The bus route feature hidden states $h_t (t \in [1, T])$ are taken as the *keys* and *values* of the attention mechanism. To be specific, the attention mechanism is formulated as:

$$Q = H_{otemp}, \tag{3}$$

$$K_t = h_t, \tag{4}$$

$$V_t = h_t, \tag{5}$$

$$f(Q, K_t) = \frac{Q^\top \cdot K_t}{\sqrt{d^{(H)}}}, \tag{6}$$

$$\alpha(Q, K_t) = \frac{exp(f(Q, K_t))}{\sum_{t'} exp(f(Q, K_{t'}))}, \tag{7}$$

$$Attention(Q, K, V) = \sum_{t'} \alpha(Q, K_{t'}) V_{t'}, \tag{8}$$

where the $d^{(H)}$ denotes the hidden size of the *keys* and *values*. Then, the dynamic correlation between the bus route interval features and temporal features can be encoded as $H_{oatt} = Attention(Q, K, V)$ by Eq. (8).

Multitask Learning. Intuitively, the departure interval changes over time and has a great significance on waiting time estimation. Staged approaches estimate bus departure schedule separately, which may introduce cumulative error. Therefore, we designed a multi-task structure to reduce the cumulative error while fully leveraging the bus interval information. More specifically, we estimate bus waiting time and each departure interval of a bus route using a sequence model simultaneously, which is similar to the sequence labeling task in natural language processing (NLP).

Based on the bus route component, we have latent representations of the bus route feature $h_t (t \in [1, T])$ at time interval t. h_t is fed through the fully-connected layer to output new hidden state, defined as:

$$h_{to} = ReLU \left(W_{ht} h_t + b_{ht} \right). \tag{9}$$

Then, h_o is fed through the fully-connected layer to output the bus departure interval result $\hat{y}_t^{val}$, defined as:

$$\hat{y}_t^{val} = V_{hto}^{\top} h_{to} + b_{hto}, \tag{10}$$

where the W_{ht}, b_{ht}, V_{hto} and b_{hto} are the parameters to be learned. Finally, we use a linear transformation to generate the final output result.

Training and Optimization. Based on the above components, we concatenate all the latent representation layers H_{oatt}, H_{ostop} and H_{otemp} as H_f, which is then fed into the fully-connected layer to output the bus waiting time result, defined as:

$$\hat{y} = V_{hf}^{\top} H_f + b_{hf}, \tag{11}$$

where the V_{hf} and b_{hf} are the parameters to be learned. Finally, we use a linear transformation to generate the final output result.

Our proposed model aims to minimize the mean squared error (MSE) between the ground truth bus waiting time y and the estimated bus waiting time $\hat{y}$:

$$L_1 = \|y - \hat{y}\|_2^2. \tag{12}$$

In addition, the bus interval estimation auxiliary task aims to minimize the mean squared error (MSE) between the ground truth departure interval y_t^{val} and the estimated departure interval $\hat{y}_t^{val}$, defined as:

$$L_2 = \sum_{t=1}^{T} \|y_t^{val} - \hat{y}_t^{val}\|_2^2. \tag{13}$$

By considering the MSE loss and auxiliary task loss, our model aims to jointly minimize the following objective:

$$L(\theta) = L_1 + \lambda L_2, \tag{14}$$

where θ are all learnable parameters in our model, λ is the hyper-parameter controls the importance of the auxiliary task loss.

5 Experiments

A set of experiments are employed in this section to measure the performance of BusWTE and verify the effectiveness of each component in BusWTE. All of our approaches are deployed on Baidu PaddlePaddle deep learning platform [15].

5.1 Datasets

In the evaluation, we use the following 2 real datasets in the experiments. Table 2 shows the statistical details of the datasets.

Bus Trip Data: Two datasets are used to evaluate our solutions of this problem. Both of them are acquired from Baidu maps, from December 1st 2021 to December 28th 2021.

Mobility Data: We also employ sampled geolocation data and map query data from crowdsourcing data of Baidu Maps.

Traffic Data: The realtime traffic data and historical traffic data are also from Baidu Maps.

Road Network Data: The public transportation network containing the geolocation information of bus routes and stops, is acquired from Baidu Maps.

Table 2. Detail of dataset.

Data description		Xiamen City	Nanjing City
Bus trip data	Bus trip records	4,042,772	3,919,149
Road network data	Bus routes	665	870
	bus stops	16,802	19,096
Mobility data	Crowdsourcing queries	334,241	402,118
	Crowdsourcing geolocations	19,917,326	27,915,180

The ground truth of bus waiting time, bus departure interval and bus travel time are all produced by the bus trip datasets mentioned above. We use the data from December 1st 2021 to December 21th 2021 for training, and the data from December 22th 2021 to December 28th 2021 is used for testing. We also guarantee that the bus routes of test dataset are not in the training dataset.

5.2 Experimental Settings

Evaluation Metrics. We use three metrics including root mean square error (RMSE) [7], mean absolute error (MAE) [14] and mean absolute percentage error (MAPE) [8] to evaluate all tasks (e.g., bus waiting time estimation and bus interval estimation). We use second as the unit of bus waiting time. For the above-mentioned evaluation metrics, a smaller evaluation metric value means better performance in the following experiments.

Implementation Details. The time period of bus departure interval is set to an hour, which indicates the total number T of time intervals is 24. The super parameter λ in Equation (14) is set to 0.35 in our multi-task learning model. The number of hidden states in BiLSTM layer is 64. Each of the two layers has 64 neurons in the stop component the same as the temporal component. The hidden state size of the output layer is 64 in both bus waiting time task and bus interval task. To optimize the model, we choose Adam as the optimizer and set the learning rate to 0.001. Each of the two layers has 128 neurons in the DNN model. We also employ Adam as the optimizer of the DNN model, and the learning rate is set to 0.0006. We choose ReLU as the activation function of all the hidden layers.

5.3 Baselines and Variants

Baselines. We compare our proposed BusWTE with following approaches:

Historical Average (HA): The historical average waiting time of all the bus stops, covered by bus trip datasets in a time interval in the city.
Waiting Time Based Interval (WTBI): In the case of regular bus services, the average waiting time of passengers is estimated assuming that passengers arrive randomly at bus stops and passengers can be served by the earliest arriving bus [2], and is given by: $E(W) = \frac{1}{2}H$, where H is bus departure interval.
Waiting Time Based Pipeline (WTBP): We also compared BusWTE with pipeline based method, which estimates bus waiting time based on approximating the realtime locations of buses, using the estimated bus intervals and realtime travel times.
Linear Regression (LR): Linear regression is widely used to model the relationship of multiple independent variable and single dependent variable [19].
Gradient Boosting Decision Tree (GBDT): GBDT is well-known for its outstanding performance and efficiency. The XGBoost (eXtreme Gradient Boosting) is an open source gradient boosting library which also provides an optimized distributed version [4].
Deep Neural Network (DNN): We also use a two fully-connected layers neural network with ReLU activation to estimate the bus waiting time.

Variants. To evaluate each component of our proposed model, we also compare it with different variants of BusWTE:

BusWTE-noRoute: BusWTE-noRoute removes the bus route component.
BusWTE-noStop: BusWTE-noStop removes the bus stop component.
BusWTE-noTemp: BusWTE-noTemp removes the temporal component.
BusWTE-noAttn: BusWTE-noAttn removes the attention mechanism.
BusWTE-noMul: BusWTE-noMul removes the multil-task mechanism.

5.4   Overall Performance

A set of experiments compares the performance of BusWTE and several baseline methods. Table 3 shows the experimental results. From the results, we have the following observations:

(1) From Table 3, we can see that GBDT algorithm outperforms Linear Interpolation. Both Xiamen City and Nanjing City present good performance on the MAE and MAPE. Thus our features are general and robust for different cities.
(2) BusWTE significantly outperforms other methods on the two datasets. HA is a simple baseline and works the worst. The main reasons for such improvement lie in two aspects. First, we introduce several feature components and the attention mechanism to extract more useful spatial-temporal information from the designed features. Second, we propose an end-to-end multi-task network to estimate bus waiting time and bus interval simultaneously, which is able to reduce the cumulative error compared with pipeline based methods.

Table 3. Performance of BusWTE and Baseline Methods.

Methods	Xiamen City			Nanjing City		
	MAPE	MAE (sec)	RMSE (sec)	MAPE	MAE (sec)	RMSE (sec)
HA	93.9%	359.81	450.86	98.0%	328.58	407.24
LR	70.6%	231.81	286.23	71.3%	202.45	254.08
GBDT	66.1%	227.80	280.19	70.9%	200.36	252.63
DNN	54.8%	228.10	300.36	63.3%	198.46	257.01
WTBT	72.1%	231.60	288.77	75.7%	230.46	312.72
WTBP	67.0%	232.00	325.67	72.1%	228.01	348.91
BusWTE	**52.4%**	**220.28**	**276.82**	**50.2%**	**196.47**	**252.30**

5.5   Ablation Study

In this section, we conduct ablation studies on BusWTE, including model ablation and feature ablation, to further verify the effectiveness of each component. The experiments are finished for three metrics on both Xiamen City and Nanjing City datasets. Table 4 shows the experimental results of ablation study.

Feature Ablation. To examine the performance impact of feature components, we evaluate BusWTE with complete features and its three variants: BusWTE-noRoute, BusWTE-noStop and BusWTE-noTemp.

Table 4. Performance of BusWTE and Variants.

Methods	Xiamen City			Nanjing City		
	MAPE	MAE (sec)	RMSE (sec)	MAPE	MAE (sec)	RMSE (sec)
BusWTE-noRoute	61.7%	233.34	298.12	71.2%	204.46	254.08
BusWTE-noStop	59.0%	235.43	298.62	62.2%	209.31	272.31
BusWTE-noTemp	56.1%	231.47	299.05	58.2%	198.01	260.05
BusWTE-noAttn	57.8%	226.05	293.07	55.2%	196.49	272.31
BusWTE-noMul	54.9%	228.29	300.36	63.3%	198.46	257.01
BusWTE	**52.4%**	**220.28**	**276.82**	**50.2%**	**196.47**	**252.30**

Effectiveness of the Route Component: We evaluate the relevance of the route component by removing all the route features. Table 4 shows that the MAE and MAPE of BusWTE-noRoute declines significantly compared with BusWTE. The contribution of the route component is significant. The main reason is bus route interval information has a great influence on the result of waiting time estimation. In fact, in the case of regular bus services, the average waiting time of passengers is estimated by the bus departure interval [2]. As can be seen in Table 4, the results of WTBI and WTBP are also effective, which indicates that the route interval information is always beneficial for this problem.

Effectiveness of the Stop Component: We also evaluate the relevance of the stop component by removing all the stop features. As shown in Table 4, the results of BusWTE-noStop drops significantly compared with BusWTE. The contribution of stop component is important, i.e., the MAPE of Xiamen City and Nanjing City increases 12% and 23% respectively, after removing the stop component. Intuitively, there is a significant difference in average waiting time distribution between different bus stops, which is caused by the spatial-temporal factors conditions along bus route, such as dynamic traffic conditions.

Effectiveness of the Temporal Component: We also evaluate the relevance of the stop component by removing all the temporal features. Table 4 shows that the results of BusWTE-noTemp drops obviously compared with BusWTE. The contribution of temporal component is also important, i.e., the MAE and MAPE of Xiamen City and Nanjing City increase to a certain extent, after removing the temporal component. Therefore, temporal information is critical for waiting time estimation.

Model Ablation. We evaluate the performance of BusWTE and it's two variants, which are BusWTE-noAttn and BusWTE-noMul.

Effectiveness of the Attention Mechanism: We remove the attention mechanism from BusWTE to test its contribution. As illustrated in Table 4, the results of BusWTE-noAttn falls obviously compared with BusWTE. Particularly, the MAPE of Xiamen City and Nanjing City increases 9% and 10% respectively, after removing the attention mechanism. A possible reason is that temporal attention mechanism can effectively capture the realtime bus routes departure information.

Effectiveness of the Multil-task Mechanism: To evaluate the importance of multil-task mechanism, we compare BusWTE-noMul to BusWTE. As can be seen from Table 4, when the multil-task mechanism is removed, the performance declines significantly. Especially, the MAE, MAPE and RMSE of Xiamen City and Nanjing City increase in varying degrees, after removing the multil-Task mechanism. This is because the multitask mechanism can reduce cumulative error and fully leverage the valuable information of bus route interval, which is beneficial for bus waiting time estimation.

5.6 Application and Deployment

We applied BusWTE to provide the realtime bus waiting time service in Baidu Maps, in more than twenty major cities in China. We build online service based on BRPC (https://github.com/brpc/brpc), a scalable RPC framework used throughout Baidu. We can acquire the waiting time query information such as the query route, stop and current time from Baidu map app. First, we retrieve the route related features, stop related features, and temporal features from database, which are extracted in advance. Then all above features are fused into a single feature vector for the bus stop at current time. Finally, the bus waiting time is estimated by the trained model and the online service sends the estimated travel time to Baidu map app.

Table 5 presents the online efficiency of our approach, which was tested on a 64-bit server with 8-core 2.4G CPU, 64 GB RAM and NVIDIA A100 GPU. The feature processing accounts for up to more than 90% of the total online processing time.

Table 5. Efficiency study

Procedures		Time (ms)
Feature processing (per query)	Online process	6.37
Inference (per query)	BusWTE-CPU	0.76
	BusWTE-GPU	0.24

6   Conclusion

We propose BusWTE, an end-to-end multi-task model to estimate bus waiting time for those bus routes without GPS sensors. BusWTE utilizes historical bus trip data reported by a few existing buses with GPS sensors and various datasets, such as traffic condition data, map mobility data and road network data. Then we propose a temporal attention mechanism to capture the dynamic correlation between the bus route features and temporal features. Furthermore, we employ multi-task learning to estimate the bus waiting time and the bus interval simultaneously, which reduces the cumulative error caused by staged estimation. Experimental results on two real-world datasets prove the effectiveness of BusWTE. We applied it to provide the realtime bus waiting time services on Baidu Maps, serving over 20 major cities in China. In the future, we will try to model the dynamic temporal autocorrelation inside of and between bus routes (stops) with and without GPS sensors, to improve the estimation performance.

Acknowledgment. This work was supported by National Key Research and Development Program of China (2020AAA0108800), National Natural Science Foundation of China (62137002, 61721002), Innovation Research Team of Ministry of Education (IRT_17R86), and Project of China Knowledge Centre for Engineering Science and Technology.

References

1. Amin-Naseri, M.R., Baradaran, V.: Accurate estimation of average waiting time in public transportation systems. Transp. Sci. **49**, 213–222 (2014)
2. Ansari Esfeh, M., Wirasinghe, S., Saidi, S., Kattan, L.: Waiting time and headway modelling for urban transit systems - a critical review and proposed approach. Transp. Rev. **41**(2), 141–163 (2020)
3. Barnes, R., Buthpitiya, S., Cook, J., Fabrikant, A., Tomkins, A., Xu, F.: BusTr: predicting bus travel times from real-time traffic, pp. 3243–3251 (2020)
4. Chen, T., He, T., Benesty, M., Khotilovich, V., Tang, Y.: XGBoost: extreme gradient boosting (2015)
5. Chu, K., Lam, A.Y.S., Loo, B.P.Y., Li, V.O.K.: Public transport waiting time estimation using semi-supervised graph convolutional networks. In: ITSC (2019)
6. Hsu, S.: Determinants of passenger transfer waiting time at multi-modal connecting stations. Transp. Res. Part E **46**, 404–413 (2010)
7. Hyndman, R.J., Koehler, A.B.: Another look at measures of forecast accuracy. Int. J. Forecast. **22**(4), 679–688 (2006)
8. de Myttenaere, A., Golden, B., Le Grand, B., Rossi, F.: Mean absolute percentage error for regression models. Neurocomputing **192**, 38–48 (2016)
9. Politis, I., Papaioannou, P., Basbas, S., Dimitriadis, N.: Evaluation of a bus passenger information system from the users' point of view in the city of Thessaloniki, Greece. Res. Transp. Econ. **29**, 249–255 (2010)
10. Ramli, M.A., Jayaraman, V., Chee, K., Heong, T., Khoon, G., Monterola, C.: Improved estimation of commuter waiting times using headway and commuter boarding information. Physica A **501**, 217–226 (2017)
11. Rong, Y., Xu, Z., Yan, R., Ma, X.: Du-parking: spatio-temporal big data tells you realtime parking availability. In: SIGKDD. ACM (2018)
12. Sutskever, I., Vinyals, O., Le, Q.V.: Sequence to sequence learning with neural networks. In: NeurIPS (2014)

13. Wang, S., Cao, J., Yu, P.: Deep learning for spatio-temporal data mining: a survey. IEEE Trans. Knowl. Data Eng. (2020)
14. Willmott, C.J., Matsuura, K.: Advantages of the mean absolute error (MAE) over the root mean square error (RMSE) in assessing average model performance. Climate Res. **30**(1), 79–82 (2005)
15. Ma, Y., Yu, D., Wu, T., Wang, H.: Paddlepaddle: an open-source deep learning platform from industrial practice. Front. Data Comput. **1**(1), 105–115 (2019)
16. Zhang, W., Liu, H., Liu, Y., Zhou, J., Xiong, H.: Semi-supervised hierarchical recurrent graph neural network for city-wide parking availability prediction. In: Proceedings of the AAAI Conference on Artificial Intelligence, vol. 34, pp. 1186–1193 (2020)
17. Zheng, Y., Liu, F., Hsieh, H.P.: U-air: when urban air quality inference meets big data. In: SIGKDD. ACM (2013)
18. Zhou, P., Zheng, Y.: How long to wait? Predicting bus arrival time with mobile phone based participatory sensing. TMC **13** (2012)
19. Zou, K.H., Tuncali, K., Silverman, S.G.: Correlation and simple linear regression. Radiology **227**(3), 617–628 (2003). PMID: 12773666

PathOracle: A Deep Learning Based Trip Planner for Daily Commuters

Md. Tareq Mahmood[1]([✉])(iD), Mohammed Eunus Ali[1](iD),
Muhammad Aamir Cheema[2](iD), Syed Md. Mukit Rashid[1], and Timos Sellis[3](iD)

[1] Bangladesh University of Engineering and Technology, Dhaka, Bangladesh
{tareqmahmood,eunus,mukitrashid}@cse.buet.ac.bd
[2] Monash University, Melbourne, Australia
aamir.cheema@monash.edu
[3] Archimedes/Athena RC, Marousi, Greece

Abstract. In this paper, we propose a novel data-driven approach for a
trip planner, that finds the most popular multi-modal trip using public
transport from historical trips, given a source, a destination, and user-
defined constraints such as time, minimum switches, or preferred modes
of transport. To solve the most popular trip and its variants, we propose a multi-stage deep learning architecture, PathOracle, that consists
of two major components: KSNet to generate key stops, and MPTNet
to generate popular path trips from a source to a destination passing
through the key stops. We also introduce a unique representation of stops
using Stop2Vec that considers both the neighborhood and trip popularity between stops to facilitate accurate path planning. We present an
extensive experimental study with a large real-world public transport
based commuting Myki dataset of Melbourne city, and demonstrate the
effectiveness of our proposed approaches.

Keywords: Public transport · Path recommendation · Trip planning ·
Learning popular trips

1 Introduction

Almost every modern city offers a must-have trip planner (or a journey planner) [1] for the smooth and convenient daily commuting of its dwellers. A trip
planner is a web or mobile search engine application to find an optimal means
(e.g., fastest, shortest, or cheapest) of traveling between two locations in the city
using public transport, where a single trip may use a sequence of several modes
of transport. The service has become so ubiquitous that major map services such
as Google Maps integrate such trip planners with their system. These search-
based trip planners rely on the available transport networks and the timetables
of the public transport services of a city and find one or more trip options from a
source to a destination by optimizing different criteria [2], e.g., minimum travel
time or a minimum number of switches. These existing planners have the following limitations: (i) they do not support returning the preferred trip (i.e., popular

M.-R. Amini et al. (Eds.): ECML PKDD 2022, LNAI 13718, pp. 571–586, 2023.
https://doi.org/10.1007/978-3-031-26422-1_35

one) taken by the past users, which might be of interest for many users, especially tourists; and (ii) these systems rely on the transport network and fixed timetables of the transport service and, thus, do not work when timetables are not available which is the case for a large number of developing mega cities like Dhaka, Karachi, Delhi etc. To mitigate the above problems, in this paper, we take an orthogonal and a completely new data-driven approach for a trip planner that finds the most popular trip from historical trips given a source s, a destination d, and user-defined constraints such as minimum switches or preferred modes of transport.

Popular paths between a source and a destination may vary at different times of the day (or days of the week). Moreover, for the case of daily commuting, the user may want to know the details of the popular path, if the path consists of a combination of different transport modes such as bus, train, and walk. Also, the path preferences of individuals may change, e.g., some may prefer bus over tram, others may prefer a single transport mode rather than taking a combination of bus, train, tram, etc. Answering popular paths tailored for individuals based on different contexts is a challenging research problem. In 'this paper, we propose a deep learning framework that learns from historical trips to generate popular paths between a given pair of source and destination and user preferences for a trip using public transport.

There have been few efforts to solve the popular path problems using trajectory data [6,9,12], which largely falls under route planning. A route planning problem typically deals with finding a route using a single private mode of transportation such as taxis or cars. In contrast, in our trip planner, we are interested in a path that uses one or more public transport modes to reach the destination. Chen et al. [6] find the popular route between two locations using HMM. Guo et al. [9] proposed a learning to route (L2R) approach that learns the routing behavior of trajectories in a region and transfers this learning to another region where enough user trajectories are not available for answering paths. In the most recent work, Li et al. [12] use a deep probabilistic learning based framework, called DeepST, to find the popular path from historical taxi trips.

Though the above works make important contributions for finding popular routes by learning from historical taxi trajectories, they have the following major limitations in addressing our problem of interest. (i) *Transport-Mode Oblivious:* They are oblivious to the transport mode of the route, i.e., they assume that users will use a single mode of transport in their entire path, which is not the case for most of the journeys on public transport. This limits the applicability of such systems in many cities, especially in developing cities where no journey planner is available for public transport network; also, although most of the modern cities provide a journey planner for commuting from one place to another, there are a number of ways to reach from one place to another, and there is no way for the users of these planners to know which path is generally used by most of the commuters. (ii) *Context Oblivious:* Existing works assume that popular paths will remain fixed for the entire day or may only change in peak and off-peak hours. For example, a simple additional time context in the popular path queries requires both approaches [6,9] to construct separate graphs for each time range, which is costly. We argue that the model should also learn useful contexts such as time, preferences, etc., while learning the user trajectories and also reflect this learning while answering path queries in a particular context. (iii) *Fixed Preference:* Existing works do not allow users to set their preferences while generating the path from source to destination. However, users may have some personal choices for the preferred trip, e.g., an older person may prefer a bus over a train as it is more accessible to her, or a disabled person may prefer a path with a minimum number of switches. Thus, incorporating user preferences in the popular path construction will facilitate more flexibility for the user.

The key challenges of solving the problem include how to incorporate the complex multi-modal nature of user trips and other preferences, such as minimum switches or preferred mode of transport, of the users in the learning process. A straightforward way to build such a system by adapting the methodologies of existing works (e.g., [6] or [9]) may need to build a separate model for each transport mode and every conditional constraint such as time range and then answer popular paths by combining these models. Building such a large number of models, and more importantly, combining them in answering path queries tailored for individuals is infeasible. While the existing DeepST [12] model can be adapted to provide popular paths considering multi-modal transport and different departure times (which we consider as a baseline in our experimental study), none of the existing approaches can handle user preferences such as preferred mode or a minimum number of switches.

In this paper, we propose a multi-stage neural network framework, called PathOracle, that essentially learns the travel patterns of users while commuting in a city using public transport. The key intuition of PathOracle is to learn key intermediate stops to reach from a source to a destination and use these intermediate stops to generate a mostly preferred trip from historical trips. To achieve this, we build two networks, Key Stops Net (KSNet) to generate key stops on the most probable trip for a given source to a destination and Most Probable Trip Net (MPTNet) to generate trips by progressively connecting key stops to reach from the source to the destination. One of the most important features of PathOracle is the flexibility of incorporating constraints such as time, preferred mode, or trip with the minimum number of switches during query time. PathOracle achieves this flexibility by decoupling key stop generation with the popular trip generation. In short, our contributions are as follows:

- We are the first to formulate the problem of answering the most popular path query from historical trips in the context of multi-modal public transports based city commuting, which allows users to find the popular path for a given source-destination, and preferences such as time, a preferred mode of transport, and minimum switches.
- We propose a deep learning architecture, PathOracle, that consists of two major components: KSNet to generate key stops and MPTNet to generate popular path trips from a source to a destination passing through the key stops. We also introduce a unique representation of stops using Stop2Vec that considers both the neighborhood and trip popularity between stops.

– We present an extensive experimental study with a large real-world public transport based commuting dataset of Melbourne city and test the effectiveness of our proposed approaches.

2   Definitions and Problem Statement

Stop: A stop x is a location in a map where a person can get on or get off a vehicle. A stop is represented as a tuple $x = (id, lat, lon)$, where id is the stop-id, lat is the latitude and lon is the longitude of the stop. S is the set of all stops.

Mode: A mode m represents the type of a transport mode. $\mathcal{M}$ is the set of all modes. In our case, $\mathcal{M} = \{bus, train, tram, walk\}$ as we consider city based public transport in Melbourne city.

Hop: A hop $h = (u, v, m, t)$ is represented as a tuple, where a person starts from stop $u \in S$ at time t and goes to stop $v \in S$ using a transport mode $m \in \mathcal{M}$.

Trip: A trip $T = [h_i]_{i=1}^n$ is a sequence of n hops, where $h_1.u$ is the source, $h_n.v$ is the destination and $h_i.v = h_{i+1}.u$ for $i > 0$.

Stop Sequence: The stop sequence of a trip T includes starting stops of the hops and the destination. It is represented as $x(T) = \langle h_1.u, h_2.u, \ldots, h_n.u, h_n.v \rangle$.

Mode Sequence: The mode sequence of a trip T is the sequence of types of transport modes of the trip. It is represented as $m(T) = \langle h_1.m, h_2.m, \ldots, h_n.m \rangle$.

Trip Length: The length of a trip T is defined as the length of its node sequence, which is $l(T) = |x(T)|$

Mode Coverage: Mode coverage $mc(T, m)$ of a mode m in a trip T is the fraction of the distance of T travelled by m. For simplicity, in the calculation of mode coverage, we exclude walking distances as distances travelled by walk is significantly smaller compared to the distance travelled on vehicles.

Query: A query $q = (s, d, t)$ is a tuple of source $s \in S$, destination $d \in S$ and starting time t.

Most Popular Trip (MPT): Given a list of historical trips $\mathcal{H}$ and a query $q = (s, d, t)$, the MPT query predicts the most popular trip T^* that starts from stop s at time t and ends at stop d.

Most Popular Trip with Preferred Mode (MPTPM): Given a list of historical trips $\mathcal{H}$, a query $q = (s, d, t)$, a preferred mode m and mode coverage c, the MPTPM query predicts the most popular trip T^* that starts from stop s at time t, ends at stop d and the mode coverage $mc(T, m) \geq c$.

Most Popular Trip with Minimum Switch (MPTMS): Given a list of historical trips $\mathcal{H}$ and a query $q = (s, d, t)$, the MPTMS query predicts the most popular trip T^* that starts from stop s at time t, ends at stop d and has a trip length of $l(T^*) \leq l_q$ where l_q is the minimum length of all trips $T \in \mathcal{H}$ for query q, i.e., $l_q = \text{argmin}_{T \in \mathcal{H}} l(T)$.

Note that, in our deep learning based approach we do not require to define any explicit popularity metrics; rather, our approach learns from the historical trips and returns the most likely path as the most popular path. This is also recommended as, in many cases, there may not be any direct trip from s to d in the historical trips, and the proposed algorithms learn to connect s with d using parts of other existing trips to return the preferred path. Thus, we predict the most probable trip with respect to the historical trips, and also design our evaluation metrics accordingly. Please see Sect. 4.2 for the details of the evaluation metrics and how predicted trips are compared with real observations.

3   Methodology

To answer the MPT query and its variants, we propose a multi-stage deep learning architecture, namely PathOracle. PathOracle consists of two major components: the key stop generation network (KSNet), and the popular trip generation network (MPTNet). Given a source and a destination,

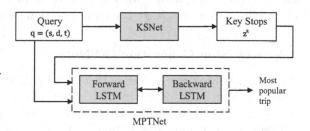

Fig. 1. The block diagram of PathOracle

and the preferred time of the trip, the KSNet generates a number of key stops through which the popular trips from the source to the destination may pass through. The key intuition of KSNet comes from the observation that most of the trips pass through key stops such as central stations or transportation hubs, and thus identifying key stops play a vital role to the popular trip generation. Based on the identified key stops, we use another deep learning network, MPTNet, that constructs the popular paths by connecting the source and the destination via the key stops.

Moreover, to generalize among stops in the same neighborhood and historical trip frequency among stops, we coin a concept called, Stop2Vec, for learning the vector representation of stops. Figure 1 shows an overview of PathOracle.

3.1   Stop Representation Using Stop2Vec

Inspired by Node2Vec [8], we propose a new representation of stops, namely Stop2Vec, which learns low-dimensional features of stops based on historical trips. Learning representations directly from trajectories may be challenging due to the data sparsity issue of rarely-visited nodes. Also, a simple application of Node2Vec will not capture underlying popularity in the historical trips. Stop2Vec addresses both of these issues. The construction of Stop2Vec works as follows. First, we build a weighted graph G from historical trips. The weight of an edge (u, v) is the frequency of hops from u to v. Then, we sample R random walks per node from G. Finally, we adopt the Skip-Gram approach of word embedding as used in Node2Vec to learn node representation $e_s(x) \in \mathbb{R}^{n_s}$ for each stop $x \in \mathcal{S}$.

3.2   Time Representation

The travel patterns of users in a city largely vary at different times of the day (peak vs. off-peak) or on different days of the weeks (e.g., weekdays vs. weekends). Also, some transports may only be available for a particular period of a day. Thus, the popular trip using multi-modal transports between two stops may change with the time of the day. Thus, to capture the impact of time in the learning of popular trips, we split a day into σ_t time windows each having an interval of $\frac{\sigma_t}{24}$ hours. We represent each of the time windows as a fixed-sized vector $e_t(t) \in \mathbb{R}^{n_t}$ of size n_t. For this, both in KSNet and MPTNet, we add embedding layers that learn the representation of time as $e_t(t)$ while training.

3.3   Key Stop Generation (KSNet)

The key intuition for KSNet is that if we can identify the key stops such as transportation hubs of a trip that comes along reaching the destination, we can predict accurate paths. Thus, KSNet finds the most probable key stops between a source and a destination for a given time. Formally, given a query $q = (s, d, t)$, KSNet estimates the probability distribution $P_z(x|q)$, which represents the probability of any stop $x \in \mathcal{S}$ being an intermediate stop of a trip from s to d at time t. To achieve this, we assign KSNet a task to predict every intermediate stop of a trip from the source, destination, and starting time of the trip. The learning objective of KSNet is to maximize the sum of log-probability of all intermediate stops of all historical trips for the respective source, destination, and starting time. This is represented by the following objective function:

$$J_\theta = \frac{1}{|\mathcal{H}|} \sum_{T \in \mathcal{H}} \left(\frac{1}{l(T) - 2} \sum_{i=2}^{l(T)-1} \log p(x_i | T.q, \theta) \right)$$

Here, $p(x_i | T.q, \theta)$ is a probability estimation of $P_z(x_i | T.q)$ based on the learnable parameter θ of KSNet. The learned probability function will produce the likelihood of a stop being an intermediate stop of a query. For KSNet, first, we generate training samples from historical trips and then use a neural network to learn the probability function.

Sample Generation. Suppose, a trip T starts at time t and has a stop sequence $\langle x_1, x_2, \ldots x_n \rangle$. Here, the source is x_1 and the destination is x_n. We generate $n - 2$ training samples from T for KSNet, where the inputs are the source, destination, and starting time, and outputs are the intermediate stops. For example, the generated samples from T will be $[(x_1, x_n, t), x_2], [(x_1, x_n, t), x_3], \ldots, [(x_1, x_n, t), x_{n-1}]$. Similarly, we generate samples for all the trips in $\mathcal{H}$.

KSNet Architecture. For a generated sample $[(s, d, t), x]$, we first obtain the embeddings of the source, destination and time. The embedding of the source and destination $(e_s(s), e_s(d))$ is obtained from the learned representation of Stop2Vec. The embedding layer e_t for time is randomly initialized and is tuned gradually while training KSNet. The core part of KSNet is a Multi-Layer Perceptron (MLP). The MLP takes the concatenation of $e_s(s), e_s(d)$, and $e_t(t)$ as input. The input is passed through hidden layers of this feed-forward network. The output layer is comprised of $|\mathcal{S}|$ neurons with LogSoftmax activation function. LogSoftmax produces the log probabilities of all stops being an intermediate stop for query q. To maximize the objective function J_θ, we use Negative Log-Likelihood Loss (NLL Loss).

Prediction. After the training phase, KSNet is able to infer the probability distribution $P_z(x|q)$ for a query q. We select a list of top K key stops (Z^q) for the trip generation task, where K is a hyperparameter.

3.4   Most Popular Trip Generation (MPTNet)

At the last step of the PathOracle, we develop a separate neural network model, MPTNet. This part of our solution is motivated by [17] that finds alternate paths. MPTNet generates the most popular trip from a source to a destination that passes through the selected key stop. MPTNet consists of two RNN units, a forward-LSTM, and a backward-LSTM, to capture the forward and backward influence, respectively, from historical trips. The output of each LSTM unit is passed through two separate MLPs to predict the stop and the mode.

To generate the most popular trip for a query $q = (s, d, t)$, we obtain the key stops from KSNet in order of their likelihood, and we use MPTNet to perform the following procedure for finding a popular trip from source to destination via the selected key stop. Let Z_i^q be a key stop. We generate two candidate trips using MPTNet for the key stop Z_i^q. First, we generate a sub-trip from Z_i^q to s using the backward-LSTM and then consider the generated sub-trip as the given past sequence to generate another sub-trip from Z_i^q to d using the forward-LSTM. Second, we generate a sub-trip from Z_i^q to d using the forward-LSTM and then treat the generated sub-trip as the future sequence (of the to be generated trip) to generate another sub-trip from Z_i^q to s using the backward-LSTM. While selecting the next stop for a sub-trip in forward-LSTM, we only consider those stops that have a hop from the current stop according to historical trips. A similar strategy is implemented for backward-LSTM too. Finally, of the two candidate trips generated above, we pick the most probable trip as the most popular trip. We use the forward LSTM to compute the probability of a trip.

3.5   Preferred Mode Constraint

PathOracle is flexible enough to incorporate the mode preference of the user. In such a case, we find the most popular trip that mostly uses the preferred mode of choice. Specifically, we allow a user to give two constraint parameters, a transport mode m and target mode coverage c. Based on this, we extend the KSNet (of Sect. 3.3) in such a way that the choice of preferred mode can influence the choice of key stops. For this, KSNet learns another probability function $P_m(x|q, m)$, which indicates the probability of x being a key stop of the popular trip from s to d at time t that mostly uses the transport mode m. The preferred mode m is passed to the MLP of KSNet through a learnable embedding layer e_m. The MLP of KSNet takes the concatenation of $(e_s(s), c_s(d), e_t(t), e_m(m))$, and gives the key stops with associated probabilities.

The sample generation for the training phase is also similar to Sect. 3.3. Suppose a trip T starts at time t, has stop sequence $\langle x_1, x_2, \ldots, x_n \rangle$ and mode sequence $\langle m_1, m_2, \ldots, m_{n-1} \rangle$. We find the mode m_p that has the most mode coverage in that trip,

$$m_p = \underset{m \in \mathcal{M}}{\text{argmax}} \ mc(T, m)$$

where $mc(T, m)$ is the coverage of m in T. Then, we generate $n - 2$ samples: $[(x_1, x_n, t, m_p), x_2], [(x_1, x_n, t, m_p), x_3], \ldots, [(x_1, x_n, t, m_p), x_{n-1}]$. From the generated samples, KSNet learns to capture the pattern of key stops depending on preferred modes.

During the trip generation phase, we obtain K key stops from KSNet. In order of their likelihood, each of the key stops is passed to MPTNet to complete the trip by connecting the source and destination to the key stop. Once we find a trip that satisfies the mode coverage constraint, we consider that trip as the most popular trip with the preferred mode.

3.6   Minimum Switch Constraint

MPTNet allows us to fix the maximum length (L) of a generated trip. Suppose, MPTNet is generating a candidate trip and it has generated the first sub-trip of length L_1 from a key stop to the source. Then, MPTNet tries to connect the key stop to the destination within a sub-trip of length $L - L_1$. Thus, MPTNet can find the most probable trip within length L. This capability facilitates MPTNet to generate trips with the minimum switch constraint. Specifically, we set L to the minimum trip length value (i.e., 2) and enforce MPTNet to generate a trip. If MPTNet fails, L is incremented gradually up to the maximum value until MPTNet generates a trip.

4   Experiments and Results

In this section, we present the experimental evaluation for our solution, PathOracle, to answer the MPT query and its variants. As there is no prior work that directly answers these problems, we compare our solution with a number of baselines that we adapted by appropriately modifying state-of-art deep learning techniques suitable for these tasks.

4.1   Experimental Setup

Dataset. We use **Myki**[1] dataset which contains real-world public transport data of Victoria, Australia. The dataset consists of *touch-on* (getting on a vehicle) and *touch-off* (getting off a vehicle) events of the first 10 weeks of 2017. The dataset has 27620 stops, 2357 routes and on average 10 million events per week. Among the 10 weeks of 2017 datasets - we consider the first 8 weeks as the training dataset, the 9th week as the validation dataset, and the 10th week as the testing dataset. Each event has the following information: *Mode, Date and time, User ID, Vehicle ID, Route ID, and Stop ID*. We extract the trips taken by various users by connecting the discrete user events. Finally, we are able to reconstruct about 18 million trips. The number of trips we use for training, validation, and testing are 14 million (first eight weeks), 2 million (9th week), and 2 million (10th week), respectively.

We define trip length as the number of stops in a trip, including source and destination. A trip length includes walking events in between changes of vehicles. For example, if a person takes a train from Clayton to Melbourne Central, then walks to a nearby tram stop and reaches the University of Melbourne using a tram, the trip length is four, whereas the number of vehicles involved is 2 (train and then tram) and the number of vehicle switches is 1 (train to tram). We exclude the trips with a trip length of more than six or a vehicle count of more than three because such trips are extremely rare in the dataset.

Baselines. As no prior works focus on finding the popular trip using multimodal public transports, we developed three baselines by adopting popular deep learning frameworks and state-of-the-art techniques.

- **LSTM:** We adapt vanilla LSTM [10] for popular trip generation using only forward influence. The output of LSTM is passed to two MLPs: one predicts the next stop, and the other predicts the next mode of transport.
- **FB-LSTM:** As a second baseline, we use both forward and backward influence with FB-LSTM (Forward-Backward LSTM) to answer our popular path queries. We separately train the two LSTM models, namely forward-LSTM for modeling forward influence and backward-LSTM for modeling backward influence. In this approach, we predict two trips from these two models and take the most probable one.
- **DeepST:** As the final baseline, we extend DeepST [12], which is the state-of-art model for finding the most probable trip for a given source, destination, traffic condition, and historical trajectories of taxi trips. We modify DeepST to predict sequences of stops and sequences of modes.

For consistency, each baseline is implemented to predict only those stops that have a hop from the current stop according to historical trips. On top of that, as there is no way to incorporate constraints during learning for the baselines, for

---

[1] https://www.ptv.vic.gov.au/tickets/myki/.

preferred mode and minimum switch constraints, we implement Beam Search for each of the baselines. We generate 20 alternate trips using Beam Search and select the most optimal one according to the constraints. We observed that these two strategies improve the performance of the baselines.

Implementation Details. In Stop2Vec, we generate $R = 80$ random walks per stop. Random walks are generated up to a length of 10. The window size of the Skip-Gram model is set to 5. For PathOracle, the sizes of stop, time, and mode embeddings are set to 256, 36, and 36, respectively. We split 24 h of a day into $\sigma_t = 4$ windows, each with a 6-hour interval. The MLP in KSNet has four layers where two hidden layers of size 128 and 32, respectively, are used. Forward and backward LSTMs of MPTNet are two single layer LSTM units with hidden size 512. The maximum allowable trip length L is set to 6 (as trips of more than six stops are extremely rare and thereby discarded from our dataset). We select top $K = 20$ key stops from KSNet. Models including baselines are implemented in PyTorch and are trained with one NVIDIA GeForce GTX 1080 GPU. Models are trained up to 30 epochs with Adam optimizer [11] and batch size 128.

4.2 Evaluation of MPT Query

In this section, we evaluate PathOracle against the baselines on the performance of generating the most popular trip for MPT queries.

Evaluation Metrics for MPT. The performance of an MPT query is evaluated based on five metrics: *stop accuracy, stop recall, mode accuracy, mode recall, and reachability*. The measurement of accuracy and recall is based on the metrics used in DeepST [12]. For a given ground-truth sequence y and a prediction sequence y^*, we can define the metrics as follows.

- *Accuracy* is the ratio of the count of correctly predicted stops/modes to the maximum length between y and y^*. Accuracy $= \frac{|y \cap y^*|}{\max(|y|,|y^*|)}$
- *Recall* is the ratio of the count of correctly predicted stops/modes from the first $|y|$ stops of y^* to the length of y. Recall is measured for both stop sequence and mode sequence. Recall $= \frac{|y \cap y^*_{1:|y|}|}{|y|}$
- *Reachability* is a boolean metric. If a predicted trip is able to reach the destination, the reachability of the trip is one. Otherwise, it is zero.

Performance Comparison. Table 1 and 2 show the performances of different approaches on predicting stop sequence and Table 3 and 4 show the performances on predicting mode sequence. Lastly, we show the performance on finding a trip to the destination. Here, we vary the trip length as 2, 3, 4, 5, and 6.

For shorter length of trips (i.e., 2–4), all models perform similarly well because it is relatively straightforward to capture short-range dependencies. As trip

Table 1. The stop sequence accuracy versus trip length

Models	Trip length				
	2	3	4	5	6
PathOracle	**0.98**	**0.97**	**0.83**	**0.80**	**0.73**
DeepST	0.97	0.96	0.82	0.76	0.63
FB-LSTM	0.96	0.94	0.75	0.69	0.51
LSTM	0.95	0.91	0.79	0.69	0.48

Table 2. The stop sequence recall versus trip length

Models	Trip length				
	2	3	4	5	6
PathOracle	**0.98**	**0.97**	**0.83**	**0.80**	**0.73**
DeepST	0.97	0.96	0.82	0.76	0.63
FB-LSTM	0.96	0.94	0.75	0.69	0.51
LSTM	0.95	0.91	0.79	0.69	0.48

Table 3. The mode sequence accuracy versus trip length

Models	Trip length				
	2	3	4	5	6
PathOracle	**0.97**	0.96	**0.90**	**0.88**	**0.84**
DeepST	0.96	0.97	0.62	0.67	0.51
FB-LSTM	0.95	0.94	0.84	0.82	0.70
LSTM	0.95	0.90	0.87	0.79	0.71

Table 4. The mode sequence recall versus trip length

Models	Trip length				
	2	3	4	5	6
PathOracle	**1.00**	**0.97**	**0.92**	**0.88**	**0.84**
DeepST	1.00	0.97	0.65	0.69	0.54
FB-LSTM	0.99	0.95	0.86	0.82	0.73
LSTM	1.00	0.91	0.91	0.81	0.75

length becomes longer (i.e. 5–6), the performances of all methods drop. This is because (i) the number of possible trips from source to destination increases rapidly with the increase of trip length, and (ii) capturing the long-range dependencies among stops in long sequences is challenging. We observe that, for lengths 5 and 6, PathOracle outperforms every other model significantly in accuracy and recall metrics. This is because PathOracle significantly reduces the number of possible trips by fixing a key stop between source and destination. The inclusion of the key stop also reduces the length of the sequence to be generated, thus, tackling the challenge of modeling long-range dependencies.

Moreover, PathOracle and FB-LSTM show significantly better reachability than others in long trips. In shorter trips, models perform similarly. However, especially for lengths 6, PathOracle and FB-LSTM are able to generate a valid trip to destination 94% times, whereas DeepST is able to generate such a trip only 83% times. Both PathOracle and FB-LSTM employ forward and backward influences together and thus have a better chance of reaching to destination compared to others, which is also evident from the results.

4.3   Evaluation of MPTPM Query

In this section, we compare the performance of models in generating the most popular trip with a preferred mode constraint. The constraint consists of a preferred mode m and a target mode coverage c.

Metric for MPTPM. The performance of a predicted trip of an MPTPM query is measured by the metric, Coverage Score. Coverage score is the ratio of the coverage of the preferred mode c_p in the predicted trip and the target coverage c. Coverage Score $= \min(1, c_p/c)$. The maximum value of a Coverage Score can be 1. Also, if the predicted trip does not reach the destination, the coverage score will be 0.

Performance Comparison. We evaluate performance for different preferred modes (bus, train, tram) with different mode coverages. Evaluating performance under this constraint is challenging because (i) there is no information about mode preferences in the dataset and (ii) a trip with random preferred transport mode and desired coverage may not be possible. So, for fair evaluation, we generate queries from the test dataset in such a way as to increase the chance of the existence of trips for those queries. The generation of queries is done in two approaches.

Firstly, we consider only the test dataset. For a transport mode m, we find the trips in the test dataset where the coverage of m is higher than other transport modes. From each of these query trips T, we query each method six times with the same source $T.s$, destination $T.d$, time $T.t$, and preferred mode m, while varying target coverage c from 0.5 to 1.0 with a 0.1 interval. We also keep track of the lengths of the trips we generated the queries from. We show the mean coverage score of MPTPM queries in Fig. 2 for different preferred modes and lengths of the query trip. As the performance of the methods largely varies for long sequence trips, we only show the results for lengths 5 and 6. Here, PathOracle consistently shows better performance than DeepST and FB-LSTM in all cases. This is because KSNet can effectively select preferred mode-specific key stops that increase the mode coverage while MPTNet generates the popular trips through them. The coverage score of each method decreases with the increase of c.

Secondly, we generate only those queries from the test dataset such that each query has a trip in the historical dataset that satisfies the constraint. Let, T is the trip in the test dataset we are currently considering and m is our preferred mode. We find the maximum coverage (c_m) of m for all trips between $T.s$ and $T.d$ at time $T.t$ in the historical dataset. If $c_m < 0.5$, we discard the trip. Otherwise, we set target coverage to c, where value of c is 0.5, 0.7 or 0.9 when c_m is within $[0.5, 0.6)$, $[0.7, 0.8)$ or $[0.9, 1.0)$, respectively. Then, we generate an MPTMP query with source $T.s$, destination $T.d$, time $T.t$, preferred mode m, and target coverage c. We keep track of the length l of the historical trip where m has the maximum coverage c_m. We generate such queries for bus, train, and tram, for length $l = 5, 6$. Figure 3 shows the mean coverage score of models for different preferred modes and coverages. We observe that the PathOracle outperforms the baselines in all cases except one. We observe a lack of pattern with the change of c. This is because in each case of preferred mode, length, and target coverage, results are coming from a particular set of queries tailored for that case.

4.4   Evaluation of MPTMS Query

In this section, we compare the capabilities of the methods in finding the most popular trip with minimum change of vehicles. In other words, we want to generate the most popular trip with a minimum trip length. Models are compared based on two experiments.

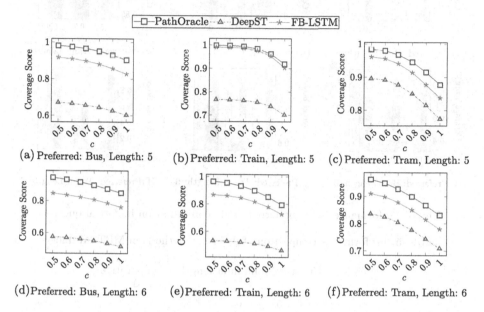

Fig. 2. Performance under preferred mode constraint on test dataset queries

In the first set of experiments, we evaluate models based on historical ground truth of minimum length. For each query $q = (s, d, t)$ in the test dataset, we find the minimum length l_m of all historical trips that start from s at t and end in d. Then each of the methods predicts its most popular minimum trip for q. Say, the length of a predicted trip is l_p. We define a metric ML Score (Minimum Length Score), that measures the ratio of l_m and l_p. ML Score $= \min(1, l_m/l_p)$. If the length of the predicted trip is less than or equal to l_m, the score is 1.

In the first four columns of Table 5, we show the mean ML scores of different methods against different l_m. For the lack of variation in the score and for space constraints, we exclude the results for shorter paths. We observe that PathOracle consistently surpasses the competing methods, especially for length 6. This is because PathOracle can effectively impose restrictions on the trip generation process by reducing L. Whereas, FB-LSTM and DeepST are producing alternate trips using Beam Search without any consideration of the constraint.

For the second set of experiments, we compare the methods in the test dataset. We define a metric, Comparative Score, which is the fraction of cases where a model generated the shortest trip compared to other methods. Comparative scores of PathOracle, DeepST and FB-LSTM in this experiment are shown in the last column of Table 5. PathOracle outperforms DeepST and FB-LSTM by a significant margin.

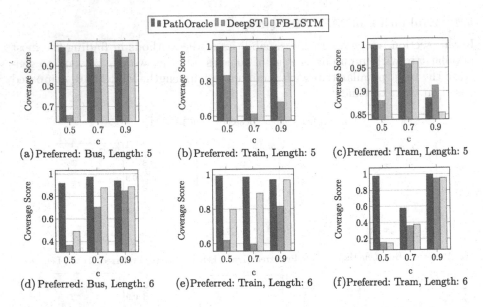

Fig. 3. Performance under preferred mode constraint on historical queries

Table 5. Performance comparison of different methods in MPTSM query

Models	Historical minimum length			Comparative score
	4	5	6	
PathOracle	**0.999**	**0.999**	**0.975**	**0.958**
DeepST	0.918	0.886	0.715	0.802
FB-LSTM	0.995	0.991	0.859	0.906

5   Related Works

Trip planners like Google maps, PTV Journey Planner [1], OpenTripPlanner [2], etc., are widely used by millions every day commuting in a city using public transport. These planners use shortest path algorithms to find the fastest (or shortest/cheapest) route on the public transport network, given the schedule of the services run on the transport network. To facilitate these planners with real-time transit data, a number of works (e.g., [3,4,20]) proposed multi-modal trip planning algorithms. All these systems and algorithms work on the provided public transport network and public transport schedules of the services to recommend a route.

Though no work exists for learning based multi-modal popular trip planning, automated route planning (that considers trips with a single vehicle, such as taxis or cars) between two locations based on historical trajectories has been studied extensively in recent years. These studies tackle a variety of route planning related tasks such as the most popular trip planning [6,12], personalized route recommendation [5,7,14], route pattern modeling [19], route cost estimation [15], travel time estimation [13,18], etc. Next, we will discuss the works on route planning and path recommendation from historical trajectories.

MPR [6] finds the most popular route between a source and a destination from historical trajectories. It works without road network data by first creating a transfer model to estimate the transfer probability of nodes. The most popular path is inferred by finding a path that maximizes the probability according to the transfer model. L2R [9] solves the problem of route planning in sparse trajectories. They learn the routing patterns between frequent regions and then transfer those patterns to regions with sparse trajectories. However, to answer time-based queries, both L2R and MPR have to create multiple models for different time ranges. MFP [16] is a search-based technique that considers the temporal context in finding the popular path. It searches the most frequent path from a source to a destination for a time frame in history. MFP processes a query by instantly building a sub-graph that captures the historical routing information for that time frame, then finds the most frequent path from the sub-graph. Being a search-based algorithm, query processing in MFP is expensive in computation and memory.

Recently, Li *et al.* [12] propose DeepST, a deep probabilistic model to learn spatial transition patterns from taxi trajectories. DeepST incorporates the impact of the past traveled route, destination, and real-time traffic condition for route generation, which shows the best performance in generating the most probable route. We have considered DeepST as one of our baselines by modifying it for the multi-modal popular path problem. To the best of our knowledge, none of the previous works can learn to generate popular multi-modal trips considering the impact of the time of the day and user preferences in a unified model.

6 Conclusion

In this paper, we have introduced the problem of answering the most popular path query by learning historical trips in the context of multi-modal public transports based city commuting. To solve this problem, we have developed a multi-stage deep learning architecture, PathOracle, that enables users to find the popular path for a given source-destination pair and the time of the travel. The PathOracle can gracefully accommodate user preferences constraints such as preferred mode of transports, and minimum number of switches in the trip. We have conducted an extensive experimental study with a large real-world public transport based commuting Myki dataset of Melbourne city. The results show that PathOracle outperforms all the baselines significantly, especially while answering longer trips involving multiple modes of public transport.

Acknowledgments. This work is done at DataLab, BUET. Muhammad Aamir Cheema is supported by ARC FT180100140.

References

1. Journey Planner - Public Transport Victoria. https://www.ptv.vic.gov.au/journey. Accessed 30 June 2022
2. Opentripplanner - Multimodal trip planning. http://opentripplanner.org/. Accessed 30 June 2022
3. Benchimol, P., Amrani, A., Khouadjia, M.: A multi-criteria multi-modal predictive trip planner: application on Paris metropolitan network. In: ISC2 (2021)
4. Borole, N., Rout, D., Goel, N., Vedagiri, P., Mathew, T.V.: Multimodal public transit trip planner with real-time transit data. Procedia-Soc. Behav. Sci. **104**, 775–784 (2013)
5. Chang, K.P., Wei, L.Y., Yeh, M.Y., Peng, W.C.: Discovering personalized routes from trajectories. In: ACM SIGSPATIAL LBSN (2011)
6. Chen, Z., Shen, H.T., Zhou, X.: Discovering popular routes from trajectories. In: ICDE (2011)
7. Dai, J., Yang, B., Guo, C., Ding, Z.: Personalized route recommendation using big trajectory data. In: ICDE (2015)
8. Grover, A., Leskovec, J.: node2vec: scalable feature learning for networks. In: ACM SIGKDD (2016)
9. Guo, C., Yang, B., Hu, J., Jensen, C.: Learning to route with sparse trajectory sets. In: ICDE (2018)
10. Hochreiter, S., Schmidhuber, J.: Long short-term memory. Neural Comput. **9**(8), 1735–1780 (1997)
11. Kingma, D.P., Ba, J.: Adam: a method for stochastic optimization. In: ICLR (2015)
12. Li, X., Cong, G., Cheng, Y.: Spatial transition learning on road networks with deep probabilistic models. In: ICDE (2020)
13. Li, X., Cong, G., Sun, A., Cheng, Y.: Learning travel time distributions with deep generative model. In: WWW (2019)
14. Liu, H., Tong, Y., Zhang, P., Lu, X., Duan, J., Xiong, H.: Hydra: a personalized and context-aware multi-modal transportation recommendation system. In: ACM SIGKDD (2019)
15. Liu, H., Jin, C., Zhou, A.: Popular route planning with travel cost estimation from trajectories. Front. Comput. Sci. **14**, 191–207 (2020)
16. Luo, W., Tan, H., Chen, L., Ni, L.M.: Finding time period-based most frequent path in big trajectory data. In: ACM SIGMOD (2013)
17. Rashid, S.M., Ali, M.E., Cheema, M.A.: DeepAltTrip: top-k alternative itineraries for trip recommendation. arXiv (2021)
18. Wang, D., Zhang, J., Cao, W., Li, J., Zheng, Y.: When will you arrive? Estimating travel time based on deep neural networks. In: AAAI (2018)
19. Wu, H., Chen, Z., Sun, W., Zheng, B., Wang, W.: Modeling trajectories with recurrent neural networks. In: IJCAI (2017)
20. Yu, L., Shao, D., Wu, H.: Next generation of journey planner in a smart city. In: ICDMW (2015)

Demo Track

Logistics, Graphs, and Transformers: Towards Improving Travel Time Estimation

Natalia Semenova[1,2(✉)], Vadim Porvatov[1,3], Vladislav Tishin[1,3], Artyom Sosedka[1,3], and Vladislav Zamkovoy[1]

[1] Sberbank, Moscow 117997, Russia
semenova.bnl@gmail.com
[2] Artificial Intelligence Research Institute, Moscow 105064, Russia
[3] National University of Science and Technology "MISIS", Moscow 119991, Russia

Abstract. The problem of travel time estimation is widely considered as the fundamental challenge of modern logistics. The complex nature of interconnections between spatial aspects of roads and temporal dynamics of ground transport still preserves an area to experiment with. However, the total volume of currently accumulated data encourages the construction of the learning models which have the perspective to significantly outperform earlier solutions. In order to address the problems of travel time estimation, we propose a new method based on transformer architecture – TransTTE.

Keywords: Graph embedding · Travel time estimation · Geospatial linked data

1 Introduction

As long as ground transport dramatically increases its quantitative presence in the cities, traffic management becomes more complex and hence less predictable for drivers. In order to handle the escalation of such a negative trend, it is important to effectively estimate the essential parameters describing traffic dynamics. One of the most important values among such quantities is the estimated time of arrival (ETA) which could be considered as the expected time expenditure for a trip between two locations. Accurate travel time estimation (TTE) is mostly challenging for cars due to the presence of the extensive limitations induced by the road network structure. These aspects of urban traffic ordinary require special spatio-temporal methods implementation to be handled. The contributions of our work are the following:

1. We proposed TransTTE model that could utilize the spatio-temporal dependencies and explored the capabilities of the transformer model application

---

Supplementary Information The online version contains supplementary material available at https://doi.org/10.1007/978-3-031-26422-1_36.

in the domain of TTE via comparison with several baselines. Computational experiments allow us to conclude that the TransTTE architecture achieves competitive performance.

2. We published a new dataset related to the city of Omsk.
3. For the needs of demonstration, we developed a web service based on the TransTTE model.

The application is available at http://transtte.online and the code could be accessed from https://github.com/Vloods/TransTTE_demo.

2   Related Work

Generally, the TTE methods could be divided into two categories related to the different approaches of ETA computing. The first one is based on the extraction of the total traveled time regarding each segment of the path [1]. Such models do not capture any global properties of the path which is explicitly reflected in their performance. The second class of methods utilizes the corresponding trip path as a whole [2]. The results achieved by these approaches defined the mainstream of current research in the domain of TTE and hence are widely established in the experiments section.

3   Framework Design

In this section, we discuss the aspects of model design and deployment as a part of a developed web service.

Task. Given an origin, destination, and departure time, our goal is to estimate the duration using the set of historical trip dataset X and the underlying road network G.

Model. The transformer architecture has recently become a prevalent approach in many domains, such as natural language processing and computer vision. Yet, it has not achieved competitive performance on popular leaderboards of graph-level prediction compared to mainstream GNN variants. Therefore, it remains a question of how transformers could perform well for graph representation learning in the TTE task.

One of the graph-oriented aspects in the Graphormer architecture [8] is a *centrality encoding* which assigns each node two real-valued embedding vectors according to its indegree and outdegree $h_i^{(0)} = x_i + z^- + z^+$, where $z^-, z^+ \in \mathbb{R}^d$ are learnable embedding vectors specified by the indegree $\deg^-(v_i)$ and outdegree $\deg^+(v_i)$ respectively. Along with centrality encoding, *spatial encoding* is used to capture the structural relation via function $\phi(v_i, v_j) : V \times V \to \mathbb{R}$ which measures the spatial relation between nodes v_i and v_j of road network G. Original choice of such function $\phi(v_i, v_j)$ is the shortest distance between v_i and v_j which further serves as a bias term in the self-attention module $A_{ij} = \frac{(h_i W_Q)(h_j W_K)^T}{\sqrt{d}} + b_{\phi(v_i, v_j)}$,

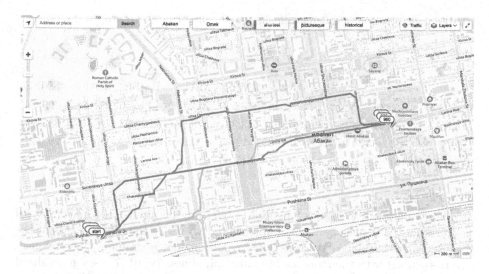

Fig. 1. Application interface.

where $b_{\phi(v_i, v_j)}$ is a learnable scalar indexed by $\phi(v_i, v_j)$ which is shared across all layers.

Data. In this paper, we use the dataset related to the road networks of Abakan and Omsk[1] which have different scales and road topology [6]. The datasets are collected in a monthly period starting from December 1, 2020. The datasets consist of a road network with corresponding to its segments features and trip part. The presence of the noisy data among the trip part of the datasets encourages us to apply filtering regarding the rebuild count feature, maximum/minimum length, and the total time of the trips.

Web Application. For the needs of model demonstration, we deployed our TTE service in the platform of the Yandex Maps project, Fig. 1. The interface allows choosing between two cities and three types of routes regarding demands of a user.

4   Results

In addition to the computing TTE for the shortest route, the framework also evaluates the routes based on the metrics of picturesqueness and historicity. Using the OpenStreetMap API, we managed to parse information about the location of historical, cultural and natural objects. The number of certain objects is used as the road segments weights for Dijkstra's algorithm $W_i = \frac{1}{1+C_r}$, where W_i is the weight for the i'th segment of the road, C_r is the number of objects within a radius r of a road segment.

We reimplemented Graphormer architecture to accelerate the training process and consider the peculiar properties of road trips. Due to caching spatial

---

[1] The full data could be requested from semenova.bnl@gmail.com.

Table 1. Evaluation of different pipelines and comparison with proposed method

Dataset	Omsk				Abakan			
Split	Train		Test		Train		Test	
	MAE	RMSE	MAE	RMSE	MAE	RMSE	MAE	RMSE
GBDT	403.921	582.011	408.644	573.559	244.119	449.250	248.862	399.534
MURAT	279.616	438.228	286.491	443.397	179.037	285.003	185.153	286.934
WDR	311.581	440.511	336.756	487.876	173.684	285.132	182.296	293.551
TransTTE	101.381	387.241	105.464	261.103	81.048	285.032	83.616	168.421

encoding values, we were able to speed up training by almost 10 times. Several baselines for TTE task were also implemented to verify the effectiveness of the proposed model, Table 1. We considered results made by gradient boosted decision trees along with the more sophisticated pipelines. WDR [7] uses generalized linear model and LSTM together to compute travel time. MURAT [3], in its turn, produces unsupervised representations due to DeepWalk [5] and applies residual feedforward blocks to predict travel time and distance.

The best result was achieved on Graphormer$_{\text{SLIM}}$ ($L = 12, d = 80$) version with reduced size of dimension. As the optimizer we used AdamW [4]. Experiments were done with 5 Tesla V100 GPUs and 460 Gb of RAM. The training time of the different configurations of TransTTE lies in the interval from 2.5 h up to 5 h which is smaller than in case of WDR (7 h) and MURAT (5.5 h).

5   Conclusion and Outlook

In this paper, we proposed the new transformer-based approach to the computing of ETA and explored its performance. The experiments revealed the perspective of graph transformer utilization in the travel time estimation. In the upcoming studies, we want to extend the current transformer architecture by virtue of extra road network features and more precise work with the temporal aspect of road trips. Future research should be devoted to the development of a joint TransTEE model which could compute travel time for rides on different city networks indeed.

References

1. Asghari, M., Emrich, T., Demiryurek, U., Shahabi, C.: Probabilistic estimation of link travel times in dynamic road networks, pp. 1–10 (2015)
2. Jin, G., Wang, M., Zhang, J., Sha, H., Huang, J.: STGNN-TTE: travel time estimation via spatial-temporal graph neural network. Future Gener. Comput. Syst. **126**, 70–81 (2022). https://www.sciencedirect.com/science/article/pii/S0167739X21002740

3. Li, Y., Fu, K., Wang, Z., Shahabi, C., Ye, J., Liu, Y.: Multi-task representation learning for travel time estimation. In: International Conference on Knowledge Discovery and Data Mining (KDD 2018) (2018)
4. Loshchilov, I., Hutter, F.: Decoupled weight decay regularization (2019)
5. Perozzi, B., Al-Rfou, R., Skiena, S.: Deepwalk: online learning of social representations. In: Proceedings of the 20th ACM SIGKDD International Conference on Knowledge Discovery and Data Mining, pp. 701–710 (2014)
6. Porvatov, V., Semenova, N., Chertok, A.: Hybrid graph embedding techniques in estimated time of arrival task. In: Benito, R.M., Cherifi, C., Cherifi, H., Moro, E., Rocha, L.M., Sales-Pardo, M. (eds.) Complex Networks & Their Applications X. SCI, vol. 1016, pp. 575–586. Springer, Cham (2022). https://doi.org/10.1007/978-3-030-93413-2_48
7. Wang, Z., Fu, K., Ye, J.: Learning to estimate the travel time. In: Proceedings of the 24th ACM SIGKDD International Conference on Knowledge Discovery and Data Mining, pp. 858–866. KDD 2018, Association for Computing Machinery, New York, NY, USA (2018). https://doi.org/10.1145/3219819.3219900
8. Ying, C., et al.: Do transformers really perform bad for graph representation? arXiv preprint arXiv:2106.05234 (2021)

Explainable Anomaly Detection System for Categorical Sensor Data in Internet of Things

Peng Yuan[1], Lu-An Tang[1], Haifeng Chen[1(✉)], Moto Sato[1], and Kevin Woodward[2]

[1] NEC Labs America, Princeton, NJ, USA
{pyuan,ltang,Haifeng,moto}@nec-labs.com
[2] Lockheed Martin Space, Denver, CO, USA
kevin.woodward@lmco.com

Abstract. Internet of things (IoT) applications deploy massive number of sensors to monitor the system and environment. Anomaly detection on streaming sensor data is an important task for IoT maintenance and operation. However, there are two major challenges for anomaly detection in real IoT applications: (1) many sensors report categorical values rather than numerical readings; (2) the end users may not understand the detection results, they require additional knowledge and explanations to make decision and take action. Unfortunately, most existing solutions cannot satisfy such requirements. To bridge the gap, we design and develop an eXplainable Anomaly Detection System (XADS) for categorical sensor data. XADS trains models from historical normal data and conducts online monitoring. XADS detects the anomalies in an explainable way: the system not only reports anomalies' time periods, types, and detailed information, but also provides explanations on why they are abnormal, and what the normal data look like. Such information significantly helps the decision making for users. Moreover, XADS requires limited parameter setting in advance, yields high accuracy on detection results and comes with a user-friendly interface, making it an efficient and effective tool to monitor a wide variety of IoT applications.

Keywords: Explainable AI · Internet of things · Sensor data · Anomaly detection

1 Introduction

Internet of things (IoT) integrates sensor devices with informational components to form a context sensitive system that responds intelligently to dynamic changes in real-world environments [9]. With rapid developments in recent years, IoT devices are widely used in different fields such as satellite, healthcare, transportation, and environment monitoring. A typical IoT application usually contains thousands of sensors to monitor its components and surrounding environment. Evaluating the streaming sensor data in real-time and detecting abnormal symptoms are critical for IoT maintenance and operation tasks.

In real applications, IoT sensors contain not only numerical readings but also categorical data representing the working status or operational mode. Unfortunately, most

© The Author(s), under exclusive license to Springer Nature Switzerland AG 2023
M.-R. Amini et al. (Eds.): ECML PKDD 2022, LNAI 13718, pp. 594–598, 2023.
https://doi.org/10.1007/978-3-031-26422-1_37

existing methods on anomaly detection are proposed to detect outliers and anomalies of numerical data [1–8]. They cannot be used on categorical data. In addition, many methods only provide a timestamp of the detected anomaly. Without enough context information, the users cannot understand such detection results. To bridge the gap, we design and develop an eXplainable Anomaly Detection System (XADS) to monitor the sensor data of IoT devices. The solution constructs a three dimensional histogram model of category, event duration, and frequency. XADS profiles the normal states by learning from historical data, and automatically determines the anomaly thresholds despite of noisy data. After training models from historical data, XADS monitors newly arrived data and detects the anomalies in real time. Once an anomaly is detected, XADS searches in the normal profiles and generates detailed reasons to explain the result. It also provides expected values as a normal baseline for comparison. With such detailed explanations, the users can understand the detected anomalies and take out correct actions.

Another major advantage of XADS is on the applicability and feasibility. The solution only requires limited parameter setting in advance and can be applied to a wide variety of IoT devices. In many real applications, it is difficult to obtain the abnormal or fault events as training data. XADS does not need such abnormal data for training. It trains the model only with normal data, which are much easier to collect. XADS can detect both seen and unseen anomalies (i.e., the types of anomalies that has not appear before) with high accuracy. The solution has been tested and applied in multiple real IoT applications including satellite and spacecraft [10, 11]. A demo of XADS can be accessed from the project page at: https://github.com/pengyuan0106/eXplainable-Anomaly-Detection-System.

2 System Description

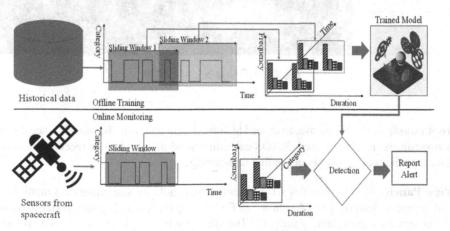

Fig. 1. System framework of XADS

As shown in Fig. 1, the overall structure of XADS is consisted of two modules: (1) offline training from historical data and (2) online monitoring for streaming data.

In offline training module, XADS segments categorical sensor data into event sequences through sliding windows of adaptive length. The window length is learned from the distribution of events. After window separation, XADS learns the features of all historical segments and generates a 3D histogram model to profile the normal data from the dimensions of category, event duration, and frequency. At last, XADS computes the anomaly threshold by running trained model on historical data.

In online monitoring module, XADS first converts streaming data into a new sliding window and transforms the window into a histogram. The new histogram is then matched with trained model to calculate an anomaly score. The system raises an alert if the score is higher than anomaly threshold.

Figure 2 shows a snapshot of using XADS to monitor the telemetry sensor data from a soil moisture active passive satellite [3]. The dashboard of XADS includes two parts: a tool panel (left) and a set of view panels (right).

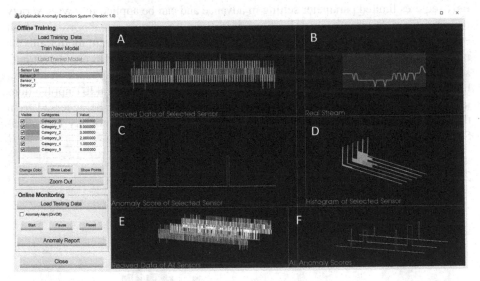

Fig. 2. Main interface of XADS

Tool Panel: It allows the user to upload historical data and train the model. Once the 3D histogram models are trained, XADS can either load testing data or receive streaming data from network and conduct online monitoring.

View Panels: XADS provides six different view panels for streaming data monitoring and anomaly detection. (1) As shown in Fig. 2 (A), the streaming data panel plots the so-far arrived sensor data by time; (2) The sliding window panel (Fig. 2 (B)) provides a zoom-in view of the current data; (3) The anomaly score panel (Fig. 2 (C)) plots the computed anomaly scores in real time. It is aligned with the streaming data panel. The period labeled by orange color are with abnormal events. (4) The 3D histogram panel (Fig. 2 (D)) shows the constructed histogram from streaming data in the new window;

(5&6) To provide a global view to the users, XADS shows all the received data in Fig. 2 (E) and anomaly scores of multiple sensors in Fig. 2 (F).

Once an anomaly is detected, the users can check more details in anomaly report panel. XADS lists out the abnormal values and context information in an anomaly explanation panel, as shown in Fig. 3 (B). Figure 3 (C) shows the histogram of abnormal data. The blue lines indicate the normal range of frequency in trained model. The orange rectangle represents the abnormal frequency of current window. Figure 3 (D) has two plots: the left one is a zoom in view of the observed anomaly, the orange color denotes the abnormal event. The right plot is a normal baseline, where the blue color denotes expected normal values during the abnormal period. In this way, XADS provides an explicit comparison to illustrate detected anomalies.

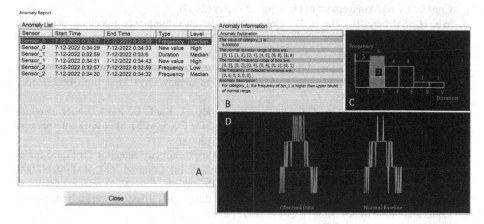

Fig. 3. Anomaly report panel of XADS

3 Conclusion and Future Work

In this paper, we present a novel eXplainable Anomaly Detection System (XADS) to monitor categorical sensors in IoT applications. XADS generates a histogram model on the dimensions of category, event duration, and frequency. It automatically determines the value's normal ranges and anomaly thresholds. The detected anomalies are reported in GUI interfaces with detailed explanations, as well as a normal baseline to help the user's understanding and decision making.

In the near future, we plan to extend XADS to complex IoT monitoring with both categorical and numerical sensors, and to test XADS on more applications such as weather forecasting and financial analysis.

Acknowledgements. The authors would like to thank Matthew Horak, Giovanni A Tobar, Sowmya S Chandrasekaran, and Sadananda Narayanappa from Lockheed Martin Space for the constructive comments and suggestions.

References

1. Li, X., Han, J.: Mining approximate top-k subspace anomalies in multi-dimensional time-series data. In: 33rd International Conference on Very Large Data Bases, pp. 447–458 (2007)
2. Gao, Y., Yang, T., Xu, M., Xing, N.: An unsupervised anomaly detection approach for spacecraft based on normal behavior clustering. In: 2012 Fifth International Conference on Intelligent Computation Technology and Automation, pp. 478–481 (2012)
3. Hundman, K., Constantinou, V., Laporte, C., Colwell, I., Soderstrom, T.: Detecting spacecraft anomalies using LSTMs and nonparametric dynamic thresholding. In: Proceedings of the 24th ACM SIGKDD International Conference on Knowledge Discovery & Data Mining, pp. 387–395 (2018)
4. Tang, L.A., Cui, B., Li, H., Miao, G., Yang, D., Zhou, X.: Effective variation management for pseudo periodical streams. In: Proceedings of the 2007 ACM SIGMOD International Conference on Management of Data, pp. 257–268 (2007)
5. Wu, H., Salzberg, B., Zhang, D.: Online event-driven subsequence matching over financial data streams. In: Proceedings of the 2004 ACM SIGMOD International Conference on Management of Data, pp. 23–34 (2004)
6. Wu, H., Sharp, G.C., Salzberg, B., Kaeli, D., Shirato, H., Jiang, S.B.: A finite state model for respiratory motion analysis in image guided radiation therapy. Phys. Med. Biol. **49**(23), 5357 (2004)
7. Wu, H., Salzberg, B., Sharp, G.C., Jiang, S.B., Shirato, H., Kaeli, D.: Subsequence matching on structured time series data. In: Proceedings of the 2005 ACM SIGMOD International Conference on Management of Data, pp. 682–693 (2005)
8. Schwabacher, M., Oza, N., Matthews, B.: Unsupervised anomaly detection for liquid-fueled rocket propulsion health monitoring. J. Aerosp. Comput. Inf. Commun. **6**(7), 464–482 (2009)
9. Tang, S., Shelden, D.R., Eastman, C.M., Pishdad-Bozorgi, P., Gao, X.: A review of building information modeling (BIM) and the internet of things (IoT) devices integration: present status and future trends. Autom. Constr. **101**, 127–139 (2019)
10. Chen, H., Horak, M., Narayanappa, S., Woodward, K.: Integrating AI into planning, diagnostic, and prescription systems for human & robotic deep space exploration missions. In: AAAI 2018 Fall Symposium Series (2018)
11. Yuan, P., Tang, L.A., Chen, H., Sato, M., Woodward, K.: 3D histogram based anomaly detection for categorical sensor data in Internet of Things. Submitted to VLDB Workshop on Very Large Internet of Things (VLIoT 2022)
12. Hodge, V., Austin, J.: A survey of outlier detection methodologies. Artif. Intell. Rev. **22**(2), 85–126 (2004)
13. Tamboli, J., Shukla, M.: A survey of outlier detection algorithms for data streams. In: 2016 3rd International Conference on Computing for Sustainable Global Development (INDIACom), pp. 3535–3540 (2006)
14. Panjei, E., Gruenwald, L., Leal, E., Nguyen, C., Silvia, S.: A survey on outlier explanations. VLDB J., 1–32 (2021). https://doi.org/10.1007/s00778-021-00721-1

AGG: An Automated Genogram Generator by Discovering Information in Clinical Texts

Nuria García-Santa[(✉)] and Kendrick Cetina

Fujitsu Research of Europe (FRE), Camino Cerro de los Gamos 1, 28224 Pozuelo de Alarcón (Madrid), Spain
{nuria.garcia.uk,kendrick.cetina}@fujitsu.com

Abstract. In Deep Learning, the use of pre-trained language models such as BERT has exploded within NLP for model fine-tuning due to the top performance results. We showcase AGG, an Automated Genogram Generator, capable of extracting relevant family data in clinical texts to generate genograms, which are hierarchical relationship diagrams of a family with special emphasis in the family health. The contributions are: (i) automated real-time genograms generation by family history data discovery in texts through language models fine-tuning; (ii) real-time customization of the visual representation of the genograms; and (iii) web service with user-friendly interactive UI. AGG allows the easy genogram creation to users without expertise and saves time in physicians work.

Keywords: NLP · Deep Learning · Family history extraction · Genogram

1 Introduction

Genograms[1] are visual family relationship representations that use the known genealogy tree structure and focus in describing family health. This is relevant for diagnosing patterns of inheritance conditions. Healthcare professionals analyze genograms to identify health risks that can be transmitted through family, supporting the anticipation and prevention of future conditions.

There are several commercial products available in the market for the creation of genograms, such as GenoPro[2], Genogram Analytics[3], or iGenogram for iPad[4]. However, current tools only provide creation of genograms manually from scratch. Therefore, users need previous healthcare knowledge, require long time for building the genogram (30mins of average), and, there is one unique way of visual representation of the genogram.

In this paper we present AGG, a novel Automated Genogram Generator tool that creates genograms in real-time by discovering relevant information in the

---

[1] https://www.sciencedirect.com/topics/medicine-and-dentistry/genogram.
[2] https://genopro.com/genogram/.
[3] http://www.genogramanalytics.com.
[4] http://www.ilogotec.com/igenogram-1-8/.

© The Author(s), under exclusive license to Springer Nature Switzerland AG 2023
M.-R. Amini et al. (Eds.): ECML PKDD 2022, LNAI 13718, pp. 599–602, 2023.
https://doi.org/10.1007/978-3-031-26422-1_38

Family Medical History of the patient from unstructured clinical documents (see demo: https://youtu.be/JNtNtwsLvbI). For the Family Medical History extraction, we use Natural Language Processing (NLP) and semi-supervised machine learning. Previous research challenges in 2018 BioCreative/OHNLP [4] and 2019 n2c2 [5] studied widely the family history extraction in clinical texts with approaches from rule-based to machine learning techniques. For the genogram generation, we use the open source software of *Graphviz*[5] to transform the family data and relationships extracted to the graph diagram visualization.

The main contribution of AGG is the exploitation of family history extraction from clinical texts through machine learning approaches to generate automatically in seconds a genogram of the patient, saving crucial time to healthcare professionals. In addition, we provide functionality for customization of the visual representation of the genograms by processing template configurations.

2   AGG Tool: System Overview

We provide a system overview of AGG, describing the features and the behind technology. AGG tool consists of three major components: (1) a family medical history discovery module; (2) a genogram manager module; and (3) an interactive UI. The first two components run on back-end services that handle the core computation. On top of such services are deployed HTTP REST APIs to communicate with the UI. Below, we provide further details of AGG components.

2.1   Family Medical History Discovery

This module receives a patient's clinical text and retrieves the family history information included. The data extracted is a list of family members; for each one we obtain the family role (mother, father, etc.) and the entities related, i.e. family side (maternal, paternal), status (healthy, deceased, etc.) and observations (any kind of condition suffered by the family member). Also, the module recognizes modalities for status and observations; positive for occurrence (e.g. *...is diabetic...*), negative in case of absence (e.g. *...is not diabetic...*).

We fine-tuned the state-of-the-art BioBERT [3] pre-trained language model to train Named Entity Recognition (NER) and Relation Extraction for the family history discovery task. We used BioBERT because is a BERT-based [1] language model with top performance results in the biomedical domain. For the dataset, we collected anonymous family history text fragments from MIMIC-III [2] clinical notes (in English language) related to section of family antecedents history. Such text fragments were not annotated. Therefore, we followed a distant supervision approach by rule-based methods for the dataset annotation of 6817 samples. In the rule-based methodology we exploited several NLP techniques such as POS tagging, dependency parser, negation detection and dictionary matching. For preliminary evaluation, we used a test set of 100 samples and we obtained,

---

[5] https://graphviz.org/.

for joint NER and Relation Extraction, an F-score of 91.2% in the BioBERT fine-tuned in contrast to 81.3% achieved in the baseline rule-based approach.

2.2 Genogram Manager

The Genogram Manager is in charge of building automatically the genograms from patients' family history information extracted. We use Graphviz Python library in back-end services to create the graph diagram visualizations. Besides the automated genogram generation, this component is provided with the following functionalities:

- **Detection of inner-relations:** Processing of family history data to detect and include the implicit family members inner relations (e.g. patient's paternal grandmother is transformed to mother of patient's father). The interpretation of this information is relevant to build an appropriate hierarchical genogram. We used a rule-based approach over known family member relations.
- **Customization of genogram visualizations:** Definition of JSON template files to configure the shapes of nodes and edges of the genograms. This includes options of customization for nodes (e.g. depending on family member gender, or, family member status to differentiate deceased people), and, for edges (e.g. line shapes in sibling relation, parent relation, etc.). Therefore, the same genogram could be visualized in different ways in real-time depending on the template file created/selected.

2.3 Interactive User Interface

The AGG user interface scenario is illustrated in Fig. 1. This UI includes a panel of synthetic text samples to be selected and show the family data extracted and the generated genograms associated to such texts. In addition, users can write new texts on-the-fly to be analysed and select different customization templates to change the visual representation of the genograms. Figure 1 shows (a) User selects the note sample *'Cancer pattern in family history'* in correspondent panel; (b) The panel TEXT outputs the family note, marking with colours the family data extracted where entities of the same colour reference relationship; (c) User selects the first template sample and panel TEMPLATE FEATURES exposes the configuration chosen; (d) Lastly, there is a panel to visualize the automated genogram generated following the representation expressed in the template attributes. Currently, AGG tool supports English and Japanese language. MIMIC-III dataset was translated to ensure a Japanese-native solution since the beginning, with adaptation of rule-based methods and fine-tuning of Multilingual BERT[6] to cover this new language.

---

[6] https://github.com/google-research/bert/blob/master/multilingual.md.

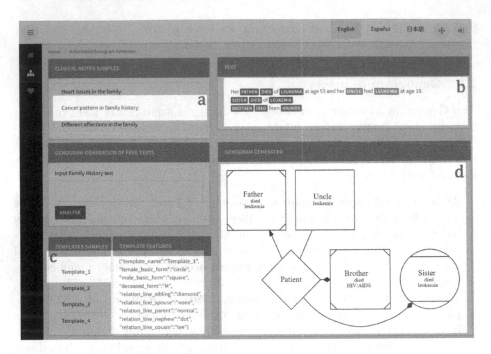

Fig. 1. UI usage scenario

3   Conclusions and Future Work

We presented AGG, an innovative framework for the real-time generation of genograms by discovering family history information in clinical texts. The intuitive UI allows easy interaction for any user and the automatisation enables to save crucial time to healthcare professionals. In the future we plan to extend the tool to other languages and incorporate more editable features for making modifications to the initial generated genogram.

References

1. Devlin, J., Chang, M.W., Lee, K., Toutanova, K.: BERT: pre-training of deep bidirectional transformers for language understanding. In: NAACL-HLT (1) (2019)
2. Johnson, A.E., et al.: MIMIC-III, a freely accessible critical care database. Sci. Data **3**, 160035 (2016). https://doi.org/10.13026/C2XW26
3. Lee, J., et al.: BioBERT: a pre-trained biomedical language representation model for biomedical text mining. Bioinformatics **36**(4), 1234–1240 (2020)
4. Liu, S., et al.: Overview of the BioCreative/OHNLP 2018 family history extraction task. In: Proceedings of the BioCreative 2018 Workshop, p. 2018 (2018)
5. Shen, F., et al.: Family history extraction from synthetic clinical narratives using natural language processing: overview and evaluation of a challenge data set and solutions for the 2019 National NLP Clinical Challenges (n2c2)/Open Health Natural Language Processing (OHNLP) competition. JMIR Med. Inform. **9**(1), e24008 (2021). https://doi.org/10.2196/24008

TAMOR: Tier-Aware Multi-objective Recommendation for Ant Fortune Financial Marketing

Xu Min, Xiaolu Zhang, Jun Zhou[✉], Changxun Fan, and Junlin Yu

Ant Group, Beijing, China
{minxu.mx,yueyin.zxl,jun.zhoujun,changxun.fcx,julian.yjl}@antgroup.com

Abstract. Online marketing recommendation is crucially important for user growth of mobile applications. However, there are currently three common challenges in designing such an efficient recommendation system. First, on the user side, users can be stratified into different layers which have distinctive user characteristics and marketing objectives. Second, on the item side, items from heterogeneous business scenarios need to be mixed together for ranking. Third, there are often multiple marketing objectives, which are even internally related to each other. In this paper, we address the above challenges by proposing a joint training system Tier-Aware Multi-Objective Recommendation (**TAMOR**). The TAMOR system leverages all tiers of data to train a unified model, while the representation learned by the model for users and items are aware of data tiers. Besides, in order to better deal with the multi-objective prediction problem, the user bias learning is designed to learn user preferences, which are then used to assist learning for user-specific tasks. TAMOR has been deployed for financial marketing of Ant Fortune, which brings a 10.67% boost for the number of daily new high-holding users.

Keywords: Tier-aware · Multi-objective · User bias learning

1 Introduction

In online marketing of mobile applications, the recommendation system plays an important role in the accurate distribution of traffic. Ant Fortune is a wealth management platform under Ant Group, where various kinds of mission cards are pushed to specific users to stimulate their investment behaviors within the app. For example, a typical sequential pattern of user actions is: impression $\rightarrow$ click $\rightarrow$ conversion $\rightarrow$ investment $\rightarrow$ large investment (single transaction > 100 yuan). The core goal of the recommendation system in financial marketing is to increase the number of users with positions over 100 yuan. Different from traditional recommendation in e-commerce like Taobao, we are confronted with the following three major challenges. (1) **Stratified Users:** Different users have different user characteristics and marketing goals. (2) **Heterogeneous Scenarios:** The items belonging to heterogeneous scenarios should be mixed together for ranking. (3) **Multiple Objectives:** There are multiple objectives to predict, which are usually related to each other.

M.-R. Amini et al. (Eds.): ECML PKDD 2022, LNAI 13718, pp. 603–606, 2023.
https://doi.org/10.1007/978-3-031-26422-1_39

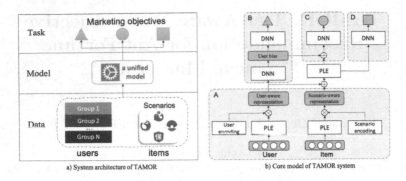

Fig. 1. System overview of TAMOR

Conventional practice in the industry is to build models individually for a certain combination of user group and business scenario. Formally, a model can hence be defined by a triple of *<user group, item scenario, objectives>*. Since it is a multi-task learning problem, we usually choose Multi-gate Mixture-of-Experts (MMoE) [1] as backbone model, which is the state-of-the-art method in multi-task recommendation. However, the amount of data in separate data tiers is relatively small and can hardly support the training of large-scale recommendation models. Besides, independent modeling blocks the information sharing between different data tiers, thus limiting the model performance.

With the above consideration, we propose a novel recommendation system TAMOR[1], namely tier-aware multi-objective recommendation, especially for cases when there are stratified users and heterogeneous scenarios, as shown in Fig. 1. TAMOR trains one model on the union dataset of all user groups and item scenarios, so that it can exploit all available data. TAMOR is able to perceive data tiers through tier-aware representation learning module. Besides, TAMOR inherits the ability of multi-task learning from MMoE, with an extra user bias learning module to facilitate the training of user-specific tasks. In a real industrial dataset of Ant Fortune, our TAMOR system achieves higher area under the ROC curve (AUC) than MMoE in all tasks on three user groups, with significant improvement ranging from 1.3% to 4.1%. Furthermore, TAMOR has been successfully applied in the financial marketing of Ant Fortune, and achieved 10.67% boost for the number of daily new high-holding users.

2   System Overview

We now present an overview of the TAMOR system for Ant Fortune financial marketing, which can be split into three levels, as is demonstrated in Fig. 1(a). (1) **Data Level.** In the bottom level of TAMOR system, we collected Ant Fortune marketing dataset. Based on business settings, we stratified users into three layers according to the amount of positions held, and clustered the items into

---

[1] An introductory video is available at https://www.bilibili.com/video/BV1CR4y1 P7qv.

six groups according to the business scenarios they belong to. (2) **Model Level.** We use one unified model as the core recommendation engine of the TAMOR system. (3) **Task Level.** We define five tasks including: 1) click, 2) conversion, 3) investment, 4) a single large investment with over 100 yuan, and 5) user total investment with over 100 yuan in recent period of time.

As is illustrated in Fig. 2, we have a special page in the APP to recommend financial mission cards to users. Users of different layers have different recommendation results. For new users, the main goal is to simply increase their daily activity, such as click, conversion and investment. Meanwhile, for existing users with low positions, the key goal is to achieve large investment to bring more high-holding users. The items exposed to users may be associated with multiple lines of business, including Huabei, Jiebei, Yuebao. These business scenarios are distinct from each other and have different business purposes. Meanwhile, together they form the product matrix of Ant Fortune, and share a common marketing purpose of user growth.

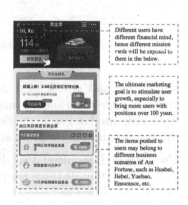

Fig. 2. An illustration of financial marketing in Ant Fortune

The core model contains three major parts as demonstrated in Fig. 1(b), including 1) A: **tier-aware representation learning** for both user side and item side, 2) B: **user bias learning**, and 3) C&D: **user-specific and common task learning**. Basically, the model adopts a joint training framework, which shares data information between different data tiers as much as possible. Bottom embedding table of raw features is shared across different user groups and item scenarios From the perspective of multi-task learning, TAMOR divides tasks into three categories according to their business relationships. First, in user bias learning (B), we focus on the task which can reflect the user preferences or characteristics, such as financial investment capacity. Second, in user-specific task learning (C), we intend to learn prediction tasks which are more relevant to the user's mind, such as investment action after click-through. Third, in common task learning (D), we predict early behaviors in the action chain, such as the click-through rate (CTR) and conversion rate (CVR) prediction tasks.

Tier-Aware Representation Learning: Tier-aware representation learning is the key component of TAMOR to realize the simultaneous modeling of multiple data tiers and retain the specific information of each data tier. In this module, the raw features of users/items are projected into a unified feature space with the stratification information. In detail, we first obtain multiple representation $V \in \mathbb{R}^{d \times g}$ from the raw features using the PLE [2] network. Second, we learn a weight $\mathbf{w} \in \mathbb{R}^g$ across groups through an encoding module. This encoding module can be either simple one-hot encoding, or soft encoding with learnable weights. Finally, we use the vector multiplication to compute the tier-aware

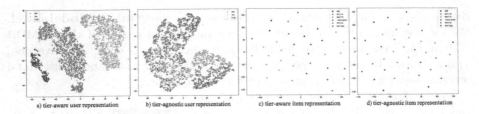

a) tier-aware user representation   b) tier-agnostic user representation   c) tier-aware item representation   d) tier-agnostic item representation

Fig. 3. Visualization of tier-aware representations vs. tier-agnostic representations

representation $V\mathbf{w} \in \mathbb{R}^d$. Empirically, we compare the tier-aware representations and the representations learned in the way which is agnostic about data tiers. As is visualized in Fig. 3, the tier-aware representations successfully discriminate the samples into separate local regions in the feature space.

User Bias Learning: User bias learning plays a key role in multi-objective recommendation, if there are predicted events that are strongly related to user preference. Specifically, in this module, the user-side data is deeply mined to model user bias to predict some item-independent tasks. The learning process is essentially item-agnostic allowing us to focus on the modeling of user features alone. Ultimately, this module is primarily intended to alleviate the learning difficulty of user-specific tasks.

User-Specific and Common Task Learning: The multiple objectives in recommendation are subdivided into common tasks, and user-specific tasks which are more dependent on user bias. Separate DNN towers are built upon the tier-aware representations to make predictions on corresponding tasks. In particular, for user-specific tasks, the user bias vector is concatenated with the input vector of their DNN towers, to enhance the user-side features.

3 Conclusion

In this paper, we propose TAMOR for stratified users and heterogeneous scenarios. TAMOR learns tier-aware representations and models the relationship among multiple objectives. We proved the effectiveness of TAMOR through its successful application in Ant Fortune financial marketing. Future work involves further refining the encoding module for tier-aware representation learning.

References

1. Ma, J., Zhao, Z., Yi, X., Chen, J., Hong, L., Chi, E.H.: Modeling task relationships in multi-task learning with multi-gate mixture-of-experts. In: Proceedings of the 24th ACM SIGKDD International Conference on Knowledge Discovery & Data Mining, pp. 1930–1939 (2018)
2. Tang, H., Liu, J., Zhao, M., Gong, X.: Progressive layered extraction (PLE): a novel multi-task learning (MTL) model for personalized recommendations. In: Fourteenth ACM Conference on Recommender Systems, pp. 269–278 (2020)

Benchmarking GNNs with GenCAT Workbench

Seiji Maekawa[1]([✉]), Yuya Sasaki[1], George Fletcher[2], and Makoto Onizuka[1]

[1] Osaka University, 1-5, Yamadaoka, Suita, Osaka, Japan
{maekawa.seiji,sasaki,onizuka}@ist.osaka-u.ac.jp
[2] Eindhoven University of Technology, P.O. Box 513, 5600 MB Eindhoven,
The Netherlands
g.h.l.fletcher@tue.nl

Abstract. We present GenCAT Workbench, an end-to-end framework
with which users can generate synthetic attributed graphs with node labels
and evaluate their graph analytic methods, e.g., graph neural networks
(GNNs), on the generated graphs. GenCAT Workbench supports various
types of graphs with controlled node attributes and graph topology. We
demonstrate the GenCAT Workbench and how it clarifies the strong and
weak points of GNN models. Our code base is available on Github (https://
github.com/seijimaekawa/GenCAT/tree/main/GenCAT_Workbench).

Keywords: Attributed graph · Graph generator · Community · Node
label

1 Introduction

Graph analytics methods, e.g., graph neural networks (GNNs), have attracted
attention from both academia and industry. To clarify their applicability or limitations, many studies address benchmarking GNNs [2,3]. Though repositories
[3] provide collections of real-world graphs with node labels, i.e., an assignment
of nodes to groups we call *classes*, the variety of available graphs is still limited.

Because of the large demands for various graphs, synthetic graphs are necessary to mitigate the insufficiency of real-world graphs. Several studies developed
benchmarking frameworks with synthetic graphs for evaluating graph analytic
methods [2]. However, these frameworks suffer from two drawbacks. First, they
use graph generators that cannot generate realistic graphs such as SBM [1]. Second, these frameworks require users to manually set an overwhelming number of
parameters of graph generators from scratch when users generate their desired
graphs. Hence, the requirements of benchmarking frameworks are 1) the flexibility of controlling the characteristics of generated graphs and 2) the usability
for setting parameters of the graph generation.

We present GenCAT Workbench, a framework satisfying both of these desired
features. First, our framework allows users to flexibly control the characteristics
of generated graphs since we adopt GenCAT [5], an attributed graph generator which supports various characteristics of real-world graphs, such as node

M.-R. Amini et al. (Eds.): ECML PKDD 2022, LNAI 13718, pp. 607–611, 2023.
https://doi.org/10.1007/978-3-031-26422-1_40

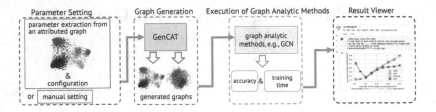

Fig. 1. Overview of the GenCAT workbench.

degree distributions, attribute distribution, and class structure. The class structure indicates the interplay between classes, attributes and topology. Second, the GenCAT Workbench can extract the parameters for its graph generation from a given graph and then allows users to configure the parameters, which reduces users' effort compared to fully manual settings. In our demonstration[1], we clarify the pros/cons of each graph analytic method across various topology structures and attribute values. Figure 1 gives an overview of our framework.

Related Work. Many studies have addressed benchmarking graph analytic methods [2,3]. However, there are no frameworks which allow users to generate various graphs and evaluate analytic methods by the graphs. For example, a recent framework uses SBM which generates graphs that are not similar to real-world graphs [2].

2   GenCAT Workbench

GenCAT [5] is the state-of-the-art attributed graph generator which allows users to flexibly control the characteristics of generated graphs. Since it captures the relationships between classes, attributes, and topology, the attributes and topology in generated graphs share the class structure. More specifically, GenCAT can flexibly generate graphs with controlled edge connection proportions between classes, called *class preference mean*. Given as inputs user specified features such as node degrees, attribute distribution, and class features (e.g., class preference mean and class size distribution), GenCAT generates graphs having similar features to these inputs.

GenCAT is the only method satisfying our requirements; supporting various class structures and extracting parameters from a given graph. Current state of the art methods [1,7] fail to support one or more features supported by GenCAT. Moreover, it can simulate existing generators in terms of class structures and node degrees. Please see more detailed and precise procedures in [5].

2.1   Features of the GenCAT Workbench

The workflow of the GenCAT Workbench is illustrated in Fig. 1. We describe the features of the GenCAT Workbench as follows.

---

[1] Our demo video is available on https://www.youtube.com/watch?v=28xVOHR DpCE.

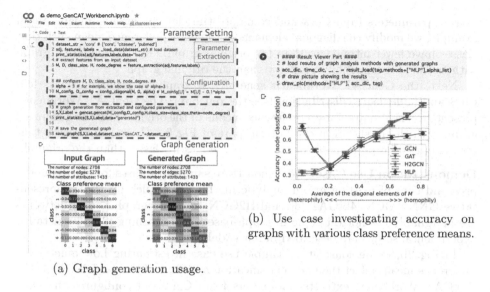

(a) Graph generation usage.

(b) Use case investigating accuracy on graphs with various class preference means.

Fig. 2. Demonstration. (Color figure online)

Easy Parameter Setting. Users can extract statistics from a given graph, and then configure the parameters to obtain their desired graphs. We present examples of Cora, Citeseer, and Pubmed, which are commonly used citation networks [4], on the GenCAT Workbench. Also, users can add other new datasets.

Benchmarking Graph Analytic Methods. Users can investigate how each parameter (e.g., class preference mean or the number of edges) affects the performance (e.g., accuracy and training time) of graph analytic methods, while keeping the rest of the parameters the same. This investigation clarifies the advantages and drawbacks of methods on various settings.

End-to-End Framework. The GenCAT Workbench provides all necessary components for benchmarking, including parameter setting (i.e., extraction and configuration), graph generation, execution of graph analytic methods, and result viewer. This enables users to easily investigate their methods in various settings.

To enhance the extensibility of the GenCAT Workbench, we implement it on Jupyter Notebook. This allows users to easily add new methods to our framework. This implementation is rather simple yet suitable for GNNs that are changing rapidly.

3   Demonstration Plan

Graph Generation Usage. We demonstrate and explain how to generate graphs by the GenCAT Workbench in Fig. 2a. First, users can choose a dataset from which they extract statistics (see the blue box). In this demonstration, we extract parameters from Cora and configure the class preference mean. As an example, we modify the diagonal elements of the class preference mean such that classes have fewer intra-edges than the original graph, i.e., we simulate a graph with the weaker homophily property than the original graph.

Next, the GenCAT Workbench generates a graph by inputting class features and node degree distribution (see the red box). The GenCAT Workbench presents the heatmaps of class preference means of the original and the generated graphs, which are shown in the bottom part of Fig. 2a. Users can observe that the generated graph actually has fewer intra-edges in classes than the original.

Demonstration Use Case. We demonstrate sample use cases for clarifying the pros and cons of existing graph analytic methods. We pick up three representative GNNs, GCN [4], GAT [6], and H2GCN [8], since graph neural networks are inarguably the hottest topic in graph-based deep learning [2]. The detailed experimental setups are described in our codebase.

In Fig. 2b, we demonstrate a sample use case investigating how much class preference means affect the node classification accuracy of the models. First, the GenCAT Workbench extracts parameters from Cora and configures the class preference means to have few intra-edges (i.e., heterophily property) from many intra-edges (i.e., homophily property). Second, the GenCAT Workbench generates graphs with the configured class preference means. Third, the framework executes GNN models on the generated graphs. To compare the models with a graph-agnostic classifier, we execute multi-layer perceptron (MLP).

Next, we discuss observations from this use case. First, GCN, GAT, and H2GCN outperform MLP on graphs with the homophily property since MLP does not use the topology information (see the bottom part in Fig. 2b). Then, H2GCN, which considers the heterophily property, performs well on graphs with the heterophily property (the leftmost points). In contrast, GCN and GAT do not perform well since they ignore the heterophily property.

In our demo video, we present two more use cases: 1) accuracy on graphs with various attribute values, and 2) training time per epoch for various numbers of edges. Through the demonstrations, we show how GenCAT Workbench can support investigations of the pros/cons of graph analytics methods on generated graphs with various class preference means, attributes, and graph sizes.

Acknowledgement. This work was supported by JSPS KAKENHI Grant Numbers JP20H00583 and JST PRESTO Grant Number JPMJPR21C5.

References

1. Abbe, E.: Community detection and stochastic block models: recent developments. J. Mach. Learn. Res. **18**, 6446–6531 (2017)
2. Dwivedi, V.P., Joshi, C.K., Laurent, T., Bengio, Y., Bresson, X.: Benchmarking graph neural networks. arXiv (2020)
3. Hu, W., et al.: Open graph benchmark: datasets for machine learning on graphs. arXiv (2020)

4. Kipf, T.N., Welling, M.: Semi-supervised classification with graph convolutional networks. In: ICLR (2017)
5. Maekawa, S., Sasaki, Y., Fletcher, G., Onizuka, M.: GenCAT: generating attributed graphs with controlled relationships between classes, attributes, and topology. arXiv (2021)
6. Veličković, P., Cucurull, G., Casanova, A., Romero, A., Liò, P., Bengio, Y.: Graph attention networks. In: ICLR (2018)
7. Wang, B., Wang, C., Feng, H.: FastSNG: the fastest social network dataset generator. In: WWW (2021)
8. Zhu, J., Yan, Y., Zhao, L., Heimann, M., Akoglu, L., Koutra, D.: Beyond homophily in graph neural networks: current limitations and effective designs. NeurIPS **33**, 7793–7804 (2020)

SLISEMAP: Combining Supervised Dimensionality Reduction with Local Explanations

Anton Björklund[✉][iD], Jarmo Mäkelä[iD], and Kai Puolamäki[iD]

University of Helsinki, Helsinki, Finland
anton.bjorklund@helsinki.fi

Abstract. We introduce a Python library, called SLISEMAP, that contains a supervised dimensionality reduction method that can be used for global explanation of *black box* regression or classification models. SLISEMAP takes a data matrix and predictions from a *black box* model as input, and outputs a (typically) two-dimensional embedding, such that the black box model can be approximated, to a good fidelity, by the same interpretable *white box* model for points with similar embeddings. The library includes basic visualisation tools and extensive documentation, making it easy to get started and obtain useful insights. The SLISEMAP library is published on GitHub and PyPI under an open source license.

Keywords: Manifold visualisation · Explainable AI

1 Introduction

In our recent manuscript [3] we introduce an algorithm, SLISEMAP, that extends [1,2] and combines manifold visualization (e.g., [6–8]) with local, model-agnostic explanations of regression or classification models (see [5] for a review). The idea of the latter is to find an interpretable *white box* surrogate model that locally approximates a complex *black box* model for a given data point.

SLISEMAP produces a non-linear embedding of the data into d dimensions (typically $d = 2$), such that data points projected nearby can, with good fidelity, be explained by the same white box model. Each data point have an embedding and an associated white box model. Together the white box models and the visual embedding provide a *global* explanation of the black box model.

In this paper we describe a Python library, called SLISEMAP, that implements the algorithm by the same name.

The SLISEMAP library can be used by all who want to explore datasets or are interested in global explanations for complex black box models.

While there are plethora of software for manifold embeddings or local explanations, none exist that combine these two.

Support by Academy of Finland (grants 320182, 346376) & Future Makers Program.

M.-R. Amini et al. (Eds.): ECML PKDD 2022, LNAI 13718, pp. 612–616, 2023.
https://doi.org/10.1007/978-3-031-26422-1_41

2   Problem Definition

Formally, input to SLISEMAP is given as a dataset of n points $(\mathbf{x}_1, \mathbf{y}_1), \ldots,$
$(\mathbf{x}_n, \mathbf{y}_n)$, where the covariates are given by real vectors $\mathbf{x}_i \in \mathbb{R}^m$ and the
responses $\mathbf{y}_i = f(\mathbf{x}_i) \in \mathbb{R}^p$, where $f : \mathbb{R}^m \to \mathbb{R}^p$ is a pre-trained black box
regression or classification model that we wish to explain. For regression problems $p = 1$ and for classification problems p is the number of classes, where $\mathbf{y}_i$
represents the predicted class probabilities.

We also need a type of easy-to-understand, *white box*, surrogate model,
$g_i : \mathbb{R}^m \to \mathbb{R}^p$, that we use to approximate the black box model f in the neighbourhood (as defined by the embedding) of the data point $i \in \{1, \ldots, n\}$. We
collect the parameters of the white box models into a matrix $\mathbf{B} \in \mathbb{R}^{n \times q}$ such
that the ith row $\mathbf{B}_{i\cdot}$ contains the parameters of the white box model g_i. As g_i for
regression problems we use a simple linear model and for classification problems a
multinomial logistic regression. Additionally, the loss function $l : \mathbb{R}^p \times \mathbb{R}^p \to \mathbb{R}_{\geq 0}$
quantifies the mismatch between the black box and white box models. We use
quadratic loss for regression problems and Hellinger loss (which is related to
log-loss) for classification problems. Formally, the SLISEMAP algorithm finds an
embedding of a given radius by solving the following computational problem.

Problem 1. [3] Given the definitions above, regularization parameters $\lambda_{lasso} \geq 0$
and $\lambda_{ridge} \geq 0$, and the radius of the embedding $z_{radius} > 0$, find the parameters
$\mathbf{B} \in \mathbb{R}^{n \times q}$ and embedding of data points $\mathbf{Z} \in \mathbb{R}^{n \times d}$ that minimise the loss given
by $\mathcal{L} = \sum_{i=1}^{n} \sum_{j=1}^{n} \mathbf{W}_{ij} \mathbf{L}_{ij} + \sum_{i=1}^{n} \sum_{j=1}^{q} \left(\lambda_{lasso} |\mathbf{B}_{ij}| + \lambda_{ridge} \mathbf{B}_{ij}^2 \right)$, where $\mathbf{L}_{ij} = l(g_i(\mathbf{x}_j), \mathbf{y}_j)$, $\mathbf{W}_{ij} = e^{-\mathbf{D}_{ij}} / \sum_{k=1}^{n} e^{-\mathbf{D}_{ik}}$, and $\mathbf{D}_{ij} = \left(\sum_{k=1}^{d} (\mathbf{Z}_{ik} - \mathbf{Z}_{jk})^2 \right)^{1/2}$,
with the constraint that $\left(\sum_{i=1}^{n} \sum_{k=1}^{d} \mathbf{Z}_{ik}^2 / n \right)^{1/2} = z_{radius}$.

This means that the local models are optimised using weights. The weights are
based on distances between the data points in the embedding. Incompatible local
models are, thus, pushed away from each other. Conversely, the constraint on
the embedding size leads to interchangable local models forming clusters.

We refer to [3] for a detailed summary of related work, description and analysis of the algorithm, as well as experimental validation.

3   The SLISEMAP Library

SLISEMAP is implemented in *Python* using *PyTorch* for the optimisation, enabling
automatic differentiation and optional GPU-acceleration. However, the library
also interfaces with standard *Numpy*. For the built-in visualisation, exploration,
and diagnostics tools we use *Seaborn*.

The design goals of the library are flexibility, performance, and ease of use.
This is accomplished through optional parameters, closures, and just-in-time
compilation, while providing extensive documentation, sane defaults, and helpful
warning messages.

The SLISEMAP library is open source and available under an MIT license at
https://github.com/edahelsinki/slisemap. The repository also includes a demonstration video and an extended version of the example discussed below in the

Table 1. Descriptions and default values for the most important parameters.

Parameter	Default Value	Description
X		Data matrix, in $\mathbb{R}^{n \times m}$
y		Response vector / matrix, in $\mathbb{R}^{n \times p}$
d	2	Number of embedding dimensions
radius	3.5	Spread of the embedding, (z_{radius})
lasso	0.0	L1 regularisation coefficient (λ_{lasso})
ridge	0.0	L2 regularisation coefficient (λ_{ridge})
local_model	Linear regression	Prediction function for the white box model (g_i)
local_loss	Least squares	Loss function for the white box model (l)

form of a *Jupyter notebook*. The package can also be installed using `pip install slisemap`.

4 Usage Example

The AUTOMPG dataset [4] is a multivariate real-valued dataset with eight attributes describing the properties of 398 distinct cars (6 rows with missing values removed). The covariates are in a (normalised) Numpy array X, that consists of seven ordinal attributes for each car. The response vector y contains the fuel consumption (miles per gallon), as estimated by a random forest regressor. Code 1 shows how we apply SLISEMAP on this dataset.

```
1  sm = Slisemap(X, y, lasso=0.01) # Slisemap object
2  sm.optimise() # Optimise the solution
3  sm.plot(title="Slisemap with local model clusters",
4          clusters=4, bars=6, jitter=0.1, variables=names)
```

Code 1. Basic SLISEMAP usage.

We make the interpretation of the local models easier by clustering (using k-means) the local model coefficients (rows of matrix **B**) and colour-code the embedding based on the cluster indices. Furthermore, we add some jitter (since some points are on top of each other), and show only the five most meaningful attributes.

The result is shown in Fig. 1.

We can now identify which attributes in a given cluster are the most important in getting the predictions correct. For example, model year is an important indicator of fuel economy for cluster 0, but it is less important in cluster 3. Further analysis of the clusters reveals that cluster 3 consists of mostly heavy, U.S.-made cars with poor fuel economy, where the weight is the primary determinant for fuel consumption. On the other hand, cluster 0 has primarily non-U.S. cars, which are, on average, newer and lighter. Here horsepower is also an important attribute in predicting fuel consumption.

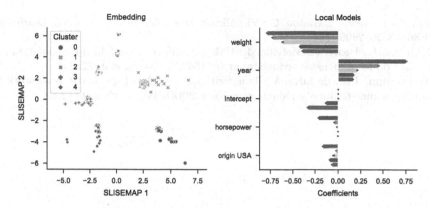

Fig. 1. Two-dimensional Slisemap embedding (left) with clusters based on *white box* surrogate models. The bar plot (right) shows the cluster centroids for the coefficients (rows of matrix **B**) of the *white box* models.

After optimising an embedding and finding local models with SLISEMAP, it is possible to investigate, with a built-in command, how new data items would be projected onto the same embedding and what their local white box models would be. This is useful for faster embedding of large datasets (using subsampling) or to detect concept drift. Also, the same command can highlight alternative explanations (locations in the embedding) for existing data points.

Classification. To use SLISEMAP for classification tasks we only have to replace the white box model (`local_model` in Table 1) with a classifier, such as logistic regression (included in the library). Alternatively we can transform the predictions of a black box model from $[0, 1]$ to $[-\infty, \infty]$ with a logit transformation, $y' = \log(y/(1-y))$, and use linear regression for the approximation. A classification example on a larger dataset is also included in the GitHub repository (https://github.com/edahelsinki/slisemap).

References

1. Björklund, A., Henelius, A., Oikarinen, E., Kallonen, K., Puolamäki, K.: Sparse robust regression for explaining classifiers. In: Discovery Science, vol. 11828, pp. 351–366 (2019)
2. Björklund, A., Henelius, A., Oikarinen, E., Kallonen, K., Puolamäki, K.: Robust regression via error tolerance. Data Min. Knowl. Discov. **36**, 781–810 (2022)
3. Björklund, A., Mäkelä, J., Puolamäki, K.: SLISEMAP: Supervised dimensionality reduction through local explanations. Mach. Learn. **112**(1), 1–43 (2023). https://doi.org/10.1007/s10994-022-06261-1
4. Dua, D., Graff, C.: UCI machine learning repository (2017)
5. Guidotti, R., Monreale, A., Ruggieri, S., Turini, F., Giannotti, F., Pedreschi, D.: A survey of methods for explaining black box models. ACM Comput. Surv. **51**(5), 1–42 (2019)

6. van der Maaten, L., Hinton, G.: Visualizing data using t-SNE. J. Mach. Learn. Res. 9(86), 2579–2605 (2008)
7. McInnes, L., Healy, J., Melville, J.: UMAP: uniform manifold approximation and projection for dimension reduction. arXiv:1802.03426 [cs, stat] (2020)
8. Tenenbaum, J.B., de Silva, V., Langford, J.C.: A global geometric framework for nonlinear dimensionality reduction. Science **290**(5500), 2319–2323 (2000)

A Camera-Based System to Detect Driver Hands on the Steering Wheel in Semi-autonomous Vehicles

Raphaël Morvillier, Christophe Prat[✉], and Saifeddine Aloui

Univ. Grenoble Alpes, CEA, Leti, 38000 Grenoble, France
christophe.prat@cea.fr

Abstract. Semi-autonomous vehicles require monitoring the driver to check if he is supervising the system and/or ready to take over. Most cars rely on steering-wheel sensors to detect hands and do not monitor the non-driving related task the driver might be performing. We present a camera-based system with a multi-branch architecture, which provides the number of hands on the steering wheel, on a tablet representing a secondary task and the tablet position. It also tackles a common issue with other camera-based systems: a free hand in front of the steering wheel can be classified as grasping it. Moreover, our system deals with cases when the driver might use a tablet on the steering wheel, as he is allowed to do in autonomous mode. These two points are critical to assess the time the driver will need to take over. Finally, combining both steering wheel and camera systems would also make vehicles harder to trick and therefore safer.

Video available at: https://www.youtube.com/watch?v=qfYOM4sdWr4

Keywords: Driver monitoring · Deep learning · Hands on steering wheel

1 Introduction

Before the advent of fully autonomous vehicles, the driver will still have to supervise the car and/or to take over the control, in order to deal with situations that the car cannot resolve. In such semi-autonomous cars, it is critical to monitor the driver, to know if he is ready to take over, with his hands on the steering wheel, or if he is engaged in a non-driving related task.

In this work, we place ourselves in the scope of such vehicles and show a system to detect if a driver has his hands on the steering wheel or on a tablet (representing the non-driving related task). An increasing number of vehicles integrate hands detection systems embedded in the steering wheel. Such systems can prove very reliable under most of the situations. However, we intend to show that camera-based systems can complement steering wheel-based systems and are critical in specific situations.

Numerous work address the detection of hands on the steering wheel with a camera. One of the most direct approach is to classify the entire image captured by the camera, like in [1], however we found it did not perform well with a small database. Systems similar to those described in [2] and [3] rely on object detection. They first detect the steering wheel, then the hands and finally determine whether the hands are on the steering wheel or not, based on their joint area. These systems have limitations, because if a hand is masking the steering wheel and not touching it, it might be classified as grasping the steering wheel. In [4], the model relies on a first object detection to detect the driver hands, and then segments them. Finally, it classifies the hands state between grasping the steering wheel, the mobile phone or no object. Such a system should distinguish between a hand grasping or overlapping the steering wheel. However, it doesn't use the rest of the image and the steering wheel and hands positions to perform the final classification. We intend to tackle these limitations with the proposed method.

2 Proposed System Demonstration

2.1 System Description

Our system consists of:

1. a steering wheel with grip sensors detecting the hands and the gripping force
2. a tablet, on its stand, on the right of the steering wheel
3. a color camera pointing towards the steering wheel and the tablet
4. a PC executing the software which processes the camera images and the grip sensor signals to output information about the driver current behavior in real-time (Fig. 1)

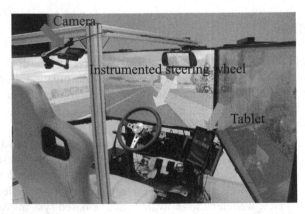

Fig. 1. The system set-up, with the steering wheel, the tablet and the camera

The software executes two models in real-time:

1. a decision tree algorithm, which processes the grip sensor signals and outputs:

    a. the hands position on the steering wheel
    b. an indicator of the gripping force

2. a deep learning model, which processes the camera images and outputs:

    a. the number of hands on the steering wheel
    b. the number of hands on the tablet
    c. if the tablet is on its stand or held by the driver

The deep learning algorithm has a multi-branch architecture: first an encoder as a common trunk and then three branches, each dedicated to one of the three tasks described above. To improve this model, we added a fourth branch which identifies the most relevant zones in the image. The advantages of this approach are that we use the entire image (the position of the relevant elements is as critical as their appearance) and the shared information between tasks (if a hand is on a tablet, it is not the steering wheel) (Fig. 2).

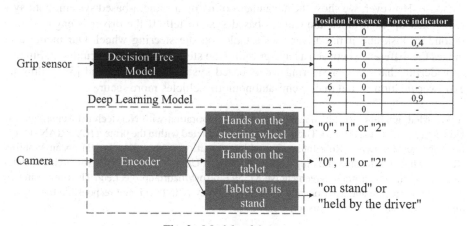

Position	Presence	Force indicator
1	0	-
2	1	0,4
3	0	-
4	0	-
5	0	-
6	0	-
7	1	0,9
8	0	-

Fig. 2. Models of the system

2.2 System in Action

In Fig. 3, we present four cases of hands detection by our system. Cases a) and b) are simple cases where most of the existing system would give accurate results. In c), most camera systems would detect that a hand is on the steering wheel even if it is only masking it. In d), the driver uses the tablet on the steering wheel. A steering wheel sensor might detect the hands but our camera system would detect the tablet usage.

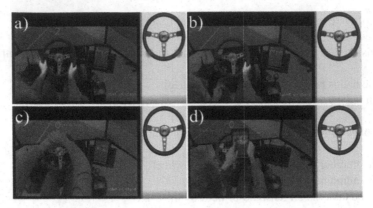

Fig. 3. Examples of hands detection by the system

3 Conclusion

We describe here a system showing the complementarity of the sensitive steering wheel and the camera-based systems. Both systems runs in parallel. Future works should focus on merging the two outputs and validating on an embedded platform with a larger database. However, we show the advantages of using a camera-based system: both systems back-up each other, the camera-based system tells if the driver is engaged in a secondary task and if the driver uses a tablet on the steering wheel. Our model also makes the difference between a hand grasping the steering wheel or occulting it. Finally, considering that most of steering wheel-based systems can be tricked [5], adding an extra verification would make semi-autonomous vehicles more secure.

Acknowledgements. Results obtained in close collaboration with Nervtech (Slovenia) and the University of Granada (Spain). This research was conducted within the project HADRIAN (Holistic Approach for Driver Role Integration and Automation - Allocation for European Mobility Needs), which has received funding from the European Union's Horizon 2020 research and innovation program under grant agreement No 875597, https://hadrianproject.eu/. The European Climate, Infrastructure and Environment Executive Agency (CINEA) is not responsible for any use that may be made of the information it contains.

References

1. Schmitz, J.-C., Tilgner, S., Kalischewski, K., Wagner, D., Kummert, A.: Hands on wheel classification based on depth images and neural networks. MATEC Web Conf. **308**, 06003 (2020). https://doi.org/10.1051/matecconf/202030806003
2. Le, T.H.N., Zheng, Y., Zhu, C., Luu, K., Savvides, M.: Multiple scale faster-RCNN approach to driver's cell-phone usage and hands on steering wheel detection. In: 2016 IEEE Conference on Computer Vision and Pattern Recognition Workshops (CVPRW), Las Vegas, NV, USA, pp. 46–53, June 2016. https://doi.org/10.1109/CVPRW.2016.13

3. Zhang, L., Yu, G., Zhou, B., Wang, Z., Xu, G.: Detection algorithm of takeover behavior of automatic vehicles' drivers based on deep learning. In: 2019 4th International Conference on Intelligent Transportation Engineering (ICITE), pp. 126–130, September 2019. https://doi.org/10.1109/ICITE.2019.8880230
4. Siddharth, Rangesh, A., Ohn-Bar, E., Trivedi, M.M.: Driver hand localization and grasp analysis: a vision-based real-time approach. In: 2016 IEEE 19th International Conference on Intelligent Transportation Systems (ITSC), pp. 2545–2550, November 2016. https://doi.org/10.1109/ITSC.2016.7795965
5. Car and Driver: It's Not Just Tesla: All Other Driver-Assist Systems Work without Drivers, Too, 11 August 2021. https://www.youtube.com/watch?v=trrmgpzPVQg. Accessed 20 Apr 2022

ADEPT: Anomaly Detection, Explanation and Processing for Time Series with a Focus on Energy Consumption Data

Benedikt Tobias Müller(iD), Marvin Ender, Jan Erik Swiadek$^{(\boxtimes)}$(iD),
Mengcheng Jin(iD), Simon Winkel, Dominik Niedziela, Bin Li(iD),
Jelle Hüntelmann(iD), and Emmanuel Müller(iD)

TU Dortmund University, Dortmund, Germany
jan-erik.swiadek@tu-dortmund.de

Abstract. Anomaly detection techniques are applicable for recognizing excessive energy consumption and device failure, thereby contributing to the maintenance of operational and sustainable energy supply systems. In this context, human decision makers can benefit from receiving explanation attempts for detected anomalies as part of a semi-automated software solution. Therefore we introduce the framework ADEPT, which comprises interfaces for processing user-supplied time series data and interactively visualizing explanatory anomaly information. Our framework features several shallow and deep machine learning algorithms for anomaly detection and explanation. We demonstrate ADEPT using energy consumption data collected from our university campus.

Keywords: Anomaly detection · Energy consumption · Explainability

1 Introduction

Conserving and efficiently utilizing energy are essential principles in sustainable development. They also reduce cost and afford greater autonomy in times of scant or uncertain energy supply. However, it is challenging to monitor energy consumption for large-scale systems because of the complexities inherent to visualizing and understanding high-dimensional time series data. Anomalous events can arise in various patterns and across all subsets of the deployed sensors, so they are hard to detect and interpret even for domain experts. On the technical side, recent methods show convincing performance in anomaly detection [1], but fully-automated solutions can't make use of human domain knowledge and lack in transparent explanations. This creates demand for semi-automated solutions offering intuitive and trustworthy anomaly explanations, which can help humans reliably find, e.g., periods of unusual consumption or sensor defects.

For the reasons stated, anomaly detection and explanation are challenging machine learning problems. Some already existing tools and frameworks make pertinent research results available to users, though they primarily focus on

M.-R. Amini et al. (Eds.): ECML PKDD 2022, LNAI 13718, pp. 622–626, 2023.
https://doi.org/10.1007/978-3-031-26422-1_43

different application domains, like eX^2 [2] for cybersecurity, DAART [8] for military purposes, and EXAD [9] for big data tracing. Other options for explainable anomaly detection include MSDA [3], a library targeting data scientists, and VADETIS [4], which does not go beyond comparative explanations. We thus propose ADEPT, a novel interactive framework providing easily accessible anomaly explanations in addition to energy consumption monitoring for homeowners and facility managers maintaining energy supply systems. Furthermore, our framework enables the research community to assess and compare machine learning methods concerning anomaly detection and explainability.

2   Framework Overview

Because our target audience is partly non-technical, a simple and easy-to-use way of comfortably and quickly assessing anomalies is needed. For this purpose we chose a microservice-based web application. That means users can access the application from every device, no calculations need to take place on the device itself, and the framework is extensible. A demonstration video of the ADEPT web application is available here: https://youtu.be/Uk28ipbJGiY.

2.1   Flexible Architecture

The framework is composed of a multitude of microservices, one for each core component. This allows researchers and developers to quickly and independently test innovative techniques, simply by adapting the appropriate component of the framework. Due to ADEPT's dynamic and flexible design, data can be read from many different sources, like real-time sensor data or static data files. These design principles extend to all parts of the software including the machine learning pipeline, which consists of normalization, feature engineering and model training as well as the detection, explanation and visualization of anomalies.

2.2   Interactive Exploration

ADEPT enables users to easily browse through and analyze existing data for anomalies without prior knowledge in data science. A screenshot of the ADEPT web interface can be found in Fig. 1. The first row contains the raw data and a configuration panel. Here users can select their desired sensors, features, a time period, and an anomaly detection algorithm. Detected anomalies are displayed in the second row. The table on the left side presents the timestamps and types of the anomalies, while the diagram on the right side features calculated anomaly likelihood scores with a threshold. Selecting one of the anomalies from the table fills the bottom row with corresponding explanation results, allowing users to analyze the anomaly in depth. The bottom left tile depicts an example-based explanation of the feature most responsible for the selected anomaly, contrasting the anomaly with normal patterns. This gives users immediate feedback on the shape of the anomaly. The bottom right tile displays the feature attribution of the anomaly, i.e., how much each feature contributes to its anomaly score.

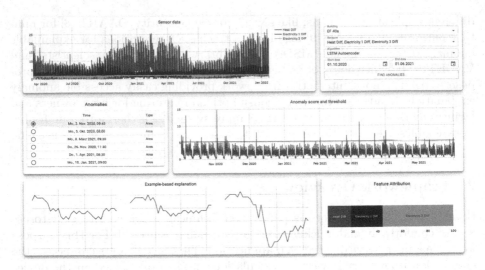

Fig. 1. Screenshot of the ADEPT web interface

3   Detection Models and Explainability Challenges

Each anomaly detection model comes with different strengths and weaknesses, which is why we need several models to detect all kinds of anomalies reliably. On a high level, models are categorized as shallow or deep models. Shallow models provide high training efficiency and are often sufficient for detecting simple anomalies, such as low-dimensional or extreme-value anomalies. Thanks to their simplicity, explanations can usually be derived directly. Meanwhile, explaining the results of deep models requires more sophisticated techniques, but their enhanced detection performance is essential for our use case because of the typically complex anomaly patterns hidden in high-dimensional energy consumption data. Among others, ADEPT makes use of the shallow algorithms Isolation Forest [5] and One-Class SVM [7] as well as the deep model LSTM Autoencoder [6]. Each model returns anomaly likelihood scores for all measurement timestamps. It is possible to train all models on-demand with user-supplied data. Shallow models can also be fitted using real-time data from the machine learning pipeline.

To facilitate human understanding and trust in the models, ADEPT includes explanation techniques that highlight anomalies by presenting normal patterns for comparison. We identify three key challenges in this regard. Firstly, a uniform normal state might not exist, as the meaning of "normal" not only depends on the respective time series, but can also vary over the course of a single time series, e.g., due to concept drifts. Secondly, the interplay of multiple time series can obfuscate the normal state and result in very complex anomalies. For instance, a slight deviation from a correlation involving a large number of dimensions is hardly noticeable. Thirdly, there are many approaches for extracting normal patterns and it has not yet been fully explored how intuitive their results are under different conditions. By implementing multiple methods for extracting normal patterns, ADEPT makes it possible to compare them. In order to find the dimension with the greatest contrast between a detected anomaly and the corresponding normal state, feature attributions are provided. In the case of LSTM Autoencoder, they are calculated using Integrated Gradients [10].

4   Evaluation and Future Work

For evaluating the detection performance of our models we use data from TU Dortmund University that consists of electricity, heat and water consumption measurements across more than 40 buildings on the university campus. This data is provided to us by the facility managers of our university, who also collaborate with us in interpreting normal states and abnormal events as domain experts. Thus far, ADEPT helped us find many events in the campus data that were confirmed by the facility managers as known anomalies, but also a few previously unknown, more subtle occurrences. These findings might enable them to optimize the energy efficiency of some buildings with abnormal energy consumption.

Considering the challenges we laid out before, there are still limits to the capabilities of ADEPT. At the same time, this creates opportunities for future research, in which our framework could help with assessing and comparing anomaly detection and explanation methods. Moreover, we plan to conduct regular stakeholder meetings for discussing its usage in the decision making process regarding the sustainability goals of our university's energy supply system.

Acknowledgements. This work was supported by the Research Center Trustworthy Data Science and Security, an institution of the University Alliance Ruhr.

References

1. Aggarwal, C.C.: Outlier Analysis, 2 edn. Springer, Cham (2017). https://doi.org/10.1007/978-3-319-47578-3
2. Arnaldo, I., Veeramachaneni, K., Lam, M.: eX2: a framework for interactive anomaly detection. In: Joint Proceedings of the ACM IUI 2019 Workshops (2019)
3. Arunachalam, A.: MSDA (2021). https://pypi.org/project/msda/
4. Khelifati, A., et al.: VADETIS: an explainable evaluator for anomaly detection techniques. In: 37th IEEE International Conference on Data Engineering, pp. 2661–2664 (2021)
5. Liu, F.T., Ting, K.M., Zhou, Z.: Isolation forest. In: Proceedings of the 8th IEEE International Conference on Data Mining, pp. 413–422 (2008)
6. Malhotra, P., Ramakrishnan, A., Anand, G., Vig, L., Agarwal, P., Shroff, G.: LSTM-based encoder-decoder for multi-sensor anomaly detection. CoRR (2016). https://arxiv.org/abs/1607.00148
7. Schölkopf, B., Williamson, R.C., Smola, A.J., Shawe-Taylor, J., Platt, J.C.: Support vector method for novelty detection. In: Advances in Neural Information Processing Systems 12, pp. 582–588 (1999)
8. Smith-Renner, A., Rua, R., Colony, M.: Towards an explainable threat detection tool. In: Joint Proceedings of the ACM IUI 2019 Workshops (2019)

9. Song, F., Diao, Y., Read, J., Stiegler, A., Bifet, A.: EXAD: a system for explainable anomaly detection on big data traces. In: ICDMW 2018, pp. 1435–1440 (2018)
10. Sundararajan, M., Taly, A., Yan, Q.: Axiomatic attribution for deep networks. In: Proceedings of the 34th International Conference on Machine Learning, pp. 3319–3328 (2017)

RE-Tagger: A Light-Weight Real-Estate Image Classifier

Prateek Chhikara(ID), Anil Goyal(✉), and Chirag Sharma

Housing.com, Gurugram, India
{prateek.chhikara,anil.goyal,chirag.sharma}@housing.com

Abstract. Real-estate image tagging is one of the essential use-cases to save efforts involved in manual annotation and enhance the user experience. This paper proposes an end-to-end pipeline (referred to as RE-Tagger) for the real-estate image classification problem. We present a two-stage transfer learning approach using custom InceptionV3 architecture to classify images into different categories (i.e., bedroom, bathroom, kitchen, balcony, hall, and others). Finally, we released the application as REST API hosted as a web application running on 2 cores machine with 2 GB RAM.

1 Introduction

Over the past few years, the demand for online real-estate tools has increased drastically due to the ease of accessibility of the internet, especially in developing countries like India. There are many online real-estate platforms (e.g., Housing.com, Proptiger.com, Makaan.com, etc.) for owners, developers, and real-estate brokers to post properties for buying and renting purposes. Daily, these platforms receive $8,000$ to $9,000$ new listings consisting of approximately $60,000$ to $70,000$ house images belonging to different categories like bedroom, bathroom, kitchen, balcony, living room, etc. To enhance the customer experience, it is necessary to organize the listing images by tagging/categorizing images into one of these categories. Generally, a team of data annotators manually tag a massive volume of images, which is both costly and time-consuming. Moreover, manual tagging introduces a delay of approximately $40\,h$ from when seller upload the images on the platform to when the listing becomes online.

To overcome these challenges and enhance the user experience, we have developed an end-to-end pipeline for real-estate image tagging (called RE-Tagger). For any input image, the RE-Tagger categorizes the image into one of the six categories, i.e., bedroom, balcony, bathroom, kitchen, hall, and others. Concretely, we have used two-stage transfer learning using the custom InceptionV3 [5] architecture for multi-class image classification problem [1]. Finally, we released the pipeline as REST API, which runs in a web browser. It requires 2 cores machine with 2 GB RAM for hosting the API and can be easily hosted on edge devices.

M.-R. Amini et al. (Eds.): ECML PKDD 2022, LNAI 13718, pp. 627–630, 2023.
https://doi.org/10.1007/978-3-031-26422-1_44

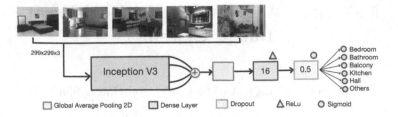

Fig. 1. Model architecture

2   Model Training and Validation

In this section, we present the proposed model architecture along with data acquisition and evaluation results.

2.1   Model Architecture

We have proposed a two-stage transfer learning approach using the custom InceptionV3 [5] model for the real-estate image classification problem. In the proposed architecture, we have replaced the final classification block of the original InceptionV3 with a global 2D average pooling layer, fully connected layer, dropout layer ($rate = 0.5$), and softmax layer. Figure 1 illustrates the proposed architecture. Please note that, we have experimentally validated that InceptionV3 architecture provides best performance as compared to ResNet [3], VGG [4] and Xception [2] architectures on real-estate image classification task. For training the architecture, we have initialized the network with ImageNet weights followed by a two-stage transfer learning approach. In the first step, we freeze the base model and only fine-tune the newly added layers (global 2D average pooling, fully connected, dropout, and softmax layers) using Housing.com data. Further, we train the complete end-to-end network on Housing.com data in the second step. We have empirically selected the input image dimensions to be $299 \times 299 \times 3$ without cropping and padding. The model training was performed for 50 epochs (both stages) using RMSProp as an optimizer with a learning rate of 0.0001 and discounting factor (ρ) to be 0.9. We have used categorical cross-entropy as a loss function and set the batch size to 64.

2.2   Data Acquisition

We have collected 3.1 million manually annotated images from Housing.com's databases. The majority of examples (approximately 73%) in the obtained dataset belong to the bedroom, bathroom, balcony, living, dining, and kitchen classes. Moreover, there is a high overlap between dining room and living room classes because residences generally do not have separate living and dining rooms in India. Therefore, we considered living and dining rooms a single class, i.e., 'hall'. The images which do not belong to any of these categories are classified as 'others.' The detailed distribution of classes is shown in Fig. 2.

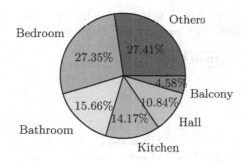

Fig. 2. The distribution of classes in obtained dataset

Table 1. Obtained precision, recall and F1-scores on the test dataset over all the classes

Class	Balcony	Bathroom	Bedroom	Hall	Kitchen	Others
Precision	0.98	0.98	0.87	0.84	0.85	0.82
Recall	0.82	0.98	0.89	0.94	0.95	0.98
F1-score	0.90	0.98	0.88	0.89	0.90	0.90

2.3 Experimental Protocol and Results

For evaluation, we reserved 100K images for testing and the remaining for training. For training the model, we randomly under-sample the samples from the majority classes such that all the classes have an equal number of images at the time of training. After under-sampling, we had 1.2 million images consisting of 200K images from each class. Furthermore, the training dataset is divided into train and validation in the ratio of 9:1. Since the classes are imbalanced, we evaluated the learning algorithm in terms of Precision, Recall, and F1-score. Finally, in Table 1, we present the obtained results over all the classes. The results show that the proposed method performs more than 88% (in terms of F1-score) over all the classes.

3 REST API and Web Application

RE-Tagger is developed in Python using Deep Learning frameworks: Keras and Tensorflow. We have released the application as REST API[1] which is hosted as a web application running on 2 cores machine with 2 GB RAM[2]. Please note that, the API can be easily hosted on edge devices as well.

In Table 2, we present the Python code snippet along with JSON response for making a HTTP POST request to REST API. The web interface of RE-Tagger is shown in Fig. 3 where a user can upload a real-estate image to receive an API response in real-time.

---

[1] The endpoint for REST API is http://52.70.157.211:5000/re-tagger.
[2] Web Interface is accessible at http://52.70.157.211:5000/.

Table 2. An example of `Python` code for making HTTP request to `RE-Tagger` API url using POST request along with output JSON response

Python Code	JSON Response
```import requests` `url='http://52.70.157.211:5000/re-tagger'` `filename = 'path_to_file'` `files =` ` {'image':(filename, open(filename, 'rb'))}` `response=requests.post(url,files=files)` `print(response.json())```	```{` `"bedroom":"score",` `"bathroom":"score",` `"balcony":"score",` `"kitchen":"score",` `"hall":"score",` `"others":"score"` `}```

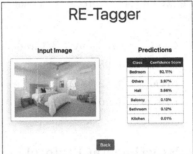

Fig. 3. Web Interface of `RE-Tagger` API with home page (left) and output page (right)

4   Conclusion

This demo paper introduces the `RE-Tagger` pipeline that classifies real-estate images into multiple categories: bathroom, bedroom, hall, etc. We proposed a two-stage transfer learning approach using a custom InceptionV3 model and released the application as REST API hosted as web application.

References

1. Abou Baker, N., Zengeler, N., Handmann, U.: A transfer learning evaluation of deep neural networks for image classification. Mach. Learn. Knowl. Extr. **4**(1), 22–41 (2022)
2. Chollet, F.: Xception: deep learning with depthwise separable convolutions. corr abs/1610.02357 (2016). arXiv preprint arXiv:1610.02357 (2016)
3. He, K., Zhang, X., Ren, S., Sun, J.: Deep residual learning for image recognition. Comput. Vis. Pattern Recognit. (2015). Google Scholar There is no corresponding record for this reference pp. 770–778 (2015)
4. Simonyan, K., Zisserman, A.: Very deep convolutional networks for large-scale image recognition. arXiv preprint arXiv:1409.1556 (2014)
5. Szegedy, C., Vanhoucke, V., Ioffe, S., Shlens, J., Wojna, Z.: Rethinking the inception architecture for computer vision. In: Proceedings of the IEEE Conference on Computer Vision And Pattern Recognition, pp. 2818–2826 (2016)

An Embedded Continual Learning System for Facial Emotion Recognition

Olivier Antoni[1]([✉]), Marion Mainsant[1], Christelle Godin[2], Martial Mermillod[3],
and Marina Reyboz[1]

[1] Univ. Grenoble Alpes, CEA, List, 38000 Grenoble, France
{olivier.antoni,marion.mainsant,marina.reyboz}@cea.fr
[2] Univ. Grenoble Alpes, CEA, Leti, 38000 Grenoble, France
christelle.godin@cea.fr
[3] Univ. Grenoble Alpes, LPNC, Grenoble, France
martial.mermillod@univ-grenoble-alpes.fr

Abstract. While being a key element of human-human communication,
face emotion recognition is an important challenge for human-computer
interactions. Feature extraction and classification methods have been
developed during the past decades in order to propose increasingly accurate emotion recognition algorithms. Nevertheless, in a changing environment where systems need to be continually adapted, the issue of catastrophic forgetting becomes a major challenge. Based on the bio-inspired
continual learning algorithm Dream Net, we propose an embedded system for face emotion recognition. This system is innovative in its ability to learn incrementally on a NVIDIA Jetson Nano platform without
catastrophic forgetting while preserving privacy and being agnostic to
data. Live demonstration of this system can be done and users can test
it in several modes of operation: emotion recognition or learning of new
emotions.

Keywords: Facial emotion recognition · Embedded deep learning ·
Continual learning

1 Introduction

Emotions are one of the cornerstones of human social interactions. Expressing
as well as understanding emotions from others is strongly needed in an environment where several people interact with each other. In today environment
where interaction with computers is increasingly common, introducing emotional
skills in technologies appears as a way to simplify human-computer interactions
[8]. Facial expressions are the most used features in non-verbal communication
[7]. Therefore, facial emotion recognition have been particularly studied in past
decades and many deep learning methods were proposed [4]. Nevertheless, as
they need a large amount of data to be correctly trained, most of the proposed models are not designed to be robust to a changing environment where

M.-R. Amini et al. (Eds.): ECML PKDD 2022, LNAI 13718, pp. 631–635, 2023.
https://doi.org/10.1007/978-3-031-26422-1_45

new emotions or new people can appear. When dealing with human emotion data, especially in the context of facial emotion recognition, privacy becomes an important concern. Another key issue of deep learning is that "classical" artificial neural network are not able to learn and fine-tune new concepts without a drastic reduction of their performances called "catastrophic forgetting". Based on this observation, Mainsant et al. [6] proposed a bio-inspired continual learning model, called Dream Net, that overcomes catastrophic forgetting, preserves privacy, and is data agnostic. Using this algorithm, we developed an embedded system able to learn and recognize face emotion of people in front of a camera. This work is part of a larger purpose to use the Dream Net algorithm in real life applications such as environmental monitoring, personalization of wearable sensors for healthcare applications or autonomous driving support.

2   Demonstration

2.1   Goal

The system is initially able to recognize five of the seven basic emotions: neutral, angry, disgust, fear and sad. The goal of the demonstration is to extend the system's knowledge to two additional emotions (happy and surprise) without forgetting the five initially learned emotions. This demonstration shows that using Dream Net algorithm allows the system to learn new emotions without storing examples of previous emotions while overcoming catastrophic forgetting.

2.2   Scenario

The demonstration begins with the evaluation of the recognition capabilities of the system. Then, some face images are placed in front of the camera to collect the necessary data for the detector to learn the last two unknown emotions. Next, Dream Net algorithm is used to teach the system these emotions. Finally, the system is updated and tested, not only with face images, but also with real faces. The tests confirm that the system is able to detect all emotions after learning.

2.3   Specifications and Related Optimizations

For the demonstration to run smoothly, the following conditions must be met. First, people seen by the camera should not experience a lag between their movements or emotional changes and the system response: the processing time of the whole system must be less than 100 ms. Second, to keep people's attention, the time it takes for the system to learn new emotions should not exceed one minute.

Such a real-time system has been achieved by using TensorFlow [1] to train the models, and TensorRT [2] to generate 16-bit floating-point optimized runtime engines for inference. Special attention has been paid to minimizing the update time of TensorRT engines once TensorFlow models are trained, and to allow both frameworks to run simultaneously on the same platform, without stepping on each other's toes. A time-memory trade-off was also found due to the small amount of memory available on the embedded platform.

2.4 Performance

The final performance of the emotion detection system is about 10 FPS and the overall learning time for happy and surprise emotions learnt together is about 45 s. There is an increase in emotion detection accuracy of 25% on average compared to a system that does not use a specific continual learning algorithm to overcome catastrophic forgetting.

2.5 Execution

Please see the demonstration video at https://youtu.be/XFVE7vq3iGk.

3 Technology

3.1 System Hardware

The system is running on NVIDIA Jetson Nano platform, featuring 128-core GPU and 4 GB memory capacity. It is a very popular low-cost embedded platform with great GPU performances, but with a relatively small amount of memory. The platform is enclosed in a metal casing equipped with IMX219-77 camera producing 1280 × 720 pixel resolution images. Finally, a monitor is connected to the HDMI output to display emotion detection results.

3.2 System Architecture

The system pipeline for emotion detection is shown on Fig. 1. The face detector is responsible for detecting faces in the camera image. Face images are cropped and resized to grayscale images of 197 × 197 pixels. These images are then fed into the features extractor that outputs feature vectors of size 2048, which are normalized and used by the emotion detector to recognize the associated emotions.

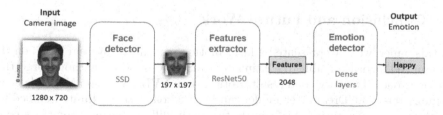

Fig. 1. Pipeline for emotion detection

The face detector model is frozen and provided by OpenCV. It was created with SSD framework [5] using ResNet10 like architecture and trained in Caffe framework. Camera images are scaled to 533 × 300 pixels, knowing that the neural network was initially trained on 300 × 300 pixel images.

The features extractor model is frozen and based on a ResNet50 architecture trained on FER2013 database by Stanford University [3] in which the emotion classifier has been removed. We evaluated the embedded emotion detector trained offline to recognize the seven emotions with this feature extractor and obtained the same accuracy value of 73% on the test set.

The emotion detector model is a hybrid architecture [6] able of replicating the input (like an auto-encoder) and classifying facial emotion in a single inference. It is composed of one input layer of size 2048, one dense layer with 1024 neurons and ReLu activation function, one 50% dropout layer to avoid over-fitting, and one output layer of size 2055 (2048 features replicated and 7 emotions classified) with a sigmoid activation function. This model was trained on FER2013 database where happy and surprise faces have been removed from the training set.

3.3   System Interface

A menu displayed in the execution window allows user to select the desired mode of operation from the three presented below.

The first mode of operation is dedicated to the recognition of live emotions of at most 10 faces simultaneously detected in the camera image. The monitor displays the detected faces enclosed by emotion-annotated bounding boxes.

The second mode of operation is dedicated to generate the "learning dataset" for the continual learning of emotions by the emotion detector. For each emotion to be learnt, several images are captured by the camera, complemented by few images from FER2013 dataset so that the emotion detector can generalize well while learning the new emotions. To preserve privacy, only the associated features are computed and stored in memory.

The third mode of operation is dedicated to learn new emotions. It implements the Dream Net algorithm proposed by Mainsant et al. [6]. The particularity of this model is that it does not store any example of emotions previously learnt because it is able to generate pseudo-examples that represent the past knowledge. New emotions are learnt using these pseudo-examples and the new examples available in the "learning dataset".

4   Conclusion and Future Work

In this paper, we have presented a face emotion recognition system based on the Dream Net algorithm, able to continually learn new emotions without forgetting previous ones. The very good results obtained on NVIDIA Jetson Nano platform demonstrate that Dream Net model can be used on resource-limited embedded platforms in order to benefit from its two main differentiating properties compared to other continual learning models, namely the agnosticity of the data and the preservation of privacy. Future work will be about bringing personalization and multimodality to the system.

Acknowledgements. This demonstrator was developed within the scope of the Carnot MIEL (Multimodal and Incremental Embedded Learning) project. It was also partially supported by MIAI @ Grenoble Alpes (ANR-19-P3IA-0003).

References

1. TensorFlow framework. https://www.tensorflow.org
2. TensorRT framework. https://developer.nvidia.com/tensorrt
3. Khanzada, A., Bai, C., Celepcikay, F.T.: Facial expression recognition with deep learning (2020)
4. Li, S., Deng, W.: Deep facial expression recognition: a survey (2020)
5. Liu, W., et al.: SSD: single shot multibox detector. In: Leibe, B., Matas, J., Sebe, N., Welling, M. (eds.) ECCV 2016. LNCS, vol. 9905, pp. 21–37. Springer, Cham (2016). https://doi.org/10.1007/978-3-319-46448-0_2
6. Mainsant, M., Solinas, M., Reyboz, M., Godin, C., Mermillod, M.: Dream net: a privacy preserving continual learning model for face emotion recognition. In: 2021 9th International Conference on Affective Computing and Intelligent Interaction Workshops and Demos (ACIIW). IEEE (2021)
7. Revina, I., Emmanuel, W.S.: A survey on human face expression recognition techniques (2018)
8. Wu, C.H., Lin, J.C., Wei, W.L.: Survey on audiovisual emotion recognition: databases, features, and data fusion strategies (2014)

CAGE: A Hybrid Framework for Closed-Domain Conversational Agents

Edward Burgin[✉], Sourav Dutta, Haytham Assem, and Raj Nath Patel

Huawei Research, Dublin, Ireland
{edwardburgin,sourav.dutta2,raj.nath.patel}@huawei.com,
hithsala@amazon.co.uk

Abstract. Current *conversational agents* are primarily designed to answer user queries based on structured pre-defined utterance-response pairs. While *question-answering (QA) systems* extracts potential answers, to queries, from unstructured texts. However, in domain-specific settings, manual creation of query-response pairs is expensive, and domain adaptation of QA platforms is crucial. To this end, we propose CAGE, a "hybrid" conversational framework seamlessly integrating structured and unstructured data to obtain precise answers for user queries – improving *user experience* and *quality-of-service*. We describe the different components combining *query matching* and *extractive question answering*, and demonstrate the multi-lingual chatbot interface provided to a user.

1 Introduction

Chatbots or "virtual agents" provide a natural dialogue interface to users, simplifying information search and assisting in domain-specific applications. As such, chatbots are increasingly used in healthcare [8], ecommerce [6], public administration [9], and education [1] – involving (i) domain understanding; (ii) anticipating question styles; (iii) query responses; and (iv) multi-linguality. This makes it more challenging than open-domain digital assistants like Google Voice, Alexa, Siri and Cortana.

Traditionally chatbots relied on IR [9] on curated FAQ utterance-responses [5] – depicting high precision, but poor recall due to vocabulary mismatch and domain specificity. Machine reading comprehension (MRC) extracts answer spans from unstructured texts [14], providing flexibility in terms of data and coverage, but lacks contextual answer generation. Light-weight chatbots using MRC [13] have been widely incorporated [10]. Unfortunately, limited efforts exist towards combining the above techniques [4], and separate channels are proposed like Google DialogFlow (chatbot and knowledge connector), Amazon Services (Lex and Kendra) and Microsoft Azure (LUIS and QnAMaker). This paper presents a *hybrid and unified* chatbot prototype for integration of both structured and unstructured domain-specific data, to seamlessly answer diverse user queries.

M.-R. Amini et al. (Eds.): ECML PKDD 2022, LNAI 13718, pp. 636–640, 2023.
https://doi.org/10.1007/978-3-031-26422-1_46

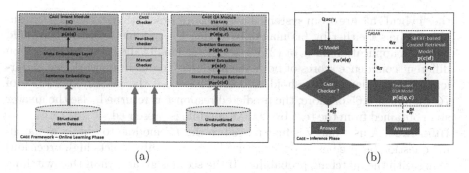

(a)   (b)

Fig. 1. (a) System architecture of CAGE with *IC* Module, QASAR Module, and Checker Module. (b) Interaction flow diagram of CAGE at interaction (inference) time.

2   CAGE Framework

We now introduce our *hybrid* conversational framework, *Closed-Domain Conversational AGEnt (*CAGE*)* (Fig. 1a). CAGE comprises **3** components, as described next.

- **Intent Classification Module (*IC*)** – This module trains a supervised learning model for *User Question Classification* based on a pre-defined structured query-response dataset, specifying questions (with a few paraphrases) along with curated answers. The trained model is used to classify an end-user's query, during inference, to one of the pre-defined questions. Internally, the *IC* module utilizes several *multi-lingual sentence encoders* to map questions into high-dimensional dense vector representations. The embeddings from the encoders are concatenated to obtain *"query meta-embedding"*. Finally, a shallow Multi-Layer Perceptron (MLP) with two hidden layer with ReLU non-linear activations and a softmax layer is used for classification. Specifically, the *IC* module implements the approach of [11], with the underlying "frozen" sentence encoders (instead of fine-tuning) to achieve (1) few-shot learning and (2) inexpensive compute requirement – making CAGE suitable for deployment as an online cloud based chatbot service using Amazon Lex or Google DialogFlow.
- **EQA Module (QASAR)** – This module fine-tunes a QA model for *self-supervised domain adaptation* by automatically generating *context-question-answer* triples from domain-specific unstructured documents. We employ pre-trained T5 model [12] for *self-learning*, wherein extracted paragraphs from a document are used to generate possible questions and corresponding answer spans – providing a set of triples that forms the synthetic training dataset for CAGE. These triples are then used to fine-tune a pre-trained SpanBERT QA model [7] for adapting it to our application domain. This provides a fully self-supervised approach with enhanced performance, especially for closed-domain datasets [2]. Currently, multi-linguality is supported via machine translation, however a multi-lingual QA model can be easily incorporated.
- **Checker Module** – The final module drives the integration for seamless transition between the *IC* and QASAR modules to extract the best answer – enabling

the "hybrid" nature of our system. The appropriate selection/triggering threshold can be set either by (a) manually setting the module selection threshold based on application data, or (2) F1-score on a small validation data based on different confidence scores of both the modules. In our framework, we empirically set the default threshold to 0.65. That is, if the match confidence of *IC* module is 0.65 or more, the predicted response is returned, else the answer span obtained from the text by QASAR module is presented.

Inference: A user query is first passed to the *IC* module to obtain a matching question (as prediction on structured data typically depicts high precision) along with the matching probability. If the score is greater than the switching threshold, the matched answer is returned. Otherwise, the query is routed to QASAR (to extract a possibly answer) along with a set of sentences (i.e., context) from the text, that might have the answer – to obtain the answer text span from QASAR. As a fall-back policy, if the EQA module is also not confident, the chatbot requests the user to rephrase the query (or flags it as out-of-scope).

3   CAGE System Demonstration

We now present snapshots of user interaction for our multi-lingual CAGE chatbot platform. CAGE was integrated with the popular *BotFront* dialogue system interface (based on Meteor app) provided by Rasa [3]. We showcase on *three* data sources – (a) chitchat data with various "small talk" and greetings; (ii) structured FAQ data on Huawei Mobile Service (HMS) with 50 different questions (and paraphrasings); and (iii) unstructured text description of HMS applications obtained from the web.

In Fig. 2(a), we show a typical user interaction wherein the user initially *greets* the system followed by a domain pertinent question. We see that our system *correctly matches*

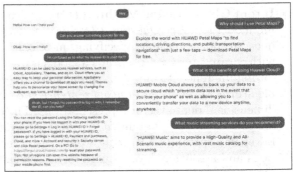

(a) User interaction with inter-play between *IC* and QASAR modules.

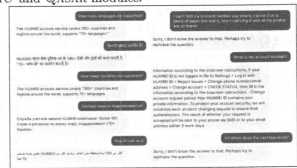

(b) Multi-lingual user query answering, rephrasing, and fall-back policy.

Fig. 2. System demonstration of CAGE framework.

the user question to the pre-defined FAQ, even for colloquially phrased user queries. Further, we see factoid-based questions are efficiently answered by the QASAR module, wherein information present in the text are retrieved along with a *longer context* for readability.

For example, for the question *'How many languages are supported?"*, CAGE is seen to report: `The Huawei account service covers 190+ countries ...`, supports `''70+ languages''`. Here, the text span in quotes provides the direct answer, while the entire response presents a well-contexted human readable response. In fact, even seemingly *objective questions* like *" Why should I use Petal Maps?"* are well answered by CAGE (`to find locations, driving directions, and public transport navigations` in this case). In Fig. 2(b), we depict the multi-linguality and *out-of-scope* scenarios of our framework. Overall, we showcase our *usability, performance and quality-of-service*. The inference time was typically less than 500 ms.

Note, a standalone question matching or question answering system would fail for many of the above queries. Thus, we empirically compare the performance on a small annotated HMS data sample; with questions half of which are answerable from the text, while the others are related to pre-defined questions. We use *F1 score* to gauge the performance, with: *True Positive* (TP) for correct answer, *True Negative* (TN) for null returned on unanswerable question, *False Positive* (FP) for incorrect matching, and *False Negative* (FN) if null response is given to a true answer.

Table 1. Accuracy results on small HMS dataset.

Method	P	R	F1
EQA	0.78	1.00	0.88
Intent	0.89	1.00	0.94
CAGE	**0.93**	1.00	**0.97**

From Table 1, we observe that our "hybrid" CAGE framework performs better than the classification and EQA system individually, precisely answering both types of user questions. For detailed results of *IC* and QASAR modules on other datasets, please refer to [2,11]. A short demo of CAGE can be found at https://youtu.be/PIzwbrmM4UU.

4   Conclusion

This paper presented CAGE, a novel *multi-lingual "hybrid"* deployable conversational system seamlessly coupling both question matching from *structured* data as well as extractive answering from *unstructured* data. CAGE combines *few-shot classification* with *domain-adapted answering* to provide high efficiency, improving quality-of-service.

References

1. Adamopoulou, E., Moussiades, L.: An overview of chatbot technology. In: AIAI, pp. 373–383 (2020)
2. Assem, H., Sarkar, R., Dutta, S.: QASAR: self-supervised learning framework for extractive question answering. In: IEEE Big Data, pp. 1797–1808 (2021)

3. Bocklisch, T., Faulkner, J., Pawlowski, N., Nichol, A.: Rasa: open source language understanding and dialogue management. In: NIPS Workshop on Conversational AI (2017)

4. Gapanyuk, Y., Chernobrovkin, S., Leontiev, A., Latkin, I., Belyanova, M., Morozenkov, O.: A hybrid chatbot system combining QA and knowledge-base approaches. In: AIST (2018)

5. Hussain, S., Sianaki, O., Ababneh, N.: A survey on conversational agents/chatbots classification and design techniques. In: Barolli, L., Takizawa, M., Xhafa, F., Enokido, T. (eds.) Web, Artificial Intelligence and Network Applications. WAINA 2019. AISC, vol. 927, pp. 946–956. Springer, Cham (2019). https://doi.org/10.1007/978-3-030-15035-8_93

6. Manzano, M.D.I., Lopez, N.V., Gonzalez, N.A., Rodriguez, C.C.: Implementation of chatbot in online commerce, and open innovations. J. Open Innov. Tech. Market Complx. **7**(2) (2021)

7. Joshi, M., Chen, D., Liu, Y., Weld, D.S., Zettlemoyer, L., Levy, O.: Spanbert: improving pre-training by representing and predicting spans. TACL **8**, 64–77 (2020)

8. Jovanovic, M., Baez, M., Casati, F.: Chatbots as conversational healthcare services. IEEE Internet Comput. **25**(3), 44–51 (2021)

9. Lommatzsch, A., Katins, J.: An information retrieval-based approach for building intuitive chatbots for large knowledge bases. In: LWDA (2019)

10. McTear, M.: Conversational AI: Dialogue Systems. Conversational Agents and Chatbots, Morgan and Claypool (2021)

11. Patel, R.N., Burgin, E., Assem, H., Dutta, S.: Efficient multi-lingual sentence classification framework with sentence meta encoders. In: IEEE Big Data, pp. 1889–1899 (2021)

12. Raffel, C., et al.: Exploring the limits of transfer learning with a unified t2t transformer. arXiv:1910.10683 (2019)

13. Yan, Z., et al.: DocChat: an IR approach for chatbot engines using unstructured documents. In: ACL, pp. 516–525 (2016)

14. Zhang, Z., Zhao, H., Wang, R.: Machine reading comprehension: the role of contextualized language models and beyond. Comput. Linguist. **1**(1), 1–51 (2020)

Cloud-Based Real-Time Molecular Screening Platform with MolFormer

Brian Belgodere, Vijil Chenthamarakshan, Payel Das, Pierre Dognin,
Toby Kurien, Igor Melnyk, Youssef Mroueh, Inkit Padhi, Mattia Rigotti,
Jarret Ross[✉], Yair Schiff, and Richard A. Young

IBM Research, Cambridge, USA
rossja@us.ibm.com

Abstract. With the prospect of automating a number of chemical tasks
with high fidelity, chemical language processing models are emerging at
a rapid speed. Here, we present a cloud-based real-time platform that
allows users to virtually screen molecules of interest. For this purpose,
molecular embeddings inferred from a recently proposed large chemical
language model, named MolFormer, are leveraged. The platform currently supports three tasks: nearest neighbor retrieval, chemical space
visualization, and property prediction. Based on the functionalities of
this platform and results obtained, we believe that such a platform can
play a pivotal role in automating chemistry and chemical engineering
research, as well as assist in drug discovery and material design tasks. A
demo of our platform is provided at www.ibm.biz/molecular_demo.

Keywords: Molecular screening · Drug discovery · Cloud platform

1 Introduction

Machine learning (ML) offers high throughput material exploration that is more
efficient than high-cost quantum chemical/empirical force-field calculations and
wet lab evaluations. In this work, we present a cloud-based platform for real-time
virtual screening of molecules, which uses a general-purpose deep learning model
of large organic small molecule libraries. Specifically, our Molecular Explorer
Platform builds on our previous work "MolFormer", a large, masked chemical language model trained on over 1.1 billion molecular string representations
known as SMILES (see [11] for details). MolFormer provides representations for
molecules that we showcase here in a platform enabling neighbor search, chemical
space visualization, and property prediction for molecules of interest.

2 Real-Time Screening Platform

Given a backend dataset, such as PubChem [4] or FlavorDB [1], we start by
embedding this database through MolFormer and obtain a latent representation of 768 dimensions. To index the database for nearest neighbor search, we

B. Belgodere, V. Chenthamarakshan, P. Das, P. Dognin, T. Kurien, I. Melnyk, Y.
Mroueh, I. Padhi, M. Rigotti, J. Ross, Y. Schiff, R. A. Young—Equal contribution.

M.-R. Amini et al. (Eds.): ECML PKDD 2022, LNAI 13718, pp. 641–644, 2023.
https://doi.org/10.1007/978-3-031-26422-1_47

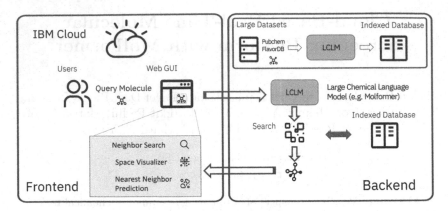

Fig. 1. Diagram of our molecular explorer platform.

start by reducing the dimensionality of MolFormer representations using Discrete Cosine Transform to 128 dimensions. We then leverage the approximate nearest neighbor search library HNSWlib [8]. with hyperparameters calibrated so that retrieval would be faster than 10 milliseconds per query with a recall of 0.99 (Fig. 1).

Our molecular platform consists of a frontend GUI that enables 3 critical molecule screening functionalities: 1) neighbor search, 2) visualizing latent space of molecules using t-SNE visualization in 2D, and 3) nearest neighbor property prediction using Sklearn [10] for moderately sized datasets and FAISS [3] for large-scale predictions. User queries are provided in the form of a line separated list or .txt file of molecule SMILES strings. An implementation of MolFormer running on OpenShift on IBM Cloud enables real-time feedforward embedding of SMILES strings, which are normalized using the RDKit library [5,6]. The obtained MolFormer representation is subsequently used to query the indexed backend database, which returns the user provided N nearest neighbors along with molecular properties, such as logP, QED, and weight, which are computed on-the-fly using RDKit. Optional call to PubChem's similarity search API is provided in our user interface allowing the user to compare it to MolFormer similarity. If a user provides property labels for each SMILES string, such as toxicity or flavor (see use case 2), the molecular platform enables visualization of the embedding space color-coded by labels in t-SNE 2-dimensional space. Finally, nearest neighbor prediction functionalities using known properties of the backend index database are also provided, along with predictions for these properties of query molecules and graphical visualization of the results.

Use Case 1: Similarity Search Among Known Drug Molecules. A typical task that arises in molecule screening/discovery is to identify similar molecules in existing chemical libraries. This is a frequent use case for medicinal chemists, for example. Our molecule explorer platform allows users to retrieve similar molecules from PubChem using the PubChem API [4] and MolFormer

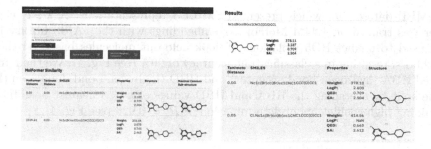

Fig. 2. Use Case 1: nearest neighbor search in large chemical embedding space.

embeddings. To achieve this, we index over 100 Million molecules from pubchem embedded in the MolFormer latent space. As an example, we show the neighbor retrieval results for known drug molecules (Table S4 from [2]) obtained using the platform in Fig. 2. The maximal common subgraph of the query molecule and closest molecules are also shown allowing a user to understand the key differences between the query molecules and its closest neighbors.

Use Case 2: Flavor Molecules Screening. The molecule explorer platform also allows a user to upload a set of molecules along with a their corresponding class (property) labels and visualize their chemical space. The user can visually explore the t-SNE [7] representation of those molecules obtained using MolFormer embeddings and check if the resulting chemical space captures the distribution of class labels for a particular application. Alternatively, a k-NN classifier can be trained on the MolFormer embeddings and performance characteristics of the classifier can be visualized as a confusion matrix. We show the application of these techniques to

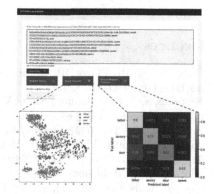

Fig. 3. Use Case 2: visualization of unsupervised MolFormer Embeddings in t-SNE space and separation of flavor molecules in that space.

molecules with different flavor descriptions from [1]. The flavor database consists of 25,595 individual flavor molecules with up to 43 different attributes. 4 basic flavors were chosen for evaluation; bitter, sweet, sour, and savory. Figure 3 shows that our chemical space map captures the different flavors and provides excellent predictive performance.

Use Case 3: Drug-like Molecules Screening. Lastly, we predict the conformity to the RO5 (Lipinski rule of five) of 1.8M molecules out of ∼2M from the

CheMBL dataset [9], which presented SMILES representations. A k-NN classifier was trained on 1.44M MolFormer embeddings with the FAISS library [3] and used to predict RO5 violations of 360k held-out molecules based on their neighbors, resulting in a classification accuracy of 90% (see Fig. 4). We then predicted HBA (hydrogen bond acceptor) and HBD (hydrogen bond donor) on the same split by averaging the HBA and HBD values of $k = 3$ nearest neighbors, obtaining high coefficients of determination of $R^2 = 0.926$ (see Fig. 4).

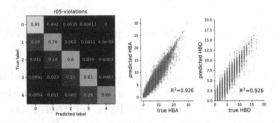

Fig. 4. Use Case 3: Retrieval of r05-violations of 1.8M drug-like molecules with 1-NN gives an average holdout prediction accuracy of 0.90 (left). HBA and HBD are also predicted with high accuracy ($R^2 = 0.926$ for both) by $k = 3$ NN-Regression (right).

References

1. Garg, N., et al.: FlavorDB: a database of flavor molecules. Nucleic Acids Res. **46**(D1), D1210–D1216 (2017)
2. Hoffman, S.C., Chenthamarakshan, V., Wadhawan, K., Chen, P.Y., Das, P.: Optimizing molecules using efficient queries from property evaluations. Nat. Mach. Intell. **4**(1), 21–31 (2022). https://doi.org/10.1038/s42256-021-00422-y
3. Johnson, J., Douze, M., Jégou, H.: Billion-scale similarity search with GPUs. IEEE Trans. Big Data **7**(3), 535–547 (2019)
4. Kim, S., et al.: PubChem in 2021: new data content and improved web interfaces. Nucleic Acids Res. **49**(D1), D1388–D1395 (2020). https://doi.org/10.1093/nar/gkaa971
5. Landrum, G.: RDKit: A software suite for cheminformatics, computational chemistry, and predictive modeling (2013)
6. Landrum, G.: Rdkit: Open-source cheminformatics (2013). https://www.rdkit.org
7. van der Maaten, L., Hinton, G.: Visualizing data using t-sne. J. Mach. Learn. Res. **9**(86), 2579–2605 (2008), http://jmlr.org/papers/v9/vandermaaten08a.html
8. Malkov, Y.A., Yashunin, D.A.: Efficient and robust approximate nearest neighbor search using hierarchical navigable small world graphs. IEEE Trans. Pattern Anal. Mach. Intell. **42**(4), 824–836 (2018)
9. Mendez, D., et al.: ChEMBL: towards direct deposition of bioassay data. Nucleic Acids Res. **47**(D1), D930–D940 (2018)
10. Pedregosa, F., et al.: Scikit-learn: machine learning in python. J. Mach. Learn. Res. **12**, 2825–2830 (2011)
11. Ross, J., Belgodere, B., Chenthamarakshan, V., Padhi, I., Mroueh, Y., Das, P.: Do large scale molecular language representations capture important structural information? (2021)

ImbalancedLearningRegression - A Python Package to Tackle the Imbalanced Regression Problem

Wenglei Wu[1] (ID), Nicholas Kunz[2] (ID), and Paula Branco[1(✉)] (ID)

[1] Faculty of Engineering, University of Ottawa, Ottawa, ON, Canada
{wwu077,pbranco}@uottawa.ca
[2] College of Engineering, Cornell University, Ithaca, NY, USA
nhk37@cornell.edu

Abstract. This package helps Python users address imbalanced regression problems. Popular Python packages exist for imbalanced classification. However, there is still little Python support for imbalanced regression. Imbalanced regression is a well-known problem that occurs across domains, where a continuous target variable is poorly represented on ranges that are important to the end-user. Here, a re-sampling strategy is applied to modify the distribution of the target variable, biasing it towards the end-user interests so that downstream learning algorithms can be trained on the most relevant cases. The package provides an easy-to-use and extensible implementation of eight state-of-the-art re-sampling methods for regression, including four under-sampling and four over-sampling techniques. Code related to this paper is available at: https://github.com/paobranco/ImbalancedLearningRegression.

1 Introduction

Imbalanced domains are characterized by having an imbalanced target variable. A model trained on an imbalanced data set cannot focus on the important regions and thus is not able to predict well the most important rare cases [2]. Research has been more intensive on the imbalanced classification problem, with a vast number of re-sampling techniques being proposed. However, this issue also occurs in regression tasks where the target variable is continuous. To define the important and unimportant ranges of the target variable, we use the notion of relevance function that can be either estimated from the data distribution or explicitly provided by the end-user [12]. In the automatic method, low-density ranges are mapped to high relevance values while high-density ranges are mapped to low relevance values. The formed ranges can be thought of as different minority (important) and majority (unimportant) classes, in a classification setting.

Implementations of a high diversity of re-sampling techniques for class imbalance are available in Python (imbalanced-learn [10]) and R (imbalance [5], UBL [1]). However, this is not the case for imbalanced regression for which some methods exist in R (UBL [1]), but only one package exists in Python that implements a single over-sampling method: SMOGN [3,9]. The proposed Python package ImbalancedLearningRegression fills this gap.

© The Author(s), under exclusive license to Springer Nature Switzerland AG 2023
M.-R. Amini et al. (Eds.): ECML PKDD 2022, LNAI 13718, pp. 645–648, 2023.
https://doi.org/10.1007/978-3-031-26422-1_48

2   The `ImbalancedLearningRegression` Package

Our package provides different re-sampling techniques for the imbalanced regression problem in Python based on the data analysis libraries `pandas`, `numpy`, and `scikit-learn`. At the current stage of development, eight re-sampling methods have been implemented, including four over-sampling methods: Random Over-sampling (RO) [4,11], SMOTE [14], Introduction of Gaussian Noise (GN) [4], ADASYN [8]; and four under-sampling methods: Random Under-sampling (RU), Condensed Nearest Neighbor (CNN) [7], TomekLinks [13], Edited Nearest Neighbor (ENN) [15]. These methods perform differently in terms of data manipulation, execution time, and the number of samples created or deleted. It is up to the user to select an appropriate method for re-sampling a specific domain. The representation of the data sets through `pandas` data frame in `ImbalancedLearningRegression` gives the end-user the flexibility to apply any pre-processing steps before and/or after the use of `ImbalancedLearningRegression`.

For the sake of usability, only two parameters are required to be specified to execute a re-sampling method in the package: (i) the data set in the form of a pandas data frame, and (ii) the name of the target variable. The remaining parameters have default values that globally correspond to the following assumptions: the less dense target variable regions are the most important ones, and the user's goal is to balance the important and unimportant cases. End-users can change any parameter to control the behavior of the re-sampling strategy. `ImbalancedLearningRegression` is organized into several modules and is therefore consistent, maintainable, and extensible. Future collaborators can take advantage of its structure to implement improvements or add more re-sampling techniques for the imbalanced regression problem. The package can be used on any OS supported by Python, including Windows, macOS, and Linux. It is fully open-source and is available under a GNU General Public License v3 (GPLv3). The source code can be found at https://github.com/paobranco/ImbalancedLearningRegression, and an introduction video is available at https://youtu.be/BanN904NyX0. The documentation can be found at https://imbalancedlearningregression.readthedocs.io/en/latest. The package can be easily installed via PyPI[1] using `pip install ImbalancedLearningRegression`.

3   Some Application Examples

We present a basic use case of re-sampling with the Ames Housing data set [6] to show how simple it is to use `ImbalancedLearningRegression`. This data set illustrates a regression task where `SalePrice` is the continuous target variable. We applied four different re-sampling methods with default parameter settings. The complete code of execution is shown below.

---

[1] https://pypi.org/project/ImbalancedLearningRegression/.

```
import ImbalancedLearningRegression as iblr
import pandas as pd

housing = pd.read_csv("housing.csv")
housing_smote = iblr.smote(data = housing, y = "SalePrice")
housing_gn = iblr.gn(data = housing, y = "SalePrice")
housing_cnn = iblr.cnn(data = housing, y = "SalePrice")
housing_enn = iblr.enn(data = housing, y = "SalePrice")
```

The first two lines import our package `ImbalancedLearningRegression`, as well as the data analysis library **pandas**. The following line loads the data from a file to a standard **pandas** data frame. Each one of the next four lines applies a re-sampling method available in the package. In this example, we selected SMOTE, GN, CNN, and ENN methods. Two parameters are necessary to be specified to run the techniques: the instance of the **pandas** data frame is assigned to the parameter **data**, and a string of the name of the target variable is assigned to the parameter y that represents the target variable. Users can also control the degree of re-sampling by setting the parameter **samp_method**, or control the threshold of classifying majority and minority by setting the parameter **rel_thres**. For more details regarding the optional parameters, please refer to the package documentation.

The original Ames Housing data set contains 1460 samples. After applying SMOTE, GN, CNN, and ENN, the number of samples in the modified data sets changed to 1974, 1459, 401, and 1428 respectively. Figure 1 shows the density distribution of our data set before and after applying the four different re-sampling techniques. We observe that the distribution of the Ames Housing data set changes considerably when SMOTE, GN, and CNN are applied, whereas it is only slightly affected when ENN is used.

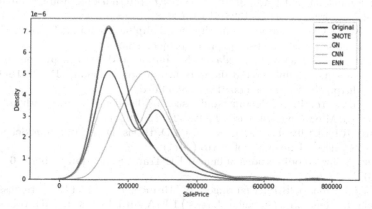

Fig. 1. Density distribution of Ames Housing data set before and after applying four re-sampling methods using `ImbalancedLearningRegression` package.

4   Conclusion

Here we introduced the `ImbalancedLearningRegression` package that allows the application of multiple re-sampling techniques to address the imbalanced problem in regression tasks in a Python environment. This package provides an easy-to-use, extensible, and freely available implementation of solutions for this problem.

Acknowledgements. We would like to thank Xinzi Hu, Lingyi Kong, and Chengen Lyu for their contributions to the re-sampling implementations.

References

1. Branco, P., Ribeiro, R.P., Torgo, L.: UBL: an R package for utility-based learning (2016). https://arxiv.org/abs/1604.08079
2. Branco, P., Torgo, L., Ribeiro, R.P.: A survey of predictive modeling on imbalanced domains. ACM Comput. Surv. (CSUR) **49**(2), 1–50 (2016)
3. Branco, P., Torgo, L., Ribeiro, R.P.: SMOGN: a pre-processing approach for imbalanced regression. In: First International Workshop on Learning with Imbalanced Domains: Theory and Applications, pp. 36–50. PMLR (2017)
4. Branco, P., Torgo, L., Ribeiro, R.P.: Pre-processing approaches for imbalanced distributions in regression. Neurocomputing **343**, 76–99 (2019)
5. Cordón, I., García, S., Fernández, A., Herrera, F.: Imbalance: Oversampling algorithms for imbalanced classification in r. Knowl.-Based Syst. **161**, 329–341 (2018). https://doi.org/10.1016/j.knosys.2018.07.035
6. De Cock, D.: Ames, iowa: alternative to the boston housing data as an end of semester regression project. J. Stat. Educ. **19**(3) (2011)
7. Hart, P.: The condensed nearest neighbor rule (corresp.). IEEE Trans. Inf. Theory **14**(3), 515–516 (1968)
8. He, H., Bai, Y., Garcia, E.A., Li, S.: ADASYN: adaptive synthetic sampling approach for imbalanced learning. In: 2008 IEEE International Joint Conference on Neural Networks, pp. 1322–1328. IEEE (2008)
9. Kunz, N.: SMOGN: synthetic minority over-sampling technique for regression with gaussian noise (2020). https://pypi.org/project/smogn
10. Lemaître, G., Nogueira, F., Aridas, C.K.: Imbalanced-learn: a python toolbox to tackle the curse of imbalanced datasets in machine learning. JMLR **18**(17), 1–5 (2017), http://jmlr.org/papers/v18/16-365.html
11. Menardi, G., Torelli, N.: Training and assessing classification rules with imbalanced data. Data Mining Knowl. Disc. **28**(1), 92–122 (2014)
12. Ribeiro, R.P.: Utility-based regression. Ph.D. thesis, Dep. Computer Science, Faculty of Sciences - University of Porto (2011)
13. Tomek, I.: Two modifications of cnn. IEEE Trans. Syst. Man Cybern. **6**, 769–772 (1976)
14. Torgo, L., Ribeiro, R.P., Pfahringer, B., Branco, P.: SMOTE for regression. In: Correia, L., Reis, L.P., Cascalho, J. (eds.) EPIA 2013. LNCS (LNAI), vol. 8154, pp. 378–389. Springer, Heidelberg (2013). https://doi.org/10.1007/978-3-642-40669-0_33
15. Wilson, D.L.: Asymptotic properties of nearest neighbor rules using edited data. IEEE Trans. Syst. Man Cybern. **3**, 408–421 (1972)

A Light Weight Cardiac Monitoring System for On-device ECG Analysis

Rohan Banerjee$^{(\boxtimes)}$ and Avik Ghose

TCS Research, Tata Consultancy Services, Mumbai, India
{rohan.banerjee,avik.ghose}@tcs.com

Abstract. In this paper, we propose a demonstrable prototype of an on-device cardiac monitoring system comprising bio-sensor module and a low-powered microcontroller. Apart from measuring physiological vitals, the proposed system can classify abnormal heart rhythms on the microcontroller itself for low-cost 24 × 7 unobtrusive monitoring. A Convolutional Neural network (CNN) is duly optimized to run on the constrained hardware platform for identification of normal, Atrial Fibrillation (AF) and other abnormal rhythms from single-lead electrocardiogram (ECG) signals. The system is successfully verified on offline dataset. It also reports promising accuracy when deployed for real-time health monitoring.

Keywords: TinyML · CNN · ECG analysis · Real-time system

1 Introduction

In recent times, the healthcare industry has seen a rapid transformation towards automation owing to the proliferation of artificial intelligence (AI) and machine learning techniques. AI-based decision support systems are even used in the intensive care units of the hospitals for various applications in cardiology like anomaly detection or prediction of intermittent abnormal rhythms from 24 × 7 electrocardiogram (ECG) recordings which are difficult to analyze manually. Machine learning algorithms are resource-hungry and hence large machine learning jobs are typically done in the cloud. Streaming of healthcare data via internet to the cloud has security and privacy risks. There may be delay in response due to network latency. The recent trend is to optimize large machine learning models to effectively run on low-powered microcontrollers.

Commercial wearable devices like fitness-bands or smartwatches typically communicate with smartphones to offload the machine learning tasks. Although user privacy is preserved, one still needs to carry the smartphone all the time which is inconvenient for continuous monitoring. In this paper, we propose a prototype system for real-time on-device cardiac monitoring using single-lead ECG and Photoplethysmogram (PPG) signals. The system can be used as a portable stand-alone device for personal healthcare and continuous monitoring at home. We design an optimized light weight Convolutional Neural Network (CNN) for ECG classification. The optimized model is ported to a small low-powered microcontroller which

M.-R. Amini et al. (Eds.): ECML PKDD 2022, LNAI 13718, pp. 649–653, 2023.
https://doi.org/10.1007/978-3-031-26422-1_49

directly communicates with the ECG sensor. Apart from predicting Atrial Fibrillation (AF) and other abnormal rhythms which are considered as early signs of a cardiac arrest, the proposed system measures heart rate and blood oxygen saturation level (SpO2) from PPG with high accuracy.

2   Proposed System for Health Monitoring

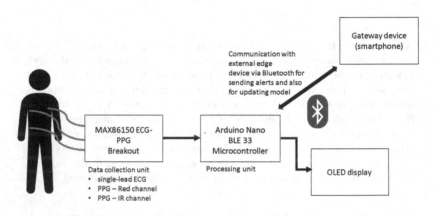

Fig. 1. Block diagram of proposed on-device health monitoring system

Figure 1 shows a high-level block diagram of our proposed on-device health monitoring system. MAX86150, an integrated PPG-ECG breakout board is used for getting the data [1]. It can simultaneously record single-lead ECG and two PPG signals using red and infrared optical emitters. Three metal electrodes, connected to the breakout board via 3.5 mm jack are used to record single-lead ECG from a person. The operating voltage is 1.8 V for the chip and 3.3 V for the LEDs. The breakout board communicates with an Arduino Nano BLE 33 Sense microcontroller for processing via I2C interface. The Arduino Nano development board is widely recommended for TinyML applications. It has an operating voltage of 3.3 V. It comes with 32-bit ARM® CORTEX®-M4 processor at a clock frequency of 64 MHz which is powerful enough to run optimized deep learning models for inference. It has 1 MB of flash memory and 256 KB of Random Access memory (RAM). The processed output is displayed on a 128 × 64 OLED display which also communicates with the Arduino board via I2C interface. The Arduino can also communicate with external devices via Bluetooth for sending of recorded data or alert messages and downloading necessary updates.

2.1 Brief Description of the Processing Algorithms

We first define a baseline deep CNN architecture for single-lead ECG classification. Subsequently, the model is optimized for microcontrollers. The baseline CNN has 4 convolutional layers. 32 filters are used in the first convolutional layer and the number of filters gets doubled in every following layer. The kernel dimension is selected as 7×1 for 1D ECG signals. Depthwise separable convolution, proposed in the Mobilenets architecture [3] is used in our network, which reduces the number of computations with a lesser number of trainable parameters for efficiently running the convolution operations on small edge devices. Each convolutional layer is associated with a maxpool layer with a pooling dimension of 2×1. Rectified Linear Unit (ReLU) is used as the activation function. The final feature-map is flattened and applied to a dense layer with 64 neurons followed by a softmax layer for classifying three classes- normal, AF and other abnormal rhythms. Length of an input signal is selected as 9 s for decision making. The baseline CNN is trained on the publicly available PhysioNet challenge 2017 database [2]. Model optimization is done in two steps. First, we apply magnitude-based weight pruning to trim the smaller insignificant weights in the baseline model. The baseline model is retrained in an iterative manner to add 40% of sparsity up to which no significant impact is found on the performance. Finally, we quantize the pruned model weights and activation from 32-bit floating point to 8-bit integer by applying post training quantization. The optimized model is 10x smaller than the baseline model with a size of 95 KB which is small enough to run on the Arduino Nano. TensorFlow 2.8.0 is used to implement the baseline model and the optimization is done using TensorFlow Lite.

Instantaneous heart rate and Sp02 are measured from PPG which measures the volumetric blood flow in blood vessels through optical sensor and photodetector. If b is the number of PPG pulses within a time-frame of T seconds, heart rate (HR) is measured in bpm as, $HR = \frac{b*60}{T}$. SpO2 is highly correlated with the ratio of modulation (R), which is given by, $R = (\frac{AC_R}{DC_R})/(\frac{AC_{IR}}{DC_{IR}})$. AC_R, DC_R, AC_{IR} and DC_{IR} are the AC and DC components of the red and infrared PPG channels. We define an equation, $Sp02 = a * R^2 + b * R + c$. The parameters a, b, c are obtained by fitting a linear regression on an in-house training dataset.

2.2 Deployment on Target Platform

Figure 2(a) shows a snapshot of our prototype system, and a sample waveform of the three simultaneously recorded signals are shown in Fig. 2(b). Three metal electrodes are placed near the chest of a person via disposable pads for recording of ECG. Red and infrared PPG are recorded by placing the tip of right hand index finger on the optical sensor of the PPG-ECG breakout. All three signals are sampled 200 Hz for processing. The Arduino Nano board is powered by a 9 V battery. Raw signals are passed through five-point moving average filter to remove the high frequency noise components. The algorithms run as continuous process. The system has a push button to start and end the process. Heart rate and SpO2 are measured and displayed in every 3 s, whereas ECG classification is

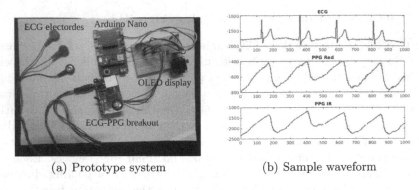

(a) Prototype system   (b) Sample waveform

Fig. 2. Our prototype system for cardiac monitoring

done in every 9 s. Average processing time of a 9 s long ECG data is measured as 185 milli-seconds on the Arduino board. A small video of the system is publicly available for viewing[1].

3   Experimental Results and Conclusion

Currently, TensorFlow Lite has a limited number of supported deep network layers for microcontrollers. Hence, the proposed network is kept simple enough for effective optimization and porting to the target platform. The baseline ECG classifier and the optimized model are evaluated on the PhysioNet Challenge 2017 database. The baseline model yields an average F1-score of 0.82 in detecting the three target classes (normal, AF and other abnormal rhythms) in a 5-fold cross validation, which is similar to other approaches reported in literature [2]. The optimized model is 10× smaller and 6× faster than the baseline model with a mere 1.5% drop in overall classification performance. The end-to-end system is successfully tested on a small population of normal and diseased people with above 90% accuracy. Regarding measurement of heart rate and SpO2, our system reports only 1% mean absolute difference with respect to an FDA-grade commercial pulse-oximeter when tested on 20 different subjects.

The proposed system can be logically extended for predicting other diseases having markers in ECG or PPG. However, PPG and single-lead ECG are highly susceptible to external noise and motion artifacts. As of now, the users are expected to remain still as much as possible while recording the data. We are working on to incorporate on-device noise cancellation at the front-end so that the system can be reliably used for measurements of physiological parameters even during exercises. Another future research aspect is to predict an abnormal cardiac rhythm well in advance which can be very useful in preventive medicine.

---

[1] https://drive.google.com/file/d/1n06lLU98wbudpCcbIzzfI9vAsh5SEErw/view?usp=sharing.

References

1. Max86150 sensor. https://datasheets.maximintegrated.com/en/ds/MAX86150.pdf. Accessed 30 Apr 2022
2. Clifford, G.D., et al.: Af classification from a short single lead ecg recording: the physionet/computing in cardiology challenge 2017. In: 2017 Computing in Cardiology (CinC), pp. 1–4. IEEE (2017)
3. Howard, A.G., et al.: Mobilenets: efficient convolutional neural networks for mobile vision applications. arXiv preprint arXiv:1704.04861 (2017)

Urban Traveller Preference Miner: Modelling Transport Choices with Survey Data Streams

Maciej Grzenda[(✉)][iD], Marcin Luckner[iD], and Przemysław Wrona[iD]

Faculty of Mathematics and Information Science, Warsaw University of Technology,
ul. Koszykowa 75, 00-662 Warszawa, Poland
{M.Grzenda,M.Luckner,P.Wrona}@mini.pw.edu.pl

Abstract. The unprecedented interest in sustainable transport modes for urban areas raises the question of what makes citizens select environmentally friendly transport modes such as public transport rather than private cars. While travel surveys are conducted to document real transport mode choices, they can also shed light on how these choices are made.

In this paper, we demonstrate a system combining survey data with complex information documenting public transport features, as perceived by individual respondents. The system relies on a combination of big data modules to collect vehicle location records and travel planning engines to calculate candidate connection features, including disruptions faced by individuals. Hence a combination of streaming and batch modules is used to transform survey data into instances used to learn classification models. This takes place while taking into account concept drift. Real-life data from the city of Warsaw, including recently collected survey data, location records of trams and buses, and planned and true schedules, are used to demonstrate the system. A video related to this paper is available at https://youtu.be/fTcxUxEMGlk.

Keywords: Public transport · Feature engineering · Stream mining

1 Introduction

The ever growing need for reduced pollution and city congestion raises the question of what makes citizens select sustainable transport modes such as public transport (PT) rather than private cars. The analysis of transport mode selection can rely on declared choices for hypothetical journeys. Another approach involves collecting travel diaries documenting actual journeys and mode choices made for these journeys by citizens during the day(s) preceding the survey. However, such a survey does not elicit the reasons for the choices made, or may collect just the subjective opinions of respondents justifying their choices.

In this work, we demonstrate the Urban Traveller Preference Miner (UTPM) system, which combines data on journeys reported by individuals with features documenting both planned and real transport availability for these journeys.

M.-R. Amini et al. (Eds.): ECML PKDD 2022, LNAI 13718, pp. 654–657, 2023.
https://doi.org/10.1007/978-3-031-26422-1_50

Importantly, citizen preferences clearly evolve over time, which is best exemplified by reduced public transport use due to COVID-19 concerns. Therefore, the UTPM system produces a stream of instances integrating survey data and transport mode features. This stream of instances can be forwarded to online learning modules capable of addressing concept drift, or used for batch learning. In both cases, classifiers are trained and used to predict mobility choices under varied circumstances, such as distance, the median number of transfers needed, and the walking time needed to reach the relevant stops. The role of the UTPM system is to provide data and findings relevant to city planners and other actors such as NGOs interested in promoting sustainable transport. We describe the way the system has been used for the City of Warsaw.

2   The Overview of the System

2.1   Data Collection

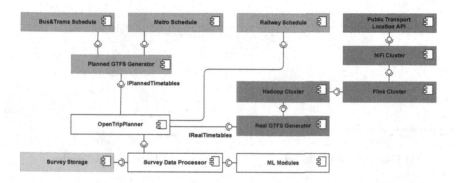

Fig. 1. High level architecture of the Urban Traveller Preference Miner

The UTPM system extends the USE4IoT architecture we proposed in [2] to enable survey data processing and mode choice modelling. Figure 1 presents the outline of the system. First of all, the Planned GTFS Generator downloads schedules and makes them available in General Transit Feed Specification (GTFS)[1] format. In parallel, every 10 s Apache NiFi makes a request to Warsaw Open Data API to get the current location of each of up to 2000 PT vehicles. The Apache Flink-based module is responsible for consuming the stream of raw location records and combining location data with timetables to calculate delays and produce a PT behaviour data stream. Hence, features like average speed, delay at the previous stop, and the difference in delay between current and previous stops are calculated. These results are stored in Apache Hadoop and then used by inter alia Real GTFS Generator for generating real schedules based on true

---

[1] https://gtfs.org.

departure times. Next, actually available public transport connections can be calculated by the OpenTripPlanner engine.

Finally, Survey Storage includes files with survey records. The Survey Data Processor is prepared to handle data from multiple surveys possibly based on heterogeneous schema, i.e. a stream of survey data sets. In particular, the surveys can use varied sets of questions and different wordings of some of the questions, as suggested by the outcomes of previous surveys.

2.2   Preparing Candidate Connections with Journey Planning Engine

OpenTripPlanner[2] (OTP) is a system which we supply *inter alia* with GTFS schedules, road network and elevation data. It calculates the time needed to reach a destination from a given origin at a given time for individual transport modes. It can also determine candidate connections with public transport, including multimodal connections such as connections combining the use of train, metro and bus.

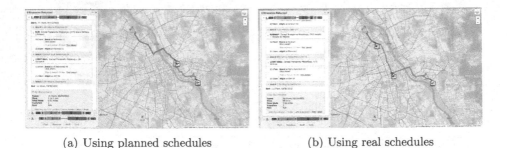

(a) Using planned schedules   (b) Using real schedules

Fig. 2. Sample public transport connections proposed by OTP

Figure 2 presents the two scenarios which we consider in the UTPM system. The first was calculated using official schedules obtained through the Planned GTFS Generator and thus corresponds to the planned behaviour of the PT system. Citizens planning their journeys, including survey respondents, are likely to take such a scenario into account when planning their journeys and making mode choices. The second was created based on real departure times and delays present in the PT behaviour data stream. This reflects the actual experience of travellers including possible disruptions and missed connections. Figure 2 shows that planned and real journeys may vary in travel time, number of transits, and even routes. Such differences bring additional information to the mode choice modelling about passengers' preliminary assumptions and travel experience influencing mode choices.

---

[2] https://www.opentripplanner.org.

2.3   Feature Engineering with Survey Data Processor

The core part of the system is the Survey data processor (SDP), which is responsible for analysing survey responses and preparing data for training classification models. For every data record present in a survey for one individual, it develops a number of composite data records (CDR). One CDR represents one journey made by the individual and includes information coming from the survey and complex aggregated OTP-based information. Out of the different methods of compositing data records from different sources discussed *inter alia* in [1], the method the SDP implements is most similar to deterministic record linkage. However, instead of linking travel data records to predefined data records describing possible PT connections, the SDP module requests such connections from OTP, based both on planned schedules and true departure-based schedules. This is because of the large number of (origin, destination) pairs, which is in the order of the squared number of addresses in the city. The features of possibly many candidate connections as well as alternatives such as the use of cycling only are aggregated to provide one vector of feature values per a CDR.

2.4   Learning Mobility Choices

Both features coming from the survey, such as departure time, and features of matching connections, such as average travel time, necessary walking distance or transfer count, are placed in CDRs. Hence, each CDR includes travel features $\mathbf{x}$ and transport mode y reported by an individual. These records are then used to build classification models. This is in order to predict the transport mode preferred for the journey under different individual, travel and available transport modes features. Both batch learning and stream mining modules can be used to develop prediction models. As real concept drift is likely to occur, i.e. $p(y|\mathbf{x})$ may change with time, one of the options is to use methods capable of adapting their models to such changes. Therefore, SDP makes CDRs available as a stream of instances sorted by the departure date of the journey. The outcomes of mode choice modelling performed by the UTPM system include decision trees and learning curves for stream mining models such as adaptive random forest. Results are based on survey and PT data for the City of Warsaw.

Acknowledgements. This work was supported by the CoMobility project. The CoMobility benefits from a 2.05 million€ grant from Iceland, Liechtenstein and Norway through the EEA Grants. The aim of the project is to provide a package of tools and methods for the co-creation of sustainable mobility in urban spaces.

References

1. Lohr, S.L., Raghunathan, T.E.: Combining survey data with other data sources. Stat. Sci. **32**, 293–312 (2017). https://doi.org/10.1214/16-STS584
2. Luckner, M., Grzenda, M., Kunicki, R., Legierski, J.: IoT architecture for urban data-centric services and applications. ACM Trans. Internet Technol. **20**(3), 1–30 (2020). https://doi.org/10.1145/3396850

Interactive Toolbox for Two-Dimensional Gaussian Mixture Modeling

Michael C. Thrun$^{(\boxtimes)}$ (iD), Quirin Stier, and Alfred Ultsch

Mathematics and Computer Science, Philipps-Universität Marburg, Hans-Meerwein-Straße 6, 35032 Marburg, Germany
mthrun@informatik.uni-marburg.de

Abstract. Research data obtained during economics or human studies experiments often displays a complex distribution. Even in the two-dimensional case, the statistical identification of subgroups in research data poses an analytical challenge. Here we introduce an interactive R-based tool called "AdaptGauss2D". It enables a valid identification of a meaningful multimodal structure in two-dimensional data. With a human-in-the-loop approach, a Gaussian mixture model (GMM) can be fitted to the data. The interactive interface allows a supervised selection of the number and parameters of the GMM based on various visualizations. Integrating a Human-in-the-loop into the process of modeling two-dimensional gaussian mixtures enables the expectation-maximization (EM) algorithm to adapt to more complex GMM compared to the standard non-interactive approach. The work demonstrates that the interactive modeling process for GMM improves the quality of the model in contrast to non-interactive modeling. The improvement is shown using the datasets of EngyTime and a large flow cytometry dataset. The R package "AdaptGauss2D" is available on GitHub https://github.com/Mthrun/AdaptGauss2D.

Keywords: Gaussian mixtures · Human-in-the-loop · Interactive ML

1 Introduction

A Gaussian mixture model (GMM) is a probabilistic model that explains the chance of detecting an event x with probability p with the assumption that underlying data is generated using the weighted sum of a finite number k of normal distributions $N(X|M_i, S_i)$ also known as modes or components, with means M_i and covariance S_i. The weighting w_i determines the relative contribution of each of these normal distributions to the mixture and is the prior probability of occurrence of the modes with $\sum_{i=1}^{k} w_i = 1$. In the two-dimensional case, a k-modal GMM is defined as $p(X|M, S) = \sum_{i=1}^{k} w_i N(X|M_i, S_i)$ where S_i is the 2×2 matrix of covariances, $X = \begin{pmatrix} x_1 \\ x_2 \end{pmatrix}$ and $M_i = \begin{pmatrix} m_1 \\ m_2 \end{pmatrix}$. The GMM calculates a "soft" assignment to the modes with the Bayes theorem, which determines the likelihood of X being allocated to one of the k modes for a given value. Parameter optimization methods such as the expectation-maximization (EM) algorithm [1]

M.-R. Amini et al. (Eds.): ECML PKDD 2022, LNAI 13718, pp. 658–661, 2023.
https://doi.org/10.1007/978-3-031-26422-1_51

are commonly utilized in various domains to fit GMMs to two-dimensional data [2–4]. However, automatic modeling of two-dimensional GMMs does not guarantee accurate findings because the EM algorithm is quite sensitive to initial values [5]. As a result, it is advisable to assess the correctness of the derived GMM model through visual means [6]. Therefore, we propose a human-in-the-loop (HIL) approach for modeling two-dimensional gaussian mixtures. Although commercial software approaches exist that provide some range of interactivity for modeling two-dimensional GMMs (e.g., https://www.originlab.com/fileExchange/details.aspx?fid=472; or https://de.mathworks.com/help/stats/tune-gaussian-mixture-models.html), to the authors' knowledge, no fully interactive user interfaces for two-dimensional GMMs have been published so far. Here, we fully integrate the EM optimization of two-dimensional GMM into the interactive adjustment of EM parameters based on visualizations and automatically estimate the number of modes using [7]. To ease the Human-the-loop (HIL) into our interactive tool, we simplify the EM parameters as described in the next section. The third demonstrates that the proposed system "AdaptGauss2D" can improve the automatic state-of-the-art EM modeling of two-dimensional GMMs.

2 System Description

The interactive tool allows the manual modification of all GMM parameters. In this work, the covariance matrix is approximated with the principal component axes (PCA) to ease interactivity for HIL connecting structure of GMM component to parameter axes and angle. Therefore, we propose to compute the principal component axis with a singular value decomposition (SVD) in the first step. Since a two-dimensional space is used, both the diagonal matrix Σ and the unitary matrices U and V^* from the SVD are square matrices. A second step computes ellipsoids based on the two axes for the two-dimensional case. The angle of the axes can be deducted from the axes' position relative to the cartesian coordinate system. The covariance matrix can be computed in a final third step based on the ellipsoid with a rotation matrix. The first step is the SVD of the matrix M resulting from the EM computation with M, U, Σ, $V^* \in \mathbb{R}^{2 \times 2}$. The square root of the singular values p_1 and p_2 denote the length of the principal component axes. The angles can be computed based on the vectors in matrix U and the standard basis vectors. Furthermore, the orientation can be determined by the smaller angle between the main axis and the first vector of the standard basis using $\alpha = \mathrm{acos}\left(\frac{\langle u_1, e_1 \rangle}{\|u_1\|}\right)$. The main axes and the angle define a unique ellipsoid on the cartesian coordinate system, which can be transformed into a symmetric positive definite matrix. A rotation matrix R needs to be defined based on the priorly computed angle and axes with

$$R = \begin{pmatrix} cos\left(\frac{alpha \cdot \pi}{180}\right) & -sin\left(\frac{alpha \cdot \pi}{180}\right) \\ sin\left(\frac{alpha \cdot \pi}{180}\right) & cos\left(\frac{alpha \cdot \pi}{180}\right) \end{pmatrix} \tag{1}$$

The rotation matrix is applied to transform the matrix P defined by the length of the principal component axes $P = \begin{pmatrix} p_1 & 0 \\ 0 & p_2 \end{pmatrix}$. The symmetric positive definite matrix C can be deployed as the covariance matrix for the original problem with $C = R \cdot P^2 \cdot R^T$. The following actions can be done by the user: 1. Select the Gaussian that you intend to edit. Add new Gaussians or remove the currently selected one. 2. Modify the parameters of the selected Gaussian. The selected Gaussian is shown in blue. 3. Use the knob slider as an alternative way to set the ellipsoids angle of the currently selected gaussian. 4. Use the interactive three-dimensional plots to understand the two-dimensional data and/or model. 5. Use one of the four two-dimensional visualizations to understand the data or model better. 6. Use the upper buttons to switch between a view of the empirical density estimation and the model, switch on or off the data's scatter, or compare the original classification (if given) of the data versus the model's classification using the Bayes Theorem. Here, the maximum of the posterior distribution is used as a hard classification. 7. Switch between the four different two-dimensional plots (upper button row) and switch on or off the ellipsoid's axis and outline the models' components, the data scatter or choose between the original classification (if given) and the model's classification. 8.

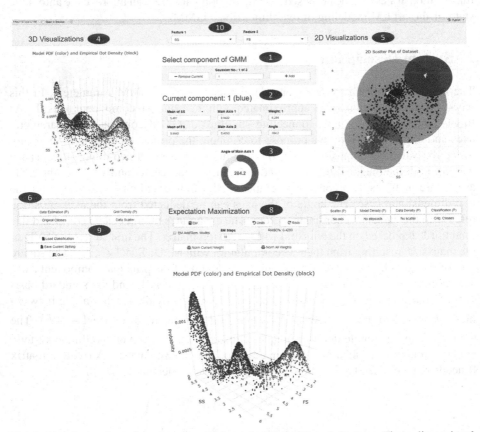

Fig. 1. Top Screenshot of the interface of the AdaptGauss2D tool. Bottom: Three-dimensional visualization of the model fitted with the interactive tool in color versus the density estimation of data in black of the flow-cytometry dataset that was interactively modeled after the usage of EM. The third dimensions indicate the density.

Execute the EM algorithm with the desired number of steps (EM Steps), allow the EM to add/remove modes or not, undo or redo any change made by the algorithm or by hand, preserve the currently selected Gaussian weight, and norm the others or norm all the Gaussian weights. 9. Load a classification to compare with the model's computed classification, save the current setting, or close AdaptGauss2D.

3 Evaluation and Application

In the video https://www.youtube.com/watch?v=MV7DVEWys_c the dataset EngyTime is used, which is described in [8]. The identification of cluster structures combined with an EM algorithm yields a root mean square deviation (RMSD) of 20%. A manual fitting of the initialized results from the automatized adaptation reduced RMSD to 5%. Comparing both solutions to the ground truth shows an improvement of accuracy from 0.921 to 0.965. Figure 1 presents a flowcytometry sample file of blood with N = 296.755 measured event. In a flow cytometer, each cell rapidly passes through a laser beam one by one. Two light scatter and several surface parameters can be measured for each event. Figure 1 (top) presents the forward scatter FS versus side scatter SS in which three modes are visible in the shiny interactive app. However, the EM algorithm is unable to fit the Gaussians to the data, as Fig. 1 (top) shows. Here, the identification of cluster structures combined with an EM algorithm yields an RMSD of 0.4233%. A manual fitting by a HIL of the initialized results from the automatized adaptation reduced the RMSD to 0.0605%. The result of the interactive modeling is presented in Fig. 1 bottom as a three-dimensional plot for which the density of the model (colors) and data (black) is shown in the third dimension.

References

1. Baggenstoss, P.M.: Statistical modeling using Gaussian mixtures and HMMS with matlab. Naval Undersea Warfare Center, Newport RI (2002)
2. Yoshida, E., Kimura, Y., Kitamura, K., Murayama, H.: Calibration procedure for a DOI detector of high resolution PET through a Gaussian mixture model. IEEE Trans. Nucl. Sci. **51**(5), 2543–2549 (2004)
3. Yu, J.: Bearing performance degradation assessment using locality preserving projections and Gaussian mixture models. Mech. Syst. Signal Process. **25**(7), 2573–2588 (2011)
4. Wang, et al.: Efficient volume exploration using the Gaussian mixture model. IEEE Trans. Vis. Comput. Graph. **17**(11), 1560–1573 (2011)
5. Yang, M.-S., Lai, C.-Y., Lin, C.-Y.: A robust EM clustering algorithm for Gaussian mixture models. Pattern Recogn. **45**(11), 3950–3961 (2012)
6. Ultsch, et al.: Identification of molecular fingerprints in human heat pain thresholds by use of an interactive mixture model R toolbox (AdaptGauss). Int. J. Mol. Sci. **16**(10), 25897–25911 (2015). https://doi.org/10.3390/ijms161025897
7. Thrun, M.C., Stier, Q.: Fundamental clustering algorithms suite SoftwareX **13**(C), 100642 (2021). https://doi.org/10.1016/j.softx.2020.100642
8. Thrun, M.C., Ultsch, A.: Clustering benchmark datasets exploiting the fundamental clustering problems. Data Brief **30**(C), 105501 (2020). https://doi.org/10.1016/j.dib.2020.105501

Demonstrator on Counterfactual Explanations for Differentially Private Support Vector Machines

Rami Mochaourab[1]([✉]), Sugandh Sinha[1], Stanley Greenstein[2],
and Panagiotis Papapetrou[3]

[1] Digital Systems Division, RISE Research Institutes of Sweden, Stockholm, Sweden
{rami.mochaourab,sugandh.sinha}@ri.se
[2] Department of Law, Stockholm University, Stockholm, Sweden
stanley.greenstein@juridicum.su.se
[3] Department of Computer and Systems Sciences, Stockholm University,
Stockholm, Sweden
panagiotis@dsv.su.se

Abstract. We demonstrate the construction of robust counterfactual explanations for support vector machines (SVM), where the privacy mechanism that publicly releases the classifier guarantees differential privacy. Privacy preservation is essential when dealing with sensitive data, such as in applications within the health domain. In addition, providing explanations for machine learning predictions is an important requirement within so-called high risk applications, as referred to in the EU AI Act. Thus, the innovative aspects of this work correspond to studying the interaction between three desired aspects: accuracy, privacy, and explainability. The SVM classification accuracy is affected by the privacy mechanism through the introduced perturbations in the classifier weights. Consequently, we need to consider a trade-off between accuracy and privacy. In addition, counterfactual explanations, which quantify the smallest changes to selected data instances in order to change their classification, may become not credible when we have data privacy guarantees. Hence, robustness for counterfactual explanations is needed in order to create confidence about the credibility of the explanations. Our demonstrator provides an interactive environment to show the interplay between the considered aspects of accuracy, privacy, and explainability.

Keywords: Counterfactual explanations · Support vector machines · Differential privacy

1 Motivation

Machine learning algorithms have proven to be powerful for learning from data and making decisions with high accuracy. In particular, they are able to outperform humans on many specific tasks. However, such data-driven technologies are

---

Demonstrator video is available under: https://rami-mochaourab.github.io/papers/2022-ECML/demo-video.mp4.

M.-R. Amini et al. (Eds.): ECML PKDD 2022, LNAI 13718, pp. 662–666, 2023.
https://doi.org/10.1007/978-3-031-26422-1_52

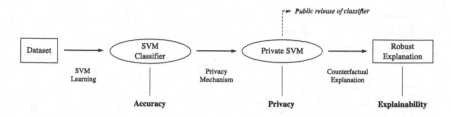

Fig. 1. The considered relationship between accuracy, privacy, and explainability.

seldom value-neutral to the extent that they include social and ethical values. Even when such values are integrated into the models they may be mandated by regulatory frameworks, such as traditional laws or policy documents. The goal of our work, reported in [2,3], is to demonstrate in a technical context the link between three social and ethical values advocated by the General Data Protection Regulation (GDPR), namely, *explainability*, *privacy*, and *accuracy*.

Figure 1 gives an overview on how the three mentioned social values are related within this work: **Accuracy** is targeted when learning an SVM classifier. **Privacy** is guaranteed using a differentially private mechanism for the classifier [4]. Afterwards, the private SVM version is made publicly available. **Explainability** for private SVM is done by designing counterfactual explanations [5] which take into account the characteristics of the classifier and privacy mechanism [3].

The innovative aspects of this work correspond to the simultaneous analysis of these three desired aspects, namely, accuracy, privacy, and explainability. The application domains of our work include those with sensitive data, such as within health, as well as within high risk applications as referred to by the EU AI Act, where explainability for data driven predictions is needed. To the best of our knowledge, there does not exist other work that studies explainability for privacy-preserving machine learning models.

The target users of our work are both machine learning researchers, working on explainable AI, as well as AI regulatory bodies interested in understanding the interplay between machine learning based decision-making, privacy guarantees, and explainability of machine learning predictions.

2   Demonstrator

Our demonstrator provides an interactive environment to understand the effects of privacy guarantees on the classification accuracy and counterfactual explanations. We use two datasets for this purpose as is shown in the snapshots from the demo in Fig. 2 and Fig. 3.

Figure 2 shows the optimal linear SVM (solid line) and its private version (dashed line). The first sliding bar corresponds to the differential privacy parameter [1] which affects the extent of privacy guarantees. A low value means larger

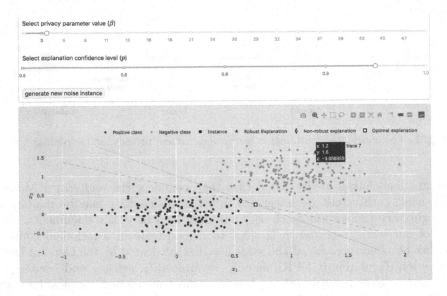

Fig. 2. Demo snapshot for explanability of linear SVM classifications on data generated from two bivariate Guassian distributions.

privacy. Consequently, larger perturbations on the classifier weights are performed when constructing the private SVM. Counterfactual explanations are the closest points to the selected instance (•) that lie on the decision boundaries. Non-robust explanation (◊) may have the same class as the instance with respect to the optimal (unknown) SVM, as is shown the screenshot. Hence, non-robust explanations are not credible and therefore we construct robust explanations (⋆) that provide confidence in explanation credibility.

The second sliding bar at the top corresponds to the confidence in the credibility of the counterfactual explanations. A large confidence means that we are more certain that the explanation has a different classification compared to that of the instance. However, a larger confidence level comes at a cost in terms of a larger distance between the explanation and the instance we want to explain. In other words, we have a tradeoff between the explanation credibility and the smallest changes needed to alter the classifier decision from the instance.

Figure 3 demonstrates similar functionality as above but on the publicly available UCI Breast Cancer Wisconsin (Diagnostic) dataset. Here, we use a feature mapping generated using a Radial Basis Function (RBF) kernel approximation (see details in [3]). Due to the high number of features, the demo allows to visualize in two dimensions by selecting pairs of features through a drop-down menu. In order to identify the classifier errors, we mark the false positives and false negatives for both optimal and private SVM. In this way, we can see the extent of errors for different privacy parameter values. In addition, at the top-right corner we show the classification of both the selected instance and the

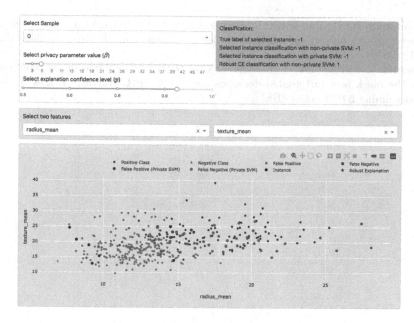

Fig. 3. Demo snapshot for explainability of kernel SVM classifications on the UCI Breast Cancer Wisconsin (Diagnostic) dataset.

explanation. This, highlights the diverse miss-classification possibilities inherent in the machine learning models.

The calculation of robust counterfactual explanations for kernel SVM is based on the bisection method aided by prototypes, as is detailed in [3]. A prototype for a specific data class is a typical case for that class known by the domain expert. By increasing the explanation confidence level, we can visualize how the explanations move towards the prototype at the center of the desired data class.

Acknowledgements. The authors would like to thank Luis Quintero and Zhendong Wang for their help in developing the demonstrator. This work has been supported by the Digital Futures center (https://www.digitalfutures.kth.se) within the project "EXTREMUM: Explainable and Ethical Machine Learning for Knowledge Discovery from Medical Data Sources".

References

1. Dwork, C., Roth, A.: The algorithmic foundations of differential privacy. Found. Trends Theor. Comput. Sci. **9**(3–4), 211–407 (2014)
2. Greenstein, S., Papapetrou, P., Mochaourab, R.: Embedding human values into artificial intelligence. De lege 2021: Law, AI and Digitalisation, pp. 91–115 (2022)
3. Mochaourab, R., Sinha, S., Greenstein, S., Papapetrou, P.: Robust counterfactual explanations for privacy-preserving SVMs. In: International Conference on Machine Learning (ICML 2021), Workshop on Socially Responsible Machine Learning (2021)

4. Rubinstein, B.I.P., Bartlett, P.L., Huang, L., Taft, N.: Learning in a large function space: privacy-preserving mechanisms for SVM learning. J. Priv. Confidentiality **4**(1) (2012)
5. Wachter, S., Mittelstadt, B., Russell, C.: Counterfactual explanations without opening the black box: automated decisions and the GDPR. Harvard J. Law Technol. Forthcoming **31**(2), 841 (2018)

Correction to: Recognizing Cognitive Load by a Hybrid Spatio-Temporal Causal Model from Multivariate Physiological Data

Zirui Yong, Guoxin Su, Xiaohu Li, Lingyun Sun, Zejian Li, and Li Liu

Correction to:
Chapter "Recognizing Cognitive Load by a Hybrid Spatio-Temporal Causal Model from Multivariate Physiological Data" in: M.-R. Amini et al. (Eds.): *Machine Learning and Knowledge Discovery in Databases*, LNAI 13718, https://doi.org/10.1007/978-3-031-26422-1_20

In the originally published version of chapter 20, there was an error in the name of the author Li Liu; first name and last name had been swapped erroneously. This has been corrected.

The updated original version of this chapter can be found at
https://doi.org/10.1007/978-3-031-26422-1_20

Author Index

M.-R. Amini et al. (Eds.): ECML PKDD 2022, LNAI 13718, pp. 667–669, 2023.
https://doi.org/10.1007/978-3-031-26422-1

Printed in the United States
by Baker & Taylor Publisher Services